BUSINESS STUDIES

Fourth Edition

Dave Hall–Rob Jones–Carlo Raffo–Alain Anderton

Edited by Ian Chambers and Dave Gray

CP

Acknowledgements

Dedication
To Elaine, Holly, Caitlin, Amanda Jane, Mandy, Sandra, Georgina, Rebecca, Jan, Natalie, Holly and Nicole for all their love and support in the writing of this book.

Cover design by Tim Button, illustration provided by Shutterstock.
Graphics by Caroline Waring-Collins, Kevin O'Brien and Anneli Jameson.
Photography by Andrew Allen and Dave Gray.
Typing by Annette Birchall
Proof reading by Sheila Evans-Pritchard, Sue Oliver and Heather Doyle.

The publishers would like to thank the following for the use of photographs and copyright material. Other copyright material is acknowledged at source.

Alvey & Towers p491(c), Corel p 199, DigitalVision pp 488, 491(b), 653, 657, 666, Image 100 p 685, John Powell/Rex Features p 633, Manganese Bronze Holdings p 104, Paula Sollaway/Photofusion p 146, PhotoDisc pp 105, 318, 400, 414, 425, 435, 448, 610, 635, Philippe Hays/Rex Features p 346, Rex Features p 733, Richard Burns/Reuters/Popperfoto p 110, Shutterstock pp 9, 10, 12, 14, 15, 17, 20, 21, 28, 40, 47, 56, 60, 66, 68, 74, 97, 107, 129, 130, 135, 137, 139, 148, 149, 152, 155, 160, 166, 172, 188, 190, 203, 210, 215, 220, 228, 230, 243, 255, 258, 261, 269, 273, 278, 281, 282, 288, 301, 304, 312, 315, 320, 321, 322, 326, 328, 336, 337, 343, 345, 356, 361, 367, 373, 380, 384, 388, 390, 394, 421, 428, 442, 455, 456, 476, 483, 484, 490, 495, 496, 502, 511, 523, 529, 542, 548, 549, 556, 583, 589, 597, 606, 622, 631, 641, 643, 646, 649, 652, 668, 669, 670, 673, 678, 680, 684, 689, 693, 696, 699, 721, 740, 744, 746, 754, Sam Morgan/Rex Features p 462, Stockbyte pp 91, 213, 218, 352, 362, 389, 397, 407, 411, 431, 491(t), 611, 654, 656, 658, 663, 715, Suma p 469.

British Library Cataloguing in Publication Data
A catalogue record for this book is available from the British Library.

ISBN 978 1 4058 9231 5

Pearson Education
Edinburgh Gate, Harlow, Essex CM20 2JE

1st edition 1993
2nd edition 1999
3rd edition 2004
4th edition 2008.
Reprinted 2009, 2010
10 9 8

Typesetting by Caroline Waring-Collins, Waring Collins Ltd. www.waringcollins.com
Printed and bound in China (CTPSC/08)

Contents

Preface

Business Studies does not provide a step-by-step guide to how to be 'good at business'. There is no simple set of rules that can be applied at all times which will always be successful. However, by being analytical, rigorous and critical it may be possible to develop skills and approaches which can be useful, at certain times and in certain situations, when making business decisions. It is possible that different approaches will be used by different people in business and there may be disagreement as to which approach to take.

Business Studies is integrated and different areas of business are interdependent. There are links, for example, between:
- what is being produced and the funds available to pay for it (production and finance);
- the selling of the product and ethical considerations (marketing and ethics);
- the type of business and many aspects of its operation.

Being aware of these aspects of business will help us to understand how and why business decisions are made, and how they affect a variety of people, both within and outside the business. The aim of **Business Studies (Fourth Edition)** is to help those studying Business to understand business decisions and to be analytical, rigorous and critical in their business thinking. A number of features are included in the book which we believe will help this task.

Comprehensive course coverage The book contains material that should meet the demands of a wide range of courses. These include AS Level, A Level, IB, Higher Grade, Applied Business, Higher Education and professional courses. The book is organised into short units, across seven sections.
- Business organisation and development.
- Marketing.
- Accounting and finance.
- People in organisations.
- Operations management.
- Objectives and strategy.
- External influences.

There is a development in the units contained in each section which reflects progress throughout the course. In addition, there are four units on collecting and presenting data, analysing data, study skills and assessment at the end. Guidance on how the book can be used for specific courses is given in Business Studies Teachers' Guide (Fourth Edition).

Flexible unit structure The unit structure allows lecturers and teachers freedom to devise the course. Business Studies teachers and lecturers often teach different aspects of the course in different orders. So, whilst there is a logical order to the book, it has been written on the assumption that teachers or lecturers and students may also piece the units together to suit their own teaching and learning needs and the requirements.

Accessibility The book has been written in a clear and logical style which should make it accessible to all readers. Each unit is divided into short, easily manageable sections.

A workbook The text is interspersed with questions. The questions which appear as part of the units mostly refer to preceding information. Answers in most cases are expected to be relatively short. Questions are based on a variety of case studies, data, articles, photographs, etc. They should allow the student and teacher/lecturer to assess whether the information has been understood. Shorter 'knowledge' questions provide a means of revising each unit. A longer case study appears at the end of each unit. It draws on information contained in the whole unit and answers are expected to reflect this. The questions asked reflect the type which are set in examinations. They help students to develop knowledge, application, analysis and evaluation - the criteria used in examinations to assess responses. **Business Studies Teachers' Guide (Fourth Edition)** provides suggested answers and mark schemes for the activities and questions that appear in this book.

Use of business examples, case studies and data Modern technology has allowed much of the book to proceed from manuscript to book form in a very short period. This has meant that we have been able to use the latest statistics and business examples available. The materials used have been chosen to demonstrate appropriate arguments and theories. They should, therefore, allow students to answer questions which require knowledge of what has happened 'in recent years' or 'over the past decade', as well as questions which deal with current debates.

Skills At the end of the book there is a skills section. The units on collecting and presenting data, and analysing data, allow students to learn and practice the presentation and analysis of business data. The last two units in the book provide guidance on how to study and the methods of assessment used in Business Studies. They are presented in the form of a manual and are designed to be used at various stages throughout the course.

Key terms Many units contain a key terms section. Each section defines new concepts, which appear in capitals in the text of the unit. Taken together, they provide a comprehensive dictionary of business terms.

Presentation Great care has been taken with how the book has been presented. It is hoped that the layout of the book, the use of colour and the use of diagrams will help learning.

Critque At appropriate points in the book there are sections which highlight that the accepted views and theories in an area of Business Studies are not without their critics. Students are encouraged to be aware that there are sometimes alternative opinions and to consider and evaluate alternatives.

Support MyBusSpace.co.uk is an online support resource for use by teachers and students using the book. It includes an online student book, an accurate graphing tool, questions from the student book that can be answered and marked online, links to key websites providing access to latest economic data and a regular updated news section.

We would like to thank the following for their efforts in the preparation of the three editions of this book: Richard Dunill, for keeping the debate sharp and yet accessible; Ingrid Hamer and Annette Birchall for their long hours of typing; Nigel Lewis; Michael J. Forshaw and Chris Sawyer for bringing a 'real' accountant's view to the book; all staff and students at Bolton Sixth Form College, King George V College, Loreto College, and Manchester University School of Education; Diane Wallace and Steve Robertson for working on the early development of the book; everyone who has proof read earlier editions.

Dave Hall Rob Jones Carlo Raffo Alain Anderton
Ian Chambers Dave Gray

1 The nature of business

What is business activity?

In 2008, Kelly Watson and her daughter Ruth opened a cafe in Coventry. Both had previous experience in catering. Kelly had spent the last seven years working in a school canteen, whilst Ruth had been employed by McDonald's when she was a sixth form student. Kelly invested £9,000 to help fund the setting up of the business. They called the cafe 'The Cathedral', due to its location near to the city's famous landmark. They planned to target the student market and cathedral visitors. Before trading began they had to:

- obtain a £3,000 bank loan;
- obtain a five year lease on a suitable property;
- line the kitchen with aluminium panels to conform with health and safety regulations;
- obtain a fire certificate;
- decorate the cafe area;
- buy furniture and kitchen equipment;
- find suppliers of fresh food;
- advertise the cafe in the local university.

Kelly and Ruth had different roles to play in the business. Kelly was responsible for dealing with suppliers and preparing the food. Ruth ran the cafe area. This involved waiting on tables, taking money and socialising with the customers. Ruth and Kelly worked very long hours. The cafe opened from 8.00 a.m. to 7.00 p.m., every day of the week except Sunday. However, it was worth it because the business became successful. The Cathedral developed a reputation for good value food and a great atmosphere. After six months they were able to employ two university students to help during busy periods.

The above case illustrates many features of business activity.

- Business activity produces an output – a good or service. A cafe service is being provided by Kelly and Ruth.
- Goods and services are consumed. Cafe customers consume the service provided by Kelly and Ruth.
- Resources are used up. Money, food and drinks, furniture, staff, gas and electricity are just a few of the resources used by Kelly and Ruth.
- A number of business functions may be carried out. Administration (the paper work), managing staff (human resources) and decisions about marketing, finance and production are some examples.
- Businesses can be affected by external factors. The government's commitment to increasing the numbers of students in higher education may have boosted the number of students in Coventry.

Figure 1: The nature of business activity

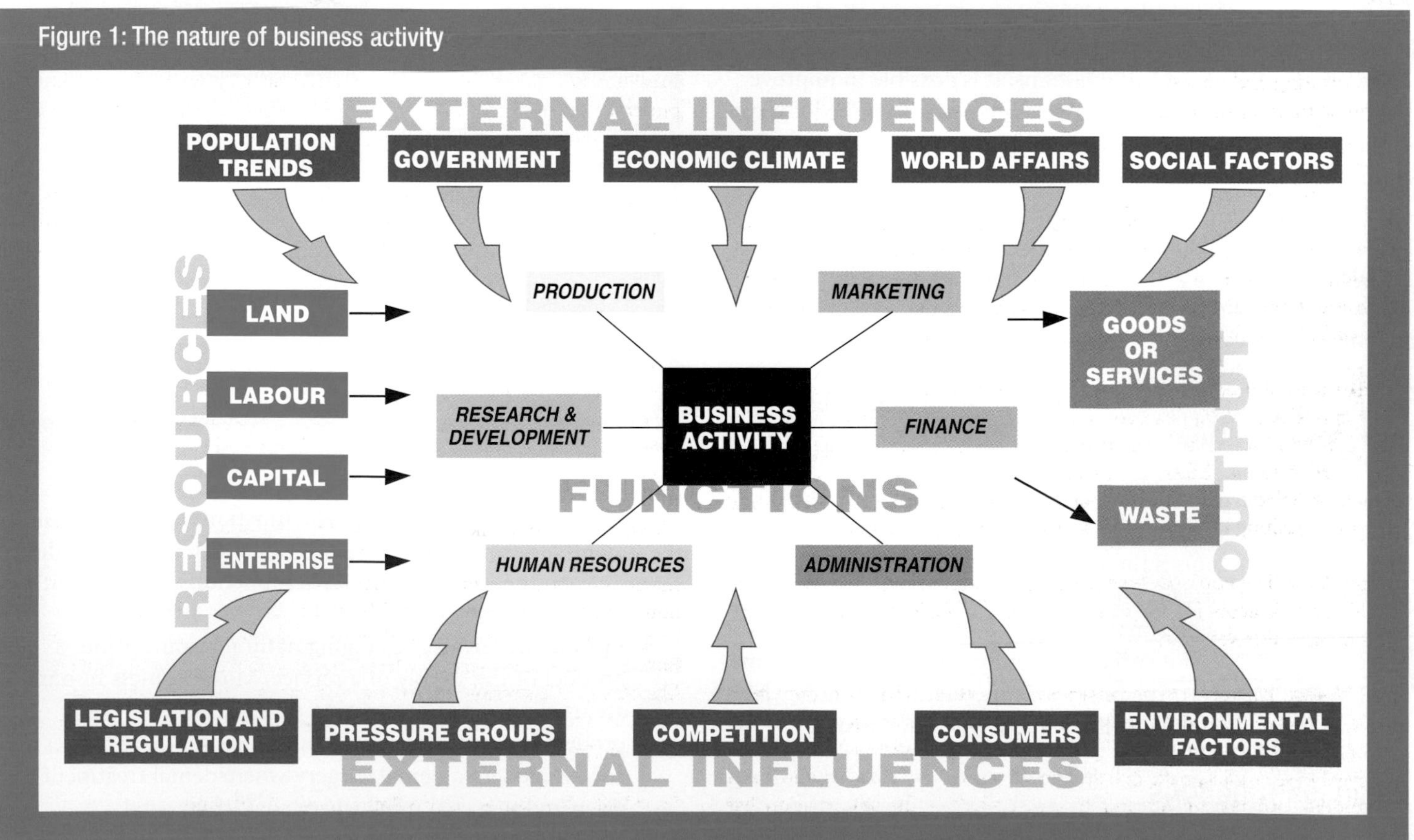

Figure 1 shows a diagram which illustrates the nature of business activity. All types of business may be represented by this diagram – a building society, a window cleaner, a multinational chemical company, a shoe manufacturer or the BBC.

Business resources

Businesses use resources or FACTORS OF PRODUCTION in business activity. These are usually divided into four groups.

Land Land is not just a 'plot of land' where business premises might be located. It also includes natural resources, such as coal, diamonds, forests, rivers and fertile soil. The owners of land receive rent from those who use it. Business activity uses both renewable and **non-renewable** resources. Renewable resources are those like fish, forests and water which nature replaces. Examples of non-renewable land resources are mineral deposits like coal and diamonds, which once used are never replaced. There has been concern in recent years about the rate at which renewable resources are being used. For example, overfishing in the North Sea has led to claims by the International Council for the Exploration of the Sea that cod stocks are now so low that fishing should stop until they recover. The number of young cod in the North Sea in early 2003 was the lowest in 20 years.

Labour Labour is the workforce of business. Manual workers, skilled workers and management are all members of the workforce. They are paid wages or salaries for their services. The quality of individual workers will vary considerably. Each worker is unique, possessing a different set of characteristics, skills, knowledge, intelligence and emotions. It is possible to improve the quality of **human resources** through training and education. Human resources become more productive if money is invested by business or government in training and education.

Capital Capital is sometimes described as the artificial resource because it is made by labour. Capital refers to the tools, machinery and equipment which businesses use. For example, JCB makes mechanical diggers which are used by the construction industry. Capital also refers to the money which the owners use to set up a business. Owners of capital receive **interest** if others borrow it.

Enterprise Enterprise has a special role in business activity. The **entrepreneur** or businessperson develops a business idea and then hires and organises the other three factors of production to carry out the activity. Entrepreneurs also take risks because they will often use some personal money to help set up the business. If the business does not succeed the entrepreneur may lose some or all of that money. If the business is successful, any money left over will belong to the entrepreneur. This is called **profit**.

Business functions

Figure 1 showed that business activity involves a number of functions. A business is a SYSTEM – it has parts that work together to achieve an objective. The functions are all parts of the system. A business is also part of other systems such as the economic and political systems. What functions does a business carry out?

- **Production** involves changing natural resources into a product or the supply of a service. Most business resources are used up in the production process. Examples of production can be seen on a building site where houses are constructed, in a dental surgery where dental treatment is given and in a coal mine where coal is extracted.
- **Marketing** has become very important in recent years due

Question 1.

Caffè Nero Group Plc is currently the largest independent coffee retailer in the UK, with over 330 Caffè Nero stores from Brighton to Glasgow. Inspired by his favourite European haunts while writing his PhD, Gerry Ford set out to bring the continental coffee experience to Britain. He founded this coffee-house group in 1997 and floated it on the London Stock Exchange four years later. He then teamed up with Paladin, the venture-capital company he also co-founded, to buy it back in February in a deal valuing the business at a reported £225m. Ford hopes to take the Caffè Nero brand to northern Europe and the Middle East, building on the allure of Italian espresso coffee and deli-style food. He is also looking to expand in Britain from 300 to 450 shops by 2010. The company's profits have grown 77% a year from £1.6m in 2003 to £9.1m in 2006.

Caffè Nero provides a high quality food offering, which is based on freshness and superior ingredients. Its product range is similar to that of a deli. It serves gourmet handmade sandwiches (including panini, focaccia, and wraps), traditional pastas featuring the recipes of the well-known chef Ursula Ferrigno, soups, pizza, salads, biscotti, fresh pastries, and cakes. Many of the food recipes are unique to Caffè Nero, and cannot be found elsewhere. Its approach is to use fresh, high quality natural ingredients and to avoid all additives and colourants whenever possible.

Source: adapted from www.fasttrack.co.uk and www.caffenero.com.

(a) Using this case as an example, explain what is meant by an entrepreneur.

(b) Suggest examples of land, labour and capital that Caffè Nero may be using.

to an increase in competition in business. It is concerned with identifying consumer needs and satisfying them. Examples of marketing activities are market research, advertising, packaging, promotion, distribution and pricing.
- The **finance** department is responsible for the control of money in a business. It has a number of important duties. This includes recording transactions, producing documents to illustrate the performance of the business and its financial position and controlling the flow of money in the business.
- Dealing with enquiries, communicating messages and producing documents for the workforce are all examples of **administrative** tasks.
- The **human resources** function involves the management of people. The personnel department looks after the welfare of the workforce, and is responsible for such things as recruitment, selection, training, appraisal, health and safety, equal opportunities, payment systems and worker disputes.
- **Research and development (R&D)** involves technical research, for example, research into a new medicine or a new production technique. R&D can be very expensive. Consequently, many businesses do not have a R&D department but rely on adapting new products and new technology developed by other companies.

In a large business these functions should be easy to identify. However, a self-employed window cleaner will also carry out these functions.
- Production – cleaning windows.
- Marketing – distributing business cards to potential customers.
- Administration – dealing with enquiries from potential customers and recording their personal details in preparation for a first visit.
- Human resources management – recruiting and supervising part time helpers during busy periods.
- Finance – keeping records of all financial transactions.

Business activity is highly **integrated**. For example, production is heavily influenced by marketing activities. If marketing is effective and more of the product is sold, then more will have to be produced. Also, the finance department, for example, will carefully watch the amount of money used by other departments.

What does business activity produce?

All business activity results in the production of a good or a service. CONSUMER GOODS are those which are sold to the general public. They fall into two categories.
- **Durable goods** such as cookers, HD televisions, ipods, books, cars and furniture can be used repeatedly for a long period of time.
- **Non-durable** goods such as food, confectionery, newspapers and shoe polish are used very soon after they are purchased. Some of these goods are called **fast moving consumer goods**, such as soap, crisps and cornflakes.

CAPITAL GOODS are those goods purchased by businesses and used to produce other goods. Tools, equipment and machinery are examples of capital goods.

The supply of **services** has grown in recent years. Banking, insurance, hairdressing, leisure, transport and gardening are examples of this type of business activity.

Business activity also results in the production of waste materials. Most waste is useless and some waste, like radioactive nuclear waste, is very dangerous and expensive to dispose of. Some production techniques result in **by-products** which can be sold. For example, the brewing process generates yeast which is used by the producers of Marmite.

External factors

Business activity is affected by a number of external forces, some of which are shown in the diagram in Figure 1. These are beyond the control of the individual business. In some cases they constrain a firm's decisions and may prevent its growth and development.
- The **government** has a great deal of influence over business activity. In most countries the government will be in favour of business development. A **legal framework**, where all individuals abide by the law and offenders are punished, will help this. A country also needs an infrastructure including roads, railways, telecommunications, schools and hospitals. Some of these items may be provided by the state. Government policy can also influence business. For example, profits and many goods and services which businesses produce are taxed.
- The **economic climate** can have an impact on business activity. For example, over the period 1993-2007 the UK economy was relatively stable. Interest rates and price increases were relatively low, while unemployment fell steadily. These stable economic conditions allowed business activity to flourish. During this time the best performing economy in the EU was the UK's.
- **World events** can influence business activity. The attack on the Twin Towers in New York in 2001 and the military action against Iraq in 2003 affected a number of industries. There was a fall in the number of passengers travelling by air in many countries. This affected the aviation industry. There was also a fall in the number of holidaymakers which affected the tourist industry. It often takes many years for businesses to recover from such events. In some cases they may fail to survive and go bankrupt.
- Some individuals form **pressure groups**. For example, Transport 2000 is a pressure group that promotes ways of reducing the environmental and social impact of transport. It aims to reduce the use of cars and encourages individuals to use public transport, walk and cycle. If Transport 2000 is influential, the car industry is likely to be adversely affected.

- **Consumers' tastes** change. In recent years there has been an increase in demand for garden products. Gardens and gardening have been popularised by a number of television programmes on gardening. There has also been a rise in demand for vegetarian and vegan foodstuffs. Increasing numbers of people are opting for non-meat diets.
- **Changes in population** can affect the demand for products and the supply of workers. For example, the ageing of the population in the UK has meant increasing numbers of people aged 60 or over still looking for work. It has also given opportunities to businesses with products aimed at this age group, such as Saga holidays.
- Most businesses face **competition** from other firms. Rivals' activities often have an influence on their operations. In recent years the manufacturing sector in particular has been hit by very fierce competition from countries in Asia – China and India for example.
- **Social factors** may influence business activity from time to time. For example, the roles of women in society have changed considerably in recent years. This has meant that more women have become involved in business management and business ownership. Some businesses have also been prepared to offer crèche facilities as women have returned to work.
- **Environmental factors** have had a major effect on businesses in recent years. Some now use recycled materials in their manufacturing processes to reduce costs. Certain businesses have tried to manufacture products which are environmentally friendly in order to boost sales.
- **Legislation** and **regulation** may influence business activity. This may be in the form of government imposed laws, EU regulations, independent bodies set up by government to regulate industry or industry self-regulation. For example, the smoking ban introduced in 2007 has had an impact on a large number of businesses – particularly pubs and bars.

Question 2.

In common with most other countries, the UK has an ageing population. The proportion of people aged 65 and over is projected to increase from 16 per cent in 2006 to 22 per cent by 2031. This is an inevitable consequence of the age structure of the population alive today, in particular the ageing of the large numbers of people born after the Second World War and during the 1960s baby boom.

One business which is likely to benefit from this population trend is Barchester Healthcare. Having experienced difficulties in finding a good quality care home for two relatives, Mike Parsons wanted to create a better alternative for others looking for care. He found Moreton Hill, a 17th century farm with stunning views over the Cotswolds, which he converted into a unique care setting. On opening the home, Mike was aiming to provide high quality care and environments for residents and to invest in staff. In 1994 Moreton Hill was awarded the Care Home Design Award and Barchester started from there. Since then Barchester has grown to provide quality care throughout the UK but the focus on residents' individual needs and providing them with a home from home environment has not changed. Today, the Barchester group cares for over 10,000 people at more than 160 different locations.

Source: www.fasttrack.co.uk and www.barchester.com.

(a) Using this case as an example, explain what is meant by an external factor.

(b) Barchester Healthcare is a tertiary sector business. Explain what this means.

Satisfying needs and wants

The success of a business activity depends on many factors. The most important is to supply a product that consumers want to buy. Businesses must satisfy consumers' NEEDS and WANTS to be successful. People's needs are limited. They include things which are needed to survive, such as food, warmth, shelter and security. Humans also have psychological and emotional needs such as recognition and love. Wants, however are infinite. People constantly aim for a better quality of life, which might include better housing, better health care, better education, longer holidays, and more friends.

Markets

The goods and services produced by businesses are sold in MARKETS. A market exists when buyers and sellers communicate in order to exchange goods and services. In some cases buyers and sellers might meet at an agreed place to carry out the exchange. For example, many villages and towns have regular open air markets where buyers and sellers exchange goods and services. Also, buying and selling can be carried out over the telephone. For example, the First Direct banking facility allows customers to conduct nearly all of their banking business over the telephone. Buying and selling can also take place in shopping centres, in newspapers and magazines, through mail order, and more recently, through television and the Internet.

The goods and services of most businesses are bought by CUSTOMERS and used by CONSUMERS to satisfy their wants and needs. A business may be interested in some of the following markets.

- Consumer goods markets – where products like food, cosmetics and magazines are sold in large quantities.
- Markets for services – these are varied and could include services for individuals, such as banking, or services for industry, such as cleaning.
- Capital goods markets – where items used by other businesses are bought and sold, such as machinery.
- Labour markets – where people are hired for their services.
- The housing market - where people buy and sell properties.
- Money markets – where people and institutions borrow and lend money, such as commercial banks.
- Commodity markets – where raw materials such as copper and coffee are bought, mainly by business.

Specialisation

One feature of modern businesses is SPECIALISATION. This is the production of a limited range of goods by an individual, firm, region or country. Specialisation can take place between firms. For example, McDonald's provides a limited range of fast foods, Ford manufactures cars, Heinz processes food products and MFI manufactures and sells furniture products. Examples of regional specialisation might be Kidderminster, which specialises in carpet production, Stoke-on-Trent, which produces pottery and Kent, which is one of the country's main hop growers. Different countries also specialise. For example, it could be argued that Scotland specialises in the distilling of whisky, Saudi Arabia in oil extraction and South Africa in the supply of gold.

Specialisation within a firm is an important part of production. Departments specialise in different activities, such as marketing, purchasing, personnel and finance. People specialise in different tasks and skills. This is called the DIVISION OF LABOUR and allows people to concentrate on the task or skill at which they are best. In business, production is divided among workers, who each concentrate on a limited range of tasks. For example, the building of a house involves an architect to draw up the plans, a bricklayer to build the structure, a joiner to undertake woodwork, a roofer to lay the tiles etc. It is argued that the division of labour raises the productivity and efficiency of business and the economy. There is a number of reasons for this.

- Workers can concentrate on the tasks that they do best, leaving other tasks to more specialist workers.
- People's skills are improved by carrying out tasks over a long period of time. It is also possible to develop a brand new skill.
- Time is saved because workers are not constantly changing tasks, moving from one area to another or collecting new tools.
- The organisation of production becomes easier and more effective.

Specialisation, however, does have disadvantages.

- Work can become tedious and boring. This can result in poor worker motivation with the likelihood of a higher rate of absenteeism and increased staff turnover.
- Problems can also occur when one stage of production depends on another stage. If one stage breaks down, production might be halted.
- Over-specialisation can pose problems when there is a change in demand. If people are only competent in one skill they may have to retrain, causing delays in production. Some are not able to retrain and become unemployed.

The importance of money

MONEY is anything which is generally accepted as a means of exchange. It is essential for the smooth exchange of goods and services in markets and helps specialisation.

Without money goods have to be exchanged using a BARTER SYSTEM. This involves swapping goods directly, which is inefficient. It is necessary for the wants of individuals to be perfectly matched. Searching for the perfect match in a barter deal can be very time consuming. It is also difficult to value different goods without money. In addition, giving change can be a problem when the values of the goods being exchanged do not match exactly. Money also has a number of other functions. It:

- allows individuals to save some of their income and buy goods and services at a later date;
- enables all goods and services to be valued in common units, for example, a house which costs £200,000 is worth exactly 10 times more than a car which is valued at £20,000;
- allows payments to be deferred, i.e. goods can be bought and payment made at a later date.

There is no single definition of the money supply. No financial asset has all the characteristics or fulfils all the functions of money perfectly. In the UK the main measure monitored by the government and the Bank of England is M4. This measure is made up of notes and coins, and deposits by households, businesses and financial institutions with banks and building societies.

Classification of business activity

Business activity is often classed by the type of production that takes place.

- PRIMARY PRODUCTION includes activity which takes the natural resources from the earth, i.e. the extraction of raw materials and the growing of food. Mining, fishing, farming and forestry are examples of primary business activity.
- SECONDARY PRODUCTION involves manufacturing, processing and construction which transform raw materials into goods. Car production, distilling, baking, shipbuilding and office construction are examples of secondary sector activity.
- TERTIARY PRODUCTION includes the provision of services. Hairdressing, distribution, security, banking, theatre and tourism are all examples of business activity in this area. Other methods of classifying business include by:
  - size;
  - geographical area;
  - sector;
  - ownership.

What are the trends in business activity?

Business activity does not follow a constant pattern. Different industries grow and decline over time. In the UK some major changes have occurred in the structure of the economy. Before the Industrial Revolution most of the UK's resources were used for primary production. This included industries such as agriculture and mining. During the nineteenth century, secondary production expanded rapidly. The Industrial Revolution resulted in a growing quantity of resources being employed in manufacturing.

Over the last sixty years tertiary production has grown at the expense of secondary production. The decline in manufacturing is often called DE-INDUSTRIALISATION. The process of de-industrialisation has resulted in the decline of some once prosperous industries, such as shipbuilding, textiles, steel and engineering. Certain reasons have been put forward to explain the decline including:

- changes in consumer demand;
- a lack of competitiveness among UK manufacturers;
- increasing competition from overseas manufacturers;
- a lack of investment in manufacturing;
- trade union restrictive practices;
- unhelpful government policy.

In contrast, service industries now account for around 80 per cent of the UK's national income. Financial services, personal services, household services and the leisure industry are just some growth areas. For example, in the 1990s and 2000s the profile of the football industry was raised significantly. A number of clubs floated on the stock exchange and the amount of money flowing into the industry rose. Since then many of the premier league clubs have been bought by other wealthy business people, including Chelsea, Manchester United and Manchester City, Liverpool and Aston Villa. Media interest increased, attendances at matches in the Premier League were high and commercial activities began to flourish.

The overall trend in business activity suggests a growth in services at the expense of primary and secondary production. Care needs to be taken when identifying trends from figures. For example, output in one particular service industry may be growing but employment figures may be falling. This could be because businesses in the industry are replacing workers with technology or are reorganising to reduce the workforce. However, employment figures do show clearly the changing patterns of business activity.

KEYTERMS

Barter system – a system of exchange which involves the swapping of goods between individuals.

Capital goods – goods used to produce other goods, such as tools, equipment and machinery.

Consumers – individuals who use or 'consume' goods and services to satisfy their needs and wants.

Consumer goods – goods produced for general use by the public. They can be durable and non-durable.

Customers – individuals, or other businesses, that buy goods and services supplied by businesses.

De-industrialisation – the decline in manufacturing.

Division of labour – specialisation in specific tasks or skills by individuals.

Factors of production – resources used by business to produce goods and services.

Markets – anywhere that buyers and sellers communicate to exchange goods and services.

Money – any substance which is generally accepted as a means of exchange.

Needs – human requirements which must be satisfied for survival.

Opportunity cost - the benefit of the next best option foregone when making a choice between a number of alternatives.

Primary production – activities which involve the extraction of raw materials from the earth and the growing of food.

Secondary production – activities such as manufacturing which transform raw materials into finished goods.

Specialisation – in business, the production of a limited range of goods.

System – parts that work together to achieve an objective; a system can be a communications system, a business, an economic or a political system.

Tertiary production – activities which involve the provision of services.

Wants – human desires which are unlimited.

The basic economic problem

Business activity involves satisfying consumers' needs and wants. Businesses aim to satisfy these wants and needs by producing goods and services. When food is produced or a bus service is provided **resources** (land, labour, capital and enterprise) are used up. These resources are scarce relative to needs and wants. In other words, there are not enough resources to satisfy all consumers' needs and wants. This is known as the BASIC ECONOMIC PROBLEM. This means businesses, individuals and the government must make **choices** when allocating scarce resources between different uses. For example, a printer may have to choose whether to buy a new printing press to improve quality or some new computer software to improve administrative efficiency.

Economics is the study of how resources are allocated in situations where they have different uses. The choices faced by decision makers can be placed in order of preference. For example, a business may be considering three investment options but can only afford one. The decision makers might decide that the order is:

1. a new computer system;
2. a fleet of cars for the sales force;
3. a warehouse extension.

The business will allocate resources to the purchase of the new computer system. The other two options are **foregone** or given up. The benefit lost from the next best alternative is called the OPPORTUNITY COST of the choice. In this example it would be the benefit lost by not having a fleet of new cars.

KNOWLEDGE

1. What are the four factors of production?
2. What is the financial reward paid to each factor of production?
3. Why is capital said to be an artificial resource?
4. Describe six functions involved in business activity.
5. Why is business activity highly integrated?
6. Explain the difference between needs and wants.
7. What is the difference between capital and consumer goods?
8. What is meant by specialisation in business?
9. State:
   (a) three advantages of specialisation;
   (b) three disadvantages of specialisation.
10. Briefly describe the role of money in business.
11. List ten business activities in your local town. State which of these are examples of:
    (a) primary production;
    (b) secondary production;
    (c) tertiary production.
12. What are the possible causes of de-industrialisation?
13. What is the basic economic problem?
14. What might be the opportunity cost of buying a machine for a business?

Case Study: Cumbrian Seafoods Ltd

Cumbrian Seafoods, set up ten years ago on the Solway Firth, provides fresh fish and seafood to Tesco and Morrisons. Its wide range of products include value added seafood lines such as Smoked Haddock with Cheese and Chive Melt and Cod in a Mornay Sauce, reduced-fat prawn cocktail and oat-coated mackerel, sold under Morrisons' Eat Smart label. As well as buying a number of companies in Cumbria and Northumberland, founder and chairman Peter Vassallo has invested in an Icelandic cod and haddock fishery. The company's profits have grown 73 per cent a year from £1.2 million in 2003 to £6.3 million in 2006.

The company owns a new state of the art factory at the Foxcover Industrial Park, Seaham. It was chosen after a thorough analysis of 19 sites lying between North Northumberland and South Yorkshire. As well as its proximity to its customers' radial distribution centres it was attractive because of its access to a large pool of available and naturally talented workforce, willing to share the company's vision of developing a genuinely world leading seafood operation.

From the outset, both in the building and the fitting out of the factory, Cumbrian Seafoods has worked hard to reduce its carbon footprint from practical measures, rather than subscribing to 'offsets'. Winning planning permission for 2 wind turbines on the site has allowed it to reach a position where it will achieve energy neutrality in its first year of activity.

Cumbrian Seafood Ltd understand the importance of conservation of marine stocks. In recent years sustainability has become a very hot topic, with high profile protests from a number of environmental groups highlighting local and global concerns. Throughout the life of the company and that of its predecessor, Vassallo Seafoods of Newcastle, it has pioneered a sustainable purchasing policy going back more than 20 years. It continues to source from suppliers who meet or exceed the requirements of this policy. These are some of the key points from Cumbrian Seafoods' sustainable purchasing policy:

- It promotes eco-friendly line-caught fishing for its selection of mature fish and minimal by-catch.
- It educates customers to avoid the use of species from the 36 most heavily depleted stocks on the Marine Conservation Society (MCS) black list.
- It has invested heavily in developing legitimate, sustainable aquaculture projects across a widening range of species, to meet continuing growth in consumer demands.
- It has full traceability back to vessels with evidence that catch falls within quota.

To Cumbrian Seafoods, sustainability is not only just about how, where and when it was caught? It is about the impact it has on the community, the eco-system and environmental issues. The company recognises the work of the MCS and Marine Stewardship Council and remains aware of the concern held by some sections of the industry that where certain areas have been certified, this may lead to an intolerable strain on the resource. In addition, it also recognises that wild caught fish is limited to current world catch levels, so it has invested heavily in developing legitimate, sustainable aquaculture projects across a widening range of species to meet continuing growth in consumer demand.

Source: adapted from www.fasttrack.co.uk and www.cumbrian-seafoods.co.uk

(a) Describe the market Cumbrian Seafoods Ltd sells into. (4 marks)
(b) Explain the type of business activity Cumbrian Seafoods Ltd is involved in. (6 marks)
(c) Explain the role of the: (i) marketing; (ii) finance departments at Cumbrian Seafoods Ltd. (12 marks)
(d) To what extent is Cumbrian Seafoods Ltd influenced by external factors? (18 marks)

2 Enterprise

Small businesses

There are over 60 million people living in the UK today. In 2006, according to official government statistics, there were 4.5 million private business enterprises. This means there was approximately one business for every 13 people in the country. Here are three more statistics about UK business.

- Three quarters of these businesses were small businesses where there was only one person working in the business.
- Almost all other businesses were also small businesses where there were between 2 and 49 people working in the business.
- There were only 33,000 businesses in the UK which were classified as medium or large where there were 50 or more people employed. This can be compared to the 4.27 million small businesses that existed.

A BUSINESS or ENTERPRISE is an organisation whose purpose is to produce goods and services. Of the 4.5 million UK businesses, some extract oil from the North Sea and some produce the carrots you eat on your plate. Others manufacture cars, provide taxi services or are local shops. The word 'business' comes from the word 'busy'. 'Enterprise' also comes from the idea that the organisation has a purpose, providing comes what they want to buy.

Entrepreneurs

Small businesses are run by ENTREPRENEURS. An entrepreneur is someone who:

- **owns** the business and has provided the money to start it up and possibly to expand it;
- **organises** the business, from hiring and buying inputs like raw materials and workers to producing the finished product for sale;
- has to be a **risk taker** because the business could perform poorly or even fail; the entrepreneur can lose money in a business as well as make it.

So the **role** of the entrepreneur is to provide at least some of the finance for the start up, run the business but take the risk of success or failure.

There are some famous entrepreneurs. Richard Branson, for example, has built a business empire from small beginnings publishing a magazine called 'Student' at the age of 15. Today he owns a string of companies from airlines to mobile phone companies to record companies. However, Richard Branson is exceptional. The more typical entrepreneur running one of the 4.27 million small businesses in 2006 is someone who is self employed.

- They are painters and decorators, plumbers or owners of a corner shop. They are farmers, architects or doctors.
- They may run their business full time. Or they may have an ordinary job working for someone else and run their business on the side, part time.
- They are likely to have started the business themselves but in some industries like farming it is common for the entrepreneur to have inherited the business from parents. Also some entrepreneurs may buy existing mature businesses.
- They may take on a lot of risk in their business or the business may have little risk attached.
- Entrepreneurs may be at the cutting edge of innovation. Or they may be providing traditional services like decorators cutting wallpaper or owners of a hairdressing salon cutting hair.

Risks, rewards and opportunity cost

According to the CBI, approximately 200 000 new businesses are started each year. But 10 per cent of these have ceased trading within 12 months. One third have been closed within three years of starting to trade. Less than half are still trading after five years. Starting up a new business offers the potential for high rewards. Some entrepreneurs, like Richard Branson, have become rich through developing their own businesses. Starting a new business also offers a chance for many people to do something different. If nothing else, it means working for yourself rather than for someone else.

However, being an entrepreneur is risky. The downside of success is business failure. If the business fails, it may leave debts to be paid off. The entrepreneur might have borrowed money to start the business or to finance growth. Getting back into a normal job may also be difficult, especially if the entrepreneur left a well paid job in the first place. The risk of failure is a major motivator for entrepreneurs to carry on and made a success of their enterprise even when the going is tough.

Success and failure have an opportunity cost. The opportunity cost of an activity is the benefits lost from the next best alternative. For example, an entrepreneur who has just started up a business might have left a job earning £40,000 a year. Part of the opportunity cost of setting up the business would then be the benefits gained from earning £40,000 a year. They would only be part of the opportunity cost because the job would probably have had other benefits too, including the satisfaction from doing the job. For a successful entrepreneur, the opportunity cost of being an entrepreneur is likely to be lower than the benefits of owning a business. For an unsuccessful entrepreneur, the opportunity cost is likely to be higher. This is why the unsuccessful entrepreneur is likely to close the business and move on to something else.

Characteristics of entrepreneurs

Starting your own business is very common. Hundreds of

thousands of small businesses are started each year. People give up their jobs to work for themselves or they start a new business alongside a normal full-time job. Not everyone is suited to becoming an entrepreneur either because they lack the skills needed or because they don't want to cope with the risk involved in setting up a business. Business Link, the government agency which encourages business start ups, identifies seven characteristics of successful entrepreneurs.

Self-confidence Successful entrepreneurs are people who believe that they are going to succeed. They think they have a winning formula for their business. They can persuade other people, for example, to buy the product or help finance the business.

Self-determination Successful entrepreneurs are ones who think they can take control of events going on around them. They can influence those events and turn them into something which will benefit their business.

Being a self-starter Many people work best when being told what to do. But to be a successful entrepreneur, you have to be a self-starter. Entrepreneurs are able to work independently and can take decisions. They have their own ideas about how things should be done and they are able to develop those ideas.

Judgment The business environment is changing all the time. A successful entrepreneur is one who is taking in information and listening to advice. At the same time, they are able to see where the business might go in the future and what they want out of the business. This helps them to make judgements and decisions.

Commitment Many people think when starting up a business that it is going to be easier than working for someone else. All the evidence shows that entrepreneurs work longer hours than those with a normal job. Running your own business can sometimes be more stressful because of the risks that are always present. So successful entrepreneurs are ones who are committed to what they do.

Perseverance All businesses have successes and failures. There is always an element of risk that their business could perform poorly or even fail. Therefore, successful entrepreneurs have to show perseverance. They have to be able to get through the bad times and the setbacks.

Initiative Successful entrepreneurs are able to take the initiative in situations. They don't allow events to overwhelm them by doing nothing. They are able to change and be proactive.

Not every successful entrepreneur has all of these characteristics. Few entrepreneurs are strong in every area. But people who run their own businesses tend to show different characteristics from people who work for someone else.

Question 1.

John Baker set up his business after working for an airline. As security manager, he was given an office with a box full of foreign coins collected from the on-board duty free sales of products like whisky and cigarettes. He thought that his airline might not be the only organisation which had boxes full of assorted foreign coins. When he left the airline, he set up his own business, Coin Co International, to collect, sort and cash coins.

His most lucrative years were when the euro was introduced and replaced the currencies of 12 different countries. There were a lot of old currency coins which needed to be exchanged for new euros. In 2001, he collected and exchanged more than 3,500 tonnes of cash and employed 110 people with offices in Germany, Canada and Australia. But this bonanza didn't last and within a couple of years, he had cut his workforce in half and sales were tumbling.

Today he is exploring new lines of business. He has already won contracts to collect the drivers' cash boxes on London buses, sort the coins and then bank them. He would like to win contracts to empty parking meters.

Source: adapted from the *Financial Times*, 7.7.2007.

(a) **An entrepreneur is someone who owns a business, runs it and takes risks. Explain why John Baker is an entrepreneur.**

(b) **Suggest what might have been the opportunity cost for John Baker of setting up his own business.**

(c) **John Baker is thinking of retiring and would like to pass the business on to his two children who already work in the business. (i) Think of ONE possible problem that could occur for the business if he did this. (ii) Compare TWO possible ways round this problem and suggest which would be the best solution to the problem.**

Motives for becoming an entrepreneur

People start their own business for a variety of different reasons.

Financial reward When people work for someone else, there is a limit to what they can expect to get paid. But owning a business gives someone the opportunity to earn much more. In practice, entrepreneurs tend, if anything, to earn less per hour than those in a paid job. Entrepreneurs have to work longer hours to earn their money. But there is always the possibility that you will become the next Richard Branson.

Independence Entrepreneurs tend to enjoy being independent and in control. They prefer to be in charge of their day to day work affairs rather than having an employer telling them what to do. In practice, this independence is limited. Work has to be done. Taxes have to be paid. Those financing the business, like a bank giving a loan, have to kept satisfied that the business is doing well. But those who own their own business, in general, do have more independence than employees working for someone else.

Building a business Entrepreneurs get satisfaction from having built their own business. Creating a successful business is a deeply satisfying experience and can help people to meet higher level goals in life.

Job satisfaction Many entrepreneurs start a business because they think they will get greater job satisfaction by working for themselves. It could be that they prefer working on their own. Or they might be able to change the sort of work they do compared to a normal job.

The product Many entrepreneurs have an interest in what they sell. They are passionate about brewing beer or selling goth clothes or providing high quality care for the elderly.

Different entrepreneurs are motivated by different factors. Some are highly motivated by financial rewards. Others are highly motivated by the job satisfaction they get from running their own business. Equally for some, also, running a business is little different from working for someone else.

Question 2.

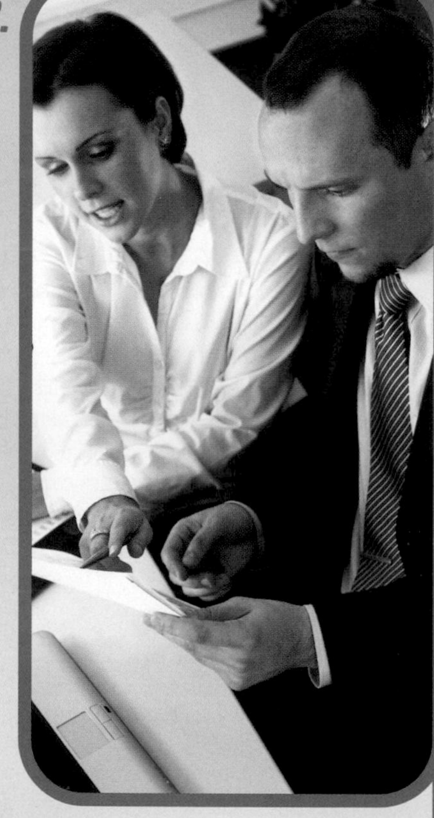

Joshua Roberts has worked for three years as the sales representative for a small print company. It employs ten people and serves the needs of local businesses in a market town and the surrounding rural areas. It prints everything from brochures and posters to invitations, specifications and flyers.

Joshua is ambitious and would like to set up his own business so that he can earn substantially more money. Over the past three years, he has been disappointed with his earnings. He has consistently failed to meet sales targets set for him by the company and so his bonuses have been negligible. In the next market town, there is no print company. By setting up there, he hopes to be able to carve out a profitable market niche.

Joshua's boss couldn't deny that he has enormous self-confidence. He is always talking about what sales he will achieve over the next few weeks and months. When he doesn't win sales contracts, he always picks himself up and gets on with the next job. In his appraisals, however, his boss is constantly pointing out that his timekeeping could improve. He can be late into the office and almost never in the office at closing time. Joshua always says he is seeing a client at that time. A quick check in his diary shows he never makes appointments to see clients outside of office hours. Joshua's boss, Natalie, thinks he tends to only see those clients who he is fairly certain will give him work. Once or twice, she has pointed out that Joshua is not pursuing sufficiently large contracts. He doesn't seem to listen, though, to this constructive criticism.

(a) Do you think Joshua would be successful if he set up his own business? In your answer, consider whether Joshua has the right characteristics to be an entrepreneur.

Government support for enterprise and entrepreneurs

The government promotes the creation of small businesses. It knows that small businesses are vital to the success of the economy. Nearly half of all jobs in the private sector are in small businesses and they produce one third of private sector output. Small businesses are essential for the future success of the economy because many of tomorrow's large businesses will come from today's small businesses. They are also linked to new ideas and new products. They provide an essential competitive dynamism in the economy.

To help new small businesses, the government has set up **Business Link**. Controlled by Regional Development Agencies, different areas of the country have their own Business Link organisation. They provide advice and support to business start-ups and to existing small businesses. They aim to provide a single point of contact on a wide variety of issues from finance and sales to tax and employment.

More generally, the government offers grants and subsidised services through a variety of schemes. For example, new start-ups might be eligible for grants if the entrepreneur is unemployed, or setting up in a rural area. More support is likely to be available in areas where unemployment is relatively high or incomes below the national average.

KEYTERMS

Business or enterprise - an organisation whose principal economic purpose is to produce goods and services.
Entrepreneur - an individual who, typically, sets up and runs a business and takes the risks associated with this.

KNOWLEDGE

1. How many businesses are there in the UK?
2. What is the role of an entrepreneur?
3. Why is profit and risk important for a business?
4. What might be the opportunity cost for you of studying Business Studies?
5. Outline two characteristics of successful entrepreneurs.
6. What might motivate someone thinking of starting up their own business?
7. What support does government give to entrepreneurs?

Case Study: Annabel Karmel Group

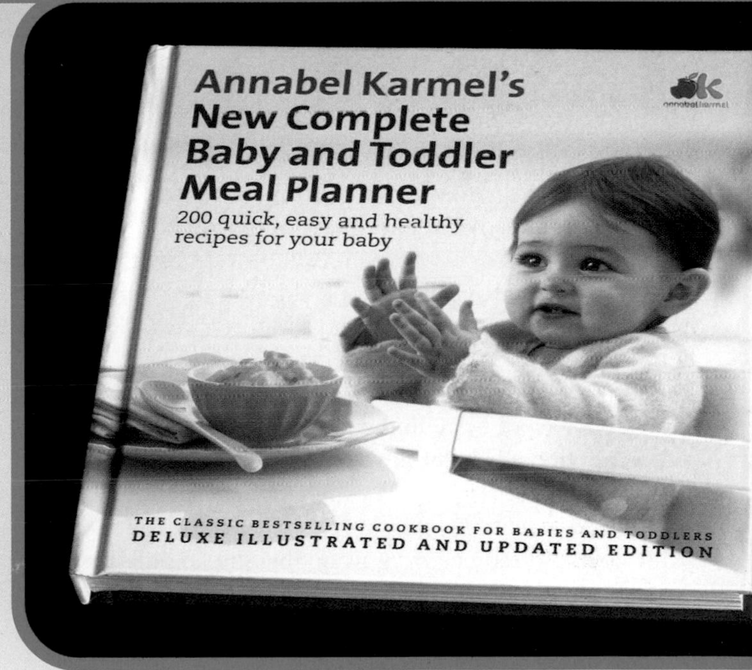

Annabel Karmel is a highly successful entrepreneur. She started her working life as a professional harpist, performing in concerts, appearing on television and recording CDs. She wrote her first book after the death of her first child from a viral infection. Her second child was not eating well and she decided to write a cookery book for feeding children. 'I didn't know anything about it,' said Annabel Karmel.' I didn't even know how to type. But I thought it would be good therapy.' Two and half years later, the book was finished and she sent it to 15 publishers who all turned it down. Then a friend took it to Europe's biggest book fair in Frankfurt and she finally found a publisher to take it on. The book, The Complete Baby and Toddler Meal Planner, has since sold more than 2 million copies. 'You do need luck', she said. 'But you should never give up.' Since then, she has written another 14 books about feeding children.

After her success, she was approached by Boots, the high street chemist chain, to design a range of cookery equipment which could be used to prepare food for children. When the range was a commercial success, this set her thinking about developing a range of ready-prepared meals. 'I was approached by a lot of very large companies to work with them and I think I lost time by talking to them. Eventually I realised that, to begin with, it would be better to do it by myself because I wanted to be in control of what I was doing.'

In 2007, her new range was launched after an investment of £350,000. It is now stocked by J Sainsbury and Ocado. Total sales from her books, meals and cooking equipment are expected to be £14 million in 2008.

'If you have a vision, you have to trust yourself. Don't let other people put you off. And don't be worried about doing something by yourself', said Annabel. 'I was worried about doing a food range by myself. I though I had to have a big company behind me, but actually it has been okay doing it by myself and very rewarding. Sometimes you think that everyone else is an expert and you are not, but if you have a passion, then go with it.' Success has come partly by working long hours. 'I regularly stay up until 3 a.m. just to finish something off. I don't sleep much and I usually work the whole weekend. I gave up my social life for several years.'

Source: adapted from *The Sunday Times*, 20.5.2007.

(a) **'Annabel Karmel is a highly successful entrepreneur.' Explain, using Annabel Karmel as an example, what is meant by an 'entrepreneur'. (15 marks)**

(b) **What might have been the opportunity cost for Annabel Karmel of writing her first book? (5 marks)**

(b) **Analyse what characteristics are likely to be make an entrepreneur successful. In your answer, use Annabel Karmel as an example. (15 marks)**

(c) **To what extent do you think Annabel Karmel has been motivated by the financial rewards of running her own business? (15 marks)**

3 Business ideas

Finding an initial idea

Each year, hundreds of thousands of people set themselves up in business. Instead of working for someone else, they become the owner. Or, they move from owning one business to owning another business. If they are successful, they may start to own and set up a string of businesses. But how do most would-be **entrepreneurs**, (those who risk their own capital in setting up and running a business) find a business idea? There are a number of ways.

Business experience For most people starting a small business, the business idea comes from their existing job. A plumber might work for a plumbing company and decides to set up on her own. A marketing consultant working for an advertising agency sets up his own marketing agency. This is likely to be the most risk free way of setting up a business because the would-be entrepreneur already has knowledge of the market.

Personal experience Some people draw on their personal experience outside of work to find a business idea. Some turn a hobby into a job. An amateur cyclist might buy a cycle shop. A keen gardener might set up a nursery. Some use their customer experience to spot a gap in the market. A mother might find it difficult to find a baby product and so sets up up a business to provide it.

Skills Some entrepreneurs draw on their broad skills base to start a business. A person with an administration job might judge that they have good 'people skills' and decide to set up a business in selling. A plumber might judge that in his area electricians can charge more for their work. So he gets training as an electrician and set himself up as a self employed electrician.

Lifestyle choices Some business areas attract people who want to make a lifestyle change. They might want to move to the country and invest in a small holding. They might always have wanted to run a pub and so buy a pub. Or they might be retiring from a full-time job but still want to carry on working on their own. So they invest in a seasonal Bed and Breakfast (B&B) business.

Identifying a product or market niche

For most entrepreneurs, identifying a broad business idea is relatively easy. But it becomes much more difficult to turn a vague idea into a practical reality. What will be the exact product to be made? What will be the market niche to be occupied?

For example, a painter and decorator setting up on his own may have to decide whether to go mainly for domestic work or for contract work with companies. Will he specialise in indoor work or outdoor work? Someone setting up in the B&B business has to decide whether to go upmarket or downmarket. Do they want to convert their own home into a B&B or will they buy new premises? Will the B&B be aimed mainly at holiday makers or people on business?

The process of identifying an exact product or market niche can take a long time. A process might be used where a lot of different ideas are discussed. Then ones which are worth exploring can be selected and worked on further. Sometimes, would-be entrepreneurs start out with an initial idea. As they explore it further, they realise it won't work but something very similar might be better. A whole range of options might be explored as each idea is considered, rejected but opens up a further idea.

Question 1.

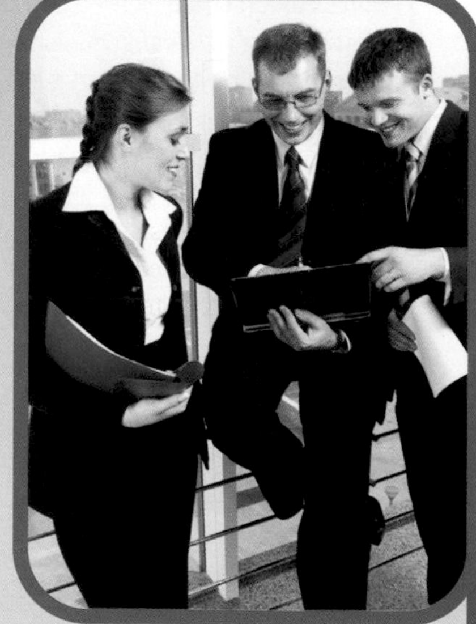

Claire Brynteson is an entrepreneur who found the right idea. She was working in a high powered job in the City of London. She noticed that there were plenty of people around her earning very large salaries but worked such long hours that they didn't have the time to organise the ordinary, everyday things in life. So she founded Buy Time, a lifestyle management service for businesses and individuals.

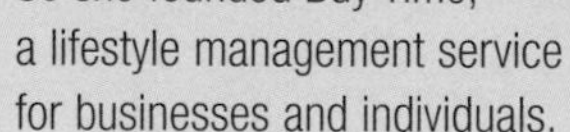

The business gives clients access to a personal assistant. The personal assistant will do everything from organising a parking permit, to getting broadband connected, to buying flowers for a partner, to getting a leaking tap fixed to organising a foreign holiday. The current 300 customers of Buy Time are either individuals or businesses which buy the service on behalf of their top employees. It employs 12 staff.

Claire Brynteson said: 'I could see that people round me were suffering from a lack of time and really needed this service. With women increasingly working the same hours as men, there was nobody at home to take care of anything.'

Source: adapted from *The Sunday Times*, 20.7.2007.

(a) How did Claire Brynteson get the idea for her business?

(b) Business Link sets out a number of criteria for checking against a possible business idea (see top of page 13). How well does Claire Brynteson's idea do when compared to this list of criteria?

Business Link, the government organisation set up to help small businesses, suggests that each business idea needs to be checked out against a number of criteria.

- What can the would-be entrepreneur bring to the business in terms of relevant experience and expertise?
- Is there a market for the product? Does it serve a need and will customers will pay for it?
- How big is the market and how can it be reached?
- What will be the main competitors in the market?
- Is there something special about the idea? Or will it be a similar product to what is already in the market place?
- How will the business be funded?
- What are the risks involved and what can go wrong?

Franchises

Starting up your own business carries a lot of risk. Most new start-ups have ceased to exist after five years of trading. One way of possibly reducing this risk is to buy a FRANCHISE. The **franchisor** is a company which owns the franchise. It has a track record of running a successful business operation. It allows another business, the **franchisee**, to use its business ideas and methods in return for a variety of fees. In the UK, there are a large number of franchise operations including Dairy Crest, Domino's Pizza, Dyno-Rod, McDonald's, Subway and Tumble Tots.

The franchisor provides a variety of services to its franchisees.

- Its gives the franchisee a licence to make a product which is already tried and tested in the market place. This could be a physical product but is far more likely to be a service.
- The franchisor provides a recognised brand name which customers should recognise and trust. This helps generate sales from the moment the franchise starts trading.
- The franchisor will provide a start-up package. This will include help and advice about setting up the business. The franchisor might provide the equipment to start the business. It might help find a bank which will lend money. It will provide training for the new franchisee.
- Many franchises provide materials to use to make the product. A company like McDonald's, for examples, sells food ingredients to its franchisees. If the franchisor doesn't directly sell to the franchisee, it might organise bulk-buy deals with suppliers to cut costs for all its franchise operation.
- It is likely to provide marketing support. For example, it might have national advertising campaigns. It may provide marketing materials like posters to place in business premises or leaflets to circulate to customers.
- There should be ongoing training. This will be linked to issues such as maintaining standards, sales and new products.
- There is likely to be a range of business services available at competitive prices. For example, the franchisor might negotiate good deals on business insurance or vehicle leasing with suppliers.
- Many franchises operate exclusive area contracts. This is where one franchisee is guaranteed that no franchise deal will be signed with another franchisee to operate in a particular geographical area. This prevents competition between franchisees and so helps sales.
- Over time, the brand should be developed by the franchisor. For example, new products should be developed to appeal to customers.

In return for these services, the franchisee has to pay a variety of fees.

- There will be an initial start-up fee. Part of this will cover the costs of the franchisor in giving advice or perhaps providing equipment. Part of it will be a payment to use the franchise name.
- Most franchisors charge a percentage of sales for ongoing management services and the ongoing right to use the brand name.
- Franchisors will also make profit on the supplies they sell directly to their franchisors.
- There may also be one-off fees charged for management services such as training.

The benefits and costs for franchisors and franchisees

There are a variety of benefits and costs to both franchisors and franchisees of the franchise model.

Benefits to franchisees For the franchisee, franchising could be a relatively safe way to start a business. Partly this is because the franchisor has vetted potential franchisees and rejected applications from individuals it thinks will fail. Partly this is because the franchise already has a successful business formula which has succeeded in the past. So the new franchisee only has to copy the performance of others. The cost of setting up the franchise is predictable. Too many start-ups have grossly over-optimistic forecasts of how little they can spend to get the business up and running on a sound financial footing. The franchisor also provides ongoing support and will provide help to franchisees which are underperforming.

Costs to franchisees Franchisees have to pay a variety of fees to the franchisor. These costs vary from franchise to franchise but franchisees are likely to lose at least 10 per cent of their revenues. This can have a significant impact on profit margins. Franchisees are locked into contracts. If they fail to keep to the contract, they can lose the franchise and as a result lose most, if not all, of their investment in the business. In some cases, contracts allow franchisors to take away a franchise without any compensation simply because it is in their commercial interests to do so.

Benefits to franchisors Many businesses are highly successful. But they find it difficult to expand because of finance and control. Finance is a problem because banks are not always

Question 2.

Domino's Pizza is a highly successful worldwide franchise operation. It provides a pizza delivery service, taking pizzas to your door. In the UK, in 2008 it had over 500 outlets owned by franchisees.

According to www.whichfranchise.com, franchisees pay a royalty to the franchisor of 5.5 per cent on sales plus 5 per cent of sales to pay into a national advertising fund. The minimum initial investment to open a single store for a franchisee is £240,000 + VAT. However, for this initial investment, Domino's Pizza provides all the equipment needed and finds premises. New franchisees are given three weeks initial training (the Franchise Development Programme) and further training on an ongoing basis. The brand is supported by national advertising campaigns. In recent years, this has included sponsoring The Simpsons on television. Franchisees are monitored for quality of service by the franchisor.

Antony Tagliamonti is a franchisee who now owns three outlets. He says: 'I never get bored and, even after ten years, I am still finding new ways of operating, recruiting team members, increasing sales and pushing the business forward.'

With information from www.franchise.com; www.thebfa.org.

(a What is the difference between a franchisor and a franchisee?

(b) What might be the advantages and disadvantages to an entrepreneur of buying a Domino's Pizza franchise rather than setting up their own pizza delivery service?

(c) What might be the advantages to the American company which owns the Domino's Pizza franchise of using a business franchise model?

prepared to lend for growth. Even if they do, it might be too little money to take the business in the right direction. Control is a problem because employees don't necessarily have the same motivation for success as the entrepreneur who founded the business. A franchise model is one way of getting round these problems. Finance for growth comes from franchisees who pay most of the cost of expanding the business. Franchisees also have the motivation to succeed. The franchisor is harnessing the skills and enthusiasm of another entrepreneur, the franchisee. Another benefit to the franchisor is that it reduces risks from failure. If the franchise proves a failure, much of the cost is borne by the franchisee rather than the franchisor.

Costs to franchisors In successful franchises, some of the profit goes to the franchisee. The franchisor, therefore, might have been better off with a traditional business expansion model rather than turning the business into a franchise operation. Running a franchise can increase costs because franchisees have to be supported in various ways. Franchisees can also be a problem. Some franchisees will fail to work hard enough or show sufficient business skills. Their franchises will underperform or fail and this will hit the profits of the franchisor. Other franchisees will not operate according to the franchise formula. For example, if it is a fast food franchise, some franchisees might cut costs by not cleaning the premises sufficiently and not keep the furniture and decor in good condition. This could tarnish the brand image of the whole chain of franchises.

Franchising associations claim that franchising is a much safer business model for an entrepreneur than opening their own business. They claim the failure rate for franchisees is much lower than for other business start-ups. Some academic research, however, suggests that franchisees, if anything, are more likely to fail than if they set up independently. This is mainly because the cost base of franchisees is higher since they have to pay a percentage of their sales to the franchisor. Successful franchises are ones where being a franchisee generates substantially more sales than if the business were independent.

Trademarks, copyright and patents

Every business has a name which is crucial to its business success. If another business starts using your business name to sell the same goods or services in the same markets, then you may be able to sue them and stop them using your business name. Businesses can further protect their name, or the names of their products, by registering them as a TRADE MARK. In the UK, this is done by registering them with the Intellectual Property Office (UK-IPO). Other businesses are then not allowed in law to use that trademark name. Trade mark protection can also be applied to signs, symbols, logos, words, sounds or music.

Business start-ups should also think about whether they want an Internet domain name (i.e. a web address). Unique domain names can be registered so that no one else can use that address. For example, no one can use www.tesco.com because it has already been registered by Tesco, the supermarket chain. Common popular names are likely to have been taken already. So a start-up business might have to use a less obvious name for their web address.

A small number of business start-ups are linked to selling a new, innovative product which can be protected through copyright and patents. COPYRIGHT is given for original artistic works such as music, films, photographs, plays and books. PATENTS are given for inventions. Both copyrights and patents have to be registered with the Intellectual Property Office.

Trademarks, copyrights and patents aren't just there to protect a business from others copying their ideas. They can be

KEYTERMS

Copyright – legal ownership of material such as books, music and films which prevents these being copied by others.

Franchise – an agreement where a business (the franchisor) sells the rights to other businesses (the francisees) allowing them to sell their products or use the company name.

Patents – right of ownership of an invention or process granted by government for a fixed period of time to the individual or business which registers the original invention or process.

Trade mark – signs, symbols, logos, words, sounds or music that distinguish the products and services of one business from those of competitors.

used to generate income by **licensing** them to other businesses. These other businesses then pay **royalties** to copy the idea legally. Businesses can also generate income from their intellectual property by selling it. So the rights to a song, for example, can be sold by one record company to another record company. The patent on a new drug can be sold by one pharmaceutical company to another pharmaceutical company.

KNOWLEDGE

1. How might would-be entrepreneurs find a business idea?
2. What criteria might an entrepreneur use to judge whether an idea can be turned into a successful business?
3. Explain what a franchisee and a franchisor might gain from a franchising arrangement.
4. Explain what a franchisee and a franchisor might lose from a franchising arrangement.
5. What is the difference between a trade mark, copyright and a patent?

Case Study: Business ideas

The Rolla Washa

A Wolverhampton firm, Washa Ltd, has developed a revolutionary new device for cleaning paint rollers. The Rolla Washa is 'designed to save users time, effort and water' according to Brett Smart, Wash's managing director. Rollers, rather than paint brushes, are used by painters and decorators for walls and ceilings. But rollers take time to clean properly and normal cleaning takes a lot of water. The Rolla Washa is a plastic container into which rollers are put for cleaning. Water mains pressure cleans dirty rollers quickly and easily. Far less water is used making it environmentally friendly.

The Rolla Wash is a now it its final stage of development and a patent has been applied for. It is currently on trial with two of Europe's leading paint manufacturers for their endorsement.

Business advisors have put a potential value on Washa Ltd of £2.5 million assuming the invention takes off.

Source: adapted from the *Express & Star*, 18.6.2007.

Red Star Natural Liquid Soaps

A Staffordshire couple, who started their business in their kitchen, are looking to sell their products globally. After two years of formulating and selling handmade soap in their spare time, Tim and Elaine Woodley launched their business product in 2004. Red Star soaps are made using cruelty and animal product free soaps. 'We're determined to make soaps from scratch using the original, constituent natural ingredients that contain no animal products and involve no animal testing,' said Tim.

The Red Star range includes liquid soap products for people, dogs and most recently, horses. 'The jewel in our crown is the new Red Star Pony Polish,' said Tim. 'It's the only horse shampoo on the market that's both natural and free from animal products and we worked with horse owners around the country to make sure it's right.'

The soaps are mainly sold online direct to customers, but the business is steadily building a distributor network both in the UK and overseas with products regularly exported to Europe and the Americas. They are even talking to the camel racing community in Arabic countries to develop a specialist shampoo for camels.

Business Link West Midlands, the government agency, have helped Tim and Elaine to develop their business model. It has ensured that steps were taken to protect intellectual property, including the business name and logo.

Source: adapted from the *Express & Star*, 18.6.2007.

(a) What is distinctive about the products described in the data which might make them stand out against competing products? (5 marks)

(b) Explain how the developers of each idea might have checked that their innovate product could be turned into a successful business. (10 marks)

(c) What is meant by 'intellectual property'? (10 marks)

(d) To what extent was it important for both businesses to protect their intellectual property? (15 marks)

4 Business plans

Why write a business plan?

Research shows that start-up businesses which have prepared a BUSINESS PLAN are more likely to survive than ones which have not. The business plan is a plan of how the business will develop over a period of time, like one or two years. Writing a business plan is important for a potential start-up business for three main reasons.

- Writing the plan forces the would-be entrepreneur to look at every key aspect of the future business. It is easy to concentrate on some aspects of running a business, like the product to be sold or its location. Most start-ups have some idea about what might give the business a **competitive advantage** against other businesses But other aspects are often not thought out well, such as finance or tax. The business plan forces the entrepreneur to consider every aspect equally.
- If the business is to borrow money from a bank, it will expect there to be a business plan. It uses the business plan to judge whether the business is likely to be creditworthy.
- The plan is useful once the business has started to trade. The actual operation of the business can be compared to the forecasts contained in the plans. This will highlight problems that are occurring. The business owner can then take steps to overcome the problem.

The contents of a business plan

The outline of a business plan can be obtained from any of the major banks in leaflets they produce on starting up a business. They give a very detailed list of points which must be addressed in the plan. These include the following.

An executive summary - this is an overview of the business start-up. It describes briefly the business opportunity to be exploited, the marketing and sales strategy, operations and then finance. According to the government organisation, Business Link, many lenders and investors make judgements about the business on this section alone.

The business and its objectives - the name of the business, its address, its legal structure and is aims and objectives.

The business opportunity - a description of the product or range of products to be made, the quantity to be sold and the estimated price;

The market - the size of the potential market and a description of the potential customers, the nature of the competition, marketing priorities, all backed up with evidence from market research.

Personnel - who will run the business, how many employees if any there will be, the skills, qualifications and experience of those in the business.

Buying and production - where the business will buy its supplies, production methods to be used, the cost of production.

Premises and equipment - the premises to be used, equipment which needs to be obtained and financed.

Financial forecasts - a variety of financial forecasts need to be included. They include a **sales forecast** showing how the value of sales will change over time; a **cash flow forecast** which shows how money will move into and out of the business on a week to week or month to month basis; a **profit and loss forecast**, showing when the business might move from making a loss to making a profit and how big a profit; and a **break-even analysis**, showing at what level of sales the business will make zero profits or losses.

Question 1.

Robert Crampton is a journalist who had a great idea for a business. He called it the Bobstacle: a soft play area, a cross between an obstacle course and an assault course with slides, trapezes and nets. It would aimed not just at children but at teenagers and adults too.

He took his idea to the television cult show, Dragons' Den. On this show, five multimillionaires who have already successfully run their own businesses, act as a panel. Would-be entrepreneurs have to 'pitch' their ideas. If any one of the multimillionaires likes the idea, then they say they are prepared to put their own money into the start-up and help it become established.

The panel of multimillionaires quickly punched huge holes in Robert Crampton's business plan. Robert hadn't thought through his future sales or costs. He found it difficult to state accurately how any money put into the business at the start would be spent. He hadn't thought through how many staff he would need, let alone what qualities he would be looked for in them. He also hadn't thought through what would be his competitive advantage.

By the end of the interview, Robert was thinking to himself that he still liked the idea of the Bobstacle. The adventure and the risk were attractive as would be the profits. But he wouldn't want to work there himself. At that point, he gave up on any dream of becoming an entrepreneur. Perhaps a career in journalism was attractive after all.

Source: with information from *The Times*, 3.2.2007.

(a) What is the advantage for a would-be entrepreneur, like Robert Crampton, to write a business plan? Use the passage to help you write your answer.

(b) Is it a waste of time of time to write a business plan when afterwards you decide not to go ahead with the business idea?

Finance - where the finance to start-up and run the business will come from, including savings of owners and borrowing.

Sources of information and guidance

Entrepreneurs setting up a business can turn to a wide variety of sources of help.

Friends, family and work colleagues Initially, would-be entrepreneurs are likely to talk about their ideas to friends, family and work colleagues. They may just provide common sense advice. But some could have specialist business knowledge. They might have started up a business themselves in the past. They might be running a successful business now. Networking, talking to a wide variety of individuals or organisations, will generate ideas and identify obstacles to be overcome.

Bank managers All the major banks offer banking services to start-up businesses including loans. They have specialist teams of advisors who assess applications for loans from those wanting to start a new business. They will give advice about preparing a business plan and identify strengths and weaknesses in the plan. Their aim is to lend to a start-up which will be strong enough financially to repay any loans taken out.

Accountants There are many accountancy firms which specialise in preparing the accounts for small and medium sized businesses. They will sell advice to start-up businesses. They will be particularly good at providing advice on the finance side of the business.

Small business advisors Would-be entrepreneurs can buy advice from a wide range of small business advisors. They will help with everything from writing a business plan, to market research to recruiting workers.

Business Link The government provides help and advice to small businesses through Business Link. Each region in the UK has its own Business Link organisation. They provide a wide range of written resources, including a website. They also have business advisors who will provide help on a one-to-one basis. They run seminars and courses for would-be entrepreneurs. They also provide advice as the business grows. For the most part, these services are free.

Local Enterprise Agencies These are non-for-profit companies whose primary objective is to help new and growing businesses. Like Business Link, they provide a wide variety of resources and help to business start-ups including consultancy and training. Their funds come mainly from local authorities and other bodies.

Question 2.

Tahira Hussein wants to open her own beauty salon which would offer a range of beauty treatments. She is in the process of drawing up a business plan and has just written down her objectives. These are as follows.

Objectives

1. By the third month of opening, to have sales of £25 000 per month offering 20 treatments per day.
2. By the sixth month of opening, to have sales of £40 000 per month offering 32 treatments per day.
3. By the end of 12 months, to have sales of £50 000 per month offering 40 treatments per day.
4. At the end of 12 months, to have 80 per cent of clients as repeat clients and 20 per cent as new clients.
5. By the end of 12 months, to be making a profit before tax of £1 000 per month.
6. By the end of 3 years to be in a position to open a second beauty salon.

(a) List six other items that might be found in a business plan apart from objectives.

(b) Suggest why it might be important to list business objectives in a business plan for a start-up company.

The Prince's Trust and Shell LiveWIRE The Prince's Trust and Shell LiveWIRE are two organisations which provide help to young people starting up in business. They will not only provide advice, but they will also give limited financial support for new businesses.

KEYTERMS

Business plan - a plan for the development of a business, giving details such as the products to be made and sold and forecasts such as costs and cash flow.

KNOWLEDGE

1. 'Writing a business plan helps identify the problems with a business idea.' Explain what this means.
2. What might be contained in the part of a business plan which deals with personnel for a start-up (a) restaurant; (b) local grocery store; (c) biological research company?
3. Where could a would-be entrepreneur find advice in writing a business plan which (a) would be free of charge; (b) would have to be paid for.

Case Study: AKC Home Support

Darren Jones launched his care business, AKC Home Support Services, in 1991 with his wife Sharron. One of the first things they did was to write a business plan. But they saw it more as just one more form to fill in. 'When we started the firm, I knew we needed a business plan but saw it more as a document for everyone else than something to help us.'

They got help to write the business plan from their local enterprise centre. 'We looked at examples from other businesses and a template from the bank. We mixed and matched bits from these sources because not everything applied to us. For example, because we were going into a new market, we couldn't write about our competitors but needed a lot of information about the market for care services.'

The business plan contained their financial and strategic goals - what they wanted to achieve with the business. This helped them early on when they were offered work in another county. Looking at their business plan, they realised that they could get into short-term financial difficulties if they took on too much work. This was because they would have to pay out costs like wages months before they themselves might get paid by the client.

They regularly update their business plan. This helped them four years ago when they wanted a loan from the bank to buy a residential unit care home. Carefully working out how the loan could be repaid from the extra revenues coming into the business impressed the bank.

Their business plans also helped them get support from Shell LiveWIRE. They were awarded prizes twice which brought into both publicity for the business and extra money. Their business plan essential because you have to have a business plan to enter the competition.

Their advice when drawing up a business plan is to get as much help and advice as possible. 'Show the plan to an independent third party - such as friends or family who have run their own businesses - who will be able to point out if anything is missing. It's much better to make mistakes on a practice run than when it really matters.'

Source: adapted from www.businesslink.gov.uk.

(a) Explain, using AKC Home Support Services as an example, what might be contained in a business plan. (15 marks)

(b) How might outside organisations help a would-be entrepreneur write a business plan? (10 marks)

(c) 'Writing a business plan is a waste of time. You are better off starting your business as quickly as possible.' To what extent do you think this is correct? Use AKC Home Support Services as an example in your discussion. (15 marks)

5 Evaluating business starts-ups

Success or failure?

Most business start-ups will have ceased to trade after five years. Starting your own business is therefore risky and the chances are that the business will not be successful enough to be worth running in the long term.

'Success' for a start-up is likely to be made up of a number of factors.

- The business generates enough profits to make it attractive for the entrepreneur to continue trading. It is not just that the business has to at least break-even. The entrepreneur could be earning money elsewhere, for example in a paid job. The financial reward from trading must be enough to prevent the entrepreneur from giving up and doing something else.
- The satisfaction gained from running a business must be greater than realistic alternatives. Some people enjoy the independence and control that running a business gives. They like being their own boss and building a business. Others find these aspects too challenging. They prefer the security that an ordinary paid job gives. Businesses may be financially successful but entrepreneurs may still close them down because they don't enjoy running their own business.
- The entrepreneur must be comfortable with the risk involved in running a business. All economic activity has an element of risk. If you have a paid job, you could be made redundant tomorrow. However, starting a business is likely to carry greater risks than working for someone else. There is so much more that could go wrong: sales might be disappointing, costs might be higher than predicted or banks may refuse to provide loan finance at a crucial point. Some entrepreneurs find that that they are uncomfortable with the amount of risk they have taken on. They close the business and decide to go back to a lower risk environment by getting a paid job.

It is very important to remember that many start-ups are very small scale and run on a part-time basis. Parents staying at home to care for young children might start a small business needing just a few hours a day to run. Or a worker might start a business on top of their ordinary every day job. It should also be understood that running your own business is far more common in some industries than in others. Agriculture, retailing and professional services are examples.

Why businesses fail

Some businesses are successful in the long run. Others are not successful enough for the entrepreneur to continue running the business. Other businesses fail financially. There are a number of possible reasons for financial failure.

Lower than expected revenues Many start-ups don't generate enough sales revenues. Either they don't sell enough or the price they get for what they sell is too low. For example, in its business plan, a hairdressing salon might have predicted that it would have 150 customers a week each paying on average £20. Its sales revenue was therefore predicted at £3,000 per week. By the end of its first year, the salon is only attracting 100 customers a week each paying on average £15. Sales revenue is therefore only £1,500, half of what was predicted. If revenues are too low, the business could make a loss which would lead to its failure. Or it may make insufficient profit for the entrepreneur to want to carry on in business. For example, the owner of the hairdressing salon might make £10,000 a year from the business. But if she could make £20,000 a year working for someone else, there would be a strong financial incentive for her to close her business and go back to an ordinary paid job.

Higher than expected start-up costs The majority of start-ups underestimate the cost of the start-up. For example, for a new restaurant, the cost of fitting out a building is likely to be higher than expected. Or an entrepreneur setting up a recruitment agency might underestimate the amount of time needed to comply with regulations. Some entrepreneurs simply run out of money at this stage and the start-up fails to get off the ground. Most will find extra money often by borrowing more from the bank. But then they have higher than expected loan repayments to make. If their revenues aren't high enough to cover these, the business will fail.

Higher than expected operating costs Many business plans underestimate the day-to-day running costs of the business. Sometimes this is because costs are simply not included in the business plan. More often, it is because actual costs are higher than predicted costs. If costs are too high, profits will be too low or the business might make a loss. In the long term, this is likely to lead to the closure of the business.

Unexpected shocks Some businesses fail because of unexpected shocks. In 1988, for example, the UK was experiencing an economic boom. The government was encouraging people to set up their own businesses. Within two years, the economy was in recession. Unemployment doubled, interest rates doubled and house prices fell. Not surprisingly, many new start-ups failed too because they couldn't generate enough sales to survive. Also their cost of borrowing was substantially more than they had expected. Another example of an unexpected shock is flooding. In recent years, a number of areas of the UK have experienced unexpected flooding. Some businesses have failed as a result. They have lost orders and equipment. Some have been uninsured and haven't had the financial capital to be able to restart.

Reliance on a few large customers Small businesses are

Question 1.

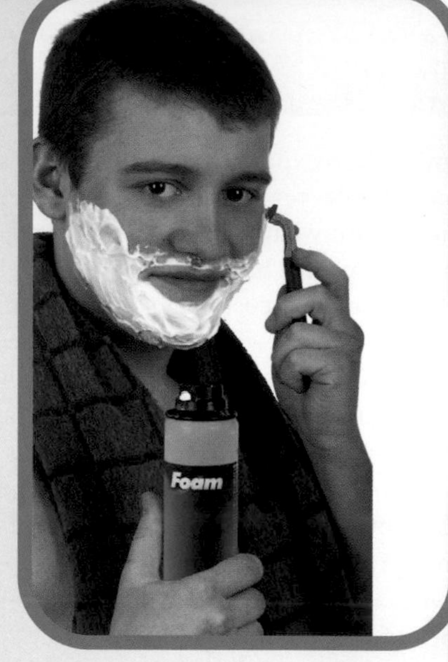

Drawing up a business plan is no guarantee of success as Chris Watkins found out. Chris Watkins was the production manager for a firm which produced mainly own label toiletries for some of the big supermarket groups. It was in a competitve market and profit margins were wafer thin. Chris was continually being asked to cut costs at the factory or risk facing redundancy along with the rest of the production staff. He decided that he had had enough and would start his own business manufacturing toiletries. His business idea was that he would go up-market to avoid price competition. He would sell mainly to smaller stores and avoid dealing with the major supermarket chains.

He did some market research, contacting a number of small local stores, and they all said that they would definitely be interested in buying his products. He produced samples and did some costings based on buying some second-hand equipment and renting a unit on an industrial estate. The financial figures looked good and there was a substantial margin between revenues and costs, even in the first year of operation. But he had trouble borrowing the £100,000 he needed as start-up capital. Three banks refused him an ordinary business loan saying that his business plan was weak. In the end, he remortgaged his house for the £100,000 he needed.

He was full of hope when he started operations. He had some small orders for his products but he intended to launch his real marketing campaign once he had sorted out production. The problem was that the marketing campaign was a disaster. He ended up with four weeks of unsold stock and no cash left to continue. He was forced to close the business.

(a) Explain three reasons for the failure of Chris Watkins' business.

(b) 'The most important reason why the business failed was the weak business plan.' To what extent to do you agree with this?

vulnerable if they rely on just a few customers for most of their orders. For example, a new start-up business may have landed a contract which accounts for 40 per cent of its orders. It borrows a substantial amount of money to buy equipment to fulfill the contract. Then, suddenly, the customers cancels the contract. Forty per cent of sales immediately have gone. But the repayments on the loans for the equipment have to be kept up. In these circumstances, a new business start-up can go from being profitable to being loss making and subsequently fail.

Operational problems Some start-ups fail because of operational problems. For example, a business may suddenly find it very difficult to find supplies. Perhaps an existing supplier discontinues a product and the start-up business then can't find an alternative supplier. Or it takes much longer to do a job than expected.

Cash flow problems Cash flow through a business is the difference between the money coming in and the money going out on a day-to-day, month to month basis. Start-ups can be profitable but fail because of cash flow problems. One reason for this is the system of credit operated by businesses. When a business sells to another business, it typically has to give at least 30 days' credit. So it won't get paid for 30 days after the work has been completed. Even then, many businesses pay late. So it could be 60 days or 90 days before the start-up business is paid. On the other hand, many costs have to be paid now. Rents, loan repayments, cost of supplies and wages have to be paid on a regular basis. A start-up can simply run out of cash and then fail.

Lack of profitability Some start-ups fail because they are loss making. They make a loss on their day-to-day operations and on top of that the entrepreneur will have spent money on starting up the business. Entrepreneurs can lose tens of thousands of pounds if not more on a new business venture. Some have mortgaged their houses to raise the money to start the business and are forced to sell the house to repay the debts. Most start-ups, however, cease trading because they are not sufficiently profitable. Running your own business has many advantages. But most entrepreneurs work much longer hours running their own business than they would if they were in a normal paid job. If then they are getting much less financially from their business than they would as a wage, they are likely to give up their business. Entrepreneurs have to weigh up the **opportunity cost**, the benefits from their next best activity, of running their own business. If the opportunity cost is too high, because they could be earning £30,000 a year in a job but the profits on their business are only £3,000 a year, then they are likely to close down their business.

Strengths and weaknesses of a business plan

Research evidence shows that business planning is crucial to the success or failure of a start-up business. A good business plan is one which has three characteristics.

- It is comprehensive and has been well researched. It covers all aspects of the business and each aspect has been explored thoroughly.
- It is realistic. The objectives of the business must be realistic. So too must the assumptions built into the plan. One key reason why business start-ups fail is because the would-be entrepreneur is far too optimistic about sales, costs and profits. It is very easy to get carried away with an idea and overestimate sales or underestimate costs.
- It is coherent. So one part of the business plan must fit with another part of the plan. For example, a would-be entrepreneur might develop a business plan for football coaching for 5-11 year olds. If one part of the business plan says that there will be 40 children attending between

10 and 11 o'clock on a Saturday morning, but another part of the business plan states that he will not be employing anyone to help him, then the business plan is not coherent. One person legally cannot look after 40 children.

Weak business plans are over-optimistic, poorly researched and not properly thought through. Many start-ups, particularly when the business is small and is operated on a part-time basis, have never had a business plan. Where the business is very simple, and there are few costs and revenues, this probably won't matter. But effective business planning helps sort out complex issues. It allows the owner to align the goals of the business with its operations. It considerably reduces the risk of failure because potential problems and opportunities have been identified.

KNOWLEDGE

1. Why might the owner of a business decide to close it despite the fact that it is making a profit?
2. Explain two sources of risk for a start-up business.
3. 'The typical business start-up is a company where owners work full time and inject large amounts of their own money with the aim of rapidly becoming the next Richard Branson'. Explain whether this is true.
4. A business can fail because sales are lower than expected or costs are higher than expected. Explain why.
5. Business failure can sometimes occur because of unexpected events. Give two examples of such events and explain why they might force a business to cease trading.

Case Study: RD Servicing and Repairs

Rosie and Dean Spencer have just finished their first year of trading and it has been an unimaginable success. Dean worked for 20 years as a driver and then a mechanic of HGVs (heavy goods vehicles). Rosie had worked in the same garage as a car mechanic. For a long time, they felt that the business they worked for was inefficient. It didn't seem to care about its customers. Prices were high and the quality of workmanship was not always very good. Two years ago, they decided they wanted to set up on their own. Their business idea was to offer a better quality of service at lower prices than other firms in the area.

They spent a year drawing up their business plan. Two of their financial objectives were for sales revenue to be £200,000 in their first year and for the business to break even after Rosie and Dean had been paid a salary of £20,000 each. A third objective was to get an overdraft facility of £10,000 and a bank loan of £50,000 to cover start-up costs.

Having resigned from their jobs where between them they were earning £50 a year, they started operations. The first year of operation was hectic. The first month, Rosie and Dean spent a great deal of time marketing their new HGV maintenance and repairs service to local customers. Then, as the work built up, over the next couple of months, Dean was forced to spend all his time as the mechanic. The business plan anticipated that the company would have to take on two more mechanics at the end of the sixth month of operation. In fact, he had to take on three mechanics. By the end of the twelfth month they were employing thirteen staff, including seven mechanics. By that stage, the first year's sales turnover was £370,000.

However, this growth had not been without its problems. Half way through the year, it became apparent that they were running out of cash. Bills were having to be paid faster than customers were paying their invoices. The £10,000 overdraft was going to be breached. What's more, customers were asking for services which needed equipment the business didn't have. They went back to the bank to ask for £30,000 in loans, but the bank refused them saying they were too risky at this stage. They then turned to a local government funded business development agency which stepped in with the £30,000 loan. The crisis was averted, but only just.

Another major problem occurred when they had to move premises after six months. Because of their unexpected expansion, they found their initial premises on an industrial estate were too small. They arranged to move to larger premises on the same industrial estate. On the Friday night before they were due to move on the Saturday, vandals burnt down the industrial unit they were to occupy. Equipment had been packed and three working days cleared of all appointments. The move had to be put back by two months until another industrial unit became available. Not only was time lost, but customers had to wait longer for an available appointment and it took more time to do the work because of the lack of space.

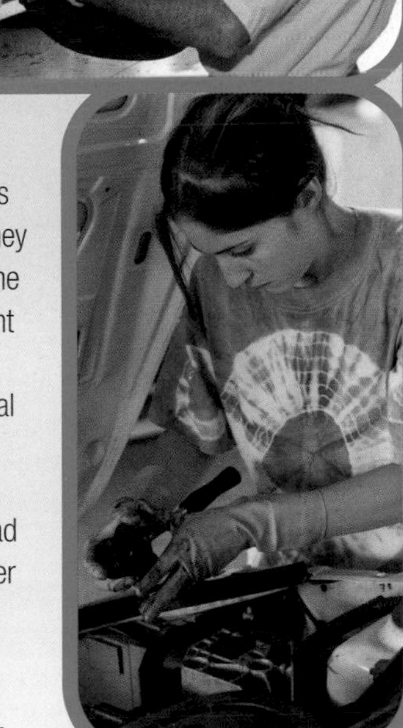

(a) Briefly explain why drawing up a business plan is important for a business start-up. (10 marks)

(b) Evaluate the risks that Rosie and Dean Spencer took in starting their business. (15 marks)

(c) 'Rosie and Dean's business plan was poor because it failed to identify how quickly the business would grow and the risks that it might face.' To what extent do you agree with this statement? (15 marks)

6 Stakeholders

Stakeholder perspectives

Businesses vary from very simple organisations where there is only one person working in the business to very complex organisations spanning five continents and with hundreds of thousands of employees. Businesses also operate in an **external environment**. They have to deal with customers, suppliers and governments for example.

STAKEHOLDERS in a business are any individual or group which is affected by the business and so has an interest in its activities. The main stakeholders in a business, shown in Figure 1, are likely to be the owners (the shareholders, in the case of a company), managers and directors in a company, the employees, the customers, the suppliers and local communities politically represented by local government. Large businesses may impact on national communities represented by central government, and international communities represented by a variety of organisations such as the United Nations. Environmental issues also point to other animals and plants possibly being stakeholders as well as future generations of human beings. **Stakeholder perspectives** (i.e. how each of these groups of stakeholders might view a business) will now be considered in turn.

The owners of a business The owners of a business are stakeholders because they have put up the capital which runs the business. Their reward is the gain they make from owning the business. In a company, this is a mix of their share of the profits made and the capital gain from any increase in the value of shares (the **shareholder value**). With a sole trader and partnership, it is a mix of the drawings from the business (part wage, part profit) together with any increase in value of business assets, such as shop or factory premises. If owners were unable to get any reward for investing in the business, no one would bother to invest. So owners are vital to the workings of a market economy. Without owners, the whole capitalist economic system in the western world would collapse.

Figure 1: Stakeholders in business

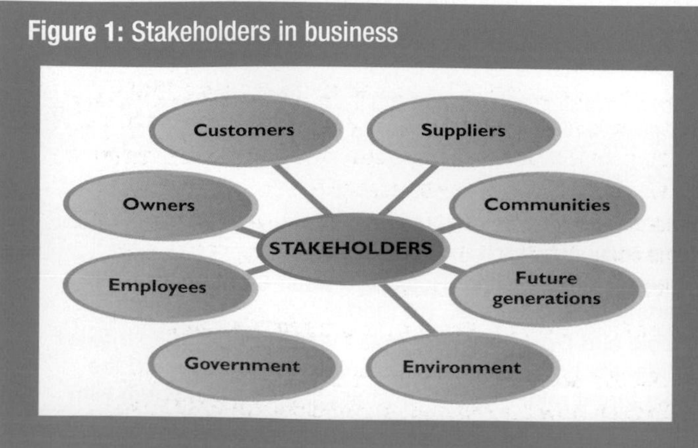

Directors and senior managers In a small business, the owner or owners are likely to run the business on a day-to-day business. But the larger the business, the more likely it is that owners will appoint managers to do this. In a company, there will be a board of directors, some of whom will be the senior managers in the company (called **executive directors**) and others who will have nothing to do with the day-to-day running of the business (called **non-executive directors**). The board of directors will be responsible for corporate strategy. The executive directors, the senior managers of the company, are stakeholders because how the business performs has a direct impact on them. If it performs poorly, they could be made redundant. If it performs well, they might be rewarded with higher salaries, promotion or bonuses.

Workers Employees from middle management downwards have a stake in the business for which they work. For example, the business pays them a wage on which they have to live. It might also give them a variety of **fringe benefits** such as pensions. Job security is important because workers have bills to pay in the future such as a mortgage. Jobs can give workers satisfaction and a sense of self worth. The success of the business is important to employees. If the business is performing poorly, they may lose their jobs. A successful business in one where there are likely to be more opportunities for promotion and for gaining pay rises.

Customers Customers are important stakeholders in the business. On the one hand, businesses need customers to survive. Without customers there would be no sales and no revenues coming into the business. The business then could not buy the factors of production needed to make goods and services. On the other hand, customers need businesses because they want to buy goods and services. Businesses provide them with the food they eat, the houses they live in and the services such as entertainment which they enjoy.

Suppliers Suppliers are stakeholders in a business because they depend upon that business for sales. Equally, the business is dependent on its suppliers. If it can't get supplies, it will be forced to cease production. As with customers, there is a mutual dependence between a business and its suppliers.

Local, national and international communities Local, national and international communities can be stakeholders in a business in a variety of ways.

- The economic prosperity of a community is dependent upon particular businesses. For example, businesses provide jobs in the local community, which in turn support other businesses such as shops where wages are spent. In some communities, a single business may provide a large proportion of the jobs. The prosperity of the local community can then become totally dependent upon one employer. This can be true of nations too. In Africa, for example, some small countries are highly dependent on single mining companies or oil companies.

- A few businesses play important roles in their communities by supporting local charities or getting involved with schools and colleges. In the past in the UK, and in some countries today, businesses have also built and owned the housing in which their workers live. The Rowntrees in York or the Cadbury's in Birmingham were examples.
- Some businesses, such as McDonald's or The Body Shop, have a very high media profile and, arguably, have had an important influence upon the way we live. McDonald's outside of the USA has been accused of being the face of American capitalism. In France, it has been accused of destroying traditional cuisine by encouraging people to eat fast food. The Body Shop, by its ethical stance, has arguably encouraged other businesses to be more ethical.

The environment and future generations In recent years, there has been a growing awareness that environmental issues are important to stakeholding. The stakeholders are sometimes human beings who are affected by the impact that a business has on the environment today. For example, a business might be responsible for noise or visual pollution. Some would argue that animals and plants are also in some sense stakeholders because business activity has an impact on them. Equally, future generations are stakeholders of todays' businesses. For example, building a nuclear power plant today means, almost certainly, that future generations will be left clearing up the nuclear waste created. Taking a barrel of oil from the ground today means that it will not be available to people 200 years from now. Sending a lorry to deliver goods 100 miles away probably contributes to global warming, a problem that will be faced mainly by people living 50 to 100 years from now.

The conflicting objectives of stakeholders

Different stakeholders in a business have different objectives. They want different things from the business.

Owners When owners play no part in the running of the business, their objective is usually to maximise their returns. Typically, this occurs when the business is a medium to large sized company owned by shareholders. Shareholder returns come from being able to sell their shares for a higher price than they paid for them and from receiving dividends, a share of the company profits.

Directors and managers Directors and managers of large companies have a mixture of motives. On the one hand, they have been appointed to look after the interests of shareholders. Their job is, therefore, to maximise returns for shareholders. On the other hand, maximising returns to shareholders may not coincide with maximising their own returns. Top management work partly to maximise their own pay and remuneration package. So there can be a conflict of interest between senior management and owners. This problem is often referred to as one which comes from the 'divorce of ownership from control'.

Workers Ordinary workers from middle management down have little interest in the objectives of the owners of the company. They come to work for a variety of motives including pay and job satisfaction. When it comes to agreeing the annual pay rise, their objective is to have to the highest rise possible. But this could lead to lower profits. Improved working conditions could lead to higher costs again damaging profits. On the other hand, it is not in the workers' interests to see the business fail. There are many examples where too high labour costs have led to the closure of a business or a business operation. So workers have to be careful about pushing their claims too far.

Customers Customers want the best prices with the highest quality at these prices. They want good service. This may conflict with other stakeholders' interests. For example, spending more on research and development to create new products might lower the amount payable in dividends to

Question 1.

EADS, the European manufacturer of aeroplanes and maker of Airbus, in partnership with the US company Northrop Grumman, has won a $35 billion contract to supply refuelling tankers for the US airforce. The deal is for 179 aircraft together with service and support. What's more, the group is now in a strong position to capture a large share of the remaining 400 aircraft tankers the US airforce needs to replace, a contract which could ultimately be worth $100 billion.

A number of groups will benefit from the order. EADS plants in France, Spain and Germany will supply some of the parts. The wings for all the planes will be manufactured at the EADS plant at Broughton in Wales, which already employs 6,000 people. A number of British companies will also supply parts. For example, Cobham plc will produce equipment to transfer fuel between planes, a contract that will be worth $1 billion in sales over the life of the programme.

To secure the deal, EADS and Northrop Grumman had to locate 60 per cent of the work by value in the United States. One of the main beneficiaries will be the city of Mobile in Alabama where the aircraft will be assembled. More than 1,000 jobs will be created.

The loser has been the US aircraft manufacturer, Boeing, which was the main rival to EADS. Not only has it lost sales and profits, but it will have to restructure some of its operations. The assembly line at its plant in Everett, Washington, is now likely to close by about 2012 because there will no longer be any work for it to do. Around 600 production workers and other support staff will lose their jobs, almost more will probably be offered jobs elsewhere in Boeing. But the area has lost out on 2,000 jobs that would have been created had Boeing won the order. A further 4,000 jobs elsewhere in the USA have also been lost due to Boeing's failure to win.

Source: adapted from *The Financial Times*, 3.3.2008, 4.3.2008.

(a) List the possible stakeholders in EADS and Boeing.
(b) Explain how the different stakeholders in EADS and Boeing have gained and lost because EADS won the contract to build refuelling tankers.

shareholders today. Improving quality might lead to higher costs and lower profits, adversely affecting shareholders. Sunday opening for banks or shops might be unpopular with workers but be very popular with customers.

Suppliers Suppliers want to charge high prices to the business so as to maximise their profits. On the other hand, the business wants to minimise the price it pays to suppliers, also to maximise profit. A whole range of other issues such as quality, delivery times and service may also lead to conflicting objectives between suppliers and the business.

The community and government The communities in which a business operates have a variety of objectives with regard to businesses. On the one hand, they tend to welcome the jobs, taxes and prosperity which businesses can bring to an area. On the other hand, they don't like the environmental damage that businesses can cause. These objectives can conflict with those of the business. For example, a business might want to put up a building as cheaply as possible in order to minimise cost. But the local authority may insist on a variety of 'improvements' which increase the cost of the build. Businesses in general tend to lobby against the introduction of new regulations by government because they tend to raise costs.

Environmental groups Environmental groups tend to see business as a necessary evil. Clearly businesses have to exist to provide human beings with goods and services. But every business damages the environment in some way simply by using energy or by occupying buildings which stand on land which was once populated by animals and plants. Businesses tend to want to see fewer environmental regulations and more spending on infrastructure like roads and airports. Environmental groups tend to lobby against business expansion.

Question 2.

Northumbrian Water Group (NWG) is a local water company in the North East and South East of England. It provides water and sewerage services, supplying clean water to businesses and to homes and treating their sewage waste.

On its website in 2008, it stated that 'NWG is a business with significant resources - notably employees, water and land. We believe it has a responsibility to use those resources for the benefit not only of customers and shareholders, but also for the wider community.'

'Our recognised stakeholders include customers, employees, investors, suppliers, Government and the wider local community. NWG tries to balance social, environmental and economic priorities to ensure that, whilst maintaining economic stability, the environment is protected and society is enhanced. Stakeholders expect a secure supply of water - a basic necessity for health - and they expect us to protect or enhance the environment when we return waste to that environment. Stakeholders also expect NWG to

- behave fairly and responsibly
- use resources wisely
- improve quality of life
- contribute to economic development.

Source: adapted from www.nwg.co.uk.

(a) Compare the possible objectives of customers, investors and 'the wider community' in NWG.

(b) Do you think that stakeholders apart from shareholders should have more influence over the running of a water company like NWG than an engineering company which manufactures parts for the automobile industry?

Costs and benefits to businesses of adopting a stakeholder approach

In the UK, adopting a 'stakeholder approach' means giving less importance to the interests of owners and more importance to other stakeholders than the typical business. The costs and benefits to businesses of adopting such an approach tend to be measured in terms of their impact on profits, sales, revenues and accounting costs. The advantages include the following.

- Having good employment policies will tend to attract better applicants for posts and help motivate and retain existing staff. Improved motivation and retention should lead to increased profits.
- Effective customer care policies should lead to higher sales and hence higher profits.
- Working well with suppliers should enable the purchaser to get value for money. It should be much easier to sort out problems of late deliveries or defective work with suppliers with whom there is a good relationship.
- Putting something into the community, such as giving to local charities, taking on workers or backing training projects should give the business good public relations. This might help sell products or attract good applicants for jobs.
- Being environmentally friendly could lead to lower overall costs. For example, recycling heat in a boiler might cost money for new equipment but quickly save money because of the lower fuel inputs needed. Being seen as environmentally friendly may help sales of products and thus increase profit.
- For some high profile companies such as Shell or BP, becoming more socially responsible deflects the criticisms of pressure groups. As companies such as Monsanto (over GM crops) or Nike (over poor conditions of work in factories making Nike trainers in the Third World) have

KNOWLEDGE

1. List the major stakeholders in a typical business.
2. Explain two ways in which the interests of the owners of a large business might conflict with the interests of its workers.
3. Explain two ways in which the interests of the senior management of a large business might conflict with the interests of environmental groups.
4. Why might the owners of a large business benefit rather than suffer by (a) giving their workers a large pay rise and (b) spending £1 million on environmental projects?
5. How might (a) workers and (b) the owners of a large business exert pressure to influence decision making within the business?

found, bad publicity can affect sales. In the mid -1990s, Shell faced a consumer boycott of its petrol filling stations over its plans to dispose of a North Sea oil platform by sinking it in the middle of the Atlantic ocean. Spending money on becoming more socially responsible is a way of reducing the risks to sales and profits that would come from bad PR.

The main disadvantage of the stakeholder approach is that, in practice, it tends to add to costs and thus lower profits for most businesses. If this weren't the case, every employer would increase the benefits given to workers, or give money to local charities or devote resources to pursuing environmentally friendly policies. Only some businesses benefit from a 'stakeholder approach'.

KEYTERMS

Stakeholder – an individual or group which is affected by a business and so has an interest in its activities.

Case Study: The Body Shop

On its website in 2008, The Body Shop stated: 'The Body Shop International plc is a global manufacturer and retailer of naturally inspired ethically produced beauty and cosmetics products. Founded in the UK in 1976 by Dame Anita Roddick, we now have over 2,100 stores in 55 countries,with a range of over 1,200 products, all animal cruelty free, and many with fairly traded natural ingredients.'

High Street beauty products retailer Body Shop has been taken over by French cosmetics giant L'Oreal in a deal worth £625 million. L'Oreal makes a wide range of cosmetics, including Ambre Solaire sun cream and Lancome lipsticks. Body Shop – with its ethically-sourced products – was one of the icons of the High Street in the 1980s. Its fortunes have been hit in recent years as rivals started making similar products. Body Shop will be operated as a stand-alone company by L'Oreal rather than being fully integrated into the L'Oreal business.

The sale has attracted criticism because L'Oreal is 26 per cent owned by the Swiss multinational Nestlé, which has long been embroiled in controversy about the sale of baby milk in Third World countries.

Source: adapted news.bbc.co.uk 17.3.2006; www.independent.co.uk 10.4.2006.

In its 2007 Values Report, The Body Shop stated that: 'We are committed to running a commercially successful, sustainable business, and using resources responsibly withy due regard for the needs of future generations. We do not believe that there is any conflict between commercial success and social or environmental responsibility. The greater our economic performance the more credible example we can set for other businesses, the wider ethical choice we can offer to consumers and the stronger our voice for the causes we champion.'

In its 2007 Values Report, The Body Shop stated that its stakeholders were:

Figure 1: The Body Shop: stakeholders

- customers: 'We know from our customer surveys and focus groups that 80 per cent of our customers shop with us because of our Values';
- employees and consultants: 'The Body Shop International plc directly employs 10, 034 people but there is a total of 31, 000 people globally working in our stores, in offices and warehouse operations and as The Body Shop At Home™ consultants.
- NGOs (non-governmental organisations): NGOs are mainly charities such as Greenpeace, WWF (World Wildlife Fund), Friends of the Earth and local groups in countries in which The Body Shop operates;
- franchisees: 'Our franchisees are responsible for the largest part of our business and their contribution to building our brand and Values is significant';
- suppliers: 'Our engagement with suppliers takes a range of different forms. We visit each of our Community Trade suppliers at least every two years, and assess our product suppliers annually. .... For example, we have been in close contact with our packaging suppliers to increase the use of recyclate, and work with other suppliers to use new natural ingredients or find alternatives to chemicals of concern.'
- Other companies and multi-stakeholder networks: 'We want to share what we have learned with other companies, as well as understand how others have made progress. We are therefore a part of a number of formal networks which include progressive companies, both within and outside our sector.'

Soruce: adapted from www.thebodyshopinternational.com.

(a) **Evaluate whether the objectives of the different stakeholders in The Body Shop must inevitably conflict with each. (40 marks)**

(b) **Assess the costs and benefits to The Body Shop of adopting a stakeholder approach to business. (40 marks)**

7 Legal structure - sole traders and partnerships

What is a business organisation?

Businesses are often referred to as organisations. An ORGANISATION is a body that is set up to meet needs. For example, the St. John's Ambulance organisation was originally set up by volunteers to train the public in life saving measures.

Business organisations satisfy needs by providing people with goods and services. All organisations will:
- try to achieve objectives;
- use resources;
- need to be directed;
- have to be accountable;
- have to meet legal requirements;
- have a formal structure.

Private sector business organisations

One method of classifying businesses is by **sector**. The PRIVATE SECTOR includes all those businesses which are set up by individuals or groups of individuals. Most business activity is undertaken in the private sector. The types of business in the private sector can vary considerably. Some are small retailers with a single owner. Others are large multinational companies such as Cadbury Schweppes. Businesses will vary according to the legal form they take and their ownership.
- **Unincorporated businesses.** These are businesses where there is no legal difference between the owners and the business. Everything is carried out in the name of the owner or owners. These firms tend to be small, owned by either one person or a few partners.
- **Incorporated businesses.** An incorporated body is one which has a separate legal identity from its owners. In other words, the business can be sued, can be taken over and can be liquidated.

Figure 1 shows the different types of business organisation in the private sector, their legal status and their ownership. These are examined in the rest of this unit.

Sole traders

The simplest and most common form of private sector business is a SOLE TRADER or SOLE PROPRIETOR. This type of business is owned by just one person. The owner runs the business and may employ any number of people to help.

Sole traders can be found in different types of production. In the primary sector many farmers and fishermen operate like this. In the secondary sector there are small scale manufacturers, builders and construction firms. The tertiary sector has large numbers of sole traders. They supply a wide range of services, such as hairdressing, retailing, restaurants, gardening and other household services. Many sole traders exist in retailing and construction, where a very large number of shops and small construction companies are each owned by one person. Although there are many more sole traders than any other type of business, the amount they contribute to total output in the UK is relatively small.

Setting up as a sole trader is straightforward. There are no legal formalities needed.

However, sole traders or self-employed entrepreneurs do have some legal responsibilities once they become established. In addition, some types of business need to obtain special permission before trading.
- Once turnover reaches a certain level sole traders must register for VAT.
- They must pay income tax and National Insurance contributions.

Figure 1: Business organisations in the private sector

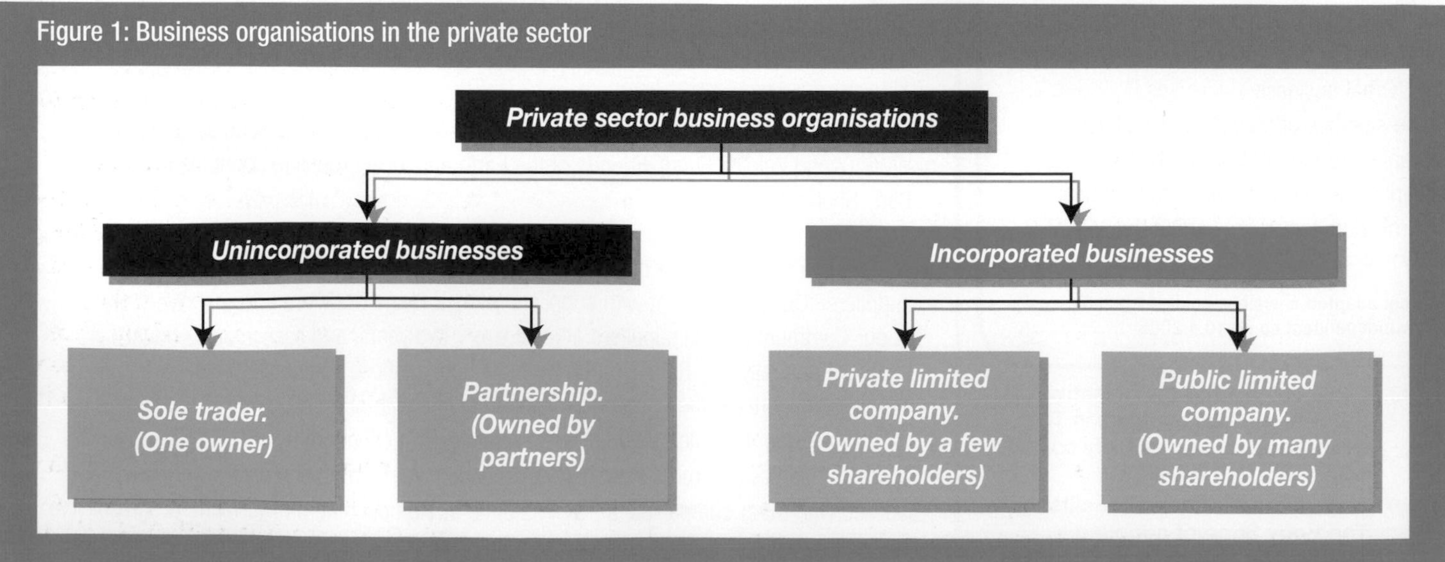

Question 1.

Joanna Carter owns Joanna Carter Contemporary Flowers in Wallingford. She attracts customers in three areas - weddings, corporate work for local business and flowers for private homes. Despite only setting up in July last year, demand has soared thanks to Joanna's growing reputation for creative arrangements. She set up as a sole trader after leaving her job to raise a family. 'After leaving my personnel job to have my children, now aged nine and six, I had time to think about where I really wanted to go in my career. I was keen to develop my passion for flowers with proper training and so I took a two-year part-time course at Abingdon and Witney College'. She also gained work experience working one day a week in a florists' shop in Wallingford. When she graduated, she had already received a number of offers from people wanting her to do private arrangements for them. So she left the shop to run her own business from home.

Joanna approached the local Business Link, a free and impartial guide to business advice, resources and information shortly after setting up the business. 'I've been able to book a place on an advanced bridal skills course with highly respected London florist Jane Packer in May. The course costs £900 and half of the cost will be paid for through the Skills Development Team at Business Link. I am also looking into a broadband grant so I can provide a slide show of my work for potential corporate customers and wedding bookings. I'm in the process of applying for an Enterprising Woman grant run by Surrey University which will give me £350-worth of funding'.

Source: adapted from www.businesslink.gov.uk.

(a) As a sole trader Joanna Carter has unlimited liability. What does this mean?

(b) Explain two advantages to Joanna Carter of operating as a sole trader.

(c) How did Business Link help Joanna Carter in running her small business?

- Some types of business activity need a licence, such as the sale of alcohol or supplying a taxi service or public transport.
- Sometimes planning permission is needed in certain locations. For example, a person may have to apply to the local authority for planning permission to run a fish and chip shop in premises which had not been used for this activity before.
- Sole traders must comply with legislation aimed at business practice. For example, legally they must provide healthy and safe working conditions for their employees.

Advantages of sole traders

Sole traders have a number of advantages.

- The lack of legal restrictions. The sole trader will not face a lengthy setting up period or incur expensive administration costs.
- Sole proprietorships can be set up with little or no money in the business. They don't cost anything to set up. So the capital cost of creating a sole proprietorship can be minimal.
- Any profit made after tax is kept by the owner.
- The owner is in complete control and is free to make decisions without interference. For many sole traders independence is one of the main reasons why they choose to set up in business.
- The owner has flexibility to choose the hours of work he or she wants and to take holidays. Customers may also benefit. Sole traders can take individual customers' needs into account, stocking a particular brand of a good or making changes to a standard design, for example.
- Because of their small size, sole traders can offer a personal service to their customers. Some people prefer to deal directly with the owner and are prepared to pay a higher price for doing so.
- Such businesses may be entitled to government support.

Disadvantages of sole traders

However, there are also disadvantages of sole traders.

- Sole traders have UNLIMITED LIABILITY. This means that if the business has debts, the owner is personally liable. A sole trader may be forced to sell personal possessions or use personal savings to meet these debts.
- Sole proprietorships can be risky for their owners. If the business is unsuccessful, sole traders can end up working for nothing or even subsidising the business out of their own private resources. Also, because the business is the sole trader, long term illness can have a devastating effect on it. Becoming an employee is less risky and is one reason why workers may not want to work for themselves.
- Sole proprietorships face continuity problems. Will the business survive if the sole trader dies, takes retirement or decides to do something different? Some sole traders run family businesses where parents tend to pass on their business to their children. Farming is an example. However, many sole traders will not pass their businesses on to family members. So these businesses will disappear.
- The money used to set up the business is often the owner's savings. It may also come from a bank loan. Sole traders may find it difficult to raise money. They tend to be small and lack sufficient **collateral**, such as property or land, on which to raise finance. This means money for expansion must come from profits or savings.
- Independence is an advantage, but it can also be a disadvantage. A sole trader might prefer to share decision making, for example. Many sole traders work very long hours, without holidays, and may have to learn new skills.
- In cases where the owner is the only person in the business, illness can stop business activity taking place. For example, if a sole trader is a mobile hairdresser, illness will lead to a loss of income in the short term, and even a loss of customers in the long term.
- Because sole traders are unincorporated businesses, the owner can be sued by customers in the event of a dispute.
- Large businesses can employ specialist workers. A sole trader often has to be purchaser, driver, accountant, lawyer and

labourer to run the business. Allowing workers to specialise can lead to lower costs of production per unit. So sole traders can be at a disadvantage competitively which they are forced to make up for by paying themselves lower wages.

- Sole proprietorships are usually small businesses. So they are unable to gain reductions in unit costs of production as the volume of output rises, known as **economies of scale**. Sole traders tend to be concentrated in industries such as farming, where economies of scale are limited.

Partnerships

A PARTNERSHIP is defined in **The Partnership Act, 1890** as the 'relation which subsists between persons carrying on business with common view to profit'. Put simply, a partnership has more than one owner. The 'joint' owners will share responsibility for running the business and also share the profits. Partnerships are often found in professions such as accountants, doctors, estate agents, solicitors and veterinary surgeons. After sole traders, partnerships are the most common type of business organisation. It is usual for partners to specialise. A firm of chartered accountants with five partners might be organised so that each partner specialises in one aspect of finance, such as tax law, investments or VAT returns.

There are no legal formalities to complete when a partnership is formed. However, partners may draw up a DEED OF PARTNERSHIP. This is a legal document which states partners' rights in the event of a dispute. It covers issues such as:

- how much capital each partner will contribute;
- how profits (and losses) will be shared amongst the partners;
- the procedure for ending the partnership;
- how much control each partner has;
- rules for taking on new partners.

If no deed of partnership is drawn up the arrangements between partners will be subject to the Partnership Act. For example, if there is a dispute regarding the share of profits, the Act states that profits are shared equally among the partners.

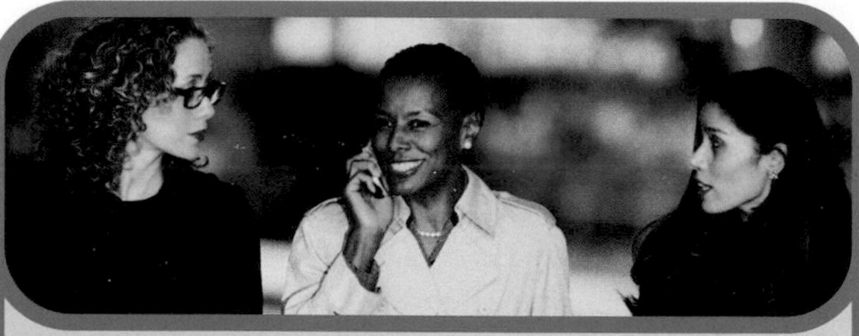

Question 2.

Sarah Otaka, Gillian Peters and Maria Ampat run a dental practice in Scunthorpe. They operate as a partnership. They undertake work for the NHS, but an increasing amount of their income comes from private work. The partnership was established in 2003. The three dentists each contributed £20,000 to provide start-up capital. A further £20,000 was borrowed from a bank. The money was used to convert a property into dental surgeries and buy equipment. The business employs four other staff – three dental assistants and a receptionist.

After three successful years in business together a problem arose. Gillian wanted to attract more private clients, particularly those requiring cosmetic work which is usually very lucrative. Sarah and Maria were more committed to NHS work. They were not in it just for the money. After a period of disagreement, where communications deteriorated, a partners' meeting was held to find a solution. Gillian, however, felt that the only way forward was for her to break away from the partnership.

(a) **At the end of the third year a profit of £180,000 was made by the practice. How much is each partner likely to get if there is no deed of partnership?**

(b) **Explain two advantages to the dentists of operating as a partnership.**

(c) **How does this case illustrate one of the main disadvantages of partnerships?**

Advantages of partnerships

Partnerships have a number of advantages.

- There are no legal formalities to complete when setting up the business.
- Like a sole proprietorship, an ordinary partnership does not need to publish any accounts which may be seen by the public. Only the tax authorities must have access to the accounts of a partnership. In contrast, the accounts of a company are available to anyone who asks to see them via Companies House. The accounts of a limited liability partnership are open to inspection by the public, but in a less detailed format than those of a company.
- Each partner can specialise. This may improve the running of the business, as partners can carry out the tasks they do best.
- Since there is more than one owner, more finance can be raised than if the firm was a sole trader.
- Partners can share the work. They will be able to cover each other for holidays and illness. They can exchange ideas when making key decisions. Also, the success of the business will not depend upon the ability of one person, as is the case with a sole trader.
- Since this type of business tends to be larger than the sole trader, it is in a stronger position to raise more money from outside the business.

Disadvantages of partnerships

- The individual partners have unlimited liability. Under the Partnership Act, each partner is equally liable for debts.
- Profits have to be shared among more owners.
- Partners may disagree. For example, they might differ in their views on whether to hire a new employee or about the amount of profit to retain for investment.
- The size of a partnership is limited to a maximum of 20 partners. This limits the amount of money that can be introduced from owners.
- The partnership ends when one of the partners dies.
- The partnership must be wound up so that the partner's family can retrieve money invested in the business. It is

normal for the remaining partners to form a new partnership quickly afterwards.
- Any decision made by one partner on behalf of the company is legally binding on all other partners. For example, if one partner agreed to buy four new company cars for the business, all partners must honour this.
- Partnerships have unincorporated status, so partners can be sued by customers.

Limited partnerships

The Limited Partnerships Act 1907 allows a business to become a LIMITED PARTNERSHIP, although this is rare. This is where some partners provide capital but take no part in the management of the business. Such a partner will have LIMITED LIABILITY - the partner can only lose the original amount of money invested. A partner with limited liabillity cannot be made to sell personal possessions to meet any other business debts. This type of partner is called a **sleeping partner**. Even with a limited partnership there must always be at least one partner with **unlimited liability**. The Act also allows this type of partnership to have more than 20 partners.

The Limited Liability Partnership Act, 2000 allows the setting up of a LIMITED LIABILITY PARTNERSHIP. All partners in this type of partnership have limited liability. To set up as a limited liability partnership, the business has to agree to comply with a number of regulations, such as filing annual reports with the Registrar of Companies.

KNOWLEDGE

1. What is the difference between a corporate body and an unincorporated body?
2. State three advantages and three disadvantages of being a sole trader.
3. What is the advantage of a deed of partnership?
4. State three advantages and three disadvantages of partnerships.
5. What is meant by a sleeping partner?

KEYTERMS

Deed of Partnership - a binding legal document which states the formal rights of partners.
Limited liability - where a business owner is only liable for the original amount of money invested in the business.
Limited Liability partnership - a partnership where all partners have limited liability.
Limited partnership - a partnership where some members contribute capital and enjoy a share of profit, but do not participate in the running of the business. At least one partner must have unlimited liability.
Organisation - a body set up to meet a need.
Partnership - a business organisation which is usually owned by between 2-20 people.
Private sector - businesses that are owned by individuals or groups of individuals.
Sole trader or sole proprietor - a business organisation which has a single owner.
Unlimited liability - where the owner of a business is personally liable for all business debts.

Case Study: Oxford Vintage cars

Hristo Petrov runs a small business buying and selling vintage cars. He buys cars at auctions and from dealers and currently sells them on Ebay. At the moment Hristo does not undertake any renovation work on the cars. He just buys them and sells them on. Last year he made a profit of £37,000. However, Hristo is ambitious.and wants to set up his own website and operate from a car showroom in Oxford. A lot of the cars he sells are MGBs and MGAs. These cars were originally made in Oxford and Hristo likes the idea of locating a showroom in their home city. He also wants to employ a team of mechanics to renovate them. He knows that premium prices are paid for well restored vintage cars.

Unfortunately Hristo can only raise £50,000 of the £100,000 needed to develop the business. He has approached several banks but has not been able to secure funding as he has a poor credit rating after having his house repossessed. A friend of his, however, is keen to get involved in the business. Mark Watkins bought a car from Hristo three years ago and the two have remained in touch ever since. Mark is happy to provide the other £50,000 if he can become an equal partner.

Hristo has eventually accepted Mark's offer and the new showroom is due to open very shortly. The partnership, called Oxford Vintage Cars, has a smart website which contains details of all the cars in stock and other useful information for enthusiasts.

After a deed of partnership was drawn up Hristo said 'At first I did not want to go into partnership, but now I think it will work. Mark is as committed as me and has come up with some good ideas. For example, he reckons we can rent out some of the cars in stock for special occasions such as weddings. I hadn't even though of that. He will also be good on the restoration side and he will be able to supervise the mechanics more effectively than me. I will concentrate on the buying and selling, that's what I'm good at'.

(a) Using this case as an example, explain what is meant by a partnership. (4 marks)
(b) Oxford Vintage Cars is an unincorporated business. What does this mean? (6 marks)
(c) How does this case highlight one of the problems of operating as a sole trader? (6 marks)
(d) Why do you think Hristo did not want to enter a business partnership? (8 marks)
(e) To what extent will the partners be able to specialise in the business? (12 marks)

8 Legal structure - limited companies

Companies

There are many examples of LIMITED COMPANIES in the UK. They range from Garrick Engineering, a small family business, to British Airways which has many thousands of shareholders. One feature is that they all have a separate legal identity from their owners. This means that they can own assets, form contracts, employ people, sue and be sued in their own right. Another feature is that the owners all have **limited liability**. If a limited company has debts, the owners can only lose the money they have invested in the firm. They cannot be forced to use their own money, like sole traders and partners, to pay business debts.

The **capital** of a limited company is divided into **shares**. Each member or **shareholder** owns a number of these shares. They are the joint owners of the company and can vote and take a share of the profit. Those with more shares will have more control and can take more profit.

Limited companies are run by **directors** who are appointed by the shareholders. The board of directors, headed by a **chairperson**, is accountable to shareholders and should run the company as the shareholders wish. If the company's performance does not live up to shareholders' expectations, directors can be 'voted out' at an **Annual General Meeting** (AGM).

Whereas sole traders and partnerships pay income tax on profits, companies pay corporation tax.

Forming a limited company

How do shareholders set up a limited company? Limited companies must submit some important information to the Registrar of Companies.

Memorandum of Association The Memorandum sets out the constitution and gives details about the company. The Companies Act 1985 states that the following details must be included.

- The name of the company.
- The name and address of the company's registered office.
- The objectives of the company, and the scope of its activities.
- The liability of its members.
- The amount of capital to be raised and the number of shares to be issued.

A limited company must have a minimum of two members, but there is no upper limit.

Articles of Association The Articles of Association deal with the internal running of the company. They include details such as:

- the rights of shareholders depending on the type of share they hold;
- the procedures for appointing directors and the scope of their powers;
- the length of time directors should serve before re-election;
- the timing and frequency of company meetings;
- the arrangements for auditing company accounts.

Form 10 This form gives details of the first directors, secretary and the address of the registered office. Directors must give their names and addresses, dates of birth, occupations and details of other directorships they have held within the last five years.

Form 12 This form is a statutory declaration of compliance with all the legal requirements relating to the incorporation of the company. It must be signed by a solicitor who is forming the company, a director or the company secretary.

These documents will be sent to the **Registrar** at **Companies House**. If they are acceptable, the company's application will be successful. It will be awarded a **Certificate of Incorporation** which allows it to trade. The Registrar keeps these documents on file and they can be inspected at any time by the general public for a fee. A limited company must also submit a copy of its **Annual Report and Accounts** to the Registrar each year. The accounts will include information such as the balance sheet and income statement or profit and loss accounts of the business. Finally, the shareholders have a legal right to attend the AGM and should be told of the date and venue in writing well in advance.

Question 1.

MD Chris Lay re-mortgaged his house to launch Gigasat Limited in 2000. The business was incorporated on 16.10.2000 and the registered address is 12 Rylands Mews, Lake Street, Leighton Buzzard, Bedfordshire. The company's registration number is 04090608. The company develops satellite communications equipment, such as lightweight, carbon-fibre antennas, and vehicles installed with satellite systems. Clients include the news channels CNN and Al Jazeera. They use Gigasat technology for live television coverage. The equipment has also been adopted by the government and the military for secure satellite transmissions. For example, its equipment allows troops posted abroad to access the Internet and talk to loved ones. Sales have grown 67 per cent a year from £2 million in 2003 to £5.7 million in 2005.

Source: adapted from Tech Track 100 and information from Companies House.

(a) What evidence is there in the case to suggest that Gigasat is a private limited company?

(b) What legal obligations will Gigasat Limited have to: (i) shareholders and (ii) the Registrar of Companies each year?

(c) Discuss two advantages to the owners of Gigasat Limited of operating as a private limited company.

Private limited companies

Private limited companies are one type of limited company. They tend to be relatively smaller businesses, although certain well known companies, such as Reebok and Littlewoods, are private limited companies. Their business name ends in **Limited** or **Ltd**. Shares can only be transferred 'privately' and all shareholders must agree on the transfer. They cannot be advertised for general sale. Private limited companies are often family businesses owned by members of the family or close friends. The directors of these firms tend to be shareholders and are involved in the running of the business. Many manufacturing firms are private limited companies rather than sole traders or partnerships.

Advantages of private limited companies

There are certain advantages in setting up a business as a private limited company.

- Shareholders have limited liability. As a result more people are prepared to risk their money than in, say, a partnership.
- More capital can be raised as there is no limit on the number of shareholders.
- Control of the company cannot be lost to outsiders. Shares can only be sold to new members if all shareholders agree.
- The business will continue even if one of the owners dies. In this case shares will be transferred to another owner.
- There may be tax advantages for the owners, particularly if owners are currently paying the higher rate of income tax. Profits can be retained by the company and distributed to the owners at a later date, for example when they retire.
- Some businesses may not deal with unlimited businesses or businesses that are not registered for VAT. This is because they think that limited companies registered for VAT are more likely to be run well, since, they have to keep proper accounts and tend to use the professional advice of accountants and solicitors.

Disadvantages of private limited companies

There are some disadvantages in setting up a business as a private limited company.

- Profits have to be shared out among a much larger number of members.
- There is a legal procedure in setting up the business. This takes time and also costs money.
- Firms are not allowed to sell shares to the public. This restricts the amount of capital that can be raised.
- Financial information filed with the Registrar can be inspected by any member of the public. Competitors could use this to their advantage.
- If one shareholder decides to sell shares it may take time to find a buyer.

Public limited companies

The second type of limited company tends to be larger and is

Question 2.

Burton's Foods, famous for its Wagon Wheels and Jammie Dogders biscuits, was bought by the private equity company, Duke Street Capital in 2007. Burton's, the UK's second largest biscuit producer, employs 3,000 people on five sites in the UK. Founded in the 1930s it became part of Associated British Foods in 1949 before being sold to Hicks, Muse, Tate & Furst seven years ago. The deal was said to be worth around £200 million. However, just two months later the new owners announced that biscuit production would cease at its factory in the Wirral, with the loss of 660 jobs. The announcement of the job cuts sparked an angry reaction from unions.

Tony Woodley, joint general secretary of the newly-created Unite union, said: 'We are not going to just roll over and accept this. We will be urgently consulting with our members about a strategy to keep the factory open and will meet management on Monday to hear their rationale for this body-blow to Merseyside manufacturing'.

The factory in Moreton is the biggest employer in the Wirral after Vauxhall cars. Mr Woodley said the job losses would 'devastate the community'. The company is to stop making biscuits, at the site but will continue to manufacture chocolate and assemble seasonal assortments at the factory. It is thought 330 jobs will remain on the site. Paul Kitchener, chief executive of Burton's Foods, said that while the company 'sincerely' regretted the loss of jobs, the changes were needed because of overcapacity in the biscuit market.

Source: adapted from *The Guardian*, 19.3.2007.

(a) Using this case as an example, explain what is meant by a private equity company.

(b) What evidence is there in the case to suggest that the private equity company is pursuing ruthless efficiency gains?

called a **public limited company**. This company name ends in plc. There were around 1.85 million registered limited companies in the UK in 2006. Only around 1 per cent were public limited companies. However, they contributed far more to national output and employed far more people than private limited companies. The shares of these companies can be bought and sold by the public on the stock exchange.

When 'going public' a company is likely to publish a **Prospectus**. This is a document which advertises the company to potential investors and invites them to buy shares before a FLOTATION. An example of a company floated on the stock exchange in 2006 is Styles & Wood. It supplies property services to retailers such as Waitrose and B&Q. 'Going public' can be expensive because:

- the company needs lawyers to ensure that the prospectus is 'legally' correct;
- a large number of 'glossy' publications have to be made available;
- the company may use a financial institution to process share applications;
- the share issue has to be underwritten (which means that the company must insure against the possibility of some shares remaining unsold) and a fee is paid to an underwriter who must buy any unsold shares;
- the company will have advertising and administrative expenses;
- it must have a minimum of £50,000 share capital.

A public limited company cannot begin trading until it has completed these tasks and has received at least a 25 per cent payment for the value of shares. It will then receive a **trading certificate** and can begin operating, and the shares will be quoted on the **Stock Exchange** or the **Alternative Investment Market** (AIM).

A stock exchange is a market where second hand shares are bought and sold. A full stock exchange listing means that the company must comply with the rules and regulations laid down by the stock exchange. Many of these rules are to protect shareholders from fraud. The AIM is designed for companies which want to avoid some of the high costs of a full listing. However, shareholders with shares quoted on the AIM do not have the same protection as those with 'fully' quoted shares.

Advantages of public limited companies

Some of the advantages are the same as those of private limited companies. For example, all members have limited liability, the firm continues to trade if one of the owners dies and more power is enjoyed due to their larger size. Others are as follows.

- Huge amounts of money can be raised from the sale of shares to the public.
- Production costs may be lower as firms may gain economies of scale.
- Because of their size, plcs can often dominate the market.
- It becomes easier to raise finance as financial institutions are more willing to lend to plcs.
- Pressures from the financial media and financial analysts, as well as the danger that the plc might be taken over by another company, encourage executives and managers to perform well and make profits. These pressures do not exist for private limited companies.

Disadvantages of public limited companies

There are also disadvantages in setting up a public limited company.

- The setting up costs can be very expensive - running into millions of pounds in some cases.
- Since anyone can buy their shares, it is possible for an outside interest to take control of the company.
- All of the company's accounts can be inspected by members of the public. Competitors may be able to use some of this information to their advantage. They have to publish more information than private limited companies.
- Because of their size they are less able to deal with their customers at a personal level.
- The way they operate is controlled by various Company Acts which aim to protect shareholders.
- There may be a divorce of ownership and control which might lead to the interests of the owners being ignored to some extent.
- It is argued that many of these companies are inflexible due to their size. For example, they can find change difficult to cope with.

Some public limited companies are large and have millions of shareholders and a wide variety of business interests all over the world. They are known as **multinationals**, which means that they have operations in a number of different countries. For example, Kellogg's is an American based multinational company with a production plant and head office situated in Battle Creek, USA. It has also had factories in Manchester, Wrexham, Bremen, Barcelona and Brescia.

Exiting the stock market

Sometimes a business operating as a public limited company is taken back into private ownership. This may be called 'exiting the stock market'. Why does it happen?

- The people responsible for running the business might no longer be willing to tolerate interference from the external shareholders. For example, shareholders such as financial institutions may demand higher dividends when the senior managers would prefer to reinvest profits to generate more growth.
- Sometimes businesses lose favour with the stock market. This may happen when city analysts publish unhelpful or negative reports about companies failing to reach profit targets for example. Such publicity often has the effect of lowering the share price very sharply.
- A business currently operating as a plc may be bought

CRITIQUE

Private equity companies have been criticised for a number of reasons. It is argued that they are often too ruthless when pursuing efficiency gains and that job losses nearly always follow an acquisition by a private equity company. Private equity investors pay very little tax on the profits of their sales. Businesses bought by private equity companies are often saddled with huge debts and some private equity companies have been accused of asset stripping. However, many of the businesses bought by private equity companies are badly managed and in need of change. Some are also undervalued by the stock market and it is suggested that the owners are not getting value for their investment. It is also argued that being taken into private ownership removes unnecessary costs such as compliance and accountancy. Finally, under private ownership the business can focus on the longer term.

outright by a private individual. For example, Philip Green, bought Bhs, the high street clothes retailer, from Storehouse in 2000. He also bought Arcadia in 2002 for a reported £770 million. Both of these companies were part of a plc organisation until purchased.

Private equity companies

An increasing number of businesses are owned by PRIVATE EQUITY COMPANIES. These are organisations that borrow money from banks, add a little of their own, and then use the cash to buy a business. Usually, the businesses they buy are public limited companies, although not always. This often means that public limited companies are taken into private ownership. Three key features of the way in which private equity companies operate are:

- they tend to put the debt used to buy the business into the company. This usually means the company will now have more debt than before it was purchased;
- since they stand to gain all of the profit made by the business, they aim to make ruthless efficiency gains;
- they tend to sell the business after about three years.

How does a private equity deal work? Assume a private equity company borrows £90 million to buy a company worth £100 million, and puts up £10 million of its own money. Its investment is heavily geared. If it can create a 5 per cent increase in the value of the company, it adds £5 million to it. But, because it keeps the whole increase in value for itself, the initial £10 million investment has not risen by 5 per cent, but by 50 per cent - a fantastic return. Some examples of private equity companies include Bain Capital, Apollo Management, Terra Firma, Blackstone Group and Apax Partners. One example of a deal involving a private equity company was the purchase of Alliance Boots, the owner of the 158-year-old high street chemists chain. Boots was bought by Stefano Pessina and his backers, Kohlberg Kravis Roberts (KKR), for £11 billion.

Holding companies

Some public limited companies operate as HOLDING COMPANIES. This means that they are not only companies in their own right, but also have enough shares in numerous other public limited companies to exert control. This type of company tends to have a very diversified range of business activities. For example, in the UK the TTP Group plc is a holding company for a number of technology businesses. These include TTP LabTech, which supplies products to the healthcare and pharmaceutical sectors, and Acumen Bioscience, which develops and provides screening instruments for the drug discovery industry.

The main advantage of this type of company is that it tends to have a diverse range of business activities. This helps protect it when one of its markets fails. Also, because it is so large, it can often gain financial economies of scale. The main disadvantage is that the holding company may see the businesses it owns only as a financial asset. It may have no long-term interest in the businesses or its development.

KNOWLEDGE

1. What is the role of directors in limited companies?
2. What is the difference between the Memorandum of Association and the Articles of Association?
3. What is a Certificate of Incorporation?
4. Describe the advantages and disadvantages of private limited companies.
5. What are the main legal differences between private and public limited companies?
6. State four financial costs incurred when forming a public limited company
7. What is meant by a statutory declaration?
8. Describe the advantages and disadvantages of plcs.
9. How is a company prospectus used?
10. State one advantage and one disadvantage of a holding company.

KEYTERMS

Flotation - the process of a company 'going public'.
Holding companies - public limited companies which owns enough shares in a number of other companies to exert control over them.
Limited company - a business organisation which has a separate legal entity from that of of its owners.
Private equity company - a business usually owned by private individuals backed by financial institutions.

Case Study: ImmuPharma plc

ImmuPharma plc, a drug discovery and development company, floated on the Alternative Investment Market (AIM) at the beginning of 2006. The main purpose of the float was to raise money to finance initial clinical trials on ImmuPharma's drugs for severe pain and MRSA-related infections. At the forefront of ImmuPharma's drug pipeline is a product that targets Lupus, a disease for which there is currently no cure or specific treatment. By 2010 there will be an estimated 1.4 million patients diagnosed with Lupus in the seven key markets. The proceeds of the flotation, together with certain grants, are expected to fund the Phase I trial and a Phase II study for the Lupus product. The flotation involved placing 67.8 million shares with institutional and private investors at the price of 42.5p a share.

Lupus is a chronic, potentially life-threatening autoimmune disease. An estimated one million people worldwide have been diagnosed with this inflammatory disease, which attacks multiple organs such as the skin, joints, kidneys, blood cells, heart and lungs. There is currently no cure or specific treatment and Immupharma's drug, IPP-201101, has a mechanism of action aimed at modulating the body's immune system so it does not attack healthy cells without causing adverse side effects. It has the potential to halt the progression of the disease in a substantial proportion of patients.

According to a Datamonitor report, the currently unique ImmuPharma drug, IPP-201101, has an 'achievable' peak market share of 50 per cent. The report also suggests that the drug could sell at a similar cost to interferon, the multiple sclerosis treatment - around $10,000 a year per patient. Immupharma have stated that due to the nature of the disease and lack of treatments, the US Food and Drug Administration may permit a fast track development and approval process for Phase III once the Phase II study is finished in the first quarter of 2007. If approved, the drug could be available on the market as early as 2010.

Source: adapted from www.drugresearcher.com and ImmuPharma, *Annual Report and Accounts 2006.*

Table 1: Financial Information for ImmuPharma

	2006*	**2005****
Turnover	£44,818	£25,409
Loss	(£1,860,038)	(£2,482,778)

*1/4/06 – 31/12/06.
**13/1/05 – 31/3/06.

(a) Why do you think ImmuPharma has decided to become a public limited company? (6 marks)

(b) What is the main advantage of floating on the Alternative Investment Market? (4 marks)

(c) Calculate how much money the flotation will raise for ImmuPharma. (6 marks)

(d) What might be the disadvantages to ImmuPharma of operating as a public limited company? (10 marks)

(e) Evaluate the potential for the success of ImmuPharma in the future. (14 marks)

9 Legal structure - not-for-profit organisations

Not-for-profit organisations

A number of organisations are run according to business principles, but do not aim to make a profit. They are known as NOT-FOR-PROFIT ORGANISATIONS. Their proceeds or surpluses from trading may be shared with employees and customers or passed on to a third party. Such organisations may be involved in a range of business activities. They may also employ staff, raise finance, buy resources, sell goods or services, market themselves, have a formal structure and be required to meet the needs of different stakeholders. They have to operate within the law and may also be faced with competition. Not-for-profit organisations include the following:

- public sector organisations;
- co-operatives;
- mutual organisations;
- charities;
- pressure groups.

Co-operatives

The origins of Co-operatives The UK Co-operative Movement grew from the activities of 28 workers in Rochdale, Lancashire. In 1844 they set up a retail co-operative society - The Rochdale Equitable Pioneers Society. With capital of just £28 they bought food from wholesalers and opened a shop, selling 'wholesome food at reasonable prices'. The surplus (or profit) made was returned to members of the society in the form of a 'dividend'. The dividend was in proportion to how much each member had spent. The principles of the society were:

- voluntary and open membership;

Figure 1: The Co-operative's business activities

Food The largest community food retailer in the UK with more than 2,200 stores, over 52,000 employees.

Healthcare Has more than 700 outlets and 5,000 employees. It is the third largest pharmacy business in the UK.

Travel The UK's most diverse retail travel business, with more than 450 high street branches, strong internet, call centre and home working businesses as well as significant cruise, franchise and business travel operations.

Funeralcare The UK's largest funeral business with over 800 funeral branches and in excess of 3,500 employees.

End of Life Planning A newly established End of Life Planning business which aims to grow its stake in the funeral planning market.

Sunwin Motors One of the top 25 motor businesses in the UK, with a turnover of £250million and 22 dealerships in Yorkshire, Lancashire and the East Midlands.

Cash in Transit Provides services for over half of The Co-operative Bank's ATM estate.

E-Store Operates several e-commerce sites and provides electrical buying, warehousing and distribution services for the Co-operative Movement.

The Co-operative Legal Services Offers free advice and legal help for members of The Co-operative Group on everything from buying or selling a property to will writing.

Property Responsible for property assets including an investment portfolio which is largely invested in the retail and commercial property sectors.

The Co-operative Farms The largest farmer in the UK with over 70,000 acres of farmland in England and Scotland. They supply products such as soft fruit, cider, potatoes and packet flour to The Co-operative food stores.

Shoefayre A leading footwear and accessories retailer with over 1,700 employees and 240 stores throughout the UK.

Mandate A leading designer, manufacturer and distributor of corporate clothing.

Co-operative Financial Services (CFS) An Industrial and Provident Society, which brings together Co-operative Insurance (CIS), The Co-operative Bank and the internet bank Smile under common leadership.

The Co-operative Bank A bank famous for its ethical stance and high standards of customer service.

CIS/Co-operative Insurance A major life assurance and general insurance business with over four and a half million customers.

Smile An award-winning full-service internet bank.

Source: adapted from www.co-operative.co.uk.

- democratic ownership - one member, one vote;
- the surplus allocated according to spending (the dividend);
- educational facilities for members and workers.

Modern co-operatives Most modern co-operatives operate as CONSUMER or RETAIL CO-OPERATIVES. They are owned and controlled by their members. Members can purchase shares which entitles them to a vote at Annual General Meetings. The members elect a board of directors to make overall business decisions and appoint managers to run day to day business. Co-operatives are run in the interests of their members. Any surplus made by the co-operative is distributed to members as a dividend according to levels of spending. Shares are not sold on a stock exchange, which limits the amount of money that can be raised.

On Sunday 29 July 2007, the two main arms of the Co-op, The Co-operative Group and United Co-operatives, merged The new society, called 'The Co-operative', is the world's largest consumer co-operative with a turnover of more than £9 billion, 4.5 million members and 87,500 employees. The new organisation operates over 4,500 trading outlets throughout the UK. Figure 1 gives a summary of The Co-operatives' business activities.

Worker co-operatives

Another form of co-operation in the UK with common ownership is a WORKER CO-OPERATIVE. This is where a business is jointly owned by its employees. A worker co-operative is an example of a producer co-operative where people work together to produce a good or service. Examples might be a wine growing co-operative or a co-operative of farmers producing milk.

In a worker co-operative employees are likely to:

- contribute to production;
- be involved in decision making;
- share in the profit (usually on an equal basis);
- provide some capital when buying a share in the business.

In 2006 there were less than 400 worker owned and controlled co-operatives in the UK according to Co-operatives UK. One example is the Edinburgh Bicycle Co-operative, a cycle retailer. One advantage of a worker co-operative is that all employees, as owners of the business, are likely to be motivated. Conflict will also tend to be reduced as the objectives of shareholders and employees will be the same. Worker co-operatives can involve the local community, either by giving donations to local bodies or even having them as members of the co-operative. However, there may be problems when operating as a worker co-operative.

- It is often difficult to persuade other workers to join a worker co-operative because it is much easier to set up a partnership.
- Some workers, new ones for example, may not want to join. They may not be able to afford the share.
- Successful worker co-operatives often get sold to companies and the workers are happy to 'sell out' due to the lucrative offers made.
- Fresh capital cannot be raised by recruiting new shareholders. This often limits growth.
- Difficulties might be encountered when trying to recruit highly skilled and qualified staff. They may want more money then the equal wages being paid to existing members.

Question 1.

Suma is an independent wholefood wholesaler-distributor. It specialises in vegetarian, fairly traded, organic, ethical and natural products and also has its own successful brand of food and non-food products. Suma operates as a workers' co-operative and has a truly democratic system of management that isn't bound by the conventional notions of hierarchy that often hinder progress and stand in the way of fairness. It uses an elected Management Committee to implement decisions and business plans but the decisions themselves are made at regular General Meetings with the consent of every co-operative member. There's no chief executive, no managing director and no company chairman. In practice, this means that their day-to-day work is carried out by self-managing teams of employees who are all paid the same wage, and who all enjoy an equal voice and an equal stake in the success of the business.

Source: adapted from www.suma.co.uk.

(a) Using this case as an example, explain what is meant by a workers co-operative.

(b) Explain the likely effect on worker motivation at Suma of operating as a workers co-operative.

Building and friendly societies

Most building societies and friendly societies in the UK are MUTUAL ORGANISATIONS. They are owned by their customers, or members as they are known, rather than shareholders. Profits go straight back to members in the form of better and cheaper products. Friendly societies began in the 18th and 19th centuries to support the working classes. Today friendly societies offer a wide range of 'affordable' financial services. These include savings schemes, insurance plans and protection against the loss of income or death. They also provide benefits such as free legal aid, sheltered housing or educational grants to help young people through university. These extra benefits are distributed free of charge, paid for by trading surpluses. The government gives friendly societies special tax treatment, which reduces the amount of tax that members pay.

Building societies used to specialise in mortgages and savings accounts. Savers and borrowers got better interest rates than those offered by banks. This was possible because building societies were non-profit making. In the 1980s building societies began to diversify and compete with banks. In the late 1990s a number of building societies, such as Halifax, Alliance and Leicester, and Northern Rock, became public limited companies.

The main reason for this was that mutual organisations are restricted by law from raising large amounts of capital which might be used to invest in new business ventures. This demutualisation process involved societies giving members 'windfall' payments, usually in the form of shares, to compensate them for their loss of membership.

Charities

Charities are organisations with very specialised aims. They exist to raise money for 'good' causes and draw attention to the needs of disadvantaged groups in society. For example, Age Concern is a charity which raises money on behalf of senior citizens. They also raise awareness and pass comment on issues, such as cold weather payments, which relate to the elderly. Other examples of national charities include Cancer Research Campaign, British Red Cross, Save the Children Fund and Mencap.

Charities rely on donations for their revenue. They also organise fund raising events such as fetes, jumble sales, sponsored activities and raffles. A number of charities run business ventures. For example, Oxfam has a chain of charity shops which sells second hand goods donated by the public.

Charities are generally run according to business principles. They aim to minimise costs, market themselves and employ staff. Most staff are volunteers, but some of the larger charities employ professionals. In the larger charities a lot of administration is necessary to deal with huge quantities of correspondence and to handle charity funds. Provided charities are registered, they are not required to pay tax. In addition, businesses can offset any charitable donations they make against tax. This helps charities when raising funds.

Pressure groups

PRESSURE GROUPS are groups of people that attempt to influence decision makers in politics, business and society. There is a wide variety of pressure groups since they can differ significantly in their aims, objectives and size. For example, a very small pressure group might be made up of residents in a small locality that are campaigning for traffic-calming measures in a particular street to be taken by the council. Such a group would then disband if the council did take acceptable measures. Some groups are quite large and operate as registered charities. Examples include Greenpeace and Friends of the Earth – big environmental pressure groups. Such groups may have formal structures, operate from central offices, employ staff, use large quantities of resources (for example, Greenpeace own a large boat) and promote themselves actively. Some generate large amounts of revenue through donations, fund-raising activities and other sources. Some pressure groups even represent businesses. For example, The Confederation of British Industry (CBI) represents the interests of a wide variety of British companies.

Factors affecting the choice of organisation

Age Many businesses change their legal status as they become older. Most businesses when they start out are relatively small and operate as sole traders. Over time, as needs change, a sole trader may take on a partner and form a partnership. Alternatively, a sole trader may invite new owners to participate in the business, issue shares and form a private limited company. Public limited companies are often formed from established private limited companies that have been trading for many years.

The need for finance A change in legal status may be forced on a business. Often, small businesses want to grow but do not have the funds. Additional finance can only be raised if the business changes status. Furthermore, many private limited companies 'go public' because they need to raise large amounts for expansion.

Size The size of a business operation is likely to affect its legal status. A great number of small businesses are usually sole traders or partnerships. Public limited companies tend to be large organisations with thousands of employees and a turnover of millions or billions of pounds. It could be argued that a very large business could only be run if it were a limited company. For example, certain types of business activity, such as oil processing and chemical manufacturing, require large scale production methods and could not be managed effectively as sole traders or partnerships.

Limited liability Owners can protect their own personal financial position if the business is a limited company. Sole traders and partners have unlimited liability. They may, therefore, be placed in a position where they have to use their own money to meet business debts. Some partnerships dealing with customers' money, such as solicitors, have to have unlimited liability in order to retain the confidence of their clients.

Degree of control Owners may consider retaining control of their business to be important. This is why many owners choose to remain as sole traders. Once new partners or shareholders become a part of the business, the degree of control starts to diminish because it is shared with the new owners. It is possible to keep some control of a limited company by holding the majority of shares. However, even if one person holds 51 per cent of shares in a limited company, the wishes of the other 49 per cent cannot be ignored.

The nature of the business The type of business activity may influence the choice of legal status. For example, household services such as plumbing, decorating and gardening tend to be provided by sole traders. Professional services such as accountancy, legal advice and surveying are usually offered by partnerships. Relatively small manufacturing and family businesses tend to be private limited companies. Large manufacturers and producers of consumer durables, such as cookers, computers and cars, are usually plcs. The reason that these activities choose a particular type of legal status is because of the benefits they gain as a result. However, there are many exceptions to these general examples.

KEYTERMS

Consumer co-operative – a business organisation which is run and owned jointly by the members, who have equal voting rights.

Mutual organisation – businesses owned by members who are customers, rather than shareholders.

Not-for-profit organisation – organisations that are run according to business principles, but that do not aim to make a profit.

Pressure groups – groups of people that attempt to influence decision makers in politics, business and society.

Public sector – business organisations owned and controlled by central or local government.

Worker co-operative – a business organisation owned by employees who contribute to production and share in profit.

KNOWLEDGE

1. What is meant by a not-for-profit organisation?
2. How might a trading surplus' be used by a not-for-profit organisation?
3. State three features of a consumer co-operative.
4. Why do charities promote themselves?
5. Who are the owners of a mutual organisation?

Case Study: Claire House

Claire House is a registered charity. It cares for children aged between 0-18 years with life threatening or life limiting conditions and their families from Merseyside, Cheshire, North Wales and the Isle of Man. Claire House runs a children's hospice on the Wirral which is dedicated to enhancing the quality of life, providing specialist respite, palliative, terminal and bereavement care. The hospice facilities include a multi-sensory room, jacuzzi, hydrotherapy pool, teenage room, art and craft area and physiotherapy/ complementary therapy. There is also a multi purpose room where they provide music therapy, group activities or quiet reflection.

The charity has demanding financial needs. Claire House has to raise £120,000 every month to keep the doors of the hospice open. For example, £2,500 is needed each month to pay for a nurse, £1,750 for physiotherapy, £1,500 for medical cover, £550 for family and bereavement support, £400 for pharmacy and sundry expenses and so on. A further £2 million is also needed to build, equip and run the new teenager wing for 12 months.

Claire House has a number of income sources. It relies heavily on donations from the public. For example, it has a web site where donations can be made online. A proportion of income is generated by organising special fundraising events. Examples for 2007 include a beer festival, a golf tournament, a sponsored parachute jump, a comedy night, a garden party, a charity ball and sponsored treks to Brazil and Nepal. It also runs around 20 charity shops in the region. It sells a range of second-hand items, such as unwanted clothes, books, toys, DVDs/videos and ornaments, that have been donated by the general public. It can also take suitable items of furniture for resale at a shop in Mold. Finally, like many charities, Claire House enjoys the support of a number of celebrities. The comedian and actor Norman Wisdom, the actress Patricia Routledge, the Tranmere Rovers goalkeeper Eric Nixon, 60s pop legend Gerry Marsden and the entertainer Claire Sweeney are just a few of the region's celebrities that support Claire House.

Source: adapted from www.claire-house.org.uk.

(a) 'Charities have specialised aims'. Explain what this means using the case as an example. (6 marks)
(b) Describe how Claire House finances its activities. (6 marks)
(c) Examine the role that the celebrities mentioned in the case play in the running of Claire House. (8 marks)
(d) Explain how Claire House faces competition. (8 marks)
(e) Analyse the ways in which Claire House resembles a profit-making organisation. (12 marks)

10 Legal structure - public sector organisations

Public sector organisations

The PUBLIC SECTOR is made up of organisations which are owned or controlled by central or local government or public corporations. They are funded by the government and in some cases from their own trading 'surplus' or profit. The amount of business activity in the public sector has decreased over the last 35 years as a result of government policy. Some public sector businesses have been transferred from the public to the private sector. However, the public sector still has an important role to play in certain areas of business activity.

Which goods and services does the public sector provide?

It has been argued that certain PUBLIC GOODS and MERIT GOODS need to be provided by public sector organisations.

Public goods have two features.

- Non-rivalry – consumption of the good by one individual does not reduce the amount available for others.
- Non-excludability – it is impossible to exclude others from benefiting from their use.

Take the example of street lighting. If one person uses the light to see her way across the street, this does not 'use up' light for someone who wants to look at his watch. Also, it is impossible to stop using the light shining across the street. This means that it would be unlikely that people would pay directly for street lighting. If you paid £1 for light to cross the street, someone else could use it for free! If people will not pay, then businesses cannot make a profit and would not provide the service. Other examples of public goods may include the judiciary, policing and defence, although in some countries private policing does exist. These public goods are provided free at the point of use. They are paid for from taxation and other income.

Some argue that certain merit goods should be provided by the public sector. Examples include education, health and libraries. These are services which people think should be provided in greater quantities. It is argued that if the individual is left to decide whether or not to pay for these goods, some would choose not to or may not be able to. For example, people may choose not to take out insurance policies to cover for unexpected illness. If they became ill they would not be able to pay for treatment. As a result it is argued that the state should provide this service and pay for it from taxation. The provision of merit goods is said to raise society's standard of living.

Government/publicly owned organisations

Government or publicly owned organisations may take a number of forms.

Public corporations PUBLIC CORPORATIONS are organisations set up by law to run services or industries on behalf of the government. Each corporation is run by a chairperson and board appointed by a government minister. The board is responsible for the day-to-day running of the corporation, but is accountable to the minister. The minister has the right to approve investment and to issue directions to the organisation in relation to matters which affect the public interest.

The **BBC** (**British Broadcasting Corporation**) is an example of a public corporation. It was given a royal charter to provide 'broadcasting services as public services'. It is run by a board of directors nominated by the Prime Minister, which is politically independent, although the government might try to influence its operations informally. The BBC is financed mainly though licence fees paid by television owners. However, an increasing amount of money is being raised from the sale and production of programmes for other TV companies, such as overseas businesses.

The Post Office Postal services in the UK have been provided by the public sector for many years. However, there has been a number of changes in the structure of the organisation during that time. In March 2001 the Post Office became a plc, but one wholly owned by the UK government. The change was brought about by the Postal Services Act 2000. It aimed to create a commercially focused company with a more strategic relationship with the government. In November 2002 the name of the company was changed from Consignia to the Royal Mail Group plc. In the UK the business operates under three brands - Royal Mail, Post OfficeTM and Parcelforce Worldwide.

- **Royal Mail** provides postal services. The company has a statutory duty to provide a letter delivery service to every one of the 27 million addresses in the UK, at a uniform price, whatever the distance travelled. It must also carry out at least one daily collection from all letterboxes. Royal Mail is now being threatened by competition from the increasing use of email and other electronic messaging and the continuing use of faxes. Other postal operators can now obtain licences to deliver mail but Royal Mail still has a huge monopoly.
- **Post OfficeTM** consists of a retail network with more than 14,400 branches, the combined UK total of the four major building societies and six banks. Only 500 branches are owned by Post Office Ltd, the operator of the branches. The rest are owned by the people who run the branches, including franchisees and sub-postmasters and mistresses. The retail network offers more than 170 products, including financial services, travel services, government information and retail products such as greetings cards and stationery. Post OfficeTM claims that 94 per cent of

people in the UK live within one mile of a post office branch, with 28 million people paying a visit at least once a week.

- **Parcelforce Worldwide** provides a time-guaranteed and next day parcel delivery service. It has the world's largest delivery network, covering more than 99.6 per cent of the world's population and reaching 239 different countries.

Network Rail In 1996 British Rail, the former nationalised rail industry, was broken up and sold off in parts. The largest part was Railtrack, the rail infrastructure which included the railway lines, stations, bridges, signals and property. Passenger transport services on the railway lines were provided by private train operators such as Virgin, Stagecoach and North Western. These businesses bid for operator's licences from the government and paid Railtrack for using the network.

In 2002, after Railtrack was declared bankrupt, ownership was transferred to the not-for-profit company Network Rail. Network Rail is run by 100 'members' drawn from train operators, unions, passengers' groups and the public. There is perhaps some dispute about its legal status. The Office for National Statistics (ONS) classified Network Rail as a private corporation since its spending on track maintenance is not included on the national accounts. However, since the government is guaranteeing Network Rail's debt, the company cannot really 'go bust'. Network Rail is accountable to the Office of Rail Regulation (ORR) for compliance with the obligations under its network licence, which authorises it to operate the main rail network. The ORR acts as the railway industry's economic and safety regulator and is independent of the government.

The Bank of England

The Bank of England is a former privately owned business that was taken into public ownership in 1946. It has a special role in the monetary system. In 1997 it was given powers by the government to decide what the level of interest rates should be in the UK. It is headed by a governor, who is accountable to the Chancellor of the Exchequer.

Local authority services

Some services in the UK are supplied by local authorities.

- Education. Local authorities are responsible for distributing most of the money allocated by the government to primary and secondary schools in the UK. However, some schools which have had problems have been taken out of local authority control and funded by central government.
- Recreation. Sports halls, libraries, swimming pools and parks are all examples of recreation services provided by local government.
- Housing. This includes the provision of council housing, amenities for the homeless, sheltered accommodation and house renovation. The importance of this provision has diminished because of the purchase of council houses by tenants.
- Environment and conservation. Refuse collection, litter clearance, pest control, street cleaning and beach maintenance are examples of these services. However, an increasing number of councils is employing private sector businesses to carry out these services, such as Onyx Environmental Group plc.
- Communications. The provision of essential services to isolated towns and villages is one responsibility under this heading. Others include road maintenance and traffic control.
- Protection. This involves the provision of fire and police services, local justice, and consumer protection. Local authorities also employ trading standards officers and environmental health officers to investigate business practice and premises.
- Social services. Local government is also responsible for providing services such as community care, social workers and children's homes.

Most of the funding for the above services comes from central government grants. However, there is some scope for independent funding. For example, local authorities raise revenue from the council tax. Charges are also made for the supply of services like swimming pools and football pitches.

There are reasons why such services are provided by local rather than central government. First, it is argued that the local community is best served by those who are most sympathetic to its needs. Thus, local authorities should have the knowledge to evaluate those needs and supply the appropriate services.

Question 1.

(a) Is the example in the photograph above a public or a merit good? Explain your answer.

(b) Explain why either the private sector or the public sector may provide such a facility.

Second, central government is made up of large departments which often have communication problems. The decentralisation of many services should help to improve communication between the providers of services and the public. Finally, local councillors are accountable to the local electorate. If their policies are unpopular in the local community it is unlikely that they will be re-elected.

Central government departments

Central government departments supply some important services. These departments are also used to implement government policy.

- **The Treasury**. Responsible for the government's economic strategy. It has many aims, including maintaining a stable economy with low inflation and sound public finances, promoting UK economic prospects and a fair and efficient tax and benefit system, ensuring a fair, competitive and efficient market in financial services which is in the public interest, improving the quality and the cost effectiveness of public services and achieving regularity and accountability in public finance.
- **The Ministry of Defence**. Responsible for the provision and maintenance of the armed forces in the UK and in other parts of the world.
- **The Department for Work and Pensions.** This has a number of functions. It is responsible for providing benefits for those in need and other payments including child benefit, disability allowance, income support and housing benefit. It assesses benefit claims and allocates payments. It also provides help, support and benefits for people who are out of work, looking for work, returning to work or looking to start their own business.
- **The Department for Business, Enterprise and Regulatory Reform (BERR)**. Created on 28 June 2007. It employs around 2,500 staff, plus 4,000 in its executive agencies. Its annual budget is just over £3 billion. Half of this is spent on nuclear decommissioning; the rest on a range of issues from trade promotion to energy security supply, to championing entrepreneurial businesses through the Regional Development Agencies.
- **The Department of Health (DH)**. Responsible for the National Health Service (NHS) in the UK. It provides guidance and leadership for a variety of NHS organisations including regional health authorities, NHS trusts and Care Trusts. These organisations help to deliver local health care in the UK, such as hospitals, surgeries and health centres.
- **The Department for Children, Schools and Families**. The Department for Children, Schools and Families leads work across Government to ensure that all children and young people stay healthy and safe, secure an excellent education and the highest possible standards of achievement, enjoy their childhood, make a positive contribution to society and the economy and have lives full of opportunity, free from the effects of poverty.
- **The Department for Environment, Food and Rural Affairs (Defra)**. Operates in a number of areas. For example, it seeks to limit global environmental threats, such as global warming, and safeguard people from the effects of poor air quality or toxic chemicals. It has the power to penalise those who break environmental legislation. It also aims to ensure animal health and welfare and clean and healthy water supplies, to help the food industry grow, and to protect the UK from harmful and illegal food imports.
- **The Department for Transport**. Implements the government's transport policy. It aims to oversee the delivery of a reliable and safe transport system which does not harm the environment. This includes areas such as road building, traffic safety and congestion, national railways, the operation of the London Underground, aviation, shipping and ports.
- **The Department for International Development (DFID)**. Works to promote sustainable development and eliminate world poverty.

Much of the work carried out by central and local government departments also benefits businesses in the private sector. For example, the Department for Transport gives contracts to large construction companies like Wimpey and Costain, to build roads and motorways.

Quangos

Some activities carried out by the government are said to be politically non-controversial. These are controlled by QUANGOs (quasi autonomous non-governmental organisations). They tend to be specialised bodies providing services which central and local government does not have the resources or the expertise to carry out. QUANGOs receive funding from and are accountable to different government departments, depending on their area of specialism. Some well-known QUANGOs in the mid-2000s included Investors in People and the Equal Opportunities Commission.

According to the UK government, which defines QUANGOs more narrowly only as non-departmental government bodies (NDGBs), there were are 529 QUANGOs in 2005. QUANGOs spend many billions of pounds of taxpayers money. For example, in 2005 the Legal Service Commission spent £2.1 billion, the Scottish Education Funding Council £800 million, the Northern Health and Social Services Board £550 million and the Teacher Training Agency £514.6 million.

In recent years they have received a certain amount of criticism. It is argued that they are not entirely non-political and can be influenced by government to achieve its objectives. It has also been suggested that members appointed by government may be biased towards its stance on certain issues. The efficiency of their operations has also been criticised and some have argued that they duplicate each others efforts.

Executive agencies

Executive agencies have become well established since their

introduction in 1985. They are responsible for the supply of services previously provided by government departments. Examples include:

- the collection of government data – The Office for National Statistics;
- the processing of passport applications – The Passport and Records Agency;
- the administering of written driving tests – The Driver and Vehicle Licensing Agency;
- the operation of state pensions – The Pensions Service;
- the granting of patents – The Patents Office.

These have been separated from the policy making bodies which used to deliver them.

Executive agencies are headed by chief executives who are accountable to a government minister. Many of these leaders are recruited from the private sector. They are encouraged to introduce business principles when delivering services. The general policy of the government departments remains the responsibility of the permanent secretaries and senior civil servants.

Since the introduction of executive agencies the efficiency of services has improved considerably. For example, it now takes seven days on average to process a passport application, compared with as much as 30 days at times in the past. Also, many benefit payments are now much cheaper to administer.

Privatisation

PRIVATISATION is the transfer of public sector resources to the private sector. It was an important feature of government policy in the 1980s and 1990s, as shown in Table 1. It is still seen by some as a means of improving efficiency and further privatisation is always a possibility. For example, the UK rail line carrying Eurostar trains to the continent is to be sold off, the government confirmed in November 2007. It was always the intention to sell off the track and stations, known as High Speed 1, after the line to London St Pancras was completed. It is currently managed by the London and Continental Railways consortium, which also owns the accompanying land and the UK's stake in Eurostar. Network Rail may make an offer, although foreign buyers could also bid. Privatisation has taken a number of forms.

Table 1: Sale of state-owned companies since 1979

Date begun			
1979	British Petroleum	1986	British Gas
	ICL	1987	British Airways
	Ferranti		Rolls Royce
	Fairey		Leyland Bus
1981	British Aerospace		Leyland Truck
	British Sugar		Royal Ordnance
	Cable and Wireless		British Airport Authority
	Amersham International		
1982	National Freight Corporation	1988	British Steel
	Britoil		British Leyland
1983	Associated British Ports	1989	British Water Authorities
	British Rail Hotels	1990	Electricity Area Boards
1984	British Gas Onshore Oil	1991	Electricity Generation
	Enterprise Oil	1994	British Coal
	Sealink Ferries	1995	British Rail
	Jaguar Cars	1996	British Energy
	British Telecom		Railtrack
	British Technology Group	2001	Nats (air traffic control)

The sale of nationalised industries NATIONALISED INDUSTRIES played an important role in the UK before 1980. They included organisations such as British Rail, British Airways, British Steel and British Telecom. These were public sector organisations which, it was argued, should be owned and controlled by the state for a number of reasons.

- To supply services which were unprofitable, such as railways in isolated areas.
- To avoid the wasteful duplication of resources where a NATURAL MONOPOLY existed.
- To control strategic industries such as energy and transport.
- To prevent exploitation by monopoly suppliers.
- To save jobs when closure threatened.

These businesses were sold off to private buyers. They became private sector businesses, owned by private shareholders.

The sale of parts of nationalised industries Some nationalised industries were broken up by parts being sold off. The Jaguar car company, which was part of the then state-owned British Leyland, was sold for £297 million. Sealink, a part of British Rail, was sold for £40 million.

Deregulation This involves lifting restrictions that prevent private sector competition. The deregulation of the communications market has allowed Mercury and cable companies to compete with British Telecom. Deregulation has also allowed bus services to be run by private sector businesses.

Contracting out Many government and local authority services have been 'contracted out' to private sector businesses. This is where contractors are given a chance to bid for services previously supplied by the public sector. Examples include the provision of school meals, hospital cleaning and refuse collection. For example, Wolds Remand Centre, run by the Group 4 security company, was Britain's first privately run prison service. In the early 1990s local authorities were forced into compulsory competitive tendering (CCT). Private businesses had to be asked to quote on contracts for services, bidding against council services. The contract was awarded to the most efficient, least cost service. In 2000 the Labour government replaced this. Tendering would not be compulsory and contracts would be awarded for 'best value' – based also on effectiveness and quality as well as efficiency.

The sale of land and property Under the 1980 Housing Act, tenants of local authorities and New Town Development Corporations were given the right to buy their own homes. Tenants were given generous discounts, up to 60 per cent of the market value of the house, if they agreed to buy. During the 1980s, for example, about 1.5 million houses were sold. The sale of land and properties has raised almost as much money as the sale of nationalised industries.

The reasons for privatisation

During the 1980s and 1990s governments transferred a great deal of business activity from the public sector to the private sector. Different reasons have been put forward for this.

- The sale of state assets generates a great deal of income for the government. Figure 1 shows the revenue raised by privatisation between 1979 and 2002.
- Nationalised industries were inefficient. They lacked the incentive to make a profit, since their main aim was arguably to provide a public service. As a result their costs tended to be high and they often made losses. Also, many believed that they were overstaffed. Supporters of privatisation argued that if they were in the private sector, they would be forced to cut costs, improve their service and return a profit for the shareholders.

Figure 1: Revenue from privatisation

£bn

0 1 2 3 4 5 6 7 8 9

1981 1984 1987 1990 1993 1996 1999 2002

Source: adapted from HM Treasury.

Question 2.

Jobcentre Plus is one of the largest of the executive agencies employing around 100,000 people. Jobcentre Plus supports people of working age from welfare into work, and helps employers to fill their vacancies. It is part of the Department for Work and Pensions (DWP). Some of the aims of Jobcentre Plus are outlined below.

- Increase the supply of labour by helping unemployed and economically inactive people move into employment.
- Pay customers the correct benefit at the right time and protect the benefit system from fraud, error and abuse.
- Provide high-quality and demand-led services to employers, which help fill job vacancies quickly and effectively with well-prepared and motivated employees.
- Help people facing the greatest barriers to employment to move into and remain in work.
- Ensure that people receiving working age benefits fulfil their responsibilities.
- Increase Jobcentre Plus' overall productivity, efficiency and effectiveness.

Jobcentre Plus is under pressure to perform efficiently. Its performance is monitored by setting targets. For example, targets are set for helping people into work, cutting fraud, helping employers to recruit workers and the time taken to process benefits. In 2006-07, the target for helping people into work was 13,500,000 points (Points are awarded for each category of person finding employment. For example, 12 points are awarded for a lone parent and 8 points for a person on job seekers allowance). In 2006-07, the number of points actually scored was 9,986,476. This is about 81 per cent of the target.

Source: adapted from www.jobcentreplus.gov.uk.

(a) Using this case as an example, explain what is meant by an executive agency.

(b) What evidence is there in the case to suggest that Jobcentre Plus has adopted business principles?

- As a result of deregulation, some organisations would be forced to improve their service and charge competitive prices. For example, in many areas, private firms began to compete for passengers on bus and train routes. Electricity and gas prices and telephone charges have also been reduced, arguably as a result of competition. Consumers would benefit from this and should also have greater choice. In addition, it is argued that there would be more incentive to innovate in the private sector.
- Once these organisations had been sold to the private sector there would be little political interference. They would be free to determine their own investment levels, prices and growth rates. In the past government interference has affected the performance of nationalised industries.
- Privatisation would increase share ownership. It was argued that this would lead to a 'share owning democracy' in which more people would have a 'stake' in the success of the economy. For example, if you bought shares in BT, you would be a part owner of the company and get a dividend each year. Workers were encouraged to buy shares in their companies so that they would be rewarded for their own hard work and success.
- Privatisation should improve accountability. The losses made by many of these nationalised industries were put down to the fact that they were operating a public service. In the private sector these industries would be accountable to shareholders and consumers. Shareholders would expect a return on their investment and consumers would expect a quality service at a fair price. For example, if shareholders were not happy with the dividends paid, they could sell their shares.

Figure 2: Year trends in household water bills: actual and projected average household bills 1991-2010

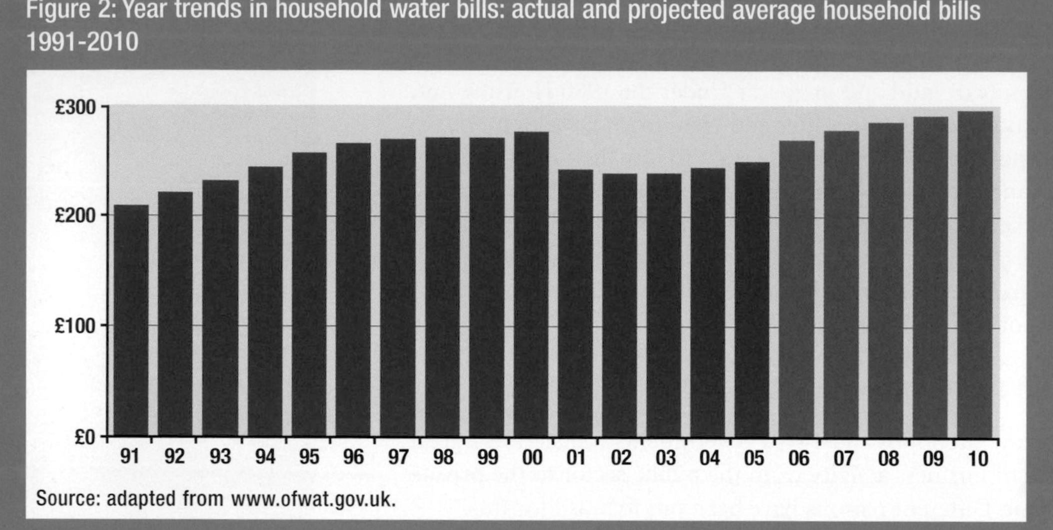

Source: adapted from www.ofwat.gov.uk.

Impact of privatisation on business

How have businesses changed after transferring to the private sector?

- Achieving a surplus or profit has become a more important objective. For example, the profits of BT increased from around £1,000 million in 1984, when the company was first privatised, to around £3,000 million in 1996, to nearly £3,200 million in 1998. In recent years, however, profits have fallen due to competition and poor acquisitions.
- In some cases prices have changed. In a number of cases they have fallen. Most analysts would agree that charges made for some telephone services, gas and electricity have fallen since privatisation, for example. However, prices of rail travel and water, for example, have risen sharply. Figure 2 shows the increase in water bills since privatisation.
- Some of the newly privatised businesses have cut back on staffing levels. For example, the Rail, Maritime and Transport Union suggested that there were 20,000 to 30,000 job losses as a result of rail privatisation. British Energy shed a quarter of its workforce before privatisation.
- Many companies increased investment following privatisation. For example, many of the water companies raised investment levels to fund new sewerage systems and purification plants. Immediately after privatisation investment rose by about £1,000 million in the water industry. However, more recently some figures suggest that investment levels are falling.
- Some of the companies have begun to offer new services and diversify. For example, North West Water (now United Utilities) offers a Leakline service which promises to repair any leaks on a customer's property provided they are outside the house.
- There has been a number of mergers and takeovers involving newly privatised companies. For example, Hanson bought Eastern Electricity and an American railway company bought the British Rail freight service. North West Water and Norweb joined together to form United Utilities and Scottish Power bought Manweb.

Arguments against privatisation

Arguments against privatisation have been put forward on both political and economic grounds. Most of the criticisms below are from the consumer's point of view.

- Privatisation has been expensive. In particular, the amount of money spent advertising each sale has been criticised.

The money spent on expensive TV advertising was at the taxpayer's expense.

- It has been argued that privatisation has not led to greater competition. In some cases public monopolies with no competition have become private monopolies. These companies have been able to exploit their position. This has been a criticism levelled at gas and electricity companies. Also Railtrack (now Network Rail) managed to pay shareholders significant dividends, arguably at the expense of essential investment.
- Nationalised industries were sold off too cheaply. In nearly all cases the share issue has been over-subscribed. This shows that more people want to buy shares than there are shares available. When dealing begins on the stock market share prices have often risen sharply. This suggests that the government could have set the share prices much higher and raised more revenue. For example, there was an £11 billion rise in the value of electricity companies between privatisation in 1990 and 1996.
- Natural monopolies have been sold off. Some argue that they should remain under government control to prevent a duplication of resources.
- Once part of the private sector, any parts of the business which make a loss will be closed down. This appears to have happened in public transport. Some bus services or trains on non-profitable routes have been cut or stopped completely since deregulation.

Question 3.

It is common now for private sector businesses to get involved in the provision of public sector services. Construction company Balfour Beatty is one example. Balfour Beatty has a number of public sector revenue streams that contribute towards the company's turnover of £5.852 million. It builds schools, hospitals, social housing and roads and has a high involvement in the rail sector. One recent contract, a 25-year deal to look after street lights for Derby City Council, brought in a useful £36m for Balfour Beatty.

The sheer range and size of Balfour Beatty makes it a strong contender in many different public sector markets. It is a major builder of hospitals and schools through PFI contracts. Experts say the firm is involved in PFI because that's the government's preferred way of doing business; whatever the financial mechanism, Balfour Beatty would still be working for the public sector. But Balfour Beatty's expertise in the UK PFI market has given it confidence; in 2006, for the first time, the firm began bidding for PFI work outside the UK. In its UK public sector work, the company has a strong order book with both central and local government and there is a consensus that Balfour Beatty is 'a good player'.

Source: adapted from *The Guardian* 1.6.2007.

(a) What type of good is street lighting?
(b) What is a PFI contract?
(c) What might be the benefits to the government of offering companies like Balfour Beatty PFI contracts?

- Share ownership arguably has not increased. Many who bought shares sold them very quickly after. In addition, a significant number of new shareowners only own very small shareholdings in just one company.
- Many of the nationalised industries are important for the development of the nation. To put them in private hands might jeopardise their existence. For example, one of the reasons why British Steel was nationalised was to save it from possible closure. If business conditions change for the worse a private company may not guarantee supply. Also, since the shares are widely available, it is possible for overseas buyers to take control of strategic UK firms.

Regulation of privatised industries

One criticism of privatisation was that dominant industries, which were previously state owned, now operated as private sector businesses. They may be able to exploit their position by increasing their prices or reducing services. Because of this they must be controlled. Control of private sector firms is nothing new. The Competition Commission was set up to monitor firms which might act against the public's interest. It investigates cases where large dominant firms or firms merging might act to exploit their position.

Because privatisation created some private monopolies, the government set up specialist 'watchdog' agencies to protect the public. Regulatory bodies were set up to monitor and control the activities of public utilities such as gas and electricity, the organisation known as Ofgem, and the telecommunications industry, the organisation known as Ofcom.

Private Finance Initiative (PFI) and Public Private Partnerships (PPP)

The PRIVATE FINANCE INITIATIVE (PFI) was introduced in 1992, but did not really take off until the end of the 1990s. PFI is one of a range of initiatives which fall under the Public Private Partnerships (PPP) umbrella. These involve the private sector in the operation of public services. The PFI is the most frequently used. Under a PFI scheme, a capital project such as a school, hospital or housing estate has to be designed, built, financed and managed by a private consortium, under contracts that typically last for 30 years. The private consortium will be paid regularly from government funds according to its performance during that time period. If the consortium misses performance targets it will be paid less. One example of an area where PFI has been used extensively by the government is in the construction of hospitals. The government had approved 15 acute hospital PFI schemes in England by 2003. The main advantages of PFI include the following.

- The government does not have to fund expensive one-off payments to build large-scale projects that may involve unpopular tax increases.
- The risk involved in funding large-scale projects is transferred to the private sector. For example, if a construction company goes out of business before a

project is completed the government does not have to meet any extra costs that might accrue, they are borne by the private consortium.
- Since the government is not funding the cost of projects the amount spent does not cause public borrowing to rise.

PFI does have its critics. For example, trade unions in the public sector often describe PFI as creeping privatisation of public services. Some possible disadvantages of PFI may include the following.
- As with any other forms of hire purchase the cost of the asset over a long period of time is greater than the capital cost. In particular the government can borrow money more cheaply than the private sector.
- There is a question mark over how much risk is genuinely transferred to the private sector given the government's record of bailing out private companies managing troubled public services.
- Concern has been expressed about the true cost of PFI. Public sector accountants claim that hospitals and schools would be cheaper to build using traditional methods of funding. The national audit office described the value for money test used to justify PFI projects as 'pseudo-scientific mumbo jumbo'.
- There is the worry that once private firms get involved in providing public services, the quality of provision falls as profit is pursued.
- Evidence suggests that PFI may be politically unpopular. In an election a government minister in the safe Labour seat of Wyre Forest was defeated by an independent candidate who stood as a protest against a new PFI hospital.

It may be another 20 years or more, when the first PFI contracts have been completed, before the real cost of PFI can be judged. However, the Institute of Public Policy Research, which argued that there should be no restriction on the private provision of public service, has since expressed its doubts.

KEYTERMS

Merit goods – goods which are underprovided by private sector businesses.
Nationalised industries – public corporations previously part of the private sector which were taken into state ownership.
Natural monopoly – a situation where production costs will be lower if one firm is allowed to exist on its own in the industry, due to the existence of huge economies of scale.
Privatisation – the transfer of public sector resources to the private sector.
Private Finance Initiative (PFI) – a scheme where private businesses build hospitals and schools, for example, funded by government.
Public corporations – organisations set up by law to run services on behalf of government.
Public goods – goods where consumption by one person does not reduce the amount available to others and, once provided, all individuals will benefit.
Public sector – business organisations which are owned or controlled by central or local government, or public corporations.
QUANGOs – Quasi Autonomous Non-Governmental Organisations.

KNOWLEDGE

1. What is meant by a public corporation?
2. What is meant by non-rivalry and non-excludability when describing public goods?
3. Why are certain merit goods provided by the public sector?
4. Why do local authorities provide some public sector services?
5. How are local authority services funded?
6. Describe the responsibilities of three government departments.
7. Explain the difference between deregulation and contracting out as methods of privatisation.
8. What are the disadvantages of privatisation?
9. What is the function of Ofgem and Ofcom?
10. State three advantages and three disadvantages of PFI.

Case Study: Royal Mail

Royal Mail delivers letters and packages throughout the whole of the UK. It is a one-price-goes-anywhere universal service. Every working day Royal Mail processes and delivers 83 million items to 27 million addresses. These items pass through a network of 70 mail centres, 8 regional distribution centres (for customer sorted mail) and 3,000 delivery offices. Then a fleet of over 30,000 red vehicles and 33,000 bicycles help it to deliver them to their final destination.

Royal Mail also provides business customers with a range of mail-related data tools to improve their marketing performance and increase the effectiveness of mail as a communication medium. Through more efficient database maintenance and well-targeted customer contact management, it can help customers achieve better response rates and a higher return on their investment.

Royal Mail has also developed an online shopping facility. Online retailing is estimated to reach 15 per cent of retail sales by 2010 – a market worth over £40 billion. Over Christmas 2005 it delivered a record breaking 70 million items ordered online – 15 million more than the same period last year. Books, videos and DVDs remain the favourite low-ticket items, but bigger-ticket items are becoming more popular, such as clothing, which now accounts for 10 per cent of total online sales.

Royal Mail is unique in designing and producing the UK's stamps and philatelic products to celebrate anniversaries and momentous occasions. It also offers electronic stamps to use as a novel and eye-catching promotional aid for businesses. Stamps can be personalised with a favourite photo, to share with friends and family for invitations, birthday greetings and letters.

In 2007, Royal Mail's revenue was static at £6.86 billion. The business faces difficult times ahead.

- The mail market in the UK is declining by around 2.5 per cent per year;
- Royal Mail is losing 40 per cent of bulk business mail to rival postal operators;
- Overall this year, rivals will handle one in five of all letters posted in the UK;
- Rivals are 40 per cent more efficient not because their people work harder but because they have already modernised and have much more technology;
- Rivals pay their people 25 per cent less than the Royal Mail.

In 2007, Royal Mail had to deal with strike action taken by workers – the first time in a decade. The long-running postal dispute eventually came to an end in October after union leaders agreed to more flexible working and a weaker pension plan. Royal Mail said the union's agreement would mean that the company could go ahead with modernisation plans that include more flexible working. The deal also involves closing the company's final salary pension scheme to new members from January 2008, and moving the company's retirement age to 65 from 2010. The Royal Mail chief executive, Adam Crozier, said: 'All along we have been clear that to become competitive we needed flexibility to modernise and we needed to reform our pension scheme because the costs were crippling the company'. 'Change is always difficult for everyone but it is vital if Royal Mail is to be able to thrive in the competitive market and build a successful future. I know that if we all work together we can achieve that success.' The union had argued that Royal Mail's original proposals would have led to the loss of up to 40,000 jobs.

Source: adapted from *The Guardian* 22.10.07 and www.royalmail.com.

(a) What sort of business organisation is the Royal Mail? (4 marks)
(b) How does the Royal Mail generate revenue? (8 marks)
(c) Analyse the threats faced by Royal Mail. (10 marks)
(d) It has been argued that Royal Mail should be privatised. Discuss the possible impact of such a move. (18 marks)

11 The nature of marketing

What is marketing?

A **market** is any set of arrangements that allows buyers and sellers to exchange goods and services. It can be anything from a street market in a small town to a large market involving internationally traded goods. But what is meant by the term MARKETING?

Marketing is not just about selling products to customers. Before selling products, many businesses carry out a range of activities to find out consumer preferences, including market research and testing of products on consumers. Similarly, marketing and advertising are not the same. Advertising is just one of a number of promotion methods used by businesses. Other methods involve giving 'free' gifts and running competitions.

A widely accepted definition of marketing, from the Institute of Marketing, is that 'Marketing is the management process involved in identifying, anticipating and satisfying consumer requirements profitably.' Some others are shown in Table 1.

Table 1: Marketing definitions

Marketing is about supplying the right products, to the right customers, at the right price, in the right place, at the right time.
Anon

'The basic function of marketing is to attract and retain customers at a profit.'
P. Drucker, The Practice of Management (1993)

'Marketing is the process of planning and executing the conception, pricing, promotion and distribution of ideas, goods and services to create exchange and satisfy individual and organisational objectives.'
American Marketing Association (1985)

The purpose of 'Marketing is to establish, maintain and enhance long term customer relationships at a profit, so that the objectives of the parties involved are met. This is done by mutual exchange and fulfilment of promises.'
C. Gronroos, 'Marketing redefined', Management Decision, 1990.

Marketing effectively

Effective marketing will have certain features

- **A process.** It does not have a start and an end, but is ongoing all the time. Businesses must be prepared to respond to changes that take place. This is shown in Figure 1. For example, a business marketing office furniture would be unwise not to take into account consumers' reactions. If the business sold modern designs, but sales were poor, it might consider designs for offices that had a traditional look.
- **A business philosophy.** It is not just a series of activities, such as advertising or selling. It is more a 'way of thinking' about how to satisfy consumers' needs. A business selling good quality products, cheaply, may be unsuccessful in its marketing if it has dirty, badly organised or poorly lit facilities. Retailers such as Ikea and Asda have large 'superstores' with restaurants and play areas for children. They could be said to cater for all their consumers' shopping needs.
- **Building relationships with customers.** Profitable businesses are often built upon good customer relations. This might involve dealing with customer complaints in a considered manner. Customers, as a result, are likely to develop a favourable view of the business and buy its products over a long period of time. RELATIONSHIP MARKETING is now used by some businesses, such as Tesco. This is an approach to marketing which stresses the importance of developing relationships with customers which last longer than the short-term.

The purposes of marketing

There is a number of reasons why businesses carry out marketing.

To satisfy consumers A product has a far greater chance of being a success if it satisfies consumers' needs. Businesses which make satisfying their customers a main concern are more likely to be effective at marketing. Marketing should affect all aspects of a business. A production department, for example, would not continue making a product that did not satisfy the needs of the

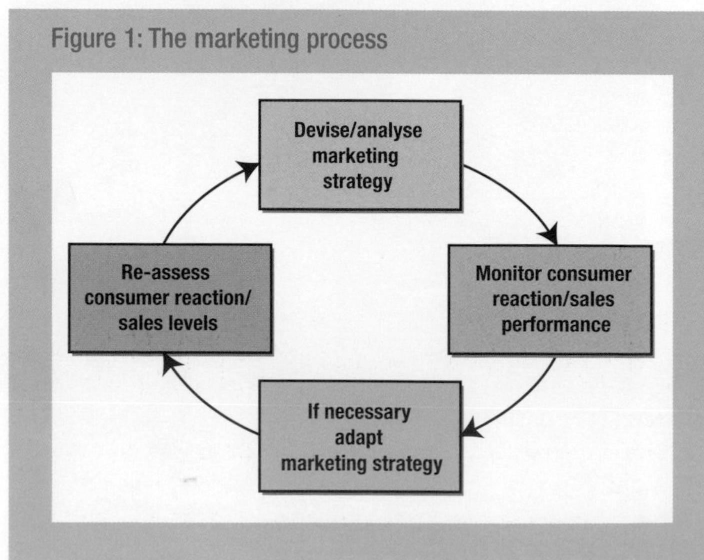

Figure 1: The marketing process

consumers at whom it was aimed.

To identifying consumer requirements Marketing should find out what consumer needs and requirements are and make sure that products meet them. Market research is often used by businesses for this purpose. Managers, however, also place stress on having a 'feel' for the market.

To anticipate consumer requirements Businesses have to understand what customers want in advance. In some cases this is easy. For example, supermarkets and butchers stock up with turkeys before Christmas. In other cases it is more difficult. What colours of clothes will be fashionable this year? A chain of stores with the wrong colours might find it difficult to sell its stock. Tastes and fashions in today's markets are changing faster than ever before. Marketing must anticipate and respond to these changes. Toy manufacturers, for example, try to be aware of the next 'craze'. In addition, rapid technological change has taken place in recent years and continues to do so. Firms constantly invent, design and launch new and advanced products onto the market. One example is the electronics industry which has introduced DVD players, digital camcorders, MP3 players and high definition televisions to the market in recent years.

To compete effectively The number of products competing for the consumer's attention is constantly increasing. Businesses today are finding it easier to change their products and enter new markets. Also, there has been increased competition from foreign products in UK markets. This means that businesses have to work even harder to be competitive. Effective marketing should help a business to achieve this.

To make a profit Most businesses today regard making a profit as their main aim. Businesses must make a profit in the long run to survive. Those that do not will cease to operate. Marketing that satisfies consumers' needs profitably is therefore essential. Even when profit is not the main objective, marketing has a vital role to play. Charities, such as Oxfam, and many public sector organisations such as colleges and hospitals, adapt and change the marketing of their services to satisfy their consumers' needs.

Consumer and business to business marketing

CONSUMER MARKETING is where a business is marketing to consumers. There are numerous examples of consumer marketing, including the marketing of the vast majority of products sold in retail outlets such as supermarkets, department stores and high street clothing stores.

BUSINESS TO BUSINESS MARKETING is where one business is engaged in marketing its products to another business. Examples of business to business marketing might include:

- an office furniture manufacturer marketing to business users;
- a car manufacturers providing company cars to a business;
- a local newspaper offering advertising space to local businesses;
- a software supplier providing software geared up to the needs of businesses.

Question 1.

Levens Farm is a fruit farm in Sussex. It allows customers to 'pick your own fruit'. But increasingly it is selling to retailers, encouraged by the news that Britain is fast becoming a nation of berry lovers.

Sales of British strawberries, blackberries and raspberries broke records in 2007 and many suppliers were struggling to keep up with demand. The soft fruits, which are credited with staving off cancer, saw sales of £204 million in the UK. 'It's because people are becoming more aware of the health benefits of eating fresh fruit, especially berries,' said Laurence Olins, the chairman of British Summer Fruits (BSF), which represents nearly all of Britain's soft fruit growers.

Strawberry sales accounted for £165 million, a 5 per cent sales increase from the previous year. In comparison, sales of blackberries shot up by 31 per cent to £4 million while raspberry sales were up 26 per cent to £35 million. Such is the demand that none of Britain's home-grown fruit is exported. And in July and August, when demand was at its highest, berries had to be imported from Europe.

Source: adapted in part from *The Independent*,18.12.2006.

(a) Explain why Levens Farm is selling to (i) consumer markets and (ii) business to business markets.

(b) Explain how the information in the article might help Levens Farm to: (i) identify customer requirements, (ii) anticipate customer requirements; (ii) make a profit.

Product and market orientation

Some businesses are said to be relatively product orientated or market orientated.

Product orientation Many businesses in the past, and some today, could be described as PRODUCT ORIENTATED. This means that the business focuses on the production process and the product itself. It puts most of its efforts into developing and making products which it believes consumers want and which will sell well.

In the past, businesses producing radios and televisions could be said to have been relatively product orientated. It was their novelty and the technical 'wonder' of the product that sold them. There were few companies to compete against each other, and there was a growing domestic market. There were also few overseas competitors. The product sold itself.

Some industries today are still said to be product orientated. The machine-tool industry, which produces machines used in the production of other goods, has to produce a final product which exactly matches a technical specification. However, because of increased competition, such firms are being forced to take consumers' needs into account. The technical specification to which a machine-tool business produces might be influenced by what customers want, for example.

Product orientated businesses thus place their emphasis on developing a technically sound product, producing that product and then selling it. Contact with the consumer comes largely at this final stage. There will always be a place for product orientation. A great deal of pure research, for example, with no regard to consumers' needs, still takes place in industry, as it does in the development of pharmaceuticals.

Market orientation A business that is MARKET ORIENTATED business is one which continually identifies, reviews and analyses consumers' needs. It is led by the market. A market orientated business is much more likely to be engaged in effective marketing if it is market orientated. Henry Ford was one of the first industrialists to adopt a market orientated approach. When the Ford motor company produced the Model T, it did not just design a car, produce it as cheaply as possible, and then try to sell it to the public. Instead, in advance of production, Ford identified the price at which he believed he could sell large numbers of Model Ts. His starting point was the market and the Model T became one of the first 'mass-market' products. This illustrates the market orientated approach - consumers are central to a firm's decision making. Sony is one of many modern businesses that has taken a market orientated approach. The Sony Bravia High Definition television is an example of a product being developed in response to the wishes of consumers.

Question 2.

Beverly Morgan started her home-based business, Kitz 4-U Inc. in Hamilton, Ontario, by selling first aid kits to fundraising organisations. She has also developed three other affordable 'Everything You Need In A Pinch' kits - the Bowling Kit, the Golf Kit, and the Travel Kit. The kits are also unique gifts and promotional items. Companies buy the kits to give away as a 'Thank You' to clients or as appreciation gifts to staff.

The challenges Beverly faced starting Kitz 4-U Inc. were those that every new business faces, including product development and defining the market. To produce the kits, she had to find the answers to questions such as, 'What will I put in each kit? What will the packaging look like? Where will I purchase the products I need? Who will do the graphic design? Who will make the packaging?'

To determine which products her potential customers would like to see in the kits, she carried out several market surveys, which she describes as 'very time consuming, but very important.' Once the product list was set, she had to find suppliers, which also took some searching. 'Some wouldn't sell to me, while others took a chance.'

Beverly prepared and rejected several designs before deciding on the final product. The graphic design for the packaging took the longest. Beverly almost went to print before she found the information she needed on packaging laws, which would have been an expensive lesson. Just in time, she discovered that everything was incorrect and the entire design had to be redone.

Source: adapted from http://sbinfocanada.about.com.

(a) Explain why Kitz 4-U Inc is likely to be selling to a niche market.

(b) Examine two problems that the business may have faced operating as a niche market.

(c) Discuss whether the business might grow to become a mass marketing organisation in future.

A more market orientated business may have several advantages over one which is more product orientated.

- It can respond more quickly to changes in the market because of its use of market information.
- It will be in a stronger position to meet the challenge of new competition entering the market.
- It will be more able to anticipate market changes.
- It will be more confident that the launch of a new product will be a success.

What effect will taking a market orientated approach have on a business? It must:

- consult the consumer continuously (market research);
- design the product according to the wishes of the consumer;
- produce the product in the quantities that consumers want to buy;
- distribute the product according to the buying habits and delivery requirements of the consumer;
- set the price of the product at a level that the consumer is prepared to pay.

The business must produce the right product at the right price and in the right place, and it must let the consumer know that it is available. This is known as the **marketing mix**.

The adoption of a market orientated approach will not always guarantee success. Many well-researched products have been failures. Coloroll was a business which started in the wallpaper market and expanded into home textiles and soft furnishings. Its attempt to enter the DIY burglar alarm market, however, was a failure. The company's reputation and design skills had little value in that section of the DIY market compared with other companies, whose reputations were based on home security or electronics. Whether a business places a greater emphasis on the product or on the market will depend on a number of factors.

The nature of the product Where a firm operates in an industry at the edge of new innovation, such as bio-technology, pharmaceuticals or electronics, it must innovate to survive. Although a firm may try to anticipate consumer demand, research is often 'pure' research, i.e. the researcher does not have a specific end product in mind.

Policy decisions A business will have certain objectives. Where these are set in terms of technical quality or safety, the emphasis is likely to be on production. Where objectives are in terms of market share or turnover, the emphasis is likely to be on marketing.

The views of those in control An accountant or a managing director may place emphasis on factors such as cash flow and profit forecasts, a production engineer may give technical quality control and research a high priority and a marketing person may be particularly concerned with market research and consumer relations.

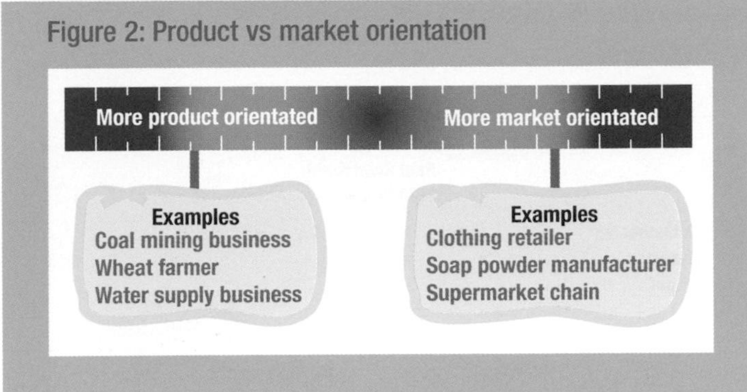

Figure 2: Product vs market orientation

The nature and size of the market If production costs are very high, then a company is likely to be market orientated. Only by being so can a company ensure it meets consumers' needs and avoid unsold goods and possible losses.

The degree of competition A company faced with a lack of competition may devote resources to research with little concern about a loss of market share. Businesses in competitive markets are likely to spend more on marketing for fear of losing their share of the market.

The distinction between product and market orientation could better seen as a spectrum, as in Figure 2. Most business are somewhere along the spectrum. For example, supermarkets may be more market orientated and a copper mining company more product orientated.

Asset-based or asset-led marketing

Both market and product orientated approaches have their limitations. Many businesses have failed because they have offered a high quality product, but have not met the needs of their customers. Perhaps the product was too expensive or the business failed to persuade enough retailers to stock it. Equally, market orientated businesses might fail because they put great effort into certain aspects of marketing, but fail to get the right product to the customer.

Another approach is ASSET-LED or ASSET-BASED MARKETING. A business which is asset-led is responsive to the needs of the market. But equally it takes into account its own strengths and weaknesses when producing a good or providing a service. Its strengths, for example, might include its product, production techniques, goodwill and branding, experience and knowledge.

A tobacco company, for example, might come up with the idea of offering life insurance to smokers. It could offer lower premiums (prices) to its customers than other insurance companies which group smokers and non-smokers together. It also might have a large customer database of users who could be contacted to advertise the insurance. However, selling insurance is a very different business from manufacturing and selling cigarettes. There are likely to be few **synergies**, or links, between the different businesses. The tobacco company has great expertise in the production of cigarettes, but little in selling insurance. Simply because market research shows there is a potentially profitable business opportunity does not mean to say that a business should take it up.

Mass and niche marketing

In order to undertake effective marketing a business needs to consider whom it will be aiming its products at. One way of thinking about this is in terms of niche and mass marketing.

Mass marketing MASS MARKETING occurs when a business offers almost the same products to all consumers and promotes them in almost the same way. Examples of products that are generally mass marketed include Coca-Cola and Microsoft computer software. Mass marketing has a number of features and benefits. Products are usually sold to large number of consumers. They may also be marketed in many different countries, a process known as **global marketing.** This means that a business can manufacture large quantities and the average costs can be reduced as the business gains **economies of scale.** High sales and lower average costs can lead to high profits.

However, there can be problems. It is often expensive to set up production facilities to provide mass marketed products. Such products also face competition in parts of the market from producers who might be more effective in targeting market segments. So mass marketing does not necessarily guarantee profitable products.

Niche marketing NICHE MARKETING involves a business aiming or **targeting** a product at a particular, often small, segment of a market. It is the opposite of mass marketing, which

CRITIQUE

Supporters or marketing argue that it benefits both businesses and their consumers. Businesses that market effectively make profits. Customers who buy the products of these businesses have their requirements met. But some argue that businesses don't seek to meet consumer requirements as their first objective. Instead, they are more interested in profits. They point to the way that some businesses are alleged to 'harm' their customers. Examples might be businesses that make profits by selling foods that may possibly contribute to a poor diet or to obesity.

Critics of marketing would also question the extent to which businesses respond to consumer needs as opposed to creating them. Many would argue that businesses actively work to create the need to consume more, rather than just responding to what consumers want and need. They suggest that consumer needs in general would be better met if businesses encouraged them to spend less rather than more. So while marketing may make sense for individual businesses and their relationships with individual consumers, it does not necessarily work at a wider level. One consequence of this so-called pressure on consumers is that individuals spend beyond their means. This has led to many people taking on more debt than they can manage. Another consequence is more rapid use of the world's resources and the creation of higher levels of environmental damage.

Question 3.

Mark Boyd works as an electrical engineer and plays guitar in groups at weekends. His ambition has been to build and sell his own guitars. After years of testing he has designed a new style of pick-up for a guitar which will reduce noise. Together with his friend Tony, who currently makes hand made acoustic guitars, he wants to build hand made electric guitars which incorporate these new pick-ups. They have some interesting ideas for modern designs, but the guitars will be very labour intensive to build.

After researching the market, Mark and Tony produced the perceptual map shown in Figure 3. They have included mass manufactured guitars with traditional designs by Fender, modern designs such as Parker, and hand made designs by TCM Guitars.

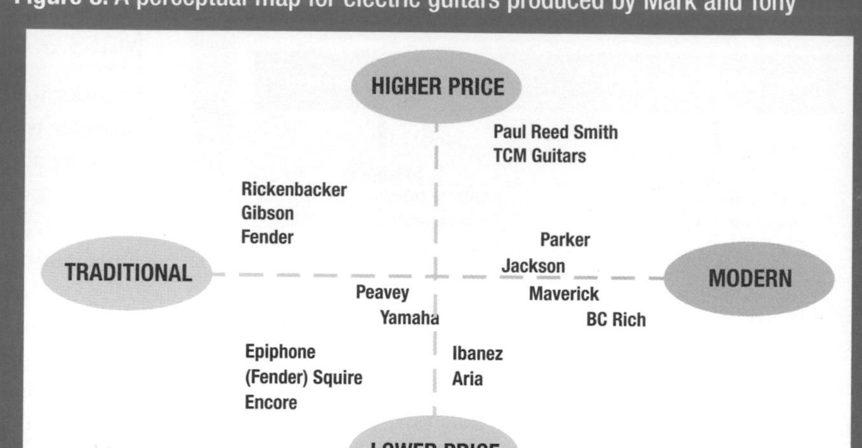

Figure 3: A perceptual map for electric guitars produced by Mark and Tony

(a) How might Mark and Tony have collected the information to produce the perceptual map of electric guitars?
(b) Explain how the information in the perceptual map might help Mark and Tony when they are making marketing decisions about their new products.

involves products being aimed at whole markets rather than at particular parts of them. Why do firms attempt niche marketing?

- Small firms are often able to sell to niche markets which have been either overlooked or ignored by other firms. In this way, they are able to avoid competition in the short run at least.
- By targeting specific market segments, firms can focus on the needs of consumers in these segments. This can allow them to gain an advantage over firms targeting a wider market.

There is, however, a number of problems with niche marketing.

- Firms which manage successfully to exploit a niche market often attract competition. Niche markets, by their very nature, are small and are often unable to sustain two or more competing firms. Large businesses joining the market may benefit from economies of scale which small firms are unable to achieve.
- Many small firms involved in niche marketing have just one product aimed at one small market. This does not allow a business to spread its risks in the way that a business producing many goods might be able to.
- Because niche markets contain small numbers of consumers, they tend to be faced by bigger and more frequent swings in consumer spending than larger markets. This may mean a rapid decline in sales following an equally rapid growth in sales.

Perceptual maps

The positioning of a brand is influenced by customer perceptions rather than by those of businesses. For example, a business may feel its brand is a high quality, up-market product. But if customers see it as low quality and down-market, it is their views that will influence sales.

So, if a business wants to find out where its brand is positioned in the market, it might carry out market research. This will help it to understand how customers see the brand in relation to others in the market.

A business may also wish to launch a new brand. Having decided the target market, market research might show what characteristics the brand must have to succeed in that market. It could reveal the price that customers are prepared to pay. It could also suggest what sort of promotional support will be needed. For example, will a national television advertising campaign be used? Will promotion to retailers be a better strategy?

The results of market research can be displayed on PERCEPTUAL MAPS (sometimes also called MARKET MAPS or POSITIONING MAPS). Typically, the maps are drawn in two

Figure 4: A perceptual map for cars

HIGHER PRICE
Bentley
Rolls Royce
Mercedes
Ferrari
TVR
Morgan
BMW
Jaguar
Audi
TRADITIONAL
SPORTY STYLE
Ford
Vauxhall
Cateram
Fiat
LOWER PRICE

dimensions, as in Figure 4. This allows two of the attributes of the brand to be shown visually. More maps need to be drawn if more than two attributes are shown.

Figure 4 shows a perceptual map for cars. Two characteristics are displayed - the price of a new car and its 'sportiness'. So Bentley cars might be highly priced, but considered traditional. Morgans might be less costly, but considered more sporty. Cateram produces cheaper sporty 'kit cars' which must be self-assembled.

Drawing maps can help a business make marketing decisions about new or existing brands. Market mapping reveals the extent to which brands are similar to or different from those of rivals. A business can then choose to emphasise those similarities or differences through promotion. Or it can change the characteristics if current sales are poor. It could, for example, change its price or its method of promotion. Perhaps the brand itself needs redesigning. Changing the characteristics will help **reposition** the brand in the market.

KEYTERMS

Asset-led or asset-based marketing – where a business combines its knowledge of the market with an understanding of its strengths and weaknesses to decide what products to bring to market.

Business to business marketing – where a business markets its products to other businesses.

Consumer marketing – where a business is marketing to consumers.

Marketing – the management process involved in identifying, anticipating and satisfying consumer requirements profitably.

Market orientation – an approach to business which places the requirements of consumers at the centre of the decision making process.

Mass marketing – the marketing of a product to all possible consumers in the same way.

Niche marketing – the marketing of products to a particular, small segment of the market.

Perceptual maps, positioning maps or market maps – typically a two dimensional diagram which shows two of the attributes or characteristics of a brand and those of rival brands in the market.

Product orientation – an approach to business which places the main focus of attention upon the production process and the product itself.

Relationship marketing – an approach to marketing which seeks to strengthen a business's relationships with its customers.

KNOWLEDGE

1. What is meant by the term marketing?
2. What are the features of effective marketing?
3. Distinguish between marketing and advertising.
4. Why is marketing described as a process?
5. Why might product orientation still be important today?
6. What are the main advantages of a market orientated approach?
7. Why might a market orientated approach still be unsuccessful?
8. What is the difference between mass and niche marketing?

Case Study: House on the Hill Software

House on the Hill Software is a highly successful software business based in Marple near Manchester. The company was established by Iain and Trudy Broadhead in 1993 with the aim of helping businesses to manage their help desks through the use of specialised cost effective computer software. In the fast changing world of IT they provide customers with regular updates, which can be collected from the House on the Hill website and make every effort to adapt and amend their software in response to customer enhancement requests.

In the 14 years the business has been in existence House on the Hill Software has developed a large, diverse customer base spanning over 40 countries. Iain Broadhead explained the reasons for the success of the business as follows: 'Initially our software was developed based upon our own experience of working in the IT business, with sometimes only a partial understanding of the needs of our different customers groups. Gradually, however, we have come to understand what our customers want from our products. Accordingly we've been very careful to respond to these wishes. I think this has been central to our success. We've also never stood still and we are always looking for new ways of developing our products and meeting the evolving needs of our customers'.

One of the biggest selling items produced by House-on-the-Hill is a piece of software called SupportDesk. The driving force behind the continuing development of SupportDesk has been customer feedback based upon longstanding relationships with customers who appreciate the prompt and friendly support offered by the company.

The businesses House on the Hill supply products to are wide and varied and include manufacturing businesses, further education colleges, providers of adventure skills programmes and medical research institutes. House on the Hill maintains regular and close contact with its customers and has become aware of a number of key features it is looking for in SupportDesk. These include functionality (doing what it says it can do), value for money, allowing help desks to become more efficient, enabling help desks to provide quicker responses and being at the forefront of technology.

The business has discovered that one of the main ways in which it gains new business is through word of mouth recommendations from existing customers. 'Our customers are important to us and we pride ourselves on the individual care and attention that we provide. We have long-standing relationships with our customers' said Trudy Broadhead.

Source: www.houseonthehill.com and networkcomputing.co.uk.

(a) Identify whether House on the Hill is engaged in business to business or consumer marketing. Explain your answer. (3 marks)

(b) (i) Explain whether House on the Hill is selling to a niche or mass market. (3 marks) (ii) Explain TWO benefits of this approach to the business. (6 marks)

(c) Examine the factors that may have affected the change in approach to marketing at the business. (8 marks)

(d) Discuss whether the approach to marketing at House on the Hill is effective. (10 marks)

12 Market research

What is market research?

Business activity will only be successful if the output produced can satisfy people's wants and needs. Information about the things people want and need will help businesses to decide what to produce. This information is often found through MARKET RESEARCH.

Market research can be defined as the collection, collation and analysis of data relating to the marketing and consumption of goods and services. For example, a business might gather information about the likely consumers of a new product and use the data to help in its decision-making process. The data gathered by this research might include:

- whether or not consumers would want such a product;
- what type of promotion will be effective;
- the functions or facilities it should have;
- what style, shape, colour or form it should take;
- the price people would be prepared to pay for it;
- where people would wish to purchase it;
- information about consumers themselves - their ages, their likes, attitudes, interests and lifestyles;
- what consumers buy at present.

Some, mainly smaller or local, businesses have just a few customers who are well known to them. For these businesses, information about their markets can be relatively easy to find. This may be through personal and social contact with their customers. Such businesses, however, must be careful that they do not misread their customers' views and actions. Other businesses, both small and large, have a more distant relationship with their customers. This may be because they have a large number of customers, operate in a range of different markets or market their products in international as well as national markets. For these businesses, market information may be less easy to come by. Such businesses often find that in order to gather marketing information they need to use sophisticated marketing research methods.

The terms **market research** and **marketing research** are usually used interchangeably in business books and in the media. This is the approach taken in this book. Some have suggested a distinction between the two terms. Market research, they argue, is about researching consumers' preferences and tastes. Marketing research is a wider term, which also includes the analysis of marketing strategies, for example the effect of promotions such as advertising.

The uses of market research

A market is anywhere that buyers and sellers come together to exchange goods and services. Markets are in a constant state of change. As a result, a business is likely to use market research on a regular basis for a number of reasons.

Descriptive reasons A business may wish to identify what is happening in its market. For example, a brewery may want to find trends in its sales of various types of beer over a certain period, or to find out which types of customer are buying a particular beer.

Predictive reasons A business may wish to predict what is likely to happen in the future. For example, a travel company will want to discover possible changes in the types of holiday that people might want to take over the next two to five years. This will place it in a better position to design new holiday packages that will sell.

Explanatory reasons A business may want to explain a variety of matters related to its marketing. This may include sales in a particular part of the country. A bus company, for example, might wish to research why there has been a fall in the number of passengers on a specific route.

Table 1: The scope of market research

Area of research	Possible elements to be considered
The market	Identifying market trends Discovering the potential size of the market Identifying market segments Building up a profile of potential/actual consumers Forecasting sales levels
Competition	Analysing the strengths and weaknesses of competitors Identifying relative market shares Identifying trends in competitors' sales Finding information on competitors' prices
Promotion	Analysing the effectiveness of promotional materials Deciding upon choice of media for promotions
The product	Testing different product alternatives Identifying consumer wants Developing new product ideas Assessing consumer reaction to a newly launched product
Distributing the product	Identifying suitable retail outlets Exploring attitudes of distributors towards products
Pricing the product	Discovering the value consumers place on the product Identifying the sensitivity of the demand for the product to changes in its price

Exploratory reasons These are concerned with a business investigating new possibilities in a market. For example, a soft drinks manufacturer could trial a new canned drink in a small geographical area to test customer reaction before committing itself to marketing the product nationally.

Once a business has decided how it wishes to use market research data, the next stage is to identify the aspects or areas that it wants to concentrate on. Table 1 shows the different areas that could be researched and some possible elements that might be considered in each.

Secondary research

SECONDARY or DESK RESEARCH involves the collection of SECONDARY DATA. This is information which **already exists** in some form. It can be internal data, from records within the business or external data, from sources outside the business.

Internal data This may be collected from existing business documents or other publications, including the following.

- Existing market research reports.
- Sales figures. The more sophisticated these are the better. For example, sales figures which have been broken down according to market segments can be particularly useful.
- Reports from members of the sales force resulting from direct contact with customers.
- Annual Report and Accounts published by businesses.
- Businesses increasingly make use of company intranets to provide up-to-date information. These are restricted to company employees. But some information may be available on the Internet on company websites.
- Stock movements. These can often provide the most up-to-date information on patterns of demand in the market. This is because they are often recorded instantly, as opposed to sales figures, which tend to be collected at a later date.

External data Secondary data will also be available from sources outside the business. Individuals or other organisations will have collected data for their own reasons. A business might be able to use this for its own market research. Examples are given below.

- Information from competitors. This may be, for example, in the form of promotional materials, product specifications or price lists.
- Government publications. There are many government publications that businesses can use. These include general statistical publications such as *Social Trends*, the *Census of Population* and the *Annual Abstract of Statistics*. Many are now online.
- Data from customer services on complaints which have been received about a product.
- The European Union. The EU now provides a wide range of secondary data which can be highly valuable to businesses operating within EU countries. Such publications include *Eurostatistics*, which is published by Eurostat (the Statistical Office of the European Union).
- International publications. There is a huge amount of information about overseas marketing published each year by organisations such as the World Bank and the International Monetary Fund.
- Commercial publications. A number of organisations exist to gather data about particular markets. This information is often highly detailed and specialised. Mintel, Dun & Bradstreet and Verdict are examples of such organisations.
- Retail audits. The widespread use of Epos (electronic point of sale) has meant that it is now much easier to collect detailed and up-to-the-minute data on sales in retail outlets such as supermarkets and other retail chains. Retail audits provide manageable data by monitoring and recording sales in a sample of retail outlets. Businesses find these audits especially helpful because of the way in which they provide a continuous monitoring of their performance in the market. A well known example is data on the best selling records or CDs which make up weekly music charts. This information is collected from retail outlets in the UK.

Table 2: Advantages and disadvantages of secondary or desk research

Advantages

- It is relatively easy, quick and cheap to collect, especially if the sources that exist are known. This makes it very useful for smaller businesses.
- Several sources may be used. This allows the data to be checked and verified.
- Historical data may be used which can show a trend over time.
- It can be used before carrying out secondary research, which helps to establish the most useful questions to be asked in questionnaires.

Disadvantages

- Data is not always in a form that a particular business would want because it has been collected for another purpose. Adapting it may take time and become expensive.
- Data may be out of date and not relevant, especially in fast changing markets.
- Researchers must be aware of bias. For example, company reports and accounts may show figures in the best possible light to satisfy shareholders.
- There may have been problems with the research. For example, the footnotes to research may state that the sample used was too small and that the results may be inaccurate as a result.

- General publications. A business may use a range of publications widely available to members of the public for its market research. These include newspaper and magazine articles and publications such as the *Yellow Pages.*
- Internet website pages. Increasingly businesses make use of the Internet to search for secondary data outside of their own organisations. Many of the sources of secondary information above (including, for example, government publications) can now be found on the Internet.

Primary research

PRIMARY or FIELD RESEARCH involves collecting PRIMARY DATA. This is information which did not exist before the research began. In other words, it has to be collected by the researcher. It can either be carried out by a business itself or by a **market research agency**. Because of the high costs of using the services of a market research agency many small businesses choose to conduct market research themselves.

Most primary information is gathered by asking consumers questions or by monitoring their behaviour. The most accurate way to do this would be to question or observe all consumers of a particular product (known as the population). However, in all but a few instances this would be either impractical to carry out or expensive. It is usual to carry out a SURVEY of a SAMPLE of people who are thought to be representative of the total market. Methods of choosing samples are dealt with in the next unit.

Methods of primary research

There is a number of different field research methods a business can use. Many of these methods make use of QUESTIONNAIRES. A questionnaire is a series of questions designed to find out the views and opinions of a respondent. It must be designed to meet the needs of the business carrying out the survey. A poorly designed questionnaire may not obtain the results the business is looking for. There are certain features of questionnaires which are important in their design.

- The balance between **closed** and **open** questions. Closed questions, such as 'How many products have you bought in the last month?', only allow the interviewee a limited range of responses. Open questions, however, allow interviewees considerable scope in the responses which they are able to offer. Open questions allow certain issues to be investigated in great detail, but they do require a high degree of expertise from the interviewer. For example, an open question might be 'Suggest how the product could be improved'.
- The clarity of questions. The questions used must be clear and unambiguous so that they do not confuse or mislead the interviewee. 'Technical' language should be avoided if possible.
- The use of leading questions. Leading questions are those which encourage a particular answer. For example, a small shop wanting to find out about its consumer preferences for Coke and Pepsi should avoid the question: 'Do you

Question 1.

The local gym could be the new place for match making. A survey by Mintel found that around 19 per cent (1 in 5) of members have met good friends or partners there. Around 25 per cent (1 in 4) see it as a place to meet people with similar interests. 'Health and fitness clubs are now so much more than just somewhere to exercise and get fit... . Clubs could look to organise more networking and evening socials for their members, while major dating agencies might like to consider acquiring a strategic stake in health and fitness clubs as a base for their activities,' said Mark Brechin, senior leisure analyst at MINTEL.

After a number of years of facing rising costs and competition MINTEL predicted a 9 per cent rise in revenue in 2006, compared with around 5 per cent in the recent past. The size of the market for leisure services was predicted to reach £2.5 billion, with more than 5 million visitors, and one in ten as club members. Most revenue (76 per cent) was from membership fees, but a growing amount comes from bars and personal treatments. This grew 32 per cent between 2002 and 2006. MINTEL's research also showed that among those adults who have never been to a health and fitness club, 8 per cent would be interested in using one. MINTEL also forecast impressive growth. The market value was predicted to reach £3.4 billion by 2012, increasing almost 40 per cent over the next five years, with the number of members set to reach 7.6 million. ' Competitive pressures and energy prices have eased off from their peak at the end of 2005 and the start of 2006. Meanwhile, consolidation within the industry has removed a lot of the discounting on membership and joining fees among the leading club chains,' explained Mark Brechin.

Source: adapted from www.mintel.com.

(a) If a health club seeking to research its market found the above report on the Internet would this be an example of primary or secondary research? Explain your answer.

(b) Explain, using examples from the article, how a health and fitness club might use the research conducted by Mintel for: (i) descriptive reasons; (ii) predictive reasons; (iii) explanatory reasons.

think that Diet Pepsi is better than Diet Coke?' A better question would be: 'Which brand of diet cola do you prefer - Pepsi or Coke?'

- The questionnaire can provide **quantifiable** information. For example, it might tell a business that 75 per cent of its sales are to people below the age of 25 and only 25 per cent are to over-25s. It may be able to use this information to make decisions.
- Whether it is to be completed by the person carrying out the survey or completed by the respondent.

Personal interviews These involve an interviewer obtaining information from one person face-to-face. The interviewer rather than the interviewee fills out the responses to questions on a questionnaire, which contains mainly 'open' questions. The main advantage of interviews is that they allow the chance for interviewees to give detailed responses to questions that concern them. Long or difficult questions can also be explained by the interviewer and the percentage of responses that can be used is likely to be high. If needed, there is time and scope for answers to be followed up in more detail. Interviews, however, can be time consuming and tend to rely on the skill of the interviewer. For example, a poorly trained interviewer asking questions on a product she did not like may influence the responses of the interviewees by appearing negative.

IT-based research Advances in IT have led to the development of new ways in which businesses can carry out field research.

- Businesses are increasingly making use of Internet and email surveys, where customers can provide data on a business website or email directly to businesses' email addresses.
- Retail audits consist of information collected by retailers about consumers, usually at the point at which a purchase is made. Epos (electronic point of sale) data can be used, for example, to analyse patterns and trends in sales. Data gathered from retail audits is also valuable for identifying the types of consumers purchasing particular products.
- In the UK many shopping centres have devices installed which record where customers shop. Recorders have been developed which 'count' the number of customers entering a shop and some even differentiate between adults, children and pushchairs. The technology provides information which allows shops to see which areas of the centre attract most shoppers. It can also be used to compare shopping centres.
- Interactive methods can also be used to gather information. Consumers may be able to express their views via Internet websites or digital television. Information can be collected when orders are placed directly via the Internet or a digital television link.
- Spending patterns may be analysed from the use of credit cards and store loyalty cards. Loyalty cards allow customers to obtain a certain amount of benefits and discounts with each purchase they make within a shop or supermarket.

Question 2.

Vegran is a company that has developed a healthy lunch bar made from carob and oats. Initially, it has decided to sell the bar in the South West for a trial period, before launching the product throughout the country. Before this, however, it wants to collect views of consumers on the taste and appearance of the bar. It is particularly interested to find out whether consumers would notice a difference in taste between chocolate and carob and their views on the bar's size and packaging. Vegran is only a small company with a limited budget for its marketing projects.

(a) What potential advantages might test marketing have for Vegran?

(b) How useful might:
(i) postal surveys; (ii) consumer panels;
(iii) personal interviews; (iv) Internet surveys;
be to the business?

Telephone interviews This method allows the interview to be held over the telephone. It has the advantage of being cheaper than personal interviewing and allows a wide geographical area to be covered. However, it is often distrusted by the public and it is only possible to ask short questions.

Postal surveys These involve the use of questionnaires sent to consumers through the post. It is a relatively cheap method of conducting field research. It also has the advantage that there is no interviewer bias and a wide geographical area can easily be covered. Unfortunately, the response rate to postal questionnaires can be poor and responses can take as long as six weeks. In addition, questions must be short, so detailed questioning may not be possible. Questionnaires must also be well designed and easy to understand if they are to work.

Observation Observation is often used by retail firms 'watching' consumers in their stores. Observers look out for the amount of time consumers spend making decisions and how readily they notice a particular display. Its advantage is that a tremendous number of consumers can be surveyed in a relatively short space of time. However, observation alone can leave many questions unanswered. For example, it may reveal that a particular display at a supermarket is unpopular, but provide no clues as to why this is the case.

Focus groups These involve a group of customers being brought together on one or a number of occasions. They are asked to answer and discuss questions prepared by market researchers. The groups contain a range of individuals who are thought to be representative of the customers of the business or of a particular segment of customers. Because they only involve a small number of customers, focus groups are a relatively cheap and easy way of gathering marketing research information. A problem is that the views of a fairly small number of customers may not reflect the views of the market or the market segment in which the business is interested.

Consumer panels These involve a group of consumers being consulted on their reactions to a product over a period of time. Consumer panels are widely used by TV companies to judge the reactions of viewers to new and existing programmes. Their main advantage is that they can be used to consider how consumer reaction changes over time. Firms can then build up a picture of consumer trends. Their disadvantage is that it is both difficult and expensive to choose and keep a panel available for research over a long period.

Test marketing Test marketing involves selling a product in a restricted section of the market in order to assess consumer reaction to it. Test marketing usually takes place by making a product available within a particular geographical area. For example, before the Wispa chocolate bar was marketed nationally, it was test marketed in the North East of England.

The benefits of market research

A business may benefit in a number of ways from carrying out market research.

An aid to decision making Perhaps the main benefit of market research is that it allows a business to make more informed decisions. This is especially important in fast-changing markets. Businesses operating in such markets constantly need to adjust their marketing activities.

Reducing risk While the reliability of market research information cannot be guaranteed, it does reduce risk for a business. Without market research, a business might spend large sums developing and launching a new product, which could prove to be unsuccessful. Businesses are less likely to waste resources on failed activities if careful marketing research is carried out.

Providing a link with the outside world Without market research might businesses operate in a vacuum. They would have little or no way of finding out the views of their actual and potential customers. They would also find it difficult to identify future trends in their existing markets and the markets in which they plan to operate in future.

Estimating the size of markets As markets become ever larger and as new markets open up, market research becomes ever more important. As markets get larger it becomes more difficult for businesses to operate without detailed information about the needs of their customers. This is because of differences in their tastes.

Public relations Carrying out market research may be good for the image of a business. Consumers may feel that their views are being considered. They may also think that the business is concerned that its customers are happy. This may lead to 'corporate' brand loyalty.

Table 3: Advantages and disadvantages of primary or field research

Advantages
• Data can be collected that directly applies to the issue being researched. Secondary data will be data collected for another purpose.
• The business which initially collects the data will be the only organization with access to it. It can be used to gain marketing advantages over rival firms.
• Secondary data may be unavailable in a certain area.

Disadvantages
• It can be expensive to collect and may take longer than desk research
• The sample taken may not represent the views of all the population.
• If the research method is flawed, the findings will also be flawed. For example, a badly worded questionnaire may not provide the data a business requires.

The problems of market research

If market research was totally dependable, businesses could use it when introducing or changing products and be completely confident about how consumers would respond to them. This would mean that all new products launched onto the market, which had been researched in advance, would be a success. Similarly, no products would flop because businesses would receive advance warning from their research and take any necessary measures.

In reality, things can be different. It has been estimated that 90 per cent of all products fail after they have been initially launched. Some of this may be put down to a lack of, or inadequate, market research. However, a number of businesses that have conducted extensive research among consumers before committing a product to the market place have launched products which have failed. Given estimates which suggest that the minimum cost of launching a new product nationally is £1 million, this is a risky business. Famous examples of thoroughly researched products which have turned out to be flops include the Sinclair C5, a cheap vehicle with more stability than a moped and lower costs than a car. In research, consumers enthused over this vehicle. In reality, it was almost impossible to sell. Similarly, when Coca-Cola launched 'New Coke' with a new formula flavour onto the market, research suggested it would be a huge success. In practice, 'New Coke' was quickly withdrawn from the shops.

Businesses want to be sure that the data they collect is reliable. One way of checking the reliability of data is to pose the question, 'If this information was collected again would the same or broadly similar results be obtained?' Businesses acting upon research data need to be sure that they can depend upon it. There is a great deal of debate among researchers about the reliability of different research methods. There is a number of reasons why **primary research** does not always provide reliable information for businesses.

- Human behaviour. Much marketing research depends upon the responses of consumers who participate in the collection of primary data. While the responses of consumers may be honest and truthful at the time, it does not mean that they will necessarily respond in the same manner in future. This is because all human behaviour, including the act of consuming and purchasing goods, is to some extent unpredictable.
- Sampling and bias. When carrying out market research, it is usual to base the research upon a sample of the total population. This is because it would be impossible and costly to include every person when dealing with a large population. It is possible, however, that results from the sample may be different from those that would have been obtained if the whole population had been questioned. This is known as a sampling discrepancy. The greater the sampling discrepancy, the less reliable will be the data obtained.
- As mentioned earlier, questionnaires need to be carefully constructed to avoid the problem of encouraging particular responses from consumers through the use of leading questions. Similarly, the behaviour of interviewers can affect the outcome of interviews.

Businesses must also be careful when using **secondary data**. For example, businesses may use a government publication to estimate the size of markets in which they might wish to operate. However, these market sizes may not always accurately match the product market being researched.

Quantitative and qualitative research

Data collected through desk and field research can be either quantitative or qualitative in nature. QUALITATIVE RESEARCH involves the collection of data about attitudes, beliefs and intentions. Focus groups and interviews are common methods used to collect qualitative data. An example of qualitative research could be face-to-face interviews with 100 purchasers of new Land Rover Discoveries to find out why they prefer this product to similar four wheel drives sold by other car manufacturers. The information collected through qualitative research is usually regarded as being open to a high degree of interpretation. This means that there are often disagreements within businesses about the significance and importance of qualitative research data.

QUANTITATIVE RESEARCH involves the collection of data that can be measured. In practice this usually means the collection of statistical data such as sales figures and market share. Surveys and the use of government publications are common methods of collecting quantitative research data. An example of quantitative research would be a survey of four wheel drive owners in West Derbyshire to establish their places of residence, ages, occupations, incomes and gender. The information collected through quantitative research is usually regarded as being open to less interpretation than that collected through qualitative research.

KEY TERMS

Confidence level – a statistical calculation which allows a business to gauge the extent of its confidence in the results of research.
Market or marketing research – the collection, collation and analysis of data relating to the marketing and consumption of goods and services.
Primary data – information which does not already exist and is collected through the use of field research.
Primary or field research – the gathering of 'new' data which has not been collected before.
Qualitative research – the collection of data about attitudes, beliefs and intentions.
Quantitative research – the collection of data that can be quantified.
Questionnaire – a series of questions designed to find out the views and opinions of a respondent.
Sample – a selection of part of the population, which must be representative of the population to be effective.
Secondary data – data which is already in existence. It is normally used for a purpose other than that for which it was collected.
Secondary or desk research – the collection of data that has already been collected for another purpose.
Survey – where respondents provide information to researchers about their actions, habits, attitudes and perceptions.

KNOWLEDGE

1. Why is market research important to businesses?
2. Explain the difference between:
   (a) descriptive research;
   (b) predictive research;
   (c) explanatory research.
3. State five areas that market research could concentrate on.
4. What is meant by desk research?
5. What is meant by field research?
6. Why might field research be of benefit to a business?
7. In what circumstances might:
   (a) postal surveys;
   (b) questionnaires;
   (c) observation;
   be useful?
8. Suggest three benefits of market research to a business
9. What is the difference between qualitative and quantitative market research?

Case Study: Beer sales plunge as Britons stay at home

Sales of beer dropped to their lowest level since the 1930s, according to figures released today. The British Beer and Pub Association (BBPA), which represents the brewing and pub industry, revealed that 14 million fewer pints are being sold daily in pubs today - a slump of 49 per cent since the peak in 1979. Part of the long-term trend has been the move towards drinking at home. In the late 70s, 90 per cent of beer was drunk in pubs, but the figure now stands at 58 per cent. While the biggest casualties of Britain's increasing preference for wine and spirits have been the pubs, they are, however, not alone: overall beer sales have plunged by 22 per cent from the peak 1979 level.

The BBPA says the situation is exacerbated by rising production costs as the prices of barley, malt, glass, aluminium and energy increase. It also feels that taxes on beer in the form of a duty imposed by the Treasury is making matters worse. Since 1997, beer duty has risen by 27 per cent while consumption has fallen by 11 per cent. Wine duty, meanwhile, has increased by just 16 per cent, while wine-drinking has gone up by 46 per cent. It's a similar story with spirits. Although consumption has risen by 20 per cent over the last decade, duty has increased by only 3 per cent.

Major British brewers saw their profits tumble by 78 per cent between 2004 and 2006. Last week, two major brewers - Scottish & Newcastle UK and Carlsberg UK - warned pubs that rising costs and a poor summer meant that big rises in wholesale beer prices were likely.

A senior executive at S&NUK told the pub trade paper *The Morning Advertiser* that prices would probably increase 'way above the rate of inflation' during the first part of next year. He said that rising cereal, crude oil and aluminium prices meant that brewers would be forced to charge more to recoup their losses.

Beer is not only falling victim to the growing fondness for wine among Britons. Its popularity is also suffering because of a cultural shift to drinking at home. In 2005, 60 per cent of all the wine sold in the UK was bought in supermarkets. And the wine and champagne market, which is now worth more than £10.2 billion, increased by 26 per cent between 2002 and 2006. Over the same period, sales of spirits and liqueurs went up by 16 per cent. However, some sections of the brewing industry are performing well, and real ale has enjoyed a quiet revival over recent years as consumers develop a taste for more authentic, natural and traditional products.

'This comes against a backdrop of a slump across the whole beer market,' said Owen Morris, a spokesman for the Campaign for Real Ale, a pressure group seeking to promote sales of traditionally brewed beers. 'But we've seen a 7.5 per cent year-on-year growth in sales of regional beers. People are enjoying regional beer more, even though the large breweries are forgetting about traditional beers and pushing lagers.' Mr Morris also referred to the threat posed by the supermarkets, which use cheap beer as a loss leader.

Table 4: The UK beer market

Table 4: The UK beer market
1930s The last time the volume of beer sold through pubs was this low
22 per cent The amount by which the total beer market has fallen since its peak in 1979
49 per cent The amount by which pub beer sales have fallen since 1979, equivalent to 14 million fewer pints every day
78 per cent The fall between 2004 and last year in the profits enjoyed by the major British brewers
Source: adapted from the *Guardian*, 20.11. 2007.

Consider the research above from the perspective of the owner of an independent pub.

(a) Is the research referred to in the article primary or secondary research? Explain your answer. (4 marks)

(b) Outline the reasons why a pub owner may find the research in the above article useful. (6 marks)

(c) Explain the various ways in which a pub owner might seek to collect primary data to complement the data provided in the article above. (10 marks)

(d) Analyse the potential usefulness of the data provided in the article for a pub owner. (10 marks)

13 Sampling

What is a sample?

Sometimes a business or market research organisation may be able to carry out market research by means of a **survey** of all its target POPULATION. The **target population** is those people whose views it wants to find out. For example, a business making components might only supply five companies with parts. So it should be fairly easy to survey all of its customers. But in most cases it is impractical to survey the whole population. It would take too long and would be too costly to gather and process the information.

Instead, researchers take a sample of the population. Samples should be REPRESENTATIVE. They should have the same characteristics as the whole population. If they don't, results from the sample which are generalised to the whole population may be inaccurate. For example, a survey may be carried out by a food company to find out how many people would buy a new, up-market product. If it only asked pensioners on low incomes, it would almost certainly find that the survey predicted fewer sales than would actually be the case. This is because the sample chosen did not accurately reflect the whole population. In this case SAMPLING BIAS is present. **Questionnaires** are often used to gather data from a sample.

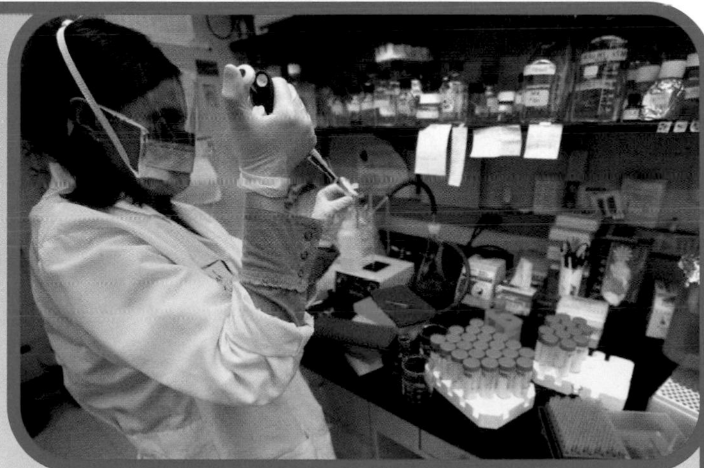

Question 1.

A pharmaceutical (drugs) company wanted to commission a study on male health worldwide. The results would be used to make major marketing decisions. A market research agency was commissioned to carry out the study. It set about conducting a two phase research project using survey techniques. In the first phase, 20,000 interviews were completed with target respondents in eight countries. A combination of phone and web interviewing was used. In the second phase, a random selection of about 5 per cent of the initial respondents for participation in a second interview were identified. These interviews were conducted on the Internet for those with access or through the use of a paper questionnaire.

The research methods used meant that the same questions were put to all respondents and answers collated in the same manner.

(a) Explain the type of sampling method used by the business.

(b) The market research agency interviewed 20,000 males in eight countries. Suggest why it interviewed (i) males only; (ii) respondents in eight countries rather than one country only and (iii) 20,000 people rather than 1,000 or 500,000.

(c) How much statistical bias would you expect to see in the findings from this research?

Size of sample

The SAMPLE SIZE will influence how representative the sample is of the population. Larger samples tend to be more representative. For example, say that the target population is 10,000 customers. If the sample were the same size as the target population, 10,000, it would be totally representative. A sample of 9,000 people is more likely to reflect the characteristics of the target population than 10 people surveyed on the street. So decisions based on the results of the larger sample are more likely to be accurate. There is a number of ways in which a sample can be chosen.

Type of sample

There are different types of sample and sampling methods that can be used by a business carrying out primary research.

Random sampling RANDOM SAMPLING gives each member of a group an equal chance of being chosen. In other words, the sample is selected at random, rather like picking numbers out of a hat. Today computers can be used to produce a random list of numbers, which are then used as the basis for selecting a sample. The main advantage of random sampling is that bias cannot be introduced when choosing the sample. However, it assumes that all members of the group are the same (homogeneous), which is not always the case. A small sample chosen in this way may not have the characteristics of the population, so a very large sample would have to be taken to make sure it was representative. It would be very costly and time consuming for firms to draw up a list of the whole population and then contact and interview them.

Systematic sampling One method sometimes used to reduce the time taken to locate a random sample is to choose every tenth or twentieth name on a list. This is known as SYSTEMATIC SAMPLING. It is, however, less random.

Stratified random sampling This method of sampling is also random. However, unlike the types of random sampling described above, STRATFIED RANDOM SAMPLING is where the sample is divided into **segments** or **strata** based on previous knowledge about how the population is divided up. For example, a business may be interested in how employment status affected the demand for a food product. It might divide the population up into different income groups, such as higher managerial and professional occupations, small employers and 'own account' workers etc. A random sample could then be chosen from each of these groups, making sure that there were the same proportions of the sample in each category as in the population as a whole. Therefore, if the population had 10 per cent upper class males, so would the sample. Stratified sampling is often preferred by researchers as it makes the sample more representative of the whole group and is less likely to privilege particular sub-groups than random sampling.

Quota sampling QUOTA SAMPLING involves the population being segmented into a number of groups which share specific characteristics. These may be based on the age and sex of the population. Interviewers are then given targets for the number of people out of each segment who they must interview. For example, an interviewer may be asked to interview 10 males between the ages of 18 and 25, or 15 females between the ages of 45 and 60. Once the target is reached, no more people are interviewed from that group. The advantage of this sampling method is that it can be cheaper to operate than many of the others. It is also useful where the proportions of different groups within the population are known. However, results from quota sampling are not statistically representative of the population and are not randomly chosen.

Snowballing SNOWBALLING is a highly specialised method of sampling. It involves starting the process of sampling with one individual or group and then using these contacts to develop more, hence the 'snowball' effect. This is only used when other sampling methods are not possible, due to the fact that samples built up by snowballing cannot be representative. Businesses operating in highly secretive markets, such as the arms trade, may use this method of sampling. Similarly, firms engaged in producing highly specialised and expensive one-off products for a very limited range of customers may need to rely upon snowballing when engaged in marketing research. Examples might include firms engaged in the nuclear and power generating industries.

Cluster sampling CLUSTER SAMPLING involves separating the population into 'clusters', usually in different geographical areas. A random sample is then taken from the clusters, which are assumed to be representative of the population. This method is often used when survey results need to be found quickly, such as in opinion polls.

Multi-stage sampling This involves selecting one sample from another sample. So, for example, a market researcher might choose a county at random and then a district of that county may be selected. Similarly, a street within a city may be chosen and then a particular household within a street.

Factors affecting the sampling method and size of sample

Businesses will take account of a number of key factors when making their choice as to which sampling method to deploy:

Finance available For some small businesses this means that random sampling can be beyond their means. Larger businesses, however, may have the resources to undertake market research methods that give more random results and use larger sample sizes.

The nature of the product The nature of a product produced by a business can affect the sampling method chosen during market research. This relates, in particular, to whether a product is the same for all consumers (uniform) or carefully adapted to meet the needs of individual consumers or very small groups of consumers (bespoke). For products that are uniform, a business will need to ensure that all of the population are properly represented in a sample and will need to ensure that little or no statistical bias is introduced in the sample. This is likely to mean a relatively large sample size. For products that are 'one-offs', bespoke or made to order, the population is likely to be very small or confined to just one person or business. In this case sampling is likely to be very straightforward and rely upon a relatively small sample, without the accompanying need for

Question 2.

Graham Hunter is a farmer in Cambridgeshire, producing a range of vegetables. All of his supplies go to three large supermarket chains and he and his farm have been featured on the packaging at one of these supermarkets. In making decisions about what vegetables to grow in the forthcoming year, Graham has decided to undertake some market research. His research will be based upon speaking to the Head Buyer at each of these supermarkets and asking their opinions.

(a) **Explain why Graham Hunter can be said to have used a sample.**
(b) **Explain TWO factors that may have influence Graham's choice of sample.**
(c) **How reliable do you think the results of his research might be?**

Question 3.

DPX is a market research company. In 2003, it completed a report for a manufacturer of building materials and fittings which had seen an unexpected fall in sales over the previous 12 months. The manufacturer wanted to find out how its immediate customers, DIY chains such as B&Q and Wickes, and the larger number of builders' and plumbers' merchants, viewed its products. For example, it wanted to find out whether customers saw its products as giving value for money compared to those of competitors, whether the fittings were reliable and whether the range of products was large enough. It also wanted information about sales and profits of rival businesses to see if they had experienced a similar downturn.

DPX devised a telephone questionnaire for customers. In its sample, it interviewed all the large DIY chains. But it only conducted 30 interviews with smaller builders' and plumbers' merchants. The sample of 30 was judged to be representative of all smaller builders' and plumbers' merchants and a 95 per cent confidence level was given for the responses.

The research showed that a major rival company had completely updated its range over the previous 24 months. The products of the manufacturing company commissioning the research had lost competitiveness as a result. For example, they were said by respondents to be giving less good value for money than before.

(a) Explain what is meant by 'a 95 per cent confidence level was given for the responses' from the smaller plumbers' and builders' merchants.

(b) How might the business reduce the chance that its results did not reflect the views of all small builders and plumbers' merchants?

(c) Discuss ONE strategy the manufacturing company might develop to reverse the decline in its sales.

sophisticated sampling techniques such as those described above.

The risk involved The greater a risk a business is taking, the more reliable it would like its results to be. Thus a business taking a large risks for example financially, or in terms of the business's future survival, would want to use the most reliable and sophisticated sampling method available to it. This would for many businesses mean a relatively larger sample size. It would reduce the risk of statistical bias and increase the reliability of the findings from the sample. By way of contrast, a business taking a small risk might be prepared to go ahead with less reliable and, possibly, informal sampling methods such as talking to a few customers. A small ice cream business that has one shop, for example, might introduce a new flavour of ice cream after asking the views of, or in response to requests from, just a few customers. If the new flavour doesn't prove popular with customers, it could be rapidly withdrawn and replaced by another. Little would be lost by the business. A large ice cream manufacturer, on the other hand, selling products to millions of customers, would be unlikely to change its production processes on the basis of such a small sample. This is because the risk associated with a wrong decision would be so great.

The target market The nature of a product's target market will influence the sampling undertaken as part of market research. For example, if there is a small target market for a product, then the sample chosen will be smaller. Similarly, if the characteristics of a products' target market are similar or the same and they are in a particular market segment, then this will influence the sampling method. In such cases businesses may use cluster or quota sampling. For products aimed at mass markets with a range of consumers, the sampling methods chosen will need to reflect this diversity and this is likely to mean a larger sample size.

Sample results and statistical significance

The only way to get an accurate picture of a population is to have all relevant data about that population. But this takes time and is expensive. So researchers take a sample and the results obtained from the sample are then applied to the whole population. But how confident can a business be about the results of such a survey? When analysing data from a sample, researchers are interested in certain statistics.

- The mean. This is the average result For example, the average amount spent on a Monday by a shopper may be £10. On Saturday it may be £20.
- The STANDARD DEVIATION. This tells researchers about the spread of results. Standard deviation measures the average difference (deviation) of each item of data from the mean. For example, the standard deviation from the average amount spent may be £2 on Monday and £5 on Saturday. Comparing the means shows that shoppers spent

Figure 1: A normal distribution

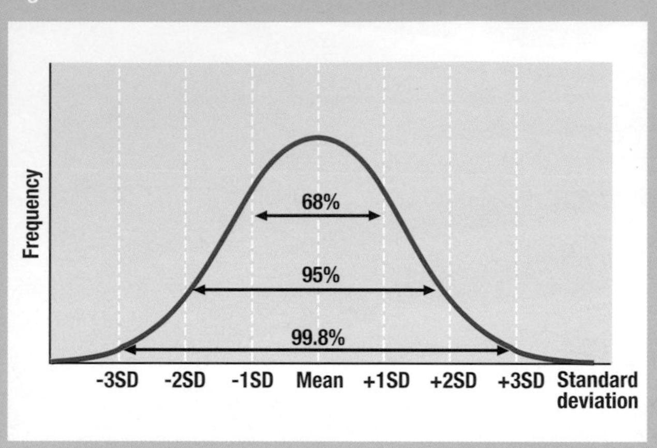

Figure 2: Setting a 95 per cent confidence level

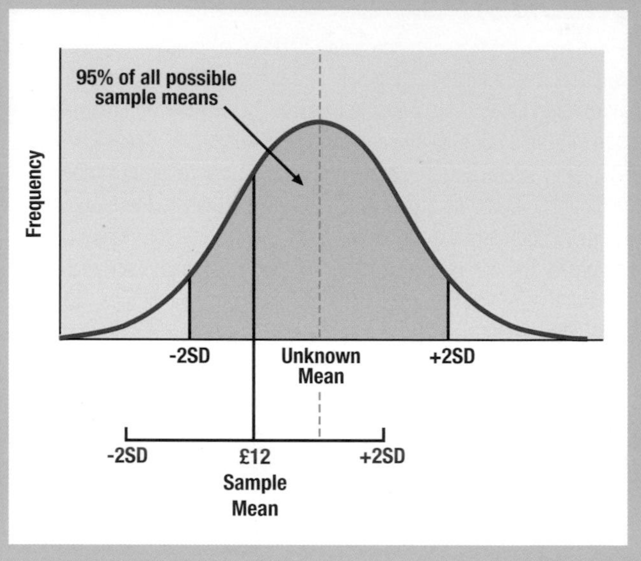

twice as much on Saturday than on Monday. The standard deviations show that the spread of amounts spent was greater on Saturday than on Monday. So, on Monday, the amounts spent by shoppers varied less and were generally closer to the mean.

- Researchers also make use of a NORMAL DISTRIBUTION curve. This is a 'bell shaped' frequency distribution. It shows the results that can be usually be expected when the whole population is surveyed.

There is a relationship between the normal distribution, the mean and the standard deviation. The mean is in the centre. Most results cluster around the mean, with a few high and low values away from the mean. The data is symmetrically distributed around the mean, so that 50 per cent of results lie either side of the mean, as in Figure 1. In a normal distribution:

- about 68 per cent of values lie within 1 standard deviation of the mean on either side;
- about 95 per cent of values lie within 2 standard deviations of the mean on either side;
- about 99.8 per cent of values lie within 3 standard deviations of the mean on either side.

Look at Figure 2. What if a business did not know the mean (average) spending, but a sample found that it was £12? How would it know whether this was an accurate reflection of the population? To do this a range of values must be taken either side of £12, which will hopefully include the unknown mean spending. A 95 per cent CONFIDENCE LEVEL could be set, where values of 2 standards deviations either side of the mean are included. The business would then know that in 95 out of

KEYTERMS

Cluster sampling – where respondents are chosen for interview in a few locations, to reduce the cost of research, rather than being spread evenly across the population.

Confidence level – expresses as percentages an indication of how likely results obtained from a sample can be applied to the population. A 95 per cent confidence level, for example, indicates that the results will be representative 95 times out of 100.

Normal distribution – a naturally occurring frequency distribution where many of the values cluster around the mean, and where there are few high and low values away from the mean.

Population – the total number of consumers in a given group.

Questionnaire – a list of questions, given to a number of respondents to answer, which provide data.

Quota sampling – where respondents are selected for interview in a non-random manner in the same proportion as they exist in the whole population.

Random sampling – where respondents are selected for interview at random.

Representative (sample) – a sample which has the same characteristics as the population.

Sampling bias – where the sample chosen is not representative of the population studied.

Sample size – the number of people chosen for the sample from the whole population.

Snowballing – a non-random method of market research, where a small number of selected respondents are asked to nominate further potential respondents for interview and so on.

Standard deviation – a measure of the average difference (deviation) of each result from the mean.

Stratified random sampling – a method of quota sampling where respondents are chosen at random.

Systematic sampling – a non-random method of sampling, where a researcher chooses respondents by taking every nth name on a list.

100 (19÷20) cases the unknown mean would fall within the range either side of the £12 sample mean. If it wanted to reduce the margin of error, it could set a confidence level of 99 per cent. This would involve a larger range of results. So the business could be more certain that the sample reflected the population.

Researchers often use 95 per cent and 99 per cent confidence levels. For a normal distribution, a 95 per cent confidence level spans 2 standard deviations either side of the population mean. A 99 per cent confidence level spans just under 3 standard deviations either side of the mean.

What about sample size? In terms of time and cost, the smaller the sample, the better. But to give meaningful results from random or stratified samples, researchers argue that the size of the sample should be over 30. As the sample gets larger, the variance of results decreases. So there is less chance that there would be a 'distorted sample', which would give an inaccurate picture of the population.

KNOWLEDGE

1 Why do most surveys involve a sample of a population rather than all the population?
2 What is the difference between a random sample and a systematic sample?
3 What is the difference between stratified random sampling and cluster sampling?
4 What does standard deviation show?
5 Explain the meaning of 'confidence levels'.

Case Study: Public transport in South West England

In 2006 Synovate Ltd, a market research company, published a report that it carried out on behalf of the Competition Commission. The report was based upon an investigation into the attitudes of the public towards transport links in the South West of England. They focused upon rail and bus services and the customers of the two main companies operating in the area at the time of the research: Wessex Rail and First Group buses. They wanted to know why people chose particular transport services and to establish whether they considered other possible services as realistic transport alternatives.

The research was based upon questionnaires. The questionnaires were conducted by researchers who boarded trains and buses between 7.00 a.m. and 7.45 p.m. Reply paid envelopes were provided where passengers did not have sufficient time to complete the survey during their journey. The sample size was 10,111 with 482 FirstGroup passengers and 529 Wessex passengers.

Table 1: Respondent Profile

		FirstGroup	Wessex Trains
		Base: 482	*Base: 529*
Age (Q26)	16-34	48%	50%
Excludes 'not answered'	35-54	23%	35%
	55-64	13%	9%
	65+	14%	4%
Gender (Q25)	Male	33%	49%
Excludes 'not answered'	Female	65%	50%
Employment (Q28)	Employed	58%	78%
Excludes 'not answered'	(FT/PT/self)		
	Retired	17%	5%
	Other	24%	16%
Number of Adults	One	72%	75%
in Group (Q27)	Two	15%	14%
Excludes 'not answered'	Three +	6%	4%

Some of the key findings of the research were as follows.

- Over a third of Wessex passengers are heading to work (36%) compared to just 17% of FirstGroup passengers.
- 31% of FirstGroup passengers travel on the bus route three or more times a week compared to 41% of Wessex Trains passengers.
- The factors of most importance to passengers of FirstGroup are 'stops at convenient station/stop', 'frequency of service' and 'cost of ticket', which are identified as the top three factors of importance.
- Wessex Trains passengers identify the 'short journey time', 'departure time' and 'stops at convenient station/stop' as most important.
- 'Space for luggage' is of least importance to passengers on both FirstGroup buses and Wessex Trains. In terms of how easy it would be to permanently change their mode of transport, no more than half of the FirstGroup or Wessex passengers identify any alternatives as quite or very easy to change to.
- FirstGroup passengers would find it easiest to change to 'train' (48% saying it would be quite or very easy) and Wessex Trains passengers would find it easiest to change to using a 'car as a driver' (48% saying quite or very easy).

Source: adapted from www.competition-commission.org.uk.

1 Explain what is meant by the terms:
(a) 'sample size'; (3 marks)
(b) 'questionnaire'. (3 marks).
2 Explain TWO reasons why the research was commissioned. (6 marks)
3 Explain the sampling method used by Synovate Ltd. (8 marks)
4 How useful might the owner of a taxi business in the South West of England find the research? (10 marks)

14 Market segmentation

Market segments

Market research provides a variety of information about the people who may be interested in buying a business's products. For example, it might tell a business that a new car will mainly be bought by women aged 18-35. It might indicate that older people have bought more copies of a magazine than younger people in the last year. Producers may use this information to identify people with similar needs. Breaking down a market into sub-groups with similar characteristics is known as MARKET SEGMENTATION. A business can then target these groups and develop products and services for each of them.

Health clubs in the UK make use of segmentation. For example, daytime users tend to be younger mothers with children and older retired people. Clubs often provide facilities such as crèches for such members. Members who visit in the evening tend to be people who work in the day and want to exercise at night.

The benefits of market segmentation

There is a number of benefits of market segmentation that lead businesses to attempt to identify different market segments.

- Successful market segmentation should allow a business to sell more products overall and perhaps increase its profit.
- By identifying different MARKET SEGMENTS, a business should understand its consumers better. Greater knowledge about its customers will allow a business to vary its products to suit their needs better.
- It might enable a business to target particular groups with particular products.
- It can help to prevent products being promoted to the wrong people. This would be wasteful of resources and might possibly lead to losses.
- It might allow a business to market a wider range of differentiated products.
- Customers may feel that their needs are being better targeted and develop loyalty to the business.

Types of market segmentation

There are four main ways in which consumers tend to be segmented:

- geographically - by where they live;
- demographically - by their gender, social class, age, income, ethnicity or religion;
- psychographically - by their lifestyle and personality;
- behaviourally - by how they act, for example whether they make repeat purchases, buy on impulse or want high quality products.

Question 1.

One of the most commonly targeted groups for advertisers are ABC1s. In the past commercial radio was not seen as a useful way of reaching such audiences. However, recently there has been a growth in the number of 'medium' ABC1s which are part of the listenership. During a typical week, 65 per cent of ABC1s tune in or listen to commercial radio. Over a month its reach rises to 83 per cent. ABC1s tend to listen for extended periods of time, around 12 hours a week. They also have high loyalty levels to their favourite stations. On average they tune in to 2.6 different stations a week. Even younger ABC1s, who might be more experimental, tend to stay loyal to one or two stations. This information is particularly useful for advertisers using a mixed media to promote products. ABC1s often avoid TV advertising.

Main listening periods tend to take place in the morning. In a typical week 61 per cent of ABC1 adults tune in to commercial radio. nineteen per cent listen on Saturdays and 15 per cent on Sundays. Around a fifth of time spent listening to commercial radio by ABC1s is in the car. Most is done at breakfast and when going home.

Source: adapted from www.rab.co.uk.

Figure 1: ABC1 profiles

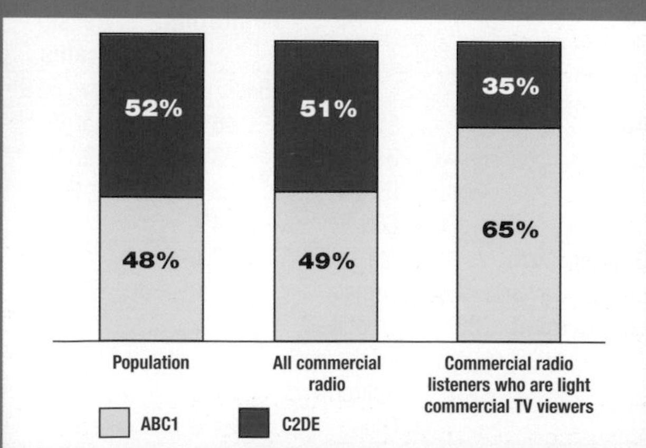

(a) Examine the reasons why commercial radio might be a useful promotional medium for small and medium sized businesses aiming at ABC1s.

(b) Suggest how a small to medium sized business might appeal to ABC1s most effectively using this medium.

Geographic segmentation

This might include considering the region of a country where consumers live and the nature of the region, e.g. rural, urban, semi-rural or suburban. It may also consider the type of house, road or area of a city that people live in. This method can be especially useful in large or highly culturally diverse markets, where buying patterns are influenced by region. Businesses selling into the EU are likely to break this area down into more manageable segments. Many large businesses selling into global markets have different products for different countries or areas. For example, Nestlé has sold refrigerated profiteroles in France and a fortified drink called Milo with a malted taste in Japan. The Maggi and Crosse & Blackwell soups are adapted to suit different tastes, by varying the ingredients from one country to another. It may also be possible for a company to price goods differently in different markets. For example, car manufacturers sell the same cars at different prices in different countries in the European Union. The prices will depend, in part, on what they think customers are prepared to pay.

A drawback of geographic segmentation is the evidence that consumer tastes are becoming more uniform across geographic boundaries. This can mean that regional boundaries and national boundaries become less important in determining tastes. For example, 30 years ago the vast majority of supporters of Manchester United or Liverpool FC could be found within a 30 mile radius of the clubs. Today supporters of these clubs and consumers of their products can be found in large numbers in other locations such as the South East of England, Asia or Southern Africa.

Demographic segmentation

DEMOGRAPHY is the study of population. Demographic segmentation splits people up into different groups according to different characteristics.

Age Many businesses pay attention to the age of their customers. For example, the over-65s could be seen as one segment, while teenagers aged 14-18 could be seen as another. R&B CDs might be marketed to teenagers, whilst a 'Hits of the 1960s' CD may be more likely to be attractive to older buyers. The over-60s are of particular interest to business as this segment is

Table 1: Socio-economic groups – IPA classification

Social grade	Social status	Head of household's occupation
A	Upper middle class	Higher managerial, administrative or professional such as doctors, lawyers and company directors
B	Middle class	Intermediate managerial, administrative or professional such as teachers, nurses and managers
C1	Lower middle class	Supervisory or clerical and junior managerial, administrative or professional such as shop assistants, clerks and police constables
C2	Skilled working class	Skilled manual workers such as carpenters, cooks and train drivers
D	Working class	Semi-skilled and unskilled manual workers such as fitters and store keepers
E	The poorest in society	State pensioners or widows, casual or lower grade workers, or long-term unemployed

Table 2: Socio-economic groups – Registrar General's classification

Class 1	Higher managerial and professional occupations **1.1** Employers in large organisations *(eg corporate manager)* **1.2** Higher professionals *(eg doctor or barrister)*
Class 2	Lower managerial and professional occupations *(eg journalist, actor, nurse)*
Class 3	Intermediate occupations *(eg secretary, driving instructor)*
Class 4	Small employers and own account workers *(eg publican, taxi driver)*
Class 5	Lower supervisory, craft and related occupations *(eg plumber, butcher, train driver)*
Class 6	Semi routine occupations *(eg shop assistant, traffic warden)*
Class 7	Routine occupations *(eg waiter, road sweeper)*
Class 8	Never worked/long-term unemployed

Table 3: Financial Services and ABC1s

- More than one-third of ABs and more than three in ten C1s borrow more than they save. Those with children are nearly twice as likely as those without to owe more than they have saved.
- ABs and C2s find saving easier than C1s, Ds and Es.
- Just over two-thirds of ABs, and almost two-thirds of C1s, expect to fund their children out of savings and investments.
- Around one-third of ABs and one-fifth of C1s have bought savings plans, investments or insurance over the telephone. Only three ABs and two C1s in 100 have bought them over the Internet.
- Only one AB in eight, and one C1 in 16, sets aside more than £200 a month to save for a retirement pension, in addition to National Insurance contributions.
- Almost one in five ABs, and nearly one in four C1s, puts less than £50 a month into a pension.
- ABs are less worried than other social groups about the accessibility of bank or building society branches, and so are less worried about branch closures.

Source: adapted from www.researchmarkets.com.

growing as a proportion of the total population. The marketing of financial services for older people has become popular in recent years. So has a number of other products and service areas, ranging from specialist holidays to the development of retirement housing.

Gender Businesses may target either males or females. This is because men and women often have different spending patterns. Some car producers, for example, have targeted women in their promotional campaigns for smaller hatchbacks. Manufacturers of perfumes and related products have realised the growing market for personal care products among men. Major brand names such as Armani and Yves Saint Laurent, as well as sports companies, have produced a range of products geared towards males. Mobile phone manufacturers target a growing number of females buying the latest 'technological gadgets', by designing accessories to suit their requirements.

Social class Markets are often divided by social class. Tables 1 and 2 show two measures of social class used in the UK. For the 2001 population census, the Registrar General divided social class into eight areas. Classes are based on employment status and conditions. This division is usually used in government reports and surveys. The Institute of Practitioners in Advertising (IPA) divides social class into six categories. These are used to decide which group to target for promoting a product. Because of regular changes in the pay and status of different occupations, these categories are revised from time to time. For example, the

Question 2.

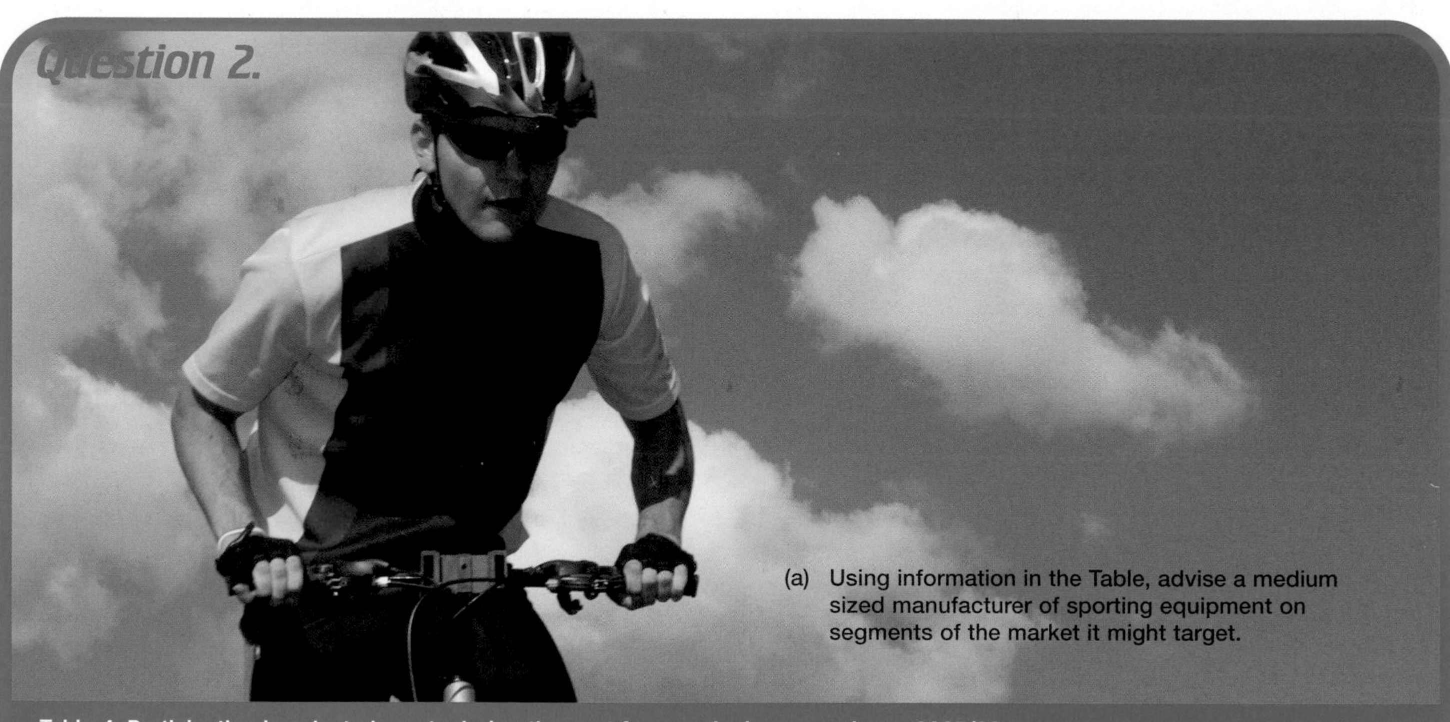

(a) Using information in the Table, advise a medium sized manufacturer of sporting equipment on segments of the market it might target.

Table 4: Participation in selected sports during the past four weeks by sex and age, 2005/06

England — Percentages

	Men					Women				
	16-24	25-44	45-64	65 and over	All aged 16 and over	16-24	25-44	45-64	65 and over	All aged 16 and over
Indoor swimming or diving	*16*	*18*	*10*	*5*	*13*	*23*	*24*	*16*	*6*	*18*
Health, fitness, gym or conditioning activities	*22*	*18*	*9*	*4*	*13*	*19*	*16*	*13*	*3*	*13*
Recreational cycling	*16*	*16*	*11*	*4*	*12*	*8*	*9*	*6*	*1*	*6*
Snooker, pool, billiards	*34*	*13*	*7*	*4*	*13*	*12*	*3*	*1*	-	*3*
Keep fit, aerobics, dance exercise	*4*	*4*	*4*	*3*	*4*	*13*	*12*	*10*	*5*	*10*
Outdoor football	*43*	*14*	*3*	-	*12*	*5*	*1*	*1*	-	*1*
Golf, pitch and putt, putting	*10*	*9*	*9*	*9*	*9*	*1*	*1*	*2*	*1*	*1*
Jogging, cross-country, road running	*11*	*10*	*4*	-	*7*	*6*	*5*	*2*	-	*3*
Tenpin bowling	*9*	*4*	*3*	*1*	*4*	*8*	*4*	*2*	-	*3*
Darts	*16*	*6*	*3*	*1*	*6*	*4*	*2*	*1*	*1*	*2*

Source: *Taking Part: The National Survey of Culture, Leisure and Sport*, Department for Culture, Media and Sports.

Registrar General's classification previously had only five classes.

Research often breaks these categories down even further. For example, AB, C1, C2, D and E are sometimes used to highlight the differences between levels of management, and skilled and unskilled manual workers. The media often refers to ABC1s. It is suggested that some businesses are particularly interested in people who might fall into this category as they tend to have higher incomes and levels of spending. Table 3 shows information from a study about the attitudes of people in the ABC1 group to financial services. This could be used by banks, insurance or pension companies to decide which customers to target.

Income Although linked to some extent to the 'social classes' described above, income groups can be different. For example, a self-employed skilled manual worker, such as an electrician, may receive the same income as a middle manager. Similarly, a self-employed builder may receive the same income as or more than a professional. However, because of his or her occupation the two people will be in different social classes.

The population can be split up into income groups and targeted accordingly. So a Cartier watch, for example, is likely to be marketed at the highest income groups.

Religion Businesses may divide markets by religious groups. Food producers, for example, may specialise in producing Kosher food for Jewish people. Digital television has seen the growth of American style Christian television channels in the UK.

Ethnic grouping Markets can sometimes be segmented by country of origin or ethnic grouping. Radio stations have been geared towards African-Caribbean groups. Some products, such as clothing or hair accessories, are also geared towards this grouping.

A drawback of demographic segmentation is that consumers try to defy consumption patterns associated with their demographic groups. For example, young people from lower income groups may seek out expensive high status products, such as certain brands of designer clothes, that were initially marketed at high income groups.

Psychographic segmentation

Geographic and demographic segmentation have limitations. For example, there is a wide variety of spending patterns among females aged 16-18 living in Manchester. Yet people in this consumer group share the same gender, age and location. An alternative way of grouping customers is through psychographic segmentation. This groups customers according to their attitudes, opinions and lifestyles.

- Sports products may be aimed at those who are interested in 'extreme' sports such as skiboarding.
- Chocolate manufacturers have identified two categories of chocolate eaters. 'Depressive' chocolate lovers eat chocolate to unwind predominantly during the evening. 'Energetic' chocolate eaters eat chocolate as a fast food and live life at a fast pace.
- People's attitudes to life may also be used to segment the market. Some pension funds are geared towards those who only want investments in 'ethical' businesses.
- Clothes may be geared at those who are interested in 'retro' fashions from earlier decades.
- Mobile phones provide services such as Internet access for business travellers.
- Travel companies target holidays at families with younger children.
- Certain newspapers are geared towards Labour voters, while others are geared towards Conservative voters.

One of the drawbacks of psychographic segmentation is that it can be difficult for businesses to collect data about the beliefs, attitudes and lifestyles of consumers. In order to do this they may require the help of specialist businesses.

Behavioural segmentation

Behavioural segmentation attempts to segment markets according to how consumers relate to a product. There is a number of different methods of behavioural segmentation:

Usage rate This is when consumers are categorised according to the quantity and frequency of their purchases. One example of this is British Airways, which established an 'Executive Club' to encourage and develop the custom of regular business travellers.

Loyalty Consumers can be categorized according to their product loyalty. The Tesco Clubcard, for example, which offers discounts to regular customers of Tesco supermarkets seeks to reward and encourage loyalty to Tesco and its products.

Time and date of consumption Consumers often consume particular products at particular times and dates. Businesses can take advantage of this in order to improve their marketing. So, for example, manufacturers of breakfast cereals, while recognising that their product will be primarily consumed in the morning, encourage consumers also to consume their products in the evening. Similarly, many bars and clubs seek to encourage different groups of consumers according to the night of the week. For example, Thursday nights are often for older singles and Friday nights for younger consumers in many such establishments.

Like other segmentation methods, a drawback of behavioural segmentation is that on its own it may fail to adequately capture a target market for a business. For this reason, in many cases a business might employ a **variety** of the segmentation methods explained above. So, for example, a manufacturer of luxury apartments may be interested in segments that included single men or women with no children, in the 30-40 age range, with high incomes that fall into social class AB. Because of the likely one-off nature of such a purchase, behavioural segmentation would be less important in this instance.

Market segmentation and strategy

Certain businesses make little use of market segmentation. Some simply adopt an **undifferentiated strategy** towards marketing. They try to promote their product to the entire market, rather than to a segment. For example, a local newsagents will want to sell to the entire market. The nature of the service it offers means that this market will be local. But the newsagents won't try to target young customers at the expense of old age pensioners, or professional customers at the expense of unskilled manual customers.

Equally, many businesses have little need to segment their markets. If a business is producing a **commodity** sold in bulk, like wheat, copper or oil, there is no need to produce specific products for specific segments of the market. Customers want to buy a standard product. It could also be that the cost of producing different products or services to satisfy different market segments far outweighs what customers are prepared to pay for the differentiation. Customers might prefer to buy a cheap undifferentiated product rather than an expensive one tailored precisely to their needs.

Some businesses even deliberately produce brands to appeal to all customers. They want to capture as much of the market as possible with an undifferentiated product. For example, in the UK tea brands such as PG Tips or Typhoo Tea are aimed at the mass market.

However, many businesses develop marketing strategies for particular segments of a market. A **differentiated strategy** would aim to target different market segments with different marketing strategies. A detergent manufacturer might sell cleaning products to consumers and to cleaning companies. But it could use different packaging for the two markets and offer cleaning companies much larger packs. It could also use different advertising and other promotion in the two market segments.

Another alternative is to focus on just one market segment. This **concentrated marketing** is used, for example, by luxury brands such as Dior or Gucci. Dior does not attempt to sell clothes to consumers in every segment of the clothing market. It concentrates on selling to consumers with high incomes by producing high quality, expensive clothing.

Segmentation, targeting and positioning

The stages through which a business might plan a differentiated or concentrated marketing strategy are shown in Figure 1.

Segmenting the market The business will try to identify how it might segment its markets.

Developing customer profiles The business will find out exactly who its customers are in each market segment. This might be done through **market research**. It might then draw up a CUSTOMER PROFILE (or CONSUMER PROFILE if the buyers are consumers). This is an analysis of the characteristics of customers in the market or market segment. It could include age, income, budgets, **channels** through which purchases are made and reasons why customers buy the product.

Evaluating market segments The business then needs to evaluate which market segments it is worthwhile targeting. A manufacturer of vacuum cleaners may find that 30 per cent of households have not bought a new cleaner in 15 years. But there might be little point in targeting these customers if three quarters of them are in the bottom 40 per cent of the income range. This might indicate that most would not have the income to buy a new vacuum cleaner. On the other hand, it might find out that young people aged 20-30 are three times as likely to buy a vacuum cleaner as old age pensioners. With higher average incomes too, young people might be worth targeting.

Selecting market segments to target Once a business has evaluated its market segments, it must then choose which will be its **target market**. The vacuum cleaner manufacturer might decide to target more affluent young people as the most promising way of increasing sales.

Positioning the product for the target segment Having chosen which market segments to target, the business must now make decisions about **positioning** its products within that market. In particular, it must consider the competition it faces and how it will differentiate its product from others.

Developing a marketing mix for each target segment Finally the business must develop a **marketing mix**. This would take into account the product, price, promotion and place suited to the market segment. By doing this, the business will have responded to the needs of the market and its customers, i.e it

Figure 1: Planning a marketing strategy

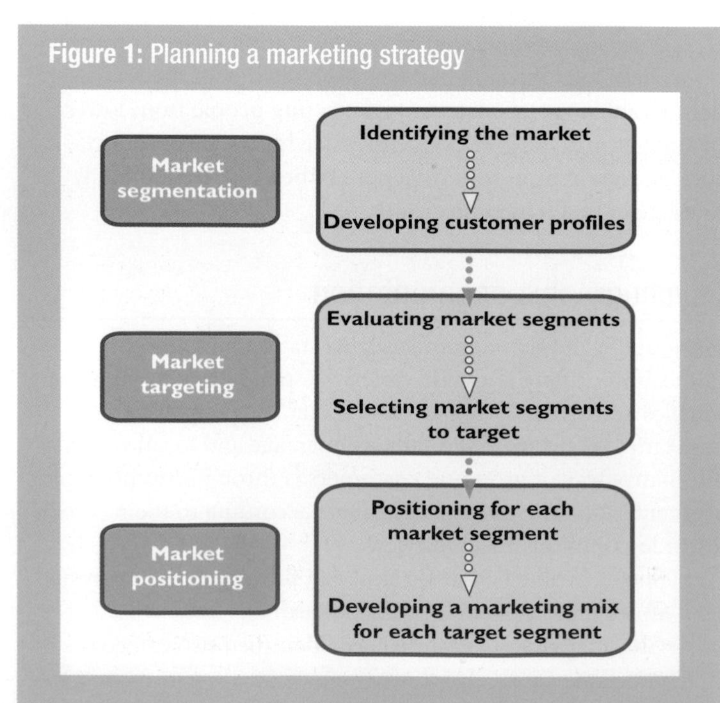

would be **market orientated.**

Identifying the target market can be more complicated. Sometimes the buyer might not be the main influence on the choice of product. An increasing example of this is the effect of PESTER POWER. This is where children constantly 'nag' to persuade their parents to purchase products. They might be the latest brand of clothing that is worn by their friends at school, buying Sky television and its many channels or a fast food burger meal when shopping. It has been suggested by some researchers in the UK that pester power results in a purchase in around two-thirds of cases.

CRITIQUE

When researching teenagers and their tastes in music *The Observer Music Monthly* struggled to develop categories into which teenagers might fit. All the teenagers they spoke to were happy to admit that their taste was diverse with what might be described as an iPod shuffle attitude to pop. It didn't bother teenagers whether they were 'meant' to like a track, or a band; whether such-and-such were cool or if a particular type of music was originally made for them. Such categories were irrelevant to them. The general view was 'it's only adults that analyse these things. Teenagers just act on instinct'.

Source: adapted from the *Observer Music Monthly*, 17.7.2007.

KNOWLEDGE

1. How can a market be segmented geographically?
2. Explain three ways in which the spending patterns of females aged 25-35 with children who are in paid employment might differ from those of males aged 55-65 who have taken early retirement and whose children have left home.
3. (a) What is meant by 'social class'?
   (b) Give two ways in which the spending of social class A households might differ from that of social class D.
4. How might understanding the personalities of different groups of consumers help in the marketing of a product?
5. Briefly explain five ways in which consumers might be segmented on a behavioural basis.
6. What is the difference between a differentiated marketing strategy and a concentrated marketing strategy?
7. How might a business plan concentrated marketing strategy?

KEYTERMS

Customer (or consumer) profile - an analysis of the characteristics of customers (or consumers) in a market or market segment, e.g. by their age, income or where they shop.
Demography – the study of population, its composition and how it is changing over time.
Market segment – part of a whole segment which contains a group of buyers with similar characteristics, such as age, income, social class or attitudes.
Market segmentation – breaking down a market into sub-groups which share similar characteristics.
Pester power - the constant requesting by one group of another to buy products. It often applies to children 'nagging' parents to make purchases.

Case Study: The power of the Muslim pound

Marian Salzman is one of the world's foremost trend-spotters. She can see something coming before others have even raised their heads to look and the next big thing in marketing she argues is the 'Muslim pound'. According to Mintel, a market research company, the estimated spending power of Muslim people in the UK is £20.5 billion. There are more than 5,000 Muslim millionaires in the UK, with combined assets worth more than £3.6 billion.

'It's a unique market with a unique set of needs, for example in the banking area,' says Salzman, the executive vice president and chief marketing officer of consultancy JWT. 'Under sharia law (which governs how Muslims can borrow money), different kinds of mortgages need to be written in order for someone who is Muslim to acquire a home. And there's halal law (which is concerned with the way in which animal are slaughtered) which affects consumption of food, beauty and healthcare products.'

This trend may provide demographic segmentation opportunities for business. There has been a huge surge in marketing to Muslims this year, according to Salzman. 'I think it is a recognition of the size of the market,' she says. 'Another thing I believe has been driving it is all the coverage of whether Turkey will be part of the EU, which has also raised the visibility of the question about the sheer percentage of the European population that is Muslim.' Muslims are also more sensitive about the moral attributes of brands and the way in which they are marketed according to research. Fifty-nine per cent agreed that there was too much suggestiveness or immodesty in most advertising compared to 28 per cent of the general sample.

Their buying behaviour is also heavily influenced by expert endorsement and opinion. In the survey, almost two-thirds agreed with the statement, 'I feel reassured if a product has been endorsed by an expert' – almost twice as many as the general sample. Muslims also have a higher level of trust in expert opinions and reviews than non-Muslims: 75 per cent compared to 56 per cent.

Source: adapted from *The Independent*, 9.7. 2007.

(a) What is meant by (i) market segmentation (3 marks) and (ii) demographic segmentation in the article? (3 marks)
(b) Explain why a small business offering financial services might benefit from market segmentation. (8 marks)
(c) Examine how targeting Muslim customers might affect a business marketing financial services. (6 marks)
(d) Discuss the extent to which selling to one market segment, such as people of a particular religion, is likely to be a successful marketing strategy for a small business offering financial services. (10 marks)

15 Market size, share and growth

Market size

The size of a market can be estimated or calculated by the total sales of all businesses in the market. Market size is usually estimated in a number of ways.

Value This is the total amount spent by customers buying products. For example, it was estimated that fast food products in the UK accounted for sales worth £8.38 billion in 2004. This included branded fast food chains and independent outlets selling hot or cold eat-in food without table service, or takeaway food.

Volume This is the physical quantity of products which are produced and sold. For example, global crude steel production was over 1.1 billion tonnes in 2005, the highest ever. The UK produced around 12 million tonnes. Some estimates of volume are based on the number or percentage of users, subscribers or viewers. This is often the case in markets for services, such as the number of mobile phone users, the number of television viewers or the percentage of households with digital television.

Different markets are likely to differ in size. For example, sales of chilled desserts like cream cakes, cheesecakes and trifles were £390 million in 2006. On the other hand over £1.9 billion was spent by British consumers on increasingly popular holiday cruises.

Market growth

Markets can grow either rapidly or slowly, or they might contract and get smaller. Take the example of the market for sandwiches in the UK. Between 2002 and 2006 average year on year growth in sandwich sales was 3.5 per cent, but from 2006-2007 growth was 9 per cent, almost three times that of previous years. Similarly, the value of the UK budget hotel market increased by 38 per cent between 2002 and 2006, to reach £1 billion. This growth was three times that of the overall UK hotel market (worth £11.2 billion), which increased by just 12 per cent over the same four year period. On the other hand the market for sales of ties fell from £158 million in 1999 to just £154 million by 2004. It was suggested that the fall was due to the growing trend amongst men for dressing down at work.

What factors are likely to influence whether a market gets bigger or becomes smaller and the rate of growth or decline?

- **Economic changes.** An increase in income, for example, can affect different markets. Rising incomes might help the growth of the market for high class restaurants or specialist furniture makers.
- **Social changes.** Changes in society can lead to a growth or a decline in markets. The decline in the number of marriages, an increase in the proportion of working

Question 1.

Ormskirk is a town in Lancashire. It has a market on Thursdays and Saturdays every week which attracts customers from both the town and local counties. Traditionally it has had local teashops and a few restaurants. But over the period 2000-2007 the market for shops providing food has increased. There are now retailers selling ready made sandwiches and meals. There are takeaways. There are Chinese, Indian, Italian, French and Tapas restaurants. There are wine bars selling food in the daytime as well as the traditional teashops. There are regular rail and bus Links to Liverpool and Preston. In 2005 after 120 years of providing education, Edge Hill was granted university status. In 2007, the university had 17,000 students. It planned to spend £220 million from its own coffers to provide extra student accommodation, new teaching buildings and facilities. A study to assess its impact on the area found that it contributed £77 million a year to the North West of England's economy. This figure was predicted to rise to £172 million by 2022. The study also showed that the number of jobs supported by the university is anticipated to rise from its current level of 2,650 to 4,850. In 2007 a planned bypass was being proposed, linking the M58 to the Ormskirk to Southport main road.

Source: adapted in part from http://info.edgehill.ac.uk, http://news.bbc.co.uk.

(a) Suggest factors that might affect the size and growth of the market in which an Ormskirk restaurant operates.

(b) Discuss whether this market will grow in future.

Question 2.

Commercial radio stations have found it difficult to match the listener numbers of BBC. In 2007 the BBC attracted 54.5 per cent of listening, up 0.3 percentage points on 2006 Commercial radio was 0.3 percentage points down to 43.3 per cent. Radio 1 gained listeners, partly due to the stability of the weekday DJ line-up and the extension of Chris Moyles' breakfast show to start half an hour earlier at 6.30a.m. Radio 2's audience was up by a quarter of a million people and market share was up from 15.5 per rcent to 15.8 per cent, attracted by long-standing, popular programmes such as Terry Wogan's breakfast show.

Johnny Vaughan, at Capital Radio, made a strong gain in number of listeners, adding 246,000 with market share holding steady. The worry for Capital is that its new listeners can easily change to other stations. Capital must build on its gains if the station is to catch up with Heart and Magic. Both have opened up and sustained a sizeable lead in London. Radio 1 and Radio 2 have also both increased their listener base in the capital in the past 12 months.

The decline in total listening to local commercial stations has been the trend for two years. This continues, with a drop in the past year from 32.6 per cent to 31.7 per cent of total listening. Stations such as Radio City in Liverpool, Clyde 2 in Glasgow and Smooth Radio in North-West England were among those to lose audience. But not all stations lost out. Choice FM in London gained 111,000 new listeners, taking the station to a new record of 611,000 listeners. Xfm Manchester increased its weekly audience by 33 per cent, lifting its market share by a third.

Source: adapted from the *Guardian*, 29.10.2007.

(a) Outline the changes in the share of the market of (i) Radio 2, (ii) national commercial and non-commercial radio stations and (iii) local commercial radio stations.

(b) Explain two factors that may influence the share of the market of radio stations.

women and the growth in the number of one parent families is linked to a growth in the market for child care and other child support services, and for housing.

- Technological changes. Changes in technology can cause a rapid growth in certain markets and a decline in others. The DVD market has expanded rapidly in recent years at the expense of the video market. The growth in iPods and other MP3 players and the downloading of music from the Internet are associated with a decline in CD sales.
- Demographic changes. Changes in the age structure of the population can affect markets. The ageing of the UK population has led to a growth in products aimed at people aged over 50, such as specialist holidays, mobility aids and insurance products.
- Changes in legislation. Changes in the law governing the use of radio frequencies has enabled a large growth in the number of commercial radio stations.

Figure 1: UK market share, supermarkets, %, 17 June 2007

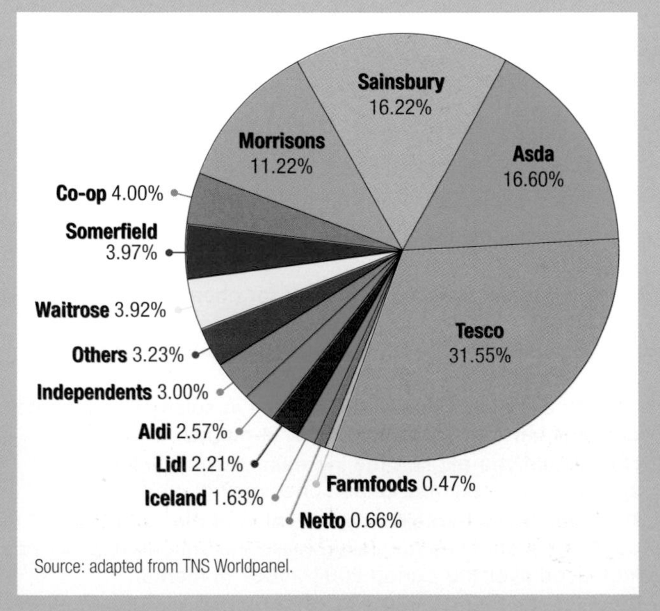

Source: adapted from TNS Worldpanel.

Market share

MARKET SHARE or MARKET PENETRATION is the term used to describe the proportion of a particular market that is held by a business, a product, a brand or a number of businesses or products. Market share is shown as a percentage. The market share of a business can be calculated as:

$$\frac{\text{Sales of a business}}{\text{Total sales in the market}} \times 100\%$$

Why might the measurement of market share be important? It might indicate a business that is a market leader. This could influence other companies to follow the leader or influence the leader to maintain its position. It might influence the **strategy** or **objectives** of a business. A business that has a small market share may set a target of increasing its share by 5 per cent over a period of time. It may also be an indication of the success or failure of a business or its strategy.

Figure 1 shows the market shares of supermarkets in the UK in June 2007. It shows, for example, that the market leader was Tesco and that three quarters of the market sales were accounted for by the 'big five' supermarket chains. However, care must be taken when interpreting the market share of businesses.

- The share of the market can be measured in different ways. Market share is calculated as the sales of a business as a percentage of total market sales. Sales can be calculated in a number of ways. They might be the value of sales, such as £100 million a year. Or they might be calculated by the number or volume of sales, for example, 6 million products sold each year or 10 million visitors to attractions owned by a theme park company.

- The market and the time period chosen can affect the results. For example, in 2004 Safeway was taken over by Morrisons. This significantly increased Morrison's market share from below 10% to over 11% as shown in Figure 1.
- The type of product and business included might also affect the results. For example, in 2007 it was reported that Scottish and Newcastle plc had 26 per cent of the beer market. However, in the UK drinks market, beer made up only 35 per cent of drinks spending. So the market share of the UK drinks market of Scottish and Newcastle plc would be less than 26 per cent because the drinks market would include the sales of other drinks manufacturers such as Coca-Cola (carbonated soft drinks) and Tetley GB Ltd (tea).

KEYTERMS

Market share or market penetration – the proportion of total sales in a particular market for which one or more businesses or brands are responsible. It is expressed as a percentage and can be calculated by value or volume.

KNOWLEDGE

1. Explain two ways in which the size of a market can be calculated.
2. What is meant by a market that is (a) growing and (b) declining?
3. Give four factors that might influence market growth.
4. What is the formula used to calculate market share?
5. Give three examples of the problems of measuring market share.

Case Study: British cheese

When it comes to cheese, continental varieties such as Brie and Emmental were once the height of sophistication. Research from Mintel has found that cheese buyers are increasingly opting for British regional cheeses, such as Lancashire, Cheshire and Red Leicester. Sales of specialist British cheese increased by as much as 16 per cent between 2004 and 2006, to reach £220 million. Growth has outpaced the likes of soft and continental cheese.

'With growing interest in environmental and ethical concerns we are becoming increasingly interested in the origin of our food. As a result we are seeing a growing trend towards "buying British", which has provided a huge boost for sales of British regional cheese,' comments David Bird, Senior Consumer Analyst. 'Many varieties of regional British cheese have extended their ranges by adding fruits, liqueurs and even curry. This has really caught the imagination of cheese customers and has lead to the rise in sales of locally produced cheese,' he adds.

Although sales by volume of continental cheese have continued to rise, the value of sales has not. Market value fell 7 per cent between 2004 and 2006 to £340 million. 'Continental cheese such as Brie used to be seen as a luxury for special occasions. But today many continental varieties are now more an everyday staple than an occasional treat. This has inevitably brought prices down and as a result market value has declined, despite rising volume sales,' explains David Bird.

Specialist British regional cheese has seen the greatest growth. But cheddars, which are not classified as specialist cheeses, from the UK and abroad accounted for over half (52 per cent) of all cheese sales in the UK last year, having grown 7 per cent between 2004 and 2006 to reach £985 million. What is more, this year sales of the humble block of cheddar will hit the £1 billion mark for the first time ever. 'Cheddars have clearly stood the test of time and are now still very much a British staple. The market has done well to see growth despite heavy discounting and many buy-one-get-one-free offers in the supermarkets,' comments David Bird.

The British cheese market was worth £1.9 billion in 2006, having increased 4 per cent between 2004 and 2006. Sales are set to rise to £1.93 billion this year. This is no mean feat considering the trend towards healthy eating.

Source: adapted from www.mintel.com.

(a) Outline the features of the market for cheeses in the UK. (4 marks)

(b) (i) Calculate the size of the market for British cheese in 2004. (4 marks)

(ii) Calculate the value of the decline in sales of continental cheeses between 2004 and 2006. (4 marks)

(c) How would you explain the increase in sales volume of specialist and regional British cheeses? (8 marks)

(d) How would you explain why the value of the sales of continental cheeses has fallen while the volume of sales has increased over the period 2004-2006? (8 marks)

(e) Examine the factors that may affect the size of the market for Cheddar cheeses in the UK in future. (8 marks)

16 The marketing mix

The markting mix

In order to market its products effectively a business must consider its MARKETING MIX. The marketing mix refers to those elements of a firm's marketing strategy which are designed to meet the needs of its customers. There are four parts to the marketing mix - product, price, promotion and place. These are often known as the four 'Ps', as illustrated in Figure 1. To meet consumers' needs and to create an effective marketing mix, businesses must produce the right product, at the right price, make it available at the right place, and let consumers know about it through promotion.

Product Businesses must make sure that their products are meeting the needs of their customers. This means paying close attention to a number of features of the product.

- How consumers will use the product. A furniture manufacturer, for example, would market different products for home use than it would for office use. Products created for the office would need to be sturdy, functional, able to withstand regular use and be long lasting. Products created for the home would need to stress features such as the quality of the fabric, the design and the level of comfort.
- The appearance of the product. This is likely to involve a consideration of such things as colour. Food manufacturers, for example, go to great lengths to ensure that their products have an appealing colour. In some cases this means adding artificial colourings to alter the appearance. There are many other factors to be taken into account during the product's design. These include shape, taste and size. Deodorant manufacturers and toilet cleaning fluid producers among others might also consider aroma.
- Financial factors. There is little point in a firm producing a product which meets the needs of consumers if it cannot be produced at the right cost. All things being equal, a good produced at high cost is likely to be sold for a high price. Unless consumers are convinced that a product is value for money, they are unlikely to purchase it. They might take into consideration factors such as the quality of the product or after-sales service.
- The product's life cycle. After a period of time the sales of all products rise and then later start to fall. A business must decide whether to allow the product to decline and cease its production or to try to revive it in some way.
- A product's UNIQUE SELLING POINT or PROPOSITION. This is the aspect or feature of the product that may differentiate it from its rivals. It may help a business to gain a competitive advantage over competitors.
- Market position. This is the view that consumers have of a product compared to that of its competitors. For example, a product might be seen as 'up-market' or alternatively 'low cost' by buyers.

Figure 1: Elements of the marketing mix

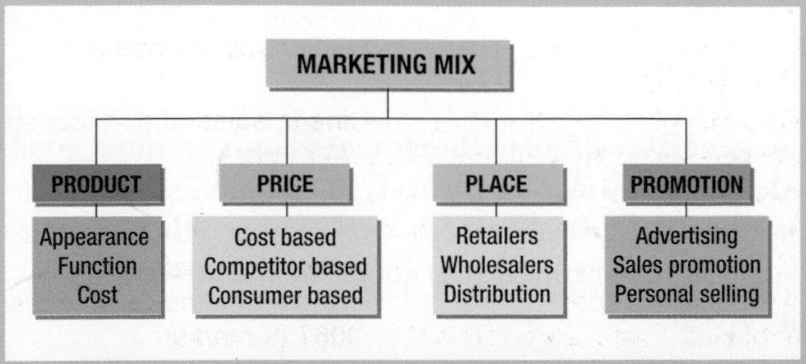

MARKETING MIX			
PRODUCT	PRICE	PLACE	PROMOTION
Appearance Function Cost	Cost based Competitor based Consumer based	Retailers Wholesalers Distribution	Advertising Sales promotion Personal selling

Price The pricing policy that a business chooses is often a reflection of the market at which it is aiming. Prices will not always be set at the level which will maximise sales or short-run profits. For example, a business may charge a high price because it is aiming to sell to consumers who regard the product as exclusive rather than because production costs are high. However, factors such as production costs can also influence pricing.

Promotion There is a number of promotional methods a business can use including above the line promotions, such as TV advertising, and below the line promotions such as personal selling. A business will choose a promotion method it feels is likely to be most effective in the market in which it operates. For example, methods such as '10 per cent off your next purchase' are used with 'fast-moving consumer goods', such as canned food and packets of biscuits. National television advertising will only be used for products with a high sales turnover and a wide appeal.

Place This refers to the means by which the product will be distributed to the consumer. The product must get to the right place, at the right time. This means making decisions about the way in which the product will be physically distributed, i.e. by air, sea, rail or road. It also means taking into account how the product is sold. This may be by direct mail from the manufacturer or through retail outlets such as supermarkets.

Sometimes **packaging**, used to protect and brand a product, is also included.

When considering the marketing mix of services, other

Question 1.

Biome Lifestyle is an online shopping site (www.biomelifestyle.com) that offers eco-friendly and ethically-sourced products for the home. The emphasis of the business is upon products that are carefully chosen for how they look and for being made from recycled, sustainable, organic or fairly-traded materials. The business has grown rapidly since its launch in December 2005, but its founder Alexandra Bramham says it has not been easy. She spent the year before the official launch developing the idea and then had to wait for the public to cotton on. 'When we first started I was a bit naïve and thought people would flock to it. I quickly found that you have to develop ways of reaching the public,' she says.

One of those ways is a recently launched wedding list service for the eco-conscious couple. Another is online advertising. Although there are frustrations, Bramham insists she is enjoying trying to get the business off the ground. For the moment, she is keeping control of costs by outsourcing elements such as design and web development, but she has big plans. 'I want to be a one-stop shop for ethical products,' she says. The business' products are not always at low prices and include handmade recycled teddy bears for £32. There are also Eco Shopper Bags for £6 and recycled wrapping paper at £1.50 per sheet.

Source: adapted from the *Independent*, 5.7.2007 and www.biomelifestyle.com.

(a) Identify elements of the marketing mix from the article.
(b) Explain how these elements might help Biome Lifestyle to gain a competitive advantage over its rivals.

factors are also considered in the marketing mix. The importance of the following is also stressed.

- The **people** involved in providing the service.
- The **process**, i.e. the mechanisms, activities and procedures involved in delivering the services, such as delivery time of a meal.
- **Physical evidence**, such as the appearance of the environment in which the service is provided.

Choice of marketing mix

Each business must decide upon its own marketing mix. It is important that the right balance between price, product, promotion and place is achieved if this is to be as effective as possible. It could be argued that as businesses become more market orientated all elements are important. However, at times businesses may stress one or more elements of the mix. What is important for a business is that its marketing mix is integrated. This means that the different parts of the marketing mix must fit together well .

Take, for example, a business launching a new range of hand-made, luxury organic cheeses priced at over 50 per cent higher than rival cheeses, promoted in specialist food magazines, packaged by hand in high quality materials and with a taste, texture and smell positively commented upon by food experts. It would not make sense to distribute such cheeses through discount supermarkets, such as Aldi and Netto, or through discount cheese stalls at local street markets. Such a strategy would suggest a marked lack of integration between the product, price and promotion on the one hand and place on the other. Instead, if it is to be effective, each element of the marketing mix should support the other. In the example above it may mean distributing the cheeses through high quality specialist cheese shops and delicatessens. The marketing mix a business chooses will depend upon certain factors.

Finance available Some new products are launched onto the market with the backing of large businesses and with huge financial back-up. There is a huge range of choice as to the components of the marketing mix to be used to support these products. Other businesses with more restricted finances have far fewer options available to them.

Technological developments Technological developments have enabled businesses to adapt and develop their marketing mixes in ways that wouldn't previously have been possible. For example, the use of the Internet and mobile phone texts are relatively recent additions to the promotional techniques available to businesses. Information technology developments have allowed businesses to develop much more sophisticated pricing strategies, with prices rising and falling according to demand. This has been a particular feature of airline and rail travel businesses. In addition, the Internet has revolutionised the place many products are sold. Many consumer goods are now more likely to be purchased on the Internet than they are in shops.

The findings from market research As well as informing consumers about the nature of a product itself, market research can also help a business to decide on the make up of its marketing mix. Indeed, it is likely that an effective marketing mix will have been informed by market research. For example, market research may allow a business to find out about how consumers will respond to different prices and where a product should be made available.

The type of product it is selling For example, a business marketing highly technical products is likely to emphasise its products' qualities rather than giving a free good as a promotion. However, a business marketing a product very similar to that of its competitors may wish to emphasise a lower price or use some method of promotion.

The market it is selling to Businesses selling consumer goods aimed at the mass market are likely to emphasise the promotional and pricing aspects of their marketing mix. Firms selling machinery or industrial goods are likely to stress the product itself.

The degree of competition A business operating in a

competitive market, with many close rivals, is likely to stress the importance of price in its marketing mix. In less competitive markets price might not be seen as being so important.

The marketing mix of competitors Businesses cannot afford to ignore the mix chosen by competitors. For example, confectionery manufacturers lay particular emphasis upon the availability of their products in a wide range of retail outlets. These include petrol stations, newsagents, off-licences and DIY stores. The emphasis here is on place. Any business wishing to compete in this market would, therefore, be unable to overlook the importance of place in its marketing mix.

The position of a business within an industry Businesses that are leaders within their industries tend to have a greater degree of freedom over the particular marketing mix which they choose. Such businesses include Nike and Coca-Cola. Other businesses are in less strong positions, but may operate in industries with strong market leaders. Where this occurs the relatively weaker businesses often choose to 'mimic' the marketing mix of the dominant business.

The marketing mix and the scope of business activity

A wide range of organisations is engaged in marketing activities. Marketing is not confined to well-known businesses, such as BMW and PepsiCo, operating in a national and international environment. It is also used by smaller firms operating in local markets. However, the size of a business and the extent to which it operates in the private or public sector can affect its marketing mix.

The marketing mix and small businesses For many small businesses, particularly sole proprietors, sophisticated marketing strategies are beyond their means. As indictated above, financial factors restrict their choices in terms of creating an effective marketing mix. They often have so much work keeping their businesses ticking over on a day-to-day basis, they do not get the chance to think strategically about their marketing.

Nevertheless, it is vital that even small business consider all aspects of their marketing mix. For example, a cake maker employing two staff would still need to think carefully about:

- the type of cakes, the **product**, that consumers would buy in the local area and how these migth be different form those of competitors;
- a **price** that would encourage local business to buy from a local business rather than a national distributor, but still allow the business to make a profit
- the type of **promotion** that is effective. Certain elements of the marketing mix may be more important for small business owners. For example, a survey by Barclays Bank found that 60 per cent of small businesses depend upon word of mouth to promote themselves.
- how to distribute to local shops and restaurants (**place**), for example, directly.

Question 2.

In 2003 Jenny Bodey set up the smallest of small businesses in a single shop. It was a wedding shop in Bootle, Liverpool, called The Bridal Lounge. By Christmas 2003 and January 2004 she had experienced record days of sales. Perhaps this was due to her choice of business. The profit margins on products in this market are very high. Dresses that are bought for £119 can be sold for £449 and still remain competitive. In the first year sales were predicted to be £56,000 but turned out to be nearer £80,000. She could now easily look at opening a second shop within a couple of years, although she needed to be careful because the area where her current shop is sited had very low overheads.

Jenny also has some advice for others looking to start up. She says budding entrepreneurs should not be too keen to offer discounts and promotions. 'I was giving people £100 of accessories with certain deals, but I've halved that. People don't expect a deal to be so generous. She also says 'I did quite a lot of advertising from regional based wedding magazines to wedding brochures and the local press. If I had a stall at a wedding fair I would take an advert in the brochure as everyone who visited my stall would take the brochure away with them.'

Source: adapted from *en*, February, 2004.

(a) Suggest reasons why the marketing mix of this business has been successful.

Non-profit making organisations There has been a huge increase in the marketing activities in which non-profit organisations such as schools and colleges, charities and hospitals engage. One of the reasons for this is that non-profit organisations in the public sector increasingly need to compete with other similar businesses for their customers (who are still usually called patients, students, clients or other appropriate terms by these organisations). The funding of such organisations is now usually linked to their ability to attract 'customers'. For example, if a college student chooses to attend College A to study for a course, rather than College B, College A will receive funding for this student and College B will not. This provides an incentive for public sector organisations to attract students. Not surprisingly they have employed marketing strategies and techniques to help them meet consumer needs and gain an advantage over rival organisations.

For many non-profit organisations, particularly those in the public sector, price may be less important as a component of the marketing mix than for other businesses. There are two reasons for this. First, such organisations often do not receive any money directly from their customers. For example, colleges and hospitals receive their money through funding organisations set up by the government. Second, the price which their customers are charged is often set by the government and is, therefore, out of the control of individual organisations. For charities, pricing is also likely to be a less important element of the marketing mix. This is because they do not have a priced product in the sense that many other businesses do. Instead they rely on donations from individuals and groups.

Question 3.

In 2003 Jenny Bodey set up the smallest of small businesses in a single shop. It was a wedding shop in Bootle, Liverpool, called The Bridal Lounge. By Christmas 2003 and January 2004 she had experienced record days of sales. Perhaps this was her choice of business. The profit margins on products in this market are very high. Dresses that are bought for £119 can be sold for £449 and still remain competitive. In the first year sales were predicted to be £56,000 but turned out to be nearer £80,000. She could now easily look at opening a second shop within a couple of years, although she needs to be careful because the area where her current shop is sited has very low overheads.

Jenny also has some advice for others looking to start up. She says budding entrepreneurs should not be too keen to offer discounts and promotions. 'I was giving people £100 of accessories with certain deals, but I've halved that. People don't expect a deal to be so generous. She also says 'I did quite a lot of advertising from regional based wedding magazines to wedding brochures and the local press. If I had a stall at a wedding fair I would take an advert in the brochure as everyone who visited my stall would take the brochure away with them.'

Source: adapted from en, February, 2004.

(a) **Suggest reasons why the marketing mix of this business has been successful.**

KEYTERMS

Marketing mix – the elements of a business's marketing that are designed to meet the needs of its customers. The four elements are often called the 4 'Ps' – price, product, promotion and place.
Unique selling point or proposition – the aspect or feature of the product that differentiates it from its rivals.

KNOWLEDGE

1. Identify the four main elements of an effective marketing mix.
2. What is a unique selling point?
3. What features of a business's product are important in the marketing mix?
4. Explain the difference between price and place in the marketing mix.
5. State five factors that influence a business's choice of marketing mix.
6. 'The size of a business is likely to affect its marketing mix.' Explain this statement.
7. Why might advertising be less important to a supplier of industrial equipment than personal contact with customers?

Businesses operating in business to business markets Such firms have other businesses as their consumers. For example, the manufacturers of fork lift trucks do not market their products for use in consumers' homes. Instead, they are aimed at businesses who are interested in buying these products, such as warehouses. The differences between consumer and business to business markets mean that the marketing mix for businesses operating in these two areas may vary a great deal. Whereas the marketing mix for many mass market consumer goods often places emphasis upon advertising campaigns in the media, business to business marketing relies more upon personal contacts and the role of personal selling. International shows or fairs are important events, where producers can make contact with actual or potential customers.

Consumer markets Many marketing theories and concepts have been developed to explain the behaviour of consumer markets, especially those for high sales, mass market goods (commonly known as fast-moving consumer goods or FMCGs). Most businesses operating within such markets tend to focus upon all aspects of the marketing mix, paying a great deal of attention to every element.

International marketing Businesses engaged in international marketing will often vary their marketing mix from one country or region of the world to another. Product names, product specifications, prices, distribution networks and promotional campaigns may all be different. For example, car and paper prices can be lower in Europe than in the UK.

Case Study: A woman's own story

Woman's Own has relaunched at the age of 75. The average age of its readers is 48. It is one of dozens of women's weeklies fighting for the over-35s in the UK national market. How has it survived? Forty seven per cent of the total magazine market in the UK is taken up with women's weeklies. They entertain readers with friendliness and real-life dramas. *Woman's Own* is a major brand, but not one that, up to now, has captured the 'excitement pushing-up circulation figures' elsewhere. All that, according to the title's publishers, IPC Connect, is about to change. The magazine, which was launched in 1932 with a cover showing three wraps of wool, relaunched in April, 2007 with a £2 million marketing budget that was to include TV and billboard advertising.

The new *Woman's Own* is the result of eight months of research into the sort of woman who buys the title and what she wants out of it. Its editor, Karen Livermore, and her team found a 'gap' between how the readers, typically women aged 35-plus, saw themselves (confident, outgoing, loves to gossip and shop) and how they saw other *Woman's Own* readers (settled, middle aged, mumsy, loves cooking and is a loyal friend and neighbour). This is the attitude gap Ms Livermore intends to tackle. But she has a battle on her hands, as these old-fashioned perceptions of the title are almost certainly shared by the wider marketplace. In fact, though more restrained than many rivals, *Woman's Own* has not been 'mumsy' and 'middle aged' for years. If it had, sales would have dropped even further than they have. Circulation has fallen in the past 10 years, from 808,311 in 1996 to 356,811 in December 2006. Despite this, it is still the 21st biggest-selling magazine on the UK news-stand.

In the late Eighties, two German companies, Bauer and Gruner and Jahr, launched their own titles into the UK market. *Best* and *Bella*, brought shorter, snappier stories and a new, 'value-for-money' feel. In 1990 Bauer launched *Take a Break*, and suddenly 'real-life stories were the undisputed currency of women's weeklies. *Woman's Own* responded by relaunching with its own strong true-life stories. Further competition came with the launch in 2002 of Emap's Closer, with its celebrity gossip and paparazzi pictures. When *Grazia* came along a few years later, calling itself a 'weekly glossy', yet another genre was born. For traditional titles to survive, reinvention has been the name of the game for the past 20 years. So what is so different about the relaunched *Woman's Own*?

'*Woman's Own* had lost connections with its readers. Their median age is 48 and that hasn't changed – what has changed is that women in their 40s are very different now. Yes, lots of our readers are housewives and they have homes to run, but they don't want to be reminded of it. Weekly readers can be an unforgiving lot. They are no one's fools – they are savvy and clued up. They're sick of tired old magazine speak – if they're on a diet, they don't want to be told to get off the bus one stop early for the exercise. Our challenge has been to launch the magazine as if it's launching for the first time in 2007. 'We have completely pulled it apart. We'd develop a section, try it out at two or three customer focus groups and then use the information to redesign it and test a different version the following night,' says Ms Livermore.

Last week's issue definitely looked different, with bolder colours and cleaner, fresher lines. The cover is a glamorous shot of Sharon Osbourne. The content is not so different, but somehow the tone of the magazine is livelier, brighter and cheekier. The cover price has risen from 78p to 85p, the paper stock has been upgraded and there is a new, seven page section of news, views and celebrity gossip. Where magazines used to compete for reader loyalty, these days research shows that women are buying across the market, picking up several titles each week, a practice termed 'repertoire buying' by the marketing teams.

So is there room for the all-new *Woman's Own* in today's crowded market? The biggest hurdle is not so much producing a great magazine. It's getting across to the reader that *Woman's Own* is no longer about knitting a nice sweater and finding a good recipe for dinner.

Source: adapted from the *Independent* 22.4.2007.

(a) What is meant by the term marketing mix? (3 marks)

(b) How would you describe *Woman's Own's* unique selling point? (4 marks)

(c) Identify elements of *Woman's Own's* marketing mix using examples from the article. (6 marks)

(d) Using evidence from the article, explain the factors that may have influenced *Woman's Own's* marketing mix. (10 marks)

(e) Discuss whether IPC connect should place so much emphasis in its marketing mix upon the nature of *Woman's Own* as a product. (10 marks)

17 The product life cycle

The product life cycle

Product is one part of the marketing mix. For marketing to be effective a business must be aware of its PRODUCT LIFE CYCLE. The product life cycle shows the different stages that a product passes through over time and the sales that can be expected at each stage. By considering product life cycles businesses can plan for the future. Most products pass through six stages - development, introduction, growth, maturity, saturation and decline. These are illustrated in Figure 1.

Figure 1: The product life cycle

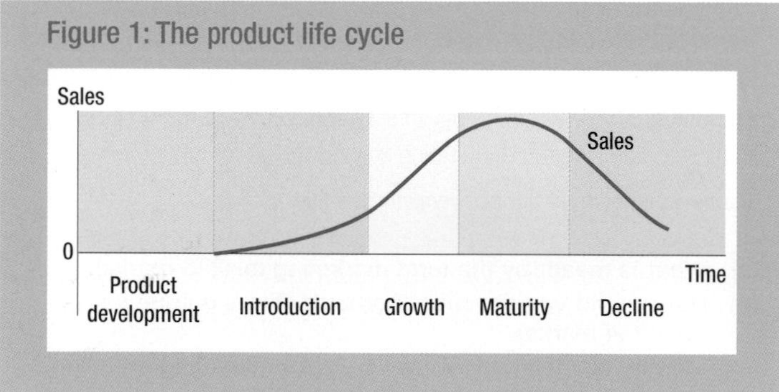

Development During the development stage the product is being **researched** and **designed**. Suitable ideas must be investigated, developed and tested. If an idea is considered worth pursuing then a prototype or model of the product might be produced. A decision will then be made about whether or not to launch the product. A large number of new products never progress beyond this stage and will **fail**. This is because businesses are often reluctant to take risks associated with new products. During the development stage it is likely that the business will spend to develop the product and **costs** will be high. As there will be no sales at this stage, the business will initially be spending but receiving no revenue

Introduction At the start of this stage the product will be **launched**. As the product is new to the market. sales initially are often slow. Costs are incurred when the product is launched. It may be necessary to build a new production line or plant, and the firm will have to meet promotion and distribution costs. A business is also likely to spend on **promotion** to make consumers aware of the new product. Therefore, it is likely that the product will still not be profitable. **Prices** may be set high to cover promotion costs. But they may also be set low in order to break into the market. Few outlets may stock products at this stage. The length of this stage will vary according to the product. With brand new technical products, e.g. computers, the introduction stage can be quite long. It takes time for consumers to become confident that such products 'work'. At first the price of such products may be quite high. On the other hand, a product can be an instant hit resulting in very rapid sales growth. Fashion products and some **fast moving consumer goods** may enjoy this type of start to their life.

Growth Once the product is established and consumers are aware of it, sales begin to grow rapidly, new customers buy the product and there are repeat purchases. Costs may fall as production increases. The product then becomes **profitable.** If it is a new product and there is a rapid growth in sales, **competitors** may launch their own versions. This can lead to a slowdown of the rise in sales. Businesses may need to consider their **prices and promotion**. For example, a high price charged initially may need to be lowered, or promotion may need to increase to encourage brand loyalty.

Maturity and saturation At some stage the growth in sales will level off. The product has become established with a stable market share at this point. Sales will have peaked and competitors will have entered the market to take advantage of profits. As more firms enter the market, it will become saturated. Some businesses will be forced out of the market, as there are too many firms competing for consumers. During the maturity and saturation stages of the product life cycle many businesses use extension strategies to extend the life of their products. These are discussed below.

Decline For the majority of products, sales will eventually decline. This is usually due to changing consumer tastes, new technology or the introduction of new products. The product will lose its appeal to customers. At some stage it will be withdrawn or sold to another business. It may still be possible to make a profit if a high price can be charged and little is spent on promotion or other costs.

Different product life cycles

Many products have a limited life span. Their product life cycles will look similar to that shown in Figure 1. For some products there is a very short period between introduction and decline. They are sometimes called **fads**. The slope of the product life cycle in the introduction and growth period will be very steep and the decline very sharp. Examples of such products include Micropets in 2003, Heelies in 2006 and Pokemon cards in 2005. Once consumers lose interest in a product and sales fall, a business may withdraw it from the market. It may be replaced with another new product. Sometimes poor selling products are withdrawn in case they damage the image of the company. However, businesses must take care not to withdraw a product too early. Over time, certain products have become popular again. For example, skateboards, which were popular in the 1980s regained popularity in the mid-1990s and the early 2000s.

Question 1.

Figure 2

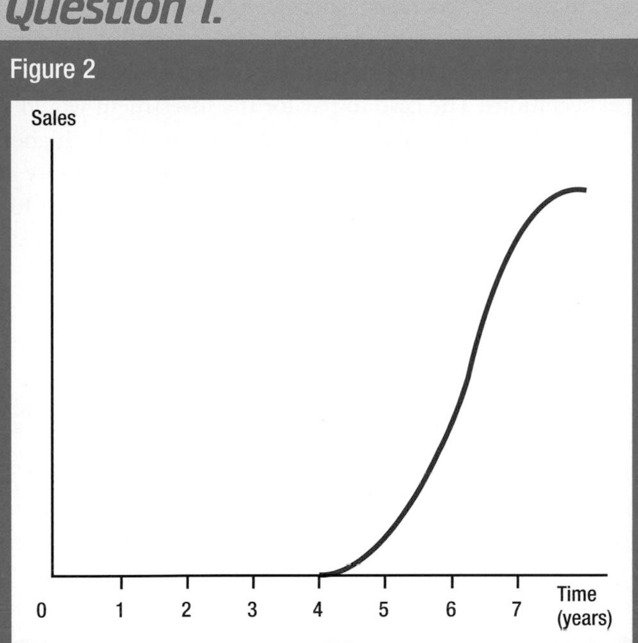

Figure 3

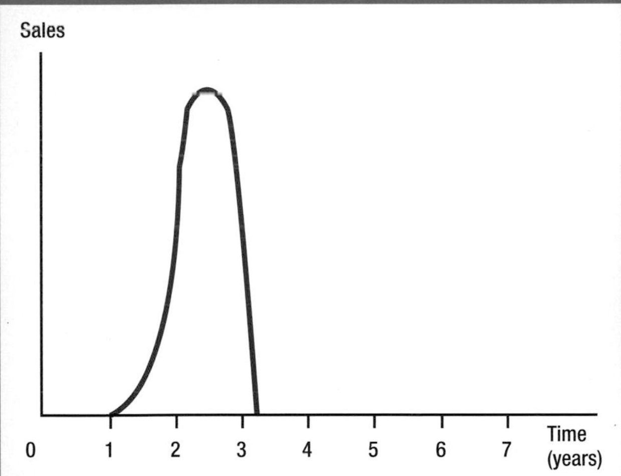

(a) Examine Figures 2 and 3. For each of these, name a product which you think might have a similar product life cycle.

(b) Why do some products have a very long life cycle (greater than 50 years)?

(c) Sketch the current product life cycle of three of the following products:

(i) A compact disc or downloadable song by a leading performance artist/group (you will need to specify the name of the song and the performance artist);

(ii) Walkers cheese and onion crisps;

(iii) Coca-Cola;

(iv) Hovis bread;

(v) Rice Krispie bars;

(vi) Golden Compass DVD;

(vii) the Facebook website;

(viii) a football strip of a Premier League team (you will need to specify the team).

Some businesses still enjoy profits from products which were launched many years ago. The Oxo cube was launched in 1910, Kellogg's Cornflakes were launched in 1906 and Theakston's Old Peculier, a strong ale, was launched in the eighteenth century. These products still sell well today in a form fairly similar to their original.

Because of the high cost of investment, car producers often set product life cycles of ten years for their models. For many products, life cycles are getting shorter, especially in areas like electronics. In the computer industry, some models and software have become obsolete within a very short period as new versions appear which are more technically advanced. For example, in 1995 Microsoft launched its operating software Windows 95. It was later replaced by Windows 98, Windows 2000 and Windows XP.

Extension strategies

It is clear from the product life cycle that the sales of products decline, although at different rates. Firms can attempt to extend the life of a product by using EXTENSION STRATEGIES. They may decide to use one or more of the following techniques.

- Finding new markets for existing products. Over the last 20 years there has been a boom in the sales of sports clothing. This has been largely due to the use of sports clothing as fashion wear.
- Developing a wider product range. Lucozade was originally sold as a product to those recovering from an illness. By extending the product range to include a 'Sports' version, a huge increase in sales has been achieved. Lego constantly develops new versions of a product that started out as a plastic set of building blocks.
- Gearing the product towards specific target markets. Mobile phone companies have packages geared to the needs of teenagers. Banks have accounts for young people.
- Changing the appearance, format or packaging. Coca-Cola is available in individual cans, in glass or plastic bottles, or in multipacks. Chocolate bars such as Toblerone are sold in standard sizes, in large bars or in mini sizes.
- Encouraging people to use the product more frequently. Manufacturers of what were previously known as 'breakfast cereals' have used promotional campaigns to encourage the use of their products at different times throughout the day.
- Changing the ingredients or components. Many microwaveable food products are available as 'weight watchers' or 'low fat' meals, as well as more traditional meals. Many cars are equipped with CD or MP3 players and air conditioning as standard.
- Updating designs. Car manufacturers regularly update models. Makers of computer gaming systems bring out new versions after a period of time.

The effect that an extension strategy can have on the product life cycle is shown in Figure 4. As the market becomes saturated and sales begin to fall, the decline in sales is delayed by the use of

Figure 4: Extensions strategies

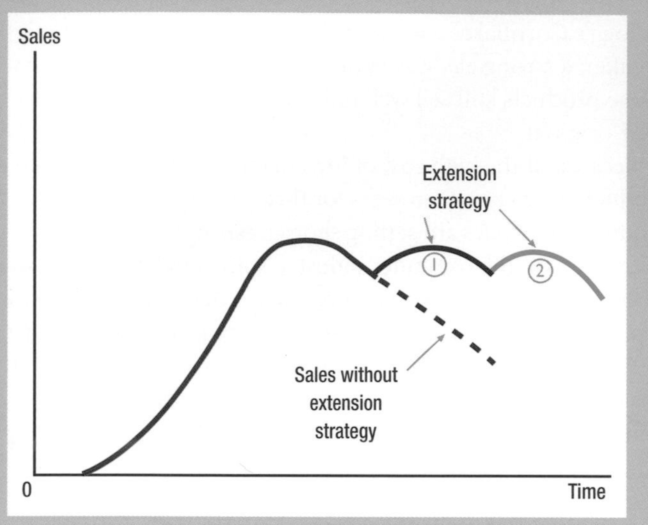

an extension strategy. It would be sensible for a business to try to extend the life of a mature product before sales start to decline. Firms that can predict falling sales from market forecasts may attempt to use extension strategies before the decline takes place, i.e. in the maturity stage.

The product life cycle and capacity

Capacity utilisation is the extent to which a business uses the capacity that it has to produce a particular product. It is the relationship between what a business actually produces and what it is capable of producing. A business working at full capacity that is unable to produce any more of a product will be at maximum capacity utilisation. A business that can still produce more with its existing technology and machinery is likely to be working at less than full capacity.

The product life cycle is linked to capacity utilisation.

- At launch, sales of a product are likely to be limited. So a business will have spare capacity.
- When a product is at its growth stage a business will often be expanding its production and using up spare capacity to meet the rising demand for the product.
- When a product is in its maturity stage a business may be operating at full capacity. If sales continue to grow it must decide whether to invest to expand capacity.
- In the decline stage the capacity that a business has to produce a product will often be underutilised. This is because sales and therefore production may be cut back.

So during the development, growth and growth phases a business will have to make decisions over its capacity.

Creating new capacity A business may decide to build new capacity to deal with sales of a new product. New capacity could be created as sales grow. This would delay outflows of cash until they were needed. There would be less risk that the new capacity would be greater than sales. But, if sales were higher than expected, the business might find it difficult to invest quickly enough to prevent shortages. Alternatively, new capacity could be created before sales take place. But this carries the risk that the investment would be wasted if sales did not grow in line with expectations. The cash to pay for the investment would flow out of the business earlier. Average costs would be higher too, because the cost of creating and running spare capacity at launch would have to be paid for. However, it would easier to deal with unexpectedly high sales than if investment took place when sales actually happened.

Utilising existing capacity There is less risk if a business uses existing capacity. If a business is operating at less than full capacity, it could use the spare capacity to launch a new product. This would help reduce cash outflow associated with new products. Or a business may be working at full capacity, but have products which are at the end of their life cycle. These could be taken out of production and replaced by the new lines.

A problem with this approach is that the average costs of

Question 2.

Rachel's is a manufacturer of organic dairy products. The business is very much a farm based enterprise. In 1952, Brynllys, a farm in Wales, began the process which made it into the first organic farm in the UK. Initially, its dairy production was confined to selling organic milk. But in 1982 it branched out into making and selling cream and butter, initially sold locally. 1984 saw the first commercial production of yoghurt. By 1987, Marigold, a leading London health food supplier, was an enthusiastic buyer and, in 1989, Rachel's yoghurts were on sale in Harrods.

In 1990, the owners of the business, the husband-and-wife team of Gareth and Rachel Rowlands, decided to expand. They borrowed the money, using their farm as collateral, to build a state-of-the-art dairy. It was capable of processing not just the 330,000 litres of organic milk a year from their farm, but 3 million litres - the entire organic output of Wales. Their decision to take this risk was helped by their first large contract to supply a supermarket chain, Sainsbury.

In 1999, they sold the business to Horizon Organic, the biggest wholly organic dairy supplier in the US. Horizon has introduced three new yoghurt flavours: low fat vanilla, whole-milk with maple syrup and Greek-style with honey. This month sees the debut of Rachel's organic fat-free yoghurt and a Welsh butter with bilingual packaging. However, Horizon promised not to alter Rachel's yoghurts in content or concept.

Source: adapted from *The Financial Times*, 24.11.2001.

(a) Discuss whether the introduction of (i) organic yoghurt in 1984 and (ii) organic fat-free yoghurt in 2001 were examples of a new product being brought to the market or an extension strategy for an existing product.

(b) Discuss the cash flow requirements of Rachel's yoghurts during and after the decision in 1990 to build a new state-of-the-art dairy.

production, excluding the cost of any investment, may be higher than if new capacity had been built. For example, it may cost 60p to produce an item on old machinery but only 40p if the latest equipment is used. The decision about whether to buy new equipment will depend upon the relationship between the cost of the new equipment and the saving on running costs. If a business only saves £10,000 a year on running costs by buying £100,000 of new equipment, then it probably won't buy. If it saves £90,000 on running costs for an investment of £100,000, it will probably purchase the new equipment.

As explained above, average costs of production may be higher at launch and during the growth phase if existing capacity to cope with high levels of sales is set aside for use at launch. But again, if sales exceed expectations, the business is more likely to cope if there is spare capacity.

The product life cycle and cash flow

Figure 5 shows the cash flow of a business over a product life cycle.

- Before product launch a business will spend to develop the product and yet no money is coming into the business from sales. So cash flow is likely to be negative.
- At launch, at point A, a product begins to sell. Cash flowing out of a business is still likely to be greater than cash flowing in, so cash flow will be negative. Sales have yet to take off and a business might be spending on promoting the product.
- In the growth period, eventually revenue from the product will be greater than spending (point B) and so cash flow becomes positive. This is because sales will be increasing and average costs may be falling as output increases.
- In the maturity stage cash flow will be at its highest. The product will be earning its greatest revenue.
- In the decline stage, sales will fall and so cash flow will decline.

Uses and problems of the product life cycle

Why might a business be interested in analysing the product life cycle of its existing products or anticipating the life cycle of new products?

- It will illustrate the broad trends in revenue that a product might earn for the business.
- It will identify points at which businesses may need to consider launching new products, as older ones are in decline.
- It will identify points at which extension strategies may need to be introduced.
- It may help a business to identify when and where spending is required, e.g. on research and development at the start, or on marketing at the introduction and when extension strategies are required.
- It may help to identify points at which a business should no longer sell a product.
- It will help a business to manage its product portfolio - its mix of products. This is discussed in the next section.
- It will give an indication of the profitability of a product at each stage in its cycle.
- It will allow a business to plan different styles of marketing that a product might need over its life cycle.

Figure 5: Cash flow, sales and the product life cycle

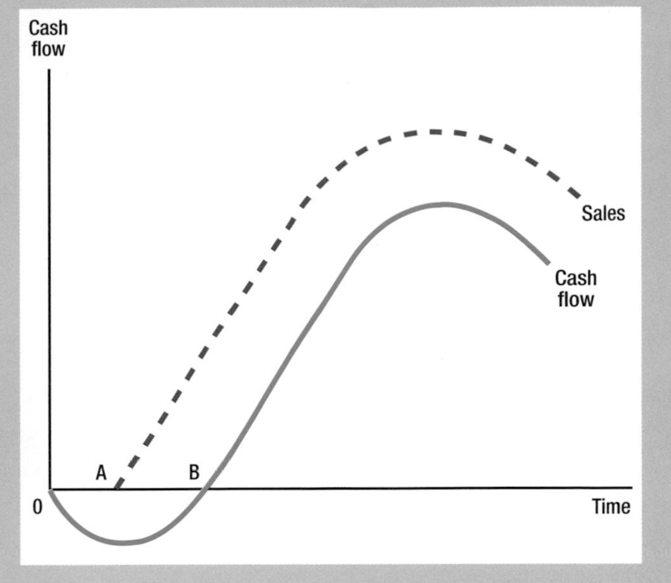

There may be problems, however, when using this model. It can be used to show changes over the life of a product. But it may not be effective in **predicting** the future sales of a product and how sales will change in future. In practice, every product is likely to have a slightly different product life cycle. Furthermore, it is important that the model does not **determine** decisions. For example, a product that is in the decline stage does not automatically have to be withdrawn. Sales may be falling due to a lack of promotion or poor distribution. The decline in sales may be more to do with management decisions than where the product is in its life cycle.

KEYTERMS

Extension strategies – methods used to extend the life of a product.

Product life cycle – shows the different stages in the life of a product and the sales that can be expected at each stage.

KNOWLEDGE

1. Briefly describe the various stages in the product life cycle.
2. Why might a product have a 'steep' life cycle?
3. Name three uses of the product life cycle.
4. How can a firm extend the life of its products?
5. State three ways in which the product life cycle is linked to capacity utilisation.
6. Name three links between the product life cycle and cash flow.

Case Study: The KitKat

The KitKat was launched as Rowntree's Chocolate Crisp in 1935 and renamed KitKat in 1937. The following year it was the company's most popular product. It first became a national favourite in the war years of the 1940s, when the government endorsed it as a healthy, cheap food. Ever since it has been the most popular chocolate bar in the UK. It was one of the main reasons behind the takeover of Rowntree by Nestlé in 1989. It maintained its supremacy even when faced with competition from Nestlé's own Smarties and Black Magic. According to the KitKat website, 47 bars are eaten every second in the UK and a year's production would stretch around the London Underground more than 350 times.

However, in 2003 sales fell by 5 per cent from nearly £123 million in 2002 to £116 million by the end of 2003. 'Saying the business is in crisis is extreme', argued a consumer brands analyst at the time, 'but maintaining its position in the UK confectionery market is going to be a challenge. It's a cut-throat market.' There was concern that saturation point had been reached.

Nestlé fought back by introducing a number of variants to the KitKat market as from 2004. These included an orange and mint flavour, a lemon and yoghurt flavour and a Halloween variant, Blood Orange. In addition, in 2005 a caramac KitKat was launched and the KitKat Dark has now established itself as a permanent addition to the KitKat range. Both the two and four finger versions of the KitKat have remained popular and they have been joined by the KitKat Chunky as mainstays of the KitKat product range.

There are many different variants upon the KitKat theme in those countries where the product remains popular. In Malaysia there is a hot weather version that is less likely to melt in the heat and in Japan a range of flavours, including green tea, passion fruit and lemon cheesecake, have been introduced. Japanese school children regard the KitKat as a lucky charm for exams and tests and take them into school on test days.

In England, health scares regarding childhood obesity have led to a school ban on vending machines selling crisps, chocolate and fizzy drinks as part of what has been termed the 'great KitKat clampdown'. These and other health moves have seen food manufacturers such as Nestle criticized for encouraging youngsters to eat what are seen as unhealthy foods. Health campaigners have also singled out the KitKat chunky for particular criticism.

Source: adapted from *The Guardian* 10.9.2007, *The Independent*, 15.2.2004; www.nestle.co.uk and www.news.bbc.co.uk

(a) Using information from the article, draw and label the product life cycle for KitKat. (3 marks)

(b) Identify significant periods in the product life cycle of KitKat using examples from the article. (6 marks)

(c) Using information from the article, explain the product extension strategies used by Nestle in relation to the KitKat. (8 marks)

(d) Discuss how changes made in the future might affect the product life cycle of KitKat. (8 marks)

18 New product development and product portfolio analysis

The nature of products

A PRODUCT is anything that can be exchanged and is able to satisfy customers' needs. It might be a tangible physical GOOD, such as a car or a packet of peas. Or it might be an intangible, non-physical SERVICE, such as a foreign holiday, a medical examination or defence.

A distinction can be made between PRODUCER (or INDUSTRIAL) PRODUCTS and CONSUMER PRODUCTS. Producer products are used to make other goods and services or in the operation of A business. For example, a coffee machine and a building are two producer products used by Starbucks to make a cup of coffee served to consumers. Producer products are sold by one business to another through business to business marketing. The cup of coffee is a consumer product because it is bought by individuals or households for personal use. A car bought from a dealer by an individual would be a consumer product bought in a consumer market. In contrast, a car bought by a business for use as a company car would be a producer product.

Consumers buy products because of the benefits given by these attributes. TANGIBLE BENEFITS are benefits which can be measured. For example, the benefit of a train journey might be that it gets you from London to Glasgow in four hours. The benefit of a washing machine might be that it will wash for five years without breaking down. INTANGIBLE BENEFITS are benefits which, though present, cannot be measured. Some products are bought because of the image they convey. For example, wearing a t-shirt in the colours of a national football team might have been considered fashionable during the World Cup of 2006. Other intangible benefits might be pleasure or peace of mind. Cadbury's advertisements stress the pleasure gained from eating a Cadbury's Flake. Insurance to cover funeral expenses is often sold to give peace of mind to the person who is going to die.

What are the characteristics of a 'good' product?

- It should be functional and fulfil the needs of customers. For example, food should taste good. A train service should be fast, frequent and reliable. A television set should give good quality pictures. A lawn mower should cut grass well.
- It should be aesthetically pleasing. Good design is not just about working properly. It is also about how a product looks to the customer. In some industries, such as clothing, cars and kitchen equipment, aesthetics and design have a great effect on how consumers spend their money.
- It should be affordable. Many people would like to take a journey into space, but at present it is too expensive for all but a few. On the other hand, a furniture company like Ikea has become extremely successful because it sells goods which are affordable to most. So the product should be capable of being produced within the purchasing budgets of the target market.
- The product must conform to legal requirements. Toys, for example, should not contain lead paint. Food sold to people should be fit to eat.
- Ideally, products should be environmentally and socially friendly. Increasingly, products are being bought by consumers on the strength of their 'ethical' credentials. For example, people want paper made from recycled paper. They might also refuse to buy trainers made in factories with poor working conditions in low income countries.

Unique selling points of products

Successful products will have a **unique selling point** or **unique selling proposition** (USP). This is a characteristic of a product that makes it different from other products. The USP is often promoted by businesses to customers as being the 'best'. For example, cars may be advertised as being the safest, giving the smoothest ride or having the most space. Identifying and promoting the USP of a product can have a number of benefits.

- For consumers, it helps them to differentiate one product from others, which can make choices easier.
- For businesses, it helps differentiate its products from others. It will aim to show consumers that it is offering something that other products are not. This can increase sales and help to build up BRAND LOYALTY.

The product portfolio

Product life cycle analysis, outlined in the previous unit, shows businesses that sales of products eventually decline. A well organised business with one or more products will attempt to phase out old products and introduce new ones. This is known as managing the PRODUCT PORTFOLIO or PRODUCT MIX. The product portfolio will be made up of PRODUCT LINES. A product line is a group of products which are similar. For example, televisions are a product line including flat screen, HD widescreen and portable televisions. With a constant launch of new products, a business can make sure a 'vacuum' is not created as products reach the end of their life.

Figure 1 shows how a business can manage its product portfolio. Say that a business over a particular time period aims to launch three products. By organising their launch at regular intervals, there is never a gap in the market. As one product is declining, another is growing and further launches are planned. At point (i), as sales of product X are growing, product Y has just been launched. This means that at point (ii), when sales of product X have started to decline, sales of product Y are growing and product Z has just been launched.

This simple example shows a 'snapshot' of three products only. In practice, a business may have many products. It would hope that existing products remain in 'maturity' for a long period. The profit from these mature products would be used to 'subsidise' the launch of new products. New products would be costly at first, and would make no profit for the business.

Examples of businesses that have successfully managed their product portfolios are sweet manufacturers. Companies such as Nestlé produce a wide range of products, including KitKat, Milky Bar and Yorkie, and constantly look to launch new products.

Figure 1: Managing the product portfolio

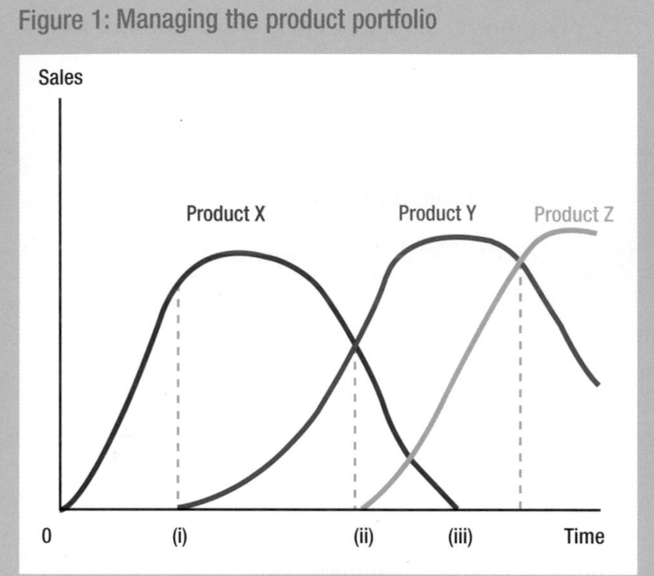

Product portfolio analysis and the Boston Matrix

One problem for firms when planning their product portfolios is that it is very difficult in practice to tell what stage of the life cycle a product is at. Also, there is no standard lifetime for products. For example, young people's fashion clothing has life cycles which can be predicted with some certainty. Other poducts are less reliable. Who, for example, could have predicted the lengthy life cycles of products such as Heinz baked beans and the VW Beetle, or the short life cycle of products such as the Sinclair C5 – a sort of 'mini-car' introduced in the 1980s?

A useful technique for allowing firms to analyse their product portfolios is the Product Portfolio Matrix developed by the Boston Consulting Group. It is sometimes called the BOSTON MATRIX. This is shown in Figure 2. Products are categorized according to two criteria.

- **Market growth.** How fast is the market for the product growing? The market may be declining or it may be expanding. Sales of a product in a fast expanding market have a better chance of growing than a product in a stagnant or declining market.
- **Relative market share.** How strong is the product within its market? Is it a market leader that other products follow? Is it a product that is twelfth in terms of sales? To measure this the market share of a product is compared with the strongest rival product. For example, if Product X had a market share of 10 per cent and the market leader had 40 per cent then the relative market share of Product X is 0.25 (10 per cent ÷ 40 per cent). If Product Y is a market leader with 50 per cent market share and the next most important product had a market share of 25 per cent, the relative market share of product Y is 2.0 (50 per cent ÷ 25 per cent).

Using these criteria the products of a business can be placed into one of four categories on the Boston Matrix.

Stars A star is a product with a high market growth and a relatively high market share. Stars are valuable to businesses. The product will be in a strong position in its market as it has a high market share and the business can take advantage of a fast growing market. A star is already likely to be **profitable** as it has a relatively high market share. But a business will need to **invest** in the product to cope with a growing market and growing sales. This could mean investing in new production facilities or promotion to fend off competition. **Cash flow** may be nearly zero. This is because although profits will be high, bringing money in, spending will also be high, leading to outflows.

Question 1.

Lokotronics is small business that produces a range of electrical products used for measuring and testing in the construction industry . Table 1 shows the sales from just four of its products over the period 2000 to 2008.

- Product A is a portable hand held machine for testing damp in houses.
- Product B is a patented tape measure that allows the accurate measurement of curves and irregular shapes to more highly accurate distances than other measuring devices.
- Product C measures the weight of small amounts of materials
- Product D is a device to test the tolerance and breaking strength of materials.

Table 1

					Sales (000)
Year	Product A	Product B	Product C	Product D	All products
2000	2	8	-	-	
2001	4	10	-	-	
2002	8	6	9	-	
2003	12	3	15	-	
2004	18	1	18	2	
2005	20	-	16	6	
2006	22	-	11	15	
2007	22	-	10	20	
2008	21	-	8	25	

(a) Calculate the total sales of all products in each year.
(b) Explain why Products B has a unique selling point.
(c) Discuss whether the product portfolio was well managed over the period.

Cash cows A cash cow is a product with a relatively high market share. It is therefore well positioned in the market and likely to be **profitable**. But the market it is in will have weak growth. So there will be little chance of increasing sales and profits in future. There will be little need for **investment**. With slow growth in sales there should be little need for new premises for example. Cash cows have strong positive **cash flow**. Money coming into the business from profits will not be taken out via investment.

Problem children Problem children, also know as question marks or wildcats, are products with a relatively low market share in a fast growing market. This can be a problem for a business because it is unclear what should be done with these products. If a product is performing weakly it is unlikely to be **profitable**. But as it is in a fast growing market, there is potential to turn it into a star. **Cash flow** is likely to be zero or negative. Weak relative market share means that it will not be profitable. But **investment** will be needed to cope with expanding sales in a fast growing market.

Dogs These are products with a relatively low market share in a market with low growth. Dogs have poor prospects for future sales and **profits**. They may generate some **cash flow** because they will need little **investment** but may earn some profit. But if they make little or no profit, cash flow may be zero or even negative.

Businesses can make use of the Boston Matrix to manage their product portfolios.

Balancing product lines Businesses must ensure that their product portfolios do not contain too many items within each category. Naturally, they do not want lots of 'Dogs', but they should also avoid having too many 'Stars' and 'Problem children'. Products on the top of the Boston Matrix are in the early stages of the product life cycle and are in growing markets. But the cost of developing and promoting them will not yet have been recovered. This will drain resources. Balancing these with 'Cash cows' will mean that the revenue from the 'Cash cows' can be used to support products in a growing market. The development cost of 'Cash cows' is likely to have already been recovered and promotional costs should be low relative to sales. This does not mean though that a business would want lots of 'Cash cows' and few 'Problem children' and 'Stars'. This is because many of the 'Stars' and perhaps some 'Problem children' might become the 'Cash cows' of the future.

Taking appropriate decisions Products in different categories in the Matrix may require different approaches.

- Stars have great future potential. They are future cash cows. A business will need to **build** the brand of these products so that sales increase and competition is fought off successfully.
- Cash cows might be **milked** for cash, which can then be used to develop other products. Or the business may decide to spend just enough on promotion and development to maintain sales and market share, known as **holding**.
- For problem children a business has choices. It can **build** the brand, hoping to turn it into a star, **harvest** the product by raising price and cutting promotion so that profits are increased, or **divest** itself of the product, withdrawing it or selling it because it is not making a profit.
- Dogs may be divested if they are not making a profit or in some cases harvested.

Figure 2: The Boston Matrix

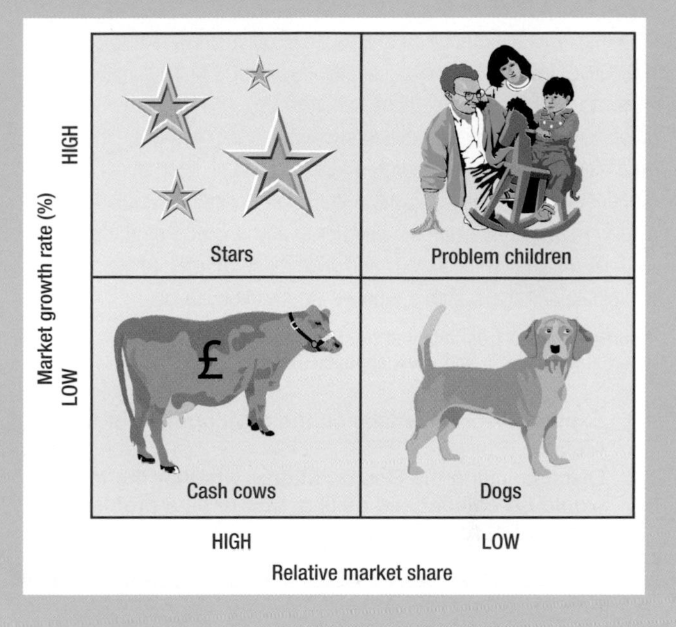

New product development

Planning the product portfolio requires the continual development and launch of new products. New products are needed to replace products coming to the end of their life cycles and to keep up with changes in the market. This is called **new product development**.

In some business sectors the need to plan ahead is very important. In the chemical industry, development work is done on products which might not reach the market for over ten years. In the motor industry many cars take over five years to develop. New products normally pass through five stages when they are being developed.

Generating ideas The first stage is when firms generate ideas. Ideas for new products come from a variety of sources.

- Identifying gaps in the market, perhaps through market research. An example of this has been the development of vegetarian microwave dishes by food producers. An important issue here for businesses is in identifying the unique selling point of a product.
- Scientific research. Pharmaceuticals businesses devote huge

Question 2.

The origins of the iPhone can be found in Steve Job's (the Apple Chief Executive) instruction to Apple engineers in 2003 to investigate touch screens. He believed that mobile phones were going to become important devices for portable information access and was determined to create a device that integrated a mobile phone, Internet access and an iPod. When it was launched in the UK in November, 2007 it was widely regarded as being far superior to anything else on the market with its multitouch technology and wide range of uses. Apple anticipate selling 10 million iPhones worldwide by 2008.

Source: adapted from adapted from *The Guardian*, 5.11.2007, www.wikipedia.org and www.apple.co.uk

(a) Explain TWO influences on the development of the iPhone.

(b) Discuss, using the Boston Matrix. whether the Iphone would be categorised as (i) a star or (ii) a problem child in future.

amounts to research and development expenditure. As a result they have developed products to tackle a range of ailments from heart disease through to cancer.

- Generating creative ideas through open discussions. Products such as the jet engine have come about as a result of this.
- Analysing other products. When developing new products many businesses will analyse products manufactured by competitors. They aim to include, adapt or improve upon the best features of these products in their own designs. Some businesses adapt their own successful products to make new products.

Analysis The second stage is the analysis of those ideas generated in the first stage. There are a number of questions a firm might ask. Most importantly, it must find out if the product is marketable - if enough consumers wish to buy it to allow the firm to make a profit. Businesses must also decide if the product fits in with the company's objectives, if it is legal and if the technology is available to produce it.

Development The third stage is the actual development of the product. This may involve technical development in the laboratory or the production of a prototype. Such work will be carried out by the research and development department. An important part of this process is the actual design of the product. Some preliminary testing may be carried out to find out whether or not the product actually meets consumers' needs.

Test marketing TEST MARKETING occurs when a new product is tested on a small, representative section of the total market. The test market area should share characteristics which are similar to those found in the market as a whole. The benefit of test marketing is the high degree of reliability of results gained. It is carried out because of the high cost and risk of launching a product in a large, usually national, market. Test marketing can itself be costly, but not as expensive as a national launch which fails. One problem is that it allows competitors to see the new product and gives them the chance to take counter-action before a national launch.

Commercialisation and launch The final stage is the launch and commercialisation. Here any problems found during test marketing must be solved. The firm will then decide on the 'marketing package' it will use to give the product launch the greatest chance of success.

At each of the five stages, many ideas are rejected. This means that very few ideas generated in the first stage will actually end up as a product launched onto the market. In Figure 3, an example is shown where 40 ideas were put forward for a new product. In this company the majority of ideas do not get beyond the first stage. The pass rate at this stage is only 1 in 5, with 4 out of 5 ideas being rejected. After that, the number of ideas which survive from one stage to the next increases as the pass rate falls from 1 in 5 ideas to 1 in 2. At the end of the process, only 1 out of a total of 40 ideas has survived to be launched onto the market.

Influences on new product development

There is a wide range of influences on businesses developing new goods and services. These influences may encourage a business to go ahead with a new product or, alternatively, restrict the development of one or more new products.

Figure 3: New product development

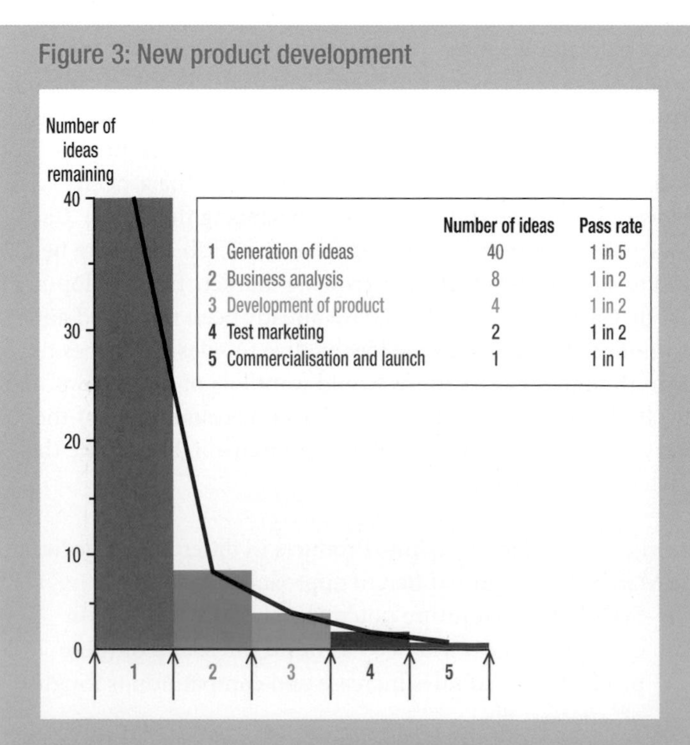

	Number of ideas	Pass rate
1 Generation of ideas	40	1 in 5
2 Business analysis	8	1 in 2
3 Development of product	4	1 in 2
4 Test marketing	2	1 in 2
5 Commercialisation and launch	1	1 in 1

Availability of finance and resources In highly competitive markets businesses find that their profit margins are squeezed. This means that financial and human resources are often not available to develop new products. An example of this is in the market for budget fashion clothing. Businesses in this market tend to copy products developed for designer labels. Other businesses may find that they have a number of mature products generating a healthy stream of income. Such businesses may invest this income in new product development, hoping to create the 'cash cows' of the future.

Technology The development of technology can affect the type of product or service provided. One hundred years ago computers did not exist. Today they are sold in a variety of ways to different businesses. Internet cafes and laptop computers are now standard products for a range of consumers. There are now many opportunities for new goods and services, such as the online retailing of music that are linked to these new technologies. Just ten years ago such opportunities for new products like these did not exist.

Cost Even when businesses have resources, the cost of developing new products may be prohibitive. The development of products in the electronics market can cost millions of pounds. As technological boundaries have been pushed forward, the cost of even modest new product development has risen sharply. Also, in many markets products have increasingly shorter life spans. This means that less time is available to recover development costs. Conversely, in those markets, such as the market for computer games consoles where technological developments are moving at a fast pace, there can be enormous rewards for successful new products. This creates a clear incentive for new products even when the costs are high.

Competitors' actions The behaviour of a business' competitors can strongly influence new product development. In some cases an innovatory competitor can act as a spur to other businesses in the same sector in their efforts to create new products. Some would argue, for example, that the new products produced by the Apple Corporation, such as the iPhone and iPod, have caused competitors to raise their game. Other businesses respond to innovatory competitors by copying, as far as possible within copyright and patent laws, their competitors' products.

Market constraints There is little point in a business developing a new product unless consumers are prepared to purchase it at a price which can cover development and production costs. Many so-called 'tremendous ideas' for new products have been abandoned. This is because firms believe they cannot find a profitable market for the product. In addition, consumers can be resistant to change. This is often because of the time and effort consumers need to spend in getting to know how new products 'work'. There is also evidence that consumers are resistant to new products which represent a radical departure from existing products. New versions of existing products are sometimes more popular with consumers than totally new ideas for this reason.

Entrepreneurial skills of managers and owners Some businesses are more likely to engage in new product development because of the skills and attitudes of their managers and owners. More entrepreneurial managers and owners of businesses are likely be more inclined to take risks rather than continue doing what they know best. Steve Job, for example, Chief Executive of the Apple Corporation, has been widely credited as being the driving force behind the revolutionary new products produced by Apple, including the iPod, iMac and iPhone.

Legal constraints Firms cannot develop whatever new products they wish. Legislation must be taken into account. For example, a pharmaceutical company wishing to develop a new product must be sure that it adheres to health legislation.

KNOWLEDGE

1. What is a product?
2. What is the difference between a consumer and a producer product?
3. Explain how a business can prevent a 'vacuum' in its product portfolio.
4. What is meant by a product line?
5. What is meant by the Boston Matrix?
6. How can the Boston Matrix help a business to manage its product portfolio?
7. What is meant by new product development?
8. State two ways in which a business can generate new product ideas.
9. State six factors that can influence the development of new products.

KEYTERMS

Brand loyalty – the extent to which customers of a brand repeat purchases of that brand rather than others.
Boston Matrix – a 2 x 2 matrix model which analyses a product portfolio according to the growth rate of the market and the relative market share of products within the market.
Consumer products – goods or services sold to individuals to households for personal consumption.
Goods – physical products.
Intangible benefits (of a product) – benefits that cannot be measured.
Producer or industrial products – goods or services that are sold by one business to other businesses.
Product line – a group of products which are very similar.
Product portfolio (product mix) – the particular portfolio of products which a firm is marketing.
Product – anything that can be exchanged and is able to satisfy customers' needs.
Services – non-physical products.
Tangible benefits (of a product) – benefits that can be measured.
Test marketing – testing out a product on a small section of a market prior to its full launch.

CRITIQUE

Critics of the Boston Matrix argue that the Matrix can cause businesses to focus too much upon pursuing increases in market share as opposed to, for example, attempting to consolidate market share or improve other aspects of the performance of a product. It is also suggested that the model fails to take account of the way in which products within a business can support one another. For example a business might sell a dog, but this might affect sales of other products it supports which could be stars or cash cows. Cash flow and profit can also be different for individual products. A dog may have strong cash flow and be profitable despite falling sales. A star might have negative cash flow if there is fierce competition.

Case Study: Stubble trouble

The Fusion Power Stealth is a razor with five pivoting blades and one at the back, a lubrication strip,a rubber guard to stretch the skin, a battery to make it vibrate and a microchip to control the level of vibration. It will also tell you when the battery's flat. It has a striking black and orange box to house the rubberised handle. Sports stars sell it to you, including David Beckham and Roger Federer. And it has a killer name.

It is, claims Gillette, the closest shave a man can get. They did, of course, say that about the last thing they came up with before Fusion Power Stealth - the one just called Fusion Power. Before that, it was just primitive old Fusion. And they said the same for the Mach3 Power, which came after Mach3 Turbo, which followed Mach3, and overtook Sensor Excel, Sensor, Atra Plus and Tracll Plus. The latter appeared in 1971 and seems positively primeval; it was smooth, it was safe, it meant you didn't leave the sink covered in blood and your face speckled with tissue paper. Nothing could better it, for a while at least.

The Fusion Power Stealth, which began appearing at chemists and supermarkets in September 2007, will probably only be 'the best' shaving system for a couple of years. After that, Gillette have other plans, which they are not keen to divulge as 'other people may be reading your story,' says Kevin Powell, Gillette's laboratory director, by which he means Wilkinson Sword. Gillette has 74 per cent of the total razor market in the UK, followed by Wilkinson Sword.

The razors aren't just thrown together by a marketing department in an attempt to sell us something we didn't know we needed. They are the result of years of called cutting-edge science and the endeavours of biologists, dermatologists, physicists, polymer scientists, biometricists and neurologists. There is a team concerned solely with how to make a razor vibrate just the right amount, and other people employed to optimise handle grip in a slippery bathroom environment. Only when these people have done their work (Fusion Power Stealth has taken four years to appear from the initial prototype), do the people who design the packaging and advertising slogans go to work.

Before the concept of the Fusion system went to Gillette's global HQ in Boston, it was tested on about 9,000 men throughout the world. When Fusion was tested against its predecessor Mach3, 30 per cent of men in the trials said they preferred their existing system. But the majority preferred it in 69 respects, including 'giving the closest shave without irritation'; 'blades shaving as close on the first stroke as the last'; 'the colour of the razor'; 'the texture of the handle'; and 'ease of rinsing'.

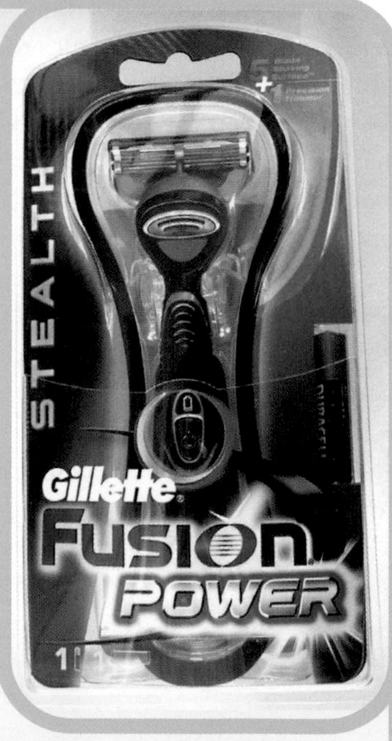

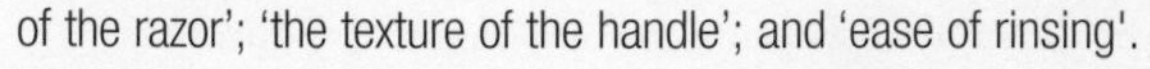
Source: adapted from *The Guardian*, 23.11.2007.

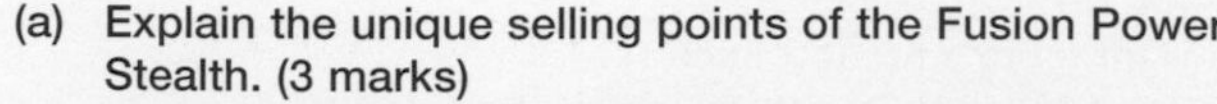

(a) Explain the unique selling points of the Fusion Power Stealth. (3 marks)
(b) Using information from the article, explain TWO influences on the development of the Fusion Power Stealth. (6 marks)
(c) Examine, using the Boston Matrix, the position in the market of the Fusion Power Stealth a couple of years after its launch and the decision about the product that Gillette may face. (8 marks)
(d) Discuss whether Gillette should have launched the Fusion Power Stealth when it had 74 per cent of the total razor market in the UK. (10 marks)

19 Price - influencing the market

Influences on pricing

The pricing strategies used by a business may be influenced by a number of factors.

Objectives The pricing strategy chosen by a business is likely to reflect the extent to which it wants to maximise profits or sales. A business seeking to maximise short-term profits may use more aggressive and perhaps risky pricing strategies.

The marketing mix The price chosen by a business must complement the marketing mix. This means that the price must fit in with the nature of the product itself and the way in which it is being promoted and distributed to consumers. For example, a low quality product being sold in retail outlets at the bottom end of the market is likely to be sold at a fairly low price.

Costs A business which cannot generate enough revenue over time to cover its costs will not survive. In the long run, a business must charge a price which earns enough revenue to cover its total cost of production at any level of output. This means that businesses must take account of all of their costs when setting price. In the short run a business may not expect to cover the fixed costs of its factory or machinery. Providing its price is high enough to generate revenue that covers its variable costs, the firm will stay in business. Revenue below this will cause the business to cease production. As a result businesses may have greater flexibility in the short term when making pricing decisions.

Competition Competition can affect pricing decisions For a market trader, the price of her goods is largely determined by prices on nearby stalls selling similar goods. Such a trader will have little room for manoeuvre compared to a business which faces less competition. A monopolist that dominates the market may be able to charge higher prices.

Demand The higher the price set the lower the quantity sold. The effect that a higher prices has on sales is dealt with in the unit titled 'Elasticity of demand'.

Consumer perceptions Businesses must pay attention to what consumers think a product is worth. A product priced above what consumers consider its value to be may generate low sales because of doubts about its value for money. A product priced too low may also generate low sales. This is because consumers often suspect that such products have something wrong with them or that they are of inferior quality. In some cases businesses actually encourage consumers to think of their products as expensive to encourage high income earners to buy them.

Market segment Businesses that produce a range of products are likely to have some aimed at particular market segments. This is true, for example, of all major car manufacturers. They are, therefore, likely to charge different prices for each segment. However, the price which they charge to one segment of the market will affect the prices charged to other segments. A product competing in the top end of the market will need to have a different price from one aimed at the middle or bottom end of the market.

Laws and regulations The price of a number of products is affected by government. Taxes can raise the price above the level that might have been set by manufacturers. Products affected greatly by taxation include cigarettes, alcoholic drinks and petrol. There is also a number of products which are offered to consumers below the price that producers would normally charge. Such products are subsidised by the government. Maximum prices can also be set. For example, the price of products such as water and gas in the UK are determined by regulatory bodies.

Question 1.

The price of each product in a market will be influenced by a variety of factors. For some products, the ability of a business to set its price is limited. For others, there will be more scope for a business to set the price it wants to charge.

(a) **What factors may have influenced the prices of the products in the photographs?**

Pricing strategies

A strategy is a set of plans designed to meet objectives. PRICING STRATEGY is part of the marketing strategy of the business. Other strategies such as product and distribution strategy also make up a marketing strategy. Marketing strategy is then part of the corporate strategy of the business. Other strategies include production and financial strategy.

Pricing strategy is therefore a set of plans about pricing which help a business to achieve its marketing and corporate objectives. For example, a corporate objective might be to double in size over the next five years. A marketing objective to achieve this might be to take the products of the business 'up-market'. The pricing strategy developed from this could be to increase the average price of the products made by the business.

- Some pricing strategies can be used for **new products**, such as market skimming or penetration pricing.
- Some strategies may be more suitable for **existing products**.

Cost based pricing

All businesses are influenced by their costs when determining prices with costs acting as a 'bottom line' when choosing a price. But some use COST BASED PRICING as their strategy for price setting. Businesses using cost-based pricing are those where the influence of cost is more important than other factors such as market conditions or competitors' pricing. The local garage repair business or domestic repair services like electricians and plumbers are likely to take a cost-based approach.

There is a number of methods that businesses use to set their prices which are based upon particular costs.

Cost plus pricing This involves setting a price by calculating the average cost of producing goods and adding a MARK-UP for profit. If a business produces 10,000 goods costing £50,000, the average cost would be £5.00. A mark up of 20 per cent would mean goods would cost an extra £1.00 and the price would be £6.00 per product. Retailers often use this method of pricing. Say that a department store buys a colour TV from wholesalers for £200 and its mark-up to allow for a profit is 100 per cent. The retail price to consumers will be £400.

Figure 1: Cost plus pricing

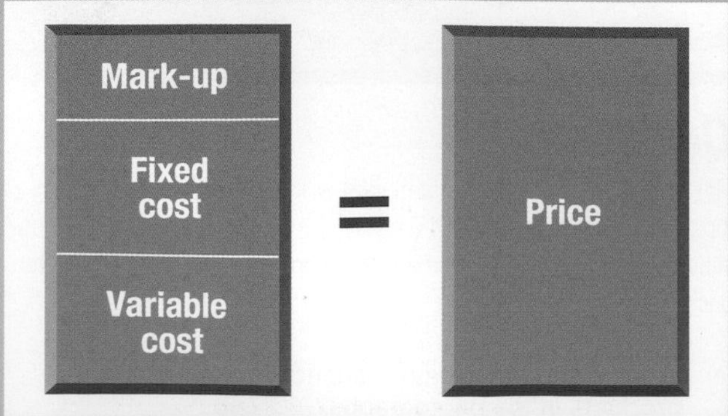

Figure 2: Contribution pricing

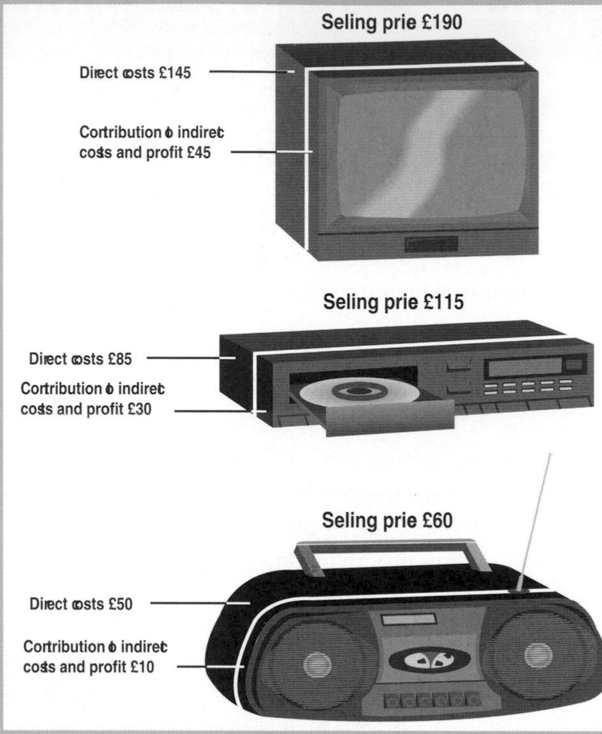

The attractiveness of cost plus pricing is that it is a quick and simple way of setting a selling price. It also ensures that sales revenue will cover total costs and generate profit. A criticism, however, is that a fixed mark-up does not allow a business to take market needs into account when setting prices. In addition, no attempt is made to allocate indirect costs to particular products. This means they do not reflect the resources being allocated by the business to that particular product or product range.

Contribution pricing This method takes into account that different products within a company might need to be priced using different criteria. For each product, a price is set in relation to the **direct costs** of producing that product and any **contribution** that the business wants that product to make towards covering its **indirect cost** and towards profit. Thus for a manufacturer of electrical goods, some prices might be as set out as in Figure 2.

No one product will be **expected** to account for all the indirect costs of the business. Each product's selling price would make some contribution to meeting indirect costs. If the producer expected to sell 100 items of each product and had to cover indirect costs of £6,500 and generate profit of £2,000 (£8,500) then:

Product A	£45 x 100 = £4,500	contribution
Product B	£30 x 100 = £3,000	contribution
Product C	£10 x 100 = £1,000	contribution
	£8,500	

Figure 3: Absorption/full cost pricing

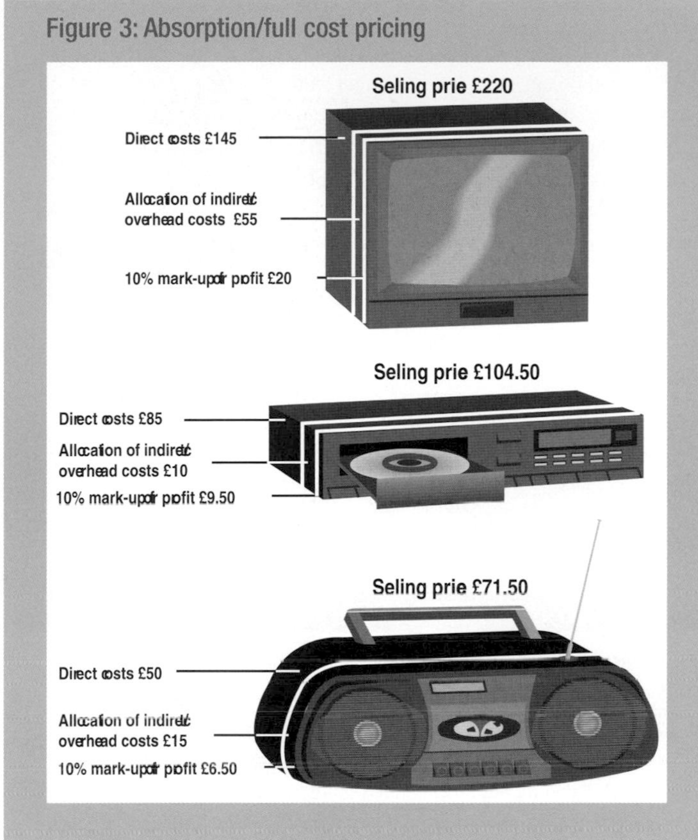

Figure 4: Target pricing

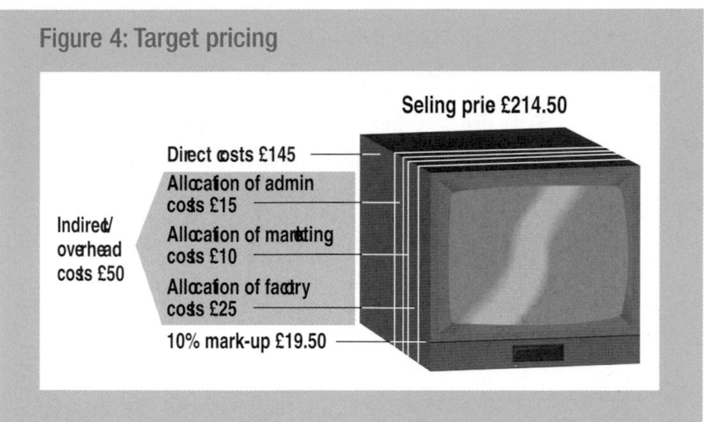

This allows businesses more flexibility than the cost plus approach. Successful products can be priced to make a large contribution. Less successful products or new products can be priced more competitively, as they need only to make a lower contribution to overheads and profits. Indeed, new products might even be making a negative contribution, ie their price does not even cover the **marginal cost** of production. Demand factors as well as cost factors are now being taken into account.

Absorption cost/full cost pricing A business may attempt to take into account the indirect costs that can be attributable to a particular product in deciding on a price. This is known as absorption or full cost pricing. In its simplest form an arbitrary method is used to allocate indirect costs to each product, for example, a percentage of total sales or total direct costs. The electrical goods manufacturer might charge the prices in Figure 3. A mark-up is then added for profit.

A more sophisticated method of allocation can also be used. Using this method to allocate indirect costs, each element of the cost will be treated separately. This means the selling price of a product will absorb elements of each overhead cost.

As we can see from Figures 3 and 4 the price of the TV is different according to the method used. A different costing formula will lead to a different final price. Under the arbitrary method a larger allocation of indirect/overhead costs was made to the television's final price.

Target pricing This is sometimes known as **target profit pricing.** It involves businesses setting prices that will earn them a particular level of profit, which has been clearly targeted. When setting a target price (or profit) businesses make use of break-even analysis. Figure 5 shows the break-even chart for a small business producing leather briefcases. It is based upon a selling price of £90, fixed costs of £30,000 and variable costs of £30 per briefcase. In order to break-even the business must produce and sell 500 briefcases. If, however, it wishes to target a profit of £30,000 then it must produce and sell 1,000 briefcases. Using break- even analysis in this way businesses can target a particular level of profit for their product.

The price which is charged for a product affects the demand for a product. The precise relationship between demand and price is measured by price elasticity of demand. Thus the briefcase manufacturer may wish to estimate the demand for its briefcases at various price levels. It can then choose a price and associated sales which will enable it to make the profit that it wants. This is shown in Table 1. Table 1 shows that the business would not benefit at present from either lowering or raising its price from £90.

Problems of cost based pricing

Cost based pricing does have a number of problems. It is a

Figure 5: A break-even chart for a briefcase manufacturer

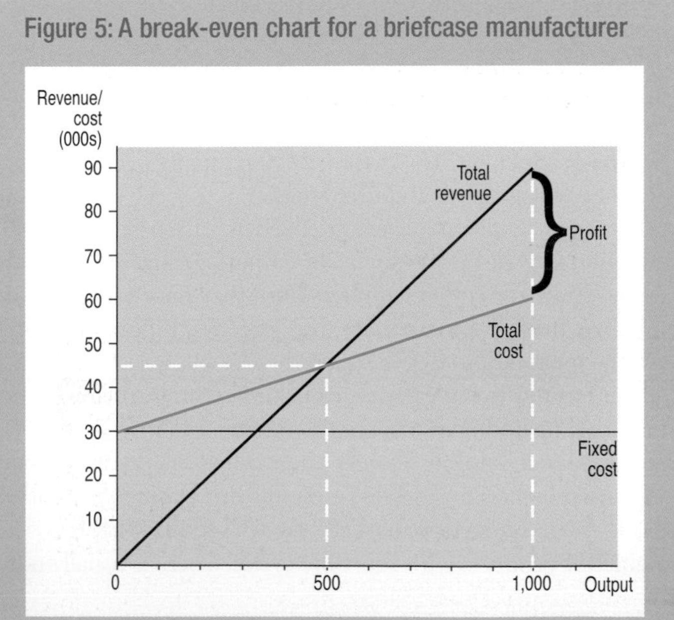

Table 1: Profits and break-even at different price levels for a briefcase manufacturer

Price	Estimated demand at given price	Total revenue	Total costs (Fixed costs = £30,000 variable costs = £30)	Break-even point	Profit
(£)		(£)	(£)		(£)
80	1,100	88,000	63,000	600	25,000
90	1,000	90,000	60,000	500	30,000
100	800	80,000	54,000	429	26,000

product and cost orientated approach which does not refer to consumers' wishes or flexibility. Contribution pricing does, however, allow more flexibility than cost plus pricing for a particular marketing strategy. Full or absorption cost pricing may result in prices being set too high or too low in relation to consumers' wishes or competitors' prices. They are also inflexible in response to market changes, as these would not necessarily be reflected in the costs of a company. The more sophisticated the costing method used when pricing, the more accurate is the allocation of costs to a product, but the further the price might be from what the market will bear.

Market orientated pricing

MARKET ORIENTATED PRICING methods are those which are based upon an analysis of the conditions in the market at which a product is aimed. As such, they are much better suited to market orientated businesses.

Penetration pricing This is used by businesses seeking to gain a foothold in a market, either with new products or with established products being placed in new markets. It involves pricing a product at a low level so that retailers and consumers are encouraged to purchase the product in large quantities.

There are two main reasons why businesses use penetration pricing.

- Consumers are encouraged to develop the habit of buying the product, so that when prices eventually begin to rise they will continue to purchase it.
- Retailers and wholesalers are likely to purchase large quantities of the product. This should mean that they will not buy from other suppliers until they have sold most of their stock. Businesses can thus gain a significant slice of the market.

Penetration pricing, because of its high cost, is often used by large firms operating in mass markets, such as those selling biscuits, sweets, washing powder and canned drinks. It is also a policy used by new businesses or established businesses in other areas to break into a new market. It is not a policy that is suitable for products with short life cycles. There is usually not enough time to recover the cost of lost revenue from the initially low price. One exception to this is new CD singles. They are sometimes launched at a lower price in the first few weeks of release before being raised to their full price.

Market skimming Market skimming involves charging a high price for a new product for a limited period. The aim is to gain as much profit as possible for a new product while it remains unique in the market. It usually means selling a product to the

Question 2.

Patel and Co has been manufacturing aluminium ladders since the business was set up in 2000. Its sales up to now have been based upon two products, a 10 metre and a 15 metre folding ladder. The business has adopted a cost plus method of pricing for each ladder, as illustrated in Table 2.

Table 2

10 metre ladder	Average cos per unit £92	20% mark-up to cover profit £18.40	Selling price to trade £110.40
15 metre ladder	Average cost per unit £125	20% mark-up to cover profit £25.00	Selling price to trade £150.00

Because of the success of these two products and pressure from competition, the company has developed a new product, a ladder which would allow people to gain constant access to their lofts, but which will be permanently attached to the loft entrance. With a third product, the company's accountant felt that a contribution pricing approach should now be used to price each of their products. He set out some initial calculations of their likely prices, as in Table 3.

Table 3

	Direct costs per unit	Contribution to indirect cost and profit	Price
10 metre ladder	£80	£35	£115
15 metre ladder	£105	£40	£145
Loft ladder	£185	£5	£190

The pricing for the loft ladder was set at a level which was in line with the price of competitors, which was £190.00.

(a) Identify the benefits to the company of using a contribution pricing approach compared to a cost plus approach for their ladders.

(b) Is the loft ladder a viable product for the company to produce given the figures produced by the accountant? Explain your answer.

most profitable segment of the market before it is sold to a wider market at a lower price.

There are two reasons why businesses adopt market skimming. They may try to maximise revenue before competitors come into the market with a similar product. Often new techniques or designs mean that entirely new products, or new versions of a product can be offered. Examples include new fashions in clothes, new childrens' toys and new inventions. When first launched, a basic digital watch could cost as much as £50 or £60. Now they often sell for as little as a few pounds. Market skimming can also be used to generate revenue in a short period of time so that further investment in the product can be made. Companies in the electronics and pharmaceutical industries often use skimming for this reason.

Customer value pricing This involves charging the price that consumers are prepared to pay. Products which have prestige names attached to them, such as Rolex, may be able to command a higher price because of the status of these names. Products for one-off events, such as music festivals or sports finals, may be given a high price because they are unique.

Loss leaders LOSS LEADERS are products priced at very low levels in order to attract customers. The price of a loss leader is set lower than the average total cost of producing the product. The company selling the product makes a 'loss' on each product sold. Businesses use this pricing technique because they expect the losses made on the loss leader to be more than compensated for by extra profits on other products. It is often used by larger supermarkets which sell everyday products such as baked-beans, bananas and corn flakes for very low prices. They aim to attract more customers into their stores, drawn in by the low prices. The 'captive' customers will then buy more highly priced and profitable items.

Psychological pricing Many businesses seek to take account of the psychological effect of their prices upon consumers. This is known as psychological pricing. A common example is the use of prices just a little lower than a round figure, such as £199.99 rather than £200, or £29.99 rather than £30. Businesses using these slightly lower prices believe that they will influence the consumers' decision as to whether or not to purchase. Such slightly lower prices also suggest that consumers will be looking for value for money. For this reason, the producers of high status products such as prestige cars or designer clothing tend to avoid such prices. Instead, they often choose prices which psychologically match their consumers expectations of higher quality. So, for example, a price of £100 may be charged for a designer shirt rather than £99.99.

Price discrimination Price discrimination occurs when a firm offers the same product at different prices when consumers can be kept separate. An example is BT's policy of charging different prices to business and residential users at different times of the day and the weekend. This allows BT to take into account the differences in cost which exists at peak and off peak times. So, for example, calls may be charged at a higher rate on Monday to Friday, 8am-6pm, than at weekends.

This price discrimination is **time based**. The price you pay for a phone call is based upon the time of day or the day of the week when you use the service. Other businesses which use this policy are rail companies (cheaper off peak travel), and holiday firms which charge higher prices for their product during school holidays.

Price discrimination can also be **market based**. This involves offering different market segments the same product at different prices. An example of this is students being given discounts on coach and bus travel.

Discounts and sales These tend to support the pricing strategies used by businesses. They often mean a reduction in the standard price for particular groups of consumers. A very common form of discount is the seasonal 'sales' of retailers. The aim is to encourage purchasers at times when sales might otherwise be low and to clear out of date and out of fashion stock. Discounts may also be given to those customers who buy in bulk or in large quantities.

Competition based pricing

With COMPETITION BASED PRICING it is the prices charged by competitors which are the major influence on a producer's price. It is used mostly by businesses which face fierce and direct competition. As a rule, the more competitive the market and the more homogeneous the products competing in that market, the greater the pressure for competition based pricing. Markets similar to the model of oligopoly will often use this form of pricing. For example, soap powder producers tend to be influenced by the price of competitors' products.

Going rate pricing This occurs in markets where businesses are reluctant to set off a price war by lowering their prices and are concerned about a fall off in revenue if prices are raised. They examine competitors' prices and choose a price broadly in line with them. It also occurs when one dominant business establishes a position of **price leadership** within a market. Other firms will follow suit when the price leader changes its prices. This type of policy can be seen when a petrol company changes the price of a gallon of petrol or when banks and building societies change interest rates.

Companies which operate in markets where going rate pricing occurs will often be frustrated by their inability to control their prices more closely. A strategy often used in such circumstances is to establish a strong **brand** identity for your product and to differentiate it from others on the market. This would be through unique design features or quality of service. An oil company's decision to upgrade all of its service stations is an example of an attempt to achieve this. A strong brand identity and unique product features allow firms much greater scope for choosing their own price levels.

Destroyer pricing The aim of destroyer pricing is to eliminate opposition. It involves cutting prices, sometimes greatly, for a period of time long enough for your rivals to go out of business. It could be argued that the offering of low price airline tickets by Ryanair and EasyJet in the 1990s was designed to drive out competition from the national European airline carriers and force some of them out of business. Some, like BA and KLM, responded by setting up their own low-price carriers and cutting prices. Others, like Sabena and SwissAir, did go out of business.

Closed bid pricing This method of pricing occurs when firms have to TENDER a bid for work which they are going to carry out. This is common practice for firms dealing with the government or local authorities. For example, if a new road is to be built firms will be invited to put in a bid to win a contract for the work. Firms will clearly need to pay very close attention to the price at which they expect their competitors to bid. Sometimes, when a number of firms bid for a contract, those with the highest prices are likely to be rejected. Another example of this type of pricing are the bids that the government organises for the National Lottery. In 2004 Camelot had won both the rounds of bidding against rival companies, including Richard Branson's Virgin group.

KNOWLEDGE

1. State 5 pricing strategies a business might use.
2. Identify 4 different pricing tactics that a business might use.
3. What are the main factors affecting a firm's pricing decisions?
4. Explain the difference between cost plus pricing and contribution pricing.
5. State one advantage and one disadvantage of cost plus and contribution pricing for a firm.
6. What is meant by absorption cost pricing?
7. Why might a firm use penetration pricing?
8. What is market skimming?
9. What types of firm might use market skimming as a pricing strategy?
10. Why might a business sell a product as a loss leader?
11. What is meant by psychological pricing?
12. What is meant by price discrimination?
13. Under what circumstances might a firm use competition based pricing?
14. Explain the terms:
    (a) going rate pricing;
    (b) destroyer pricing;
    (c) closed bid pricing.
15. Give 2 examples of tendering.

Pricing tactics

Once a business has decided upon its overall pricing strategy, it can also use price as a tactical promotional tool. This will usually involve temporary, short-term changes in prices to attract customers to specific products for a period. These PRICING TACTICS may include the following.

- Special promotional offers, such as buy one, get one free (BOGOF). Bookshops offer three books for the price of two and supermarkets offer two packets of meat for the price of one for example.
- Deliberately setting the price of a product at a low level in order to attract customers into a store to buy the product and hopefully others as well. These products are often referred to as loss leaders.
- Offering discounts on normal prices. This might be for a period of time, such as just after Christmas, for regular customers, such as offers on loyalty cards, for buying larger quantities, such as schools getting discounts for stationery, or for cost-effective purchasing, such as buying over the Internet.
- Making introductory offers. This is where the price a customer pays for the first purchase is lower than subsequent purchases. Examples include lower prices for monthly Broadband payments for the first few months or a lower price for the first issue of a magazine.

KEYTERMS

Competition based pricing - methods of pricing based upon the prices charged by competitors.
Cost based pricing - methods of pricing products which are based upon costs.
Loss leaders - products with prices set deliberately below average total cost to attract customers who will then buy other, more profitable, products.
Market orientated pricing - methods of pricing based upon the pricing conditions in the market at which a product is aimed.
Mark-up - that part of a price which seeks to provide a business with profit as opposed to covering its costs. It is used in cost plus pricing.
Pricing strategies - the pricing policies or methods of pricing adopted by businesses.
Tender - a bid to secure a contract for work.
Pricing tactics - ways of using price as a promotional tool usually over a short period of time.

Case Study: Finding a deal that will float our boat

With the summer travel season approaching, another ferry service is being introduced across the English Channel, raising the prospect of a price war on the more expensive western routes into France. LD Lines, which will run from Newhaven to Le Havre from May, is offering summer return prices from £142 for a family plus car. This route into Normandy costs less than a third of peak season prices into the Brittany ports further west along the coast.

It might only be a narrow strip of water, but there are huge variations in the cost of taking a car across - with some routes seven times more expensive for a crossing on the same day. Long criticised for their complex charging structures, ferries have become much more like airlines - with websites showing a much more transparent range of port-to-port prices. And after years in the doldrums, ferries have been making a modest revival, boosted by the soaring number of French holiday homes bought by Britons and by a disenchantment with the overcrowding and stress of airports in summer. While ferries might be a more relaxing way to travel, they can also be extremely expensive.

The great divide in this cross-channel market is between the west and the east. On the 'eastern' route, there are the short ferry crossings from Dover and the tunnel crossing at Folkestone into north-eastern France and the Pas de Calais. And on the 'western Channel' routes there are longer crossings to St Malo and Cherbourg.

These are two different holiday markets - one about high-volume, price-sensitive shuttling of passengers; the other a more leisurely, more expensive trip, with restaurants and cinemas.

On the highly competitive Dover route, passenger numbers are rising. Last year, 13.7 million people travelled through the port to Calais, Boulogne and Dunkirk. And the arrival of operators such as Speedferries and Norfolk Line has brought the budget airline pricing model, with one-way crossings for a car plus five passengers from £15.

A car with two adults and two children could travel off peak on the P&O Dover-Calais ferry route for £85 return. And depending on how flexible you could be about crossing times, there are still Eurotunnel summer fares for £98.

But on the western Channel routes it's been a different story, with Brittany Ferries dominating after competitors such as P&O pulled out. And the strategy has been to go upmarket rather than compete with the budget airlines. In terms of prices, the off-peak fare for a return trip from Portsmouth to St Malo, for two adults and two children, can be £300. And for some overnight sailings, accommodation is an additional, compulsory part of the booking. If you were travelling from the west country on the Plymouth to Roscoff route, a summer return could cost £689, if a cabin was included.

Spokesperson Steve Tuckwell says that rather than only focusing on price, passengers are ready to pay a premium for 'floating hotel' services. And although the budget airlines have 'eaten into our business' for short break trips, he says for longer summer holidays people prefer to take their cars on the ferry.

Source: adapted from *The Guardian*, 17.3.2007.

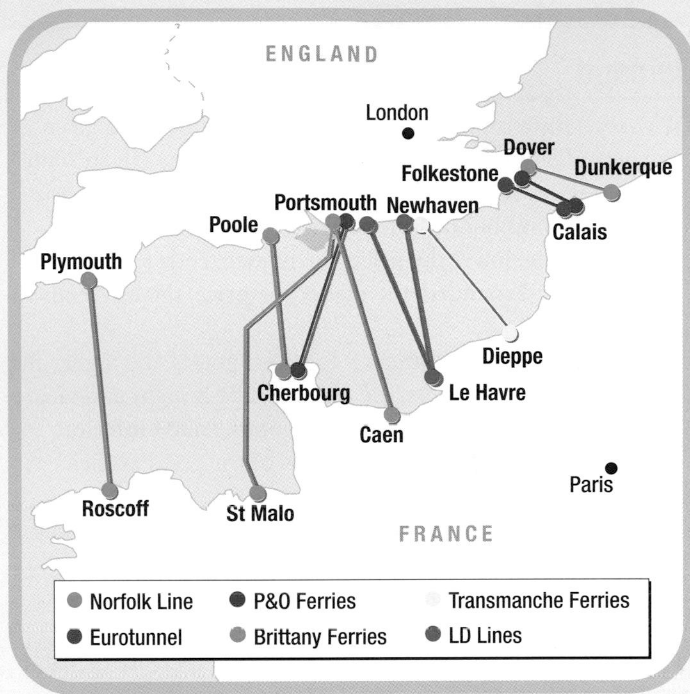

Source adapted from www.drive-alive.co.uk

(a) Using examples from the article, explain what is meant by:
   (i) price discrimination. (3 marks)
   (ii) cost-plus pricing. (3 marks)

(b) Explain the pricing strategy used by Brittany Ferries on its 'western' routes. (6 marks)

(c) Explain, using examples, why prices are higher on the 'western routes' than on the 'eastern' routes across the channel. (8 marks)

(d) Discuss how budget airlines might respond to the strategies used by their ferry competitors. (10 marks)

20 Price - the influence of demand

Demand

DEMAND for a product is the quantity bought over a given time period. For example, demand for cars in the UK in 2006 was 2.4 million vehicles. The quantity bought of a product is affected by a number of factors. These include:

- price - the lower the price, the higher tends to be the quantity demanded; the higher the price, the less tends to be bought;
- the income of customers - for most goods, the higher the income of customers, the more will be bought and vice versa. However, there are some goods, called **inferior goods**, where customers buy less of the good as their incomes rise;
- the price of other goods - for example, if one chocolate bar goes up in price by 10 per cent, demand for other chocolate bars is likely to increase if their price remains constant;
- advertising - successful advertising can increase demand for a product;
- seasonal factors - many goods, from ice creams and beer to toys and foreign holidays are affected by the time of year and the weather. For example, hot summer weather increases demand for ice creams and beer. The run up to Christmas is the peak selling time for toys and clothing.

Price and demand

Businesses operate in markets where they produce and sell, or **supply**, products that consumers want and are able to buy, or **demand**. The interaction of supply and demand can determine the price of a product. This unit considers the factors affecting the demand for an individual business's products and the way in which these factors can influence the price that the business might charge.

The demand curve of a business

Businesses need to understand how the demand for a product can affect the price that they can charge for it. This relationship can be shown by a demand schedule and a demand curve. For most products the relationship between demand and price is inverse. As the price goes up, the quantity demanded goes down. As the price goes down, the quantity demanded goes up. So, for product A shown in Figure 1, a rise in price from OP to OP_1 (£20 to £40) will lead to a fall in the quantity demanded from OQ to OQ_1 (£5,000 to £3,000).

Some products have a demand curve which looks different to that shown in Figure 1. 'Prestige' perfumes are designed to appeal to wealthy consumers. A low price might put off consumers of such a product, given the association made between a higher price and high quality. This means that the quantity demanded over lower price ranges may increase as price rises for such a product. This would create an entirely different demand curve. Figure 2 shows the demand curve for such a product. An increase in price from OP to OP_1 causes the quantity demanded for this perfume to increase from OQ to OQ_2. However, an increase in price from OP_1 to OP_2 causes the quantity demanded to fall from OQ_2 to OQ_1. In this part of the curve a more normal relationship between demand and price exists. An increase in price leads to a fall in the quantity demanded. Speculative goods are also said to have upward sloping demand curves. As prices rise people buy more of them, hoping to sell them for a profit at a later date.

Other factors influencing the demand for a business's products

Other than price there is a range of factors affecting the demand for an individual business's products. A change in any of these factors can cause a shift in the whole demand curve (as opposed to a change in price which causes a movement along the

Table 1: The demand schedule for Product A

Price (£)	Quantity demanded
10	6,000
20	5,000
30	4,000
40	3,000
50	2,000

Figure 1: The demand curve for Product A

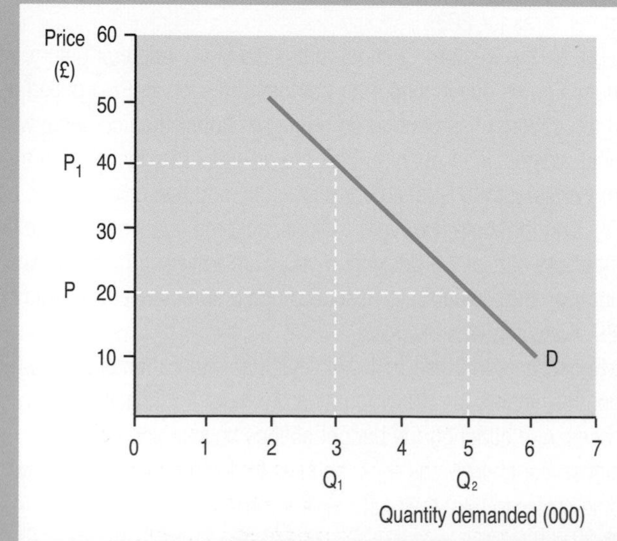

Figure 2: The demand curve for a prestige perfume

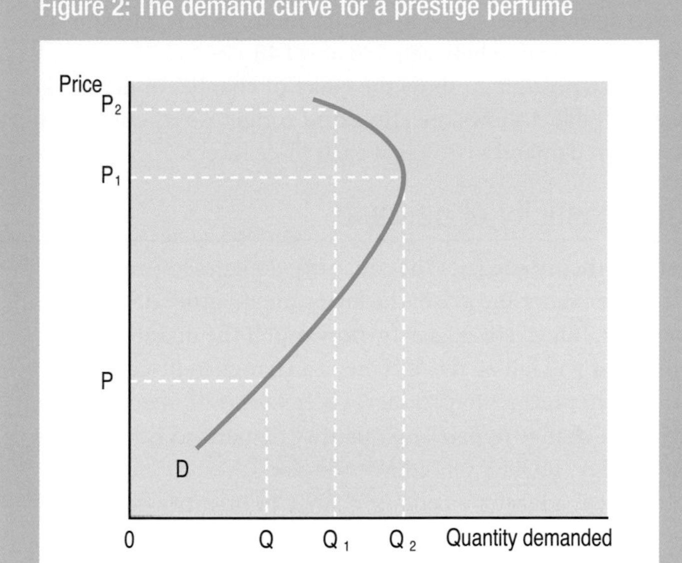

Figure 3: An increase and a decrease in demand

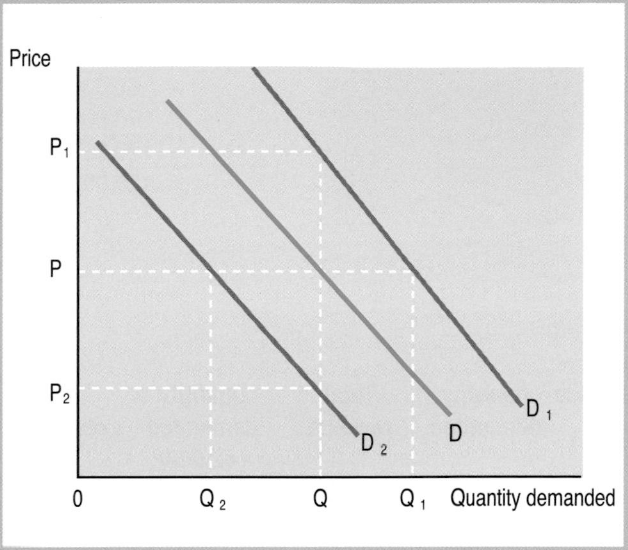

demand curve). Figure 3 shows an increase in the demand for a product by the demand curve moving outwards from D to D_1. A decrease in the demand for the product is shown by the demand curve shifting inwards, from D to D_2. What factors might lead to a change in demand and how will this affect a particular business?

- The consumers at which the product is aimed may experience an increase in income. The business may be able to sell more of the product at a given price ($OQ - OQ_1$) or charge a higher price ($OP - OP_1$). If incomes fall, the demand curve shifts inwards and the quantity demanded may fall ($OQ - OQ_2$) or the price may fall ($OP - OP_2$). An example may be increased demand for Bosch dishwashers as incomes increase.
- The price of a rival's goods may change. If a rival's price goes up, customers may be more willing to buy more of this product. If a rival's prices fall customers may reduce demand for this product. An example may be a fall in demand for one newspaper as another cuts its price.
- The price of a complementary product may fall. For example, if the price of DVD players falls, people may buy more of these and so the demand for DVDs themselves could increase. A rise in the price of a complementary product may lead to a fall in demand for the related product.
- Changes in tastes and fashion. There has been a change in the type of food products that have become popular in recent years. Examples include organic foods bought from supermarkets, flavoured and specialist coffees from shops such as Starbucks, and cholesterol reducing spreads such as Flora Proactive and Benecol.
- Marketing campaigns. Asda, for example, has pursued a low pricing marketing campaign and is often found to have the lowest supermarket prices in studies. It has supported this with the 'Asda price' adverts on television showing people saving money.
- Changes in population. A large shopping mall such as the Trafford Centre in Manchester is likely to find an increase in demand if offices and housing are drawn close to its location.
- Government legislation and regulation can affect demand. Local pubs and breweries, for example, may find a fall in demand as a result of a reduction in the legal alcohol limit for drinking and driving.

How businesses use demand curves

Demand curves are useful tools to businesses in terms of analysing and planning their marketing activities. In particular they enable businesses to:

- calculate revenue to be earned for any given price change;
- predict the likely reaction of consumers to price changes;
- predict the likely impact upon revenue of price changes.

Calculating revenue

One of the reasons why businesses are interested in their demand curve is because it enables them to calculate revenue that may be earned for a particular price that is charged. Revenue can be calculated using using a simple formula:

Price x quantity demanded = total revenue

Table 2 reproduces Table 1 showing the revenue that a business will earn for product A at different prices, given its demand schedule.

So, for example, the revenue of the business at a price of £30 would be £30 x 4,000 = £120,000. If the price were to change to £20 the revenue would be £20 x 5,000 = £100,000. Thus we can

Table 2: The demand schedule for Product A

Price (£)	Quantity demanded (Q)	Total revenue (P x Q)
10	6,000	60,000
20	5,000	100,000
30	4,000	120,000
40	3,000	120,000
50	2,000	100,000

Table 3: The demand schedule for Product A

Price (£)	Quantity demanded (Q)	Total revenue (P x Q)	Quantity demanded (+2,000) (Q)	Total revenue (P x Q)
10	6,000	60,000	8,000	80,000
20	5,000	100,000	7,000	140,000
30	4,000	120,000	6,000	180,000
40	3,000	120,000	5,000	200,000
50	2,000	100,000	4,000	200,000

see that a change in price from £30 to £20 has led to a fall in revenue from £120,000 to £100,000, a fall of £20,000.

This process can help a business to identify the point on the demand curve and the price at which revenue is maximised. This can be seen from Table 2. At prices below £30 the business actually increases the revenue by raising its price. At prices above £40 revenue falls as prices are increased. The business earns most revenue between £30 and £40.

It is also possible to show the effect of changes in demand on revenue. Table 3 shows the effect on Product A's revenue of an increase in demand of 2,000 at each price level.

Question 1.

A stationery shop selling fibre tipped pens has estimated the following demand schedule for its products.

Table 4: Demand for fibre tipped pens

Price (£)	Quantity demanded
2	800
3	600
4	500
5	400
6	350
7	300
8	260
9	225
10	200

(a) Calculate the change in total revenue for fibre tipped pens of:
(i) an increase in price from £2 to £3;
(ii) an increase in price from £7 to £10;
(iii) a decrease in price from £5 to £3.

(b) Explain why the business might be reluctant to raise prices above £7 per pen.

Price elasticity of demand

Demand theory suggests that quantity demanded varies with price. The higher the price, the lower the quantity demand and vice versa. But it doesn't say by **how much** the quantity demanded will fall or rise if there is a change in price. This varies from product to product. The relationship between the effect of a change in price on quantity demanded is known as PRICE ELASTICITY OF DEMAND.

If there is a **large** percentage change in quantity demanded when price changes by a small percentage, there is said to be ELASTIC DEMAND. The word 'elastic' is used to give an idea that there would be a large response. Think of an elastic band. When you pull it, can you easily double its length? Then it is 'elastic'. But if it is thick, it may be difficult to change its length. It is 'inelastic'. This is also the case with price elasticity. If a large percentage change in price brings about only a **small** percentage change in quantity demanded, there is said to be INELASTIC DEMAND.

Take the example of a Mars Bar made by Mars Corporation. If it puts up the price by 10 per cent, and there is a fall in quantity demanded of 30 per cent, then the demand for Mars Bars is elastic. The percentage change in quantity demanded of Mars Bars is much bigger than the percentage change in price which caused it. But if quantity demanded fell only 5 per cent when prices went up by 10 per cent, then there would be inelastic demand. The percentage change in quantity demanded is smaller than the percentage change in price.

It is important to realise that price elasticity compares **percentage** changes in quantity and price. Percentages allow the relative changes to be measured and compared.

The formula for price elasticity of demand

The exact value of price elasticity of demand can be calculated by using the formula:

$$\text{Price elasticity of demand} = \frac{\text{\% change in quantity demanded}}{\text{\% change in price}}$$

For example, say that the price of Mars Bars increases by 10 per cent.

- If the quantity demanded falls by 20 per cent as a result of the 10 per cent price rise, then price elasticity of demand is:

$$\frac{\text{-20 per cent}}{\text{+10 per cent}} = -2$$

- If the quantity demanded rises by 5 per cent as a result of the 10 per cent price fall, then price elasticity of demand is:

$$\frac{+5 \text{ per cent}}{-10 \text{ per cent}} = -0.5$$

Price elasticity of demand is always negative. This is because a rise (+) in price is always followed by a fall (-) in quantity demanded and vice versa. A plus divided into a minus is a minus. Because it is always minus, the sign is normally left out when talking about price elasticity of demand.

Elastic and inelastic demand

It is possible to give a more precise definition of elastic and inelastic demand using the formula for price elasticity.

Price elastic demand Demand is **price elastic** when it is **greater than 1**. This means that the percentage change in quantity demanded (on the top of the formula) is greater than the percentage change in price (on the bottom of the formula). A 12 per cent rise in quantity demanded resulting from a 10 per cent fall in price would give a price elasticity of +12 per cent ÷ -10 per cent or -1.2. This would be an example of elastic demand.

Price inelastic demand Demand is **price inelastic** when it is **less than 1**. This means that the percentage change in quantity demanded (on the top of the formula) is less than the percentage change in price (on the bottom of the formula). An 8 per cent fall in quantity demanded resulting from a 10 per cent rise in price would give a price elasticity of -8 per cent ÷ +10 per cent or -0.8. This would be an example of inelastic demand.

Estimating price elasticity

There is no easy way to find out the exact price elasticity of demand for a particular product. The business environment is constantly changing. So when the price of a product changes, it is likely that other factors will change too. For example, competing businesses may all change their prices at roughly the same time.

One way of estimating the price elasticity of demand is to assume that all these other factors remain the same. Then a business could consider the impact of its price changes on demand in recent years. If it has changed price four times in four years, it could estimate the impact this has had on quantity demanded each time and calculate a price elasticity figure for each price change. These four figures might be averaged to provide an approximate price elasticity.

Alternatively, a business could use market research. It could ask customers how much they would buy of a product at different prices. Price elasticity of demand for the sample could then be calculated. A problem is that what respondents actually do can be different from what they say they will do in a survey.

A business could consider the behaviour of its customers. For example, the price elasticity of demand for the gas that British Gas sells to households might be inelastic. A 10 per cent rise in price is likely to have little effect on quantity demanded. This is because households tend not to turn off their central heating when the price of gas rises. Most customers, also, won't switch to another gas company.

In contrast, a small clothing manufacturer might face elastic demand. All its work could come from larger companies that only want limited quantities of dresses or trousers. There are many UK businesses doing this sort of work and others in countries like India or China. So if it quotes a slightly higher price for a contract it is unlikely to get the order. In this industry, businesses find it difficult to raise their prices without losing many customers.

Price elasticity and sales revenue

Price elasticity of demand is important when developing a **pricing strategy**. This is because the price of a product affects **sales revenue**. Sales revenue is the amount a business receives from the sale of its products. It is calculated by multiplying the price of the product by the quantity sold. For example, a business selling 1 million products at £10 each would have sales revenue of £10 million (£1 million x £10).

Sales revenue is affected by the price at which a product is sold and price elasticity of demand. Assume that the product sold at £10 has a price elasticity of 2.

- This means that a 10 per cent increase in price would lead to a fall in quantity demanded (and therefore sales) of 20 per cent. Sales revenue would then fall from £10 million (1 million x £10) to £8.8 million (800 000 x £11).
- If, on the other hand, price was lowered by 10 per cent, quantity demanded (and therefore sales) would rise by 20 per cent. Sales revenue would then rise from £10 million (1 million x £10) to £10.8 million (1.2 million x £9).

This is an example of a more general rule. If demand is price elastic, then putting up price will lead to a fall in sales revenue. The increase in price will be more than offset by a decrease in sales. Conversely, lowering price when demand is price elastic will lead to a rise in sales revenue. The fall in price will be more than offset by an increase in sales.

Equally, the opposite relationship applies if price is inelastic. A rise in price will lead to a rise in sales revenue whilst a fall in price will lead to a fall in sales revenue. For example, if price elasticity of demand is 0.7, then a 10 per cent rise in price leads to a 7 per cent fall in sales. This leads to an approximate 3 per cent rise in sales revenue. This relationship between price elasticity and sales revenue is shown in Table 5.

Changing the price can therefore affect sales revenue. But the exact effect, and whether it leads to an increase or decrease,

Table 5: Effect on sales revenue of a change in price

	Elastic demand	Inelastic demand
Price increase	Revenue down	Revenue up
Price decrease	Revenue up	Revenue down

depends on the price elasticity of demand.

Price elasticity and profit

Price elasticity also has an effect on **profit**. Profit is calculated as sales revenue minus costs. Costs are likely to change with sales. The more that is produced, the higher the costs.

If demand is price inelastic, a rise in price will lead to lower sales but increased sales revenue as explained earlier. But the lower sales will mean lower costs. So profits will increase, not just from higher sales revenue but also from lower costs.

If demand is price elastic, an increase in sales revenue can be achieved by lowering price and raising sales. But higher sales also mean higher costs. In this situation, higher profits will only occur if the increase in sales revenue is greater than the increase in costs.

Factors affecting price elasticity of demand

The value of price elasticity of demand for a product is mainly determined by the ease with which customers can switch to other similar SUBSTITUTE PRODUCTS. A number of factors is likely to determine this.

Time Price elasticity of demand tends to fall the longer the time period. This is mainly because consumers and businesses are more likely to turn to substitutes in the long term. For example, fuel oil is highly price inelastic in the short term. If the price of petrol goes up 20 per cent in a week, the fall in quantity demanded is likely to be only a few per cent. This is because car owners have to use their cars to get to work or to go shopping. But over a ten year period, car owners will tend to buy more fuel-efficient cars. Businesses with boilers using fuel oil may replace these with gas boilers. Homeowners with oil-fired central heating systems might install more insulation in their houses to cut running costs or change to gas boilers. As a result, demand for oil in the long run is likely to be price elastic.

Competition for the same product Some businesses face highly price elastic demand for their products. This is because they are in very competitive markets, where their product is either identical (i.e. are perfect substitutes) or little different from those produced by other businesses. Farmers, for example, when selling wheat or potatoes are in this position. If they push their prices above the market price, they won't be able to sell their crop. Customers will simply buy elsewhere at the lower market price.

Branding Some products are **branded**. The stronger the branding, the less substitutes are acceptable to customers. For example, many buyers of Kellogg's corn flakes do not see own label brands, such as Tesco or Asda cornflakes, as good substitutes for Kelloggs. They will often pay 50 per cent more to buy Kelloggs rather than another brand. Successful branding therefore reduces the price elasticity of demand for the product.

Product types vs the product of an individual business Most products are made and sold by a number of different businesses. Petrol, for example, is processed and sold by companies such as Shell, Esso and Total. The major supermarkets also sell petrol which they have bought from independent refiners. The demand for petrol is price inelastic in the short term. But the demand for Shell petrol or Esso petrol is price elastic. This is because petrol has no real substitutes in the short term. But Esso petrol is a very good substitute for Shell petrol. In general, a product category like petrol, carpets or haircuts has a much lower price elasticity of demand than products within that category made by individual businesses.

However strong the branding and however little the competition that an individual product faces, it is still likely that a business will sell at a price where demand is price elastic. To understand why, consider a product which has inelastic demand. As explained above, raising the price of the product would increase sales revenue. It would also reduce sales and costs of production would fall. So profits would rise. A profit maximising firm should therefore continue raising price until demand is price elastic.

If demand is price elastic, raising price leads to a fall in sales revenue, but also a fall in costs because less is sold. At the profit maximising point, any further increase in price would see the fall in sales revenue being greater than the fall in costs.

This would suggest that even strongly branded goods, such as Coca-Cola or McDonald's meals, have a price elasticity of demand greater than one at the price at which they are sold. It also suggests that luxury brands, such as Chanel or Gucci, also have elastic demand at their current price.

Problems of measuring price elasticity of demand

There may be problems for small businesses in calculating the price elasticity of demand for their products.

Collecting data A business wanting to know about the price elasticity of its products would need to collect data on demand changes in relation to price for its own products to know the price elasticity of demand for these products. This would mean that they would need to experiment with price changes and to monitor consumer reaction. For many small businesses,

Question 2.

Kaldor Ltd manufactures reproduction juke boxes which play CDs. Jukeboxes that play old 45 records can cost around £1,000 or a great deal more. Large jukeboxes in pubs can cost thousands of pounds as well. But Kaldor had seen other 'reproduction' jukeboxes that did not cost as much and were far smaller. It decided to manufacture smaller jukeboxes that stand on a table. They sold for £200 and hold three CDs at a time. The jukeboxes have been selling well and so the business raised the price to £240. As a result sales fell from 800 to 600 per month. Kaldor is now questioning the decision to raise the price.

(a) Discuss whether or not the decision to raise the price was a good choice by the business.

especially those with a very small number of customers this would be impractical. The dangers of experimenting in this way could lead to a loss of business that would be difficult to recover. Small businesses also often do not have the time or resources to research such matters.

Predicting human behaviour Human behaviour is notoriously difficult to predict and the way that people respond on one day of the week, for example, may be different to how they will respond on others. In addition, consumers do not always act as they say they will. For this reason small businesses attempting to research their price elasticity of demand by observing and talking to their customers may not always find it easy to collect reliable data.

Interpreting data When seeking to research their price elasticity of demand it is not always easy for small business to make sense of the data they collect. Take, for example, a small business selling ice cream from one retail outlet. Were this business to trial a new higher price for its ice creams on one particular day it might find that sales actually rose. They might conclude from this that their ice cream is relatively price inelastic. However, on this same day there could have been because several large coachloads of pensioners swelling the total number of potential consumers and especially high temperatures also inflating demand. In this case it would be difficult for the business to isolate the effect of the price change.

For these reasons many small business estimate their price elasticity of demand rather than calculate it based upon actual research. They will do so based upon their observations of how their customers behave, information from similar businesses and actual sales levels.

Income elasticity of demand

INCOME ELASTICITY OF DEMAND is a measure of the sensitivity of demand to changes in income. It can be calculated using the formula:

$$\frac{\text{Percentage change in quantity demanded}}{\text{Percentage change in income}}$$

Businesses will want to know the income elasticity of demand for their products. This will help them to judge the effect of a change in their consumers' income on the demand for their products.

- If a rise in income leads to a relatively greater rise in quantity demanded then income elasticity of demand is positive and greater than one.
- If a rise in income leads to a relatively smaller rise in quantity demanded then income elasticity is positive but less than one.
- If a rise in income leads to no change in quantity demanded then income elasticity of demand is zero.
- If a rise in income leads to a fall in quantity demanded then income elasticity of demand is negative.

Advertising elasticity of demand

ADVERTISING ELASTICITY OF DEMAND is a measure of the responsiveness of demand to changes in advertising expenditure. It is measured by the following formula:

$$\frac{\text{Percentage change in quantity demanded}}{\text{Percentage change in advertising expenditure}}$$

Businesses need to be able to measure the effectiveness of their advertising campaigns. One way of doing this is to consider the impact on consumer demand of spending on advertising. This can provide businesses with valuable data which can enable them to judge how far consumers are influenced by advertising campaigns. It also allows businesses to evaluate the relative success of advertising campaigns. If the percentage increase in quantity demanded is a great deal larger than the percentage increase in advertising spending, then advertising elasticity of demand is strong and positive. This may tell a business that advertising is effective in influencing consumers.

Cross elasticity of demand

The CROSS ELASTICITY OF DEMAND shows the response of quantity demanded of one good to a change in the price of another. It allows a business to gauge how demand for its products will react if the price of either rival's products or complementary goods change. It can be calculated using the formula:

$$\frac{\text{Percentage change in quantity demanded of good X}}{\text{Percentage change in price of good Y}}$$

- Goods which are substitutes and compete with each other have a positive cross elasticity. An increase in the price of one newspaper (good Y) should lead to a fall in demand for this product and an increase in demand for another newspaper (good X). Both changes are positive. A fall in the price of good Y will lead to a fall in the demand for good X. Two negatives cancel out to make a positive.
- Goods which are complements to each other have a negative cross elasticity. An increase in the price of an electrical product (good Y) should lead to a fall in demand for this product and a fall in demand for batteries (good X). One change is positive, the other is negative.

Limitations of demand curves

It is often very difficult for an individual business to develop its own demand curve. This is because many businesses do not have sufficient information to construct their individual demand curves. They do not have the market research data to enable

Question 3.

Bill Finch is a London taxicab driver. Towards the end of 1999, all the talk amongst taxicab drivers was about the new Millennium - whether they were going to drive or be out partying on New Year's Eve. In November 1999, the government, which sets London taxicab fares, announced that London taxis would be able to charge double rate for journeys taken between 8 pm on December 31 and 6 am on January 1st. Those taking journeys long enough to cost more than an ordinary fare of £25 would have to pay a flat rate £25 supplement. This compared to the usual New Year supplement of £3 per journey.

Bill decided he would drive on the Millennium eve, expecting that demand would be highly price inelastic. But he was disappointed with his takings. Many party goers had decided to stay at home because restaurants, pubs and clubs as well as taxis were charging double or more on the night. There was a general feeling amongst the public that they were going to be ripped off if they went out. Where journeys were necessary, many took a private car and agreed in advance which of the party goers would be the non-drinking driver. Bill Finch found that he carried 30 per cent fewer passengers than he typically did on a normal Saturday night in the winter months. None of his journeys on the Millennium eve exceeded the £25 limit.

(a) Explain what is meant in the passage by 'demand would be highly price inelastic'.

(b) Explain (i) why it was expected that demand for taxi cab rides would rise on Millennium eve;
(ii) how this might have affected the ability of travellers to get a taxi cab ride on that night if fares had NOT risen from their normal levels.

(c) Using the concepts of price elasticity of demand, revenue and profit, discuss whether Bill made the right decision to drive on Millennium eve.

them to assess the likely demand for their products over a given range of prices. Often this is because of the high cost of collecting such market information. Such businesses tend to develop a PERCEIVED DEMAND curve. This is a demand curve based upon the 'feel' which managers and owners have for their market. It will involve rough estimations of the likely impact upon demand of upwards or downwards changes in prices.

Some larger businesses with access to detailed market information are in a much better position to develop demand curves which can assist them in making more informed decisions about their prices. However, even for such businesses the demand curve may be of limited value. This is because the demand curve can only provide information about the likely response of consumers to a change in the price of a particular product at a given point in time. In fast changing markets such information may quickly go out of date and will be of limited value unless it is regularly updated.

Normal and inferior goods

Most products have a positive income elasticity. When income rises, so too does demand for the product. These products are called NORMAL GOODS.

However, for some products, a rise in income leads to a fall in their demand. Their income elasticity of demand is negative (because in the formula there is a plus sign on the top and a minus sign on the bottom or vice versa). These products are called INFERIOR GOODS. Examples of inferior goods might include:

- bread - as incomes rise, consumers eat less bread and more expensive foods;
- bus transport - as incomes rise, travellers tend to use trains or cars;
- sugar - increased income tends to be associated with a better diet and a greater awareness of the problems of having too much sugar.

Most products are normal goods. However, some products have a higher income elasticity than others. For example, over the past 20 years, with rising incomes, the demand for services has increased faster than the demand for goods. Services, such as holidays and meals out, have expanded particularly fast.

KEY TERMS

Advertising elasticity of demand – the responsiveness of demand to a change in advertising expenditure.

Cross elasticity of demand – the responsiveness of the demand of one product to a change in the price of another.

Demand – the quantity of a product bought over a given time period.

Income elasticity of demand – the responsiveness of demand to a change in income.

Inferior goods – products which have a negative income elasticity. When incomes rise, the quantity demanded falls and vice versa.

Normal goods – products which have a positive income elasticity. When incomes rise, the quantity demanded rises and vice versa.

Perceived demand – the demand which businesses believe exists for their products in a particular market.

Price elasticity of demand – the responsiveness of quantity demanded to changes in price. It is measured as percentage change in quantity demanded ÷ percentage change in price.

Price elastic demand – when price elasticity is greater than 1, which means that the percentage change in quantity demanded is greater than the percentage change in price which caused it.

Price inelastic demand – when price elasticity is less than 1, which means that the percentage change in quantity demanded is less than the percentage change in price which caused it.

Substitute product – a product which has similar characteristics to another good. For example, gas is a substitute for oil as a fuel in heating systems. Shell petrol is a good substitute for BP Amoco petrol for use as a fuel in cars.

KNOWLEDGE

1. Explain, without using the formula, what is meant by 'price elasticity of demand'.
2. 'The demand for journeys taken on the London Underground is price inelastic.' Explain what this means.
3. (a) What is the formula for price elasticity of demand?
   (b) How does it differ from the formula for income elasticity of demand?
4. How can a business estimate the price elasticity of demand for one of its products?
5. Explain why a rise in price would lead to higher revenues if demand for the product were price inelastic.
6. Explain the link between price elasticity of demand and profit.
7. Explain why strongly branded goods such as Coca-Cola or Chanel perfumes are likely to be price elastic at the price at which they are currently sold.
8. Why might a business be interested in its advertising elasticity of demand?

Case Study: Bodyline

Bodyline is a small firm based in the West Midlands which manufactures womens' swimwear. Its products are distributed through four main types of outlet - mail-order catalogues, department stores, womens' clothing chains and independent retailers.

The business was set up in early 2005. The two women, Elaine and Penny, who started up the firm had originally been friends at University. One had studied for a degree in Art and Design, the other in Business Studies.

Their main product was to be a swimsuit, the Californian, which had been designed in a wide range of dazzling colours. Their marketing strategy had been to aim for the bottom end of the market, offering a cheap, but fashionable garment which would be within the reach of a wide number of consumers' pockets. Marketing research into the demand for the Californian showed that sales at different prices were likely to be as in Table 6.

Elaine and Penny found that they were able to sell all of their production at a price of £18. They sold Californians at this price for six months and made a fair profit. The market was fairly stable at this time and few sudden changes were expected in the near future. Penny felt that by reducing the price a little they would be able to capture more of the market. Elaine was not so sure and the two debated the decision over the next six months without taking any action.

By early 2007 a number of rival businesses developed similar product lines using bright colours, having seen the initial success of Bodyline in the market. As Elaine had commented, one of the worst things about the new products was that 'the Californian designs no longer stood out in the shops and are the same as other products now available'. In what had seemed like a short period of time to these two entrepreneurs, their niche in the market had all but disappeared.

After their initial success many of the new businesses had attempted to undercut Bodyline's prices. The effect on the demand curve for the Californian is shown in Table 7.

(a) What is the relationship between price and demand for Californians shown in Table 6? Use examples in your answer. (6 marks)

(b) Calculate the elasticity of demand for Californians for a reduction in price from:

(i) £18 to £16;

(ii) £16 to £14.

(6 marks)

(c) Explain whether demand for Californians is elastic or inelastic and how this would affect price and demand. (6 marks)

(d) Using Table 7, explain the idea of cross elasticity of demand for Californians. (10 marks)

(e) Assess whether you think Penny was right to suggest a reduction in price using your answer to (b) and total revenue calculations. (12 marks)

Table 6: Demand for Californians

Price	Quantity of Californians
£14	18,000
£16	14,000
£18	10,000
£20	6,000

Table 7: Effect of a change in competitors' prices on the demand for Californians

Price of other products	Quantity of Californians
£14	16,200
£12	12,600
£10	9,000
£8	5,400

21 Promotion

What is promotion?

PROMOTION is the attempt to draw attention to a product or business in order to gain new customers or to retain existing ones. There are many different forms of promotion. One way of distinguishing between these different forms is in terms of whether or not a business is promoting its products via independent media such as newspapers and TV. ABOVE-THE-LINE promotion is through independent media, such as television or newspapers. These allow a business to reach a wide audience easily. Most advertising is carried out 'above the line'. Some advertising, however, is carried out by methods over which a firm has direct control, such as direct mailing and branding. Such methods are known as BELOW-THE-LINE promotions.

The objectives of promotion

A business must be clear about exactly what it is trying to achieve through its promotion. The main aim of any promotion is to obtain and retain customers. However, there is a number of other objectives, some or all of which any successful campaign must fulfil.

- To make consumers aware or increase awareness of a product.
- To reach a target audience which might be geographically dispersed.
- To remind consumers about the product. This can encourage existing consumers to repurchase the product and may attract new consumers.
- To show a product is better than that of a competitor. This may encourage consumers to switch purchases from another product.
- To develop or improve the image of a business rather than a product. Much corporate advertising is carried out with this in mind, and is dealt with later in this unit.
- To reassure consumers after the product has been purchased. This builds up confidence in the product and may encourage more to be bought at a later date.
- To support an existing product. Such promotions may be used to remind consumers that a reliable and well thought of product is still available.

Businesses sometimes consider their promotion using **models**.

- AIDA is a method used to consider advertising. It suggests that effective advertising will raise Awareness (A) and encourage Interest (I), Desire (D) and Action (A), so that consumers buy the products.
- The DAGMAR (Defining Advertising Goals for Measured Advertising Results) model is also used to measure the effect of advertising. A business can measure how far the group that is targeted has progressed along the scale:

  Unawareness...Awareness...Comprehension...
  Conviction...Action
- A similar model by Lavidge and Steiner suggests six stages - awareness, knowledge, liking, preference, conviction and purchase.

Above-the-line promotion

Above-the-line promotion is ADVERTISING. Advertising is often placed into different categories.

- INFORMATIVE ADVERTISING is designed to increase consumer awareness of a product. Examples include the classified advertisements in local newspapers, new share offers, grants available to small firms and entries in the *Yellow Pages*. New products may be launched with informative advertising campaigns to make consumers aware of their presence. It is argued that this type of advertising helps consumers to make a rational choice as to what to buy.
- PERSUASIVE ADVERTISING tries to convince consumers to purchase a product, often by stressing that it is more desirable than others. It is argued that this type of advertising distorts consumer buying, pushing them to buy products which they would otherwise not have bought. In reality, a great deal of advertising is persuasive to some extent.
- REASSURING ADVERTISING is aimed at existing customers. It tries to persuade them that their purchase was correct and that they should continue to buy the product. Banks and building societies often use this method to assure customers that their investments are safe.

There is a wide range of ADVERTISING MEDIA that firms can choose from in order to make consumers aware of their products including:

- commercial television, whether terrestrial such as ITV1 or Channel 4, or satellite such as BSkyB;
- commercial radio, which in the UK is local radio;
- national newspapers, such as *The Sun* or *The Times*;
- regional newspapers, such as the *London Evening Standard* or the *Birmingham Evening Post*;
- magazines, such as *Cosmopolitan* or *Loaded*;
- trade newspapers and journals, such as *The Grocer* or *Accountancy Age* which are read by workers or businesses in a particular industry, trade or profession;
- directories, including the telephone directories *Yellow Pages* and *Thomson Directory*;
- posters and transport, such as billboards by the side of the road or advertisements on the side of buses;
- the Internet.

The medium that is chosen will depend on a variety of factors including:

- **Cost** – most businesses could not afford television adverts, for example. Cost also has to be measured against effectiveness – how much extra new business will be generated by each £1 of advertising expenditure?
- **Media reach** – what media will best get to the audience the advertiser wishes to reach?
- **Delivery of the chosen message** – what media would best persuade consumers to change their brand of washing powder, for example, or give customers a telephone number to call if their washing machine broke down?
- **The marketing mix** – an advertising campaign may be part of a wider campaign using other elements of the marketing mix, such as below-the-line promotion or pricing. These other elements may help determine which media to use for advertising.
- **The law** – there are legal restrictions on the use of different media for advertising certain products, such as cigarettes.

Types of advertising media

There is a wide range of advertising media that business can choose from in order to make consumers aware of their products.

Television Because of its many advantages, television advertising is often used by businesses marketing consumer goods to a mass market. The fast-changing trends in television were likely to provide opportunities for television advertising after the year 2000. 99 per cent of males and females watch television in the UK. The growth of cable, satellite and digital television may attract companies to advertise on television. Businesses may be particularly attracted to advertise on satellite television as packages on Sky, for example, may be subscribed to by higher earning and spending groups.

Newspapers and magazines Newspapers and magazines are an important medium for the advertising of mass market products. In 2007 it was estimated that 84 per cent of UK adults read a national newspaper on a monthly basis. This amounts to 26 million readers on weekdays and 31 million readers at weekends. Newspapers and magazines can also be useful for targeting a particular audience or market segment. For example, businesses selling riding equipment might advertise in Horse and Hound or a business selling musical equipment might advertise in Total Guitar. Newspaper advertising can also be useful for smaller businesses which may make greater use of regional and local newspapers such as the Manchester Evening News and the South Manchester Reporter.

Cinema Cinema attendances fell from a high of around 1.4 billion in 1951 to reach a low of 53 million in 1984. The 1990s, however, saw a revival in attendances, partly as a result of the better facilities offered by large multiplex cinemas. This revival was sustained into the 21st Century. As a result, advertisers began to pay greater attention to this medium. Firms such as Wrangler have even produced advertisements principally designed for use on large cinema screens. Of all the advertising media available to a business, the cinema has the greatest potential for having a strong impact on its audience.

Radio In recent years there has been a growth in the number of independent radio stations in the UK. These include local stations, such as Capital in London and XFM in Manchester, national stations such as Virgin and Talk Radio and specialist stations such as Smooth FM and Classic FM. For advertisers this has meant an increase in both the number and type of radio stations on which they can advertise. There has been an increase in the number of people listening to radio. This trend may be likely to continue with the development of digital radio and Internet radio stations. Both large companies such as Cunard

Question 1.

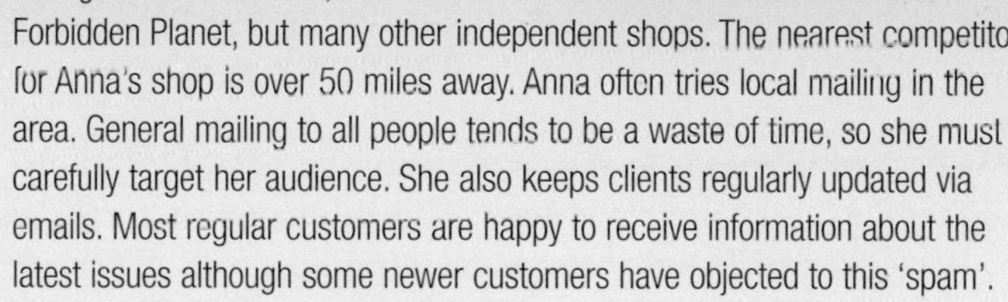

Anna Lever runs a shop which sells imported comics and graphic novels from the USA and Europe. She stocks well known comics by Marvel and DC, such as X-Men and Batman, and also a small line of European comics. Anna also sells comics by independent publishers in the UK. The market for comic sales in the UK tends to be a niche market, selling to specialist collectors, teenagers, students and children, and older people who Anna argues 'want to recapture their youth, by reading the stories they read when they were children and teenagers.'

There is a small number of chains selling comics in the UK, such as Forbidden Planet, but many other independent shops. The nearest competitor for Anna's shop is over 50 miles away. Anna often tries local mailing in the area. General mailing to all people tends to be a waste of time, so she must carefully target her audience. She also keeps clients regularly updated via emails. Most regular customers are happy to receive information about the latest issues although some newer customers have objected to this 'spam'.

Every month Anna makes the trip to the nearest city and puts up a stall in the comic mart on Sundays. She tends to see the same faces there all the time, and can build up contacts. There may also be people coming to 'have a look' on their day off and some have become regular clients. She has also occasionally taken a stand at the large fair held at the NEC in Birmingham a few times a year. She finds the trip is tiring, takes a lot of time out of her week and does not always pay for itself.

Source: adapted from company information.

(a) Why might it be important for Anna's business to use a trade fair as part of its promotional mix?

(b) Assess whether a trade fair might be more successful than direct mail advertising in promoting and selling comics.

Figure 1: Internet access

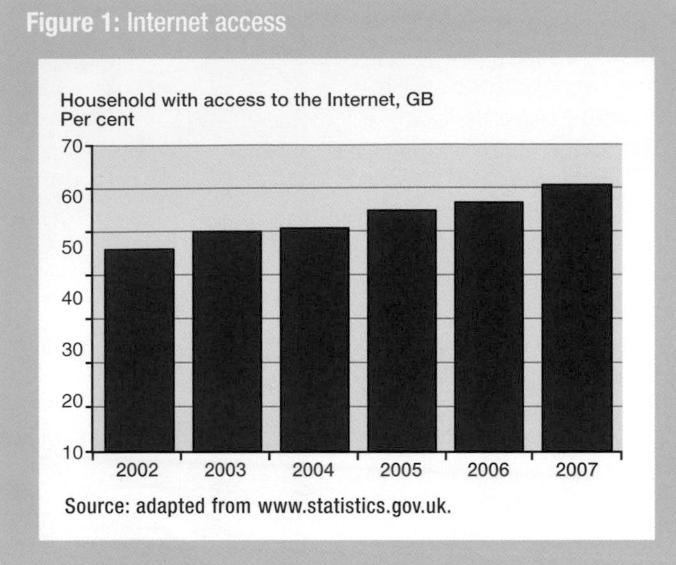

Source: adapted from www.statistics.gov.uk.

and Kleenex Tissues, as well as smaller businesses, have found radio effective in reaching target customers.

Posters or billboards Posters appear in a variety of locations and tend to carry short messages. This is because motorists and pedestrians usually only have a few seconds to consider them. An effective poster is likely to be large, attention grabbing and placed in a site where it is highly visible to large numbers of people. The development of electronic screens containing 'posters' with rotating advertisements is a development in this area which may attract businesses.

The Internet Figure 1 shows the dramatic increase in the importance of the Internet as an advertising medium in the UK. In 2007, 15.23 million UK households had Internet access. This represented 61 per cent of households and an increase of nearly 1 million households, or 7 per cent, since 2006. It was also an increase of 13 per cent since 2003. In 1998 the figure was just 9 per cent of households. As a result, businesses have shown a growing interest in advertising via websites on the Internet. One major advantage is that websites can be accessed by consumers all over the world, giving companies a worldwide market. The vast majority of companies now have their own websites to advertise products and some even allow customers to purchase online using credit cards. By 2003 over half of UK Internet users were using websites to buy goods and services.

Promotion below the line

Promotion below the line is any promotion that is not advertising. Above-the-line advertising in newspapers means that the promotion is seen by most of the readers, even though some will not be interested. With below-the-line promotions, firms aim their message at consumers who are either known to them or who have been chosen in advance, and who are interested. For example, businesses promoting through exhibitions, such as the Boat Show, can be certain that the majority of those attending will be interested in the products on show.

There may be problems that result from below-the-line promotions. As with advertising, they are expensive and their outcome can be difficult to predict. Also, they are often 'one-off' events, which have an impact for a limited period. Further, some types of promotion, such as direct mail and direct selling, are disliked by consumers.

Public relations PUBLIC RELATIONS is a attempt by a business to communicate with groups that form its 'public'. Such groups may include the government, shareholders, employees and customers. The aim is to increase sales by improving the image of the business and its products. This can be done directly by the business itself through a public relations activity or a television programme or a newspaper could be used. Because of the importance of maintaining good relations with the media, a business may appoint a **publicity manager**. As well as promoting favourable press stories, publicity managers must respond to criticisms and try to ensure that there are no unfavourable press notices.

Consumers appear to attach great importance to messages conveyed through public relations. For example, a new restaurant may promote a positive image of itself through promotional materials. Such communications may be taken 'with a pinch of salt' by consumers. However, a good write-up in a newspaper or restaurant guide is likely to be taken much more seriously by consumers. Businesses use a variety of methods to attract publicity.

- **Press conferences.** These might involve inviting journalists to a company presentation, where they are given information. The business may take the opportunity to launch a new or updated product. Sometimes, businesses provide free products for conference members to try out. Conferences may also be used for presentations to trade customers.
- **Press releases.** These are written accounts of events or activities which may be considered newsworthy. For example, new multi-million pound contracts gained by firms such as British Aerospace are announced on TV news bulletins. Such news stories usually originate from press releases issued by businesses.
- **Donations.** These can range from a small contribution to a college mini bus appeal to a large donation to Comic Relief's 'Red Nose Day' or the 'Children in Need' appeal . While some make payments anonymously, others take advantage of the opportunity for a good public relations event. The approach of a business to such an event is likely to be determined by its particular ethical stance.
- **Sponsorship.** This is popular in the sporting world. Examples have included the links between Coca-Cola and the Olympic Games, McDonald's and the World Cup, and Nike and Tiger Woods. Other types of sponsorship take place in the arts world with ballet, opera and theatre being sponsored by businesses.
- **Company visits.** Jaguar Cars and Warburtons Bakeries

have allowed members of the public to visit their manufacturing and research plants as part of their public relations activities.

Merchandising MERCHANDISING is an attempt to influence consumers at the POINT OF SALE. The point of sale is anywhere that a consumer buys a product. It may be, for example, a supermarket, a department store, a bank or a petrol station. Consumers are intended to buy based on 'what they see' rather than from a sales assistant. The aim of merchandising is to encourage sales of a product and therefore to speed up the rate at which stocks are turned over. There is a number of different features of merchandising.

- **Display material.** A good display should attract attention, enhance certain aspects of a product and encourage the 'right frame of mind' to make a purchase. Department stores lay great stress on window displays. Banks make sure that the services which they offer, such as insurance and loan facilities, are well displayed in their branches.
- **The layout of products at the point of sale.** Many retail outlets, such as supermarkets, design the layout of their stores very carefully. Their aim is to encourage consumers to follow particular routes around a store. Retail outlets often place popular items at the back or sides of a store. Consumers, on their way to these, are encouraged to walk past other items which they might buy. Another tactic is to place related products next to each other, so consumers buy both.
- **Stocks.** A firm must make sure that stock levels are maintained and shelves are quickly restocked. Shelf space is usually allocated according to the amount of a product which a business expects to sell. For example, a supermarket will give more space to products on special offer.
- **Appropriate lighting and the creation of desirable 'smells'.** Generally lighting is kept soft where browsing is encouraged and bright where there is a need to suggest cleanliness as, for example, at a cosmetics counter. Smells are used to encourage the right atmosphere. Bread smells are often wafted into supermarkets and food retailers.

Sales promotions SALES PROMOTIONS are the incentives offered to consumers to encourage them to buy goods and services. They are used to give a short-term 'boost' to the sales of a product. This is different to building up brand recognition and loyalty, which may be a longer-term aim. There is a variety of sales promotions that a business can use, as shown in Table 2. Why have these methods become popular?

- Sales promotions can be used as a method to break into a new market or introduce a new product into an existing market. They can also be used as a means of extending the product life cycle of an existing product.
- They encourage consumers to sample a good or service which they might not have bought otherwise. Once the initial good has been purchased it is likely that further goods will be bought. Many magazines offer free gifts ranging from CD ROMS to make-up in their first issues hoping that their consumers will continue to buy.
- Customers feel 'rewarded' for their custom. They may, as a result, develop a loyalty to a particular product or business.
- Customers identify products or businesses with things that they like or are attracted to. A customer is therefore more likely to purchase a product.
- Sales promotions provide businesses with feedback on the

Question 2.

How many copies of the *Sunday Times* can a delivery boy or girl carry? The answer is five. The reason for this is the polybags that now accompany newspapers. For newspapers delivering news is not enough. Added value is required in the form of supplements, additional sections and gifts. During 2006 the *Daily Mail* added 37,000 new customers. This was largely ascribed to a drive to increase homesales deliveries but was also linked to the free gift of two major DVDs per month. In the same year the *Sun* experienced a 0.6 per cent rise in readers partly linked, it is thought, to a 20p price cut in the South of England. The *Daily Mirror*, by contrast, suffered a 4.7 per cent drop in readers over the same period despite its free collection of 13 classic Ladybird books. The *Daily Star Sunday* leaped by 12 per cent as it music CD series continued, while the *People* plummeted by 12 per cent despite offering free cross channel ferry tickets.

Source: adapted from *The Independent*, 12.11.2007.

(a) Identify the diferent promotional methods described in the article.

(b) Explain whether the methods are above-the-line or below-the-line methdos of promotion.

(c) Discuss whether a local newspaper should use this type of promotional method.

Table 1: Sales promotions

- **Coupons and loyalty cards** involve either providing money off or refunds on specific purchases or allowing savings to be made over time for being a loyal customer. The Nectar card which includes Sainsbury's and PC World is now used by hundreds of retailers in this way.
- **Competitions**. Prizes are sometimes offered for competitions. To enter, consumers must first buy the product. Tabloid newspapers often use this type of promotion. They try to attract customers through large cash prizes in their 'bingo' competitions.
- **Product endorsements** are widely used by a range of manufacturers, where well-known personalities are paid to use products. For example, sports products companies will sign up teams and successful sports personalities to promote their products. The competition between sports companies has often been reflected by the teams they supply - Real Madrid has worn Adidas while Manchester United and Barcelona have worn Nike.
- **Product placing** involves a firm paying for product brands to be placed on the sets of films and TV programmes. Car manufacturers are often eager to see their vehicles driven by Hollywood stars in popular movies.
- **Free offers**. A free 'gift' may be given with the product. An example of might be music magazines, which regularly offer readers free CDs of featured artists.
- **Special credit terms** have been increasingly used by firms. They include offers such as interest free credit and 'buy now pay later' schemes.

impact of their marketing expenditure, for example, through the number of coupons returned or the amount spent on loyalty cards.

Sales promotions are not without problems. The free flight offer of Hoover in 1992 is one example. It offered two free flights to the US with the purchase of products worth over £200. The company misjudged the number of people taking advantage of the offer. This meant extreme pressure on the company to produce the goods consumers were demanding. Also many consumers did not receive the holidays on dates or at times they wished. By 1993 there were so many complaints that Maytag, Hoover's US parent company, had to intervene to make sure flights or compensation were provided. It was estimated that the cost of dealing with these problems was £21.1 million.

Direct selling Direct selling or personal selling occurs when a company's sales team promotes a product through personal contact. This can be done over the telephone, by setting up meetings, in retail outlets, or by 'knocking on doors'. In general, the more highly priced, technically complex or individual the product, the greater the need for personal selling. Most firms supplying industrial markets rely upon personal selling in the form of sales representatives. The main reason for using personal selling rather than other methods is that individuals can be given personal attention. Most forms of promotion tend to deliver a 'standard message' to a 'typical' consumer. With personal selling the individual consumer's needs can be dealt with and the product shaped to meet these needs. There are other reasons for using direct or personal selling.

- Creating awareness of and interest in a product.
- Explaining the functions and technical aspects of a product.
- Obtaining orders and, in some cases, making deliveries.
- Encouraging product trials and test marketing.
- Providing rapid and detailed feedback from the consumer to the producer via the sales representative.

A disadvantage with personal selling is that it can be expensive. The cost of maintaining a team of sales representatives can be very high. Another problem is the dislike of 'callers' by consumers. There are also legal and ethical issues about the way products are sold that need to be considered.

Direct mailing Direct mailing involves sending information

Question 3.

A firm from Walsall in the West Midlands has won an order to provide electrical wiring for the world-beating Subaru rally cars raced by drivers such as Richard Burns. Teepee Electrical Systems said that the wiring had been subjected to extensive testing to ensure it met the standards of reliability and performance needed for rally cars. Teepee Electrical Systems sells electrical wiring to other businesses. It is involved with a range of industries, from railway rolling stock, to conveyor belt systems at airports and even the submarine controls in a James Bond film. Kevin Jones, managing director of the company, put the success of the company down to the skills its workers bring to the business. 'A wiring loom is a wiring loom, but our people add engineering skills from widely diverse fields.'

Source: www.teepee-electrical.co.uk and www.expressandstar.com.

(a) In what ways might branding benefit Teepee Electrical Systems.

(b) Suggest why Teepee might find it difficult to establish a strong brand in this market.

about a product or product range through the post. The consumer can usually buy the product by placing an order by post or telephone. Although sometimes unpopular with the public, direct mail is a fast growing area of promotion. It has proved very effective for firms trying to reach a target audience. Some companies use direct e-mailing, where consumers or businesses receive product information through their email inbox. Systems, however, exist for unwanted emails to be blocked as this method of selling has proved unpopular for some people. Direct mail is one means of **direct marketing**, which is often seen as part of a firm's distribution network.

Packaging A product's packaging is important in its overall marketing. This is because consumers often link the quality and design of a product's packaging with the quality of the product itself. Unsuitable packaging may affect sales. What factors should firms consider when deciding upon how to package their product?

- **Weight and shape.** These can affect the cost of distributing a product. For example, bulky packaging may mean high distribution costs.
- **Protection.** Products must not be damaged in transit or in storage. They must also be protected against light, dust and heat.
- **Convenience.** The packaging must be easy to handle by the consumer and distributors.
- **Design.** The design of the packaging should be eye-catching and help the consumer to distinguish it from others. It should also fit in with the overall marketing of the product and project the brand image. Colour is likely to be important here.
- **Information.** It is likely that the package will contain information required by the consumer. For technical products, the packaging will need to include information about how the product should be used. For food products, there are legal requirements about the information that must be on the package, such as details of the ingredients contained.
- **Environmental factors.** Manufacturers are facing increasing pressure to cut down on the amount and type of packaging placed around products. Consumers and pressure groups stress the wastefulness of this and its impact upon the environment. The response of some manufacturers to this pressure has been to use recyclable materials.

Exhibitions and trade fairs Exhibitions and trade fairs are used by firms to promote their products. They are visited by both industrial and ordinary consumers. Examples of better known fairs and exhibitions include the Motor Show, the Boat Show, the Ideal Homes Exhibition and BETT (the British educational technology exhibition). Why do businesses find them useful?

- They give the chance to show how a product actually works. This is important in the case of bulky or complex technical products. Business to business marketing, including the promoting of industrial and agricultural machinery is often done through trade fairs.
- Consumer reaction to a product can be tested before it is released onto the market.
- Some trade fairs and exhibitions are held overseas. They can form a part of a firm's international marketing strategy.
- A fair or exhibition may attract press coverage. New products may be launched to take advantage of this. The Motor Show is widely used for this purpose.
- They allow customers to discuss a product with members of the management team. It is not unusual for the managing directors of a business to attend a trade fair. For industrial consumers, in particular, this can be a valuable point of contact.
- Technical and sales staff are available to answer questions and discuss the product.

The promotional mix

Businesses usually use a range of different types of the promotional methods described above at any one time. This range is the PROMOTIONAL MIX employed by the business. For example, a business launching a new product might advertise it on television, but also send press releases to newspapers and magazines that it thinks might cover the story. There is a number of influences on the promotional mix that a business decides to employ.

The type of product Some products are better suited to some promotional methods than others. For example, trade fairs and exhibitions are strongly suited to business to business marketing and, in particular, for the promoting of business specific products such as machinery, equipment and software. On the other hand fast moving consumer goods are often better suited to different forms of advertising so that their qualities can be communicated to a wide audience.

The type of market This includes it size, geography, socio-economic characteristics and whether it is a consumer or business to business market. For example, a small business such as a small decorating business might rely upon an occasional advertisement in a local newspaper or a listing in the *Yellow Pages*. This is partly because such a business restricts its operations to a small locality and so promotional methods designed to reach a regional or national market would not be appropriate.

Cost Many small businesses find that they are restricted by considerations of cost when deciding upon use of promotional methods. Many forms of advertising, such as in national newspapers or on television or radio may not be affordable to such businesses. This means that their choice of promotional method will be strictly limited by considerations of cost.

The promotional mix of competitors If competitors are spending a great deal on advertising, for example, a competitor may feel the need to match this. Many small businesses restrict their promotions to word of mouth and personal selling, but the use of other methods by a competitor may cause a business to reconsider this strategy.

The stage of a product in its life cycle The promotional needs of a product at its launch may be very different from those used in its decline stage. Many business, both small and large, make use of public relations when first launching a product on to the market.

Legal and social constraints There is a variety of legislation that affects promotion, particularly advertising, which may influence the choice of media by a business.

- There are laws which affect the nature of advertisements. For example, the **Trade Descriptions Act 1968** states that products must correspond to claims made for them on advertisements.
- The **Advertising Standards Authority** (**ASA**) is the main independent body in the UK which regulates and controls advertising. It ensures that business correspond with the **British Code of Advertising, Sales promotion and Direct Marketing**, the CAP code. If the ASA finds that an advertisement breaches the code it will ask the business to withdraw the advertisement, to which they usually comply. Although it has no legal powers to force the business to withdraw the advertisement it can put pressure on it by publishing its findings or ask the media to refuse the carry the advertisement. It can also refer the advertisement to the Office of Fair Trading.
- Certain **pressure groups** seek to influence advertising. FOREST, for example, campaigns for the right of people to smoke. ASH, on the other hand, seeks to make public the health risks of smoking.
- People may resent certain types of promotion. Email campaigns are often resented by people with computers.

Advertising, society and ethics

Advertising has the potential to affect the lives of many people. This is because, for most, regular exposure to advertising is almost unavoidable. How might advertising affect individuals?

- It adds to the cost of marketing products. This money could have been spent on improving products or price reductions. It is likely that consumers will pay more of any advertising costs than firms.
- It is argued that advertising encourages people to buy products which they might not otherwise have purchased. This may, perhaps, lead to a society where people are judged according to how much they consume rather than their value as human beings.
- Environmentalists are concerned about high levels of consumption and the role of advertising in encouraging this. They doubt whether the earth's resources can sustain current levels. There is a growing trend amongst consumers to look at the type of goods they buy and also how much they consume, as they become more aware of long term problems.
- Advertising can encourage people to buy products which are regarded as being damaging to society.
- Advertisements often encourage behaviour which might be to the detriment of society as a whole. An example is the fast 'macho' driving often seen in advertisements for cars and related products.

In its defence, the advertising industry would point to a number of arguments to justify its role.

- Advertisements offer a choice to consumers which allows them to make more informed consumption decisions.
- Advertisements give valuable information to consumers which might otherwise be difficult to come by.
- Advertisers respond to and reflect the needs, wishes and attitudes of consumers; they do not 'create' them.
- Advertising earns revenue for television and radio and allows newspapers and magazines to be sold at lower prices.
- The advertising industry employs large numbers of people. They are employed directly, through advertising agencies, and indirectly through jobs that may result from a successfully advertised product.

KEYTERMS

Above-the-line promotion – promotion in the form of advertising.
Advertising – a form of communication between a business and its customers where the business uses visual, oral or pictorial images in the media to encourage the purchase of products.
Advertising media – the various means by which advertisements can be communicated to the public.
Informative advertising – advertising which primarily seeks to provide consumers with information about a product.
Below-the-line promotion – promotion that is not media advertising.
Merchandising – a promotion specifically at the point of sale of a product.
Persuasive advertising – advertising which seeks to influence and persuade consumers to buy a product.
Pester power – the ability of children to persuade parents to buy products.
Promotion – an attempt to retain and obtain customers by drawing attention to a firm or its products.
Promotional mix – the mixture of promotional techniques used by a business to promote its products.
Point of sale – any point where a consumer buys a product.
Public relations – an organisation's attempts to communicate with interested parties.
Reassuring advertising – a method used to assure consumers about their purchases and encourage them to make repeat purchases.
Sales promotions – methods of promoting a product in the short term to give a boost to sales.

KNOWLEDGE

1. What is above the line promotion?
2. What choices of advertising media do firms have?
3 What is below the line promotion?
4. What is direct mailing?
5. Why do businesses promote their products at trade fairs and exhibitions?
6. Identify four different types of sales promotions.
7. Identify five features that a brand might have.
8. Where is merchandising likely to take place?
9. Which aspects of their merchandising should businesses pay attention to?
10. What is the main advantage of personal selling?
11. What is public relations?
12. Identify five factors that might influence the promotional mix.

CRITIQUE

Critics of marketing question the extent to which businesses respond to consumer needs as opposed to creating them. Promotion is a major part of this. Many would argue that promotions actively seek to create the need to consume more, rather than just responding to what consumers want and need. They suggest that consumer needs in general would be better met if businesses encouraged them to spend less rather than more. So whilst promoting their products strongly may make sense for individual businesses and their relationships with individual consumers it does not necessarily work at a wider level. One consequence of this so-called pressure on consumers is individuals spending beyond their means. This has led to many people taking on more debt than they can manage. Another consequence is more rapid use of the world's resources and the creation of higher levels of environmental damage.

Case Study: Advertising

Retailers signalled a big push for Christmas sales in 2007 with the launch of TV advertising campaigns. Leading the way was Marks & Spencer, which signed up A-list movie star Antonio Banderas to front adverts that recreate memorable moments from classic Hollywood films. But competing for screen space will be retailers who traditionally do not use TV advertising such as John Lewis and Next. Many retail chiefs have forecast trade is going to be tough this Christmas and they are pouring cash into advertising to persuade shoppers to part with their cash. Last year's M&S Christmas campaign had a James Bond theme and starred Dame Shirley Bassey. Banderas - who starred in the Mask of Zorro - will appear with M&S's usual roster of models: Twiggy, Erin O'Connor, Laura Bailey, Lizzie Jagger and Noemie Lenoir. M&S's advertising, masterminded by marketing director Steve Sharp, has been credited with helping to rebuild the reputation of the retailer.

Next week also sees the launch of a John Lewis advertising campaign. It is spending more than £6 million to promote the 27-strong chain of department stores - three times last' year's advertising spend - and will be using TV adverts for only the second time in its history. The move is the brainchild of the company's new marketing director, Gill Barr, who joined the company in January and was made a member of the board in June. The television advertisement, which is set to 'Morning Serenade', the theme from Prokofiev's ballet Romeo and Juliet, is deliberately understated to contrast with other retailers' celebrity focused Christmas ads. It shows a diverse group of people carefully arranging John Lewis products in such a way that the combined shadow casts the outline of the person for whom the gifts are intended. The image will also be used for billboards and press and in cinema and online advertising. The spend – up from £1.75 million last year – signifies a departure for the department store chain which has traditionally invested little on advertising, believing the brand has grown essentially through word of mouth and that it was not necessary to 'boast about it'.

Ms Barr, a former business development director at Woolworths, said that when she joined the company there wasn't a tradition of advertising, but there was 'an ambition to be more articulate about the brand and to talk to customers more'. She added: 'This campaign is directional for the John Lewis brand. "The creative execution is stylish, intriguing and intelligent. The media plan is more comprehensive than ever before, reinforcing the core idea with three different shadows in press and outdoor. The TV advertisement will also run in cinemas.'

Next recently unveiled its first national television advertising campaign for more than a decade. It is pouring £20 million into advertising this year - double last year's marketing budget. Chief executive Simon Wolfson said recently that he was 'acutely aware that the full effect of recent interest rates has not yet filtered through to our customers' and despite the advertising push forecasts a dip in sales of up to 3.5 per cent, compared to last year, over the current six months. She added that the ad intended to use the extent of the company's range, which includes 350,000 products, to inspire customers with their Christmas shopping. The television ad, which will run from next Tuesday, differs widely from the glitzy ads of Marks & Spencer, which star Shirley Bassey, Twiggy and Myleene Klass, and Next, which launched its first major television ad campaign in September. Next is spending £18 million more than usual on advertising this year, including £2 million more on its Christmas window displays.

Source: adapted from *The Guardian*, 3.11.2007 and the *Independent*, 2.11.2007.

(a) Identify the different promotional methods used in the case study. (6 marks)

(b) Explain, using examples, how the methods of promotion might be made:
(i) persuasive; (ii) informative; (iii) reassuring;
for customers of the businesses. (6 marks)

(c) Examine the factors which might affect the choice of promotional method for each business. (10 marks)

(d) In the light of the information in the article, evaluate the potential promotional methods available to a small independent fashion clothing business. (12 marks)

22 Place

Place and the marketing mix

Place is one of the 4Ps of the marketing mix. It is no less important than the other Ps of product, price and promotion. However good the product, if it isn't available to customers to buy at the right place and at the right time, it won't sell.

The right place Products need to be available to customers in the place where they want to buy. For example, 75 per cent of all groceries in the UK are now bought from large supermarket chains. So if a grocery product is not available in a supermarket, its sales will be severely restricted. Equally, a car manufacturer might insist that parts are delivered to its plant by the component manufacturer. Unless the business agrees to deliver, it won't get the order.

The right time Products need to be available to customers at the time they want to buy. For example, often at Christmas there is a toy which becomes popular. Supplies may run out in shops. The manufacturer of the toy knows that unless it can increase supply to meet demand before 25th December, the sales it could have made will be lost. Equally, if there is a strike at the printers of a daily newspaper and a day's production is lost, those sales will never be recovered. Nobody will want to buy yesterday's newspaper today.

Coca-Cola has become the world's largest soft drinks distributor by making sure that its drinks are available to consumers not just in the right place, but also at a time when consumers want to buy. Coca-Cola vending machines, for example, are part of this strategy.

Distribution channels in consumer markets

The DISTRIBUTION CHANNEL for a product in a **consumer market** is the route it takes from manufacturer to the consumer. Figure 1 shows some common channels of distribution. They can be distinguished by the number and type of intermediary involved. A MARKETING INTERMEDIARY is a business or individual which acts as a link between the producer and customer.

Manufacturers to consumers DIRECT MARKETING involves a business selling its product straight to consumers. A manufacturer might advertise its products directly for sale to the public through advertisements in magazines. It might also operate a mail order catalogue or offer online ordering through a website on the Internet. It might even sell via its own sales representatives. Some manufacturers have factory shops where consumers can buy products. **Services** are also usually distributed straight to the customer, for example solicitors or accountants.

Manufacturers to consumers via retailers A RETAILER is a service business which sells goods to consumers. Retailers are typically called **shops**. But there are many other names for retailers, such as department stores, supermarkets and hypermarkets, superstores and convenience stores. Jewellers, butchers, grocers and hardware stores are also examples of shops.

Retailers provide certain services. First, they BREAK-BULK. They buy large quantities from suppliers and sell in smaller quantities to consumers. For example, a supermarket chain might buy 1 million packets of butter from a food manufacturer, but sell butter to consumers in single packets. Breaking-bulk is a service both to manufacturers and consumers. Most manufacturers don't want to sell in small quantities to consumers. Equally, consumers don't want to buy large quantities from manufacturers.

Figure 1: Examples of channels of distribution

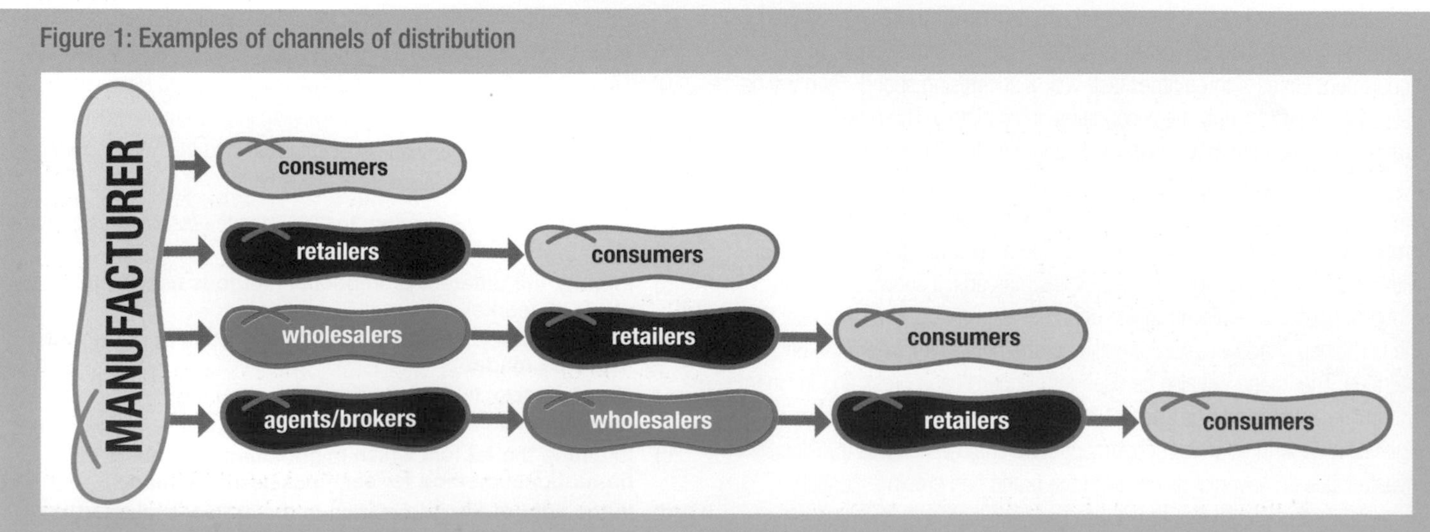

Retailers also sell goods in locations which are convenient to consumers. A yoghurt manufacturer may have a plant in Wales, for example. But consumers in London don't want to travel to Wales every time they want to buy a yoghurt.

Retailers also provide other services which add value to the good being sold. These may include home delivery, repair services, extra guarantees and gift wrapping.

Manufacturers selling to customers via retailers is a **one level channel** because there is a single intermediary between manufacturers and consumers.

Manufacturers to consumers via wholesalers and retailers
A WHOLESALER is a business which buys goods from manufacturers and sells them to retailers. Some wholesalers call themselves a **cash-and-carry** because their customers, usually small shops, visit the premises and take away what they have purchased. In most cases, though, wholesalers deliver to retailing customers.

Like retailers, wholesalers provide two main services. They break-bulk and they are located or deliver to a location which is convenient to the retailer. They may also offer services such as trade credit.

The use of wholesalers is an example of a **two level channel** because there are two intermediaries between manufacturers and consumers.

Manufacturer to consumers via agents and/or wholesalers and retailers A manufacturer may use an intermediary called an AGENT or BROKER. They bring buyers and sellers together. Agents are often used when selling into a foreign country. They often have better knowledge of the laws, needs of consumers and trading conditions in that country.

Question 1.

KFM Ltd manufactures interactive whiteboard software. Interactive whiteboards are used in education to support teaching and in business for conferences and presentations. KFM started as a small operation selling direct to customers from an industrial estate in Milton Keynes. It would place adverts in specialist magazines and often tailor products to the specific needs of customers.

Recently the business has expanded and now wants to sell more standardised products in greater quantities. KFM has been approached by a retail chain which wants to stock its product range in stores under the 'business and education' section. The retailer feels that the growing market in interactive whiteboards means that more customers will be looking for this type of software. KFM has also been looking to expand in the USA. It is interested in adapting its products for the US market. However, it is aware that legislation might affect its product specification and also that it lacks knowledge about the US market. It has considered a number of alternatives - using an agent to find a retail chain to stock the products, selling to a warehouse business or licensing the product to a US manufacturer.

(a) Examine the factors that might affect KFM's channel of distribution:
(i) as a small operation; (ii) as it expands in the UK;
(iii) as it expands abroad.

(b) Which channel of distribution would you advise KFM to use? Explain your answer.

The choice of distribution channel

Which distribution channel is used depends upon a variety of factors.

Cost The longer the supply chain, the greater may be the cost to the final consumer. This is because each intermediary has its own costs to cover and wants to make a profit. Large supermarket chains often reduce these costs by cutting out the wholesaler and buying directly from the manufacturer.

However, in some cases short supply chains can be more costly than long supply chains. For example, a small upmarket food manufacturer may find that supermarkets will not stock its goods. To survive, it might have to supply directly to the customer, by mail order or the Internet. But the cost of a catalogue, an Internet site and delivery may be far more than the cost of supplying through a retailer. Some businesses employ sales representatives to sell directly. These can also be very costly.

Distribution Manufacturers may find it difficult to reach large numbers of consumers without an intermediary. This might be because the manufacturer lacks resources. It may not be able to afford to run a sales team, for instance. Equally, a manufacturer such as Heinz or Kellogg's may want to sell to every household in the country. The only way it can achieve this might be to use the large network of retailers, including supermarket chains.

Another factor may be knowledge of the market. A UK company that wants to sell a small quantity of goods to Australia may know nothing about this market. By using an agent to sell the goods, it will gain the agent's expertise.

Control Some manufacturers want to control the distribution channels they use carefully. For example, manufacturers of luxury goods or up-market brands, such as Chanel or Levis, don't want their goods being sold in supermarkets. This is because the place of sale can give important messages to consumers about the product. Expensive perfumes or jeans sold in Tesco or Asda detract from the exclusive image of the brand, according to their manufacturers. It is then going to be more difficult to sell these luxury goods at a high price and high profit margin.

Safety may be another issue. Some products require careful installation or maintenance. The manufacturer may find it easier to control safety aspects if it sells directly to the customer.

Legal factors The law may affect how a product is distributed. For example, drugs which need a doctor's prescription can only be sold through licensed chemists.

Question 2.

Sales of CDs slumped by 8 per cent in the UK in the first half of 2007 but strong growth in legally downloaded music helped offset some of the decline. The collapse in CD and DVD sales on the UK high street has come into focus after music chain Fopp closed its 81 outlets last week. Retailers such as HMV and Virgin have come under intense pressure from low-cost online competitors as well as illegal downloading of music. However, the overall decline in CD sales was not quite as dramatic as the music retailers' woes suggest. The latest data from the BPI, the UK music industry trade body, showed that 60 million albums were sold in the first half of the year, down from 65 million in the same period in 2006. Nearly 97 per cent of those albums were sold as CDs.

Geoff Taylor, the BPI chief executive, said: 'CDs remain very attractive to consumers because of the flexibility and outstanding value for money they offer, and for this reason they represent the overwhelming majority of sales. Consumers vote with their pay packets and 58 million CD album sales in just six months is a very significant number indeed.'

The UK market for CDs is holding up better than other markets such as the US, helped by strong sales of UK artists such as Amy Winehouse and the Kaiser Chiefs. The BPI said that UK music fans buy more CDs per capita than anywhere else in the world, with the UK market accounting for more than 150 million sales for four years running.

The BPI also said the UK was 'ahead of the curve' in terms of legally downloaded music, with digital album sales partially offsetting the decline in physical sales. It said that 2.1 million albums were downloaded in the first half, with more than 100,000 sales a week achieved during June. Digital sales have also breathed life into the flagging singles market, helping to drive a 23 per cent increase in single sales in the first half of the year.

Source: adapted from *The Independent*, 11.7.2007.

(a) Identify the channels of distribution for music referred to in the article.

(b) Analyse the possible responses of a small UK based record shop/CD retailing business to the information in the article.

Distribution channels in business to business markets

The distribution channel for a good in a **business to business market** is the route it takes from the manufacturer to another business. As in consumer markets, there can be none, one or more intermediaries. For example, some businesses sell directly to others using their own 'sales reps'. Small tradespeople and businesses in the building industry, such as plumbers or carpenters, often buy from builders' merchants or building wholesalers. These intermediaries distribute products for the building industry. Agents might also be used by a producer dealing with a manufacturer in a foreign country.

Services are often distributed straight from one business to another, for example cleaning services, or through an agent, such as secretarial help.

The number of intermediaries depends upon a variety of factors, including cost and ease of distribution.

Distribution targets and objectives

A business that wants to be successful is likely to have clear **marketing objectives**. These are the goals that the business wants to achieve through its marketing, such as increasing sales.

When choosing which distribution channels it will use, a business will set DISTRIBUTION TARGETS. These are plans which might include, for example, the quantity to be sold over a future time period and to whom products will be sold. They will take into account marketing objectives. For example, a toy manufacturer that has the objective of increasing sales may set a target of selling 5,000 extra toys a month. It might decide that the best way to do this is to sell in bulk to wholesalers. Or a new computer magazine may want to target computer users. It may decide to sell directly over the Internet for a charge, allowing buyers to download and print out the magazine.

Physical distribution

Physical distribution is the movement of products from one place to another. It is an important part of the marketing process for two main reasons.

- Failure to deliver a product in the right quantities, at the right place and at the right time can damage an effective marketing effort.
- The cost of physical distribution can be high – in some cases higher than the cost of actually producing the product.

Two aspects of physical distribution are important to a business – holding stocks and transporting products.

Holding stocks Ideally a business would be able to guarantee every customer the product they wanted, whenever they wanted it. To do this a firm would have to hold huge amounts of stock. Holding excessive amounts of stock is very costly. Holding very low stock levels, however, could mean turning down orders.

The solution is for a business to assess the level of stocks needed to maintain an agreed level of customer service. This often means holding enough stock to satisfy regular orders, but not enough to deal with sudden changes in demand. This will depend on the market in which the product is selling.

Transporting products This is concerned with how goods can be physically delivered to markets. Firms need to consider the relative costs and speed of transporting their goods by road, rail, sea or air. For example, aeroplanes are faster than ships when transporting exports from the UK. However, firms must decide whether this advantage outweighs the costs which result from using this mode of transport. There are times when the nature of a product dictates the transport. For example, an Orkney Islands based firm which sells freshly caught lobsters to Paris restaurants has little choice but to fly this product to France.

When transporting goods, firms must also consider possible

damage to or deterioration of goods. Packaging may help to reduce damage and deterioration, for example, if vacuum packs are used.

Retailing

Retailers are intermediaries in the distribution of products to customers. They are responsible for the sale of final products to the consumer. They can have a major role to play because they have the ability to reach huge numbers of consumers, in different markets over a wide area. Examples of retailers include:

- supermarkets, selling mainly food products, fast-moving products and products with a short SHELF LIFE such as Sainsbury's, Tesco and Asda in the UK;
- superstores or hypermarkets, which are large stores often found on the outskirts of town selling a range of products under one roof, such as PC World, B&Q and Marks & Spencer;
- multiple shop organisations, which are businesses with a number of stores or a group of specialist shops dealing with a particular group of products, such as Oddbins, the wine, spirits and beer merchants and The Carphone Warehouse, the mobile phone retailer;
- department stores, which are large stores found in city centres selling a variety of different goods, such as Harrods in London or Debenhams;
- the Co-operative Group in the UK which has a variety of retail stores including food shops, travel agents and pharmacies;
- independent retailers, such as newsagents, local food stores or specialist retailers in sound systems for example;
- online retailers, that sell products only via the internet.

Direct marketing

Direct marketing takes place when sales occur without the use of intermediaries being involved. For consumers, this involves being bale to make purchases from their home. This type of marketing has advantages for businesses as there are no intermediaries to reduce profits. The producer is able to control its own marketing and can reach customers who may not have been reached through shops. Direct marketing can take a number of forms:

- The Internet. Customers can order and purchase goods online via sites on the Internet. This is dealt with in the unit titled 'E-commerce'.
- Direct mail. This involves sending promotional materials to people's homes. Consumers then place orders and receive products at their home address. This is dealt with in the unit titled 'Promotion'. It allows businesses to target customers and provide detailed information about products, although people often resent direct mail and the fact that businesses have their personal details.
- Direct response advertisements. These are advertisements placed in newspapers and magazines or on television and radio. Consumers fill in a coupon or make a call to purchase the product.
- Direct selling. This is where sales are made directly to people in their homes. It is dealt with in the unit titled 'Promotion'.
- Mail order catalogues. These involve a range of products being included in a catalogue, which people can read through at home and place orders via the phone or in writing, for when example ordering from the Next Directory.

KNOWLEDGE

1. Explain why it is important for businesses to have goods available for sale (a) at the right price and (b) at the right time.
2. What is the difference between a zero level channel of distribution and a two level channel of distribution?
3. Explain why a mail order catalogue is an example of direct marketing.
4. What is the difference between a retailer and a wholesaler?
5. What services do retailers provide to consumers?
6. What services do wholesalers provide to retailers?
7. What factors determine which channel of distribution is used by a manufacturer?
8. What channels of distribution might there be in producer markets?
9. Why are distribution targets important for achieving marketing objectives?
10. What is the difference between direct mailing and direct marketing.
11. Why might a business be reluctant to use direct mailing?
12. Explain four trends in retailing and their effect on business.

KEYTERMS

Agent or broker – an intermediary which arranges contracts for the sale of products between a supplier and a customer.
Break-bulk – dividing a larger quantity of goods ordered from a supplier and selling them in smaller quantities to customers. A key function of retailers and wholesalers is to break-bulk.
Direct marketing – selling by manufacturers direct to consumers without passing through retailers or wholesalers.
Distribution channel – the path taken by a product as it goes from manufacturer to the ultimate customer.
Distribution targets – goals set by a business for future sales of goods, for instance, through particular channels of distribution.
Marketing intermediary – a business or individual which acts as a link between the producer and customer.
Retailer – a type of business which buys goods from manufacturers and wholesalers and sells them, typically in smaller quantities and in a place convenient to the buyer, to customers.
Wholesaler – a type of business which buys goods from manufacturers and sells them in smaller quantities to retailers.
Shelf life – the average length of time it takes for a product to be sold, once it has been displayed by a retailer.

Trends

Retailing and direct selling have changed greatly in the last 20 years. Some of the main trends include:

- the enormous growth in e-commerce, ordering goods online via the Internet, and making use of online services such as banking and searching for quotes;
- the development of large, American-type shopping centres such as the MetroCentre in Gateshead, The Mall in Bristol and The Trafford Centre in Manchester. They contain a variety of shops, restaurants and services such as theatre booking in one place;
- the use of call centres to sell products such as insurance and airline tickets and deal with customer issues, such as telephone or computer information;
- the development of retail parks such as Fosse Park near Leicester, which are usually found on edge of town or city sites and contain large superstores, supermarkets and restaurant chain stores. They allow customers to park easily and purchase from a number of stores on one site
- changes in the selling patterns of supermarkets, including selling non-food items, later opening hours and own-brand products. The Co-operative has also opened late stores to allow shopping at more convenient times;
- the setting up of charity shops, such as Age Concern, and discount stores selling cheap products, such as The Works which sells stationery and books;
- the diversification of services offered by retailers, including Tesco selling insurance, Marks & Spencer offering financial services and petrol stations selling coffee and microwave meals;
- the growth of digital television shopping channels, such as QVC.

Case Study: Sunny side of the street

Kamil Soud is the proprietor of Matrix Mobiles a business selling mobile phones through their website cheaphonesonline.co.uk. 'With e-retailing you are always fighting to provide the lowest price, so I thought it might be good to get a shop' explains Soud.

'I could tell from the traffic on my website what type of people bought from us', Soud said and he had considered setting up in Brighton, but had some strong reservations, 'Brighton was just not right for that client group. There are a lot of lifestyle businesses which are set up there which really never make enough money to survive, so there is a high turnover of businesses, but they drive the cost of shops up,' he explained.

Not only is 'location, location, location' the retailing mantra - but renting a shop on the wrong side of the street can be the difference between healthy profits and commercial disaster. This is where the big multiples have the edge. They spend thousands of pounds analysing local retailing environments before deciding where to locate. In particular, they use software that enables them to compare their knowledge of their existing customers with the demographic profile of a new investment area.

Until recently, it has been very difficult – and very expensive – for a new, small independent trader to match this expertise. Consequently, a large proportion of independent retailers close in their first year of trading. And the mistake of many, perhaps most, is that good ideas are ruined by opening in the wrong place.

To help him with his decision about where to open a shop Soud employed the services of a business called Cartogen. They did an analysis of the areas where he had thought about opening a shop. As any business advisor will say, saving a firm from making a bad decision is just as important as helping one make a good choice. And retailers that understand much more about their potential locations are likely to make much better commercial decisions.

Cartogen gives clients a clear indication of the mix of customer types within a catchment area, their behaviour and purchasing habits. Demographic data such as age, ethnicity, family structure, employment status and housing type in any location is held on the database, along with behavioural information indicating the local population's lifestyle and spending habits. The database also provides information on potential competitors.

The service is offered across commercial retailing sectors - including bars, cafés, restaurants, health clubs and salons. 'It works for all sectors, especially for customer profiling information,' says Kennedy. But what makes the service particularly attractive is its affordability – a basic survey costs just £95, rising to £450 or £750 for more comprehensive information. Cartogen is keeping its charges low in the hope that initial surveys will lead to continuing retail consultancy services.

In the end Matrix Mobiles decided not to open a shop in Brighton after receiving advice from Cartogen. Paul Jukes is managing director of Vivid Design & Print, one of Cartogen's first customers. 'It's great,' he says. 'I moved into my premises two years ago.' But he remained concerned about the quality of his local market analysis, which he admits was "amateurish'. 'Cartogen checked all the area for me to check that my research was correct,' explains Jukes. As a result, Jukes is able to commit more strongly to his existing marketing strategy, knowing that he chose the correct location for his business.

Source: adapted from *The Independent* 3.7.2007.

(a) Identify the distribution channels:
(i) currently used by Matrix Mobiles; (3 marks)
(ii) under consideration by Matrix Mobiles. (3 marks)

(b) Explain TWO reasons why finding the most suitable method of distribution is so important for Matrix Mobiles (6 marks)

(c) Examine the factors influencing Matrix Mobile's decision to open a shop. (8 marks)

(d) Discuss whether Matrix Mobile should open its own shop. (10 marks)

23 Branding

What is a brand?

A BRAND is a name, term, sign, symbol, design or any other feature that allows consumers to identify the goods and services of a business and to differentiate them from those of competitors. So a recognised brand might be:

- the use of the 'Mc' name by McDonald's in its products such as the Egg McMuffin or Chicken McNugget;
- the Nike 'swoosh' logo;
- the three stripes design on Adidas sports products;
- the use of the colour orange in promotions by the Orange communications company or B&Q;
- the 'tune' which accompanies references to Asda supermarkets in television advertisements.

A brand might be one product, a family or range of products or the actual business itself. So, for example, a Nestlé KitKat is an individual product produced by Nestlé. KitKat Chunky and KitKat Chunky Peanut Butter are also part of the KitKat family. Nestlé is the name of the company which produces KitKats, other confectionery products such as Milky Bar and Smarties, and foods such as breakfast cereals.

Brands are important assets for businesses which have them. They will generate high revenue, promotion and repeat purchases. Sometimes they can be sold at a high price. For example, when Nestlé bought Rowntree for $2.5 billion in 1988 it acquired a number of brands including KitKat and After Eight.

BRAND NAMES are the parts of the brand that can be spoken, such as the name of the product, e.g. Heinz Baked Beans or Barbie doll. A BRAND MARK is the design or symbol used in the brand, such as the apple used on Apple Macintosh computers. It is possible to protect the use of a TRADEMARK by copyright. A company might use its TRADE NAME as a brand, such as Virgin, Disney or Starbucks. In some cases the company name might be as well known as its products or even more well known. The name Sony would be familiar to many people, as might its Sony Vaio range of laptop computers, but many other products in its organisation might not be so well known. Table 1 shows the most valuable UK grocery brands in 2007 and Table 2 shows the world's top ten brands.

Developing a brand

There is a number of important features in developing and maintaining a successful brand for a business.

Being the first or filling a gap It is suggested that successful brands are often the first in the market. This might mean being the first products to reach target customers or to use new technology. It might also mean taking advantage of a gap in the market or new developments. Examples may include financial services sold over the Internet or organic or environmentally friendly food brands.

Choosing the right brand name It is important to choose an effective brand name. It should:

- be easy to pronounce and spell, especially if a company is operating in international markets, for example Lego;
- be short and to the point so it is easy to remember, for example, Nike;
- indicate something about the benefits of the product or its uses, for example Flora Pro-active;
- help the customer to identify when buying, for example Shout magazine
- be distinctive, for example Virgin;
- be different from other brand names, so that it can be registered as a trademark.

Finding a USP Brands which are successful have a unique selling

Table 1: The most valuable UK grocery brands in 2007

1.	Coca-Cola
2.	Warburtons
3.	Cadbury Dairy Milk
4.	Lucozade
5.	Hovis
6.	Nescafé
7.	Robinsons
8.	Andrex
9.	Heinz Baked Beanz
10.	Pepsi

Source: adapted from www.intangiblebusiness.com.

Table 2: The world's top ten brands.

1. Google
2. General Electric
3. Microsoft
4. Coca-Cola
5. China Mobile
6. Marlboro
7. Wal-Mart
8. Citi
9. IBM
10. Toyota

Source: adapted from bbcnews.co.uk april 2008.

point or proposition (USP). This is what makes them different from other products and what makes people want to buy them. The USP take in many forms. For example, a Volvo car might have an attribute, such as being 'safe for passengers'. The Volvo might have a benefit to the customer, such as not breaking down because it is reliable. A Cartier watch might have a value for customers, such as 'prestige'. A pair of Vans trainers might appeal to teenagers' personalities by having 'street credibility'.

Positioning the brand A brand must be positioned in the right place in the market for it to be successful. A business, for example, might sell a 'high quality' brand. It is more likely to be successful if the target market is people with high incomes looking for a superior product rather than those looking for a bargain. The marketing mix of the business is important to positioning the brand. So, for example, high quality jewellery is likely to be:

- a product manufactured from high quality materials and design;
- sold at a premium price;
- promoted in a way that reflects the status of the product;
- sold in places that reflect the product's features, such as high quality jewellery stores.

Brand protection Brands must be protected by the use of trademarks and copyright. Brands are bought because of the features that customers perceive them to have. However, if cheap, counterfeit copies flood the market, brands may loose their credibility. Also, if all businesses were able to copy the designer logo of a well known brand, then it would lose its effectiveness.

Types of brand

Brands can come in a number of forms.

Manufacturer brands MANUFACTURER BRANDS are brands created by the producers of goods and services. The goods or services bear the producer's name. Examples might be Kellogg's Corn Flakes, Gillette razors or Dell computers. The manufacturers are involved in the production, distribution, promotion and pricing decisions of these products.

Own-label brands OWN-LABEL BRANDS (also known as DISTRIBUTOR or PRIVATE BRANDS) are products which are manufactured for wholesalers or retailers by other businesses. But the wholesalers and retailers sell the products under their own name. Examples of products containing the retailer's name

Question 1.

Table 3: Most valuable brands

2007 Rank	2006 Rank	Brand	Country of origin	Sector	2007 Brand value ($m)	Change in brand value
1	1	Coca-Cola	US	Beverages	65,324	-3%
2	2	Microsoft	US	Computer Software	58,709	3%
3	3	IBM	US	Computer Services	57,091	2%
4	4	GE	US	Diversified	51,569	5%
5	6	Nokia	Finland	Consumer Electronics	33,696	12%
6	7	Toyota	Japan	Automotive	32,070	15%
7	5	Intel	US	Computer Hardware	30,954	-4%
8	9	McDonald's	US	Restaurants	29,398	7%
9	8	Disney	US	Media	29,210	5%
10	10	Mercedes	Germany	Automotive	23,568	8%
11	11	Citi	US	Financial Services	23,443	9%
12	13	Hewlett-Packard	US	Computer Hardware	22,197	9%
13	15	BMW	Germany	Automotive	21,612	10%
14	12	Marlboro	US	Tobacco	21,283	0%
15	14	American Express	US	Financial Services	20,827	5%
16	16	Gillette	US	Personal Care	20,415	4%
17	17	Louis Vuitton	France	Luxury	20,321	15%
18	18	Cisco	US	Computer Services	19,099	9%
19	19	Honda	Japan	Automotive	17,998	6%
20	24	Google	US	Internet Services	17,837	44%

Source: adapted from www.interbrand.com.

(a) Describe the main changes in the most valuable brands between 2006 and 2007.

(b) Suggest reasons to account for
(i) companies that have changed rank;
(ii) companies that have not changed rank.

include Tesco baked beans or Marks & Spencer food. Sometimes the retailer will create its own brand name, for example, Florance and Fred clothes sold at Tesco. These products allow a retailer to buy from the cheapest manufacturer, reducing its cost. It will hope to promote its own products effectively to shoppers in its outlets.

Generic brands Some GENERIC BRANDS are products that only contain the name of the actual product category rather than the company or product name. Examples might be aluminium foil, carrots or aspirin. These products are usually sold at lower prices than branded products. They tend to account for a small percentage of all sales.

Branding strategies

Individual branding A business may attempt to brand individual products with individual brand names. An example might be the large number of washing powder brands sold by Procter & Gamble and Unilever including Daz, Bold, Tide, Dreft, Omo, Radion, Surf, Persil and Ariel. The main advantage of this is that individual brands can be developed for particular market segments. Also, failure by one brand will not have an adverse effect on another.

Family branding Family branding is where a business has a brand name which includes a number of different products. For example, Cadbury's has the brand name 'Crunchie' which is used on the original crunchie bar and which has also been extended to include crunchie ice cream, crunchie cheese cakes and crunchie snack size. The advantage of this branding method is that the benefits of the brand name are spread across a wider variety of products.

Corporate branding CORPORATE BRANDING is also known as COMPANY BRANDING. It occurs when a business' name is used as the brand name. So, for example, Heinz uses its business name to brand its products including baked beans, spaghetti and soups. The advantage of this strategy is that marketing campaigns can be spread across a range of products and a business can gain marketing economies of scale. Also, a customer might have bought one product and, as a result of confidence in the brand name, might buy other products.

Brand extensions or stretching BRAND EXTENSIONS are when an existing brand name is used for a new brand in a similar market. Examples of this might include Coca-Cola producing Diet Coke, Cola-Cola with lemon or 'light versions' of beers. BRAND STRETCHING is when an existing brand name is taken into unrelated markets. An example might be the Virgin brand name which has been used for a variety of businesses operations, including music shops, trains, financial services, travel and holidays. The advantage of this strategy is that new businesses may find it easier to establish new products.

Question 2.

Liverpool nut company, Trigon, was looking to rebrand in association with the business magazine en and MAT:designers. Three designs were shortlisted.

- MCN Food Company Limited. Trigon food products are mainly nuts. But it was important that any brand did not restrict future development of products. So an abbreviation of the warning on some nuts products - may contain nuts - seemed perfect. This was used as a logo which gave a strong corporate identity. There was also an element of humour which could be exploited in promotion.
- Lightly Salted Food Company. To add value, the word food rather than snacks was incorporated into the name. However, it was important to include a clue to Trigon's original business. So a description of the flavour was used - 'lightly salted'. Animals eating nuts were to be used on stationery to create a sense of humour.
- Elephant - The Big Snack Company. An elephant is a large, likeable animal that is identified with nuts. It gave an abstract solution. The design and logo proposed looked as if they had been developed over the years on snack packets. This gave a sense of history to the design and to the company.

Source: adapted from en.

(a) What is meant by rebranding?
(b) What factors have influenced the new brand of the business?
(c) Which new brand do you think the business might choose? Explain your answer.

Reasons for branding

There is a number of reasons why businesses use branding.

- To create brand loyalty. Consumers often have a high degree of loyalty to popular, well established, brands. In many markets it can be very difficult for firms to compete unless they have a strong brand identity.
- To differentiate the product. It is especially important, in markets where products are fairly similar, that a firm's own products can be clearly distinguished from others. A clear brand identity can help to achieve this.
- To gain flexibility when making pricing decisions. The greater the loyalty of consumers to a particular brand, the more room for manoeuvre a firm will have in its pricing decisions. A survey by Business Marketing Services found that consumers were reluctant to switch from well known brands in the hotel, car hire, computer and transatlantic flights markets. For example, in the car hire market pricing discounts of over 20 per cent were required to persuade consumers to switch from Hertz or Avis to one of the lesser known companies.
- To help recognition. A product with a strong brand identity is likely to be instantly recognised by most consumers. This may mean that consumers trust the product and are therefore more willing to buy it. Some

brand names are used to describe whole classes of products, such as Sellotape and Hoover.
- To develop a brand image. It is argued that customers respond to brand images with which they identify. For example, ice-cream eaters may identify to a greater or lesser extent with either the alternative image of Ben and Jerry's or the rural identity of Loseley Farm or the implied luxury of Haagen-Dazs. Some consumers respond to brands that allow them to pursue multiple goals. Range Rover, for example, stresses that its vehicles not only allow the user to escape to remote places, but also to do so in comfort. When consumers identify strongly with a brand or have a strong desire to be associated with a brand, they are often prepared to go to great lengths, including paying significant price premiums, in order to get the brand of their choice.

Branding in a global market

Branding can be of particular importance to businesses operating in global markets for a number of reasons.
- Brands with international appeal can be marketed in a range of different countries. For example, Coca-Cola is a brand name recognized throughout the world. This enables the product to be marketed throughout the world with only limited modifications to its marketing strategy. Significant marketing based economies of scale are associated with this
- Consumers with strong brand loyalties are able to travel around the world without missing out on opportunities to consume their favourite products. An individual who likes to eat Big Macs, for example, would find very few major cities in the world where he/she was unable to consume this product. Given the frequency and distance of international travel commonly undertaken by consumers this can significantly increase sales.

Problems with branding

Branding might not always be a successful strategy for some businesses for a number of reasons.
- As explained earlier, some products are generic. This can make it difficult to establish an effective brand.
- Not all markets are suited to brands. It has been suggested, for example, that people buy wine based on the name of the grape or the region where wine is produced rather than on the brand name.
- It can be expensive to promote and maintain a brand. Establishing a successful brand in a competitive market can be very costly. Small business may not be able to afford this.

KEYTERMS

Brand - a name, term, sign, symbol, design or any other feature that allows consumers to identify a firm's goods and services and differentiate them from those of competitors.
Brand extensions - when the brand name is used for new products in related markets.
Brand mark - the design or symbol used in the brand.
Brand name - the part of the brand that can be spoken, such as the name of the product.
Brand stretching - when the brand name is used for new products in unrelated markets.
Corporate brand or company brand - when the name of the business is used as the brand name.
Family branding - where a business has a brand name which includes a number of different products
Generic brands - products that only contain the name of the product category rather than the company or product name.
Manufacturer brands - brands created by the producers of goods and services.
Own-label or distributor or private brands - products which are manufactured for wholesalers or retailers by other businesses.
Trademark - the sign, symbol or other feature of a business that can be protected by copyright.
Trade name - the registered name of the business, which can sometimes be used as a brand name.

KNOWLEDGE

1. Identify five features that a brand might have.
2. Why might a brand be worth a lot to a business?
3. When might a business be able to measure the value of its brands?
4. Suggest five features of an effective brand name.
5. Why is brand protection important?
6. State three types of brand.
7. Suggest four types of brand strategy.
8. State five benefits of branding to a business.
9. State three situations where branding may not be effective.

Case Study: Hewlett-Packard

By 2008 Hewlett-Packard (HP) had regained its position as the world's biggest seller of personal computers. Just two years earlier critics were clamouring for the company to get out of the PC business altogether. Credit for this transformation went to Chief Executive Officer Mark Hurd, who told his executives that Hewlett-Packard Co. had to stop building and marketing the PC as if it were a commodity. Designing PCs that consumers actually wanted was, of course, the starting point. Besides making them more attractive, HP included such features as the ability to check emails and appointments without wasting precious minutes booting up.

The marketing team then went about pitching Hewlett Packard Personal Computers (HPPCs) as a personal reflection of consumers' desires and needs. Hence the slogan: 'The computer is personal again.' Last summer the company rolled out ads showing hip-hop mogul Shawn 'Jay-Z' Carter mixing music and planning tours using an HPPC. Rising sales and market share show that customers increasingly see HP's products, particularly its laptops, as cooler, hipper, and just plain better than Dell Inc.'s.

Hurd also has focused on HP's sprawling global operations, using the same marketing strategy it is employing in the US to ramp up consumer sales in emerging markets. In Russia, for example, HP has recently started mass advertising and selling PCs through retailers.

Burberry

When British soccer fans began donning Burberry hats en masse about five years ago, it became clear that the fashion icon had lost some of its prestige. The same happened when a British soap opera star appeared in the tabloids with her new baby swaddled head to toe in the iconic plaid pattern. When holiday sales tanked in 2004, Burberry knew that it was on its way to becoming overexposed. It was time to retrench. Since then, Burberry has walked a careful line, moving beyond plaid without disrespecting its fashion history.

In 2006, to mark its 150th anniversary, Burberry mined its design archives and launched the Icons collection, comprising luxury handbags, shoes, boots, trench coats, and small leather goods. The collection combined the classic Burberry look with such flourishes as quilted linings. Customers applauded. 'It's a blend of old and new, functional yet fashionable,' said Chief Financial Officer Stacey Cartright.

Meanwhile, Burberry began to do away with lower-end products, such as hats and scarves that retailed for less than $50. Originally these were aimed at winning younger shoppers who would trade up later on. But Burberry decided that they undermined the brand and were too easy for counterfeiters to copy.

So far, the new direction is paying off. Burberry shares were up almost 40 per cent in 2007. With its brand on the mend, Burberry is branching out into jewellery, such as bracelets that employ leather to mirror the brand's style.

Source: adapted from www.businessweek.com.

(a) What type of brand best describes (i) Burberry and (ii) Hewlett-Packard? (4 marks)

(b) Explain how the branding strategies being used by Burberry and Hewlett-Packard can benefit the businesses. (6 marks)

(c) Examine why each brand had suffered damage in recent years. (10 marks)

(d) Discuss the extent to which branding is likely to be successful for Burberry and Hewlett-Packard. (12 marks)

24 The market

Demand

Demand is the amount of a product that consumers are willing and able to purchase at any given price. Demand is concerned with what consumers are actually able to buy (what they can afford to and would buy), rather than what they would like to buy. So, for example, we could say that the demand for cars in the UK market at an average price of £9,000 might be 130,000 a year.

Table 1 shows a **demand schedule** for button mushrooms. These figures can be used to draw a **demand** curve as in Figure 1 In practice, demand **curves** are not a straight line, but are usually drawn in this way for simplicity.

The curve shows the quantity of a good or service that will be demanded at any given price. As with nearly all such curves, it slopes downwards from left to right. This is because the quantity demanded is likely to be higher at lower prices and lower at higher prices – **ceteris paribus** (assuming no other things change). In Table 1 more button mushrooms are bought at a price of £0.50 than at a price of £2.50.

Table 1: The demand schedule for button mushrooms

Price per kilo (£)	Quantity demanded (000 kilos)
0.50	100
1.00	80
1.50	60
2.00	40
2.50	20

A change in the price of a good or service will lead to a change in the quantity demanded. This is shown on the demand curve as a movement along (up or down) the curve. In Figure 1, a fall in price from £1.50 to £1, for example, will result in a movement along the curve from point X to point Y.

This will result in a rise in the quantity demanded from 60,000 to 80,000 kilos. The demand curve itself has not moved from its original position. Price changes only lead to an **extension** (rise) or **contraction** (fall) in the quantity demanded.

Changes in demand

As well as price, there is a number of other factors which might affect the demand for a product. Unlike price, a change in any of these factors might cause the whole demand curve to **shift**. This might result in an increase in the demand for a good. The result is that more of a product will be demanded at any given price. Alternatively, it may result in a fall in demand, so less is demanded at any given price.

Income It is reasonable to assume that the higher the incomes of consumers, the more they will be able to buy. When incomes in the country as a whole increase, the demand for products will increase. However, the rise in income is unlikely to be the same for everyone. Some consumers will have large increases in income. Others will find that their incomes do not increase at all. Thus, demand for a product will only increase if the incomes of those consumers buying the product increase.

Assume that consumers of DVDs have had a rise in their

Figure 1: The demand curve for button mushrooms

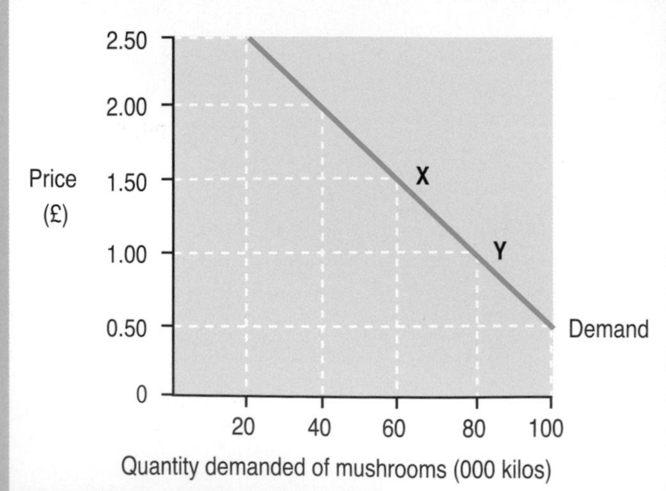

Figure 2: The effect of changes in income on the demand curve for DVDs

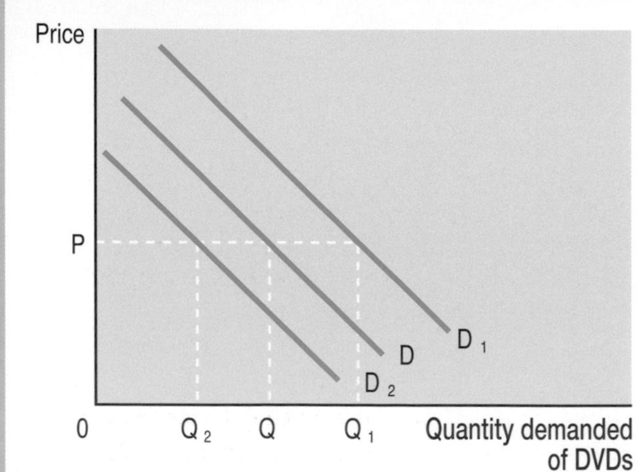

income. The demand for DVDs increases as a result. This is shown in Figure 2 as a shift to the right of the demand curve from D to D_1. The demand for DVDs has increased at any given price level. In Figure 2, demand has risen from OQ to OQ_1. On the other hand, if consumers' incomes were to fall, this would cause the demand for DVDs to fall at any given price. The result of this would be a shift of the demand curve to the left from D to D_2 in Figure 2. Demand will have fallen from OQ to OQ_2.

The price of and demand for other goods The demand for one product often depends on the price of and demand for another. For example, the demand for one brand of tea bags can be influenced by the price of other brands. A rise in the price of one brand is likely to cause an increase in the demand for others. This is often true of products which have close **substitutes**, such as canned drinks. A fall in the price of films online or on digital television may result in a shift in demand from D to D_1 in Figure 2. More online films may be bought if prices fell, leading perhaps to reduced demand for DVDs.

Complementary goods are those which are used together. Examples include cars and petrol, and DVD players and DVDs. An increase in the price of one will affect the demand for the other. A fall in the price of DVD players may lead to a shift in demand from D to D_2 in Figure 2. More players would be bought and so the quantity demanded of DVDs would also rise.

Changes in tastes and fashions Some products are subject to changes in tastes and fashions. Skateboards, for example, were bought in huge quantities in the1970s. They then went out of fashion for a number of years only to come back into favour again. It is more usual for a company to stop producing products which have gone out of fashion altogether. Other products have shown more gradual changes in demand. In recent years, the demand for red meat has gradually declined as tastes have changed, often in response to health concerns. This has caused the demand curve for red meat to shift to the left. This means that at any given price, less red meat is now demanded than in previous years. The growth in DVD sales over the last decade has shifted the demand curve to the right.

Changes in population As well as changes in population levels, changes in the structure of population can affect demand. The increase in the proportion of over 65s in the population of Western industrialised countries will have an effect upon the demand for a number of products. They include winter-sun holidays, sheltered housing and leisure facilities. This means that, other things staying the same, the demand curve for products associated with the old will shift to the right, with more being demanded at any given price.

Advertising Successful advertising and promotion will shift the demand curve to the right, with more being demanded at any given price. A successful advertising campaign for DVDs could have this effect.

Legislation Government legislation can affect the demand for a product. For example, a law requiring all cyclists to wear helmets would lead to an increase in the demand for cycling helmets at any given price.

This section has examined the market demand for goods and services. This is a summing or totalling of the demand curves for individual businesses' products. So, for example, the market demand curve for DVDs, which has been much discussed in this unit, is a totalling of the individual demand curves of all the businesses which produce DVDs.

Supply

SUPPLY is the amount of a product which suppliers will offer to the market at a given price. The higher the price of a particular good or service, the more that will be offered to the market. For example, the amount of button mushrooms supplied to a market in any given week may be as shown in Table 3.

These figures have been plotted onto a graph in Figure 3, which shows the supply curve for button mushrooms. The supply curve slopes up from left to right. This is because at

Question 1.

Table 2 shows the monthly demand schedule based on the average price of ice creams at a local theme park. It has been predicted that the following changes to the market will occur:

- incomes will rise so that there will be 500 more bought at each level;
- the prices of substitute goods (ice lollies etc.) are likely to rise so that there would be another 500 bought at each price level.

(a) Draw the original demand curve from the figures in the table.
(b) Show the combined effect on the demand curve of the changes in the market.

Table 2: The demand schedule for ice cream at a local theme park

Price (£)	Quantity demanded
0.80	2,000
0.90	1,600
1.00	1,200
1.10	800
1.20	400

Table 3 The supply schedule for button mushrooms

Price per kilo (£)	Quantity supplied (000 kilos)
0.50	20
1.00	40
1.50	60
2.00	80
2.50	100

Figure 3: The supply curve for button mushrooms

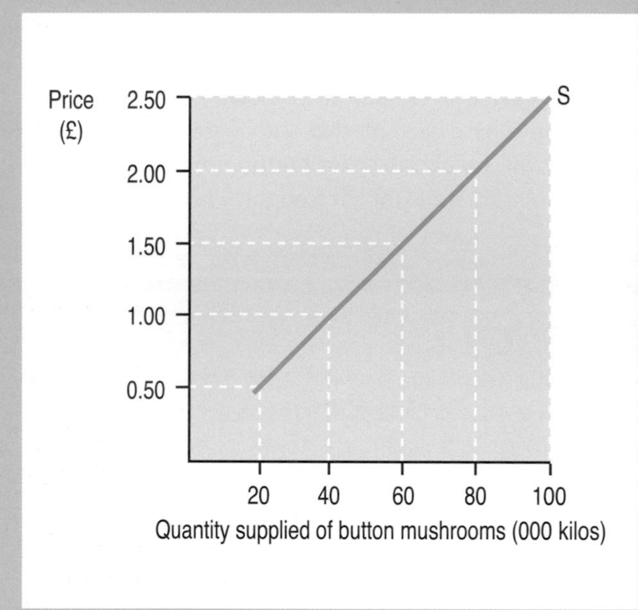

Figure 4: Shifts in the supply curve

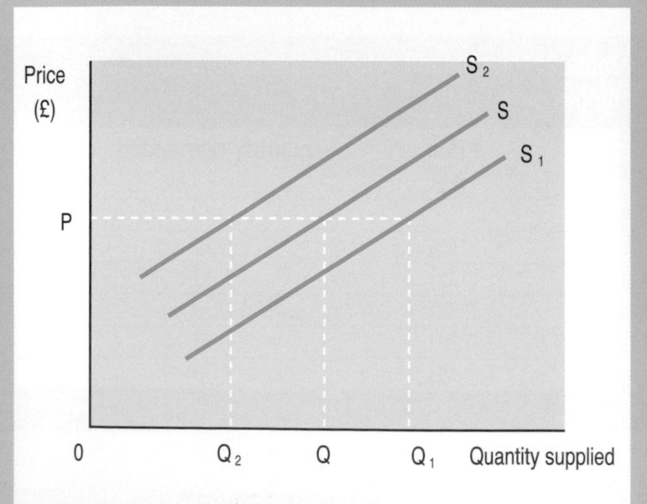

higher prices a greater quantity will be supplied to the market and at lower prices less will be supplied.

A change in price will cause a movement either up or down the supply curve. The curve will not change its position assuming that all other factors remain the same. There is a number of other factors that may affect supply other than price. Changes in these factors will cause the whole supply curve to shift.

Costs of production A fall in the costs of production due, for example, to new technology will mean that more can be offered at the same price. This will cause the supply curve to shift to the right as shown in Figure 4, from S to S_1. A rise in the costs of production would cause the supply curve to shift to the left, from S to S_2. A rise in raw material costs or wage costs could lead to such a shift.

Changes in production Where it is possible to shift production from one area to another, the price of other products can influence the quantity supplied. For example, many farmers are able to produce a wide range of crops on their land. A rise in the price of broccoli, might encourage farmers not only to produce more broccoli, but less of other crops such as turnips. The broccoli price change has affected the quantity of turnips supplied to the market. So a rise in the price of broccoli would shift the supply curve for turnips to the left, in Figure 4 from S to S_2.

Legislation A new anti-pollution law might increase production costs causing the supply curve to shift to the left. Similarly, a tax on a product would shift the supply curve to the left.

The objectives of firms Firms might seek to increase their profit levels and their market share. This might reduce the overall level of supply as other firms are forced out of business. The result of this would be a shift of the supply curve in Figure 4 from S to S_2.

Expectations If businesses expect future prices to rise they may restrict current supplies. This would be shown as a shift to the left of the supply curve in Figure 4, from S to S_2. Similarly, if businesses expect worsening trading conditions they might reduce current supply levels in anticipation of this.

The weather The weather can influence the supply of agricultural products. For example, in the UK a late spring frost can reduce the supply of strawberries, from say S to S_2 in Figure 4.

It was shown earlier in this unit that the market demand curve is a summing of individual firms' demand curves. Similarly, the market supply curve is an adding up of the supply curves of individual firms.

Price and output determination

How does the interaction of demand and supply determine the market price and output? Market prices are set where the plans of consumers are matched with those of suppliers. The point at which the demand and supply curves intersect is known as the EQUILIBRIUM PRICE. This is shown in Figure 5. The equilibrium price of button mushrooms is £1.50. The figure is drawn from Tables 1 and 3. At this price 60,000 mushrooms will be produced.

Changes in demand and supply

Shifts in the demand or supply curves will cause a change in the market price.

Changes in demand Assume that there has been a rise in income which has resulted in an increase in demand. The effect of this, as shown in Figure 6a, is a shift in the demand curve to the right, all things remaining the same, from D to D_2. This leads to an increase in quantity demanded from OQ to OQ_1. This increase in demand raises the equilibrium price from OP to OP_1. As a result, the quantity supplied extends as well, as producers will supply more at the higher price.

If demand falls, due to lower incomes, from D to D2, this leads to a fall in quantity demanded from OQ to OQ_2. The equilibrium price falls from OP to OP_2 and at this lower price suppliers will supply less.

Figure 5: The demand for and supply of button mushrooms

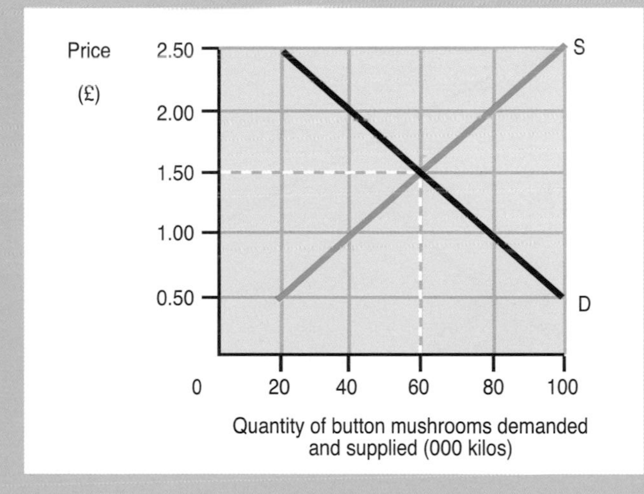

Changes in supply Figure 6b shows the effect on the equilibrium price of changes in supply. An increase in supply may have been as a result of lower labour costs. This shifts the supply curve from S to S_1. The equilibrium price falls from OP to OP_1 as the supply curve shifts from S to S_1. Consumers are more willing and able to buy goods at the lower price and so the quantity demanded rises as well from OQ to OQ_1.

If supply is cut, the supply curve moves to the left from S to S_2. The equilibrium price rises from OP to OP_2. Consumers are less willing to buy products at this higher price and so the quantity demanded falls from OQ to OQ_2.

Excess demand and excess supply

EXCESS DEMAND occurs when the demand for a product is greater than its supply. This can be illustrated using the demand for and supply of mushrooms shown in Figure 7. At a price of £0.50 per kilo, 100,000 kilos of button mushrooms are demanded, but only 20,000 kilos are supplied by businesses. This means that there is an excess demand of 80,000 kilos (100,000 - 20,000). This excess demand will result in a shortage of mushrooms, with many consumers being left disappointed.

EXCESS SUPPLY occurs when the supply of a product is greater than the demand for it. In Figure 7, at a price of £2.50, 100,000 kilos of button mushrooms are supplied by businesses, but only 20,000 are demanded. This means that there is an excess supply of 80,000 kilos of button mushrooms. This excess supply will result in a surplus (sometimes referred to as a glut)

Figure 6: The effect on equilibrium price of an increase in demand and supply

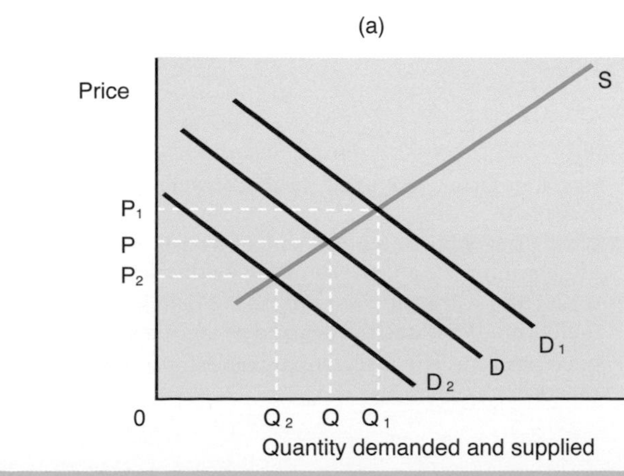

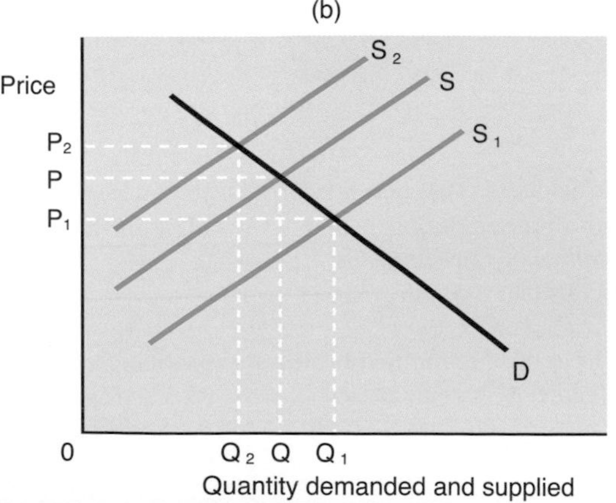

of button mushrooms. This will mean a huge quantity of unsold button mushrooms for businesses, with no immediate buyers.

It can be seen in Figure 7 that it is only at the equilibrium price, £1.50, that there is no excess demand or supply. At this price all products supplied to the market are purchased and all buyers able to afford the price of £1.50 per kilo will be able to purchase their intended quantity.

Figure 7: The excess demand for and supply of button mushrooms

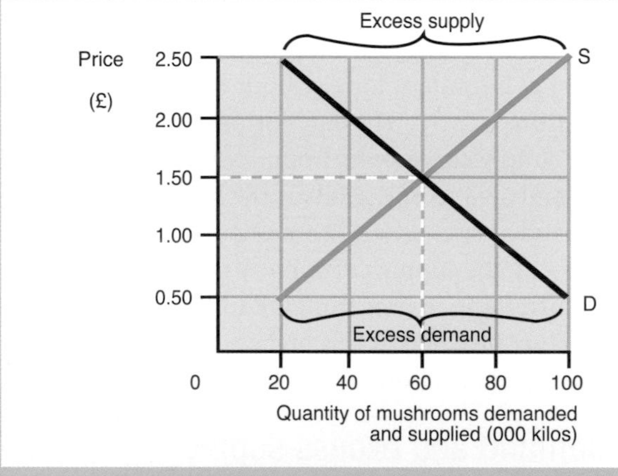

KEY TERMS

Excess demand – a situation where the quantity demanded of a product is greater than the quantity supplied at a given price.
Excess supply – a situation where the quantity supplied of a product is greater than the quantity demanded at a given price.
External environment – the factors outside a business that may influence its decisions.
Supply – the quantity of products which suppliers make available to the market at any given price.
Equilibrium price – the price at which the quantity demanded is equal to the quantity supplied.

Question 2.

(a) What is the equilibrium price of organic broccoli?
(b) Explain the effect that the following factors will have on: (i) the equilibrium price of organic broccoli; (ii) the demand for organic broccoli or the supply of organic broccoli by businesses in the market.

- A reduction in the average incomes of consumers purchasing organic vegetables.
- Improved organic farming methods leading to a reduction in the cost of producing organic broccoli.
- All types of organic vegetables becoming increasingly popular with greater health consciousness amongst food consumers.
- A fall in the price of non-organic broccoli.

Figure 8: The demand curve for button mushrooms

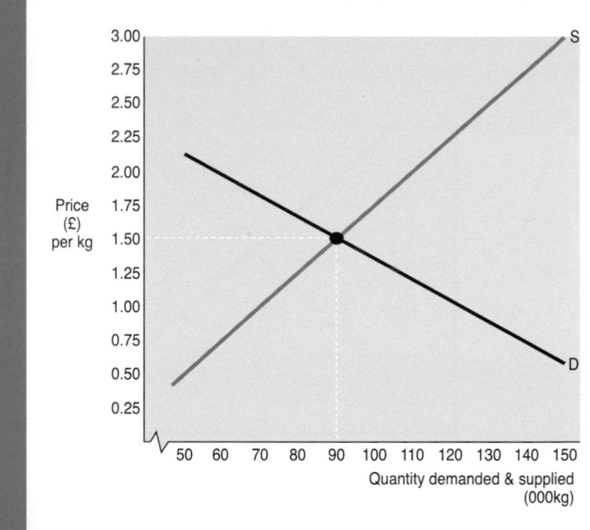

KNOWLEDGE

1. State six external factors that may affect a business's decisions.
2. What happens to the amount consumers are willing and able to buy as the price of a product falls?
3. State four factors that cause the market demand to move to the right.
4. What happens to the amount that businesses are willing to offer to the market as price increases?
5. State four factors that cause the market supply curve to shift to the left.
6. What effect will a shift in demand to the left have on equilibrium price and the supply by businesses in a market?
7. What effect will a shift in supply to the right have on equilibrium price and the demand by consumers in a market?
8. What problems will excess supply cause for some businesses in a market?

Case Study: The price of oil, 1990-2003

Figure 9 shows how the price of oil has fluctuated between 1990 and 2003. The price of oil on world markets is affected by many factors, as shown in the Figure.

One of the factors is the actions of OPEC, the Organisation of Petroleum Exporting Countries. This is an organisation made up of countries around the world which produce oil and sell it to businesses and other organisations in other countries. It has eleven members including Iran, Iraq, Saudi Arabia, Venezuela, Nigeria and Libya, whose economies rely heavily on income from oil exports. OPEC's primary mission is to 'achieve stable prices which are fair and reasonable for producers and consumers.'

OPEC countries meet to agree on the amount of production and supply of oil onto the world market. For example, in February 2004 OPEC agreed to stop overproducing crude at once, and then cut quotas by 1 million barrels. One problem with this is that countries do not always agree. Even when they do, some countries go back on the agreement. Another problem is that countries producing oil who are not OPEC members, such as Russia or Norway, might expand production when OPEC is trying to cut it.

Source: adapted from OPEC website and www.cbsnews.com.

(a) Who are likely to be the (i) demanders and the (ii) suppliers of oil? (6 marks)

(b) Suggest factors which are likely to affect the (i) demand for and (ii) supply of oil in world markets. (10 marks)

(c) Explain, using examples from the data, how changes in demand and supply over the period 1990-2003 have:
(i) raised the price of oil;
(ii) reduced the price of oil. (12 marks)

(d) Assess the extent to which OPEC is likely to be able to influence the world price of oil. (12 marks)

Figure 9: Business organisations in the private sector

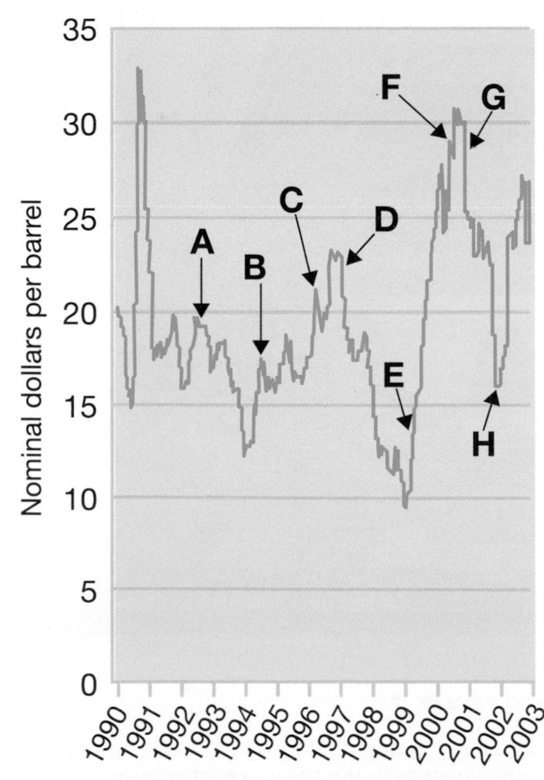

A OPEC production reaches 25.3 million barrels per day, the highest in over a decade.

B Nigerian oil workers' strike.

C Extremely cold weather in the US and Europe.

D Iraq begins exporting oil under United Nations Security Council Resolution 986.

E OPEC pledges additional production cuts for the third time since March 1998. Total pledge cuts amount to about 4.3 million barrels per day.

F USA releases 30 million barrels of oil from the Strategic Petroleum Reserve (SPR) over 30 days to bolster oil supplies, particularly heating oil in the Northeast.

G Weak world demand largely as a result of economic recession in the United States and OPEC overproduction.

H OPEC oil production cuts, unrest in Venezuela, and rising tension in the Middle East.

25 Competition and business

Markets and competition

There are many different markets in the UK. Markets might be divided by geographical boundaries, for example:

- local markets, such as the market for housing in South London;
- regional markets, such as the market for entertainment in the North West of England;
- national markets, such as the market for national newspapers in the UK;
- international markets, such as foreign exchange markets.

On the other hand they could be markets differentiated by use such as:

- highly specialised markets, such as the market for water polo playing equipment;
- non-specialised markets, such as the market for carrots.

Assessing the level of COMPETITION faced by business in a market may not always be straightforward. For example, two businesses operating on a local bus route may seem to have little competition but each other. However, they may actually face competition from other forms of transport, such as taxis, cars and trains

The degree of competition in a market will affect the **marketing mix** of a business. It will influence the:

- **prices** charged by the business;
- nature of the **products** offered by the business for sale;
- **promotion** used by the business to make consumers aware of the product and influence their spending;
- **places** where the products are for sale.

Determinants of competitiveness

Not all markets are the same. Different markets have different features and characteristics. The features and characteristics of markets are known as MARKET STRUCTURES. It is these market structures that largely determine how competitive a market is.

The number and relative size of businesses in the market In some markets, such as farming, a large number of businesses compete with each other. None of these businesses is particularly large compared to other businesses in the market. So the market share of any single business is small.

In other markets, a few businesses dominate the market, even though there might be a large number of other small firms. For example, in the UK washing powder and liquid detergent market, two businesses (Unilever and Procter & Gamble) have over 80 per cent of the market between them.

In some markets, there is only one business, a monopolist. For example, on most railway routes in the UK, there is only one train company operating a service.

The extent of barriers to entry In some markets, it is easy for a new business to set up. Many people each year set up small shops selling everything from groceries to clothes to toys. This is because the BARRIERS TO ENTRY are low. It doesn't cost much to open a shop. The amount of knowledge of the industry required is fairly little. In most cases, there are no special licences or other legal obstacles in the way. In certain markets, barriers to entry are high. In the rail transport industry or mobile telephone industry, the government gives licences to a limited number of businesses to operate. In the drug industry, newer drugs are protected by patent. This prevents other businesses from copying them.

In other markets, the costs of starting up a business are large. Car manufacturing, aeroplane production or oil refining are examples. In the perfume industry, the main companies devote a large proportion of their costs to marketing. Any new entrant then has to be able to afford to spend millions of pounds launching its new product.

Where barriers to entry are high, competition tends to be lower. One consequence of this is that businesses often compete on issues other than price. This means that they tend to emphasise the non-price elements of the marketing mix, such as promotion and place.

Potato supplier
Bank
Small cafe
Water supplier

Question 1.

(a) Explain the factors that may influence competition for the businesses in the photographs above.

The extent to which products can be differentiated In some markets, products are homogeneous. This means that they are the same whichever business produces them. Typically, there are standards to which products conform. So nine carat gold is the same quality whatever business produces it. Homogeneous products are often found in raw materials markets and in basic manufacturing, such as steel. Where products are homogenous competition tends to be largely based upon price with this element of the marketing mix emphasised.

In other markets, products differ according to which business makes them. A McDonald's meal is different from a Burger King meal. Ford cars differ from Volkswagen cars. Heineken lager is different from Budweiser lager. Individual products or product ranges can then be branded. The stronger the perceived difference, the stronger the brand. Where product differentiation is strong the non-price elements of the marketing mix such as promotion tend to be emphasised by businesses.

The knowledge that buyers and sellers possess In some markets, buyers and sellers have access to all the information they need to make rational decisions. Buyers, for instance, would be able to find out the best price in the market. Sellers would have open access to the most efficient methods of production. This is known as having perfect knowledge. Where knowledge is perfect, price is strongly emphasised in the marketing mix.

In other markets, knowledge is not available to all. One business might not be able to find out how much a rival business is charging for its products. A consumer might not know which of 20 cars will be most environmentally friendly. If there is imperfect information in the market, this can give a competitive advantage to some businesses over others. Where knowledge is imperfect businesses will tend to place a great deal of importance upon non-price elements of the marketing mix such as the product and promotion.

Degree of interrelationship In some markets, the actions of one business have no effect on another business. Businesses are independent of one another. In farming, the decision by one farmer to plant a field with carrots has no impact on a nearby farm in terms of the price it will receive or how much it produces.

In other markets, such as car production, increased sales by one business will mean reduced sales by another business if the size of the market remains the same. Businesses are then interdependent.

Legal factors Competition between businesses is generally seen as being in the best interests of customers. They can shop around between businesses offering the same or similar products for the best deal. This means that businesses have to offer what the customer wants or face closing down through lack of customers.

In contrast, monopoly is usually argued to be bad for customers. They are forced to buy from one supplier whatever the quality of the product and whatever the prices. The monopolist has enormous power over customers and acts to maximise the benefits to itself.

Monopolies, therefore, tend to be controlled by governments. In the USA, they are illegal. In the UK and the rest of the European Union they are **regulated.** A monopolist exists where there is only one firm in a market. However, firms in a market can act as if they were a monopoly by COLLUDING. This means they get together, usually to fix prices and output in a market. They then have formed a CARTEL. For example, a group of firms making vitamins may fix a high price between themselves at which they will sell vitamins to customers. Then they have to restrict output between themselves to sustain those high prices.

Question 2.

It isn't difficult to set up in the grocery industry. A few tens of thousands of pounds will give you a grocery store on a little parade of shops giving personal service to the local inhabitants. But don't expect to survive or make a large profit because the grocery industry today is dominated by just a few supermarket chains.

Supermarket chains are valued in the billions of pounds. They do change hands from time to time. Asda, for example, was bought by the US giant Wal-mart in the late 1990s. Safeway was the subject of a fierce takeover battle in 2003 and was eventually bought by Morrisons. Somerfield made a huge mistake when it took over the KwikSave chain in the mid-1990s. However, it would be almost impossible now for a new chain to set up from scratch because it is so difficult to acquire sites for large new supermarket stores.

There is no rocket science involved in running a supermarket. Success is about making a few key decisions. What mix of goods are you going to sell? How are your stores going to present the goods for sale? How much are you going to charge and how much will you make in profit on each item? How are you going to organise your supply chain? What price will you offer your suppliers? Different supermarkets offer different mixes. Asda, for example, combines groceries with other goods such as clothes. Its market share has increased in recent years due both to this and to its low price policy.

(a) What is the relative size of businesses in the grocery industry?
(b) What barriers to entry exist?
(c) How do supermarkets differ in what they offer?
(d) To what extent is knowledge about how to run a supermarket chain available to all grocery store and supermarket owners?
(e) If Tesco increases its sales, what could be the impact on Asda?

The degree of competition and the marketing mix

Markets may be classified into a number of different types according to their mix of characteristics. The market conditions in which a business operates and the degree of competition it faces will affect its market mix.

Perfect competition PERFECT COMPETITION is a situation where there is a large number of small businesses, producing almost exactly the same product. Consumers are aware of what is being offered by all businesses. There are no barriers to prevent businesses setting up. Businesses are **price-takers**. They have no influence over the price they charge. If a firm charged a higher price than others, customers would know exactly where to go to buy an alternative. An example of this type of competition is found in agricultural markets. There are often many small farmers, each with a relatively small market share, producing almost identical products.

Businesses operating under these conditions have little or no scope to determine their prices. Therefore, they may have to consider other elements of the marketing mix, such as promotion methods or how distribution channels can be used. For example, some farms have attempted to sell directly to customers through farm shops, but others through national supermarket chains. Some farms have promoted themselves as free range or organic producers.

Monopolistic competition MONOPOLISTIC COMPETITION is a situation where there is a large number of relatively small businesses in competition with each other and there are few entry barriers. Each business has a product that is differentiated from others through **branding**. But the brand identity of products is weak. A business will face competition from a wide range of other businesses in the market with similar, but differentiated, products. Businesses operating under these conditions are not price-takers. But they will only have a limited degree of control over the price they charge. Examples of this type of competition in the UK might include legal service providers and certain types of clothing retailing.

Given limited scope for price changes, businesses operating under monopolistic competition may stress other elements of their marketing mix, such as product, place and promotion. So a business might use promotional techniques that help to compete against other businesses. For example, a financial services advisor might promote its services aimed at business investors. A clothing retailer may stock clothes aimed at a particular market, such as young people, older people or taller men and women.

Oligopoly When there are many firms, but only a few dominate the market, OLIGOPOLY is said to exist. Examples include the markets for petrol, beer, detergents, paint and sweets. The majority of businesses in the UK operate under this type of competition.

Under oligopoly, each firm will have a differentiated product, often with a strong brand identity. Several brands may be competing in the same market. Brand loyalty amongst customers is encouraged by advertising and promotion. Firms in such markets are often said to compete in the form of non-price competition. Prices are often stable for long periods, disturbed only by short price wars.

Although brand loyalty does allow some price control, businesses often follow the price of the market leaders. This means that they tend to be interdependent.

Barriers to entry exist. If it was easy for new firms to enter the industry, they would set up and take the market share of the few large producers. Examples of barriers to entry might be:

- legal restrictions, such as patents which prevent other businesses copying products for a period of time;
- high start-up costs, such as the cost of manufacturing;
- the promotion or advertising required, for example, in the tobacco or soap powder industries;
- arrangements between businesses, for example in the 1990s newsagents could not stock ice creams by other producers in certain manufacturers' freezers (known as freezer exclusivity);
- collusion between businesses in cartels, which act together to prevent new entrants.

Businesses operating under oligopoly emphasise promotion in order to maintain their brand. They promote heavily in order to develop and maintain brand loyalty. However, pricing may also be an important feature of the marketing mix. A strong brand may enable a business to charge a relatively high price for a product if, for example, it has a market leading brand. Customers loyal to the brand will continue to buy the product rather than switching to another.

Monopoly MONOPOLY occurs when one business has total control over a market and is the only seller of the product. This

Question 3.

In January 2004 TelePassport Telecommunications, the first private telephone operator in Cyprus, pledged to reduce call rates by 15 per cent after gaining approval from the Telecommunications Regulator. Previously the only telephone company had been CyTA, a government controlled company.

TelePassport's president, Socratis Hasikos, said 'Statistics show that in 1998 CyTA made a profit of £50 million which increased to £62 million in 1999 and in 2001 reached £91 million. According to CyTA they expected to reap a profit of £107 million from the period 1998-2002, yet they earned a profit of £218 million. How can this be possible if they are not over-charging their customers? Now, they must present their costs and expenses to the Telecommunications Regulator, who has given them 15 days to do so.' He believed that CyTA delayed presenting its expenses because 'they have been paying out too much money and need to earn it back by charging more, or they have simply been ripping off customers'.

It was suggested that the entry of Cyprus into the EU would open the door to healthy competition for CyTA. Hasikos argues 'Our aim is not to attack CyTA, but to offer customers a better service at cheaper rates. Competition need not be negative, but could push CyTA into also lowering their prices.'

Source: adapted from www.xak.com.

(a) Identify and explain the type of competition before the entry of TelePassport Telecommunications into the market in Cyprus.

(b) Examine how (i) businesses and (ii) consumers are likely to be affected by the change in competition that is taking place in Cyprus.

pure monopoly should not be confused with a **legal monopoly**, which occurs in the UK when a firm controls 25 per cent or more of a market.

Monopolists are likely to erect barriers to prevent others from entering their market. They will also exert a strong influence on the price which they charge for their product. However, because monopolists are the only supplier of a product, it does not mean that they can charge whatever they want. If they raise the price demand will fall to some extent. Because of the influence monopolists have on their price, they are often called **price-makers**.

In the past, in the UK, certain businesses have come close to exerting pure monopoly power. For example, British Gas used to enjoy a monopoly position in the gas market. It was the sole supplier of piped gas in the UK. On the other hand, it could be argued that British Gas was operating in the energy market and therefore faced competition from electricity and oil companies. One of the main reasons why one gas company no longer exerts control over the market for gas is that the government introduced **legislation** to increase competition in markets where monopolies previously existed.

Today, the markets for water, power, rail and communications are regulated by **regulatory bodies** such as Ofcom (communications), Ofgem (gas and electricity) and Ofwat (water). Former state monopolies have been **privatised**. Limits are placed on their price increases. So telecommunications businesses offer an ever-expanding range of services and water and power companies promote to home-owners to attract their custom. In the absence of regulation monopolies may stress pricing as part of their marketing mix. Being the only provider of a product, they may seek to set a price that will maximise sales revenue. So the only supplier of a boat repair service in a harbour area, which has a **local monopoly**, may be able to regularly increase prices and not lose customers as there is no alternative service.

Methods of improving competitiveness

The market structure a business is operating within does determine to a large extent the competition that a business faces. However, businesses also adopt a range of strategies intended to increase their own competitiveness. The intention of such strategies is that they can compete more effectively within this given market structure. What businesses generally seek is to gain a **competitive advantage** over competitors.

Methods of improving competitiveness may be **marketing methods**. This will involve adapting and developing the marketing mix. The marketing mix is fundamental to a business' ability to compete effectively within a given market. By amending and developing its marketing mix a business can become more competitive. For example, a business marketing a fast-moving consumer good in an oligopolistic market might develop a new national advertising campaign that captures the imagination of consumers. This would enable the business to boost sales in the short term and, if other aspects of the marketing mix were developed to support this campaign, it might form the basis for a medium- and/or long-term increase in sales.

However, the methods used may be **non-marketing** methods.

Reducing costs Businesses use a range of strategies to reduce costs, including the setting of new budgets, changes in management processes and procedures, renegotiating contracts with suppliers, reducing staffing and employing a range of measures to improve efficiency and productivity.

Improving quality For manufacturing businesses this means producing a product that consumers recognise as being of higher quality. For service providers it means improving consumer perceptions of the quality of service that they receive. For businesses other than those operating under perfect competition improving quality enables a business to increase its competitiveness in a given market.

Staff training Staff training is a key component in a business' efforts to manage their competitiveness. A well trained and efficient staff responsive to the needs and wishes of customers can enhance competitiveness considerably. This is true in all business sectors but it is especially the case in those service industries, such as personal services like hairdressing, where responding effectively to customers on a daily basis is at the heart of the business' activities.

Porter's five forces analysis

The models of competition outlined above provide a useful means of describing markets. It can be argued, however, that they project businesses as being largely passive, simply accepting the constraints of their market structures. Michael Porter (1980) in his book *Competitive Strategy*, suggested that in certain circumstances businesses can influence the markets in which they operate. He outlined five forces that determine the extent to which businesses are able to manage competition within their markets.

Rivalry among competitors Porter argues that competitive rivalry is the main force that affects the ability of businesses to influence markets. This includes:

- the number of competitors - the more competitors the less likely it is that a business will be able to have influence;
- their ability to differentiate products - a promotional campaign by a business to differentiate its product will increase its influence;
- the rate of growth of the market - in a fast growing market competition may be less intense and individual firms will have more scope to influence the market;
- the existence of barriers to exit - competition may be intense in markets where businesses are deterred from leaving the market. Exit barriers may include the costs of high redundancy payments or losses as a result of having to sell machinery at reduced prices.

The threat of new entrants The number of businesses in a market may not always be a useful guide to competition in that market. This may also depend on the ability of businesses to enter the market. If it is easy for businesses to enter markets then competition is likely to be greater. This will restrict the ability of a business to influence the market. It is possible that businesses may be prevented or deterred from entering markets due to barriers to entry. For example, the need to invest heavily in new plant and machinery or to match high levels of promotional spending could deter new businesses from entering a market.

The threat of substitute products This depends upon the extent to which businesses can differentiate their products from those of competitors. A business which struggles to differentiate its products is likely to face intense competition. This is why businesses spend large sums of money attempting to make their products different or seem different from those of competitors. For example, the success of a chain of pizza restaurants may depend on its ability to appear to offer a style of pizza that others do not.

The bargaining power of customers Where customers are strong, there is likely to be more competition between producers and their influence will tend to be weaker. The factors affecting the power of consumers may be:
- the number of customers;
- whether they act together;
- their importance, for example, large supermarket chains have had great influence over food manufacturers;
- their ability to switch products;
- regularity of purchases, for example, consumers on holiday are often 'one-off' purchasers prepared to pay a higher price.

Question 4.

In 2003 *The Guardian* reported on the rivalry between glossy magazines. *Glamour* magazine is leader of the women's monthly magazine market. Its closest rival, *Cosmopolitan*, is one pound more expensive. *Glamour* is seen by many as being younger, funkier and more celebrity orientated, with stars such as Jennifer Lopez on its front cover. *InStyle* and *Company*, although experiencing sales increases, cannot match the 537,474 sales achieved by *Glamour*. The older women's market is not looking quite so healthy with declining or static sales for *Good Housekeeping* and *Prima*. The so-called 'middle youth market' has *Red*, *She* and *Eve* competing for customers, while the market for more intelligent upmarket women's glossies is fought for between *Marie Claire* and *Vogue*.

Source: adapted from *The Guardian*, 13.2.2003.

(a) Using Porter's five force analysis, examine Glamour's ability to manage competition in the market for women's monthly magazines in 2003.

KEYTERMS

Barriers to entry – factors which make it difficult or impossible for businesses to enter a market and compete with existing producers.
Cartel – a group of businesses (or countries) which join together to agree on pricing and output in a market in an attempt to gain higher profits at the expense of customers.
Collusion – in business, where several businesses (or countries) make agreements among themselves which benefit them at the expense of either rival businesses or customers.
Competition – rivalry between businesses offering products in the same market; competition may take forms such as price competition, distinctive product offerings, advertising and distribution.
Market structures – the characteristics of a market, such as the size of the barriers to entry to the market, the number of businesses in the market or whether they produce identical products, which determine the behaviour of businesses within the market.
Monopolistic competition – a market structure where there is a large number of small businesses producing differentiated, branded products, where barriers to entry are low and businesses are price-setters.
Monopoly – a market structure where there is a single business in the market and there are barriers to entry.
Oligopoly – a market structure where a few large businesses dominate the market producing differentiated, branded, products, where barriers to entry are typically high and where businesses are price-setters.
Perfect competition – a market structure where there is a large number of small businesses producing identical products, where barriers to entry are low and where businesses are price-takers.

KNOWLEDGE

1. How do businesses compete with each other?
2. Explain three possible barriers to entry into a market.
3. Explain two ways in which businesses can engage in unfair competition.
4. In what ways might the marketing mix of a business operating under perfect competition and a business operating under oligopoly differ?
5. State three non-monetary methods of improving competitiveness.
6. State the five forces that can affect competitiveness according to Michael Porter.

The bargaining power of suppliers Powerful suppliers can increase the costs of a business and decrease the extent to which it can control its operations. The power of suppliers is likely to depend upon the number of suppliers able to supply a business and the importance in the production process of the product being supplied. For example, if a JIT manufacturer can easily switch supplier, the producer will have greater control of the production process.

Case Study: UK sandwich sales

Are British workers losing their taste for the traditional sandwich as their favourite midday snack? New research suggests that this may be so. Office or manual workers are more likely to have a ready-chilled curry in their lunchbox, rather than a cheese sandwich. Almost three-quarters told researchers for Geest, an own-label manufacturer of convenience foods for supermarkets, that they were fed up with sandwiches and about half said they looked forward to something hot to give them a boost. Some 30 per cent of the 919 employees questioned said they bought ready-chilled supermarket soups or meals to take to work and heat up in a microwave, taking a bite out the sandwich market. The survey also found that 17 per cent thought lunch was the 'highlight' of their working day. But a quarter described colleagues with plastic lunch boxes as 'very sad'.

The market for sandwiches in the UK is shared between a range of operators of varying size. These range from the supermarkets such as Tescos and Sainsbury's and large specialist bakers such as Greggs through to small independent bakers' shops and specialist sandwich shops found mainly in town and city centres. Important arrivals on the UK sandwich market in recent years have included sandwich chains such as Pret a Manger which is largely focused in big cities such as London and Manchester.

Bakers' shops have seen their share of the sandwich market slip in the past year with competition from sandwich and snack bars and supermarkets increasing, according to a new report from market research company Key Note. The report says bakers' shops (a category that includes the Greggs chain) are still the dominant player in UK sandwich sales but their market share in terms of the value of sandwich sales value fell from 28.6 per cent in 2005/06 to 26.4 per cent over the year to May 2007. At the same time, supermarkets have increased value sales up from 12.2 per cent to 13.4 per cent over the same period. Sandwich chains had a 9.8 per cent value share of the market, with Subway the dominant player with a 7.2 per cent share of sandwich sales by value, up 4.2 per cent.

Figures on total sandwich sales don't entirely correspond with the research conducted for Geest. Total sandwich sales were £3.73 billion in the year ending May 2007, up from £3.61 billion the year before, although the 2.46 billion packs sold in 2007 was less than the 2.54 billion the previous year. The report also says that 51 per cent of sandwiches sold are wedges, 17 per cent rolls and baps, 13 per cent baguettes and 5 per cent sub rolls. Other sandwich carriers, such as pittas and wraps, accounted for 10 per cent of volumes.

Retailers say there are no signs of customers turning their backs on the humble British sandwich. Marks & Spencer, which claims to be the leading retailer in this sector, says it is 'an extremely buoyant market'. Its most popular sandwiches include chicken salad, prawn and mayonnaise and chicken tikka. However, the retailer says it has noticed an upturn in sales of foods which can be heated up, such as stuffed naans. M&S is also expanding its range of lunch foods and as recently as six weeks ago launched a line of sushi in response to customer demand.

Upmarket sandwich chain Pret a Manger also denies the threat of the ready meal to its sandwich business, saying people always turn to hot food in winter. The company adds that it is planning to increase its total number of shops in England to 200 from its present 74 over the next two years.

Source adapted from www.bbcnews.co.uk and www.bakeryinfo.co.uk.

(a) Explain what is meant by the terms (i) competition (3 marks) and (ii) dominant player. (3 marks)

(b) How would you classify the UK sandwich market? Justify your answer. (6 marks)

(c) Examine TWO factors that might influence the competitiveness in the Uk sandwich market. (6 marks)

(d) Explain how a small retailer might improve its competitiveness in the sandwich market. (8 marks)

(e) Discuss whether a small business could grow to dominate over 50 per cent of sales in the UK sandwich market. (10 marks)

26 Marketing objectives

Marketing objectives

When businesses construct their marketing strategies they will usually engage in a number of different activities. These include:

- analysing the markets in which they operate;
- setting marketing objectives;
- selecting marketing tactics and strategies;
- developing and implementing marketing plans.

This unit focuses upon MARKETING OBJECTIVES. These are the **goals** that a business is trying to achieve through its marketing. Marketing objectives are often more effective if they have a target and a time limit. For example, a marketing objective might be to increase market share by 10 per cent in the next three years. Business marketing objectives commonly focus upon the following areas.

Growth and profitability A business might want to increase sales, revenue, profit through marketing. It might be able to increase its revenue by selling more products. Or it might be able to charge a higher price. Both should lead to higher profits. So might launching new products. Businesses aiming to grow often attempt to create a competitive advantage over their rivals Marketing can help a business to do this. Examples of businesses that have grown rapidly as a result of marketing include the low-cost flight companies EasyJet and Ryanair.

Gaining and maintaining sales and market share A business may attempt to prevent losses and declining sales, and maintain market share, through its marketing. There are reasons why a business might do this.

- When a new product is launched. New products often require marketing and promotion to break into the market and for sales to take off.
- To develop over the long term. Some products have very long life cycles such as the Mini motor car and Heinz Beans. They have sold continuously over many years as a result of marketing extension strategies designed to maintain sales. Extension strategies are often used in the mature stage of the product life cycle to prevent a decline in sales.

Product differentiation It is possible to differentiate products from those of competitors by changing the marketing mix, such as charging a lower or higher price, changing the packaging, design and ingredients of the product, advertising and other forms of promotion, or selling the product in different types of retailer. Examples might be the change in the name and advertising of the sweets Opal Fruits to Starburst or the setting up of a website by BA to sell flights through the Internet.

Product introduction The marketing objective of a business might be to launch new products onto the market. Market research could have indicated that this product would be successful. Some businesses introduce products regularly, such as new versions of computer software and games. Car producers regularly introduce newer versions of cars to replace older models. For example, the Ford Mondeo replaced the Sierra and the Ford Focus replaced the Escort.

Product innovation Some products are genuinely new and innovative. It might be that new technology has created a new product or research has found a new medicine, for example.

Consumer knowledge Consumers need to know what products are available from businesses. Without awareness they may not buy products. Raising the awareness of products, for example

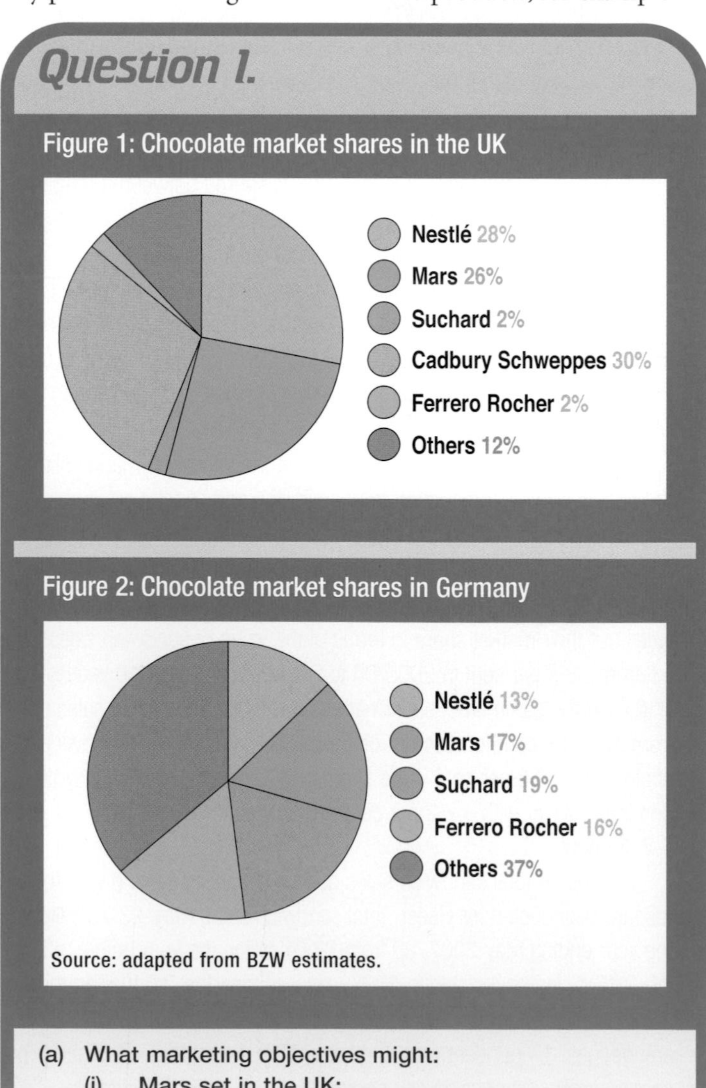

(a) What marketing objectives might:
   (i) Mars set in the UK;
   (ii) Cadbury Schweppes set in the UK;
   (iii) Ferrero Rocher set in the UK;
   (iv) Cadbury Schweppes set in Germany?

through a variety of promotion measures, can therefore be an important objective.

Consumer satisfaction Consumers also need to be happy about the products they buy. Businesses which have satisfied consumers are more likely to gain brand loyalty.

There is a relationship between the different marketing objectives. For example, in the early 1990s Adidas found its market share under threat in the European sports shoe market. This was a partly as a result of a successful promotional campaign by Nike. Adidas attempted to regain market share by its own marketing campaign, with the objective of differentiating its product. It promoted its trainers as having 'street credibility'. After the year 2000, Adidas launched a number of product ranges with a 'retro' 1970s look in an attempt to increase sales and win market share.

There is also a relationship between the marketing objectives of a business and its MARKETING TACTICS. Marketing tactics are short-term, small-scale methods a business might use to achieve its marketing objectives. For example, a furniture business with the objective of increasing sales revenue after Christmas might have a 30 day offer where customers can choose a free chair with any three seater sofa they buy.

It is argued that the marketing objectives a business sets should be SMART in the same way as the overall objectives of the business They should be specific, stating exactly what is trying to be achieved, able to be measured to decide if they have been achieved, which usually involves setting targets, agreed by everyone involved, realistic and able to be achieved within the constraints of the business and time specific, stating exactly when they should be achieved.

Question 2.

In 2004 Kodak announced it would cease production of traditional 35 mm cameras in the US and Europe at the end of the year. Sales in America fell below 8 million in 2003, a 20 per cent fall since 2002. The decision was based largely on the runaway success of digital cameras. Sales of film for traditional cameras had fallen by £2 billion in two years.

Kodak was betting its future on digital photography, printing and health imaging. The President of Kodak's digital and film imaging systems said 'We will focus our film investments on opportunities that provide faster and attractive returns'. But Kodak did not intend to halt production of traditional cameras totally. There were plans to expand manufacturing in Asia, Latin America and Eastern Europe where demand was still growing. It would also continue to produce disposable 35 mm cameras.

Kodak also announced plans to cease production of its Advanced Photo System cameras, launched in 1996, which gave wide-shot capability. Demand had failed to live up to expectations.

Digital cameras are now outselling traditional cameras. Previously they had been more expensive, produced poorer quality pictures and needed large amounts of battery power. However, the quality of digital cameras sold for less than £200 has now improved greatly. Statistics show that only 14 per cent of pictures taken on digital cameras are printed. The rest are downloaded, emailed or deleted.

Supporters of traditional cameras argue that their photographs are still superior to those of digital cameras, particularly in the depth of colour.

Source: adapted from the *Daily Mail*, 14.1.2004.

(a) Carry out a marketing audit of Kodak to identify the (i) internal factors and (ii) external factors affecting its marketing objectives.

Internal influences on marketing objectives

There is a number of influences that affect the marketing objectives set by a business. Some may be internal factors, from within the business itself.

Corporate aims and objectives A company's marketing objectives will be influenced by the corporate aims and objectives of the business. For example, the aim of a DVD and video rental chain might be to become the most well known name in the UK. Its objective might be to increase sales turnover by 20 per cent over two years to achieve this. So its marketing objectives could be to spend an extra £1 million on promotion to teenagers in magazines and product 'tie-ins' to make them more aware of the service.

Finance The availability of finance will influence what it is that a business aims to achieve. It may be difficult to launch new products, for example, if a business lacks funds. Similarly, a business with limited finances and access to only small pools of additional finance may find that some marketing objectives are beyond its realisable ambitions.

Operational and organisational issues The operation and organisation of a business may influence its marketing. A business which does not, for example, have a specialised marketing department might have a different marketing strategy from to one which does. A business operating in many countries might market differently from one in a local or national market.

Human resources To some extent the nature of a business's marketing objectives will reflect the human resources of that business. For example, a new business staffed by recent graduates may well opt for marketing methods different to a

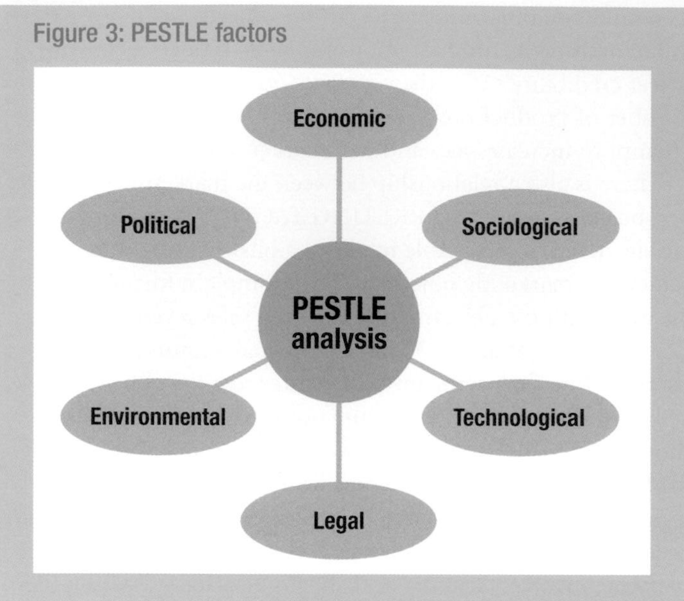

Figure 3: PESTLE factors

more established business with a wider range of employees.

External influences on marketing objectives

Factors outside the business can also influence its marketing objectives.

Competitors' actions The actions of competitor businesses may well affect the marketing objectives of a business. Take the example of a large and dominant business operating in a market where it is seeking to gain market share. In such conditions a less dominant business may seek to defend and maintain its market share.

Technological change Businesses operating in markets characterised by fast-changing technologies are likely to set themselves ambitious marketing objectives possibly with large increases in sales volume. This is because such markets are often relatively open with new businesses able to gain large slices of market share quickly. Many web-based networking businesses such as Facebook have been able to realise ambitious marketing objectives in this way. By way of contrast businesses operating in relatively slow-changing markets with few technological changes are more likely to set modest marketing objectives reflecting their belief that future circumstances may be likely to resemble in many ways those already experienced.

Market factors One of the main market factors influencing a business' marketing objectives is the degree of competition faced by a business. In a mature market with little or no room for new entrants, businesses are likely to set modest marketing objectives given that they are constrained by the intensity of competition and the relatively few opportunities to grow significantly. The global market for cars, for example, is saturated with many producers competing. This means that car businesses cannot expect to see the kind of growth experienced by Google when they entered a new market, for Internet searches, with few competitors.

External factors influencing marketing objectives also include a range of factors shown in Figure 3 known as PESTLE factors.

- **Political factors.** This may include political pressure from bodies that can exert political pressure, such as government agencies, or at local level, such as town councils.
- **Economic factors.** Increases in consumer spending, falls in interest rates and low inflation can all improve the chances of a business increasing its sales and profit. An increase in the number of new businesses may reduce the market share of a company that is dominant.
- **Social factors.** Changes in tastes can affect spending by consumers. Fashionable products can often increase sales rapidly.
- **Technological factors.** New products may be created as technology develops. The Internet has also helped to increase consumer awareness of products.
- **Legal factors.** This can include legislation from government. For example laws might restrict the type of advertising used for a product in an attempt to differentiate it from those of rivals. It would also include
- **Environmental factors.** These can often influence the type of product that a business produces, such as the development of businesses selling managed wood as an alternative to other wood or plastic products.

These factors are often found by carrying out a MARKETING AUDIT. This is an analysis of the internal organisation and procedures of the business and the external factors which affect its marketing decisions. It will also help to identify the strengths, weaknesses, opportunities and threats faced by the business, called SWOT analysis.

KEYTERMS

Marketing audit – an analysis of the internal organisation and procedures of the business and the external factors which affect its marketing decisions.
Marketing objectives – goals that a business attempts to achieve through its marketing.
Marketing tactics – short-term, small-scale methods a business can use to achieve its marketing objectives.

KNOWLEDGE

1. Identify five marketing objectives.
2. Explain the difference between an internal and external marketing audit.
3. State four internal factors influencing a business' marketing objectives.
4. Name three external factors affecting a business' marketing objectives.
5. What are the PESTLE factors?

Case Study: Recovery Kitchens Ltd

Recovery Kitchens Ltd is owned and run by Elle Jeffers and Arturo Vasques. The business manufactures kitchens using recycled and reclaimed wood. It sells mainly to two types of customer – those who are concerned about the environment and want to see wood recycled rather than destroyed, and those who want a genuinely 'old'-looking and aged kitchen to fit in with the style of their house. The business operates from a workshop in the North West of England which has enough space for its current needs but little room for expansion.

The kitchens do not come cheap. There is a tremendous amount of work involved in reclaiming old wood and making it suitable for production. Sources of wood have to be found. The wood has to be sanded, prepared and recut. Sometimes wood that has been bought turns out not to be suitable.

The business has been operating for about three years and now has a strong loyalty from customers who want this type of product. They tell their friends, who also buy kitchens. And sales have started to pick up in other areas of the country, particularly East Anglia, where the style of kitchen suits a great deal of older housing which is relatively cheaper than nearer to London.

Recovery Kitchens Ltd has been thinking of making some changes. It is concerned about its long-term position. It is facing competition from some local businesses that offer cheaper pine products which can look very similar to reclaimed wood kitchens or more expensive 'Shaker-type' kitchens which have a simple style and traditional feel. And it feels that it can take the idea of the environmental image of the business further by making kitchens from managed wood. This is wood where the supplier guarantees to replant trees for all those cut down. Recovery Kitchens Ltd can then use this in its promotion to further enhance its green image and offer something a little different to customers wanting kitchens for older properties. It is also considering whether it should reduce its price a little. It has asked local people for their views on the prices charged by some kitchen manufacturers and their knowledge of the company name. The business is concerned about whether it will have the finance to buy the managed wood. It might have to borrow, and interest rates look set to rise.

Source: adapted from independent research.

(a) What are the target markets of the business? (4 marks)

(b) Based upon the information in the article explain TWO marketing objectives of Recovery Kitchens Ltd. (6 marks)

(c) Explain the internal and external factors that might affect the marketing objectives of the business. (12 marks)

(d) Discuss the possible objectives of the business in moving to managed wood kitchens. (12 marks)

27 Marketing budgets

Marketing budgeting

A budget is a plan of operations for a future accounting period. A MARKETING BUDGET is therefore a plan of operations for a future accounting period which relates to the marketing department. As with all budgets, the marketing budget is:

- **quantifiable**, i.e. expressed in numerical terms;
- linked to the **objectives** of the business;
- a **plan** showing what the business wants to achieve and is different from a forecast.

For example, a **sales budget** sets sales targets over a period of time. Table 1 shows part of a sales budget for two different medicine products, Lynix and Polix, within a company's product range. Sales targets are set for each month over a six month period. They are expressed in terms of the physical number of products sold, the average sale price, the value of total sales and the market share for each product. Sales budgets can also break down targets in a variety of other ways. For example, it might be broken down by area or region, by distribution channel, or type of customer.

Other parts of the marketing budget are concerned with expenditure. These set out how the marketing department plans to spend resources allocated to them over a time period. For example, the marketing department has to plan how much to spend on above-the-line and below-the-line promotion. This is not just spending on advertising but also, for example, on market research, direct sales promotion or the sales force.

Methods of setting budgets

There is a variety of methods which a business might use to set its marketing budgets.

Historical budgeting HISTORICAL BUDGETING (sometimes called INCREMENTAL BUDGETING) is where the budget in the next time period is based on the outcome of the previous time period. For example, if sales were £220,000 this year, the budget might allow for a 5 per cent increase in sales to £231,000. Historical budgeting tends to rely upon looking at past trends and projecting them forward. This can have its problems because past trends are not always accurate predictors of future events. For example, changing inflation rates, changes in competition or a boom in the economy can alter the value of sales.

Affordable budgeting Businesses have many costs, including raw material costs and labour costs. The AFFORDABLE BUDGETING method bases planned marketing expenditure on what is left over after all these other more essential costs have been paid. The impact of affordable budgeting can be seen when an economy moves from boom to recession. Marketing expenditure is then often badly hit. This is because businesses typically cut their marketing spending before they cut costs such as staffing.

The advantage of affordable budgeting is that businesses only spend on marketing what they can afford. The disadvantage is that there is no attempt to match marketing spending with its effects on sales and profits. In a downturn in the economy, for example, it might make more sense to increase marketing to stabilise sales or minimise their fall. Increased marketing in a recession might also allow a business to gain market share at the expense of businesses which have cut their marketing budgets. Instead, the affordable budgeting method would see a typical business cutting its marketing spending.

Sales-based budgeting SALES-BASED or SALES-RELATED budgeting is a method used for marketing expenditure budgets. Marketing expenditure on individual products, product ranges or sales areas in the budget is based on sales achieved. For example, a product which sold £1 million would have ten times the amount of marketing expenditure allocated to it than a product which only sold £100,000.

The **percentage of past sales method** uses past sales to determine the marketing expenditure budget. In contrast, the **percentage of future sales method** uses the figures for future sales. Sometimes, businesses use the **advertising: sales ratio** as a method for planning advertising expenditure. The advertising: sales ratio is the proportion of sales which is spent on advertising. If the advertising: sales ratio were 10 per cent, for example, then for every £10 of sales, there would be £1 spent on advertising.

Sales-related budgeting methods are simple

Table 1: A six month sales budget for two products of a pharmaceuticals company

	January	February	March	April	May	June
Lynix						
Number of sales (000s)	75	73	72	75	77	79
Average price	1.21	1.24	1.24	1.25	1.26	1.26
Sales value (£000)	90.75	90.52	89.28	93.75	97.02	99.54
Market share (%)	9.6	9.6	9.7	9.7	9.8	9.8
Polix						
Number of sales (000s)	167	162	160	167	170	174
Average price	0.46	0.48	0.48	0.49	0.5	0.5
Sales value (£000)	76.82	77.76	76.80	81.83	85	87
Market share (%)	15.8	15.8	15.9	16.1	16.2	16.2

Question 1.

Look at the six month sales budget in Table 1.

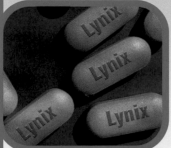

(a) Explain whether the data in Table 1 represents actual sales, forecast sales or target sales.
(b) Discuss which product, Lynix or Polix, has been set the more ambitious sales target over the six month period.

to understand and implement. They also allocate scarce marketing resources towards more successful products. However, it is a crude way of planning marketing spending. For example, more sales might be generated by spending an extra pound of advertising on a product with 50,000 sales per week than one with 500,000 sales per week. Advertising a highly successful product may have little impact on sales. Advertising a product with far fewer or declining sales may generate a large number of extra sales. Also, marketing expenditure is not just about gaining extra sales. It is about gaining extra profitable sales. Spending money on promoting high profit margin niche products may be far more profitable than expenditure on the promotion of low profit margin mass market products.

Competitor budgeting COMPETITOR BUDGETING (also known as COMPETITOR-BASED or PARITY BUDGETING) allocates marketing expenditure according to what rival businesses are spending on competing products. For example, a soap powder manufacturer may spend £10 million a year on advertising because a rival soap powder manufacturer is spending this amount.

Competitor budgeting has the advantage that it takes into account market forces. Marketing expenditure clearly has an impact on sales and profits of the average product. It is also simple to understand as a method. However, like sales-related budgeting, it is not necessarily true that matching rivals' spending is the optimal way to allocate scarce marketing resources. If a rival spends 20 per cent more on advertising a particular product, it may be better for the business not to match this even if sales decline. Instead, there may be more profitable ways of allocating spending where the decline in sales is more than matched by increases in sales and profits on other products. Also, businesses may find it difficult to identify exactly how much rivals spend. Finally, the planned spending may not help the business to achieve its objectives set out in the marketing plan.

Objective and task budgeting OBJECTIVE AND TASK BUDGETING allocates marketing expenditure according to the objectives of the business and the tasks that must be carried out to meet those objectives. For example, if an objective is to increase sales of a product by 20 per cent over three years, then extra marketing resources will probably have to be allocated to that product in the budget. A mature product may need little marketing support if sales growth is not an objective. In contrast, a new product may need heavy marketing to get it past its launch stage successfully. At its most sophisticated, a marketing department may have to justify its spending by calculating its rate of return. Then it can be compared with other possible spending such as investment in training of workers, or investment in new machinery. When marketing departments refer to 'investment in marketing', they are implying that such comparisons can be made.

Objective and task budgeting most clearly ties marketing spending in with objectives and the tasks needed to ensure that those objectives are met. As such, it is often seen as the most effective way to plan a budget. However, it requires a sophisticated approach to marketing where no simple rules apply. There is also no guarantee of success. Products launched at considerable marketing expense may fail. Mature products with little marketing expenditure back-up may suddenly go into the decline phase of the product life cycle because a rival business launches a better competing product.

Setting the budget

In practice, the marketing budget in a medium to large sized business is likely to be set by the marketing manager or director together with the managing director. It is the managing director, perhaps with the board of directors, who will determine the overall size of the budget and possibly set the targets for sales and profits. The marketing director will determine how spending is allocated between different products and different types of marketing. In a large marketing department, parts of setting the budget may be delegated further down the chain of command to budget holders. A **budget holder** is an employee responsible for a particular budget area.

How much involvement middle managers will have in preparing the budget will vary from business to business. In a centralised organisation, it is more likely that budgets will be drawn up by those higher up the organisation. In a more decentralised organisation, aspects of preparing the budget may be pushed down the hierarchy. In a centralised organisation, senior management may wish to keep a tight control on decision making, using their expertise to draw up budgets which will further the objectives of the business. In a more decentralised organisation, employees may be more motivated if they have been part of the decision making process. On the other hand, they may deliberately choose undemanding targets, or inflate their expenditure budgets. If planned sales, for

Question 2.

TPG is a magazine publisher with a wide range of titles in the UK, France and the USA. One of its most successful magazines is Got Ya!, part of the 'lads mags' segment of the market. Sales of Got Ya! in established markets has been declining for the past five years, part of the overall trend for all lads mags magazines. TPG has been unwilling to increase the marketing budget for Got Ya! in recent years because it feels that an increased marketing spend would have little impact on sales. The problems with the magazine relate to the decline in the market, the strong product offering of competing magazines and the inability to find a new angle on the product format. Its research also shows that there has been little if any increase in marketing spend by competing magazines.

However, the Chinese market has recently been liberalised, with Western publishers able to sell titles to a potential 1.3 billion customers. TPG has decided to launch a Chinese version of Got Ya!. It aims to have initial sales of 250,000 magazines per month rising to 500,000 within three years. It expects the magazine to break even within 6 months and thereafter to have a net profit margin of 20 per cent. It has allocated an extra £800,000 to the marketing budget for Got Ya! for the six month period after the launch. It will then review the budget and decide whether further spending is required for the magazine to achieve its sales and profit goals.

Source: adapted from the Financial Times, 13.5.2004.

(a) Using a diagram, explain where Got Ya! is in its product life cycle (i) in the UK and (ii) in China.

(b) Discuss what methods of setting marketing budgets are being used by TPG.

example, are targeted to grow by 1 per cent in the budget when sales have been growing at 5 per cent per annum over the last five years, then the marketing department is likely to achieve its 1 per cent target easily. They can then get the credit for achieving their target even though it was far too low in the first place. Equally, departments have a tendency to inflate their planned costs. It then becomes much easier to stay within budget. It also allows departments to spend on their favourite projects even if it is unlikely that this will benefit sales or profits.

Factors influencing the marketing budget

A number of factors might influence the marketing budget set by a business.

Business aims and objectives The marketing budget must be planned with the corporate aims of the business in mind and its business objectives. For example, if the business aims to grow in future, it is likely that the marketing budget will plan for an increase in sales, perhaps brought about by an increase in promotion expenditure. The marketing budget is also constrained by other budgets. A business might want to spend an extra £50,000 on promotion. However, if there is a need to employ more specialist workers, then funds might be diverted to the budget of the human resources department.

Rewards The level of reward is likely to affect the marketing budget. For example, a business might be faced with a choice when expanding. It might have the alternative of spending more on marketing or alternatively on reorganisation of production. If the rewards gained by the reorganisation are likely to be greater then the business might decide not to increase promotion. Similarly, if a business might decide to spend more on marketing a new product because it predicts that it will be very profitable.

Behaviour of competitors The actions of rival businesses can affect marketing. Large increases in spending on marketing by competitors might have to be matched if a business wants to remain competitive. Some businesses could not compete with others if they did not have enormous marketing budgets, such as in the motor car industry.

Nature of the market and customers Some markets do not require large amounts of promotion. For example, a wholesale business selling imported cycle parts to cycle shops might simply need to send out regular price lists and product descriptions or use a website. Businesses selling to customers around the world, such as Coca-Cola or McDonald's, are likely to spend vast amounts on marketing. Businesses also sometimes spend large amounts to launch new products on the market. They might reduce marketing spending later in the product life cycle as sales decline to gain greater profit.

Benefits and problems of marketing budgeting

There are certain benefits of marketing budgets for a business.
- They provide a business with a means of controlling marketing costs.
- They can be used to identify where costs have been too high or where marketing has been ineffective in raising sales.
- They can be used to plan the future of the business with some certainty, so other decisions can be made.
- They can be used by other departments to coordinate strategies to make the business more efficient.
- They set targets for the marketing department, which can be used to motivate employees and identify improvements in productivity.

However, there may also be problems.
- They might be too much of a straightjacket on decision making. This is particularly important if there are sudden and unexpected changes in the market.
- They might be seen by employees as a means by which a business can judge them if targets are not met, and so could be demotivating.
- They might lead to poor decision making if they are inaccurate.

- They might conflict with other objectives of the business. Different stakeholders often have different objectives. Managers, for example, might attempt to 'empire build' by trying to obtain large budgets.
- They can be constraining on other business decisions. For example, managers might over or understate budget requirements, fearing they will lose their budget or may be given too great a target next year.

KEYTERMS

Affordable budgeting – a budgeting method where planned marketing expenditure is based on what is left over after all other more essential costs have been paid.

Competitor budgeting (or competitor-based budgeting or parity budgeting) – a budgeting method where marketing expenditure is allocated according to what rival businesses are spending on competing products.

Historical budgeting (or incremental budgeting) – where the budget in the next time period is based on the outcome of the previous time period.

Marketing budget – a plan of operations for a future accounting period which relates to the marketing department.

Objective and task budgeting – where the budget is set according to the objectives of the business and the tasks that must be carried out to meet those objectives.

Sales-based budgeting (or sales-related budgeting) – where the size of the marketing budget is determined by the level of sales achieved and where the allocation of the marketing budget between different products, product ranges or sales areas is based on their relative sales.

Question 3.

Holland & Knight is a large law firm. It has more than 1,200 attorneys in 333 offices and over 100 practice areas. The marketing budget is derived from the annual strategic plans drawn up by the business. Each year there is a clean plan and a new budget. Expenditure is evaluated on the return on investment (ROI). A high ROI signals a good marketing investment. Marketing expenditures are constantly evaluated by both the attorney and marketing staff during the year.

Holland & Knight is a very client-orientated business. It relies heavily on relationship marketing, including client events, sponsorship, newsletters and seminars. It also spends on web development but not a great deal on advertising. During the past several years around 2.5-3 per cent of turnover has been allocated to marketing budgets.

There is an emphasis on 'cross marketing' within the business. Clients are 'owned' by the whole business rather than one member of the business. So the whole business is accountable for each client. This helps it to identify other services which might be useful for the client.

Source: adapted from www.firmmarketingcentre.com.

(a) Explain reasons why marketing budgeting is likely to be important for this business.

(b) Examine the factors that are likely to affect the marketing budget of the business.

KNOWLEDGE

1. What might be contained within a marketing budget?
2. What is the difference between a budget set using the historical budgeting method and one set using the affordable budgeting method?
3. What is the difference between a budget set using the sales-based budgeting method and one set using the competitor budgeting method?
4. How might a business set a marketing budget using the objective and task method?
5. Who might be involved in setting a marketing budget in a large company?
6. What are the advantages and disadvantages of involving middle managers in the marketing budget setting process?
7. Explain the advantages and disadvantages to a business of marketing budgetary control.

Case Study: Haffner plc

Haffner plc is an international cosmetics company. It has four main ranges described in more detail in Figure 1. To fix the marketing budgets for its products, it uses the percentage of past sales method. Since 2000, it has allocated 20 per cent of last year's sales to the marketing budget for the current year. Sales and marketing budgets are shown in Table 2.

Table 2: Annual sales and marketing budgets for Haffner's four main product ranges, £ million

	Emme		Gee		Vee		Cee	£ million
	Sales	Marketing budget	Sales	Marketing budget	Sales	Marketing budget	Sales	Marketing budget
2005	10.6	1.98	23.4	4.74	50.2	10.18	36.8	7.24
2006	10.8	2.12	23.2	4.68	49.2	10.04	37.8	7.36
2007	12.6	2.16	21.8	4.64	47.8	9.84	40.2	7.56
2008	16.6	2.52	20.4	4.36	46.2	9.56	44.6	8.04

Figure 1: Main product ranges

Emme is an exclusive cosmetics range aimed at high income customers. Launched in 1996, it has seen solid growth. Profit margins are the highest of all the four ranges. Market research has shown that a significant minority of target customers have low awareness of the range. Partly, it concluded, this is because the advertising:sales ratio is about half that of competitors. Partly it is because Haffner has found it difficult to get key retailers, such as department stores, to stock the range or to give sufficient space to the range if it is stocked.

Gee is a budget cosmetics range. First launched in 1982, it proved very popular for its low prices and relatively large number of products within the range. Advertising has been highly successful, targeting customers in this niche market. However, much of the marketing budget has been spent on in-store promotions and selective discounting to key retailers. Since the late 1990s, sales have been falling. Market research has suggested that customers have been trading up to more expensive product ranges as their purchasing power has increased. With relatively low profit margins on relatively high sales, Haffner has increasingly come to see Gee as a cash cow.

Vee is the brand name for the original range of cosmetics with which the company was launched in 1955. It is a mass market range. The advertising:sales ratio has traditionally been above the average for similar ranges in the industry. Price promotions have played little part in the marketing spend. Instead, the company has built up an impressive sales force which ensures that the range is sold in a wide variety of outlets, from small chemists to almost every department store to large chains of supermarkets. Profit margins have been average for the industry in this segment of the market.

Cee was launched in 1990 to cater for the 20-40 year old office worker segment of the market. Market research, prior to the launch of Cee, indicated that Vee was less attractive to 20-30 year olds than to older customers. Some young women felt that Vee was the brand their mothers would buy and therefore was not for them. Haffner has consistently used advertising to target its customers for Cee. Many of the advertising campaigns have won industry awards for their innovation and success. Cee was deliberately priced at a small premium to the Vee range to emphasise its quality and exclusivity. However, frequent price promotions are used to win customer loyalty in the target market. Profit margins are average for the industry.

(a) Showing all your workings, and assuming that the method of setting budgets remains the same, calculate
(i) the total marketing budget for Haffner in 2008;
(ii) total sales for Haffner in 2008;
(iii) sales of Cee in 2004;
(iv) the marketing budget for Vee in 2009. (8 marks)

(b) Discuss how marketing budgets might have been different if Haffner had used a percentage of forecast sales method to determine marketing budgets over the period 2004-2009. (12 marks)

(c) To what extent could Haffner increase its overall profitability if it used a different method of setting budgets than the percentage of past sales method? (20 marks)

28 Marketing planning

Components of a marketing plan

A MARKETING PLAN is a set of proposed marketing actions to be undertaken over a period of time which, if carried out, should enable the business to achieve its marketing objectives. The marketing plan is likely to contain the following, which have been outlined in the previous units.

- **Marketing objectives.** An objective could be to increase market share by 5 per cent over the next year. To accompany this a set of actions may be detailed, such as 'extend local advertising to the North West region' or 'ensure product is competitively priced'. In addition, responsibilities may be allocated between departments, sections and individuals.
- **A marketing budget.** A budget will be set which details how the marketing department will spend its funds.
- **Sales forecasts.** For example, based upon the forecasting techniques employed a business may forecast that sales will increase by 20 per cent over a two year period.
- **Marketing strategies.** Many of these will centre around the marketing mix. Price, product, promotion and place will be at the core of the actions detailed in the marketing plan.

In a large business, the marketing plan is likely to be developed in outline as part of the overall strategic or corporate plan. A small group of senior marketing managers are likely to be responsible for drawing up the plan. Once this has been agreed, detailed plans will be made within the marketing department. Managers at all levels may be involved in drawing up these more detailed plans.

In a small business, the owner/manager may have drawn up a written marketing plan. This is usually necessary if the business approaches a bank for extra loans or a larger overdraft facility. The marketing plan would be a part of the overall business plan. Often, though, the marketing plan is not written down. The entrepreneur has the plan in his or her head. Equally, the owner may have no marketing plan but may simply react to events as they arise. Using 'hunches' for decision making can be effective if the entrepreneur has a good intuitive understanding of the business environment.

Targets within the marketing plan

Targets should be set within the marketing plan. These should be measurable and understood by those operating the plan. These targets can then form part of the evaluation of the marketing plan. A business could use a number of different criteria.

Sales Sales targets can be set in many forms. For example, sales targets might be set by value (i.e. total sales x average selling price) or by volume (i.e. the number of sales made). Sales targets could be given for different areas of a country or different countries or continents. A multinational company might have sales targets for North America, Europe, Asia and the rest of the world for example. Sales targets are also likely to be set by product. For example, one product might have a sales growth target of 10 per cent per annum, while another might have one of 2 per cent.

Market share Market share can be an important target indicator of competitiveness. A business which aims to increase market share in its marketing plan is attempting to become more competitive relative to other businesses over time. A business which aims to limit loss of market share is likely to take into account that other businesses are going to become more competitive. As with sales targets, market share targets can be split down into market share by product and by region.

Marketing spending and market profitability analysis One criticism of marketing spending is that it is impossible to work out whether it has had an effect on sales, sales revenues and profits. For example, a business might spend £1 million on an advertising campaign and sales values might rise by 2 per cent. It could be that the £1 million spending caused the 2 per cent sales rise. But if at the same time the overall economy had grown by 3 per cent, it could be that the rise in sales was simply due to greater customer spending power. Or the 2 per cent rise in sales values could have been caused by new products entering the product range.

Market profitability analysis is concerned with the relationship between profits and costs. In the context of marketing planning, profitability analysis is calculated by subtracting the marketing costs of a product from the revenue gained from the product:

MARKETING PROFIT = sales revenue of a product (quantity sold x price) - marketing costs marketing research, advertising, distribution, promotion etc.)

Thus a product with high revenue and relatively low marketing costs will be highly profitable. In contrast, a product with low sales revenue and relatively high marketing costs will be less profitable.

The main benefit of calculating marketing profitability is that it can highlight some of the most and least profitable markets. Take the example of a business seeking to increase sales of a particular product by moving into two new markets, A and B. In market A, an increase in sales of 10 per cent can be achieved with additional marketing costs of 5 per cent. In market B, an increase in sales of 45 per cent can be achieved with additional marketing costs of 5 per cent. This business may wish to focus

Question 1.

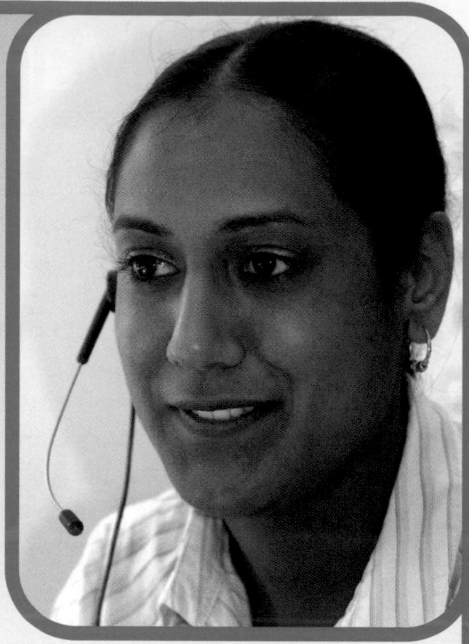

According to the 2001 census, ethnic minorities make up 9 per cent of England's population. Consumers with an ethnic minority background are typically younger and more likely to own a business than other people. They also tend to live in large urban centres, such as London or the West Midlands conurbation, creating opportunities for cost-effective local marketing. Yet British businesses are only beginning to think seriously about the needs of ethnic minority consumers.

One business area which is taking its ethnic minority customers seriously is financial institutions such as banks and building societies. Banks and building societies with branches in the West Midlands conurbation serve large numbers of customers from ethnic minority backgrounds. Some have developed policies of providing help to such customers. For example, some produce leaflets about saving and mortgage products in a number of different languages including Punjabi. Some also employ people from ethnic minorities who are able to talk to customers in their own language. This means, for example, that a Punjabi speaker can arrange a mortgage by talking to a customer adviser who will conduct the interview in Punjabi.

The financial institutions involved have benefited from this approach. Many ethnic groups have a close-knit character that makes word of mouth a powerful force to be reckoned with. Alexandria Hough, a customer services adviser at the Smethwick branch of the West Bromwich Building Society, says 'recommendation is hugely important. A lot of mortgages we sell to Sikh customers come about through parents telling their children about us.'

Source: adapted from the *Financial Times*, 28.3.2003.

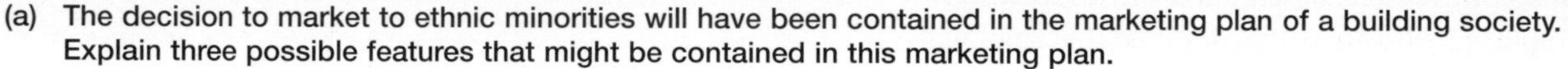

(a) The decision to market to ethnic minorities will have been contained in the marketing plan of a building society. Explain three possible features that might be contained in this marketing plan.

(b) Suggest how a building society in the West Midlands could evaluate the part of its marketing plan relating to ethnic minorities.

upon the more profitable market B.

The problem with calculating marketing profitability is that it is often difficult to calculate the marketing costs of particular products. For example, many promotional activities, such as trade fairs and corporate advertising, cannot be easily apportioned to individual products in businesses with a range of products.

Satisfaction surveys Many businesses undertake analysis of their customer satisfaction surveys. These are detailed surveys designed to identify the reactions of customers to their products. They use this data to assess the extent to which marketing plans are leading to increases or decreases in customer satisfaction.

Number of enquiries generated Many businesses pay very careful attention to the numbers of enquiries generated in particular aspects of their business. For example, financial service businesses monitor and evaluate the enquiries generated by direct mailshots as a means of evaluating the success of such promotions.

It is possible to produce clear data in some areas. For example, a bank which sends out half a million direct mail letters offering loans can measure the proportion of customers who respond. In turn, the proportion of customers finally given a loan can be calculated. So the cost per loan given or the cost per £1 loaned as a result of the direct mailing can be calculated. Equally, a business which is advertising on the Internet can measure the number of 'clicks' on an advert which take a potential customer from the advert to a website. Or the number of 'hits' on a website can be measured and the proportion which leads to a sale on the Internet can be calculated.

But the number of areas where there is such a clear link between marketing spending and sales is limited. Some businesses attempt to get around this problem by using sophisticated mathematical techniques which use correlation techniques to strip out the effect of changes in other variables. Targets for the effect on sales and profits of marketing spending can then be set. However, most businesses would not set such targets in their marketing plan because of the difficulty of getting accurate and reliable data.

Evaluating a marketing plan

A marketing plan should be evaluated at different stages.

At the start While it is being written, managers need to consider whether:
- it meets the objectives set in the marketing strategy and fits in with the corporate strategy of the business;
- the actions described in the marketing plan and their outcomes are realistic;
- the marketing department will be given a sufficiently large budget to carry out its plan.

In operation While the plan is operational, it should be monitored. A number of factors might lead to the plan failing.
- The external environment might become much harsher. For example, it may be difficult to increase sales in a recession.

- Other parts of the overall corporate plan might fail. For example, if the production department planned to increase output by 6 per cent a year, but only managed 2 per cent, then a planned 6 per cent increase in sales is unlikely to come about.
- There might be unforeseen cuts in the marketing budget.
- The original plan may have been too optimistic about the relation between changes to the marketing budget and changes in sales. For example, an expensive advertising campaign may not lead to the increase in sales hoped for. Equally, the marketing plan may have been too pessimistic. For example, the external environment may prove far more favourable than anticipated or an advertising campaign may work far more successfully than predicted.

When a marketing plan clearly is not on target while it is operational, managers should adjust the plan to take account of the new realities facing them. If they don't, they risk the plan becoming useless for operational purposes, as the predictions of the plan become more and more out of line with what is actually happening.

At the end The marketing plan should also be evaluated at the end of the plan. This evaluation should help those drawing up the next plan to see what has been successful and what has gone wrong with the existing plan. They can then build these insights into the new plan.

Co-ordinating the marketing plan with the other business functions

Marketing plans should not be written in isolation from the plans of other departments. In a large business, co-ordination is essential if plans are not to conflict with each other. For example, the marketing department might plan to set up an Internet site and require extra staff to run and develop the operation over the next three years. But the human resources department could be planning to reduce overall staff numbers in the business to achieve greater efficiency. These two plans may conflict. Therefore it is important that both departments agree on a plan which has the same effects.

Co-ordination in a large business is often difficult to achieve. Different departments have different and often conflicting agendas. It may need strong and charismatic leadership from the top of the organisation to get a whole business moving in the same direction. Planning can help achieve this unity of direction, but it is unlikely to be a business solution for problems of poor co-ordination.

Internal influences on marketing plans

There is a number of possible factors that may influence a marketing plan. These include both **internal** and **external** factors. Internal factors are those factors within the business that affect its marketing plans.

The marketing mix Of great importance will be an examination of the effectiveness of the marketing mix. This will include an analysis of each element of the marketing mix. For example, projections regarding the life span and future profitability of each of the firm's products may be carried out. It should also include an analysis of how well the elements of the marketing mix fit together, for example, the extent to which distribution channels are compatible with the promotions may be considered.

Finance Firms can set themselves ambitious marketing goals. However, unless finance is available to fund plans, such goals are unlikely to be achieved. Consequently, the availability of finance can act as an important constraint upon a business' capacity to realise its marketing plan. For example, the so-called 'credit crunch' experienced by many businesses in 2007-08 meant that for some businesses, most particularly those operating in the property market, the necessary finance to realise marketing plans was not available.

Operational issues There is a number of operational issues internal to a business that can impact upon marketing plans. Two important operational issues in this respect include a business' production processes and the people it employs. Any marketing plan must take into account whether the firm can produce the product. There is little point in planning to increase market share unless enough of the product can be produced to achieve this. A firm cannot plan to launch a new product if it cannot manufacture it. Similarly, a huge range of people will be involved in devising and implementing marketing plans. The objectives of these people will determine the targets set in the plan. Also, the skills and abilities of those people working for a firm will determine whether targets can be met.

External influences on marketing plans

There is also a range of external factors that can influence marketing plans. These are factors outside the business that affect its marketing plans. A major factor can be **competitor's actions**. The behaviour of rival businesses can be an important influence upon a business' marketing plan. For example, the entry into a market of an aggressive new competitor might mean that an existing business within that same market scales down its forecasts for sales growth. On the other hand a rival business exiting a market as a result, for example, of bankruptcy, might open up new opportunities for an existing business.

It is possible to analyse external influences using the PESTLE ANALYSIS. This includes the political, economic, social, technological and environmental factors which affect a business's performance.

- **Political.** This can include the effect of pressure groups or other political organisations. For example, ASH is a pressure group which aims to 'eliminate the harm caused by tobacco'. It might provides information on its website about the effects of smoking and lobbies government to introduce legislation to limit the effects of smoking.

- **Economic.** A wide range of economic factors may affect a business's marketing plans. A buoyant economy, for example, may lead to increased demand for products, higher incomes and the possibility of price increases. Growing unemployment may lead to a fall in future levels of demand. Marketing plans should also take into account the pricing, promotion, distribution and product policies of rival businesses.
- **Social.** Changes in society can have consequences for marketing planning. The decline of the so-called nuclear family and the changing role of women may influence how a business promotes its product. The ageing of the population may influence the types of products which are developed and the channels of distribution used to deliver products to customers.
- **Technological.** Changes in technology can affect marketing plans in a variety of ways. It may make it possible for businesses to manufacture products that were previously thought to be too costly. It may also lead to greater obsolescence and shorter product life cycles. New technological developments, such as interactive television and the Internet, may change the promotional methods that a business uses.
- **Legal factors.** There is an increasing amount of legislation and regulation that may affect the marketing plans of a business. It can vary from controls on the ingredients of products to restrictions on price changes of public utilities, such as water and gas. Much of the legislation affecting the UK comes from the European Union.
- **Environmental factors.** Environmental factors are playing an increasing role in the operation of businesses. Legislation on pollution and emissions might influence production. The expectations of consumers about packaging and ingredients might affect marketing. Pressure groups can affect decisions. Taking into account the effects of operations on the environment can increase business costs, but may also increase sales.

Marketing audits and SWOT analysis

Examining the external and the internal and external factors that affect the marketing of a business is part of a marketing audit as explained in the unit 'Understanding marketing objectives'. The marketing audit should identify the internal strengths (S) and weaknesses (W) of the business. It should also identify the external opportunities (O) and threats (T). SWOT ANALYSIS outlines these factors. Table 1 gives an example of a SWOT analysis for a soft drinks manufacturer.

The advantages of marketing planning

There are advantages to a business of planning its marketing effectively.

- The process of drawing up a marketing plan forces a business to think about how it will act in the future. It can therefore be proactive in its marketing and not just

Table 1: SWOT analysis of a soft drinks manufacturer

STRENGTHS (the strong points of the business)
• Current products are market leaders in some countries in terms of sales and market share.
• Brand loyalty to products and to the corporate identity.
• Effective promotion.
• Flexibility in production methods.
• Excellent distribution network.
• Constant R&D leading to new ideas.
WEAKNESSES (the problems it has at present)
• Age of the life cycle of certain products.
• Restricted product range could cause problems if sales suddenly fall.
OPPORTUNITIES (that may arise in future)
• Expansion into newer markets such as sports drinks, low calorie drinks and drinks with new flavours.
• Expansion into new geographical areas such as Eastern Europe.
• Development of a global brand and possible global marketing.
• Possible growing demand for soft beverages.
• Legislation on drink driving may encourage growth of soft drink sales.
THREATS (that may arise and should be avoided/prevented if possible)
• Growing competition from supermarket own brands.
• Increasing competition from competitors bringing out new products.
• Competition from producers of alcoholic beverages and non-alcoholic beers and lagers.
• Legislation on ingredients could force changes in production.

reactive. The larger the business, the more likely it is that successful marketing will only come about through careful planning.

- Because a wide range of employees should be involved in drawing up the marketing plan in a large company, there is more chance that workers will be committed to ensuring that the goals of the company are achieved. It is a way of motivating and informing staff.
- A thorough planning process will mean that the marketing plan is co-ordinated with other plans in the business. Therefore all departments will be pulling in the same direction.
- Marketing plans are drawn up in the light of the objectives of a business. There is therefore more chance that these objectives will be achieved than if there were no plans.

Question 2.

Paul Rossington had just been appointed Marketing Manager of SBC plc, a firm which had forty years' experience of supplying a range of instrumentation and components to the aircraft industry. Paul had decided that his first act would be to involve a range of managers in drawing up a marketing plan. To this end, he called a meeting requesting the presence of all senior managers within the firm. At the meeting, he began with a short presentation outlining the advantages to SBC plc of marketing planning. He then invited comments from all those assembled. The sales manager chipped in with the first comment; 'It's about time we started advertising more heavily in trade journals and stopped turning out products with the wrong specifications'. The production manager came next; 'I don't know why you dragged me up here to this meeting. You concentrate on the marketing and I'll get on with the production side. So long as you keep me informed of developments we'll be happy down in production.'

Paul was beginning to feel uncomfortable, but it wasn't until the senior accountant's remark that he really felt worried about having accepted this new post. 'I suggest you go away and write this plan and then call another meeting when you're in a position to discuss it with us', she had said.

(a) What advantages of marketing planning would you have advised Paul to mention in his brief presentation?

(b) From the comments made at the meeting, explain any problems which you think SBC plc will have with marketing planning.

The problems of marketing planning

However, marketing planning can also have certain problems.

- Scarce resources, for examples in terms of management and employee time, are used up in creating a marketing plan. Those resources could have been used elsewhere. There is therefore an opportunity cost in drawing up a marketing plan.
- Too many marketing plans are poorly drawn up. They may fail to take account of the objectives of the business. They may be created by a few individuals who see them as 'paper-pushing' exercises. The marketing plan may be filed away and never used. Those creating the plan may include actions which the business could never do, or may be far too cautious in their approach. The marketing plan may not be co-ordinated with other plans in the business.

KEYTERMS

Marketing planning – the process by which marketing activities are identified and decided upon.

Marketing plan – a set of proposed marketing actions to be undertaken over a period of time which, if carried out, should enable the business to achieve its marketing objectives.

PESTLE analysis – an analysis of the external political, economic, social, technological, legal and environmental factors affecting a business.

SWOT analysis – analysis of the internal strengths and weaknesses of a business and its external opportunities and threats.

KNOWLEDGE

1. State four aspects of the marketing plan.
2. In a large company, who might be involved in writing a marketing plan?
3. What targets might be set within a marketing plan?
4. State three internal and three external factors that may affect a marketing plan.
5. State three benefits of marketing planning.
6. State three problems of marketing planning.

Case Study: The XBox, 2001-2007

Xbox launch, 2001

Microsoft launched its XBox video game console in 2001. It spent $500 million on the launch of the new product, including spending on marketing, advertising and support to retailers and software makers.

Prior to the launch, the senior vice president of the company's games division said 'We have to build demand for this to be successful.'

The new product, which would include DVD drive and Internet access, was part of the plans of the business to move beyond the PC market. Microsoft also planned to tap into the market for devices that combine television and the Internet, and to offer online gaming.

Microsoft was developing 30 video games inhouse and approving many games from other software developers. It was suggested that the XBox would have three times the performance of Sony's PlayStation 2 (PS2). By the time the XBox was released, Sony's PS2 and Sega's Dreamcast would already have been on the market for a year.

2002-2004 One down, three to go. In February 2002 Sega announced that it would cease production of the Sega Dreamcast games console and quit the hardware business. Instead it decided to produce games for other games consoles. The three left remaining were Sony's PS2, Microsoft's XBox and Nintendo's GameCube. In 2002 there were 30 million PS2 consoles worldwide (as well as 90 million old PS1 consoles). Contrast that to the 4 million XBoxes worldwide.

The Internet gaming market is growing. It was estimated at the time that it would be a $20 billion industry by 2005. In 2002 Sony's PS2 and Microsoft's XBox were planned to be linked to the Internet for interactive gaming. However, unlike the XBox, the PS2 would require additional equipment to be bought. Previously people could play games through their PCs on the Internet. But now they could take advantage of the stunning graphics of games consoles.

2002-2003 Between August 2002-03 Microsoft's XBox was the only gaming console to show positive market share growth in the US. It was suggested that sales increased 6 per cent in the US, giving it a 27 per cent market share. In comparison sales of Sony's PS2 fell to 36 per cent and Nintendo's GameCube fell to 22 per cent. In May 2003 the price of the XBox was cut in the US from $199 to $179 in response to a similar cut in the price of Sony's PS2. XBox sales have been fuelled by the success of its almost 400 software games, including Star Wars games. XBox Live, Microsoft's online gaming service, had over half a million subscribers.

In October 2003 Nintendo reduced the price of its GameCube to $99 in the US. Within 35 days it was suggested that it had doubled its market share in the US from 19 to 37 per cent as a result, becoming a strong second in the market.

2004 In 2004 Sony announced that it had shipped over 50 million consoles since the launch of PS2 in 2000. This compared to nine million sales worldwide of Microsoft's XBox. This gave XBox 15 per cent of the global market, a long way from Sony's estimated 70 per cent global market share. The majority of XBoxes are in the US (6 million), with 2.2 million in Europe. Microsoft admits it is weak in Asia, where it has struggled to make an impact in Japan in particular.

Analysts suggested that Microsoft loses $100 on every XBox it sells. Yet the company has strong relationships with retailers and is pinning many of its hopes on the broadband market. It is particularly concentrating its marketing on areas of the world where broadband penetration is high, such as South Korea. This gives great possibilities when XBox Live is launched in these countries.

2007 The balance of power in the games console market has tipped towards Nintendo and away from Microsoft and Sony after the phenomenal success of the Wii gaming console helped the Kyoto-based company almost triple its profits in the first half of the year.

The reversal of fortunes within the games console sector has been stunning and highly unexpected given Nintendo's Wii was tipped to struggle to compete with its competitors. Sony – which had achieved unparalleled success with the first two incarnations of its PlayStation machine – and Microsoft were widely expected to dominate the market for next-generation consoles with state-of-the-art machines.

Nintendo stuck to its guns and despite concerns that the Wii would be another also-ran compared with the top-end Play-Station 3 and Xbox 360, the console has sold like wildfire and proved the doubters wrong. It has outsold the PS3 three-to-one in the Japanese market and five-to-one in the US and has taken the PS2's mantle as the fastest selling console in history in the UK after shifting 1 million machines in just eight months. The Wii has reinvigorated the video games sector by appealing to consumers outside the 'hard-core' gaming market, particularly female gamers and families. While titles such as the ultra-violent Grand Theft Auto: San Andreas and Resident Evil sold well to traditional fans who lust after eye-boggling graphics and more complex adventures, Nintendo recognised that there was a vast untapped market of people who wanted more simple and fun games. The Wii's motion-sensor-based controllers revolutionised the market by allowing consumers to physically play simple games, such as tennis and ten-pin bowling, on the screen. The games are far more basic than the likes of Halo 3 that boast the best graphics, but that has not deterred consumers from outside the traditional video games audience.

David Yarnton, managing director of Nintendo UK, said the decision to target non-traditional gamers with the Wii has led to household penetration of consoles rising for the first time in 25 years.

Sources: adapted from www.instat.com., news.com., asia.cnet.com,and www.forbes.com., xcox.the maingroup.com, www.ciol.com, abcnews.go.com., *The Independent* 23.11.2007.

(a) **Using examples from the information, outline the benefits of marketing planning for businesses in the game consoles market. (6 marks).**

(b) **Examine the external and internal factors affecting businesses in the game consoles market. (12 marks)**

(c) **Carry out a SWOT analysis of X-Box's position in the market. (12 marks)**

(d) **Evaluate the success of marketing planning by Microsoft for X-Box. (20 marks)**

29 Marketing strategies

Marketing strategy

A MARKETING STRATEGY is a set of plans about marketing which are designed to fulfil the objectives of a business. A marketing strategy might, for example, set out plans about product development, pricing and promotion to achieve marketing objectives, such as breaking into new markets or increasing sales of existing products.

A marketing strategy is a set of plans about the future. A successful marketing strategy must have plans which are achievable and realistic. Marketing plans in practice may simply be the 'wish lists' of the marketing department, which have little chance of success. For example, at the moment it may be unrealistic for Waitrose to have as its marketing strategy 'the growth of the business so that it becomes the number 1 supermarket chain in the UK within two to three years'. It is so far behind the current number 1, Tesco, that within three years it is highly unlikely that it would achieve this. But a realistic strategy could be to 'increase market share at the expense of small independent grocery retailers'.

Marketing strategy will differ from one business to another. Partly this is because there are many different markets and industries in which they operate. But even businesses in the same market adopt different marketing strategies. For example, the marketing strategy of Aldi and Netto in the grocery market is to offer goods at lower prices than larger rivals, such as Sainsbury's or Tesco. The marketing strategy of Sainsbury's and Tesco places more importance on their product ranges and the quality of their products.

Another reason why marketing strategy differs is because no two businesses have identical resources. Jaguar cars, for example, has expertise in developing, producing and marketing luxury cars. Vauxhall in the UK may have more expertise in the family car market. So their marketing strategies are likely to be different.

Figure 1: The stages of preparing a marketing strategy

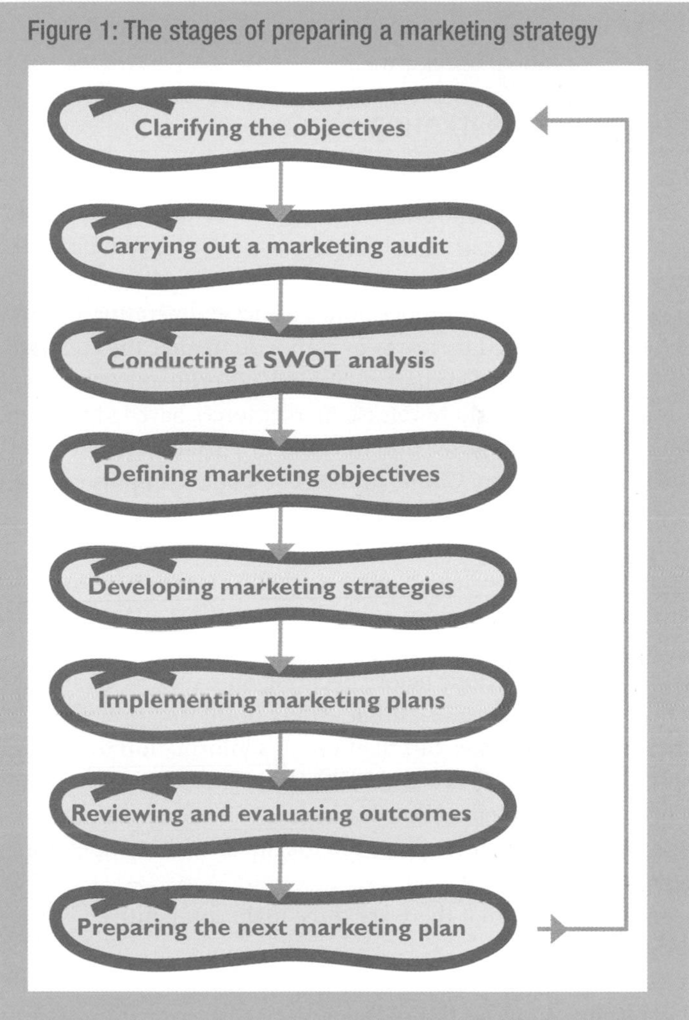

Developing a marketing strategy

There are many ways in which a marketing strategy can be developed.

For a small, established business, a marketing strategy could be simply to continue as before. Only if circumstances change might a business change its marketing strategy. This is an example of a rational marketing strategy, if the objective is to continue making the same level of profit. Developing a marketing strategy requires time and resources. It also involves predicting how a market will develop, which could be wrong. Formal planning, therefore, would be costly and could be of little value.

Similarly, in businesses where there are charismatic leaders, planning may be pointless. The leader may be constantly making decisions as events change. These decisions might have little to do with a prepared strategy.

A more rigorous approach, often used by larger businesses, is where:

- assumptions are made and objectives are set;
- information is gathered;
- a hypothesis or theory is put forward;
- this is tested using quantifiable data;
- then it is reviewed.

This approach is similar to the testing of theories used in subjects like science. In business, a multinational company aiming for growth, based on market research information could hypothesise that the market for sales in China will grow greatly during the next five years. It could test market products in China to verify its ideas. The business might then decide to target its products and marketing at the Chinese market as a result. This approach is sometimes referred to as the **marketing model.**

It is often suggested that such an approach reduces the risk that decisions will be incorrect and strategies will fail. However, this does not mean that gut feeling decisions cannot be effective, but they may be more risky. Large businesses might not be prepared to take this type of risk. Small businesses might not want to either. But they may have no choice if they do not have the time or resources to carry out detailed decision making techniques.

The stages a business may follow in preparing a marketing strategy are shown in Figure 1.

Competitive marketing strategies

Many businesses are finding that the markets in which they operate are increasingly competitive. Two factors might explain this. First, the increasing internationalisation of trade means that many markets that were dominated by domestic business are now open to foreign competition. Businesses operating within the EU experienced increases in competition after the creation of the single European market. Second, government attempts throughout the world to release market forces have led to many markets being privatised and liberalised. This has often led to greater competition. China, in the 2000s, opened up its economy so that foreign business could operate in the country.

These changes have led businesses to pay careful attention to their competitors when creating marketing strategies. Businesses often carry out competitor analysis. Competitor analysis allows a business to develop a knowledge and understanding of its competitors' behaviour before deciding on a suitable strategy. This provides businesses with a variety of information about their rivals. Businesses can then use this information to develop suitable COMPETITIVE MARKETING STRATEGIES. Competitive strategies allow businesses to compete most effectively with their rivals and to maximise their competitive advantage.

It is suggested that there are three main competitive strategies.

Cost leadership The aim of following a cost leadership strategy is to gain a cost advantage over competitors. This **low cost** advantage can then be passed on to consumers in the form of lower prices. Businesses can gain a cost advantage by having higher levels of productivity and more efficient supplier and distribution networks. Amstrad is an example of a business which has pursued this strategy. It provides electrical goods cheaper than those of competitors. The main problem with cost leadership is that it focuses upon costs of production and lower prices rather than the needs of customers. This may create certain problems. For example, consumers might not always wish to purchase the lowest priced product as it may have been perceived as being of lower quality.

Differentiation This strategy is where a business offers consumers something different from that which is offered by its competitors, in order to gain a competitive 'edge' over them. The difference can be in terms of something real, such as a technical difference in the product itself, or perceived, such as a strong brand identity developed through a promotional campaign. In the latter case, consumers must actually believe the perceived difference. Guinness, for example, has been differentiated both in terms of its smooth consistency and taste, and through marketing campaigns which promote it as an 'intelligent' drink.

Question 1.

Travel giants, such as Thomas Cook and JMC, slashed the prices of Spanish holidays by an average £150 in 2004. This was almost unheard of. But it was in response to the growing impact made by cut price airlines. It was seen as a deliberate attempt to win back custom from the low cost airlines.

It was the first time that the major companies felt that they had to cut the cost of ordinary family holidays to popular destinations. Two adults travelling to Majorca with Thomas Cook would save £120. Five adults going to Gran Canaria with JMC would save £210. Cosmos introduced a 'two kids free' deal to seven family resorts.

Bookings for holidays in popular resorts such as Spain had been sluggish. However, resorts outside the eurozone, such as those in the eastern Mediterranean, were doing well.

Source: adapted from *The Daily Mail*, 26.1.2004.

(a) Analyse the competitive strategies and market positions of the businesses in the travel industry using examples from the data.

Focus Businesses adopting focus strategies concentrate upon particular market segments rather than on the market as a whole. They attempt to meet effectively the needs of a clearly defined group of consumers. By following this strategy, a business seeks to gain a competitive advantage over other businesses which spread their efforts over a wider range of consumers. For example, there is a small but thriving market for hand made, made-to-measure suits.

Market positioning

Another set of competitive marketing strategies is based upon the 'position' which a business wishes to occupy in relation to other businesses operating in the same market.

Market leader strategies In many markets there is one business which is generally recognised as the market leader. Market leaders tend to have the largest share of a particular market. Market leaders may also be businesses which lead the market in terms of price changes and promotional spending. An example of a market leader might be Microsoft in the software market. There is a number of strategies which market leaders can adopt to improve or maintain their market leadership.

- Expanding the total market. As holders of the largest market share, market leaders stand most to gain by expanding the market. Expanding the market can be achieved by attracting new product users, promoting new uses for the product or encouraging greater product usage. For example, breakfast cereal manufacturers have tried to get consumers to eat cereal at different times of the day.
- Expanding market share. Market leaders may use the range of elements in the marketing mix to expand their current market share at the expense of competitors'. For example, Microsoft increased its share of the computer software market by establishing its product as the standard PC operating system.
- Defending current market share. The aim here is to prevent competitors from increasing their market share at the expense of the market leader. Most market leaders take the view that defending market share can best be achieved by continually improving the way in which they meet consumer needs. Often this is achieved with the use of complex and sophisticated marketing strategies. For example, some commentators have seen the development by Nestlé of a range of brands in the instant coffee market not only as an example of meeting new needs, but also as a sophisticated form of defence. The development of the Alta Rica, Cap Colombie and Blend 37 brands can be seen as a defence of Nescafé and Gold Blend against competitors seeking to damage Nestlé's share of this market by gaining a foothold in smaller segments.

Market challenger strategies MARKET CHALLENGERS are those businesses with a substantial share of the market. However, they hold second, third or lower positions in the market in relation to the market leader. Not all businesses with lower market shares than the leader are market challengers. To be defined as market challengers businesses must be in a strong enough position to challenge the leader and be willing to adopt strategies to win more market share. There are three main types of strategy that market challengers can adopt.

- Direct attacks on the market leader. Here the market challenger must be prepared to directly compete in terms of the market leaders' strengths and also to match its marketing mix. To do this the market challenger must be able to match the resources of the market leader and to respond to retaliatory actions by the market leader. Such retaliatory actions often take the form of price cutting and aggressive promotion and distribution campaigns.
- Indirect attacks on the market leader. Because of the problems involved in mounting a direct attack upon a market leader, many market followers choose to adopt less confrontational strategies. One of the most common is to identify areas in which the market leader is less strong and to develop products designed to address these weaknesses. For example, businesses have attempted to compete with the crisp manufacturer Walkers by offering exotic snack foods, such as popadums and Chinese rice crackers.
- Attacking firms other than the market leader. This allows a business to increase its market share by attacking relatively weaker businesses. For example, many of the larger brewing businesses have increased their market share in this way in the UK by taking over smaller breweries.

Market follower strategies Many businesses occupying lower positions in a market do not wish to challenge the market leader. Challenges to a market leader often lead to retaliatory action and cause expensive battles, which often hurt challengers more than they do leaders. For this reason many businesses choose to follow the strategies of market leaders. There are three main types of MARKET FOLLOWERS.

- Those who imitate market leaders. Own-brand products in supermarkets fall into this category, as do canned drinks such as Virgin Cola. In more extreme cases imitation may lead to cloning. This occurs when one business seeks to copy the market leaders' products without originating anything itself.
- Innovative businesses. Such businesses lack the resources to challenge market leaders. They tend to willingly follow moves made by market leaders so that they do not change the structure of the market.
- Businesses incapable of challenging market leaders, which are content to satisfice. It is not unusual to find such businesses in the take-away food market. These businesses have little competitive advantage. They tend to be vulnerable to changes in the market and may fail as a consequence.

Market niche strategies Market niches are very small segments of the market. They are sometimes described as segments within segments. The majority of businesses which operate in niche markets tend to be small and medium sized. However, some larger businesses have divisions specialising in market niches. Niches can be based upon geographical location, specific

Figure 2: The Ansoff Matrix

		PRODUCT	
		Existing	New
MARKET	Existing	Market penetration	Product development
	New	Market development	Diversification

product differentiation, customer group or product type. Examples of businesses adopting market niche strategies include Tie Rack, Reuters and TVR, the sports car manufacturer.

Marketing strategies for growth

Many businesses operate in or intend to move into markets where business growth is both desirable and possible. Businesses operating in such markets will tend to emphasise growth in their corporate and marketing objectives. Growth may be in the form of increased sales revenue or turnover, greater profits, increased capital or more land and employees. There is a range of marketing strategies that growth orientated businesses can adopt. Growth orientated marketing strategies are not suited to all businesses, however. In shrinking markets, for example, a business may wish to maintain previous sales levels or just survive rather than aim for growth.

The ANSOFF MATRIX is a useful tool for businesses aiming for growth. The Ansoff Matrix shown in Figure 2 illustrates both existing and new products within existing and new markets. Four possible marketing strategies to achieve growth are revealed by the Matrix.

Market penetration As suggested by the Ansoff Matrix, the purpose of market penetration is to achieve growth in existing markets with existing products. There is a number of ways in which businesses can achieve this.

- Increasing the brand loyalty of customers so that they use substitute brands less frequently. Well known brands such as Kellogg's Corn Flakes make use of this strategy.
- Encouraging consumers to use the product more regularly. An example might be encouraging people to drink canned drinks at breakfast.
- Encouraging consumers to use more of the product. An example might be a crisp manufacturer producing maxi sized crisp packets rather than standard sized crisp packets.

Product development This is concerned with marketing new or modified products in existing markets. The development of the Ford Focus, intended to act as a replacement for the Ford Escort, is an example of product development. Confectionery manufacturers, such as Cadbury and Nestlé, regularly use this strategy in order to stimulate sales growth.

Market development This involves the marketing of existing products in new markets. For example, the Halifax has extended its banking activities to the Spanish market and Harvey Nichols, a retail outlet previously limited to London, has opened branches in Leeds and Manchester.

Diversification This occurs when new products are developed for new markets. Diversification allows a business to move away from reliance upon existing markets and products. This allows a business to spread risk and increase safety. If one product faces difficulties or fails, a successful product in another market may prevent the business overall facing problems. However, diversification will take a business outside its area of expertise. This might mean that its performance in new markets is relatively poor compared to more experienced operators. The move by Mercedes Benz into the market for small, high volume cars and the move by Virgin into financial services and the air passenger business are perhaps examples of this marketing strategy.

Factors affecting marketing strategies

There is a number of factors that may influence a business's marketing strategy.

The objectives of the business The marketing strategy that a business uses must reflect the objectives of the business as a whole. Marketing strategies must therefore be consistent with the wider corporate objectives of the organisation. For example, a business which is aiming to reduce the number of countries in which it operates should not develop international marketing strategies which go against this wider, corporate strategy. However, marketing strategies are not always secondary to corporate objectives. In some businesses, marketing information and strategies often have a strong influence upon corporate objectives and strategies. A growing market for ethical customers, for example, may persuade the business to deal only with those businesses that conform to certain ethical principles.

The strategies of competitor businesses As shall be seen later in this unit, many businesses take account of the strategies of their competitors when setting their own marketing strategies. For example, if a competitor promotes all of its company products on the Internet successfully, other businesses may follow.

The structure of the market Marketing strategies will be influenced by the level of competition and the degree of change within different markets. In less competitive markets, with relatively little change, for example, businesses may find that their strategies require only minor adjustments from one period to another. In more competitive and dynamic markets businesses may find that marketing strategies require far reaching changes on an annual basis. For example, a manufacturer of active wear clothing aimed at 16-24 year olds may need to constantly monitor changes in tastes.

The attitudes of key decision makers within businesses Marketing strategies are likely to be influenced by the attitudes of decision makers towards matters such as the desirability of risk and change. Such attitudes are not only influenced by the environment within which a business operates, but also by the views of managers and directors and the culture of the business itself. For example, new managers aiming to alter the 'direction' of a business may decide to change the entire distribution network to mail order and to sell off its retail outlets, because this has worked successfully in other businesses.

The size of the business Larger businesses are likely to be strongly influenced by one or more of the above factors when making decisions about their marketing strategies. Smaller and medium-sized businesses, however, often find strategic decision making more challenging. This is because the owners and managers of such businesses are often so immersed in the operational side of their work that they take few opportunities to adopt a strategic outlook. As a result, marketing strategy may be influenced by 'intuition' and responses to daily pressures.

The strengths of the business Asset-based or asset-led marketing is where a business develops those products that make the best use of its 'core competences'. These are the major strengths of the firm. It produces goods or services that make the best use of its resources. Many businesses see brand loyalty or goodwill as a major **intangible asset**.

The marketing strategy adopted by such businesses will therefore attempt to develop products that can be associated with the brand names of its successful products. Many food manufacturers have followed this marketing strategy in recent years. Examples have included ice cream Mars Bars and Kit Kat Chunky. One of the most successful companies in the world, the Walt Disney Company, has perhaps followed this strategy into a number of areas. The launch by Ikea of a new range of furniture or a construction company moving into house renovation might be other examples. Examples in the service industry might include travel companies buying cottages to let for holidays or buying ships to sell cruise holidays.

Question 2.

In 2004 Levi's went back to the drawing board with its classic Levi 501 jeans. They were recut in a bid to attract a new generation of wearers. Too many young people were put off by 'middle aged men' such as Top Gear presenter Jeremy Clarkson, who continued to wear jeans. The company planned to spend £10 million on the new jeans aimed at the under 25s rather than over 40s. The jeans would retail at £50 a pair and would resemble the original denim work trousers designed and marketed by Levi Strauss in 1873. A TV campaign would support the launch. The company suggested that the 501s on general sale in the UK were very eighties and nineties and had begun to look dated. Levi's had faced competition from a wide variety of jeans manufacturers. These included own-brand jeans from shops such as Gap and 'designer' jeans from Firetrap, Armani and Ted Baker, as well as from traditional jeans manufacturers such as Wrangler.

In the USA everybody's heard of Levi's jeans, but not enough people are buying them. Instant brand recognition is not enough. It had some success in wooing women, particularly with its new low waist jeans for young women. People know that Levi's make good quality jeans, but want more than a box fit. Research has shown that its image perception is improving, but it needs to react more quickly to fast changing trends in the fashion scene.

Source: adapted from *The Daily Mail*, and www.mercurynews.com.

(a) Identify the factors that may have contributed to the changes in marketing strategy by Levi's.

(b) To what extent do you think that Levi's might make use of its assets in its new strategy?

Marketing strategy issues

Over time many issues arise that business must take into account when developing their marketing strategies. Over the last decade a number of issues have become increasingly important.

Social marketing SOCIAL MARKETING was first analysed by Kotler and Zaman in 1971. It was defined as 'the design, implantation and control of programs to influence the acceptability of social ideas involving considerations of product planning, pricing, communication, distribution and market research'. In the late 1990s it was agreed by many researchers that it involved the use of marketing techniques to bring about changes in behaviour that benefit society. So social marketing makes use of the tools of commercial marketing, such as market research, segmentation, branding and the use of the marketing mix.

Examples of social marketing might include a reduction in tooth decay by improved dental hygiene, an improvement in people's health by changing their diet, a reduction in disease by improved medication or an improvement in the water system by the use of fluoride.

Social marketing is not the same as businesses being socially responsible. These tend to be businesses that consider the effect on the environment etc., but are ultimately judged on profit for shareholders. Social marketing is different because its success is judged on the benefit to society rather than commercial goals. Nor is it the same as ethical businesses that are concerned about fair and socially acceptable business practices.

However, some profit orientated businesses do engage in social marketing. Procter & Gamble, for example, contributed to a major social marketing drugs prevention initiative in the North East of England.

Green marketing Today the world faces a 'green' problem – the need to make the environment sustainable and yet still develop. This provides a number of challenges for marketing. GREEN MARKETING has been defined as 'the management process responsible for identifying, anticipating and satisfying customers and society in a profitable and sustainable way'. It involves using resources in a way that is sustainable, so they can be replenished or replaced in future. It also involves reducing pollution and waste which can be absorbed into the environmental system.

The adoption of green marketing policies can have implications for marketing strategy. Businesses must try to identify 'green consumers' through market research. Businesses will only be able to satisfy their needs if they can find out the concerns of these consumers. Products and packaging must be environmentally friendly. They must be designed for re-use or recycling. Promotion may need to change. Advertising must be chosen to present a green image. Discounts may need to be given to persuade people to change to more environmentally friendly products. Sponsorship must be carefully chosen. Pricing might also be affected. Sometimes consumers might pay a slightly higher prices for free range products, for example. Distribution channels must be chosen which reduce pollution and congestion.

It has been suggested that effective green marketing will be successful if businesses have marketing strategies which follow the 7 Cs.

- Customer orientated, taking into account the views of customers about the environment.
- Commercially viable, so that products will meet consumer needs but still make a profit.
- Credible to customers, but also to other stakeholders, such as shareholders or government.
- Consistent with marketing and other business aims and objectives.
- Clear and not hidden in technical jargon.
- Co-ordinated with other business strategies.
- Communicated effectively, both internally to employees and others in the business and externally, to consumers and other stakeholders outside the business.

The impact on businesses of adapting more environmentally policies is explained in unit 112.

Question 3.

A successful buzz campaign hinges on finding the right message carriers. Ford was aware of the importance of this to its strategy when replacing the well loved Escort with the Ford Focus. The idea was to position the Focus as a hip, young person's car and help it win the war against competitors such as the market leading Honda Civic.

Ford looked for its style gurus in the New York youth marketing boutique Fusion Five. It was able to identify 120 influential buyers in five markets – New York, Miami, Los Angeles, Chicago and San Francisco. Each of the 120 people were given a Focus to drive for 6 months. They kept a record of where they went and what they did.

So did it work? Well certainly for Joe Regner, a 21 year old operations manager in Miami. He spotted a yellow Focus parked near the hip hop station WEDR and stopped to check it out. The Focus had been loaned to a DJ at the station, Jill Tracey. Joe ordered his and persuaded his girlfriend to switch from buying a Honda Civic. Ford sold over 200,000 cars in its first full year.

The person who ignites the buzz depends on the product. ConAgra Foods' Hebrew National Unit searched 12 US cities for 250 PTA presidents, Hispanic community leaders and Jewish mothers to serve on 'mom squads'. They drive around in yellow vehicles with a Hebrew National logo, hosting backyard hot dog barbecues and passing out discount coupons. The company vice chair of marketing said that even a loved American food like hot dogs can benefit from 'viral marketing'.

Source: adapted from www.businessweek.com.

(a) Explain why this strategy might be known as viral marketing.

(b) Examine the factors that might lead to the success of this type of marketing.

Internet marketing The growth of the Internet has led many businesses to consider the use of INTERNET MARKETING STRATEGIES. These are the marketing approaches used by a business selling products over the Internet. They may be similar to those used by businesses using other methods of distribution. However, there are some specific factors relating to marketing via the Internet that a business might need to consider when deciding on an Internet marketing strategy.

- Targeting the market. The target market might be regarded as restricted or larger. For example, the target market might be only people using the Internet. So a business selling an online magazine to older people in a particular area of the country might have a smaller target market than usual. However, a magazine about a topic that appeals to all people, no matter what age, region or country they come from might gain a larger market from the Internet because it is a worldwide web.
- Market research. It may be possible to gain research information about the market from the Internet. For example, some businesses download cookies and spyware onto computers to find out information about users of websites. There is software available to prevent this, so information may be restricted.
- The website. The main point of contact with the company on the Internet is the website. Image management is important. A well designed website that operates efficiently will present a good image. People like pictures, but text is more important. Users must be able to find their way around the website easily.
- Promotion. There is a variety of forms of promotion that businesses can use for their website on the Internet. They can buy advertising on other sites. They can make sure their site is included on search engines. They can also use bulletin board systems (BBSs). A BBS is like a storage facility that allows people to send and receive messages through their computers, as well as to send and receive files. They can be used to gather information about a topic or to buy and sell products. Many businesses use BBSs to send electronic mail to distributors and to talk to business prospects. Mail order businesses, banks and travel agents

often make use of BBSs.

- The nature of the product for sale can influence the website. Some products are sold online or can be downloaded, such as subscriptions to sites or written information. Others sell products which are sent to customers.
- Methods of payment. Businesses must decide how customer will pay for products. Some allow purchasers of products to pay online using credit cards. Businesses must be aware and comply with legislation about privacy of financial information. And they must comply with data protection legislation regarding information they keep about customers.
- Co-ordination. Internet marketing must be coordinated with other forms of marketing. For example, it is often useful to include the website address with other forms of publicity such as leaflets or advertisements.

Buzz or viral marketing BUZZ MARKETING is where businesses attempt to generate a positive image or 'buzz' about products through non-traditional marketing methods. It is a form of 'stealth' strategy. It usually involves businesses using word of mouth to promote a product. A business might employ groups to talk about products in appropriate places, for example software games in Internet cafés. People who are thought to be 'trend setters' might be employed to ride around in vehicles, eat food in public or wear particular clothing. For example, DaimlerChrysler generated pre-launch promotion for its PT Cruiser in the USA by placing cars in rental fleets around the trendy Miami Beach area.

The advantage of this type of marketing is that it can be a cheap and effective method for a narrow range of products, which have a target market and which people care about. It may also be useful for younger target audiences who have yet to develop brand loyalties. However, it is argued that it might be less effective for products that people have less interest in, such as washing powder. It might also lose its effectiveness if all businesses are attempting to generate a buzz for their products.

This is also sometimes referred to as VIRAL MARKETING. A 'buzz' is created about a product and this is passed from one person to another, like a virus. It can be by word of mouth. Increasingly businesses are making use of the Internet to aid marketing. Sites such as YouTube and blogs on members' sites can be helpful in creating a buzz about a particular product. People who are pleased with a product will write about it and this will be viewed by others. However, some businesses have been criticised for their viral marketing campaigns when people have found out that a blog is not genuinely from a buyer, but written by the business itself.

KEYTERMS

Ansoff Matrix – a model which identifies growth strategies for businesses based on an analysis of their products and their markets.

Buzz or viral marketing – a strategy which uses word of mouth and peer group approval to market products.

Competitive marketing strategies – marketing strategies directly based upon particular approaches to dealing with competitors.

Green marketing – a strategy which takes into account the effects of marketing on the environment.

Internet marketing strategies – the use of the worldwide web to market and sell products.

Market challengers – businesses which are in a position to threaten the market leader.

Market follower – a business which mimics or copies the strategies of the dominant businesses or businesses in the market.

Marketing strategy – a set of plans designed to achieve the marketing objectives of a business.

Social marketing – a strategy where the success of marketing is evaluated on the extent to which society benefits.

KNOWLEDGE

1. What is meant by a strategic marketing decision?
2. Outline the stages in developing a marketing strategy.
3. State the three aspects of competitor analysis.
4. Explain the difference between a cost leadership and a differentiation strategy.
5. Suggest three ways in which a market leader might protect its market position.
6. Suggest three ways in which a market challenger might improve its market position.
7. What four methods of growth strategy are suggested by the Ansoff Matrix?
8. How might a business gain greater penetration in an existing market with an existing product?
9. What are the 7Cs that might make green marketing effective?
10. State five ways in which Internet marketing might affect the marketing strategy of a business.

Case Study: Coca-cola

Figure 2: Coca-Cola and Pepsi Worldwide market share, 2006

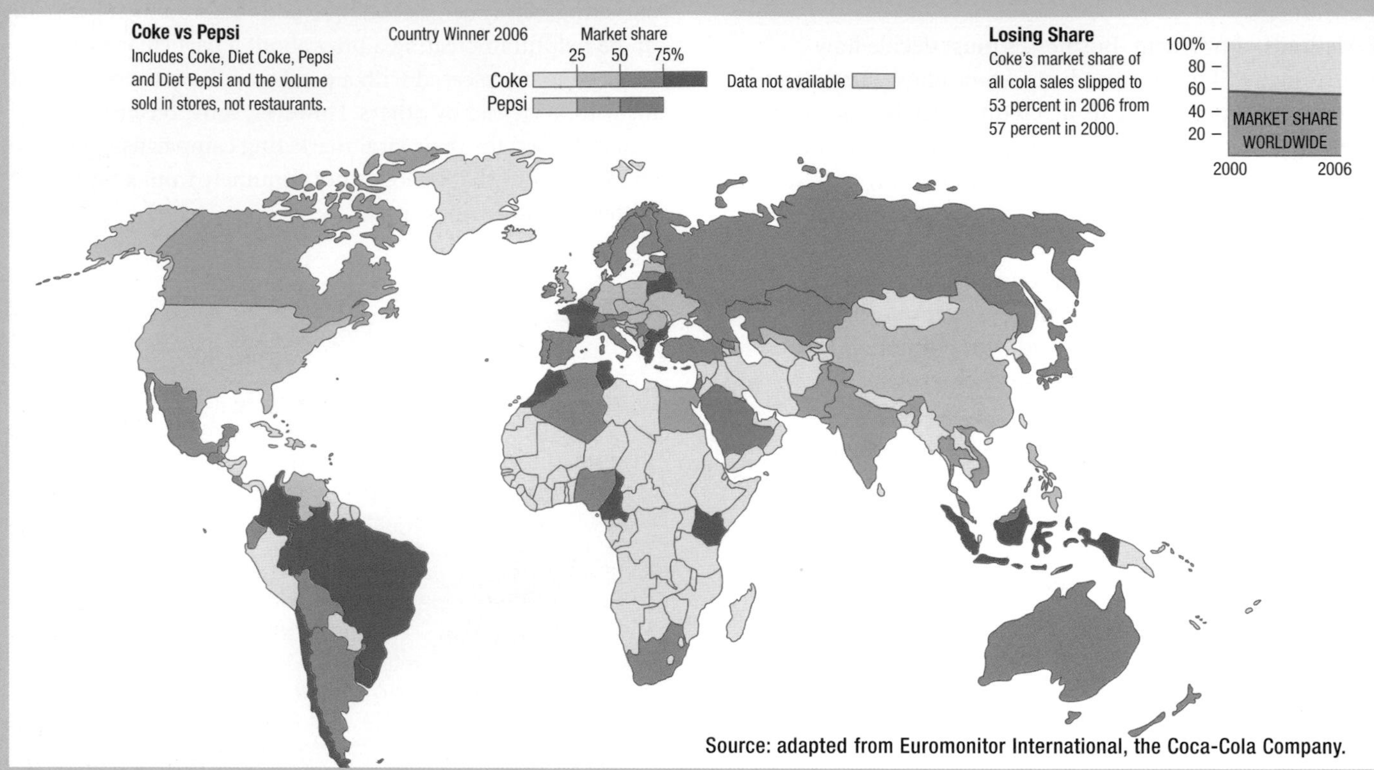

Source: adapted from Euromonitor International, the Coca-Cola Company.

In early 2007 it was reported that both Coke and Pepsi were struggling to increase sales and market share for their carbonated soft drinks in the US as more health-conscious consumers bought to energy drinks and bottled water products. A report in *Beverage Digest* showed that Coke and Pepsi both saw their share of the soda market fall in 2006 for the second straight year, led by weak sales of Coke Classic and regular Pepsi. Coke's US market share fell to 42.9 per cent in 2006 from 43.1 per cent in 2005.

In the first quarter of 2007 sales increased by 6 per cent. This was driven mainly by drinks sales in emerging markets, including China, Russia, South Africa, Nigeria, Eastern Europe and Southern Eurasia. In July 2007 expansion of Coca-Cola in China and India led to the best sales growth for almost nine years. By the second quarter of the year sales rose by 19 per cent compared with the year before. Sales of soft drinks in China, such as Diet Coke and Qoo, a vitamin C children's drink, represented the best-performing part of the group's business. But sales of carbonated drinks in the US fell by 3 per cent during the same period.

Looking ahead, Coke was pinning hopes on Coke 'Zero' a calorie-free variation of Coca-Cola launched in 2005, its new 'Diet Coke Plus' drink, energy soda beverages like 'Vault Red Blitz', flavoured waters and ready-to-drink coffee drinks to increase sales in the US. 'Zero' had double-digit growth in the US and it was suggested that the company would work on more 'extensions' around 'Zero' in future.

Source: adapted from money.cnn.com, business.timesonline.co.uk.

Table 3: Coca-cola annual income statements

	2007	2006	2005
Revenue ($m)	28,857	24,088	23,104
Gross profit ($m)	18,451	15,924	14,909

Source adapted from www.hoovers.com.

(a) Explain the different marketing positioning strategies that might be used by (i) Coca-Cola; (ii) other businesses in the soft drinks market in the US. (6 marks)

(b) Using Ansoffs' Matrix, examine the marketing strategies of Coca-Cola. (8 marks)

(c) Examine the reasons that may have influenced the marketing strategy of Coca-Cola. (12 marks)

(d) Discuss whether the marketing strategies of Coca-Cola have been successful. (12 marks)

30 International marketing

The importance of international marketing

At one time businesses may have thought that marketing products overseas was an adventurous act. It was generally undertaken by large businesses which had grown too big for domestic markets. Today, however, the world has 'shrunk' due to, amongst other things, rapid changes in international transport and telecommunications. One effect of this is that a business now needs to consider the threat from foreign competition and the opportunities which might be gained from marketing internationally.

For many firms international marketing is no longer an option. It is necessary if a business is to survive in a competitive business environment. For British firms this was the case after trade barriers between European Union nations were lifted in 1992 and perhaps with the expansion of the EU in 2004 and 2007. The increase in the size and number of multinationals has contributed to the increase in international trading. The globalisation of business activity has also affected business marketing strategy.

Why might businesses market their products internationally?

- Profits. By selling in overseas markets, a business might have the potential to increase its profits through an increase in sales. Overseas markets may be more lucrative than domestic ones. Manufacturing and distribution costs may be lower abroad. The product might also sell at a higher price on foreign markets than in the home market.
- Spreading the risk. If a business only produces in one country then it may face problems caused by downturns in demand due to recession. The more countries a firm operates in, the less vulnerable it is to changes in the business climate of any single country.
- Unfavourable trading conditions in the domestic market. Businesses often find that the market for a product is saturated or in decline. One option for a firm is to try and breathe new life into the product by introducing it into an overseas market. This is an example of an **extension strategy**. British American Tobacco industries, for example, have started to sell in developing countries as domestic market sales have declined.
- Legal differences. Legal restrictions on the sale of products vary from one country to another. For example, developing countries have fewer restrictions on which drugs can be offered for sale. Some pharmaceutical companies (in what many regard as unethical practice) have sold drugs banned on health grounds in the UK to these nations.

Why the overseas market is different

There can be many rewards for a business entering an overseas market.

One problem that it will face, however, is that market conditions will be different to those in the domestic market. This makes selling abroad very risky. What are the differences that are likely to affect the success of foreign sales?

Political differences A firm must take into account the political stability of the country in which it plans to sell. Political instability can make trading almost impossible. Also, a change of government can bring about a change in attitude towards foreign companies. A firm thinking of investing a large sum in its operations abroad will need to weigh up the political situation carefully. A number of businesses, for example, were affected by the change in government in Hong Kong in 1997 as ownership of the area was transferred from the UK to China.

Cultural differences One difference which, in the past, may have caused problems for British businesses is that English was not the main or even the second language in many countries. In Eastern Europe, for example, German and Russian may have been more widely spoken than English. Th eexpansion of the EU has led to English being spoken in more countries, helping to solve this problem to some extent.

Other cultural differences may influence the way a product is marketed. For example, a product name suitable in one country may have a totally different meaning in another – the French lemonade Pssschit would require a new name were it to be sold in the UK. Colours have different meanings throughout the world. In the Far East, white rather than black is associated with mourning. In India fashion models of the sort used to promote products in the West are considered too thin. In some countries, what may be regarded as a 'bribe' in the UK is common business practice. Payments to government or industry officials may be required to get things done, from electricity connection to securing contracts.

Differences in legislation Such differences can affect the way in which a business produces and markets its products.

- Product labelling. US laws are far more stringent than UK laws about the amount of information which should be included on food labels.
- Product safety. Some countries have very strict legislation governing safety standards on childrens' toys. Others are less strict.
- Environmental impact. Some countries have restrictions on car emissions, for example.
- Advertising. Cigarette advertising on television is outlawed within EU countries.

Economic and social differences Some of the economic factors which businesses must consider include levels of income, levels of sales and corporation tax, how income is distributed, the use

Question 1.

Café culture has taken a firm grip on India's cities, and coffee shops spring up almost daily. Technopak, a consultancy specialising in Indian consumer businesses, argues that 40 per cent-a-year growth is 'conservative'. Not surprisingly foreign chains have begun to scent the profits. Costa Coffee was the pioneer, launching its first coffee shop in Delhi two years ago. John Derkach, UK managing director, says: 'The growth in the young Indian middle classes is driving massive growth in the coffee shop market at the moment.'

Costa now has 32 outlets in Delhi and is close to opening its second in Mumbai. It plans to have 300 outlets in India within five years, half as many as it has in the UK. But its UK rival Caffè Nero is also planning an entry. Last year it held talks with Dubai's Landmark Group on a franchise agreement, but Landmark wanted a partner with international experience. This September it was back for a second try, holding discussions with a new potential partner.

Another UK brand, Caffè Ritazza, part of travel food services group SSP, has an outlet in Mumbai airport and wants to set up shop across Indian airports and rail stations as they are updated and overhauled.

America's Starbucks, meanwhile, is struggling. Its entry, planned for this autumn, was postponed in July after the Indian government rejected its application for a second time.

Other countries' chains are also getting in on the act. Italy's Lavazza took the most decisive step in March, buying out Barista, India's second-largest chain. Landmark will choose one of two US chains as a partner by mid-December and Gloria Jean's Coffees is expected to arrive by the end of the year.

But no foreign entrant comes close to matching the growth rate of Cafe Coffee Day, India's largest chain, which is backed by Asia's largest coffee-growing business. It is churning out 20 new cafés a month and plans to grow from 480 today to 750 by the end of 2008, and to hit 1,400 in five years. Mr Derkach thinks the chains are thriving in India because they are meeting a previously untapped need: 'Despite India's reputation as a tea-drinking nation, there is no real heritage of tea shops as places for people to sit. Coffee shops are filling a complete gap in the market.'

Simrin Sablok, head of marketing at Cafe Coffee Day, agrees, adding that the parental tight reins on Indian teens makes cafes their only option. 'In India, there's really no place for the youth to hang out, and a cafe is a place where there's no alcohol served, so the parents are happy.'

Mr Singhal is convinced the Indian market is so huge that it can easily accommodate the 10 or more international chains looking to take the plunge. 'While the premium locations have been taken up, India is expanding in every direction. If I was them, I'd feel there's no urgency or hurry.'

Source: adapted from *The Independent on Sunday*, 2.12.2007.

(a) Explain how foreign coffee businesses have entered the Indian market.

(b) What factors might influence the success of these businesses in the Indian market?

of tariffs or other import barriers and the level and growth of population. For example, many foreign businesses took advatage of investment opportunities in China in 2004 after the country 'opened up' its economy and its trading arrangements.

Social factors which firms may need to consider include literacy levels, the role of women, religious attitudes, readiness to accept new ideas, and the habits and attitudes of social groups.

Differences in business practice The usual amount of time it takes to receive payment may vary in different countries. Other differences include accounting techniques, company ownership (most British companies are relatively independent whereas those in other EU nations are often controlled by families or banks) and distribution (in many EU countries greater use is made of rail transport than in the UK).

Adapting products to fit in with local, national and regional needs can be costly. It is cheaper to have one product with one brand name and a promotional package which fits all markets. Businesses must attempt to cater for national consumer tastes, whilst trying to gain economies of scale from operating in international markets.

Methods of entering overseas markets

Once a business has made the decision to enter an overseas

market, it must decide the best way to do this.

Exporting This is often the first step for a business wishing to enter an overseas market. It involves manufacturing products at home but selling them abroad. The great advantage of exporting is that it minimises the risk of operating abroad. It can also be used as a means of testing out the ground.

Sometimes, the business may have little or no control over how the product is actually marketed in the countries to which it is sent. For this reason many firms exporting abroad make use of overseas agents. These agents are able to play an active role in the marketing of the product.

Franchising This involves one business selling a licence to others. The licence allows one firm to use another's name, product or service in return for an initial payment and further commission or royalties.

This is a quick and relatively easy way into foreign markets and it allows the franchiser a high degree of control over the marketing of its product. However, a share of the profit does go to the franchisee. Firms such as PizzaExpress and Budget Rent-a-Car have used this as a way of entering overseas markets.

Licensing This is similar to franchising. Franchising is used in service industries, such as fast foods and car hire. Licensing, however, involves one firm producing another's product and using its brand name, designs, patents and expertise under licence. This means that goods do not have to be physically moved abroad. Instead they are produced abroad by the foreign licensee. Also, it means that firms can avoid operating overseas. The main disadvantage is that the success or failure of the venture is largely in the hands of the licensee.

Joint ventures This involves two companies from separate countries combining their resources. One new enlarged company is formed to launch a product onto one market. An example of this is the Royal Bank of Scotland's alliance with Banco Santander of Spain to provide banking and financial services throughout Europe. Joint ventures are increasingly being used by businesses wishing to enter Eastern European markets.

One advantage of this form of venture is that the risks are shared between two firms. Also, each business can draw on the strengths of the other. One business may have research and development strengths, for example, while others may have strengths in manufacturing. However, many joint ventures have broken down due to conflicts which occur.

Direct investment Direct investment requires the setting up of production and distribution facilities abroad. They can be obtained by merger or takeover, or they may be built for this specific purpose. It is an increasingly common way for firms to reach overseas markets. For example, many Japanese manufacturers such as Nissan and Toyota set up plants in the UK in the 1990s. It was argued that there were a number of advantages to these businesses of direct investment.

- They could avoid paying import duties that were placed on foreign products entering the EU.
- They could take advantage of the relatively low costs and availability of relatively cheap labour in the UK.
- They could take advantage of government and EU incentives to invest in the area.
- There would be lower distribution costs.
- They could take advantage of local knowledge.

Mergers or takeovers Buying a business in another country may allow a company to produce and sell its products more easily. This method of entering foreign markets has similar advantages to direct investment and is most often used by **multinationals**.

The ethics of international marketing

The behaviour of some businesses in their international marketing activities has been questioned. Concerns have been raised about businesses from wealthier countries operating in areas such as Africa, Asia and South America. For example, some tobacco companies have focussed their marketing efforts on countries with lower incomes. With health concerns about smoking and laws being passed to reduce smoking there has been a decline in the number of cigarettes purchased in western Europe and North America. One response of tobacco companies has been to focus their efforts upon poorer countries where attitudes to smoking are less negative. Also, some food companies have engaged in selling what many regard as unnecessary products to poorer consumers. Examples include sales of baby milk to mothers when breast feeding babies would be a cheaper and healthier option.

KNOWLEDGE

1. Give five reasons why international marketing can be so important to firms.
2. How does entering an overseas market allow a firm to spread its risks?
3. State three differences between overseas and domestic markets.
4. How can an agent help a business to export its products?
5. In what ways can a business enter an overseas market?
6. What is meant by licensing?
7. What is the difference between direct investment and joint ventures?
8. List two concerns about businesses marketing their products overseas.

Case Study: Tesco in China

In 2006 Tesco unveiled its first profit from China of £2 million. It hoped for more in future. Potentially China is the world's biggest retail market, with 1.3 billion customers. The Happy Shopper store is a 17,000 square-metre mix of traditional eastern wet market and modern western hypermarket in Tianjin's industrial zone. It is one of 39 Chinese stores that Tesco operates with its local partner and Taiwanese food supplier, Ting Hsing. Since the signing of the joint venture (Hymall) in 2004, the firm has expanded its workforce by 20 per cent. In 2006 it planned to open 12 more hypermarkets, including one in Beijing.

Unlike its overseas rivals, Tesco seems unconcerned about building on its established brand. Carrefour and Wal-Mart sell under their own names. But there is nothing in Hymall's Happy Shopper that suggests a British link. The colour scheme is orange. All managers and shop floor staff are Chinese and there are few brands on the shelves familiar to a UK shopper. 'We are going into local markets in a local fashion,' said Lucy Neville-Rolfe, group corporate affairs director. 'It doesn't seem to be essential to use the Tesco name.' The UK side provides expertise in IT, food safety and retail management. But the shops are distinctly Chinese, with lots of live fish tanks inside and bicycle parking areas outside. With less than one expatriate for every 1,000 Hymall staff, Tesco appears to have a hands-off approach to its Chinese investment. This has gone down well with the local staff. 'When we heard that a British firm had bought a stake in the company, everyone was a bit worried that it would mean big changes, but so far there hasn't been anything that noticeable,' said one staff member. 'The middle managers are all Chinese. Only the most senior executives are British.'

Shoppers in Tianjin did not seem to notice that there local store was partly owned by a British firm. Liu Honghua, who spends about 100 yuan on her daily trips to Happy Shopper, said the only change she had noticed in the past year was an increased variety of products. 'I guess that is because the competition is increasing,' she said. 'Does Happy Shopper have a British owner? I didn't know.'

Huge layoffs and cost-cutting were never likely. This is partly because wages are low (supermarket salaries in China are usually less than £70 for a 160-hour month). But, also, high staff numbers are needed to provide service to customers who shop more frequently, but spend less than shoppers in Britain. Hymall stores in 2006 had about 2.3 million customers a week. Each spent less than £1 a visit.

The market in 2006 was worth $240 billion (£135billion). It was growing at double digit pace. But Tesco's position was a long way from the company's dominance in Britain, where Tesco took one in every eight pounds spent at supermarket checkouts. Even if business increases, the company is unlikely to be a household name in China. All foreign companies lag behind the domestic leader, Hualian, which runs nearly 2,000 stores.

Source: adapted from *The Guardian*, 26.4.2006.

(a) (i) Explain how Tesco entered the market in China. (4 marks)
(ii) What might have been the main attraction to the business in entering this market? (4 marks)

(b) Examine TWO features in the Chinese market that might be different from Tesco's market in the UK. (8 marks)

(c) Explain how Tesco's strategy in China would need to change as a result of differences in the market. (8 marks)

(d) Discuss whether operating in the Chinese market was likely to be a successful strategy for Tesco after 2006. (16 marks)

31 E-commerce

What is E-commerce?

E-COMMERCE or ELECTRONIC COMMERCE is concerned with the buying and selling of products using electronic systems. Although these electronic systems refer to any computer network, in reality the majority of E-commerce is conducted via the Internet. There are many examples of E-commerce as shown in Figure 1.

E-commerce arguably began in the 1970s when Electronic Data Interchange and Electronic Funds Transfer allowed businesses to transfer funds and documents, such as purchase orders, electronically. With the growth of the Internet in the 1990s E-commerce flourished. The Internet enabled anyone with access to a computer to carry out electronic transactions.

Types of E-commerce

There are two main types of E-commerce.

Business to consumers (B2C) E-commerce is an established part of the marketing activities of many new and existing businesses. Businesses marketing to consumers in this way can gain many benefits. These are described later in this unit.

Business to Business (B2B) E-commerce is also a well-established part of the business world. Like businesses selling to consumers, B2B organisations gain many benefits from E-commerce. However, E-commerce also enables those engaged in B2B to benefit from more efficient and cost-reducing financial transactions, that would not otherwise be possible. Such benefits include:

- receiving and issuing purchase orders online;
- paying and receiving payments for invoices online;
- establishing private electronic markets, often accessible only to those with suitable passwords, where specialist goods and services can be exchanged.

Figure 1: Examples of E-commerce

The buying and selling of:
- ✔ music on the iTunes website;
- ✔ organic vegetables on specialist organic websites;
- ✔ travel insurance policies on insurer websites;
- ✔ banking services via online banks;
- ✔ tax discs on the driver and vehicle licensing website;
- ✔ second hand cars on eBay;
- ✔ rail tickets on trainline.com;
- ✔ books on amazon;
- ✔ photograph printing services on a variety of relevant websites;
- ✔ grocery items on websites of the large supermarket chains.

Some E-commerce is conducted entirely electronically. For example, an individual downloading a movie to watch on their iPhone or iPod would take part in a transaction that involved no physical movement of a good. Likewise, the purchasing of access to a premium website would not involve any physical exchange. However, much E commerce continues to involve the movement of physical goods. So, for example, an individual might buy a new camera from a specialist website which would then be delivered some days later to their home address. E-TAILING is the term used to describe online retailing. There are now few large retailing businesses that do not offer their customers opportunities to purchase their goods online.

The benefits of E-commerce

There are benefits and advantages of E-commerce for both businesses and consumers.

Businesses For businesses there may be certain benefits.

- For a business involved in international trade, a website offering goods and services to consumers enables that business to reach a global market. For example, a business based in Oldham selling sunglasses could sell its products to consumers across the world using the website to reach consumers and a postal or parcel service to distribute their products. Without E-commerce, such a business would face a number of obstacles in reaching consumers beyond a national market.
- E-commerce means that a B2C business does not need to be physically close to its consumers. This means that businesses using E-commerce can choose to locate in a much wider range of locations. For example, a website design business might be able to locate in a rural area without harming its capacity to access customers.
- Businesses may benefit from longer 'opening hours', which may increase sales. There is access to business websites 24 hours a day. For example, Helpful Holidays, a business offering holiday cottages to let, was previously only able to offer a telephone based service for 12 hours per day to consumers. With its website consumers can book holiday cottages whenever they choose.
- Many B2C businesses are able to reduce their costs via the use of E-commerce. For example, an E-tailer with a

Question 1.

If you are still unsure about leaving the real world behind you, an easy first step on the web is to find the website of your favourite high-street names. A huge number of retailers have now jumped on to the worldwide bandwagon and become E-tailers. In many cases their prices online are much more competitive than the ones you'll get in store. Argos is a giant in this field, integrating its online ordering facilities with the bricks and mortar stores, allowing you to pre-order items before going into the store to pick them up in person. Sites such as marksandspencer.com, tesco.com, next.co.uk, currys.co.uk and hmv.co.uk are among the most popular high street names with successful web businesses.

Source: adapted from the *Independent*, 1.12.2007.

(a) Using an example from the article explain what is meant by an 'E-tailer'.
(b) For what reasons might the prices of the High Street retailers be cheaper online?

successful website may find that it is able to reduce the number of high street stores that it has. Banks have been able to reduce the number of branches that they have with the growth of online banking.

Consumers The main advantage of E-commerce for consumers is the ease with which they are able to access and purchase goods and services. Consumers can now clothe themselves, book holidays, do their weekly shopping and purchase tickets for a range of entertainments from home, work or anywhere that they are able to access the Internet. The latest developments in mobile phones means that such access can be gained wherever a mobile phone signal is available. The rise of E-commerce has given those consumers with access to information and communication technologies unparalleled choices and opportunities.

The costs of e-commerce

There are also costs, problems and disadvantages of E-commerce for businesses and consumers.

Businesses For businesses there may be certain difficulties involved in E-commerce.

- The Internet has meant that competition has become ever more fierce. Consumers wanting to buy a mountain bike on the Internet, for example, are faced with a wide array of options. In such circumstances it can be difficult for a business to stand out from its competitors. For businesses wishing to maintain consumer interest, regular updates to websites are necessary, perhaps even on a daily basis.
- E-tailers, in particular, are highly dependent upon the services of speedy and efficient delivery services. An E-tailer that is not able to deliver to consumers rapidly is likely to lose out to more conventional retailers. When operating in international markets such delivery can be even more difficult. Some businesses have to ship their goods across continents. This can lead to delays which may be off-putting to consumers.
- There is a number of dangers to businesses operating on the Internet. These include viruses, that can harm business websites, and hackers, who can gain access to sensitive information by breaking into protected computer networks. In order to protect themselves against such activities businesses need to invest in sophisticated software designed to ward off viruses and establish strong security measures on their websites. Online banks, for example, need to be careful to ensure that individuals do not breach protected parts of their website and remove funds from their customers.

Consumers For consumers there are also some problems with E-commerce. Choosing from the huge number of rival businesses offering the same or similar goods and services can be time-consuming and frustrating. Those consumers who do not have access to credit or debit cards and/or information and communications technologies are, in effect, excluded from this form of consumption. In addition, waiting for goods to be delivered and arranging for goods to be dropped off by E-tailers can be a frustrating experience. For these reasons some consumers prefer to buy many goods and services by conventional means.

The effects of e-commerce on the marketing mix

Businesses engaged in e-commerce need to consider the impact of their e-business activities on each element of the marketing mix.

Price Businesses must be sure that their product is priced competitively in relation to its E-commerce rivals. This is especially the case for those businesses with products that are difficult to distinguish from those of competitors.

Promotion The focus of promotional activities for businesses engaged in E-commerce is much more likely to revolve around the Internet. This is likely to include the use of email alerts to potential customers. For many E-businesses the use of emails as the principal promotional tool will replace or at the very least complement more conventional advertising campaigns.

Product Because of the intense competition faced by many businesses engaged in E-commerce, it is especially important that one business is able to distinguish its products from others marketing the same good or service. This means establishing a clear unique selling point (USP).

Place Businesses engaged in E-commerce often have greater freedom of choice over where they locate their businesses because the principal point of contact with consumers is the Internet. So, for example, an E-tailer mainly targeting the UK market might have its central office in Glasgow and its distribution centre in Sheffield. There is no need for the business to locate, as has been the convention for many businesses, close to its customers.

KEYTERMS

E-commerce - the buying and selling of products using electronic systems

E-tailing - the term used to describe online retailing

Question 2.

Domino's Pizza notched up record profits last year thanks to a very wet British summer and a leap in orders over the Internet and via text messages. The UK's leading pizza delivery chain said sales were boosted by new pizzas such as the Meateor and the rugby-themed Scrummy as well as a 'back-to-basics focus' on the classic Pepperoni Passion. New ways of ordering paid off, with E-commerce sales, orders online and by mobile phone texts, up by 60.5 per cent. The scooter delivery specialist predicted this trend for ordering food would continue this year.

Source: adapted from *The Guardian*, 19.2.2008.

(a) **Explain the reasons why Domino's Pizzas E-commerce sales have risen by 60.5 per cent.**

KNOWLEDGE

1. State five examples of E-commerce.
2. What is the difference between B2C and B2B E-commerce?
3. Explain whether or not E-commerce involves only the physical movement of goods.
4. Identify five costs to businesses of engaging in E-commerce.
5. Identify five advantages to businesses of engaging in E commerce.
6. Why might consumers prefer purchasing goods and services using E-commerce?
7. In what ways might Ecommerce influence a business' marketing mix?

Case Study: Sales of CD slump

CD sales were facing a catastrophic decline, according to figures. The BPI, which represents the UK music industry including businesses such as EMI, Sony and Warner revealed that sales of albums plunged by 10.8 per cent in 2007. When compilations and soundtracks were taken out of the figures the fall was an even more dramatic (14.3 per cent on the previous year), which in turn was nearly three per cent down on 2005 sales.

Despite the success of UK acts such as Amy Winehouse and Leona Lewis, whose albums Back to Black and Spirit sold four million albums between them, 2007 was far from a vintage year for new releases. Sixteen million fewer albums were sold than in 2006. Figures were boosted by the appeal of compilations such as the Now That's What I Call Music 68 and the two High School Musical soundtrack albums.

The BPI said album sales were still well above 1990s levels and that singles, fuelled by the soaring growth in downloads, enjoyed the third biggest year on record. But the popularity of digital music was blamed for hurting the performance of albums. Many fans now prefered to download individual tracks, often recommended by reviewers, rather than buying an entire album.

The industry was pinning its future on the ability to generate

Figure 2: UK album sales

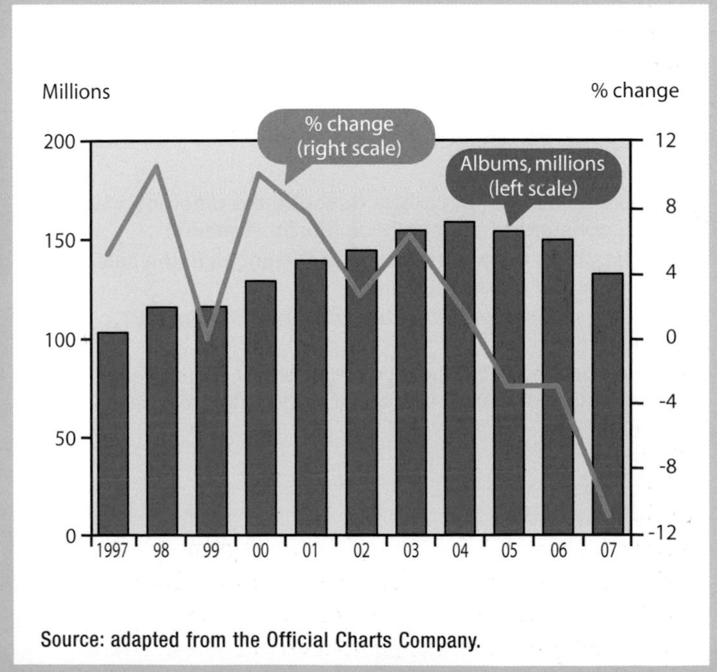

Source: adapted from the Official Charts Company.

new talent and new formats, particularly online and on mobile phones. The BPI chief executive, Geoff Taylor, said: 'The UK market remains a strong performer internationally and the pace of growth in digital sales is encouraging. Music in all its forms is more popular than ever and the recorded music sector will reap the benefits as the online market matures.'

Source: adapted from *The Independent* 9.1.2008.

(a) Using examples from the article describe the different ways in which consumers can purchase music. (4 marks)

(b) Using data from the article outline the changes in the sales of albums in CD format. (6 marks)

(c) Explain the reasons why CD sales declined during 2007. (6 marks)

(d) Examine how music businesses might adapt and develop their marketing mix to take account of declining CD sales. (10 marks)

(e) Evaluate the costs and benefits for music businesses such as EMI of expanding the E-commerce aspects of their marketing. (12 marks)

Table 1: Industry data

- Global album sales volume declined by 34.8 per cent from 2000 to 2006.
- The BPI estimates that more than 3.1 billion CDs have been sold in the UK since their introduction in 1983.
- The UK has 2.7 million album sales a week on average.
- 90 per cent of singles are now sold digitally. Digital sales grew the market by 30 per cent in 2007. In 2007 there were over 86.6 million singles sold.

32 Interpreting sample results

Sample results

Businesses carry out market research to find out what their customers want. It is highly unlikely that a business will be able to carry out market research on everyone in the population. So businesses tend to choose a **sample** of people to survey. There is a variety of sampling techniques that can be used. These vary from completely random samples, where everyone has an equal chance of being chosen, to quota sampling, where the population is segmented into groups with similar characteristics and a certain number of people are selected out of each segment.

Market research will provide a wide variety of information about the people in the sample. Businesses then analyse this data to find out the significance of the sample results. For example, a business may be interested to know the likely proportion of the population that would pay between £10 and £20 for its product or whether a new promotional campaign has increased the sales of its product.

To analyse sample market research data, businesses make use of probability, average and standard deviation calculations and the normal distribution.

Probability and sampling

The reason why businesses carry out surveys and take samples is to try to reduce the risk and uncertainty that exists in every business decision. PROBABILITY is a technique that helps a business to quantify risk and it forms a basis for the analysis of sampling data.

A probability is a simple ratio between the event the business is interested in and the total number of events that could occur, i.e.:

$$\text{Probability (P)} = \frac{\text{Required event}}{\text{Total events}}$$

Take an example of a card drawn from a pack of 52 playing cards. The probability of drawing a 'Heart' would be:

$$\text{P(a Heart)} = \frac{13}{52} = \frac{1}{4} = 0.25$$

Similarly, for drawing a card that is from one of the other suits:

$$\text{P(a Club)} = \frac{13}{52} = \frac{1}{4} = 0.25$$

$$\text{P(a Diamond)} = \frac{13}{52} = \frac{1}{4} = 0.25$$

$$\text{P(a Spade)} = \frac{13}{52} = \frac{1}{4} = 0.25$$

There are three important laws of probability.

- The sum of the probabilities of all the possible events will equal 1. Thus the probability of drawing a Heart, a Club, a Diamond or a Spade will equal 1 (0.25 + 0.25 + 0.25 + 0.25 = 1).
- To obtain the probability of one event or another event occurring, **add** the probabilities (the addition rule). Thus the probability of drawing a Diamond or a Spade = 0.25 + 0.25 = 0.5.
- To obtain the probability of one event and another occurring, multiply the probabilities (the multiplication rule). Thus the probability of drawing a Diamond and a Spade on two successive draws = 0.25 x 0.25 = 0.0625.

Two examples can be used to illustrate how probability might affect a business. The first example considers its use in marketing. However, it is possible to use probability in other areas of the business, such as production or stock control. The second example shows how the business might evaluate problems arising in its administration department.

To quantify the risk associated with making a decision Say that a business has the following information about the launch of a new product.

- Probability of gaining a high demand = 0.6, expected return £6 million.
- Probability of gaining a medium demand = 0.2, expected return £3million.
- Probability of gaining a low demand = 0.2, expected return £1 million.

This information about the likelihood of high, medium or low demand would have been derived from market research. The likely outcome from the decision to launch the new product will be:

- 0.6 probability of a return of £6m = 0.6 x £6m = £3.6m;
- 0.2 probability of a return of £3m = 0.2 x £3m = £0.6m;
- 0.2 probability of a return of £1m = 0.2 x £1m = £0.2m.

Given that these are the only three outcomes possible (the sum of the three probabilities = 1), then the average return the company can expect from the launch of such a product = £3.6m + £0.6m + £0.2m = £4.4m. If, for example, the cost to the business of launching such a product is £3m, then by the laws of probability, such a launch would be worth the risk. This use of probability is found in decision trees.

To establish the possible range of events that might occur in business situations Say an estate agency has three photocopiers in operation. The photocopiers are known to break down one day in every ten. What is the chance that all three are out of operation at once? There is a number of alternative combinations to consider.

- All three copiers are working.
- Two copiers are working and one is faulty.
- One copier is working and two are faulty.
- All three copiers are faulty.

If a working copier is (w) and a faulty copier is (f), the possible combinations amongst the three machines are:

Machine	1	2	3	
	w	w	w	All three machines are working
	w	w	f	Two are working and one is faulty
	w	f	w	
	f	w	w	
	w	f	f	One is working and two are faulty
	f	w	f	
	f	f	w	
	f	f	f	All three machines are faulty

If the probability of a working machine (p) is 0.9 then the probability of a faulty machine (q) is 0.1. It is possible to work out the probability of all these combinations.

- All three machines working = 1 x 0.9 x 0.9 x 0.9 = 0.73 (or 73%).
- Two machines working and one faulty = 3 x 0.9 x 0.9 x 0.1 = 0.24 (or 24%).
- One machine working and two faulty = 3 x 0.9 x 0.1 x 0.1 = 0.027 (or 2.7%).
- All three machines are faulty = 1 x 0.1 x 0.1 x 0.1 = 0.001 (or 0.1%).

In algebraic terms the probabilities are worked out using the binomial expansion:

$$p^3 + 3p^2q + 3pq^2 + q^3 = 1$$

Thus for this business there is only a 0.001 chance (0.1 per cent) of all three machines being out of action at once. But there is a 0.24 (24 per cent) chance of at least one machine being out of action, which might be a problem for the company. Although three machines have been used in this example, a business might need to look at combinations involving two, four or more machines. Probabilities would then be worked out using, for example:

$$p^2 + 2pq + q^2 = 1 \text{ (for two machines)}$$

$$p^4 + 4p^3q + 6p^2q^2 + 4pq^3 + q^4 = 1 \text{ (for four machines)}$$

The normal distribution

The normal distribution is a statistical model that will tell a business what the expected range of outcomes from a particular population will be. It is used where businesses have been carrying out large-scale sampling, for example in market research or in quality control, where they want to find out what range of results to expect.

The normal distribution occurs in many different contexts. For example, if a large group of sixth form students, representing the full ability range, took a Business Studies examination, then the frequency distribution of their marks may resemble a normal distribution, as shown in Figure 1. Some students will do very well, some students will do very badly, but the majority of students will fall close to and either side of the average (mean) score.

The resulting NORMAL DISTRIBUTION CURVE shows all the possible outcomes (range of marks) and the frequency at which they occurred (number of students at each mark). It is 'bell-shaped' and symmetrical about the mean value.

Normal distributions will differ in their shallowness or steepness. The weights of people in a population are likely to be quite evenly spread as in Figure 2(a), while IQ scores in a population are likely to be more closely bunched around the

Question 1.

Littlehurst is a manufaturer of electronic sensor equipment. Its most popular product is a sensor device that is used to test corrosion in metal on equipment. It has tested two new hand held sensor devices with a sample of its customers and has found the following information.

Test product A
Probability of success - 0.3 Expected revenue - £200,000
Probability of failure - 0.7 Expected revenue - £50,000
Cost of launch - £90,000

Test product B
Probability of success - 0.5 Expected revenue - £120,000
Probability of failure - 0.5 Expected revenue - £30,000
Cost of launch - £80,000

(a) Calculate:
(i) the returns that the company can expect from each product;
(ii) the profit or loss that the company can expect from each product.

(b) Suggest which product the company the company should launch based on the above information alone.

(c) If the cost of the launch of product B fell to £65,000, how might this affect your answer to (a)?

Figure 1: A normal distribution

Figure 2: Normal distributions showing different amounts of steepness

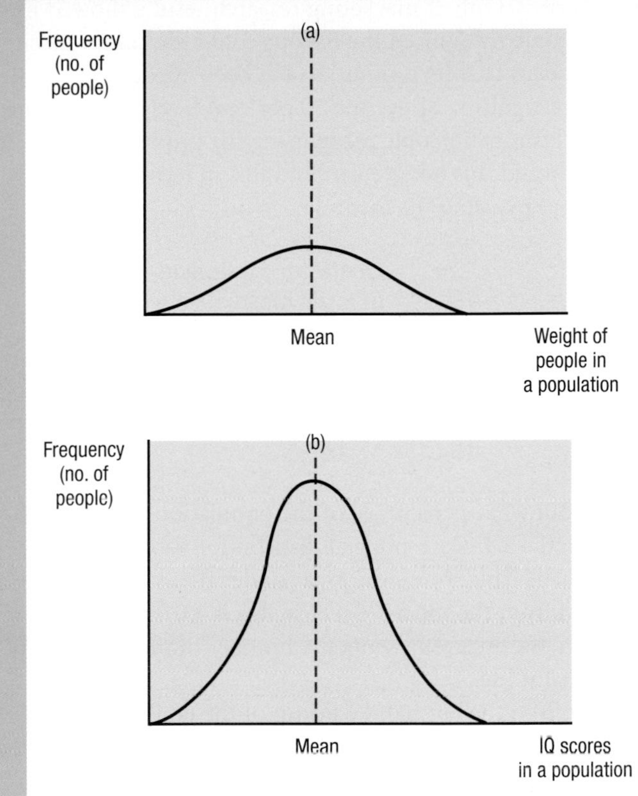

Figure 3: A normal distribution showing standard deviations

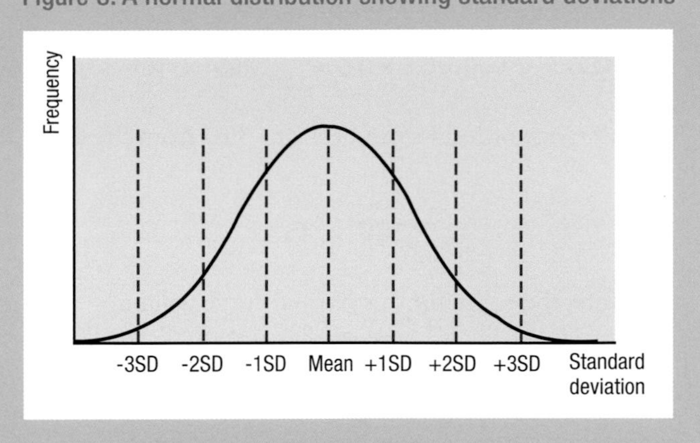

average, with few high or low scores as in Figure 2(b). It is the spread of the data that determines the curves' steepness or shallowness. This spread can be measured by the use of standard deviations.

Whatever the spread of the normal distribution curves, they have particular features in common.

- The curve is symmetrical about the mean.
- The mean, mode and median of the distribution is equal.
- Fifty per cent of all values lie either side of the mean value.
- The curve can be divided into 3 standard deviations (SDs) either side of the mean.
  68 per cent of the population will lie between + or - 1 SD.
  96 per cent of the population will lie between + or - 2 SDs.
  99.8 per cent of the population will lie between + or - 3 SDs.

Thus nearly all results will lie within + or - 3 SDs of the mean. A small proportion (0.2 per cent) will lie outside this range, but this is so small businesses are not concerned about it in practice. The exact distribution of the range of results possible is shown in Figure 3. The normal distribution has a certain predictability. Therefore any results that lie outside the expected range become significant and unexpected.

Using the normal distribution

One business context where the normal distribution can be used is in the analysis of market research data. A business might ask, 'was the result of a survey possible purely by chance or was there a significant difference between the actual result and the expected one?'

Say that a company which manufactures potato crisps has used a market research company to discover whether their new 'Sweet and Sour' flavour, which has been heavily promoted since its launch, is well known by the public. On average, the company would expect 50 per cent of those asked to recognise a flavour, but following the promotion they would expect a higher recognition. If the market research company asks 900 consumers, what results might the company expect to get to measure whether the promotion was successful?

The first stage in the use of normal distribution to answer this question involves the calculation of the expected RANGE OF RESULTS from such surveys. To do this it is necessary to calculate the mean and the standard deviation for this particular distribution.

The mean for a normal distribution can be calculated using the formula:

$$\text{mean} = n \times p$$

where n = the sample size
and p = the probability of an event occurring.

The standard deviation for a normal distribution can be calculated using the formula:

$$1 \text{ standard deviation (1SD)} = \sqrt{npq}$$

where n = the sample size;
p = the probability of an event occurring;
and q = the probability of an event not occurring.

For the market research on the 'Sweet and Sour' crisps:

$n = 900$
$p = 0.5$
$q = 0.5$

Therefore, for such surveys as this:

mean = 900 x 0.5 = 450

$$1SD = \sqrt{900 \times 0.5 \times 0.5} = \sqrt{225} = 15$$

The full range of results can be + or - 3SD from the mean where:

2SD = 30
3SD = 45

Therefore, the range for this normal curve will be:

450 + or - 45 = 405 to 495.

The normal curve can now be drawn based on this information as in Figure 4. For the company, this normal curve provides a tool to help it analyse any market research results.

- 68 per cent of all results will show that between 435 and 465 people recognise the flavour (given a mean of 450).
- 96 per cent of all results will show that between 420 and 480 people recognise the flavour.
- 99.8 per cent of all results will show that between 405 and 495 people recognise the flavour.

These percentages are usually referred to as **confidence levels**.

Figure 4: A normal distribution and standard deviations

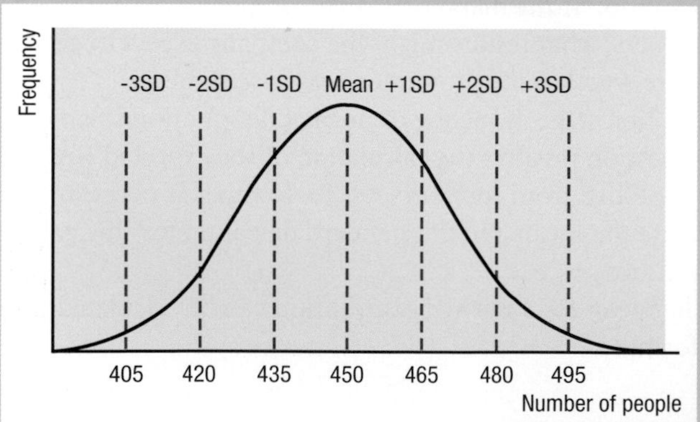

Question 2.

A manufacturer of dental products is particularly interested in the hygiene habits of its customers. The business expects that the average length of time people take before changing their toothbrush is 90 days and the standard deviation is 20 days.

(a) **Draw a normal distribution. Assuming that the information is normally distributed, calculate and plot onto the graph:**
   (i) **the expected average length of time people take to change their toothbrush;**
   (ii) **the range of results between minus 3 and plus 3 standard deviations (in days).**

(b) **What percentage of its customers might the business expect to change their toothbrush:**
   (i) **after 70 days; (ii) after 130 days?**

Confidence levels

Look again at the previous example about sweet and sour flavoured crisps. Only if marketing research results showed more than 495 people recognised the flavour could the company be totally confident that its promotion has been effective in increasing recognition above the 50 per cent level. Suppose the actual result was 486 people recognising the product? How significant would this be? We can find this in terms of standard deviations (z) by using the formula:

$$z = \frac{x - m}{s}$$

where x = the value
m = the mean
s = the standard deviation

so:

$$z = \frac{486 - 450}{15} = \frac{36}{15} = 2.4 \text{ SDs from the mean}$$

To find out what percentage of the population lies between the mean and +2.4SDs, a normal distribution table, as in Table 1, can be used. This shows the areas under the standard normal distribution from the mean. Because this is a frequency distribution, the area represents the number in the population between each value.

Reading from the left hand column of the table, 49.18 per cent (or 0.4918) of the population will lie between the mean and +2.4SDs. To include all values up to and including 486 it is necessary to add this to the 0.5 or 50 per cent on the other side of the mean. This gives a total of:

0.5 + 0.4918 = 0.9918 or 99 per cent

This is shown as a shaded area on Figure 5. The company can therefore be 99 per cent certain that a result of 486 represents an improvement over the 50 per cent average. If it wanted to be even more certain, it would need to take three standard deviations (rather than 2.4) into account.

Limitations of the normal distribution

As with all models used in business decision making, there are possible problems with its use.

- The sample size has to be large otherwise it is unlikely that

Figure 5: A normal distribution showing standard deviations

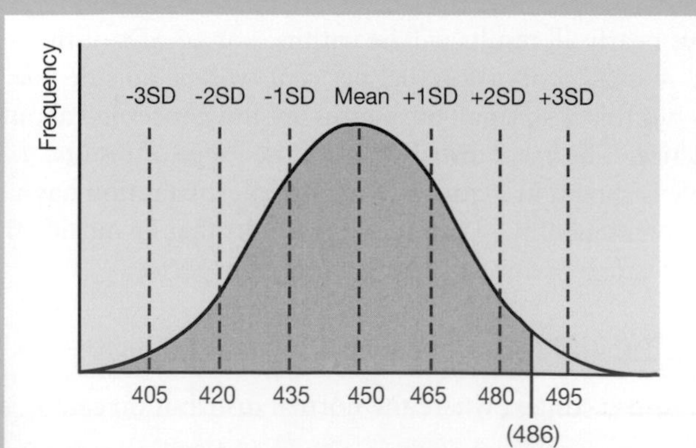

Table 1: Table of standard normal curve areas

(z)	.00	.01	.02	.03	.04	.05	.06	.07	.08	.09
0.0	.0000	.0040	.0080	.0120	.0160	.0199	.0239	.0279	.0319	.0359
0.1	.0398	.0438	.0478	.0517	.0557	.0596	.0636	.0675	.0714	.0753
0.2	.0793	.0832	.0871	.0910	.0948	.0987	.1026	.1064	.1103	.1141
0.3	.1179	.1217	.1255	.1293	.1331	.1368	.1406	.1443	.1480	.1517
0.4	.1554	.1591	.1628	.1664	.1700	.1736	.1772	.1808	.1844	.1879
0.5	.1915	.1950	.1985	.2019	.2054	.2088	.2123	.2157	.2190	.2224
0.6	.2257	.2291	.2324	.2357	.2389	.2422	.2454	.2486	.2517	.2549
0.7	.2580	.2611	.2642	.2673	.2704	.2734	.2764	.2794	.2823	.2852
0.8	.2881	.2910	.2939	.2967	.2995	.3023	.3051	.3078	.3106	.3133
0.9	.3159	.3186	.3212	.3238	.3264	.3289	.3315	.3340	.3365	.3389
1.0	.3413	.3438	.3461	.3485	.3508	.3531	.3554	.3577	.3599	.3621
1.1	.3643	.3665	.3686	.3708	.3729	.3749	.3770	.3790	.3810	.3830
1.2	.3849	.3869	.3888	.3907	.3925	.3944	.3962	.3980	.3997	.4015
1.3	.4032	.4049	.4066	.4082	.4099	.4115	.4131	.4147	.4162	.4177
1.4	.4192	.4207	.4222	.4236	.4251	.4265	.4279	.4292	.4306	.4319
1.5	.4332	.4345	.4357	.4370	.4382	.4394	.4406	.4418	.4429	.4441
1.6	.4452	.4463	.4474	.4484	.4495	.4505	.4515	.4525	.4535	.4545
1.7	.4554	.4564	.4573	.4582	.4591	.4599	.4608	.4616	.4625	.4633
1.8	.4641	.4649	.4656	.4664	.4671	.4678	.4686	.4693	.4699	.4706
1.9	.4713	.4719	.4726	.4732	.4738	.4744	.4750	.4756	.4761	.4767
2.0	.4772	.4778	.4783	.4788	.4793	.4798	.4803	.4808	.4812	.4817
2.1	.4821	.4826	.4830	.4834	.4838	.4842	.4846	.4850	.4854	.4857
2.2	.4861	.4864	.4868	.4871	.4875	.4878	.4881	.4884	.4887	.4890
2.3	.4893	.4896	.4898	.4901	.4904	.4906	.4909	.4911	.4913	.4916
2.4	.4918	.4920	.4922	.4925	.4927	.4929	.4931	.4932	.4934	.4936
2.5	.4938	.4940	.4941	.4943	.4945	.4946	.4948	.4949	.4951	.4952
2.6	.4953	.4955	.4956	.4957	.4959	.4960	.4961	.4962	.4963	.4964
2.7	.4965	.4966	.4967	.4968	.4969	.4970	.4971	.4972	.4973	.4974
2.8	.4974	.4975	.4976	.4977	.4977	.4978	.4979	.4979	.4980	.4981
2.9	.4981	.4982	.4982	.4983	.4984	.4984	.4985	.4985	.4986	.4986
3.0	.4987	.4987	.4987	.4988	.4988	.4989	.4989	.4989	.4990	.4990

Question 3.

High Style is a manufacturer of clothing for tall people. It provides a bespoke leg length service. It will turn up trousers to suit the leg length specified on an order. On average, it expects the people buying its trousers to have an inside leg length of 35 inches with a standard deviation of 0.5 inches.

(a) **Assuming the leg lengths of its customers are normally distributed, what range of lengths would the business expect its customers to have? Plot these figures onto a normal distribution.**

(b) **If the business tested a sample of 100 people, what percentage would it expect to be:**

(i) above 36.5 inches;

(ii) between 35 inches and 36 inches;

(iii) between 35 inches and 35.8 inches;

(iv) below 34.2 inches?

Use Table 1 to answer this question.

Figure 6

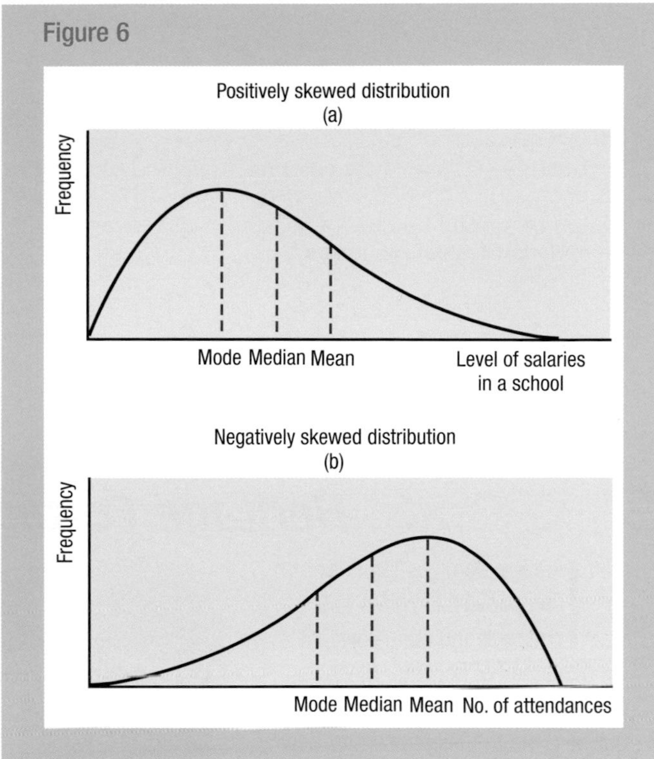

the distribution will be normally distributed. A large sample size helps to smooth out the peaks and troughs in smaller frequency distributions.

- The calculation of the mean and the standard deviation are based on probability figures that themselves might be based upon estimates rather than exact figures. In the example of market research, the 0.5 probability used to calculate the likely response to the market research on crisps was an estimate based upon previous experience.
- Especially in the area of quality control, a 'one-off' reading which is a long way from the expected mean may not be sufficient to reject a batch or shut down a machine. Further sampling would be important to confirm the evidence of the first sample before costs are incurred by the business.
- Not all large distributions will resemble the normal distribution. The distribution might be skewed and therefore not symmetrical about the mean. Figure 6(a) shows a positively skewed frequency distribution, which might represent the distribution of teachers' salaries in a school or college. In a positively skewed distribution, the mode will have a lower value than the median, which will have a lower value than the mean. Figure 6(b) shows a negatively skewed frequency distribution, which might represent the number of people per day attending a successful cinema over a period of time. In a negatively skewed distribution, the mode will have a higher value than the median, which will have a higher value than the mean. Normal distribution analysis could not be used with such skewed distributions.

KEYTERMS

Normal distribution curve – a graphical representation of the normal distribution.

Probability – a quantification of the likelihood of an event occurring.

Range of survey results – the highest and lowest results from market research surveys.

KNOWLEDGE

1. What statistical concepts are used to analyse market research data?
2. What does probability measure?
3. Why is the normal distribution a useful tool for businesses to use in analysing data?
4. What are the distinguishing features of a normal curve?
5. What is the difference between a normal distribution and a skewed distribution?

Case Study: Heritage Cottages Ltd

Heritage Cottages Ltd is a company which hires out cottages and bungalows in various areas of England. Most customers book directly with the business via the telephone and view properties in the company brochure which shows the cottages that are available. The brochure is produced each November and Heritage has traditionally advertised the availability of the brochure in a range of weekly magazines between December and April. The management was always careful to analyse the responses that resulted from these advertisements each week. Over a five year period it calculated that the mean number of responses was 1,500 each week with a standard deviation of 125.

For the 2007-08 season Heritage decided to shift its advertising over the December to April period to the Sunday papers, such as *The Sunday Times* and *The Observer*. It wanted to see if this resulted in a significant increase in the number of customer enquiries. It carried out a survey of the responses over the twenty week period that it ran the advertisements. Heritage found that the mean level of response had risen to 1,800 for the 2007-08 season. The company was pleased with the outcome and decided, on the basis of these figures, to continue advertising in the Sunday papers for the following season.

(a) What is meant by the terms (i) mean number of responses and (ii) significant increase in customer enquiries? Use examples from Heritage Cottages in your explanation. (6 marks)

(b) Explain why the results from the five year analysis by Heritage Cottages of responses to a magazine advertisement might be normally distributed. (8 marks)

(c) (i) Draw a normal distribution curve which shows the full range of responses that the company achieved. (6 marks)

(ii) How many standard deviations from the mean did the 1,800 responses from the Sunday newspaper advertisements represent? (6 marks)

(d) Was the business right to be pleased with the outcome from the switch to newspaper advertisements? Consider the normal distribution diagram from your answer to (c) and other factors that Heritage Cottages might need to take into account in evaluating the move from magazine to newspaper advertising. (14 marks)

33 Forecasting and analysing markets

Forecasting

Businesses are keen to know about what might happen in the future. Anything they can predict accurately will reduce their uncertainty and will allow them to plan. Predictions may be based on a variety of data. They could be based on current information provided by managers. Most forecasts are based on **backdata** gathered from a variety of marketing research techniques. The accuracy of forecasts will depend on the reliability of the data.

What might a business like to predict with accuracy? Some examples might include:

- future sales of products;
- the effect of promotion on sales;
- possible changes in the size of the market in future;
- the way sales fluctuate at different times of the year.

A variety of techniques can be used to predict future trends. One of the most popular is **time series analysis**, which is discussed in the next section.

Time series analysis

TIME SERIES ANALYSIS involves predicting future levels from past data. The data used are known as time series data - a set of figures arranged in order, based on the time they occurred. So, for example, a business may predict future sales by analysing sales data over the last ten years. The business, of course, is assuming that past figures are a useful indicator of what will happen in the future. This is likely to be the case if trading conditions are **stable** or if the business needs to forecast trends in the short term. Time series analysis does not try to explain data, only to describe what is happening to it or predict what will happen to it.

There are likely to be four components that a business wants to identify in time series data.

- **The trend**. 'Raw' data can have many different figures. It may not be easy to see exactly what is happening from these figures and so a business often tries to identify a trend. The trend shows the pattern that is indicated from the figures. For example, there may be a trend for sales of a new product to rise sharply in a short period as it becomes very popular.
- **Cyclical fluctuations**. For many businesses there may be a cycle of 'highs and lows' in their sales figures, which rise over a number of years and then fall again. It is argued that these are a result of the recession-boom-recession of the trade cycle in the economy. In a recession, for example, people have less money to spend and so the turnover of a business may fall in that period.
- **Seasonal fluctuations**. Over a year a business is unlikely to have a constant level of sales. The seasonal variations are very important to a business such as a travel agent or a 'greetings card' producer, where there may be large sales at some times but not at others.
- **Random fluctuations**. At times there will be 'freak' figures which stand out from any trend that is taking place. An example may be the sudden boost in sales of umbrellas in unusually wet summer months or the impact on consumers' spending of a one-off event such as a summer music festival.

Identifying the trend

An analysis of figures will tell a business whether there is an upward, downward or constant trend. Identifying the trend allows the business to predict what is likely to happen in future. The first step is to smooth out the raw data. Take an example of a toy manufacturer, whose yearly sales over ten years are shown in Table 1.

Table 1: Yearly sales of a toy manufacturer (£000)

2000	2001	2002	2003	2004	2005	2006	2007	2008	2009
300	500	600	550	600	750	850	1,100	800	1,100

It is possible to calculate a trend by using a MOVING AVERAGE. The average can be taken for any period the business wants, such as a year, a month or a quarter. For now we will assume the toy manufacturer uses a three year average.

The average of sales in the first three years was:

$$\frac{300 + 500 + 600}{3} = \frac{1,400}{3} = 466.7$$

The first year's sales 'drop out' and the next year's sales are added to give a moving average. The average for the next three years was:

$$\frac{500 + 600 + 550}{3} = \frac{1,650}{3} = 550$$

If the business continues to do this, the results will be as shown in Table 2. Notice that the moving average is placed at the centre of the three years (i.e. the average for 2000-2002 is plotted next to 2001).

What if the firm had used a four year period instead of three years? No one year is the centre point and simply placing the figure in between two years may result in misleading predictions in future. The solution is to use CENTRING. This uses a four and eight year moving **total** to find a mid point. So, for

Table 2: Three year moving average for sales of a toy manufacturer (£000)

2000	2001	2002	2003	2004	2005	2006	2007	2008	2009
300	500	600	550	600	750	850	1,100	800	1,100
	466.7	550	583.3	633.3	733.3	900	916.7	1,000	

example, in Table 2:

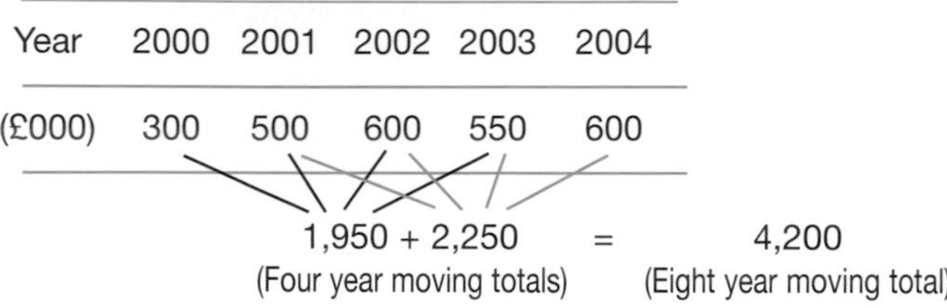

Year 2000 2001 2002 2003 2004
(£000) 300 500 600 550 600
1,950 + 2,250 = 4,200
(Four year moving totals)
(Eight year moving total)

This can then be used to find the mid-point, which is 2002. The **trend** or **four period centred moving average** can be found by dividing the eight year moving total by 8, the number of years, as shown in Table 3.

Plotting the four period centred moving average figures onto a graph (as shown in Figure 1) shows the trends in the figures. It is clear to see that sales appear to be rising over the period. The trend line is 'smoother' than the line showing the actual sales figures. It eliminates any fluctuations in sales each year and gives a more obvious picture of the trend that has been taking place.

Question 1.

A business has recently gathered data on its sales revenue as shown in Table 4, and wants to calculate a three and four period moving average.

Table 4: Sales revenue

(£000)

Period	1	2	3	4	5	6	7	8	9	10
Sales revenue	100	130	160	175	180	190	190	180	220	250
3 period moving average		130	155							
4 period moving average		151.3								

(a) Calculate the three and four period moving averages for as many years as you can to complete the table.

(b) Plot the sales figures and both trend lines onto a graph on graph paper and explain the relationship between the trend and the actual sales revenue figures.

Table 3: Calculating a four year moving average for a toy manufacturer

£000

Year	Sales	Four year moving total	Eight year moving total	Trend (Four year centred moving average = Eight year moving total ÷ eight)
2000	300			
2001	500	1,950		
2002	600	2,250	4,200	525.00
2003	550	2,500	4,750	593.75
2004	600	2,750	5,250	656.25
2005	750	3,300	6,050	756.25
2006	850	3,500	6,800	850.00
2007	1,100	3,850	7,350	918.75
2008	800			
2009	1,100			

Figure 1: Annual sales of a toy manufacturer

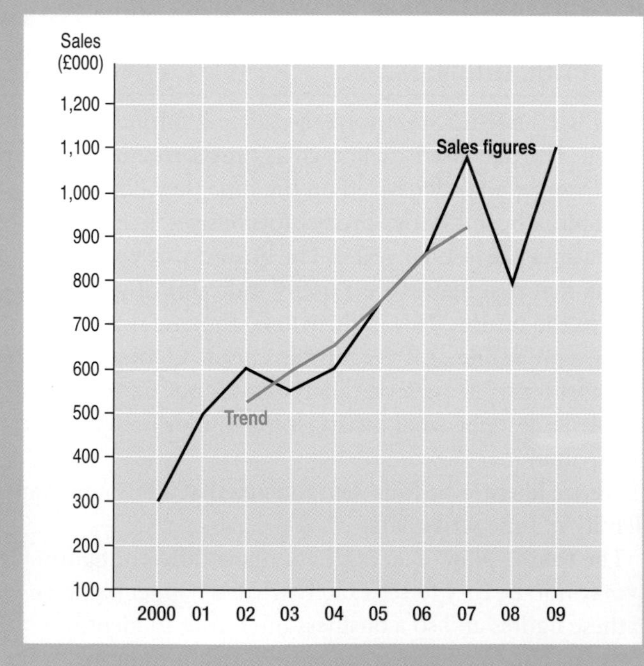

Predicting from the trend

Having identified a trend that is taking place the business can now predict what may happen in future. Figure 2 shows the trend data from Figure 1, but with a line drawn to predict the likely sales in 2010. The graph shows that sales of the toy manufacturer's goods may reach about £1,160,000.

The business has made certain assumptions when predicting this figure. First, no other factors were likely to have changed to affect the trend. If other factors changed, resulting in different sales figures, then the prediction is likely to be inaccurate.

Second, the sales figures are predicted by drawing a line through the trend figures and extending it to the year 2010. The broken line through the trend in Figure 2 is called the LINE OF BEST FIT. It is the best line that can be drawn which matches the general slope of all points in the trend. The line is an average, where points in the trend on one side of the line are balanced with those on the other. In other words, it is a line which 'best fits' all points in the trend.

It is possible to draw the line of best fit by plotting the trend figures on graph paper accurately and then adding the line of best fit 'by eye', so that points fit equally either side of the line. Extending the line carefully should give a reasonable prediction.

To help draw the line, it should pass through the coordinates $(\bar{X},\bar{Y})$ where $\bar{X}$ is the average of the years and $\bar{Y}$ is the average sales. These coordinates can be calculated using the figures in Table 3.

$$\bar{X} = \frac{\Sigma X \text{ (the total years)}}{N \text{ (the number of years)}} = \frac{2002+2003+2004+2005+2006+2007}{6} = \frac{11{,}997}{6} = 1999.5$$

$$\bar{Y} = \frac{\Sigma Y \text{ (the total sales in the trend)}}{N \text{ (the number of years)}}$$

$$= \frac{£525{,}000 + £593{,}750 + £656{,}250 + £756{,}250 + £850{,}000 + £918{,}750}{6} = \frac{£4{,}300{,}000}{6}$$

$$= £716{,}667$$

This point is shown on Figure 2. The actual predicted figure for the year 2010 is £1,162,550. This can be found by a method known as 'the sum of least squares'. Computer software can be used by businesses to calculate the line of best fit and to predict from the trend.

Variations from the trend

How accurate is the prediction of **around** £1,160,000 sales of toys by the year 2010? Even allowing for the assumptions above, the prediction may not be accurate because it is taken from the trend, and the trend 'smoothed out' variations in sales figures. To make an accurate prediction, the business will have to find the average variation over the period and take this into account.

We can find how much **variation** there is from the trend by calculating:

Actual sales - trend.

So, for example, the **cyclical** variation in Table 3 would be as shown in Table 5. The average of the variations over the period 2000-2009 is (in £000):

$$\frac{+75 -43.75 -56.25 -6.25 +/-0 +181.25}{6} = \frac{+150}{6} = +25 \text{ (or } +£25{,}000)$$

If the predicted value based on the trend was £1,160,000, then adding £25,000 may give a more accurate predicted figure of £1,185,000.

Figure 2: Annual sales of a toy manufacturer

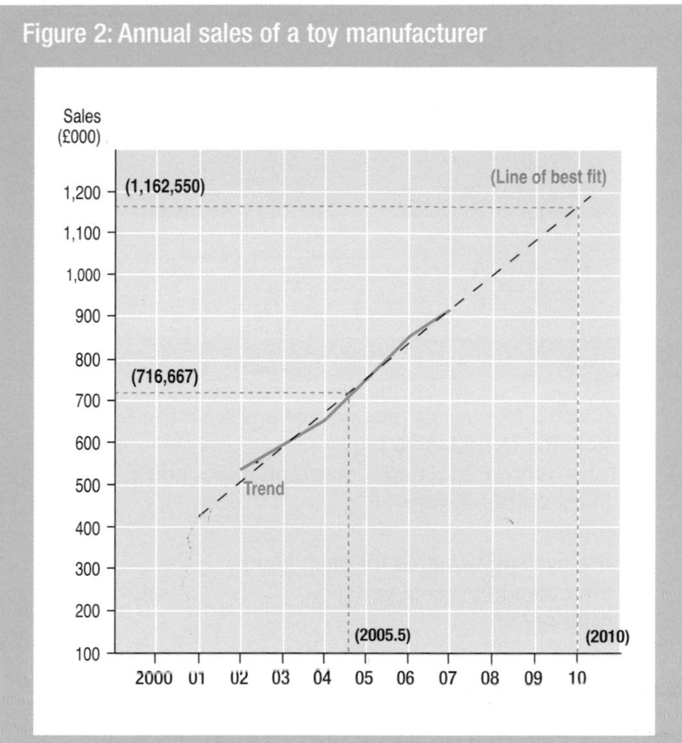

Table 5 Cyclical variations

Year	Sales	Trend (4 year centred moving average)	(£000) Variation in each year
2000	300		
2001	500		
2002	600	525.00	+75.00
2003	550	593.75	-43.75
2004	600	656.25	-56.25
2005	750	756.25	-6.25
2006	850	850.00	+/- 0
2007	1,100	918.75	+181.25
2008	800		
2009	1,100		

Seasonal variations

Earlier it was stated that a business may be interested in variations in any one year. It is possible to predict from a trend and use **seasonal** variations to make a more accurate prediction. Table 7 shows sales of a business over a three year period, including sales in each quarter. A four quarter moving average has been calculated and also the variation in each quarter.

Carrying on the trend to predict the sales for the fourth quarter of the year 2009 might give a figure of £470,000. (It would be possible to find this by drawing and extending a line of best fit through the trend.) As we know, this is a 'smoothed out' figure. A more accurate prediction might be to calculate the **average**

Question 2.

Table 6 shows the yearly sales figures of a furniture manufacturer over a period of ten years.

Table 6:

										units
Period	1	2	3	4	5	6	7	8	9	10
Sales	5,000	5,200	5,800	6,000	5,800	7,000	8,200	7,400	7,600	8,400

(a) Calculate a four yearly moving average from the figures to show the trend taking place.
(b) Plot the trend onto a graph on graph paper and predict the likely output in year 11.
(c) Calculate:
(i) the cyclical variation for each year;
(ii) the average cyclical variation over the period.

seasonal variation in the fourth quarter, for example (in £000):

$$\frac{-97.125 - 117.5}{2} = \frac{-214.625}{2} = -107.313$$

By subtracting £107,313 from the total of £470,000, this gives a more accurate prediction of £362,687.

The reliability of forecasts

Forecasts are likely to be more reliable when:

- the forecast is for a short period of time in the future, such as six months, rather than a long time, such as five years;
- they are revised frequently to take account of new data and other information;
- the market is slow changing;
- there is plenty of backdata from which to produce a forecast;
- market research data, including test marketing data, is available;
- those preparing the forecast have a good understanding of how to use data to produce a forecast;
- those preparing the forecast have a good 'feel' for the market and can adjust the forecast to take account of their hunches and guesses about the future.

No forecaster is accurate all the time. Even in slow moving markets, sales can change by a few per cent for no apparent reason. One way to take this into account is to produce a forecast range. Forecasters might, for example, prepare three sets of figures – an optimistic forecast, a pessimistic forecast and a central forecast. The two outlying forecasts would have low probabilities of occurring but would indicate a best and worst case scenario. The central forecast would be the forecast which had the highest probability of occurring. Supplying these forecasts to other departments, such as production, would give them an indication of the possible variations they might have to face. They could then prepare their own plans for these eventualities. In a very sophisticated forecast there would be a whole range of possible outcomes, each with a probability attached to its occurring.

Even though forecasts are rarely 100 per cent accurate, they do provide an indication of likely future trends. As such, they are important tools for any planning or budgeting.

Table 7 Seasonal variations

Year	Quarter	Sales	Four quarter moving average	(£000) Variation
2006	3	460		
	4	218		
2007	1	205	328.5	-123.5
	2	388	346.0	+42.0
	3	546	358.25	+187.75
	4	272	369.125	-97.125
2008	1	249	383.625	-134.625
	2	431	396.625	+34.375
	3	619	404.0	+215.0
	4	303	420.5	-117.5
2009	1	277		
	2	535		

Causal modelling

Time series analysis only describes what is happening to information. Causal modelling tries to explain data, usually by finding a link between one set of data and another. For example, a business may want to find whether there is a link between the

Table 8 Advertising and sales data

Period	Advertising expenditure (£000) X	Sales (000) Y	(£million) X^2	(million) Y^2	(£million) XY
A	1.0	3.2	1.0	10.24	3.2
B	2.0	4.5	4.0	20.25	9.0
C	3.0	1.8	9.0	3.24	5.4
D	4.0	3.0	16	9.0	12.0
E	1.5	1.8	2.25	3.24	2.7
F	2.5	1.6	6.25	2.56	4.0
G	3.5	5.8	12.25	33.64	20.3
H	1.2	4.7	1.44	22.09	5.64
I	2.7	5.9	7.29	34.81	15.93
J	3.0	3.5	9.0	12.25	10.5
K	3.6	3.1	12.96	9.61	11.16
L	7.0	3.5	0.49	12.25	2.45
			$\Sigma X^2 = 81.93$	$\Sigma Y^2 = 173.18$	$\Sigma XY = 102.28$

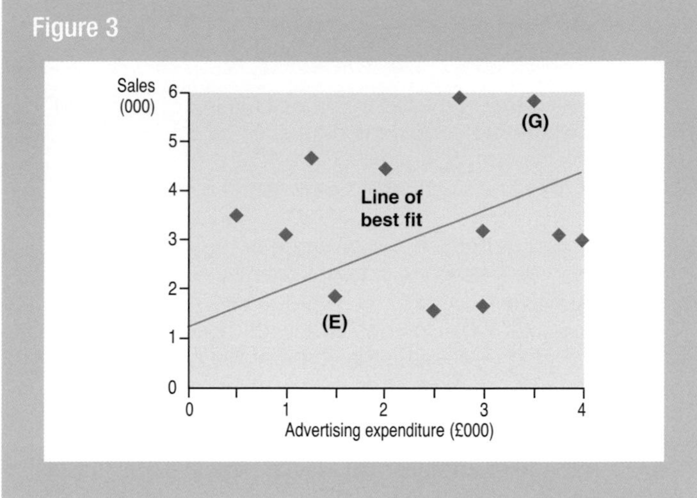

amount that it spends on advertising and its sales.

Table 8 shows data that have been collected about advertising and sales by a business at different times. The data in the table are plotted onto a SCATTER GRAPH in Figure 3. Advertising (the **independent** variable) is shown on the horizontal (X) axis. Sales (the **dependent** variable) are shown on the vertical (Y) axis. The figure shows, for example, that in one period (E) the business had advertising spending of £1,500 and sales of 1,800 units. In another period (G) the business had advertising spending of £3,500 and sales of 5,800 units.

Looking at the graph, there appears to be a positive CORRELATION between the two variables. The more that is spent on advertising, the higher the level of sales. The line of best fit is drawn through the data to show this relationship better. It is also possible to calculate the extent of the relationship by means of a CORRELATION COEFFICIENT, using the formula:

$$r = \frac{\Sigma XY}{\sqrt{(\Sigma X^2)\ (\Sigma Y^2)}}$$

Using the data in Table 8, the correlation coefficient for advertising and sales can be calculated as follows.

$$r = \frac{£102.28m}{\sqrt{£81.93m \times 173.18m}}$$

$$r = \frac{£102.28m}{£119.117m}$$

$$r = +0.86$$

- A correlation coefficient of +1 means that there is an absolute positive relationship between the two variables. All points in the scatter graph fall on the line of best fit and the line slopes upwards from left to right. As the values of the independent variable increase, so do the dependent variable values.
- A correlation coefficient of 0 means that there is no relationship between the variables.
- A correlation coefficient of -1 means that there is an absolute negative relationship between the two variables. All points in the scatter graph fall on the line of best fit and the line slopes downwards from left to right. As the values of the independent variable increase, the values of the dependent variable fall.

The formula itself does not show **positive** and **negative** values. However, it is easy to see whether the relationship is positive or negative from the graph. A positive coefficient of 0.86 suggests a strong correlation between the spending on advertising and the level of sales. As advertising increases, so do sales. This information could help a business in future when making decisions about its marketing. It is suggested that if the figure falls below 0.7 it becomes difficult to see any correlation from the scatter graph. An example of a negative correlation might be the relationship between prices and customers' demand. As prices rise, demand falls. Examples of different correlations are shown in Figure 4.

Businesses must be careful when basing decisions on such calculations.

- A large quantity of sales in any period may be due to factors other than advertising, such as other forms of promotion.
- There are sometimes examples of 'nonsense correlations'. These are correlation coefficients that appear to show a strong relationship between two variables, when in fact the relationship between the figures is pure coincidence.

Figure 4 A weak positive correlation, a strong negative correlation and little or no correlation

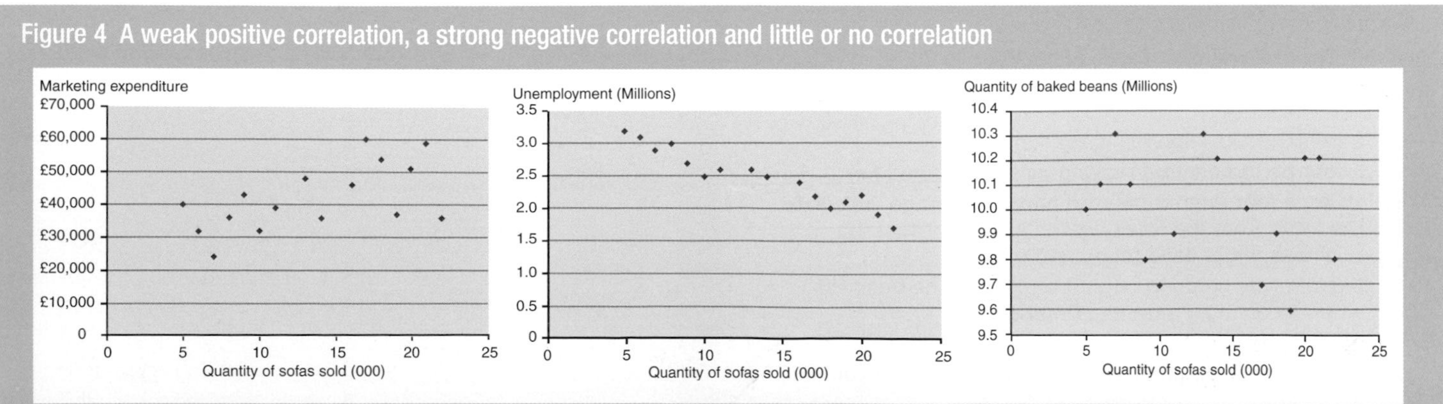

Qualitative forecasting

Qualitative forecasting uses people's opinions or judgments rather than numerical data. A business could base its predictions on the views of so-called experts, or on the opinions of experienced managers in the marketing or production department. Such methods are usually used by businesses:

- where there is insufficient numerical data;
- where figures date quickly because the market is changing rapidly.

Question 3.

Denten Limited is a manufacturer of bins and other storage equipment. It exports a large amount of its products abroad. It makes use of direct sales to customers and also employs some overseas agents. The managing director has asked the marketing department to examine the relationship between the number of agents it employs and sales of three of its most popular products and make recommendations. The research found the following information.

Product 1 $\Sigma Y^2 = 5,360$ $\sum XY = 2,720$
Product 2 $\Sigma Y^2 = 17,360$ $\sum XY = 3,200$
Product 3 $\Sigma Y^2 = 25,080$ $\sum XY = 3,240$
Agents $\Sigma X^2 = 1,400$

(a) Calculate the correlation coefficients to show the relationship between spending on overseas agents and products 1, 2 and 3.
(b) Explain the relationship between the variables in each case.
(c) What advice do you think the marketing department should give the managing director concerning agents from this information?

KEYTERMS

Centring – a method used in the calculation of a moving average where the average is plotted or calculated in relation to the central figure.
Correlation – the relationship between two sets of variables.
Correlation coefficient – a measure of the extent of the relationship between two sets of variables.
Line of best fit – a line plotted through a series of points which balances those on one side with those on the other, and best represents the slope of the points.
Moving average – a method used to find trends in data by smoothing out fluctuations. It involves calculating an average for a number of periods, then dropping the first figure and adding the next to calculate the average that follows.
Scatter graph – a graph showing the performance of one variable against another independent variable on a variety of occasions. It is used to show whether a correlation exists between the variables.
Time series analysis – a method which allows a business to predict future levels from past figures.

KNOWLEDGE

1. Why might a business want to predict the future?
2. What are the four components of time series data that a business might be interested in?
3. What does a trend show?
4. How might a business use the calculation of a trend?
5. What is meant by causal modelling?

Case Study: Jamesons

Jamesons is a retail outlet which specialises in selling outdoor clothing and equipment. This includes walking boots, shoes and weatherproof clothes and also skiing and mountain equipment. Its sales have been increasing over the past two years as increasing numbers of people are becoming interested in outdoor activities and are taking holidays involving sports and exercise. Sales tend to be best in winter months, although recently it has introduced a range of lightweight clothing that seems to have sold well in summer. Table 9 shows its sales revenues over a period from 2006 to 2009.

(a) What is meant by:
(i) a trend in sales figures; (2 marks)
(ii) a four period centred moving average? (2 marks)
(b) (i) Using a four quarter centred moving average, calculate the trend from the sales figures in Table 9 that the business might have found. (10 marks)
(ii) Explain why centring might be used by the business when calculating a trend. (4 marks)
(c) Calculate:
(i) the seasonal variation for as many quarters as you can; (6 marks)
(ii) the average seasonal variation for the fourth quarter. (4 marks)
(d) Plot the trend line onto a graph. Using the trend line and the average seasonal variation for the fourth quarter, predict the sales in the fourth quarter of 2009. State the assumptions that you have made in your prediction. (12 marks)

Table 9 Jamesons sales revenue, 3rd quarter 2006 to 2nd quarter 2009, (£000)

Year	Quarter	(£000) Sales revenue
2006	3	100
	4	180
2007	1	140
	2	60
	3	180
	4	220
2008	1	180
	2	100
	3	220
	4	260
2009	1	220
	2	180

34 Sources of finance

The need for funds

Firms need money to get started, i.e. to buy equipment, raw materials and obtain premises. Once this initial expenditure has been met, the business can get under way. If successful, it will earn money from sales. However, business is a continuous activity and money flowing in will be used to buy more raw materials and settle other trading debts.

If the owner wants to expand, extra money will be needed over and above that from sales. Expansion may mean larger premises, more equipment and extra workers. Throughout the life of a business there will almost certainly be times when money has to be raised from outside.

The items of expenditure above fall into two categories – CAPITAL EXPENDITURE or REVENUE EXPENDITURE. Capital expenditure is spending on items which may be used over and over again. A company vehicle, a cutting machine and a new factory all fall into this category. Capital expenditure will be shown in a firm's balance sheet because it includes the purchase of fixed assets. It also includes the maintenance and repair of buildings and machines.

Revenue expenditure refers to payments for goods and services which have either already been consumed or will be very soon. Wages, raw materials and fuel are all examples. It also includes the maintenance and repair of buildings and machines. Revenue expenditure will be shown in a firm's profit and loss account or income statement because it represents business costs or expenses.

Internal sources of finance

Figure 1 shows how sources of finance are either internal or external. Internal sources can only be used when a business is established because money cannot be taken out of a business until revenue has been generated by trading activities. Although most of this unit focuses on external sources of finance, internal sources are very important. This is because internal sources are cheap. A business does not have to pay interest, for example, if it uses its own money to fund activities.

There are three important internal sources of finance.

Profit Retained profit is profit after tax that has not been returned to the owners. It is the single most important source of finance for a business. Around 65 per cent of all business funding comes from retained profit. It is the cheapest source of finance, with no financial charges such as interest, dividends and administration. However, there is an opportunity cost. If retained profit is used by the business it cannot be returned to the owners. This may lead to conflict if the shareholders of a public limited company, for example, see that dividend payments have been frozen because the directors have used the profit in the business.

Working capital It may be possible to 'squeeze' working capital to provide extra finance for the business. One way of doing this is to operate a 'tighter' credit policy. For example, a business might reduce the trade credit period, so that money is received

Figure 1: Sources of funds

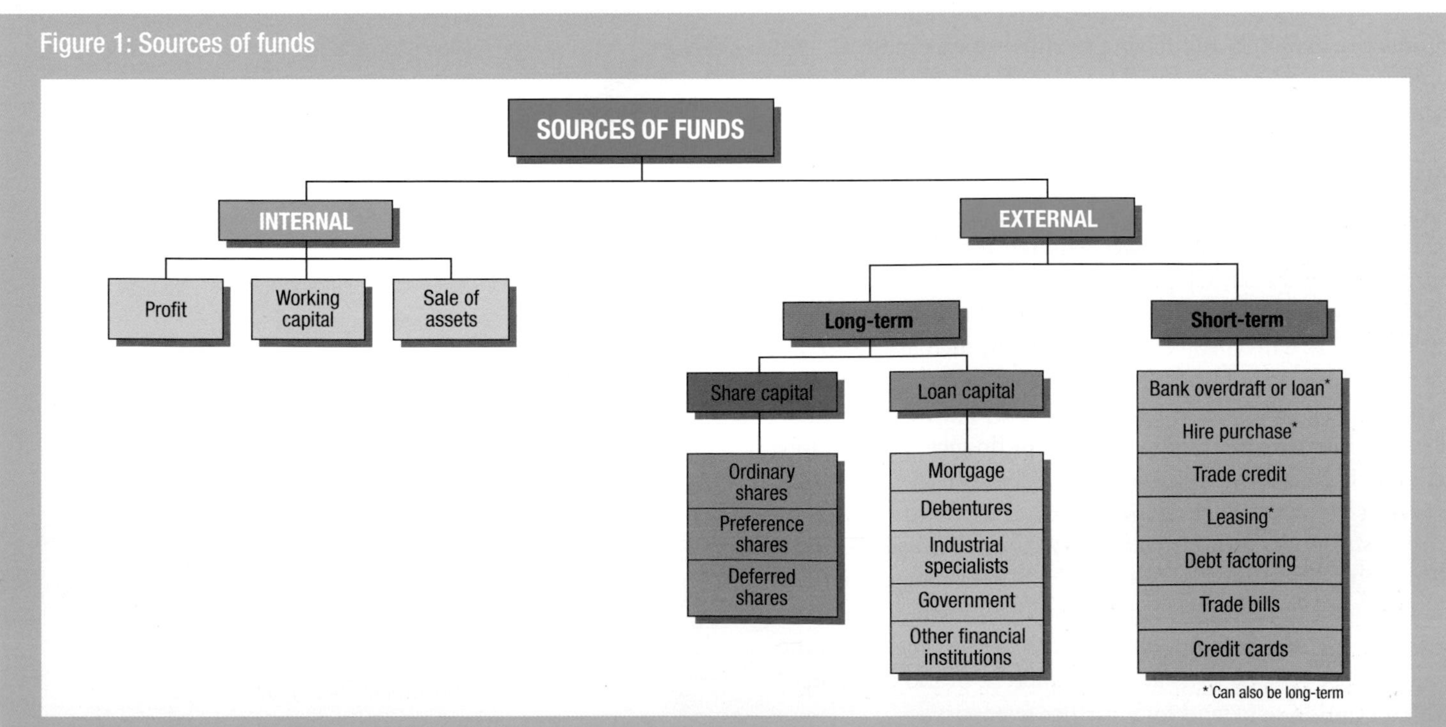

Question 1.

Godwin's Ice Cream is located in Weston-on-the-Green, Oxfordshire. The business has an ice cream factory and shop attached to a working farm. The business's activities include ice cream manufacture from the farm's own milk, sale of ice cream on-site and sale through a limited number of shops and restaurants. The aim of the business was to replace lost income from falling product prices, through adding value to the existing product. Before setting up the owners wrote a business plan and made an application for a Rural Enterprise Scheme (RES) grant. There were initial problems with the grant due to different interpretations by DEFRA staff of which aspects of the business were eligible for the RES grant. However, it was felt this was probably a teething problem with the scheme as they were one of the first applicants and the forms and guidance are now clearer. The grant was eventually awarded to Godwin's. The other main source of finance for the business is a bank overdraft.

Source: adapted from www.southeast-ra.gov.uk.

(a) **What is the advantage to Godwin's Ice Cream of obtaining a grant to help fund the business?**

(b) **Why do you think it is important to write a business plan when applying for funds?**

(c) **One of Godwin's main sources of finance is a bank overdraft. Explain (i) why this is an external source of finance and (ii) why this will be a flexible source of finance to Godwin's.**

from customers more quickly. Or a business might collect long-standing debts by applying more pressure to customers. Both these options might result in a loss of orders and damage customer relations. Another approach is to reduce stock holding. Money tied up in stocks is unproductive. If a business can reduce stock, money is released and can be used for more productive activities. But having too little stock can be a problem. For example, a business might find it difficult to cope with a surge in demand if stocks are too low.

Sale of assets An established business may be able to sell some unwanted assets to raise finance. For example, machinery, land and buildings that are no longer required could be sold off. Large companies can sell parts of their organisation to raise finance. Another option is to raise money through a SALE AND LEASEBACK. This involves selling an asset, such as property or machinery, that the business still wants to use. The sale is made to a specialist company that leases the asset back to the seller. This is an increasingly popular source of finance. For example, in 2007, HSBC agreed the sale and leaseback of its head office building in Canary Wharf, London for £1.09 billion. A wholly-owned subsidiary of Metrovacesa, S.A., one of Europe's most respected property companies, and HSBC exchanged contracts on the deal which sees the bank retain full control of occupancy while Metrovacesa takes a 998-year lease. HSBC has leased the building back for 20 years at an annual rent of £43.5 million with an option to extend for a further five years.

External long-term sources of finance

External long-term capital can be in the form of share capital or loan capital.

Share capital For a limited company SHARE CAPITAL is likely to be the most important source of finance. The sale of shares can raise very large amounts of money. ISSUED SHARE CAPITAL is the money raised from the sale of shares. AUTHORISED SHARE CAPITAL is the maximum amount shareholders want to raise. Share capital is often referred to as PERMANENT CAPITAL. This is because it is not normally redeemed, i.e. it is not repaid by the business. Once the share has been sold, the buyer is entitled to a share in the profit of the

Table 1: Summary and explanation of the ways in which new shares can be made available to investors on the stock exchange

INITIAL PUBLIC OFFERING (IPO)	
Public issue	Potential investors might apply to an ISSUING HOUSE, such as a merchant bank, after reading the company prospectus. This is an expensive method, but suits big issues.
Offer for sale	Shares are issued to an issuing house, which then sells them at a fixed price. This is also expensive but suits small issues.
Sale by tender	The company states a minimum price which it will accept from investors and then allocates shares to the highest bidders.
PLACING	
Private placing	Unquoted companies (who do not sell on the Stock Exchange) or those with small share sales approach issuing houses to place the shares privately with investors.
Stock exchange placing	Less popular issues can be placed by the stock exchange with institutional investors, for example. This is relatively inexpensive.
AN INTRODUCTION	Existing shareholders get permission from the Stock Exchange to sell shares by attracting new shareholders to the firm. No new capital is raised.
RIGHTS ISSUE	Existing shareholders are given the 'right' to buy new shares at a discounted price. This is cheap and simple, and creates free publicity. Issues can be based on current holdings. A one for five issue means that 1 new share is issued for every five currently held.
BONUS ISSUE	New shares are issued to existing shareholders to capitalise on reserves which have built up over the years. No new capital is raised and shareholders end up with more shares, but at lower prices.

company, i.e. a dividend. Dividends are not always declared. Sometimes a business makes a loss or needs to retain profit to help fund future business activities. A shareholder can make a CAPITAL GAIN by selling the share at a higher price than it was originally bought for. Shares are not normally sold back to the business. The shares of public limited companies are sold in a special share market called the STOCK MARKET or STOCK EXCHANGE, dealt with later in this unit. Shares in private limited companies are transferred privately. Shareholders, because they are part owners of the business, are entitled to a vote. One vote is allowed for each share owned. Voting takes place annually and shareholders vote either to re-elect the existing board of directors or replace them. Different types of shares can be issued.

- **Ordinary shares.** These are also called EQUITIES and are the most common type of share issued. They are also the riskiest type of share since there is no guaranteed dividend. The size of the dividend depends on how much profit is made and how much the directors decide to retain in the business. All ordinary shareholders have voting rights. When a share is first sold it has a nominal value shown on it - its original value. Share prices will change as they are bought and sold again and again.
- **Preference shares.** The owners of these shares receive a fixed rate of return when a dividend is declared. They carry less risk because shareholders are entitled to their dividend before the holders of ordinary shares. Preference shareholders are not strictly owners of the company. If the company is sold, their rights to dividends and capital repayments are limited to fixed amounts. Some preference shares are cumulative, entitling the holder to dividend arrears from years when dividends were not declared. Some are also redeemable, which means that they can be bought back by the company.
- **Deferred shares.** These are not used often. They are usually held by the founders of the company. Deferred shareholders only receive a dividend after the ordinary shareholders have been paid a minimum amount.

When a company issues shares there is a variety of ways in which they can be made available to potential investors as shown in Table 1.

Loan capital Loan capital may come from a number of sources.

- **Debentures.** The holder of a debenture is a creditor of the company, not an owner. This means that holders are entitled to an agreed fixed rate of return, but have no voting rights. The amount borrowed must be repaid by the expiry date.
- **Mortgages.** Only limited companies can raise money from the sale of shares and debentures. Smaller enterprises often need long-term funding, to buy premises for example. They may choose to take out a mortgage. A mortgage is usually a long-term loan, from, say, a bank or other financial institution. The lender must use land or property as security on the loan.

Figure 2: A hire purchase agreement and the parties involved in the three way transaction

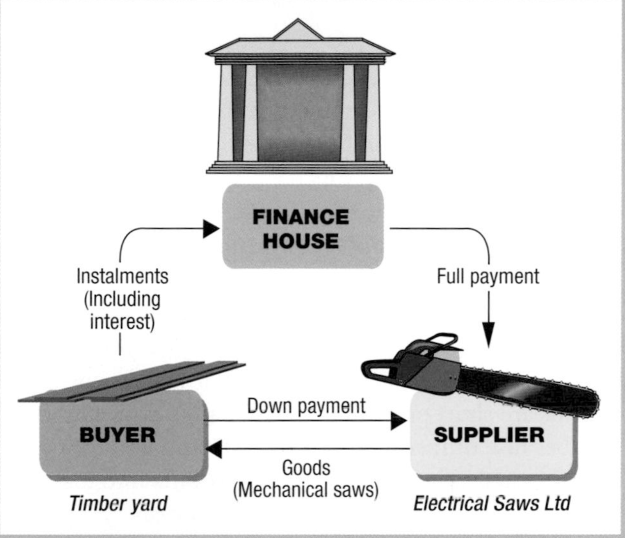

- **Industrial loan specialists.** A number of organisations provide funds especially for business and commercial uses. These specialists tend to cater for businesses which have difficulty in raising funds from conventional sources. In recent years there has been a significant growth in the number of VENTURE CAPITALISTS. These provide funds for small and medium sized companies that appear to have some potential, but are considered too risky by other investors. Venture capitalists often use their own funds, but also attract money from financial institutions and 'Business Angels'. Business Angels are individuals who invest between £10,000 and £100,000, often in exchange for an equity stake. A typical Angel might make one or two investments in a three year period, either individually or together with a small group of friends, relatives or business associates. Most investments are in start-ups or early stage expansions. There are several reasons why people become Business Angels. Many like the excitement of the gamble involved, or being part of a new or developing business. Others are attracted by the tax relief offered by the government. Some are looking for investment opportunities for their unused income, such as retired business people.
- **Government assistance.** Both central and local government have been involved in providing finance for business. Business start up schemes can provide a small amount of income for those starting new businesses for a limited period of time, providing they meet certain criteria. Financial help is usually selective. Smaller businesses tend to benefit, as do those setting up in regions which suffer from heavy unemployment.
- **Other financial institutions.** Banks, for example might under certain conditions give a business a long-term loan

which will be repaid over a number of years. The bank may require some form of collateral on the loan, and a business may need to present a business plan to secure the loan.

External short-term sources of finance

Bank overdraft This is probably the most important source of finance for a very large number of businesses. Bank overdrafts are flexible. The amount by which a business goes overdrawn depends on its needs at the time. Interest is only paid by the business when its account is overdrawn.

Bank loan A loan requires a rigid agreement between the borrower and the bank. The amount borrowed must be repaid over a clearly stated time period, in regular instalments. Most bank loans are short or medium term. Banks dislike long term lending because of their need for security and liquidity. Sometimes, banks change persistent overdrafts into loans, so that firms are forced to repay at regular intervals.

Hire purchase This is often used by small businesses to buy plant and machinery. Sometimes, a hire purchase agreement requires a down payment by the borrower, who agrees to repay the remainder in instalments over a period of time. FINANCE HOUSES specialise in providing funds for such agreements. Figure 2 illustrates the working of an agreement and the parties involved. The buyer may place a down payment on a machine with the supplier and receives delivery. The finance house pays the supplier the amount outstanding and collects instalments (including interest) from the buyer. The goods bought do not legally belong to the buyer until the very last instalment has been paid to the finance house. If the buyer falls behind with the repayments the finance house can legally repossess the item. Finance houses are less selective than banks when granting loans. Hence their interest rates are higher. They add a servicing charge for paying in instalments which also leads to higher rates. Hire purchase agreements can sometimes be for longer periods.

Trade credit It is common for businesses to buy raw materials, components and fuel and pay for them at a later date, usually within 30-90 days. Paying for goods and services using trade credit seems to be an interest free way of raising finance. It is particularly profitable during periods of inflation. However, many companies encourage early payment by offering discounts. The cost of goods is often higher if the firm does not pay early. Delaying the payment of bills can also result in poor business relations with suppliers.

Leasing A LEASE is a contract in which a business acquires the use of resources such as, property, machinery or equipment, in return for regular payments. In this type of finance, the ownership never passes to the business that is using the resource. With a finance lease, the arrangement is often for three years or longer and, at the end of the period, the business is given the option of then buying the resource. In accounting, the payments are treated as capital expenditure. With an operating lease, the arrangement is generally for a shorter period of time, and the payments are treated as revenue expenditure.

There are some advantages of leasing.

- No large sums of money are needed to buy the use of equipment.
- Maintenance and repair costs are not the responsibility of the user.
- Hire companies can offer the most up to date equipment.
- Leasing is useful when equipment is only required occasionally.
- A leasing agreement is generally easier for a new company to obtain than other forms of loan finance. This is because the assets remain the property of the leasing company.

However:

- over a long period of time leasing is more expensive than the outright purchase of plant and machinery;
- loans cannot be secured on assets which are leased.

Factoring When companies sell their products they send invoices stating the amount due. The invoice provides evidence

Question 2.

A mobile phone-based information service, 82Ask, launched by one of Britain's top rising female entrepreneurs, is aiming to float on the stock market early next year after raising £1.3 million in funds. The company, which is changing its name to Texperts, is led by Sarah McVittie, a former UBS investment banker. Texperts allows users to text a question to a team of research experts who promise to provide an answer within five minutes. Users are charged £1 per question only if the inquiry is fully completed. The service, which has close to 400,000 users, has a network of 220 experts answering questions on anything from trivia and entertainment to recommending restaurants, providing travel information and sending maps to people's mobile phones.

Odey Asset Management (an industrial loan specialist), is understood to have provided most of the new funding and now has a stake of around 14 per cent in Texperts. McVittie and co-founder Thomas Roberts, each have about a 15 per cent stake. Over the past four years, Texperts has raised £2.5 million, mainly from wealthy individuals in three fundraising rounds. About £1 million of the £1.3 million from the latest round of fund raising is earmarked for advertising and marketing. This is well above the £200,000 spent to date.

Source: adapted from the *Sunday Times*, 19.8.2007.

(a) Why is Texperts raising finance?

(b) How much of the business is owned by the original founders?

(c) Describe the two key sources of finance used by Texperts?

(d) Discuss the drawback to the founders of Texperts of using this type of finance.

Table 2: Advantages and disadvantages of being high geared and low geared

	Advantages	Disadvantages
Low geared	The burden of loan repayments is reduced. The need for regular interest payments is reduced. Volatile interest rates are less of a threat.	Dividend payments have to be met indefinitely. Ownership of the company will be diluted. Dividends are paid after tax.
High geared	The interest on loans can be offset against tax. Ownership is not diluted. Once loans have been repaid the company's debt is much reduced.	Interest payments must be met. Interest rates can change, which causes uncertainty. Loans must be repaid and may be a burden, increasing the risk of insolvency.

of the sale and the money owed to the company. Debt factoring involves a specialist company (the factor) providing finance against these unpaid invoices. A common arrangement is for a factor to pay 80 per cent of the value of invoices when they are issued. The balance of 20 per cent is paid by the 'factor' when the customer settles the bill. An administrative and service fee will be charged.

Trade bills This is not a common source of finance, but can play an important role, particularly in overseas trade and commodity markets. The purchaser of traded goods may sign a **bill of exchange** agreeing to pay for the goods at a specified later date. Ninety days is a common period. The seller of the goods will hold the bill until payment is due. However, the holder can sell it at a discount before the maturity date to a specialist financial institution. There is a well developed market for these bills and all holders will receive payment at the end of the period from the debtor.

Credit cards Businesses of all sizes have uses for credit cards. They can be used by executives to meet expenses such as hotel bills, petrol and meals when travelling on company business. They might also be used to purchase materials from suppliers who accept credit cards. Credit cards are popular because they are convenient, flexible, secure and avoid interest charges if monthly accounts are settled within the credit period. However, they tend to have a credit limit. This may make them unsuitable for certain purchases.

The choice of the source of finance

A number of factors are important when choosing between alternative sources of finance.

Cost Businesses obviously prefer sources which are less expensive, both in terms of interest payments and administration costs. For example, share issues can carry high administration costs while the interest payments on bank overdrafts tend to be relatively low.

Use of funds When a company undertakes heavy capital expenditure, it is usually funded by a long-term source of finance. For example, the building of a new plant may be financed by a share issue or a mortgage. Revenue expenditure tends to be financed by short-term sources. For example, the purchase of a large amount of raw materials may be funded by trade credit or a bank overdraft.

Status and size Sole traders, which tend to be small, are limited in their choices of finance. For example, long-term sources may be mortgages and perhaps the introduction of some personal capital. Public and private limited companies can usually obtain finance from many different sources. In addition, due to their size and added security, they can often demand lower interest rates from lenders. There are significant economies of scale in raising finance.

Financial situation The financial situation of businesses is constantly changing. When a business is in a poor financial situation, it finds that lenders are more reluctant to offer finance. At the same time, the cost of borrowing rises. Financial institutions are more willing to lend to secure businesses which have **collateral** (assets which provide security for loans). Third World countries which are desperate to borrow money to fund development are often forced to pay very high rates indeed.

Gearing GEARING is the relationship between the loan capital and share capital of a business. A company is said to be **high geared** if it has a large proportion of loan capital to share capital. A **low geared** company has a relatively small amount of loan capital. For example, two companies may each have total capital of £45 million. If the first has loan capital of £40 million and share capital of only £5 million it is high geared. The other company may have share capital of £30 million and loan capital of £15 million. It is relatively low geared.

The gearing of a company might influence its finance. If a business is high geared, it may be reluctant to raise even more finance by borrowing. It may choose to issue more shares instead, rather than increasing the interest to be paid on loans.

Table 2 shows the advantages and disadvantages of being low or high geared.

Capital and money markets

Businesses have to look to external sources for their finance. Financial intermediaries are the institutions responsible for matching the needs of savers, who want to loan funds, with those of investors, who need funds. These groups do not naturally communicate with each other. Intermediaries provide the link between them.

A number of financial institutions hold funds for savers, paying them interest. In addition, they make finance available to investors who, in turn, are charged interest. Some deal in capital, i.e. permanent and long-term finance, while others deal in money, i.e. short-term loans and bills of exchange. They offer a variety of commercial and financially related services.

The stock market The capital market is dominated by the London Stock Exchange, which deals in second-hand shares. The main function of a stock exchange is to provide a market where the owners of shares can sell them. If this market did not exist, selling shares would be difficult because buyers and sellers could not easily communicate with each other. Savers would be less inclined to buy shares and so companies would find it more difficult to raise finance through the issue of shares.

A stock exchange enables mergers and takeovers to take place smoothly. If the price of a company's shares begins to fall due to poor profitability, a predator may enter the market and begin to build up a stake in that company. Once the stake is large enough a predator can exert control over the company.

A stock exchange also provides a means of protection for shareholders. Companies which have a stock exchange listing have to obey a number of Stock Exchange rules and regulations, which are designed to safeguard shareholders from fraud.

Finally, it is also argued that the general movement in share prices reflects the health of the economy. However, there are times when share price movements could be very misleading. For example, they fell very sharply in 2003 just before the Iraq war when the UK economy was quite stable.

Insurance companies, pension funds, investment trusts, unit trusts and issuing houses (merchant banks) are some of the institutions which trade in shares.

Banks and other financial institutions The money market is dominated by the major commercial banks, such as NatWest or the HSBC. They allow payments to be made through the cheque system and deal in short-term loans. Savings banks and finance corporations also deal in short-term funds. Building societies also provide a source of finance. They have tended to specialise in long-term loans for the purchase of land and property.

At the heart of this highly complex market system is the **Bank of England**. This plays a role in controlling the amount of money loaned and interest rates.

In recent years many of the above institutions have changed in nature. Due to competition, changes in legislation and mergers there has been a great deal of diversification. In particular, there is now little real difference between the role of a building society and that of a bank.

The Alternative Investment Market and the PLUS Markets Group In June 1995 the Alternative Investment Market (AIM) was established. Its purpose was to give small, young and growing companies the chance to raise capital and trade their shares more widely, without the cost of a full stock market listing. In order to join the market, a nominated adviser must be appointed, such as a stockbroker, banker or lawyer. The adviser must supervise the admission procedure and be responsible for ensuring that the company complies with AIM regulations. The admission procedure takes three months. The cost of a listing is about £100,000. Another market, called the PLUS Market Group (previously called OFEX), was set up by J.P. Jenkins, the specialist market-maker in small company shares. It is not regulated by the stock exchange, but only stock exchange member firms can deal directly on the PLUS Market Group. It offers a market place for the shares of unlisted companies that have no interest in joining AIM. Two of Britain's biggest private companies, Rangers Football Club and Jessops, the camera retailer, both feature on the PLUS Market group. The market also acts as a 'feeder' to AIM because flotation and other costs are less at the initial stages.

Capital structure

The CAPITAL STRUCTURE of a business refers to the different sources of funds a business has used. Capital structures can vary considerably depending on the type of business. For example:

- sole traders will not have any share capital in their capital structure;
- firms which have funded expansion by reinvesting profits may not show any long-term loan capital in their capital structure;
- debt-laden companies may have large amounts of loan capital in their capital structure.

KNOWLEDGE

1. Why do businesses need to raise finance?
2. State the internal sources of finance.
3. State the main advantage of using internal finance.
4. What is the difference between ordinary, preference and deferred shares?
5. Why would someone want to become an Business Angel?
6. State the advantages to a business of a bank overdraft compared with a bank loan.
7. What is trade credit likely to be used for?
8. Which is likely to be more expensive, a bank loan or HP?
9. What is the difference between a finance lease and an operating lease?
10. What factors affect the choice of source of finance?

KEYTERMS

Authorised share capital – the maximum amount which can be legally raised.
Capital expenditure – spending on business resources which can be used repeatedly over a period of time.
Capital gain – the profit made from selling a share for more than it was bought.
Capital structure – the way in which funds are raised by a business.
Equities – another name for an ordinary share.
Finance houses - specialist institutions which provide funds for hire purchase agreements.
Gearing – the relationship between funds raised from loans and from issuing shares.
Issuing house – any institution that deals with the sale of new shares.
Issued share capital – amount of current share capital arising from the sale of shares.
Lease – a contract to acquire the use of resources such as property or equipment.
Permanent capital – share capital which is never repaid by the company.
Revenue expenditure – spending on business resources that have already been consumed or will be very shortly.
Sale and leaseback – the practice of selling assets, such as property or machinery, and leasing them back from the buyer.
Share capital – money introduced into the business through the sale of shares.
Stock market or stock exchange – a market where second-hand shares are bought and sold.
Venture capitalists – providers of funds for small or medium sized companies that may be considered too risky for other investors.

Case Study: Gamingking

Gamingking plc was established in 1993 and floated on the Alternative Investment Market (a market for shares) in 1996. In May 2005 Gamingking acquired its largest competitor, Kelly's Eye (No. 1) Ltd. In doing so the Group became the leader in the provision of lotteries and game play products and services to the registered members' club marketplace. The Group now has a client base of around 5,000 clubs in the UK. The Group comprises three main wholly-owned trading subsidiaries:

Kelly's Eye No. (1) Kelly's Eye, based in Hemel Hempstead, is responsible for all sales and marketing activities related to lottery and game play products. The Kelly's Eye salesforce operates nationwide and is able to supply the wide-ranging product portfolio into clubs quickly and efficiently.

Lotteryking Ltd. Lotteryking was the original business providing vending machines; pull-tab lottery tickets and online lottery solutions to the private members' clubs.

Following the acquisition of Kelly's Eye, Lotteryking is now focused on the provision of technical support services, manufacturing, R&D, and purchasing.

Logoking Ltd. This division supplies logo-embroidered leisure and workwear to a wide market including the substantial staff and sports needs of the private members' clubs.

In 2006, Gamingking made a profit of £51,000 and retained the entire sum. It did the same in 2005 when profit was £38,000. At 30 April Gamingking had a loan facility of £800,000 from Barclays Bank much of which was used to buy Kelly's Eye (No.1) Ltd. This loan was due to mature on 15th April 2010. Also, at 30th April 2006, Gamingking had authorised share capital of £5 million and issued share capital of £2.907 million. Other sources of finance used by Gamingking include trade credit and hire purchase.

Source: adapted from www.gamingking.co.uk.

(a) Explain the difference between authorised and issued share capital. (6 marks)

(b) How will floating on the Alternative Investment Market (a stock market) affect Gamingking's ability to raise finance? (8 marks)

(c) (i) Why did Gamingking borrow £800,000 from Barclay's Bank? (4 marks)

(ii) How will this loan affect the gearing of the company? (8 marks)

(d) Discuss the advantages and disadvantages to Gamingking of retaining all of its profit in 2005 and 2006. (14 marks)

35 Costs, revenue and profit

The costs of production

A business needs accurate and reliable cost information to make decisions. A firm that is aiming to expand production to meet rising demand must know how much that extra production will cost. Without this information it will have no way of knowing whether or not it will make a profit. You will be familiar with your own costs. These are the expenses you have, such as travel costs to school or college. Similarly, businesses have expenses. These might include wages, raw materials, insurance and rent.

Economists usually think of costs as opportunity costs. The **opportunity cost** is the value that could have been earned if a resource was employed in its next best use. For example, if a business spends £40,000 on an advertising campaign, the opportunity cost might be the interest earned from depositing the money in a bank account. A business is also concerned, however, with ACCOUNTING COSTS. An accounting cost is the value of a resource used up in production. This is shown in the business accounts as an asset or an expense. For example, if a firm buys some fuel costing £5,500, this is shown as an expense in the accounts.

It is also important to understand how a firm's costs change in the SHORT RUN and the LONG RUN.

- The short run is the period of time when at least one factor of production is **fixed**. For example, in the short run, a firm might want to expand production in its factory. It can acquire more labour and buy more raw materials, but it has a fixed amount of space in the factory and a limited number of machines.
- In the long run, all factors can vary. The firm can buy another factory and add to the number of machines. This will increase **capacity** (the maximum amount that can be produced and begin another short run period.

Fixed costs

Costs which stay the same at all levels of output in the short run are called FIXED COSTS. Examples might be rent, insurance, heating bills, depreciation and business rates, as well as **capital costs** such as factories and machinery. These costs remain the same whether a business produces nothing or is working at full capacity. For example, rent must still be paid even if a factory is shut for a two week holiday when nothing is produced. Importantly, 'fixed' here means costs do not change as a result of a change in **output** in the short run. But they may increase due to, say, inflation. Figure 1 shows what happens to fixed costs as a firm increases production. The line on the graph is horizontal which shows that fixed costs are £400,000 no matter how much is produced.

What happens over a longer period? Figure 2 illustrates

Figure 1: Fixed costs

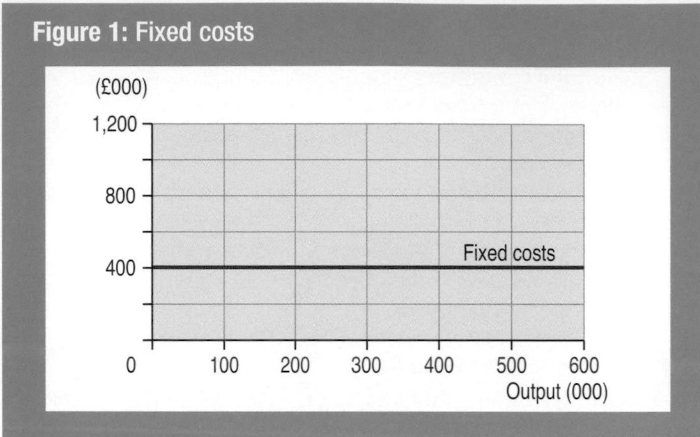

Figure 2: Stepped fixed costs

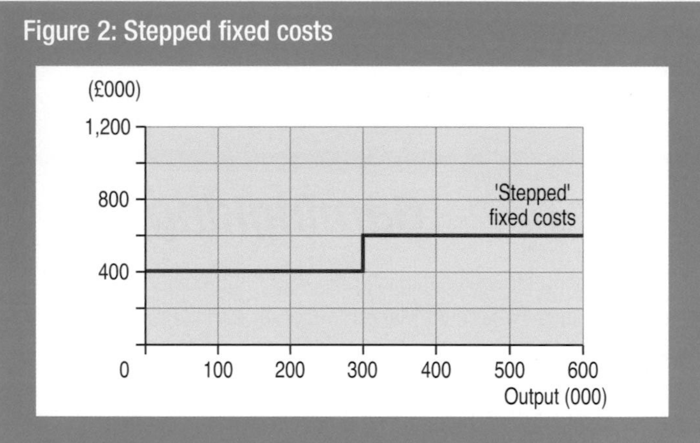

'stepped' fixed costs. If a firm is at full capacity, but needs to raise production, it might decide to invest in more equipment. The new machines raise overall fixed costs as well as capacity. The rise in fixed costs is shown by a 'step' in the graph. This illustrates how fixed costs can change in the long run.

Variable and semi-variable costs

Costs of production which increase directly as output rises are called VARIABLE COSTS. For example, a baker will require more flour if more loaves are to be produced. Raw materials are just one example of variable costs. Others might include fuel, packaging and wages. If the firm does not produce anything then variable costs will be zero.

Figure 3 shows a firm's variable costs. Assume that the firm buying new machinery in Figure 1 produces dolls and that variable costs are £2 per doll. If the firm produces 100,000 dolls it will have variable costs of £200,000 (£2 x 100,000). Producing 600,000 dolls it will incur variable costs of £1,200,000 (£2 x 600,000). Joining these points together shows the firm's variable costs at any level of output. As output increases, so do variable costs. Notice that the graph is **linear**. This means that it is a straight line.

Figure 3: Variable costs of a doll manufacturer

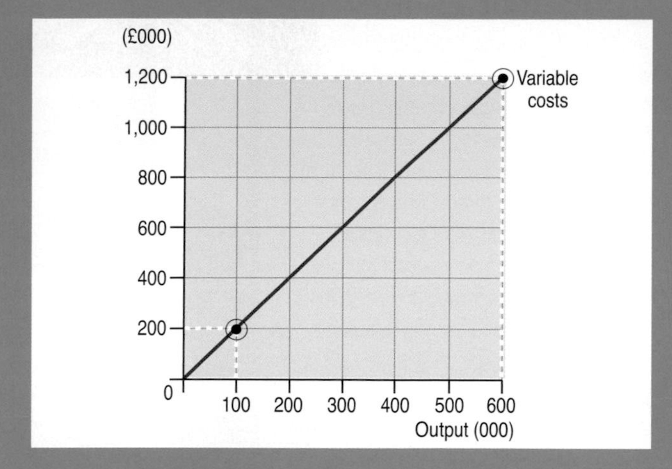

Some production costs do not fit neatly into our definitions of fixed and variable costs. This is because they are not entirely fixed or variable costs. Labour is a good example. If a firm employs a member of staff on a permanent basis, no matter what level of output, then this is a fixed cost. If this member of staff is asked to work overtime at nights and weekends to cope with extra production levels, then the extra cost is variable. Such labour costs are said to be SEMI-VARIABLE COSTS. Another example could be the cost of telephone charges. This often consists of a fixed or 'standing charge' plus an extra rate which varies according to the number of calls made.

Total costs

If fixed and variable costs are added together they show the TOTAL COST of a business. The total cost of production is the cost of producing any given level of output. As output increases total costs will rise. This is shown in Figure 4, which again shows the production of dolls. We can say:

Total cost (TC) = fixed cost (FC) + variable cost (VC)

The business has fixed costs of £400,000 and variable costs of £2 per doll. When output is 0 total costs are £400,000. When output has risen to 300,000 dolls, total costs are £1,000,000, made up of fixed costs of £400,000 and variable costs of £600,000 (£2 x 300,000). When output is 600,000, total costs are

Table 1: Summary of cost information for the doll manufacturer

000			£000
Output	Fixed cost	Variable cost	Total cost
0	400	0	400
300	400	600	1,000
600	400	1,200	1,600

Figure 4: Total costs of a doll manufacturer

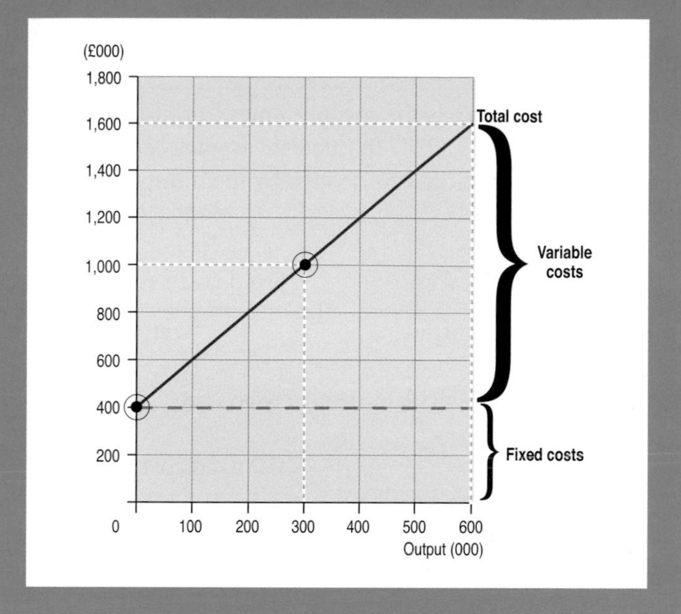

£1,600,00 made up of fixed costs of £400,000 and variable costs of £1,200,000 (£2 x 600,000). This information is summarised in Table 1. Figure 4 shows the way that total costs increase as output increases. Notice that as output increases fixed costs become a smaller proportion of total costs.

Direct and indirect costs

Costs can also be divided into direct and indirect costs. DIRECT COSTS are costs which can be identified with a particular product or process. Examples of direct costs are raw materials, packaging, and direct labour. INDIRECT COSTS or OVERHEADS result from the whole business. It is not possible to associate these costs directly with particular products or processes. Examples are rent, insurance, the salaries of office staff and audit fees. Indirect costs are usually fixed costs and

Question 1.

Dale Roberts runs EdMedia, an education and training services company based in Stevenage, Hertfordshire. EdMedia produces online and video information films about workplace issues, from disability discrimination to bullying and harassment. Orders have soared as new employment laws create demand for staff training. Large contracts with high profile clients have helped to boost sales from £1.1 million in 2005 to £3.9 million in 2007. In 2006, Dale had to hire a new photocopier. The monthly hire rate was £100. Other costs associated with the photocopier were toner, paper and electricity. These costs amounted to £1 per 100 copies.

(a) Using the photocopier as an example, explain the difference between fixed and variable costs.

(b) Calculate the total annual cost of the photocopier if 68,000 copies were made during the year.

(c) Explain why the total cost of the photocopier is an indirect cost for EdMedia.

direct costs variable costs, although in theory both direct and indirect costs can be fixed or variable.

Average and marginal costs

The AVERAGE COST is the cost per unit of production, also known as the UNIT COST. To calculate average cost the total cost of production should be divided by the number of units produced.

$$\text{Average cost} = \frac{\text{Total cost}}{\text{Output}} \quad \text{or} \quad \frac{\text{Fixed cost + variable cost}}{\text{Output}}$$

It is also possible to calculate average fixed costs:

$$\text{Average fixed cost} = \frac{\text{Total fixed cost}}{\text{Output}}$$

and average variable costs:

$$\text{Average variable cost} = \frac{\text{Total variable cost}}{\text{Output}}$$

Take the earlier example of the doll manufacturer with fixed costs of £400,000 and variable costs of £2 per unit. If output was 100,000 units:

$$\text{Average fixed cost} = \frac{£400{,}000}{100{,}000} = £4$$

$$\text{Average variable cost} = \frac{£2 \text{ x } 100{,}000}{100{,}000} = £2$$

$$\text{Average total cost} = \frac{£400{,}000 + (£2 \text{ x } 100{,}000)}{100{,}000}$$

$$= \frac{£600{,}000}{100{,}000} = £6$$

MARGINAL COST is the cost of increasing total output by one more unit. It can be calculated by:

$$\text{Marginal cost} = \frac{\text{change in total cost}}{\text{change in output}}$$

For example, if the total cost of manufacturing 100,000 dolls is £600,000 and the total cost of producing 100,001 dolls is £600,002, then the marginal cost of producing the last unit is:

$$\text{Marginal cost} = \frac{£600{,}002 - £600{,}000}{100{,}001 - 100{,}000} = \frac{£2}{1} = £2$$

Question 2.

Carefabric is a home-based business run by Margaret Parry. She makes a small range of towelling and other products for children. The products are advertised on her website and she distributes about 50 per cent of output to retailers in the southwest on a sale or return basis. Recently she has concentrated more on design and has employed someone full time to do most of the manufacturing - although Margaret still helps out when the orders pile up. One of the new products Margaret has recently added to her line is a skin-friendly suit for small children. Made from natural materials, the costs for each suit are given below.

Fabric	£5.60 per unit
Other materials	£2.40 per unit
Packaging	£1.00 per unit
Machining	£11.00 per unit
Fixed overheads	£50 per month

When setting the price for her products Margaret just adds on 50% of costs. This method has generated good sales and profits in the past and she has no reason to change a successful strategy. Margaret plans to produce 400 suits in the next trading year.

(a) Calculate: (i) total fixed cost; (ii) total variable cost; (iii) total costs (iv) average cost; (v) price.

(b) During the year Margaret managed to sell just 250 suits. Calculate the total revenue.

The problems of classifying costs

There is a number of possible ways in which costs can be classified.

- By type. This involves analysing business costs and deciding whether they are **direct** or **indirect**.
- By behaviour. Economists favour this method. They classify costs according to the effect that a change in the level of output has on a particular cost. **Fixed**, **variable**, **semi-variable**, **average and marginal costs** all fall into this category.
- By function. It is possible to classify costs according to the business function they are associated with. For example, costs could be listed as **production**, **selling**, **administrative** or **personnel**.
- By nature of resource. This involves classifying costs according to the resources which were acquired by a business, for example, **materials**, **labour** or **expenses**.
- By **product**, **job**, **customer** or **contract**. A multi-product manufacturer, such as Heinz for example, might classify costs according to the product line (beans, soups,

Figure 5: Total revenue

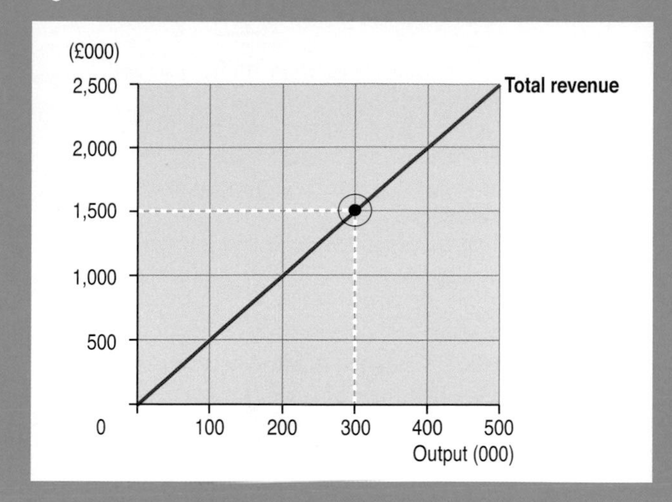

puddings) they are associated with. Solicitors might classify costs by identifying them with particular clients.

The classification of costs is not always straightforward. In some cases the same business cost can be classified in several ways. For example, the earnings of a full-time administrative assistant may be classified as a fixed cost, if they do not vary with output, and an indirect cost, if they are not associated with a particular product. The costs of a worker earning piece rates might be a direct cost if they can be associated with a particular product and a variable cost if they rise as the output of the worker increases.

Another problem relating to costs concerns the allocation of indirect costs. When calculating the cost of producing particular products it is necessary to allocate indirect costs to each of the different products a business manufactures. In practice this may be difficult.

The way in which costs are classified will depend on the purposes for which the classification is being undertaken and the views of the management team.

Long-run costs

Most of the costs discussed so far in this unit have been short-run costs, ie the time period where at least one factor of production is fixed. In the long run, all factors of production are likely to be variable.

Total revenue

The amount of money which a firm receives from selling its product can be referred to as TOTAL REVENUE. Total revenue is calculated by multiplying the number of units sold by the price of each unit:

Total revenue = quantity sold x price

For example, if the doll producer mentioned earlier sells 300,000 dolls at a price of £5 each:

Total revenue = 300,000 x £5 = £1,500,000

Figure 5 shows what happens to total revenue as output rises. Notice that the graph is linear.

Profit and loss

One of the main reasons why firms calculate their costs and revenue is to enable them to work out their **profit** or **loss**. Profit is the difference between revenue and costs.

Profit = total revenue - total costs

For example, if the doll manufacturer in the earlier example produces and sells 300,000 dolls, they sell for £5, fixed costs are £400,000 and variable costs are £2 per unit, then:

Profit = £5 x 300,000 - (£400,000 + [£2 x 300,000])

= £1,500,000 - (£400,000 + [£600,000])

= £1,500,000 - £1,000,000

= £500,000

It is possible to calculate the profit for a business at any level of output using this method.

KEYTERMS

Accounting cost - the value of an economic resource used up in production.

Average cost or unit cost - the cost of producing one unit, calculated by dividing the total cost by output.

Direct cost - a cost which can be clearly identified with a particular unit of output.

Fixed cost - a cost which does not change as a result of a change in output in the short run.

Indirect cost or overhead - a cost which cannot be identified with a particular unit of output. It is incurred by the whole organisation or department.

Long run - the time period where all factors of production are variable.

Marginal cost - the cost of increasing output by one more unit.

Semi-variable cost - a cost which consists of both fixed and variable elements.

Short run - the time period where at least one factor of production is fixed.

Total cost - the entire cost of producing a given level of output.

Total revenue - the amount of money the business receives from selling output.

Variable cost - a cost which rises as output rises.

But if the variable costs were £4 per unit, the business would make a loss.

Loss = £5 x 300,000 - (£400,000 + [£4 x 300,000])

= £1,500,000 – (£400,000 + £1,200,000)

= £1,500,000 – £1,600,000

= - £100,000

KNOWLEDGE

1. What is the difference between opportunity costs and accounting costs?
2. How do you account for a 'stepped' fixed cost function?
3. Why are some costs said to be semi-variable?
4. What happens to variable costs as a proportion of total costs when output rises?
5. Explain the difference between direct and indirect costs.
6. How is: (a) average fixed cost; (b) average variable cost; calculated?
7. How is total revenue calculated?
8. What information is required to calculate a firm's profit?
9. What problems might there be when classifying costs?

Case Study: Wilkins

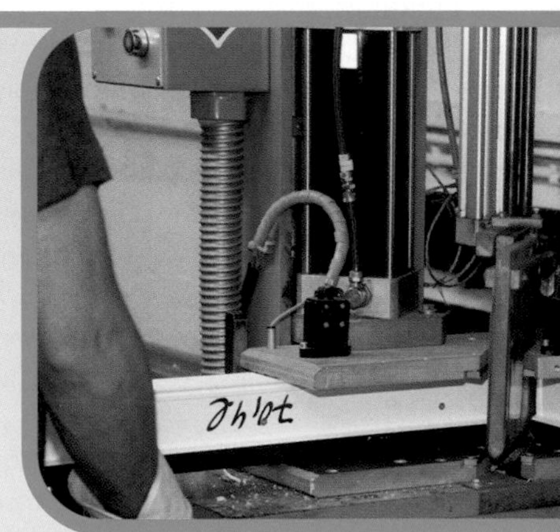

Wilkins manufactures and supplies a range of PVC products such as windows, doors, door canopies, conservatories, garage doors and porches. It is a north eastern company and operate from a factory in Gateshead. The company is committed to high quality standards and as a result gets regular work from large building contractors. Wilkins uses a number of control procedures which are outlined briefly below.

- **The Environmental Test Chamber** uses computer technology to reproduce the conditions of a warm living room and more extreme weather conditions.
- **Weather Cycle Tests** are carried out using data from studies undertaken with the Met Office over the last 30 years, and subjecting our samples to similar patterns.
- **Weld Testing Equipment** is used to check the quality of welds, and a Salt Spray Cabinet ensures that the metal fittings are of the highest quality.
- **Security Test Rig** simulates the damage that a burglar might inflict and the results are assessed to ensure high standards of security in our products.

Wilkins' management system is registered to BS EN ISO 9001-2000 and all products are covered by British and European Standards.

Wilkins is about to start work on a large contract in Newcastle. The contract is to supply 100 standard conservatories on a new housing development. The variable costs for manufacturing and supplying the conservatories are £4,000 each. The fixed costs for the contract are £20,000. An incomplete cost schedule is shown in Figure 6. Wilkins will receive £6,000 for each conservatory.

(a) Give two examples of variable costs that Wilkins is likely to incur when manufacturing and supplying the conservatories. (4 marks)
(b) Complete the cost schedule in Figure 6. (10 marks)
(c) Plot the: (i) fixed cost; (ii) variable cost; (iii) total cost functions on a graph. (12 marks)
(d) Calculate the profit that Wilkins will make on the contract. (8 marks)
(e) How will this profit be affected if fixed costs rise to £35,000? (6 marks)

Figure 6: Cost information for Wilkins

	0	10	20	30	40	50	60	70	80	90	100
Fixed cost	£20,000										
Variable cost											
Total cost											

36 Contribution

What is contribution?

Craig Eckert sells second-hand cars. His last sale was £990 for a Golf GTI. He bought the Golf at a car auction for £890. The difference between what he paid for the car and the price he sold it for is £100 (£990 - £890). This difference is called the CONTRIBUTION. It is not profit because Craig has fixed costs to pay such as rent, insurance and administration expenses. Contribution is the difference between selling price and variable costs. In this case the selling price was £990 and the variable cost was £890. The £100 will **contribute** to the **total fixed costs** of the business and the profit.

Contribution per unit and total contribution

A business might calculate the contribution on the sale of a single unit, or the sale of a larger quantity, such as a whole year's output.

Unit contribution In the above example the unit contribution was calculated. It was the contribution on the sale of one unit, a single car. The formula for calculating the unit contribution is:

Contribution per unit = selling price - variable cost
= £990 - £890
= £100

Total contribution When more than one unit is sold the total contribution can be calculated. For example, a textile company receives an order for 1,000 pairs of trousers. The variable costs are £7.50 a pair and they will be sold for £9.00 a pair. The total contribution made by the order is:

Total contribution = total revenue - total variable cost
= (£9.00 x 1,000) - (£7.50 x 1,000)
= £9,000 - £7,500
= £1,500

Table 1: Variable cost and selling price of cars in January

Description	Variable cost	Selling price	Contribution (£)
Nissan Micra	900	1,100	200
VW Polo	1,100	1,450	350
Fiat Tipo	780	900	120
Volvo 740 SE	1,400	1,700	300
Seat Ibiza	670	700	30
Astra Auto	2,300	2,700	400
Nissan Primera	3,100	3,600	500
BMW 318i	6,900	8,000	1,100
Escort estate	560	620	60
Golf GTI	890	990	100
Total	**18,600**	**21,760**	**3,160**

The £1,500 in this example will contribute to the textile company's fixed costs and profit. The total contribution can also be calculated by multiplying the unit contribution by the number of units sold.

Total contribution = unit contribution x number of units sold
= (£9.00 - £7.50) x 1,000
= £1.50 x 1,000
= £1,500

Contribution and profit

Contribution can be used to calculate profit. Take the example again of Craig Eckert the car salesperson. He wants to calculate the profit his business makes in January. Table 1 shows the variable cost and selling price of cars in January.

The fixed costs of the business in the same month are also shown in Table 2.

The total contribution from car sales in January was £3,160. This is calculated by subtracting the total variable costs, ie the cost of purchasing the cars, from the total revenue (£21,760 - £18,600). Total revenue is the amount of money received from the sale of the 10 cars during January. The profit for January 2007 is:

Profit = total contribution - fixed costs
= £3,160 - £1,160
= £2,000

So the business made £2,000 profit in January.

Profit can be calculated by subtracting total costs from total revenue. If this method is used here, the profit made by Craig Eckert's business in January is:

Profit = total revenue - total cost
= total revenue - (fixed cost + variable cost)
= £21,760 - (£1,160 + £18,600)
= £21,760 - £19,760
= £2,000

Table 2: Monthly fixed costs for Craig Eckert

Description	(£)
Office rent	700
Insurance	60
Telephone	100
Administrative expenses	300
	1,160

Figure 1: The relationship between fixed costs, variable costs, profit and contribution for Craig Eckert's business in January

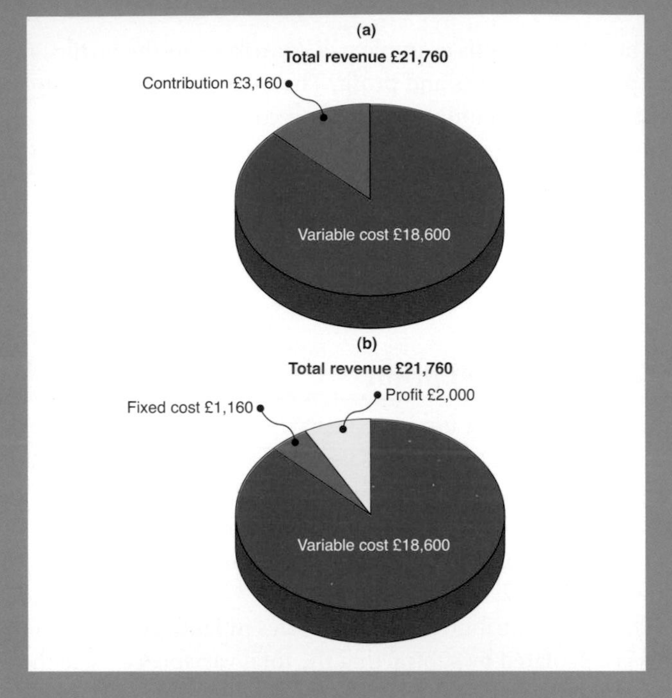

The answer is the same as before, £2,000. However, the contribution method can often be quicker than this method because there is slightly less calculation.

Fixed costs, variable costs, contribution and profit

The relationship between fixed costs, variable costs, profit and contribution is shown in Figure 1. The pie charts show information from Craig Eckert's business in January.

Figure 1(a) shows how the total revenue of £21,760 is divided between the variable cost (£18,600) and contribution (£3,160). Figure 1(b) shows how total revenue of £21,760 is divided between variable cost (£18,600), fixed costs (£1,160) and profit (£2,000). Note that the value of contribution (£3,160) is equal to the value of fixed cost (£1,160) and profit (£2,000) added together.

Contribution costing

How can a business make use of contribution calculations? Calculating the contribution to fixed costs and profit that a product makes might help a business in decision making. This is known as contribution costing. For example, say that a design business has limited time and resources. It has been approached by two clients who want a new corporate logo and image designing this week. The prices and variable costs and contribution are shown below.

- Design 1 – Price £3,000, variable costs £2,500, contribution per unit £500 (£3,000 - £2,500)
- Design 2 – Price £3,000, variable costs £800, contribution per unit £2,200 (£3,000 - £800)

So the business might choose the second design as it contributes more to fixed costs and profit.

Contribution pricing

Some businesses use contribution when setting their price. This approach involves setting a price for orders or individual products which exceeds the variable cost. This means that a particular order or product will always make a contribution when sold. This approach ignores fixed costs since a single order or product may not generate enough contribution to cover fixed cost. This approach needs to be used with caution. Obviously, to make a profit fixed costs have to be covered. Contribution pricing is most likely to be used when fixed costs are low or when a business knows through experience that fixed costs will be covered.

Table 4 shows some financial information for R G Edwards, an engineering company, that receives four big orders in a particular month. The table shows the price charged, the variable cost and contribution for each order. The total contribution is £35,500. Through experience R G Edwards knows that these prices will cover fixed costs. Fixed costs are £10,000 per month. Therefore the profit for the month is £25,500 (£35,500 - £10,000).

Contribution can be used to calculate the break-even output of a business. This is covered in the next unit.

Contribution pricing is also a useful approach for multi-product firms. Some businesses produce such a wide range of products that standard pricing is inappropriate. Therefore, for each product or order they charge a price that exceeds variable costs. Obviously, such an approach can only be used if the business is confident that all costs will be covered and a profit is generated. The use of contribution to help businesses choose viable products and make decisions is sometimes called **contribution analysis**.

Question 1.

AblePrint Ltd is a medium-sized printing company based in Worcester. It offers professional quality-controlled printing with a clear and competitive pricing policy. Examples of its servcies include the printing of business cards, compliment slips, brochures and price lists. AblePrint Ltd has received an order from a local tour operator. It wants 1,000 brochures printed to supply travel agents. The business has agreed a price of £540 for the job.

(a) Calculate the total contribution for the job.
(b) Calculate the profit from the job.

Table 3: Print costs

Fixed costs	£100
Variable costs	
Paper	15p per brochure
Ink	10p per brochure
Other variable costs	10p per brochure

Table 4: Financial information for R G Edwards

	Price	Variable cost	Contribution (£)
Order 1	45,000	32,000	13,000
Order 2	23,000	21,000	2,000
Order 3	49,000	39,500	9,500
Order 4	58,000	47,000	11,000
Total	175,000	139,500	35,500

KEY TERMS

Contribution – the amount of money left over after variable costs have been subtracted from revenue. The money contributes towards fixed costs and profit.

KNOWLEDGE

1. A product sells for £10 and the variable costs are £8.50. What is the contribution per unit?
2. A clothes retailer buys 240 jumpers for £27. The jumpers are sold for £39 each. What is the total contribution made by the jumpers?
3. What is the formula for calculating profit using contribution?
4. If the total contribution is £120,000 and fixed costs are £96,000, what is the profit?
5. If the total variable costs are £450,000 and contribution is £225,000, what is the total revenue?
6. State three ways in which contribution can be used by a business to help make decisions.

Question 2.

Laura Wooding runs a catering company. She provides dinner parties for people in their own homes. Laura has built up an excellent reputation in her local town and only has to work four nights a week to make a very comfortable living. Most of her costs are variable. These include the cost of food, wine, dining accessories such as table decorations and napkins and the hire of glassware and eating utensils if necessary. Laura uses her client's kitchen and cooking utensils when working. The fixed costs of the company are only £100 per week. Laura uses contribution pricing. The price is influenced by the number of diners and the choice of food. Table 5 shows some financial information for a typical week.

(a) **What is meant by contribution pricing?**
(b) **Calculate the week's profit made by Laura's company using the information in Table 5.**
(c) **Why should contribution pricing be used with caution?**

Table 5: Financial information for Laura's company

	Price	Variable cost	Contribution (£)
Party 1	240	155	85
Party 2 (basic)	140	70	70
Party 2 (gourmet)	320	180	140
Party 3	200	60	140

Case Study: Timmings Ltd

Timmings Ltd is a family business set up in 2001 when Frank Timmings, a plastics factory manager, decided that he no longer wanted to work for someone else. Frank set up a small production facility to manufacture transparent plastic containers for storage of documents. He was surprised by the demand because he thought that most documents were stored electronically now. His main customers are office suppliers and large businesses.

Sales have grown from £1.1 million in 2003 to £3.64 million in 2006. Timmings Ltd is operating at almost full capacity. At the moment Frank has no plans to expand and is content with current profit levels. But Frank does have to turn work down. When faced with a choice of orders he only accepts those which make the largest contribution. One week in February 2007 he received the four orders outlined in Table 6. The factory can only meet the demands of two.

Table 6: Details of four orders for Timmings Ltd

	Butlers	A & P Ltd	VC Singh	VWD plc (£)
Number of units	20,000	30,000	25,000	20,000
Contract price per unit	£8.00	£8.50	£7.00	£10.50
Material costs per unit	£2.20	£2.00	£2.40	£3.00
Labour costs per unit	£3.40	£4.20	£2.10	£3.80
Other variable costs per unit	£1.00	£1.40	£1.20	£1.30
Fixed costs	£5,000	£5,000	£5,000	£5,000

(a) **State three possible fixed costs for Timmings Ltd. (3 marks)**
(b) **Using the Butlers order as an example, explain the difference between unit contribution and total contribution. (6 marks)**
(c) **Calculate the total contribution made by each of the four orders. (8 marks)**
(d) **(i) Which two orders should Timmings accept? (2 marks)**
(ii) Calculate the profit made by the two orders. (6 marks)
(e) **What might be the long-term effect on Timmings Ltd of selecting orders in this way? (8 marks)**

37 Break-even analysis

The break-even output

Businesses, particularly those that are just starting up, often like to know how much they need to produce or sell to BREAK-EVEN. If a business has information about fixed costs and variable costs and knows what price it is going to charge, it can calculate how many units it needs to sell to cover all of its costs. The point where **total costs** are exactly the same as **total revenue** is called the BREAK-EVEN POINT. The level of output a business needs to produce so that **total costs** are exactly the same as **total revenue** is called the BREAK-EVEN OUTPUT.

For example, if a business produces 100 units at a total cost of £5,000, and sells them for £50 each, total revenue will also be £5,000 (£50 x 100). The business will break-even at this level of output. So the break-even output is 100 units. It makes neither a profit nor a loss.

Calculating break-even using contribution

It is possible to calculate the break-even output if a firm knows the value of its fixed costs, variable costs and the price it will charge. Take an example of a small producer, Jack Cadwallader, who has just set up a business making wrought iron park benches. His fixed costs (FC) are £60,000 and variable costs (VC) £40 per bench. He sells the benches to local authorities across the country for £100 each.

The simplest way to calculate the break-even output is to use **contribution**. Contribution is the amount of money left over after the variable cost per unit is taken away from the selling price. For Jack's park benches, the contribution is:

Contribution = selling price - variable cost
Contribution = £100 - £40
Contribution = £60

To calculate the number of benches Jack needs to sell to break-even, the following formula can be used:

$$\text{Break-even output} = \frac{\text{Fixed costs}}{\text{Contribution}}$$

$$= \frac{£60{,}000}{£60}$$

$$= 1{,}000 \text{ benches}$$

Jack Cadwallader's business will break-even when 1,000 park benches are sold.

Calculating break-even using revenue and costs

Another way of calculating the break-even output is to use the total cost and total revenue figures. In the case of Jack Cadwallader:

Total cost = fixed cost + variable cost
or TC = £60,000 + £40Q
and Total revenue = price x quantity sold
or TR = £100Q

where Q is the quantity produced and sold, ie the number of park benches. A firm will break-even where total cost is equal to total revenue. Therefore we can write:

TC = TR
£60,000 + £40Q = £100Q

To find Q we can calculate:

$$60{,}000 = 100Q - 40Q$$
$$60{,}000 = 60Q$$
$$\frac{60{,}000}{60} = Q$$
$$1{,}000 = Q$$

It is possible to check if this answer is correct by calculating total cost and total revenue when 1,000 benches are produced. If the answers are the same, the break-even output is correct.

TC = £60,000 + (£40 x 1,000) = £60,000 + £40,000 = £100,000
TR = £100 x 1,000 = £100,000

Both TC and TR are equal to £100,000, so the break-even output is 1,000 benches. This also confirms that the answer using the contribution method was correct.

Total cost and total revenue figures can be used to calculate the amount of profit or loss the firm will make at particular levels of output.

- At any level of output below the break-even output the firm will make a **loss**.
- Output produced above the break-even level will make a **profit**. If the bench manufacturer were to produce 1,200 benches, profit would be:

Profit = TR - TC
= (£100 x 1,200) - (£60,000 + [£40 x 1,200])
= £120,000 - (£60,000 + £48,000)
= £120,000 - £108,000
Profit = £12,000

Figure 1: Break-even chart for Jack Cadwallader

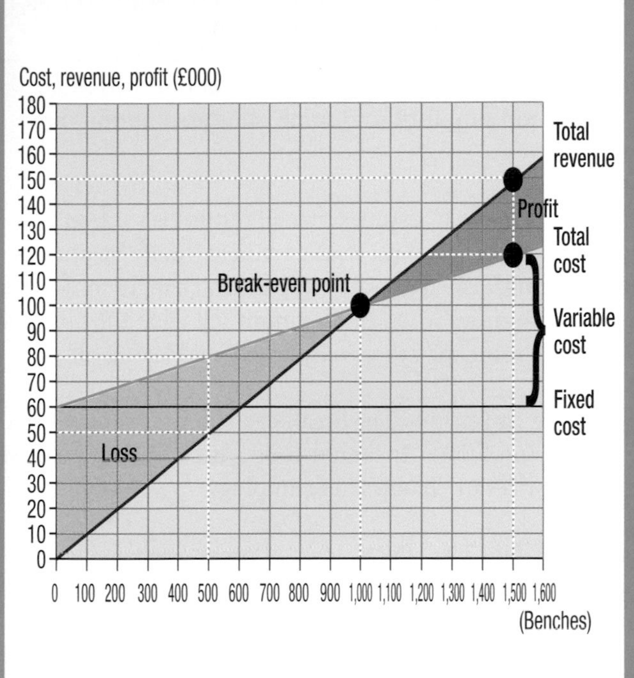

Question 1.

Jun Shan produces Chinese rugs using traditional techniques and sells them online. The rugs are high in quality and made from natural materials. The rugs sell for £105 and variable costs are £65 per rug. Jun Shan's fixed costs are £2,000 pa.

(a) Calculate how many rugs Jun Shan needs to produce and sell to break-even.

(b) How much profit will Jun Shan make if 500 rugs are sold during a year?

(c) How many rugs will Jun Shan need to sell to break-even if the price is increased to £115?

Calculating break-even using break-even charts

The use of graphs is often helpful in break-even analysis. It is possible to identify the break-even point and break-even output by plotting the total cost and total revenue equations on a graph. This graph is called a BREAK-EVEN CHART. Figure 1 shows the break-even chart for Jack Cadwallader's business.

Output is measured on the horizontal axis and revenue, costs and profit are measured on the vertical axis. What does the break-even chart show?

- The value of total cost over a range of output. For example, when Jack produces 1,500 benches total costs are £120,000.
- The value of total revenue over a range of output. For example, when Jack produces 1,500 benches total revenue is £150,000.
- Break-even charts can show the level of fixed costs over a range of output. For example, the fixed costs for Jack's business are £60,000.
- The level of output needed to break-even. The break-even point is where total costs equal total revenue of £100,000. This is when 1,000 benches are produced. So the break-even output is 1,000 benches.
- At levels of output below the break-even output, losses are made. This is because total costs exceed total revenue. At an output of 500 a £30,000 loss is made.
- At levels of output above the break-even output, a profit is made. This profit gets larger as output rises. At an output of 1,500 a profit of £30,000 is made.
- The relationship between fixed costs and variable costs as output rises. At low levels of output fixed costs represent a large proportion of total costs. As output rises, fixed costs become a smaller proportion of total costs.
- The profit at a particular level of output. If Jack produces 1,500 benches, profit is shown by the vertical gap between the total cost and total revenue equations. It is £30,000.

The margin of safety

What if a business is producing more than the break-even output? It might be useful to know by how much sales could fall before a loss is made. This is called the MARGIN OF SAFETY. It refers to the range of output over which a profit can be made. The margin of safety can be identified on the break-even chart by measuring the distance between the break-even level of output and the current (profitable) level output. For example, Figure 2 shows the break-even chart for Jack Cadwallader. If Jack produces 1,200 benches the margin of safety is 200 benches. This means that output can fall by 200 before a loss is made. If Jack sells 1,200 benches the chart shows that total revenue is £120,000, total cost is £108,000 and profit is £12,000.

Businesses prefer to operate with a large margin of safety. This means that if sales drop they still might make some profit. With a small margin of safety there is a risk that the business is more likely to make losses if sales fall.

Figure 2: Break-even chart showing the margin of safety for Jack Cadwallader's business

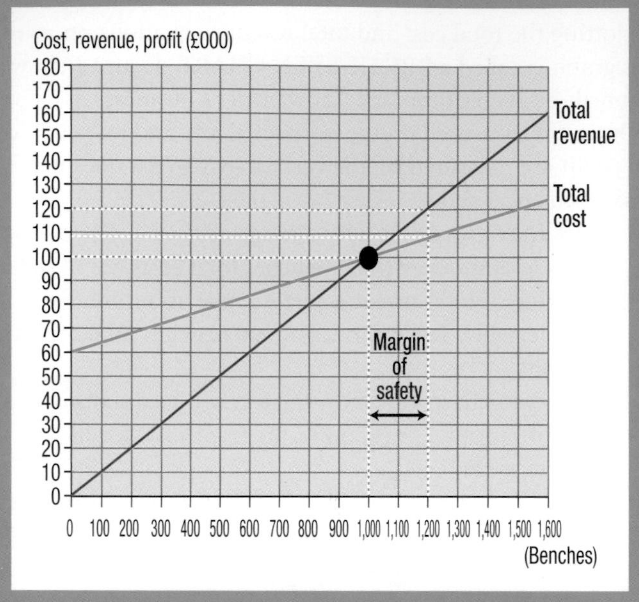

Using break-even analysis

Break-even analysis is used in business as a tool to make decisions about the future. It helps answer 'what if' questions. For instance:

- if price went up, what would happen to the break-even point?
- if the business introduced a new product line, how many would the new product have to sell to at least break-even?
- if the business is just starting up, what has to be the level of output to prevent a loss being incurred?
- what will happen to the break-even point if costs are forecast to rise?
- would the break-even point be lower if components were bought in from outside suppliers rather than being made in-house?

Break-even analysis is also found in business plans. Banks often ask for business plans when deciding whether or not to give a loan. So break-even analysis can be vital in gaining finance, especially when starting up a business.

KEYTERMS

Break-even – where a business sells just enough to cover its costs.
Break-even chart – a graph containing the total cost and total revenue lines, illustrating the break-even output.
Break-even output – the output a business needs to produce so that its total revenue and total costs are the same.
Break-even point – where total revenue and total costs are the same.
Margin of safety – the range of output between the break-even level and the current level of output, over which a profit is made.

Weaknesses of break-even analysis

Break-even analysis does have some limitations. It is often regarded as too simplistic and some of its assumptions are unrealistic.

Output and stocks It assumes that all output is sold, so that output equals sales, and no stocks are held. Many businesses hold stocks of finished goods to cope with changes in demand. There are also times when firms cannot sell what they produce and choose to stockpile their output to avoid laying off staff.

Unchanging conditions The break-even chart is drawn for a given set of conditions. It cannot cope with a sudden increase in wages and prices or changes in technology.

Accuracy of data The effectiveness of break-even analysis depends on the quality and accuracy of the data used to construct cost and revenue functions. If the data is poor and inaccurate, the conclusions drawn on the basis of the data are flawed. For example, if fixed costs are underestimated, the level of output required to break-even will be higher than suggested by the break-even chart.

Non-linear relationships It is assumed that the total revenue and total cost lines are linear or straight. This may not always be the case. For example, a business may have to offer discounts on large orders, so total revenues fall at high outputs. In this case the total revenue line would rise and then fall, and be curved. A business can lower costs by buying in bulk. So costs may fall at high outputs and the costs function will be curved.

Multi-product businesses Many businesses produce more than one single product. It is likely that each product will have different variable costs and different prices. The problem is how to allocate the fixed costs of the multi-product business to each individual product. There is a number of ways, but none is perfect. Therefore, if the fixed costs incurred by each product is inaccurate, break-even analysis is less useful.

Stepped fixed costs Some fixed costs are stepped. For example, a manufacturer, in order to increase output, may need to acquire more capacity. This may result in rent increases and thus fixed costs will rise sharply. Under these circumstances it is difficult to use break-even analysis.

KNOWLEDGE

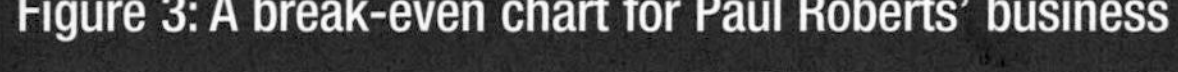

1. How can the contribution be used to calculate the break-even level of output?
2. How can the break-even level of output calculation be checked?
3. State five things which a break-even chart can show.
4. What effect will a price increase have on the margin of safety?
5. What effect will a fall in fixed costs have on the margin of safety?
6. State three uses of break-even analysis.
7. State three weaknesses of break-even analysis.

Question 2.

Paul Roberts makes Spanish guitars from a rented room in a rural business park. Figure 3 shows a break-even chart for his business.

(a) What is the total revenue of the business at an output and sales level of (i) 0 (ii) 20 guitars?
(b) What are the fixed costs of the business?
(c) (i) What is the break-even level of output? (ii) What are the revenue and costs at this level?
(d) What is the margin of safety if the business sells (i) 12 guitars; (ii) 20 guitars?
(e) If the business produces and sells 15 guitars, what would be the: (i) total revenue; (ii) total costs; (iii) profit or loss (iiii) total variable costs; (v) variable cost of each guitar?

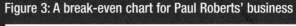

Figure 3: A break-even chart for Paul Roberts' business

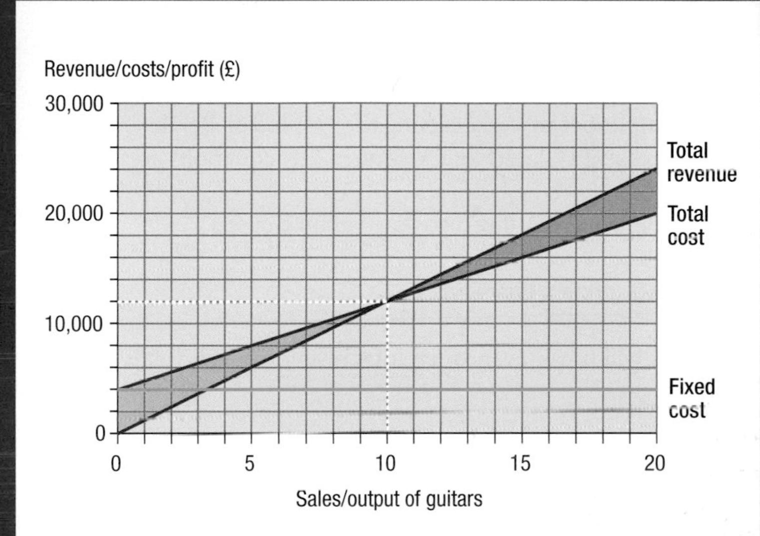

Case Study: Carl Hurst Balti Pies

After following his football team to an away fixture at Villa Park last year, Carl Hurst discovered Balti pies on sale at half-time at the ground. These are pies, filled with chicken balti, a curry dish for which Birmingham is famous. Carl decided that Balti pies could provide him with a new and successful opportunity. He thought he could make the pies himself and sell them in the north-west.

Carl did some research and found that there were few outlets in the north-west where Balti pies were sold. He made some pies at home and took them to various retailers, pubs and clubs to see whether they would be interested. People who liked curry (an overwhelming majority) loved them. Those that had no taste for curry were uninterested.

But Carl was sure he had a winner. He found a disused kitchen unit in Wigan, previously used for pie-making. A week before he signed a 12 month lease for the unit, Carl put some figures together to help him assess the possible profitability of the venture. Carl planned to produce pies in batches of 100 and sell pies for 50p each. He also prepared a business plan to help in the setting-up process. Some financial information is shown below.

Fixed costs	
Lease	£2,500 per year
Other fixed costs	£500 per year
Variable costs	
Food ingredients	£14 per batch
Fuel	£2 per batch
Other variable costs	£4 per batch

(a) Calculate the contribution per batch of pies. (4 marks)
(b) How many batches would Carl need to produce in his first year of trading to break-even? (6 marks)
(c) How much profit would Carl make if he sold 55,000 pies in his first year? (6 marks)
(d) In the second year of trading the landlord raised the lease for the kitchen unit to £4,500 per year. Carl responded to this by raising the price of his pies to 70p each. What effect would this have on the break-even level of output? (6 marks)
(e) To what extent will break-even analysis be useful to Carl Hurst? (18 marks)

38 Applications of break-even analysis

Constructing break-even charts

A break-even chart can be constructed by plotting the total cost and total revenue lines on a graph. The graph should measure output on the horizontal axis and costs, revenue and profit on the vertical axis. Consider Reidle Bros, a small canoe manufacturer. It incurs fixed costs of £20,000 per annum and variable costs of £75 per canoe. The canoes are sold for £125 to agents and wholesalers. The following steps can be used to construct a break-even chart.

Calculating the break-even output It is helpful to calculate the break-even output before constructing the graph. For Reidle Bros the total costs (TC) and total revenue (TR) equations are:

TC = £20,000 + £75Q (fixed costs + variable costs)

TR = £125Q (price x quantity)

Reidle Bros will break-even when total revenue equals total costs. This is where:

$$
\begin{aligned}
£20{,}000 + £75Q &= £125Q \\
£20{,}000 &= £125Q - £75Q \\
£20{,}000 &= £50Q \\
\frac{£20{,}000}{£50} &= Q \\
400 &= Q
\end{aligned}
$$

Therefore, Reidle Bros will break-even when it manufactures 400 canoes.

Calculating revenue and total cost Both the total cost and total revenue lines are linear or straight. Therefore the lines can be drawn by joining two points which lie on each function. To plot total revenue choose two levels of output and calculate the total revenue at each level. Any two levels of output could be chosen but 0 is often chosen as one of the points. Choose a second value which is twice that of the break-even point, such as 800 (2 x 400) in the case of the canoe manufacturers. This will ensure that the break-even point is in the centre of the chart, improving presentation. The value of total revenue at each of these output levels is shown in Table1. This is based on fixed costs of £20,000, variable costs of £75 per canoe and a sale price of £125.

Figure 1: Break-even chart for Reidle Bros

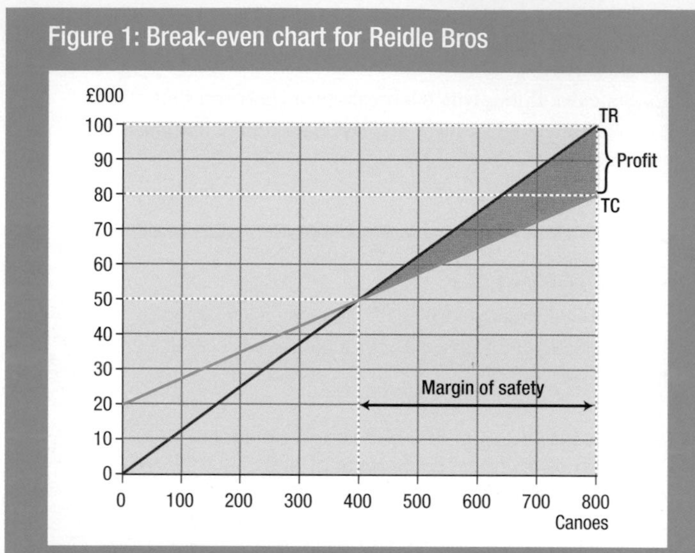

Plotting total revenue Total revenue (TR) can now be plotted on the graph. The output axis should run from 0 to 800 canoes and the other axis from 0 to £100,000. Using the information in Table 1, the two points, or co-ordinates, on the total revenue line are (0, 0) and (800, £100,000). If these are plotted on the graph and joined up the total revenue will appear as shown in Figure 1.

Plotting total costs To plot total costs, calculate the total cost at two levels of output. It is useful to use the same values as those used for total revenue, ie 0 and 800. From Table1 the two points which lie on the total cost line are (0, £20,000) and (800, £80,000). If these are plotted on the graph and joined up the total cost line will appear as shown in Figure 3. Total costs do not start at co-ordinates 0,0. At an output of zero, the business still has fixed costs of £20,000.

Analysis from the diagram The break-even chart is now complete. An analysis of certain points on the diagram can be made.

The break-even output can be identified and plotted. It is usual to draw lines to show the number of canoes Reidle Bros

Table 1: Values of TR and TC at two levels of output for Reidle Bros

Output (£)	Fixed costs (£)	Variable costs (£)	Total costs (£)	Total revenue (£)	Profit /loss (£)
0	20,000	0	20,000	0	-20,000
800	20,000	60,000 (800 x £75)	80,000	100,000 (800 x £125)	+20,000

Figure 2: Break-even chart – an increase in price

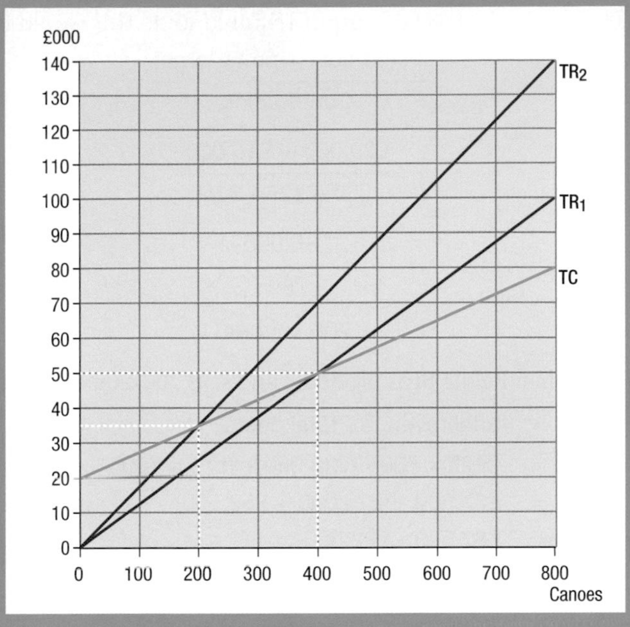

must sell to break-even (400), and the value of TR and TC at this level of output (£50,000). The break-even output should coincide with the calculation made in the first step, ie 400 canoes.

- The profit at certain levels of output may be indicated. For example, at an output of 800 canoes, the profit is £100,000 - £80,000 = £20,000.
- The margin of safety can be indicated. This is the difference between the current output of the business and the break-even point. At an output of 800 canoes it is 800 - 400 = 400 canoes.

Figure 3: Break-even chart – an increase in fixed costs

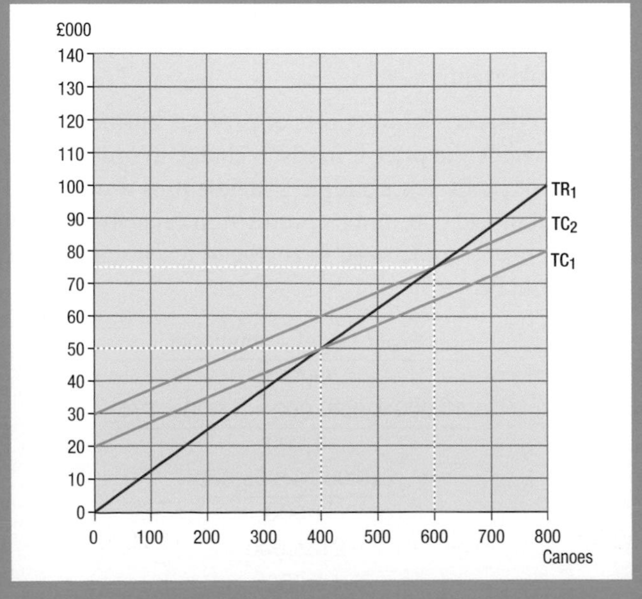

Question 1.

Ryestairs is a Benedictine monastory which earns part of its living by running The Haven, a guest house and retreat centre. It charges £80 per day for full board and overnight stay per person. The variable costs of items such as food and laundry cleaning come to £30 per day per visitor. The fixed costs of running the business venture are £50 000 per year.

(a) Draw a break-even diagram for The Haven. The horizontal axis will be the 'number of overnight stays per year'. Label the axis up to 1,500 overnight stays per year. Mark on it the break-even level of output.

(b) The management of The Haven decide to raise the price to £110 per day. (a) Draw a new total revenue function on your diagram for question 1. (b) Show on the diagram what has happened to the break-even level of output.

(c) If prices remained at £80 per day and variable costs are still £30, but The Haven cut its fixed costs to £40,000 per year, what would happen to the break-even level of output? Illustrate your answer by drawing a new diagram.

(d) Prices remain at £80 per day and fixed costs remain at £50,000, but The Haven manages to reduce its variable costs to £20. Explain, using a diagram, the effects of this on: (a) the break-even point, (b) the margin of safety assuming the number of overnight stays is 1,200 a year.

Changes in variables

Break-even charts provide a visual means of analysing the effect of changes in output on total cost, total revenue, profit and the margin of safety. The effects of changes in fixed costs, variable cost and price on profit and the margin of safety can also be shown. These will help a new or existing business to make decisions.

Changes in price Figure 2 shows the effect of an increase in price from £125 to £175 for Reidle Bros. This causes the total revenue line to become steeper, shifting from TR_1 to TR_2. This shows that total sales revenue has increased at all levels of output. The higher price means that the business will break-even at a lower level of output. This is 200 canoes. It will also mean higher levels of profit (or lower losses) at every level of output.

Figure 4: Break-even chart – an increase in variable costs

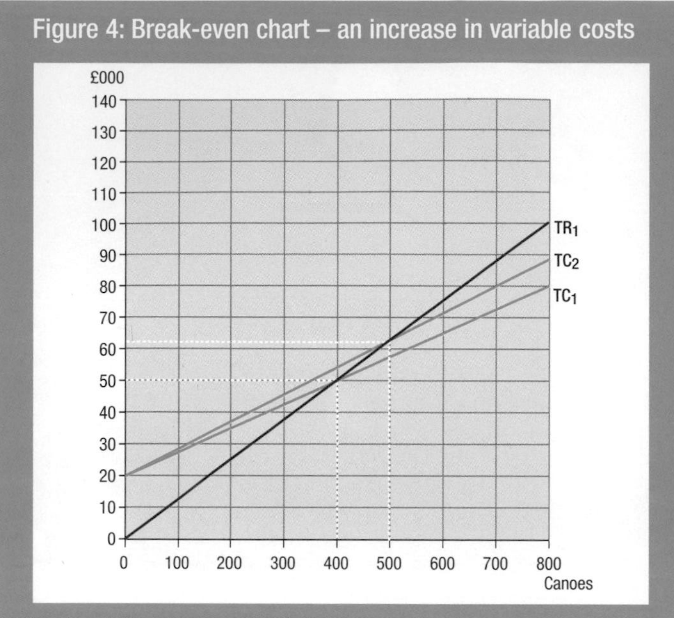

The margin of safety will also increase assuming an output of 800 canoes is produced. This is not shown in Figure 2.

For a price reduction, the total revenue line would become flatter. This would raise the break-even level of output and reduce the margin of safety. At a lower price more canoes would have to be sold to break-even.

Changes in fixed costs Figure 3 shows the effect of an increase in fixed costs from £20,000 to £30,000 for Reidle Bros. The total cost function makes a parallel shift upwards from TC_1 to TC_2. This occurs because a rise in fixed costs causes total cost to increase by the same amount at every level of output. As a result the break-even level of output rises to 600 canoes. At all levels of output profit falls (or losses rise). The margin of safety has also fallen assuming production remains at 800 canoes. This is not shown in Figure 3.

If fixed costs fell, the total cost function would make a parallel shift downwards. This would lower the break-even level of output and raise the margin of safety. Fewer canoes would need to be sold to break-even.

Changes in variable costs An increase in variable costs will increase the gradient of the total cost function. This is illustrated in Figure 4 by a shift from TC_1 to TC_2 when variable costs rise from £75 to £85 per canoe. The break-even level of output for Reidle Bros rises to 500 canoes. Assuming that production remains at 800 canoes, the margin of safety will fall.

If variable costs fell the total cost function would become flatter. This would lower the break-even level of output and raise the margin of safety. With lower variable costs, fewer canoes need to be sold to break-even.

Other uses of break-even charts

Target rate of profit Break-even analysis can be used to calculate the amount of output needed to generate a certain level of profit. For example, if Reidle Bros wanted to make £15,000 profit, the level of output required to do this would be:

$$\frac{\text{Fixed cost + profit target}}{\text{Contribution}}$$

$$= \frac{£20,000 + £15,000}{£50\ (£125 - £75)}$$

$$= \frac{£35,000}{£50}$$

$$= 700 \text{ canoes}$$

Thus, when Reidle Bros produces and sells 700 canoes profit is:

Profit = total revenue - total costs
= £125 x 700 - (£20,000 + [£75 x 700])
= £87,500 - (£20,000 + £52,500)
= £87,500 - £72,500
= £15,000

Break-even price Sometimes a business may want to know how much to charge for its product to break-even. In these circumstances a business must know how much it is going to produce and sell. For example, assume Reidle Bros aimed to sell 500 canoes and its objective was to break-even at that level of output. The price it should charge to break-even would be:

$$\text{Break-even price} = \frac{\text{Total cost}}{\text{Output}}$$

$$= \frac{£20,000 + (500 \times £75)}{500}$$

$$= \frac{£20,000 + £37,500}{500}$$

$$= \frac{£57,500}{500}$$

$$= £115$$

Thus, if output was 500, Reidle Bros must charge £115 per canoe to break-even.

Price needed to reach a target rate of profit A business may want to determine the price it needs to charge in order to reach a target rate of profit. For example, if Reidle Bros wanted to make a profit of £40,000, and its production capacity was 1,000 canoes, the price it would need to charge to reach this target rate of profit would be:

$$\text{Price} = \frac{\text{Profit target + total cost}}{\text{Output}}$$

$$= \frac{£40,000 + (£20,000 + 1,000 \times £75)}{1,000}$$

$$= \frac{£40,000 + £95,000}{1,000}$$

$$= \frac{£135,000}{1,000}$$

$$= £135$$

Question 2.

Julia Robinson owns a large farm and supplies apples to cider producers. Apple production is only part of the farm's output. Most of the profit is generated from milk production. Julia is happy if apple production breaks-even each year. The orchard was inherited from her grandfather and Julia does not wish to cease apple production for sentimental reasons, even though it is generally unprofitable. Whether she achieves her aim depends on how many apples she harvests and the going market price. At the end of the season Julia had picked 60,000 kilos. The fixed costs associated with apple production were £6,000 for the year. Variable costs were 40p per kilo.

(a) **Calculate the price per kilo Julia would need to receive in order for apple production to break-even.**

(b) **Calculate the profit Julia would make from apple production if the market price was: (i) 48p per kilo; (ii) 51p per kilo.**

Figure 5: A total cost function subject to the law of diminishing returns

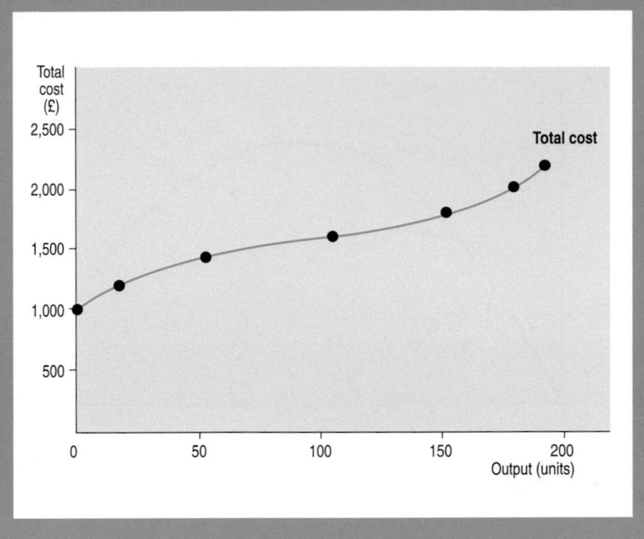

Thus, Reidle Bros would have to charge £135 for each canoe in order to make £40,000 profit if it produced and sold 1,000.

Accounting for changes in costs and revenues

One of the weaknesses of break-even analysis is the assumption that the total cost and total revenue functions are **linear**. This indicates that as output increases, total cost and total revenue rise by the same proportion. What actually happens to total costs and total revenue as output increases can affect the decisions a business makes based on its break-even analysis, given a fixed amount of capital.

Total cost Assume a factory is built for 1,000 workers. As more workers are employed they can specialise in different tasks. 500 workers are likely to be more productive than one, for example. At some point, however, the opportunity to take advantage of specialisation may be used up and although total output will continue to rise, each extra worker will be less productive. For example, if 2,000 workers were employed in the above factory, there would not be enough machinery available for all workers to be usefully employed. This is called the law of DIMINISHING RETURNS. It states that as more of a variable factor (labour here) is added to a fixed factor (say capital) the output of the extra workers will rise and then fall. In other words output will rise but at a diminishing rate. In extreme cases output may even fall. This is called negative returns.

Table 2: The effect on output and total cost as a firm employs more workers given a fixed amount of capital

Capital (machines) costing £100 each	Labour (workers) costing £200 per week	£ Fixed costs (machinery)	£ Variable costs (labour)	Total cost (£)	Output (units)
10	0	1,000	0	1,000	0
10	1	1,000	200	1,200	20
10	2	1,000	400	1,400	54
10	3	1,000	600	1,600	105
10	4	1,000	800	1,800	152
10	5	1,000	1,000	2,000	180
10	6	1,000	1,200	2,200	192

Figure 6: A break-even chart with non-linear total cost and total revenue functions

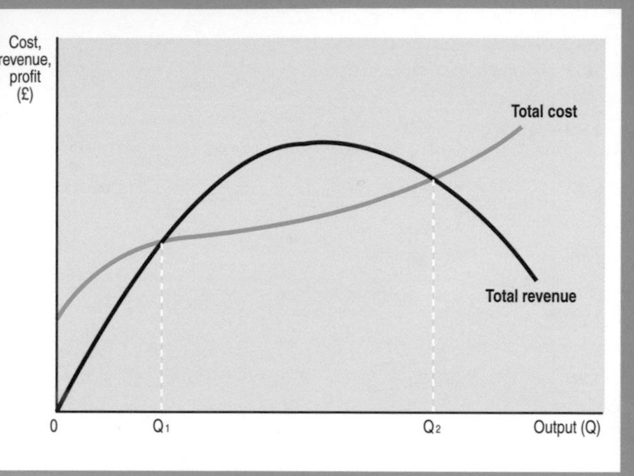

How does this affect the costs of a business? Table 2 shows the effect on output and total cost of hiring labour at £200 per week with fixed capital costs of £100 per machine. The output per worker always rises, but eventually at a diminishing rate. For example, when the fourth worker is employed output rises by 47 units, but the fifth worker adds only 28 units. Total costs rise as the firm employs more labour. The effect of diminishing returns on the firm's total cost function is shown in Figure 5. Notice that it is non-linear.

Total revenue The total revenue function drawn earlier in this unit assumed that each unit would be sold for the same price. In reality, it is unlikely that a firm can continually sell its output for the same price. There comes a point where additional sales can only be made if the price is lowered, for example a business may offer lower prices to customers who buy larger quantities. Figure 6 shows that as the price is lowered to encourage more sales the total revenue earned by the business falls.

The graph also shows a total cost function subject to diminishing returns. Notice that there are now two break-even points, Q_1 and Q_2. When linear functions are used on a break-even chart, as output is increased beyond the break-even level of output, profit continues to increase indefinitely. When non-linear functions are used profit can only be made over a particular range of output, i.e. between Q_1 and Q_2. If production is pushed beyond Q_2 losses are made.

KNOWLEDGE

1. When constructing a break-even chart, why is zero always used as one of the levels of output?
2. What does the vertical distance show between TC and TR on a break-even chart?
3. What happens to the break-even level of output if price is increased?
4. What effect will a fall in variable costs have on the break-even level of output?
5. What happens to the margin of safety if fixed costs fall?
6. What happens to the margin of safety if price is cut?
7. How is break-even price calculated?
8. How might the law of diminishing returns affect the break-even point of a business?

KEYTERM

Diminishing returns – the eventual decline in output each extra worker adds to total output when the opportunity to specialise is used up.

Case Study: Organic Hampers

Amelia Hume and Julia Nuttall worked in a food factory, but wanted to start their own business. They had seen adverts for organic hampers. Having bought one, they found it was 'all show and presentation' as Amelia put it. The food was unimaginative and inadequate for a large family. The hamper was also expensive at £120. Amelia and Julia both felt they could improve easily on this and exploit the current trend in organic food. They decided to set up a business selling organic picnic hampers from a website.

After estimating demand and finding suppliers to use they were able to come up with some costs. These are outlined below. The fixed costs included items like website design, advertising, insurance and a variety of setting-up costs. These fixed costs were for the first year of trading. They were expected to fall in future years. Examples of the food they planned to include in the hampers were cheese, antipasta, pickles, pasta salad, rice salad, pitta breads, olives, fresh fruit, a bottle of organic wine and milk, and fruit juice.

Fixed costs = £4,000	
Wicker hamper	£12
Food	£39
Utensils	£2
Delivery	£3
Other variable costs	£4

Amelia and Julia decided they would sell the hampers for £80. This was lower than many of their competitors. At this price it was felt that 400 hampers could be sold in the first year of trading. Before making the final decision to launch the business, Amelia insisted that they work out how many hampers they would need to sell to break-even. Amelia and Julia also agreed that they should not give up their jobs at the factory until the business was established.

(a) Using this case as an example, explain what is meant by break-even. (4 marks)

(b) (i) Construct a break-even chart for Organic Hampers. (10 marks)
(ii) How many hampers need to be sold to break-even in the first year? (2 marks)

(c) (i) Show the margin of safety if annual sales meet the 400 sales target. (2 marks)
(ii) How much profit is made at this level of sales? (2 marks)

(d) In the second year, it was expected that fixed costs would only be £2,000.
(i) Why are fixed costs likely to fall in the second year of trading? (4 marks)
(ii) Show the new break-even output on the chart. (2 marks)
(iii) If 500 hampers were sold in the second year, could Amelia and Julia leave their factory jobs? (Show any necessary calculations). (6 marks)

(e) What measures could be taken to lower the break-even output in this case? (8 marks)

39 Cash flow

The importance of cash

Cash is the most LIQUID of all business assets. A business's cash is the notes and coins it keeps on the premises and any money it has in the bank, for example. Cash is part of, but not the same as, working capital. Working capital contains other assets, such as money owed by debtors, which are not immediately available if a business needs to pay bills, for example.

Why is cash so important to a business? Without cash, it would cease to exist. There is a number of reasons why firms fail. The most common tend to be:

- lack of sales;
- inadequate profit margins;
- poor choice of location;
- reliance on too small a customer base;
- poor management of working capital;
- poor cash flow.

According to a Confederation of British Industry (CBI) survey, 21 per cent of business failures are due to poor cash flow or a lack of working capital. Even when trading conditions are good, businesses can fail. Many of these businesses may offer good products for which there was some demand. They have the potential to be profitable and yet still went into RECEIVERSHIP. Probably the most likely cause of this is that they ran out of cash.

The role of cash in a business is shown in Figure 1. It shows a simple CASH FLOW cycle. Cash flow is the continuous movement of cash into and out of a business. Initially, cash is used to buy or hire resources. These resources are converted into goods or services which are then sold to customers in exchange for cash. Some of the money from sales will be used to finance further production. In a successful business, this flow of cash is endless. If this flow of cash ceases at some stage then the business will be unlikely to continue.

Figure 1: Continuous cash flow into and out of a business

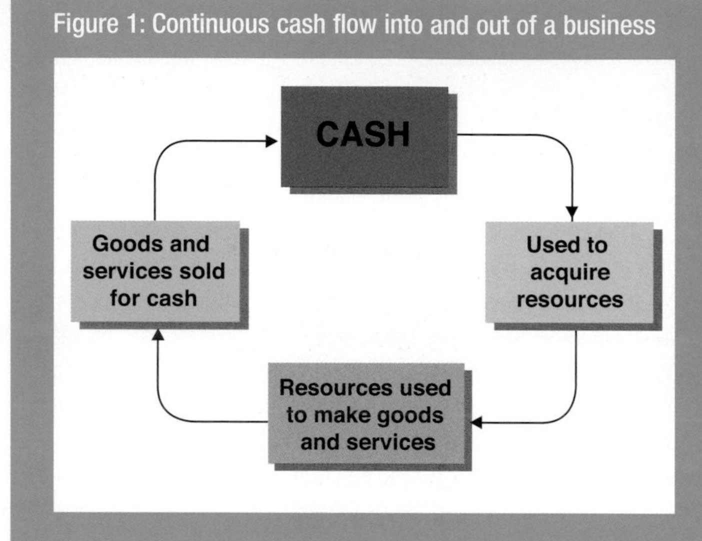

Table 1: Cash flow forecast for Fishan's Ltd

(£000s)

	Jan	Feb	Mar	Apr	May	Jun	Jul	Aug	Sep	Oct	Nov	Dec
Receipts												
Cash sales	451	360	399	410	490	464	452	340	450	390	480	680
Capital introduced									300			
Total receipts	451	360	399	410	490	464	452	340	750	390	480	680
Payments												
Goods for resale	150	180	150	180	150	180	150	180	150	180	220	250
Leasing charges	20	20	20	20	20	20	20	20	20	20	20	20
Motor expenses	40	40	40	40	40	40	40	40	40	40	40	40
Wages	100	100	100	100	100	100	100	105	105	105	125	125
VAT			126			189			187			198
Loan repayments	35	35	35	35	35	35	35	35	35	35	35	35
Telephone		11				12			12			14
Miscellaneous	20	20	20	20	20	20	20	20	20	20	20	20
Total payments	365	406	491	395	377	584	365	412	557	400	474	688
Net cash flow	86	(46)	(92)	15	113	(120)	87	(72)	193	(10)	6	(8)
Opening balance	11	97	51	(41)	(26)	87	(33)	54	(18)	175	165	171
Closing balance	97	51	(41)	(26)	87	(33)	54	(18)	175	165	171	163

Brackets show minus figures.

Controlling cash flow

It is important that a business continually monitors and controls its cash flow. It must ensure that it has enough cash for its immediate spending. However, it should avoid holding too much cash because cash is an unproductive asset. Holding cash means that the business might lose out on the profit from investing the cash. A business will have more effective control over its cash flow if it:

- keeps up to date business records;
- always plans ahead, for example by producing accurate cash flow forecasts;
- operates an efficient credit control system which prevents slow or late payment.

The need to keep up to date records of business transactions is very important. The quality of decision making is better if accurate information is available when choosing between different courses of action. Problems can arise if decisions are based on inadequate or inaccurate information. For example, say a business fails to record that a £20,000 payment has been made to a supplier. A manager may go ahead with the purchase of a new machine costing £30,000 believing that the firm's cash position is better than it actually is. The business may not have enough money in the bank to cover a cheque given in payment.

Advances in information technology have enabled businesses to keep more up to date records and access information very quickly. However, mistakes can still occur if computer operators fail to input information correctly.

Cash flow forecasts

Most businesses produce a regular CASH FLOW FORECAST. This lists all the likely receipts (**cash inflows**) and payments (**cash outflows**) over a future period of time. All the entries in the forecast are estimated because they have not occurred yet. The forecast shows the planned cash flow of the business month by month. Table 1 shows a twelve month cash flow forecast statement for Fishan's Ltd, a grocery wholesaler located in Ipswich.

What is predicted to happen to cash flow at Fishan's over the twelve month period?

January The company will have an opening cash balance of £11,000 in January. In January receipts are expected to be £451,000 and payments £365,000. This means that an extra £86,000 (£451,000 - £365,000) will be added in this month - a positive NET CASH FLOW. The closing balance should be £97,000 (£11,000 +£86,000).

February In February expected payments (£406,000) are greater than expected receipts (£360,000). This means that there will be a negative net cash flow of £46,000 in February. However, the opening balance of £97,000 will cover this and the business will not have a cash flow problem. It ends the month with a positive closing balance of £51,000 (£97,000 - £46,000).

March In March payments again will be greater than receipts,

The **receipts** of the business are the monthly inflows of cash. For Fishan's, cash sales result from the sale of groceries to local retailers and other customers. The sales figures are probably based on the previous year's. In September the owners have introduced £300,000 of fresh capital to the business. The total amount of cash a business expects to receive each month is shown as total receipts. Some businesses sell goods on credit. If this is the case, the figures in the statement should show cash actually received in that month and not the value of goods sold.

Payments are the outflows from the business. Some payments are for the same regular amounts, such as leasing charges (£20,000) and loan repayments (£35,000). Other payments vary, such as purchases of goods for resale. Some payments such as telephone charges are made on a quarterly basis. It is also possible for payments to be annual such as accountancy fees. These do not appear for Fishan's, perhaps because they employ their own accountant. The total amount of cash a business expects to pay out each month is shown as total payments. If a business buys goods on credit, cash payments made to suppliers are included when they occur and not the value of goods received in a particular month.

Net cash flow for a month is found by subtracting total payments from total receipts. If receipts are greater than payments, net cash flow is positive. If payments are greater than receipts, net cash flow is negative - shown by brackets around a figure.

- The **opening balance** in January will be the value of December's closing balance in the previous year.
- The **closing balance** for a month is found by adding or subtracting the net cash flow for the month from the opening balance.
- The closing balance of one month becomes the opening balance of the next month. It can be a positive or negative figure.

giving a negative net cash flow of £92,000. However, this is now greater than the opening balance of £51,000. This means that the business faces a negative closing balance of £41,000 and will have a cash flow problem. It would have to find some way to finance this, perhaps by borrowing from a bank.

March to May The business will have cash flow problems in March and April, when it faces negative closing balances, even though in April receipts are greater than payments (a positive net cash flow). In May, however, the negative opening balance of £26,000 is outweighed by the positive net cash flow of £113,000. The business will have a positive closing balance of £87,000 and no cash flow problem.

June to December In June and August, but not July, the business would have cash flow problems. From September onwards, when there will be positive closing balances every month, there appear to be no cash flow problems. This is because the owners plan to introduce £300,000 into the business in September.

Why do businesses prepare cash flow forecasts?

Businesses draw up cash flow forecast statements to help control and monitor cash flow in the business. There are certain advantages in using statements to control cash flow.

Identifying the timing of cash shortages and surpluses A forecast can help to identify in advance when a business might wish to borrow cash. At the bottom of the statement the monthly closing balances are shown clearly. This will help the reader to identify when a bank overdraft will be needed. For example, Table 2 showed that Fishan's would need to borrow money in March, April, June and August. In addition, if a large cash surplus is identified in a particular month, this might provide an opportunity to buy some new equipment, for example. A business should try to avoid being overdrawn at the bank because interest is charged. If certain payments can be delayed until cash is available, this will avoid unnecessary borrowing.

Supporting applications for funding When trying to raise finance, lenders often insist that businesses support their applications with documents showing business performance, outlook and solvency. A cash flow forecast will help to indicate the future outlook for the business. It is also common practice to produce a cash flow forecast statement in the planning stages of setting up a business.

Enhancing the planning process Careful planning in business is vital. It helps to clarify aims and improve performance. Producing a cash flow forecast is a key part of the planning process because it is a document concerned with the future.

Monitoring cash flow During and at the end of the financial year a business should make comparisons between the predicted figures in the cash flow forecast and those which actually occur. By doing this it can find out where problems have occurred. It

Question 1.

Norfolk-based Longacre Farm is owned by the Durrant family. The farm has a shop and one weekend a number of customers asked Janet Durrant if they sold homemade soup. This set Janet thinking. She approached her father with the idea of a new business activity - making soup and selling it in the farm shop. She explained that vegetables produced on the farm could be used. Janet produced a business plan with a cash flow forecast. Her father said he would lend Janet £1,000 if she could match the amount to provide start-up capital for Janet's new business venture, Longacre Farm Homemade Soups. A copy of the nine month forecast is shown in Table 2.

Table 2: Cash flow forecast for Longacre Farm Homemade Soups

									(£)
	May	Jun	Jul	Aug	Sep	Oct	Nov	Dec	Jan
Receipts									
Loan from Mr Durrant	1,000								
Own capital	1,000								
Cash	200	400	500	400	500	600	900	800	1,200
Total receipts	2,200	400	500	400	500	600	900	800	1,200
Payments									
Cooking equipment	900								
Other setting up costs	700								
Vegetables	50	100	125	100	125	150	225	200	300
Other food ingredients	60	80	90	80	90	100	150	130	180
Packaging	50	100	125	100	125	150	225	200	300
Overheads	100	100	100	100	100	100	100	100	100
Total payments	1,860	380	440	380	440	500	700	630	880
Net cash flow	140	20	60	20	60	100	200	170	320
Opening balance	0	140	160	220	240	300	400	600	770
Closing balance	140	160	220	240	300	400	600	770	1,090

(a) Using examples from the month of June, explain how Janet would calculate:
(i) total payments;
(ii) net cash flow;
(iii) closing balance.

(b) Why is the opening balance in May zero?

(c) Explain what is happening to the cash balance resulting from Janet's soup venture.

Question 2.

Kieran Venkat runs an off-licence in the Manchester suburb of Rusholme. He has recently extended his premises into the property next door and is looking to acquire a wider range of stock. The cost of the extension has completely exhausted the business of its cash reserves and Kieran needs to borrow some money to buy stock. He needs to borrow £5,000 for nine months. In order to support his application for a bank loan he drew up the nine month cash flow forecast shown in Table 3. The forecast assumes that the loan has been granted and repayments are included.

Table 3: Cash flow forecast statement for Kieran Venkat

									(£)
	Jul	Aug	Sep	Oct	Nov	Dec	Jan	Feb	Mar
Receipts									
Cash sales	3,800	4,000	5,000	?	6,000	9,000	7,000	3,000	3,500
Bank loan	5,000								
Total receipts	8,800	4,000	5,000	?	6,000	9,000	7,000	3,000	3,500
Payments									
Stock	7,000	3,000	3,400	3,400	4,000	6,100	4,800	2,000	2,400
Loan repayments	620	620	620	620	620	620	620	620	620
Casual labour	200	200	200	200	200	400	200	200	200
Miscellaneous costs	100	100	100	100	100	100	100	100	100
Drawings	500	500	500	500	500	500	500	500	500
Insurance				450					
Advertising	370								
Telephone			170			200			210
Total payments	8,790	?	4,990	5,270	5,420	7,920	6,220	3,420	4,030
Net cash flow	10	(420)	10	(270)	580	1,080	780	(420)	(530)
Opening balance	(90)	(80)	(500)	(490)	(760)	(180)	?	1,680	1,260
Closing balance	(80)	(500)	(490)	(760)	?	900	1,680	1,260	730

(a) **Calculate the following figures for Kieran's cash flow forecast.**
  (i) **Cash sales and total receipts for October.**
  (ii) **Total payments for August.**
  (iii) **Closing balance for November.**
  (iv) **Opening balance for January.**

(b) **As well as supporting his application for a bank loan, how else might this cash flow forecast help Kieran in running his business?**

(c) **On the basis of this cash flow forecast alone, discuss whether a bank would grant Kieran a loan.**

could then try to identify possible reasons for any significant differences between the two sets of figures. For example, it might be that an overpayment was made. Constant monitoring in this way should allow a business to control its cash flow effectively.

Improving forecasts

Cash flow forecasts may not be helpful if they are inaccurate. Very inaccurate forecasts could lead to businesses getting into trouble and running out of cash. How can a business improve the accuracy of its cash flow forecasts?

Accurate data A cash flow forecast is based on anticipated flows of cash into and out of the business. Some of these flows will be known for certain. For example, a business usually knows what some of its overheads will be next year, such as rent, rates and insurance. Other costs such as wages may have been negotiated for the next year. Variable costs such as raw materials are may be more difficult to predict. This is because output might fluctuate unexpectedly or suppliers may change their prices.

Generally, cash outflows are easier to predict than cash inflows. Most of the cash coming into the business is from sales. It can sometimes be difficult to estimate what sales will be exactly in future. Some businesses have advanced orders, such as firms in the holiday industry, which will help to improve accuracy. Others do market research, while many rely on projections based on the previous year's figures. When cash inflows and outflows are unknown it is better to overestimate costs and underestimate revenues. New businesses have particular problems when producing forecasts. This is because they have no past data on which to base projections. They also tend to underestimate costs and over-estimate revenues.

Biased forecasts Businesses sometimes manipulate cash flow forecasts. For example, a business may overestimate cash inflows to improve the strength of the business on paper. It might do this if it was borrowing money from a bank. A manager may overestimate costs and underestimate sales so that credit can be taken when the real figures are better. If forecasts are biased they are not likely to be accurate.

Coping with external factors Cash flow forecasts could be improved if business managers could predict future events such as changes in interest rates, the weather and the behaviour of competitors. One way to allow for unforeseen events is to have **contingency funds** built into the cash flow forecast. For example, a business may make a monthly allowance for unexpected costs, including it as a cash outflow. Another approach could be to make regular adjustments to cash flow forecasts during the trading period. If forecasts are updated regularly, predictions may be more accurate. It is also possible to produce a series of forecasts. For example, a business might produce three, a 'worst case', a 'best case' and one in the 'middle'. This could show the business what is likely to happen to its cash position in different situations.

Cash flow statements

The management of funds is easier if there is documented information on business performance. The balance sheet shows the assets and liabilities of a business at a point in time. The profit and loss account or income statement shows how the year's profit is distributed. In 1991, the Accounting Standards Board (ASB) published its first Financial Report Standard, FRS 1 'Cash flow Statements'. The new standard required companies to publish a CASH FLOW STATEMENT in the annual accounts. Note that this is not the same as a cash flow forecast. Cash flow statements may include receipts and payments from the previous two years. These may not be disclosed elsewhere in published financial statements. Another advantage is that a cash flow statement must be shown in a standardised presentation. This allows a comparison between different companies.

FRS 1 requires cash flows to be disclosed under standard headings. These are:

- operating activities;
- returns on investments and servicing of finance;
- taxation;
- investing activities;
- financing;

in that order.

Table 4 shows a cash flow statement for the Restaurant Group plc, owners of Frankie & Benny's, Chiquito, Garfunkel's and Bluebeckers. The key entries in the cash flow statement are explained as follows.

- In 2006 the cash inflow from operating activities was £63.374 million. The way in which the business generated this is shown in Table 5.
- From this £2.906 million is subtracted and £0.068 added.

Table 4: The Restaurant Group plc, cash flow statement

	Year ended 31 December 2006 £ 000	Year ended 1 January 2006 £ 000
Cash flows from operating activities		
Cash generated from operations	**63,374**	55,484
Interest received	**68**	219
Interest paid	**(2,906)**	(2,076)
Tax paid	**(9,656)**	(8,199)
Net cash flows from operating activities	**50,880**	45,428
Cash flows from investing activities		
Acquisition of associate	**–**	(10,186)
Acquisition of subsidiary, net of cash acquired	**–**	(26,889)
Disposal of business, net of cash disposed	**(1,455)**	32,982
Disposal of subsidiary, net of cash disposed	**–**	5,630
Integration of business	**(584)**	–
Purchase of property, plant and equipment	**(40,775)**	(39,767)
Proceeds from sale of property, plant and equipment	**58**	708
Net cash used in investing activities	**(42,756)**	(37,522)
Cash flows from financing activities		
Ney proceeds from issue of ordinary share capital	**1,096**	604
Net proceeds from issue of bank loan	**36,000**	4,000
Dividends paid to shareholders	**(44,283)**	(9,277)
Net cash used in investing activities	**(7,187)**	(4,673)
Net increase in cash and cash equivalents	**937**	3,233
Cash and cash equivalents at start of year	**(1,419)**	(4,652)
Cash and cash equivalents at end of year	**(482)**	(1,419)

Brackets show minus figures.

Table 5: The Restaurant Group plc, cash flow from operating activities

		(£000s)
	2006	**2005**
Profit before tax	**21,579**	26,458
Net finance	**2,609**	2,003
Loss and provision for loss on disposal of fixed assets	**–**	2,594
Release of accrual forproperty exit costs	**–**	(1,700)
Loss on integration of DPP (net of operating cash flow)	**4,101**	–
Provision against carrying value of loan note from associate	**9,500**	–
Share of loss made by associate	**917**	600
Non cash charge reversed in reserves	**1,059**	508
Depreciation	**16,458**	18,606
Increase in stocks	**(229)**	(439)
Increase in debtors	**(1,295)**	(2,451)
Increase in creditors	**8,675**	9,305
Cash flows from operating activities	**63,374**	55,484

Brackets show minus figures.

This is the interest paid on loans and the interest received from money invested, respectively.
- During the year the Restaurant Group paid the Inland Revenue £9.656 million in corporation tax.
- The **net cash flows** from operating activities is now £50.880 million.
- In 2006 the Restaurant Group spent a net amount of £42.756 million on capital expenditure. The main item of expenditure was on £40.775 million on property, plant and equipment.
- In 2006 the key sources of finance for the Restaurant Group was a bank loan for £36 million and proceeds from the sale of shares for £1.096 million. £44.283 million was paid to shareholders in the form of dividends. The net cash used in financing activities was £7.187 million.
- In 2006 the amount of net cash generated by the Restaurant Group was £0.937 million.
- At the end of the financial year the Restaurant Group still had a negative cash balance of £0.482 million. However, this was less than the beginning of the year when it was negative £1.419 million.

CRITIQUE

The inclusion of cash flow statements helps to clarify the cash position of a business. However, there are some criticisms of cash flow statements.

- In practice, little new information is shown in the statements. The law encourages disclosure but does not enforce it.
- Small limited companies are not bound to publish a cash flow statement because they are owner managed. However, medium sized firms are. This seems to lack a little logic since most medium sized firms are also owner managed.
- Cash flow statements are based on historical information. It is argued that cash flow statements based on future predictions are more useful.

KEYTERMS

Cash flow – the continuous movement of cash in and out of the business.

Cash flow forecast – the prediction of all expected receipts and expenses of a business over a future time period which shows the expected cash balance at the end of each month.

Cash flow statement – a financial statement which shows sources and uses of cash in a trading period.

Liquid asset – an asset which is easily changed into cash.

Net cash flow – cash inflows minus cash onflows over a period of time.

Receivership – the liquidation (selling) of a firm's assets by an independent body following its collapse.

KNOWLEDGE

1. Explain the operation of the cash flow cycle.
2. Why is it important that a business: (i) does not hold too much cash; (ii) holds sufficient cash?
3. Briefly explain what a cash flow forecast includes.
4. How does a cash flow forecast indicate whether a business faces cash flow problems in future?
5. Explain why a business prepares a cash flow forecast.
6. What are the advantages of businesses preparing cash flow statements?
7. How is it possible for a profitable business to collapse?

Case Study: Kay Jones Garden Designs

Having completed a HND in Landscape Construction and Garden Design, Kay Jones wanted to run her own garden design business. The design process would involve Kay meeting with a client to discuss their needs and carrying out a survey. A second meeting would establish a more precise brief and a budget. Kay would then put together a 3D masterplan, showing drawings and materials. In addition to design, Kay also planned to do all the construction work. She felt that people might spend between £500 and £5,000 on a new garden design in her local area.

Kay did not have very much capital of her own, so she needed a bank loan. To obtain a loan she would have to draw up a business plan, including an accurate and realistic cash flow forecast. Kay knew that she would stand a better chance of a loan if she had some orders. She decided to get a job and save, develop some orders in her spare time and then launch the business in April. She lived at home and thought she could save £2,000 before the launch.

By February Kay had 5 definite orders for garden designs. She was sure that once she got started people would see her work and orders would follow. However, she did plan to market the business and applied for a listing in *Yellow Pages*. Table 4 shows the predicted revenue for the first nine months of her business. The following financial information was also gathered.

- A bank loan of £3,000 would be needed.
- Kay would contribute £2,000 of her own savings as capital in April.
- A van for £2,000 would be purchased in April.
- Tools and equipment for £3,400 would be purchased in April.
- A laptop computer with specialist design software for £600 would be purchased in April.
- A *Yellow Pages* listing will cost £100 in May.
- General overheads would be £400 per month.
- Advertising will be £100 in alternate months starting in May.
- Kay would take out £800 per month starting in June.
- Loan repayments will be £200 per month.

(a) Explain the meaning of the term 'cash flow forecast'. (4 marks)

(b) Draw up a nine month cash flow forecast for Kay Jones Garden Designs. (12 marks)

(c) (i) Comment on the cash position of the business during the nine month period. (4 marks)
(ii) What would you expect to happen to the cash position of the business in early 2008? Explain your answer. (4 marks)

(d) Once Kay was 'up and running' she had some bad news at the end of April. The van she bought needed some urgent repairs to the value of £1,200. A client with a firm £1,300 order in June cancelled. Produce an amended cash flow forecast. (6 marks)

(e) Do you think the bank would grant a loan based on the amended forecast? (10 marks)

Table 6: Predicted revenue for Kay Jones Garden Designs (first nine months)

(£)

	Apr	May	Jun	Jul	Aug	Sep	Oct	Nov	Dec
Predicted revenue	2,000	2,100	2,000	2,500	2,500	2,000	1,000	500	0

NB The predicted revenue is net of the cost of plants and other materials used in the construction of the gardens.

40 Improving cash flow

Cash flow and financial management

One crucial aspect of financial management is making sure that the business has enough cash when it is needed. If a business runs out of cash it will find it difficult, if not impossible, to trade. It will probably have to close down. In 2007, music retailer Fopp closed down after an 'extraordinary stock take'. It revealed that it had run out of cash after the company overreached itself through the purchase of the ailing Music Zone group in February. In July receivers were called in and it was announced that all 105 of its stores would be closed at the expense of 700 jobs.

This example illustrates the importance of careful financial management. Prudent owners and managers may use budgets, cash flow forecasts and credit control systems to manage financial resources effectively. Effective financial management will ensure that the business has enough cash when it is needed.

Causes of cash flow problems

Shortages of cash in a business often result from a number of errors in the control of financial resources.

Overtrading Young and rapidly growing businesses are particularly prone to OVERTRADING. Overtrading occurs when a business is attempting to fund a large volume of production with inadequate cash. Established companies trying to expand can also face this problem.

Investing too much in fixed assets In the initial stages of a business, funds are limited. Spending large amounts quickly on equipment, vehicles and other capital items drains resources. It may be better to lease some of these fixed assets, leaving sufficient cash funds.

Stockpiling Holding stocks of raw materials and finished goods is expensive. Money tied up in stocks is unproductive. Stocks may become obsolete. In addition, stocks of raw materials in particular cannot easily be changed into cash without making a loss. Stock control is an important feature of managing liquid resources. Firms should not buy in bulk if discounts are not enough to compensate for the extra cost of holding stocks.

Allowing too much credit A great deal of business is done on credit. One of the dangers is that businesses allow their customers too long to pay their bills. This means that they are waiting for money and may actually be forced to borrow during this period. Failure to control debtors may also lead to bad debts. Taking early action is the key to the effective control of debtors. At the same time businesses must maintain good relations with customers. Small firms are particularly vulnerable if they are owed money by much larger companies. Powerful businesses are often accused of endangering smaller companies by delaying payments to them.

Taking too much credit Taking more credit might appear to help a firm's cash position since payments are delayed. However, there are some drawbacks. Taking too much credit might result in higher prices, lost discounts, difficulties in obtaining future supplies and a bad name in the trade. At worst, credit might be withdrawn.

Overborrowing Businesses may borrow to finance growth. As more loans are taken out, interest costs rise. Overborrowing not only threatens a firm's cash position, but also the overall control of the business. It is important to fund growth in a balanced way, for example by raising some capital from share issues. Examples of overborrowing are not uncommon in the mortgage market. Sometimes people 'overstretch' themselves. They take out mortgages to buy houses that they can't really afford. In the worse cases, people are not able to meet interest payments and their houses are repossessed. The same could happen to businesses if they borrow too much. If they are not able to meet interest payments, their businesses could be wound up.

Underestimating inflation Businesses often fail to take inflation into account. Inflation raises costs, which can cause cash shortages. This is often the case if higher costs, such as wages or raw materials, cannot be passed on in higher prices. Inflationary periods are often accompanied by higher interest rates which place further pressure on liquid resources. Inflation is also a problem because it is difficult to predict future rates. Although it can be built into plans, firms often underestimate it. In the last ten years inflation has not been a real problem. However, sharp increase in the price of certain raw materials, such as oil, has put pressure on some businesses, particularly those that rely heavily on oil.

Unforeseen expenditure Businesses are subject to unpredictable external forces. They must make financial provision for any unforeseen expenditure. Equipment breakdowns, tax demands, strikes and bad debts are common examples of this type of emergency expense. In the early stages of business development, owners are often hit by unforeseen expenditure. This might be because they lack experience or have not undertaken sufficient planning.

Unexpected changes in demand Although most businesses try to sustain demand for their products, there may be times when it falls unexpectedly. Unpredicted changes in fashion could lead to a fall in demand. This could lead to a lack of sales and cash

Question 1.

In July 2007, Kwik Save the supermarket chain, collapsed after it ran out of cash. Most of its workers had not been paid for up to six weeks. Kwik Save was founded in 1959 as one shop in Rhyl, north Wales, and floated on the stock exchange in 1970. By the 1990s it had more than 1,000 stores and recently became part of Somerfield. However, it was sold on to a new firm, BTTF, headed by Mr Niklas, in February 2007. Some new cash was injected into the business but it was not enough to save the chain.

The firm collapsed due to a combination of tough competition from the big supermarkets which have slashed prices, foreign low-cost rivals such as Aldi and Lidl, and bad management. In May suppliers halted bread and milk deliveries saying that there were considerable difficulties getting paid by Kwik Save. Just before the company collapsed 81 stores were closed and 700 people lost their jobs. A further 90 stores were closed on the day it collapsed with around 1,100 people being laid off. However, it was hoped that some of the stores would be bought by other retailers and that some people would be kept on. Amanda Higgins, the former deputy manager of a store in Ellesmere Port that has been closed down, heard the news on television, while the company remained silent. 'It's diabolical,' she said. 'I just don't know what to do.'

She phoned the Little Sutton store near her home and was told by staff there that the shop had been shut down. Staff were also told that if they came in and handed over the store in a rational manner they would be paid a week's wages, but Ms Higgins could not believe it.

Source: adapted from *The Guardian*, 6.7.2007 and www.a2mediagroup.com

(a) Using this case as an example, explain the importance of cash when running a business.
(b) Explain how: (i) employees and (ii) the owner will be affected by the collapse of Kwik Save.
(c) Analyse the possible causes of the collapse of Kwik Save.

flowing into a company. Travel companies in the UK have faced this problem in the past. Companies have to 'buy' holidays before they are sold. External factors, including a recession, may have led to many of these holidays remaining unsold as consumers changed their holiday buying patterns. Firms may also have lost revenue if holidays were discounted in an attempt to sell them.

Seasonal factors Sometimes trade fluctuates for seasonal reasons. In the agriculture industry, cereal farmers have a large cash inflow when their harvest is sold. For much of the year, though, they have to pay expenses without any cash flowing in. This situation requires careful management, although it is possible to predict these changes.

Poor financial management Inexperience in managing cash or a poor understanding of the way cash flows into and out of a business may lead to cash flow problems. For example, if a business plans to spend heavily just before it receives large amounts of cash from customers who have bought on credit, it is likely to face problems. It is not prudent to spend cash when it is not definitely there.

Methods of improving cash flow

Cash flow problems can be prevented by keeping a tight control on financial resources. The use of budgets and cash flow forecasts will improve the financial management of the business. Inevitably, though, there will be occasions when firms run short of cash. When this does happen the firm's main aim will be survival rather than profit. The following measures might be used to either generate cash or save it.

Use of overdraft facilities If a business is not able, or does not wish, to use the options listed above, an obvious option is to borrow money. Most businesses have an overdraft facility with their banks. An overdraft is a type of flexible loan. The borrower can choose to borrow up to a certain sum of money agreed with the bank, called the overdraft limit. But they are free to pay back part of the money borrowed at any time and do not have to be borrowing money to have an overdraft facility. A business can increase its cash by borrowing more money on its overdraft. For example, it might have an overdraft limit of £5,000. It is currently borrowing £3,000. So it could borrow up to £2,000 extra.

There is more of a problem if a business is already borrowing up to its overdraft limit. Then it has to negotiate with its bank to that limit. There is no guarantee that the bank will do this. A business experiencing cash flow problems could well be a business in difficulties. The bank will not want to increase lending to a business which could cease trading in the immediate future. The bank is likely to want to see a cash flow forecast to judge whether or not the business will be able to pay the interest on the overdraft and the overdraft itself in the future.

Negotiate additional short-term or long-term loans A business may be able obtain a short-term loan from a bank to inject some extra cash. If a business feels that extra money will be needed for a longer period of time a long-term loan might be considered. A business could pay back smaller installments over a longer period of time to help cash flow. However, once it is known that a business is short of cash, banks and other money lenders may be reluctant to provide cash for fear of the business collapsing.

Sell off or reduce stocks Sometimes it may be possible to sell stocks of raw materials, components or semi-finished goods for cash. To generate cash quickly they can be sold cheaply in a sale or below cost if necessary. Some stocks may be quite specialised and prove difficult to sell quickly.

A business might simply reduce the amount of stocks it holds. A machine manufacturer may buy in fewer stocks of components to make machines. Stocks cost money to hold. So fewer stocks can increase cash in the business. The danger is that stocks will not be available to make products that are required for sale.

Use a factoring company An alternative to pressurising customers for money is to sell the debts to a specialist **debt factor**. A factor is a business that will provide finance to another business against its debts for a fee. It often pays a certain amount to the business 'up front' and the remainder once debts are collected. Debt factors give businesses cash immediately and take the responsibility for collecting the debt. However, they make a charge for this and the debts must be good.

Sell off unwanted or non-vital fixed assets A business may be able to sell off unwanted or non-vital fixed assets like vehicles, machines and property. Unfortunately, to sell assets like these quickly they are likely to be sold at auctions and they may be sold below their true value.

Use of sale and leaseback Businesses are increasingly using sale and leaseback to raise cash. Assets like property and machinery can be sold to specialists in the market, such as Arnold Clark and Lease Direct. The assets are then leased back to the seller. This means that cash can be raised and the business can continue to use the assets. However, it may take a while to set up such agreements and can be an expensive way to fund assets in the long term.

Stimulate sales for cash Many businesses, retailers for example, can generate cash by offering large discounts for customers who pay in cash. In the example at the beginning of this unit, Fopp tried to generate cash in this way by selling records, CDs and other stock for cash only. Unfortunately, the measure was not enough to save the business.

Mount a rigorous drive on overdue accounts This involves a business putting pressure on its customers to pay back what they owe more quickly. Allowing customers to receive products and pay for them at a later date is called TRADE CREDIT. The DEBTORS of a business are those customers (individuals or businesses) that owe a business money. However, pressurising customers in this way may mean that they find other suppliers.

Only make essential purchases It obviously makes sense during a cash crisis to postpone or cancel all unnecessary spending. A business should only buy resources for cash when it absolutely has to.

Delaying payments A business may simply delay payments. It then keeps this cash in the business for a longer period of time. It will only make payments when it is put under pressure to do so by CREDITORS – businesses that are owed money.

Extend credit with selected suppliers It will help a business to save cash if it can delay paying suppliers for goods and services that have already been bought. It may be able to extend its credit payment period from 30 to 60 days, for example. However, delaying for too long could mean that suppliers withdraw their credit facilities or refuse to deliver goods in the future.

Reduce personal drawings from the business Owners who regularly take cash from the business for their own personal use could attempt to take less. Obviously some cash might be needed for living expenses, but making a reduction in drawings is a quick way to stop cash leaving the business.

Introduce fresh capital Owners may be able to provide some new capital to improve cash flow. For example, small businesses may be able to use savings or take out loans using personal possessions as security. A small business may be able to persuade friends or relatives to invest in it – new partners might be taken on for example. Larger companies may be able to sell shares to raise fresh capital. However, attracting fresh capital might be very difficult if the business is struggling. It is likely to be up to the current owners to provide more capital.

In all the above cases, action must be taken quickly. If the business survives the cash crisis, it is important to identify the causes and to make sure it does not happen again. It is also

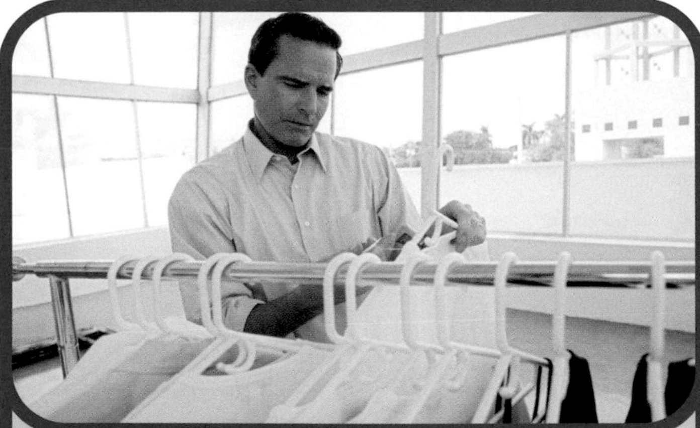

Question 2.

Adrian Talbot owns and runs a small garment manufacturing business. He employs 12 workers, using rented premises in London. Cash flow is always a problem for him. The businesses that buy from him often pay late while the profit margins he earns are wafer thin in an industry notorious for cut throat competition. At least finished stock is never a problem. He makes a sample and wins orders based on that. As soon as an order is complete, it is sent out to the purchaser.

(a) Suggest and explain THREE ways in which Adrian Talbot could possibly improve his cash flow situation.

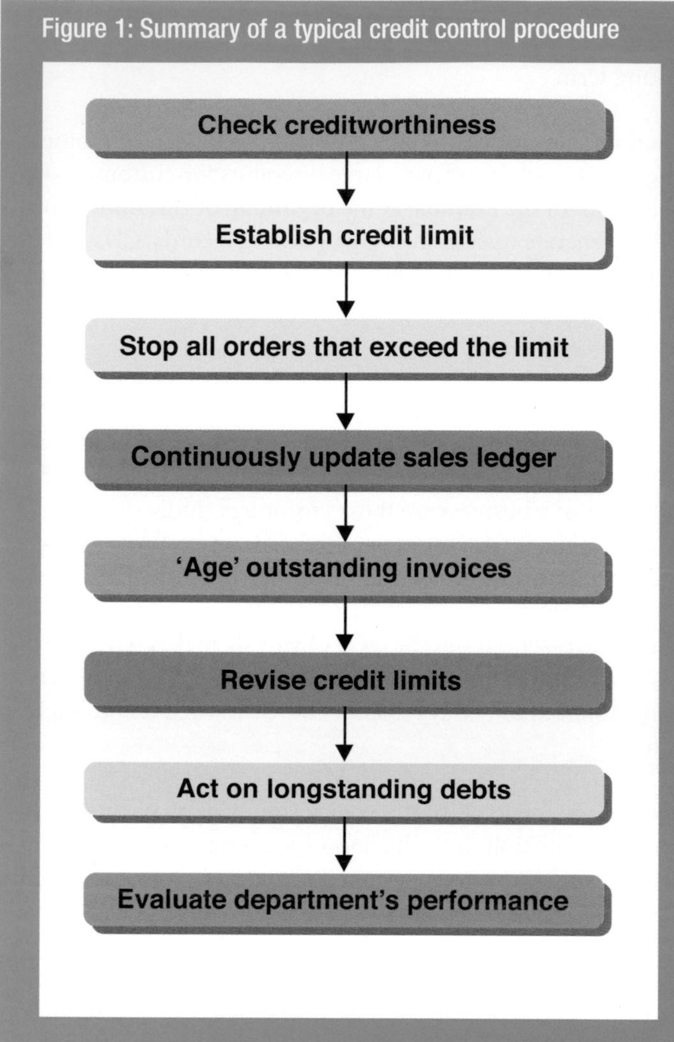

Figure 1: Summary of a typical credit control procedure

evident that measures taken to alleviate a cash crisis are likely to reduce profits. For example, selling goods at a discount to raise cash will reduce profit margins; selling off assets and leasing them back can reduce profit in the long term; borrowing money from banks will incur interest charges; inviting new members to provide capital will dilute ownership.

Credit control

Most businesses have some sort of CREDIT CONTROL system, so that cash that is owed can be collected quickly and easily. A 'tight' or 'easy' credit policy may be adopted. Tight credit terms may be used to improve liquidity, reduce the risk of bad debts, exploit a seller's market or maintain slender profit margins. Easy credit terms may be designed to clear old stocks, enter a new market or perhaps help a regular customer with financial difficulties.

The company accountant and the sales manager often work closely with the credit controller, since credit policy will affect the financial position of the firm and its sales. Between them they set targets for the credit control department, such as the maximum value of bad debts or the length of time it takes to collect debts.

Firms have procedures to help credit control. Figure 1 shows an example.

- Many firms will not do business with new customers until their creditworthiness has been checked. This can be done by asking for references from a supplier, a banker's reference or a credit-rating agency's report. From this information the credit controller can set a credit limit based on the risk involved.
- When an order exceeds the credit limit, the credit controller should investigate. This may result in a stop being placed on the order, requesting the customer to pay any outstanding debt or simply allowing the order to go ahead.
- Credit control records, which show customer orders and payments, must be up to date. Every month, outstanding invoices must be 'aged' to identify customers who owe money over 30, 60 and 90 days.
- If there are persistent debts, the credit controller must take action. A statement of the account should be sent, followed by a second one with a letter. Next, a telephone call to the debtor should be followed by a personal visit. Finally, as a last resort, it may be necessary to take legal action to recover the debt.
- Some firms use an independent **debt factor** to assist in credit control. There has been quite a growth in this type of business in recent years. A factor is a business that will provide finance to a business against its debts for a fee. It often pays a certain amount to a business' up front' and the remainder as debts are collected.

KEYTERMS

Creditors – those to whom a business owes money for goods or services delivered but not yet paid for.
Credit control – the process of monitoring and collecting the money owed to a business.
Debtors – those who owe a business money for goods or services delivered but for which they have not yet paid.
Overtrading – a situation where a business does not have enough cash and other liquid resources to support its production and sales.
Trade credit – given when a supplier allows a customer to receive goods or services but pay for them at a later point in time. Typically, trade credit is given for 30 days.

KNOWLEDGE

1. What might happen if a business runs out of cash?
2. What methods might a business use to manage its financial resources effectively?
3. Explain why young and rapidly growing businesses are prone to overtrading.
4. Explain how: (i) stock piling (ii) overborrowing and (iii) underestimating inflation can cause cash-flow problems.
5. State four ways in which a business can improve cash flow.
6. Why might it be difficult to extend a bank overdraft to generate more cash?
7. What is meant by 'credit control'?

Case Study: **Hotel Condor**

Hotel Condor is a 45 room hotel, with conference facilities, a restaurant and a bar. It is located in north London, about 35 minutes drive from Heathrow Airport. The hotel business, which includes the property, is owned by Asif and Ashraf Hussain. The hotel uses a booking agent in the USA and about 80 per cent of the hotel's guests are American business travellers and tourists. The hotel has many facilities, including coffee makers in the room, room service, safe deposit boxes, televisions with cable and high-speed Internet connection.

The hotel has not performed particularly well in the last couple of years. The flow of American guests has dwindled due to the strength of the pound against the dollar. Occupancy rates have fallen from 82 per cent in 2005 to less than 50 per cent in 2006. To keep the business going, the owners put in £20,000 cash, in the hope that the exchange rate would eventually reverse. £4,000 of the money was spent on obtaining some listings in hotel directories. Although this did generate some more business, it was nowhere near as much as promised. £4,000 was spent relaunching the restaurant, but unfortunately the appointment of a new head chef, and a change in the menu, did not attract many more customers. By the end of 2006, the hotel had £5,600 in the bank and cash flow forecasts showed that more cash would need to be injected in June 2007 unless business picked up significantly.

The hotel was contacted by a British company that was undertaking some work in the north London area. The company wanted to book 25 rooms for three months (May to July) to accommodate their employees. They also wanted to make regular use of the conferencing facilities. A price was agreed, a deposit was received, and it looked as though the hotel was about to get back on an even keel. However, as luck would have it, the hotel was forced to close for two weeks in April after a visit from health and safety inspectors. Hygiene conditions in the large kitchen, which served both the hotel and the restaurant, were not up to standard. About £15,000 of work needed to be done before it could reopen. There was £9,200 in the bank.

(a) Using this case as an example, explain what is meant by a cash flow problem. (4 marks)

(b) Explain how external factors have contributed to cash flow problems in this case. (12 marks)

(c) Ashraf and Asif have invited a relative of theirs to become a sleeping partner in the business and contribute £50,000 capital. Do you think the relative should accept the invitation? (14 marks)

(d) Evaluate the measures the Hotel Condor might take to resolve its cash crisis. (20 marks)

41 Setting budgets

What is a budget?

The control of a business becomes more difficult the larger it is. A new, small business setting up may be run informally. The owner is the manager, who will know everyone, be aware of what is going on and will make all decisions. In medium sized and larger firms, work and responsibility are delegated, which makes informal control impractical. To improve control, budgeting has been developed. This forces others to be accountable for their decisions.

A BUDGET is a plan which is agreed in advance. It must be a plan and not a forecast. A forecast is a prediction of what might happen in the future, whereas a budget is a planned outcome which the firm hopes to achieve. A budget will show the money needed for spending and how this might be financed. Budgets are based on the objectives of businesses. They force managers to think ahead and improve co-ordination. Most budgets are set for twelve months to coincide with the accounting period, but there are exceptions. Research and Development budgets, for example, may cover several years.

Information contained in a budget may include revenue, sales, expenses, profit, personnel, cash and capital expenditure. In fact, budgets can include any business variable (known as a budget factor) which can be given a value. One well known budget is 'The Budget'. The Chancellor of the Exchequer prepares a budget for a particular period. It will take into account the government's spending plans and how these plans will be financed by taxes and other sources of funds.

The reasons for setting budgets

There is a number of reasons why a business sets budgets.

Control and monitoring Budgeting helps control a business. It does this by setting objectives and targets. These are then translated into budgets for, say, the coming year. Success by the business and the workforce in achieving those targets can be found by comparing the actual results with the budget. The reasons for failing to achieve the budget can then be analysed and appropriate action taken.

Planning Budgeting forces businesses to think ahead. Without budgeting, people might work on a day-to-day basis, only dealing with opportunities and problems as they arise. Budgeting, however, plans for the future. It anticipates problems and their solutions.

Co-ordination As a business grows in size its organisation becomes more complicated. There may be different departments or different production and administrative sites. A multinational company will have workers spread across the world. Budgeting is one way of co-ordinating the activities of areas of the business.

Communication Planning allows the objectives of the business to be communicated to its employees. By keeping to a budget, employees have a clear framework within which to operate. So budgeting removes an element of uncertainty within decision making throughout the business.

Efficiency In medium sized or larger businesses it may be difficult for one person to make every decision. Budgeting gives financial control to those workers who are best able to make decisions in the business.

Motivation Budgeting should act as a motivator to employees. It provides workers with targets and standards. Improving on the budget position is an indication of success. Fear of failing to reach budgeted targets may make workers work harder.

The preparation of budgets

The way in which a budget might be prepared is shown in Figure 1. It is a step-by-step process.

Figure 1: A summary of the stages involved in budget preparation

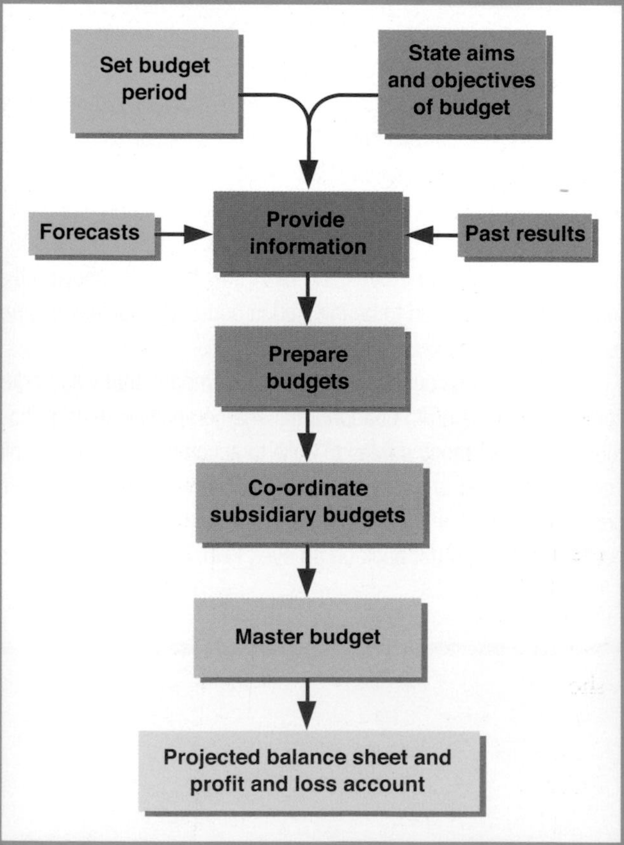

Set budget period
State aims and objectives of budget
Forecasts
Provide information
Past results
Prepare budgets
Co-ordinate subsidiary budgets
Master budget
Projected balance sheet and profit and loss account

Table 1: Planned sales figures for Emerald Artwork

	Feb	Mar	Apr	May
AD23	100	100	100	100
AD24	50	80	80	100
AE12	40	50	40	50
AE13	30	30	50	50

- Decide on a budget period and state the objectives and targets which are to be achieved. The budget period may vary according to the type of budget. One month or one year is usual. Targets for performance, market share, quality (provided it can be quantified) and productivity are all examples.
- Obtain information upon which to base the budget. A new business setting up will not be able to base its budgets on its own historical information. So it will need to estimate future figures. It may do this from market research. Some business variables are easier to estimate than others. It may be easier to quantify future costs than future sales, for example. This is because sales levels are subject to so many external factors. Once the business has traded for a period, budgets can be based on past figures.
- Prepare budgets. Two important budgets are the sales budget and the production budget. These budgets are related and affect all other budgets. For example, sales targets can only be met if there is productive capacity. Also, a firm would be unlikely to continue production if it could not sell its products. The sales budget will contain monthly sales estimates, expressed in terms of quantities per product, perhaps, and the price charged. From the sales budget, and with knowledge of stock levels, the production budget can be determined. This will show the required raw materials, labour hours and machine hours. At this stage the business should know whether or not it has the capacity to meet the sales targets. If it is not possible, then it may be necessary to adjust the sales budget.
- Draw up subsidiary operating budgets. These are detailed budgets usually prepared by medium sized and larger businesses. Budgets can be broken down, so that each person in the hierarchy can be given some responsibility for a section of the budget.
- The MASTER BUDGET is a summary statement of all budgets. For example, it shows the estimated income, anticipated expenditure, and, thus, the budgeted profit for the period. The cash budget can be prepared when all other budgets are complete. This budget is particularly useful since it shows the monthly flows of cash into and out of the business. It will help to show whether future cash flow problems might occur.
- Prepare the projected balance sheet and profit and loss of the business. These show the financial position that will result from the firm's budgets.

Table 2: A sales revenue (income) budget for Emerald Artwork

				(£)
	Feb	Mar	Apr	May
AD23	1,200 (12 x 100)	1,200 (12 x 100)	1,200 (12 x 100)	1,200 (12 x 100)
AD24	1,000 (20 x 50)	1,600 (20 x 80)	1,600 (20 x 80)	2,000 (20 x 100)
AE12	1,000 (25 x 40)	1,250 (25 x 50)	1,000 (25 x 40)	1,250 (25 x 50)
AE13	900 (30 x 30)	900 (30 x 30)	1,500 (30 x 50)	1,500 (30 x 50)
Total	4,100	4,950	5,300	5,950

Income or sales revenue budget

An INCOME or SALES REVENUE BUDGET shows the planned income or revenue for a period of time. Emerald Artwork produces four products, AD23, AD24, AE12 and AE13. They sell for £12, £20, £25 and £30 respectively. The planned sales levels for a four month period are shown in Table 1.

The budget is prepared by showing the planned income or sales revenue in each month. This is calculated by multiplying the predicted sales levels by the prices. The sales revenue budget is shown in Table 2.

Table 3: A production budget for Emerald Artwork covering production of all 4 products

				(£)
	FEB	MAR	APR	MAY
Cost of materials (£3 per unit)	660 (3 x 220)	780 (3 x 260)	810 (3 x 270)	900 (3 x 300)
Direct labour costs (£4 per unit)	880 (4 x 220)	1,040 (4 x 260)	1,080 (4 x 270)	1,200 (4 x 300)
Indirect labour costs (£2 per unit)	440 (2 x 220)	520 (2 x 260)	540 (2 x 270)	600 (2 x 300)
Production Overheads (10% of direct & indirect costs)	1,320 x 10% = 132	1,560 x 10% = 156	1,620 x 10% = 162	1,800 x 10% = 180
Total	2,112	2,496	2,592	2,880

Table 4: An expenditure budget for Emerald Artwork

				(£)
	Feb	**Mar**	**Apr**	**May**
Materials	660	780	810	900
Direct labour	880	1,040	1,080	1,200
Indirect labour	440	520	540	600
Production overheads	132	156	162	180
General overheads	300	600	200	700
Capital expenditure	2,000	0	200	1,700
Total expenditure	4,412	3,096	2,992	5,280

Table 5: Profit budget for Emerald Artwork

				(£)
	Feb	**Mar**	**Apr**	**May**
Income (sales revenue)	4,100	4,950	5,300	5,950
Expenditure	2,412	3,096	2,792	3,580
Profit	1,688	1,854	2,508	2,370

Production budget

Once Emerald Artwork has produced a sales budget, it is possible to calculate its production budget. The example in Table 3 assumes stock levels stay the same throughout the four month period. The figures are based on expected sales in Table 1.

Expenditure budget

An EXPENDITURE or TOTAL COST BUDGET shows how much money a business is expected to spend for a period of time. It is based on the production budget. Expenditure might include raw materials, labour, production overheads, general overheads and capital expenditure such as new machinery. An expenditure budget is shown for Emerald Artwork in Table 4. It is based on the production budget but includes all other business expenditure for the four month period.

Profit budget

A PROFIT BUDGET shows the amount of profit a business is expected to make over a period. It contains information on all income generated by the business and all expenditure. However, the profit budget would not include capital expenditure. A profit budget for Emerald Artwork is shown in Table 5. Note that capital expenditure has been excluded. In the profit budget, expenditure is subtracted from income to get the monthly profit.

Problems of setting budgets

Businesses may sometimes find that there are problems when setting budgets.

Question 1.

Hannah Ngilo and David Saunders run Penzance Motor Services. The business generates revenue in a number of ways. It sells petrol, a limited range of grocery and confectionery items, car accessories and a few second-hand cars. The garage also carries out servicing, motor repairs and MOT testing. An income budget for a six month period is shown in Table 6.

(a) Complete the income budget for Penzance Motor Services by calculating the total monthly income.

(b) Hannah and David set sales targets for each source of income. What role will setting budgets play when setting such targets?

(c) Explain how the information in this budget might be used in a profit budget.

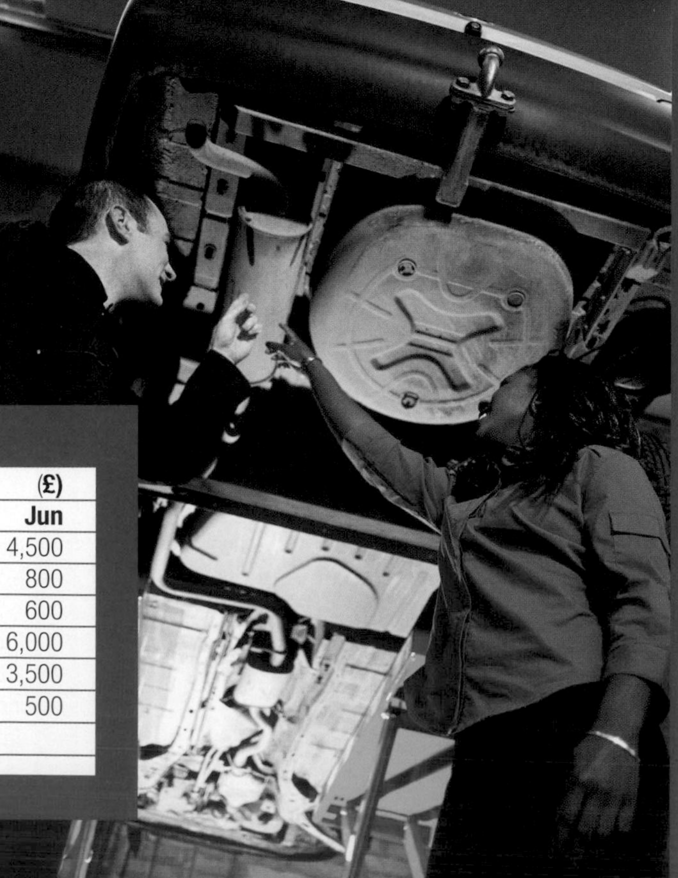

Table 6: Income budget for Penzance Motor Services

						(£)
	Jan	**Feb**	**Mar**	**Apr**	**May**	**Jun**
Petrol sales	3,400	3,500	3,400	3,600	4,000	4,500
Grocery sales	650	650	700	700	750	800
Car accessories	450	500	500	550	550	600
Car sales	1,000	1,500	2,000	4,000	5,000	6,000
Servicing and repairs	4,300	4,800	5,000	4,500	4,000	3,500
MOTs	400	500	450	550	600	500
Total income						

Question 2.

Melanie Croft runs the Motherwell Leisure Centre, a private leisure facility for residents in the Motherwell and Hamilton areas of Scotland. The centre has about 900 members and offers a range of facilities. In order to keep control of costs Melanie sets expenditure budgets every six months for the various departments within the complex. An expenditure budget for the first six months of 2007 is shown in Table 7.

(a) **Complete the expenditure budget shown in Table 7 and calculate the total expenditure for the sixth month period.**
(b) **What might account for the pattern of expenditure for the café bar over the time period?**
(c) **Explain how using an expenditure budget could help Melanie control costs in the business.**

Table 7: Expenditure budget for the Motherwell Leisure Centre – January to June 2007

						(£)
	Jan	**Feb**	**Mar**	**Apr**	**May**	**Jun**
Sports Hall	1,400	1,600	1,700	1,700	1,500	1,300
Swimming pool	2,300	2,400	2,400	2,500	3,000	3,500
Games room	600	700	600	500	400	200
Fitness centre	3,200	3,500	3,600	3,600	3,400	3,200
Outdoor activities	500	400	500	600	800	1,000
Massage & beauty treatments	5,300	5,300	6,000	6,000	7,000	7,000
Administration	2,000	2,000	2,000	2,000	2,000	2,000
Café bar	3,200	3,500	3,700	4,000	5,000	7,000
Total expenditure						

Using planned figures Problems tend to arise because figures in budgets are not actual figures. Planned figures may be inaccurate. The most important data in the preparation of nearly all budgets is sales data. If sales data are inaccurate, many of the firm's budgets will be inexact. The accuracy of sales data might be improved if market research is used However, it may be difficult to estimate sales of new products for a future period.

Collecting information The setting of budgets in some businesses may require a great deal of co-ordination. This is because different parts of the business may provide information for budgets. Some medium sized and larger businesses appoint a budget officer. This person is responsible for collecting data and opinions, keeping managers to the budget timetable and carrying out budgetary administration.

Conflict The setting of budgets may lead to conflict between staff. For example, a business may only have limited funds. One person may want to spend this on marketing, but another may feel that new machinery is needed.

Cost The time spent setting budgets could have been spent on other tasks. This is very important for a small, new business with limited resources.

Over-ambitious objectives Sometimes businesses set over-ambitious objectives. When this happens, the budgeting process is pointless because budgets are being drawn up for targets which are unachievable. The budget then ceases to become a benchmark with which to compare the outcome.

External influences In some industries, it is difficult to plan ahead because of large and unpredictable changes in the external environment. In farming, for instance, there can be variations in price from year to year and the weather can have large effects on output. This doesn't mean that businesses in such industries should not draw up budgets. However, it can be difficult to analyse outcomes against the budget. It may be unclear if external influences or the way in which a business is run have affected whether a budget is achieved or not.

KNOWLEDGE

1. How might a budget improve employee accountability?
2. Why is the sales budget such an important budget?
3. How might budgets motivate staff?
4. State examples of three types of budget.
5. Why might a business manipulate a budget?
6. What costs are incurred when setting budgets?

KEYTERMS

Budget – a quantitative economic plan prepared and agreed in advance.
Income or sales revenue budget – shows the planned income or revenue for a period of time.
Expenditure or total cost budget – shows how much money a business is expected to spend for a period of time
Profit budget – shows the amount of profit a business is expected to make over a period.
Master budget – a summary statement which brings together information from budgets.

Case Study: Agarka Mini Market

Agarka Mini Market is a small supermarket serving residents in the Poole area of Dorset. The store is divided into a number of sections.

- Dairy – maintains refrigerated products such as milk, cheese, other dairy products, smoothies and fruit juices.
- Delicatessen – serves cold meats, olives, fresh pickles, dips and other delicatessen products.
- Fresh produce – is responsible for all fruit and vegetables.
- Grocery – is the largest department and is responsible for all food products in cans and packets, household goods such as cleaning materials, drinks, confectionery and products which do not fall neatly into other departments.
- Meat – stocks pre-packaged refrigerated meat products for customers and prepares many of these packages for sale. Also cuts meat to order for customers.
- Liquor – this is a new department since a liquor licence was only granted in 2006. However, it is expected to grow rapidly. A wide range of wines, beers and spirits are offered.

Six members of the Agarka family work in the store and a further nine people are employed part-time. In order to monitor the progress of different parts of the business profit budgets are set for every department. The head of each department is paid a six month bonus of 5 per cent of profit if the profit targets are reached. The income and expenditure budgets are shown in Tables 8 and 9.

(a) **Explain what is meant by the term budget. (2 marks)**

(b) **Produce separate profit budgets for each of the sections at the Agarka Mini Market. (18 marks)**

(c) **(i) Which section has the poorest profit record over the time period? (4 marks)**

(ii) How might you account for the poor profit record of the section identified in (i)? (4 marks)

(d) **(i) How will profit budgets serve to motivate staff in the store? (6 marks)**

(ii) Calculate the six month bonus due to the person responsible for the Grocery department. (4 marks)

(e) **Discuss three problems which might be encountered by the Agarka family when setting budgets for their Mini Market. (12 marks)**

Table 8: Income budget for Agarka Mini Market

						(£)
	Jul	**Aug**	**Sep**	**Oct**	**Nov**	**Dec**
Dairy	7,500	7,500	8,000	8,000	8,000	9,000
Delicatessen	9,000	9,000	9,500	9,500	9,500	12,000
Fresh produce	5,700	6,000	6,000	6,500	6,000	8,000
Grocery	27,000	28,000	29,000	29,000	30,000	34,000
Meat	8,000	8,000	8,500	8,500	9,000	12,000
Liquor	3,000	4,000	5,000	6,000	8,000	17,000

Table 9: Expenditure budget for Agarka Mini Market

						(£)
	Jul	**Aug**	**Sep**	**Oct**	**Nov**	**Dec**
Dairy						
Goods for resale	5,000	5,000	5,200	5,300	5,300	6,100
Wages and other costs	1,300	1,200	1,600	1,600	1,500	1,700
Delicatessen						
Goods for resale	6,000	6,000	6,100	6,200	6,000	7,500
Wages and other costs	2,000	2,000	2,100	2,100	2,200	3,000
Fresh produce						
Goods for resale	4,300	4,400	4,700	5,300	5,200	6,300
Wages and other costs	1,000	1,000	1,000	1,000	1,000	1,300
Grocery						
Goods for resale	19,000	19,500	20,000	20,500	20,600	21,200
Wages and other costs	4,200	4,200	4,300	4,300	4,500	6,000
Meat						
Goods for resale	5,100	5,000	5,100	5,300	5,400	7,100
Wages and other costs	1,400	1,400	1,400	1,600	1,600	2,100
Liquor						
Goods for resale	1,800	2,200	3,000	3,500	5,200	10,000
Wages and other costs	500	500	700	700	900	1,200

42 Using budgets

Managing finance

Once a business is established the owners will generally want to improve its performance. In the early stages of business development the emphasis is often on survival. But once the business is through this stage, other issues become important. Owners will probably want to grow their businesses and improve their effectiveness. One aspect of improving the effectiveness of a business is financial management. This involves managing the financial resources of the business. In most businesses this means:

- making sure that costs are kept down;
- ensuring that there is enough money to buy resources;
- ensuring that customers pay for what they have bought;
- measuring and monitoring financial performance indicators, such as profit and returns on capital.

Businesses have developed a number of systems to help manage financial resources and one of these is budgeting.

Using budgets

BUDGETARY CONTROL or BUDGETING involves a business using budgets to look into the future, stating what it wants to happen, and then deciding how to achieve these aims. The control process is shown in Figure 1.

Figure 1: Stages in budgetary control

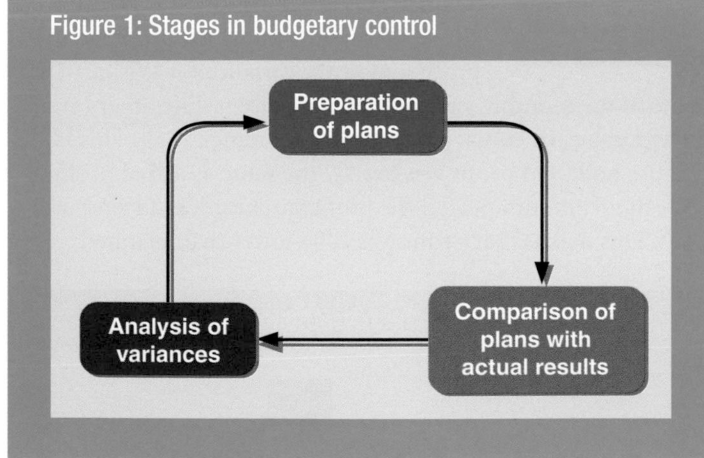

Preparation of plans All businesses have objectives. If the sales department increases sales by 10 per cent, how does it know whether or not this is satisfactory? Targets are usually set which allow a business to determine whether its objectives have been met. The results it achieves can then be compared with the targets it sets.

Comparisons of plans with actual results Control will be effective if information is available as quickly as possible. Managers need budgetary data as soon as it is available. Recent developments in information technology have helped to speed up the supply of data. For budgeting purposes the financial year has been divided up into smaller control periods - usually four weeks or one calendar month. It is common to prepare a budget for each control period. At the end of the period the actual results can then be compared with targets set in the budget.

Analysis of variances This is the most important stage in the control process. VARIANCE ANALYSIS involves trying to find reasons for the differences between actual and expected financial outcomes. Variances are explained in the next section. A variance might be the result of some external factor influencing the business. In this case the business may need to change its business plans and adjust the next budget.

Variances

A VARIANCE in budgeting is the difference between the figure that the business has budgeted for and the actual figure. Variances are usually calculated at the end of the budget period, as that is when the actual figure will be known.

Variances can be **favourable** (F) or **adverse** (A). Favourable variances occur when the actual figures are 'better' than the budgeted figures.

- If the sales revenue for a month was budgeted at £25,000, but turned out to be £29,000, there would be a £4,000 favourable variance (£29,000-£25,000) as sales revenue was higher than planned.
- If costs were planned to be £20,000 and turned out to be £18,000, this would also be a favourable variance of £2,000, as actual costs were lower than planned.

Adverse variances are when the actual figures are worse than the budgeted figures. Actual sales revenues may be lower than planned, or actual costs may be higher than planned. Managers will examine variances and try to identify reasons why they have occurred. By doing this they might be able to improve the performance of the business in the future.

Types of variance

Variances can be calculated for a wide range of financial outcomes. Most budgets are set for expenditure (costs) and income (sales revenue). Consequently, variances will also focus on a firm's expenditures and income. This suggests that variance analysis provides a very good way of monitoring business costs. Examples of variances could be wages, materials, overheads and sales revenue. Variances can also be calculated for volumes. For example it is possible to calculate a sales variance or a labour hours variance. One of the most important variances of all is the profit variance. The profit variance is influenced by all other variances. A change in any variance will affect profit. This is

Table 1: Income budget, actual income and income variances for Wishart Ltd

							(£)
	Jan	**Feb**	**Mar**	**Apr**	**May**	**Jun**	**Total**
Budgeted income	16,500	17,000	17,500	18,000	19,000	20,000	108,000
Actual income	16,600	17,400	17,900	17,700	18,500	20,800	108,900
Variance	**100F**	**400F**	**400F**	**300A**	**500A**	**800F**	**900F**

Table 2: Budgeted expenditure, actual expenditure and expenditure variances for Wishart Ltd

							(£)
	Jan	**Feb**	**Mar**	**Apr**	**May**	**Jun**	**Total**
Budgeted expenditure	11,400	11,900	12,500	13,000	14,000	15,000	77,800
Actual expenditure	11,500	11,600	12,700	13,500	14,200	15,600	79,100
Expenditure variances	**100A**	**300F**	**200A**	**500A**	**200A**	**600A**	**1,300A**

Table 3: Budgeted profit, actual profit and profit variance for Wishart Ltd

							(£)
	Jan	**Feb**	**Mar**	**Apr**	**May**	**Jun**	**Total**
Budgeted profit	5,100	5,100	5,000	5,000	5,000	5,000	30,200
Actual profit	5,100	5,800	5,200	4,200	4,300	5,200	29,800
Profit variances	**0**	**700F**	**200F**	**800A**	**700A**	**200F**	**400A**

because all variances relate to either the costs or the revenue of a business, both of which affect profit levels. The number of possible variances is equal to the number of factors which can influence business costs and revenue.

Income or sales revenue variances

Table 1 shows the budgeted income, actual income and income variances for Wishart Ltd, a bamboo and wicker furniture manufacturer. Four of the monthly variances are favourable while two are adverse. The biggest variance occurred in June. In this month actual income was £800 greater than the budgeted income. The variance for the whole six month period is also shown. Over the period the total income variance was £900. Wishart Ltd's shareholders are likely to be pleased with this.

Possible causes of the favourable income variance over the six months in this case might be the result of:

- the ability to charge higher prices;
- an increase in demand due to a marketing campaign;
- improvements in the quality of the product;
- an increase in consumer incomes;
- a change in consumer's tastes in favour of bamboo and wicker furniture.

Expenditure or cost variances

Table 2 shows the budgeted expenditure, actual expenditure and expenditure or total cost variances for Wishart Ltd over the six month period. Most of the monthly expenditure variances are adverse over the time period. For example, in April the variance was £500A. This means that costs were £500 higher than planned. Over the whole six month period the expenditure variance was adverse at £1,300. There is a number of possible reasons for such adverse variances.

- Costs might be higher because production was higher.
- Suppliers may have raised prices.
- There may be some inefficiencies in production.
- Wages may have been higher due to wage demands by workers.

Profit variances

The most important of all variances is the profit variance. This is shown in Figure 2. Differences between actual profit and planned profit will be of particular interest to business owners, managers and other stakeholders. The performance of most businesses is often measured by profit. Table 3 shows the budgeted profit, actual profit and profit variance for Wishart Ltd. Some of the monthly variances are favorable while others are unfavourable. In January there was no variance at all. This is because budgeted profit was exactly the same as actual profit. Over the six month period the profit variance was adverse at £400. This means that profit was £400 lower than planned.

Figure 2: A summary of the key variances

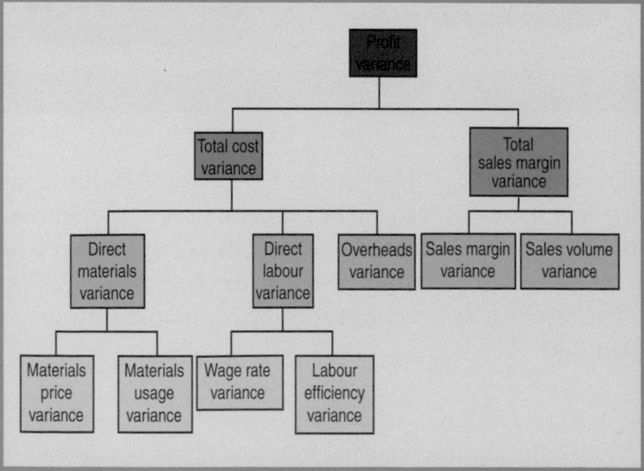

Question 1.

FT Office Supplies sells office equipment and computer accessories such as printers, toners, computer cables, port hubs and laptop bags. It used to operate three stores in the south of England, but it recently closed the stores and now conducts all business online. To monitor sales the business sets budgets every six months. Table 4 shows an income (sales revenue) budget for the first six months of 2007. Actual income figures are also shown.

Table 4: Income budget and actual income for FT Office Supplies

							(£000)
	Jan	**Feb**	**Mar**	**Apr**	**May**	**Jun**	**Total**
Budgeted income	1,200	1,300	1,400	1,400	1,500	1,600	8,400
Actual income	1,140	1,190	1,430	1,400	1,390	1,450	8,000

(a) Calculate the sales revenue variances for each month and the total sales revenue variance for the whole budget period.

(b) Explain the variance in April.

(c) Analyse two possible reasons for the pattern of variances for FT Office Supplies over the six month time period.

The main reason for Wishart's adverse profit variances over the six month period is the adverse cost variance of £1,300. Costs have been higher than planned. Higher costs may have been caused by a number of factors, such as those listed in the examples above.

Direct materials variance

Figure 2 shows that the total cost variance can be influenced by several cost variances. One of these is the direct materials variance. This is the difference between budgeted direct materials costs and actual direct materials costs. Direct materials include raw materials, components and any other resources used directly in production. For example, a biscuit manufacturer may use flour as one of its raw materials. Table 5 shows the budgeted and actual price of flour and the budgeted and actual usage of flour in a particular budget period. According to the table, the budgeted direct materials cost of the flour is £3,000. However, the actual direct materials cost is £2,860. This gives a favourable direct materials variance of £140 in this budget period.

The favourable variance in Table 5 is influenced by two other variances.

Table 5: Cost and usage of flour for a biscuit manufacturer

	Price (per kilo)	Usage (kilos)	Direct materials cost
Budgeted	£1.50	2,000	£3,000
Actual	£1.30	2,200	£2,860
Direct materials variance			£140 (F)

Materials price variance This will result when the actual price of direct materials is different from the budgeted or standard price. In Table 5 this is calculated by:

Materials price variance = (budgeted price - actual price) x actual usage

= (£1.50 - £1.30) x 2,200

= £0.20 x 2,200

= £440 (F)

The materials price variance is favourable because the actual cost is lower than the budgeted cost. This variance may be the responsibility of the purchasing department. Materials price variances could arise for a number of reasons, for example:

- materials may be obtained at a special discount;
- a new supplier might have been found;
- unexpected inflation may raise prices;
- a price war may have broken out in the market.

Materials usage variance A materials usage variance is found by comparing the actual usage of materials and the budgeted usage. The difference is valued at the budgeted price. For the biscuit manufacturer above the variance is:

Materials usage variance = (budgeted usage - actual usage) x budgeted price

= (2,000 - 2,200) x £1.50

= -200 x £1.50

= £300 (A)

The materials usage variance is adverse because the actual usage is greater than the budgeted usage. The effect will lead to lower profit. This variance might be the responsibility of the production manager. Materials usage variances might arise because materials are:

- wasted in production due to sloppy or careless work;
- wasted because they are inferior;
- used more efficiently because staff take more care in their work;
- wasted due to a machine malfunction.

The direct materials variance for the biscuit manufacturer is £140 (F). It is influenced by both the materials price variance, which is favourable, £440, and the materials usage variance, which is adverse, £300. Notice that the adverse usage variance is outweighed by the favourable price variance.

Question 2.

Armstrong Ltd makes components for games machines in arcades. The company operates from an industrial estate in Slough. It has experienced some problems in recent months due to worn out machinery. An expenditure budget and actual expenditure are shown in Table 5.

Table 6: Budgeted costs and actual costs for Armstrong Ltd

							(£000)
	Jan	Feb	Mar	Apr	May	Jun	Total
Budgeted direct costs	2,300	2,500	2,500	2,600	2,600	2,700	15,200
Budgeted overheads	200	200	200	300	300	300	1,500
Budgeted total cost	2,500	2,700	2,700	2,900	2,900	3,000	16,700
Actual direct costs	2,200	2,450	2,400	2,550	2,600	2,600	14,800
Actual overheads	210	220	190	890	750	320	2,580
Actual total cost	2,410	2,670	2,590	3,440	3,350	2,920	17,380

(a) Calculate the following variances: (i) direct cost (ii) overheads and (iii) total cost.
(b) Analyse the variances calculated in (a).

Direct labour variances

The direct wage bill is the amount of money paid to workers involved in production. A direct labour variance will occur when the budgeted direct wage bill is different from the actual direct wage bill. In the case of the biscuit manufacturer, the budgeted wage rates and actual wage rates, and the budgeted number of labour hours and the actual number of labour hours used in a particular budget period, are shown in Table 7. The planned direct wage bill is £7,500. However, the actual wage bill is £8,320. This results in a £820 adverse variance. The direct labour variance is influenced by two other variances.

Wage rate variances A wage rate variance will result if there is difference between the budgeted wage rate paid to workers and the actual wage rate paid. In the case of the biscuit manufacturer the wage rate variance is:

Wage rate variance = (budgeted wage rate - actual wage rate) x actual hours
= (£5.00 - £5.20) x 1,600
= - £0.20 x 1,600
= £320 (A)

Table 7: Budgeted and actual wage rates and labour hours for the biscuit manufacturer

	Wage rate	No. of labours hours	Direct wage bill
Budgeted	£5.00	1,500	£7,500
Actual	£5.20	1,600	£8,320
Direct labour variance			£820 (A)

The wage rate variance is adverse because the actual wage rate is higher than the budgeted wage rate. The personnel manager may be responsible for this variance. The factors which might influence wage rates could include:

- trade union pressure;
- shortages of skilled labour;
- using a different type of labour;
- government legislation, such as raising the minimum wage.

Labour efficiency variances There will be a labour efficiency variance if there is a difference between the budgeted number of labour hours required in a budget period and the actual number of labour hours used. In the case of the biscuit manufacturer, the labour efficiency variance is:

Labour efficiency variance = (budgeted hours - actual hours) x budgeted wage
= (1,500 - 1,600) x £5.00
= - 100 x £5.00
= £500 (A)

The labour efficiency variance is adverse because the actual number of hours worked is greater than the budgeted number. The production manager may be responsible for this variance. The factors which might influence the number of labour hours used might include:

- the productivity of workers;
- the reliability of machinery used by workers;
- how well trained workers are.

The direct labour variance for the biscuit manufacturer is £820 (A). It is influenced by the wage rate variance, £320(A), and the labour efficiency variance, £500 (A).

Overheads variances

Overheads variances arise when planned overhead costs are different from the actual overhead costs. Overheads are the general expenses incurred by a business. Table 9 shows the annual budgeted and actual overheads for the biscuit manufacturer. The overhead variances are also shown. The total overheads variance is adverse (£4,200). The main reason for this is the adverse distribution variance of £7,000. Some of the overheads in Table 9 do not have any variances. This is because the budgeted figures are exactly the same as the actual figures. This may happen when a business pays some of its bills in advance. For example, a business will normally know what rent is going to be

Question 3.

Wallace & Co. makes a range of swimwear which it sells to retailers in the UK. It operates six monthly budget periods. The direct labour budget is shown in Table 8. The actual figures for 2008 are also shown. Although swimwear is subject to seasonal demand, Wallace & Co. prefers to keep production fairly constant and build up stocks during the winter. This has helped to maintain good industrial relations in the past.

Table 8: Direct labour budget and actual figures for Wallace & Co, 2008

	Jan		Feb		Mar		Apr		May		Jun	
	B	A	B	A	B	A	B	A	B	A	B	A
Labour (hours)	800	**810**	800	**820**	800	**810**	800	**200**	800	**800**	800	**810**
Wage rate	£5	**£5**	£5	**£5**	£5	**£5**	£5	**£5**	£5	**£5**	£5	**£5**
Direct labour costs (£)	4,000	**4,050**	4,000	**4,100**	4,000	**4,050**	4,000	**1,000**	4,000	**4,000**	4,000	**4,050**

B = Budgeted **A** = Actual

(a) For the six month budget period calculate: (i) the wage rate variance; (ii) the labour efficiency variance; (iii) the direct labour variance.
(b) Explain what is likely to have caused the direct labour variance.

charged in the next 12 months. This helps businesses to produce more accurate budgets.

Sometimes a business might separate overheads into fixed and variable costs. A business could then calculate the fixed overhead variance and the variable overhead variance. Overhead variances might be caused by:
- excessive or under-utilisation of a service, such as wasteful or uneconomic use of a service;
- price changes for a service, such as an increase in accountancy fees;
- a change in the nature of a service, such as using oil for heating instead of electricity.

Table 9: Annual budgeted and actual overheads for the biscuit manufacturer

Description	Budgeted	Actual	Variance
Rent	£60,000	£60,000	0
Rates	£5,500	£5,500	0
Insurance	£1,200	£1,300	£100 (A)
Maintenance	£16,000	£15,000	£1,000 (F)
Distribution	£78,000	£85,000	£7,000 (A)
Telephone	£1,700	£1,600	£100 (F)
Administration	£64,000	£62,000	£2,000 (F)
Accountancy fees	£4,500	£4,700	£200 (A)
Depreciation	£20,000	£20,000	0
Total	**£250,900**	**£255,100**	**£4,200 (A)**

Sales margin variances

A sales margin variance will arise if there is either a change in the price charged by the business or a change from the budgeted volume of sales. Table 10 shows budgeted and actual prices and budgeted and actual sales volumes for cases of biscuits in a particular budget period. The budgeted value of sales is £20,000. However, the actual sales value is £21,320. This generates a favourable sales margin variance of £1,320 in this budget period.

The favourable variance shown in Table 10 is influenced by two other variances.

Sales margin price variance This will occur if the actual price charged by a business is different from the budgeted price. For the example above this is:

Sales margin price variance = (actual price - budgeted price) x actual sales
= (£2.60 - £2.50) x 8,200
= £0.10 x 8,200
= £820 (F)

The sales margin price variance is favourable because the actual price charged is higher than the budgeted price. This variance may be the responsibility of the sales or marketing department. Such variances might arise due to:
- the chance to charge premium prices;
- sales in non-planned markets with different prices;
- changes in market conditions, such as a rival leaving the market.

Sales volume variance This will occur if the actual level of sales is different from the budgeted sales. For the biscuit manufacturer this is:

Sales volume variance = (actual sales - budgeted sales) x budgeted price
= (8,200 - 8,000) x £2.50
= 200 x £2.50
= £500 (F)

Table 10: Budgeted and actual prices and sales volumes for cases of biscuits

	Price (per case)	Sales (cases)	Sales value
Budgeted	£2.50	8,000	£20,000
Actual	£2.60	8,200	£21,320
Sales margin variance			£1,320 (F)

Question 4.

Bromford Motors is a large car dealership based in Wimbledon, London. It sells cars for a Japanese car manufacturer. The company operates a very strict budget regime. The five sales staff have a fraction of their pay linked to budget performance. Table 11 shows the budgeted and actual prices and volume of cars sold for a particular budget period.

Table 11: Budgeted and actual prices and sales of cars for Bromford Motors

	Average price	Volume	Sales value
Budgeted	£9,500	250	£2,375,000
Actual	£9,325	269	£2,508,425

(a) For the budget period calculate the: (i) the sales margin price variance; (ii) the sales volume variance; (iii) sales margin variance.
(b) Explain the possible causes of the variances in (a).

The sales volume variance is favourable because the actual number of sales is greater than the budgeted number. This variance is likely to be the responsibility of the marketing department or the sales manager. Sales volume variances may arise due to:

- changes in the state of the economy;
- competitors' actions;
- changes in consumer tastes;
- government action, such as a cut in income tax;
- changes in the quality of the product;
- changes in marketing techniques.

The sales margin variance for the biscuit manufacturer is £1,320 (F). It is influenced by both the sales price margin variance, £820 (F), and sales volume variance, £500 (F).

Cash variances

One variance not shown in Figure 2 is the cash variance. This is because cash and profit are not the same. Cash budgets are concerned with liquidity, not profitability. A cash variance will show the difference between budgeted cash flows and actual cash flows. Table 12 shows the budgeted and actual cash flows for a carpet retailer in a three month budget period. The cash variances are also shown. A favourable cash variance arises when more cash flows in than was planned and if cash outflows are lower than planned. An adverse cash variance is caused by more cash flowing out than budgeted or less cash flowing in. In Table 12 all the closing balance cash variances are adverse. This means that the amount of cash actually left at the end of each month was lower than budgeted. For example, in January it was planned to have £5,500 at the end of the month. However, the actual closing balance was £3,900 giving an adverse variance of £1,600.

Cash variances can be caused by many factors. Some examples include:

- lower or higher than expected cash sales;
- customers not settling their accounts on time;
- unexpected costs;
- unexpected inflation.

Using variances for decision making

The final stage in budgetary control is the analysis of variances. It is important to identify the reasons why variances have occurred. If variances are adverse it will be necessary to take action to ensure that adverse variances are avoided in future. If variances are favourable the business can learn from understanding the reasons why this has occurred and can introduce strategies and systems to help sustain performance improvements in the future.

When making decisions about how the business should be run, information about the causes of variances will be very helpful. For example, if a business has an adverse cost variance, it might discover that the cause was higher prices charged by suppliers. The business might then decide to look for new

Table 12: Budgeted and actual cash flows for a carpet retailer (£)

	JANUARY			FEBRUARY			MARCH		
	Budgeted	Actual	Variance	Budgeted	Actual	Variance	Budgeted	Actual	Variance
Cash receipts	25,000	25,600	600F	26,000	27,100	1,100F	30,000	29,800	200A
Cash inflow	25,000	25,600	600F	26,000	27,100	1,100F	30,000	29,800	200A
Purchases	15,000	17,000	2,000A	15,000	16,000	1,000A	20,000	22,000	2,000A
Wages	6,500	6,600	100A	6,500	6,700	200A	8,000	7,600	400F
Overheads	2,000	2,100	100A	2,000	1,800	200F	2,500	2,000	500F
Cash outflow	23,500	25,700	2,200A	23,500	24,500	1,000A	30,500	31,600	1,100A
Net cash flow	1,500	(100)	1,600A	2,500	2,600	100F	(500)	(1,800)	1,300A
Opening balance	4,000	4,000	0	5,500	3,900	1,600A	8,000	6,500	1,500A
Closing balance	5,500	3,900	1,600A	8,000	6,500	1,500A	7,500	4,700	2,800A

suppliers. A favourable sales revenue variance might be the result of an effective advertising campaign. The business might decide to make more use of the same or similar campaigns in the future. Variance analysis can help business decision-makers because of the information they provide about financial outcomes and their causes.

Zero-based budgeting

The financial information used in most budgets is based on **historical** data. For example, the cost of materials in this year's production budget may be based on last year's figure, with perhaps an allowance for inflation. Production and manufacturing costs, such as labour, raw materials and overheads, are relatively easy to value and tend to be controlled using methods such as standard costing.

However, in some areas of business it is not so easy to quantify costs. Examples might be certain marketing, administration or computer services costs. Where costs cannot be justified then no money is allocated in the budget for those costs. This is known as ZERO-BASED BUDGETING (ZBB) or ZERO BUDGETING. A manager must show that a particular item of spending generates an adequate amount of benefit in relation to the general objectives of the business in order for money to be allocated in a budget.

This approach is different to the common practice of extrapolating from past costs. It encourages the regular evaluation of costs and helps to minimise unnecessary purchases. The concept of **opportunity cost** is linked to ZBB. Opportunity cost is the cost of the next best alternative. When choices are made, businesses try to minimise the opportunity cost. ZBB also involves a cautious approach to spending, so that costs are minimised. Both approaches include an element of 'value for money'.

The main advantages of ZBB are that:

- the allocation of resources should be improved;
- a questioning attitude is developed which will help to reduce unnecessary costs and eliminate inefficient practices;
- staff motivation might improve because evaluation skills are practised and a greater knowledge of the firm's operations might develop;
- it encourages managers to look for alternatives.

ZBB also has some disadvantages.

- It is time consuming because the budgeting process involves the collection and analysis of quite detailed information so that spending decisions can be made.
- Skilful decision making is required. Such skills may not be available in the organisation. In addition, decisions may be influenced by subjective opinions.
- It threatens the status quo. This might adversely affect motivation.
- Managers may not be prepared to justify spending on certain costs. Money, therefore, may not be allocated to spending which could benefit the business.

To deal with these possible problems, a business might give each department a 'base' budget of, say, 50 per cent. Departments could then be invited to bid for increased expenditure on a ZBB basis.

Benefits of using budgets

Monitoring performance Budgets allow managers to monitor the performance of a business as a whole, as well as different sections. For example, analysing departmental cost variances may allow a business to find out why certain departments are incurring high costs. Alternatively, it allows businesses to identify good practice and discover why some costs are lower.

Identifying factors affecting performance Prompt variance analysis allows managers to assess whether variances are caused by internal or external factors. Once causes have been traced, they can be corrected.

Improved plans in future By identifying variances and their causes managers may be able to produce more accurate budgets in future. This will aid planning and perhaps improve the performance of the business.

Improved accountability Budgetary control in general helps to improve accountability in businesses. It can also be linked to performance-related pay. For example, budget holders may receive a bonus payment at the end of the budget period if they can show favourable variances. Consequently motivation in a business can be improved.

Drawbacks of using budgets

Motivation In some businesses, workers are left out of the planning process. If workers are not consulted about the budget, it will be more difficult to use that budget to motivate them. Budgets which are unrealistic can also fail to motivate staff.

Manipulation Budgets can be manipulated by managers. For example, a departmental manager might have great influence over those people co-ordinating and setting budgets. The manager may be able to arrange a budget which is easy to achieve and makes the department look successful. But the budget may not help the business achieve its objectives.

Rigidity Budgets can sometimes constrain business activities. For instance, departments within a business may have different views about when it is best to replace vehicles. The more often vehicles are replaced, the higher the cost. However, the newer the vehicle, the lower the maintenance cost and the less likely it is to be off the road for repairs. The budget may be set so that older vehicles have to be kept rather than replaced. But this may lead to customer dissatisfaction and lost orders because deliveries are unreliable.

Short-termism Some managers might be too focused on the current budget. They might take actions that undermine the future performance of the business just to meet current budget targets. For example, to keep labour costs down in the current budget period, the manager of a supermarket might reduce staffing on customer service. This might save costs now, but it could lead to customers drifting away over time due to poor service. Consequently the long-term performance of the business would suffer.

KNOWLEDGE

1. What is meant by financial management?
2. Describe the three steps in budgetary control.
3. Explain how a variance is calculated.
4. What is meant by an adverse variance?
5. State two possible causes of a favourable sales revenue variance.
6. State two possible causes of an adverse cost variance.
7. State four benefits of using budgets.
8. What might cause a direct materials variance?
9. What is the difference between the wage rate variance and the labour efficiency variance?
10. What might cause a direct labour variance?
11. Why might some overhead variances be 0?
12. Explain the difference between the sales margin price variance and the sales volume variance.

KEYTERMS

Budgetary control or Budgeting – a business system which involves making future plans, comparing the actual results with the planned results and then investigating causes of any differences.

Variance – the difference between actual financial outcomes and those which were budgeted.

Variance analysis – the process of calculating variances and attempting to identify their causes.

Zero-based budgeting or zero budgeting – a system of budgeting where no money is allocated for costs or spending unless they can be justified by the fundholder (they are given a zero value).

Case Study: Cynplex.com

Cynplex.com, founded and owned by Josh Howarth, develops software for e-transactions including payments, document distribution and account verification. Cynplex.com, based in Glasgow, has a good proportion of the UK market for electronic funds transfer with over 10,000 business customers. Cynplex.com's software provides a range of integrated e-business solutions for businesses of any type and size. The software is designed to improve efficiency by reducing the time and expense of manual day-to-day business processes. The products include:

- payment solutions – for processing transactions such as payroll and supplier payments;
- electronic data interchange – for streamlined communications between trading partners;
- collections management – for managing multiple Direct Debit and credit card transactions;
- e-document distribution – for fast, efficient distribution of financial documents such as purchase orders and invoices.

Josh has grown the business successfully since it was setup five years ago. He employs an accountant who is responsible for the financial management of the business. He uses variance analysis to monitor income, expenditure and profit. Some financial information is shown in Table 13 for Cynplex.com.

Table 13: Financial information for Cynplex.com

			(£000)
	2007	**2006**	**2005**
Budgeted income	4,500	3,800	3,200
Budgeted expenditure	3,900	3,350	2,800
Budgeted profit	600	450	400
	2007	**2006**	**2005**
Actual income	4,890	4,010	3,600
Actual expenditure	4,050	3,400	3,100
Actual profit	840	610	500

(a) Using this case as an example, explain what is meant by a favourable variance. (3 marks)

(b) Calculate the income, expenditure and profit variances for Cynplex.com for each year. (9 marks)

(c) Why is the profit variance probably the most important of all? (4 marks)

(d) Analyse the variances calculated in (c). (10 marks)

(e) Josh is hoping to float the company on the stock market in order to raise finance to break into overseas markets. How might the profit variances influence this decision? (10 marks)

(f) Evaluate the drawbacks to Cynplex.com of using budgets as a means of financial management. (14 marks).

43 The role and objectives of accounting

Business transactions

Business activity involves purchasing resources, such as raw materials, labour and machinery, and selling goods or services that have been produced using these resources. The purchase of resources from suppliers and the sale of products to customers are examples of BUSINESS TRANSACTIONS. Other examples include borrowing money from a bank and the payment of taxes. For a small business, such as Robinson's fish and chip shop, examples of business transactions might include:

- the purchase of potatoes from a wholesaler for £250;
- the sale of fish and chips to a customer for £5.30;
- the payment of £140 interest to a bank;
- the sale of a portion of chips and curry sauce to a customer for £3.90;
- a payment of £220 to an employee.

It is important for a business to keep accurate records of these transactions. Every single transaction should be recorded. In this example the sales made by the fish and chip shop are likely to be recorded on a till roll. The value of purchases may be written in a book. During the year such a business may be involved in possibly thousands of individual transactions.

In contrast, for a very large business such as BT, the number of transactions that take place in a year is immense. Every telephone call made using the BT network is recorded as a separate transaction. Such transactions are recorded electronically and their value is calculated by computer. BT's customers receive quarterly statements summarising these transactions. BT must also record details of its expenditure, such as payments to its employees and purchases of telecommunications equipment.

Figure 1: Stages in the accounting process

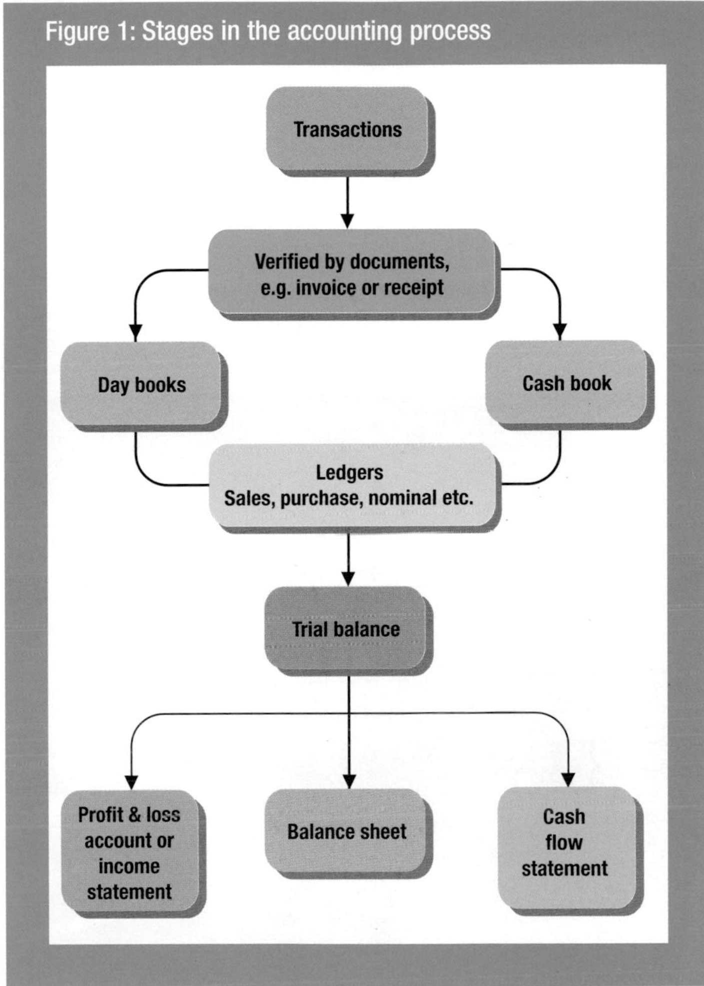

Recording business transactions and the accounting process

BOOKKEEPERS are responsible for recording business transactions. They play an important role in the ACCOUNTING PROCESS. This involves recording, classifying and summarising business transactions. The aim of the process is to generate useful financial information that can be communicated to a range of users such as business stakeholders and the media. Details of all users are discussed below. Many sole traders keep their own records because they cannot afford bookkeepers. As a firm grows, it may become cost effective to take on a bookkeeper, part-time perhaps. In large businesses, with their own finance departments, bookkeepers will work under the supervision of accountants. It is also likely that most of their work will be done on a computer.

Figure 1 illustrates the stages in the accounting process. When a transaction takes place, it should be verified by a **document** – an invoice, receipt or cheque stub perhaps. From these documents entries are made in the company's books. The first entries are likely to be made in the books of **prime entry**, where details of all transactions may be recorded almost as they happen. The **day books** will contain records of purchases and sales, while the **cash book** lists the flows of money into and out of the business. At the end of the month, entries in these books will be totalled and recorded in ledgers. The main purpose of these subsidiary books is to avoid overloading the **ledgers**.

Ledgers form the basis of any book-keeping system. A ledger contains details of individual business accounts. The **sales ledger** records transactions with customers and the **purchase ledger** records those with suppliers. The accounts of customers and suppliers are called personal accounts. All others are impersonal and are recorded in the nominal ledger. The headings in the nominal ledger might include:

- the wages account, which records the wages paid to employees;
- the purchase account, which records all business purchases from suppliers;

- the sales account, which records all business sales.

From time to time a company may wish to check that all previous entries were made correctly. This can be done by producing a **trial balance**. Finally, various accounts can be produced using the information gathered from book-keeping. These are outlined below.

What are accounts?

All businesses produce ACCOUNTS. These are statements that provide financial information about a business. A statement might include information about the revenue, costs and profit that a business records during the year. This is called a **profit and loss account** or **income statement**. Another statement, called a **balance sheet**, provides information about debts, capital and the assets of a business. Finally, a **cash flow statement** shows the flows of cash into and out of the business during the year. Table 1 shows a simplified profit and loss account or income statement for J Conrad, a sole trader who is a manufacturer of leather shoes.

Table 1: Simple profit and loss account for J Conrad 2008

J Conrad
Profit and loss account 2008

	£	£
Sales revenue		201,511
Cost of sales		125,870
Gross profit		**75, 641**
Wages	18,300	
Rent	20,000	
Heat & Light	5,900	
Other overhead costs	25,320	
		69,520
Net profit		**6,121**

What does the account show?

- That £201,511 was generated from the sale of shoes during the year.
- A total of £125,870 was paid for costs of sales, including materials and other production costs.
- The profit after the costs of sales are deducted is £75,641.
- Other costs included £20,000 for rent and £5,900 in heat and light. The total of these overhead costs during the year were £69,520.
- The net profit made during the year was £6,121. This is calculated by subtracting all costs, £125,870 and £69,520 (i.e. £195,390) from the sales revenue of £201,511.

Businesses produce accounts because they are legally obliged. For example, a sole trader will need information from accounts to help complete a self-assessment declaration for the Inland Revenue. This is used to calculate how much income tax the sole trader must pay. Larger companies need to produce accounts to provide information for external users such as shareholders and creditors. Accounts may also be used internally. For example, they might be used by managers to assess the performance of the business. The use of accounts made by all stakeholders and other users is discussed in the next section.

Who uses accounts? – internal needs

Figure 2 shows the groups that may need the financial information produced by a business. The users are divided into two groups. Internal users are those people within the business.

Question 1.

Isabel Ortiz runs a music business and is also a professional musician. She makes part of her income from hiring her services to touring bands who want a musician to play on a few songs, but not to be a permanent band member. Sometimes she is paid in a lump sum after a gig. Other times she is paid regularly over a period of time.

Another part of her business involves, selling instruments to collectors. She is a regular visitor to the USA and she has a number of contacts there who can find her old instruments from people's houses. They try to hunt down 'finds' in attics or garages that might be worth something. Isabel can fix these up and then sell them to shops or to specialist collectors.

A final part of her services is the teaching of music. She will often buy in music notation paper for her students, reeds for instruments and DVDs and videos to show playing techniques.

(a) Identify the business transactions that take place in Isabel Ortiz's music business.

(b) Explain why the business might find it difficult to keep accurate records of transactions.

Figure 2: The need for financial information

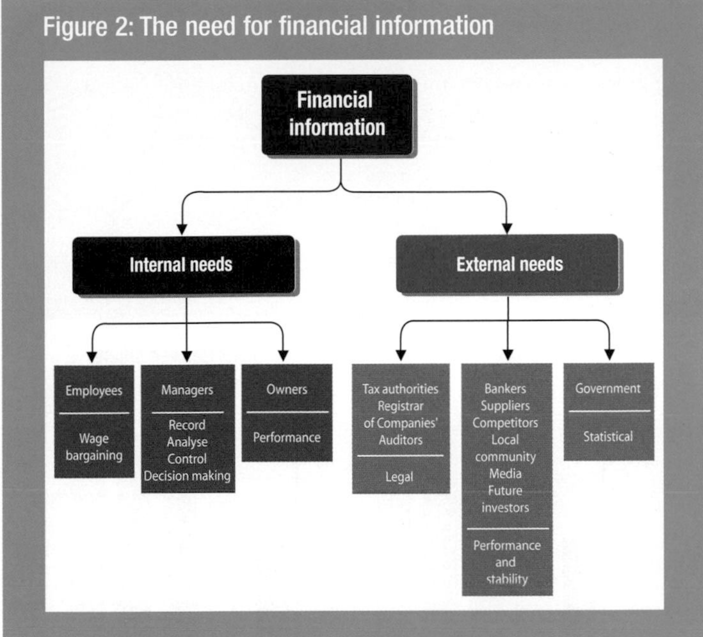

Management The main users of financial information are likely to be management. Up-to-date and accurate financial data will help to improve the running of the business. It can also be used for a number of other activities.

- **Recording.** The values of all of a company's resources and lists of its transactions can be recorded by hand or on computer. The records can then be used to show company assets, liabilities and capital, for example. Here it is enough to say that assets are the resources of the business, such as equipment, liabilities are amounts of money owed by the business, such as a bank loan, and capital is the money introduced into the business by the owners.
- **Analysis and evaluation.** It is possible to evaluate the performance of the company, make comparisons with competitors and keep a record of the firm's progress over a period of time.
- **Control.** Financial information helps the control of money flowing in and out of the business. This becomes more important as the firm grows and the amounts of money used increase.
- **Decision making.** One of the most important reasons why businesses need financial information is to help managers make decisions. Financial information is quantitative data which is very useful when making decisions. For example, managers might use cost information contained in profit and loss accounts to help identify targets for cost-cutting in the organisation. Financial information might be used to help decide whether part of the business should be sold off. Finally, managers might use financial information in the balance sheet to help decide on a future funding strategy for the business. Financial information is likely to be helpful when making a very wide range of business decisions.

Employees Employees are another group of people who might need financial information. During wage bargaining, information about the profitability, liquidity and financial prospects of the business could be used to decide if management can meet a particular wage demand.

Owners The owners (internal or external, or both) will have a vested interest in the company's financial position. They will naturally assess its performance. For example, shareholders will decide whether any dividend is satisfactory or not. On the other hand, a sole trader might look at the annual profit and decide whether or not they could earn more from another activity. Owners might also use accounts in a business plan. For example, if a group of entrepreneurs are planning to set up a new business, they might produce a business plan when applying for a bank loan. In that plan the bank might want to see some **projected accounts**. These are accounts based on financial information, such as costs and revenue, that the owners plan to achieve in a future trading period.

Who uses accounts? – external needs

Certain external parties, from time to time, need financial information about a company. Companies are legally obliged to provide information to the following institutions.

Tax authorities The Inland Revenue may require proof of income when assessing the tax liabilities of businesses and business owners. Accounts can be used to provide confirmation of income. Customs and Excise may require access to business accounts when calculating VAT and excise duties owed by businesses. The Department for Social Security may require accounts to check whether a business has paid enough National Insurance contributions.

Auditors Every year the accounts of limited companies have to be checked by an independent firm of accountants and registered auditors. The process of checking the authenticity of accounts is called AUDITING, explained in the next section.

Registrar of Companies All limited companies have to register with the Registrar of Companies when they are formed. One of the conditions of registration is that they submit a copy of their final accounts every year. Copies of these accounts are made available to the general public on demand.

A number of external groups are interested in the performance and financial stability of businesses.

Bankers When deciding whether to lend money to a business, bank managers will want to base their decisions on a range of up-to-date information. Financial information, such as accounts, provide managers with an insight about whether a business is capable of meeting loan and interest payments. Existing businesses will probably have to submit accounts from several years trading. New businesses may have to provide projected accounts.

Question 2.

Next is a UK-based retailer offering stylish, good quality products in clothing, footwear, accessories and home products. Next distributes through three main channels:

- Next Retail – a chain of around 480 stores in the UK and Eire;
- Next Directory – a direct mail catalogue and transactional website with more than 2 million active customers;
- Next International – a chain of more than 140 stores overseas.

Next also has other businesses such as Next Sourcing, which designs, sources and buys Next and Lime branded products; and Ventura, which provides customer services management to clients wishing to outsource their customer contact administration and fulfilment activities. Next has enjoyed a great deal of success in recent years. Figure 3 shows some financial information for Next.

Source: adapted from Next, Annual Report and Accounts, 2007.

(a) Explain how (i) the media; (ii) potential investors might use the financial information in the case.

(b) In your view, based on the financial information in the case, might investors be interested in buying shares in Next?

(c) How might Next make use of IT in their accounting process?

Figure 3: Financial information for Next plc

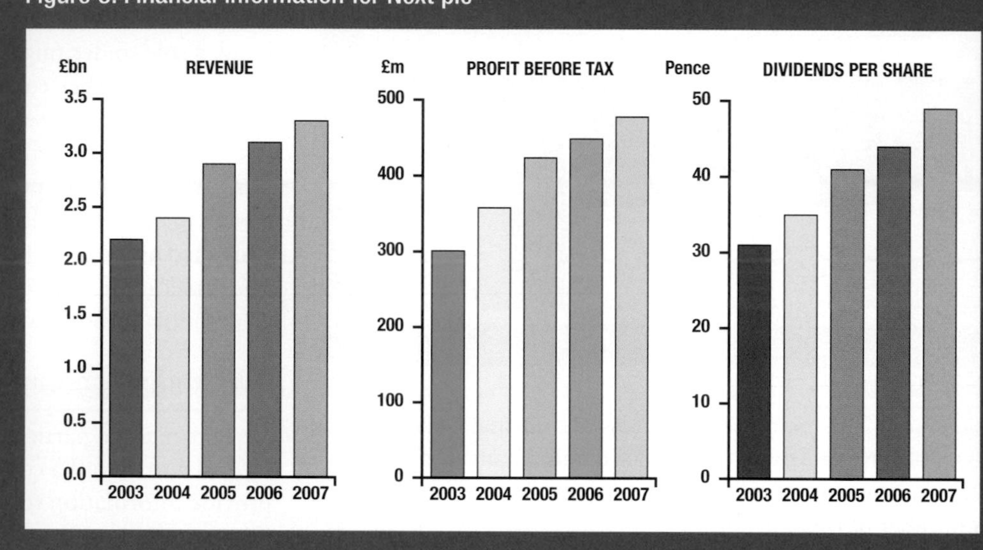

Suppliers Many businesses buy goods and services using trade credit. However, before a supplier allows a new customer to buy on credit a credit search may be undertaken. This involves analysing a range of information relating to the financial circumstances of the business. Accounts may provide suppliers with some useful information regarding the ability to pay for goods bought on credit.

Competitors The accounts of limited companies are available for public scrutiny. Therefore competitors may wish to analyse them in order to make comparisons. For example, a supermarket chain may look at its competitor's accounts to see whether their turnover and profit has grown as fast. Also, if a competitor is contemplating an aggressive takeover it can use the information to help make a decision.

Local community Sometimes people might show an interest in a business that is located in their community. For example, the local community might use accounts to see if the company has any expansion plans that might create jobs in the area. Quite often the well-being of local businesses is vital for the prosperity of local economies.

The media Business and commerce is often the subject of newspaper, TV and radio reports. There are specialists that focus on business information. For example, *The Financial Times* is a newspaper devoted almost entirely to business and financial reports. Also, *Working Lunch* on BBC, provides daily updates on company news and financial markets. Company accounts give valuable information to journalists and producers when writing their reports and making programmes. Some sections of the media provide information services on personal finance. Company accounts might be used to help give audiences and readers advice on buying shares for example.

Investors and financial analysts The accounts of public limited companies are produced mainly to inform shareholders about the progress and performance of the company. However, accounts are also used by potential investors and financial analysts. They might be used to help make decisions when purchasing shares in different companies. For example, pension funds and insurance companies employ financial analysts to manage the money collected from pension contributions and insurance premiums. A lot of this money is invested in shares and analysts will use accounts to help them decide which companies to invest in.

Government The government may have an interest in a company's financial information. The Office for National Statistics gathers a wide range of business and financial information which it makes available to the public. Some of the data will be extracted from company accounts. It is usually summarised and published in journals such as the Annual Abstract of Statistics. This information is used by the government to monitor the progress of the economy and help evaluate the success of its economic policies. It might also be used by students, for example, when doing research.

Who produces accounts?

Accountants are responsible for supplying and using financial information. They are employed by businesses specialising in accountancy, or by large firms which have their own financial departments. Accountancy specialists sell their services to small and medium-sized firms as well as self-employed individuals. They use the transactions recorded by these groups to produce final accounts. They may also advise clients on various financial matters such as taxation and investment.

Another function of these specialists is auditing. Businesses which produce their own final accounts must by law have them checked for authenticity by an independent firm of accountants. This audit is performed annually.

Accountants also carry out internal audits of businesses. These are audits which check that internal procedures are being carried out correctly. For example, a business may audit its pension fund arrangements to prevent misuse of funds.

There are two branches of accounting – FINANCIAL ACCOUNTING and MANAGEMENT ACCOUNTING. The role of financial accountants is to make sure that a company's accounts are a 'true and fair' record of its transactions. They supervise the book keeping process, which involves recording the value of every single business transaction. From time to time they summarise these records and convert them into statements which may be used by those parties described earlier in the unit.

Financial accountants are concerned with the past. They need to know about accounting techniques, company law, auditing requirements and taxation law.

Management accountants are more concerned with the future. They do need knowledge of accounting concepts and methods, but they also require training in economics and management science. Such accountants are involved in decision making and problem solving in the business. They are responsible for producing cost and financial data, interpreting financial statements and preparing forecasts and budgets. They act as 'information servants' to the management team, but also help in planning and control.

A subsidiary of management accounting is cost accounting. Cost accountants carry out detailed costing projects. This involves working out the cost of particular business activities, such as calculating the cost of opening a new store, launching a new product or changing working practices.

Business statements

At the end of a trading year all businesses produce final accounts. A profit and loss account or income statement and a balance sheet generally form the basis of these accounts, although public limited companies publish a full annual report which contains a wider range of financial statements and reports.

Balance sheet A balance sheet provides information about the company's funds and how they are used in the business. It lists the assets, liabilities and capital of the business and, to some extent, shows the wealth of the company. A balance sheet describes the financial position of a business at a particular point in time.

Profit and loss account or income statement The profit and loss account provides a summary of the year's trading activities, stating the revenue from sales (the turnover), business costs, profit/loss and how the profit is used.

Cash flow statement Certain companies are required to produce cash flow statements in their accounts. A cash flow statement shows the flows of cash into and out of a business in a trading year.

Notes to the accounts The balance sheet and profit and loss account show summarised information. 'Notes to the accounts' are a more detailed analysis of some entries in these statements.

Directors' report This statement, written by the directors, is required by law. It contains information which might not be shown in other financial statements, such as the number of employees, changes of personnel on the board of directors and any special circumstances arising.

Chairperson's statement One of the chairperson's roles is to communicate with the shareholders. This can be done by making a statement in the annual report. The chairperson discusses the company's general performance and comments on events during the trading year which might be of interest to the shareholders. Future prospects are also discussed and shareholders are encouraged to remain loyal to the company.

Auditor's report Auditors must make a brief report to confirm that the accounts give a 'true and fair view' of the firm's financial position, assuming, of course, that they do!

Statistics Companies often include tables and graphs in their annual report. They can be used to illustrate trends and comparisons. They might show turnover, profit, dividends or earnings per share, for example.

Finally, limited companies are required to publish financial information by law. There are a number of rules which outline the way accounts should be presented and what sort of financial information should be included. This is discussed in more detail in the unit on accounting concepts.

The use of IT in accounts

Many businesses now use information technology (IT) in their accounts department. A number of companies, such as Sage, provide fully integrated software packages which handle the whole accounting function. Such packages are very sophisticated and, provided details of all transactions are entered into the

Question 3.

Figure 4: A job advertisement

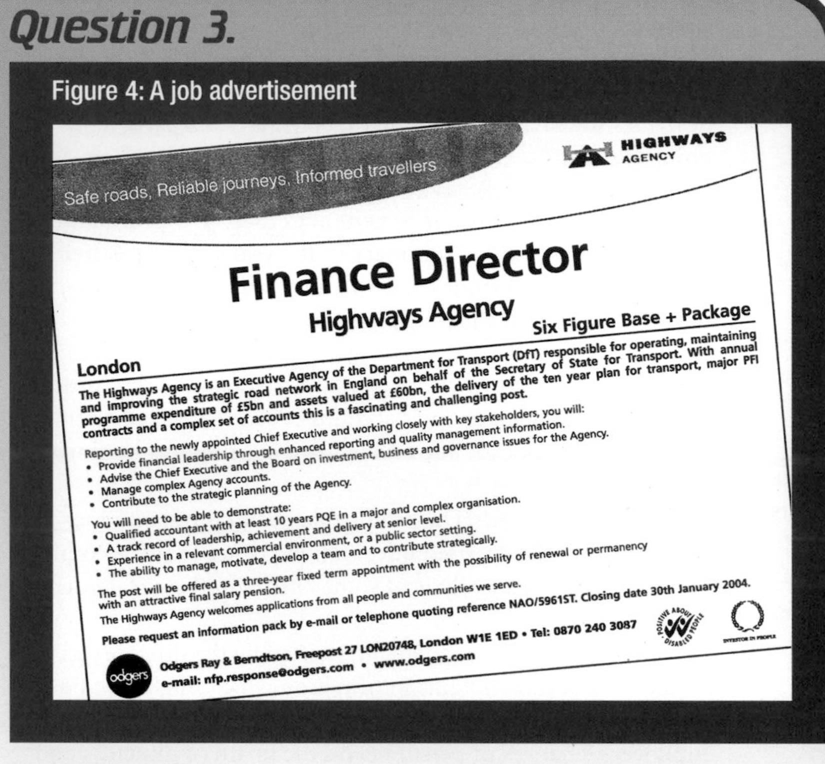

Source: Highways Agency.

(a) What evidence is there in the advert to suggest that the Highways Agency is trying to recruit a management accountant?

system, they are capable of numerous tasks. These might include:

- keeping records of transactions with all customers showing up-to-date balances on all accounts;
- keeping records of transactions with all suppliers showing up to date balances on all accounts;
- producing daily, weekly, monthly or annual sales figures;
- producing an aged debtors list;
- producing an aged creditors list;
- producing trial balances;
- producing profit and loss accounts;
- producing balance sheets;
- calculating staff wages and producing wages slips;
- producing stock details.

Advantages of computerised systems

There are certain advantages to a business in having computerised accounting systems.

- **Speed.** Large numbers of transactions can be processed much more quickly in computerised than in manual systems.
- **Capacity.** Some businesses conduct billions of transactions each year. If records of these transactions were stored in manual systems a huge quantity of resources would be required. In addition, access to information stored in a computer is very easy. From the billions of transactions that might be recorded, an operator can instantly call up details of any one single transaction.
- **Efficiency.** Because large volumes of data can be processed quickly, computer systems require a smaller workforce than manual systems. Therefore the cost of collecting and recording transactions can be reduced.
- **Data handling.** Information can be input and accessed from different locations around the country or the world. For example, a supermarket chain might have several hundred branches in the UK, each with twenty or more checkouts. The sales information from all of these sources eventually goes to one central processing unit where it is sorted and stored in the appropriate accounts. Information from every store can be retrieved and monitored from head office. Electronic data exchange may be used to transmit information in this way.
- **User friendly.** The design of accounting programmes means that staff do not need a detailed knowledge of bookkeeping and accounts to be able to input and retrieve data. Consequently, training costs could be lower and a business might employ non-specialist staff in the accounts department to keep labour costs down.
- **Accuracy.** Computerised systems are more accurate than manual systems when processing data. Partly this is because computers do not become distracted or tired when performing large numbers of routine operations.
- **Security.** By using a system of passwords, it is possible to restrict access. This prevents the unauthorised use of sensitive information. Intranets, which allow one computer to communicate with another like the larger Internet, may be also used by larger businesses. However, with intranets the communication is confined to computers within a business, therefore, outsiders are prevented access.

Disadvantages of computerised systems

The widespread use of computerised accounting systems suggest that the benefits outweigh the drawbacks. However, there are certain disadvantages.

- **Cost.** The cost of purchasing and then upgrading computer hardware and software can be expensive. Staff training costs can also be high. It is sometimes necessary to employ specialist IT staff to monitor the system. This adds to the cost.
- **Technical problems.** There is a wide range of computer systems and it is not always easy for a business to choose the most appropriate package. If an incorrect choice is made the mistake may be costly. Problems often arise when

a new computer system is installed. It might not run smoothly because of 'bugs' in the system. Other difficulties arise if a 'virus' is downloaded from the Internet or via an email, or if inexperienced staff cause the system to crash. When this occurs, it can lead to problems and delays to staff, customers and suppliers.

- **Industrial relations.** The use of computerised systems may cause industrial relations problems. If staff see technology as a threat to their jobs or status, they might not co-operate with management when systems are installed This can result in delays and friction between managers and employees.
- **Security.** Although security can be increased by the use of passwords, employees or outsiders might be able to 'hack' into the system. This unauthorised access might be used by a disgruntled employee to sabotage the business, or by a competitor who hopes to gain an advantage.
- **Operator error.** Computer systems are only effective if data is inputted correctly. If inaccurate data is entered, the reports that are generated will also be inaccurate, misleading and of little use. This problem is sometimes described as 'GIGO', ie garbage in, garbage out.

Social auditing

For many businesses social responsibility is becoming a more important issue. In an effort to become better corporate citizens some businesses carry out a SOCIAL AUDIT. This is a way of measuring and reporting on an company's social and ethical performance. It is a move away from the traditional method of evaluating performance which measures accounting information such as revenue, profit or dividends. Businesses that undertake social audits are accountable to a wider range of stakeholders and are also committed to following the audit's recommendations. Social accounting may look at the firm's impact on the environment, the workforce, suppliers or the wider community.

Social accounting might use the following process.

- Identify the stakeholders who are affected by its activities. These could be employees, suppliers, customers or local communities.
- Select a range of indicators that can be used to measure social performance. For example, to assess the impact a firm has on the environment it might measure factory emissions, water usage, fuel usage, waste generation or the use of recycled materials. Some businesses set targets which they hope to achieve.
- Gather information and report on the company's performance. This is an ongoing process and involves monitoring the indicators selected in the previous stage. Both quantitative and qualitative data may be gathered.
- Arrange for a social audit to be carried out. This might be done internally by assessing whether performance targets have been met from the previous year. Alternatively a business might employ an independent social auditing consultant. This acts as a safeguard against misleading information and can protect the interests of stakeholders.

Critics argue that social accounting is just a public relations exercise and a means of improving its corporate image. However, companies that have adopted social accounting, such as BP, Shell, the Co-op and Body Shop, would probably say that it helps them to satisfy the needs of a wider range of stakeholders. It makes them aware of the impact the business has on society.

KEYTERMS

Accounts – financial statements that provide information about a firm's financial circumstances.
Accounting process – the process of recording, classifying, and summarising business transactions with the aim of providing useful financial information for a range of users.
Auditing – an accounting procedure which checks thoroughly the authenticity of a company's accounts.
Bookkeepers – people involved in the recording and classifying of business transactions.
Business transactions – an event that affects the finances of a business, for example, the purchase of resources from suppliers and the sale of products to customers.
Financial accounting – the preparation of company accounts from business records.
Management accounting – the preparation of financial statements, reports and data for use by managers.
Social auditing – collecting information and reporting back on the impact of the business on society and the environment.

KNOWLEDGE

1. Why is it important for managers to have access to information?
2. Which users have a legal right of access to accounts?
3. State the internal users of accounts.
4. How might the media use accounts?
5. Explain the importance of accounts to shareholders and potential investors.
6. What might be the role of a management accountant in business?
7. State five advantages and five disadvantages of using IT in accounts.
8. Explain the significance of the term GIGO when using computers in accounts?
9. Explain how a business might undertake a social audit.
10. List the financial statements that might appear in the Annual Report and Accounts of a public limited company.

Case Study: easyJet

Based at Luton Airport, easyJet is one of the largest low-fare airlines in Europe. It operates domestic and international scheduled services on over 250 routes between around 80 key European cities. In 2007 easyjet carried over 37 million passengers. It is committed to the provision of low cost 'no frills' air services. easyJet is able to offer cheap flights because it keeps costs down. For example, to cut administration costs nearly all bookings are processed automatically online. In 2006 the company increased its revenue by 21 per cent to £1.6 billion and profit before tax by 56 per cent to £129 million. Some financial information is shown below.

Source: adapted from easyJet, *Annual Report and Accounts*, 2006

Figure 5: Revenue, profit and net cash flow for easyJet 2002 - 2006

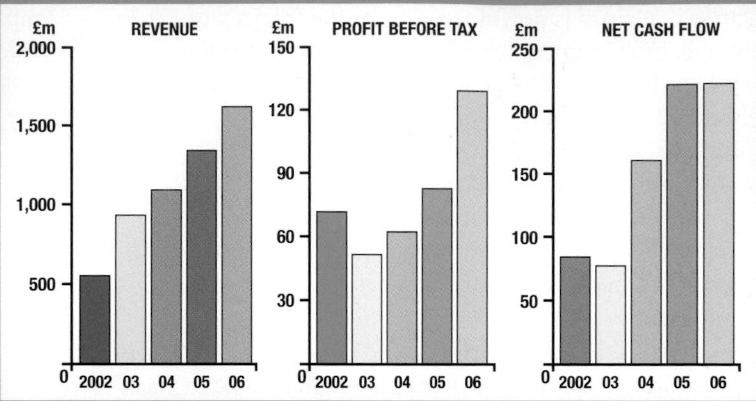

Table 2: A summarised income statement for easyJet

	2006 £m	2005 £m
Revenue	1,619.70	1,341.40
Operating costs	1,341.20	1,134.90
Depreciation and leasing costs	160.7	140.3
Operating profit	117.8	66.2
Interest and other financing income	35.4	27.2
Interest and other financing charges	-24.1	-10.9
Profit before tax*	129.2	82.6

* Also after share of profit after tax of associate (£0.1m)

Table 3: An analysis of operating costs for easyJet

	2006 £m	2005 £m
Ground handling charges, *including salaries*	144.1	130.5
Airport charges	258.4	230.1
Fuel	387.8	260.2
Navigation charges	121.2	108.6
Crew costs, including training	160	136.2
Maintenance	109.5	119.2
Advertising	38.2	32.8
Merchant fees and incentive pay	17.9	15.6
Aircraft and passenger insurance	15.8	19.3
Other costs	88.3	82.4
	1341.2	**1134.9**

Figure 7: Extracts from easyJet's Annual Report

Health and safety Safety is the number one priority for the business. easyJet aims to provide a safe and efficient work environment for all its people. Beyond those engaged in office-based work, the large majority of people are aircrew. They have been one of the mainstays to easyJet's success, giving a great deal of effort to their role. easyJet is continuing to invest substantial effort and money into rostering practices and systems. easyJet is committed to the development of an industry leading Fatigue Risk Management System (FRMS) for its pilots, as an integral part of the airline's safety management processes. The aim of the programme is to detect any sources of fatigue risk within the airline operation and act upon them.

Ethical easyJet is committed to the highest standards of corporate behaviour from its Directors and employees. easyJet requires all of its people to perform their duties with efficiency and diligence and to always behave to customers and other people alike with courtesy and decorum. easyJet's procurement process has strong controls to ensure that any dealings are open and transparent, and avoids any suspicion of conflicts of interest. In particular, easyJet has specific clauses in each employee's contract of employment, which set tight rules in respect of accepting gifts or gratuities.

Figure 6: Extracts from easyJet's corporate and social responsibility report

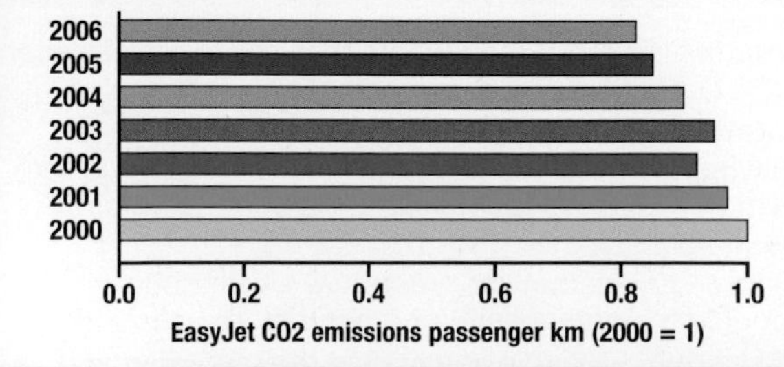

(a) Briefly outline the role of a financial accountant employed at easyJet. (6 marks)

(b) How might the financial information in Figure 5 and Table 2 be used by competitors? (8 marks)

(c) How might the financial information in Table 3 be used by the management at easyJet? (8 marks)

(d) To what extent does easyJet carry out social accounting? (10 marks)

(e) Discuss the advantages and disadvantages to easyJet of using IT in their accounting process. (16 marks)

44 Balance sheets

Using financial data to measure and assess performance

Many of the performance indicators used by businesses are financial in nature. This means they are measured in **money** terms. In order to compile a range of performance indicators such as sales revenue, profit, return on capital employed, working capital and dividend payments, it is necessary to gather appropriate financial data. One way in which businesses gather such data is to prepare financial statements and **accounts**. Financial statements such as **balance sheets** and **profit and loss accounts** or **income statements** are important examples. ACCOUNTING is 'the process of identifying, measuring and communicating information to permit informed judgments and decisions by users of the information' according to the American Accounting Association.

Balance sheets

What does a BALANCE SHEET show? It is like a photograph of the financial position of a business at a particular point in time. The balance sheet contains information about the assets of a business, its **liabilities** and its **capital**.

- ASSETS are the resources that a business owns and uses. Assets are usually divided into current assets and fixed assets. Current assets are used up in production, such as stocks of raw materials. They can also be money owed to a business by debtors. Fixed assets, such as machinery, are used again and again over a period of time.
- LIABILITIES are the debts of the business, ie what it owes to other businesses, individuals and institutions. Liabilities are a source of funds for a business. They might be short term, such as an overdraft, or long term, such as a mortgage or a long-term bank loan.
- CAPITAL is the money introduced by the owners of the business, for example when they buy shares. It is another source of funds and can be used to purchase assets.

Figure 1: The assets, liabilities and capital of a private limited company

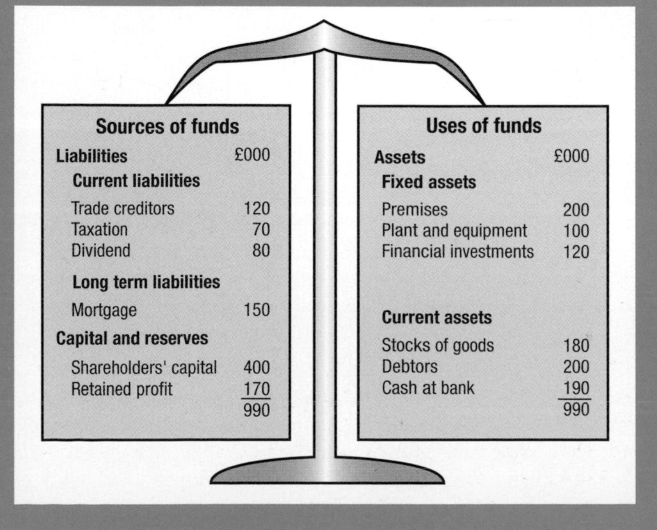

Sources of funds
Liabilities £000
Current liabilities
Trade creditors 120
Taxation 70
Dividend 80
Long term liabilities
Mortgage 150
Capital and reserves
Shareholders' capital 400
Retained profit 170
990
Uses of funds
Assets £000
Fixed assets
Premises 200
Plant and equipment 100
Financial investments 120
Current assets
Stocks of goods 180
Debtors 200
Cash at bank 190
990

In all balance sheets the value of assets (what a business uses or owns) will equal the value of liabilities and capital (what the business owes). Why? Any increase in total assets must be funded by an equal increase in capital or liabilities. A business wanting to buy extra machinery (an asset) may need to obtain a bank loan (a liability), for example. Alternatively, a reduction in credit from suppliers (a liability) may mean a reduction in stocks that can be bought (an asset). So:

Assets = capital + liabilities

This is shown in Figure 1. The diagram shows the types of asset and liability that might appear on the balance sheet of a private limited company. There are differences in the assets and liabilities shown in the balance sheets of sole traders and limited companies. This is explained later in this unit.

Presenting the balance sheet

Table 1 on the next page shows the balance sheet of Breakout Ltd. It is a business that owns a small chain of nightclubs. It is presented here in a vertical format. The balance sheet is a record of the company's assets, liabilities and capital.

One advantage of presenting the balance sheet in this format is that it is easy to see the amount of **working capital** (current assets - current liabilities) that a business has. This is important because the working capital shows whether a business is able to pay its day-to-day bills. The net assets (total assets - current liabilities - long-term liabilities) of a business are also clearly shown.

The balance sheets of public limited companies

In 2005 all publicly traded EU companies were required to present their balance sheets in a slightly new format. This change, along with others in the preparation and presentation of accounts, was introduced to bring Britain and other EU countries into line with international accounting standards. Table 3 shows the balance sheet for Bridgeford Holdings, an engineering company. It is presented according to the new international standards and reflects the type of transactions of a public limited company.

Non-current assets The term NON-CURRENT ASSETS replaces the term fixed assets. Non-current assets are any assets

Table 1: Balance sheet of Breakout Ltd

BREAKOUT LTD
Balance sheet as at 31 August 2008

	£000	£000
Fixed assets		
Premises	1,200	
Fixtures and fittings	1,100	
Equipment	700	
		3,000
Current assets		
Stocks	800	
Debtors	500	
Cash at bank	400	
	1,700	
Current liabilities (Creditors amounts falling due within one year)		
Trade creditors	200	
Dividends	200	
Other liabilities	300	
	700	
Net current assets (working capital)		1,000
Total assets less current liabilities		4,000
Creditors: amounts falling due after one year		
Bank loan	200	
Mortgage	1,100	
		1,300
Net assets		**2,700**
Capital and reserves		
Ordinary share capital (2,000,000 shares at £1)	2,000	
Retained profit	700	
		2,700

FIXED ASSETS are assets with a lifespan of more than one year. They might include the buildings, musical and lighting equipment, drinks equipment behind the bar, tables and seating.

CURRENT ASSETS are assets that are likely to be changed into cash within one year. For Breakout they might include:

- ***stocks*** of goods such as cigarettes and drink – in a manufacturing business this would include stocks or raw materials, semi-finished goods and finished goods;
- customers or businesses that owe money to Breakout Ltd – the ***debtors*** of the business;
- *cash* 'in hand' at the business or deposited in the bank.

Current assets are liquid assets. The liquidity of an asset is how easily it can be changed into cash.

CURRENT LIABILITIES are debts that have to be repaid within 12 months. They are sometimes called Creditors: amounts falling due within one year. In this case they might include:

- money owed to suppliers of drinks or food, telephone companies or suppliers of electricity that have provided goods or services to Breakout Ltd – these are the ***trade creditors*** of the business;
- ***dividends*** – payments to shareholders out of profit which has been announced but is yet to be paid. Other current liabilities might be:
- ***taxation*** – this may be corporation tax or employees' income tax owed to the tax authorities;
- ***overdrafts*** – monies borrowed from banks which are repayable within 12 months;
- ***short-term loans*** – typically loans from banks or similar financial institutions which must be repaid within 12 months;
- ***leases*** – any lease agreements, on machinery or property for example, are classified as a current liability.

The value of **NET CURRENT ASSETS** or ***working capital*** can be found by:

Current assets – current liabilities

Calculating working capital is important for a business. The working capital a firm has indicates whether or not it can afford to pay its day-to-day bills.

The value of ***total assets less current liabilities*** can be found by:

(Fixed assets + current assets) – current liabilities

LONG-TERM LIABILITIES Creditors: amounts due after one year are the LONG-TERM LIABILITIES of the business. These are the debts that a business owes that do not need to be paid for at least 12 months. They might include:

- a ***loan*** from a bank or other financial institution;
- a ***mortgage*** – a loan taken out to purchase buildings;
- a long-term ***lease*** or ***hire purchase*** agreement, such as a five year contract to lease or buy machinery, although Breakout Ltd does not have this.

The value of **NET ASSETS** can be found by:

(Total assets less current liabilities) – long-term liabilities

CAPITAL AND RESERVES The capital and reserves figure is equal to the value of net assets. The total of capital and reserves is sometimes called capital employed or shareholders' funds. Capital and reserves are a liability for a business – money that it owes. They include:

- share capital – the amount of money put into the business by investors buying shares. It is the value of shares when first sold, not the current market value;
- retained profit – the amount of profit that the business has made in previous years. It is money which is owed to the owners. However, it has been retained in the business to buy equipment or to help cash flow rather than distributing it as a dividend.

Question 1.

The Maltings is a care home for the elderly based in Colchester. It accommodates up to 22 elderly people and has a waiting list for places due to its good reputation in the area. The care home is run by a family and the business operates as a private limited company. A balance sheet for the company is shown in Table 2 (some information is excluded).

Table 2: Balance sheet for The Maltings as at 31.12.08

The Maltings Balance sheet as at 31.12.08	
Fixed assets	
Property	1,200,000
Fixtures & fittings	21,000
Equipment	16,000
	1,237,000
Current assets	
Stocks	2,300
Debtors	6,400
Cash at bank	31,000
	39,700
Current liabilities	
Trade creditors	4,500
Other liabilities	12,900
Dividends proposed	5,400
	22,800
Net current assets	********
Total assets less current liabilities	1,253,900
Long-term liabilities	
Mortgage	500,000
Other liabilities	22,000
	522,000
Net assets	********
Capital and reserves	
Share capital	500,000
Other reserves	45,100
Retained profit	********
	731,900

(a) Suggest two examples of: (i) fixtures and fittings; (ii) trade creditors; that the business might have.

(b) Complete the balance sheet above by calculating: (i) Net current assets; (ii) Net assets; (iii) Retained profit.

(c) Why is the value of net current assets an important figure in the balance sheet?

which are not expected to be sold within 12 months. A number of entries are likely to be found in this section of the balance sheet.

- **Goodwill** is likely to be shown as a separate item. This is the amount the business is worth above the value of net assets. Goodwill exists if a company has built up a good reputation and its customers are likely to return. Goodwill is an **intangible asset**. This is a non-physical asset of a business.
- **Other intangible assets** may appear in some plc balance sheets. Examples include brand names, copyrights, trademarks and patents. There is no entry for this on the Bridgeford balance sheet.
- **Property, plant and equipment** are the **tangible assets** which the business owns. In this case it might be a factory and machines used in engineering by Bridgeford. Tangible assets are the physical assets of a business.
- **Investments** are the financial assets owned by the company. An example might be shares held in other companies. If investments are listed under non-current assets it means that they are not expected to be sold for at least 12 months. If investments are likely to be sold within 12 months they should be listed under current assets.
- **Deferred tax assets** relate to the prepayment of tax. Deferred tax assets can be created if a company is likely to offset losses against tax in future years. Details of this will be explained in the **notes to the accounts**.

Current assets Most current assets in a plc balance sheet are the same as those found in other types of balance sheet. However, some different terminology is used.

- **Inventories** refers to stocks of raw materials and components, stocks of finished goods and work-in-progress.
- **Trade and other receivables** are trade debtors, prepayments and any other amounts owed to the business that are likely to be repaid within 12 months.
- **Cash at bank and in hand** is the same as in other types of balance sheet.

Current liabilities Again, most current liabilities in a plc balance sheet are the same as those in other balance sheets but have different names.

- **Borrowings** is a new term that relates to any short-term loans or bank overdrafts taken out by the business.
- **Trade and other payables** refer to trade creditors and other amounts owed by the business to suppliers of goods, services and utilities, for example.
- **Current tax liabilities** refers to corporation tax, employees' income tax and any other tax owed by the business that must be repaid within 12 months.

Non-current liabilities The long-term liabilities of a plc are called NON-CURRENT LIABILITIES. Any amount of money

Table 3: Balance sheet for Bridgeford Holdings – a plc

Bridgeford Holdings
Balance sheet as at 31.12.08

	2008 £m	2007 £m
Non-current assets		
Goodwill	12.4	10.8
Property, plant & equipment	15.7	14.5
Investments	3.8	3.4
Deferred tax assets	2.1	2.3
	34.0	31.0
Current assets		
Inventories	5.6	4.9
Trade and other receivables	8.6	7.8
Cash at bank	2.4	2.7
	16.6	15.4
Total assets	50.6	46.4
Current liabilities		
Borrowings	2.1	2.2
Trade and other payables	6.7	6.9
Current tax liabilities	1.9	1.8
	10.7	10.9
Net current assets	5.9	4.5
Total assets less current liabilities	39.9	35.5
Non-current liabilities		
Other loans and borrowings	5.8	6.2
Retirement benefit obligations	10.1	9.6
Provisions	2.9	3.1
	18.8	18.9
Net assets	21.1	16.6
Equity		
Called up share capital	6.2	5.0
Share premium account	5.6	4.8
Other reserves	4.1	3.2
Retained earnings	5.2	3.6
Total equity	21.1	16.6

Table 4: Balance sheet for Joanna Cullen as at 31.5.2008

Joanna Cullen
Balance sheet as at 31 May 2008

2007 £		2008 £	2008 £
	Fixed assets		
10,000	Car		8,000
7,900	Fixtures and fittings		7,000
17,900			15,000
	Current assets		
30,000	Stocks	35,000	
4,000	Debtors and prepayments	5,000	
3,000	Bank account	4,000	
1,000	Cash in hand	1,000	
38,000		45,000	
	(less) **Current liabilities**		
20,000	Creditors and accrued charges	25,000	
18,000	Working capital		20,000
35,900	**NET ASSETS**		35,000
	(FINANCED BY)		
30,000	**Opening capital**		35,900
-	Capital introduced		4,500
48,100	*(add)* Net profit		59,600
78,100			100,000
42,200	*(less)* Drawings		65,000
35,900			35,000

owed for more than one year will appear in this section of the plc balance sheet.

- **Other loans and borrowings** refers to money owed by the company that does not have to be repaid for at least 12 months. Examples would be long-term bank loans and mortgages.
- **Retirement pension obligations.** Plcs must now show any money owed to past employees in the form of pension obligations.
- **Provisions.** Provisions have to be made if a company is likely to incur expenditure in the future. Such expenditure might arise as a result of agreements in contracts or warranties. Repairing some machinery sold to a customer might be an example. If these provisions are short term they will appear under current liabilities.

Equity The bottom section of the plc balance sheet shows the amounts of money owed to the shareholders. Most of the entries are the same or similar to those found in the capital and reserves of a private limited company balance sheet.

- **Share capital** is the amount of money paid by shareholders for their shares when they were originally issued. It does not represent the current value of those shares on the stock market. Share capital is not usually repaid to the shareholders in the lifetime of a company.
- **Share premium account** shows the difference between the value of new shares issued by the company and their nominal value. For example, the nominal value of a share may have been £1. The company may decide to issue

Question 2.

Melanie Cooper is a sole trader and runs a gift shop in Brighton. She sells gifts, souvenirs and novelty products to day-trippers and other visitors to the seaside town. Melanie has been successful in recent years and her balance sheet for 2008 is presented in Table 5.

Table 5: Balance sheet for Melanie Cooper as at 31.7.08

Melanie Cooper Balance sheet as at 31.7.08	2008 £	2007 £
Fixed assets		
Fixtures & Fittings	8,000	9,000
Equipment	3,000	3,500
Vehicle	4,000	5,000
	15,000	17,500
Current assets		
Stock	18,600	16,500
Debtors and prepayments	2,900	3,500
Cash in hand & at bank	12,900	10,100
	34,400	30,100
Current liabilities		
Trade creditors	9,800	9,500
Other current liabilities	6,300	5,600
	16,100	15,100
Working capital	18,300	15,000
Net assets	33,300	32,500
Financed by:		
Opening capital	32,500	26,400
Net profit	29,600	32,100
	62,100	58,500
Less drawings	28,800	26,000
Closing capital	**33,300**	**32,500**

(a) Explain why the value of fixed assets has fallen over the two years.
(b) How is the opening capital calculated in 2008?
(c) Why do you think drawings has increased over the two years?
(d) What is the value of Melanie's business?

2 million new shares. If the company sold them for £3, each new share is now worth £2 more than the nominal price. In total this would be £4 million (£2 x 2 million). This £4 million would be entered on the share premium account in the balance sheet.

- **Revaluation reserve** sometimes appears under capital and reserves to balance an increase in the value of fixed assets. A business may buy a building for £100,000. Later it may be worth £160,000. This £160,000 would be included in the tangible assets figure. However only £100,000 would appear under capital and reserves as this was the original amount spent. Capital and reserves have to be revalued by £60,000 so that assets still equal liabilities plus capital and reserves. There is no revaluation reserve for Bridgeford.
- **Other reserves** refer to any amounts owing to the shareholders not covered by the other entries under equity.
- **Retained earnings** is the same as retained profit. It is the amount of profit retained by the business to be used in the future, for example to fund investment projects.

Company law requires both **private and public limited** companies to show both this year's and last year's figures in published accounts. This allows comparisons to be made.

Sole trader balance sheets

Earlier it was mentioned that sole trader balance sheets will be different to those of limited companies. Take the example of Joanna Cullen, a sole trader running a retail outlet that sells computers. Her balance sheet is shown in Table 4. There is a number of differences between a sole trader and a limited company balance sheet.

- The sole trader has a capital account rather than a 'capital and reserves' section. Sole traders are set up with the personal capital introduced into the business by the owner. Joanna Cullen introduced a further £4,500 into the business during 2007, according to the balance sheet in Table 4.
- It is likely that a sole trader will need to withdraw money from the business for personal reasons during the year. This is subtracted from the capital account and is shown as DRAWINGS in the balance sheet. The balance on the capital account is the amount owed to the owner. This is equal to the assets of the company.
- A limited company has many sources of capital and reserves. However, all companies will show shareholders' funds (often listed as capital and reserves), which will not be in a sole trader's balance sheet.
- The shareholders of a limited company are paid a dividend. This appears in the figure for current liabilities. As sole traders do not have shareholders no such figure will be included in their accounts.

Assessing performance and potential

Balance sheets can be used to evaluate the performance and potential of a business.

- In general, it provides a summary and valuation of all business assets, capital and liabilities.
- The balance sheet can be used to analyse the asset structure of a business. It can show how the money raised by the business has been spent on different types of asset. The balance sheet for Breakout in Table 1 shows that £3 million was spent on fixed assets in 2007. Current assets, however, accounted for only £1.7 million.

- The balance sheet can also be used to analyse the capital structure of a business. A business can raise funds from many different sources, such as shareholders' capital, retained profit and long-term and short-term sources.
- Looking at the value of working capital can indicate whether a firm is able to pay its everyday expenses or is likely to have problems. The value of working capital is the difference between current assets and current liabilities. It shows the money left over after all current liabilities have been paid that can be used to settle the day to day debts of the business. In the balance sheet for Breakout the value of working capital was £1 million.
- A balance sheet may provide a guide to a firm's value. Generally, the value of the business is represented by the value of all assets less any money owed to outside agents such as banks or suppliers. The value of Breakout in 2007 was £2.7 million.

However, there are limitations to using balance sheets to assess performance.

- The value of many assets listed in the balance sheet may not reflect the amount of money the business would receive if it were sold. For example, fixed assets are listed at cost less an allowance for depreciation. However, the depreciation allowance is estimated by accountants. If estimates are inaccurate, the value of assets will also be inaccurate.
- Many balance sheets do not include intangible assets. Assets such as goodwill, brand names and the skills of the workforce may be excluded because they are difficult to value or could change suddenly. If such assets are excluded, the value of the business may be understated.
- A balance sheet is a static statement. Many of the values for assets, capital and liabilities listed in the statement are only valid for the day the balance sheet was published. After another day's trading, many of the figures will have changed. This can restrict its usefulness.
- It could be argued that a balance sheet lacks detail. Many of the figures are totals and are not broken down.

KEYTERMS

Accounting – the process of identifying, measuring and communicating information to permit informed judgments and decisions by users of the information.
Assets – resources used or owned by the business in production.
Balance sheet – a summary at a point in time of business assets, liabilities and capital.
Capital – a source of funds provided by the owners of the business used to buy assets.
Current assets – assets likely to be changed into cash within a year.
Current liabilities – debts that have to be repaid within a year.
Drawings – money withdrawn by a sole trader from the business for personal use.
Fixed assets – assets with a lifespan of more than one year.
Liabilities – the debts of the business which provide a source of funds.
Long term liabilities – debts that are payable after 12 months.
Net assets – the value of total assets minus current liabilities minus long-term liabilities. The value is equal to capital and reserves on the balance sheet.
Net current assets – current assets minus current liabilities. Also known as working capital.
Non-current assets – the long-term assets of a plc which are not expected to be sold within 12 months/a year.
Non-current liabilities – the long-term liabilities of a plc – any amount of money owed for more than 12 months/a year.

KNOWLEDGE

1. What is a balance sheet?
2. Why is a balance sheet a static business document?
3. Why must the value of assets on a balance sheet be equal to the value of liabilities plus capital?
4. What is the difference between fixed and current assets?
5. State three examples of the fixed assets that a business might have.
6. State three examples of the current assets that a business might have.
7. What is the difference between tangible and intangible fixed assets?
8. What is the difference between current and long-term liabilities?
9. State three current liabilities that a business might have.
10. Why is revaluation of assets sometimes included under capital and reserves?
11. How does depreciation affect the balance sheet?
12. Suggest three uses of balance sheets for a business.
13. Suggest three limitations of balance sheets.

Case Study: Winters Timber Ltd

Winters Timber Ltd is a timber merchant. The business originally started out as timber merchants, supplying to manufacturers. However, the company realised that it could expand by making its own timber products. A major area of the business is the manufacture of fencing panels, pallets and landscape products. This is now a major part of the business and 90 per cent of the stock in this area is made on site. Winters Timber has recently installed a panelmaster system for the manufacture of fence panels. One of the reasons why the business is successful is because it holds a wide range of stock. Table 6 shows a balance sheet for Winters Timber.

Table 6: Winters Timber balance sheet as at 31 December 2008

WINTERS TIMBER LTD
BALANCE SHEET AS AT 31.12.08

	2008	2007
Fixed assets	**£000s**	**£000s**
Equipment and machinery	1,200	1,400
Vehicles	340	310
	1,540	1,710
Current assets		
Stock	230	160
Debtors	65	80
Cash at bank	180	100
	475	340
Creditors: amounts falling due in one year		
Trade creditors	120	105
Accruals	20	25
Taxation	100	80
	240	210
Net current assets	**235**	**130**
Creditors: amounts falling due after one year		
Mortgage	(500)	(500)
Net assets	**1,275**	**1,340**
Capital and reserves		
Share capital	200	200
Other reserves	115	540
Retained profit	960	600
	1,275	**1,340**

(a) Why does a business like Winters Timber produce a balance sheet? (4 marks)

(b) Using examples from this case, explain what is meant by fixed assets. (4 marks)

(c) Explain why: (i) retained profit; (ii) vehicles; has increased in the balance sheet over the two years. (8 marks)

(d) How would you describe the financial situation of Winters Timber Ltd? (8 marks)

(e) Evaluate the usefulness of this balance sheet to the shareholders of Winters Timber Ltd. (16 marks)

45 Business assets and depreciation

Assets

Assets are the **resources** used by business. A company will use the funds it earns to purchase assets which add value to a company. Most assets are physical in nature and are used in production. However, there are some, such as goodwill, which do not fall into this category, although they still add value. They are called intangible assets because they are non-physical. One of the functions of a **balance sheet** is to provide a summary of all business assets and their values. Assets are usually valued at their original cost, less a deduction for depreciation. This is to take into account that they wear out over a period of time and are worth less.

Fixed assets

Resources with a lifespan of more than one year are called **fixed assets**. Fixed assets, such as machinery, can be used again and again until they wear out. Some fixed assets like land and property do not depreciate, although they have to be maintained. In the balance sheet, fixed assets are divided into **tangible**, **intangible** and **financial assets**. Each of these are dealt with in detail in the following sections.

Tangible assets

TANGIBLE ASSETS are physical assets that can be touched. The most long term or the least **liquid** of these assets (the most difficult to turn into cash) appear at the top of the list of fixed assets on the balance sheet. For a farmer or a small manufacturing company these are likely to be the most important and largest fixed assets, if owned.

Land and property can either be **freehold** or **leasehold**. Freehold property is owned outright by the business. It is valued on the balance sheet at its original cost, less depreciation. In the past, inflation has resulted in soaring property prices. Accountants have advised many companies to revalue their land and property so that the accounts reflect more accurately a 'true and fair view' of the company. When assets are revalued in this way on the assets side of the balance sheet, an equivalent entry must be made on the liabilities side in reserves to balance the accounts. This is called a revaluation.

Leasehold land and property is rented from an owner and is a company asset. Any capital amount paid for the lease appears separately as 'leasehold property'. This amount is **written off** over the period of the lease. This means the value of the lease is reduced by an amount each year as it depreciates.

Fixed assets which are not land or property are referred to as plant, machinery and equipment. Again, they are valued at cost less depreciation. Large companies often have vast amounts of these assets. The balance sheet will, in this case, not list separate assets, but give only a total.

Intangible assets

Some fixed assets are not tangible, but are still valuable, income-generating resources. These are INTANGIBLE ASSETS.

Goodwill Over many years of trading companies build up goodwill. They may have gained a good reputation, which means that customers will use their services or purchase their products. If the company is to be sold in the future, some value needs to be placed on this goodwill and included in the purchase price. From an accountant's point of view, goodwill is equal to the amount by which the purchase price of a business exceeds the **net assets** (total assets - total liabilities).

Take the example of Amanda Storey, a young, newly qualified accountant, who decides to set up in business. She considers renting an office, advertising her services in the local press and distributing business cards. However, she is approached by Geoff Horrocks, an accountant who is considering retirement. Clearly it would pay Amanda to buy Geoff's list of established clients. The agreed price would represent goodwill.

Before 2005, the value of purchased goodwill was shown on the balance sheet and then depreciated (or amortised) over its expected useful economic life. Since the introduction of international accounting standards in 2005, plcs are expected to show intangible assets on the balance sheet and write them off over a much longer period. Many companies choose a period of 20 years.

Patents, copyrights and trade marks If a company or an individual invents and develops a unique product, a patent can be obtained from the patent office. This is a licence which prevents other firms from copying the product. Patents have been granted in the past for products as diverse as catseyes in 1935 and Polaroid cameras in 1946.

Copyright prevents the reuse of published works, such as books, plays, films and music without the author's consent. Michael Jackson allegedly paid £48 million for a back catalogue of 250 Beatles' songs, out-bidding former Beatle Paul McCartney. Substantial fees are paid to copyright owners of music used in TV advertisements. Occasionally, certain magazines will allow a part of their publication to be used free of charge. Trademarks generally signify a manufacturer's name. The right to sell another company's products may have to be registered if they carry a trade mark and a fee may be charged.

Research and development Normally research and development (R&D) costs are classified as revenue expenditure. However, if a project is expected to earn a substantial income in the future, its costs may be recorded as capital expenditure and included as an intangible asset in the balance sheet. The costs are written off over the period when income is generated.

Brand names Many companies enjoy successful brand names. Recently, some of these companies have debated the inclusion of these intangible assets in the balance sheet because they generate income for a lengthy period of time in some cases. This means that the amount a successful brand name is estimated to be worth should be included as an intangible asset on the balance sheet, so that the true value of a company's assets is made clear.

When an intangible asset is written off it is described as **amortisation** rather than depreciation.

Financial assets

These are often called **investments** in the balance sheet. They usually refer to shares held in other companies. If the shareholding in a particular company is more than 50 per cent then that company is classified as a **subsidiary**. If the holding is between 20 per cent and 50 per cent then the company is described as an **associated company**. Finally, any holdings of less than 20 per cent are called trade investments.

There is a number of motives for holding shares in other companies. These are shown in Figure 1. Some companies hold shares to earn income. Holding companies such as Kingfisher, for example, specialise in buying and controlling other companies. In some cases, businesses are bought, broken up, and parts sold at a profit. This activity has been described as **asset stripping**.

Figure 1: Motives for holding shares in other companies

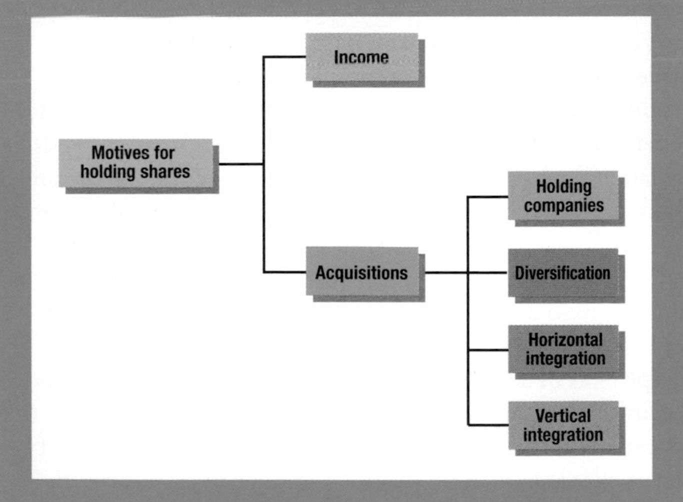

Another motive for holding shares is to diversify in order to reduce risk. Companies also buy firms in the same line of business to exploit economies of scale, ie horizontal integration. They may also seek to buy out their suppliers or distribution networks, ie vertical integration.

Finally, other financial investments might include government bonds or deposits of foreign currency. All financial assets are listed at cost in the balance sheet.

Current assets

Short-term assets which can be changed into cash within one year are called **current assets**. There is a number of common current assets.

Stocks Most businesses hold stocks of finished goods. Stocks are classed as current assets because the business would hope to sell them within 12 months. The quantity of stocks held by a company will depend on the nature of the company.

Work-in-progress is also classified as stock. It represents partly finished goods, e.g. half-built properties. We also include stocks of raw materials and components in **current assets**. The business would expect to change them into finished goods which would then be sold, hopefully within a year.

Debtors In some lines of business, when a sale is made, it is common to receive payment at a later date. Any amounts owing by these customers at the end of the financial year are listed as **debtors** in the balance sheet. In order to speed up the payment of bills some firms offer cash discounts. In addition, debt factors offer a debt collecting service.

Related to debtors is another current asset - **prepayments**. A prepayment is a sum, such as insurance, rent or uniform business rate, which is paid in advance. At the end of the financial year any service which has been paid for but not fully consumed is listed in the balance sheet as a prepayment.

Cash at bank Most businesses deposit their takings in a bank. From the bank account various business expenses are paid for. If the bank balance is positive at the end of the trading year the amount will be shown as a current asset in the balance sheet.

Cash in hand Many businesses have cash on their premises. This is often called **petty cash**. Cash is used to pay for small or unexpected transactions, e.g. the purchase of toilet paper.

Together, cash at bank and cash in hand represent the firm's most **liquid resources**. Businesses need to hold just the right amount of cash. Too much cash means business opportunities are being wasted as the money could be invested in other assets. Too little cash may prevent the business from making urgent purchases.

Investments Some investments held by businesses may be short term. They may include shares in other companies, bonds or deposit accounts. If it is possible to convert these investments into cash within 12 months they are listed as investments under current assets.

Liquidity

Liquidity refers to the speed or ease with which assets can be converted into cash without suffering any capital loss. For example, a house is an illiquid asset. It could be sold for cash for, say, £100, but the owner would be likely to lose money. In the balance sheet the least liquid assets (fixed assets) are listed at the top and the most liquid (current assets) are placed at the bottom.

Question 1.

Corbridge Engineering Limited was established in 1981 as a sub-contract supplier of pressed components and metal pressings to customers' own specifications. It manufactures bespoke presswork and metal pressings, using ferrous and non-ferrous metals in sheet coil or tube form. Corbridge also offers a range of ancillary processes such as sub-assemblies, spot welding, surface finishing, thread rolling and tube sawing.

During 2006 the company began to experience cash flow problems. The directors felt that too much money was tied up in stock and many customers were taking too long to pay. At the beginning of 2007 some measures were taken to improve cash flow by addressing the stock and debtor problems. Table 1 shows the current assets for Corbridge Engineering Ltd for 2006 and 2007.

Table 1: Current assets for Corbridge Engineering Ltd

	2007 £	2006 £
Current assets		
Stocks of raw materials	134,000	135,600
Work-in-progress	321,900	342,600
Stocks of finished goods	238,900	243,100
Debtors	289,600	438,000
Prepayments	34,000	36,400
Cash in hand and at bank	187,600	2,900
	1,206,000	**1,198,600**

(a) **Explain what is meant by current assets.**
(b) **To what extent has Corbridge Engineering Ltd improved its cash flow over the two years?**

Fixed assets like land and buildings tend to be very illiquid. It can sometimes take a long time to sell such assets. Possibly the most illiquid of all assets is a highly specialised item of machinery, ie a machine which has been especially made for a company. This type of capital good will prove very difficult to sell since demand will be limited. Some fixed assets may be much easier to sell and are therefore more liquid. Vehicles, non-specialised machinery like a cement mixer or a JCB, and standard tools and equipment, which have a variety of uses, are all examples.

The least liquid of the current assets is stock. Stocks of finished goods are expected to be sold, but business fortunes change and sales can never be guaranteed. The liquidity of raw material stocks can vary. Non-specialised materials like coal will be more liquid than specialised components since they are easier to sell. Debtors are more liquid than stocks because goods have been sold and the business is legally entitled to payment. However, money has not yet been received so it cannot be spent. In addition, there are times when firms cannot pay and so the debt has to be written off (known as bad debts).

Cash at the bank and cash in hand are obviously the most liquid assets of all.

Asset structure

The ASSET STRUCTURE of a business refers to the amount of capital employed in each category of asset. Asset structures will vary according to the nature of the industry in which a business is competing. Manufacturing companies will tend to have a large amount of capital tied up in plant, machinery and equipment. Construction firms will have a significant amount of work-in-progress. Businesses which face seasonal demand may hold large stocks of finished goods at particular times of the year. In the retail trade, public houses and restaurants will have very few debtors, or even none.

A profit maximising company will want to purchase those assets which yield the greatest return. Fixed assets are the productive assets of a business, so firms will want to invest as much of their capital as possible in these. However, some capital must be kept in current assets to fund day to day expenditure. It is not possible to conduct business activity without current assets. Some firms may exist with very little capital employed in fixed assets. Retailers often have a large proportion of current assets if they rent premises (stock in particular).

Valuing assets

One of the problems in financial accounting is how to place a value on assets. Accountants value assets at **historical cost**, ie the cost of the asset when it is first purchased. There are reasons why assets should be valued in this way. Business transactions are entered into records as they occur. For example, if a firm buys a vehicle for £15,000 and pays cash, two entries will be made in the records. Also, accountants would argue that historical cost can be checked. It is based on actual costs and is better than methods which involve estimates. Other methods of valuation, such as those which take into account inflation, are also used. As yet, though, a suitable replacement has not been found.

One problem with historical cost accounting is how to put a value on fixed assets like property. In recent years there have been times when the values of land and buildings have risen sharply - as much as 30 or 40 per cent in one year. Unless the accounts are amended, they will not reflect the true value of the business. It is common now to revalue assets such as property every few years. Inflation distorts the value of assets and any other value which is measured in money terms.

Depreciation

Fixed assets are used again and again over a long period of time. For example, a milling machine might be used for many years to produce metal components. A motor business would expect automated production lines to run for many years. During their operation fixed assets are consumed and their value is 'used up'. This measure of consumption or any other reduction in the useful economic life of a fixed asset is known as DEPRECIATION. Figure 3 shows the possible causes of depreciation.

Question 2.

FRD Ltd is a small haulage company owned by Mandy Armstrong and her partner John Entwhistle. The business has a small office in Lincoln and provides haulage services to farmers in the county. FRD Ltd owns two Scania trucks and three specialist trailers to cope with a variety of agricultural loads. It also employs one other driver.

Allens is an electrical goods cash and carry based in Stoke-on-Trent. The store employs three staff and stocks a very wide range of electrical goods such HD TVs, sound systems, computers and white goods. Figure 2 shows the asset structure of the two businesses.

Figure 2: The asset structure of FRD Ltd and Allens

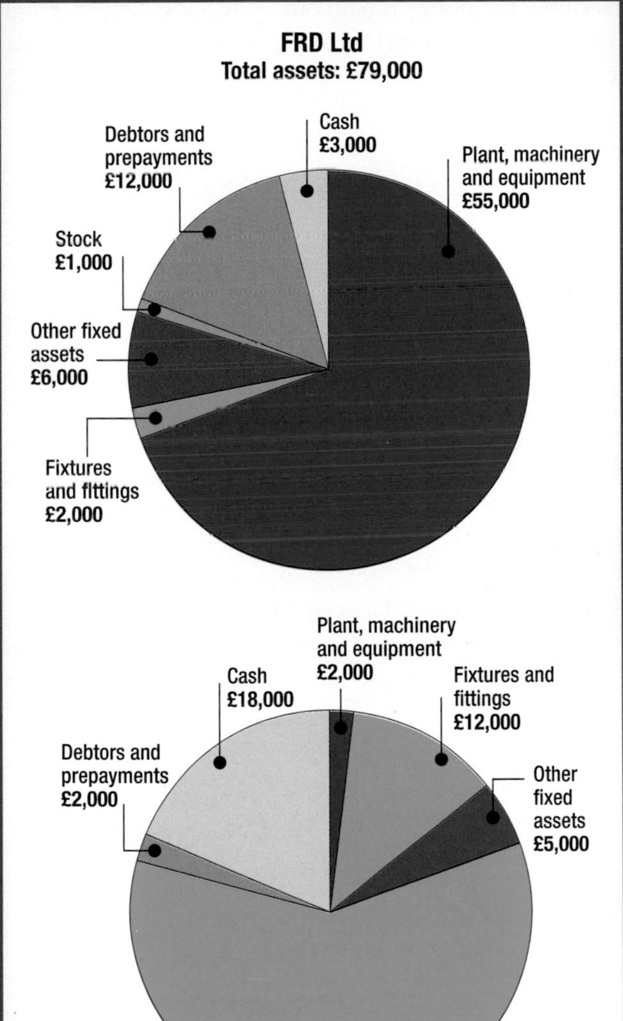

(a) Account for the differences in the asset structures of FRD Ltd and Allens.

(b) Which of the two businesses would have the largest annual depreciation charge? Explain your answer.

- Machinery, tools and equipment all suffer wear and tear when they are used. They deteriorate, which can sometimes affect their operation or effectiveness. Eventually they will have to be replaced.
- Changing technology can often make assets OBSOLETE. Although a machine may still work, it may not be used because a new machine is more efficient.
- Capital goods which are hardly used or poorly maintained may depreciate quickly. The life of machinery can be prolonged if it is 'looked after'.
- The passing of time can also lead to depreciation. For example, if an asset is leased, the 'buyer' can use the asset for a period of time. As the expiry date gets close, the lease becomes worth less and less.

Figure 3: Possible causes of depreciation

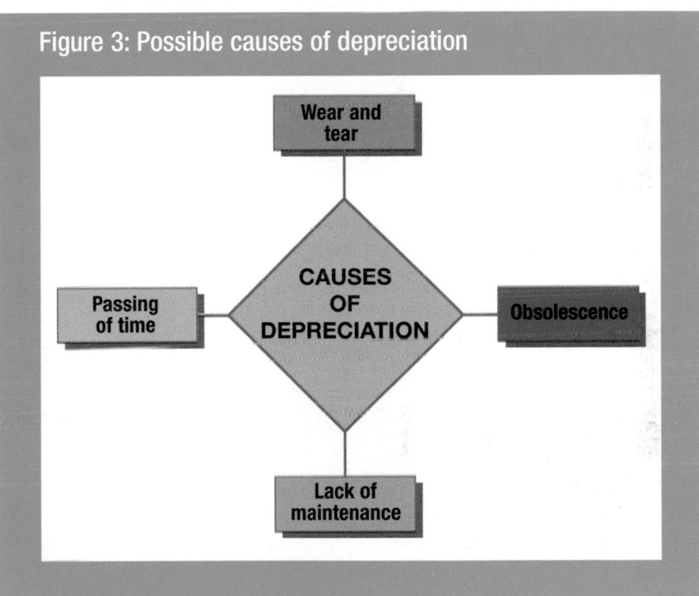

Depreciation and the accounts

Each year accountants must work out how much depreciation to allow for each fixed asset. This can then be used in the balance sheet and the profit and loss account. The **balance sheet** will show the NET BOOK VALUE of assets. This is their original value minus depreciation. So if a piece of machinery is bought for £10,000 and depreciates by £2,000 in the first year, its net book value in the first year would be:

£10,000 - £2,000 = £8,000.

The net book value falls each year as more depreciation is deducted. So in the second year the net book value would be:

£8,000 - £2,000 = £6,000

This simple method of calculating depreciation is called the **straight line method** as the same value for depreciation is used each year. Another method, the **reducing balance method**, involves depreciating fixed assets by a fixed percentage each year.

Depreciation is shown in **profit and loss accounts** or **income statements** under expenses. This indicates that part of the original value is 'used up' each year (known as revenue expenditure). Eventually the entire value of the asset will appear as expenses, when the asset depreciates fully. This process of reducing the original value by the amount of depreciation is known as writing off.

Intangible assets are also depreciated or **amortised**, as explained earlier in this unit. For example, a business may 'write off' the value of its goodwill over a 20 year period.

The importance of depreciation

There are good reasons why a business should allow for depreciation each year in its accounts.

Accurate accounts If it does not, the accounts will be inaccurate. If the original value of assets was placed on the balance sheet this would overstate the value. The value of assets falls each year as they depreciate. If the value of assets on a balance sheet is inaccurate, then any financial analysis based on the balance sheet will be flawed. For example, ratio analysis would be ineffective.

Valuing the business The value of a business is represented by the net assets on a balance sheet. Clearly, if assets have not been depreciated then the value of the business would be overstated.

Matching benefits with costs Fixed assets generate profit for many years. It seems logical to write off the value of the asset over this whole period, rather than when it is first bought. This matches the benefit from the asset more closely with its cost.

Provision A sensible firm will know that assets must be replaced in future and allow for this. Even though depreciation appears as an expense on the profit and loss account, it is actually a PROVISION. Expenses involve paying out money. In the case of depreciation, no money is paid out. A business simply recognises that assets have to be replaced and 'provides' for this by placing a value in the accounts.

KEYTERMS

Asset structure – the proportion of capital employed in each type of asset.
Depreciation – the measure of wearing out, consumption or other reduction in the useful life of a fixed asset.
Intangible assets – non-physical business assets.
Net book value – the historical cost of an asset less depreciation accumulated every year.
Obsolete – an asset that is no longer any use to a business.
Provision (in relation to depreciation) – an allowance made in the accounts for depreciation.
Tangible assets – assets which are physical in nature.

KNOWLEDGE

1. What is the difference between tangible and intangible assets?
2. How is it possible to calculate the value of goodwill?
3. Distinguish between a subsidiary, an associated company and a trade investment.
4. What is meant by asset stripping?
5. What is the difference between debtors and prepayments?
6. What is the difference between a liquid and an illiquid asset?
7. Why is a specialised machine an illiquid asset?
8. What is the main determinant of a firm's asset structure?
9. State four causes of depreciation.
10. Why is depreciation a provision?

Case Study: Domino's Pizza

Domino's Pizza Group Limited is a wholly owned subsidiary of Domino's Pizza UK and Irl plc and holds the master franchise licence to own, operate and franchise Domino's pizza stores in England, Scotland, Wales and Ireland. Domino's Pizza Inc. founded in the United States in 1960, is recognised as world leader in the delivery of freshly-made, home-delivered high quality pizza. The first UK store opened in 1985 and Domino's now has 451 stores operating in the UK and Ireland.

2006 was a record breaking year for Domino's Pizza. Store sales, store count and e-commerce all reached record levels. Store sales rose 19.7 per cent to £240.1 million, 46 new stores were opened and e-commerce sales were up 43.8 per cent to £20.1 million.

One of the reasons for Domino's continued success is its commitment to reducing 'out-the-door' time. This is the time it takes for a pizza order to leave the store after receiving an order. Domino's displays the 'real-time' average speed of the pizza making and baking process in their stores. By using this approach it has been able to improve the number of orders leaving the store in under 15 minutes by 34 per cent. The 'real-time' screens show the national average as well as the individual store. This has introduced a competitive spirit in the organisation which has helped to improve efficiency. Table 2 shows some information on fixed assets and depreciation for Domino's Pizza.

Table 2: Fixed assets and depreciation for Domino's Pizza 2006

	Freehold land and buildings	Leasehold improvements	Equipment	Total
Cost:	£000	£000	£000	£000
At 1 January 2006	8,245	1,315	9,655	19,215
Additions	38	311	1,945	2,294
Disposals		(206)	(317)	(523)
At 31 December 2006	**8,283**	**1,420**	**11,283**	**20,986**
Depreciation:				
At 1 January 2006	648	116	4,858	5,622
Provided during the year	124	170	1,377	1,671
Disposals		(5)	(82)	(87)
At 31 December 2006	**772**	**281**	**6,153**	**7,206**
Net book value:				
At 31 December 2006	**7,511**	**1,139**	**5,130**	**13,780**

Source: adapted from Domino's Pizza, *Annual Report and Accounts*.

(a) What is meant by the term 'wholly owned subsidiary' in the case. (4 marks)

(b) Using examples from this case, explain what is meant by tangible assets. (4 marks)

(c) What might account for the additions to equipment of £1,945,000 in 2006? (4 marks)

(d) Explain how the net book value of fixed assets (£13,780,000) is calculated. (6 marks)

(e) (i) Why do businesses provide for depreciation? (6 marks)
(ii) What might cause Domino's fixed assets to depreciate? (6 marks)

(f) In 2006, Domino's had £773,000 of goodwill shown in the balance sheet. Explain what is likely to happen to the net book value of Domino's goodwill in the future. (10 marks)

46 Calculating depreciation and stock values

Calculating depreciation

There is a number of methods which can be used to calculate a value for depreciation. Each method has its own advantages and accountants are free to choose the method they prefer. Four methods are outlined below.

The straight line method

The STRAIGHT LINE METHOD is the most common method used by businesses to work out depreciation. It assumes that the net cost of an asset should be written off in equal amounts over its life. The accountant needs to know the cost of the asset, its estimated residual value, i.e. its 'scrap' value after the business has finished with it, and its expected life in years. The formula used is:

$$\text{Depreciation allowance (each time period)} = \frac{\text{Original cost - residual value}}{\text{Expected life (years)}}$$

Assume a delivery van costs £28,000 to buy and has an expected life of four years. The residual value is estimated at £4,000.

$$\text{Depreciation allowance} = \frac{£28{,}000 - £4{,}000}{4 \text{ years}}$$

$$= \frac{£24{,}000}{4}$$

$$= £6{,}000$$

When calculating depreciation it is helpful to draw up a table to show how an asset is written off over its lifetime. Table 1 shows the depreciation allowance charged to the profit and loss account each year, and the net book value which is listed in the balance sheet. We can illustrate this on a graph as shown in Figure 1. These are some advantages of using this method.

Table 1: A summary of the annual depreciation allowance and book value of the delivery van using the straight line method

Year	Depreciation allowance (each year) £	Net book value £
1	6,000	22,000
2	6,000	16,000
3	6,000	10,000
4	6,000	4,000

Figure 1: A graph illustrating the book value of the delivery van over its lifetime (straight line method)

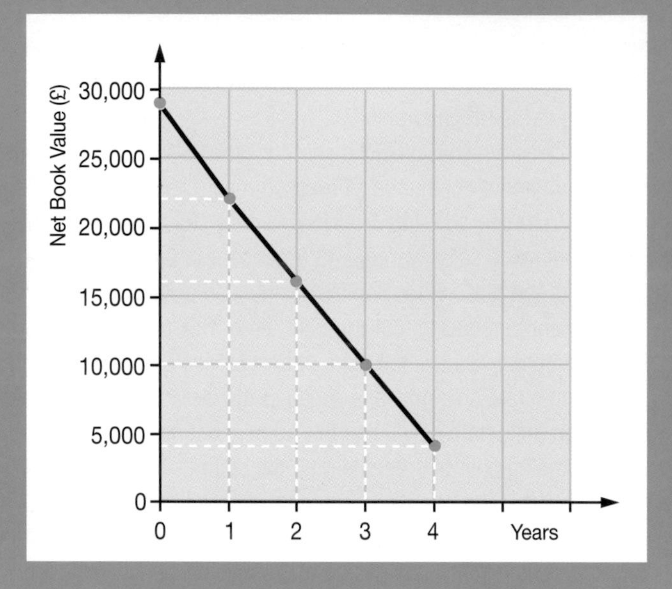

- It is simple. Little calculation is needed and the same amount is subtracted from the book value each year.
- It is useful for assets like a lease, where the life of the asset and the residual value is known precisely.

The reducing balance method

The REDUCING or DECLINING BALANCE METHOD assumes that the depreciation charge in the early years of an asset's life should be higher than in the later years. To do this, the asset must be written off by the same percentage rate each year. This means the annual charge falls.

Assume a vehicle is bought for £28,000 and has a life of four years. Table 2 shows how the vehicle can be written off using the

Table 2: A summary of the annual depreciation allowance and book value of the vehicle using the reducing balance method

Year	Depreciation allowance (each year) £	Net book value £
1	11,200 (28,000 x 40%)	16,800
2	6,720 (16,800 x 40%)	10,080
3	4,032 (10,080 x 40%)	6,048
4	2,419 (6,048 x 40%)	3,629

reducing balance method. A 40 per cent charge will be made each year and the firm expects a **residual value** of £3,629. Table 2 shows the depreciation allowance in the profit and loss account in each of the four years. It also shows the book value which would be listed in the balance sheet. Notice that the depreciation allowance falls every year. This is shown in Figure 2. What if the business expected the residual value to be £4,000? The depreciation charge for this can be calculated using the formula:

$$\text{Depreciation rate} = \left[1 - \sqrt[n]{\frac{\text{Residual value}}{\text{Cost}}}\right] \times 100$$

Where n = estimated life of the asset, i.e. four years, so:

$$\text{Depreciation rate} = \left[1 - \sqrt[4]{\frac{4{,}000}{28{,}000}}\right] \times 100 = 38.52\%$$

There are some advantages to using the reducing balance method.

- It takes into account that some assets, machinery for example, lose far more value in the first year than they do in the fifth year, say. So the book value reflects more accurately the real value of the asset in the balance sheet.
- For many assets, maintenance and repair costs grow as the asset ages. Using the declining balance method results in a more equal total expense each year for fixed assets related costs. For example, at the end of year 1 the depreciation charge for a machine might be £4,500 with only a £500 maintenance charge. In year 5 the depreciation charge might have been £1,500 and repairs and maintenance may have been £3,000. Although the two totals are not the same (£5,000 and £4,500), as the depreciation charges fall the maintenance and repair costs rise.

Figure 2: A graph illustrating the book value of the vehicle over its life time (reducing balance method)

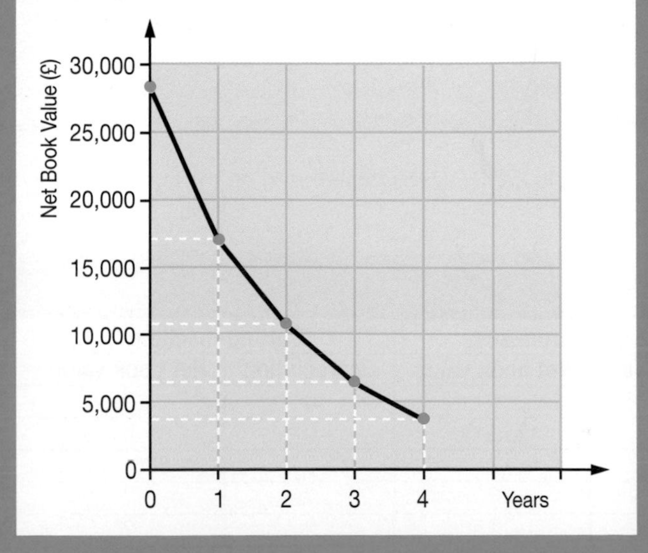

Question 1.

A Liverpool wheel manufacturer is currently building a £2 million robotic paint plant. The investment is needed to satisfy growing demand for alloy wheels worldwide. It is also further developing its site and is spending £500,000 on buying the freehold of a factory adjoining its site. It continues to invest in its fleet of delivery vehicles. This year it will spend £60,000 on new vehicles.

The manufacturer has a policy of depreciating its assets on a straight-line basis over their estimated useful economic lives as follows.

- Freehold property - 50 years.
- Plant and machinery - 10 years.
- Vehicles - 3 years.

Assume that the expenditure on each of the three items mentioned in the data is recorded at its full historic cost value in the accounts of the company at 31 December 2008.

(a) Calculate the depreciation in the first year on (a) the freehold property; (b) the robotic paint plant; (c) the vehicles; (d) the total of all three items.

(b) What is the net book value of each item at 31 December 2009?

(c) What is the net book value of each item after four years at 31 December 2012? Show all your workings.

Other methods of calculating depreciation

The **sum-of-the-years' digits method** assumes that fixed assets depreciate quicker in the early years. The calculation is based on the sum-of-the-years' digits, given the expected life of an asset, less the residual value. For an asset which has an expected life of 4 years the sum-of-the-years' is 10, i.e. 4+3+2+1 = 10. The depreciation charge for the first year will be 4/10 of the original cost, the second year it will be 3/10 of the original cost and so on.

Assuming a cost of £28,000, a life span of four years and a residual value of £4,000, the net value of the asset is £24,000 (£28,000 - £4,000). We can draw up a table to show the annual depreciation charge and the book value each year (Table 3). Table 3 shows that the depreciation allowance falls in a similar way to the reducing balance method.

Table 3: A summary of the annual depreciation allowance and book value of the asset above, using the sum-of-the-years' digits method

Year	Depreciation allowance (each year) £	Net book value £
1	9,600 (24,000 x 4/10)	18,400
2	7,200 (24,000 x 3/10)	11,200
3	4,800 (24,000 x 2/10)	6,400
4	2,400 (24,000 x 1/10)	4,000

Another method called the **usage method** or **machine hour method** takes into account that some assets wear out more rapidly the more they are used. Thus, depreciation is based on the number of hours a machine, for example, is used during the accounting period. It is not a method that is often used by firms.

The disposal of assets

The book value of assets rarely reflects their precise value. So if an asset is sold, a business usually makes a profit or a loss. This is likely if the asset is sold before the end of its expected life. For example, if a machine is bought for £100,000 with an expected life of 10 years and residual value of £15,000, the depreciation allowance each year will be £8,500 (using the straight line method). If the firm decides to sell the machine at the end of year 7 and receives £44,000, it earns a profit of £3,500 because the book value at the end of year 7 is £40,500. A firm must show this in the accounts. It is common practice to deal with profit or loss on disposal by adjusting that year's depreciation charge. If a profit is made, the depreciation charge will be reduced by the amount of the profit. If a loss is made, the depreciation charge will be increased by the amount of the loss. If the profit or loss is very large then it will be treated as an exceptional item in the accounts.

Stock valuation

When accounts are produced, a firm must calculate the quantity and value of the stocks which it is holding. The value of stocks at the beginning and the end of the trading year, i.e. the opening stock and the closing stock, will affect the gross profit for the year. This is because the cost of sales in the trading account is adjusted for changes in stock. If, for example, the closing stock is overvalued, then the cost of sales will be lower and the gross profit higher. This is shown in Tables 4 and 5. In Table 4 the closing stock is £11,300, the cost of sales (adjusted for stock) is £57,400 and gross profit is £40,500.

Table 4:

	£	£
Turnover		97,900
Opening stock	12,300	
Cost of sales	56,400	
	68,700	
Less closing stock	11,300	
		57,400
Gross profit		40,500

Table 5:

	£	£
Turnover		97,900
Opening stock	12,300	
Cost of sales	56,400	
	68,700	
Less closing stock	14,100	
		54,600
Gross profit		43,300

In Table 5 the closing stock is now valued at £14,100 instead of £11,300, so the cost of sales (adjusted for stock) is lower at £54,600 and the gross profit higher at £43,300.

A **stock take** can be used to find out how much stock is held.

Question 2.

Laser Prompt is a London based sub contract laser cutting firm. From its state of the art plant, it will laser cut materials for a wide variety of uses in manufacturing. To retain its competitive edge, it is constantly investing in the latest technology. Two years ago, it bought a £500,000 cutting machine. This month it is about to take delivery of a £600,000 machine. It moved into its new £800,000 freehold premises just one year ago.

It has a policy of depreciating its assets on a reducing balance basis over their estimated useful economic lives as follows.

- Freehold property - 5 per cent per annum.
- Plant and machinery - 20 per cent per annum.

All plant and machinery is written off after five years.

(a) **Complete the following table based on the information in the data.**

Table 6: Laser Prompt depreciation, £

	Cutting machine		Freehold premises		Cutting machine	
Year	Depreciation	Net book value	Depreciation	Net book value	Depreciation	Net book value
2008	0	500,000	0	0	0	0
2009	100,000	400,000	0	800,000	0	0
2010	?	?	?	?	0	600,000
2011	?	?	?	?	?	?
2012	?	?	?	?	?	?
2013	?	?	?	?	?	?

Question 3.

During a trading period the following stock transactions were recorded for a company:
01.7.08 50 units were bought @ £2 per unit.
03.8.08 100 units were bought @ £2.20 per unit.
19.8.08 100 units were issued.
23.9.08 200 units were bought @ £2.30 per unit.
25.9.08 150 units were issued.

(a) Assuming that the opening stock was zero, calculate the value of closing stock using the:
(i) FIFO method; (ii) LIFO method; (iii) AVCO method. Present your answers in tables using a spreadsheet.

(b) If the stock listed in the transactions above was perishable, which of the three methods is most suitable for the physical issuing of stock? Explain why.

(c) Why do you think that the LIFO method is the least favoured by firms?

This involves making a list of all raw materials, finished goods and work-in-progress. Stock valuation is more difficult. The 'prudence' concept in accounting does not allow selling prices to be used because profit is only recognised when a sale has been made. So stocks are valued at historic cost or net realisable value, whichever is the lower. Normally stocks would be valued at cost. But there are circumstances when net realisable value is lower. If goods are damaged in stock, they may sell for a lot less than they cost to produce. Also, some products face severe changes in market conditions. Clothes tend to fall in value when fashions change, and may need discounts to sell them.

What happens to stock valuation when the cost of stock changes over time? Say a business buys some goods at the start of the year, but finds that half way through their cost of replacement has gone up. How are they valued? Three methods can be used.

- FIFO (first in first out).
- LIFO (last in first out).
- Average cost.

First in first out

The FIRST IN FIRST OUT method assumes that stock for production is issued in the order in which it was delivered. Thus, stocks that are bought first are used up first. Any unused stocks at the end of the trading year will be those most recently bought. This ensures that stocks issued for production are priced at the cost of earlier stocks, while any remaining stock is valued much closer to the replacement cost. Assuming that the opening stock is zero, consider the following stock transactions in Table 7.

On 1.6.08 a business receives 100 units of stock at £5, which means it has £500 of goods in stock. On 4.6.04, an extra 200 units at £6 (£1,200) are added, making a total of £1,700. On 25.6.08, 100 units are issued from stock for production. As it is first in first out, the goods are taken from the 1.6.08 stock, priced at £5 – the first stock to be received. This means £500 is removed from stock, leaving 200 units valued at £6 (£1,200) left in stock.

By using the FIFO method, the value of stocks after all the transactions is £650.

Last in first out

The LAST IN FIRST OUT method assumes that the most recent deliveries are issued before existing stock. In this case, any unused stocks are valued at the older and probably lower purchase price. Table 8 shows how the previous transactions are adjusted for a LIFO stock valuation. On 1.6.08, 100 units of stock are received at £5, meaning £500 of goods are in stock. On 4.6.08 an extra 200 units of stock valued at £6 are added (£1,200) – a total of £1,700. When 100 units of stock are issued on 25.6.08 they are taken from the most recent (last) stock received, priced at £6. So £600 of stock is removed. This leaves 100 units at £5 and 100 units at £6 in stock – a total of £1,100.

This time the value of stocks remaining after the transactions is £500. If the value of stocks is rising, the LIFO method gives a lower finishing stock than the FIFO method.

Table 7: A record of stock transactions showing how a closing stock figure is calculated using the FIFO method of stock valuation

Date	Stock received and price	Stock issued and price	Stock valuation	
			Goods in stock	Total
				£
01.6.08	100 @ £5		(100 @ £5 = £500)	500
04.6.08	200 @ £6		(100 @ £5 = £500)	
			(200 @ £6 = £1,200)	1,700
25.6.08		100 @ £5	(200 @ £6 = £1,200)	1,200
02.7.08		100 @ £6	(100 @ £6 = £600)	600
12.7.08	200 @ £6.50		(100 @ £6 = £600)	
			(200 @ £6.50 = £1,300)	1,900
23.7.08		100 @ £6	(200 @ £6.50 = £1,300)	1,300
24.7.08		100 @ £6.50	(100 @ £6.50 = £650)	650

Table 8: A record of stock transactions showing how a closing stock figure is calculated using the LIFO method of stock valuation

Date	Stock received and price	Stock issued and price	Stock valuation	
			Goods in stock	Total
				£
01.6.08	100 @ £5		(100 @ £5 = £500)	500
04.6.08	200 @ £6		(100 @ £5 = £500)	
			(200 @ £6 = £1,200)	1,700
25.6.08		100 @ £6	(100 @ £5 = £500)	
			(100 @ £6 = £600)	1,100
02.7.08		100 @ £6	(100 @ £5 = £500)	500
12.7.08	200 @ £6.50		(100 @ £5 = £500)	
			(200 @ £6.50 = £1,300)	1,800
23.7.08		100 @ £6.50	(100 @ £5 = £500)	
			(100 @ £6.50 = £650)	1,150
24.7.08		100 @ £6.50	(100 @ £5 = £500)	500

Average cost

This method involves recalculating the average cost (AVCO) of stock every time a new delivery arrives. Each unit is assumed to have been purchased at the average price of all components. In practice the average cost of each unit is a weighted average and is calculated using the following formula:

$$\frac{\text{Existing stock value + value of latest purchase}}{\text{Number of units then in stock}}$$

Using the same stock transactions as before we can find the closing stock by drawing up Table 9. This time the weighted average cost method is used.

When the AVCO method is used the value of stock following the transactions is £622. This stock figure lies closer to the FIFO method of stock valuation. It is often used when stock prices do not change a great deal. In practice it is the FIFO and average cost methods which are most commonly used by firms. Indeed, the LIFO method does not conform to the accounting standard SSAP, nor is it acceptable for tax purposes with the Inland Revenue. Once a method has been chosen it should conform to the 'consistency' convention and not change. This is also true for calculating depreciation.

Table 9: A record of stock transactions showing how a closing stock figure is calculated using the weighted average cost method of stock valuation

Date	Receipts	Issues	Weighted average cost £	Stock valuation	Total £
01.6.08	100 @ £5		5.00	(100 @ £5 = £500)	500
04.6.08	200 @ £6		5.67	(300 @ £5.67 = £1,701)	1,701
25.6.08		100	5.67	(200 @ £5.67 = £1,134)	1,134
02.7.08		100	5.67	(100 @ £5.67 = £567)	567
12.7.08	200 @ £6.50		6.22	(300 @ £6.22 = £1,866)	1,866
23.7.08		100	6.22	(200 @ £6.22 = £1,244)	1,244
24.7.08		100	6.22	(100 @ £6.22 = £622)	622

KEYTERMS

First in first out (FIFO) – a method of stock valuation which involves issuing stock in the order in which it is delivered, so that the remaining stock is valued closer to its replacement cost.

Last in first out (LIFO) – a method of stock valuation which involves issuing more recent deliveries first, so that closing stock is valued at the older and possibly lower purchase price.

Reducing or declining balance method – a method used to calculate the annual depreciation allowance which involves writing off the same percentage rate each year.

Straight line method – a method used to calculate the annual depreciation allowance by subtracting the estimated scrap value from the cost and dividing the result by the expected life of the asset.

KNOWLEDGE

1. Why is it necessary to provide for depreciation?
2. What are the main differences between the straight line and reducing balance methods of calculating depreciation?
3. State two advantages of the straight line method of calculating depreciation.
4. State two advantages of the reducing balance method of calculating depreciation.
5. What is meant by opening stock and closing stock?
6. Explain the difference between the LIFO and FIFO methods of stock valuation.
7. Why is stock not valued at its selling price?

Case Study: Glencoe Service Station

Stella McDonald runs the Glencoe Service Station in the Scottish Highlands. Most of the revenue is generated from the sale of petrol to tourists and other motorists passing through Glencoe on the busy A82. The garage also carries out minor motor repairs and provides a breakdown service. Movements of petrol stocks for July 2008 are shown in Table 10.

In 2008 Stella purchased a new breakdown truck for the business. The cost was £30,000 and the truck was expected to have a useful life of ten years. At the end of ten years it was estimated that the truck would have a residual value of £4,000.

Table 10: Petrol stock movements - July 2008

Date	Purchases (Litres)	Stocks used (Litres)
04.07.08	400,000 @ 100p	
07.07.08		350,000
07.07.08	400,000 @ 100p	
12.07.08		410,000
14.07.08	400,000 @ 100p	
18.07.08		360,000
19.07.08	400,000 @ 105p	
23.07.08		460,000
24.07.08	400,000 @ 105p	
28.07.08		410,000

(a) Calculate the value of closing stock at the end of July 2008 using the FIFO method. (8 marks)

(b) Assuming that petrol sales for July 2008 were £2,133,000, calculate the gross profit for the month. (Gross profit is turnover minus cost of sales. Cost of sales can be calculated using opening stock, closing stock and purchases. Assume opening stock for the month is zero.) (6 marks)

(c) (i) Calculate the closing stock using the LIFO method. (8 marks)

(ii) Show the effect on gross profit at the end of July. (4 marks)

(d) Using the straight line method of depreciation, calculate: (i) the annual depreciation provision for the breakdown truck; (4 marks) (ii) the book value of the breakdown truck at the end of each year. (4 marks)

(e) If Stella sold the breakdown truck for £12,000 at the end of year 6, what would be the profit or loss on disposal? (6 marks)

47 Working capital

What is working capital?

WORKING CAPITAL, sometimes called circulating capital, is the amount of money needed to pay for the day-to-day trading of a business. A business needs working capital to pay expenses such as wages, electricity and gas charges, and to buy components to make products. The working capital of a business is the amount left over after all current debts have been paid. It is:

- the relatively liquid assets of a business that can easily be turned into cash (cash itself, stocks, the money owing from debtors who have bought goods or services); *minus*
- the money owed by a business which needs to be paid in the short term (to the bank, to creditors who have supplied goods or services, to government in the form of tax or shareholders' dividends payable within the year).

In the balance sheet of a company working capital is calculated by subtracting current liabilities from current assets:

Working capital = current assets - current liabilities

The amount of working capital a business has is an important issue. It can reflect how well a business is performing. For example, a business that is struggling and threatened with closure is likely to have low levels of working capital. Consequently, if a balance sheet shows a low level of working capital, this should act as a signal that the business may be in trouble.

The working capital cycle

Managing working capital in a business is crucial. In many types of business, particularly manufacturing, delays or **time lags** exist between different stages of business activity. For example, there is a lag between buying materials and components and changing them into finished goods ready for sale. Similarly, there may be a delay between finishing the goods and the goods being sold to a customer. The WORKING CAPITAL CYCLE, shown in Figure 1, helps to illustrate the intervals between payments made by a business and the receipt of cash. The cycle shows the movement of cash and other liquid resources into and out of a business.

Time lags can occur at a number of stages in the working capital cycle.

Lag 1 Businesses usually purchase resources such as raw materials, components, fuel and other services from suppliers on credit. This means that a business can obtain resources without having to pay for them immediately. There might be a lag of up to 90 days before payment to suppliers has to be made. The length of the lag depends on suppliers' conditions. When a business is first set up, trade credit may not be granted until that business has proved to be creditworthy.

Lag 2 The next lag may occur as resources are turned into products using fixed assets, such as equipment. Work-in-progress (partially finished goods) is created and other costs are incurred, such as wages. The production process can take a long time depending on the nature of business activity. For example, for a cereal farmer this time lag could be about nine months. This would be the time it takes for corn seeds to be planted, grow into plants and eventually ripen so that the corn can be harvested. Alternatively, a furniture manufacturer might take about four to six weeks to make two armchairs and a settee for a customer.

Lag 3 Even when production is complete, a time lag can exist. Businesses may store their finished goods before they are sold to customers. This can be expensive. There may be warehousing costs and opportunity costs. However, storage enables a business to cope with unexpected increases in demand and allows continuous production. In recent years many businesses have adopted just-in-time manufacturing methods. Goods are only produced to order. This minimises stock holdings and reduces this time lag. When goods are distributed to customers further costs result, such as transport and handling costs.

Lag 4 A fourth time lag occurs when goods have finally been sold to customers. It is common business practice to allow customers to pay their bills over 30-90 days. However, depending on the nature of the business activity, this time lag can vary. For example, in many areas of retailing, goods are sold for cash only and this time lag is eliminated. Once cash has been

Figure 1: The working capital cycle

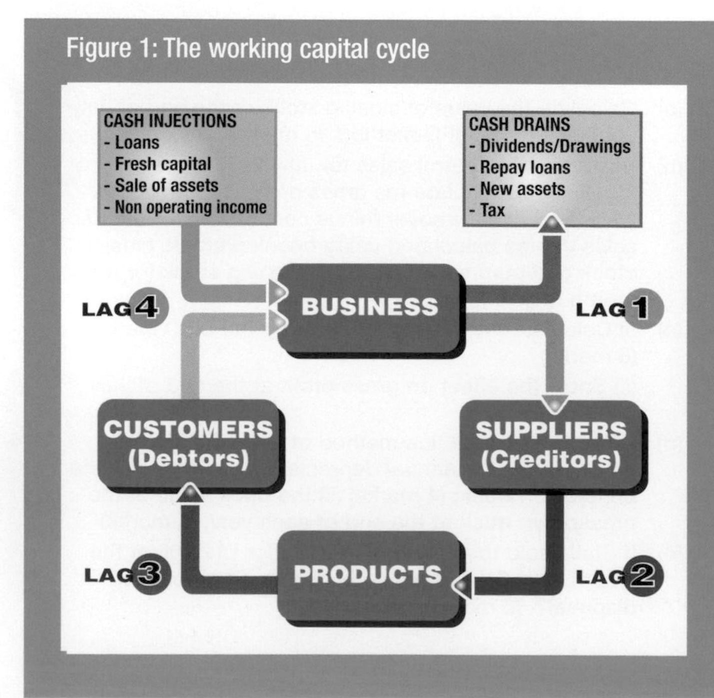

collected from customers much of it is used to keep the process going, for example buying more materials and paying wages.

Figure 1 also shows that a business can enjoy injections of cash from sources other than the sale of products. Loans, the sale of assets and new capital are common examples. However, at the same time there will be cash drains from the business. Cash will leak from the cycle to pay dividends or drawings, to pay tax, to repay loans and to purchase new fixed assets.

The length of time lags can be crucial when managing the working capital cycle. Business managers must attempt to prolong the first time lag by delaying payments to suppliers. However, this requires careful judgment because a business would not want to damage relations with valuable suppliers. Also, if payments are delayed for too long this could cause hardship for suppliers and eventually contribute to their downfall. Managers would ideally want to reduce:

- production time;
- the storage time of finished goods before they are dispatched to customers, by reducing stock holdings or encouraging just-in-time manufacturing, for example;
- the time it takes for customers to settle their bills, by monitoring and checking late payments or offering discount for early settlement, for example.

Different working capital needs

Different businesses have different working capital needs.

- **Size of business.** Sales typically generate a need for stocks, trade credit and cash. Hence the larger the business, the larger the amount of working capital there is likely to be. Equally, expanding businesses are likely to need growing amounts of working capital.
- **Stock levels.** Businesses in different industries have different needs for stocks. A window cleaning business is unlikely to carry much stock. A retailer is likely to carry considerable amounts of stock. Businesses which are able to adopt just-in-time techniques will carry lower stocks than other businesses. The more stocks a business needs, the higher will be its working capital, all other things being equal.
- **Debtors and creditors.** The time between buying stock financed by trade credit and selling finished products can influence levels of working capital. For example, a builder may need high levels of working capital because the time between starting a project and receiving payment from the client may be long.

At the other extreme, large supermarket chains can often operate with negative working capital (i.e. the current assets are less than their current liabilities). This happens because they buy in stock from suppliers and do not pay them for at least 30 days. The stock though is sold quickly on supermarket shelves, often within days of delivery from suppliers. Customers pay cash. So large supermarket chains can operate safely owing suppliers large amounts, but having very few debtors. The result is negative working capital.

Few businesses are fortunate enough to be able to operate with negative working capital. The textbook rule is that the typical business needs around twice the amount of current assets as current liabilities to operate safely. This means that its current ratio is between 1.5:1 and 2:1. This is how we can measure whether the business is performing effectively with regard to working capital.

Question 1.

Williams & Son

Williams & Son is a small property development company in Bradford. It buys plots of land or derelict properties and then builds houses or small apartment blocks. The business aims to complete one or two developments each year. Williams & Son incurs legal costs and pays architects fees before any building can begin. Most of the materials used by Williams & Son are bought on 60 days' credit from local builder's suppliers. Sometimes the new properties are not sold until after they have been completed. The business employs two other workers.

Tina's Taxi Service

Tina McKenna leases two minibuses and operates an airport taxi service in Gloucester and Cheltenham. She employs two drivers and also drives herself. The 24 hour service is successful, but competition is tightening in the area. Drivers are paid 25 per cent of their fares and get to keep their tips. They are paid weekly. All journeys are booked through Tina and drivers are instructed to accept only cash when collecting fares. In addition to the drivers' wages the main variable cost is diesel. Tina has an account with a local garage and is given 30 days' credit.

(a) Analyse the differences in the working capital cycles of the two businesses above.

The importance of keeping adequate levels of working capital

Businesses need to keep adequate levels of working capital. If they keep too little (ie current assets are too low and current liabilities are too high) they will start to encounter trading problems.

- If a business does not carry enough stocks of raw materials, it could find that production is halted when items run out of stock. If it does not carry enough finished stock, it might be unable to fulfil orders on time.
- If there is not enough cash in the business, it might not be able to pay its bills on time.
- If it has borrowed too much through trade credit, so it owes too much to creditors, it might be unable to pay invoices when they are due.

On the other hand, a business does not want too much working capital (ie current assets are too high and current liabilities are too low).

- Stocks are costly to keep. The more stock, the higher the cost of physically storing and handling it. The stock will

Question 2.

F&H Welding Products is a Black Country business which specialises in high-value high-specification welding contracts. The company has recently been through difficult times but has emerged stronger and financially more prudent.

The company had always tended to live from hand to mouth financially. There never seemed to be enough cash to pay the bills. Each month, the company would have to put off paying some bills that were due, or would be putting pressure on its bank to increase its overdraft facility. Two years ago, the company took on four large contracts, all of which were completed at roughly the same time. The company offered its customers 45 days credit but was buying from suppliers which were only offering 30 days credit. None of the customers for the four large contractors paid their invoices on time. After 60 days the company was on the verge of going into liquidation because it had exhausted all its sources of cash.

Frank Smith, the managing director, then went to see the four customers personally. He explained his dire situation. Two of the customers paid within 48 hours, enough to stave off the crisis. The other two said they would pay immediately, but in fact took another 30 days to pay.

The crisis had been made worse because the company had ordered extra stock in the belief that there would be an increase in new orders. In fact, orders fell 20 per cent over six months due to fierce competition from overseas suppliers.

Having sought advice, Frank Smith changed the way the company operated. He changed all customer contracts to give only 30 days free credit. He also offered a 5 per cent discount on the invoice for paying on time, which was paid for mainly by raising prices. He refused to accept orders from customers who were persistent late payers. He also reduced his stock levels and moved to ordering from suppliers who were prepared to deliver at short notice. Although the number of orders fell by one third, turnover only fell 15 per cent and profits were hardly down at all.

(a) 'F&H Welding Products suffered from poor credit control and overstocking.' Explain this statement.
(b) Examine how the company overcame these problems.
(c) 'F&H Welding Products simply didn't have enough working capital.' Discuss whether or not this was the case.

need to be insured while it may be liable to shrinkage (a business term for theft, usually by employees). Stock is also financially expensive because money tied up in stock could be used to reduce borrowing and so save interest for the business.

- Too much cash is also a problem because the cash is unlikely to be earning very high rates of interest. It could be used, perhaps, to pay back debts or to invest in higher interest long-term investments.
- If the number of debtors is high, the company could be allowing its customers too long to pay their invoices. If customers are taking 45 days on average to pay their bills when they only have 30 days credit given, the business would be losing the interest that could be earned on 15 days of credit. They also might have to spend scarce time chasing up late payments. In the UK, according to a 2004 survey by Intrum Justitia, invoices in the UK were on average paid 18 days late. Forty-seven per cent of all invoices are paid late, with 89 per cent of businesses saying that they suffered from late payments. Small businesses are more likely to suffer from late payment of invoices than large companies. The cost to British businesses of late payment was an estimated £20 billion, although many businesses benefit from themselves paying late.

Reasons for working capital problems

Many businesses find themselves in difficulties over working capital for a variety of reasons.

Poor control of debtors Too many businesses fail to control their debtors effectively. Partly this is because they fail to collect debts on time. Partly, it is because they give credit to businesses which fail, leaving the debt unpaid. For a small business, a bad debt, one which will not be paid, can be devastating. If large enough, it can lead to the business itself failing. Credit control systems can help avoid these problems. When a new customer approaches a business wanting trade credit, it should run a credit check on the customer. This could involve getting a bank reference from the customer, checking at Companies House to get the latest accounts of the customer or getting a credit rating agency report. A credit rating agency is a business which specialises in investigating and reporting on the creditworthiness of businesses. The business then has to decide whether to trade with the potential customer and if so set a maximum amount of **trade credit** that will be extended to it at any one time. Once a customer has received trade credit, the business should chase any overdue payments. This may involve a mixture of telephone calls or emails requesting payment, warning letters and in the last resort taking the customer to court. Customers who are too overdue with payments should be refused any new credit.

Overstocking and understocking Many businesses carry too much stock. Overstocking may arise because the business is being run inefficiently. Managers or owners have failed to realise the business could run with less stock, or they have failed to put in place systems which would minimise stock levels. A less common problem is understocking, where businesses carry too little stock. This leads to production problems. For instance, if a shop runs out of a line which is selling well, then it will lose sales.

Overtrading A common problem faced by small growing businesses is overtrading. This is when a business has insufficient working capital for its level of turnover. For example, a business might accept orders but then run up against trade credit limits set by its suppliers. It therefore can't order enough stock to complete the orders. It could turn to its bankers to get a higher overdraft limit, but its bankers may refuse because of the risk of failure of the business. The great danger in this situation is that one of the creditors of the business could take legal action to recover debts outstanding. Then the business may be forced to close even though its order book is profitable.

Overborrowing Businesses can borrow too much in the short term. For example, they can take too much trade credit. This might push them up against trade credit limits, risking a refusal to supply on extra orders. If the business fails to pay on time because it does not have the cash to pay, this can lose the business discounts for paying on time. Borrowing on overdraft from the bank also carries risks. If the business experiences trading difficulties, its bank may demand repayment of the overdraft afraid that the overdraft will not be repaid in the future. Being constantly at overdraft limits also doesn't allow for the unexpected. A small extra bill then could force the business to close because it does not have the cash to pay it.

Downturns in demand When the economy goes into recession, the number of business failures increases. Often this is because of problems with working capital. In a recession, orders and sales fall. Businesses often fail to react quickly enough. They allow stocks of finished goods to increase, causing overstocking. They then experience cash flow problems as they have to pay invoices from suppliers but don't have enough cash from sales of their own goods or services. In a recession, debtors also become more of a problem. If all businesses are experiencing difficulties, they will often try to solve short-term cash problems by delaying paying their bills. Recessions may also be associated with higher interest rates, as was the case in 1990-92. This increases the cost of running overdrafts and causes further cash flow problems.

Seasonal demand Businesses which face seasonal demand have to be careful that they have enough working capital at times of both peak demand and off-peak demand. A toy shop, for instance, may not have enough stock in the run up to Christmas, losing potential sales. On the other hand, it may have too little cash to pay for invoices in August when sales are likely to be very low.

Solving working capital problems

Businesses experience problems with working capital either because they have the wrong amount of working capital or because there is an imbalance between the different constituents of working capital. What tactics and strategies might a business use to try to deal with such working capital problems?

Too little or too much working capital in total What if the business does not have enough working capital to operate efficiently? There is a number of solutions to this.

- Raise more long-term finance. This could be long term loans, a share issue or putting new retained profit into working capital assets for example.
- A business unable to do this may choose to reduce its size to cope. By turning away orders and reducing sales, for example, it will need less stock and will reduce its debtors. In many cases, not enough working capital causes cash flow problems. Typically, a business with this sort of problem is continually short not just of cash but also of stocks and credit with suppliers.
- In some cases, management may manipulate working capital so that there is enough cash in the business. However, cash may be generated by running down stocks to crisis levels, or by increasing overdraft borrowings.

Sometimes businesses have too much working capital. They then need to identify which elements of working capital it would be best to reduce. The cash raised could then be used, for example, to pay off long-term debts, increase investment in the business or to pay a higher dividend to the owners.

An imbalance in the constituents of working capital Sometimes businesses have enough working capital in total, but it is badly allocated. For example, a business may not have enough cash to pay its weekly bills. But it may be holding more stock than it needs to operate efficiently. Reducing stock levels could increase the amount of cash in the business and so resolve the problem.

Similarly, a liquidity problem might occur at the same time as a business has an excessive amount of debtors. Chasing up debtors and getting more to pay on time through better credit control will inject cash into the business.

Improving cash flow may not be the problem though. It could be that a business has too much cash but too little stock. Management might be too cautious and hold excessive amounts of cash leading to production problems as stock levels are too low. Equally, management may turn away orders to avoid having to give trade credit to customers when it has more than enough cash to finance an expansion of sales.

Working capital and cash flow

It might be assumed that working capital problems are the same as cash flow problems. Although cash flow and working capital are interlinked, and many working capital problems are cash flow problems as well, they are not the same.

For example, one way of dealing with a cash flow problem is to increase borrowing through an overdraft facility or a short-term bank loan repayable within one year. Borrowing more in the short term will lead to an increase in cash, a current asset. So it could solve a cash flow problem. But it will not increase working capital. This is because such borrowing also increases current liabilities. The money borrowed is, in theory, repayable within 12 months. Another way in which a business can solve a cash flow problem is to run down its stocks. Not reordering stock means that less cash is leaving the business. But improving cash flow in this way leaves the amount of working capital exactly the same. On the balance sheet, all that happens immediately is that the value of stocks falls whilse the value of cash rises. Equally, a common short-term way of dealing with a cash flow problem is for a business to delay paying its bills. This increases the amount of cash in the business. But it also increases the amount of creditors. There is no change in overall working capital.

However, a business with persistent cash flow problems is likely to have a shortage of working capital. The most likely solution to both problems is to increase the equity in the business or to borrow more in the long term.

Working capital and profit

Loss making businesses are likely to have working capital problems. But so do some profitable businesses. Working capital and profit are not the same. For example, a business might be offered a contract which would be highly profitable. However, it may be unable to take it because it does not have enough working capital. Payment for the contract might only arrive in four months' time, one month after completion. In the meantime, stocks need to be paid for, wages of extra workers will be owed and other costs will be incurred. If the firm's suppliers will not extend any more credit and if the firm's bank will not extend its overdraft, the finance for these expenses will not be available.

In general, businesses which are unprofitable run into working capital problems. Losses drain cash away from the business. This ultimately leads to both cash flow problems and therefore inadequate levels of working capital. However, a business may get around this by raising long-term finance. An unprofitable business can survive if long-term finance is being used to top up its working capital.

Late Payment of Commercial Debts

Small businesses complain that larger organisations use their power to exploit smaller firms by making them wait before payment is made. This can create working capital problems for small businesses, particularly when the large firm is the only customer of the small firm. The government recognised the problem and introduced the **Late Payment of Commercial Debts (Interest) Act 1998** and the **Late Payment of Commercial Debts Regulations 2002** to give small firms help. Legislation financially penalises late payers. It gives all businesses a right:

- to charge interest on unpaid debts;
- to claim reasonable debt recovery costs;
- to challenge contractual terms that do not provide a substantial remedy against late payment;
- for representative bodies to challenge contractual terms that are grossly unfair to SMEs (small and medium-sized enterprises).

Only time will tell whether legislation will be effective. Its critics say that the worst thing a business can do when a customer can't or won't pay is ask for even more money.

KEYTERMS

Working capital – the funds left over to meet day-to-day expenses after current debts have been paid. It is calculated by current assets minus current liabilities.
Working capital cycle – the flow of liquid resources into and out of a business.

KNOWLEDGE

1. How is the value of working capital calculated?
2. At what point does a business have sufficient working capital to avoid a problem?
3. State four time lags that exist in the working capital cycle.
4. State two ways in which time lags can be reduced.
5. State three examples of cash drains from the working capital cycle.
6. Why can some businesses operate with negative working capital?
7. Can a business have too much working capital? Explain.
8. Explain the link between working capital and profit.

Case Study: LED Ltd and Hopes Ltd

LED Ltd

LED Ltd is a family company and manufactures gears for conveyer belt systems. Some examples of their products are shown below.

- **Worm gears** – gears which offer protection against corrosion.
- **Bevel gears** – used to redirect the shaft from a horizontal gas turbine engine to the vertical rotor.
- **Ring gears** – gears which increase or decrease motion.
- **Helical gears** – gears which allow motors to be installed at right angles to the axis of equipment.
- **Bevel helical gears** – used as a storage and retrieval unit.

LED Ltd operates in a fairly stable market and uses just-in-time (JIT) manufacturing techniques. It holds very little stocks of raw materials, components, work-in-progress or finished goods. Most of LED's sales are on 90 day trade credit. In 2007 the company increased its turnover to £3,640,000 and made a profit of £221,000.

Table 1: Financial information for LED Ltd and Hopes Ltd, 2008

	LED Ltd (£)	Hopes Ltd (£)
Turnover	3,640,000	3,786,000
Profit before tax	221,000	289,000
Current assets		
Stocks	10,000	460,000
Debtors	385,000	112,000
Cash at bank and in hand	343,000	123,000
	738,000	**695,000**
Current liabilities		
Short term bank loan	0	200,000
Trade creditors	369,000	387,000
Dividend proposed	50,000	60,000
Corporation tax	45,000	53,000
Other creditors	22,000	45,000
	486,000	**745,000**

Hopes Ltd

Hopes Ltd is a large independent DIY store located in Edinburgh. Its product range is fairly typical for a DIY store and includes paint, wall coverings, tiles, bathroom units, kitchen units, kitchen appliances, tools, building materials, fittings, flooring, garden tools and furniture and heating and plumbing materials. It has managed to maintain its independence and compete with some of the larger DIY stores such as B&Q by offering exceptional levels of customer service. For example, Hopes will deliver orders for customers free of charge. The company also offers trade credit to a selection of regular customers (although most sales are still for cash). Hopes buys its stock from a wide range of manufacturers and wholesalers and on average enjoys 45 days trade credit.

In 2008, Hopes Ltd took out a short-term loan to pay for the construction of a large greenhouse adjacent to the store. This allowed the company to grow and stock a wider range of plants and similar products.

(a) Explain what is meant by working capital. (4 marks)

(b) Describe the cash injection into Hopes' working capital cycle in 2008. (4 marks)

(c) Explain two possible reasons why Hopes Ltd has a much higher figure for stocks than LED Ltd. (8 marks)

(d) What difficulties might LED Ltd encounter operating with such a low level of stocks? (6 marks)

(e) Calculate the working capital for LED Ltd and Hopes Ltd. (6 marks)

(f) Account for the differences in working capital between the two companies. (12 marks)

48 Profit and loss accounts and income statements

The nature of profit

Profit is the driving force in most businesses. There are few, if any, which attach no importance to making profit, the exceptions perhaps being charities. Even state run industries, whose major objective has been to provide a comprehensive service, have pursued profits in recent years.

Profit has a number of functions. The prospect of making profit motivates people to set up in business. Without profit there would be little incentive for individuals to commit their time and personal resources to business activity. Economists often refer to **normal profit**. This is the minimum reward an entrepreneur must receive in order to maintain interest in the business. If the business does not earn this amount of profit the owner will pull out and pursue other opportunities.

Profit also helps resource allocation in market economies. Businesses that make profits are able to purchase more raw materials and labour in order to expand production. Investors are attracted to those businesses that are likely to give the greatest financial reward. Economists call this abnormal profit - the amount by which total profit is greater than normal profit.

The amount of profit that a business makes is a measure of how well it is performing. Those firms that supply quality products which are efficiently produced and sold at prices which are attractive to consumers will tend to be more profitable. However, there are other factors which affect the performance of a business, such as the competition a business faces. From an accountant's point of view, profit is the amount of money left over in a particular trading period when all business expenses have been met. Profit can then be:

- retained;
- used to pay tax;
- distributed to the owners of the company.

If expenses exceed sales revenue in a trading period then there will be a loss. It is the accountant's definition of profit which we will be referring to in this unit.

Measuring profit

At the end of the trading year most owners like to see how well their company has performed. One initial indication of performance is the amount of profit (or loss) that the business has made during that year. Figure 1 illustrates how profit (and loss) is measured. It is the difference between turnover and business costs.

Businesses measure their profit by compiling a PROFIT AND LOSS ACCOUNT or an INCOME STATEMENT. These provide a summary of a company's profit or loss during any one given period of time, such as a month, three months, or one year. Before January 2005 all businesses produced profit and loss accounts. After, public limited companies were required to adopt international accounting standards (IAS) and produce an income statement. This has a slightly different format to a traditional profit and loss account. Other types of businesses continue to use profit and loss accounts.

Figure 1: Profit and loss

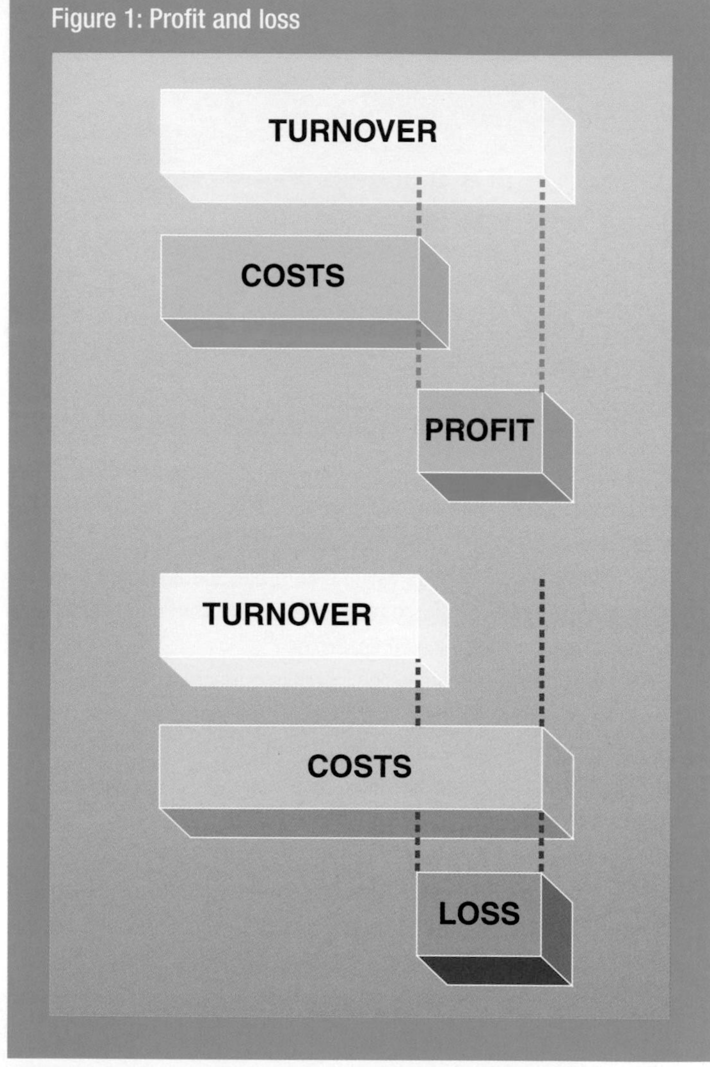

Profit and loss account

A profit and loss account for the year ending 31 January 2008 is shown in Table 1. It shows the business transactions for Virginian Carpets Ltd, a carpet wholesaler which specialises in Moroccan carpets. It is divided into three sections: the TRADING ACCOUNT; the PROFIT AND LOSS ACCOUNT; the PROFIT AND LOSS APPROPRIATION ACCOUNT.

The trading account

The trading account shows the revenue earned from selling products (the turnover) and the cost of those sales. Subtracting

Table 1: The profit and loss account for Virginian Carpets Ltd for the period ending 31.12.08

	VIRGINIAN CARPETS LTD Profit and loss account for the year ended 31 January 2008	£
	Turnover	900,000
(less)	Cost of sales	500,000
	Gross profit	400,000
(less)	Expenses	300,000
	Operating profit	100,000
(plus)	Non-operating income	20,000
	Profit on ordinary activities before interest	120,000
(plus)	Interest receivable	5,000
(less)	Interest payable	15,000
	Profit on ordinary activities before taxation/ Net profit	110,000
(less)	Corporation tax	27,500
	Profit after tax	82,500
(less)	Dividends	40,000
	Retained profit for the period	42,500

one from the other gives **gross profit**. In Table 1, Virginian Carpets Ltd made a gross profit of £400,000 in the year ending 31.1.08.

The **turnover** or **sales revenue** figure shows the income from selling goods or services. For the year ending 31.1.08, Virginian Carpets Ltd had sales revenue of £900,000. According to the **realisation concept** a sale is made only when goods are delivered to customers. This is important because profit must be **included** in the same trading period as sales. Goods which have been manufactured but not sold to customers are **excluded** and goods which have been sold and payment not received are **included**. The final turnover figure may have to be adjusted for a number of reasons.

- Businesses must exclude indirect taxes such as VAT from the turnover figure. VAT is added to the sale price of goods. It is paid by consumers to businesses, which then hand it over to the government. Including VAT would overstate a firm's turnover.
- Sales of goods which are returned because they are faulty or unwanted must be removed from the turnover figure. Turnover will be overstated if their value were included.

Table 2: Cost of sales adjusted for stock

Opening stock 1.2.07	80,000
Purchases during the year	600,000
	680,000
less Closing stock 31.1.08	180,000
Cost of sales	500,000

- Errors often occur on invoices - documents which tell the purchaser how much is owed for the goods that are purchased. If there is an error which overstates the value of a sale, an adjustment must be made to turnover. Businesses usually send a credit note to cover the exact amount that the purchaser has been 'overcharged'.
- Sometimes a customer who has bought goods on credit is unable to pay for them. The turnover figure is usually left unchanged. However, businesses do record the value of an unpaid sale as a business expense in the profit and loss account as a bad debt.

The second figure listed in the trading account is the **cost of sales**. This refers to all costs of production. It will include direct costs such as raw materials, the wages of labour and other indirect costs or **overheads** associated with production (known as production overheads) such as fuel and rent.

It is often necessary to adjust the cost of raw materials for changes in stock. The cost of sales for Virginian Carpets Ltd in Table 1 is £500,000. This is mainly the cost of buying carpets for resale from Morocco. However, it is likely that during the trading year some of the carpets sold were bought in previous trading years and held in stock. Also, some of the carpets bought during the trading year will remain unsold and so the cost of sales must be adjusted.

In Table 2, at the beginning of the trading year, Virginian Carpets had £80,000 worth of carpets in stock. During the trading year £600,000 worth of new carpets were imported from Morocco. At the very end of the trading year the stock of carpets unsold was valued at £180,000. Therefore the cost of sales was £500,000. Only purchases of goods for resale are included in 'cost of sales' figures. Expenditure, such as stationery, that is not for resale is not included.

The gross profit of £400,000 in Table 1 is found by subtracting the cost of sales from the turnover.

The profit and loss account

The **profit and loss account** is an extension of the trading account. In practice, there is no indication of where the trading account ends and the profit and loss account begins. However, once a business has calculated its **gross profit** it can then calculate how much profit (or loss) it has made by adding any extra income it has earned and subtracting its expenses and tax.

Question 1.

Berry Ltd is a stockist of metals. The company is based in Telford and supplies a wide range of customers such as engineers and metal fabricators in the local area. Some of its stock items include metal tubes, angle iron, plate and sheet metal, galvanised, corrugated and cladding metal sheet, perforated metals, square and rod metals and stair treads.

Table 3: Trading account for Berry Ltd, year ending 31.12.08

Berry Ltd
Trading account for year ending 31.12.08

	£	£
Turnover		780,400
Cost of sales		
Purchases	489,300	
Plus opening stock	******	
	554,600	
Less closing stock	71,300	
		483,300
Gross profit		******

(a) What is the purpose of a trading account?
(b) Complete the trading account in Table 3 by calculating opening stock and gross profit.
(c) Explain why Berry's turnover will be exclusive of VAT.

Table 4: Operating (administrative) expenses for Virginian Carpets Ltd

	£	£
Expenses		
Wages and salaries (admin.)	110,000	
Rent and rates	40,000	
Heating and lighting	30,000	
Advertising	15,000	
Motor expenses	24,000	
Telephone	8,000	
Printing and stationery	13,000	
Insurance	9,000	
Accountancy fees	4,000	
Provision for bad debts	12,000	
Depreciation	35,000	
		300,000

In Table 1 the **profit after tax** earned by Virginian Carpets Ltd for the year ended 31 January 2008 was £82,500.

The first item to be subtracted from the gross profit figure is **expenses.** Expenses are those overheads or indirect costs that are not involved in production of goods and services. They include advertising and promotion, wages of the administration staff and depreciation. Table 4 gives a breakdown of the expenses incurred by Virginian Carpets Ltd during the trading year. They reflect the type of costs associated with companies. The breakdown of these figures is normally shown in the notes to the accounts or a separate Trading and Profit and Loss Account.

Subtracting expenses from gross profit gives a figure for OPERATING PROFIT. Operating profit is often regarded by businesses as the key indicator of trading performance. It is generally defined as the profit made by a company as a result of its ordinary trading activities.

The company will then add any non-operating income to its operating profit. Non-operating income is income which is not earned from the direct trading of the company. This could include dividends from shares held in other companies or rent from property that is let out.

The next stage is to add or subtract interest. Interest is received by a business from deposits in financial institutions and is paid out on borrowings. If any interest is receivable it is added. If any interest is paid out it is subtracted. This is sometimes shown as one figure. It is called **net interest receivable** if interest received is more than interest payable. However, for Virginian Carpets (Table 1) the figure would be **net interest payable** of £10,000 as £5,000 has been received but £15,000 is payable.

When this final adjustment has been made the resulting figure is the **profit on ordinary activities before tax** (sometimes known as **net profit**) of £110,000. In the notes to the accounts there are often further details of expenses incurred during the year. For example, by law, the notes must show the directors' rewards, ie salaries, the auditor's fee, depreciation of fixed assets, donations and the number of employees receiving payments.

The final entry in the profit and loss account is the profit after taxation, £82,500. All limited companies have to pay corporation tax on profits over a certain amount to the government. The amount paid by Virginian Carpets Ltd is £27,500.

The profit and loss appropriation account

The final section in the profit and loss account is the **appropriation account.** This shows how the company profit or loss is distributed. Any profit made by a company is distributed in a number of ways. In Table 1, the profit of Virginian Carpets Ltd is distributed as follows:

- £27,500 is paid to the HR Revenue and Customs for corporation tax;
- £40,000 is paid to shareholders in the form of a dividend;
- £42,500 is retained by the business for the year (2008) for internal use in future periods. The business is also likely to have profit from previous years. If, for example, it had £127,500 retained profit from previous periods then it would have £127,500 plus £42,500 or £170,000 profit to **carry forward** to future years.

Most companies retain a proportion of profit for investment

or as a precaution. The amount paid out in dividends is determined by the board of directors and approved by the shareholders at the Annual General Meeting. Although the business is not legally obliged to pay dividends, shareholders may be dissatisfied if they are not paid.

Sole trader accounts

Table 5 shows the trading and profit and loss account for Joanna Cullen, a retailer selling computers. The differences and similarities between the profit and loss account of a sole trader and a limited company can be illustrated from Table 5. The profit and loss account of a sole trader normally shows how the year's purchases are adjusted for stock by including opening and closing stocks. In addition, a more detailed list of expenses is included. This allows a comparison with the previous year. A profit and loss appropriation account is not included since there is only one owner and all profit is transferred to the capital account in the balance sheet.

The presentation of a sole trader profit and loss account can vary quite significantly. Variations occur due to the nature of the business and preferences in the style of presentation.

Table 5: The profit and loss account for Joanna Cullen, a sole trader

JOANNA CULLEN
Trading and profit and loss account for the year ended 31.5.08

2007			2008
£		£	£
130,000	**Turnover**		150,000
25,000	Opening stock	30,000	
65,000	Purchases	70,000	
90,000		100,000	
30,000	*less* Closing stock at selling price	35,000	
60,000			65,000
70,000	**Gross profit**		85,000
	less:		
1,000	Casual labour	2,000	
2,500	Motor expenses	3,000	
800	Telephone	1,000	
2,500	Printing, stationery & advertising	3,000	
1,300	Electricity	1,500	
8,000	Rent and rates	9,000	
400	Insurance	500	
2,500	Bank interest & charges	2,500	
2,000	Depreciation - car	2,000	
900	Depreciation - fixtures & fittings	900	
21,900			25,400
48,100	**Net profit**		59,600

Question 2.

The Frozen Food Centre is owned and run by Imran Rasul, a sole trader. The store is located in a busy shopping centre in Bournemouth. The business is very profitable but Imran believed that the store had the capacity to at least double its turnover. In 2008 Imran invested heavily in marketing. He advertised the store on local radio and followed this up with the distribution of regular monthly leaflets. The profit and loss account for the Frozen Food Centre is shown in Table 6.

Table 6: The Frozen Food Centre

Profit and loss account year ending 31.12.08

	2008	2007
	£	£
Turnover	785,600	529,700
Opening stock	37,300	36,900
Purchases	498,400	369,100
	535,700	406,000
Less closing stock	38,100	37,300
Cost of Sales	497,600	368,700
Gross profit	288,000	161,000
Less:		
Wages	45,300	44,100
Motor expenses	10,600	15,900
Telephone	900	800
Electricity	2,300	2,100
Rent & rates	12,000	12,000
Advertising	10,800	400
Insurance	2,300	2,100
Accountancy fees	1,600	1,500
Depreciation	6,500	6,500
	92,300	85,400
Net profit	195,700	75,600

(a) Explain how the profit and loss account distinguishes between gross profit and net profit.

(b) Explain one main difference between the sole trader account shown in Table 6 and that of a private limited company.

(c) Explain the change in turnover between 2007 and 2008.

(d) Comment on the performance of the Frozen Food Centre over the two years.

Public limited company accounts

Public limited companies have similar accounts to those of private limited companies, such as Virginian Carpets. They must also publish their accounts by law. In 2005, plcs were required to replace the profit and loss account with an **income statement**. The income statement records all revenues for a business during this given period. It also shows the operating expenses for the business. It is very similar to the profit and loss account of a private limited company. Table 7 shows the income statement for J Sainsbury plc. The following points should be noted.

- Plcs must show separately profit from continuing operations (businesses they currently own) and discontinued operations (businesses that were sold during the year). In this case J Sainsbury does not have any discontinued operations.
- The term 'revenue' is used instead of turnover or sales.
- The terms 'finance income' and 'finance costs' are used instead of interest received and interest paid.
- The income statement does not show dividends or retained profit. It just shows the profit attributable to the equity holders of the parent company (the shareholders of Sainsbury) and minority interests (shareholder groups with a very small interest).

Table 7: Income statement for J Sainsbury plc

J Sainsbury plc Group Income Statement
For the 52 weeks to 24th March 2007

	2007 £m	2006 £m
Continuing operations		
Revenue	17,151	16,061
Cost of sales	(15,979)	(14,994)
Gross profit	1,172	1,067
Administrative expenses	(669)	(839)
Other income	17	1
Operating profit	520	229
Finance income	64	30
Finance costs	(107)	(155)
Profit before taxation	477	104
Tax	(153)	(46)
Profit for the financial year	324	58
Attributable to:		
Equity holders of the parent	325	64
Minority interests	(1)	(6)
	324	58
Earnings per share	Pence	Pence
Basic	19.2	3.8
Diluted	18.9	3.8

Source: adapted from J Sainsbury, Annual Report and Accounts, 2007.

- Plc accounts show the **earnings per share** (EPS) at the bottom of the income statement. This is calculated by dividing the profit after tax by the total number of issued shares. The earnings per share gives an indication of a company's performance. The higher it is the better. The EPS is always shown for the basic shareholding and the fully diluted shareholding (the diluted shareholding includes shares which may be purchased as a result of share option schemes the company has).
- From time to time business may make a 'one-off' transaction. An example of an **exceptional item** might be a very large bad debt which is deducted as normal in the profit and loss account, but disclosed separately in the notes. In recent years some of the commercial banks have had to make such entries after incurring bad debts from Third World countries. An example of an **extraordinary item** might be the cost of management restructuring. Generally they arise from events outside the normal business activities and are not expected to occur again. The expenditure would normally be listed in the profit and loss account, below the line showing profit after tax.
- Limited companies often produce consolidated accounts. This happens when a business group is made up of several different companies or divisions. Each company is likely to retain a separate legal identity and produce its own accounts. However, the group is also obliged to produce accounts for the whole organisation. These consolidated accounts are produced by adding together the results of all the individual companies.

Assessing performance and potential

Profit and loss accounts and income statements can be used to evaluate the performance and potential of a business.

Overall profit Business owners are keen to see how much profit they have made at the end of the trading year. The size of the profit may be a guide to the performance of the business. A comparison is also possible because a profit and loss account will show the previous year's figures. It is possible to calculate the gross profit margin and net profit margin from the profit and loss account.

Controlling costs A profit and loss account can be used by managers to see how well a business has controlled its overheads. If the gross profit is far larger than the net profit, this would suggest that the company's overheads are quite high. However, if there is little difference between the two this could suggest that a business has controlled its overheads.

Measuring growth A business can use the profit and loss account to help measure its growth. A guide to a business's growth may be the value of turnover compared with the previous year's. If the turnover is significantly larger than the previous year's, this could suggest that the business has grown.

Benefits to shareholders The earnings per share is also shown on the profit and loss account for limited companies. This shows shareholders in a limited company how much each share has earned over the year. However, this is not necessarily the amount of money which they will receive from the company. This is the dividends per share.

Benefits to other stakeholders Other stakeholders may also use the profit and loss account. For example, workers may use it to argue for improvements in their pay and conditions of service. Banks are likely to ask to see the profit and loss account if a business wishes to borrow money. Suppliers may check the profit and loss account of a business to decide whether or not to give trade credit. Potential investors in the business may use the profit and loss account as one indication of whether the business is likely to do well in the future. The tax authorities use the profit and loss account to calculate some taxes on businesses. All businesses, including sole traders who are self-employed, have to keep records of financial transactions. Finally, the media may publish stories about businesses using accounts as a source of information.

However, there are certain limitations when using profit and loss accounts and income statements to assessing performance.

Other financial data The profit and loss account only gives data about revenue, costs, profit and how the profit is used. Much more financial data is needed to assess accurately the performance of a business. For example, the cash flow position of the business is a vital indicator of performance. So too is the size of the borrowings of the business.

Other business data The profit and loss account gives data about the finances of a business. But it does not say anything about the environmental or social impact of the business and only indirectly gives information about new product development or efficiency of production. Financial data is only one source of data for evaluating the overall performance of a business.

Past, present and future The profit and loss account is a record of the past performance of a business. So it can be used as one piece of evidence to evaluate the performance of the business in the past. But it is not necessarily a good indication of present or future performance. Much can happen within six months or a year to a business. The economy might go into recession. There might be a sudden fall in demand for the products of a business. A new competitor might enter the market and be highly successful. A business whose profit and loss accounts show a period of ten years of successful growth in revenues and profits might suddenly see a fall in turnover and a slump into loss in the eleventh year.

Trends The profit and loss account for a single year is of limited value when judging performance. It gives an indication of the profitability of the business. But one year's figures would not indicate whether the business is growing or declining, or whether the profit is unusually high or low. The more periods of data available, the more reliable any evaluation can be.

The level of detail in the account The more detail in the profit and loss account, the more information available to be analysed.

Question 3.

Ultra Electronics is a defence and aerospace company specialising in the design, manufacture and support of electronic and electro-mechanical systems, sub-systems, products and services for aircraft, ships, submarines armoured vehicles, surveillance and communication systems, airports and transport systems. Table 8 shows the company's income statement for 2006.

Table 8: Income statement for Ultra Electronics 2006

Ultra Electronics
Income statement for year ending 31.12.06

	2006	2005
Continuing operations	**£000**	**£000**
Revenue	377,040	342,410
Cost of sales	(274,466)	(250,160)
Gross profit	102,574	92,250
Other operating income	1,505	4,805
Distribution costs	(810)	(825)
Administrative expenses	(48,569)	(48,393)
Other operating expenses	(753)	-
Operating profit	53,947	47,837
Investment revenue	4,939	553
Finance cost	(3,874)	(7,688)
Profit before tax	55,012	40,702
Tax	(15,404)	(11,292)
Profit attributable to equity holders of the parent company	39,608	29,410
Earnings per share (pence)		
Basic	58.8	43.9
Diluted	58.3	43.5

Source: adapted from Ultra Electronics, Annual Report and Accounts, 2006.

(a) Give two possible examples of administrative expenses for Ultra Electronics
(b) What is meant by the term 'finance cost' in the income statement above?
(c) What is meant by 'continuing operations' in the above statement?
(d) Comment briefly on the performance of Ultra Electronics over the two years.

Companies tend to give the minimum information required by law. So anyone looking at published accounts will not necessarily pick up important trends or features within the accounts. Far more background information will, however, be available to managers within the company if they are using profit and loss figures to assess performance. Sole traders and partnerships should have full access to all the detail behind the final profit and loss account drawn up.

'Window dressing' the accounts For sole traders and partnerships, profit and loss accounts are typically prepared for the tax authorities. There may be a temptation to minimise profit, for example by not putting some revenue 'through the books' or exaggerating costs. This will then reduce the amount of tax that has to be paid. Companies too may manipulate their accounts to present a better picture than is actually the case.

Special characteristics of individual accounts Profit and loss accounts can have special features which need to be noted in evaluating performance. Occasionally a business will change its tax year. Accounts might for a single period be presented for 9 months or 15 months, say, instead of the usual 12 months. An increase in profit would be expected if the accounts covered 15 months rather than 12 months. Exceptional and extraordinary items should also be carefully studied. Some businesses are constantly taking over and closing down businesses. Every year they may record extraordinary items in their account as a result. This makes it very difficult to judge performance over time from the profit and loss account. Equally, the costs and revenue sources of these businesses are constantly changing. It becomes very difficult to judge from the profit and loss account whether the operations of the business are being well managed because so much of the profit is coming from new parts of the business.

The importance of profit utilisation and profit quality

When making decisions using financial data one of the key financial indicators used is profit. Most businesses pursue profit and generally businesses will choose the course of action that is likely to generate the most profit. However, it will be necessary to consider PROFIT QUALITY. It is possible for a business to earn a high level of profit due to exceptional or extraordinary circumstances. For example, in a particular year a large proportion of the profit made by a company may be the result of selling part of its business for a much higher than expected price. In this year the profit quality would be considered low. It is important to analyse the profit of a business over a period of time – at least five years, say. High quality profit is profit that can be sustained by the normal trading activities of a business over a period of time.

It is also necessary to consider PROFIT UTILISATION. The profit after tax made by a business may be **utilised** in two ways. Most businesses return some of the profit to the owners. In the case of limited companies the shareholders are likely to be paid dividends from the profit. Clearly, if the owners of the business do not receive a fairly regular 'financial payback', they are likely to withdraw their interest. In the case of plcs this may involve investors selling their shares. If this happens on a large enough scale the share price will fall and the company could become the target of a takeover. This might mean that the directors could be replaced.

Any profit remaining after owners have been compensated is retained by the business. This may be used for investment purposes – to expand operations, for example. Alternatively it may be placed in reserve to be used when the business has an urgent need for such funds. It might even be used to pay dividends in a year when profits are low.

How much profit should be retained? In plcs it is the job of directors to find the 'right balance' between dividends and retained profit. Using retained profit to fund investment in the business is a very cheap source of finance. However, shareholders may be more interested in the shortterm gains from holding shares. Directors will have to use their judgment when deciding how much profit to retain and how much to give back to shareholders.

KEYTERMS

Operating profit – the profit made by a business as a result of its ordinary trading activities.

Profit and loss account or income statement – a financial document showing a company's revenue/income and costs/expenditure over a particular time period, usually one year.

Profit and loss account – shows net profit after tax by subtracting business expenses and taxation from operating profit.

Profit and loss appropriation account – shows how the profit after tax is distributed between shareholders and the business.

Profit quality – occurs when profits are sustained over a period of time; there is low profit quality if profit in one time period is mainly due to some one-off factor which is not sustainable.

Profit utlisation – the way in which profit made by a business is distributed.

Trading account – shows operating profit by subtracting the cost of sales from turnover.

KNOWLEDGE

1. What is meant by profit from an accountant's point of view?
2. What is likely to happen to a business if normal profit is not made?
3. Distinguish between gross and operating profit.
4. What adjustments might need to be made to turnover during the year?
5. Why is it necessary to adjust purchases for changes in stock levels?
6. What is meant by non-operating income?
7. How might a limited company appropriate its profits?
8. How are earnings per share calculated?
9. What is the difference between an extraordinary item and an exceptional item?
10. How might the profit and loss account of a sole trader be different from that of a limited company?
11. How might the profit and loss account be used by a business?
12. How might a business calculate its: (a) gross profit ratio; (b) net profit ratio?

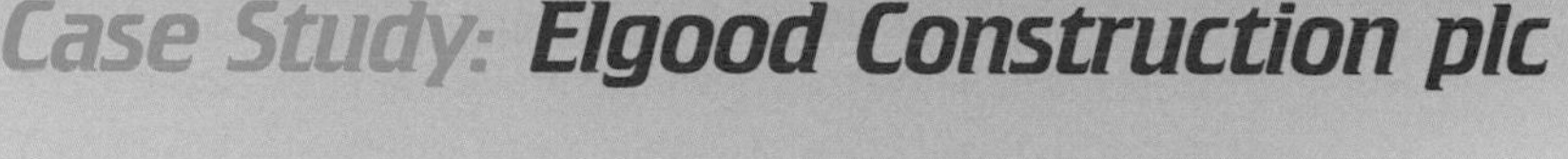

Case Study: Elgood Construction plc

Table 9: Income statement for Elgood Construction plc

Elgood Construction plc
Income statement for the year ending 31.12.08

	2008	2007
Continuing operations	£m	£m
Revenue	*******	1,980
Cost of sales	920	810
Gross profit	1,380	1,170
Distribution expenses	600	500
Admin expenses	230	250
Operating profit	550	420
Finance costs	30	********
Profit on ordinary activities before tax	520	390
Taxation	******	80
Profit attributable to equity holders	420	310
Earnings per share		
Basic	23.6p	18.9p
Diluted	22.1p	17.7p

Elgood Construction plc is a large construction company. Located in South Wales, it is a well-established business, which offers a wide range of construction services and undertakes large construction projects for the Welsh government and other high profile customers. The company has been trading for over 25 years and takes pride in the provision of a reliable, professional service and has a reputation for quality workmanship. The company is also a member of the Guild of Master Craftsmen. Throughout the life of the company it has never spent money on advertising or promotion. According to Arthur Elgood, the company chairman, 'We rely on client recommendations to build our business, so you can bet we are never happy with our services until you are'. The income statement for Elgood Construction plc is shown in Table 9.

(a) Complete the income statement by calculating (i) revenue in 2008; (ii) finance costs in 2007; (iii) taxation in 2008. (6 marks)

(b) Explain what is meant by (i) earnings per share; (ii) cost of sales; shown in the account. (6 marks)

(c) Who might be interested in Elgood's income statement? (8 marks)

(d) Analyse the performance of the company over the two years. (10 marks)

(e) Discuss the drawbacks to Elgood Construction plc of using the income statement to analyse the performance. (20 marks)

49 Measuring and increasing profit

Measuring profit

Business owners and financial managers will monitor the profitability of a business very carefully. Profit is perhaps the most important performance indicator. This is because, for most businesses, making profit is the main aim.

The actual size of profit is not always a true indicator of performance. In 2007, Next, the high street clothes retailer, made a profit of £478 million and BA, the airline, made a profit of £611 million. In contrast, Wetherspoons, the pub chain, made a profit of just £62 million.

Does this mean that BA was the best performing business out of the three? It may do but not necessarily. A number of other factors have to be taken into account. For example, how much money was invested in the business and how much profit was made in relation to turnover? A closer examination of more financial information would be required before a conclusion could be drawn about which company had performed the best.

Profit margins

One way of measuring profit is to calculate a PROFIT MARGIN. A profit margin expresses profit as a proportion of turnover, usually as a percentage. A profit margin can be used to compare the performance of a business in different periods when turnover changes. It can also be used to compare the performance of different sized businesses. There are two common profit margins.

Gross profit margin GROSS PROFIT is the amount of profit a business makes after direct costs have been subtracted from turnover. It can be calculated using the formula:

$$\text{Gross profit} = \text{turnover} - \text{cost of sales}$$

It is the profit before overheads (indirect costs) are subtracted. For a retailer gross profit would be turnover minus the cost of buying goods for resale. For a manufacturer it would be turnover minus the costs of raw materials, components and direct labour.

The GROSS PROFIT MARGIN or MARK-UP is the gross profit expressed as a percentage of turnover. It is calculated using the formula:

$$\text{Gross profit margin} = \frac{\text{Gross profit}}{\text{Turnover}} \times 100$$

Table 1 shows some financial information for Prior's, a large independent electrical goods store. Figures are shown for 2006 and 2007. The gross profit margins for the two years are calculated as follows.

$$\text{For 2007 Gross profit margin} = \frac{£550{,}000}{£1{,}230{,}000} \times 100 = 44.7\%$$

$$\text{For 2006 Gross profit margin} = \frac{£450{,}000}{£1{,}100{,}000} \times 100 = 40.9\%$$

Higher gross profit margins are preferable to lower ones. However, it is difficult to say what a 'good' margin is likely to be. Gross profit margins will vary in different industries. For example supermarkets, which generally have a fast stock turnover, will have lower gross profit margins than, say, a car dealer, which will operate with a much slower stock turnover. The gross profit margins for Prior's have increased over the two years from 40.9 per cent to 44.7 per cent. This shows that performance has improved. Margins of around 40 per cent for

Table 1: Financial information for Prior's

	2007	(£) 2006
Turnover	1,230,000	1,100,000
Cost of sales	780,000	650,000
Gross profit	550,000	450,000
Overheads	340,000	280,000
Net profit	210,000	170,000

Question 1.

Goodalls is a small chain of butchers operating in Kent. It has a shop in Dover, Ashford and Canterbury. Table 2 shows some financial information for Goodalls for 2007.

Table 2: Financial information for Goodalls

	Dover	Ashford	(£) Canterbury
Turnover	158,000	142,000	197,000
Cost of sales	102,000	101,000	146,000
Gross profit			
Overheads	31,000	29,000	33,000
Net profit			

(a) Complete the table by calculating gross profit and net profit.

(b) Calculate the net profit margins for the three shops.

(c) (i) Which shop has performed the best in 2007?
(ii) How will these figures assist Goodalls in the financial management of the business?

an electrical goods retailer are probably acceptable.

Net profit margin NET PROFIT is the amount of profit after all costs have been subtracted from turnover. It is calculated as:

Net profit = gross profit - overheads

Or

Net profit = turnover – cost of sales - overheads

The NET PROFIT MARGIN is net profit expressed as a percentage of turnover. The net profit margin shows how effectively a business has controlled its overheads and its cost of sales. The net profit margin is calculated by:

$$\text{Net profit margin} = \frac{\text{Net profit}}{\text{Turnover}} \times 100$$

When calculating the net profit margin it is important to use net profit before tax and interest. The net profit margins for Prior's in 2006 and 2007 are calculated as follows.

$$\text{For 2007 Net profit margin} = \frac{£210,000}{£1,230,000} \times 100 = 17.1\%$$

$$\text{For 2006 Net profit margin} = \frac{£170,000}{£1,100,000} \times 100 = 15.5\%$$

Again, higher margins are better than lower ones. The net profit margin for Prior's has improved over the two years from 15.5% to 17.1%. This suggests that the business has been able to control its overheads slightly more effectively in 2007.

Return on capital

Another way to measure the profitability of a business is to calculate the RETURN ON CAPITAL. Capital is the money invested in a business by the owners. The return on capital is the amount of profit expressed as a percentage of the capital invested in a business. Owners can use this measure to see how well their investment in the business is doing. The return on capital is:

$$\text{Return on capital} = \frac{\text{Net profit}}{\text{Capital}} \times 100$$

In 2007, the amount of capital invested in Prior's, the electrical goods retailer in the example above, was £1 million. The same amount was invested in 2006. The return on capital for 2007 and 2006 is shown below.

$$\text{For 2007 Return on capital} = \frac{£210,000}{£1,000,000} \times 100 = 21\%$$

$$\text{For 2006 Return on capital} = \frac{£170,000}{£1,000,000} \times 100 = 17\%$$

Clearly, the return on capital increased over the two-year period. In 2006 the owners of Prior's got a 17 per cent return on their £1,000,000 investment. This rose to 21 per cent in 2007. One way to determine whether 21 per cent is a good return or not, is to make a comparison with another electrical goods retailer. However, it may not be possible to obtain the information required to do this. A 21 per cent return does look good when compared with the return the owner might get if the £1,000,000 was deposited in a bank. This would have been about 6 per cent in 2007 (£60,000). Clearly, the money is generating a much bigger return when it is invested in the business. However, the £1,000,000 invested in the business is at risk and investors would expect a bigger return to compensate for this risk.

Finally, when comparing profit measures between businesses, it is important to compare 'like with like'. The profit margins and returns on capital may vary from industry to industry and from business to business. Fair comparisons can only be made between businesses if they operate in the same industry and have the same characteristics. For example, comparing the rate of return of a shoe manufacturer with that of a bank may not be appropriate.

Question 2.

Leonard & Co manufactures glassware in Hereford. It employs 45 staff and has a reputation for high-quality wine glasses, vases and crystalware. The company has won awards for innovation in recent years but is facing pressure from overseas competitors.

Simpsons plc is a sheet glass retailer. It operates from a huge site in Bradford and mainly serves traders such as builders and glaziers. In the last year it has taken over a local rival and the integration of the two businesses raised costs for the year.

Argo Ltd makes a range of glass products such as glass tables, show cases and cabinets. It employs seven staff and operates from an industrial unit in Sunderland. The company was bought from the previous owner by the present manager two years ago. Some financial information for the three companies is shown in Table 3.

Table 3: Financial information for Leonard & Co, Simpsons plc and Argo Ltd

			(£)
	Leonard & Co	**Simpsons plc**	**Argo Ltd**
Capital invested	2,340,000	7,800,000	1,400,000
Net profit	245,000	466,000	156,000

(a) Explain what is meant by return on capital.
(b) Calculate the return on capital for the three businesses in the case.
(c) Comment on and compare the returns calculated in (b).
(d) How useful are the comparisons made in (c)?

Methods of improving profitability

All businesses will want to improve their performance. An improved performance is likely to benefit all stakeholders. The returns on capital can be increased by making more profit with the same level of investment. This might be achieved by growth funded externally. This means the business increases sales using fresh capital.

Increasing profit margins will also improve performance. If profit margins can be raised, the business will make more profit at the existing level of sales. The profit margins can be improved in two ways.

Raising prices If a business raises its price it will get more revenue for every unit sold. If costs remain the same then profitability should improve. However, raising price might have an impact on the level of sales. Generally, when price is raised demand will fall. However, if demand is not too responsive to changes in price, the increase in price will generate more revenue even though fewer units are sold. Raising price is always risky because it is never certain how competitors will react.

Lowering costs A business can also raise profit margins by lowering its costs. It can do this by buying cheaper resources or using the existing resources more effectively.

- **Using existing resources more efficiently.** It might be possible to buy raw materials and components from new suppliers that offer better prices. It may also be possible to find new providers of essential services such as telecommunications, electricity, insurance and IT support. For example, there has been increased competition recently in the supply of gas, electricity and telecommunications. Another option might be to find ways of using cheaper labour. For example, some businesses have moved overseas to take advantage of cheap labour in places like China and eastern Europe. However, these measures may have drawbacks. When taking on new suppliers the possibility that they are cheaper because they are not as good should be considered. The quality of raw materials might be inferior, they may be unreliable and supply might not be guaranteed. For example, a number of new, and cheaper, broadband providers have not been able to guarantee supply. Moving abroad to take advantage of cheap labour may be disruptive. It may also damage the image of the company if it lays off large numbers of staff in the UK. Consequently, when looking to acquire cheaper resources, a business must be cautious and understand the pitfalls.
- **Buying cheaper resources.** Making better use of current resources will improve efficiency and lower costs. A business might do this by introducing new working practices or training staff. This would help to raise labour productivity. It could upgrade its machinery by acquiring newer, more efficient models. This would raise capital productivity. A business might be able to reduce waste by recycling materials, for example. Some of these measures might also have drawbacks. For example, the workers might resist new working practices and new technology often has teething problems. This could disrupt the business.

The difference between cash and profit

It is important for businesses to recognise the difference between cash and profit. At the end of a trading year it is unlikely that the value of profit will be the same as the cash balance. Differences between cash and profit can arise for a number of reasons.

- During the trading year a business might sell £200,000 worth of goods with total costs of £160,000. Its profit would be £40,000. However, if some goods had been sold on credit, payment by certain customers may not yet have been received. If £12,000 was still owing, the amount of cash the business had would be £28,000 (£40,000-£12,000). Thus, profit is greater than cash.
- A business may receive cash at the beginning of the trading year from sales made in the previous year. This would increase the cash balance, but would not affect profit. In addition, the business may buy resources from suppliers and not pay for them until the next trading year. As a result its trading costs will not be the same as cash paid out.
- Sometimes the owners might introduce more cash into the business. This will increase the cash balance, but will have no effect on the profit made. This is because the introduction of capital is not treated as business revenue in the profit and loss account. The effect will be the same if a business borrows money from a bank.
- Purchases of fixed assets will reduce cash balances, but will have no effect on the profit a company makes. This is because the purchase of assets is not treated as a business cost in the profit and loss account.
- Sales of fixed assets will increase cash balances but will have no effect on profit unless a profit or loss is made on disposal of the asset. This is because the cash from the sale of a fixed asset is not included in business turnover.
- The amount of cash at the end of the year will be different from profit because at the beginning of the year the cash balance is unlikely to be zero. If, at the beginning of the year, the cash balance for a business is £23,000, then the amount of cash a business has at the end of the year will exceed profit by £23,000.

It is possible for a business to trade for many years without making a profit. For example, Oxford Biomedica, a biopharmaceuticals company, began trading in 1995 and has never made a profit. The company survives because it has been able to generate cash. Extra cash has been introduced by shareholders on several occasions (a total of £117 million over the life of the company). In 2006 the company lost £17.62 million. However, the company had £33 million in liquid assets - including about £8 million in cash.

On the other hand it is possible for a profitable business to collapse if it runs out of cash. This is likely to happen if a business has to meet some substantial unexpected expenditure or if a bad debt occurs.

KEYTERMS

Gross profit – total sales revenue or turnover minus cost of sales, the direct costs of production.
Gross profit margin or mark-up – gross profit expressed as a percentage of turnover.
Net profit – total sales revenue or turnover minus cost of sales and overheads.
Net profit margin – net profit expressed as a percentage of turnover.
Profit margins – profit expressed as a percentage of turnover.
Return on capital – the amount of profit expressed as a percentage of the capital invested in a business.

KNOWLEDGE

1. How reliable is the size of profit as a performance indicator?
2. Explain the difference between net profit and gross profit.
3. What does an increase in the net profit margin tell a business?
4. Why would an investor expect a greater return on capital when investing in a business compared with depositing money in a bank?
5. What might be a negative impact of raising price to improve the net profit margin?
6. State two ways in which a business can lower costs.
7. State two reasons why profit and cash may not be the same in a business.

Case Study: Compton Foods

Compton Foods is a food-processing company. It buys fresh fruit and vegetables from farmers and produces a wide range of packaged products, including mangetout, beans, baby carrots, mushrooms and bean sprouts. It adds value to some products by slicing and dicing fruit and vegetables before packing. It also produces variety packs where several vegetables or mixed vegetables are combined in the same pack. All of Compton Foods' products are sold to supermarkets in the south of England.

The processing plant is located in Reading. Around 50 people are employed in the plant, most of whom are unskilled. In 2006, the company's shareholders provided an injection of fresh capital. £300,000 was raised to pay for a computerised packing machine and the introduction of new shift patterns. Unfortunately, this resulted in seven staff being laid off, affecting the relationship between the owners and the workers. The workers benefited financially from the new shift patterns, but they resented their colleagues being laid off. This was the first time in the history of the company that staff had been made redundant. A worker representative said 'Working here will never be the same. There used to be an atmosphere of a family company, but that's all changed now. The company is dominated by the accountants.'

Table 4: Financial information for Compton Foods

				(£)
	2004	**2005**	**2006**	**2007**
Turnover	2,440,000	2,820,000	3,190,000	3,210,000
Net profit	235,000	242,000	246,000	331,000
Capital invested	1,500,000	1,500,000	1,500,000	1,800,000

(a) Calculate the net profit margins for the four years. (8 marks)
(b) Using this case an example, explain why the size of profit might be misleading when measuring the performance of a business. (6 marks)
(c) How might you account for the changes in the net profit margin between 2006 and 2007? (8 marks)
(d) At the end of the trading year in 2007, Compton Foods had £378,000 in the bank. Explain the difference between cash and profit for the year. (8 marks)
(e) Calculate the returns on capital between 2006 and 2007. (8 marks)
(f) Do you think the measures taken to improve the performance of the company were worthwhile? (12 marks)

50 Financial data and performance

Using financial data for comparisons

When evaluating the performance of a business it is necessary to make comparisons. Comparisons will help a business to gauge more effectively how well it has performed. Three types of comparisons are common:

- interfirm comparisons;
- comparisons over time;
- interfirm comparisons over time.

Interfirm comparisons

A business can get a good idea of how it has performed by comparing its results with those of another company in the same industry. For example, Sainsbury might want to compare its results with those of Tesco or Morrisons. These businesses are all supermarket chains. Therefore a comparison would be meaningful. It is important to compare 'like with like' when making interfirm comparisons. Comparing the net profit margin of a supermarket with that of a chemical engineering company is not likely to be appropriate. This is because the two businesses have many different features.

Interfirm comparisons might highlight particular strengths or weaknesses. For example, a bus company with a turnover of £12.4 million might think its £2.1 million profit is satisfactory. Another bus company might have made a £2 million profit on a turnover of just £7.5 million. Assuming the two firms are similar and operate in similar circumstances, the relative profit of the first business is not as good.

Table 1: Revenue and net profit of two construction companies, 2006

	Bellway £000	George Wimpey* £000
Revenue	1,240,193	3,147,400
Net profit	155,742	256,000
Net profit margin	12.60%	8.10%

* Before exceptional items.

Table 1 shows financial information of two construction companies Bellway and George Wimpey. Bellway homes are designed, built and marketed by local teams operating from regional offices managed and staffed by local people. George Wimpey also builds homes and has been trading for around 125 years. Table 1 shows revenue, net profit and net profit margin for 2006 for both companies. The Bellway figures are for the year ending 31.7.2006 while the George Wimpey figures are for the year ending 31.12.2006.

George Wimpey has generated the most turnover and profit. For example, George Wimpey's net profit is 64 per cent larger than Bellways. However, it could be argued that Bellway is the better performer. This is because the net profit margin is higher for Bellway. This means that Bellway has generated more profit per pound of turnover. But it must be noted that the two companies have different year ends so the figures may not be 100 per cent comparable.

Comparisons over time

Looking at performance indicators for a single year is not always helpful. This is because one year's trading figures may not reflect what has been going on over a longer time period. Most accounts show figures for the current year and the previous year. This is helpful but only up to a point, even two years' figures could disguise the long-term trend. A more thorough evaluation of a company's performance can be undertaken by looking at many years' figures. This is called TREND ANALYSIS. Trend analysis involves looking at data over a long period of time and spotting patterns in data. Most public limited companies publish key performance data for five years in their annual report and accounts.

Table 2: Revenue and net profit of Punch Taverns

(£ million)	2006	2005	2004	2003	2002
Revenue	1,546.10	770.1	637.6	429	391.8
Profit after tax	194.8	167.2	121.5	97.6	67.9
Net profit margin	7.90%	21.70%	19.10%	22.50%	17.30%

Table 2 shows financial information of Punch Taverns. It operates over 8,400 pubs and has grown rapidly in recent years through a series of acquisitions. For example, in 2006 the company bought Spirit Group, a 1,830 pub estate, for £2.7 billion. Table 2 shows revenue, profit after tax and the net profit margin for a five year period.

The data show clearly that the company has grown spectacularly over five years. Turnover has increased from £391.8 million in 2002 to £1,546.1 million in 2006. This is a very strong trend. Profit has also increased impressively between 2002 and 2006 – from £67.9 million to £194.8 million. The net profit margin has fluctuated and is at its lowest in 2006. This might be due to the large acquisition made in this year. There may have been some high costs associated with this – financing perhaps. Trend analysis shows that Punch Taverns is a rapidly growing and profitable company.

Interfirm comparisons over time

Using a combination of the two methods above we can make interfirm comparisons over time. This means that more meaningful comparisons can be made between businesses in the same industry. It also means that trends in a particular industry might be identified. Enfield Publishing and Durrant Press are both medium-sized publishers. They have similar financial circumstances and compete in the same markets. Table 3 below shows the capital employed and net profit margins of the two companies.

Table 3: Financial data, Enfield Publishing Ltd and Durrant Press Ltd

	2006	2005	2004	2003	2002
Enfield Publishing Ltd					
Return on capital employed	11.50%	12.60%	14.10%	15.10%	15.90%
Net profit margin	9.20%	8.90%	9.90%	10.50%	11.20%
Durrant Press Ltd					
Return on capital employed	12.30%	13.20%	12.50%	13.90%	14.10%
Net profit margin	10.50%	11.10%	11.90%	12.60%	13.00%

The financial data shown suggest that Durrant Press Ltd is the best performing company. Its return on capital employed is higher than Enfield's for the whole time period. The same pattern is evident with the net profit margin. Durrant Press has higher margins in every year. It is also clear from the data that over the time period the performance of both companies has worsened. For example, the ROCE for Enfield has fallen from 15.9 per cent to 11.5 per cent. Similarly, the ROCE for Durrant has fallen (although not so sharply) from14.1 per cent to 12.3 per cent. The net profit margins also show a decline. This suggests that the industry has suffered over the time period. Perhaps it has become more competitive.

Using data for decision making

One of the reasons for producing accounts and compiling other forms of financial data is to help make business decisions. When choosing between different courses of action a business will want to gather as much relevant information as possible. Having relevant and accurate information is likely to help businesses make more informed decisions. It is also helpful to have a range of quantitative information because it is easier to analyse. Financial data falls into this category. Financial data is likely to be used to help make the strategic decisions outlined below.

Acquisitions Many companies grow through acquisitions. However, before a company takes over another business it needs to look very closely at the financial circumstances of that business. A wide range of financial data will be analysed before a bid can be made. The size of the bid is likely to depend on the results of this financial analysis. In some cases a company might employ a specialist to carry out this work, such as a merchant bank.

Investment All businesses have to invest from time to time. Making an investment decision is fraught with uncertainty. Businesses are likely to use quantitative appraisal methods when choosing between different investment projects. Financial data will have to be gathered in order to carry out such detailed appraisals.

Strategy A business will use financial data when deciding its corporate strategy. For example, if a business is considering a venture into overseas markets for the first time, it will have to evaluate the impact such a venture would have on the financial position of the business.

Product portfolio Developing and launching new products is a highly risky activity. In order to minimise the risk businesses will consider carefully the impact such a move would have on the financial standing of the business. A wide range of financial data might be analysed when making such a decision. If a new product fails, the effect on the performance of the company could be severe and far reaching.

When making strategic decisions like the ones outlined above, a wide range of financial information and performance indicators might be considered. Examples might include profit, earnings, return on capital employed, sales revenue, sales volumes, costs, working capital and debt. Much of this information can be extracted from the financial statements produced by a business – the profit and loss account or income statement and balance sheet for example.

Assessing strengths and weaknesses of financial data in judging performance

The importance of using financial data to assess the performance of a business is clear. Performance indicators such as the net profit margin and return on capital employed can go along way to show how effectively a business is performing. Such indicators have clarity and can be used to make direct comparisons. These are key strengths when using financial data to judge performance.

However, financial data can be imperfect. For example, accounts can be 'window dressed' to distort the true financial circumstances of a business, much financial data is historic and is of limited use when looking into the future and inflation can distort financial values. It must also be remembered that qualitative data can be of use when judging performance. Using questionnaires to assess the views of other stakeholders such as employees, customers and environmentalists, can also help to judge performance. These issues and many others are discussed in more detail in the units on the balance sheet, profit and loss account and limitations to ratios.

KEYTERMS

Trend analysis – looking for patterns in data over a period of time.

KNOWLEDGE

1. Why might businesses compare their performance with rivals?
2. State two problems of using one year's figures to assess the performance of a business.
3. Briefly explain the value of trend analysis to a business.
4. State two ways in which financial data might be used to make decisions in business.
5. State two problems a business should be aware of when using financial data to judge performance.

Sainsbury's and Tesco

Sainsbury's and Tesco are two of the major supermarket chains in the UK. Tesco has operations overseas but about 80 per cent of its revenue is generated in the UK. Tesco employs about 250,000 people in the UK in 1,779 stores. Tesco has four store formats. In order of size starting with the smallest these are Express, Metro, Superstore and Extra. Much of Tesco's growth in recent years has come from the development of the smaller stores. Growth has also come from extending the product range into more and more non-food items.

Sainsbury is the smaller of the two groups but is still a leading UK food retailer with interests in financial services. It consists of Sainsbury's Supermarkets, Sainsbury's Local, Bells Stores, Jacksons Stores and JB Beaumont, Sainsbury's Online and Sainsbury's Bank. It employs 148,000 people and operates 788 stores. In addition to its grocery stores Sainsbury has a joint venture with HBOS. It offers financial services such as savings, loans and credit cards. Table 4 shows some financial data for the two supermarkets.

Table 4: Financial data for Sainsbury and Tesco

					(£000)
	2003	2004	2005	2006	2007
Sainsbury					
Revenue	18,144	18,239	16,573	17,317	18,518
Profit	695	675	254	267	380
Profit margin					
Tesco					
Revenue	26,004	30,814	33,974	39,454	42,641
Profit	1,401	1,708	2,029	2,277	2,545
Profit margin					

Source: adapted from Sainsbury and Tesco, *Annual Report and Accounts*, 2007.

(a) Calculate the profit margins for Tesco and Sainsbury's. (10 marks)

(b) What type of comparison can be made using the financial data in Table 4? (4 marks)

(c) (i) Explain why trend analysis allows a more meaningful comparison between two businesses. (4 marks)

(ii) Compare the financial data for the two supermarkets and explain which has performed the best over the five year period. (10 marks)

(d) Explain how the two supermarkets might use financial data to help make decisions? (12 marks)

51 Accounting concepts

The need for accounting concepts

The accounts of a business should reflect a 'true and fair' view of its financial position. To achieve this accountants apply a series of 'rules' or ACCOUNTING CONCEPTS. These are also known as conventions or principles. In the USA, and increasingly in the UK, the expression GAAP is used to refer to 'generally accepted accounting principles'.

By using agreed concepts when analysing and presenting financial information, accountants can avoid confusion and inconsistency. There is also less scope for presenting misleading financial information and the accounts of different businesses can be compared more easily.

The concepts or principles have developed over time as a framework within which accountants operate. In the UK, the Accounting Standards Committee (ASC) was established in the 1970s. This committee issued a number of Statements of Standard Accounting Practice (SSAPs). The ASC described four 'fundamental accounting concepts' in its Statements of Standard Accounting Practice (SSAP 2). These are the:

- going concern concept;
- consistency concept;
- prudence concept;
- accruals or matching concept.

Since 1990, the regulation of accounting in the UK has passed over to the Accounting Standards Board (ASB). SSAPs still exist, but any new standards are now called Financial Reporting Standards (FRSs). During 2001, the Financial Reporting Standard Accounting Policies (FRS 18) was introduced to replace SSAP 2. These are:

- relevance;
- reliability;
- compatibility;
- understandability.

FRS 18 states that a business should regularly review its accounting policies to ensure they remain the most appropriate to the business's circumstances. Specific disclosure about the policies used, and any changes to the policies, must be made.

In addition to the fundamental concepts listed above, a number of others are generally accepted. These include objectivity, business entity, money measurement, historical cost, dual aspect, realisation and materiality.

Objectivity

As far as possible accounts should be based on verifiable evidence rather than on personal opinion. In other words they should be **objective** rather than **subjective**. So, for example, an accountant should value a transaction on the basis of an invoice rather than his or her own personal opinion. This avoids bias. Consider what might happen if two accountants were asked their opinion on the value of a particular transaction, for example the purchase of new premises. They might disagree because value can be measured in many different ways. However, if they were asked to value the transaction according to the invoice, they would likely record exactly the same value.

Historical cost

This concept states that accounting should be based on the original costs incurred in a transaction. So, for example, assets

Question 1.

Emily Jones set up a small production operation in a rented unit in Brentford. She purchased some specialised equipment and began making high quality, Belgian style chocolates. The business started well and in the first six weeks of trading, which included the busy Christmas period, Emily made a small profit. Unfortunately the novelty of her products wore off and trade dwindled. After poor summer sales, Emily was wondering whether the business would have to cease trading. She had some ideas for a new business which she might be able to finance by selling the assets from the existing business. The balance sheet for Emily's business is shown Figure 1.

Figure 1: Balance sheet for Emily Jones

Emily Jones
Balance sheet as at 31.10.07

	£	£
Assets		3,500
Machinery		1,700
Packaging equipment		1,500
Van		1,400
Stocks		150
Cash at bank		8,250
Less Liabilities		
Bank loan	4,000	
Trade creditors	1,900	
		5,900
		2,350
Financed by:		
Capital		2,350
		2,350

(a) Explain how an accountant might have valued Emily Jones's fixed assets if the business was a going concern.

(b) If Emily did decide to close down her business and sell off the fixed assets. How would they be valued?

such as machinery should be valued at their HISTORICAL COST, i.e. the cost when purchased. The historical cost can be verified by documentary evidence such as an invoice or receipt. This should allow the valuation to be objective.

There are some disadvantages of using historical cost as a basis for valuation. The price of some assets such as property and land can rise or fall. For example, in the late 1990s and early 2000s, property prices rose quite sharply. For example, a business property bought for £50,000 in 1999 may have been worth £160,000 in 2007. This means that the value of the asset would be understated in the accounts in 2007.

The rise in the general price level is called **inflation**. If the value of assets does increase significantly due to inflation businesses may arrange to have assets revalued. By arranging a professional revaluation of assets, the balance sheet will reflect more accurately the true and fair value of the business.

A further problem with inflation is that money becomes unreliable as a measure of value when prices are rising very rapidly in the economy. Over the past decades, inflation has caused a rise in the monetary value of most assets. For example, the average price of a house in Britain in 1970 was £5,000. By the year 2000, this had risen to around £100,000. So care must be taken when comparing monetary values in different time periods.

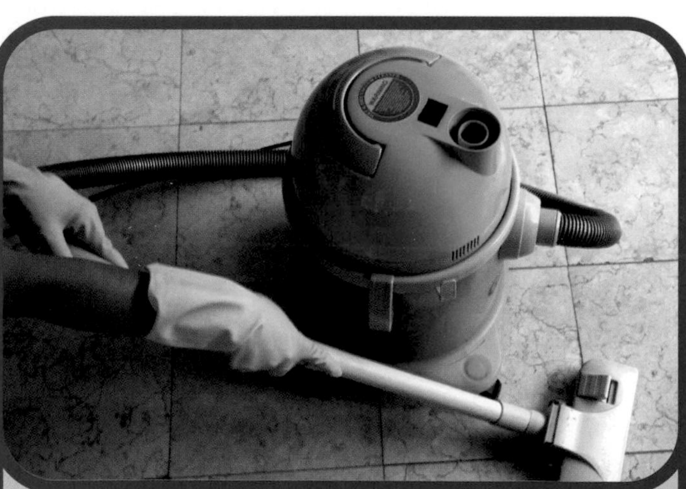

Question 2.

Impact Cleaning Ltd was set up by Lisa Scarrot in July 2007. The company has a number of cleaning contracts with businesses in the Swansea area. Just before the business was launched Lisa purchased the resources listed below.

- Van £3,200
- Industrial vacuum cleaner £2,300
- Laptop computer £800
- Four buckets £3.00
- Mop £5.50
- Broom £3.95

Lisa expects that all of these resources will be used for a number of years. However, she is not sure whether some or all of this expenditure should be treated as capital expenditure.

(a) **Using the materiality concept, suggest which of these resources might be listed as fixed assets in the balance sheet.**

(b) **Suggest a method that Lisa might use to classify future spending as revenue expenditure or capital expenditure.**

Going concern

The GOING CONCERN concept assumes that a business will carry on trading for the foreseeable future. In other words, it is not expected to be closed down or be sold. This concept affects how the assets are valued. For a going concern, it is reasonable to value assets at their historical cost. However, if a business is about to close down, assets should be valued at their NET REALISABLE VALUE. This is the amount that they would sell for if the business closed and all the assets were sold off. Under most circumstances it is likely that the net realisable value (second-hand value) of assets like machinery and stock will be lower than their historical cost. However, in the case of property and land, the opposite might be true and on the break up of a business these assets might be sold for more than their historical cost.

Realisation

The REALISATION concept states that revenue should not be recognised until the exchange of goods or services has taken place. In other words revenue should not be recorded until it has been **realised**. For example, if a wholesaler supplies £4,000 of goods on a 'sale or return' basis, the customer might return some, or all, of the goods at a later date. According to the realisation concept, the £4,000 should not be recorded as revenue at the time the goods were supplied. If the customer returns £700 of the goods two months later and buys the remainder, revenue of £3,300 would be recorded.

Accruals or matching

These two concepts have slightly different meanings, but their effect is similar so they are generally considered together.

The ACCRUALS concept states that revenue should be recorded when it is earned and not when the money is received. This distinction can be illustrated by considering a business transaction in which goods are sold on credit. Suppose a business sells the goods in December and receives payment for them in March. Even though the payment is not received until March, it should still be recorded as revenue received in December. The same principle applies to purchases made by a business. Costs should be recognised when they are incurred and not when payment is made.

The MATCHING concept states that in calculating profit, revenue should be matched against expenditure incurred in earning it. To illustrate this, consider a toy retailer who buys 100 teddy bears for £10 each in May. During the month, 70 of these teddy bears are sold for £15 each. According to the matching concept, the profit in May is determined by calculating the cost of buying 70 teddy bears and offsetting this expense against the revenue generated from their sale. This is shown as follows.

Revenue (70 x £15)	£1,050
Less	
Expenses (70 x £10)	£700
Profit (for May)	£350

Only the cost of acquiring the 70 teddy bears should be matched with the sales revenue. The 30 unsold teddy bears are treated as an asset (stock) and not as an expense. If they are eventually sold, the profit would be calculated by subtracting the purchase cost of 30 teddy bears from the revenue raised when selling them.

In practice, it is not always possible to match precisely the revenue and costs for every item sold. This is particularly the case in manufacturing where a wide range of raw materials and components are used to produce different products. It is for this reason that most accountants take the view that revenue and costs should be matched 'so far as these costs are material and identifiable'.

Consistency

The CONSISTENCY concept states that the accounts of a business should be prepared on the same basis every year. In other words, there should be consistent treatment of similar items within each accounting period and from one period to the next. This allows a more meaningful comparison of accounts in different time periods. If accountants are not consistent in their policies, it is unclear whether changes in reported profits or the value of assets are the result of changes in business conditions or of changes in accounting practice. For example, changes in the way stock is valued can lead to changes in the value of profit made by the business. The result is that accounts create a misleading impression about the performance of the business.

The consistency concept does not mean that a business cannot ever change its accounting policies. However, if it decides to adopt a new policy, it is normal for the business to report this in its final accounts. Sometimes a business might change its accounting techniques deliberately to convey a false impression. The practice of manipulating accounts is known as 'window dressing'.

Prudence and caution

The PRUDENCE concept states that accountants should be cautious when reporting the financial position of a business. It is therefore better to understate profits or the value of assets than to overstate them. In general, when applying the concept of prudence the guidelines below should be followed.

- Revenue and profit should not be recorded unless it is certain, i.e. realised.
- Anticipate all possible losses and record them as soon as they are known.
- Choose the lowest value when faced with a choice of asset values or revenue.
- Choose the highest value when faced with different estimates of costs.

Question 3.

Chaminda de Silva operates as a sole trader and runs an employment agency in Leicester. He rents an office in a city centre office complex and specialises in the market for catering staff such as chefs, waiters and bar staff. He has a large number of contacts with the city's hotels, pubs, bars and restaurants. One of Chaminda's important assets is his laptop computer which he bought for £1,200. On average he uses the computer for 8 hours a day, 5 days a week for business purposes. However, during the evenings and at weekends the computer is used by Chaminda for personal reasons. On average he uses the laptop at home for 20 hours a week.

(a) **With reference to Chaminda de Silva's business, explain what is meant by the business entity concept.**

(b) **Suggest what proportion of the computer cost should be attributed to Chaminda's business.**

For example, if a business buys a vehicle at an auction for a bargain price of £4,500, and then discovers that it is actually worth £5,700, the lower value should be recorded. This is a cautious or 'conservative' valuation and also conforms to the historical cost concept.

A similar prudent approach should be adopted with bad debts. If goods have been sold on credit and the customer goes bankrupt, payment for the goods is not likely to be received. The money owed is classified as a 'bad debt' and therefore recorded as such immediately. In accounting terms, introducing a 'provision for bad debts' is treated as an expense on the profit and loss account or income statement.

Materiality

Accountants should avoid wasting time trying to accurately record items of expenditure which are trivial. For example, a business might purchase a waste paper bin for the office for £1.50. This bin might last for 15 years or more, however, the bin is not a 'material' item. Even though it is expected to be used for many years the purchase should be recorded once and treated as an expense in the year it was bought. No attempt should be made to 'write off' the expenditure over the period of time the bin is in use. This avoids cluttering up the balance sheet with trivial items.

Unfortunately there is no law or formal guideline which governs MATERIALITY. Different firms may use a variety of arbitrary methods to determine which items of expenditure are material and which are not. For example, a business may decide that all items of expenditure under £50 should be treated as expenses in the period for which they were bought, even if some items are actually used for many years. The method of assessing materiality will be selected by accountants using their judgment.

Business entity or separate entity

The BUSINESS ENTITY concept states that the financial affairs of a business should be completely separate from those of the owner. The business is treated as a **separate entity**. This means that personal transactions must not be confused with business transactions. Difficulties can arise, however, if resources are used jointly by both the business and the owner. Suppose, for example, that a van is used during the week for business purposes and at the weekend for personal use. From an accounting point of view, the costs associated with the van must be divided as accurately as possible between the business and the owner. One approach might be to split the costs so that 5/7 (i.e. five days out of seven) of the van's costs are charged to the business and 2/7 to the owner.

The business entity concept does not conform with the legal position of sole traders and partnerships. In these cases the law does not distinguish between a business and its owners. So, for example, a sole trader is liable, i.e. responsible, for all the debts of the business. However, in the case of limited companies, there is a separation of identity between the owners and the business itself. The owners are not liable for the debts of the business. They have limited liability. For accounting purposes, these legal distinctions are not relevant. In all cases, a business and its owners are treated as separate entities.

Money measurement

The MONEY MEASUREMENT concept states that financial records, including the value of transactions, assets, liabilities and capital, should be expressed in monetary terms. There are two key reasons for recording financial information in this way.

- Most transactions have an agreed monetary value and are expressed in monetary terms. Few transactions are carried out by barter or 'swapping' , i.e. with no money involved.
- The different values of products and assets can be more easily compared in money terms. For example, the relative value of two buildings that cost £300,000 and £950,000 is more clearly expressed in monetary terms than a descriptive term such as 'medium' price and 'high' price.

However, the use of money to record financial information does have some limitations. One problem is that some information cannot be expressed in money terms. As a result it might be ignored. Therefore, the accounts might not reflect a 'true and fair' view of the business. For example, a business might have a poorly motivated workforce with high rates of absenteeism. This information cannot easily be expressed in money terms. However, clearly it is important and when taken into account, would have an impact on the business.

Dual aspect

The DUAL ASPECT concept states that every transaction has two effects on the business's accounts. Suppose, for example, that a business buys some goods on credit. Assets, increase, because stocks increase, and liabilities also increase because money is owed to a creditor. Similarly, if the business repays a loan of £1,000 to a bank, there is a dual aspect. Liabilities decrease, because the loan is repaid, and assets decrease because the business has less money. In accordance with the dual aspect concept, each transaction is recorded twice by bookkeepers.

KEYTERMS

Accounting concepts, principles or conventions – rules or guidelines that accountants follow when drawing up accounts.
Accruals – an accounting concept that distinguishes between the exchange of goods in one time period and the payment for those goods in another.
Business entity – an accounting concept which states that the financial affairs of a business should be completely separate from those of the owners. An entity is a business organisation.
Consistency – an accounting concept that requires accountants, when faced with a choice between different accounting techniques, not to change policies without good reason.
Dual aspect – the idea that every transaction has two effects on the accounts.
Going concern – an accounting concept that assumes a business will continue to trade in the foreseeable future.
Historical cost – the value of an asset when purchased, i.e. the amount paid.
Matching – an accounting concept that ensures that revenues are associated with their relevant expenses.
Materiality – an accounting concept which states that accountants should not spend time trying to record accurately items that are trivial or immaterial.
Money measurement concept – an accounting concept which states that all transactions should be expressed in money terms.
Net realisable value – the value of an asset when sold, i.e. the amount received.
Prudence – an accounting concept that requires accountants to recognise profit and revenue only when they are realised.
Realisation – an accounting concept that states that revenue should be recognised when the exchange of goods and services takes place.

KNOWLEDGE

1. What is meant by GAAP?
2. What are SAPPs?
3. What are the fundamental concepts which aim to make the accounts a 'true and fair' view of the firm's financial position?
4. How might the historic cost of a new asset be verified?
5. What is the relevance of the business entity concept to a sole trader?
6. Explain the difference between historical cost and net realisable value.
7. How might inflation undermine the historical cost concept?
8. How might assets be valued if a business closes down?
9. What is meant by the concept prudence and caution?
10. At what stage in a transaction should revenue be recognised?

Case Study: Jon Peters

Jon Peters operates as a chiropractor in the town of Wheatly, near Oxford. Chiropractors who are members of the British Chiropractic Association offer expert advice, pain relief, and hands-on pain management for a wide range of aches and pains. Chiropractic care is centred primarily upon the body's nervous system. As a major part of that nervous system pathway, Chiropractic focuses on the spine and its associated structures as common causes of pain and disability. What's more, chiropractic care is a completely natural solution – no drugs, and no invasive surgery.

Jon's business is very successful. One reason is because there is very little competition in the local area. However, he also has a good reputation and most of his clients now come from recommendations. Jon enjoys running his own business but like many small business people he is not so keen on the paper work and keeping financial records in particular. Jon keeps records of all payments and receipts on computer. At the end of the financial year he pays a local accountant to produce accounts. At the end of 2007 five transactions were giving Jon some concern.

- One month before the end of the financial year Jon paid his quarterly rent of £15,000. However, Jon decided not to include the payment in his records because the majority of it related to the next year.
- One of Jon's clients had sent a cheque for £230 by mistake when settling his account. The actual amount due was £210. Jon is not sure which figure to enter.
- Another of Jon's clients owes £150 for a course of treatment. However, after trying to contact the client for several months it appears that the client has left town and cannot be traced. Jon is not sure what to do.
- Jon purchased some stationery for £560 in the last month before the end of the financial year. He does not expect to pay for it for three months. Jon thinks that the goods purchased should not be entered in the books yet.
- Some equipment purchased by Jon during the year cost £2,500. However, two months after he purchased it he saw an advert in a medical journal offering exactly the same equipment for just £1,500. Jon is not sure which value to record.
- During the year Jon used his car both for business use and personal use. Total motor expenses for the year were £12,800. He estimated that 8,000 miles were attributable to the business and 2,000 for personal use. Jon is not entirely sure whether all of the expenses can be attributed to the business.

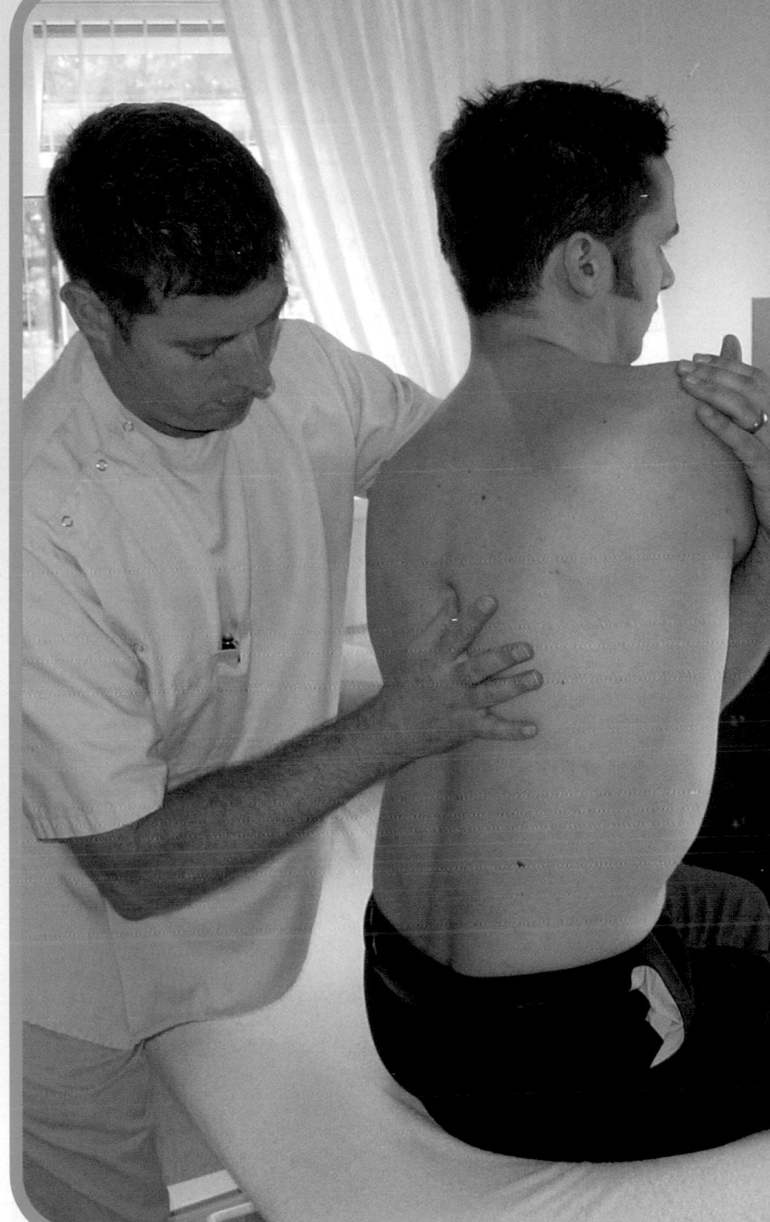

(a) Explain why it is necessary for Jon's accountant to adopt accounting concepts when preparing his final accounts. (4 marks)

(b) Explain why objectivity is important to Jon's accountant when preparing the final accounts. (6 marks)

(c) Explain why all of Jon's transactions are recorded in money terms. (6 marks)

(d) Explain how Jon should treat each of the above transactions according to the appropriate accounting concepts. (24 marks)

52 Costing methods

What is costing?

The process of measuring the likely consequences of a business activity is called COSTING. Costing systems benefit a business in a number of ways. They provide managers with financial information on which to base decisions. They help to identify the profitable activities, avoid waste and provide information for cost cutting strategies. Costing can also assist the marketing department in setting the price of products.

Examples of costing exercises include:

- measuring the cost of manufacturing individual products;
- calculating whether or not it would be more economical to contract out a particular business operation, e.g. security;
- determining the cost of moving to a new business location;
- estimating the cost of decorating the office.

What costing methods might be used by firms? Methods include absorption, standard and marginal costing.

Absorption costing

ABSORPTION COSTING is also known as FULL COSTING or TOTAL COSTING. The main principle of absorption costing is that all the overheads or indirect costs are 'absorbed' by cost centres. In other words, all overheads are included when calculating the cost of producing particular items. The main problem is how to allocate a firm's overheads between different cost centres. One simple approach is to use an arbitrary method. For example, a manufacturer which makes two metal components code named ZX 1 and ZX 2 may have the direct costs of producing 100,000 of each component shown in Table 1.

Table 1: Direct costs of two components

			£000
Component	ZX 1	ZX 2	Total
Direct cost	200	300	500

Assume that total indirect costs are £300,000. We need to calculate the percentage each component contributes to total direct cost.

$$\text{For ZX 1} = \frac{200}{500} \times 100 = 40\%$$

$$\text{For ZX 2} = \frac{300}{500} \times 100 = 60\%$$

The £300,000 indirect costs can now be allocated to each component.

For ZX 1 indirect costs = 40% x £300,000 = £120,000
For ZX 2 indirect costs = 60% x £300,000 = £180,000

The total cost or full cost of producing 100,000 of each component can now be calculated. This is done by adding the allocated indirect costs to the direct costs.

For ZX 1 full cost = £120,000 + £200,000 = £320,000
For ZX 2 full cost = £180,000 + £300,000 = £480,000

This approach is often criticised for the arbitrary way it

Question 1.

Bantom Ltd manufactures motorbikes in its Bristol factory. It makes three models:

- the Fury – a racing bike with a 1000 cc engine;
- the Trialmaster – a popular trials bike;
- the XL10 – a standard 500 cc road bike.

Details of the direct production costs are shown in Table 2. Bantom also incurs indirect costs of £600,000 per month. The company manufactures 100 of each bike per month.

Table 2: Direct costs for Bantom Ltd

			(£ per bike)
	Fury	**Trialmaster**	**XL10**
Direct labour	250	150	200
Raw materials	150	.120	100
Components	400	300	340
Other direct costs	200	130	160

(a) Calculate the direct costs of producing 100 of each motorcycle.
(b) Allocate the indirect costs of production to each product as a percentage of direct costs.
(c) Calculate the full cost of producing 100 of each bike.

Table 3: Bases for apportioning overheads

Indirect costs	Basis
Rent and rates	Floor area of cost centres
Heating and lighting	Floor area, the volume or size of cost centres
Personnel costs (i.e. health & welfare)	Number of staff employed by each centre
Buildings insurance	Floor area or book value of buildings in each centre
Machinery & equipment insurance	Book value of machinery used by each centre
Depreciation (plant, machinery & tools)	Book value of assets used by each centre
Maintenance	Book value of assets used by each centre
Supervisory costs	Number of staff, or hours worked by supervisor in each centre
Staff canteen	Number of staff employed by each centre
Administration	Number of staff employed by each centre

allocates indirect costs. It could result in misleading costings because the allocation of indirect costs is not based on any actual indirect costs incurred.

To improve the accuracy of absorption costing a business may prefer to apportion overheads or indirect costs. This involves allocating a certain percentage or proportion of indirect costs to each cost centre. A business must decide on what basis to apportion indirect costs. The basis depends on the nature of the indirect cost. Table 3 shows how a selection of overheads might be apportioned.

To illustrate absorption costing take the example of Dudley Car Exhausts which manufactures three types of exhaust systems, the E1, E2, and E3. Factory time and direct cost details (per system) are shown in Table 4. Annual indirect costs include rent, selling costs, overheads and administration. These are £12,000, £18,000, £24,000 and £4,000 respectively. Rent is apportioned according to the factory time used by each system. Selling costs and overheads are apportioned equally between all systems. Administration is apportioned according to the labour input of each system (most administration costs in this case are labour related, e.g. wages). Dudley Car Exhausts produces 1,000 of each system every year.

Using the absorption costing method it is necessary to allocate every single business cost to the production of the three systems. For E1 the total direct cost is calculated by adding labour, materials and fuel, ie (2 + 3 + 1 = £6). To apportion rent to the production of one E1 system it is necessary to take into account the amount of factory time one E1 system uses, i.e. one sixth of the total time and also the number of E1 systems produced, ie 1,000 during the year. The following calculation must now be performed:

Table 4: Factory time and direct costs for Dudley Car Exhausts

System	Labour (£)	Materials (£)	Fuel (£)	Factory time (hrs)
E1	2	3	1	1
E2	2	4	2	3
E3	4	4	2	2
Total	**8**	**11**	**5**	**6**

Rent apportioned to one E1 system

$$= £12{,}000 \times \frac{1}{6} \times \frac{1}{1{,}000}$$

$$= \frac{£12{,}000}{6{,}000}$$

$$= £2$$

Selling costs and overheads are split equally between each system, so that selling costs are £6 and overheads £8 for each system. Administration costs are apportioned according to the amount of labour used to make each system. For the E1 system the allocation can be calculated as follows.

Administration costs apportioned to one E1 system

$$= £4{,}000 \times \frac{£2}{£8} \times \frac{1}{1{,}000}$$

$$= £4{,}000 \times \frac{1}{4} \times \frac{1}{1{,}000}$$

$$= \frac{£4{,}000}{4{,}000}$$

$$= £1$$

The complete cost schedule for all three systems is shown in Table 5. Some businesses use the absorption method to set the price of their products. Once the cost of each unit has been calculated a profit percentage is added to determine the selling price.

Table 5: The cost of producing the three exhaust systems using the absorption method of costing

						(£)
System	**Direct**	**Rent**	**Selling**	**Overheads**	**Admin.**	**Total**
E1	6	2	6	8	1	23
E2	8	6	6	8	1	29
E3	10	4	6	8	2	30
Total	24	12	18	24	4	82

Advantages and disadvantages of absorption costing

There are certain advantages to a business in using the absorption cost method of apportioning indirect costs.

- It ensures that all costs are fully recovered. This means that businesses will cover their costs as long as the actual costs and level of activity are similar to the budgeted figures. Therefore if a business uses a cost-plus pricing policy, it knows that the prices charged will generate a profit.
- It is fair provided overheads are not allocated in an arbitrary way. This is because costs are apportioned to those activities that actually incur them.
- The method conforms to the accounting standard SSAP 9 *Stocks and work-in-progress.* This states that absorption costing should be used when valuing stocks in the final accounts. This is because absorption costing includes a share of the fixed costs. It therefore recognises these fixed costs in the same period as revenues, and so conforms to the 'matching' principle.

However, the method does have some limitations.

- Cost information used might be inaccurate. This is because the figures are generally based on historical data which may not reflect future costs or activity levels. As a result, businesses might **underabsorb** or **overabsorb** their overheads and could set prices that are too low or too high.
- In practice, absorption costing can be complex, time consuming and expensive to gather detailed information from different cost centres. This is particularly the case for small firms that do not employ specialist cost accountants.
- Some costs are difficult to apportion exactly to a particular cost centre. For example, how can a business apportion electricity costs to different cost centres accurately if there is only one meter?

Standard costing

Some businesses focus on standard costs. A standard cost is a planned or 'target' cost. It is normally associated with a specific activity or a particular unit of production. For example, a business manufacturing cans of fizzy drink may say that the standard cost per can is 17p. This means that the usual cost per can is 17p. STANDARD COSTING involves calculating the usual or planned costs of an activity and then comparing these with the actual costs incurred. The difference between the standard cost and the actual cost is called a **variance**. Standard costing helps businesses to monitor and control costs. For example, the standard cost and actual cost of making a circuit board for an electronics company is shown in Table 7.

In this example the actual cost is 50p more than the standard cost. This means that there is a variance of 50p. Such a variance is likely to result in the business carrying out an investigation to determine why the actual cost of manufacturing the circuit board was higher than expected, i.e. higher than the standard cost. In this case the actual cost is higher because the labour cost was £4 compared with an expected labour cost of £3.50. This may have been caused by, say, a new recruit working a little more slowly than a fully experienced operative.

Table 7: The standard cost and actual cost of producing a circuit board

Description	Standard cost	Actual cost
Materials	90p	90p
Components	120p	120p
Labour	350p	400p
Indirect costs	140p	140p
Total	**700p**	**750p**

Question 2.

Renfrews is a small department store in Leeds. It has five departments and each one is operated as a cost centre. This helps to monitor the costs of running the business. A newly appointed cost accountant has suggested that the current method of apportioning overheads is inappropriate and should be reviewed. Table 6 shows the direct costs and some other details relating to the various cost centres. An analysis of overheads is also given. The value of overheads in 2008 was £500,000.

Table 6: Information for each cost centre operated by Renfrews, 2008

	Food Hall	Women's wear	Men's wear	Electrical goods	Toys	Total
Direct costs	£400,000	£200,000	£100,000	£200,000	£100,000	£1,000,000
Staff employed	12	8	4	6	6	36
Floor space	800m^2	600m^2	600m^2	400m^2	200m^2	2,600m^2

Overheads	
Rent and electricity	= £300,000
Administration	= £200,000
Total	**= £500,000**

(a) Suggest suitable bases for apportionment for the overheads. Explain your answer.

(b) Using the bases of apportionment shown in (a), calculate the full or total cost of operating each department at Renfrews in 2008.

Advantages and disadvantages of standard costing

There are certain advantages to a business in using standard costing.

- By comparing standard costs with actual costs a business can identify areas of weakness and inefficient practice. For example, large adverse variances on materials costs might suggest that materials are being wasted in production. Standard costing is likely to be used as a means of controlling costs in a business.
- Staff can be motivated if they achieve cost targets which they are involved in setting. In some cases staff might be rewarded financially if they reach or exceed targets.
- Standard costs may represent the best estimate of what a product should cost to make. So, by using standard costs, estimates of costs for products and price quotations for orders are likely to be more reliable.

However, there may also be disadvantages.

- Like absorption costing, standard costing requires a business to gather a large amount of information. This process can be time consuming and expensive. Also, since standard costs are updated regularly, this cost is ongoing.
- The method may be inappropriate if certain management methods are used. For example, if kaizen is adopted, where workers are expected to strive for continuous improvement, standards might become a barrier to innovation. Employees might regard standards as 'ceilings' and therefore the incentive to improve further is removed.
- Standard costing may encourage staff to strive for favourable variances, even if this harms the firm's overall objectives. For example, staff may take short cuts to reduce costs. This might reduce the quality of the product and lead to a fall in sales.

Contribution or marginal costing

CONTRIBUTION or MARGINAL COSTING ignores fixed costs and focuses on variable costs. The method involves looking at the amount of contribution a product or order makes.

Table 8: Sales revenue, variable costs and contribution for two orders received by Thompson Engineering

		(£)
	Metal panels	**Metal brackets**
Revenue	**12,000**	**17,000**
Variable costs		
Materials	3,000	5,500
Direct labour	4,200	6,900
Other variable costs	1,700	3,000
Total variable costs	**8,900**	**15,400**
Contribution	**3,100**	**1,600**

Contribution can be calculated as selling price minus variable cost for a unit. Total contribution is the revenue from units sold (price x quantity) minus the total variable costs. Generally, if the revenue from products or orders exceeds the variable costs, i.e. the contribution is positive, then managers are likely to consider them for production.

A situation where contribution costing might be helpful is when choosing which orders to accept from customers. For example, Thompson Engineering has received two late orders and only has the resources to accept one. One is for 1,000 metal panels and the other for 800 metal brackets. Details of the revenue, variable costs and contribution are shown in Table 8.

In this example, where only one order can be accepted, Thompson Engineering is likely to accept the order for the metal panels. This is because the panels make the largest contribution out of the two orders. Even though the metal brackets generate more revenue, the panels' contribution is £1,500 higher (£3,100 - £1,600). Note that the marginal costs of the orders are £8,900 for the panels and £15,400 for the brackets. In each case they are the same as the total variable costs.

In this case fixed costs have been ignored. This is because accepting either of the orders had no effect on Thompson Engineering's fixed costs. However, in circumstances where accepting orders results in additional fixed costs, they must be taken into account.

Special order decisions

Sometimes businesses receive orders which are unexpected, from a new customer or for a new product perhaps. On these occasions a business has to decide whether or not to accept the order. The business will consider whether or not the order is profitable. However, even if the order is not profitable it may still be accepted. This may be because the business is considering the size of the **contribution** when making the decision to accept the order.

For example, Powerfire Ltd makes high speed powerboats for the luxury boat market.

- Its **fixed costs** are £500,000 per annum and **variable costs** £18,000 per boat.
- The **price** of the boats is £23,000 each and last year the business **produced and sold** 120 boats.
- The **total costs** of the business are £500,000 + (£18,000 x 120) = £2,660,000.
- The **total revenue** of the business is £23,000 x 120 = £2,760,000.
- This generated a **profit** of £2,760,000 - £2,660,000 = £100,000.

What if, unexpectedly, the business received an order from a new customer for 10 boats, for which the customer was only willing to pay £19,000 each? The contribution that this order would make is:

revenue of 10 x £19,000 (£190,000) minus
variable costs only of 10 x £18,000 (£180,000)
= £10,000.

Note that only the variable costs are taken into account for

Question 3.

Blackburn Mouldings Ltd makes a range of plastic products such as buckets, washing up bowls, clothes baskets, kitchen utensils, plastic toys and plastic components. The standard cost and actual cost of making a new plastic toy are shown in Table 9.

Table 9: Standard and actual cost of making a new toy

Description	Standard cost	Actual cost
Materials	65p	70p
Labour	180p	230p
Machinery	210p	205p
Overheads	50p	50p

(a) Using this case as an example, explain what is meant by a standard cost.

(b) (i) Calculate the total variance.
(ii) Explain possible reasons for the variance.

(c) Outline two advantages of standard costing to Blackburn Mouldings Ltd.

the order of ten extra boats because the fixed costs have been covered by production of the original 120 boats. Sale of the extra ten boats at £19,000 would help to raise profit to £110,000 assuming last year's figures (£100,000 plus £10,000). If Powerfire sold all 130 boats for £19,000 it would make a **loss** of £370,000. This is found by revenue of £2,470,000 (£19,000 x 130) minus costs of £2,840,000 (£500,000 + [130 x £18,000]).

The single unexpected order is worth accepting on financial grounds because the contribution is positive and annual profit rises. However, it would only be accepted if the price of all other boats is unchanged. A number of non-financial factors might also be considered before accepting the order.

- **Capacity.** A business must ensure that it has enough resources to complete the order. For example, are workers prepared to work extra hours? Is there enough space in the factory? Will it replace other, more profitable, production?
- **Customer response.** If existing customers find out that products have been sold to others for lower prices this might cause resentment. It might damage the image of the company and lead to lost sales in the future.
- **Future orders.** Sometimes unprofitable orders are accepted in anticipation of future, more profitable orders, from the new customer.
- **Current utilisation.** An unprofitable order may be accepted to keep staff occupied. It may be better to have permanent staff employed completing orders with small contributions rather than doing nothing.
- **Retaining customer loyalty.** A business may accept an unprofitable order from a regular customer as a favour in order to retain their loyalty.

Advantages and disadvantages of contribution costing

There are advantages to a business in using the contribution costing method.

- It is simple to operate. Unlike absorption costing, the difficulty in sharing fixed costs between different products or cost centres is avoided. There is the advantage that under or overabsorption of overheads does not occur.
- It is a useful decision making tool. It can be used when ranking products or choosing between orders. It is also useful when deciding whether to make or buy-in a particular product or component.

However, there are some disadvantages.

- In some industries contribution costing is inappropriate, particularly when fixed costs represent the majority of a firm's costs. For example, the cost to a train or bus operator of carrying one more passenger is almost zero. Most of the operator's costs are fixed and the variable cost of transporting one more passenger is perhaps just the cost of issuing the ticket. If most customers only pay fares that cover the low variable costs, a business will make a loss because it will not cover the huge fixed costs. However, this does explain the benefit of filling empty seats at discount fares, as long as fixed costs are already covered. The money earned from these passengers adds a lot more to revenue than it does costs.
- When valuing stocks in final accounts, SSAP 9 *Stocks and work-in-progress*, states that the absorption method should be used and not the marginal costing method.
- It can lead to bias in costing calculations. For example, a cost centre that uses a high proportion of overheads may be making a positive contribution. However, when the amount of overheads is taken into account that same centre may be making a loss for the business.

The relationship between marginal and average cost

The average total cost and marginal cost curves are shown in Figure 1. Notice that the marginal cost curve cuts the average cost curve at its lowest point. Why? Consider a business building houses with an average cost of £150,000.

- If another house is built (the marginal house) with a higher than average cost, the average cost will rise;
- if the marginal house cost less than the average cost, the average cost would fall;
- if the marginal house cost £150,000 (the same as average cost) then the average cost would remain the same.

So the marginal and average costs are equal when average costs are constant. On a U-shaped average cost curve this is only at the one point, the lowest point. At all other points the average cost curve in Figure 1 is either rising or falling.

The closing-down point

In the short run it may be worth continuing production of a

Figure 1: Average total cost and marginal cost

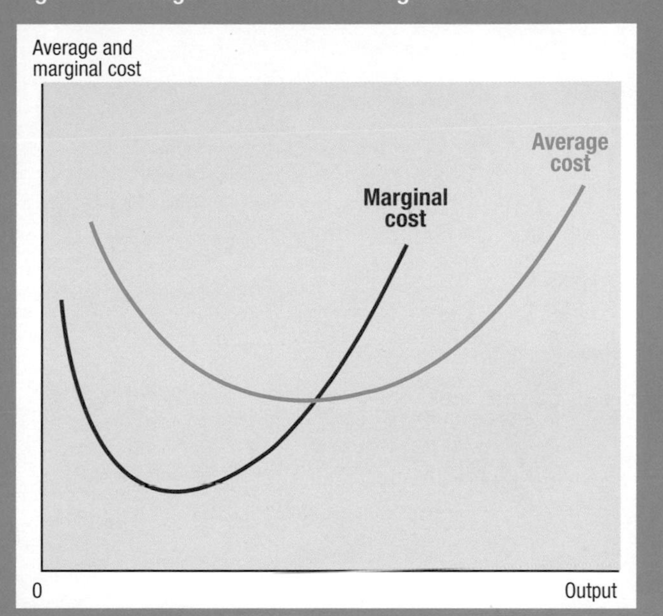

Figure 2: The firm's short run closing-down point

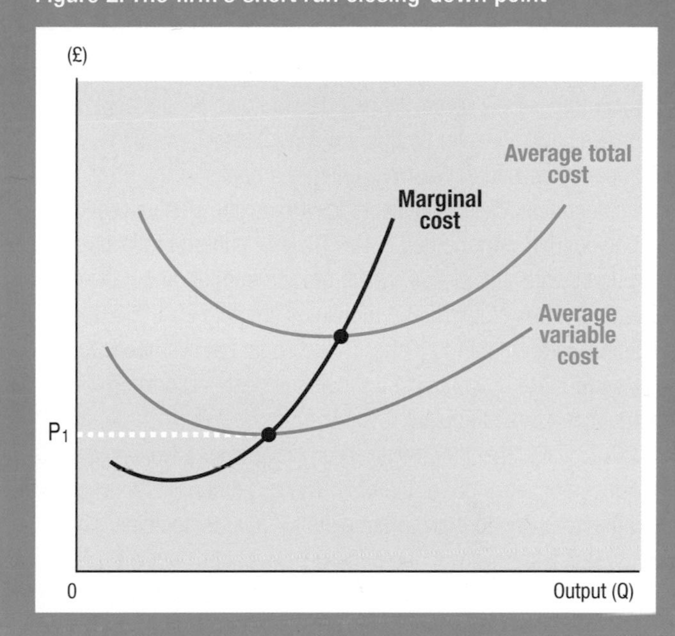

Table 10: Cost and revenue information for a shop

	Open	Closed
		£
Fixed cost	1,000	1,000
Variable cost	500	-
Total cost	1,500	1,000
Total revenue	700	-
Loss	800	1,000

product even when a loss is being made. This can be shown for a whole company as well. Consider the case of a shop whose present cost and revenue conditions are shown in Table 10. If the shop remains open it incurs total costs of £1,500 and generates £700 in sales revenue. This results in a loss of £800. However, if the shop closes this loss is increased to £1,000. Although total costs fall to £1,000 because there are no variable costs to pay, total revenue falls to zero because there are no sales. Thus, in the short run it pays the shop to remain open because losses are lower. However, when revenue is incapable of covering variable costs the firm should close down.

Diagrammatically, the CLOSING-DOWN POINT can be shown by combining the average total cost, average variable cost and marginal cost curves, as in Figure 2. The closing-down point is where marginal cost is equal to average variable cost. When the price falls below P1 on the diagram, the firm can no longer cover its variable costs. At this point the firm may decide to close down.

KEYTERMS

Absorption costing or full costing or total costing – a method of costing which involves charging all the costs of a particular operation to a unit of output.

Closing-down point – the level of output in the short run where a firm should cease its operations, i.e. where marginal cost is equal to average variable cost.

Costing – the process of measuring the likely economic consequences of a particular business activity or operation.

Contribution or marginal costing – the process of costing the production of one more unit of output.

Standard costing – the process of calculating the costs of a specific activity and then comparing them with the actual costs incurred.

KNOWLEDGE

1. Describe the benefits of costing.
2. How might the following indirect costs be apportioned: (a) office wages; (b) corporate advertising; (c) factory insurance?
3. What is the main advantage of absorption costing?
4. In what way is the absorption method limited?
5. How are fixed costs treated in contribution costing?
6. What is meant by standard costing?
7. What are the advantages and disadvantages of contribution costing?
8. When might a loss making contract be accepted?
9. Explain when a firm should close down in the short run.

Case Study: Dave Shepherd Ltd

Dave Shepherd set up a limited company after operating as a sole trader for 7 years. He and his wife own 80 per cent of the shares and Malcolm Wright, a business angel, owns the rest. The company is based in West Wylam on the banks of the River Tyne and manufactures steel components for a Tyneside shipbuilder. Most of the engineering work carried out by Dave Shepherd Ltd involves making underwater 'templates' which provide support and protection to pipes and valves of ships. The templates are sold for £250,000 and take around a month to make. The total annual overheads for the company are £280,000. Table 11 shows the costs associated with the production of one template.

In 2007, Dave Shepherd received an order from a Norwegian shipbuilder, completely out of the blue. The customer, D L Jensholm, wanted the company to make a template for a large container ship they were building. However, the price D L Jensholm was willing to pay did not appear to be attractive. It wanted the template for £185,000. Dave was reluctant to accept the order because he felt that the contribution it would make would be too small. On the other hand, the factory was operating below full capacity and it was an opportunity to start exporting. The costs of producing the template for D L Jensholm are shown in Table 12.

Table 11: Cost information relating to the production of one template

Variable costs	£
Materials and components	34,500
Direct labour	111,200
Subcontracting	29,400
Other variable costs	23,600

Table 12: Costs associated with producing the template for DL Jensholm

Variable costs	£
Materials and components	26,400
Direct labour	98,500
Subcontracting	32,000
Other variable costs	22,500

(a) Calculate the contribution made by the production of one template. (4 marks)

(b) If 12 of these templates are made during the year, calculate the annual profit generated by Dave Shepherd Ltd. (4 marks)

(c) Calculate the contribution that would be made by the order from D L Jensholm. (4 marks)

(d) Discuss whether or not Dave Shepherd Ltd should accept the Norwegian order. (14 marks)

(e) Dave Shepherd's accountant has suggested that the company should use absorption costing rather than marginal costing. Discuss the advantages and disadvantages of this proposition. (14 marks)

53 Investment appraisal

The nature of investment

Investment refers to the purchase of capital goods. Capital goods are used in the production of other goods, directly or indirectly. For example, a building contractor who buys a cement mixer, some scaffolding, a lorry and five shovels has invested. These goods will be used directly in production. If the contractor buys a computer, a filing cabinet and a photocopier for the firm's office, this is indirect investment. Although these items will not be used in production the business would not run as efficiently without them.

Investment might also refer to expenditure by a business which is likely to yield a return in the future. For example, a business might spend £20 million on research and development into a new product or invest £10 million in a promotion campaign. In each case, money is being spent on projects now in the hope that a greater amount of money will be generated in the future as a result of that expenditure.

Types of investment

Investment can be placed into various categories.

- Capital goods. This includes the purchase of a whole variety of mechanical and technical equipment. Vans, lathes, computers, robots, tools, vehicles and information technology are examples.
- Construction. This includes spending on new buildings that are bought or constructed by the firm. Factories, shops, warehouses, workshops and offices are examples.
- Stocks. This is a less obvious item of investment, since it does not fit neatly into the earlier definition. However, because stocks of finished goods and work-in-progress will earn income in the future when they are sold, they are classed as investment.
- Public sector investment. Central and local government fund about 25 per cent of all investment in the economy. Examples of public sector investment include the building of schools, motorways, hospitals and expenditure on goods like buses, dustcarts and equipment for the civil service. The factors which influence the level of public sector investment are often very different from those which affect private sector investment. This is dealt with later in this unit.

Reasons why businesses invest

One of the main reasons why businesses invest is because they have to. Most businesses use plant, machinery, equipment, vehicles, tools and other capital goods. Without capital goods most businesses could not operate. Consequently a lot of investment may take place when a business is setting up. However, even when a business is established investment will continue. Eventually some of the capital goods bought by a business will wear out or become obsolete. These will have to be replaced. This type of investment is called **autonomous** investment.

Most businesses will also carry out **induced** investment which is new investment. Such investment is usually undertaken to help achieve the **functional objectives** of the business. Some examples are given below.

- If the business wants to increase its market share a big investment in a national marketing campaign might be planned.
- Some businesses are committed to lengthy research and development programmes. For example, Oxford Biomedica invested £19.523 million in research and development in 2006. Such investment in research and development is very common in pharmaceutical companies like Oxford Biomedica.
- Some businesses invest in new technology to minimise costs or improve quality, for example. Investment in automation will help to reduce labour costs and improve consistency in production, for example.
- It is common for business to invest in new capacity to help the business grow organically. For example, in 2007, Royal Dutch Shell and a Saudi Arabian partner pledged to invest $7 billion in doubling the size of their refinery in Texas.
- Many business commit investment funds to the acquisition of other businesses. This helps the company to grow faster. For example, in 2006, Ultra Electronics, a defence and aerospace company, invested £7.8 million buying Polyflex Aerospace Ltd and Winfrith Safety Systems.

Investment criteria

Figure 1 shows the factors which might affect private sector investment decisions.

Motives To begin with, firms must have a reason to invest.

- All firms have to replace worn out equipment.
- To be competitive on costs, price and quality, firms may have to invest or risk losing customers to their rivals. Much investment is related to the company's functional objectives.
- The availability of new technology may persuade firms to invest. When technology becomes available, firms are often keen to use it if they can afford to.
- Firms may wish to grow, to be more profitable or to increase their market influence. Growth involves investment in more plant, equipment and other productive assets.

Return If firms have a reason to invest, they must then decide

Figure 1: Investment criteria

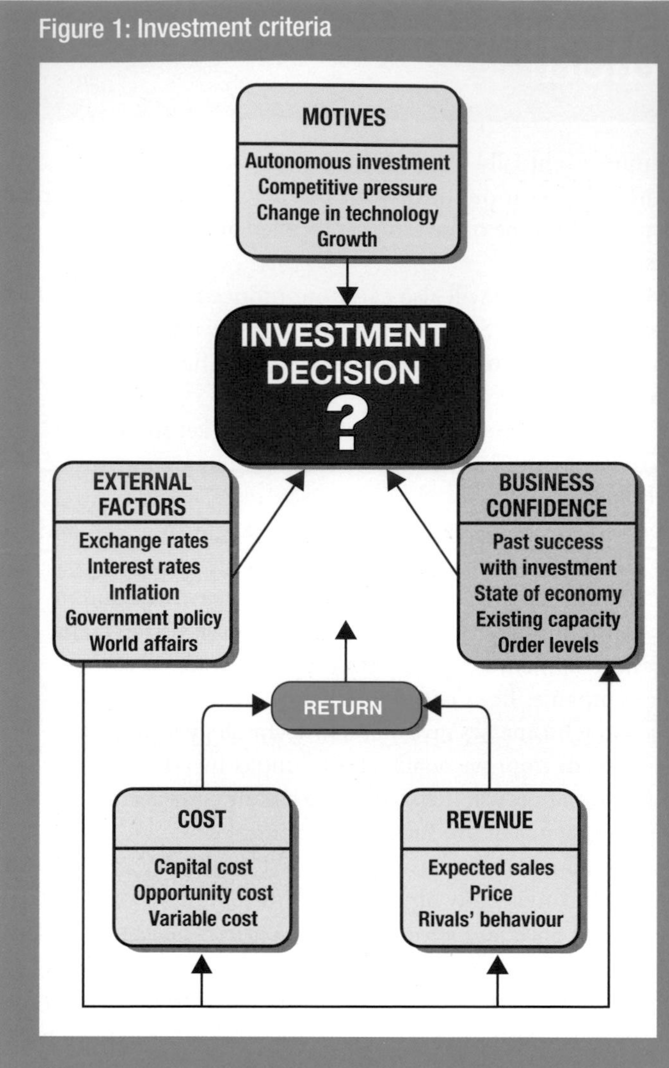

whether it is worthwhile. One influence on this is the return on the investment. The return on an investment project can be found by subtracting the cost of the project from the expected revenue. There are three major costs. Capital costs might be the cost of a new factory. Opportunity costs are the foregone alternatives the investment funds might have been used for, e.g. higher dividends to shareholders. Direct variable costs include the running costs of the project, e.g. labour or fuel costs.

Calculating the expected revenue is not easy. Expected sales are hard to predict with accuracy because many factors affect them. Market research can only predict sales to some extent. Sales can also be influenced by the price set by the business in the future and by rivals' behaviour. Both of these factors are unpredictable.

Business confidence Entrepreneurs and managers will be either optimistic or pessimistic about the future of their businesses. Confidence may be influenced by a range of factors. These include whether or not previous investment has been a success, the state of the economy, the existing level of capacity and future order levels. A pessimistic business person may be less likely to invest than an optimistic one.

External factors External influences can be direct or indirect. For example, high interest rates may directly affect the cost of investment. If money is borrowed the business will pay back more. This can indirectly affect confidence. Inflation could affect costs, revenue and confidence.

The factors affecting public sector investment

What factors influence investment by central government and local authorities?

- Investment in new schools, roads and hospitals, for example, will be influenced by national and local needs. As the demands of the population grow, more of these facilities will be needed.
- Political factors may also influence the quantity and type of investment. In recent years, the government has invested heavily in education and the NHS.
- The availability of government funds and the opportunity cost of investment spending. If revenue from taxes is falling, there may be fewer investment funds. If the opportunity costs of investment projects are high, then they may be cancelled. The state of the economy will be important. For example, falling unemployment in the late 1990s and early 21st century reduced government spending on unemployment benefit. This perhaps meant that extra funds were available for spending on health or education.

Assessing the risks and uncertainties of investment decisions

The decision to invest by business is the most difficult it has to make because of the risk involved. There is often a number of alternative choices. A firm buying a new fleet of cars for its sales staff has to decide which model of car will suit the company best of all. There may also be a considerable choice of projects. For example, a firm may need to choose whether investment in a new packaging machine which increases efficiency would be more profitable than a new computer system.

If all cost and revenue data upon which a decision would be based was accurate, there would not be a problem. However, revenue information in particular comes from predictions. It may be based on forecasts of future demand and conditions in the economy. Even costs, which are perhaps easier to predict, can vary.

Most investment decisions are uncertain because they are long-term decisions, where resources are committed for a period of time. Investment projects have failed both in the private sector and the public sector. For example, in the private sector, independent TV production company, the Television Corporation, had to write off £13 million on Californian subsidiary Pacifica in 2003. The company was still reeling from a failed bid to set up a Formula One version of power boating. The company had already written off £2.6 million, including £400,000 in the previous year. In the public sector, the government spent a lot of money on equipment which was used in the development of the Concorde aircraft. This also proved to be commercially unsuccessful. Concorde services were stopped in 2004.

Investment is also said to be risky because it is often funded with borrowed money. This means that the return on any investment project must also cover the cost of borrowing. Also, if the investment project fails the company may be left with a heavy debt burden and possibly without the means to repay it. The Channel Tunnel project experienced such problems in the late 1990s. Around £5 billion was owed to several hundred banks following the construction of the tunnel link. Although the company was covering its operating costs, it has ceased interest payments to the banks. It was suggested that it unlikely ever to be able to repay the original £5 billion borrowed. This was still the case in 2007.

Investment appraisal and net cash flows

INVESTMENT APPRAISAL describes how a private sector business might objectively evaluate an investment project to determine whether or not it is likely to be profitable. It also allows businesses to make comparisons between different investment projects. There is a number of quantitative methods that a business might use when evaluating projects. However, they all involve comparing the **capital cost** of the project with the **net cash flow**.

- The capital cost is the amount of money spent when setting up a new venture.
- The net cash flow is the amount of money the business expects to receive each year over the life of the investment project, less the estimated running costs.

Consider a haulage company that invests in a new lorry. Table 1 shows the capital cost, the estimated revenue, the estimated running costs and the net cash flow each year over the life of the lorry. The lorry is expected to last for five years. The capital cost is the £80,000 paid to the vehicle supplier. The lorry is purchased in year 0, i.e. 'now'. The net cash flow by the end of year 1 is £19,000. This is found by subtracting the estimated running costs, such as fuel, drivers' wages and insurance, from the estimated revenue generated by the lorry from carrying goods (£56,000 - £37,000). In this example the business would compare the capital cost of £80,000 with the total net cash flow of £87,000 (£19,000 + £21,000 + £22,000 + £15,000 + £10,000),

Table 1: Capital cost and net cash flow from an investment

						£000
	Yr 0	**Yr 1**	**Yr 2**	**Yr 3**	**Yr 4**	**Yr 5**
Capital cost	80	0	0	0	0	0
Estimated revenue	0	56	60	62	58	55
Estimated running costs	0	37	39	40	43	45
Net cash flow	-80	19	21	22	15	10

when evaluating the investment. It may use one of the appraisal methods discussed in this unit.

Payback period

The PAYBACK PERIOD refers to the amount of time it takes for a project to recover or pay back the initial outlay. For example, an engineer may invest £500,000 in new cutting machinery and estimate that it will lead to a net cash flow (after operating costs) over the next five years, as in Table 2.

Table 2: Expected net cash flow from some new cutting machinery

						£000
	Yr 0	**Yr 1**	**Yr 2**	**Yr 3**	**Yr 4**	**Yr 5**
Net cash flow	(500)	100	125	125	150	150
Cumulative net cash flow	(500)	(400)	(275)	(150)	0	150

Here the payback period is four years. If we add together the net cash flows from the project in the first four years it amounts to £500,000 (i.e. 100 + 125 + 125 + 150).

The payback period can also be found by calculating the **cumulative net cash flow**. This is the cash flow each year taking into account revenue and operating costs (net cash flow) and the initial cost of the machine. When the machine is first bought, in year 0, there is negative cash flow of minus £500,000, the cost of the machine. Next year the revenue minus operating costs are £100,000. So the cumulative net cash flow is -£500,000 +

Table 3: Expected net cash flow from three investment projects

									£000
	Yr 0	**Yr 1**	**Yr 2**	**Yr 3**	**Yr 4**	**Yr 5**	**Yr 6**	**Total net cash flow**	**Payback period**
A Net cash flow	(70)	10	10	20	20	30	40	60	4 yrs 4 mths
A Cumulative cash flow	(70)	(60)	(50)	(30)	(10)	20	60		
B Net cash flow	(70)	20	20	20	20	20	20	50	3 yrs 6 mths
B Cumulative cash flow	(70)	(50)	(30)	(10)	10	30	50		
C Net cash flow	(70)	30	30	20	10	10	10	40	2 yrs 6 mths
C Cumulative cash flow	(70)	(40)	(10)	10	20	30	40		

Table 4: Advantages and disadvantages of payback method

Advantages

- This method is useful when technology changes rapidly, such as in the agriculture industry. New farm machinery is designed and introduced into the market regularly. It is important to recover the cost of investment before a new machine is designed.
- It is simple to use.
- Firms might adopt this method if they have cash-flow problems. This is because the project chosen will 'payback' the investment more quickly than others.

Disadvantages

- Cash earned after the 'payback' is not taken into account in the decision to invest.
- The method ignores the profitability of the project, since the criterion used is the speed of repayment.

£100,000 = -£400,000. In year 4 it is zero, so all costs have been covered.

When using this method to choose between projects, the project with the shortest payback will be chosen. Assume a business is appraising three investment projects, all of which cost £70,000. The net cash flow expected from each project is shown in Table 3.

In this example project C would be chosen because it has the shortest payback time, i.e. two years and six months. How is this calculated? In years 1 and 2 the net cash flow is £30,000 + £30,000 = £60,000. To pay for an investment of £70,000 the remaining £10,000 (£70,000 - £60,000) comes from year 3's net cash flow. This is £20,000, which is more. So the number of months in year 3 it takes to pay the £10,000 can be calculated as:

$$\frac{\text{Amount required}}{\text{Net cash flow in year}} \times 12 = \frac{£10{,}000}{£20{,}000} \times 12 = 6 \text{ months}$$

Project A's payback is four years four months and project B's is three years and six months. Note that total cash flow is not taken into account in this method. In fact project C has the lowest total return over the six years. The advantages and disadvantages of the payback method of appraisal are shown in Table 4.

Average/accounting rate of return

The AVERAGE RATE OF RETURN or ACCOUNTING RATE OF RETURN (ARR) method measures the net return each year as a percentage of the capital cost of the investment.

$$\text{Average rate of return (\%)} = \frac{\text{Net return (profit) per annum}}{\text{Capital outlay (cost)}} \times 100$$

For example, the capital cost and expected net cash flow from three investment projects are shown in Table 6.

A business would first calculate the profit from each project by subtracting the total net cash flow of the project from its capital cost, ie £70,000 - £50,000 = £20,000 for project X. The next step is to calculate the profit per annum by dividing the profit by the number of years the project runs for, ie £20,000 ÷ 5

Question 1.

Delrose Associates is a full service digital marketing agency. The company offers a blend of consultancy and creativity, resulting in fully managed, highly successful online marketing campaigns. Delrose has clients in a variety of sectors including consumer, corporate, commercial, retail and not-for-profit. Their main work is developing targeted campaigns to drive quality traffic to websites using highly cost-effective methods.

In 2007 the managing director of the company recognised the need for a new computer system. She carried out some research into three new systems and put together the financial information shown in Table 5.

(a) Explain what is meant by 'expected net cash flow'.

(b) Calculate the payback period for each system and state which system Delrose Associates should select.

(c) Explain one reason why Delrose used the payback method of investment appraisal in this case.

Table 5: Capital costs and expected net cash flows from three new computer systems

								£000
Computer system	**Capital cost**	**2007**	**2008**	**2009**	**2010**	**2011**	**2012**	**Total**
System A	24,000	6,000	6,000	6,000	6,000	6,000	6,000	36,000
System B	37,000	8,000	8,000	9,000	9,000	6,000	6,000	46,000
System C	12,000	4,000	4,000	4,000	2,000	1,000	1,000	16,000

= £4,000 for X. Finally, the ARR is calculated by using the above formula, i.e.

$$\text{ARR (Project X)} = \frac{£4{,}000}{£50{,}000} \times 100$$

$$= 8\%$$

The results for all three projects are shown in Table 7. Project Y would be chosen because it gives a higher ARR (10 per cent) than the other two. Table 8 outlines the advantages and disadvantages of the ARR method.

Table 6: The capital cost and net cash flow from three investment projects

	Project X	Project Y	Project Z
Capital cost	£50,000	£40,000	£90,000
Return Yr 1	£10,000	£10,000	£20,000
Yr 2	£10,000	£10,000	£20,000
Yr 3	£15,000	£10,000	£30,000
Yr 4	£15,000	£15,000	£30,000
Yr 5	£20,000	£15,000	£30,000
Total net cash flows	£70,000	£60,000	£130,000

Table 7: The ARR calculated for three investment projects

	Project X	Project Y	Project Z
Capital cost	£50,000	£40,000	£90,000
Total net profit (ncf - capital cost)	£20,000	£20,000	£40,000
Net profit p.a. (profit ÷ 5)	£4,000	£4,000	£8,000
ARR	8%	10%	8.9%

Table 8: Advantages and disadvantages of the ARR method

Advantages

The advantage of this method is that it shows clearly the profitability of an investment project. Not only does it allow a range of projects to be compared, the overall rate of return can be compared to other uses for investment funds. In the example in Table 7, if a company can gain 12 per cent by placing its funds in a bank account, it might choose to postpone the investment project until interest rates fall. It is also easier to identify the opportunity cost of investment.

Disadvantages

The method does not take into account the effects of time on the value of money. The above example assumes that, for project X, £10,000 of income for the firm in two years' time is the same as £10,000 in one year's time. Some allowance must be made for the time span over which the income from an investment project is received for it to be most useful.

Question 2.

Hastings Group focuses on the development, production, installation and support of electrical, electronic, and mechanical components for aircraft, helicopters, missiles and targeting systems. The company has a leading position in the field of aircraft and helicopter services, customisation and modification. Hastings' employees are engineers and skilled workers. In 2007 the directors identified three investment projects that would benefit the company:

- R & D project;
- Marketing campaign;
- Some new CNC machinery.

The capital cost and expected cash flows for the investment projects are shown in Table 9.

(a) (i) Calculate the average rate of return for each project.
(ii) Explain which project should be selected.

(b) Explain the advantages to Hastings Group of using this method of appraisal.

Table 9: Capital cost and expected cash flows for three investment projects

£000

Investment project	Capital cost	2008	2009	2010	2011	2012	2013	Total
R & D	9,600	0	0	2,500	4,600	5,000	5,500	17,600
Marketing campaign	9,000	5,000	4,000	3,000	2,000	1,000	1,000	16,000
New CNC machinery	7,800	2,000	2,000	2,000	2,000	2,000	2,000	12,000

Table 10: Value of £100 invested over five years at 10 per cent per annum compound interest

Year	1	2	3	4	5
Value of £100	£110	£121	£133	£146	£161

Discounted cash flow (DCF)/net present value (NPV)

Present value and DCF When making an investment decision a business might take into account what cash flow or profit earned in future is worth now. Look at Table 10. This shows that £100 invested today at a compound interest rate of 10 per cent would be worth £161 in five years' time.

- In one year's time, the investment would be worth £110. Of this, £10 would be the interest and £100 would be the initial investment.
- In two years' time, it would be worth £121. With compound interest, the interest is based not on the initial investment but on the investment at the end of the first year. So interest is 10 per cent of £110, making £11. Then this has to be added to the £110 value at the end of the first year to make a total of £121 for the second year.

This carries on until the value after five years is £161.

If £100 today is worth £161 in five years' time, it must be true that £161 in five years' time is worth just £100 today. This is an example of an important insight of DISCOUNTED CASH-FLOW techniques. Money in the future is worth less than the same amount now (the PRESENT VALUE). This is because money available today could be invested and it could earn interest.

Note that this is a completely different idea to the fact that money in the future can also become devalued due to the effects of inflation. Inflation does indeed affect future values of money. So there are two effects on the value of future money. Discounted cash-flow techniques just deal with one of these, the effect of interest rates.

Discount tables can be used to show by how much a future value must be multiplied to calculate its present value. Table 11 shows a discount table with five different rates of interest. If an investment project were predicted to give a net cash flow of £10,000 in three years' time, and the discount rate were 10 per cent, then reading off the table, the £10,000 would need to be multiplied by 0.75. To arrive at its present value the calculation would be:

£10,000 x 0.75 = £7,500

So £10,000 received in five years' time at a discount rate/interest rate of 5 per cent is worth £7,500 today. Cash flow or profit of £15,000 from an investment project received in five years' time, a discount/interest rate of 20 per cent, would be £15,000 x 0.40 or £6,000.

The discount table shown in Table 11 also shows two features of discounting.

Table 11: Discount table

				Rate of discount	
Year	5%	10%	15%	20%	25%
0	1.00	1.00	1.00	1.00	1.00
1	0.95	0.91	0.87	0.83	0.80
2	0.91	0.83	0.76	0.69	0.64
3	0.86	0.75	0.66	0.58	0.51
4	0.82	0.68	0.57	0.48	0.41
5	0.78	0.62	0.50	0.40	0.33
6	0.75	0.56	0.43	0.33	0.26
7	0.71	0.51	0.38	0.28	0.21
8	0.68	0.47	0.33	0.23	0.17
9	0.64	0.42	0.28	0.19	0.13
10	0.61	0.39	0.25	0.16	0.10

- The higher the rate of discount, the less the present value of cash flow in future. This is the reverse of saying that the higher the rate of interest, the greater will be the value of an investment in the future.
- The further into the future the cash flow or earnings from an investment project, the less is their present value. So £1,000 earned in five years' time is worth less than £1,000 earned in one year's time. Again this is simply the opposite way of saying that £1,000 invested today at a fixed rate of interest will be worth more in five years' time than in one year's time.

Calculating NPV The NET PRESENT VALUE method makes use of discounted cash flow. It calculates the rate of return on an investment project taking into account the effects of interest rates and time. Using discount tables, it is possible to calculate the net present value of an investment project.

Table 12 shows three investment projects. The initial cost of each investment project is £50,000, shown in the Year 0 row. In years 1 to 10, each produces a stream of net cash flow. When added up, these come to far more than the initial £50,000. So it might appear that each investment project is profitable. However, if the net cash flow is discounted using a discount rate of 20 per cent, the picture is very different.

- **Project A.** The sum of the present values in years 1-10 for Project A is just £41,700. The net cash flow each year is constant at £10,000. But the present value of each of those £10,000 falls the further away it is received. By year 10, the present value of £10,000 discounted at 20 per cent is just £1,600. The net present value can be calculated simply by totalling the present value figures in years 0-10, including subtracting the initial cost. Or it can be calculated using the formula:

Net present value = present values - initial cost = £41,700 - £50,000 = - £8,300.

So project A is unprofitable according to discounted cash-flow techniques.

Table 12: Net present value of three investment projects discounted at 20 per cent

Year	Project A Net cash flow £	Project A Present value £	Project B Net cash flow £	Project B Present Value £	Project C Net cash flow £	Project C Present Value £	Discount table Rate of discount at 20%
0	(50,000)	(50,000)	(50,000)	(50,000)	(50,000)	(50,000)	1.00
1	10,000	8,300	5,000	4,150	20,000	16,600	0.83
2	10,000	6,900	8,000	5,520	16,000	11,040	0.69
3	10,000	5,800	10,000	5,800	14,000	8,120	0.58
4	10,000	4,800	12,000	5,760	12,000	5,760	0.48
5	10,000	4,000	12,000	4,800	12,000	4,800	0.40
6	10,000	3,300	12,000	4,000	12,000	4,000	0.33
7	10,000	2,800	12,000	3,360	12,000	3,360	0.28
8	10,000	2,300	14,000	3,220	10,000	2,300	0.23
9	10,000	1,900	16,000	3,040	8,000	1,520	0.19
10	10,000	1,600	20,000	3,200	5,000	800	0.16
Total net cash flow before discounting	50,000		71,000		71,000		
Present values years 1-10		41,700		42,850		58,300	
Net present value (NPV)		(8,300)		(7,150)		+8,300	

- Project B. The total net cash flow before discounting is higher than for Project A, £71,000 compared to £50,000. But once discounted, there is little difference in the sum of the present values. This is because net cash flow in Project B is weighted towards later years. The net present value of this project is £42,850 - £50,000 = - £7,150. Again, Project B is unprofitable according to discounted cash flow techniques.
- Project C. The total net cash flow before discounting is the same as with Project B. Indeed, the pattern of net cash flow is an exact reverse of those of Project B. Here, the higher net cash flow figures are concentrated at the start and fall off towards the end. This means that the total present value is much higher than with Project B. The net present value of Project C is £58,300 - £50,000 = £8,300. This is the discounted profit that the business will make on this project.

The net present value method would suggest that a business should go ahead with any investment projects that have a positive net present value. If a business has to make a choice between investment projects for whatever reason, it should go for those with the highest net present value. So in this case it would choose Project C.

Calculating present value using a formula

It is possible to calculate accurately the present value of a sum of money to be received in the future. For example, what is the present value of £100 in 3 years? It can be found by the formula:

$$\text{Present value} = \frac{A}{\left(1 + \frac{r}{100}\right)^n}$$

Table 13: Advantages and disadvantages of net present value method

Advantages

- The net present value method, unlike the payback method and the average rate of return, correctly accounts for the value of future earnings by calculating present values.
- The discount rate used can be changed as risk and conditions in financial markets change. For example, in the 1990s, the cost of bank borrowing for many businesses fell from over 15 per cent to 7-8 per cent. Investment projects therefore did not need to make such a high rate of return to be profitable and so the rate of discount could be lowered.

Disadvantages

- Calculating discounted cash flow is the most complex of the three methods. It certainly can't be done 'on the back of an envelope' as can the other two methods. As such, it is rarely used by small businesses.
- The rate of discount used is critical in determining what is and is not profitable. The higher the discount rate, the fewer investment projects are likely to be profitable.

where A = amount of money, r = rate of interest and n = number of years. The present value of £100 received in three years' time is (assuming a 10 per cent interest rate):

$$\text{Present value} = \frac{£100}{\left(1+\frac{10}{100}\right)^3} = \frac{£100}{(1.1)^3} = \frac{£100}{1.331} = £75.13$$

This shows that £100 received in three years' time is worth less than £100 today. How much less depends on two things.

- Interest rates. If interest rates rise to 20 per cent then present value would be:

$$\frac{£100}{\left(1+\frac{20}{100}\right)^3} = £57.87$$

- The length of time. If £100 was received in 25 years' time the present value would be:

$$\frac{£100}{\left(1+\frac{10}{100}\right)^{25}} = £9.23$$

It is also possible to calculate the net present value of an investment project using the formula. Assume an investment project costs £100,000 and yields an expected net cash flow over a three year period - year 1, £30,000; year 2, £40,000; year 3, £50,000. The rate of interest remains at 10 per cent over the time period. The present value of the future income stream using the technique described above will be:

$$\text{Present value} = \frac{£30,000}{(1+0.1)^1} + \frac{£40,000}{(1+0.1)^2} + \frac{£50,000}{(1+0.1)^3}$$

$$\text{Present value} = \frac{£30,000}{(1.1)^1} + \frac{£40,000}{(1.1)^2} + \frac{£50,000}{(1.1)^3}$$

$$\text{Present value} = \frac{£30,000}{1.1} + \frac{£40,000}{1.21} + \frac{£50,000}{1.331}$$

$$\text{Present value} = £27,272 + £33,057 + £37,565 = £97,894$$

The above investment project is not viable since the present value of the net cash flow (£97,894) is less than the cost (£100,000). The net present value of this investment project is:

$$\begin{aligned}\text{NPV} &= \text{Present value of return - cost}\\ &= £97,894 - £100,000 = -£2,106\end{aligned}$$

Question 3.

Gethings is a garment manufacturer in London. It is considering making an investment in one of two machines, A and B. The projected net cash flows for each machine are shown in Table 14.

Table 14: Expected net cash flow from two investment projects

						£000	
Year	0	1	2	3	4	5	6
	Initial cost						
Machine A							
Net cash flow	(600)	100	150	200	300	200	100
Discounted cash flow							
Machine B							
Net cash flow	(600)	200	300	200	150	100	100
Discounted cash flow							

(a) Calculate the discounted cash flow for each machine and each year using a discount rate of 15 per cent from the discount table, Table 11.

(b) Calculate the net present value for each machine.

(c) Explain why Gethings might buy Machine B if it uses the net present value method of decision making.

Internal rate of return

This technique also makes use of discounted cash flow. To decide on the INTERNAL RATE OF RETURN (IRR) a firm must find the rate of return (x) where the net present value is zero. This internal rate of return is then compared with the market rate of interest to determine whether the investment should take place. Assume an investment project costs £10,000 and yields a one year return only of £13,000. The market rate of interest is 14 per cent. To calculate the IRR (x):

$$\begin{aligned}\text{Cost} &= \frac{A}{(1+x)^1}\\ 10,000 &= \frac{13,000}{(1+x)^1}\\ (1+x) &= \frac{13,000}{10,000}\\ 1+x &= 1.3\\ x &= 1.3 - 1\\ &= 0.3 \text{ or } 30\%\end{aligned}$$

Since the IRR (x) of 30 per cent is greater than the market rate of interest (14 per cent) the firm should invest in the project. When this is applied to projects over a longer period the calculation becomes more complex. However, the method remains the same.

An alternative approach is to use trial and error. This means choosing a discount rate, calculating the net present value (NPV) and seeing whether it equals zero. If it does not then another rate must be chosen. This process is continued until the correct rate is found. For example, assume that an investment project costs £50,000 and earns a five year return.

Table 15: The net present value of an investment project at three different discount rates

Year	Net cash flow	Present value of income at: 10%	7.5%	5%
1	5,000	4,545	4,651	4,762
2	5,000	4,132	4,325	4,555
3	10,000	7,513	8,045	8,643
4	20,000	13,661	14,970	16,447
5	20,000	12,442	13,828	15,661
Total	60,000	42,273	45,919	50,048
NPV		-7,727	-4,081	48

Table 15 shows the actual return and the present value of the return over the five year period at different discount rates. If a 10 per cent discount rate is used the NPV is less than zero, i.e. -£7,727. Also, if a 7.5 per cent discount rate is used the NPV is less than zero, ie -£4,081. If a 5 per cent rate is used the NPV is as near to zero as is needed, ie just £48. Thus, 5 per cent is the internal rate of return. Figure 2 shows the relationship between the discount rate and the NPV. As the discount rate increases the NPV falls. The IRR is shown on the discount rate axis where NPV is zero.

Qualitative factors influencing investment decisions

In addition to the factors which might influence investment decisions already outlined in this unit, a number of other qualitative factors might be considered. These are non-financial considerations.

Human relations Some investment projects can have a huge impact on the staff in an organisation. For example, investment in plant automation might lead to mass redundancies. A business might decide to postpone plans to automate their plant if it thought the damage to human relations in the organisation would be too severe.

Figure 2: The relationship between the NPV and the discount rate

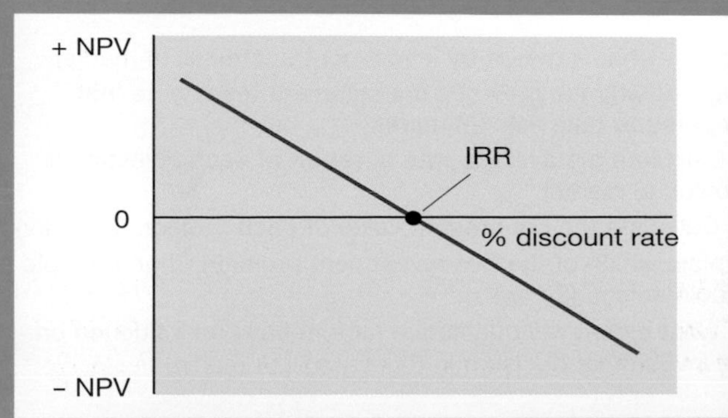

Ethical considerations Along with many other business decisions, managers are taking more of an ethical stance when choosing courses of action. For example, a chemicals producer might decide to build a new plant in a location which does not minimise financial costs but does reduce environmental damage. Such a decision might help to enhance the image of a company. Companies are increasingly keen to be seen as 'good corporate citizens'.

Corporate strategy Many businesses have long-term corporate objectives which are laid down in their corporate strategy. Such long term objectives might influence short-term investment decisions. For example, a business operating a chain of theme pubs might be considering some repairs to a fire-damaged pub. Repairs might be postponed because the pub in question was due for complete refurbishment in the next financial year.

Risk The financial position in which a business finds itself is one factor in assessing the risk of an investment project. Others include the state of the economy and the markets into which a business sells. Investment projects which have long payback periods are also riskier than ones with shorter payback periods.

Government legislation Investment may have to take place for a business to conform to government laws and regulations. So, for example, a business may have to install anti-pollution equipment to bring down its emission levels even though this investment project could make a loss for the business. Or it may have to adapt its premises to conform to various disability regulations without seeing any return on this investment.

Availability of funding A large number of investment projects fail to get started because businesses are unable to raise the necessary money to fund the project. A significant proportion of these will be small businesses which have difficulty in persuading investors and lenders to provide funding.

Business confidence Entrepreneurs, managers and businesses tend to have different attitudes and cultures from each other. One aspect of this is confidence or optimism. Some decision makers tend to be very cautious, seeing all the problems that might arise if things go wrong. Others are confident and optimistic. They see the future as much better and brighter than the average. This has a crucial impact on investment. The cautious, unconfident entrepreneur or manager may delay or abandon possible investment projects. In the same circumstances with the same investment projects, confident and optimistic managers will tend to go ahead and authorise the expenditure. So the deeply held attitudes of decision makers have an important influence on investment decision making.

KEYTERMS

Average rate of return or accounting rate of return (ARR) – a method of investment appraisal which measures the net return per annum as a percentage of the initial spending.

Discounted cash flow (DCF) – a method of investment appraisal which takes interest rates into account by calculating the present value of future income.

Investment appraisal – the evaluation of an investment project to determine whether or not it is likely to be worthwhile.

Net present value (NPV) – the present value of future income from an investment project, less the cost.

Present value – the value today of a sum of money available in the future.

Payback period – the amount of time it takes to recover the cost of an investment project.

KNOWLEDGE

1. What is meant by the term investment?
2. Explain the difference between autonomous and induced investment.
3. State the 4 types of investment.
4. Why is the investment decision risky?
5. State the factors that might influence (a) private sector and (b) public investment?
6. What is the function of investment appraisal in business?
7. Explain briefly how a business would appraise investment using the payback period.
8. What are the advantages and disadvantages of the payback method?
9. What does the average or accounting rate of return method of investment appraisal aim to measure?
10. Why is the discounted cash flow/NPV method of appraisal used in business?
11. Suggest how environmental considerations may affect an investment decision.

Case Study: Chambers plc

In 2006, Chambers plc, an ailing cylinder manufacturer, was bought by a management team for £4 million. The company employs 169 staff and operates from a factory in Tipton, West Midlands. It designs and manufactures custom high-quality, heavy-duty hydraulic cylinders for the mobile, off-highway, specialty vehicle and heavy hydraulic machinery markets.

The new management team believe they can transform the company into a profit-making concern. Last year the company lost £560,000 on sales of £13,256,000. The team believe that in the past the people running the company were not prepared to take risk. Consequently they have failed to invest in new technology and working methods and fallen behind their competitors.

Dave Williams, the new managing director, has already earmarked £5 million for investment. Initially four investment projects were identified but two were eliminated at a preliminary stage using the payback method of appraisal. The two remaining projects are now being appraised. One of these projects involves automating about 60 per cent of the production process. The other involves introducing total quality management (TQM) right across the organisation. The capital cost of the two projects and the expected cash flows are shown in Table 16. The present value of £1 receivable at the end of five years at 5 per cent is shown in Table 17.

Table 16: Capital cost and expected cash flows for Chambers investment projects

							(£m)
Investment project	**Cost**	**2007**	**2008**	**2009**	**2010**	**2011**	**Total**
Automation	5.0	2.3	2.6	2.8	3.3	3.2	14.2
Introduce TQM	4.4	2.1	2.1	2.3	2.4	2.5	11.4

Table 17: The present value of £1 receivable at the end of 5 years at 5 per cent

After	0 yr	1 yr	2 yrs	3 yrs	4 yrs	5 yrs
Present value of £1	£1.00	£0.95	£0.90	£0.86	£0.82	£0.78

The new owners of the company are very optimistic about the future direction of the company. However, the workforce does not share their enthusiasm. Most of them are worried about the proposed investment plans. The age profile of the workforce is very high. Many of the workforce joined the company when they left school and undertook apprenticeships. More than 50 per cent of the workers have never worked anywhere else and are over 55. If Chambers select the automation project about 50 staff are certain to lose their jobs. Also, an employee representative said, 'The introduction of TQM will create pressure and stress for many of the lads here'... 'Some of them just aren't up to it.'

(a) Explain what is meant by investment appraisal. (4 marks)

(b) Suggest why the previous management team were 'not prepared to take risk'. (6 marks)

(c) (i) Calculate the average rate of return of each investment project. (6 marks)

(ii) Calculate the net present value of each project. (8 marks)

(d) Explain which of the two investment projects Chambers plc should select. (2 marks)

(e) To what extent will qualitative factors have an influence on the investment decision in this case? (14 marks)

54 Selecting financial strategies

What are financial strategies?

Most businesses have financial objectives such as increasing the return on capital employed, generating cash flow or increasing shareholder value. In order to meet these objectives a business is likely to employ FINANCIAL STRATEGIES. A financial strategy is a detailed action plan designed to achieve a specific financial objective. For example, in order to increase the return on capital employed a business might try to bring down its costs. It might do this by introducing **cost centres** to make individual parts of the business more accountable. Examples of financial strategies include:

- raising finance;
- implementing cost or profit centres;
- cost minimisation;
- allocating capital expenditure.

Financial strategies may also be linked to other functions such as production, research and development and marketing. For example, there may be a need for a company to spend more on research and development to keep up with competition. If the company decides to go ahead with such an investment there will be financial implications. For example, there may be a need to raise more long-term finance.

Raising finance

The need for finance is a vital issue for businesses. There are few businesses that can self-finance all of their activities. Businesses need money to set up and get established, but the need for finance continues indefinitely. Raising finance is often a **strategic** issue. This is because it affects many aspects of the business and can have an impact over the long-term. Some of the key financing issues are outlined below.

Flotation Many businesses decide to 'go public' as a means of raising finance. This means changing the legal structure of the business from a private limited company to a public limited company. Such a move will have a huge impact on the organisation. There will be new owners of the company, legal issues to deal with and the prospect of a change in culture. However, operating as a plc means that much more finance can be raised and the profile of the business will be raised. In 2007, for example, CVS, the veterinary practice group which operates 128 small practices, floated on AIM. It raised £92.7 million after placing 45.2 million shares at 205p each. Much of this was to be used to acquire other businesses, to help the company grow.

Financial restructuring Sometimes established companies have to restructure their finances. This often means raising new finance and changing the emphasis of funding methods. The need for financial restructuring often arises when a company gets into difficulties. For example, a company might be pressured into handing over some of its equity in exchange for debt. An example of a company restructuring its finances is outlined in Figure 1.

Figure 1: Financial restructuring at Biofuels Corporation

A slump in the price of crop-based diesel and technical difficulties with its processing plant forced a fledgling biofuels company into a drastic financial restructuring. Shares slumped 40% to 7.25p as the board of Biofuels Corporation agreed to a deal under which it will hand over 94% of the company to Barclays Bank in return for retiring £40m of the company's £100m debts.

Shareholders were called to an extraordinary general meeting where they were asked to vote on the decision to dilute their equity to a tiny stake. They were warned that the company faces insolvency if the restructuring is not agreed. 'The board has undertaken a thorough review of the group's options, including seeking purchasers of the company, but the board has concluded that, given the existing financial structure, neither a trade sale nor an equity fundraising is possible,' said chairman Mike Buzzacott. Biofuels blamed their problems on US government incentives which have boosted production in America and forced down the global price of biodiesel since last September.

Source: adapted from *The Guardian* 26.6.2007.

The problems of being under capitalised Some businesses are UNDER CAPITALISED. This means that the owners have not provided enough funds to support its activities. In order for the business to survive and flourish such companies have to find new funding. Businesses must employ appropriate financial strategies to avoid being under capitalised.

- The current owners might provide more capital. If the shareholders in a company can inject more capital they will retain ownership and enjoy all the future profits made by the company. An approach might be to use a **rights issue.** This involves selling more shares to existing shareholders at a discount. However, the current owners may be unable or unwilling to do so. Consequently this option may have limited scope.

Question 1.

One of the companies aiming to take part in the biggest wave power scheme in Britain, on a site just off the northern coast of Cornwall, plans to float on AIM (the London Stock Exchange's international market for smaller growing companies). Oceanlinx, an Australian company, is hoping to raise up to £35 million to build six generators, as well as invest in research and development and hire new staff. The site was built as a pilot project but after a year in operation Oceanlinx has signed a commercial agreement to supply electricity to a local energy firm. The so called Wave Hub, 10 miles out to sea, was given planning permission last month. It is an area of 4 km by 2 km, in which wave power developers can set up plants and plug into the power grid through an undersea socket. It is expected to be operational in 2009 and will generate enough electricity for 7,500 homes. The decision to 'go public' allows Oceanlinx to raise the substantial amount of money it needs to build the generators. It will operate as a plc and have to comply with stock exchange rules. The decision to float the company will change it for ever.

Source: adapted from www.oceanlinx.com.

(a) **What is the main reason why Oceanlinx has floated the company?**

(b) **What are the advantages to Oceanlinx of raising finance in this way?**

- A business can raise more capital by inviting new owners to join and make a contribution. A limited company may decide to issue more shares. Another option is to 'go public' as explained above. Alternatively, a business might seek specialist investors such as business angels or venture capitalists.
- A business can take out more long-term funding. This might involve taking out a 25 year mortgage for example. One advantage of this is that such funding might be cheaper. Taking out longer-term funding gives the business more time to repay the amount borrowed and reduces uncertainty as the business is trying to develop.

Implementing cost and profit centres

One way in which a business might achieve its financial objectives is to implement cost or profit centres. This will help to control costs and improve accountability.

Cost centres A COST CENTRE is an individual part of the business where costs are incurred and can be recorded easily. For example, Canning Insurance has four types of insurance which it offers customers – Car Insurance, House Insurance, Holiday Insurance and Life Assurance. Each of these operates as a cost centre. The total costs incurred by the business during 2008 were £5.6 million. The costs incurred by each cost centre were:

- Car Insurance £1.2 million;
- House Insurance £2.0 million;
- Holiday Insurance £0.9 million;
- Life Assurance £1.5 million.

Canning Insurance might conclude from this information that the Holiday Insurance has the best control over its costs. However, other factors will have to be taken into account, such as the size of each department.

How can a business be divided into cost centres? There is a number of ways and the method chosen by a business will depend on its circumstances.

- **By product.** Canning Insurance, in the example above, uses this method. It means that costs are measured for each of the products of a business. So each product is a cost centre.
- **By department.** Many businesses are divided into departments such as marketing, production, accounts and human resources. Each department can be treated as a cost centre.
- **By geographical location.** A business which has operations all over the country or world might use this method. For example, a supermarket chain with stores all over the UK may treat each one as a cost centre.
- **By employee.** In some businesses it is appropriate to measure the costs incurred by individual members of staff. For example, a salesperson could be treated as a cost centre and examples of costs might be wages, National Insurance contributions, motor expenses, overnight accommodation expenses and entertaining expenses.
- **By machine.** It is possible to use a machine, such as a vehicle, as a cost centre by recording all its costs. These might be leasing charges and payments for fuel, motor tax, insurance and maintenance.

Profit centres A PROFIT CENTRE is very similar to a cost centre. The difference is that in addition to recording costs at each centre, revenues are also recorded. This allows a business to calculate how much profit each centre makes. The use of profit centres makes it much easier to compare the performance of each different part of the business. For example, a supermarket chain can identify the most profitable stores in the country by comparing the profit each centre makes. Profit centres can only be used effectively if an activity generates revenue. For example, since a research and development department does not generate any revenue directly, it is unlikely to be used as a profit centre. A business can be divided into profit centres in the same way as it would be into cost centres, provided the centre generates revenue.

Advantages of using cost and profit centres

There are certain advantages to a business of using cost and profit centres.

Improving accountability Although it is important to measure the performance of the whole business, it is also helpful to monitor the progress of different products, regions or departments, for example. Cost and profit centres can be used to hold individual parts of the business accountable. Without cost and profit centres an inefficient department might not be identified and held accountable for its poor performance.

Helping decision making To make decisions about different parts of the business managers need financial information about those different parts. Cost and profit centres help provide this information. For example, if managers are trying to decide which product to discontinue, to make way for a new product, it can use information gathered from profit centres. Managers are likely to stop supplying the least profitable product.

Improving motivation The performance of cost and profit centres is likely to depend on the quality of work done by the people employed in them. It is possible to motivate staff in centres by offering them incentives to achieve goals or targets. For example, a clothes chain might give bonus payments to staff working in stores if they achieve monthly profit targets. This should help to motivate them to produce their best work. It is also common to delegate control of cost and profit centres to middle managers. Managers may be better motivated if they are offered promotion, for example, when targets are met.

Question 2.

Frank O'Connell runs a small independent chain of bakeries in Northern Ireland. He is concerned about the problems the company is having with the bank and overdraft facility. The account is constantly in excess of its limit and so cheques are being returned. After a discussion with his bank manager it became apparent that the financial position of the business was unclear and the property valuation was not up to date. After a closer analysis of the situation, and a property revaluation, the entire finance was restructured onto a loan with an agreement that the interest rate would be reviewed after 12 months. The existing commercial mortgage and overdraft facility were converted to a new mortgage over a longer term. This released cash back into the business and reduced the monthly repayments. As this was a restructure of the business finance, an agreement was reached that the interest rate would be reviewed if the trading was better. If the bank account remained in credit then the interest rate would be reduced.

(a) **Using this case as an example, explain what is meant by financial restructuring.**
(b) **When is a company likely to use restructuring as a financial strategy?**

Tracing problems If part of the business is suffering it may be possible to trace a specific problem if cost or profit centres are used. For example, if one of the stores in a supermarket chain is suffering from a high labour turnover, its recruitment and training costs will be high. Labour productivity may also be lower. This will restrict the performance of the store and will show up as higher costs if it were operating as a cost centre. This may not come to light so easily if the costs of the entire business were recorded together.

Problems of cost and profit centres

Dividing a business into cost and profit centres might also lead to problems.

Conflict If a business is divided into individual parts, conflict between those parts may arise. Staff are likely to be more interested in the performance of their own centre than the performance of the whole business. This might lead to competition for resources and a reluctance to share valuable information. The performance of the whole business might suffer as a result.

Cost allocation Not all costs are incurred directly by a particular cost centre. Some costs are incurred by the business as a whole. For example, a chain store might spend £2 million on a national advertising campaign. How should this cost be allocated between cost or profit centres? One way might be to divide the cost equally between all the stores. But this might not be fair because a very large store may get more benefit from the campaign than a smaller store. This suggests that the larger store should bear more of the campaign's cost. In practice, the allocation of such costs between centres is difficult. When costs are not allocated fairly the performance of a particular centre can be distorted.

Factors outside the business It is common for the performance of a business to be affected by external factors such as the state of the economy, competition, the weather or pressure groups. However, it is possible that the performance of each individual cost or profit centre is not affected to the same extent. For example, a UK fast-food chain might experience intense competition in the south-west, therefore the performance of centres operating in that region will be hit. This might have a demotivating effect on staff in those centres.

Wasting resources Operating cost or profit centres may result in the business as a whole wasting money. If all centres are responsible for performing the same tasks there may be some duplication of resources. For example, it may be more cost effective if the purchasing of resources for each department in a business is done centrally. Resources may also be wasted gathering financial information from each centre. It is possible that the costs of operating cost or profit centres may not be outweighed by the benefits.

Staff pressure Some of the staff given the responsibility of running a cost or profit centre may not have the skills to do so. This might create pressure and demotivate staff. This is more likely to happen if responsibility is delegated too far down the hierarchical structure.

Cost minimisation

Many financial objectives can be aided by minimising business costs. For example, if costs are reduced, profits will be higher and shareholder value will increase. Many businesses are likely to use cost minimisation as part of their financial strategy. Some examples of approaches that might be used to reduce costs are outlined below.

Outsourcing A business may decide to outsource a particular activity because another business can do the job at a lower cost. For example, a business may use a recruitment agency to recruit staff. Not only will costs be lower but the contractor is likely to do a better job because they are specialists.

Waste reduction and recycling Many firms are looking for ways of reducing waste in their organisations. For example, they may opt for lean production techniques that are designed specifically to reduce all types of waste. An increasing number of businesses are looking to cut costs by recycling their waste. For example, businesses might call on the services of a company like Computacenter. It offers to develop more effective environmental policies for the acquisition, operation, reuse and disposal of IT equipment. Responding to increasing electricity costs and pressures to improve the corporate environmental footprint, their service will introduce significant cost savings while reducing carbon emissions and landfill usage. It is based on a series of practical steps, starting with an energy efficiency audit of a company's current IT usage.

Sourcing new suppliers Businesses often review the performance of their suppliers. Suppliers that have grown expensive may be replaced or contracts with them renegotiated. Increasingly businesses are using eSourcing to reduce the cost of buying raw materials and components. eSourcing involves using the Internet and electronic communications in the whole purchasing process. eSourcing enables buyers and suppliers to connect and contract quickly and efficiently in order to improve the company's competitiveness.

Introducing technology A business may reduce costs by automating certain processes. For example, the introduction of robotic welders in factories has cut costs significantly. New technology is often more efficient and cost effective than labour.

Downsizing Firms may minimise costs by reducing their capacity. This might involve laying off workers or closing down unprofitable divisions in the organisation. This should result in a leaner, more competitive operation made up of profitable businesses with 'no dead horses to flog'.

There are many other ways in which a business might attempt to minimise costs. The approach chosen will depend on the circumstances of the business and what their specific aims are. For example, a business with dated machinery may opt for the introduction of new technology. However, a company with an ailing division may choose to downsize by closing the unprofitable operation.

Allocating capital expenditure

Most businesses will have to undertake capital expenditure to meet financial and other objectives. Capital expenditure is spending on assets that last more than one year. It includes spending on assets such as machinery, equipment, factories or offices. For example, a supermarket chain that wants to increase shareholder value by growing will need to invest in new stores. When allocating capital expenditure a business has to consider a number of issues.

Current needs The pattern of capital expenditure for a business will often centre on the current needs of the business. The amount of money a business has for capital expenditure is often restricted and there may be multiple demands on the limited amount of money available. Consequently a business has to look at the current needs of a business and favour those which are more urgent. For example, if a business needs to urgently upgrade its IT systems it is not likely to allocate money to a speculative product development project. Financial strategies clearly have to address the company's immediate needs.

Return on investment Inevitably, when faced with a choice between alternative investment projects a business will prefer to invest in the project with the greatest return. However, calculating the return on investment projects is notoriously problematic. This is because it is so difficult to estimate future revenues and costs. However, there is a number of different quantitative investment appraisal techniques that can be used to select the most profitable project once future costs and revenues have been estimated. These are outlined in the next unit.

Risk Investment in capital expenditure is fraught with risk. This is because the return on an investment project is not certain. It is possible for an investment project to yield a negative return and even endanger the survival of a business. For example, Leeds United football club went into liquidation twice in 2006 and 2007 after its heavy investment in new players failed to bring success on the football field.

Some businesses are likely to take a lot less risk than others when allocating capital expenditure. This may be because their management team is risk averse. However, others may be prepared to take more risks. This is because the rewards for taking risk can often be very high. For example, launching a new product is often very risky. However, if it is successful the business is likely to enjoy a lengthy stream of profits. The amount of risk involved in a particular financial strategy will depend on the managements' attitude to risk.

External factors The allocation of capital expenditure may be influenced by external factors. One very important one is competition. A business may select a particular investment project because a rival's action has forced its hand. For example, television companies often invest in certain new programmes because rival television companies have launched a new and successful series. Failure to bring out a version of the programme may result in lower viewing figures and lower advertising revenue. The economic climate is also likely to affect capital expenditure. For example, during a recession a business is likely to have a more defensive financial strategy and cut back on all but necessary capital expenditure.

The range of external factors that might affect the allocation of capital expenditure in financial strategies is wide. Other examples include interest rates, exchange rates, social and political factors, changes in consumer tastes, the availability of new technology and the availability of investment funds in capital markets.

Assessing the value of strategies

Managers will select financial strategies that they think will achieve the financial and functional objectives of the business. The financial strategies chosen will depend on the circumstances of the business, the pressure from key stakeholders and the nature of the business. Different companies will have different financial strategies. However, the financial objectives of companies quoted on the stock exchange are not likely to differ very much. Most shareholders want to see an increase in shareholder value (higher dividends and higher share prices). Each company has to decide how they can best deliver this and most opt for growth. Some examples of different financial strategies are outlined below. Many are linked strongly to corporate strategies.

- The financial strategies of many pharmaceutical companies involve heavy investment in research and development. They rely on the revenue from new drugs to generate profits in the future. They protect revenue streams by patenting new drugs and treatments
- For many businesses financial strategies are based on growth through acquisitions. Investment is channelled into the purchase of new businesses which they hope to integrate effectively and push for more economies of scale.
- Some businesses restructure their activities to meet financial objectives. They may decide to focus more on core activities for example. This might involve demerging some non-core activities. Cost minimisation strategies are likely to play an important role here.
- Companies that have limited financial resources may opt for a strategy of organic growth. This might be funded from retained earnings and less so from external sources of funds.

KEYTERMS

Cost centre – an individual part of a business where costs can be identified and recorded easily.
Financial strategies – actions taken by a business to achieve its financial objectives.
Profit centre – an individual part of the business where costs and revenue can be identified and recorded easily.
Undercapitalised – where the owners have not put enough money into a business to support all of its activities.

KNOWLEDGE

1. Why do businesses need a financial strategy?
2. What is the main purpose of a flotation?
3. When might a business need to be financially restructured?
4. Explain how it is possible to use a product as a cost centre.
5. State three other ways of choosing a cost centre.
6. Explain the difference between a cost centre and a profit centre.
7. State three ways a business may reduce costs.
8. How might the current needs of a business affect the allocation of capital expenditure?
9. Why is capital expenditure so risky?
10. Why might businesses have different financial strategies?

Case Study: Ambercom plc

Ambercom plc is a multinational manufacturer of fertilisers and pesticides. It operates five divisions with plants in the following locations.

- **UK** – based in Basingstoke, employs 340 staff and supplies the entire UK market.
- **US** – based in Conneticut, employs 250 staff and supplies the North American and Canadian markets.
- **India** – based in Dehli, employs 450 staff and supplies many Asian countries such as India, Pakistan, Bangladesh, Thailand and increasingly, China.
- **Germany** – based in Dortmund, employs 320 staff and supplies the European market.
- **Australia** – based in Brisbane, employs 130 staff and supplies the Australasian market.

Ambercom plc mission statement

Building value for our shareholders is our goal. We achieve this through sustained, controlled growth – driven by a focus on providing the very best products and solutions for the worlds' food producers. We are committed to the needs of all stakeholders and believe that the development of financial strength will help meet these needs.

Table 1 shows some financial information for Ambercom plc relating to the five profit centres.

Table 1: Ambercom's profit centres 2007

(£ million)

	UK	US	Germany	India	Australia	Total
Revenue	245.9	211.8	265.9	198.7	103.8	1,026.1
Cost of sales	101.1	95.1	112.6	67.4	67.9	444.1
Gross Profit	144.8	115.7	153.3	131.3	35.9	582.0
Admin costs	87.2	54.3	91.1	54.1	32.5	319.2
Distribution costs	34.9	29.8	41.4	21.0	18.9	146.0
Total overheads	122.1	84.1	132.5	75.1	51.4	465.2
Profit before tax	**22.7**	**31.6**	**20.8**	**56.0**	**-15.5**	**115.6**

Ambercom plc operates profit centres. This helps to monitor the performance of each division. In June 2007, the directors organised a board meeting to agree on a medium-term financial strategy for the organisation. The strategy has three elements which are outlined below.

- Close down the Australian operation. Unfortunately there has been a growing resistance to the use of fertilisers and pesticides in Australia. The number of customers in the region has fallen by 40 per cent in the last three years and there is no reason to believe that the decline is about to halt. The remaining customers in the region will be served by the Indian plant.
- Invest £100 million in a new research and development centre. The main purpose of the centre will be to develop more environmentally friendly fertilisers and pesticides.
- Raise £150 million through a rights issue. The money will be used to fund the new research and development centre and help pay for the closure of the Australian division.

(a) What do you think the main financial objective is for Ambercom plc? (4 marks)

(b) Why is Ambercom plc closing down the Australian division when the company is committed to pursuing growth? (6 marks)

(c) Explain two advantages to Ambercom plc of operating profit centres. (8 marks)

(d) (i) What is meant by a rights issue? (4 marks)
(ii) What is the purpose of the rights issue in this case? (4 marks)

(e) To what extent do you think the financial strategy outlined in this case will help to achieve Ambercom's financial objective? (10 marks)

(f) Evaluate the factors that the directors may have considered before committing the company to a £100 million investment in a new research and development centre. (14 marks)

55 Interpreting published accounts - ratio analysis

The investigation process

Financial data is used by a range of stakeholders to assess the performance of a business and help make decisions. Different stakeholders are interested for different reasons. For example, shareholders may want information to assess the rewards for holding shares. Managers may try to gauge performance. This unit explains how the information in the **final accounts** can be interpreted. It is possible to base investigation on some of these figures alone. Also, information can be obtained by combining some of these figures and carrying out a RATIO ANALYSIS. The chairperson's report, the directors' report and the notes to the accounts provide extra material as well.

The investigation process is shown in Figure 1. There is a number of steps involved.

Figure 1: Steps in the investigation process

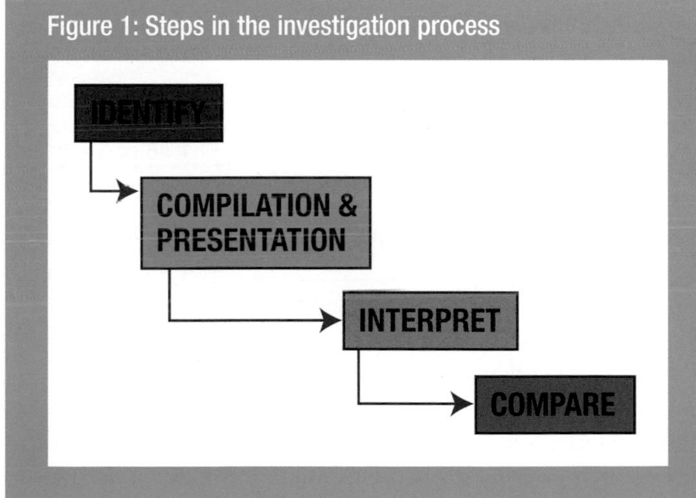

Identification Figures that are relevant must be identified from the final amounts. Suitable data must be used. For example, an accountant might need information on current assets and current liabilities, rather than total assets and total liabilities, in order to assess the solvency of the business.

Presentation Once the correct figures have been chosen they can be compiled and presented into a useful form, such as percentages.

Interpretation To interpret ratios an understanding of their significance is needed. Ratios can be used to find out the firm's financial position, assess performance, analyse capital structure and help shareholders when deciding whether to invest.

Comparison Ratios may be used by businesses to compare figures in the accounts which are related in some way. A ratio be one number expressed as a percentage of another or simply one number divided by another. For an accounting ratio to be useful the two figures must be connected, eg profit is arguably related to the amount of capital a firm uses. These comparisons might include interfirm comparisons, comparisons over time and interfirm comparisons over time. There may be other bodies or institutions which might use ratios. The media produce reports about businesses which they publish. They might use a range of ratios when reporting on particular businesses. In some newspapers the dividend yield and price/earnings ratio are actually published every day for a range of public limited companies. The Inland Revenue might also use ratio analysis when investigating the performance of a business. Some businesses collect business data and sell it to other users. For example, an agency might write a financial report on a business and part of it might consist of comments about particular ratios.

Tables 1-3 show the profit and loss account and balance sheet for Hudsons Ltd, and some additional information from the notes to the accounts. Hudsons Ltd, a large private limited company, sells electrical goods such as TVs, videos, DVD players, music systems and computers from its 130 stores. The figures shown in the accounts will be used in this unit to illustrate how ratios can be calculated and interpreted.

Table 1: Profit and loss account, Hudsons Ltd

Hudsons Ltd Profit and Loss Account
Y/E 31.7.08

	2008 £000	2007 £000
Turnover	70,000	63,000
Cost of sales	55,000	50,000
Gross profit	15,000	13,000
Operating expenses	9,500	9,000
Operating profit	5,500	4,000
Income from investments	100	80
Profit on ordinary activities before tax and interest	5,600	4,080
Net interest paid	1,100	600
Profit on ordinary activities before tax (net profit)	4,500	3,480
Taxation	1,100	680
Profit on ordinary activities after tax	3,400	2,800
Dividends	900	700
Retained profit	2,500	2,100

Table 2: Additional information, Hudsons Ltd

	2008	2007
Number of ordinary shares	40,000,000	40,000,000
Share price 31st July	135p	94p

Table 3: Balance sheet, Hudsons Ltd

Hudsons Ltd Balance Sheet
As At 31.7.08

	2008 £000	2007 £000
Fixed assets		
Tangible assets	21,000	19,800
Investments	500	400
	21,500	20,200
Current assets		
Stocks	8,500	7,100
Debtors	500	400
Cash at bank and in hand	3,000	2,100
	12,000	9,600
Creditors:		
amounts falling due within one year *(current liabilities)*	8,100	7,000
Net current assets *(working capital)*	3,900	2,600
Total assets less current liabilities	25,400	22,800
Creditors:		
amounts falling due after one year *(long term liabilities)*	(8,000)	(6,500)
Net assets	17,400	16,300
Capital and reserves		
Called up share capital	2,000	2,000
Other reserves	1,400	2,800
Profit and loss account	14,000	11,500
Shareholders' funds	17,400	16,300

Liquidity ratios

LIQUIDITY RATIOS illustrate the solvency of a business - whether it is in a position to repay its debts. They focus on short-term assets and liabilities. Creditors are likely to be interested in liquidity ratios to assess whether they will receive money that they are owed. Money lenders and suppliers, for example, will be interested in how easily a business can repay its debts. Potential investors might also have an interest in liquidity ratios for the same reason. In addition, managers might use them to aid financial control, ie to ensure that they have enough liquid resources to meet debts.

A business must make sure that it has enough liquid assets to pay any immediate bills that arise. Liquid assets include cash and assets that can be quickly switched into cash such as stocks, debtors and short-term investments. Two widely used ratios to monitor liquid assets are the current ratio and the acid test ratio.

Current ratio The CURRENT RATIO focuses on current assets and current liabilities. It is also known as the working capital ratio and is calculated using the formula:

$$\text{Current ratio} = \frac{\text{Current assets}}{\text{Current liabilities}}$$

For Hudsons, current assets were £12,000,000 in 2008 and current liabilities were £8,100,000. Both of these figures are shown in the balance sheet.

$$\text{For 2008 Current ratio} = \frac{£12,000,000}{£8,100,000} = 1.48 \text{ or } 1.48:1$$

$$\text{For 2007 Current ratio} = \frac{£9,600,000}{£7,000,000} = 1.37 \text{ or } 1.37:1$$

It is suggested that a business will have sufficient liquid resources if the current ratio is between 1.5:1 and 2:1. If the ratio is below 1.5 it might be argued that a business does not have enough working capital. This might mean that a business is overborrowing or overtrading. Operating above a ratio of 2:1 may suggest that too much money is tied up unproductively. Money tied up in stocks does not earn any return.

The current ratio for Hudsons has hardly changed over the two years, rising slightly from 1.37:1 to 1.48:1. As with other ratios, judgement on what is satisfactory depends to a large extent on comparisons within the industry. For example, retailers often have very low current ratios, perhaps 1:1 or below. This is because they hold fast-selling stocks and generate cash from sales. Since Hudsons is a retailer, it might be well satisfied with a current ratio of 1.48:1 in 2008.

Hudsons may be able to improve its current ratio by increasing its current assets relative to current liabilities, or reducing its current liabilities relative to its current assets. For example, current assets might be improved by better stock or credit control. Current liabilities might be reduced by reducing short-term creditors.

Acid test ratio The ACID TEST RATIO or QUICK RATIO is a more severe test of liquidity. This is because stocks are not treated as liquid resources. Stocks are not guaranteed to be sold and they may become obsolete or deteriorate. They are therefore excluded from current assets when calculating the ratio.

$$\text{Acid test ratio} = \frac{\text{Current assets – stocks}}{\text{Current liabilities}}$$

The information required to calculate the acid test ratio are found in Hudsons' balance sheet.

For 2008
$$\text{Acid test ratio} = \frac{£12,000,000 - £8,500,000}{£8,100,000} = 0.43 \text{ or } 0.43{:}\ 1$$

For 2007
$$\text{Acid test ratio} = \frac{£9,600,000 – £7,100,000}{£7,000,000} = 0.36 \text{ or } 0.36{:}\ 1$$

If a business has an acid test ratio of less than 1:1 it means that its current assets less stocks do not cover its current liabilities. This could indicate a potential problem. However, as with the current ratio, there is considerable variation between the typical acid test ratios of businesses in different industries. Again, retailers with their strong cash flows, may operate comfortably with acid test ratios of less than 1. Since Hudsons is a retailer and its stock is likely to be sold quite quickly, an acid test ratio of 0.43:1 may be acceptable to the business. The methods of improving the current ratio can all be used here, although changing stock levels are not an option as stocks are excluded from the calculation.

Question 1.

HR Owen operates a number of vehicle franchises in the prestige and specialist car market for both sales and aftersales, predominantly in the London area. For example, it sells Bentleys, Rolls Royce's, Maseratis, Ferraris and Lamborghinis. Bpi (British Polythene Industries) manufacture over 300,000 tonnes of polythene products in a year for a variety of applications. Table 4 shows current assets and current liabilities for the two companies.

Table 4: Current assets and current liabilities for HR Owen and Bpi

	HR Owen		Bpi	
	2008	2007	2008	2007
	£000	£000	£000	£000
Stocks	42,481	81,559	59,500	55,300
Other current assets	20,074	49,615	60,500	64,100
Total current assets	62,555	131,174	120,000	119,400
Current liabilities	53,757	136,531	68,300	75,500

Source: adapted from HR Owen and Bpi, *Annual Report and Accounts*.

(a) Calculate the: (i) current ratios; (ii) acid test ratios for both companies in 2008 and 2007.

(b) (i) Which is the more liquid of the two companies?
(ii) Suggest and explain one reason for your answer in (i).

Profitability ratios

PROFITABILITY or PERFORMANCE RATIOS help to show how well a business is doing. They tend to focus on profit, capital employed and turnover. Stakeholders such as owners, managers, employees and potential investors are all likely to be interested in the profitability and performance of a business. Competitors might also use these ratios to make comparisons of performance. The profit figure alone is not a useful performance indicator. It is necessary to look at the value of profit in relation to the value of turnover or the amount of money that has been invested in the business.

Return on capital employed (ROCE) One of the most important ratios which is used to measure the profitability of a business is the RETURN ON CAPITAL EMPLOYED (ROCE).

Table 5: Calculating ROCE using other measures of capital

ROCE (Total capital employed) Total capital may be used to calculate the ROCE. Total capital employed can be found by:

- adding together the fixed assets and the current assets. For Hudsons in 2008, fixed assets were £21,500,000 and current assets were £12,000,000, so total capital employed was £33,500,000;
- adding capital and reserves (£17,400,000), long-term liabilities (£8,000,000) and current liabilities (£8,100,000) together to give £33,500,000.

For Hudsons, the profit before tax and interest in 2008 was £5,600,000. The ROCE for 2008 can be calculated as:

$$\text{ROCE} = \frac{\text{Profit before tax and interest}}{\text{Total capital employed}} \times 100 = \frac{£5,600,000}{£33,500,000} \times 100 = 16.7\%$$

This measure of ROCE gives a lower percentage than ROCE using long term capital because the figure for capital is higher.

ROCE (Shareholders' capital or net assets) This looks at the return on the shareholders' capital, which is total share capital plus reserves. However, it is conventional to use the term net assets rather than shareholders' capital. Hudsons' balance sheet shows that shareholders' capital is £17,400,000 in 2008. This is the same as net assets. The RETURN ON NET ASSETS for Hudsons in 2008 can be calculated using the formula:

$$\text{Return on net assets} = \frac{\text{Profit before tax and interest}}{\text{Net assets}} \times 100 = \frac{£5,600,000}{£17,400,000} \times 100 = 32.2\%$$

The return on net assets gives a higher percentage than other measures of ROCE because the figure for capital is lower.

This is sometimes referred to as the primary ratio. It compares the profit, ie return, made by the business with the amount of money invested, ie its capital. The advantage of this ratio is that it relates profit to the size of the business. When calculating ROCE, it is standard practice to define profit as net profit (or operating profit) before tax and interest. This is sometimes described as earnings before interest and tax (EBIT). Tax is ignored because it is determined by the government and is therefore outside the control of the company. Interest is excluded because it does not relate to the business's ordinary trading activities. ROCE can be calculated using the formula:

$$\text{ROCE} = \frac{\text{Profit before tax and interest}}{\text{Long-term capital employed}} \times 100$$

For Hudsons the profit before tax and interest in 2008 was £5,600,000. Long-term capital employed was £25,400,000. Long-term capital employed is shareholders' funds plus any long-term loans, i.e. £17,400,000 + £8,000,000.

$$\text{For 2008 ROCE} = \frac{£5{,}600{,}000}{£25{,}400{,}000} \times 100 = 22.0\%$$

$$\text{For 2007 ROCE} = \frac{£4{,}080{,}000}{£22{,}800{,}000} \times 100 = 17.9\%$$

The return on capital employed will vary between industries, however, the higher the ratio, the better. Over the two years Hudsons has seen its ROCE increase from 17.9 per cent to 22.0 per cent. To decide whether Hudsons has performed well, this would have to be compared with another business in the same industry. An investor might also compare the ROCE with the possible return if the capital was invested elsewhere. For example, if £25,400,000 was placed in a bank account in 2008 it might have earned a 5 per cent return. So the 22 per cent ROCE in 2008 seems impressive. However, an investor in the company will also want to be rewarded for the risk involved. The £25,400,000 invested by shareholders in Hudsons is at risk if the business fails. So, for the investment to be worthwhile, the ROCE must be far greater than the return that could be earned in a 'safe' investment. Increasing profit with the existing capital employed will improve the ROCE ratio for a business. It is possible to calculate ROCE using other measures of capital, as shown in Table 5.

Gross profit margin The gross profit margin is also known as the mark-up. This shows the gross profit made on sales turnover. It is calculated using the formula:

$$\text{Gross profit margin} = \frac{\text{Gross profit}}{\text{Turnover}} \times 100$$

For Hudsons in 2008 gross profit was £15,000,000 and turnover was £70,000,000.

$$\text{For 2008 Gross profit margin} = \frac{£15{,}000{,}000}{£70{,}000{,}000} \times 100 = 21.4\%$$

$$\text{For 2007 Gross profit margin} = \frac{£13{,}000{,}000}{£63{,}000{,}000} \times 100 = 20.6\%$$

Higher gross margins are usually preferable to lower ones. It may be possible to increase the gross profit margin by raising turnover relative to cost of sales, for example by increasing price. Or cost of sales could be reduced relative to turnover. However, the gross profit margin required will tend to be different for different industries. As a rule, the quicker the turnover of stock, the lower the gross margin that is needed. So, for example, a supermarket with a fast stock turnover is likely to have a lower gross margin than a car retailer with a much slower stock turnover. Some supermarkets are therefore very successful with relatively low gross profit margins because of the regular and fast turnover of stock. The gross margin for Hudsons has improved slightly over the two years. Interfirm comparisons would help to confirm whether this was a satisfactory performance.

Net profit margin The net profit margin helps to measure how well a business controls its overheads and cost of sales. If the difference between the gross margin and the net margin is small, this suggests that overheads are low. This is because net profit equals gross profit less overheads. The net profit margin can be calculated by:

$$\text{Net profit margin} = \frac{\text{Net profit before tax and interest}}{\text{Turnover}} \times 100$$

For Hudsons in 2008 net profit before tax and interest was £5,600,000 and turnover was £70,000,000.

$$\text{For 2007 Net profit margin} = \frac{£5{,}600{,}000}{£70{,}000{,}000} \times 100 = 8.0\%$$

$$\text{For 2007 Net profit margin} = \frac{£4{,}080{,}000}{£63{,}000{,}000} \times 100 = 6.5\%$$

Again, higher margins are usually better than lower ones. The net profit margin for Hudsons has improved over the two years. This suggests that the business was able to restrict overhead spending as a proportion of turnover more effectively in 2008 than in 2007.

Financial efficiency ratios

FINANCIAL EFFICIENCY, ACTIVITY or ASSET UTILISATION RATIOS are used to measure how effectively a business employs its resources. Such ratios are likely to be used internally by managers. This is because they focus on how well a business uses its resources. For example, the performance of the credit control department could be assessed by looking at how quickly debts are collected.

Asset turnover The ASSET TURNOVER ratio measures the productivity of assets. It looks at how much turnover is generated by the assets employed in the business. The formula is:

$$\text{Asset turnover} = \frac{\text{Turnover}}{\text{Net assets}}$$

The turnover for Hudsons in 2007 was £70,000,000 and the net assets were £17,400,000.

$$\text{For 2008 Asset turnover} = \frac{£70{,}000{,}000}{£17{,}400{,}000} = 4.02$$

$$\text{For 2007 Asset turnover} = \frac{£63{,}000{,}000}{£16{,}300{,}000} = 3.87$$

The ratio shows that, in 2008, for every £1 invested in net assets by Hudsons, £4.02 of turnover was generated. Over the two years the asset turnover improved by a few pence. The asset turnover varies in different industries. In retailing, where turnover is high and the value of fixed assets is relatively low, like Hudsons, the asset turnover can be 3 or more. In contrast, in manufacturing, where there is often heavier investment in fixed assets, the ratio is generally lower. For example, it can be 1 or less. Increasing turnover using the same assets, so that assets work more effectively, is a method of improving the ratio.

Stock turnover The STOCK TURNOVER ratio measures how quickly a business uses or sells its stock. It is generally considered desirable to sell, or 'shift', stock as quickly as possible. One approach to stock turnover is to calculate how many times during the year a business sells its stock. The formula is:

$$\text{Stock turnover} = \frac{\text{Cost of sales}}{\text{Stocks}}$$

The cost of sales for Hudsons in 2008 was £55,000,000. The value of closing stocks as shown in the balance sheet was £8,500,000.

$$\text{For 2008 Stock turnover} = \frac{£55{,}000{,}000}{£8{,}500{,}000} = 6.5 \text{ times}$$

$$\text{For 2007 Stock turnover} = \frac{£50{,}000{,}000}{£7{,}100{,}000} = 7.0 \text{ times}$$

Another approach to stock turnover is to calculate the number of days it takes to sell the stock. This is found by:

$$\text{Stock turnover} = \frac{\text{Stocks}}{\text{Cost of sales}} \times 365$$

$$\text{For 2008 Stock turnover} = \frac{£8{,}500{,}000}{£55{,}000{,}000} \times 365 = 56 \text{ days}$$

$$\text{For 2007 Stock turnover} = \frac{£7{,}100{,}000}{£50{,}000{,}000} \times 365 = 52 \text{ days}$$

High stock turnovers are preferred (or lower figures in days). A higher stock turnover means that profit on the sale of stock is earned more quickly. Thus, businesses with high stock turnovers can operate on lower profit margins. A declining stock turnover ratio might indicate:

- higher stock levels;
- a large amount of slow moving or obsolete stock ;
- a wider range of products being stocked;
- a lack of control over purchasing.

So improvements to purchasing methods or better control of stock levels, for example, should improve the stock turnover ratio of a business.

Stock turnover differs considerably between different industries. Supermarkets often have a relatively quick stock turnover of around 14 to 28 days. This means that they sell the value of their average stock every two to four weeks. Manufacturers generally have much slower stock turnover because of the time spent processing raw materials. However, in recent years, many manufacturers have adopted just-in-time production techniques. This involves ordering stocks only when they are required in the production process and, therefore, stock levels tend to be lower. As a result stock turnover is faster. Businesses which supply services, such as banks, travel agents and transport operators, are not likely to hold very much stock. Therefore this ratio is not likely to be used by service industry analysts.

Over the two years, Hudsons' stock turnover has worsened very slightly. However, to determine whether a stock turnover of 56 days is good, comparisons with other electrical goods retailers would have to be made.

Creditor days (creditors' payment period) This ratio measures how quickly a business pays its debts to its suppliers and other short-term creditors. The CREDITOR DAYS or CREDITOR PAYMENT PERIOD is the average number of days it takes to pay debts. It can be calculated using the formula below.

$$\text{Creditor days} = \frac{\text{Creditors}}{\text{Cost of sales}} \times 365$$

Question 2.

Grantham Paints is an established producer of paint and other coverings. An important aspect of its manufacturing strategy is to use modern materials and technology that minimise environmental impact. It favours waterborne finishes that are low in volatile organic compounds. In 2006 the company began to experience cash-flow problems. In order to resolve the problem it devoted more resources to debt collection and renegotiated the terms of payment with some key suppliers. Table 6 shows some financial information for Grantham Paints plc.

Table 6: Financial information for Grantham Paints plc

	2008 £000	2007 £000
Revenue	102,876	98,433
Cost of sales	58,981	56,670
Value of stock	3,889	3,467
Debtors	11,870	15,600
Creditors	14,300	11,800

(a) Calculate for 2008 and 2007 the (i) debt collection period; (ii) creditor days period.

(b) To what extent do you think Grantham's measure to improve cash flow may have worked?

(c) (i) Calculate the stock turnover for Grantham Paints and comment on the change over the two years.
(ii) How might the company raise stock turnover to help improve cash flow?

According to the accounts for Hudsons Ltd, the amount owed to short-term creditors in 2008 was £8,100,000. The cost of sales for 2007 was £55,000,000.

$$\text{For 2008 Creditor days} = \frac{£8{,}100{,}000}{£55{,}000{,}000} \times 356 = 54 \text{ days}$$

$$\text{For 2007 Creditor days} = \frac{£7{,}000{,}000}{£50{,}000{,}000} \times 365 = 51 \text{ days}$$

For Hudsons, the creditors' payment period has increased slightly from 51 to 54 days. This is to their advantage because they have been able to delay paying bills for slightly longer. However, Hudsons would have to be careful not to damage relations with suppliers by delaying the payment of bills for too long.

Ideally, businesses would want to operate in a situation where the creditors payment period is higher than the debt collection period. This would improve cash flow because it would be receiving cash from customers before having to pay it to suppliers. In this case Hudsons is in a very favourable position. Its creditors' payment period is far higher than its debt collection period in both years. To improve the ratio, the creditors' payment period can be increased by negotiating a longer trade credit period with suppliers.

Debtor days (debt collection period) This ratio measures the efficiency of a business's credit control system. The DEBTOR DAYS or DEBT COLLECTION PERIOD is the average number of days it takes to collect debts from customers. It can be calculated using the formula:

$$\text{Debt collection period} = \frac{\text{Debtors}}{\text{Turnover}} \times 365$$

According to the balance sheet the value of debtors for Hudsons in 2008 was £500,000. Turnover was £70,000,000.

$$\text{For 2008 Debt collection period} = \frac{£500{,}000}{£70{,}000{,}000} \times 365 = 2.6 \text{ days}$$

$$\text{For 2007 Debt collection period} = \frac{£400{,}000}{£63{,}000{,}000} \times 365 = 2.3 \text{ days}$$

Businesses often vary the amount of time they give customers to pay for products they have bought on credit. They keep a list of **aged debtors**, showing how much is owed and over what period. Credit periods may be 30, 60, 90 or even 120 days. Businesses prefer a short debt collection period because their cash flow will be improved. Retailers will have a very low debt collection period, perhaps just a few days. This is because most of their sales are for cash. This appears to be the case for Hudsons. Although the debt collection period has risen from 2.3 days to 2.6 days over the two years, there is unlikely to be a problem. Hudsons' sales will be for cash and the debtors value on the balance sheet is likely to be for prepayments not customer debts. Improving turnover relative to debtors will improve the ratio. However, businesses often try to improve this ratio by reducing debtors relative to turnover using credit control.

Gearing ratios

GEARING RATIOS show the long-term financial position of the business. They can be used to show the relationship between loans, on which interest is paid, and shareholders' funds, on which dividends might be paid. Creditors are likely to be concerned about a firm's gearing. Loans, for example, have interest charges which must be paid. Dividends do not have to be paid to ordinary shareholders. As a business becomes more highly geared (loans are high relative to share capital) it is considered more risky by creditors. The owners of a business might prefer to raise extra funds by borrowing rather than from shareholders, so they retain control of the business. Gearing ratios can also show the relationship between fixed interest bearing debt and the long-term capital of a business.

Gearing ratios can be used to analyse the capital structure of a business. They compare the amount of capital raised from ordinary shareholders with that raised in loans and, in some cases, from preference shareholders and debentures. This is important because the interest on loans and dividends for preference shareholders are fixed commitments, whereas the dividends for ordinary shareholders are not. Gearing ratios can assess whether or not a business is burdened by its loans. This is because highly geared companies must still pay their interest even when trading becomes difficult.

Gearing ratios There are several different versions of the gearing ratio. One widely used relates the total long-term loans and other fixed cost capital to long-term capital employed. The formula is:

$$\text{Gearing ratio} = \frac{\text{Fixed cost capital}}{\text{Long-term capital}} \times 100$$

Fixed cost capital includes long-term loans from banks, certain preference shares and debentures. Long-term capital includes shareholders' funds, any reserves and long-term loans. For Hudsons in 2007 the fixed cost or interest/dividend bearing debt, according to the balance sheet, is loans of £8,000,000 (creditors: amounts falling due after one year). The value of shareholders' funds, including reserves, was £17,400,000.

$$\text{For 2008 Gearing ratio} = \frac{£8{,}000{,}000}{£17{,}400{,}000 + £8{,}000{,}000} \times 100 = 31.5\%$$

$$\text{For 2007 Gearing ratio} = \frac{£6{,}500{,}000}{£16{,}300{,}000 + £6{,}500{,}000} \times 100 = 28.5\%$$

If the gearing ratio is less than 50 per cent the company is said to be low geared. This means that the majority of the capital is provided by the owners. If the ratio is greater than 50 per cent the company is high geared. This means that a much higher proportion of total capital is borrowed. With a gearing ratio of around 30 per cent in both years, Hudsons is low geared. Although gearing rose slightly over the two years, the increase is not significant.

Another version of the gearing ratio looks at the relationship between borrowing and equity. In this context borrowing is defined as long-term loans. For Hudsons in 2007 it was the creditors: amounts falling due after one year of £8,000,000. Equity is defined as ordinary share capital plus reserves which for Hudsons in 2008 was £17,400,000. The ratio is calculated using the formula:

$$\text{Gearing ratio} = \frac{\text{Borrowing}}{\text{Equity}} \times 100$$

$$\text{For 2008 Gearing ratio} = \frac{£8{,}000{,}000}{£17{,}400{,}000} \times 100 = 46.0\%$$

When this definition of gearing is used, a ratio that is greater than 100 per cent means that debt is greater than equity. In most industries, this would be regarded as high geared and could prove to be an unacceptable risk for potential lenders. This is because, if there was a downturn in trading, a company might struggle to meet interest payments. However, this is not the case for Hudsons since the ratio is below 100 per cent. A business can improve its gearing ratio by reducing its long-term borrowing relative to its capital.

Interest cover The gearing ratio is a balance sheet measure of financial risk. INTEREST COVER is a profit and loss account measure. The ratio assesses the burden of interest payments by comparing profit and interest payments. It is calculated using the formula:

$$\text{Interest cover} = \frac{\text{Profit before interest and tax}}{\text{Interest}}$$

The profit before tax and interest for Hudsons in 2008 was £5,600,000 as shown in the profit and loss account. The amount of interest paid during the year was £1,100,000.

$$\text{For 2008 Interest cover} = \frac{£5{,}600{,}000}{£1{,}100{,}000} = 5.1 \text{ times}$$

$$\text{For 2007 Interest cover} = \frac{£4{,}080{,}000}{£600{,}000} = 6.8 \text{ times}$$

If interest cover is 1, this means that all of the firm's profit would be used to pay interest. This is obviously not sustainable in the long term. In the case of Hudsons, the cover has fallen over the two years. However, for a low geared company like Hudsons, this is still likely to be satisfactory. A figure of between 1 and 2 is likely to cause problems for a business, suggesting that it is becoming difficult for a company to meet its debt payments.

Shareholders' ratios

The owners of limited companies will take an interest in ratios which help measure the return on their shareholding. Such ratios focus on factors such as the earnings and dividends from shares in relation to their price. Potential investors will also show an interest in shareholders' ratios.

SHAREHOLDERS' RATIOS provide information to help investors to make decisions about buying or selling shares. They are often used to analyse the performance of public limited companies. However, they can also be helpful to the owners of private limited companies.

Dividend per share The DIVIDEND PER SHARE is the ratio that shows how much money ordinary shareholders receive per share.

$$\text{Dividend per share} = \frac{\text{Dividend (ordinary shares)}}{\text{Number of shares}}$$

Question 3.

Najia Khan works for a merchant bank. In 2008 she received a £50,000 performance-related bonus. She already has a large share portfolio and decided to invest the bonus in a mining company. The prices of natural resources such as oil, minerals and metals had been climbing rapidly in recent years but she felt there was further to go. Najia identified three companies which she felt might be suitable for investment. Some financial information for the three companies is shown in Table 7.

Table 7: Financial information for three mining companies

	Alum Resources	GTR plc	Aztec Mining
Dividends paid	£27.6m	£12.8m	£143.2m
Number of shares	400m	30m	600m
Share price	300p	1334p	1327p

(a) Calculate the: (i) dividend per share; (ii) dividend yield; for the three mining companies.
(b) Which company should Najia invest in? Explain your answer.
(c) Do you think there is sufficient information in the case upon which to make such a decision? Explain your answer.

For Hudsons the dividend paid to shareholders in 2008 was £900,000. This is shown in the profit and loss account. The number of shares issued by Hudsons in 2008 is shown as additional information and was 40,000,000.

$$\text{For 2008 Dividend per share} = \frac{£900{,}000}{40{,}000{,}000} = 2.25\text{p per share}$$

$$\text{For 2007 Dividend per share} = \frac{£700{,}000}{40{,}000{,}000} = 1.75\text{p per share}$$

The dividend per share paid to Hudsons' shareholders increased from 1.75p to 2.25p over the two years. This is quite a significant improvement. However, to determine whether or not this is satisfactory the dividend per share must be compared with the share price. This involves calculating the dividend yield.

Dividend yield The DIVIDEND YIELD is the dividend per share expressed as a percentage of the current share price.

$$\text{Dividend yield} = \frac{\text{Dividend per share}}{\text{Share price}} \times 100$$

For Hudsons the share price is shown in Table 2. On 31.7.07 it was 135p. The dividend per share was calculated above and was 2.25p in 2008.

$$\text{For 2008 Dividend yield} = \frac{2.25\text{p}}{135\text{p}} \times 100 = 1.7\%$$

$$\text{For 2007 Dividend yield} = \frac{1.75\text{p}}{94\text{p}} \times 100 = 1.9\%$$

Over the two years the dividend yield has fallen for Hudsons, even though the dividend per share rose significantly. The reason for this is that the share price also rose sharply. Whether a dividend yield of 1.7 per cent is adequate depends on expectations and what might be earned in other companies and other forms of investment. However, it must be remembered that dividends are not the only return on shares. Investors may make a capital gain if the shares are sold for a higher price than they were bought.

Earnings per share The EARNINGS PER SHARE (EPS) is a measure of how much profit each ordinary share earns after tax. It does not, however, show how much money is actually paid to ordinary shareholders. This is because companies usually retain some profit in reserve. The EPS is generally shown at the bottom of the profit and loss account or income statement. EPS can be calculated by:

$$\text{Earnings per share} = \frac{\text{Profit after tax}}{\text{Number of ordinary shares}}$$

For Hudsons in 2008 the net profit after tax was £3,400,000 as shown in the profit and loss account. Note that if the company had any preference shareholders, any dividends paid to them would have to be subtracted from profit. According to the additional information shown in Table 2, the number of ordinary shares issued in 2008 was 40,000,000.

$$\text{For 2008 Earnings per share} = \frac{£3{,}400{,}000}{40{,}000{,}000} = 8.5\text{p}$$

$$\text{For 2007 Earnings per share} = \frac{£2{,}800{,}000}{40{,}000{,}000} = 7.0\text{p}$$

Over the two years the EPS for Hudsons has improved. However, on its own, this does not necessarily indicate a satisfactory performance. Only when the EPS is compared with the company's share price and with the EPS of comparable companies is it possible to make a judgment. Improvements in profits relative to the number of shares will improve this ratio.

Price/earnings ratio The PRICE/EARNINGS (P/E) RATIO is one of the main indicators used by investors when deciding whether to buy or sell particular shares. The P/E ratio relates the current share price to the EPS. It is calculated using the formula below. The ratio is often expressed as the number of times by which the share price can be divided by the EPS.

$$\text{Price/earnings ratio} = \frac{\text{Share price}}{\text{EPS}}$$

In the case of plcs which are listed on the stock market, their share prices are published daily in The *Financial Times*, other newspapers and on the Internet. However, the share prices for Hudsons on 31st July are shown as additional information in Table.2. In 2008 the share price was 135p. The EPS was 8.5p as calculated above.

$$\text{For 2008 Price/earnings ratio} = \frac{135\text{p}}{8.5\text{p}} = 15.9 \text{ times}$$

$$\text{For 2007 Price/earnings ratio} = \frac{94\text{p}}{7.0\text{p}} = 13.4 \text{ times}$$

The P/E ratio of 15.9 means that the market price of the share is 15.9 times higher than its current level of earnings. Assuming that nothing changes, it would take 15.9 years for these shares to earn their current market value. The P/E ratio for Hudsons rose over the two years from 13.4 to 15.9, indicating increased confidence in the future profitability of the company. As a result, the shares rose from 94p to 135p. A P/E ratio of around 15 is generally a good sign.

Price/earnings ratios provide a useful guide to market confidence and can be helpful when comparing companies. However, a general rise or fall in share prices will affect P/E ratios, so care must be taken when interpreting changes.

Return on equity The RETURN ON EQUITY looks at the return on the money contributed by, and belonging to, the ordinary shareholders. It defines equity as the ordinary shareholders' capital plus reserves. Profit after tax is used in this calculation. Note also that any payments to preference shareholders should also be subtracted from this profit. The formula to calculate return on equity is:

$$\text{Return on equity} = \frac{\text{Profit after tax}}{\text{Equity}} \times 100$$

For Hudsons the net profit after tax in 2008 was £3,400,000. The value of ordinary share capital and reserves or shareholders' equity was £17,400,000.

$$\text{For 2008 Return on equity} = \frac{£3{,}400{,}000}{£17{,}400{,}000} \times 100 = 19.5\%$$

$$\text{For 2007 Return on equity} = \frac{£2{,}800{,}000}{£16{,}300{,}000} \times 100 = 17.2\%$$

Hudsons' return on equity has improved slightly over the two years from 17.2 per cent to 19.5 per cent. As with all ratio analysis, judgement on whether this was satisfactory depends to a large extent on comparisons with similar companies in the same industry.

Dividend cover The DIVIDEND COVER measures how many times a company's dividends to ordinary shareholders could be paid from net profit.

$$\text{Dividend cover} = \frac{\text{Profit after tax}}{\text{Dividends (ordinary shares)}}$$

For Hudsons the net profit after tax in 2008 was £3,400,000. The dividend paid to ordinary shareholders is shown in the profit and loss account and was £900,000 in 2008.

$$\text{For 2008 Dividend cover} = \frac{£3{,}400{,}000}{£900{,}000} = 3.8 \text{ times}$$

$$\text{For 2007 Dividend cover} = \frac{£2{,}800{,}000}{£700{,}000} = 4.0 \text{ times}$$

For Hudsons the dividend cover has fallen slightly over the two years. A cover of 3.8 means that dividends could have been paid 3.8 times over in 2008. If the cover is too high, shareholders might complain that too much profit is being retained and that dividends should be higher. If it is too low, it suggests that profits are low or that the business is not retaining enough profit for new investment.

It is possible for a business to pay dividends even when there is not sufficient profit in the current year to cover the payment. A company may do this to maintain shareholder loyalty. The money to cover the payment would have to come from reserves.

Question 4.

Rockhampton Quarries plc operates a number of limestone quarries in the UK. The company supplies cement manufacturers and large construction companies. Table 8 shows some financial information for the company.

Table 8: Financial Information for Rockhampton Quarries plc

	2004	2005	2006	2007	2008
Profit (after tax)	£12.5m	£13.9m	£12.8m	£12.1m	£10.4m
Share price	1229p	1100p	980p	880p	709p
Number of shares	20m	20m	21m	21m	23m
Equity	£114.2m	£116.3m	£107.1m	£107.4m	£109m

(a) Calculate the (i) EPS; (ii) P/E ratio; (iii) return on equity for Rockhampton Quarries.

(b) Discuss whether the shareholders would be happy with the performance of their shares.

KEYTERMS

Acid test ratio – similar to the current ratio but excludes stocks from current assets. Sometimes called the quick ratio.

Asset turnover – a measure of the productivity of assets.

Creditor days or credit payment period – the average number of days it takes to pay short-term debts.

Current ratio – assesses the firm's liquidity by dividing current liabilities into current assets.

Debtor days or debt collection period – the number of days it takes to collect the average debt.

Dividend cover – how many times the dividend could have been paid from the year's earnings.

Dividend per share – the amount of money a shareholder will actually receive for each share owned.

Dividend yield – the amount received by the shareholder as a percentage of the share price.

Earnings per share – the amount each ordinary share earns.

Interest cover – assesses a firm's ability to meet interest payments by comparing profit and interest payable .

Financial efficiency, activity or asset utilisation ratios – measure how effectively a business employs its resources.

Gearing ratios – explore the capital structure of a business by comparing the proportions of capital raised by debt and equity.

Liquidity ratios – illustrate the solvency of a business.

Price/earnings ratio – relates the earnings per share to its market price and reflects the return from buying shares.

Profitability or performance ratios – illustrate the relative profitability of a business.

Ratio analysis – a numerical approach to investigating accounts by comparing two related figures.

Return on capital employed – the profit of a business as a percentage of the total amount of money used to generate it.

Return on equity – measures the return on shareholders' investment by expressing the profit earned by ordinary shareholders as a percentage of total equity.

Return on net assets – expresses profit as a percentage of long term assets only.

Shareholders' ratios – provide information to help investors to make decisions about buying or selling shares.

Stock turnover – the number of times in a trading year a firm sells the value of its stocks.

KNOWLEDGE

1. Briefly describe the steps involved in the investigation process when analysing a set of accounts.
2. What is the difference between profitability and financial efficiency ratios?
3. What is the difference between liquidity ratios and gearing ratios?
4. A business has a current ratio of 6.8:1. Comment on this.
5. How do gross and net profit margins differ?
6. What do stock turnover and debt collection period measure?
7. Explain why it is preferable for a business to have a high creditor days ratio.
8. Describe the difference between the current ratio and the acid test ratio.
9. What is meant by a high geared company?
10. How is the dividend yield calculated?
11. What happens to the price/earnings ratio if the share price rises sharply?

Case Study: easyJet

easyJet is a popular low cost airline. It is based in London Luton Airport and provides cheap 'no-frills' flights to a wide range of European destinations. Since the company was launched by Sir Stelios Haji-Ioannou in 1995 it has grown from strength to strength. Some of the key business highlights for 2006 were as follows:

- Record profit before tax of £129 million, up 56 per cent from £83 million in 2005.
- Passenger numbers rose by 11.5 per cent to 33 million.
- Passenger revenues increased by 5.9 per cent or £2.13 per seat, driven by strong summer trading.
- Ancillary revenues improved significantly in all areas, rising by 34 per cent or £0.86 per seat.
- Unit costs excluding fuel fell by 1.5 per cent or £0.42 per seat from £28.78 to £28.36.
- Unit fuel costs increased by 33 per cent or £2.48 per seat.
- 58 new routes and 11 new destinations were launched, expanding the network to 262 routes and 74 airports in 21 countries.
- The fleet grew to 122 aircraft with an average age of 2.2 years, making it one of the most modern and environmentally friendly fleets in Europe.
- The balance sheet remains strong with cash of £861 million and gearing at 31 per cent.

Table 9 shows some financial information for easyJet extracted from the income statement and balance sheet in 2006.

Table 9: Financial information for easyJet – 2006

	2006 £m	2005 £m
Revenue	1,619.70	1,341.40
Profit (EBIT)	117.8	66.2
Capital employed*	1,614.60	1,215.30
Net assets	982.9	863.4
Current assets	1,087.20	890.9
Current liabilities	509	414.5

* Long-term capital employed (equity + non-current liabilities)
Source: adapted from easyJet, *Annual Report and Accounts*, 2006.

(a) Explain how ratio analysis can be used to interpret accounts. (4 marks)

(b) According to the key business highlights, gearing for easyJet was 31 per cent in 2006. Explain what this means. (6 marks)

(c) For 2005 and 2006, calculate: (i) net profit margin; (ii) ROCE; (iii) current ratio; (iv) asset turnover; for easyJet. (16 marks)

(d) To what extent do the results in (c) support the view that easyJet has 'grown from strength to strength'? (14 marks)

56 The value and limitations of ratio analysis

The value of ratio analysis

Ratio analysis is used by people such as business owners, managers, financial analysts and the media to help evaluate the performance of businesses. It is a tried and trusted approach to financial analysis and has a number of distinct advantages.

Simplicity Ratios are easy to calculate. They are generally one number divided by another, using figures that can be taken directly from the accounts (or notes to the accounts). Most ratios have a consistent formula and only a few (such as gearing) are subject to variation in definition by different users. This simplicity makes ratios easy to understand. For example, a net profit margin of 7 per cent is easily recognisable as being better than one of 4 per cent.

Speed Ratio analysis can be carried out very quickly. Once the necessary information has been gathered from annual reports the financial situation of a company can be analysed very quickly indeed. Most companies make their annual reports available on the Internet and other important information, such as share prices, can also be accessed instantly online.

Comparisons Ratios are ideal for making comparisons between companies, especially those in the same industry that operate under the same environmental conditions. They may be companies of a different size and shape but ratio analysis can be used to look at them in the same light. Interfirm comparisons, comparisons over time and interfirm comparisons over time can all be made using ratio analysis. A business might also use ratios to make internal comparisons. For example, it could compare the net profit margins for different products or the ROCE in different divisions.

Decision making Ratio analysis may be of use to decision makers in businesses. This is because ratio analysis can help to identify strengths and weaknesses in the organisation. For example, if a business discovers that its gross profit margins are very high but net margins are very low, the manager may decide to undertake a cost minimisation strategy.

Limitations to ratio analysis

Unfortunately ratio analysis is not without its problems, consequently it must be used with caution. Some of the key limitations are outlined below.

The basis for comparison A great deal of care must be taken when making comparisons using ratios. It is very important to compare 'like with like'.

- **Comparisons over time** Care must be taken when comparing ratios from the same company over time. Many companies remain broadly in the same industrial sector over time. But others can diversify and change very rapidly. Equally, some companies remain the same size over time. Others grow rapidly or shrink quickly. Such factors can affect the way in which ratios can be used as a measure of performance. The measures of performance of a small company which starts off in the defence sector and grows rapidly to become a leading telecommunications equipment manufacturer will change over time. The value of a particular ratio that is appropriate for the company will therefore change. This must be taken into account when comparing ratios.
- **Interfirm comparisons** Caution must also be used when comparing ratios between companies at a point in time. Comparing the ratios of two companies which make broadly the same products is likely to say something about their relative performance. But comparing the ratios of a supermarket chain with a cement manufacturer is unlikely to be helpful in most cases. The two companies, for example, will have different working capital needs, different profit margins and different asset turnover ratios. Even companies operating in the same industry can have 'subtle' differences. An example is shown in Figure 1.

Figure 1: Comparing 'like with like'

Tesco and Sainsbury are supermarket chains. However, Tesco is selling more and more non-food products such as electrical goods, clothing and kitchen equipment. This makes a direct comparison less meaningful. For example, the profit margins on non-food items might be much higher than those on groceries.

- **Other differences** Even when companies are well matched in their activities and operating circumstances, there may be other differences between them which must be observed. For example, two similar companies may use different accounting techniques. They may use different methods to calculate depreciation or employ different stock valuation methods. If the same accounting conventions have not been used comparisons may be misleading. Companies can also have different year-ends. For example, two companies publishing their accounts for 2008 could be presenting financial information in two quite different time periods. This would happen if one company ended its financial year on 31 December and the other on 31 July. In this case only six months of the year would be truly comparable.

Limitations of the balance sheet Because the balance sheet is a 'snapshot' of the business at the end of the financial year, it might not be representative of the business's circumstances through the whole of the year. If, for example, a business experiences its peak trading activity in the summer, and it has its year-end at a time when trade is slow, in the New Year, figures for stock and debtors will be unrepresentative.

Qualitative information is ignored Ratios only use quantitative information. However, some important qualitative factors may affect the performance of a business. Such factors may be ignored by ratio analysis. For example, in the service industry the quality of customer service may be an important performance indicator. Ratio analysis cannot easily embrace such information.

The quality of final accounts Ratios are based on financial accounts such as the balance sheet, profit and loss accounts and income statements. Consequently ratio analysis is only useful if the accounts are accurate. One factor that can affect the quality of accounting information is the change in monetary values caused by inflation. Rising prices can distort comparisons made between different time periods. For example, in times of high inflation, asset values and revenue might rise rapidly in monetary terms. However, when the figures are adjusted for inflation, there might be no increase in **real terms**. There is also the possibility that the accounts have been **window dressed**. This is discussed next.

Window dressing

Accounts must represent a 'true and fair record' of the financial affairs of a business. Legislation and financial reporting standards place limits on the different ways in which a business can present accounts. These limits are designed to prevent fraud and misrepresentation in the compilation and presentation of accounts. However, businesses can manipulate their accounts legally to present different financial pictures. This is known as WINDOW DRESSING. Businesses may want to window dress their accounts for a variety of reasons.

- Managers of companies might want to put as good a financial picture forward as possible for shareholders and potential shareholders. Good financial results will attract praise and perhaps rewards. They might also prevent criticism from shareholders and the financial press.
- If a business wants to raise new capital from investors, then it will want its financial accounts to look as good as possible.
- Where a business has experienced severe difficulties during the accounting period, it may decide to take action which will make the financial position look even worse now but which will improve figures in the future.
- Making the financial picture look worse is often a way of lowering the amount of tax that is paid.
- If the owners of a business want to sell it, the better the financial position shown on the accounts, the higher the price they are likely to get. Equally, a company which wants to avoid being taken over can discourage predators by showing flattering accounts because these accounts would make the cost of buying the company higher.

There is a number of ways of window dressing accounts explained in this unit.

Manipulating sales Increasing the level of revenue recorded on the profit and loss account or income statement will increase profit in that accounting period. This can be done in a number of ways. Some businesses, for example, are able to choose when they record a sale onto the profit and loss account. For example, a software company can choose under UK accountancy practice either to record a software licence deal when a contract has been signed or when the revenue has been received. Choosing to record a deal today will boost profits at the expense of profits in future accounting periods.

Another practice relates to stocks. At the financial year end, a business may make a special effort to dispatch all outstanding orders. This can boost sales in that accounting period and so flatter the profit and loss account figures. It also reduces stocks of finished goods. This can flatter the balance sheet figures, for example, by increasing the stock turnover ratio.

Costs and depreciation Profits on the profit and loss account or income statement can be increased if costs are reduced. One way of reducing costs is to reduce the cost of depreciation. Depreciation of assets like buildings, vehicles or machinery takes place over a number of years. Take a building initially valued at £1 million. If the business depreciates the building over 10 years using the straight-line method, then each year the cost of depreciation will be £100,000 (£1 million ÷ 10). This is a cost on the profit and loss account. What if the business were to depreciate the building over 25 years instead? Then the annual depreciation charge would be £40,000 (£1 million ÷ 25 years). For the first ten years, profits on the profit and loss account would then be £60,000 (£100,000 - £40 000) a year higher with depreciation over 25 years compared to a depreciation over a ten

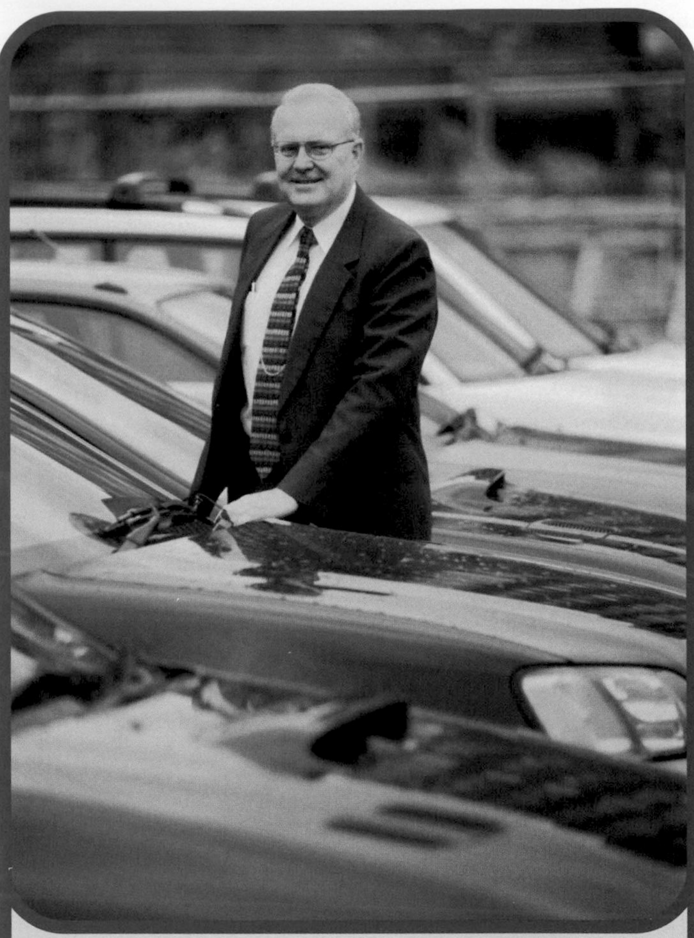

Question 1.

Pennell's plc is a medium sized car dealership in East Anglia. This year has been very disappointing for sales. Despite record sales nationally, Pennell's sales have actually declined. Senior management were worried about the impact this would have on the share price and on shareholder reaction. They therefore agreed on a strategy to boost sales in the all important last financial month of the year to 30 April.

All car sales staff were offered twice the bonus they normally received for selling cars during April so long as the customer took delivery of the car and paid for it in full by the last day of the financial year. As the end of the month approached, sales staff were having to be very persuasive to get some customers who had chosen a car and placed a deposit on it to take delivery of the car on the 30 April rather than in early May.

At the same time, employees were told to cut all unnecessary expenses. There had been a ban in place since mid-February on replacing existing staff who left. Stocks of parts were also run down as far as possible. All this led to some operating difficulties. Waiting times for a service lengthened from around 3 days to 4 days, while some customers found that their repairs took a day longer because parts, normally kept on site, had to be ordered specially from suppliers.

(a) Explain how the managers at Pennell's manipulated (a) sales and (b) costs to window dress the profits of the company at its year end.

(b) Discuss what impact this window dressing might have had on revenues, costs and profits for the next financial year.

year period. However, for years 11-25, profits would be £40 000 lower. This is because if it has been depreciated over ten years, there is no cost for years 11-25. But if it has been depreciated over 25 years, £40 000 a year is still being accounted for as a cost on the profit and loss account.

Depreciation also has an effect on the balance sheet. In the above example, depreciating the building over 25 years rather than 10 years means that profit on the profit and loss account would be higher in the first ten years because the annual depreciation charge, an expense, would be lower. In later years profit will be lower. On the balance sheet, the reverse is true. Fixed assets will tend to be higher if the asset is depreciated over 25 years rather than 10 years. For example, if the £1 million building is depreciated over 25 years, then it has a fixed asset value of £600 000 at end of year 10 (£1 million x 15 ÷ 25). But if it is depreciated over 10 years, it has £0 value at the end of year 10.

A business can also 'write off' its R&D (research and development) costs. Accounting standards allow R&D costs to be written off immediately. Or they can be 'capitalised', treated as an intangible asset and then amortised (i.e. depreciated) over a number of years. What if development costs are depreciated immediately instead of over a number of years? This will reduce profits this year on the profit and loss account but increase them in future years. For example, assume that a company has spent £10 million on R&D this year. It could write these off immediately, increasing costs on the profit and loss account by £10 million and so reducing profit by £10 million. Or it could capitalise the R&D and depreciate it over, say, 10 years. Then each year, including the first year, there would be a cost on the profit and loss account of £1 million (£10 million ÷ 10 years) reducing profit each year by £1 million.

A business must be consistent in the method of depreciation it uses. Businesses don't frequently change their method of depreciation. Indeed, accounting standards only allow a business to change methods if there are 'justifiable reasons'. However, businesses occasionally do change their method of depreciation, for instance by lengthening the period of depreciation or changing the way in which R&D is amortised. This can provide a boost to profits over a number of years and is helpful to a company which is perhaps experiencing low profits and is being criticised by shareholders.

Extraordinary items Businesses are allowed to classify some costs as **extraordinary items**. These are 'one-off' costs such as the costs associated with shutting down a factory or writing off the goodwill from the acquisition of a company. Writing off assets in this way might seem to put a business in a bad light with investors or shareholders. But some companies choose deliberately to write off assets in an accounting period when the business has done badly anyway. Getting all the 'bad news' out at once is better than having continued poor performance over a number of years.

For example, take a business which made some disastrous acquisitions in the past. The companies it bought have performed very poorly. It also paid more for the companies taken over than the value of their tangible assets. Hence, there is now, say, a £100 million entry on the balance sheet as goodwill, an intangible asset. This year, the company is due to announce a £50 million loss. So its directors decide to get all the bad news out at once by writing off the £100 million in goodwill. The loss this year then becomes £150 million. But in future years, reported profits will be higher because there will be no depreciation on the goodwill.

Writing off assets like this also improves future rates of return on capital. In the example, the company now has higher future profits from writing off the £100 million. But in future it will also have £100 million less in assets. Since the rate of return on capital is profit divided by assets, the rate of return will inevitably increase.

Bad debts A business may choose to write off some of its bad debts. This has exactly the same effect as writing off fixed assets. In the short term, profit is reduced by the value of the bad debts. But future profit figures are likely to be improved. This is because most of those bad debts would have had to be written off anyway. A few of the debts may, however, suddenly be paid. This would then be counted as part of revenue boosting profit.

Changing asset values A business can increase the value of tangible fixed assets such as land and buildings, where this is justified by property valuations. Unlike equipment, land and property can increase in value over time, rather than depreciate. A business choosing to revalue its property on the balance sheet would boost the value of its assets, possibly making the balance sheet look stronger. Note that a company which chooses to do this must make an equal and opposite adjustment under capital on the balance sheet under the revaluation reserve.

Boosting liquidity A business may be able to boost liquidity on its balance sheet. Some businesses have too little liquidity, giving rise to cash flow problems as well as working capital problems. One way to boost liquidity is to use sale and leaseback with property. By selling property to a property company and arranging for that property to be leased back to it, a business can release cash tied up in a fixed asset. In the first year, the cash benefit to the business is the value of the property sale minus the lease payment. Sale and leaseback therefore is a way of increasing liquid assets through the sale of fixed assets. If the cash generated from a sale and leaseback scheme is used to pay off long-term loans, the business will also be able to reduce its gearing. Gearing is loans ÷ equity expressed as a percentage. If equity was £20 million and loans £30 million, then gearing would be high at 150 per cent (100% x £30 million ÷ £20 million). If a sale and leaseback deal generated £8 million, loans could be reduced to £22 million (£30 million - £8 million) and gearing would fall to 110 per cent (100% x £22 million ÷ £20 million).

Current assets and liabilities Some businesses have problems with aspects of their current assets and liabilities. The year end can be a time when the business makes a special effort to improve its performance. For example, a business can improve its debtors' data by making a special effort to collect in money owed by late paying debtors. This is likely to increase the amount of cash in the business or reduce short-term borrowings on overdraft. It also improves debtors' ratios. It can attempt to improve its creditors' position by repaying as much as possible, for example by repaying early. It could also get discounts for doing this, which might help show its accounts in a better light. As explained above, a business could try to hide a problem of excessive stock levels by not ordering new stock towards the year end and by making a special effort to dispatch finished stock to customers.

KEYTERMS

Window dressing – the legal manipulation of accounts by a business to present a financial picture which is to its benefit.

KNOWLEDGE

1. Explain three advantages of using ratio analysis.
2. When making comparisons with ratios it is important to compare 'like with like'. Explain what this means.
3. Why does ratio analysis ignore qualitative information?
4. Explain why a company may want to window dress its accounts.
5. How can a company manipulate (a) its sales and (b) its costs to flatter its recorded profits on the profit and loss account?
6. How might (a) extraordinary items and (b) exceptional items be used to window dress accounts?
7. How might bad debts be manipulated to window dress accounts?
8. How might liquidity be boosted on the accounts?
9. How might a company manipulate its current assets and liabilities to window dress its accounts?

Case Study: CNV Plastics

CNV Plastics is a large private limited company based in Leeds. It is an engineering business which designs and produces pvc piping, tanks, scrubbers and hoods. In 2008 the business began to struggle financially. It was undercapitalised and needed to raise £10 million to boost working capital and provide funding for product development. A bank loan was being considered by the directors. Unfortunately the 2007 accounts did not look good. Some of the ratios used to analyse the company's performance suggested that most banks would be reluctant to lend money to the company. However, at an emergency board meeting the financial director suggested that the performance of the company could be enhanced by 'window dressing' the accounts. The managing director was dubious about this. However, the finance director reassured all board members that 'window dressing' was legal and could be used to show the company in a better light. She suggested two actions.

- The method used to calculate depreciation could be changed. This would increase profit in 2008 by £2 million from £6 million to £8 million.
- Selling its factory and leasing it back. This would boost liquidity by injecting some cash into the company. The financial director also explained that this would also help to boost working capital.

The board of directors eventually agreed with the finance director and the suggested actions were taken. Table 1 shows some financial ratios for CNV Plastics after the accounts had been window dressed in 2008.

Table 1: Financial ratios for CNV Plastics

	2008	2007
Net profit margin	5.40%	2.40%
ROCE	4.60%	1.90%
Current ratio	1.6	1.1
Gearing	42%	41%

(a) What would be the value to CNV of using ratio analysis? (8 marks)

(b) What is meant by 'window dressing' the accounts? (4 marks)

(c) What might be the danger of 'window dressing' to CNV Plastics? (6 marks)

(d) (i) Explain the effect on the net profit margin and the ROCE of changing the method used to calculate depreciation. (8 marks)

(ii) Explain the effect on the current ratio and gearing ratio of selling the factory and leasing it back. (8 marks)

(e) What might be the long-term effects on CNV Plastics of selling the factory and leasing it back? (8 marks)

57 Constructing accounts

When are accounts compiled?

The compilation of accounts involves using the information generated by recording business transactions to produce a balance sheet, profit and loss account or income statement and cash flow statement. Many businesses use computer software to compile accounts on a regular basis.

Final accounts are constructed at the end of the trading year. Small businesses such as sole traders, partnerships and small limited companies may employ chartered or certified accountants to prepare their accounts. Business owners provide records of transactions and supporting documents. Most large companies and many medium-sized companies employ their own accountants who compile accounts for the business. However, companies which produce their own accounts must get them audited by an independent firm of accountants.

Once the accounts have been compiled they can be used by the various stakeholders. Public limited companies distribute their annual reports and accounts to all their shareholders.

Compiling the balance sheet

Figure 1 shows a summary of the balance sheet structure. Accountants produce balance sheets according to accounting convention set out by the Accounting Standards Board (ASB) and the Companies Act, 1985.

A balance sheet can be compiled by inserting the appropriate information in the correct positions in the structure. Consider the financial information in Table1 for Corporate Signs Ltd, a business which makes neon signs for companies. All the information relates to the assets, liabilities and capital of the company on 31.1.2008.

Figure 1: Balance sheet summary diagram

	£	
Fixed assets	A	
Current assets	B	
Current liabilities	C	
Net current assets (working capital)	D	B-C
Total assets less current liabilities	E	(A+B)-C *or* A+D
Creditors: amounts due after one year(Long-term liabilities)	F	
Net assets	G	E-F *or* (A+D)-F
Capital and reserves (Capital employed or shareholders' funds)	H	G=H

Table 1: Financial information for Corporate Signs Ltd, 31.1.2008 (£)

Mortgage	100,000
Share capital	100,000
Other reserves	71,000
Premises	231,000
Debtors	75,000
Vehicles	87,000
Stocks and work in progress	98,000
Plant and equipment	199,000
Current liabilities	201,000
Retained profit	290,000
Cash at bank	112,000
Unsecured bank loan	60,000
Intangible assets	20,000

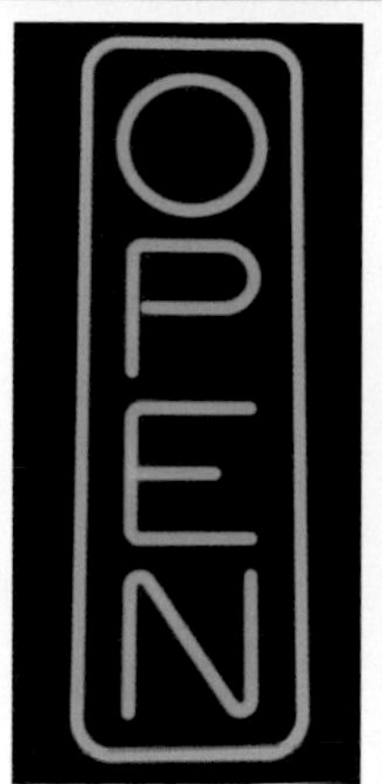

To construct the balance sheet for Corporate Signs Ltd, the following step-by-step approach might be used.

- Identify which of the items are assets, which are liabilities and which are capital and reserves.
- Write the title and date at the top of the account.
- List the fixed assets and add them up. Fixed assets are premises (£231,000), plant and equipment (£199,000) and vehicles (£87,000). All these are tangible assets (a total of £517,000). Intangible assets are £20,000. Fixed assets are therefore tangible plus intangible assets, a total of £537,000.
- List the current assets and add them up. Current assets are stocks and work-in-progress (£98,000), debtors (£75,000) and cash at bank (£112,000) which total £285,000.
- List the current liabilities and add them up. Current liabilities are stated as £201,000. These are the amounts falling due within one year.
- Enter the value for net current assets by subtracting current liabilities from current assets (£285,000 - £201,000 = £84,000).
- Enter the value for total assets less current liabilities by adding fixed assets to net current assets (£537,000 + £84,000 = £621,000).
- List the creditors: amounts falling due after one year and add them up. These are the mortgage (£100,000) and the unsecured bank loan (£60,000) which total £160,000.
- Enter the value for net assets by subtracting creditors: amounts falling due after one year from total assets less current liabilities (£621,000 - £160,000 = £461,000).
- List the capital and reserves and add them up. Capital and reserves are share capital (£100,000), other reserves (£71,000) and retained profit (£290,000) which total £461,000.

Table 2: Balance sheet for Corporate Signs Ltd, 31.1.2008

CORPORATE SIGNS LTD - BALANCE SHEET AS AT 31 JANUARY 2008	£
Fixed assets	
Tangible assets	
Premises	231,000
Plant and equipment	199,000
Vehicles	87,000
	517,000
Intangible assets	20,000
	537,000
Current assets	
Stocks and work in progress	98,000
Debtors	75,000
Cash at bank	112,000
	285,000
Current liabilities	201,000
Net current assets	84,000
Total assets less current liabilities	621,000
Creditors: amounts falling due after one year	
Mortgage	(100,000)
Unsecured bank loan	(60,000)
Net assets	461,000
Capital and reserves	
Share capital	100,000
Other reserves	71,000
Retained profit	290,000
Capital employed	461,000

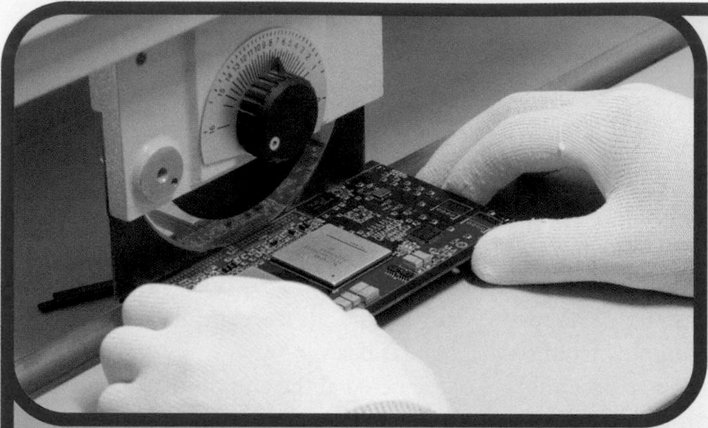

Question 1.

Munro & Thompson Ltd is a medium-sized electronic components manufacturer. The company supplies a wide range of industries. The business has enjoyed steady growth in recent years despite intense competition from Chinese manufacturers. Table 3 shows some financial information for Munro & Thompson Ltd.

Table 3: Financial information for Munro & Thompson Ltd.

	£000 2008	£000 2007
Retained profit	1,210	772
Equipment and machinery	4,450	3,600
Mortgage	200	300
Share capital	2,500	2,500
Vehicles	120	140
Cash at bank	30	20
Taxation	50	40
Other reserves	420	330
Debtors	85	80
Other long-term liabilities	340	280
Accruals	23	25
Stock & work-in-progress	145	122
Trade creditors	87	65

(a) Compile the balance sheet for Munro & Thompson Ltd using the information in Table 3. (Include 2007 and 2008.)
(b) Explain briefly the changes in the financial position of Munro & Thompson Ltd over the two years.

- Check that the value of capital and reserves (also shown as shareholders' funds or capital employed on some balance sheets) are the same as net assets. If the balance sheet has been compiled accurately, the value of net assets should be exactly the same as capital employed.

If the above steps are followed the result should be the same as the balance sheet shown in Table 2. Remember that normally both the current trading figures, and the previous year's figures, are shown in the accounts.

Transactions and the balance sheet

How might a transaction affect the balance sheet? There are two sides to every transaction and transactions can affect both assets and liabilities. For example, when a business makes a sale it will receive cash (an increase in assets) but reduce its stock of finished goods (a decrease in assets). Table 4 shows the balance sheet of Gregory Issacs Ltd, a construction company, as at 31 August 2008. How might the four transactions affect the balance sheet?

- **Transaction 1** The company buys a range of new equipment for one division of the business for £1 million. It arranges to pay by credit. This will increase fixed assets (equipment) by £1 million and current liabilities (trade creditors) by £1 million.
- **Transaction 2** A consignment of stocks is ordered costing £500,000 on credit. This will increase current assets (stocks) by £500,000 and current liabilities (trade creditors) by £500,000.
- **Transaction 3** The company repays a short-term debt of £1.8 million. This will decrease current assets (cash at bank) by £1.8 million and creditors: amounts due within one year (other liabilities) by £1.8 million.
- **Transaction 4** A debtor repays £200,000 to the company.

Table 4: The affect of transactions on the balance sheet

	Gregory Issacs Ltd. Balance sheet as at 31 August 2008	Gregory Issacs Ltd. Balance sheet as at 1 September 2008	
	£m	£m	
Fixed assets			
Tangible assets	84.8	85.8	*Equipment is a tangible asset. The value of tangible assets rises by £1m, from £84.8m to £85.8m*
Investments	0.8	0.8	
	85.6	86.6	*The value of fixed assets has also increased by £1m from £85.6m to £86.6m*
Current assets			
Work-in-progress and stocks	802.4	802.9	*The value of stocks has increased by £500,000, from £802.4m to £802.9m*
Debtors	84.4	84.2	*The value of debtors has fallen by £200,000, from £84.4m to £84.2m*
Cash at bank	10.8	9.2	*The value of cash at bank has fallen by £1.8m and then risen by £200,000, an overall fall of £1.6m from £10.8m to £9.2m*
	897.6	896.3	*The value of current assets has fallen by £1.3m, from £897.6m to £896.3m*
Creditors: amounts falling due within one year (current liabilities)			
Trade creditors	246.6	248.1	*The value of trade creditors has increased by £1m and £500,000 (£1.5m) from £246.6m to £248.1m*
Taxation	12.8	12.8	
Other liabilities	20.8	19.0	*The value of other liabilities has fallen by £1.8m, from £20.8m to £19m*
	280.2	279.9	*The value of current liabilities has fallen by £300,000 from £280.2m to £279.9m*
Net current assets (working capital)	617.4	616.4	*The value of net current assets has fallen by £1m from £617.4m to £616.4m*
Total assets less current liabilities	703.0	703.0	*The value of total assets less current liabilities, creditors due after one year, net assets and capital and reserves has not changed. This is because transactions on that particular day have not affected either long-term liabilities or capital and reserves.*
Creditors: amounts falling due after one year	(199.8)	(199.8)	
Net assets	**503.2**	**503.2**	
Capital and reserves			
Called-up share capital	91.2	91.2	
Revaluation reserve	91.5	91.5	
Retained profit	320.5	320.5	
	503.2	**503.2**	

Table 5: Financial information for a supermarket chain 1.12.2008

	£m
Turnover	3,000
Administrative expenses and distribution costs	400
Taxation	45
Cost of sales	2,500
Interest paid (net)	5
Dividends	30
Non-operating income	30

This will only affect current assets. Debtors will fall by £200,000 and cash at bank will increase by £200,000.

It is assumed here that all these transactions are carried out on 1 September 2008. The effects of these transactions are shown in Table 4.

Compiling the profit and loss account or income statement

The structure of a profit and loss account or income statement was explained in an earlier unit. Accountants produce profit and loss accounts according to accounting conventions set out by the ASB and the Companies Act. There is, however, some variation when looking at the profit and loss accounts or income statements of limited companies.

The profit and loss account will contain three key sections.

- The trading account, where gross profit is calculated.
- The profit and loss account, where net profit is calculated.
- The profit and loss appropriation account, which shows how the net profit is distributed.

Consider the financial information in Table 5, which shows the revenue and expenses incurred by a supermarket chain. The following steps could be used when compiling a profit and loss account or income statement from a set of figures:

For the trading account

- Write the title and date at the top of the account.
- Enter the value for turnover (£3,000 million).
- Enter the value for cost of sales (remember that the cost of sales must be adjusted for stock). The value of cost of sales has already been adjusted in Table 5 and is £2,500m.
- Enter the value for gross profit by subtracting cost of sales from turnover (£3,000m - £2,500m = £500m).

Table 6: Profit and loss account for the supermarket chain 1.12.2008

Profit and Loss Account
year ended 31.1.2008

	£m
Turnover	3,000
Cost of sales	2,500
Gross profit	500
Administrative expenses and distribution costs	400
Operating profit	100
Non-operating income	30
Profit before interest and tax	130
Interest paid (net)	5
Profit on ordinary activities before tax	125
Taxation	45
Profit on ordinary activities after tax	80
Dividends	30
Retained profit	50

Question 2.

Maynard Ltd is a clothes manufacturer based in Oldham. It is a successful business and prides itself on the quality of personal service it provides customers. The company produces clothes for men, women and children and can deliver articles from high-end, one-off designer niche garments, fashion items and accessories to a simple mass produced T-shirt. Maynard Ltd offer:

- Full garment design service
- Your garment design interpretation (pattern making)
- Manufacture of production samples and prototypes
- Manufacturing of one off bespoke items or production line multiple items
- Warehousing, storage and drop shipping
- Route to market consultation
- Fabric sourcing
- Accessory sourcing

Some financial information for Maynard Ltd is shown in Table 7.

Table 7: Financial information for Maynard Ltd.

	2008 £000s	2007 £000s
Admin expenses	1,560	1,800
Dividends	600	500
Taxation	580	450
Cost of sales	3,780	2,100
Turnover	7,800	5,700
Net interest payable	70	45

(a) Produce a profit and loss account for Maynard Ltd for 2008 and 2007.

(b) Comment briefly on the performance of Maynard Ltd over the two year period.

For the profit and loss account

- Enter the administrative/operating expenses underneath the gross profit (£400 million).
- Enter the value for operating profit by subtracting operating expenses from gross profit (£500 million - £400 million = £100 million).
- Enter the value of other income below operating profit (£30 million).
- Enter the value for profit before interest and tax by adding non-operating income to operating profit (£100 million + £30 million = £130 million).
- Enter the value for (net) interest payable underneath the value of profit before interest and tax (£5 million).
- Enter the profit on ordinary activities before tax by subtracting (net) interest paid from profit before interest and tax (£130 million - £5 million). This gives a total of £125 million.

For the profit and loss appropriation account

- Enter taxation underneath profit on ordinary activities before tax (£45 million).
- Enter the value for profit on ordinary activities after tax by subtracting taxation from profit on ordinary activities before tax (£125 million - £45 million) which gives £80m.
- Enter dividends underneath profit on ordinary activities after tax (£30 million).
- Enter the value for retained profit (or loss) for the financial year by subtracting dividends from profit on ordinary activities after tax (£80 million - £30 million = £50 million).

The retained profit for the financial year figure is the last entry in the accounts (although the earnings per share is usually listed in public limited company accounts underneath retained profit). If the above steps are followed then the result should be the same as the profit and loss account shown in Table 6.

Additional entries for inclusion in the profit and loss account

The profit and loss account shown here is fairly simple. Profit and loss accounts or income statements for other businesses may appear slightly different. This is because they contain additional information. Whether they do or not depends on the nature of their business and what has happened during the trading year. Some possible differences are described below.

- Exceptional items, if they occur, should be included after operating profit in the account. If the exceptional item is a cost, such as a bad debt, then it should be subtracted from operating profit. If it is revenue, it should be added.
- Sometimes the operating expenses are split into specific expenses. For example, they might be divided between distribution costs and administration expenses. It is quite normal to show these items separately and then subtract them from gross profit.
- The figure for interest paid shown here is a net figure (net interest = interest paid - interest received). The actual breakdown of interest paid and received would be shown in the notes to the accounts. Net interest can be positive or negative. Some businesses receive no interest, so the figure would simply be for interest paid. In other accounts both the figures for interest paid and received will be shown.
- Some businesses do not calculate gross profit in the account. This might be because they provide services rather than make goods. If this is the case all costs and expenses are added together and subtracted from turnover to calculate operating profit.

The list above is not definitive. In reality it is rare to find two companies with identical entries in their profit and loss accounts.

KNOWLEDGE

1. When do businesses normally compile their accounts?
2. Which assets are listed first in the balance sheet?
3. How is net current assets calculated in the balance sheet?
4. How is the net assets figure calculated in the balance sheet?
5. How is gross profit calculated in the trading account?
6. What entries will appear in the profit and loss appropriation account?
7. How are exceptional items dealt with in the profit and loss account?
8. Under what circumstances might gross profit not appear in a profit and loss account?

Case Study: Cutpricetours.com

Cutpricetours.com operates a website for bargain holidays, cheap flights and special accommodation deals. It also offers a range of travel related products from travel gear and travel clothing to car hire and insurance. The company has a call centre in High Wycombe staffed by experienced travel agents who are ready to advise and help all customers.

Cutpricetours.com is not tied to any one tour operator, it is an independent travel agent offering the chance to find the latest deals that are available online and on the high street. It has a unique database of holidays and flights and customers can search online through thousands of available destinations within minutes – from the Mediterranean to the Caribbean and from the USA to the Far East.

In 2007 the company invested around £10 million in an advertising campaign to raise the profile of the company. Market research showed that Cutpricetours.com was fairly well known in the south east but largely unknown in the midlands and the north. The business hoped to achieve national recognition through the advertising campaign. The investment was funded partly internally and partly from a bank loan. Some financial information for Cutpricetours.com is shown in Table 8.

Table 8: Financial information for Cutpricetours.com, 31.3.2008

	2008 £m	2007 £m
Other long-term liabilities	1.3	1.1
Other reserves	3.1	6.0
Other fixed assets	5.3	4.2
Other current liabilities	4.27	3.91
Retained profit	4.48	13.96
Computer equipment	14.0	16.0
Stocks	2.11	1.95
Bank loan	8.5	4.5
Taxation	2.55	1.76
Share capital	5.0	5.0
Debtors and prepayments	4.33	3.87
Trade creditors	9.44	8.49
Cash at bank	12.9	18.7

(a) Compile the balance sheet for Cutpricetours.com. (Include both 2008 and 2007 figures.) (18 marks)

(b) Comment briefly on the nature, and possible cause, of the changes shown in the balance sheet over the two years. (10 marks)

(c) On the 1.4.08 the following transactions were undertaken by Cutpricetours.com:
- **Some computer hardware was purchased for £1,000,000. Payment is not due for three months.**
- **Debtors repaid £800,000.**
- **£1,000,000 was repaid on the bank loan.**

Draw up a new balance sheet to show the effect of these transactions. (12 marks)

58 The valuation of businesses

The valuation of a business

Financial ratios can be used to investigate a company's accounts. For example, a relatively high net profit margin might show that one business has performed better than another. It might also show that its own performance has improved over time. A relatively low gearing ratio might indicate that a business has raised most of its finance from its shareholders, rather than through loans.

To some extent, calculating financial ratios can help place a VALUE on a business. For example, businesses which have adequate working capital and high profit margins and returns on capital employed will tend to have more value than those which do not. The value of a business is how much it is worth to a **stakeholder** or any other interested party, such as a potential buyer. For example, in January 2008, Andy Appleby, an American businessman, bought Derby County Football Club. The purchase price was said to be £50 million. This was the agreed value of the business at the time of the sale.

Different people might place different values on the same business. A seller is likely to place a higher value on a company than a buyer. This is sometimes called the **expectation gap**. Differences in value might also occur because a business might be worth more to one particular buyer. For example, Asda might place a higher value on an independent supermarket located in a town where it was not represented than Tesco might if they already had a store in that town. The difference in value occurs due to strategic considerations.

Reasons for valuation

There may be times when it is necessary to have some idea how much a business is worth.

Planning a sale If the owners are considering the sale of a business, it will be necessary to know its value before putting it 'on the market'. Homeowners will normally ask an estate agent to value their house before putting it up for sale. Similarly, business owners might consult an accountant to help place a value on their business. Such valuations normally provide a starting point for negotiations between buyers and sellers. In many cases the agreed sale price will be different from the original valuation.

A takeover One company may be thinking about taking over another. In this case it will need to know the value of the company it is buying in order to decide whether it has enough funds to go through with the acquisition. Sometimes a takeover can work out more expensive than anticipated. This is often the case in a hostile takeover. The current owners might resist the takeover by refusing to sell their shares. This could drive up the price. Also, another company might want to take over the same firm. This could result in a bidding war, where the price is inflated until the business is eventually sold to the highest bidder.

Merging When two companies merge, they need to know the value of each business. This is because the conditions of the merger have to be determined so that both companies can agree. For example, if one firm is twice the value of the other, it might mean that the new board of directors is made up of six representatives from the highest valued company and three from the other. It is also necessary to know the value of the merging companies so that accountants can merge their financial affairs.

Demerger or management buy-out This is very similar to the sale of a business. In the case of a demerger it is necessary to calculate the value of the company before it is divided into smaller units. This then helps to calculate the value of the new, smaller companies when demerger takes place. Valuation of the new companies is required so that the number of new shares being issued, and their price, can be determined. In the case of a management buy-out or buy-in, valuation of the business or part of the business being sold is necessary to help set the sale price.

Flotation If a business, or part of a business, is being floated on the stock exchange it is necessary to know the value. Again, this is required so that the number of shares being issued and their price can be determined. During the privatisation era of the 1980s it was suggested that many companies, such as BT and Powergen, were sold off by the government way below their true value. The government argued that it was necessary to price the share issues attractively in order for the flotation to be a success.

Securing loans When a business wants a loan the bank may require some collateral for security. If this is the case, the business, or part of the business, may be used. The bank may need to know the value of the business in order to clarify the value of the collateral.

Other reasons It may be necessary to calculate the value of the business if:

- the owner is involved in a divorce settlement, where the business is being shared out between husband and wife;
- a business has been inherited and inheritance tax is being calculated by the Inland Revenue;
- business owners or shareholders are curious about how much their business would be worth if sold;
- a business person is considering the sale of the business to retire;

Question 1.

In January 2008, the directors of Scottish and Newcastle (S & N) recommended that shareholders should accept an 800p per share takeover offer from Carlsberg and Heineken. S & N is the UK's largest brewer and one of the world's leading beer-led beverages companies with strong positions in 15 countries including leadership in the UK, France and Russia. In the last 20 years, S&N has expanded significantly from its home base to become a major international business with beer volumes growing almost tenfold. Some of its most popular UK brands include John Smiths, Newcastle Brown Ale, Fosters, Kronenbourg 1664, McKewans 80/-, Strongbow Cider and Scrumpy Jack. Four of these brands are in the top ten UK leading beer brands (see Table 1).

After the announcement, S & N warned that confirmation of the 800p a share offer, after three months of negotiations, may not be the end of the takeover battle. John Dunsmore, chief executive of S & N, said: 'We've retained our bid defence strategy intact'. S & N believes that the recent publication of its profit growth forecasts for Baltic Beverages Holding, its Russian joint venture with Carlsberg, may tempt other brewers to make rival offers.

(a) **On 26 January 2008, the price of S & N shares was 783p. At this price the company was valued at £7,418 million. What would be the market capitalisation of S & N if the tabled takeover offer was accepted?**

(b) **Why is the value of S & N an important issue in the circumstances described in the case?**

(c) **What might happen to the value of S & N if rival bids are made for the company?**

Table 1: Leading beer brands 2008

	Brand	UK brand owner
1	Carling	Coors
2	Foster's	S & N
3	Stella Artois	InBev
4	Carlsberg	Carlsberg
5	John Smiths	S & N
6	Guinness	Diago
7	Kronenbourg 1664	S & N
8	Budweiser	Anheuser-Busch
9	Tennents Lager	InBev
10	Tetley Bitter	S & N

Source: adapted from *The Financial Times* 26.1.08

- to make financial comparisons between businesses in an industry, for example, in an industrial survey.

Methods of valuation

There is a number of techniques which could be used to value a business.

Market capitalisation This can be calculated using the formula:

MARKET CAPITALISATION = the current share price x the number of shares issued

For example, on 27 January 2008, the share price for British Airways was 317.5p and the number of shares issued in the company was approximately 1,151,811,000. The value of the company could have been £3.657 billion using this measure. This method of valuation may be distorted because external factors can cause the share price to change, such as interest rates and the actions of speculators. If the share price falls by 10 per cent due to one of these factors, this does not necessarily mean that the value of the company has fallen by 10 per cent.

Capitalised earnings This method is often used to value the holdings of the majority shareholders in a business. When shareholders buy shares, they buy the right to a future stream of profits that the business will make, known as maintainable earnings. Multiplying these maintainable earnings by the price/earnings ratio of a company gives the capitalised earnings. So:

CAPITALISED EARNINGS = price/earnings ratio (P/E) x maintainable earnings

The price earnings ratio shows the relationship between the amount each share earns for the investor and the current market price of the share. The P/E ratios of plcs are published each day in newspapers such as *The Financial Times*. A discount is often applied to the P/E ratios of private limited companies as their shares are not sold openly.

Maintainable earnings are the sustainable profits, after tax, that a business is capable of generating on a recurring basis. How can a value for maintainable earnings be estimated? It is necessary to consider all factors affecting a company's ability to maintain its current level of profit. This usually means starting with profits after tax for the current financial year. Then the figure is adjusted for one-off items of income or expenditure and directors' payments in excess of the market rate. So the estimate of maintainable earnings requires some human judgment. A subjective decision needs to be made about what non-recurring income and spending to take into account.

Discounted cash flow (DCF) This method may be used to value an entire company. It may also be used as a benchmark to compare the capitalised earnings value. To calculate the DCF a business needs to forecast annual cash flows and a discount factor. The discount factor will be the purchaser's cost of capital, such as the interest rate. The unit on investment appraisal explained how it is possible, using the DCF method, to calculate the net present value of a future stream of income. This will tell a business what the value of any future income streams is worth now.

Financial institutions, such as banks and venture capitalists, tend to prefer this method. It focuses on future cash flows rather than historic profit. They argue that valuations based on forecasts of future cash flows provide a better guide to the firm's ability to repay capital than a valuation based on past profits.

Net assets This method is most suitable when assets make up a major part of the value of the business. This might be the case with property or investment companies, for example. It might also be used if the company is a loss maker and the buyer of the business intends to sell the assets and then reinvest the cash. It might be used if a business has had difficulties and is being purchased from a receiver, for example. In this case the business may be bought at a discount to the value of net assets. The net assets of a business are:

Net assets = (fixed assets + current assets) – (current liabilities + long-term liabilities)

This is quite a simple method of valuation because the value of net assets is shown clearly on all business balance sheets.

Return on investment (ROI) This method might be used, for example, when a choice has to be made about which business to buy from two alternatives. This method uses similar techniques to the calculation of capitalised earnings. However, rather than maintainable earnings after tax it uses **maintainable operating profits** (profit before interest and tax). ROI can be found by:

$$\text{ROI} = \frac{\text{Maintainable operating profit}}{\text{Purchase price}}$$

When using this method to choose between different businesses for acquisition, the business with the highest ROI will be selected. Again, a subjective judgment is required regarding non-recurring income and spending when estimating maintainable operating profits.

The pricing curve Accountants have developed a rule-of-thumb measure to determine the value of a business. The pricing curve shown in Figure 1 can be used to give some idea of a company's value. The curve is based on aggregate sales values of private companies. To use the curve it is necessary to determine the operating profits of the company before tax and interest. However, the profit figure must be adjusted to take into account factors specific to the company. For example, if the current owners are paying themselves too much money, the profit figure should be raised accordingly. Once profits have been adjusted the curve can be used to obtain a value. For example, if earnings (profits) before interest and tax were £3 million, reading from the curve, the business would be worth £35 million.

Figure 1: The PCPI Pricing Curve

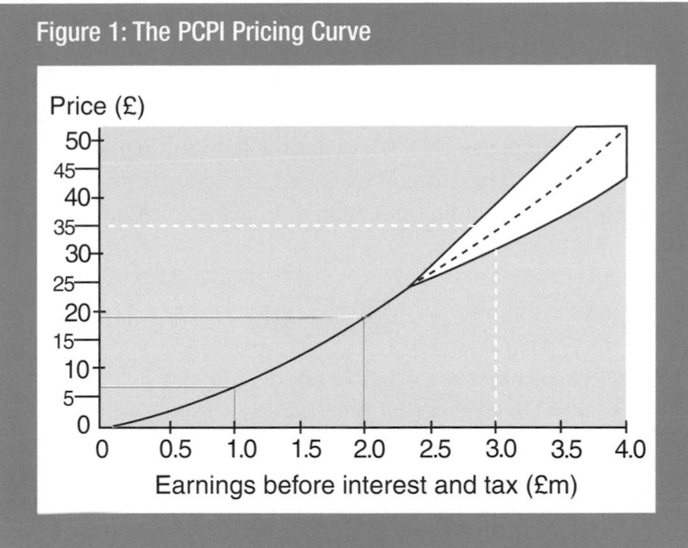

Problems of valuation

The valuation of a business is often difficult. A company's value may not be known until it is placed on the market and sold. Certain problems exist when calculating the value of the business using the methods in the last section.

- When calculating the market capitalisation of a business the current share price is used. Sometimes the share price does not reflect accurately the performance of the business. Share prices can be influenced by external factors, such as interest rates and the actions of speculators. Also, the share price of a particular company may be a lot lower than one would expect because the company is 'out of favour' with the City. If share prices do not reflect the performance of the business the valuation will be inaccurate.
- The determination of maintainable earnings and maintainable operating profit require some human judgment. They are both concerned with the sustainable profits that a business is capable of generating on a **recurring** basis. The profit figures in the current accounts therefore need to be adjusted for non-recurring income and spending. This decision about what is non-recurring is likely to vary depending on who is making it.
- The DCF method also requires some human judgment. It is necessary to predict future cash inflows. This is difficult to do because a wide range of external factors, such as

competitor's actions and the state of the economy, might influence future cash inflows.

- When using net assets to value a company, the true value of some assets may not appear on the balance sheet. These are intangible assets such as goodwill, brand names and copyrights. Therefore, if excluded, the value of the company would be understated. Many accountants choose not to include the value of intangible of assets because they are difficult to value. Also, the value of intangible assets can change quite sharply and suddenly.

To overcome some of the problems, businesses might use more than one method of valuation.

KEYTERMS

Capitalised earnings – the value of a company determined by multiplying the P/E ratio by maintainable earnings.
Market capitalisation – the value of a company determined by multiplying the share price by the number of shares issued.
Value (of a business) – the amount a business is worth to a stakeholder or any other interested party.

KNOWLEDGE

1. What is meant by the expectation gap in relation to the value of a business?
2. Explain two reasons why a hostile takeover might lead to a rise in the value of a business.
3. State five reasons for valuing a business, other than for a takeover.
4. What information is needed to calculate (i) market capitalisation and (ii) maintainable earnings?
5. How does DCF allow a business to be valued?

Case Study: TelecityGroup

TelecityGroup is a pan-European provider of network independent data centres. It offers a range of data centres and managed services to a wide range of organisations. The Group's data centres act as 'connectivity and content hubs' helping the storage, sharing and distribution of data and media. The Group's data centres also provide a secure location for organisations who want to outsource the hosting and management of their technical, web and Internet infrastructure.

With its headquarters in London, TelecityGroup operates 18 network independent data centres across seven European countries. The data centres are located in prime positions for commerce and connectivity, including Amsterdam, Dublin, Frankfurt, London, Manchester, Milan, Paris, and Stockholm. TelecityGroup combines highly-skilled engineers, an experienced management team and a commitment to customer service with sound financial support. Its customers include Sony, BBC, AOL, Skype and French Connection.

Telecity has it roots at Manchester University, where it was set up by an engineer called Mike Kelly. Floated during the dot.com boom in 2000, Telecity was valued at £1 billion before the boom turned to bust and business dried up. It bought out rivals Redbus but eventually succumbed to a £58 million buyout by 3i and California-based Oak Hill Capital in 2005. In October 2007, however, Telecity came back onto the market in a flotation that valued the company at 220p a share or £436 million. Telecity acquired Globix for $62 million (£30 million) and if the effect of Globix is folded into the figures for the whole of 2006, Telecity had annual underlying earnings of £13.2 million. In the first half of this year, it had already made £10.3 million on sales of £46.1 million. Analysts say it should be able to hit earnings of £34 million next year. The data hosting market has been taking off in recent years as the rapid take-up of broadband Internet access has boosted web usage among consumers, and increased regulation means companies have to retain their data for longer. This is all good news for Telecity. On 29.1.2008 the share price was 251p.

Table 2: Financial information for Telecity as at 31.12.2006

	£000
Non-current assets	149,887
Current assets	35,055
Current liabilities	64,765
Non-current liabilities	37,467

Source: adapted from www.telecitygroup.com and *The Sunday Times*, 28.10.2007.

(a) Why did the value of Telecity fall from £1 billion in 2000 to £58 million in 2005? (4 marks)

(b) Why is a company valuation necessary before a flotation? (4 marks)

(c) (i) What has happened to the market capitalisation of Telecity since its flotation in 2007? (The number of shares issued was 198.092 million on 29.1.2008.) (6 marks)

(ii) What might account for the change shown in (i)? (6 marks)

(d) (i) Calculate the value of net assets for Telecity on 31.12.2006. (4 marks)

(ii) How does the value of net assets shown in (ii) illustrate some of the problems of valuing a business? (16 marks)

59 Organisational structures

Organisational structures

Each business has its own ORGANISATIONAL STRUCTURE or BUSINESS STRUCTURE. The structure is the way in which positions within the business are arranged. It is often know as the **internal structure** or FORMAL ORGANISATION of the business.

The organisational structure of the business defines:

- the workforce roles of employees and their job titles;
- the route through which decisions are made;
- who is responsible and who is accountable to whom, and for what activities;
- the relationship between positions in a business;
- how employees communicate with each other and how information is passed on.

Different businesses tend to have different objectives, relationships and ways in which decisions are made. So they may have different structures. But there may also be some similarities. For example, small businesses are likely to have simple structures. Larger businesses are often divided into departments with managers.

Structure is important to all businesses. It helps them to divide work and co-ordinate activities to achieve objectives. But it may be more important for larger businesses. For example, a two person plumbing business is likely to have fewer problems deciding 'who does what' than a business operating in many countries.

One method of organising a business is where managers put people together to work effectively based on their skills and abilities. The structure is 'built up' or it 'develops' as a result of the employees of the business. In contrast a structure could be created first, with all appropriate workforce roles outlined, and then people employed to fill them. It has been suggested that the entrepreneur Richard Branson worked out a complete organisation structure for his Virgin Atlantic airline before setting up the company and then recruited the 102 people needed to fill all the positions.

Workforce roles

The positions in an organisation will have particular workloads and jobs allocated to them.

Directors Directors are appointed to run the business in the interest of its owners. In smaller businesses, owners may also be directors. But in larger businesses owned by shareholders, for example, they may be different. Directors are in overall charge of activities in an organisation. They meet, as the **Board of Directors**, to make major decisions that will affect the owners. Some directors, known as executive directors, will be involved in the running of a business. Non-executive directors may play little part in its running. The **managing director** (MD) will have overall responsibility for the organisation and have AUTHORITY over specific directors, such as the **finance** or **marketing director**.

Managers Managers are responsible for controlling or organising within the business. They often make day-to-day decisions about the running of the business. The sales manager, for example, would have responsibility for sales in the business and be responsible to the marketing director. Businesses often have **departmental** managers, such as the marketing, human

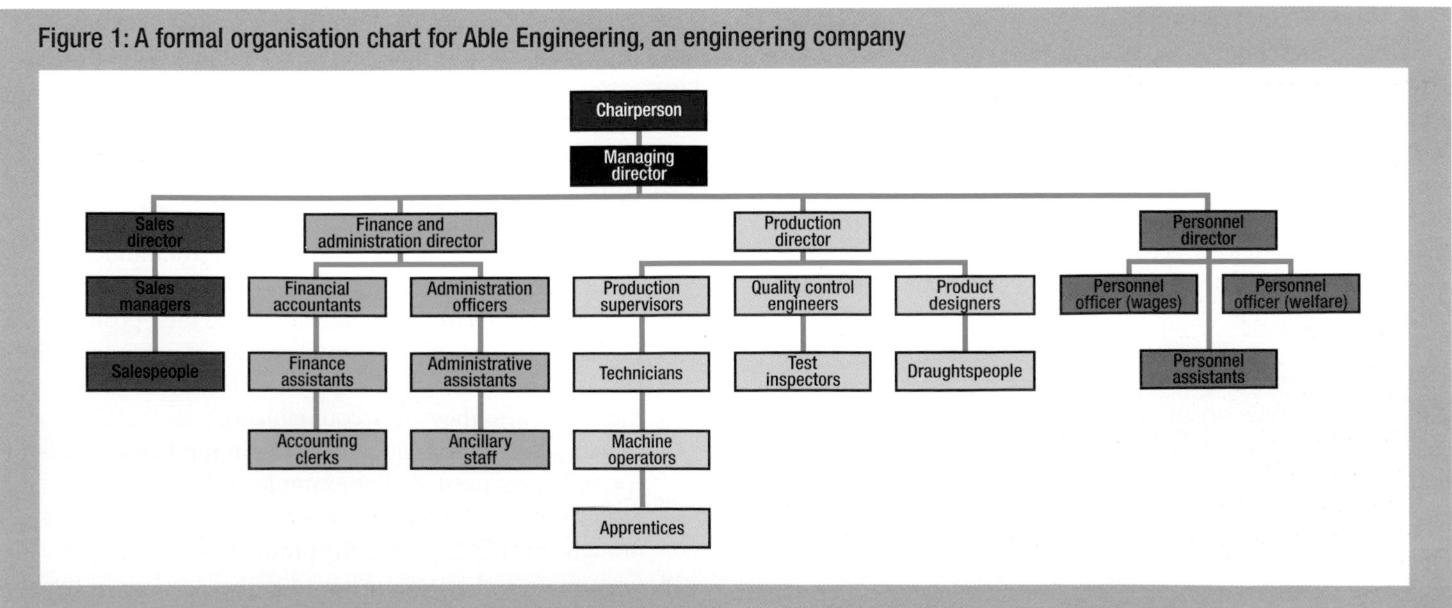

Figure 1: A formal organisation chart for Able Engineering, an engineering company

resources, finance and production manager. There may also be **regional** managers, organising the business in areas of a country or **branch** managers, organising particular branches or stores.

Team leaders Team leaders are members of a team whose role is to resolve issues between team members and co-ordinate team efforts so that the team works effectively. A team leader may be part of a permanent cell production team or a team set up for a particular job, such as investigating staff morale. A team leader may also take responsibility for representing the views of a team to the next higher reporting level, for example to report the findings of a market research team.

Supervisors Supervisors monitor and regulate the work in their assigned or delegated area, for example stock supervisor or payroll supervisor. Supervisors may be given some of the roles of managers, but at a lower level. Their roles in this case may be to hire, discipline, promote, punish or reward.

Professionals These are positions for staff with high levels of qualifications and experience. The job roles are likely to involve a degree of decision making and responsibility for ensuring that task are carried out effectively to a high standard. Examples might include doctors, architects, stockbrokers, product designers, chefs and accountants.

Operatives These are positions for skilled workers who are involved in the production process or service provision. They carry out the instructions of managers or supervisors. In their own area of activity they may have to ensure targets are met and tasks are carried out effectively. Examples of operatives in business might include staff in:
- production, for example assembling a car or manufacturing furniture;
- warehousing, for example checking invoices against goods and ensuring effective deliveries;
- IT, for example giving technical support for machinery.

General staff There is a variety of positions in business which are carried out by staff with non-specific skills. They follow instructions given by superiors to carry out particular tasks and are an essential part of the production process or service provision. Examples might include checkout staff and shelf stackers in supermarkets, cleaners and receptionists in offices. They might also include general jobs on a farm or building site, such as cleaning out.

Although there may be similar generic job roles, there will be differences between organisations in the precise nature of these roles, relationships between various job roles, how they are managed and how decisions are made.

Organisation charts

Businesses often produce ORGANISATION CHARTS. These illustrate the structure of the business and the workforce roles of people employed with the business. Figure 1 shows a 'traditional' type of chart. It is a chart for an engineering firm, Able Engineering. It illustrates the formal relationship between different workforce roles and people in the business. Why do businesses draw such charts?
- To spot communication flow problems. An organisation chart indicates how employees are linked to other employees in the business. If information is not received, the business can find where the communication breakdown has occurred by tracing the communication chain along the chart.
- Organisation charts help individuals see their position in a business. This can help them appreciate the responsibilities that have been delegated to them, who has authority over them and who they are accountable to.
- Organisation charts allow firms to pinpoint areas where specialists are needed. For example, in Figure 1 Able Engineering recognises it needs designers and draughtspeople as part of the production 'team'.
- Organisation charts show how different sections of the firm relate to each other. For example, the chart for Able

Figure 2: Different chains of command and spans of control

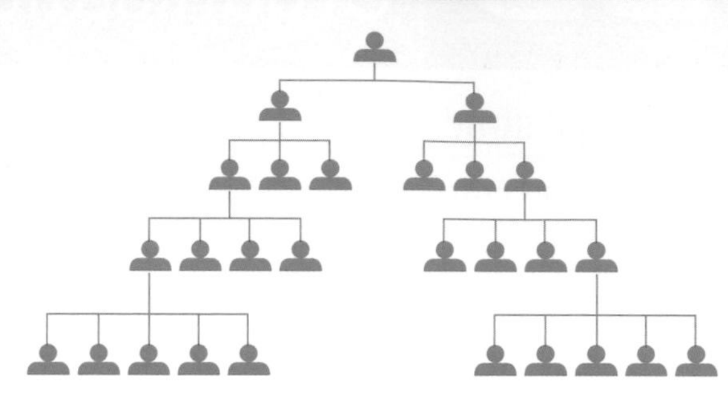

(a) A long chain of command and a narrow span of control. A production department may look like this. One manager is helped by a few assistant managers, each responsible for supervisors. These supervisors are responsible for skilled workers, who are in charge of a group of semi-skilled workers. Close supervision is needed to make sure quality is maintained. This is sometimes referred to as a tall organisational structure.

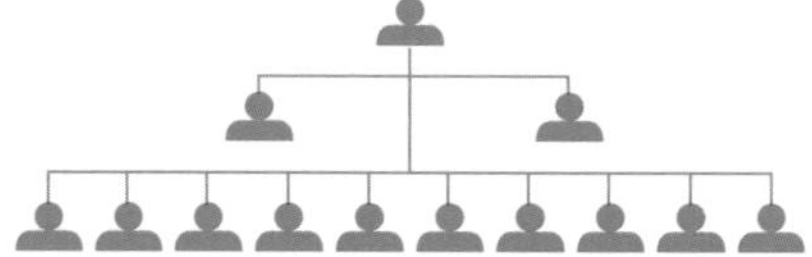

(b) A short chain of command and a wide span of control. A higher or further education department may look like this, with a 'head' of department, a few senior staff and many lecturing staff. Staff will want a degree of independence. This is sometimes referred to as a flat organisational structure.

Engineering shows the relationship between salespeople and technicians. They are both at the same level in the hierarchy, but work in different departments and are responsible to different managers.

Simply producing an organisation chart is of limited use to a business. The business will only achieve its objectives if it understands the relationships between employees and other parts of the business.

Key elements of organisational structures

Chain of command The HIERARCHY in a business is the levels of management in a business, from the lowest to the highest rank. It shows the CHAIN OF COMMAND within the organisation - the way authority is organised. Orders pass down the levels and information passes up. Businesses must also consider the number of links or levels in the chain of command. R. Townsend, in his book *Up the Organisation*, estimated that each extra level of management in the hierarchy reduced the effectiveness of communication by about 25 per cent. No rules are laid down on the most effective number of links in the chain. However, businesses generally try to keep chains as short as possible.

Span of control The SPAN OF CONTROL refers to the number of subordinates working under a superior or manager. In other words, if one production manager has ten subordinates his span of control is ten. Henri Fayol argued that the span of control should be between three and six because:

- there should be tight managerial control from the top of the business;
- there are physical and mental limitations to any single manager's ability to control people and activities.

A narrow span of control has the advantage for a firm of tight control and close supervision. It also allows better co-ordination of subordinates' activities. In addition, it gives managers time to think and plan without having to be burdened with too many day-to-day problems. A narrow span also ensures better communication with subordinates, who are sufficiently small in number to allow this to occur.

A wide span of control, however, offers greater decision-making authority for subordinates and may improve job satisfaction In addition, there are likely to be lower costs involved in supervision. Figure 2 shows two organisation charts. In the first (a), there is a long chain of command, but a narrow span of control. The second (b) shows a wide span, but a short chain.

Authority and responsibility Employees in the hierarchy will have RESPONSIBILITY and authority. However, these terms do not mean the same thing. Responsibility involves being accountable or being required to justify an action. So, for example, managers who are responsible for a department may be asked to justify poor performance to the board of directors. The personnel department may be responsible for employing workers. If a new worker was unable to do a particular job, they would be asked to explain why.

Authority, on the other hand, is the ability to carry out the task. For example, it would make no sense asking an office worker to pay company debts if she did not have the authority to sign cheques. Employees at lower levels of the hierarchy have less responsibility and authority than those further up. However, it may be possible for a superior to delegate (pass down) authority to a subordinate, eg a manager to an office worker, but retain responsibility. Increasingly, businesses are realising the benefits of delegating both authority and responsibility.

Line, staff and functional authority Line, staff and functional authority are terms used to describe the type of relationship that managers may have with others in the hierarchy.

Question 1.

Figure 3 shows part of an organisation chart for a UK engineering company.

Figure 3: Part of an organisation chart of a UK engineering company

Chief Executive
Director of Human Resources
Director of Marketing
Director of Production
Director of Finance
National Marketing Manager
Marketing Manager North West
Marketing Manager North East
Marketing Manager Midlands
Sales Rep.
Sales Rep.
Sales Rep.
Sales Rep.
Sales Rep.

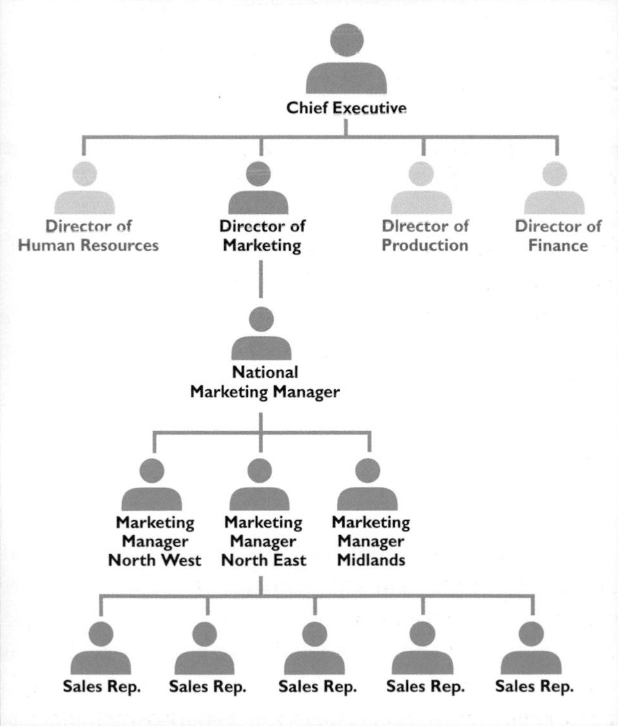

(a) The company sells into regional markets. How can this be seen from the chart?
(b) Describe the chain of command from Chief Executive to UK sales representative.
(c) How large is the span of control of the Marketing Manager?
(d) Who is immediately subordinate to the Director of Marketing?
(e) The Chief Executive is considering reducing the number of sales reps from five to three. How might this affect the Marketing Managers?

Question 2.

During 2007 BP aimed to cut overheads and re-energise the oil and gas company. Tony Hayward, the chief executive, insisted the overall strategy was not about 'cost reduction and cull', but about a radical change in culture. There were no specific numbers for how many staff would be cut, but Mr Hayward said it 'could be thousands over several years'.

The BP boss sent a message to his 100,000 staff outlining other plans to streamline the business into two basic units. This would be exploration and production on one side and refining and marketing on the other, similar to the type of structure at Exxon. The third segment, gas, power and renewables, is to be incorporated mainly into the other two.

A city analysts said, 'I think it is really good. This is copying the Exxon model of keeping things simple and ensuring unit managers are given responsibility but held accountable too.'

Mr Hayward promised that in future, corporate infrastructure would be 'rigorously' reviewed and up to four layers of management would be shed. 'Managers will be listening more acutely, particularly to frontline staff. We will make sure individuals are fully accountable for things they control,' he said.

Source: adapted from www.guardian.co.uk, 12.10.2007.

(a) Explain how the changes might affect: (i) employees at the businesses; (ii) management at the businesses; (iii) clients of the business.

(b) Discuss to what extent BP might experience resistance from managers and employees.

- **Line authority** is usual in a hierarchy. It shows the authority that a manager has over a subordinate. In Figure 1, the production director would have line authority over the designers. Communication will flow down from the superior to the subordinate in the chain of command. The advantage of this is that a manager can allocate work and control subordinates, who have a clear understanding of who is giving them instructions. The manager can also delegate authority to others if they feel this will make decision making more effective. In large organisations, the chain of command can be very long. This means that instructions given by those at the top of the chain of command may take time before they are carried out at a lower level.
- **Staff authority** might be when a manager or department in a business has a function within another department, for example, giving specialist advice. A marketing manager may give advice to the production department based on market research into a new product. Personnel managers have responsibilities for personnel matters in all departments. Although the specialist can give advice, they have no authority to make decisions in the other department.
- **Functional authority** is when a specialist has the authority to make a line manager accept his or her advice. It is different from staff authority, where the specialist can only advise. For example, the finance manager may have overall authority over the budget holder in the marketing department.

Problems may occur in a business if people do not understand where authority and responsibility rest. This means that managers must know whether their authority is line, staff or functional. Unfortunately, this can lead to friction. Line managers are sometimes thought of as 'first class citizens' and staff managers are thought of as costly 'overheads' who are not contributing anything of worth to the organisation. Also, the authority of functional managers is not accepted by line managers at times.

Delegation Managers are increasingly being asked to carry out strategic activities that affect the whole business. This has resulted in the need to DELEGATE activities for certain tasks to employees further down the hierarchy. Delegation can provide benefits to a business, as explained in the next section. When is delegation likely to be effective?

- Researchers such as Spetzer (1992) have suggested that employees need to be empowered in order to make effective decisions. They need to be given self-confidence and control of what they do.
- If managers only delegate when they are overloaded, subordinates may be resentful.
- Delegation requires planning. Managers must be clear about what needs to be done. Instead of freeing time, poor delegation may take up managers' time as they try to correct problems.
- Managers must take time to explain delegated tasks clearly. Employees may waste time or make mistakes because of lack of information. Telling subordinates why the work is important helps to create shared values.
- Allow participation. It is useful to discuss the task with those to whom it has been delegated. Subordinates will then know from the start what the task will include. It also helps managers to decide if delegation is appropriate. A person may feel they do not have the skills to carry out the task.
- The employee given a delegated task should also be given the authority and responsibility to carry it out. Managers must tell others in the business that the delegated person is acting on his or her behalf. This will avoid difficulties, such as the questioning of authority.
- Managers must avoid interfering with delegated tasks.
- Delegated tasks should be given to suitable employees. It would be inappropriate to delegate a marketing task to an employee in personnel. Employees must also have the training to carry out the task.
- Provide support and resources. If an employee is delegated a task without suitable support and resources this could lead to anxiety, frustration and the task being badly done.

Research has shown that when factors like these are taken into account, delegation was four times as likely to be successful.

Different forms of business structure

Despite the variety of formal business organisation that exists, there are four main types of structure most often found.

The entrepreneurial structure In this type of business structure, all decisions are made centrally. There are few collective decisions and a great reliance on 'key' workers. It is often found in businesses where decisions have to be made quickly, such as newspaper editing. Most small businesses also have this type of structure, as illustrated in Figure 4(a). These businesses rely on the expertise of one or two people to make decisions. Decision making is efficient up to a point because:

- decisions can be made quickly;
- subordinates understand to whom they are accountable;
- little consultation is required.

Figure 4: Alternative forms of organisation structure

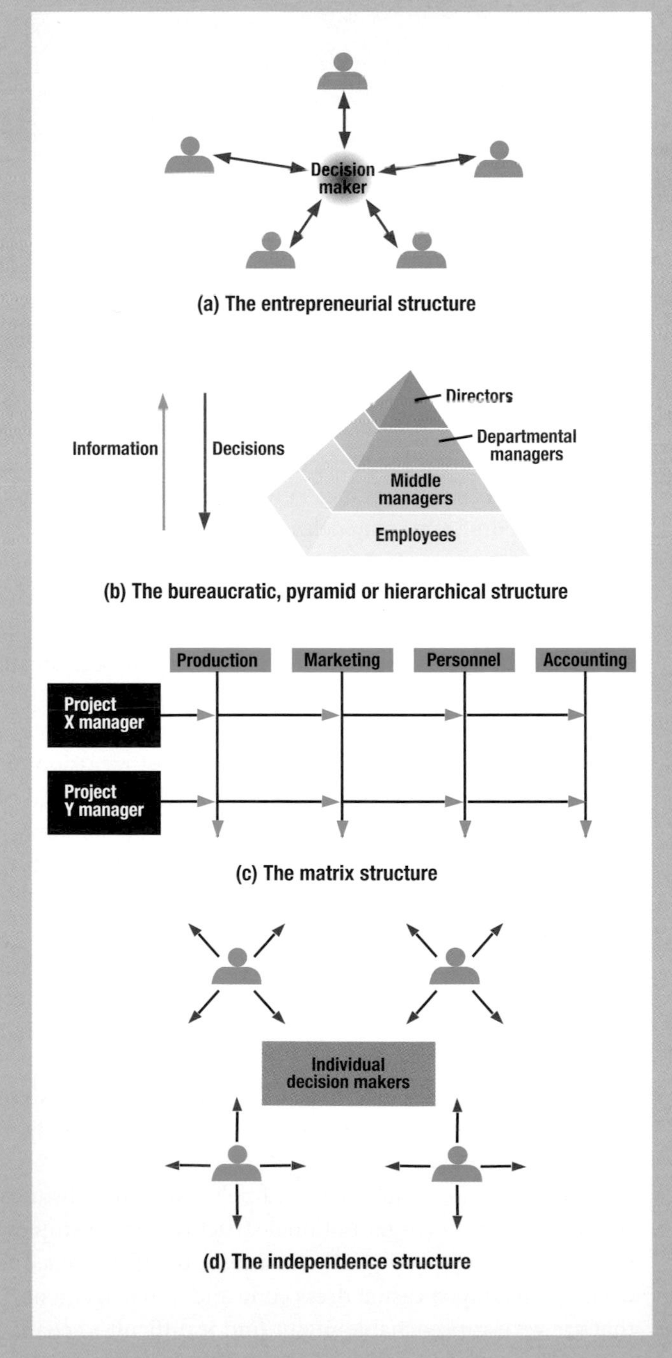

However, as the business grows, this structure can cause inefficiency as too much of a load is placed on those making decisions.

The bureaucratic, pyramid or hierachical structure This is the traditional hierachical structure for most medium-sized and large businesses and perhaps the most well known. It is illustrated in Figure 4(b). Decision making is shared throughout the business. Employees are each given a role and procedures are laid down which determine their behaviour at work. Specialisation of tasks is possible. This means that a departmental structure, with finance, personnel, production and marketing employees, can be set up. Specialisation may allow the business to enjoy economies of scale. Recently, this type of structure has been criticised for its inability to change and meet new demands.

The matrix structure This emphasises getting people with particular specialist skills together into project teams, as illustrated in Figure 4(c). Individuals within the team have their own responsibility. The matrix structure was developed to overcome some of the problems with the entrepreneurial and bureaucratic structures. Matrix management involves the co-ordinating and support of specialist teams within a matrix structure.

Managers often argue that this is the best way of organising people, because it is based on the expertise and skills of employees and gives scope for people lower down the organisation to use their talents effectively. For example, a project manager looking into the possibility of developing a new product may draw on the expertise of employees with skills in design, research and development, marketing, costing etc. A college running a course for unemployed people may draw on the skills of a number of lecturers in different departments. In this way, a matrix structure can also operate within a business that has a bureaucratic structure. The matrix model fits in with managers who have a Theory Y view of employees It is suggested that this structure improves flexibility and motivation of employees. It has recently lost favour because it often needs expensive support systems, such as extra secretarial and office staff. There may also be problems with co-ordinating a team drawn from different departments and the speed of decision making.

The independence structure This emphasises the individual and is almost a 'non-organisation'. The other three methods put together the contributions of a number of people so that the sum of their efforts is greater than the parts. All efforts are co-ordinated so that the business benefits. The independence structure is a method of providing a support system. Barristers' chambers and doctors' clinics have worked in this way. It is attractive to independent people who are confident of their ability to be successful. This form of organisation tends to be unsuitable for most types of business because of the lack of control and co-ordination.

Question 3.

The Manchester Film Association is an SME in the centre of the city's 'cultural quarter'. Its main activities are video, film and multimedia production. It employs nine full-time staff. Mike joined the company six months ago. He recently graduated, but has little work experience. However, he has proven so far in the work that he has done for clients to be innovative. He often has ideas that no-one else has considered. Shoaib has worked for the business for 15 years. He has built up considerable production and post-production skills. Lisa had previously set up her own website design and consultancy operation. She has experience in managing projects, working to deadlines and taking responsibility for clients' requests. The managing director of the business, Paula, has been approached by a fast growing leisure company to produce an innovative multimedia training programme on CD Rom for newly recruited employees. The company wants the programme to be interactive, but it must be ready within two months. Paula decided to ask Mike to look after the project.

Source: adapted from company information.

(a) Explain what type of organisational structure do you think might best reflect the business needs of Manchester Film Association.

Informal business structure

Organisation charts show the formal organisation of a business. However many relationships between employees in business are informal. The INFORMAL BUSINESS STRUCTURE is the network of relationships that develops between members on the basis of their common interests and friendships. These relationships can affect the way a business operates. A study of informal networks in the banking industry, for example, found three types of relationship.

- Advice networks - who depends on who to solve problems and provide information.
- Trust networks - which employees share potential information and back each other up in times of crisis.
- Communication networks - which employees regularly talk to each other on work related matters.

They recommended that businesses use informal structures to solve problems. For example, a study showed that a bank's task force group was unable to find ways of improving the bank's performance. The leader of the task force held a central position in the 'advice network'. Employees relied on her for technical advice. However, she only had one 'trust link' with a colleague. Management did not want to label the group as a failure or embarrass a valued employee by dismissing her as team leader. Instead, it redesigned the task force in line with the informal organisation of the business by adding a person in the trust network to share responsibility for group leadership.

Influences on organisational structures

Many businesses have traditional, hierarchical structures, with layers of management and employees. They face issues such as organising the span of control, chain of command, authority and responsibility. However, there are other organisational structures, including entrepreneurial and matrix and independence structures. A number of factors can influence the particular structure that a business might choose.

- **Size.** As a business grows, it is likely to move away from an entrepreneurial structure towards one where authority is passed to other employees. A large firm will also tend to have a longer chain of command, with more levels in the hierarchy.
- **Views of the owners or leadership styles.** If owners wish to retain control in the business, they will want a narrow span of control. Owners or managers who wish to motivate or encourage employees may delegate decision making.
- **Business objectives.** If the business decides to expand rapidly, perhaps by merger, it is likely to find that its span of control gets wider. An example might be a business setting up an operation in a foreign country or deciding to sell into a foreign market.
- **External factors.** Changes in external factors can often influence business organisation. In periods of recession or rising costs, a business may be forced to reduce its chain of command to cut costs. Similarly, in a period of economic growth, a firm may employ extra managers as specialists to gain economies of scale.
- **Changes in technology.** The introduction of new technology can change the structure of a business. For example, a new system of production may remove the need for quality controllers, or an information technology system could reduce the role of administration.
- **The informal structure.** If the informal structure does not complement and support the formal structure, this may lead to problems.
- **Corporate culture.** The norms of behaviour in a business might influence its organisational structure. For example, a business that has developed with a team based approach to decision making, a casual dress code and a management that are very approachable might find it difficult to change suddenly to a structure with layers of hierarchy and formal

decision making processes. Charles Handy in *Understanding Organisations* (1976) identified four cultures. The **power** culture is a structure with one powerful decision maker. The **role** culture is a structure where everyone in the hierarchy has a clear role. The **task** culture is a structure based on a team approach. The **person** culture is a structure with an emphasis on individuals.

Question 4.

Wesley Hains runs a card design business in Cardiff. He employs four staff - Laura, Mitchell, Kieran and Ella. Laura manages the office in Cardiff dealing with telephone and email enquiries, visitors, administration and a small amount of marketing. Mitchell, Kieran and Ella are card designers and all work from home in various parts of the country. Mitchell lives and works in a small croft in Glen Cona in North West Scotland. The designers are all linked by computer to the main Cardiff office. This ensures good communications. For example, design briefs are sent direct by Wesley using email and design copy is transmitted direct to Wesley's terminal when designs are completed. Some specialisation takes place amongst the designers. Mitchell designs birthday cards, Kieran designs postcards and Ella works on specialist projects. Wesley is occupied with customers, ensuring that design briefs are satisfied by his designers and looking for new business. He spends three days a week out of the office.

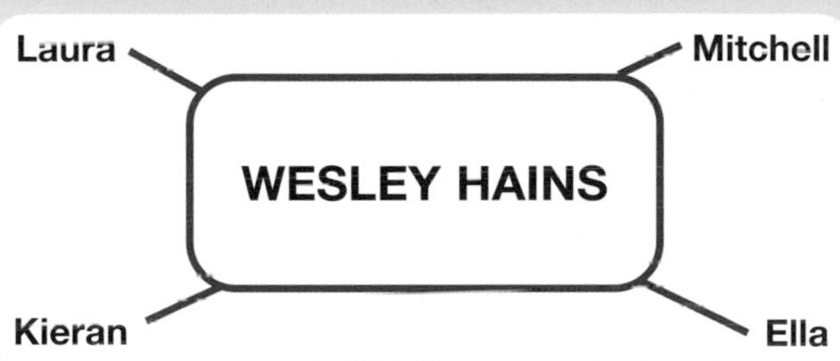

(a) In September, Wesley secured a contract with an American card manufacturer. Wesley had to recruit four more designers as a result. He decided to employ a full-time salesperson to sell designs in the US. He also bought a small printing business in Newport to print and supply cards as well as designing them. Explain why Wesley might decide to change the organisational structure of his business.

KEYTERMS

Authority - the right to command a situation, a task or an activity.
Chain of command - the way authority and power are passed down in a business.
Delegation - authority (and sometimes responsibility) to pass down from superior to subordinate.
Formal organisation - the relationships between employees and the organisational structure determined by the business, as shown in an organisation chart.
Hierarchy - the order or levels of management of a business, from the lowest to the highest.
Informal business structure - the relationships between employees that are based on the common interests of employees.
Organisation chart - a diagram which illustrates the structure of an organisation.
Organisational or business structure - the way in which a business is organised.
Responsibility - being accountable and required to justify an action.
Span of control - the number of subordinates working under a superior.

KNOWLEDGE

1. What are the features of the internal structure of a business?
2. How might an organisation chart be used in a firm's induction programme?
3. Draw a simple organisation chart showing:
   (a) a partnership with two partners and six employees;
   (b) a large company with a board of directors, six departments, and two more levels in the hierarchy.
4. What is meant by a 'wide span of control'?
5. What problems might a 'wide span of control' have for a business?
6. Explain the difference between line, staff and functional authority.
7. What factors influence effective delegation?
8. Why is empowerment important when tasks are delegated?
9. What problems might a matrix structure cause for a business?
10. What type of business might be organised with:
    (a) an entrepreneurial structure;
    (b) an independence structure?
11. Why is it important for businesses to understand their informal business structures?
12. Identify six factors that could affect the choice of organisational structure.

Case Study: Avalanche

Avalanche control operations at the Lake Louise Ski Area have a history spanning nearly 30 years. Lake Louise is in the Banff National Park in Canada. The area currently receives half a million guests per year for skiing, snowboarding and related activities. Safety is a key aspect and part of that relates to the danger of avalanches of snow burying skiers in their wake. The ski resort covers over 17 square kilometres and there are over 100 places where avalanches can occur. In addition, some skiers deliberately go outside the resort area for the thrill of skiing in uncrowded, uncontrolled areas. But this increases the number of potential avalanche areas.

In the 1980s, there were effectively three separate departments working on the mountain. The main responsibility of the Ski Patrol was pre-hospital care for skiers who had accidents. For the Warden/Ski Patrol Avalanche Crew, it was monitoring and controlling avalanches. For the Trail Crew, it was managing the slopes, including putting up fencing. However, there was overlap between the three departments. Members of the Trail Crew, for example, would organise help if they were first on the scene at an accident.

These three departments were then reorganised into one Snow Safety Department. This was partly prompted by budget costs. The previous three departments had over 40 staff in total. The new single department now consisted of just 25 staff. Efficiency gains were possible because staff were used more intensively. In particular, on the mountain, patrollers were expected to perform any of the functions which before had been the main responsibility of just one of the departments.

Under the new structure, shown in Figure 5, a Snow Safety Manager was put in charge of the whole department, answerable to the Area Manager for the ski resort. Beneath the Snow Safety Manager in the hierarchy are three Snow Safety Supervisors. Two of these are Avalanche Forecasters and one is a Patrol Leader. Working under the the Snow Safety Supervisors are four Senior Avalanche Patrollers. Their main duties are as Team Leaders in snow research and avalanche control. In addition, they have become involved in other facets of the department, such as training and acting as roving 'troubleshooters'. They are not scheduled into the daily routine of run checks and accident coverage or to patrol specific areas. In addition, there are five Senior Patrollers and 13 Patrollers who have as their primary responsibilities pre-hospital care and risk management (in the form of run checks and trail work). These 18 people also act as Avalanche Team Members on a rotating basis wherever needed. Generally, between two and five teams are used daily for research and control, depending on conditions.

Adapted from a paper by Mark Klassen, Skiing Louise Ltd, Alberta, Canada.

(a) Explain what is meant by the terms: (i) 'hierarchy'and (3 marks) (ii) 'department' (3 marks).

(b) (i) Explain what is the span of control of the Snow Safety Manager shown in Figure 5. (3 marks). (ii) Explain to whom the Patrol Leader, who is one of the three Snow Safety Supervisors, might delegate a task. (3 marks)

(c) Analyse how the change in structure between the 1980s and the 1990s described in the data has affected job roles, responsibilities and communication. (8 marks)

(d) Discuss the possible costs and benefits of delegating greater authority and responsibility further down the hierarchy. (10 marks)

Figure 5: Organisation chart: Snow Safety Department

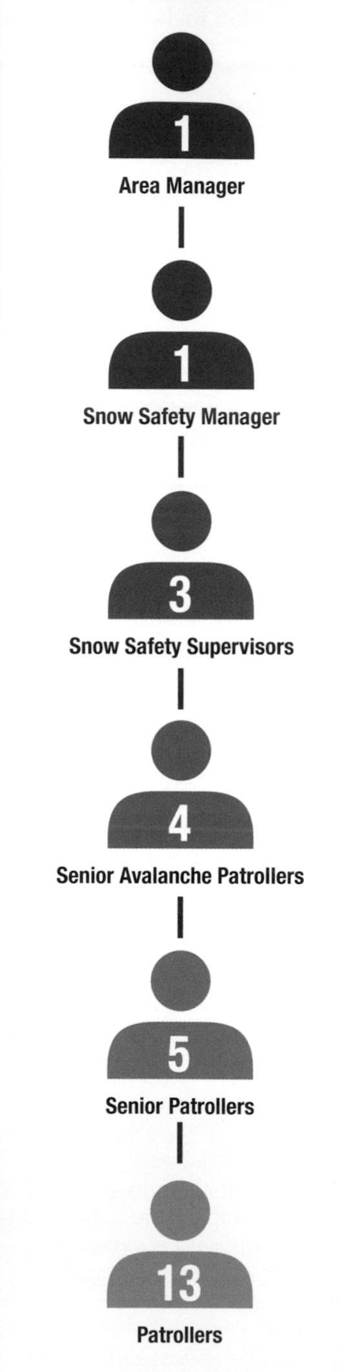

60 Business organisation

How are businesses organised?

All businesses need to organise their activities. Running a business involves planning, decision making, co-ordination and communication. In order to simplify these complex tasks it is helpful to organise the business into a number of clearly defined sections. For example, a business selling books to customers by mail order from a warehouse may be organised into a number of departments.

- Buying and marketing. This department purchases books from publishers. It also deals with advertising and handles the production of the mail order catalogue.
- Warehousing/dispatch. This department stores books delivered to the warehouse and deals with requests for books from the orders department. It is then responsible for putting together customers' orders and checking, wrapping, addressing and transporting parcels.
- Orders. This department receives orders from customers and informs the warehouse. It also processes all the paperwork involved in the buying and selling of books.
- Administration and finance. This department deals with payments and receipts of cash. It also handles all the personnel work, including staff wages.

This type of STRUCTURE is simple but effective. Staff in each department will understand their role. They will also know what other departments are doing in relation to their own. Small businesses may feel that they do not need to organise themselves in this way. However, as businesses grow, so does the need for organisation. Without this, the efficiency of a business could suffer. Communications may break down, mistakes might be made and staff may become confused about their roles.

The mail order business described here is organised by function. This is explained in the next section. There are other methods of organising a business which may be more suitable in certain situations. Large businesses often combine different methods of organisation to gain the benefits of each.

Organisation by function

One of the most common methods of organising a business is by function. This is where a business is divided into different sections or departments according to the operation undertaken. Typical functional departments in many larger businesses include production, marketing, finance and personnel. There is a number of advantages for a business in organising itself in this way.

- Specialisation. It allows each department to focus on just one business area. Specialist staff can be employed in each department. For example, the finance department may employ management and financial accountants and credit

Question 1.

Wycombe Holdings designs and manufactures hand made furniture for retailers. However, it has recently developed an Internet shopping service where members of the public can buy furniture directly from the factory online. The company is organised into departments as shown in Figure 1.

(a) Analyse the advantages to Wycombe Holdings of using the above method of organisation.

Figure 1: Wycombe Holdings, organisational structure

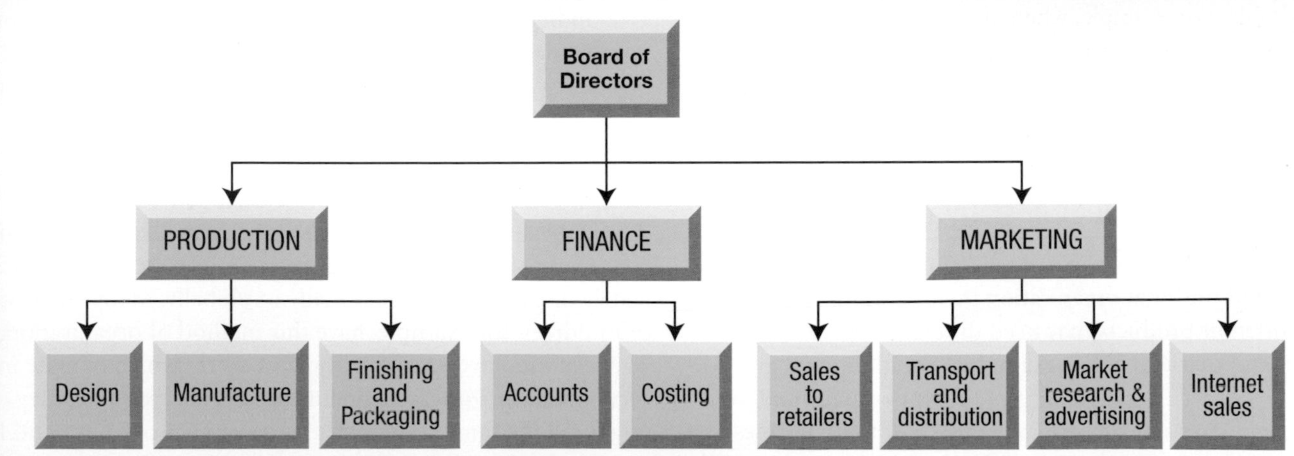

controllers. Specialisation should help to improve efficiency.
- Accountability. Each department is likely to have a manager who will be responsible for allocating departmental resources, employing staff and achieving departmental goals. The manager will be accountable to a senior executive and will be under pressure to perform. This method of organisation also allows a business to organise itself into cost or profit centres. For example, if a business decides to make one department into a cost centre, it may have to keep its costs within a limit. This will help accountability.
- Clarity. Organisation by function helps staff to understand their role and position in the business structure. For example, staff are likely to be trained in their department, will be familiar with their superiors and will know where to seek help and support.

This method of organisation will also have some drawbacks.
- Communication and co-ordination problems. When businesses are divided by function they often operate as self-contained units. Communication between departments may be limited, resulting in a lack of information sharing and some unnecessary duplication. Senior management may struggle with co-ordination if departments pursue their own objectives rather than those of the whole company. Individual departments may also be reluctant to work with other departments on projects.
- Inertia. Individual departments may become 'set in their ways' over time. They may try to resist change and prefer to continue their current practices.
- Bureaucracy. Organisations may become too bureaucratic. For example, there may be a large increase in paperwork if every communication from one department to another has to be made via memo or if transactions between departments require written confirmation. Email and company **intranets** may solve this problem to some extent. However, time may still be wasted responding to requests.
- Suitability. Very large companies with a diversified product range could find this method of organisation unsuitable. For example, when an organisation grows there will be more departments and more layers of management. In this case senior management may find it increasingly difficult to influence what is happening lower down.

Organisation by product or activity

When a business produces a wide range of different goods or services it could find that organisation by function is not effective. Different products may need different approaches to production and marketing. For example, a multinational group may operate a supermarket chain, a property company and a construction business. It is possible that each of these businesses may have different approaches to marketing which take into account the needs of their markets. It is also possible that different staff with different skills will be needed.

Large diversified companies often organise their business by grouping together different functional staff who are involved in the production of the same product lines or activities.

This method of organisation is often seen as 'a business within a business' and has a number of advantages.
- Each division is able to focus on the needs of a particular market segment. Thus, customers should find that their needs are satisfied more effectively.
- Each division is likely to operate as a profit centre. This will help to measure the performance of each division and allow comparisons in the business. Poor performing sections can be identified and action taken.
- Healthy competition may take place between each division. This could improve the overall performance of the organisation.
- There may be scope for reorganisation. Organisation by product provides some flexibility for the future. Loss making divisions can be closed down. Divisions supplying similar markets can be merged. Businesses that are bought by the company can be absorbed more easily. Divestment (selling) of parts of the business should also be easier.
- Co-operation may improve. Because each division is pursuing the same goal, e.g. profit, it is possible to share expertise and ancillary services. For example, the Burton Group, in the above illustration, might use the same transport fleet to serve all of its branches.

Disadvantages of organisation by product include the following.
- There may be a duplication of functions in different departments. For example, an accountant may be employed in each division. It may be more cost effective to employ a small team of specialist accountants for the whole organisation.
- Competition between divisions may become counter-productive. This is likely to occur when divisions compete for the organisation's resources. A division which fails to obtain resources may become poorly motivated.
- Senior management might lose control over each individual division. For example, a decision by a junior manager in one division to extend credit to customers for longer than company policy allows might go unnoticed.

Organisation by area

Some businesses prefer to organise their activities on a geographical or regional basis. This is particularly the case if a business has a large number of very similar operations which are widely dispersed either nationally or globally. Many chain stores or multiples, for example, have this method of organisation. They tend to have a large number of stores which operate in a very similar or sometimes identical way. For example, they might sell the same products, use the same procedures and look very similar. The stores are then grouped together in regions and will be accountable to a regional or area manager. Multinational businesses operating in many different countries may also organise themselves into regions of the world, such as Europe, North America and the Far East. The advantages of organising a business geographically include the following.

- Local needs. Sometimes the needs of customers, employees and the community vary in different geographical regions. If a business is organised regionally then it should be able to serve the needs of local people more easily. This is particularly the case for multinational companies. For example, the needs of Middle Eastern customers may be different from those of North American customers.
- Improved communications. Operating on a regional basis should improve communications. For example, a regional manager may be able to more easily inform local shops of a decision than all retail outlets. To some extent this benefit is not as important today as information and communication technology allows fast and easy communication around the world.
- Competition. It may be possible to encourage healthy internal competition between different regions in the organisation. For example, prizes or bonuses are sometimes awarded to those regions with the highest sales or profits. In addition, regions are often used as training grounds for senior management.

Some disadvantages of regional organisation include the following.

- Duplication of resources. As with some other methods of organisation, it may not be cost effective for each region to provide certain specialist services, such as accountancy and research and development.
- Conflict. It is possible that local managers may begin to introduce their own policies. They might argue that their local situation requires a different approach from that of the business. This might lead to conflict with senior management as they see their authority being undermined.

Question 2.

Unilever is a multinational company, which manufactures food and home and personal care products. Some of its well known brands include Knorr soups and snacks, Magnum and Cornetto ice creams, Lipton teas, Findus frozen food meals, Dove soap and OMO washing detergent. Figure 2 provides two pieces of analysis of sales.

Figure 2: Unilever, leading category positions and global presence

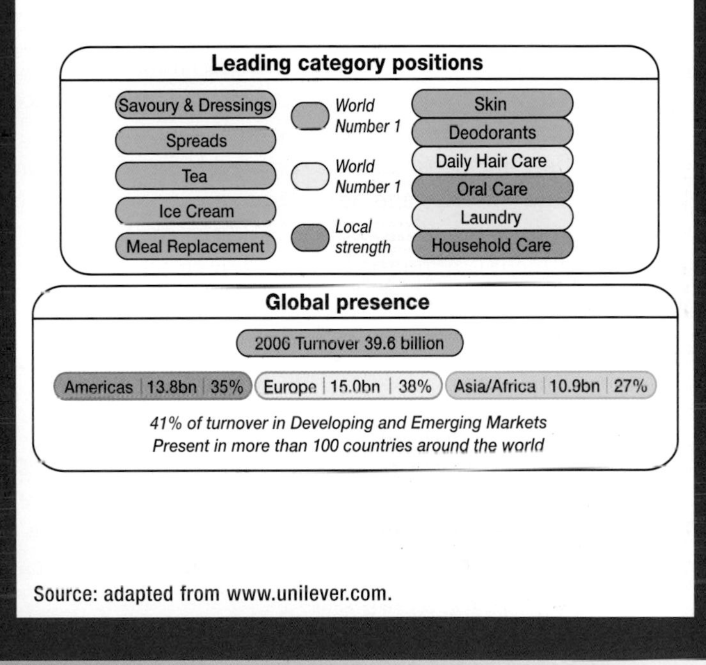

Source: adapted from www.unilever.com.

(a) What two methods of organisation are suggested by Figure 2? Explain your answer.

(b) Analyse the possible reasons why the business might have organised itself using two methods.

Organisation by customer

This method is similar to organising a business by product. It involves grouping together employees who deal with a specific customer or group. This method is particularly useful where the needs of distinct customer groups are different. For example, an advertising agency might organise itself according to customer. Senior staff may be given the accounts of the most important customers. This method of organisation has a number of advantages.

- Customer needs. The needs of different customers will be served more effectively by a department focused on one particular service. Also, customers might prefer to do business with a company that is sensitive to specific customer needs.
- Market segmentation. A business may divide its market into different market segments.

However, there may also be some difficulties.

- Customer definition. It is not always possible to clearly define a particular customer group. For example, students at university may be taking a modular course, which involves more than one faculty. This may cause problems for students if different faculties operate in different ways.
- Inefficiency. It is possible that some departments are too small because they do not have enough customers. In this case costs per customer could be high. This may affect the profitability of the whole organisation.
- Control and co-ordination. As with other methods of organisation where the company is split into discrete divisions, there may be problems of control and co-ordination. Communication between departments may be limited, individual departments may pursue their own goals and senior management may find it difficult to control the organisation.

Organisation by process

The production of some products or services requires a series of processes. Departments could be established to take responsibility for each process. For example, a clothing company manufacturing children's clothes may be divided into departments. Each department operates in its own workshop in the factory.

- The first stage in the production process may be design. This department would be responsible for designing new clothes and producing computerised patterns for the cutting department.
- In the cutting department fabrics are cut to size by computer operated machines. The cut fabrics are then taken to the sewing department. Here the separate pieces of fabric are sewn together to form clothes.
- The finishing department is responsible for adding seams, frills, buttons, zips and other accessories.
- The last process in the sequence is dispatch. This department is responsible for packing the clothes and preparing the products for distribution to retailers.

Organisation by process is very similar to organisation by function and has similar benefits. Teams of staff in each department may be more focused. The company may enjoy the advantages of specialisation. There is likely to be regular communication between each stage in the production process. Management will be able to monitor clearly the performance of each department. The main disadvantage of organisation by process is a lack of flexibility. It may be difficult to switch staff from one process to another. This may be because they are not trained to work in other departments or because they do not wish to transfer. In addition, departments will have to operate at the same pace. For example, if the cutting department slows down, resources in the sewing department may lay idle. Communications problems may also arise.

KEYTERMS

Structure of a business – the way in which a business is organised.

KNOWLEDGE

1. What is meant by organisation by function?
2. Why might a business be organised in more than one way?
3. State two advantages and two disadvantages of a functional organisational structure.
4. Describe the advantages of a company organising itself by product.
5. When is regional organisation likely to be an appropriate method of organisation for a business?
6. Why might solicitors organise themselves according to customer group?
7. What is meant by organisation by process?
8. Suggest two types of business that may organise themselves by process.

Case Study: StarCars

StarCars was formed in 1994 by Ernie Anderson. He started by purchasing a Porsche 911 and hiring it out in his home town of Oxford. Demand for the car was unbelievable. By 1996 he had bought another Porsche, a Ferrari and an Aston Martin and was beginning to develop a profitable business. By 2002 he had five car hire centres - a head office and centre in Oxford, centres in Reading and Watford, and two others in London. The business was organised as shown in Figure 3.

By 2008 StarCars had another 14 centres, as shown on Figure 4. But some serious problems had arisen.

- There were communication problems. Staff in other centres often found it difficult to sort out wage queries with Oxford. Also, when a centre had a problem, such as a customer dispute, it

Figure 3: Organisation chart for StarCars

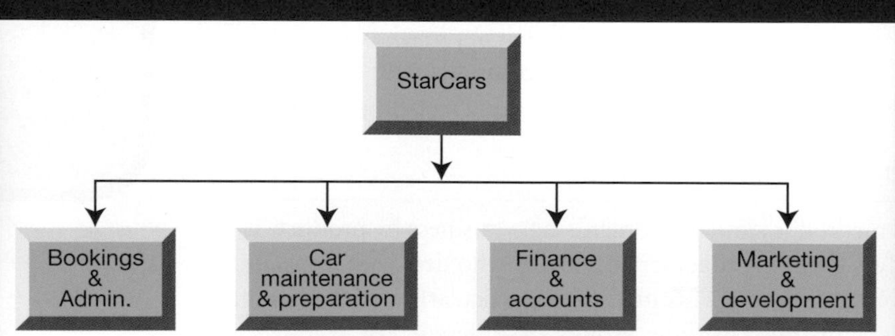

- **Bookings & Admin.** Each centre had one full-time and two part-time staff handling bookings and administration. They dealt with customers when they booked cars, picked them up and dropped them off.
- **Car maintenance and preparation.** A 'mobile' mechanic was based at Oxford, but dealt with maintenance work on all of the cars. In each centre one person cleaned the cars and prepared them for customers before they were picked up.
- **Finance and accounts.** Two people were employed at Oxford to process wages, deal with staff problems, record business transactions, produce accounts and carry out purchasing.
- **Marketing and business development.** This section was set up when the business started to expand. Ernie played an important role, but also hired two other staff to help him. This part of the business bought the cars. It was time consuming because the cars were expensive and required research, comprehensive knowledge, sound negotiation skills and careful judgment. The role of one of the staff was to advertise the business and find suitable sites for new centres.

Figure 4: StarCar centres in 2004

was difficult to settle because no one seemed to have any authority. Ernie, who made all the key decisions, was often unavailable.

- Because of the distances involved, the mobile mechanic found it impossible to maintain cars all over the country. The mechanic was overworked, even though eventually an assistant was employed.
- Ernie worried about the accountability of each centre. Although he trusted the majority of his staff, he felt that there was not enough incentive for each centre to maximise performance.
- Because of the geographical distance between centres, staff felt isolated. There was often a lack of leadership and some staff became demotivated. Staff turnover had also risen, particularly in the centres away from the South East.

Ernie felt that the solution was to organise the company geographically. Looking at Figure 5, he thought that the company could be divided into six areas. It would be necessary to appoint a manager responsible for each region and delegate a lot more responsibility. Regional managers would make daily visits to each centre in the region, recruit staff, and attend a management meeting with Ernie every two weeks in Birmingham. Managers could take decisions on behalf of their region without consulting Ernie.

Ernie decided to outsource all car maintenance to another business and to allow managers to buy cars for their region based on regional demand. However, managers would have to be carefully trained in this task. Ernie also decided to pay managers a low basic salary, but offer an incentive package based on the amount of time cars were hired out. If cars were hired out 80 per cent of the time an annual bonus of £10,000 would be paid. If this rose to 95 per cent a further £17,000 would be paid. Ernie expected all managers to reach the first target and the company would make a reasonable profit based on this performance. However, the second target was likely to be more of a challenge.

(a) **Explain why you think Ernie organised StarCars by function initially. (6 marks)**

(b) **Draw the new organisational chart suggested by Ernie, based on geographical location in Figure 4. (8 marks)**

(c) **Explain why organisation by product might be inappropriate for StarCars. (6 marks)**

(d) **Explain why accountability is likely to improve after the reorganisation. (12 marks)**

(e) **To what extent will the new organisation structure help overcome the problems StarCars is experiencing? (18 marks)**

61 Measuring the effectiveness of the workforce

Measuring personnel effectiveness

Advocates of human resource management (HRM) claim that the performance of the workforce is enhanced through adopting appropriate personnel policies. In many other areas of business, such as finance or production, there is a large number of possible measures of performance, from sales revenue to profit after tax to output per day. In personnel, there are fewer key measures. Some of these only point indirectly at key variables. For example, it is not possible to measure directly:

- the motivation of a workforce;
- the ability of a workforce to accept and implement change;
- the teamworking capabilities of workers;
- the commitment of workers to the business;
- the contribution of £1 spent on personnel such as higher pay or spending on training to profit.

However, there are a few measures which can be used, including labour productivity, absenteeism rates, labour turnover, working days lost for health and safety reasons and wastage rates.

Labour productivity

Labour productivity is defined as output per worker. As a formula:

$$\text{Labour productivity} = \frac{\text{Total output (per period of time)}}{\text{Average number of employees (per period of time)}}$$

Labour productivity is an important measure of the efficiency of a workforce. For example, if there are two teams of workers in a factory, each with identical equipment and the same number of workers, then the team with the highest productivity could be identified as the most effective team.

Figures for labour productivity need to be used with caution. For example, differences in labour productivity between factories or plants may be accounted for by differences in equipment used rather than the efficiency of the workforce. A plant with newer equipment is likely to have higher labour productivity than one with old equipment. Equally, productivity differs widely between processes within a business and between businesses in different industries. A highly automated section of a factory is likely to have much higher labour productivity than a labour-intensive packing section in the same factory using little capital equipment. Manufacturing industry may have a higher average labour productivity than service industries simply because more capital is used per employee in manufacturing.

A business wishing to improve the labour productivity of groups of workers can adopt a number of strategies.

- Improving the capital equipment with which they work.
- Changing the way in which workers are employed, for example, moving from an assembly line production system to a cell production system.
- Disappointing labour productivity may be due to a lack of training on the part of workers. Increased training may therefore raise productivity.
- Changing the reward system may increase motivation and commitment and so improve productivity. There are many other ways that motivation may be increased. These include changing the structure of the business and devolving decision making power down the chain of command.

Increasing labour productivity is generally assumed to increase the competitiveness of a business. Higher labour productivity should drive down costs, allowing a business either to lower its prices and so gain higher sales, or to keep its prices the same but increase its profit margins.

However, businesses sometimes find that they become less competitive despite increasing their labour productivity. This may occur for a number of reasons.

- Rival businesses may increase their productivity at an even faster rate.
- New rival businesses may set up which pay considerably lower wages. Many UK manufacturing businesses have become less competitive over the past ten years due to the emergence of competition from low wage, low cost businesses in the Far East and eastern Europe.
- Other factors apart from cost may change adversely for a business. For example, a rival business may bring out a far better new product. However, productive the workforce and however low the cost, customers may prefer to buy the new product rather than a cheaper old product.

Absenteeism

Absenteeism is a problem for all businesses for a number of reasons.

- Staff who are absent often claim to be ill. The business then, in most cases, has to pay sick pay.
- If temporary staff are brought in to cover for absent staff, this leads to increased costs. Equally, costs will increase if permanent staff have to work overtime and are paid at higher rates than their basic rate of pay.
- Output may suffer if workers are expected to cover for sick colleagues or if temporary staff are not as productive as the absent workers.
- Prolonged absences can lead to major disruption if the worker is key to a particular area of work or a new project.
- If production is delayed or there are problems with quality, customers can be lost.

Question 1.

The NHS Executive has introduced the labour productivity index for all NHS trusts in England. The index is a measure of the value of the output per trust employee. It is calculated by multiplying each type of activity, eg inpatients, outpatients, health visitor contacts, by its average cost, adding all these costs together and dividing the total by the number of employees in the trust. The index allows trusts to compare their labour productivity with others. It may also be a useful tool in contract negotiations. Theoretically, a trust with a labour productivity index of 6000 can be interpreted not only as being more productive than a trust with an index of 3000, but of being twice as productive.

This simple interpretation however, is not without difficulties. Major areas of activity, such as research and diagnostic services, are excluded, distorting the index. It is also assumed that those activities included are the same in each trust. This does not take into account variations in the quality or effectiveness of different contacts. Another problem is that the effort (cost, labour, etc) to produce one 'unit' of activity will vary across trusts and will depend on patient characteristics such as age or complexity. Further, only full-time staff are included but many trusts subcontract work.

Source: adapted from *British Medical Journal*, 2006.

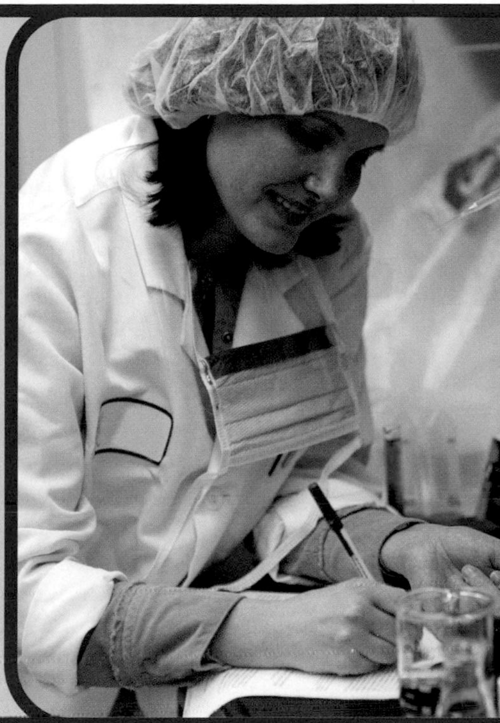

(a) How is the productivity of employees in the NHS being measured?
(b) Explain how the measurement of employees' productivity can benefit NHS trusts.
(c) Discuss how useful the labour productivity index will be in measuring NHS employees' productivity.

- Absenteeism can be demotivating to staff left to cope with the problems.
- The higher the rate of absenteeism, the more likely it is that workers will report ill. This is because a culture of absenteeism will develop where it becomes acceptable for workers to take extra days holiday by reporting in sick.

The RATE OF ABSENTEEISM or ABSENTEEISM RATE or ABSENTEE RATE can be calculated by dividing the number of staff absent by the total number of staff employed. The rate is expressed as a percentage. It can be calculated as a daily rate using the formula:

$$\frac{\text{Number of staff absent on a day}}{\text{Total number of staff employed}} \times 100\%$$

For example, if 1,000 staff are employed, and 30 are absent on a particular day, then the rate of absenteeism for that day is 3 per cent (100% x 30 ÷ 1,000). If the rate of absenteeism for a year is calculated, the total number of staff days lost through absenteeism must by divided by the number of staff days that should have been worked over the year. This is calculated using the formula:

$$\frac{\text{Total number of staff absence days over the year}}{\text{Total number of staff days that should have been worked}} \times 100\%$$

For example, assume 6,000 staff days were lost through absence. There were 500 staff, each of whom should have worked 240 days during the year. So the total number of staff days that should have been worked was 120,000 (500 x 240). The rate of absenteeism was therefore 5 per cent (100% x 6,000 ÷ 120,000).

Rates of absenteeism can be calculated for a business as a whole and compared to industry averages or national averages. They can also be compared between one part of a business and another or compared over time. Differences in rates of absenteeism occur for a number of reasons.

- Small businesses tend to have lower rates of absenteeism than larger businesses. Arguably this is because there is much more commitment and feeling of teamwork in a small business than in a large business. Workers in large businesses can feel that no-one will suffer if they take a day off work and so absenteeism is acceptable.
- Health and safety is a factor. Businesses which have good health and safety procedures will tend to suffer less illness-related absenteeism than those with poor procedures. Equally, some jobs are inherently more dangerous to health than others and so absenteeism is more likely.
- The nature of the tasks given to workers is another factor. Tasks which are fragmented and repetitive lead to low job satisfaction and demotivation. This encourages workers to report sick. Workers in jobs which are interesting and rewarding tend to have lower absentee rates.
- The culture of a workplace can cause absenteeism. Where workers are overworked, where there is a climate of intimidation and bullying by superiors of subordinates, and where the needs of workers are ignored, work-related stress becomes much more common. Workers off through stress are a particular problem because they often take months off work at a time.
- Stress-related illness is also more common where workers are oversupervised and feel that they are not trusted by their superiors to accomplish tasks.

- Workers who feel that they are grossly underpaid are more likely to take time off work. They see it as compensation for the lack of monetary reward they receive. Low pay is also a demotivator and so contributes to absenteeism.

Businesses can adopt a variety of methods to reduce absenteeism. Some assume that absenteeism is mainly caused by inappropriate or a lack of human resource management policies. Problems such as lack of commitment, low motivation, bullying, oversupervision and perceptions of low pay can be tackled through methods such as more teamwork, devolving power down the chain of command, more democratic leadership, better reward systems and policies which make bullying and harassment at work a major disciplinary offence. Health and safety issues can be addressed through the rigourous application of a well thought out health and safety policy. Adoption of lean production techniques are also likely to improve absenteeism rates.

The UK government in the early 2000s stressed the importance of a WORK LIFE BALANCE in dealing with a number of HR issues including absenteeism. Absenteeism can be caused by conflicts between work and family commitments, or work and leisure goals. A parent may phone in sick when in fact he or she is having to stay at home to look after his or her ill eight year old. Or a worker may phone in sick on a Monday morning because he can't face work after a weekend's activities. The solution is for more flexible working patterns. For example, workers may be able to take a few hours off work if they work them at some other time in the week or the month. Or workers may have a number of individual days holiday a year which can be taken without giving notice. Or a worker may have the right permanently to the number of hours worked per week, changing for example from full time to three days a week.

On the other hand, a scientific management approach would tend towards the introduction of systems of rewards and punishments. Cutting down the number of days when staff can claim sick pay is one measure. Another is for superiors to monitor closely staff who are absent. Telephoning them or even visiting them in their homes when they are off sick can be effective in deterring absenteeism. Being prepared to sack staff who abuse the system can also be an important deterrent to the rest of the workforce. Some employers offer bonuses to workers who have not had time off work due to illness. A few even offer all their staff a number of paid days off work each year which can be taken when staff don't feel like going into work or have problems with childcare arrangements.

Another policy which is frequently advocated is 'back to work' interviews. Any member of staff who has been absent has to be interviewed by a superior about why they were absent. This can be seen from a human relations school perspective as supportive of the worker. Their superior cares for them enough to want to know why they were away. Equally it can be judged from a scientific management school perspective. The superior is checking up on the worker to see whether the absence was genuine.

Question 2.

Royal Mail's cure for Britain's £1.75bn problem of absenteeism is simple - a Ford car and holiday vouchers. Its incentive scheme has improved attendance levels by more than 10 per cent in six months, equivalent to 1,000 extra staff. It is so pleased that it is extending the scheme for 12 months. Under the initial scheme staff who worked for six months without a day off work sick were entered for a prize draw. More than half of the 170,000 employees at Royal Mail and Parcelforce Worldwide qualified. Thirty-seven won a new Ford Focus car, worth £12,000 each and 75 won the £2,000 holiday vouchers. Even the 90,000 who qualified for the draw but missed out got a £150 holiday voucher.

Royal Mail will not say how much the scheme cost, but insists it makes financial and commercial sense. 'The employees like it, as a company we like it - we have 1,000 more people every day than we would otherwise have had if nothing had changed. It benefits the customers too because good attendance goes hand in glove with good quality of service', said a Royal Mail spokesperson. Some have estimated the costs at £1.9m before allowing for any discounts.

The company denies it is putting pressure on genuinely ill workers to turn up for work. Its people and operational development director, said 'We must support and reward postmen and women. They deserve it. They do a demanding job to a high standard, day in and day out, in all weathers.'

The Communication Workers Union had a more old-fashioned explanation for the fall in absenteeism - better pay and conditions. The union's deputy general secretary said: 'Giveaways are not the reason why attendance levels have improved and they are certainly not a substitute for continuing to invest in our members' overall employment package.'

Source: adapted from *The Guardian*, 26.4.2005.

(a) Why is it important for the Royal Mail to measure absenteeism rates?

(b) Examine the advantages and disadvantages of the scheme to reduce absenteeism at Royal Mail for (i) the business and (ii) its employees.

(c) Discuss whether the scheme is likely to be more effective than 'better pay and conditions'.

Labour turnover

Labour or staff turnover is another measure of personnel effectiveness. **Labour turnover** is the proportion of staff leaving a business over a period of time. It is measured by the formula:

$$\text{Labour turnover} = \frac{\text{Number of staff leaving over a period of time}}{\text{Average number of staff in post during the period}} \times 100\%$$

For example, if 20 staff left over a year and there were on average 40 on the staff, then the staff turnover would be 50 per cent (100% x 20 ÷ 40).

As with other measures of personnel performance, labour turnover differs from department to department within a business, from business to business within an industry and from industry to industry within an economy. Relatively high labour turnover is caused by a number of factors.

- Relatively low pay leads to higher labour turnover as workers leave to get better paid jobs.
- Relatively few training and promotion opportunities will encourage workers to leave their current jobs.
- Poor working conditions, low job satisfaction, bullying and harassment in the workplace are other factors.
- Some businesses are relatively poor at selecting and recruiting the right candidates for posts. Where workers are ill suited to their jobs, there is more chance that they will leave relatively quickly.
- In a recession, labour turnover tends to fall as the number of vacancies falls and workers become worried that if they leave their job without having got another one to go to, they will become part of the long-term unemployed. In a boom, when there might be labour shortages, there are far more vacancies and so labour turnover tends to rise.

Relatively high labour turnover is usually seen as a problem for businesses for a number of reasons.

- Recruiting new staff can be costly.
- It takes time for new staff to become familiar with their roles and the way in which the business operates. High labour turnover is likely to reduce the human process advantage of a business.
- Larger companies may put on induction programmes which further adds to costs.
- If the post is filled internally, there may be training needs for the worker who gets the job.

However, some labour turnover is usually beneficial to a business.

- New staff can bring in fresh ideas and experience from their work with other businesses.
- Some workers may be ineffective and need to be encouraged to leave. Getting rid of ineffective staff leads to labour turnover.
- If a business is shrinking in size, reducing the size of the workforce will lead to higher labour turnover.
- Where a business pays low wages, or where conditions of work are poor, it may be more profitable to have a constant turnover of staff rather than raise wages or improve conditions of work.

Businesses can attempt to reduce their labour turnover if they see it as a problem. Higher pay and better working conditions might be one strategy. Another might be offering better internal promotion prospects to workers. Better selection procedures would be appropriate if the problem is poor recruiting. Effective procedures against bullying and harassment could help too. For senior workers, a business might offer bonuses in the future (often in the form of share option schemes) which can only be claimed if they are still employed by the business at the point in time.

Health and safety

The safety of the working environment can be measured in a number of different ways. For example, health and safety could be measured by the number of working days lost through accidents or injuries per thousand employees over a time period.

$$\frac{\text{Number of working days lost for health and safety reasons per time period}}{\text{Total number of workers}} \times 100\%$$

For example, if there were 300 days lost through accidents or injury over a year and the workforce were 6,000, then the number of working days lost per thousand employees would be (300 ÷ 6,000) x 1,000, which is 50.

Another measure relates working days lost to the total number of working days that could have been worked over the period, expressed as a percentage.

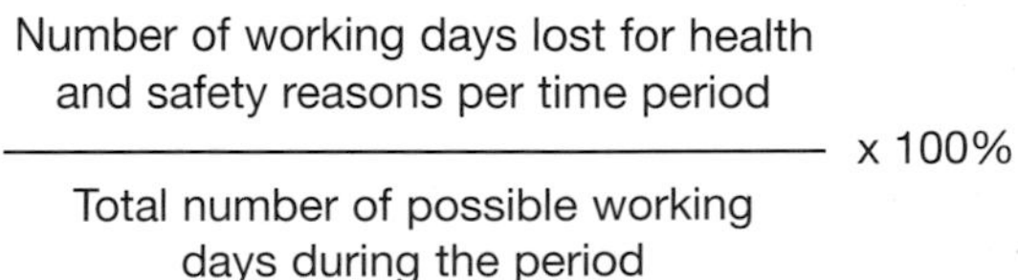

For example, if 2,000 days are lost due to health and safety reasons over a year, and the number of possible working days for the workforce over the period was 100,000, then the health and safety ratio is 2 per cent (100% x 2,000 ÷ 100,000).

A poor health and safety record may occur for a number of reasons.

- Equipment used may be dangerous. For example, it might be poorly maintained or be too old.
- The working environment itself may be dangerous. For example, unsafe levels of dangerous gases or chemicals may be found in the atmosphere in a factory building.
- There may be a lack of safety equipment. For example, workers should perhaps be wearing safety hats, but these are not provided by the employer.
- Workers may not receive sufficient health and safety training.

- The business may not enforce its own health and safety procedures. It may turn a 'blind eye' to abuses because otherwise production would be slowed down.
- Work may be contracted out to self-employed workers who prefer to disregard time-consuming health and safety procedures in order to earn more money. In the building industry, the widespread use of subcontractors is sometimes given as a reason for a poor health and safety record.

Improving a poor health and safety record may be achieved by:

- increasing expenditure on buildings and equipment to bring them up to health and safety standards;
- drawing up an appropriate set of health and safety policies and procedures;
- training all staff to ensure that they understand these policies and procedures and can carry them out;
- strictly enforcing health and safety policies, putting safety above profit and output.

Businesses which have poor health and safety records are either poorly organised and managed, or deliberately exploiting the situation to cut their costs. Lower health and safety standards is one way in which some businesses can gain a competitive advantage. One of the criticisms of globalisation is that producers in Third World countries operate under much less stringent health and safety standards than in the UK. Hence, it could be argued that they have an 'unfair' competitive advantage.

A poor health and safety record can be a disadvantage to a business.

- Poor health and safety standards are likely to lead to the demotivation of staff. Their basic needs are being threatened.
- Such businesses are liable to have their operations closed down or be open to prosecution by health and safety inspectors. Equally, they are open to being sued by workers involved in accidents or by customers if products are put at risk. At worst, such a business could be forced to close because of this issue.
- Staff absences due to accidents may have the same costs as absences due to illness, as explained in the last section. Businesses may also be fined or sued as a result of accidents.
- A poor health and safety record could contribute towards giving a business a poor reputation with customers and so it could affect sales. In the Third World, suppliers to some Western multinationals have to conform to basic standards to win and retain orders. This is because the reputation of the multinationals in their First World markets can be at stake.

Industrial relations

The management of human resources may also improve industrial relations. A business may consider that a reduction in the number of:

- industrial disputes;
- days lost through industrial action;
- grievances against the business by employees;

might indicate effective management. Improvements in staff motivation indicated in appraisal questionnaires, attitude surveys or in meetings may also be an indication of the success of the business's policy.

Relations with stakeholders

Stakeholders are all the people with an interest in the business. They include employees of the business, such as workers and managers, and shareholders who may or may not work for the business. They also include people who are affected by the activities of the business, such as clients, customers, suppliers and the general public. An indication of the success of HRM might be found in improved relations with suppliers. It may also be indicated in the views of customers about how the workforce is treated.

Profitability

The main aim of most private sector businesses is to make profit. Modern approaches to HRM suggest that the management of human resources should be geared towards improving productivity of workers, reducing costs, raising revenue and increasing profit. It is a vital part of the overall strategy of the company rather than a series of processes, such as recruitment, selection and training. Increasing profit may be a result of improvements in HRM.

One model that has been suggested to evaluate the human resources management is the '4Cs model' of the Harvard Business School. This suggests that HRM should be evaluated under four headings as shown in Table 1.

Table 1: Evaluation of human resources management

• Commitment - employees' loyalty and motivation, assessed by surveys, labour turnover and absenteeism.
• Competence - employees' skills and training - assessed through appraisal systems and skills inventories.
• Congruence - employees and managers sharing the same values, assessed by absence of grievances and conflict.
• Cost effectiveness - employees' efficiency, assessed by cost, output and profit figures

KEYTERMS

Rate of absenteeism or absenteeism rate or absentee rate – the number of staff absent as a percentage of the total number of staff employed. It can be calculated for different periods of time, ie daily rates or annual rates.

Work life balance – the relationship between time spent at work and time spent away from work or the time spent at work as a proportion of total time.

KNOWLEDGE

1. How is labour productivity calculated?
2. A component manufacturer makes 10,000 metal washers with ten workers. After employing five extra workers it makes 20,000. Calculate the effect on labour productivity.
3. List four ways in which a business may improve labour productivity.
4. How can a business calculate its rate of absenteeism?
5. List five reasons why rates of absenteeism are different in different industries.
6. State three ways in which a business might reduce rates of absenteeism.
7. What is the relationship between absenteeism and a work life balance?
8. A business finds that its labour turnover falls from 20% to 15%. Should it be concerned?
9. List four factors that might lead to high labour turnover.
10. State five problems of high labour turnover for a business.
11. State two formulae that a business might use to measure its health and safety record.
12. List five factors that may cause a business to have a poor health and safety record.
13. State five possible problems for a business with a poor record of health and safety.

Case Study: Supermarkets' labour turnover and absenteeism

First there were duvet days for staff temporarily 'sick' of work - offered by companies trying to reduce absenteeism by gentle persuasion. Then there was time off for everything from a religious festival to a child's first day at school. In 2004 Tesco, opted for the stick approach, cutting sick pay in some of its stores and tested other schemes in an attempt to cut rates of absenteeism. Tesco spokesperson Jonathan Church said that absenteeism '...impacts on our business as well as creating more work for people in the store. These trials are about encouraging people to use planned absence whenever they can. If they need to take little Johnnie to the dentist, then we will bend over backwards to make that possible.'

One scheme, introduced in two stores in the south, meant workers got no pay for the first three days off sick, but after the fourth day would get paid again with compensation for the first three days. That could encourage people to go sick for a whole week. Other options are to offer staff more holiday allowance up front, but reduce it every time they take a day off sick. Tesco said there are fewer absences in stores testing the schemes. 'Our intention is not to penalise people who are genuinely ill. It is to discourage people from taking those odd days.'

Asda offers incentives such as prizes to reward low absenteeism. 'It might be a week's extra holiday or a weekend break or vouchers. It has really helped bring absenteeism down because people think hard about whether they really need to be off.' The company already has 'carers leave' and 'first day/half day' leave for parents taking children to school.

Sick leave costs British companies around £11 billion every year through 166 million lost working days. Stress-related absence is rising, according to the Health and Safety Executive. This has prompted organisations like The Work Foundation for businesses to look more carefully at how they treat staff and the work environment.

In 2003, seasonal workers at Asda at Christmas were entitled to benefits and job security equivalent to those enjoyed by their full-time colleagues, after the supermarket created 10 000 new permanent positions for contract workers. The new 'seasonal squad' would have the same status as permanent staff but with a contract to work an annual, rather than weekly, number of hours. They could work for as little as ten weeks of the year. The contracts would cover Christmas, Easter and the school summer holidays and cover jobs such as greeters, porters, checkout operatives and warehouse workers. 'We recognise that people are looking for flexibility across the working year, not just the working week' said Caroline Massingham, Asda retail people director. 'If you're one of the many people that want to balance long periods of leave with a fulfilling job, the options are limited'. Asda hopes the initiative would encourage more over 50s to join. The supermarket said that since actively recruiting older workers, it has seen absence levels drop, customer service levels rise and labour turnover fall. The flexible working package includes one week's leave for new grandparents, five days leave for IVF treatment and up to two years for a career break. Asda is hoping to make huge savings from the initiative by reducing turnover, as it has spent around £3,500 per person in recruitment costs.

Source: adapted from *The Observer*, 16.5.2004.

(a) (i) Explain why supermarkets may want to reduce rates of absenteeism and labour turnover. (8 marks)

(ii) Examine the factors that might affect rates of absenteeism and labour turnover at supermarkets. (12 marks)

(b) Evaluate the methods used by supermarkets in the article to reduce rates of absenteeism and labour turnover. (20 marks)

62 Recruitment

The need for effective recruitment

This unit concentrates on the first stage in the management of human resources - recruitment. The personnel department will aim to attract the 'best' candidates for the job and then to choose the most suitable. If the wrong person is recruited, this can cause problems for a business. The person appointed may find the job boring or too difficult, which could lead to a lack of motivation and poor productivity. If the person leaves, there will be administration costs for the personnel department. The business will face the extra costs of advertising, interviewing and training. There will also be a settling in period until the new employee has learned the job.

Employing a suitable person should allow the business to get the most out of its human resoources. In addition, recruiting the best employees may give a business a competitive edge over rivals. To make sure the 'best' person is chosen, businesses must be clear about:

- what the job entails;
- what qualities are required to do the job;
- what rewards are needed to retain and motivate employees.

Recruitment is becoming more and more important in business. This is especially the case where employees need to be flexible or work autonomously, or where direct control over workers is difficult.

Figure 1: A job description for a cabin crew assistant with an airline

Job title
Cabin crew member.

Function
Perform ground and air duties that the company may reasonably require. Ground duties apply to any area of work connected to aircraft operational requirements.
Other duties, including boardroom functions and publicity, are voluntary.

Cabin crew must also:
- be familiar and comply with company policy and procedures;
- provide a high standard of cabin service and perform their duties conscientiously at all times;
- not behave in any way that reflects badly upon the company or harms its reputation.

Pay and expenses
Salary will be £13,000 per annum.
Payment will be one month in arrears, paid directly into the employee's bank account.
Expenses will be paid as set out in the current contract.
If flights are cancelled, you will be entitled to a reporting allowance as set out in the current contract.

Work time
You are required to work 20 days in every 28 day roster period.
Days and hours will vary according to the company's requirements.
Details of rest periods and flight time limitations are set out in the staff manual.

Job analysis

Before a business recruits new employees, the personnel department usually carries out some form of JOB ANALYSIS. Job analysis is a study of what a job entails. It contains the skills, training and tasks that are needed to carry out the job.
Job analysis can be used by firms in many ways. These include selecting employees, setting pay, disciplinary interviews, promotion and job appraisal (dealt with later in this unit). For example, if a firm was trying to choose an applicant for the post of systems analyst, it may use job analysis to find out exactly what a systems analyst does in that firm.

In order to find out about what is involved in a job, the personnel department must gather data about all the different elements in that job. It is likely that people associated with the job will have different views about what is involved.

- The occupant of the job. She will have the most detailed knowledge of what the job requires. However, she might change the information to exaggerate her own status, or leave parts of the job out because they are taken for granted.
- The job holder's superior. She will have her own view of what the job involves, but is unlikely to be fully aware of all job details.
- Subordinates and others with whom the job holder is in regular contact. They are likely to have observed the behaviour of the job holder over a period of time. Once again, any bias or error which the observer may have must be taken into account.

Figure 2: Person specification for an administrative assistant in an engineering plant

	Essential/Desirable
Aptitudes/skills/abilities	
Able to take a flexible approach to working conditions and a changing working environment	E
Self-motivated and enthusiastic	E
Ability to work on own initiative	D
Work effectively as part of a team	D
Qualifications/knowledge and experience	
4 GCSE level C or above	E
Computer literate in Word and Excel	E
Good written and verbal communication skills	E
Able to solve problems effectively	E
Planning and organisational skills	D
Experience of working in a manufacturing environment	D

Question 1.

Job Designation: Broadcast Journalist

Grade: Towers Perrin Level 5/7

Ref: 59858

JOB PURPOSE

To initiate and produce, as part of a team, a wide variety of news and current affairs material for Radio and/or Television.

KEY BEHAVIOURS

1. To carry out in-depth research to a broad brief, with minimal supervision across the whole range of Regional Broadcasting news and current affairs output.
2. To write material for programme scripts, bulletins and links, exercising editorial judgment, maintaining professional journalistic standards and adhering to BBC policy and legal and contractual guidelines.
3. To undertake interviewing and reporting duties, under broad direction in both recorded and live situations, in studio or on location, for both Radio and Television.
4. To prepare and present bulletins, including assessing incoming copy, sub-editing news copy and deploying the necessary resources.

(a) Explain what is meant by a 'job description', illustrating your answer with examples from the data.

(b) The job being advertised was for the presenter of the Good Afternoon Show on BBC Radio Leeds. Discuss whether the BBC was likely to recruit internally or externally for the post.

- Specialist observers, such as job analysts. These can provide an independent view of the work being carried out. The major problem is that the job holder, knowing she is being observed, may adjust her behaviour.

Having collected this information, it must then be analysed. This is often done by using five categories.

Task analysis This involves the study of those tasks an employee carries out when doing their job. Any job will be made up of a variety of tasks. A task is seen as a collection of activities that result in an objective being achieved. For example, an employee may have the task of reporting on stock levels in the company.

Activity analysis This is a study of the activities which make up a task. These will include physical activities and the intellectual demands of the job. So an employee whose task is to do a stock check might need to understand how to use the computerised stock control program and understand the concept of lead time.

Skills analysis This involves a study of the skills that are needed to do the job. These could be the ability to use a computer program or the ability to work with others, for example.

Role analysis This is the information gathered from the job holder, superiors and colleagues. The duties, responsibilities and behaviour expected from the job holder are discussed to produce a role description which all involved agree upon.

Performance analysis This attempts to set the criteria that will be used when evaluating how well a job holder carries out the job. It involves identifying standards and expectations. For example, an employee may need to ensure that stock wastage is kept to a certain level. This will give a target to aim at while carrying out stock control.

Job description

First, a JOB DESCRIPTION will be drawn up. This gives the title of the job. It is a statement of the tasks to be undertaken and responsibilities of the employee holding that job. The job description may describe the employee's place in the hierarchy of the business. Working conditions may also be specified, such as rates of pay or holiday entitlements. An example of a job description is shown in Figure 1. In many cases, the job description for the new recruit will simply be the job description of the person leaving the job. Large businesses, where many employees do the same job, such as a sales assistant or production line worker, might have a common job description for a particular job.

Job descriptions tell the new employee what is expected of them. It can be used when appraising the performance of a worker. If the worker fails to perform satisfactorily and is threatened with dismissal, it can also be used by the employer as evidence to support the dismissal.

Person specification

A job description can be used to draw up a PERSON SPECIFICATION. This is a description (or profile) of the personal qualities that match the requirements of the job specification. The person specification might include the educational and professional qualifications needed for the post. Previous experience required might be outlined. General skills and character traits could also be described.

The person specification can be used to 'screen' applicants. If there are many applicants, selectors will be able to discard those which don't match the person specification. If there are only a few applicants, and none match the specification exactly, the employer may have to compromise and decide which aspects of the person specification are most important. Alternatively, the employer might decide to readvertise the post. An example of a person specification is shown in Figure 2.

Job evaluation

A business can use JOB EVALUATION to compare the value of different jobs. Any job can be broken down into a number of factors. These are the skills, effort, responsibility, knowledge and tasks that the job entails. This allows the business to decide on the wages or salary for that job. If another job has greater skill or responsibility, then the business may award it a higher rate of pay.

Job evaluation has become more popular over the last decade. It has been seen by businesses as a rational way of working out why some jobs are paid more than others. It has also been used in equal pay cases. For example, if there is a dispute about equal pay, the job evaluation will help to show if employees are doing work of equal value. When using job evaluation, a business must remember certain points.

- Job evaluation is about the job and not the performance of the employee in the job.
- Experienced people decide on the value of a job. Whilst this is likely to give useful results, they are not 'perfect'.
- It allows firms to set differential rewards for jobs. This does not rule out collective bargaining to raise these rates.
- Only pay is determined, not other earnings, such as incentives.

The most popular method of job evaluation is a points scheme. A number of factors (skill, problem solving etc.) are found which are common to all jobs. Each factor is given a weighting according to its importance. A job description is then prepared and points are allocated to each factor. The total number of points determines the value of the job, and the wages or salary to be paid.

Whilst it can be useful, job evaluation is costly for firms. Also, some jobs will still be 'underpaid' or 'overpaid', as it is a matter of human judgment.

Question 2.

Pete Roghey owns and runs a small building company with 20 employees. Turnover of staff is relatively high. Skilled workers are constantly in demand and he can find that they have been poached by another company, often on short-term contracts, to work at higher rates of pay.

This week, Pete needs to hire three workers. There is a part time office cleaner's job, working in the evening from 5-7, five nights a week. He is looking for a skilled full time bricklayer. Then there is a general labourer's job, which could suit a young person just starting.

There never seems to be a right way to get hold of new staff. Sometimes, Pete advertises in the local newspaper and gets no replies. Other times, he can be spoilt for choice. More often than not, he gets approached by someone who has heard about the job vacancy from one of his workers. But there is never any guarantee that anyone will turn up this way.

(a) Discuss the advantages and disadvantages for Pete Roghey of using word of mouth to fill job vacancies compared to placing adverts in local newspapers.

(b) What might be the advantages of placing an advert in a local newsagent for the cleaner's job?

Internal recruitment

INTERNAL RECRUITMENT is recruitment from within the business. An employee may be chosen to be offered a post. Or the business may advertise internally, asking employees to apply for the vacancy. The advertisement may be sent round via email or posted on a noticeboard. Larger organisations may have regular newsletters devoted to internal vacancies or notices may be put in the company magazine or on the company website. Internal recruitment has a number of advantages compared to external recruitment.

- It is often cheaper because no adverts have to be placed and paid for at commercial rates.
- Internal recruits might already be familiar with the procedures and working environment of the business. They may, therefore, need less induction training and be more productive in their first year of employment.
- The qualities, abilities and potential of the candidates should be better known to the employer. It is often difficult to foresee exactly how an external recruit will perform in a particular work environment.
- Regular internal recruiting can motivate staff. They might see a career progression with their employer. Even for those who aren't seeking promotion, internal recruitment suggests that the employer is looking after existing staff.

External recruitment

EXTERNAL RECRUITMENT is when someone is appointed from outside the business. External recruitment has two main advantages over internal recruitment.

- The employer may want someone with new and different ideas to those already working in the business. Bringing in experience of working in different organisations can often be helpful in keeping a business competitive.
- External recruitment might attract a larger number of applicants than internal recruitment. The employer then has more choice of whom to appoint.

External recruitment requires the employer to communicate with potential employees. Ideally, every person who is suitable and who might consider the job should apply. That way, the employer will have the maximum number of candidates from which to choose. There is a number of ways in which an employer can do this.

Word of mouth A common method of hearing about a job is

through word of mouth. This means a person hearing about a job from someone else, often someone who works in the place of employment. For example, a person might hear about a vacancy for a hospital porter from their next door neighbour who works as a nurse in a local hospital.

Direct application Many jobseekers send their details to employers for whom they would like to work on the off-chance that they would have a vacancy. An employer might then use these to recruit if a vacancy arises.

Advertising The employer may place advertisements in local or national newspapers and specialist magazines and journals. The Internet is another medium for job advertisements. Advertisements may appear on a company website. The largest sector covered by Internet advertising is jobs in IT. Advertisements on a board or window on the employer's premises can also be successful. Advertisements are sometimes costly. But they can reach a wide number of potential applicants. People wanting to change their job are likely to seek out advertisements.

Private employment agencies The business may employ a private employment agency to find candidates. Private employment agencies are probably best known for finding temporary workers (temps). However, many also specialise in finding permanent staff. At the top end of the range, private employment agencies tend to call themselves executive agencies. They specialise in recruiting company executives and finding jobs for executives seeking a change or who have been made redundant. Using an employment agency should take much of the work out of the recruitment process for the employer. But it can be costly because the employment agency charges a fee. Private employment agencies sometimes have a website where specialist workers can look for jobs or advertise their services.

Headhunting For some posts, such as chief executive of a company, it may be possible to headhunt a candidate. This is where the agency draws up a list of people they think would be suitable for a job. Having cleared the list with the organisation making the appointment, the agency will approach those on the list and discuss the possibility of them taking the job. Some will say no. Others will indicate that, if the terms were right, they might take the job. A final selection is then made and one person is offered the job. Nobody has formally applied or been interviewed. Headhunting works best where there is only a limited number of people who potentially could take on the post and where the agency knows about most of those people.

Jobcentres Businesses can advertise vacancies through Jobcentres run by the government. Jobcentres are often used by the unemployed and vacancies tend to pay less than the average wage. So a cleaner's post is more likely to be advertised in a Jobcentre than a chief executive's post. For a business, this is a relatively cheap way of advertising, but it is not suitable for many vacancies.

Government funded training schemes Some businesses take on trainees from government funded training schemes. The current main scheme is called the New Deal. The schemes are designed to give the unemployed a chance to work for six or 12 months with some element of training. Businesses may choose then to offer these workers a permanent job if there is a vacancy and they have proved satisfactory.

Producing a job advertisement

As important as choosing the most appropriate media through which to advertise a vacancy is the drafting of the advertisement. The decision on what to include in a recruitment advertisement is important because of the high cost of space and the need to attract attention. Both factors will encourage the use of the fewest number of words. Some of the information that might be included is:

- the job title;
- the name and address of the employer;
- the salary and any other remuneration;
- details of the vacancy;
- the skills and experience required for the successful candidate;
- any other benefits;
- what the applicant needs to do to apply;
- where to apply and to whom.

Employee segmentation

The standard of service is increasingly important to customers buying products. Providing an excellent service means matching employees' actions to the needs of customers. So businesses are trying to answer the question 'What behaviour by employees creates greater customer satisfaction?'

One way of doing this is to segment employees into groups depending on the profile of customers. This is known as EMPLOYEE SEGMENTATION. It means that businesses must organise and recruit specific types of employees to match the profiles of their customers. So, for example, B&Q knows that its customers often want advice about products. Therefore it recruits staff with experience of DIY who can talk sympathetically to customers about its products. In call centres it has meant a change of approach to one based on relationships with customers. Employees now tailor responses to customers' needs, based on information about the customer which is shown on a computer screen. Productivity is measured not by how many calls are taken but by how many problems are resolved first time. It is argued that such an approach leads to greater customer loyalty and repeat sales for businesses.

Factors affecting recruitment

A study by Illes and Robertson (1997) of recruitment strategies identified factors which can affect recruitment and make it successful.

- The recruitment literature sent out to candidates can influence their decision about whether to apply or not. Informal sources of information, such as word of mouth and referrals, can sometimes be seen as more accurate sources of information than formal advertisements. Applicants who come through such informal routes may be more likely to stay with the business, reducing levels of labour turnover. This is because they have more realistic expectations when appointed.

- Businesses that want to recruit from under-represented groups, such as ethnic groups, the disabled or women, must ensure that their recruitment strategies are targeted, rather than using general recruitment procedures.
- The recruitment message affects applicants. Glossy, positive images may attract applicants, but can cause problems later if the job does not meet expectations. Job previews and work samples can lead to self-selection. Once experienced, a candidate may decide not to continue with the application. Site visits and opportunities to talk to colleagues can also help. Different messages may affect different groups. For example, flexible schedules can attract retired people.
- The behaviour of recruiters can affect applicants. For example, the presence of women recruiters and managers on site visits and interviews can create a positive impression.
- Applicants may respond better to recruiters who are seen as competent, informed and credible, and have interpersonal skills.
- Delays in response may put off applicants as they may indicate how they will be treated if appointed.
- Applicants may respond better to recruiters of the same gender, ethnicity, age and location as themselves or to those with whom they identify.

Legal constraints

Businesses recruiting and selecting new staff are bound by various employment laws.

- The Sex Discrimination Act 1975 and the Race Relations Act 1976 state that there must be no discrimination against applicants, whether male or female, or whatever ethnic origin. Discrimination can occur at any stage of the recruitment process. For example, an advertisement saying 'Males only need apply' might be a case of discrimination. Cases are also brought against employers through employment tribunals (courts which deal with employment law) mainly by women or those from ethnic minorities arguing that jobs were given not to the best applicant, but on gender or race grounds.
- The Disability Discrimination Act 1995 states that it is unlawful for businesses to discriminate against an applicant with a disability, unless there is justification. Justification might be shown if the employer had to take unreasonable measures to allow the person with the disability to work successfully. For example, an employer might not be able to reject a candidate in a wheelchair if there were a few steps at the entrance to the place of work because a ramp could easily and cheaply be installed. However, it might be unreasonable to expect an employer to move premises just to employ the disabled worker.
- The Age Discrimination Act 2006 gives protection against age discrimination, unless it can be justified, for example if there are saftey issues. The laws protect employees of any age against age discrnimation over recruitment, terms and conditions, promotions, transfers, dismissals and training.
- After appointment, employees must be given a contract of employment detailing their duties and their rate of pay, for example.

How recruitment and selection can improve the workforce

Good recruitment and selection procedures can help to improve the workforce of a business and ensure it works effectively. They will identify the type of person required for the a job. This means that a suitable person can be appointed. They will have the skills to do the job and labour productivity may be high. They are likely to make fewer mistakes, which can be costly and time consuming.

KNOWLEDGE

1. What is the difference between a job description and a person specification?
2. Give three pieces of information that might be on job description.
3. Give two reasons why a business might carry out job analysis.
4. Compare the advantages of recruting internally with recruiting externally.
5. Briefly explain the different ways a business may recruit externally.
6. Briefly explain the legal constraints on recruitment.
7. Identify two ways in which effective recruitment can benefit a business.

KEYTERMS

Employee segmentation – when a business recruits types of employees who match the profiles of its customers.
External recruitment – when an employee looks for applicants for a job from outside the organisation.
Internal recruitment – when an employee seeks to find applicants for a job from inside the organisation.
Job analysis – a study of what the job entails, such as skills, tasks and performance expected.
Job description – a statement of the tasks to be undertaken and responsibilities of the employee holding the job.
Job evaluation – a method used by businesses to compare the value of different jobs and perhaps set wages or salaries.
Person specification – a description (or profile) of the personal qualities that match the requirements of the job specification.

Effective procedures may also be able to identify ways in which employees can improve. For example, if training needs are highlighted at an early stage then employees' skills may improve as they are employed for a period and receive training.

If the wrong person is recruited, this can cause problems for a business. The person appointed may find the job boring or too difficult, which could lead to a lack of motivation and poor productivity. If the person leaves, there will be administration costs for the human resource department. The business will face the extra costs of advertising and interviewing. There will also be a settling in period until the new employee has learned the job. Good recruitment and selection procedures can prevent this.

Identifying the most suitable employees may give a business a competitive edge over rivals. Productive and motivated employees will help a business to operate effectively. Business may also develop a good reputation, which can help attract customers. For example, a restaurant that has attentive staff and chefs that cook to a high standard may encourage customers to return.

Case Study: Using online information in recruitment and selection

More and more employers are using the Internet in the recruitment process. A survey by *Employment Review* found that more than three-quarters of employers were convinced that making changes to the use of general job boards was the most effective way of achieving savings when attracting new candidates.The findings show that altering one or two aspects of online recruitment often yielded the most effective outcomes when trying to attract candidates. These included making greater and better use of corporate websites, general job boards and specialist job boards, improving their use of intranets to advertise jobs on them more effectively and encouraging readers of printed job ads to go onto a website to find out more information about the job and the employer.

However, the results were more varied when considering the best way to improve the suitability of candidates applying for vacancies. The majority of employers believed that taking measures to change their use of employment agencies was the best way to improve the quality of job applicants. But specialist job boards and advertising on corporate websites were also highly ranked, as well as taking steps to improve the use of search consultancies. There was also a greater interest in hosting open days for prospective applicants, with one in six employers changing their attitudes towards them in 2006 and 2007 – 47 per cent decided to make greater use of them, while 37 per cent incorporated them into their recruitment drives.

Web browsers are also being used to check out potential staff. According to one recruitment consultancy survey, one in five employers are using information from network sites such as Facebook and MySpace as an aid to recruitment. Employees used to be able to predict how prospective employers would research them, but social networking sites have changed this. Candidates may not realise the effect their websites are having on their job prospects and may not have full control over the details being posted. Employer surveys indicate the key recruitment 'turn-offs' are:

- disparaging a previous employer or disclosing confidential work information;
- disparity between the website and the CV/application form, for example, qualifications;
- intolerance of others that could cause disruption in the workplace
- criminal activity.

It can be to employers' advantage to use online information. But there are employment law risks. For example, employers could be guilty of not processing personal data fairly under the Data Protection Act 1998 or they might breach guidelines in the Information Commissioner's Employment Practices Code (DPA Code). Employers could also face potential discrimination claims. For example, employers may discriminate against people using Facebook on the grounds of age, since most users are aged between 18 and 24. Checking existing employees without good reason could breach the implied contract term of trust and confidence.

How can employers reduce the risk? The DPA Code recommends candidates are told that web-checking may be part of the recruitment process. Employers could also nominate someone removed from the decision making team to research and document information. This reduces the scope for unlawful bias. Employers could also give applicants a chance to explain discrepancies in qualifications, for example. Employers could limit checking in this way to those they intend to offer a job to rather than shortlist candidates. And they should consider carefully the information they find. They may be put off by images of drunkenness, but having too many drinks at the weekend does not necessarily mean that a person can not do their job, nor are they an alcoholic.

Employers need to weigh up what message 'web-vetting' sends out about the business. Some will see it as intrusive. Others as a legitimate way of getting a feel for how a person behaves.

Source: adapted from *www.personneltoday.com, 28.2.2008, People Management,18.10.2007.*

(a) Explain whether using the Internet as part of the recruitment process is an example of internal or external recruitment. (6 marks)

(b) Examine the reasons why a business may want to use network sites such as Facebook and Myspace in the recruitment process. (10 marks)

(c) Discuss whether the use of the Internet or hiring an employment agency is the most effective means of recruiting managers and professionals. (12 marks)

(d) Discuss the extent to which using networks might help the business recruit effectively. (12 marks)

63 Selection

Effective selection - making the right choice

Businesses need to recruit and then select the 'right' person for the job. If the candidate chosen is unsuitable, the business may be faced with the cost of poor performance by the employee. There will also be extra costs in selecting and training a replacement when that employee leaves.

Businesses have also realised the need for a fair and valid choice of candidate. The most suitable applicant will only be chosen if selection is based on ability, skills and knowledge, rather than race or gender, for example. **Equal opportunities** legislation has helped to make impartial selection more likely, although there are still arguments about the 'fairness' involved in selection.

Effective selection should lead to the most suitable candidate being employed, in terms of their skills and motivation, as well as reducing the cost of selection. Personnel managers play an important part in this. They help to prepare the job analysis, job description, and person specification, and decide exactly how to recruit. They also advise on the nature of application forms, how to SHORT LIST or LONG LIST from them, and how to conduct tests and interviews. Finally, they will influence how the information is evaluated and what decisions should be made about candidates.

Application

The first time that a business receives information about candidates for a job it is advertising is when they apply for the job. Applicants may have collected details about the job from the business itself or from a job centre, for example. Some jobs ask for a letter of application from the applicants in which they explain why they want the job. This is often accompanied by a CURRICULUM VITAE (CV). The CV is a list of the applicant's:

- personal details (name, address, nationality etc.);
- educational qualifications;
- hobbies and interests;
- past job experience;
- reasons why the candidate is suitable for the job (strengths);
- references or names and addresses of referees who will provide references. **References** are a confirmation of the abilities, skills and experience of the candidate.

Growing use is being made of application forms by businesses. They have a number of benefits. All applicants give details in a standard way, rather than the different approaches of letters of application. This makes sorting applications and short listing far easier. This task is often called 'pre-selection'. It involves the 'sifting out' of applicants who least fit the requirements of the person specification and job description. The application form is often used as the basis of the interview

Question 1

Frost Frame is a small company producing double glazed windows. It has decided to expand production. In particular, it is looking for someone with skills in working with stained glass. Having placed an advertisement in the local newspaper, the company sent out application forms. The standard application form was used which had been devised for all general workshop employees. It did not ask any questions related to the applicant's specific skills. After four weeks it has received three applications and only one candidate looks worth interviewing. However, it is unclear from his answers whether he will be entirely suitable.

(a) Identify problems that Frost Frame may have had with its application form.

(b) Analyse the possible implications for the company if it decides not to interview the candidate.

and can be a starting point for personnel records.

The application form covers the information contained in a CV above, such as personal details, education and job experience. Certain forms leave out some of the above, while others include much more. Whatever the format, the form helps applicants 'present' their case. Also, by gaining biographical information, the personnel department has a simple way of matching the applicant's qualifications, interests, past experience etc. to their person specification. This allows the firm to decide quickly which of the applicants is suitable for a job. Table 1 shows a checklist of points which can be used to help a business design an application form.

Interviews

Most people have at least one experience of being interviewed prior to employment. Few people enjoy interviews. Often this is because the interviewer appears to be more interested in finding fault than being helpful.

The personnel department is usually involved in interviewing, both in carrying them out and helping managers to adopt good interview practice. By following certain guidelines, the business hopes to employ the 'right' person for the job. It also aims to carry out the interview in a way that is fair to all candidates and well structured. These guidelines might include the following.

- The interview should allow information to be collected from candidates which can be used to predict whether they can perform the job. This can be done by comparing replies with the criteria that successful applicants should have.
- The business should give candidates full details about the job and the organisation. This will help them decide whether the job would suit them.
- The interview should be conducted so that candidates can say that they have had a fair hearing.

Table 1: Application form checklist

- Handwriting is often larger than type. Do the boxes/areas on the form give enough room for the applicant to complete the information?
- Forms that take too long to complete may be completed haphazardly or not at all. Is the time the form takes to complete appropriate to the information the employer needs?
- Some questions may be illegal, offensive, or not essential. Does the form ask only for information appropriate to the job?
- Word processing software makes it possible to produce separate application forms for each post advertised and to make them user friendly. One way of doing this is to use introductory paragraphs explaining why the information in each section is being sought.

The interview has, however, been criticised as not always being an effective 'tool'. Some of the main criticisms are:

- interviewers often decide to accept or reject a candidate within the first three or four minutes of the interview, and then spend the rest of the time finding evidence to confirm their decision;
- interviews seldom change the initial opinion formed by the interviewer seeing the application form and the appearance of the candidate;
- interviewers place more stress on evidence that is unfavourable than on the evidence that is favourable;
- when interviewers have made up their minds very early in the interview, their behaviour betrays their decision to the candidate.

The problem with these criticisms is that they do not solve the problems, only identify them. No matter what other means of selection there may be, the interview is crucial. If it is thought to be unreliable, it should not be discarded. Businesses must simply make sure they carry it out properly.

Conducting an interview

There is a number of factors which could be taken into account when carrying out interviews. The interview should be conducted around a simple plan and be based on a number of questions against which all candidates will be assessed. It is also considered good practice to prepare a suitable place for the interview, such as a warm, quiet, ventilated room. The interviewer should also ensure that the candidates have a

Table 2: Organising an interview

Organisation	Tasks	Time (minutes)
Introduction	Who are they?	2
	Who are you?	3
Body of interview	Begin questioning. Ask questions which probe what they have learnt from their experiences/qualifications /interests and how they would apply this to their new position.	10
	Let the candidate ask questions. Explain about the organisation.	5
	If any questions are left, clear them up.	5
	Tell the candidate what happens next, eg 'We will let you know in 10 days'.	3
Close of interview	Finish tidily.	
After the interview	Assess the candidate.	10/15
	Prepare for next interview.	10/15

friendly reception and are informed of what is expected of them.

An average interview may take around 30 minutes. An interview plan organises the time to cover the important areas in assessing applicants. The plan must be flexible enough to allow the interviewer to explore areas that may come up during the interview. An example is shown in Table 2.

Many recruitment handbooks spell out the 'dos and don'ts' of interviewing. Some of the 'dos' that the interviewer may take into account include the following.

- Introduce yourself to the candidate.
- Adopt a suitable manner, show respect and be friendly.
- Make sure the interview is not interrupted.
- Conduct the interview at an unhurried pace.
- Have a list of questions that need to be asked.
- Encourage the candidate to talk by using 'open' questions such as:
  'Tell me about your present/last job ...'
  'What is your opinion on ...?'
  'What do you find interesting in ...?'
- Concentrate on those areas not fully covered by the application form.
- Be alert for clues in the candidate's answer, probe where necessary, and be more specific in the questioning if you are not satisfied.
- When the interview has ended, make sure the candidate has no further questions and let the candidate know when the decision will be made, e.g. within seven days.
- Write up your assessment notes immediately.
- Prepare for the next interview.

Table 3: Criteria used in assesing candidates

Rodgers' 7 point plan	Munro-Fraser 5 point plan
Physical make-up	Impact on others
Attainments	Qualifications
General intelligence	Innate abilities
Specialised aptitude	Motivation
Interests	Emotional adjustment
Disposition	
Circumstances	

The interviewer will have gained a great deal of information from the interview. It will help the interviewer to have a checklist of the criteria used when assessing candidates. Table 3 shows two possible lists. The interviewer can make notes about candidates next to each criterion and compare the information with the person specification after the interview, to decide if the person is suitable.

Testing

Businesses appear to be taking a greater interest in testing. There are strong arguments for and against the use of tests in selection. Those in favour argue that many interviews in business are unstructured and do not really allow a business to predict performance. They also point to the greater accuracy and objectivity of test data. Those against dispute this objectivity. They also argue that predictions from test results can mislead. For example, does a high test score mean high job performance

Question 2.

- One of eight applicants applying for a trainee position was put forward largely due to the level of maturity shown. Most candidates, all university graduates, acted their age. He got the edge by being positively different. He was calm, relaxed and self assured.
- A candidate was not put forward due to the number of times he laughed during interview. Even allowing for nerves, he did not appear serious enough.
- A candidate was too rehearsed. Each question was given the same answer, which at times was not appropriate to the question being asked.
- A candidate was rejected because of her attitude towards an aptitude test. Another candidate was rejected on his attitude towards a female interviewer, when he tried to flirt.
- A candidate was rejected when his mobile phone went off during the interview. This may not be a problem in itself, but the candidate then had a lengthy telephone call.
- A candidate was recommended for second interview and offered a job. The main attribute was the candidate's honesty. She had suffered some illness with her previous employer. The candidate gave a complete and honest account of her illness and current prognosis.
- A candidate's CV was average in presentation and detail, but the enthusiasm and spirit in the covering letter encouraged the business to interview the candidate.
- A candidate gave only a satisfactory interview. However, what stood out was his approach having received a call for interview. He contacted the interviewer thanking him for the opportunity of the interview and confirming he would be attending. He then independently approached the interviewer's secretary to make sure he had the right directions and was polite to the secretary on attending the interview.

Source: adapted from www.sfrecruitment.co.uk.

(a) Using examples from the case, advise candidates of features of a successful interview.

(b) Using examples, explain how interviews might be useful for helping a business to select the most suitable candidate for a job.

and a low score mean low job performance?

There is a number of tests that are used in selection. These are often associated with different levels of staff.

- Aptitude tests measure how well a candidate can cope when faced with a business situation or problem.
- Attainment tests measure an individual's ability using skills they have already acquired. For example, a candidate for an administration post may take a word processing test.
- Intelligence tests aim to give an indication of overall 'mental' ability. A variety of questions are asked in such tests covering numeracy and literacy skills, as well as general knowledge. It is assumed that a person who scores highly will be able to retain new knowledge and to succeed at work.
- Personality tests, also known as psychometric tests, examine the **traits** or **characteristics** of employees. For example, they might indicate that a manager does not change her mind once her decision is made or that an employee is willing to experiment and adapt to change. Personality tests may allow a business to predict how hard working or motivated a employee will be or how suited she is to a job. The usefulness of such tests depends on whether the business feels that they are a suitable way of selecting employees. The business must also have qualified personnel to carry out the tests. Such tests do have problems. There is unlikely to be a standard personality profile of the 'ideal employee' to compare tests results against. The tests also rely on the individual being honest. Often, however, candidates try to pick the answer that they feel is wanted. In addition, some traits measured in the tests may not be relevant to job performance.

Question 3.

easyJet has 80 per cent of ticket sales via the Internet. So it makes sense for it to use this in its selection process. Pilots, for example, are asked to fill in a customised, online application form. All correspondence between applicants and easyJet is then carried out online. Successful applicants are invited to a pilot workshop or assessment centre. Unsuccessful ones are filed away to be contacted later when they may have more experience.

CVs and applications are picked up from the website and sent to the relevant manager. But they are also logged on to the HR system where they can be electronically screened to see how they match up to existing jobs and vacancies. This allows personnel to build up a database of potential recruits for the future.

The business can be very effective in screening out applicants that have little chance of selection. Pilots, for example, must have a number of flying hours. It is immediately obvious from the application form if a candidate does not have this experience. It also filters out speculative applications from 16-year olds wanting to be pilots.

The business is less convinced about the value of online testing. easyJet uses psychometric tests for recruiting pilots, but these are still pen and paper tests. One of the problems is the lack of feedback from candidates with online testing.

Source: adapted from recruiter.totaljobs.com.

(a) Identify the methods of selection used at easyJet.
(b) Discuss to what extent online selection methods are useful for the business in the selection of pilots.

Selection exercises

As well as interviews and tests, more and more companies are using a variety of:

- role play exercises;
- group presentations;
- PSYCHOMETRIC TESTS, which attempt to assess a candidate's personality;
- simulations;
- assessment centres, which attempt to evaluate a wider range of skills using a variety of techniques to help a business analyse the capabilities of candidates.

These allow candidates to demonstrate social skills and problem solving skills which they may need to use in the job. For example, a salesperson may show persuasive communication skills in a role play situation. The use of exercises has a number of benefits for a business.

- They allow more information to be gathered about a candidate than other methods of selection.
- They show how well candidates react to situations such as team working, responding to customers or meeting deadlines.
- They allow large numbers to be assessed and may save on costs.

Interviewing and technology

Businesses are increasingly making use of technology in selection.

Videoconferencing Some businesses use videoconferencing as an interviewing tool. For example, it can cost less than £1,000 for a recruiter in the UK to interview six candidates in the US by video link. Videoconferencing is not likely to replace the face-to-face interview because people still need the 'human touch'. However, it will help to save time and money. Glaxo-SmithKline, the pharmaceuticals company, has used video-interviewing in the initial screening of candidates. It has found this to be a way of saving on travel expenses, particularly when an interview would have involved international air travel.

Telephone interviews There is a growing trend among Companies may choose to select candidates by using the telephone. Phone interviews have a number of advantages. Savings can be made on costs and managers need to spend less time away from their desks. They can also prevent discrimination due to visual appearance. However, telephone interviews are not always suited to all types of interview situation and certain candidates may not interview well over the telephone.

The Internet The use of online questionnaires on company, websites can help in the short or long listing process. For example, it may be possible to assess a candidate's CV from answers given to a standard questionnaire. This will reduce costs greatly in the application stage. It might even be possible to given candidates an online test to assess their abilities.

The future In future, businesses might even consider using technology such as webcams and the Internet for interviews. This might be used, for example, if a candidate had to be interviewed from another country.

Evaluating selection

How can a business tell if selection has been effective? It could simply decide that if it has appointed the 'right' candidate, then its aim has been achieved. However, selection will involve costs to a business. There will be expenses in sending out application forms and perhaps travelling expenses for candidates. Staff will also have to give up time to carry out the interviews.

So, for example, if ten people were interviewed for three posts, but only one applicant was suitable, selection may not have been effective. In this case the firm would have to readvertise and interview other candidates as two posts would be unfilled. The personnel department's role would be to check all stages of selection to find out where problems had arisen. For example, when short listing, a suitable candidate may have been 'left out'. At an interview a possible candidate may have been rushed, so he was not given the chance to do his best.

Research in the 1990s and after the year 2000 suggests certain factors that lead to successful selection.

- Ability tests, job knowledge tests and situational judgement tests, where candidates are tested on how they would respond to a real business problem, have been found to be very effective in predicting future job performance.
- Personality measures and employment interviews, especially when they are structured, have emerged as stronger predictors of job performance than was previously believed.

KEYTERMS

Curriculum Vitae – a list of the applicant's personal details, experience and qualifications.
Long listing – reducing the number of total candidates to a manageable list, that might be reduced further.
Psychometric tests – methods of selection designed to assess a candidate's personality.
Short listing – reducing the original number of candidates to a small number to be interviewed.

KNOWLEDGE

1. Why has selection become increasingly important to businesses?
2. State five features covered in an application form.
3. What criteria might a personnel department take into account when designing an application form?
4. Name four types of tests that a personnel department might carry out when selecting applicants for a job.
5. What are the main problems with personality tests as a method of selection?
6. Explain the main problems with interviews.
7. State five 'dos' when conducting an interview.
8. How might a business evaluate its selection procedure?
9. How might a business make use of technology when conducting an interview?
10. What is meant by a selection exercise?

Case Study: Breaking with tradition

Looking smart and smiling at an interview may be a thing of the past. At Inkfish Call Centre anyone given an initial interview won't even have to leave home. Why? Because they are carried out by telephone. 'It's popular with candidates who often find it a lot less daunting and more relaxing than being thrown straight into a face-to-face interview' says Ruth Ebbern-Robinson, head of HR. Telephone interviews resulted from a policy to employ a wider age group. Many of the recruiters at the business were young and so 'Telephone interviewing soon proved a good way of avoiding any kind of discrimination by young folk who can think people are over the hill at 40. It worked perfectly because if you can't see someone, you don't know how old he or she is. People who are successful in the phone interview are then invited to a selection day run by company personnel representing a wide range of ages' according to Ruth Ebbern-Robinson.

Telephone interviews also avoid discrimination on ethnic grounds and disability. There are no visual clues and research has found that there's no bias towards accent. A company spokesperson at B&Q says about telephone interviews, 'We introduced it a few years ago to provide a consistent means of recruitment and one in which we couldn't, even subliminally, prejudice certain groups such as people with disabilities'. She also says 'Candidates benefit because telephone interviews can be arranged at a mutually convenient time, and time and money is saved by cutting out travel. You don't have to think about what you're going to wear and there's a good chance you won't even need to take time off from your current job'.

Businesses may also benefit. If a job involves communicating by phone, it gives employers an insight into the employee's telephone skills. Not having to find a location also means that more candidates can be interviewed, leading to a fairer recruitment process.

However, telephone interviews do have problems.

- Research shows that interviews with multiple interviewers are most fair and valid, which is not possible over the phone.
- If the job does not require any telephone communication, there is a chance that the candidate might not be comfortable with this kind of medium.
- Not everyone can find somewhere quiet in their home or at work for a phone interview.
- Interviewees may find that telephone interviews are structured, with questions which are less open ended than those asked in a face-to-face interview.
- Interviews may be through an automated system. This is rare, although it is becoming popular for secretarial, receptionist and other customer-facing positions.
- Interviewees may answer questions too quickly. Silences are more prominent over the phone and can seem longer than they really are.

Shell has used telephone interviews for graduates. Candidates may not live near a Shell recruitment centre or simply prefer to be interviewed by phone. Shell then invites successful candidates along to a follow-up interview in person. Angela Baron, employee resourcing adviser for the CIPD, believes this is essential. 'Telephone interviews are no substitute for more detailed interviewing' she says. 'Telephone interviews are particularly beneficial for applicants who switch careers.' 'Many companies would see from this person's CV that they have no direct experience for this role and bin it. Those that use telephone interviews, on the other hand, would have the chance to check out their generic skills and may wind up with a more suitable recruit.'

Source: adapted from *The Guardian*, 13.8.2003.

(a) **Explain what is meant by (i) a CV and (ii) face-to-face interview. (4 marks)**

(b) **Explain why employers might use telephone interviews for employees in sales or call centres. (6 marks)**

(c) **Examine the ways in which a business might short list candidates for telephone interviews. (6 marks)**

(d) **Explain the advantages of telephone interviewing for:**
(i) employees;
(ii) businesses. (8 marks)

(e) **Suggest the factors that a business like B&Q might need to take into account to carry out a successful telephone interview. (8 marks)**

(f) **Discuss whether telephone interviews on their own are likely to lead to a successful appointment. (12 marks)**

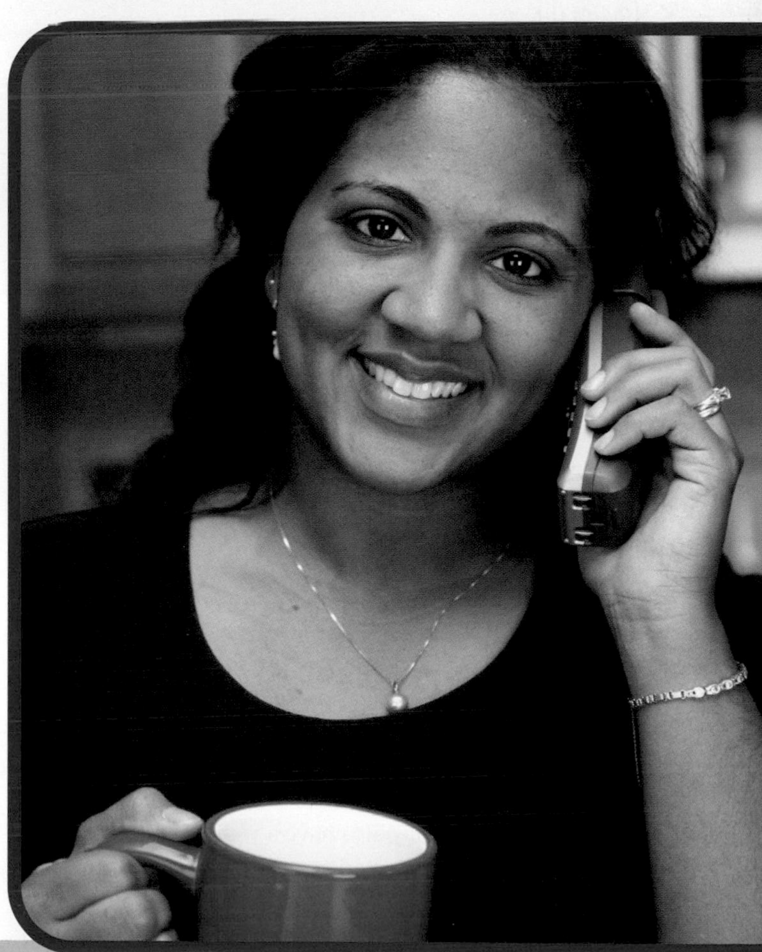

64 Appointment and termination

The contract of employment

Once a business has selected an employee, the successful candidate must be **appointed**. Once appointed, employees are entitled to a CONTRACT OF EMPLOYMENT. This is an agreement between the employer and the employee under which each has certain obligations. It is 'binding' to both parties in the agreement, the employer and the employee. This means that it is unlawful to break the terms and conditions in the contract without the other party agreeing.

As soon as an employee starts work, and therefore demonstrates that she accepts the terms offered by the employer, the contract comes into existence. It is sometimes a written contract, although a verbal agreement or an 'implied' agreement are also contracts of employment. The **Employment Rights Act, 1996** requires employers to give employees taken on for one month or more a **written statement** within two months of appointment. This written statement sets out the terms and conditions in the contract. Some common features shown in the written statement are:

- the names of the employer and the name of the employee;
- the date on which the employment is to begin;
- the job title;
- the terms and conditions of employment.

The duties and rights of employees and employers

Employees that are appointed by a business are covered by certain employment protection rights. Government legislation makes it a duty of employers to safeguard the rights of individuals at work. These are **individual labour laws**, as opposed to collective labour laws which affect all employees. They fall into a number of areas.

Discrimination Employees can not be discriminated against on grounds of gender, race or disability. So, for example, a business can not refuse to appoint a candidate for a job only because that person is female.

Pay Employees must be paid the same rate as other employees doing the same job, a similar job or a job with equal demands. They also have the right to itemised pay statements and not to have pay deducted for unlawful reasons.

Absences Employees have a right to maternity leave, time off for union or public duties and time off to look for training or work at times of redundancy. They also have a right to guaranteed payments during a period of lay off or medical suspension. Employees have a right to return to work after maternity leave. The **Employment Act, 2002** extended the rights of parents who worked. It gave working mothers and working adoptive parents paid maternity leave. It increased maternity pay as well. Two weeks paid leave were also given to working fathers.

Dismissal Employees have the right not to be dismissed or face disciplinary action for trade union activity or on health and safety grounds. They also have a right to notice of dismissal. Employers have the right to terminate contracts of employment under certain circumstances, such as misconduct. These are discussed later in this unit.

Health and safety Employers have duties to provide a safe and healthy environment in which employees can work. In the UK the **Health and Safety at Work Act, 1974** is the main legislation protecting employees. However, many other UK and EU regulations exist and are being constantly introduced to raise standards of safety at work.

The duties of employees may be set out in the written statement of the contract of employment. For example, employees may be expected to conform to standards of behaviour and conduct at work. These may include standards of attendance, punctuality, dealings with colleagues and dress. Standards of quality and accuracy of work, speed of work and safety are also likely to be expected of employees.

Vicarious liability

In certain circumstance legislation forces business to have VICARIOUS LIABILITY. This is where a business must accept responsibility for the actions of its employees. Employers are liable for the wrongful acts of employees providing these happen during the course of their employment and are connected with it. So, for example, a construction business may be liable if its workers cause damage to an adjoining building whilst carrying out repairs to a client's building. Businesses found to be vicariously liable might incur fines or other penalties.

Conditions of work and service

The written statement of the contract of employment will contain information about the conditions of work and service agreed by the employer and employee. Conditions may include the following.

The number of hours to be worked The statement will show the hours to be worked per week or over a period such as a year in the case of annualised hours. The number of hours must conform to legislation. For example, in 1998 the **European Union Working Time Directive** allowed workers to limit their working hours to a maximum of 48 hours per week, although workers such as junior doctors and senior executives were excluded. Details of the start and finish times may also be included, along with any meal or rest breaks. If an employee is expected to work 'shifts', this should be stated. Shift work is where an employee may work, for example, from 9am-5pm in the day for a week and then from 9pm-5am at night the following week.

The **Employment Act, 2002** introduced, for the first time, rights regarding flexible working. Mothers and fathers of children under 6 or disabled children under 18 have the right to request flexible working arrangements. Employers can only refuse the request if there is a clear business reason.

The designation of the job Workers may be employed in **full-time** jobs or **part time** jobs. They may also be given a **permanent** job or a **temporary** job that only lasts for a period of time. The period of employment would usually be stated in the case of a temporary job. If a worker is expected to be based in a factory or office, this place of employment should also be mentioned. Some employees may be expected to work from home or to travel. If this is the case then arrangements that cover this such as support from the employer or travel expenses should be mentioned. These are discussed in the next section.

Pay The method of payment used to reward the employee is usually included in the written statement. She might be paid a wage or a salary. Payment may be by cheque or directly into a bank account. The rate of pay would be specified, such as £5 per hour or an annual salary of £20,000 a year. There may also be an indication of any bonuses, commission or overtime, incentive schemes and deductions from wages. Pay must conform to legislation. For example, employers are bound by the **Equal Pay Act 1970**. This states that an employee must be paid the same rate as another employee doing the same job, a similar job or a job with equal demands.

Benefits Benefits that the employer is offering to the employee are usually included.

- The annual number of days paid **holiday** is often stated and any restrictions on when they can be taken. Statutory holidays are often stated as being taken.
- If the business runs its own **pension scheme** or offers to contribute to an individual or stakeholder pension, this may be stated along with contribution rates.
- There may be information on the length of time and the rate at which **sick pay** is available over and above any statutory rate.
- Any other benefits given by the business might also be included. Benefits can be wide ranging, from subsidised holidays to membership of leisure facilities to company cars.

Disciplinary procedures The written statement may indicate the immediate superior of the employee, who might be responsible for induction, training, supervision and discipline. In a larger business these are likely to be carried out by the

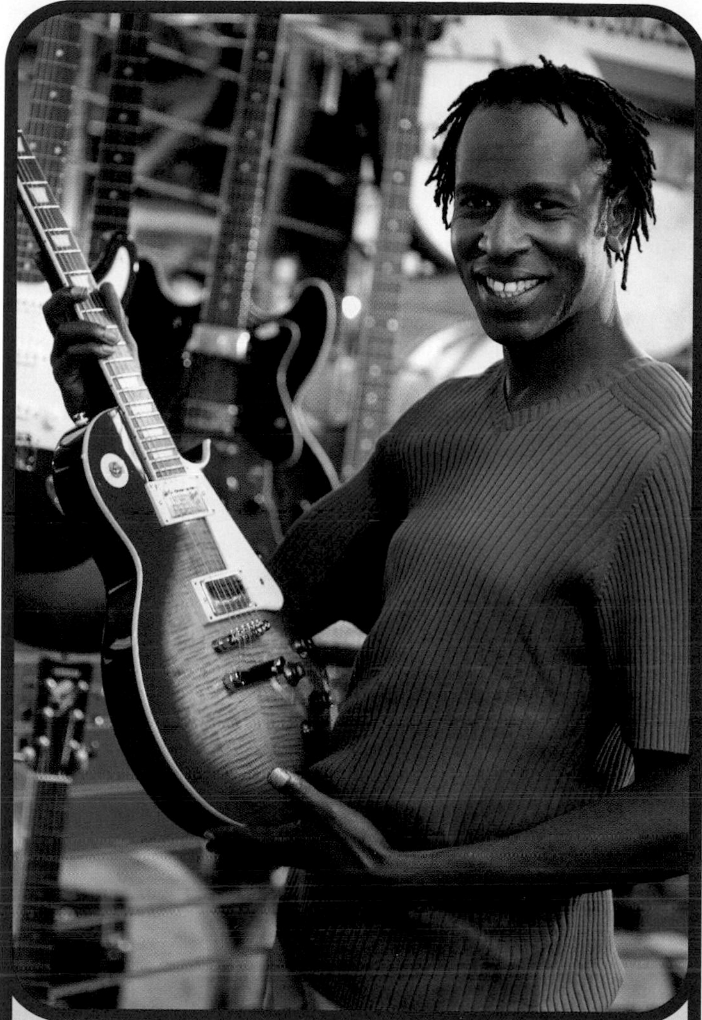

Question 1.

Micah Lampkin recently set up Picks, a guitar and musical instrument workshop in Glasgow. The business wants to offer a variety of services to its customers, including cleaning, setting up and refretting. It also offers more specialist services, including bodywork repair. Micah currently employs one full-time worker, Carla. She deals with most of the professional clients of the business, including regular work on guitars for touring bands that often need work done immediately which requires technical expertise. His other worker is part time. Kevin works in the afternoons. He helps Micah to set up guitars and takes orders that come in.

Recently more orders have come in that need to be worked on during the mornings. Micah is considering employing Ged a young school leaver who wants to learn more about the business. He will work at different times of the day to Kevin. Micah is wondering whether to employ him on a temporary contract or as a permanent part-time employee.

(a) Explain the difference between a full-time and part-time employee.
(b) Why does Micah employ Carla full-time?
(c) Explain TWO factors that might affect Micah's decision about whether to employ Ged as a temporary or permanent part-time worker.

personnel department. The **Employment Rights Act, 1996** states that employers must explain their disciplinary procedures. These are the rules that set standards of conduct at work. Employees must also be clearly informed of the consequences of breaking these rules, how this will be investigated and the rights of appeal against a decision. Employees that break rules could be liable for disciplinary action. This may be in the form of a verbal or written warning, suspension or even dismissal in some cases.

Notice Employees may leave a business to change jobs, to stop work totally or to have children. When employees do not intend to return they have to 'hand in their notice'. In other words they have to inform (or notify) the employer before they leave. The length of time that notice must be given by employees before they leave may be indicated in the written statement and must comply with legislation. This may be 'one week's notice' or 'one month's notice' for example. Similarly, the contract may state the length of 'notice' to be given by employers to employees before making them redundant or dismissing them. The length of notice will vary depending on the length of service.

Grievance procedures If an employee has a complaint against other staff or against their treatment at work then a business may have its own internal grievance procedure. Details of these procedures and who to contact in case of complaints may be included in the written statement. Employees should also be aware of how to contact an industrial tribunal, ACAS (the arbitration service) or a trade union in the case of a complaint. The **Employment Act, 2002** introduced minimum internal grievance procedures that businesses must have. They are designed to improve communication, so that employees can raise grievances, and to reduce the number of unfair dismissal claims.

Employee rights The rights of employees to union representation, time off and equality of treatment as explained above may be outlined in the written statement of the contract of employment. The **Employment Act, 2002** gave trade union representatives the right to time off for training so that they can carry our their duties.

Types of employment

A number of different definitions can be used to classify the way in which people are employed.

Employees and self-employment If an employer provides and controls work, supplies equipment and pays tax and National Insurance contributions for the worker, then the worker is an EMPLOYEE. An employee will work under the conditions of the contract of employment agreed with the employer. If the worker makes her own decisions about accepting work and conditions of work, and pays her own tax and National Insurance contributions, the worker is likely to be SELF-EMPLOYED. Working at home does not necessarily mean a worker is self-employed, as discussed in the section on homeworkers later in this unit. To be self-employed, a worker must be in business on her own account. Businesses sometimes 'contract out' work to self-employed people to save on the costs of extra employees. For example, buildings in city centres which are mainly glass may hire window cleaners rather than employing staff, even though regular cleaning may be needed.

Permanent and temporary employment PERMANENT workers are employed by a business for an indefinite period of time. For example, a flour mill may employ a full-time quality controller to check wheat as it arrives. He will work for the business until he leaves, either by choice, because he is forced to by the business or when he retires. TEMPORARY workers are employed for a limited period. For example, the mill may employ temporary workers for a period of six months to operate machines that 'mill' the wheat into flour.

In the UK, around 10 per cent of all workers are temporary workers. Businesses needing casual work at busy times employ temporary workers. So do farms, which employ seasonal workers as 'pickers' during the harvesting period. Shops employ retail assistants at Christmas for a fixed period. One advantage of temporary workers is that they no longer have to be employed once demand falls off. They can also be hired when required, for example to cover staff on maternity leave or for 'one-off' tasks. Costs may be lower because temporary workers do not receive the benefits of permanent workers. Some businesses use temporary jobs to try out workers who may later become permanent. One problem with temporary workers, businesses argue, is that they are less reliable than permanent staff.

The **Employment Act, 2002** introduced the right for fixed term employees not to be treated less favourably than similar permanent staff.

Full-time and part-time employment Workers may be employed full-time or part-time by a business. Part time workers are defined in *Labour Market Trends* published by The Office for National Statistics as 'people normally working for not more than 30 hours a week except where otherwise stated'. An advantage of part-time workers is the flexibility they provide for a business. For example, part-time workers may be employed at times of peak trade, such as in public houses at the weekend. They may be employed to allow supermarkets to stay open later in the evening.

Part-time work can also benefit employees. It allows workers such as lone parents who have difficulty working full time to be employed. Students or others with low incomes can supplement their wages. The long-term unemployed or people who are retraining may find it a way to 'get back to work'.

The **Part-time Workers (Prevention of Less Favourable Treatment) Directive 2000** and the **Employment Relations Act, 1999** ensure that part-time workers are treated no less favourably in their terms and conditions of employment than full time colleagues. For example, the Directive states that part-timers working under 30 hours a week must receive the same hourly, overtime, sickness and maternity pay, and leave and holiday entitlements as a 'comparable' full-time employee of the same employer. Equal treatment also applies to redundancies, training and access to pensions schemes. Exceptions are allowed to meet 'legitimate objectives' of employers.

Homeworkers and teleworkers A wide range of different people working in the UK might be classed as homeworkers. It may include for instance farmers, shop owners, representatives, telesales people, hotel owners and some computer operators. They may be employed by a business to work at home or they may be self-employed. They may be full-time or part-time. Teleworker homeworkers are people who work from their own home, or use it as base, and who could not do so without a telephone or computer. There were three million teleworkers in the UK in 2007.

For an employer, the use of homeworkers has a number of advantages. As these workers are not based at the place of employment, the cost of equipment is reduced and less space is needed. There are also fewer problems with absenteeism and transport delays, such as people arriving late to work or who are unable to get to work because of bad weather. People with children are able to work more easily, at times when they want. However, there may be communication problems if staff can not be contacted. Also, it is far more difficult to monitor and control the work of employees.

Flexible working arrangements Different types of workers can have flexible working arrangements. There are many different types of flexibility. Workers might have flexible working hours, having to work a number of hours in the day or week, but able to choose what hours to work. Or they might work a reduced number of days but longer hours each day. Job sharing is becoming more popular as people seek part-time work. This is where the tasks involved in a job description are divided between two people, for example. They often work at different times. Examples could be a legal secretary's job, part of which is carried out by one person from 9am to 12am and another person from 12am to 5pm, or two GPs in a doctor's practice working on different days or weeks.

A growing number of businesses are taking advantage of the use of flexible arrangements. Legislation in the UK allows certain employees to request flexibility. Flexible arrangements can be beneficial for both employees and employers. Employees can choose the times they want to work to fit in with circumstances. Employers have the chance to change work patterns to fit in with production and demand.

Termination of contracts

Why might a contract of employment come to an end? The contract may be terminated either by the employee or the employer for a number of reasons.

Changing jobs and promotion Employees may leave a business to change jobs. Their existing contract would end and they would be given a contract for their new job. As stated earlier, employees cannot usually leave immediately. They often have to work out a period of 'notice', such as one week or one month. Employees who are promoted internally are also likely to be given a new contract of employment as their terms and conditions may have changed. For example, a machine operator who was appointed to be supervisor may have different wages, benefits, deductions and leave entitlements.

Dismissal Employees may be dismissed for a number of reasons. These may be for unfair reasons, such as joining a trade union. If an employment tribunal finds that a person has been dismissed unfairly, it has the power to reinstate the employee. There are lawful reasons, however, for dismissing an employee. These may include misconduct or because an employee is incapable of doing a job. A period of notice is required, but the length will vary depending on how long the employee has worked for the business. The Employment Relations Act, 1999 reduced the qualifying period for protection against unfair dismissal to one year.

Redundancy Another lawful method of dismissing an employee is on grounds of redundancy. This is where there is no work or insufficient work for the employee to do. The **Employment Rights Act, 1996** states that employees are entitled to redundancy or SEVERANCE payments. They also need to meet other criteria. For example, they must have a contract of

Question 2.

Rue du Paris is a chain of restaurants specialising in French cuisine. It expanded rapidly in the 1990s and employed increasing numbers of employees. However, the setting up of many celebrity chef restaurants and the growing number of restaurants aimed at clients wishing to spend large amounts on meals meant that by 2003 it was facing problems. Its main aim was to change its staffing levels to suit a slimmed down organisation.

The business faced a number of staffing problems.Chefs at Rue de Paris had been moving to work for competitors at higher rates of pay. After training its employees for a number of years, they took their skills elsewhere. Some of its least experienced chefs had been 'moonlighting' at other restaurants. They had hurried their cooking, leaving early to work in other establishments and in many cases they had broken the terms of their employment contracts. A few chefs were over the age of 60. They had a great deal of experience, but perhaps the company was looking to younger people with new ideas that could really move the business forward.

Some of the newer restaurants had been set up with flexible staff because the business was unsure how they would perform. Some staff had been employed on fixed term contracts, for example. Other staff had part time contracts, with flexible hours. Two restaurants in particular had been doing very poorly and the company had to decide whether to close them.

(a) Examine the ways in which the business might terminate the contracts of its employees which may help solve the problems it faces.

employment (i.e. not be self-employed). Some people, such as members of the armed forces, The House of Commons and the House of Lords are not covered by the Act. Neither are people who are retiring over the age of 60/65 or who are coming to the end of a contract or an apprenticeship.

Retirement and early retirement Some people decide to leave work when they are entitled to this state pension. However, many take 'early retirement' and finish work before. They will then live on state benefits or a private pension which they can draw upon at an earlier age. Some employers that want to get rid of older workers or reduce staff numbers offer attractive 'early retirement' packages to encourage people to leave work. People do not have to leave work at these ages. Some employees are now seeing the benefit of employing older workers.

Illness Employers can dismiss employees if they are no longer able to do a job. However, employees may choose to leave a job themselves if they are too ill to continue. Some businesses provide private health cover for employees who need to finish work. Other employees would need to live on state benefits or private insurance benefits.

End of duration of contract Some temporary employees are only given a contract to work for a limited period of time. For example, contractors may hire construction workers to work on a large project, such as a shopping centre, for a period of two years. After the project finished the employees' contract would end.

Breach of contract

If either the employee or employer suffers a financial loss as a result of a BREACH OF CONTRACT by the other party, they may claim damages. For example, an employee on a fixed term contract who is asked to work an extra two weeks to finish the job, but is not paid, may claim as a result. Claims by employees and employers are normally taken to either the the county court or another civil court. An employee can take a claim to an industrial tribunal if an amount is outstanding when the contract is terminated and if it is not related to certain categories, such as patents. Industrial tribunals often settle claims quicker than courts but there is a limit to the amount they can award.

KEYTERMS

Breach of contract - breaking of terms agreed in the contract of employment by the employers and the employees.
Contract of employment - an agreement between an employer and an employee in which each has certain obligations.
Employee - a worker for whom an employer provides and controls work, supplies equipment and pays tax and National Insurance contributions.
Permanent employment - employment for an indefinite period of time.
Self-employed - a worker who makes his or her own decisions about accepting work and conditions of work, and pays his or her own tax and National Insurance contributions.
Severance pay - an amount payable to an employee on termination of contract.
Temporary employment - employment for a limited or finite period of time.
Vicarious liability - when employers are liable for the wrongful actions of their employees.

KNOWLEDGE

1. 'A contract of employment is an agreement that is binding to both parties.' Explain this statement.
2. What is a written statement of the contract of employment?
3. State three rights of employees of a business.
4. State three duties of employees of a business.
5. Suggest five conditions of work that may appear on the written statement.
6. Explain three differences between an employee and a person who is self-employed.
7. Why might a business employ temporary workers?
8. What is meant by job sharing?
9. What are the advantages of job sharing for an employee?
10. What is meant by a homeworker?
11. Suggest three advantages of homeworkers for a business.
12. State five reasons why a contract of employment may be terminated.

Case Study: Benefits of a virtual workforce

Small business owners may find it tough to find a balance between giving enough time to ensure success and not running themselves into the ground. They often say that the first few years are the hardest, putting a strain on life outside work. They often find it necessary to get help. But employing additional, permanent staff brings with it extra headaches. Permanent recruitment can be time-consuming. There are costs in advertising the position and time taken on interviews. A small start-up business doing this may lose valuable time making sales or winning new business. There are also training costs and time and effort spent to stay in line with employment legislation. Also there are other fixed costs like tax and National Insurance contributions.

To ease this, many businesses are outsourcing support functions, freeing up time. Virtual personal assistants (PAs), off-site staff who can work on small or large projects for a fixed fee, are an example. Xenios Thrasyvoulou, founder and chief executive of Peopleperhour.com says, 'Small companies are increasingly looking for flexible labour and need a platform on which to do that. Forums, like Peopleperhour.com, help people find skilled freelance professionals to undertake support tasks or functions on a 'per project' basis ... It functions like an online marketplace where professionals can put up their profile and companies or 'buyers' can list their requirements. Buyers then receive bids from professionals willing to carry out the work and can choose the most suitable one. We take a 10 per cent commission from the freelancers, which works out less than you'd see from an agency and it remains completely free for the buyers ... Remote support can really help small businesses and busy individuals to get projects done in an easy, cost-effective and transparent way, without the hassle and costs associated with employing someone full-time to carry out these tasks.'

A forum, he argues, cuts out intermediaries in the recruitment process. Some employees, like freelancers, are hard to find. So small businesses use a recruitment agency. But recruitment agencies often want to place people in a permanent position because they get better commission. This means they can be quite pricey.

Outsourcing is not new, but until recently it was seen as the privilege of larger companies. Small businesses didn't have the resources to outsource on the large scale needed for it to be worthwhile. Through forums, off-site staff or freelance workers could offer small companies a viable alternative to permanent recruitment.

Source: adapted from http://www.smallbusiness.co.uk/5.6/human-resources/guides/256602/the-benefits-of-a-virtual-workforce.thtml.

(a) Identify the problems of employing permanent staff. (4 marks)
(b) What does outsourcing mean? Give two examples. (4 marks)
(c) Explain how the various services of Peopleperhour.com might help a small business. (8 marks)
(d) Evaluate the potential effectiveness of using outsourcing services such as Peopleperhour.com. (12 marks)

65 Training and appraisal

Why business train their workforce

TRAINING is the process of increasing the knowledge and skills of workers so that they are better able to perform their jobs. The objectives of training differ from business to business but they include:

- making workers more productive by teaching them more effective ways of working;
- familiarising workers with new equipment or technology being introduced;
- educating workers in new methods of working, such as shifting from production line methods to cell methods;
- making workers more flexible so that they are able to do more than one job;
- preparing workers to move into a different job within the business, which could be a new job at a similar level or a promotion;
- improving standards of work in order to improve quality;
- implementing health and safety at work policies;
- increasing job satisfaction and motivation, because training should help workers feel more confident in what they are doing and they should gain self-esteem;
- assisting in recruiting and retaining high quality staff, attracted by the quality of training offered.

Sometimes, individual employees request training or undertake training without the financial or time support of their employers. For example, a manager may take an MBA university course in her own time. More frequently, training is provided by the employer. The need for training is sometimes identified in the appraisal process.

Induction training

Many businesses put on training for people starting a job. This is known as INDUCTION TRAINING. It is designed to help new employees settle quickly into the business and their jobs. Exactly what is offered differs from business to business and job to job. For example, a small business might simply allocate another worker to look after the new employee for a day to 'show them the ropes'. A young person just out of university might have a year long induction programme to a large company. They might spend time in a number of departments, as well as being given more general training about the business. But most induction training attempts to introduce workers to the nature of the business and work practices, including health and safety issues.

On-the-job training

ON-THE-JOB TRAINING is training given in the workplace by the employer. There are many ways in which this could happen.

Learning from other workers An employee might simply work next to another worker, watch that worker do a task and with their help repeat it.

Mentoring This is where a more experienced employee is asked to provide advice and help to a less experienced worker. The less experienced worker can turn for help and advice to another more experienced worker at any time.

Job rotation This is where a worker spends a period of time doing one job, then another period of time doing another job and so on. Eventually they have received the broad experience needed to do a more specialist job.

Question 1.

Michelle Hallett went from sales assistant to store manager with the help of two training courses available through Modern Apprenticeships. A basic retail training programme led to a National Vocational Qualification level 2 achievement followed by a management course tied to level 3 saw her climb the ladder with Chockers, a small Essex-based shoe retailer. Michelle, said: 'I feel I've benefited in a number of ways. I'm more confident with customers and am better at handling staff. It's all been worthwhile.' Chockers, an eight-store chain with a flagship shop in The Strand in London, is a classic example of a business faced with a training problem in a sector with a high staff turnover.

Rosanne Lewis, area manager co-ordinator, said: 'We couldn't afford to operate a training scheme of our own but now we're able to put more of our sales staff through the apprenticeship programmes.' John Gill, the founder, trained the hard way, on a market stall, before launching the business, but is now committed to using the framework to provide a comprehensive training to add some extra staff polish and performance.

There was some apprehension among young sales assistants at the start.

'Some felt it would be like going back to school but I quickly reassured them on that score. We have a staff of 50 and I want all of them to take up the training programme,' says Ms Lewis.

Michelle did on-the-job training with a supervisor monitoring progress and discussing the finer points of customer relations at the end of a day's work. Her deputy, Hayley Clarke, has followed a similar programme. She said: 'I found it a bit hard at first to fit into the routine but the others in the shop have been really helpful. Being assistant manager now means I have more responsibility.'

Source: adapted from *The Telegraph*, 18.3.2004.

(a) Using examples from the article explain what is meant by on-the-job training?
(b) Explain why there might be potential problems with training staff at Chockers.
(c) Discuss whether Chockers might offer its own training scheme in future.

Traditional apprenticeships In the past, workers in traditional skilled trades, such as carpentry or engineering, would undertake training over, say, three-five years in an apprenticeship. This would involve a mix of training methods. When the business decided they had 'qualified' they would be employed as a full-time worker. Many of these schemes died out due to the cost for the business, the decline in traditional trades, mechanisation and the need for more flexible work practices.

Graduate training Medium- to large-sized businesses may offer graduate training programmes. They are typically designed to offer those with university degrees either professional training, such as in accountancy or the law, or managerial training.

Off-the-job training

OFF-THE-JOB TRAINING is training which takes place outside the business by an external training provider like a local college or university. For example, 16-25 year olds might go to college one day a week to do a catering course or an engineering course. A trainee accountant might have an intensive course at an accountancy college or attend night classes before taking professional exams. A graduate manager might do an MBA (Masters in Business Administration) course at a Business School in the evening and at weekends.

Off-the-job training can provide courses which a business internally would be unable to provide. But it can be expensive, particularly if the business is paying not just for the course but also a salary for the time the employee is attending the course.

Training initiatives

The government promotes training through a variety of initiatives and schemes.

Learning and Skills Councils These are bodies which have been set up by government to cover the whole of the UK. Each area of the UK has its own regional Learning and Skills Council. They are responsible for promoting training and manage funding for a wide range of schemes such as modern apprenticeships (see below). They are funded by the government from taxes. But businesses taking part in training may also be required to contribute towards the cost of training which directly benefits them.

Modern Apprenticeships In the past, apprenticeships were the most common way for a school leaver to become a skilled manual worker with a qualification. In the 1970s, with a sharp decline in employment in manufacturing industry, most businesses scrapped their apprenticeship schemes. Today, the government sponsors Modern Apprenticeships. This scheme aims to give young people an apprenticeship training which will equip them for a specific job in an industry. Businesses run Modern Apprenticeships and then receive a subsidy from the government for each apprentice on the scheme. Typically the Modern Apprenticeship training runs for three years.

Question 2.

Asda operates one of the most rigorous retail training programmes in the UK. New employees spend the equivalent of 25 weeks, mainly in-house, learning how to do their job. In 2004 Asda linked its own programme with National Vocational Qualifications in retailing and Modern Apprenticeships. It hoped this would will help increase productivity, encourage a higher level of internal promotion and reduce a staff turnover rate currently running at 26 per cent. The Learning and Skills Council provided more than £500,000 to the project. Asda, rather than a training provider, would control the money which will be used to cover the cost of outside assessors ensuring that its training is in line with the NVQ programme.

Mrs Sam Smith, people development manager, said: 'We're not doing this for profit but to raise the standard of our training and provide the staff with extra qualifications which will benefit them and the company.' There was extensive discussions between the company, the Learning and Skills Council and City & Guilds to validate the Asda in-house training set-up as a retail NVQ.

Source: adapted from *The Telegraph*, 18.3.2004.

(a) What is meant by (i) a Modern Apprenticeship and (ii) in-house training?
(b) Why is training likely to be so important for a business like Asda?
(c) Discuss whether Asda rather than a training provider should provide training.

The New Deal Since the late 1970s, governments have run a variety of schemes aimed at getting unemployed workers, particularly young workers, into a job. The New Deal, for example, promises to give any young unemployed person under the age of 25 either full-time training or work experience. The New Deal also offers older long-term unemployed workers a similar package.

Investors in People (IiP) IiP is a national standard developed by industry bodies such as the CBI and TUC with the support of the Employment Department, which businesses have to meet if they wish to gain IiP accreditation. To get accreditation, they have to show that the need for training is considered at every level and in every major decision made by the business. Businesses which go through the process of gaining IiP accreditation typically find that there are inefficiencies in the way the business operates because staff have not been trained properly. These training needs then have to be addressed. Gaining IiP is a useful marketing tool for a business. This is because customers perceive that, by gaining IiP accreditation, the business is a modern, forward-thinking business where staff are properly trained to deal with their work.

Labour market failure and the need for training

It can be argued that, if left to free market forces, too little training would take place. This is an example of MARKET FAILURE. In the labour market, it occurs for two reasons.

- Businesses spend too little money on training because it is often cheaper for them to recruit new workers who have already been trained by another business or on a government training scheme.
- Individual workers don't spend enough on training themselves because they don't want to get into short-term debt. They also fail to realise how much more they could earn if they had better training.

In the past, traditional apprentices might have signed an agreement to stay with their employer a number of years after they became qualified. This meant they could not be 'poached' by a rival business. Today, linking training with staying on in the business is rare. There is nothing to stop a newly trained worker from leaving one business to take up a post at a higher salary elsewhere.

A major problem that the UK labour force has faced in the past is SKILLS SHORTAGES. This is where there is a large number of vacancies because individuals do not have the abilities, skills, experience or qualifications necessary to do the jobs that employers require.

Generally, when there is market failure, it is argued that the government should step in to correct that market failure. Governments have two broad ways of doing this.

- They can provide training themselves and pay for it from tax revenues. Currently, the UK government provides training for the unemployed through its New Deal programme for example. Training is also provided through free college or further education courses.
- The government can pay grants to industry bodies or individual businesses to undertake training. This can be funded from general taxation or by a levy on all businesses in the industry. For example, in the UK construction industry, businesses have to pay a levy (effectively a tax) to pay for the work of the Construction Industry Training Board. This provides training for construction workers.

Evaluation of training

As businesses have demanded greater value for money, it has become important to evaluate training. Evaluation is simple when the result of the training is clear to see, such as when training workers to use new technology. Where training is designed to give a certain result, such as:

- a health and safety course;
- a word processing course;
- a design course;

evaluation can be based on observed results. This may be a reduction in accidents, increased typing speed or designs with greater impact.

It is more difficult to evaluate the success of a management training course or a programme of social skills development. It is usual to use end of course questionnaires, where course members answer a number of questions. The problem is that the course will have been a break for most employees from the normal work routine. This can make the participants' view of training appear of more value than it is. Also questionnaires tend to evaluate the course and not the learning. This often means that the person attending the course is assessing the quality of the tutors and visual aids, instead of what has been learnt.

To overcome these problems a business might:

- ask participants and managers to complete a short questionnaire at the start of the course to focus their minds on what they hope to get from it;
- give out another questionnaire at the end of the course focusing on learning and what could be applied back at the job;
- give further questionnaires to review the effects of the course on performance.

This helps employees to concentrate on what has been learnt. This process may, however, be costly for the business.

Is training becoming more popular?

Ashton and Felstead (2003), in their review of research on training in the UK, suggested a number of reasons to explain the evidence of increased training in the UK over the last five years.

- There has been an improvement in the UK's skills base due to the investment by government to increase numbers in higher education.
- Some employers have played their part in improving skills. Companies with Investors in People and a commitment to training are now training all staff, including the unskilled. This has resulted in the general upskilling of employees in business.
- A group of businesses now state that strategic human resource management is central to business development, and that training is part of that strategy. In addition, a small group of 'leading edge' or high performance organisations use employees' skills as a source of

competitive advantage.

However, a group of UK businesses is still not committed to training. They only engage in formal training when they are forced, either by government legislation or customer requirements. For example, some manufacturing firms can only become suppliers to large retail firms when they obtain ISO 9000. Some argue, therefore, that the UK still appears to be struggling to catch up with competitors in Europe in its investment in training. They also suggest that it may be falling behind new competitors from South East Asia.

Appraisal

After a period of time working in a job (and regularly after), a firm may APPRAISE the employee. This is an attempt by the business to find out the qualities, usefulness or worth of its employees.

Appraisal can be used by a business to:
- improve performance;
- provide feedback;
- increase motivation;
- identify training needs;
- identify potential for promotion;
- award salary increases;
- set out job objectives;
- provide information for human resource planning;
- assess the effectiveness of the selection process.

The problem with having all of these aims is that the person carrying out the appraisal may have conflicting roles. If appraisal is designed to help performance and to act as a basis for salary awards, the appraiser would have to be both judge and helper at the same time. This makes it difficult to be impartial. It is also difficult for the person being appraised. A worker may want to discuss problems, but is likely to be cautious about what they say in case they jeopardise any possible pay rise. One way around this is for the appraisal system to review the performance of the worker only.

Many appraisal schemes have been linked to **performance appraisal**, called **performance management**. This involves observing, measuring and developing the performance of employees. Performance can be 'measured' against criteria such as output, quality and speed.

Carrying out appraisal

Appraisal has, in the past, been seen as most suitable for employees in management and supervisory positions. Increasingly, clerical, secretarial and manual staff, with skilled or technical jobs, are also being appraised.

Who carries out the appraisal? There is a number of people that might be involved in appraising an individual. Appraisers may be referred to as **raters**. These are people who 'rate' the performance of an individual.

- Superiors. Most appraisals are carried out by the employee's superior. The advantage of this is that the supervisor usually has intimate knowledge of the tasks that a worker has been carrying out and how well they have been done.
- People 'above' the immediate superior can be involved in appraisal in two different ways. They may 'approve' the superior's appraisal of the employee. A manager further up the hierarchy may also directly carry out the appraisal. This is more likely to happen when individuals decide if a worker has the potential for promotion, for example.
- Self appraisal. This is a relatively new idea and not greatly used. Individuals do carry out self appraisal in traditional appraisal schemes, although the superior's decision officially 'counts'. The ratings that the employer has given may be changed, however, in the light of the employee's comments.
- Peer appraisal. It is sometimes argued that appraisal by peers is reliable and valid as they have a more comprehensive view of the employee's job performance. The main problem, though, is that peers may be unwilling to appraise each other. This can be seen as 'grassing'.
- Subordinates. Appraisal by subordinates is another less well used method. It is limited, as subordinates will only know certain aspects of the work of other employees.
- 360 degrees appraisal. This method gathers ratings from a combination of supervisors, peers and subordinates. Self-ratings and customer ratings may also be used. It provides feedback to individuals on how their performance is viewed by business stakeholders. It also encourages individuals to self-diagnose their strong and weak areas and identifies where training is needed. The information from 360 degrees appraisal can help a business when making personnel decisions, such as who to choose for promotion.

Many firms have used appraisal systems only to find that they have to change or abandon them after a short time. Others 'battle' on with the system, but recognise that it is inadequate or disliked. What factors influence the success of an appraisal system?

- Purpose of the system. Effectiveness will be greater if all involved are clear about what the system is for.
- Control. It is vital that the system is controlled by senior and line management and isn't something done simply 'for the personnel department'.
- Openness and participation. The more feedback that appraisees are given about their ratings, the more likely they are to accept the process. Similarly, the more the employee is allowed to take part in the system, the greater the chance of gaining their commitment.
- Appraisal criteria. The criteria must be related to the job, be easy to use and appear fair to the worker.
- Training. Training may be needed in how to appraise and how to conduct interviews.
- Administrative efficiency. Appraisal must be carried out so that it causes as few problems as possible for both parties. It also needs to be confidential.
- Action. Appraisal needs to be supported by follow-up

action. Plans that are agreed by appraiser and workers must be checked, to make sure they take place.

- Selection of raters. The choice of rater should be carefully controlled to avoid, for example, individuals nominating only 'friendly raters' to provide them with feedback.
- Anonymity of raters. Ratings should be made anonymously to encourage honest appraisal.
- Training of raters. Raters should be trained to complete rating and appraisal forms accurately.

KEYTERMS

Appraisal – evaluating the usefulness of the employee to the business.
Induction training – training which occurs when a worker starts a job with a business.
Market failure – when the operation of free market forces fails to provide an optimal level of output.
Off-the-job training – training which takes place outside the business through an external training provider like a local college or university.
On-the-job training – training given in the workplace by the employer.
Skills shortages – where potential employees do not have the skills demanded by employers.
Training – the process of increasing the knowledge and skills of workers so that they are better able to perform their jobs.

KNOWLEDGE

1. List the reasons why a business might train its employees.
2. Why might a business offer induction training?
3. Explain the difference between mentoring and job rotation.
4. What is graduate training?
5. Who benefits from training through the New Deal programme?
6. What is Investors in People?
7. What is the role of Learning and Skills Councils in training?
8. Explain why businesses might spend less on training than is desirable.
9. How can training be evaluated?
10. What is meant by performance appraisal?
11. How can appraisal help a business?

Question 3.

Pettersford plc is a manufacturer of plastic cartons and other containers. It has a number of plants around the UK. In 2002 it faced rising costs and falling productivity. The business had previously used annual appraisal methods. Every year employees were reviewed to discuss their performance over the year. It was often a one way communication process, with the line manager 'telling' the employee why they had done well or badly, and how they might improve next year. At the end of the appraisal, employees were asked to make their own comments. But only a short time was left for this and usually the employee could not remember issues that had arisen up to 12 months previously.

Faced with the possibility of closure, the business introduced a quarterly performance review for all its factories. It did allow this to be amended if a plant felt that it did not want four, but the business was adamant that it needed to get away from the annual reviews. Another change was that each employee nominated two of their work colleagues to comment on their work. At first people were reluctant to criticise, but eventually, as people became more comfortable with the system, the business and employees found constructive criticism and praise useful. The dialogue also had to be more of a two way process, so that employees could express their own views.

The appraisal was backed up by regular meetings with managers, where suggestions at the appraisal could be introduced into the work environment. Employees gave a 'personal commitment' at their review and this was implemented with the help of the line manager and senior staff. Employees also felt that they could take more initiative, by making suggestions at appraisal meetings. Previously they had simply 'keep their heads down' hoping to get it all over quickly.

The business found that productivity rose as a result of the changes. One spokesperson said 'If you give people some recognition for their work, and listen to what they have to say in return, then it's not only the employee who benefits'.

(a) Explain the problems that existed in the old method of appraisal at Pettersford plc.
(b) Identify the methods of appraisal in the new system.
(c) Discuss the advantages and disadvantages of the new appraisal system for (i) employees and (ii) the business.

Case Study: Training in social housing

Kiran Singh argues that his job as a housing officer for a housing association is more than just sorting out anti-social tenants and chasing rent. When he says he works in social housing, his friends think he works with awkward tenants and council homes – a stereotypical view. However there are now many more jobs out in housing than there were 20 years ago, particularly in regeneration. Kiran is responsible for 300 homes managed by the social landlord, East Midlands Housing. Earning £20,000 a year just months after graduating with a housing degree. He hopes to carve himself a successful career in the sector. It is now common for experienced housing managers to earn a minimum £40,000, and it is not unusual for top chief executives or directors to command salaries of up to £100,000.

Unlike other public services, such as the NHS, there are few graduate training programmes in this area, although they are starting to appear in some of the larger organisations. It is not essential to have a housing degree to work in housing. But it does attract graduates from different disciplines such as social sciences, human geography, economics and politics. A Modern Apprenticeship offers another route into the sector. Apprentices are given on-the-job training, but also learn about the historical context of social housing, its management and Housing law. Roger Keller, head of education at the Chartered Institute of Housing, the professional organisation for housing, says: 'An apprenticeship offers a proper understanding of why social housing is important in a country which doesn't have enough housing and how people can get access to housing when prices are rising.' Keller says that the uptake of Modern Apprenticeships in housing is low. 'They aren't widely taken up and you could argue that the sector ought to be recommending more young people take them on.' Once in the sector, it is possible to study for a range of professional qualifications offered by the Institute. Keller estimates that around 90 per cent of people studying for a professional qualification are sponsored by their employer.

The job opportunities within social housing sector have increased over the last 30 years as it has made a greater contribution it makes to public services. In the 1980s social housing was limited, geared towards rent collection and bad neighbours and there was little money available for development. Training may have simply meant learning from a colleague. New job titles today include regeneration officers, tenant participation officers, urban designers, antisocial behaviour managers and financial inclusion officers. These jobs require people to work with agencies like health, education, the police force and the army. There is a need for appropriate people skills and an understanding of different professional perspectives, requiring training and development of staff. With 50,000 people working in social housing sector due to retire by 2014, it may be just the right time to consider a career move into the sector.

Source: adapted from *The Guardian*, 8.11.2007.

(a) What us meant by (i) Apprentices (3 marks) and (ii) a graduate training programme? (3 marks)

(b) Outline one of example of 'on-the-job training' and one example of 'off-the-job training' mentioned in the article. (6 marks)

(c) Examine the advantages to an 18 year old of accepting a Modern Apprenticeship in housing rather than doing a university degree. (8 marks)

(d) Evaluate the type of training that might be needed in the future for individuals working in housing. (10 marks)

66 Motivation theories

The satisfaction of needs

If asked, most people who work would probably say they do so to earn money to buy goods and services. However, this is not the only need that is satisfied by working. A list of people's needs that may be satisfied from work might be very long indeed. It could include, for example, the need for variety in the workplace, which may be satisfied by an interesting job. Employees may also need to feel appreciated for the work they do, which could be reflected in the prestige attached to their job.

Individuals are not the same. Therefore, it is likely that lists made by any two people of their needs and how they can be satisfied will be very different. There are some reasons for working that could apply to everyone, such as the need to earn money. However, some reasons have more importance for particular individuals than others. One employee may need to work with friendly colleagues, whereas another might be happy working on his own.

The importance of motivation

Why is it important for a business to find out what satisfies the needs of its employees? It is argued that if an individual's needs are not satisfied, then that worker will not be MOTIVATED to work. Businesses have found that even if employees are satisfied with pay and conditions at work, they also complain that their employer does not do a good job in motivating them. This applies to all levels, from the shop floor to the boardroom. It appears in many companies that employers are not getting the full potential from their employees because they are not satisfying all of their employees' needs. Figure 1 shows one example of how a business might make decisions, having first identified an employee's needs.

It is important for a business to motivate its employees. In the short run a lack of motivation may lead to reduced effort and lack of commitment. If employees are watched closely, fear of wage cuts or redundancy may force them to maintain their effort even though they are not motivated. This is negative motivation. In the long term, a lack of motivation may result in high levels of absenteeism, industrial disputes and falling productivity and profit for a business. So it is argued that well motivated employees will be productive which should lead to greater efficiency and profits for a business.

This unit examines different theories of motivation. They can be broadly categorised into two main groups – content theories of motivation and process theories of motivation. **Content theories** of motivation explain the specific factors that motivate people. They answer the question 'What drives behaviour? and include the theories of Maslow, McGregor, McClelland and Herzberg. **Process theories** are concerned with the thought processes that influence behaviour, such as the theories of Vroom, Porter and Lawler, and Adams.

Maslow's hierarchy of needs

The first comprehensive attempt to classify needs was by Abraham Maslow in 1954. Maslow's theory consisted of two parts. The first concerned classification of needs. The second concerned how these classes are related to each other. Maslow suggested that 'classes' of needs could be placed into a hierarchy. The hierarchy is normally presented as a 'pyramid', with each level consisting of a certain class of needs. This is shown in Figure 2.The classes of needs were:

- physiological needs, e.g. wages high enough to meet weekly bills, good working conditions;
- safety needs, e.g. job security, safe working conditions;
- love and belonging, eg working with colleagues that support you at work, teamwork, communicating;
- esteem needs, e.g. being given recognition for doing a job well;
- self-actualisation, e.g. being promoted and given more responsibility, scope to develop and introduce new ideas and take on challenging new job assignments.

Figure 2 can also be used to show the relationship between the different classes. Maslow argued that needs at the bottom of the pyramid are basic needs. They are concerned with survival.

Figure 1: Satisfying an individual's needs

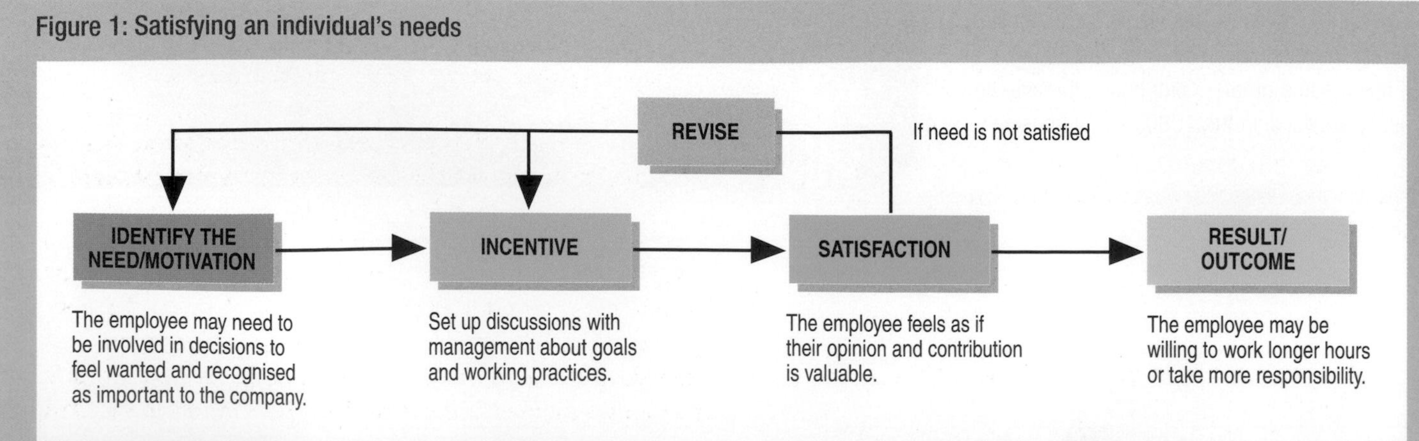

REVISE
If need is not satisfied
IDENTIFY THE NEED/MOTIVATION
INCENTIVE
SATISFACTION
RESULT/ OUTCOME
The employee may need to be involved in decisions to feel wanted and recognised as important to the company.
Set up discussions with management about goals and working practices.
The employee feels as if their opinion and contribution is valuable.
The employee may be willing to work longer hours or take more responsibility.

These needs must be satisfied before a person can move to the next level. For example, people are likely to be more concerned with basic needs, such as food, than anything else. At work an employee is unlikely to be concerned about acceptance from colleagues if he has not eaten for six hours. Once each level is satisfied, the needs at this level become less important. The exception is the top level of SELF-ACTUALISATION. This is the need to fulfil your potential. Maslow argued that although everyone is capable of this, in practice very few reach this level.

Each level of needs is dependent on the levels below. Say an employee has been motivated at work by the opportunity to take responsibility, but finds he may lose his job. The whole system collapses, as the need to feed and provide for himself and his dependants again becomes the most important need.

Maslow's ideas have great appeal for business. The message is clear – find out which level each individual is at and decide on suitable rewards. Unfortunately the theory has problems when used in practice. Some levels do not appear to exist for certain individuals, while some rewards appear to fit into more than one class. Money, for example, needs to be used to purchase 'essentials' such as food, but it can also be seen as a status symbol or an indicator of personal worth. There is also a problem in deciding when a level has actually been 'satisfied'. There will always be exceptions to the rules Maslow outlined. A well motivated designer may spend many hours on a creative design despite lack of sleep or food.

Figure 2: Maslow's hierarchy of needs

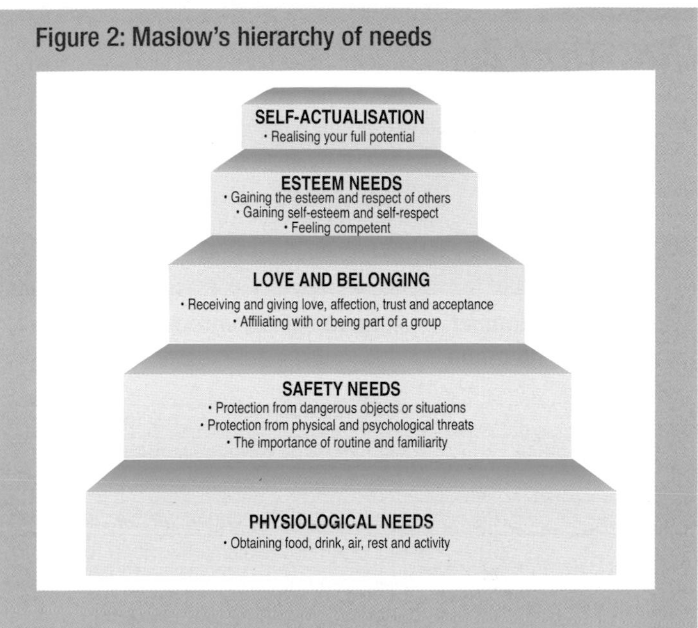

Taylor's Scientific Management

Research into the factors that motivate individuals had been carried out long before Maslow's 'hierarchy' of needs. Frederick W. Taylor set out a theory of SCIENTIFIC MANAGEMENT in his book *The Principles of Scientific Management* in 1911. Many of the ideas of today's 'scientific management school' come from the work of Taylor.

The turn of the 20th century in the USA was a time of rapid expansion. Compared to today, the organisation of work on the shop floor was left much more in the hands of workers and foremen. Workers often brought their own tools and decisions about the speed of machines were left to operators. There were few training programmes to teach workers their jobs and skills were gained simply by watching more experienced colleagues. Decisions about selection, rest periods and layoffs were frequently made by foremen.

Taylor suggested that such arrangements were haphazard and inefficient. Management did not understand the shop floor and allowed wasteful work practices to continue. Workers, on the other hand, left to their own devices, would do as little as possible. 'Soldiering' would also take place (working more slowly together so that management did not realise workers' potential) and workers would carry out tasks in ways they were used to rather than the most efficient way.

Taylor's scientific principles were designed to reduce inefficiency of workers and managers. This was to be achieved by 'objective laws' that management and workers could agree on, reducing conflict between them. Neither party could argue against a system of work that was based on 'science'. Taylor believed his principles would create a partnership between manager and worker, based on an understanding of how jobs should be done and how workers are motivated.

Taylor's approach How did Taylor discover what the 'best way' was of carrying out a task? Table 2 shows an illustration of Taylor's method. Taylor had a very simple view of what motivated people at work – money. He felt that workers should receive a 'fair day's pay for a fair day's work', and pay should be linked to output through piece rates. A worker who did not produce a 'fair day's work' would face a loss of earnings; exceeding the target would lead to a bonus. In 1899 Taylor's methods were used at the Bethlehem Steel Works in the USA,

Question 1.

Anmac Ltd is a small expanding high-tech company. It employs approximately 25 workers in two factories, one at Chester and one at Stafford. The employers organise work on a fairly informal basis. Workers work at their own pace, which often results in a variable level of output. Recently orders for their advanced micro-electronic circuit boards have increased rapidly. The firm has decided that, to cope with the orders, increased production is needed. Two suggestions have been put forward.

- Encourage the workers to work overtime at the Chester plant.
- Redeploy some of the workers from Chester to Stafford where there is a shortfall of workers.

The workers at the Chester plant are mainly married women in their twenties, many with young, school-aged children and husbands who also work.

(a) Explain how Taylor's scientific management principles might be used to solve the problems faced by Anmac Ltd.

(b) What problems might Anmac Ltd find in using such principles?

Question 2.

Table 1 shows the results of a survey carried out in Bryant and Gillie, a SME that manufactures children's clothing. The company introduced a piece rate system of work - a system where employees are paid according to the number or quantity of items they produce. Five groups were involved in the new system. Different actions were taken to introduce the system to each group. The table shows the effect on labour turnover and output of these actions.

Table 1: The effect of introducing a piece rate system into a clothes manufacturing business

Group	Number in group	Action taken to introduce system	Resignations within 40 days of introduction	Change in output
A	100	Group told the changes will take place next week	17%	-2%
B	150	Management introduces changes with the help of group to suit their needs	0%	+10%
C	200	Group told the changes will take place next week	7%	0%
D	50	Management explains the need for change to group	2%	+2%
E	100	Management explains the need for change and discusses this with the group	0%	+5%

(a) To what extent do the results support the human relations explanation of workers' motivation?

(b) Using the results of the survey in Table 1, advise the management on the likely action needed to motivate workers when changing work practices.

where they were responsible for raising pig iron production by almost 400 per cent per man per day. Taylor found the 'best way to do each job' and designed incentives to motivate workers.

Taylor's message for business is simple - allow workers to work and managers to manage based on scientific principles of work study. Many firms today still attempt to use Taylor's principles. In the 1990s for example some businesses introduced **Business process reengineering (BPR)**. This is a management approach where organisations look at their business processes from a 'clean slate' perspective and determine how they can best construct these processes to improve how they conduct business. Taylor's approach is similar in that it advocates businesses finding the best way of doing something to add value to the business.

Table 2: Taylor's method, designed to find the 'best way' to carry out a task at work

- Pick a dozen skilled workers.
- Observe them at work and note down the elements and sequences adopted in their tasks.
- Time each element with a stop watch.
- Eliminate any factors which appear to add nothing to the completion of the task.
- Choose the quickest method discovered and fit them in their sequence.
- Teach the worker this sequence; do not allow any change from the set procedure.
- Include time for rest and the result will be the 'quickest and best' method for the task. Because it is the best way, all workers selected to perform the task must adopt it and meet the time allowed.
- Supervise workers to ensure that these methods are carried out during the working day.

Problems with Taylor's approach There is a number of problems with Taylor's ideas. The notion of a 'quickest and best way' for all workers does not take into account individual differences. There is no guarantee that the 'best way' will suit everyone.

Taylor also viewed people at work more as machines, with financial needs, than as humans in a social setting. There is no doubt that money is an important motivator. Taylor overlooked that people also work for reasons other than money. A survey in America by the Robb and Myatt in 2004, for example, found that of the top ten factors motivating workers, the first three categories were a sense of achievement, having that achievement recognised, and positive working relationships. This suggests there may be needs that must be met at work, which Taylor ignored, but were recognised in Maslow's ideas which came later.

Human relations

Taylor's scientific management ideas may have seemed appealing at first glance to business. Some tried to introduce his ideas in the 1920s and 1930s, which led to industrial unrest. Others found that financial incentives did motivate workers, and still do today. However, what was becoming clear was that there were other factors which may affect workers' motivation.

The Hawthorne studies Many of the ideas which are today known as the 'human relations school' grew out of experiments between 1927 and 1932 at the Hawthorne Plant of the Western Electric company in Chicago. Initially these were based on 'scientific management' - the belief that workers' productivity was affected by work conditions, the skills of workers and financial incentives. Over the five year period, changes were made in incentive schemes, rest periods, hours of work, lighting and heating and the effect on workers' productivity was measured. One example was a group of six women assembling telephone relays. It was found that whatever changes were made, including a return to the original conditions, output rose. This came to be known as the HAWTHORNE EFFECT.

The study concluded that changes in conditions and financial rewards had little or no effect on productivity. Increases in output were mainly due to the greater cohesion and communication which workers in groups developed as they interacted and were motivated to work together. Workers were also motivated by the interest shown in their work by the researchers. This result was confirmed by further investigations in the Bank Wiring Observation where 14 men with different tasks were studied.

The work of **Elton Mayo** (and Roethlisberger and Dickson) in the 1930s, who reported on the Hawthorne Studies, has led to what is known today as the human relations school. A business aiming to maximise productivity must make sure that the 'personal satisfactions' of workers are met for workers to be motivated. Management must also work and communicate with informal work groups, making sure that their goals fit in with the goals of the business. One way to do this is to allow such groups to be part of decision making. Workers are likely to be more committed to tasks that they have had some say in.

There are examples of these ideas being used in business. The Volvo plant in Uddevalla, opened in 1989,was designed to allow workers to work in teams of eight to ten. Each team built a complete car and made decisions about production. Volvo found that absenteeism rates at Uddevalla averaged 8 per cent, compared to 25 per cent in their Gothenburg plant which used a production line system. Other examples have been:

- Honda's plant in Swindon where 'teamwork' has been emphasised - there were no workers or directors, only 'associates';
- McDonald's picnics, parties and McBingo for their employees where they were made to feel part of the company;
- Mary Kay's seminars in the USA, which were presented like the American Academy awards for company employees.

Question 3.

Larry Page and Sergey Brin graduated from America's Stanford University in computer science in 1995. They found common ground in a unique approach to solving one of computing's biggest challenges – retrieving relevant information from a massive set of data. They spent 18 months perfecting their technology, following a path that would ultimately become Google Inc. At Mountain view, California, where Google is based, there is a beach volleyball court, a dinosaur skeleton and gaudy parasols aplenty. There is an abundance of open space, courtyards, quadrangles and forums. The buildings are uncluttered, mixing functionality and hi-tech feng shui. Staff travel between buildings on electric mini-scooters. Whiteboards are dotted throughout and the famous 'help yourself' juice counters are also in evidence. Lunch is free for employees and there's more choice than one would find in a small town. Open a laptop in Mountain View anywhere and you are invited to join the free Google wi-fi network. Everywhere there are examples of the legendary 20 per cent scheme that Google operates - letting engineers spend a fifth of their time pursuing personal projects. On one plasma screen a spinning globe shows search engine queries to Google made in real time. It was created by one of the engineers in his 20 per cent time. Google also has its on-site gym, on-site dentist and on-site celebrity chef who previously served the Grateful Dead.

Source: adapted from www.matr.net, www.bbc.co.uk.

(a) Outline the various ways that Google uses to motivate its staff.

(b) Using a motivation theory, examine why Google is successful at motivating its employees.

Problems There is a number of criticisms of the human relations school.

- It assumes workers and management share the same goals. This idea of workplace 'consensus' may not always exist. For example, in the 1980s Rover tried to introduce a programme called 'Working with Pride'. It was an attempt to raise quality by gaining employee commitment. This would be achieved by greater communication with employees. The programme was not accepted throughout the company. As one manager stated: 'We've tried the face-to-face communications approach. It works to a degree, but we are not too good at the supervisory level ... enthusiasm for the Working with Pride programme is proportionate to the level in the hierarchy. For supervisors it's often just seen as a gimmick ...'
- It is assumed that communication between workers and management will break down 'barriers'. It could be argued, however, that the knowledge of directors' salaries or redundancies may lead to even more 'barriers' and unrest.
- It is biased towards management. Workers are manipulated into being productive by managers. It may also be seen as a way of reducing trade union power.

Herzberg's two-factor theory

In 1966 Fredrick Herzberg attempted to find out what motivated people at work. He asked a group of professional engineers and accountants to describe incidents in their jobs which gave them strong feelings of satisfaction or dissatisfaction. He then asked them to describe the causes in each case.

Results Herzberg divided the causes into two categories or factors. These are shown in Figure 3.

- **MOTIVATORS.** These are the factors which give workers **job satisfaction**, such as recognition for their effort. Increasing these motivators is needed to give job satisfaction. This, it could be argued, will make workers more productive. A business that rewards its workforce for, say, achieving a target is likely to motivate them to be more productive. However, this is not guaranteed, as other factors can also affect productivity.
- **HYGIENE or MAINTENANCE FACTORS.** These are factors that can lead to workers being **dissatisfied**, such as

pay or conditions. Improving hygiene factors should remove dissatisfaction. For example, better canteen facilities may make workers less dissatisfied about their environment. An improvement in hygiene factors alone is not likely to motivate an individual. But if they are not met, there could be a fall in productivity.

There is some similarity between Herzberg's and Maslow's ideas. They both point to needs that have to be satisfied for the employee to be motivated. Herzberg argues that only the higher levels of Maslow's hierarchy motivate workers.

Herzberg's ideas are often linked with **job enrichment**. This is where workers have their jobs 'expanded', so that they can experience more of the production process. This allows the workers to be more involved and motivated, and have a greater sense of achievement. Herzberg used his ideas in the development of clerical work. He selected a group of workers in a large corporation. Performance and job attitudes were low. Herzberg redesigned these jobs so that they were given more responsibility and recognition.

Problems Herzberg's theory does seem to have some merits. Improving pay or conditions, for example, may remove dissatisfaction at first. Often, however, these things become taken for granted. It is likely that better conditions will be asked for in following years. Evidence of this can be seen in wage claims which aim to be above the rate of inflation in some businesses every year. Job enrichment may also be expensive for many firms. In addition, it is likely that any benefits from job improvements will not be seen for a long time and that businesses will not be able to continue with such a policy in periods of recession.

Surveys that have tried to reproduce Herzberg's results have often failed. This may have been because different groups of workers have been examined and different techniques used. Also, there is a problem in relying too much on what people say they find satisfying or dissatisfying at work as this is subjective. For example, if things go wrong at work individuals have a tendency to blame it on others or factors outside of their control. On the other hand if individuals feel happy and satisfied when they are at work then they tend to see it as their own doing.

McGregor's Theory X and Theory Y

Douglas McGregor suggested two theories to explain why people work. Theory X assumes workers are lazy, motivated by money and will only work if coerced by management. Theory Y assumes that workers are motivated by many different factors and are responsible and committed. In this cases management should create a work environment to allow workers to show creativity and contribute at work. These views are examined in the unit titled 'Management'.

McClelland's managerial needs

David McClelland suggested that what motivates people is that they learn in early childhood that certain types of behaviour lead to 'gratification'. They develop needs based on this behaviour. For example, a girl may have a great need to achieve, encouraged by parents who help her to be successful at school. When she becomes employed, she will behave in a similar way. There are, McClelland argues, three basic needs – achievement, affiliation, power.

- The need for achievement. This is one of the keys to a company's success. People who have high achievement needs often become successful entrepreneurs. Such people like to take responsibility and risks, and want quick feedback on how they have performed. They like to set their own goals and standards and achieve these on their own. However, it is also likely that people with a need to achieve will not work well in groups.
- The need for affiliation. McClelland found that some successful people in business did not, as he expected, score high on the need to achieve. In large firms, managers' goals can often by achieved by working with others, rather than by their own efforts. Such managers have a need to relate to others and will try to gain the acceptance of their superiors and work colleagues.
- The need for power. Some individuals with high achievement and affiliation needs still had problems in influencing or controlling others, McClelland found. To be

Figure 3: Herzberg's two factor theory

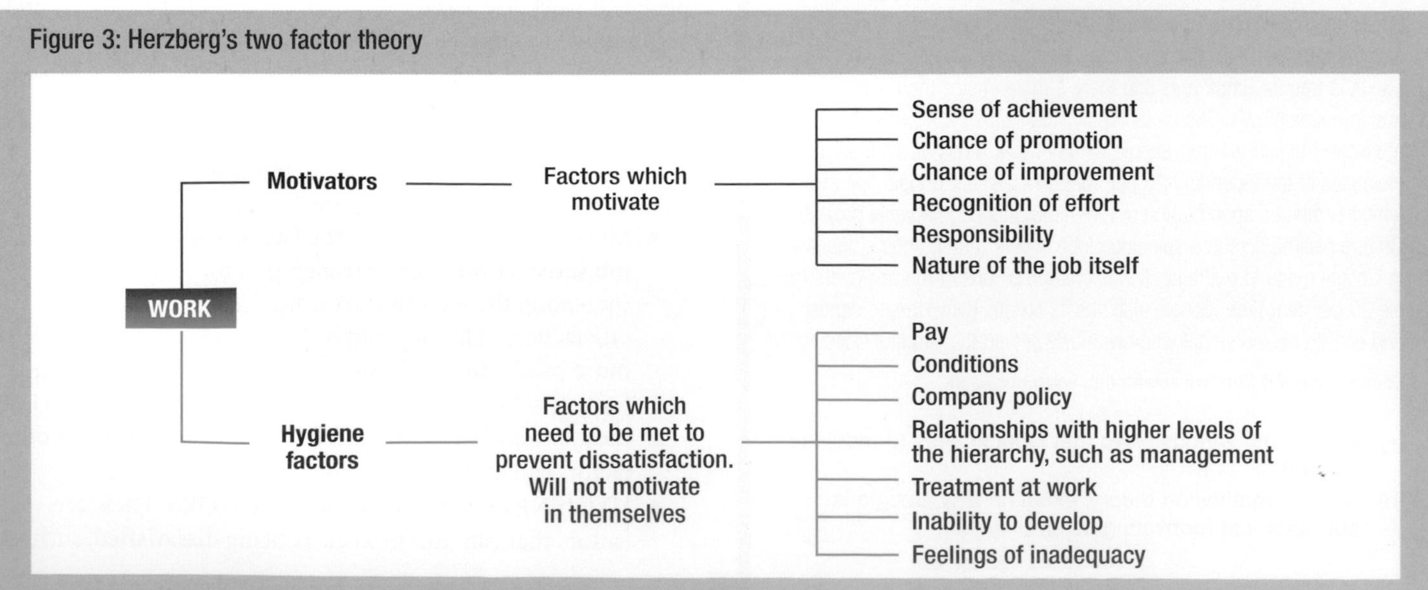

successful there was often a need to get people to work together. McClelland called this the power motive. He recognised that although the need for power is often seen as undesirable (where one person dominates others) it can also be seen in a positive light. It might reflect the ability of an individual to persuade, influence or lead people. Research suggests that people with a need for power tend to be in higher and more influential positions in business.

According to McClelland, a business needs to know how these three needs affect an individual. For example, a person who has high affiliation needs may not make a good marketing manager. Such a person would, based on the theory, constantly look for acceptance and support for all decisions. It is likely that this job would need someone who was far more self-motivated.

Vroom and Porter-Lawler expectancy theories

The theories examined so far assume that people try to meet goals and so satisfy their needs. The **expectancy theories** of Victor Vroom and L. Porter and E. Lawler argue that this relationship is not so simple. First, each individual will have different goals. Second, people only act to achieve their goals if they feel there is a chance of success. Third, the value of the goal to the individual will also affect that person's motivation. These theories might affect the way a business designs its pay and benefit systems and also the design of tasks and jobs to enable people to satisfy their needs. They take into account that people have different needs, and that some may want autonomy and responsibility at work, whereas others may not.

Adam's equity theory

John Stacey Adam's **equity theory** of motivation suggests that people are happiest in relationships where 'give and take' are about equal. If one person is getting too little from the relationship, then not only are they going to be unhappy with this, but the person getting the lion's share will also be feeling rather guilty about this imbalance. This is reinforced by strong social norms about fairness. In business, equity theory suggests that in return for an input (skills, effort, training) an employee receives an outcome (pay, status, fringe benefits). This creates a ratio of input to outcome and equity is achieved when the ratios are the same for everyone in an organisation. A manager in a finance company may know that he makes over £200,000 in revenue for the company each year and his salary is £30,000. An older executive, who performs the same job, and also brings in a revenue of £200,000 may receive a higher salary. Awareness of this lack of fairness (equity) creates demotivation among the junior employees, who feel exploited as a result.

CRITIQUE

Motivation theories may not work in practise for a number of reasons.

Different circumstances If the business is geared towards hierarchy and authority, and work is routine, people may choose to do such work in return for financial rewards, for example to enjoy themselves away from work. At other times, job interest and involvement may outweigh financial rewards. This may be true, for instance, in worker buyouts, when employees are prepared to accept lower financial rewards to maintain job security and have a say in the running of the business.

Different types of operation It is also argued that many motivation theories were developed in earlier times, when work conditions were different. Work methods did not need the advanced levels of technological knowledge and problem-solving skills that they do today. These skills change the relationship between management and the shop floor, for example by empowering workers.

Capitalism Theories of motivation based on the ideas of Marx suggest that getting people motivated will always be a problem under capitalism. This is because, although we depend on each other to produce wealth, private ownership of business allows owners to exploit those employees who must sell their labour in order to live. Though profits are only made through labour, the interests of owners and workers, diverge since labour is a cost to be minimised if profits are to be maximised.

KNOWLEDGE

1. Why is it important for business to satisfy workers?
2. Name five needs in Maslow's hierarchy that an individual might have at work.
3. What are the aims of Taylor's scientific management theory?
4. According to Taylor, how are people motivated?
5. What is meant by the human relations school of thought?
6. What, according to the human relations school, is the main motivator at work?
7. Explain the difference between Theory X and Theory Y.
8. According to Herzberg's theory, what factors are likely to: (a) increase job satisfaction; (b) reduce dissatisfaction at work?
9. What general conclusions can a business draw from the criticisms of motivation theory?

KEYTERMS

Hawthorne effect – the idea that workers are motivated by recognition given to them as a group.

Hygiene or maintenance factors – those things that can lead to workers being dissatisfied.

Motivated – being encouraged to do something.

Motivators – those things that can lead to workers being satisfied.

Self-actualisation – a level on Maslow's hierarchy where an employee realises his or her full potential.

Scientific management – a theory that suggests that there is a 'best' way to perform work tasks.

Case Study: Mendelsons

Lee Worsnip has worked as an assistant in the financial analysis department of Mendelsons Insurance for two years. He is 24 years of age and joined Mendelsons from college with good exam results. Lee also obtained some extra qualifications by taking night school courses. He started as junior clerk, and quickly moved to a more senior post, which paid a better salary. However, he has been in this post for a while now.

Lee's aim was to use the job as a stepping stone to one of the sales teams. The business was pleased that Lee looked on the job in this way, as it is in favour of encouraging people to get on. However, it is difficult to get onto one of the sales teams, particularly when the company has placed so much emphasis on its graduate recruitment. This may be one of the things that seems to be bothering Lee. Recently the Unit Trust team hired a graduate trainee instead of Lee, although he did accept that the new recruit had an advantage as she was a qualified actuary.

Until a few months ago, Lee had been an above average employee. He was always cheerful, enthusiastic and willing, and picked things up quickly. Lee used to make an excellent contribution to regular weekly meetings. And he was prepared to do one-off projects, always seeming to be able to squeeze in the extra work. He was also quite prepared to work late.

Lately, however, he seems to lack motivation. He has missed some meetings and taken days off. He complained that other members of the meetings had more senior posts and felt they did not listen to his views. He said, 'I shouldn't be treated as a worker who is satisfied just by basic physiological needs.'

The other day, Lee refused to take on a low level task. He suggested that he was fed up doing routine work and not leaving the office every day until 8 o'clock. Lee also argued that he was never allowed to make decisions and his work was always checked, as if he wasn't trusted. In the end some of these tasks had to be given to other members of staff, increasing their workload. Lee's absences have put additional pressure on the team.

Lee has also started being offhand. He was overheard several times being rude to people who asked him for information or help. Last week, at a team meeting about new procedures, Lee suggested that they had been drawn up in secret behind his back.

(a) **What is meat by the terms:**
(i) lack of motivation (3 marks) and
(ii) physiological needs. (3 marks)

(b) **Explain the problems that (i) Lee and (ii) the business might have as a result of a lack of motivation. (10 marks)**

(c) **Using a motivation theory, examine reasons why Lee may lack motivation. (12 marks)**

(d) **Suggest ways in which the business might improve Lee's motivation. (12 marks)**

67 Financial methods of motivation

Financial and non-financial rewards

A number of theories have tried to explain the factors that motivate people at work. Some of these theories stress that money is the most important factor. The scientific approach, in particular, argues that workers respond to financial rewards. It is argued that such rewards are necessary to motivate a reluctant workforce. Employees see work as a means to an end. As a result they are far more likely to be interested in **financial rewards.** In contrast, the human relations view argues that workers are motivated by a variety of factors. An employee working in a car assembly plant, for example, may be highly motivated by working as part of a team. Poor pay may lead to employees being dissatisfied, which can make other **non-financial rewards** less effective in motivating them. The next two units examine how financial and non-financial rewards can be used.

Salaries and wages

For nearly all workers, the main reason for going to work is to earn money to buy goods and services. Most workers in the UK are either paid a wage or a salary.

Wages WAGES tend to be associated with lower paid workers and BLUE COLLAR WORKERS (i.e. MANUAL WORKERS). Wages are typically expressed as hourly TIME RATES of pay, such as £5.50 an hour or £12.75 an hour. This then forms weekly rates of pay, such as £250 a week, for a fixed number of hours work, such as 38 hours. The 38 hours would then be the basic working week. Time rates are useful when a business wants to employ workers to do specialist or difficult tasks that should not be rushed. Employees can ensure that work is of a high quality without worrying about the time they take.

Waged employees often have the opportunity to work OVERTIME. These are hours worked over and above the basic working week. To motivate workers to accept overtime, employers often pay higher rates of pay. If the basic wage is £10 an hour, overtime might be paid at time and a quarter (£12.50 an hour) or time and a half (£15 an hour). Saturday or Sunday overtime working might be paid at higher rates than weekday overtime, to encourage people to work at weekends.

Salaries SALARIES tend to be associated with better paid workers, particularly WHITE COLLAR WORKERS (i.e. NON-MANUAL WORKERS). Salaried staff are typically paid each month. Some salaried staff might earn overtime because they are only expected to work a fixed number of hours per week. However, most salaried staff are paid to do a particular job. There might be a recommended number of hours work per week, like 38 hours. But they are often expected to work as many hours as it takes to complete the job. A yearly salary is usually higher than that which could be earned by workers if they were in a less senior job and paid a wage.

The main long-term factors which determine the level of wages and salaries are the forces of demand and supply. Businesses have to pay the 'market rate' for the job if they want to retain existing staff and recruit new staff. Paying below the market rate can also demotivate staff. They might feel that they are not valued by their employer. Paying above the market rate can be motivating. Workers might feel that their contribution is being rewarded by higher pay.

Workers are sometimes paid a basic wage or salary and a BONUS at the end of the year or other period if **targets** are reached, or for attendance or punctuality. Sometimes the 'best employee' over a period may be rewarded with a bonus. This is usually a money payment, although Richer sounds, the electronics retailer, has rewarded the retail outlet that performed bets over a period with the use of a classic car such as a Rolls Royce. A problem with regular bonuses is that they are often seen as part of the employee's basic pay. As a result, they may no longer act as a motivator.

Many employers have found that payment based on a fixed working week can be inflexible. For example, half the year employees may be idle after 3 p.m. every day, but are still paid for a 'full day's' work. The other half of the year they may work into the evening and be paid overtime. To cater for fluctuations in demand some employers pay staff on the basis of a certain number of hours to be worked in a year. These are known as ANNUALISED HOURS CONTRACTS. For annualised hours contracts, the number of hours to be worked each year is fixed. However, the daily, weekly or monthly hours are flexible. So employees may have a longer working day at peak times and work less when demand is slack. An employee's pay is calculated on the basis of an average working week, for example 35 hours, which is paid regardless of the actual number of hours the employee works. There are certain advantages of annualised hours. An employee has a guaranteed income each week. Employers often see this as a way of avoiding overtime, reducing costs, increasing flexibility and improving efficiency.

Piece rates, commission and fees

Not all workers are paid wages or salaries. Some are paid piece rates, commission or fees.

Piece rates Piece rates are payments for each unit produced. They are an example of PAYMENT BY RESULTS. For example, a worker might be paid £0.50 per parcel delivered or £1.00 per kilo of strawberries picked. PIECE RATES were recommended by Frederick Taylor, founder of the scientific management school. He thought they were an ideal way to motivate workers. Workers who produced more were more highly paid. However,

Question 1.

FINANCE DIRECTOR
Burton on Trent £60k + Benefits

My client is a rapidly expanding business, involved in the commercial Vehicle Leasing market. Due to the group's success they are looking to appoint a Finance Director to run the growing finance department.

Reporting to the board your remit will be to provide accurate and effective financial information, from the production of management accounts, to special ad hoc projects. You will have a strong commercial acumen, and demonstrate strong managerial skills. You will be a proactive hands on accountant, with the ability to communicate at all levels.

Supervising a team of three, you will be results driven, possess the skills to develop the finance function for future requirements.

Experience within a similar sector, or the finance sector would be advantageous, but is not essential.

For further information please forward your CV to:
Alan Webb
BENTLEY JENNISON
15-20 St Paul's Square, Birmingham B3 1QT
No agencies please.

accountemps®
Specialised Financial Staffing

Purchase Ledger Clerk - Wolverhampton
Temporary to permanent position working in a large orga sation at their Head Office. Good team player and previ purchase ledger experience essential. £7.00 per hour.

Accounts Assistant - Telford
Temporary to permanent role, working part time 30 hours week. The successful candidate will be working for a s organisation assisting the company accountant. £7.50 hour.

Finance Assistant - Wolverhampton
Maternity cover to start May 2003. General accounting d to include - cash reconciliation, budget preparatio spreadsheet work. £8.50 per hour.

Credit Controller - Telford
Solid credit controller required for a short-term assignm reduce debtor days, to start as soon as possible. £7.75 per hour.

Accounts Clerk - Shropshire
Temporary ongoing assignment, working in a large team resolving invoicing queries, previous accounting experience essential. £6.50 per hour.

Finance Manager - Shropshire
Temporary to permanent assignment to start as soon as possible, the successful candidate will be required to supervise a small team and complete all round general accounting duties. £10.00 per hour.

Payroll Clerk - Wolverhampton
Temporary to permanent assignment, the successful applicant will be responsible for a 150 monthly payroll covering all aspects. Previous payroll knowledge essential. £5.50 per hour.

For more information on these and other positions please contact Melissa Brown, Claire Marshall or Penny Witcherley on 01902 317200.

Wanted
Salespeople with or without experience

We are looking for well motivated and ambitious people aged 25-45. The successful candidates will earn over £30,000 a year and will be allowed the use of a company car. You will be given a travel allowance each week and all the training required to become a success. There is no cold calling. We provide at least 10 appointments per week. Payment is based on commission, but you can also take advantage of the great holiday incentives for you and a partner.

Call now for more details on
01112 98766 and ask for Mel Peterson

(a) Compare the different payment systems shown in the advertisements.
(b) What fringe benefits were being offered?
(c) Discuss what might happen if any of the employers advertising were offering a remuneration package which was below the market rate for the job.

piece rates are only suitable for jobs where it is easy to identify the contribution of an individual worker. It would be difficult to devise a piece rate system for, say, secretaries or managers. Piece rates have been criticised on health and safety grounds. They might encourage workers to take dangerous short cuts in a bid to reduce the amount of time taken for each item. Rushing production might also affect the quality of the product.

Commission COMMISSION is a payment system mainly used with white collar workers. Commission, like piece rates, is a payment for achieving a target. For example, car salespeople may get a commission of £100 for each car they sell. Some white collar workers are paid entirely on commission. A salesperson, for example, may be paid entirely on the basis of their sales record. Alternatively, a worker may be paid a basic salary and then receive commission on top. Commission based pay systems are intended to 'incentivise' workers by tying in pay with output.

Fees Fees are payments made to people for 'one-off' tasks. Tasks tend to be geared towards the needs of the client, rather than a standard service or product. The amount paid will depend on a variety of factors. These might include the time taken to finish the task or the difficulty of the task. Often fees are paid to people providing services, such as solicitors, performers etc.

Fringe benefits

FRINGE BENEFITS are benefits received over and above that received from wages or salaries. Fringe benefits are payments 'in kind' rather than in cash. Typical examples of fringe benefits include contributions to pensions, a company car, private health insurance, subsidised meals including luncheon vouchers, and subsidised loans or mortgages.

One reason why fringe benefits are given is because they are a tax-efficient way of rewarding employees. It may cost a business less to give the fringe benefit than the equivalent sum of money needed to buy it by the employee. Some fringe benefits help the running of the business. For example, private health care might reduce the number of days off sick by employees and give the business greater control about when an employee has an operation.

Businesses also give fringe benefits as a way of motivating staff. They can act as a motivator in two ways.

- Many satisfy the basic physiological and safety needs of workers, as outlined by Maslow. They also meet the hygiene factors as outlined in Herzberg's two-factor theory.
- The awarding of fringe benefits can be linked to achievement and promotion. Free private medical health care insurance, for example, is sometimes only available to more senior members of staff within an organisation.

Performance related pay

PERFORMANCE RELATED PAY(PRP) is a pay system designed specifically to motivate staff. Introduced in the 1980s and 1990s, it is now used widely in the UK among white collar workers,

Table 1 Examples of fringe benefits that have been used by businesses

Company	Function	Fringe benefit
Dyson Appliances	Vacuum cleaner manufacturer	Dyson cleaner at reduced rate for new employees
Text 100	PR Agency	2 'Duvet days' (unscheduled holidays) a year
Air Products	Industrial gas supplier	Free exercise classes and subsidised gym and yoga classes, free annual medical checks
Saatchi & Saatchi	Advertising agency	Company pub - 'The Pregnant Man'
Virgin Group	Travel, entertainment, media, retail and financial services	24 hour parties
Body Shop	Cosmetics manufacturer and retailer	£100 a year to 'buy' a training course in new skill of their choice
Tesco	Food retailer	SAYE tax-free share option scheme
Google	Internet search engine provider	Free meals for staff

especially in the financial services industry, such as banking, and in the public sector.

PRP gives workers extra pay for achieving targets. The extra pay may be a lump sum such as £1,000 or it could be a percentage of salary. Some PRP systems make distinctions between levels of achievement. For example, one worker may be rated 'excellent' and receive a 10 per cent bonus, another 'good' and receive a 5 per cent bonus, another 'satisfactory' and receive no bonus.

The targets are likely to be set through a system of **appraisal**. This is where the performance of individual staff is reviewed against a set of criteria. These criteria could include factors such as arriving for work on time, ability to get on with other workers, improving skills through training or achieving a particular task within the job. Staff are likely to have a performance appraisal interview where someone more senior, such as their line manager, conducts the appraisal.

PRP is widely used because it directly links performance with pay. According to the scientific management school, it should motivate workers to achieve the goals set for them by the organisation.

However, PRP and performance appraisal have been widely criticised for a number of reasons.

- The bonus may be too low to give workers an incentive to achieve their targets.
- Achieving the targets may have far more to do with the smooth running of machinery or technological systems, or how a group of workers perform than the performance of an individual. For example, a worker may set a goal of increasing forms processed by 5 per cent. But the number of forms she receives may depend on how many are processed by other members of her team or whether the printing machines are working smoothly. Where teamworking is an important management tool, it is likely to be better to give bonuses based on the output of a team rather than an individual.
- Targets may be difficult or even impossible to achieve in the eyes of workers. If this is the case, then they are unlikely to make any effort to achieve them.
- Few staff see appraisal as an independent objective procedure. Staff are quite likely to put their failure to achieve a grade in an appraisal interview down to the unfairness of the interviewer. This is particularly true when there are already problems in the relationship between, say, a worker and his or her boss. Staff who do achieve highly in appraisal interviews may be seen by others as 'favourites' of the interviewer.

Failure to receive a high enough grade in the appraisal process may act as a demotivator of staff. Instead of staff wanting to improve their performance, they may simply give up attempting to change their behaviour and attitudes. Failure to receive a PRP bonus could challenge the physiological needs of staff in Maslow's hierarchy of needs because it deprives them of money. It could also make them feel less 'loved' by the organisation, challenging their need for love and belonging. It will almost certainly knock their self-esteem.

Profit sharing

Some businesses have PROFIT SHARING schemes. In a company, profits would normally be distributed to shareholders. Profit sharing occurs when some of the profits made are distributed to workers as well as shareholders.

Profit sharing can motivate workers to achieve the objectives of the business. Shareholders want higher profits. So too do workers if they are to receive a share of them. Profit sharing therefore unites the goals of both owners and workers for extra money. Profit sharing can also be a way of showing staff that they are appreciated. In Maslow's hierarchy of needs, it may help satisfy the need for love and belonging.

However, most individual workers will have little or no control over how much profit their company makes. If they make extra effort to raise sales or reduce costs, the benefit of that extra effort will be shared between all the other workers. There is no link between individual effort and individual reward in profit sharing. Profit sharing is also unlikely to motivate financially if the amount received is fairly small.

A UK business which uses profit sharing is the John Lewis Partnership, which owns the John Lewis department stores and the supermarket chain Waitrose. The John Lewis Partnership is owned in trust for its workers. So all the profits after tax and retentions are distributed to its workers. The amount given varies according to the salary of the worker. In a good year,

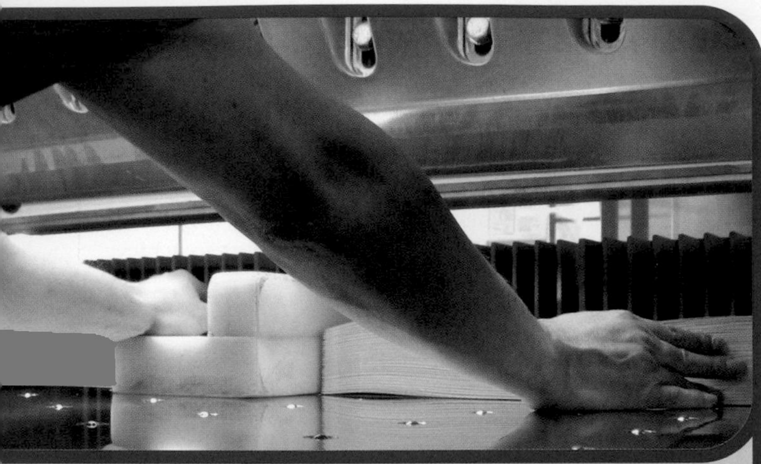

Question 2.

Nick Barnes runs a small printing company in Norwich. It prints cards, leaflets and catalogues for local businesses. It has three design staff and two staff who work as printers. The business pays all its staff the same salary, although at peaks times it might ask employees to work overtime. The business is a limited company and all the shares are owned by Paul and his brother, Wes, who is the company secretary and handles the marketing.

Recently the business has expanded into printing larger posters and designs for exhibitions. Nick has asked Natalie, his longest serving employee, if she will take responsibility for this. He knows that it will be a very profitable venture and wants someone who is experienced and motivated. He is concerned, however, that if he pays her more for the work than other staff they could become demotivated.

Paul has suggested that if this area of the business expands, Natalie could be given a small part-ownership of the business. She would be allowed to buy shares and benefit in future. Nick is still concerned that others in the business may feel that they also deserve shares, as they have all worked for a number of years, although not as long, currently, as Natalie. Nick wonders whether he should involve others in exhibition design and hopes that the revenue gained will generate enough so that he can raise all wages.

(a) Outline one advantage and one disadvantage of Nick paying his staff overtime.
(b) Explain why a financial rewards system at the business can be a problem.
(c) Discuss whether Nick should use share ownership as a means of financial incentive.

Waitrose workers will receive a profit share handout of more than 20 per cent of their salary. This is a substantial sum. Whether it motivates John Lewis Partnership workers to work harder is debatable.

Share ownership

Some have argued that workers would be motivated by owning a share of their business. They would then have an incentive to work hard because their efforts would contribute to profit. They would benefit from high profits because they would get part of those profits. The value of their shares in the business would also rise if the business were successful.

There are many ways in which employees might acquire shares. One is through **save-as-you-earn schemes**. Here, employees are able to save a regular amount of money from their pay over five years. At the end of five years, they are able to buy shares in the company at the price that they were five years previously. If the share price has gone up over the five years, the saver will make a capital gain.

The granting of **share options** has become a common way of rewarding senior managers and chief executives of large companies. A member of staff is given the option to buy shares in the company at a fixed point in the future, say three years, at a price agreed today. This price may be below, above or at the same level as today's share price. Share options are supposed to be an incentive to senior management to act in a way which will raise the share price significantly. This means that senior management have the same objective as shareholders.

Share options have been controversial. Some chief executives have been able to earn millions of pounds from **exercising** their share options (i.e. buying the shares at the end of the period and then, usually, selling them immediately, make a large capital gain). But when the stock market is rising, the performance of a company can be average and still its share price will rise. So chief executives can earn large amounts even though their company has not done particularly well.

Measured daywork

The idea of measured daywork may provide the answer to the problems of piece rate schemes. Instead of employees receiving a variable extra amount of pay depending on their output, they are paid a fixed sum as long as an agreed level of output is maintained. This should provide stable earnings and a stable output, instead of 'as much as you can, when you can, if you can'.

The first major agreement based on the principles of measured daywork was the National Power Loading Agreement in coal mining in 1966. London Docks and British Leyland both reverted to more traditional 'payment by result' methods in the late 70s. Although productivity gains may not have been great, most surveys found that measured daywork improved industrial relations and that less expenditure was spent on dealing with grievances. Furthermore, measured daywork seemed to give management a greater control over such payment schemes. In practice, the need for flexibility in reward schemes has meant that measured daywork is rarely used as an incentive scheme today.

Profit-related pay

Profit-related pay involves employees being paid a cash 'bonus' as a proportion of the annual profits of the company. In previous years a certain amount of profit-related pay has been exempt from taxation. However, this was no longer to be the case after the year 2000. Profit-related pay has a number of problems for employees. It is not linked to individual performance and rewards can fluctuate from year to year depending on the performance of the business.

Incentive schemes

The pay that employees receive often reflects the nature of the job. However, some payment systems try to relate pay to the performance or commitment that an employee makes to the business, known as incentive schemes. Businesses attempt to induce high commitment and performance from employees with high pay in order to gain the maximum output.

Incentive schemes for manual and non-manual employees Incentive payments have been widely used in the management of manual workers in the past. Today incentives are being used for administrative workers and in service industries. Productivity agreements are a form of bonus payment, where rewards are paid providing workers achieve a certain level of 'productivity'. They are usually agreed between employees' groups and management to 'smooth over' the introduction of new machinery or new techniques that workers need to learn. Incentive schemes fall into three categories.

- Individual schemes. Individual employees may be rewarded for exceeding a target. The benefit of this scheme is that it rewards individual effort and hence employees are more likely to be motivated by this approach.
- Group incentives. In some situations, like assembly lines, the need is to increase group output rather than individual output. Where one worker relies on the output of others, group incentives may also have benefits. They can, however, put great pressure on all group members to be productive. It can also be difficult for a new recruit to become part of the group, as existing members may feel they will have to compensate for his inexperience.
- Factory-wide schemes. Employees are given a share of a 'pool' bonus provided the plant has reached certain output targets. The benefit to management is that incentives are related to the final output rather than sections of the plant. Furthermore, in theory at least, employees are more likely to identify with the company as a whole. The difficulty with this type of scheme is that there is no incentive to work harder, as there is no direct link between individual effort and reward. Some employees who work hard may have their rewards reduced by others who do not – the same problem that arises with group incentives.

Incentive schemes for managers and directors Incentive schemes for managers and directors are usually linked to how well the company has performed. Share ownership schemes can be useful in motivating managers. There is evidence to suggest that management perform better if they 'own' part of a business, for example after an internal buyout. However, other research indicates that incentive schemes may not necessarily be the most important motivator at work for many managers. The Ashridge Management Index is an indicator of managers' attitudes based on a survey of 500 middle and senior managers. When asked what motivates them, 61 per cent of managers placed challenging work first. Other high-scoring motivators included 'letting people run their own show' and 'seeing the impact of decisions on the business'. These factors, along with high basic salary (35 per cent), topped the motivation league table.

Employer objectives for pay

There is a number of objectives employers will have when paying their workforce.

Motivation It has been argued that workers are motivated by money. This may be a rather simple view of workers' behaviour. Yet it is clear from the way that employers use money incentives that they believe employees react positively to the prospect of increasing their earnings. For example, many firms are attempting to link pay with performance because they believe that employees care about pay.

Employers must give consideration to any system they use. For example, if payments are made when targets are achieved, these targets must be realistic. Payment systems are often negotiated between groups, such as company representatives and trade unions.

Cost Employers are interested in the profitability or cost-effectiveness of their business. Any system that is used by the business must, therefore, attempt to keep the cost of labour as low as possible in relation to the market wage in that industry. This should enable the firm to increase its profits.

Prestige Managers often argue that it is a 'good thing' to be a good payer. Whether high pay rates earn an employer the reputation of being a good employer is arguable. What seems much more likely is that the low-paying employer will have the reputation of being a poor one in the eyes of employees.

Recruitment and labour turnover Payment rates must be competitive enough to ensure that the right number of qualified and experienced employees stay within the business. This will prevent a high level of labour turnover. This is also true of vacant posts. A business must pay rates which encourage the right quality and quantity of applicants.

Control Certain methods of payment will reduce costs and make the control of labour easier. These are examined later in this unit.

Employee objectives for pay

Employees will have their own objectives for the payment they receive.

Purchasing power A worker's standard of living is determined by the level of weekly or monthly earnings. The purchasing power of those earnings is affected by the rate of inflation. Obviously, in periods of high inflation workers are likely to seek higher wages as the purchasing power of their earnings falls. Those whose earnings fall behind the rate of inflation will face a decline in their purchasing power.

Fair pay Employees often have strong feelings about the level of payment that is 'fair' for a job. The employee who feels underpaid may be dissatisfied and might look for another job, be careless, or be absent a great deal. Those who feel overpaid may simply feel dishonest, or may try to justify their pay by looking busy.

Relativities Employees may be concerned about how their earnings compare with those of others. 'How much do I get relative to ... ' is an important question for a worker. Workers with a high level of skill, or who have trained for a long period, will want to maintain high wages relative to less 'skilled' groups. Flat rate pay increases, such as £10 a week for the whole workforce, would erode differences. A 5 per cent increase would maintain the differences.

Recognition Most people like their contribution to be recognised. Their pay gives them reassurance that what they are doing is valued.

Composition Employees often take into account the way their earnings are made up. It is argued that younger employees tend to be more interested in high direct earnings rather than indirect benefits like pensions. Incentive payments are likely to interest employees who want to increase their pay. Married women and men are generally less interested in overtime payments, for example, and regard other factors more highly.

Problems with financial rewards

There is a number of problems that financial incentives schemes have.

Operating problems For financial incentives to work, production needs to have a smooth flow of raw materials, equipment and storage space, and consumer demand must also be fairly stable. These conditions cannot be guaranteed for long. If raw materials did not arrive or ran out, for example, the worker may not achieve a target and receive no bonus for reasons beyond his control. If this happens the employee is unlikely to be motivated by the scheme, and may negotiate for a larger proportion of earnings to be paid as guaranteed 'basic' pay.

Fluctuating earnings A scheme that is linked to output must result in fluctuating earnings. This might be due to changes in demand, the output of the worker or machinery problems. As in the case above, the worker is likely to press for the guaranteed part of pay to be increased, or store output in the 'good times' to prevent problems in the 'bad'. Alternatively, workers may try to 'slow down' productive workers so that benefits are shared out as equally as possible.

Quality The need to increase output to gain rewards can affect quality. There is an incentive for workers to do things as quickly as possible and this can lead to mistakes. Workers filling jars with marmalade may break the jars if they work too quickly. This means the jar is lost and the marmalade as well, for fear of splinters. For some businesses, such as food processing, chemicals or drug production, errors could be disastrous.

Changes in payment Because of the difficulties above, employers constantly modify their incentive schemes. Improved financial reward schemes should stop workers manipulating the system and may give renewed motivation to some workers. However, constant changes mean that employees do not always understand exactly how to gain rewards.

Quality of working life Financial rewards based upon payment by results require a certain type of job design. This often means tight control by management, routine and repetition. The scientific management school argues that production will only be efficient if workers know exactly what to do in any situation and their activities are tightly controlled by management. The result of this is that boredom and staleness may set in and the worker's 'standard of life' at work may be low.

Jealousy Individual workers may be jealous of the rewards earned by their colleagues. This can lead to problems in relationships and a possible lack of motivation. Increasingly, businesses are using group or plant-wide incentives to solve this.

Measuring performance For incentives to work effectively it must be possible to measure performance. For example, a business must be able to measure the number of components made by a worker if she is paid a bonus after 20,000 are made a month.

Team-based rewards Problems may take place if rewards are based on the performance of a team, but some workers are more productive then others in the team.

Given these problems, why are financial incentive schemes still used by many firms? Managers may find a use for a certain scheme. For example, financial rewards may be used to overcome resistance to change. A business introducing new technology, such as computers, may offer an incentive for staff to retrain or spend extra time becoming familiar with the new system. Employees often see benefits in such systems of payment. They may feel that they are gaining some control over their own actions in the workplace, being able to work at their own pace if they so wish. Furthermore, many businesses believe that financial rewards ought to work as it is logical to assume that employees work harder if they are offered more money.

KEYTERMS

Annualised hours contracts – a payment system based on a fixed number of hours to be worked each year, but a flexible number of hours each day, week or month.
Blue collar (or manual) workers – workers who do mainly physical work, like assembly line workers.
Bonus – an extra payment made in recognition of the contribution a worker has made to the company.
Commission – payment made, typically for achieving a target such as a sales target.
Fringe benefits – payment in kind over and above the wage or salary paid, such as a company car or luncheon vouchers.
Overtime – time worked over and above the basic working week.
Payment by results – payment methods that reward workers for the quantity and quality of work they produce.
Performance related pay (PRP) – a payment system, typically where workers are paid a higher amount if they achieve certain targets set for them by their employer.
Piece rates – a payment system where employees are paid an agreed rate for every item produced.
Profit sharing – where workers are given a share of the profits made by the company which employs them.
Salary – pay, usually of non-manual workers, expressed as a yearly figure but paid monthly.
Time rates – rates of pay based on an amount of time, usually per hour.
Wages – payments made to employees for work done, usually given weekly to manual workers.
White collar (or non-manual) workers – workers who do non-physical work like office workers or teachers.

KNOWLEDGE

1. Explain the difference between payment systems frequently found for blue collar workers and white collar workers.
2. Explain the difference between piece rates and commission.
3. Why might fringe benefits motivate workers?
4. Explain the role of targets in performance related pay systems.
5. How might profit sharing schemes motivate workers?
6. Explain the difference between a save-as-you-earn scheme for buying shares and share option schemes.
7. State four employee objectives for pay.
8. State four employer objectives for pay.
9. Identify five problems of financial reward schemes.

Research

How effective are incentive schemes according to research?

- Pearce's and others' (1985) research into merit pay amongst managers in US Social Security Administration found little effect on organisational performance. The Institute of Personnel Development (1999) suggested that managers view merit pay as having only a modest effect on employee commitment. In a study, 53 per cent said that there had been 'no change' in such commitment.
- Gerhard and Milkovich (1992) found the use of bonuses for managers had a positive effect on the rate of return on capital employed in business.
- Kruse and Weitzman (1990) found that profit sharing schemes had a positive effect on productivity and company performance, although whether such schemes led to improved performance or whether such performance allows business run such schemes is debatable.

Question 3.

In 2007 two multimillion-pound pay deals were being put in place for the chief executives of major UK retailers. It was reported that the chief executives of WH Smith could earn £5 million as a result of a lucrative new incentive plan. Blacks Leisure appointed a new chief executive with an option package that could generate £1.8 million on top of a salary by 2011.

WH Smith said the plans had been put in place 'following concerns which had been raised by some of the company's major shareholders regarding retention of the current management team'. Under the terms of the plan, WH Smith's chief executive would be able to invest a proportion of her salary in WH Smith shares and the company would match that investment fivefold, with shares which would be handed over if targets were met over the following three years. That gave the potential to receive £3.75 million shares at current prices. Salary payments plus annual bonuses and benefits would take the total to more than £5 million.

Blacks Leisure lured its new chief executive with options over 1 million shares. The options would be payable in three equal tranches at the end of the second, third and fourth years if the share price rose above 350p, 425p and 500p respectively. The chief executive would be able to acquire the shares at about 238p, meaning his share option gains could total £1.79 million within four years. He would also be paid £300,000 a year plus bonuses.

Source: adapted from *The Guardian*, 3.12.2007.

(a) Explain why the financial rewards in the article are examples of: (i) management incentives and (ii) performance related pay.
(b) Why might the businesses use these management incentives?
(c) Discuss whether a chain of five health and fitness centres in Yorkshire should introduce performance related pay for its managers.

Case Study: Incentives for Value Added Resellers

Value Added Resellers (VARs) are businesses which take a manufacturer's product and add their own value before selling it. For example, a VAR might take an operating system, add its own specialist software for, say, architects, and then sell the bundle to architect businesses. Manufacturers offer VARs a number of incentives to sell their products.

'The best incentive is money in the pocket' said one VAR. Most incentive schemes are based on money and commissions. Other means are used, but do they work? 'Freebies' such as day trips and air miles are commonly on offer. But in the day-to-day slog of running a business, motivation to take advantage of such benefits can be hard to muster. 'We don't really bother with these schemes' said one VAR. 'They create more administration than they're worth. 'Luxury rewards are still available as part of wider packages. For example, the top performing VAR for SolidWorks, was invited to Hawaii.

Opinions on whether rewards for individuals are effective will depend on to whom you speak. There will always be salespeople who thrive on beating the competition and who want to gain recognition for doing so. Peter Dickin, marketing manager at Delcam, feels that a more inclusive approach is required. 'Incentives targeted just at salespeople neglect the contribution of others, which can be demotivating. We tend to favour schemes that foster team building.'

Incentive schemes that reward a group of high-performing VARs have to be carefully structured to create a level playing field to give companies of different sizes and locations a chance. Clearly this is not always being achieved. One disgruntled VAR said 'I have never, ever been incentivised by any scheme I have worked with in the past. Overpaid VAR managers justify their own existence, even so far as coming up with jollies that they had no prior interest in, such as driving racing cars and sailing around the Leeward Isles.'

Schemes based mainly on the volume of sales can have negative implications for all parties. 'The aims of the incentives that we work to are not those that suit our long-term business goals, nor the needs of our customers,' said one VAR. 'They are generally incentives to motivate short-term business.'

The opportunity to gain marketing funds is another regular element of incentive schemes, particularly where a business wants to make inroads into a particular market. IBM, for example, offers a special marketing fund to companies who join its Top Contributor Programme and commit themselves to selling $100,000 of software to the SME (small and medium-sized business) market.

As free trips and luxury gifts are used less, terms such as 'active business management' have crept into the language of incentives. 'We don't incentivise on volume' explains John Mitchell, Manager of Indirect Channels, Europe, PLM Solutions. 'We incentivise VARs to invest in their business and improve the quality of their service to our customers.'

Many VARs are dubious about whether the incentives on offer actually made them do anything differently. Not offering incentives doesn't go down well either. One VAR said "Our own main vendor doesn't offer any incentive schemes (or even buy drinks at the bar at sales events). So we will have to do our best focusing upon making money for ourselves.'

Source: adapted from retailsystemseller.com.

(a) What is meant by the terms:
(i) luxury rewards (3 marks);
(ii) incentivise on volume? (3 marks)

(b) Describe the different financial rewards in the article. (6 marks)

(c) Examine the advantages and disadvantages of each financial reward scheme for VARs. (10 marks)

(d) Assess which financial rewards are likely to be most motivating to VARs selling products such as computers for manufacturers to small businesses. (12 marks)

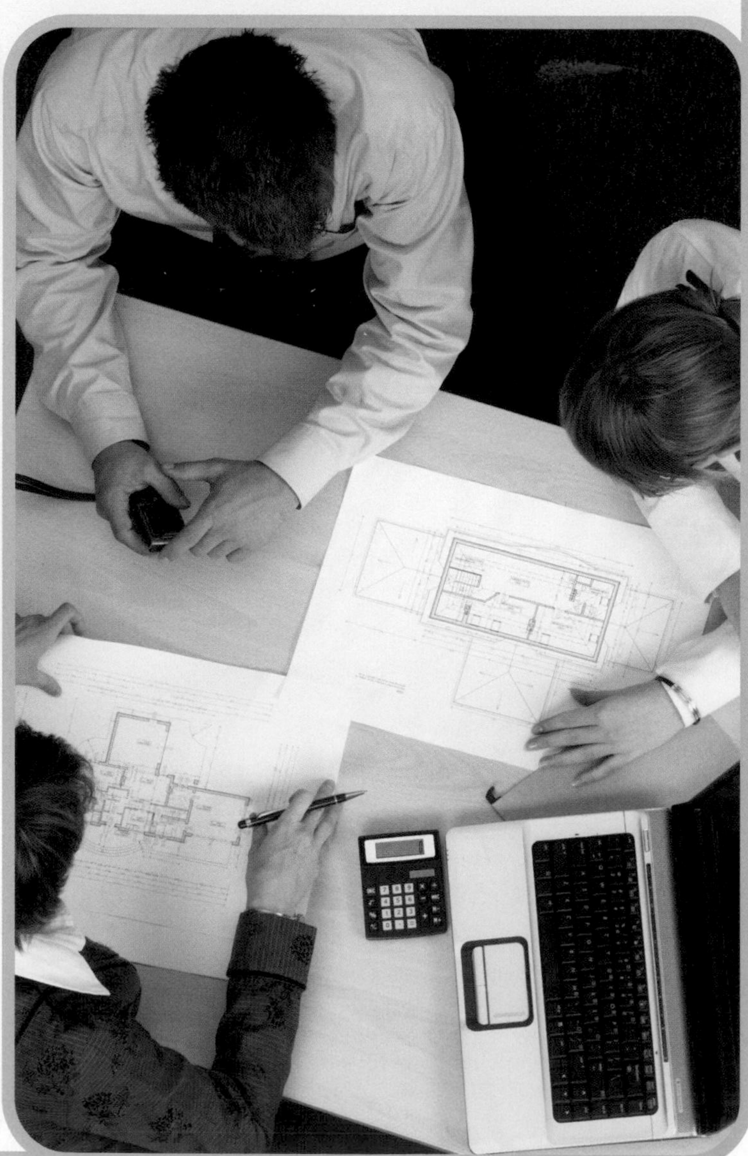

68 Non-financial methods of motivation

The need for non-financial rewards

Financial rewards have often been used in the past by firms in an attempt to motivate employees to improve productivity. However, increasingly businesses have realised that:

- the chance to earn more money may not be an effective motivator;
- financial incentive schemes are difficult to operate;
- individual reward schemes may no longer be effective as production has become organised into group tasks;
- other factors may be more important in motivating employees.

If other factors are more important than pay in motivating workers, it is important for firms to identify them. Only then can a business make sure its workforce is motivated. Figure 1 shows some of the factors that employees might consider important in their work environment. Many of these have been identified by the **human relations approach**. A business may consider introducing non-financial incentives to help employees satisfy these needs.

Job design and job redesign

The dissatisfaction with financial incentive schemes reached its peak in the 1960s and 1970s. In response the 'Quality of Working Life Movement' began to develop ideas which were based around the **human relations school**, as first outlined by the Hawthorne studies. It was argued that workers were likely to be motivated by non-monetary factors and that jobs needed to be DESIGNED or REDESIGNED to take these factors into account. Five principles were put forward which any incentive scheme needed to consider.

- The principle of closure. A job must include all tasks necessary to complete a product or process. This should ensure that work is meaningful for employees and that workers feel a sense of achievement.
- Control and monitoring of tasks. Jobs should be designed so that an army of inspectors is not needed. The worker, or the team, should take responsibility for quality.
- Task variety. There should be an increase in the range of tasks that a worker carries out. This should allow job rotation to occur and keep the workers interested in their work.
- Self-regulation. Employees should have control of the speed at which they work and some choice over work methods and sequence.
- Interaction and co-operation. The job structure should allow some social interaction and the chance for an employee to work in a group.

Various methods were devised to try and put these principles into practice. They included job enrichment, job enlargement, job rotation, quality control circles and employee participation in groups. These are examined in this unit.

Poor job design may mean that employees do not achieve their full potential. This means that the firm's output may suffer as a result. For example, an architect who is constantly having her work checked for accuracy is unlikely to be as productive as possible, due to constant interruptions. Also, jobs that do not meet workers' needs are likely to lead to poor motivation,

Figure 1: Employees' needs from the work environment

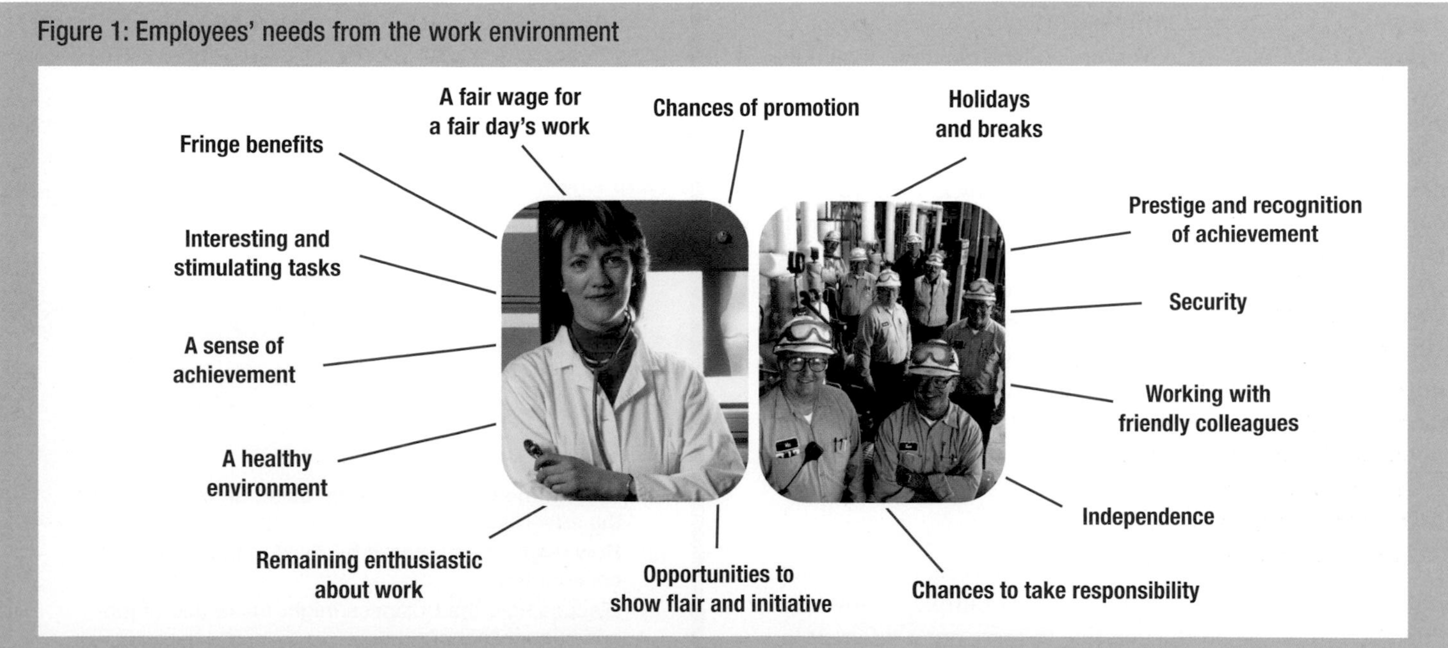

Table 1: Problems of job redesign

- Employees may be familiar with the old approach to doing a job and may resent new changes. They might not want the extra duties that result from job redesign.
- Job redesign may be expensive. New methods often require extra training. In addition, redesigned jobs might lead employees to claim extra pay for new responsibilities. There is no guarantee that the redesign of jobs will increase productivity in the long term.
- The introduction of new machinery can make job redesign more difficult. Certain jobs have had to be redesigned almost totally as new technology has changed production processes. In some cases employees have had to learn totally new skills, such as when newspaper page design on computer screens replaced old methods of cutting and pasting type onto pages. At other times skills may be made redundant.
- Effects on output and productivity. Redesigned jobs need to be evaluated to gauge whether they have actually motivated the workforce to increase output.

absenteeism and a lack of quality in work. The process of redesigning existing jobs is often difficult to carry out in practice for a number of reasons, as shown in Table 1.

Job enlargement

JOB ENLARGEMENT involves giving an employee more work to do of a similar nature. For example, instead of an employee putting wheels onto a bicycle he could be allowed to put the entire product together. It is argued that this variety prevents boredom with one repetitive task and encourages employees' satisfaction in their work, as they are completing the entire process. Job enlargement is more efficient if workers are organised in groups. Each worker can be trained to do all jobs in the group and job rotation can take place. Other forms of job enlargement include job rotation and job loading.

Critics of this method argue that it is simply giving a worker 'more of the same'. It is often called the problem of **horizontal loading** - instead of turning five screws the worker turns ten. In many businesses today such tasks are carried out more effectively by machines, where repetitive tasks can be completed quickly and efficiently without strain, boredom or dissatisfaction. It could even be argued that allowing employees to complete the entire process will reduce efficiency. This is because the fall in productivity from carrying out many tasks more than offsets any productivity gains from increased worker satisfaction.

Job rotation

JOB ROTATION involves an employee changing jobs or tasks from time to time. This could mean, for example, a move to a different part of the production line to carry out a different task. Alternatively, an employee may be moved from the personnel to the marketing department where they have skills which are common to both. From an employee's point of view this should reduce boredom and enable a variety of skills and experience to be gained. An employer might also benefit from a more widely trained workforce.

Although job rotation may motivate a worker, it is possible that any gains in productivity may be offset by a fall in output as workers learn new jobs and take time to 'settle in'. Worker motivation is not guaranteed if the employee is simply switched from one boring job to another. In fact some workers do not like the uncertainty that job changes lead to and may become dissatisfied. Although used by firms such as Volkswagen in the past, where employees carried out a variety of production tasks, job rotation has been less popular in the last decade.

Job enrichment and job loading

The idea of JOB ENRICHMENT came from Herzberg's two factor theory. Whereas job enlargement expands the job 'horizontally', job enrichment attempts to give employees greater responsibility by 'vertically' extending their role in the production process. An employee, for example, may be given responsibility for planning a task, quality control, work supervision, ordering materials and maintenance.

Job enrichment gives employees a 'challenge', which will develop their 'unused' skills and encourage them to be more

Question 1.

Instyle is a fashion design company. It has placed an advertisement on a recruitment website. Part of the advertisement included the following.

Instyle is a modern fashion design company. We want a tailor with at least one year's experience to help with making up our bespoke fashion designs. The main duties will include making up clothing such as suits, shirts, dresses and trousers, including sewing parts together, adding buttons and pressing. You will also work as part of a small team dealing directly with customers. This will involve measuring clients, making a draft of a master pattern and altering patterns to fit customers.

(a) Explain the term 'job design' using an example from the advertisement.

(b) How might the business be making use of job enlargement?

(c) Discuss how the business might make use of job enrichment techniques.

productive. The aim is to make workers feel they have been rewarded for their contribution to the company. Employees will also be provided with varied tasks, which may possibly lead to future promotion. It is not, however, without problems. Workers who feel that they are unable to carry out the 'extra work', or who consider that they are forced into it, may not respond to incentives. In addition, it is unlikely that all workers will react the same to job enrichment. Trade unions sometimes argue that such practices are an attempt to reduce the labour force, and disputes about the payment for extra responsibilities may arise. In practice, job enrichment has been found to be most successful in administrative and technical positions.

Job loading is where workers are given extra tasks when colleagues are off sick or if they have left and not been replaced. It can be particularly important in manufacturing, where absence can disrupt an assembly line for example.

Empowerment

Delegated decision making can be more successful if employees were empowered. EMPOWERMENT of employees involves a number of aspects.

- Recognising that employees are capable of doing more than they have in the past.
- Making employees feel trusted, so that they can carry out their jobs without constant checking.
- Giving employees control of decision making.
- Giving employees self confidence.
- Recognising employees' achievements.
- Developing a work environment where employees are motivated and interested in their work.

Many businesses now recognise the need to empower employees. There is a number of advantages of this for a business and for employees.

- Employees may feel more motivated. They feel trusted and feel that businesses recognise their talents. This should improve productivity and benefit the business in the long term, for example by reducing absenteeism.
- Employees may find less stress in their work as they have greater control over their working lives. This could reduce illness and absenteeism.
- Decisions may be made by those most suited to make them. Also, employees may feel less frustrated that senior staff who are less equipped to make decisions are making them.
- There may be greater employee skills and personal development.
- Businesses may be able to streamline their organisations and delegate decision making.
- Workers may feel less frustrated by more senior staff making decisions which they feel may be incorrect.

However, empowerment is sometimes criticised as simply a means of cutting costs and removing layers from the business. Passing decision making down the hierarchy might allow a company to make managers redundant. Employees are given more work to do, but for the same pay. Some businesses argue that they want to empower workers, but in practice they are unable or unwilling to do this. For example, a manager may feel insecure about subordinates making decisions that might affect his position in the business. Feeling that they may 'make the wrong decision' might lead to constant interruptions which are counter-productive. A further problem is the cost involved to the business, such as the cost of training employees or changing the workplace.

Question 2.

St Luke's Communications is a London Advertising Agency owned by its staff. It was formed on St. Luke's day 1995 and has expanded from 35 to 75 staff. It is renowned for its innovative approach to stimulating staff. Teams are a core part of what the advertising agency does. People can sit anywhere and work anytime, but it is their personal responsibility to see that their behaviour doesn't damage the team. In a more traditional structure, empowerment means the handing down of power. If the organisation is owned by everyone, then everyone can 'rise to true freedom from the concepts of authority and power'. Asserting power would seriously damage this concept, so that discipline is through peers, not from above.

Staff are encouraged to contribute to projects other than those to which they have been specifically assigned. Everyone has the right to stumble into meetings. At meetings staff can mention incomplete ideas. It is argued that such thoughts may inspire others. There is also no owned space. Computers are available to all, and if there are not enough to go around, staff may bring in their own. It has been suggested that business has a turnover rate of around 10 per cent, although only around 1 per cent go to competitors. A turnover rate of 25 per cent is typical for advertising agencies.

Source: adapted from www.flexibility.co.uk, harvardbusinessonline, www.fastcompany.com, *The Sunday Times*.

(a) Using examples from the article, explain how the business motivates employees.

(b) Explain how this will benefit (i) employees and (ii) the business

Team working

The Swedish car firm Volvo is a well quoted example of a company that has effectively introduced 'teamwork'. In both its plants at Kalmar and Uddevalla, it set up production in teams of eight to ten highly skilled workers. The teams decided between themselves how work was to be distributed and how to solve problems that arise. It is arguable whether these practices led to an increase in productivity, but the company firmly believed that this method of organisation was better than an assembly line system. A similar system has been used at Honda UK. Team working has a number of benefits.

- Productivity may be greater because of pooled talents.
- People can specialise and draw on the skills and knowledge of others in the team.
- Increasingly businesses are finding that the abilities of teams are needed to solve difficult business problems.
- Responsibility is shared. People may be more prepared to take risks.
- Ideas may be created by brainstorming.
- It allows flexible working.

However, in practice team work does not always produce the desired results. Part of the problem may lie in the way teams are organised. Members may fail to work well together for several reasons, from lack of a sense of humour to clashing goals. Studies of teams in the US have shown a number of problems with team work.

- Too much emphasis on harmony. Teams probably work best when there is room for disagreement. Papering over differences sometimes leads to vague or bland recommendations.
- Too much discord. Tension can destroy team effectiveness.
- Poor preparation. It is important that team members prepare for meetings by focusing on the facts. Members should have a detailed knowledge of the issues at hand and all work with the same information.
- Too much emphasis on individualism. For example, teams may fail to deliver results if the emphasis of the company is placed on individualism.
- A feeling of powerlessness. To work well, teams must be able to influence decisions.
- The failure of senior management to work well together. This creates problems because team members may walk into meetings with different priorities.
- Meeting-itis. Teams should not try to do everything together. Too many meetings waste the team's time.
- Seeing teams as the solution for all problems. Some tasks are better accomplished by individuals, rather than groups.

Quality control circles

QUALITY CONTROL CIRCLES or QUALITY CIRCLES are small groups of workers (about 5-20) in the same area of production who meet regularly to study and solve production problems. In addition, such groups are intended to motivate and involve workers on the shopfloor. Unlike job enlargement and job enrichment, they allow the workforce directly to improve the nature of the work they are doing.

Quality control circles started in America, where it was felt workers could be motivated by being involved in decision making. The idea gained in popularity in Japan and was taken up by Western businesses. Examples of their use can be found in Japanese companies setting up plants in the UK in the 1990s. Honda at Swindon has had 52 teams of six people looking at improvements that can be made in areas allocated to the groups, for example, safety.

Quality control circles are only likely to work if they have the support of both management and employees. Businesses have to want worker participation and involvement in decision making, and set up a structure that supports this. Workers and their representatives also need to support the scheme. Employees must feel that their views within the circle are valued and must make a contribution to decisions.

Multiskilling

MULTISKILLING is a term used to describe the process of enhancing the skills of employees. It is argued that giving individuals the skills and responsibilities to deal with a greater variety of issues will allow a business to respond more quickly and effectively to problems. So for example, a receptionist might have been trained to pass on calls to other people in a business. Multiskilling this job could mean that the receptionist now deals with more straightforward enquiries himself. This would result in a quicker response to the customer's enquiry. It would also free up time for other people to work on more demanding activities.

Certain motivation theories suggest that giving individuals more skills and responsibilities can improve their work performance. A criticism of multiskilling is that individuals are only given more skills so that they are expected to work harder without any extra pay. Problems may also result if workers are not trained adequately for their new roles.

Achieving a work-life balance

Recently there has been a stress on the need for employers to deal with the work-life balance of employees. Life is becoming faster and more complex, but without the support of communities or extended families. It is suggested that unless employers are sympathetic and supportive of employees' external needs, there could be an increase in health related absences such as stress. This could affect the operation and efficiency of the business.

Organisational structure, financial and non-financial rewards

There is a link between the motivational techniques used by managers in business and the organisational structure of a business. For example, a business with a traditional and rigid hierarchy will often make use of financial rewards. Each level of the hierarchy will have an associated level of financial reward, which is clear to employees in the organisation. Employees can see this and be motivated into working to achieve promotion or move through the levels of the business.

In a hierarchy non-financial rewards may also be motivating in certain circumstances. As workers achieve a certain living standard with which they are comfortable, they may find that other factors are more motivating, such as the ability to make their own decisions or to have flexibility in their work. These factors can be motivating for higher level posts. Job enrichment and empowerment further down the hierarchy may also be motivating to employees, especially if their jobs are repetitive and boring. However, a manger must take care when empowering workers as not all employees want to or feel able to take extra responsibility.

In other forms of organisational structure non-financial rewards may be particularly motivating. For example, in a matrix structure workers are working in teams. The support of other members of the team or respect from colleagues may be important as a motivation factor. Managers may have to generate a sense of team belonging to motivate staff. In an independent structure the ability to make decisions is likely to be very motivating to employees.

Employee involvement schemes in practice

The non-financial methods so far in this unit are examples of EMPLOYEE INVOLVEMENT SCHEMES. They can be categorised according to how involved employees are. For example, in teamworking employees are encouraged to extend the range and type of tasks undertaken at work. Employees are less involved perhaps through quality circles. This is an example of an upward problem solving scheme, designed to tap into employee's knowledge and opinions. However, studies seem to indicate that downward communication schemes are more popular. They are designed to inform and educate employees and include informal and formal communication. The level of active employee involvement here tends to be minimal. Surveys have shown that employee involvement schemes have been increasingly used by UK businesses over the last 20 years. But they have had problems. Sometimes they contradict each other and they are rarely part of a human resource strategy. Managers often lack the enthusiasm and commitment and many employers have not given enough time and resources to training supervisors to run them.

Goal setting and management by objectives

Goal setting is part of a more general theory of management by objectives (MBO). MBO was put forward by Peter Drucker in 1954 and is covered in the unit tiled 'Management and leadership'. It suggests that a business should define objectives or **targets** for an individual to achieve and revise those targets after assessing the performance of the worker. In 1984 Ed Locke wrote *Goal Setting: A motivational technique that works.* According to Locke, the idea that in order to improve job performance you need to motivate workers by making jobs more satisfying is wrong. He argued that satisfaction comes from achieving specific goals. In addition, the harder these goals are, the greater the effort and satisfaction. His message was for businesses to set specific goals that people can achieve and that have been negotiated. 'Do your best', he argued, is not specific. Employees must also have feedback on the progress they are making and then they will perform. The assumption behind the theory is that people will do what they say they will do, and then will strive hard to do it.

Organisation behaviour modification

Businesses have used the theory of organisation behaviour modification (OBMod) with management by objectives when motivating employees. OBMod assumes that workers' behaviour is determined by the consequences of their actions. For example, a worker who receives a reward as a result of increasing productivity is likely to work harder. Similarly, workers try to avoid behaving in ways that produce no reward or lead to punishment.

OBMod is based on the work of psychologists such as Thorndike and Skinner, who argue that since we cannot observe people's attitudes we should observe their behaviour. Managers should therefore observe how employees' behaviour is affected by the consequences of their actions. These consequences can be broken down into four categories.

- The employee receives something he likes.
- Something the employee dislikes is taken away.
- Something the employee likes is taken away.
- Something the employee dislikes is given.

The first two categories are known as **reinforcers**, as they lead to an increase in the behaviour that precedes them. If a junior manager gives a good presentation and receives praise (something he likes), then the behaviour that resulted in praise (the good presentation) will be reinforced. This is an example of positive reinforcement. If something the employee dislikes is taken away, this is called **negative reinforcement**.

The other two categories are kinds of **punishment**. They tend to reduce the behaviour that precedes them. For example, if a worker is constantly late and is fined (something he dislikes), he may try to reduce the number of times he is late. Examples of positive reinforcement include:

- employees in Xerox's personnel department being given 'X certificates' to pass to others in the company that they felt deserved reward. Each certificate was redeemable for $25;
- passengers being given coupons on American Airlines which they can pass on to staff who they feel deserve recognition;
- an American factory in Mexico where 15 per cent of the workforce arrived late. Management decided to reward good timekeeping by paying workers two pesos (16 cents at the time) a day extra if they started work early. Lateness fell from 15 per cent to 2 per cent, at little extra cost to the company.

Employee assistance programmes

Employee assistance programmes (EAPs) started in America in the 1950s. They began to appear in the UK in the 1990s. These schemes have been developed to help staff cope with difficulties. They may include help in areas such as drug and alcohol rehabilitation, abusive households, career planning and financial advice, housing and relocation, retirement planning; child or elder care, legal aid and advice, grief and loss of relatives and friends and workplace stress. An EAP usually consists of confidential counselling on an issue for employees and their families, paid for by employers. Employers are aware that life for individual employees is becoming more demanding. They recognise that if they want to motivate employees, they need to provide support services that cater for their more general needs. Sometimes such services are provided directly by employers, but it is more common to use a third-party supplier. Staff can then be assured of privacy and neutrality.

KEYTERMS

Employee involvement schemes – systems used to motivate employees through their participation in decision making of the business.
Empowerment – to give official authority to employees to make decisions and control their own activities.
Job design – the process of organising the tasks and activities required to perform a job.
Job redesign – changing the tasks and activities of a job, perhaps in an attempt to motivate workers.
Job enlargement – giving an employee more work to do of a similar nature.
Job enrichment – an attempt to give employees greater responsibility and recognition by 'vertically' extending their role in the production process.
Job rotation – the changing of jobs or tasks from time to time.
Multiskilling – the processes of enhancing the skills of employees.
Teamworking – Employees working in small groups with a common aim.
Quality control circles or Quality circles – small groups of workers in the same area of production which meet regularly to study and solve all types of production problems.

KNOWLEDGE

1. State five possible non-financial rewards that may be an incentive for individuals.
2. What principles would a 'good' job have according to the 'Quality of Working Life Movement'?
3. State four methods of job redesign.
4. 'Job enlargement is simply a method of horizontal loading.' Explain this statement.
5. Under what circumstances might job rotation not lead to an increase in productivity?
6. Suggest four problems of working in teams.
7. Why is job enrichment said to extend an employee's role in the firm vertically?
8. What are the advantages to an employee of quality control circles?
9. State three features of empowerment.
10. What is meant by achieving a work-life balance?
11. Show, using an example, how positive reinforcement can motivate a worker.
12. Why might a business have an employee assistance programme?

Case Study: Zinx

Zinx is an independent boutique hotel and restaurant in the South East of England. It employs 60 staff. It has always had a very traditional organisation with senior managers, departmental managers, supervisors, head waiters, bar staff, cleaners and administrators. It has read the following article about staff in independent hotels and is considering changing its operations to increase staff motivation.

'Empowerment is a frequently used buzzword, not just in the hospitality industry. Empowerment means staff can make decisions. If hotels want to remain successful, they need to be driven by their staff on customer service. Independent hotels have to go "above and beyond" and work harder in a competitive environment. This helps to ensure survival through a high percentage of repeat business, while fostering growth of new clients.

Guests appreciate dealing with people who are empowered. The last thing an arriving guest needs is to be given the runaround, going through "layers" of management to get what they need. Empowerment means, rather than becoming defensive, staff assume accountability mistakes and put them right.

Essential to empowerment is the practice of "trust, but verify". A balance is necessary because empowerment can backfire especially in the wrong application or misguided interpretation. Owners and managers cannot give responsibility to staff without empowering them. But attention should be given to training staff to be ensure empowerment works. Empowerment can work against you if you have a staff member too empowered without direction.

In the hotel industry employees should be seen as part of a team. The terms employee and management create divisions. Such a divide in organisational structure does not foster a sense of teamwork. It's a

"them and me" situation rather than a "we or us". Terms such as staff member illustrate better and reinforce working together. This creates a culture of "leadership teamwork" for the staff working with guests. Having fluid organisational structures reduce levels of management, separating President/CEO/General Manager from guests. The more layers you have, the more distant you remain from the guest and from the pulse of the staff.'

Source: adapted in part from www.hotelinteractive.com.

(a) Explain the meaning of the terms (i) empowerment (3 marks) and (ii) teamwork (3 marks).
(b) Explain TWO ways in which the organisation at Zinx might change to help motivate employees. (6 marks)
(c) Explain how greater empowerment at Zinx can affect (i) employees, (ii) clients and (ii) the business. (8 marks)
(d) Discuss whether Zinx should increase empowerment at the business. (12 marks)

69 Management

What is management?

Managers are an important group involved in business activity. It may be difficult to define exactly what is meant by 'management'. However, many agree that managers are responsible for 'getting things done' - usually through other people. The term manager may refer to a number of different people within a business. Some job titles include the word manager, such as personnel manager. Other job holders may also be managers, even though their titles do not say it. It could be argued that managers:

- act on behalf of the owners - in a company, senior management are accountable to the shareholders;
- set objectives for the organisation, for example, they may decide that a long term objective is to have a greater market share than all of the company's competitors;
- make sure that a business achieves its objectives, by managing others;
- ensure that corporate values (the values of the organisation) are maintained in dealings with other businesses, customers, employees and the general public.

The functions of management

Henri Fayol, the French management theorist, listed a number of functions or elements of management in his book *General and Industrial Administration* (1916).

Planning This involves setting objectives and also the strategies, policies, programmes and procedures for achieving them. Planning might be done by line managers who will be responsible for performance. However, advice on planning may also come from staff management who might have expertise in that area, even if they have no line authority. For example, a production manager may carry out workforce planning in the production department, but use the skills of the personnel manager in planning recruitment for vacancies that may arise.

Organising Managers set tasks which need to be performed if the business is to achieve its objectives. Jobs need to be organised within sections or departments and authority needs to be delegated so that jobs are carried out. For example, the goal of a manufacturing company may be to produce quality goods that will be delivered to customers on time. The tasks, such as manufacturing, packaging, administration, etc. that are part of producing and distributing the goods, need to be organised to achieve this goal.

Commanding This involves giving instructions to subordinates to carry out tasks. The manager has the authority to make decisions and the responsibility to see that tasks are carried out.

Co-ordinating This is the bringing together of the activities of people within the business. Individuals and groups will have their own goals, which may be different to those of the business and each other. Management must make sure that there is a common approach, so that the company's goals are achieved.

Controlling Managers measure and correct the activities of individuals and groups, to make sure that their performance fits in with plans.

Managerial roles

Henry Mintzberg in the 1980s suggested that, as well as carrying out certain functions, the manager also fulfils certain roles in a firm. He identified three types of role which a manager must play.

Interpersonal roles These arise from the manager's formal authority. Managers have a figurehead role. For example, a large part of a chief executive's time is spent representing the company at dinners, conferences etc. They also have a leader role. This involves hiring, firing and training staff, motivating employees etc. Thirdly, they have a liaison role. Some managers spend up to half their time meeting with other managers. They do this because they need to know what is happening in other departments. Senior managers spend a great deal of time with people outside the business. Mintzberg says that these contacts build up an informal information system, and are a means of extending influence both within and outside the business.

Information roles Managers act as channels of information from one department to another. They are in a position to do this because of their contacts.

Decision making roles The manager's formal authority and access to information means that no-one else is in a better position to take decisions about a department's work.

Through extensive research and observation of what managers actually do, Mintzberg drew certain conclusions about the work of managers.

- The idea that a manager is a 'systematic' planner is a myth. Planning is often carried out on a day-to-day basis, in between more urgent tasks.
- Another myth is that a manager has no regular or routine duties, as these have been delegated to others. Mintzberg found that managers perform a number of routine duties, particularly 'ceremonial' tasks.
- Mintzberg's research showed that managers prefer verbal communication rather than a formal system of communication. Information passed by word of mouth in an informal way is likely to be more up to date and easier to grasp.

Management by objectives (MBO)

In 1955, Peter Drucker, a US business adviser and writer, published a book called *The Practice of Management*. In the book, he suggested that managers had five functions:

- setting objectives;
- organising work;
- motivating employees and communicating information to them;
- job measurement - checking that tasks have been performed and objectives met;
- developing people, including organising training.

Question 1.

Alison Broomes had a typical morning as personnel manager for a company employing 750 people.

8.00 In her office dealing with her emails.
8.10 Interrupted by the production manager asking whether she had any luck in getting applications for the toolsetter's job.
8.30 Secretary arrives and they go through her diary appointments for the day.
8.40 Meeting with accounts manager to discuss the wording of an advert and job description for an accounts executive. Interrupted by mobile phone call from managing director's personal secretary confirming 3.45 meeting.
9.20 Back into the office to deal with the mail. Delegate tasks arising from the mail to her 2 assistants and 1 secretary in their open plan office.
9.40 Meeting with trade union representative to discuss disciplining of a worker for persistent lateness.
9.50 Review file for interviews taking place the following day. Interrupted by phone call from managing director's personal secretary to ask if the meeting could be moved to 4.00 p.m.
10.10 Checks progress on two job vacancies with one of her assistants.
10.30 Monthly meeting with head of marketing to discuss current personnel issues in her department.
11.30 Attendance at small ceremony where 15 employees are given their CIEH Basic Health and Safety awards.
11.50 Back in the office reading over letters and documents that are to be sent out by her secretary which require her signature.
12.10 Discussion with one of her assistants about a pay issue that has cropped up.
12.25 Accesses emails and replies to them.
12.40 Calls assistant head of production about application for training course from two of his workers.
12.55 Working lunch with her two assistants in the office.

(a) Explain what functions of management Alison Broomes has fulfilled during her morning according to (i) Fayol's theory of management and (ii) Mintzberg's theory.

Setting objectives Drucker argued that businesses could run into problems if managers and employees worked towards different objectives. For example, the marketing department might want to launch a new product. This could raise revenues, but would also increase costs. In contrast, the finance department might frustrate those plans by not agreeing to any increase in spending for the next six months. So Drucker put forward the idea that a business could be run and controlled through:

- the setting out of objectives;
- making plans to realise those objectives;
- carrying out those plans;
- monitoring whether objectives have been reached.

This is MANAGEMENT BY OBJECTIVES (MBO). It is a scientific approach to management, where the same principles can be applied to different businesses and different situations. MBO requires managers to use the skills identified by Drucker as essential to their role as managers.

Planning and MBO In a large organisation, the system to implement MBO is likely to be complex. This is because there is a large number of employees who must be involved at different levels in the hierarchy of the business. In a large organisation, objectives or goals for the whole business (corporate objectives) are set by senior managers and the directors of the company. Those objectives are derived from their aims (sometimes written out in the mission statement of the business). Senior management then has to plan how to achieve those objectives.

The next stage is to involve the next layer of management in the hierarchy. A corporate objective might be to increase sales by 30 per cent over the next three years. Senior management of a subsidiary company of the business would then be asked how they could contribute to realising that goal. Following discussions and analysis, they could agree on their objective. They might, for example, agree to an objective of increasing sales by 10 per cent. Planning is then required to map out how the 10 per cent increase will be achieved.

This might then be taken down to managers of individual departments within the subsidiary company. What objectives would those departments have to help achieve the 10 per cent increase in sales? Ultimately, it can be taken down to the level of individual workers. Through systems of performance appraisal, individual workers can be set goals, say for the next year. Achieving these goals will form a small part of the way in which the objectives of the whole business will be achieved.

Participation and MBO The MBO process should encourage participation and negotiation. Orders should not simply be

Table 1: Advantages of MBO

- Managers and workers in the organisation will know their objectives. So the business can work to a single purpose.
- Objectives and plans can be co-ordinated throughout the organisation. So one part of an organisation should not be working in a way which will frustrate the objectives of another part of the organisation.
- Clarity of purpose, negotiation and payment systems should lead to workers and managers being better motivated.
- MBO allows senior managers to control the organisation. The MBO system allows them to steer the business in the direction in which they have agreed to go.

passed down the chain of command. Instead, objectives and how to achieve them should be the subjects of discussion and negotiation. There are two main reasons for this.

- Those lower down the chain of command often have a better understanding of what is possible than those further up the chain. Their knowledge and experience should be used rather than ignored. So they should be fully involved in objective setting, planning and execution.
- Participation is likely to increase motivation. Managers and workers are likely to be committed to achieving goals which they have helped to set.

Compensation and MBO Compensation of individual workers or groups of workers can be linked into the achievement of objectives. Bonuses can be paid to managers and workers who meet targets. Bonus systems should be designed to reward those who achieve. They should therefore motivate managers and workers. Reward-based compensation systems also force businesses to be clear about whether they have achieved their objectives. Information about what has been achieved must be collected to decide whether or not bonuses are to be paid. They force everyone to concentrate their attention on what is to be achieved and what has been achieved.

Advantages and problems of MBO

Table 1 shows the benefits of a MBO approach. However, there may be some problems. Some large organisations have attempted to adopt MBO, although perhaps not as a complete management system. Others have not, for a number of reasons.

Time and resources Properly implemented, the system requires a considerable amount of time and resources to be allocated to it. Involving managers at all levels of an organisation is costly. It can be argued that these costs outweigh the benefits to be gained from implementation.

Obstruction MBO assumes that managers and workers can be moulded into employees who will understand objectives and carry out plans which will fulfil those objectives. But each manager and worker is different. Some are highly motivated and are good at seeing objectives and implementing them. Others might have less positive attitudes towards work. They might have little interest in seeing the business achieve its objectives. Equally, many workers and managers find it difficult to understand large-scale objectives and plans. In their view, getting on with familiar routine tasks is all that is important. Meetings to them are mostly a waste of time and the outcomes are usually best ignored. There are also employees who find it difficult to work in ways which are fixed by others. They are not necessarily good team members because they do things in the way which suits them. But they can be highly valuable to an organisation, particularly where individuality and creativity are needed. So, many managers and workers conform to the type of working required by the MBO system. This reduces its effectiveness.

Creativity Some argue that MBO fails to recognise the importance of creativity and spontaneity in a successful business. MBO is a system of control to ensure that managers

Question 2.

Kaplin Price is a manufacturer of scaffolding and safety equipment. It is increasingly facing stiff competition from abroad, but is not certain how best to react to this. Should it expand rapidly? Or should it rationalise to some extent? What would happen if it differentiated its products in some way from those of its competitors? Unless it makes a decision soon, it might find that its costs have escalated and it may be forced to shut down.

It has also experienced difficulties with its internal organisation. Last year it attempted to launch a new range of products with the intention of expanding its market share. It was not clear exactly what share it wanted to achieve, just that it wanted sales to grow. It set in place an incentive system for its sales representatives. Those that reached a certain target of sales would receive a bonus. However, it did not explain to the reps exactly what the target would be. This meant that they lacked motivation and whether they should be paid the bonus or not was decided by managers with a 'gut feeling' about individuals if there had been improved sales from the whole team.

(a) Using examples, examine ways in which adopting an MBO approach might solve the difficulties faced by Kaplin Price.

carry out the objectives and plans of senior management. But success in many businesses comes about because workers react as individuals to individual situations. MBO stifles that initiative and makes it more difficult for managers to react to an unpredictable environment.

A changing environment MBO assumes that the environment in which a business finds itself is likely to be fairly predictable. But in practice, the business environment can be volatile. Objectives set one month can be unrealistic the next. War, recession, collapsing markets or new competitors can completely change what is possible. So, too much planning can be a waste of resources. Even worse, it can paralyse a business when circumstances change. Managers can carry on working to old objectives and plans when these have become redundant.

In practice, all medium to large businesses have formal or informal strategies (plans to meet objectives) and systems to implement those strategies. These systems include elements of MBO. But most accept that management by objectives is not the only way to run a successful business.

Being a manager

Charles Handy, an Irish author specialising in organisational behaviour and management, has outlined what is likely to be involved in 'being a manager'.

The manager as a general practitioner Handy made an analogy between managing and staying 'healthy'. If there are 'health problems' in business, the manager needs to identify the symptoms. These could include low productivity, high labour turnover or industrial relations problems. Once the symptoms have been identified, the manager needs to find the cause of the trouble and develop a strategy for 'better health'. Strategies for health might include changing people, through hiring and firing, reassignments, training, pay increases or counselling. A manager might also restructure work through job redesign, job enrichment and a redefinition of roles. Systems can also be improved. These can include communication systems, reward systems, information and reporting systems, budgets and other decision making systems, e.g. stock control.

Managerial dilemmas Handy argued that managers face dilemmas. One of the reasons sometimes given for why managers are paid more than workers is because of the dilemmas they face.

- **The dilemma of cultures** When managers are promoted or move to other parts of the business, they have to behave in ways which are suitable for the new position. For example, at the senior management level, managers may deal more with long term strategy and delegate lower level tasks to middle management more often. If a promoted manager maintains a 'culture' that she is used to, which may mean taking responsibility for all tasks, she may not be effective in her new position.
- **The trust-control dilemma** Managers may want to control the work for which they are responsible. However, they may have to delegate work to subordinates, trusting them to do the work properly. The greater the trust a manager has in subordinates, the less control she retains for herself. Retaining control could mean a lack of trust.
- **The commando leader's dilemma** In many firms, junior managers often want to work in project teams, with a clear task or objective. This can mean working 'outside' the normal bureaucratic structure of a larger organisation. Unfortunately, there can be too many project groups (or 'commando groups') for the good of the business. The manager must decide how many project groups she should create to satisfy the needs of her subordinates and how much bureaucratic structure to retain.

The manager as a person Management has developed into a profession and managers expect to be rewarded for their professional skills. Managers must, therefore, continue to develop these skills and sell them to the highest bidder.

Theory X and Theory Y

In 1960 Douglas McGregor published *The Human Side of Enterprise*. It was an attempt to apply the implications of Maslow and the work of Taylor and Mayo on motivation to business. In the book, he gives different reasons why people work. He coined the terms Theory X and Theory Y to describe these differences. Table 3 shows the main ideas behind the two theories.

- **Theory X** THEORY X assumes that people are lazy. If this is accepted, then the only way to get people to work is by using strict control. This control can take one of two forms. One method is to use coercion - the threat of punishment if rules are broken or targets not achieved. This is often known as the 'stick' approach. The problem with threats is that they are only effective if the person being threatened believes that they will be carried out. Modern employment laws and company-wide agreements,

Table 2: Theory X and Theory Y

Theory X	Theory Y
• Workers are motivated by money	• Workers have many different needs which motivate them
• Workers are lazy and dislike work	• Workers can enjoy work
• Workers are selfish, ignore the needs of organisations, avoid responsibility and lack ambition	• If motivated, workers can organise themselves and take responsibility
• Workers need to be controlled and directed by management	• Management should create a situation where workers can show creativity and apply their job knowledge

Question 3.

In 2007 BP's new chief executive, Tony Hayward, vowed to fix the problems at the company after announcing a slide in second quarter profits. He said there would be a revamp of BP's structure and promising to rein in operating subsidiaries in favour of a more centralised management style. Previously BP's head office issued financial targets, but left divisional heads with a high degree of operational independence. Mr Hayward is thought to admire the greater 'command and control' style of industry leader Exxon Mobil. 'We are not moving to a completely functional operation,' he said, 'but there will be much stronger boundaries and standards within which to operate.'

Promising the end of 'duplication' around the group, Mr Hayward detailed cost cuts, including the redeployment of 25 per cent of head office staff into the field. Hayward has already indicated that the management style and approach that he wants to filter down to the grass roots will be less about politics and cult of personality and more focus used on profits and operations. Hayward has written of BP's failure to 'listen enough to what the bottom of the organisation is saying'. The word 'collegiate' crops up a lot in conversations with BP personnel about the management approach that Hayward aims to cultivate.

Source: adapted from the *Telegraph*, 2007.

(a) What are the potential dilemmas of a manager's role at BP?
(b) To what extent does Mr Hayward subscribe to a Theory X or Theory Y approach to management?

have made this difficult for managers. For this reason, a 'carrot' approach may be more suitable. People have to be persuaded to carry out tasks by means of promises or rewards. In many ways this theory is similar to Taylor's **scientific management** view of people at work as shown earlier in this unit.

- **Theory Y** THEORY Y, on the other hand, assumes that most people are motivated by those things at the top of Maslow's hierarchy. In other words, people are responsible, committed and enjoy having control over work. Most people, given the opportunity, will get involved in work, and contribute towards the solution of a problem that may arise. This theory is similar in some ways to the **human relations school**.

Business managers tend to say that their own assumptions are closer to Theory Y than to Theory X. But tests on management training courses tend to show that their attitudes are closer to Theory X than they might like to admit. In addition, many managers suggest that, while they themselves are like Theory Y, workers are closer to Theory X. This theory has been used by managers to organise employees in business.

In practice, it could be argued that most firms behave according to Theory X, especially where shopfloor workers are concerned. The emphasis is on the use of money and control to encourage workers to behave in the 'correct way'. The same organisations might behave according to the assumptions of Theory Y when dealing with management. A representative of a banker's union wrote in *The Independent on Sunday*, 'The lower down the ladder you are, the less control you have over your work environment. Managers can do as they please, stretch their legs whenever they want. Clerical workers, if they are working in a data-processing centre, for example doing entries for cheques or credit cards, are disciplined if they don't complete a given number of key strokes in an hour or a day. Half the time they don't know what they are doing. They don't see any end product. More and more work has been downgraded.'

KEYTERMS

Management by Objectives (MBO) – a management theory which suggests that managers set goals and communicate them to subordinates.
Theory X – put forward by McGregor, the theory that workers disliked work, were inherently unambitious, lazy, irresponsible and untrustworthy and were motivated to work mainly by earning money.
Theory Y – put forward by McGregor, the theory that workers enjoy work, want to take responsibilities and organise themselves and are motivated to work by a much wider number of factors simply than earning money.

KNOWLEDGE

1. (a) According to Fayol, what are the functions of management? (b) How do these differ from those suggested by Mintzberg?
2. What are the functions of management according to Drucker?
3. Explain what is meant by 'management by objectives'.
4. Explain the role, in management by objectives, of (a) participation and (b) compensation.
5. Compare the advantages and disadvantages of management by objectives.
6. What is the difference between the Theory X and Theory Y views of workers'?

Case Study: MBO in banking

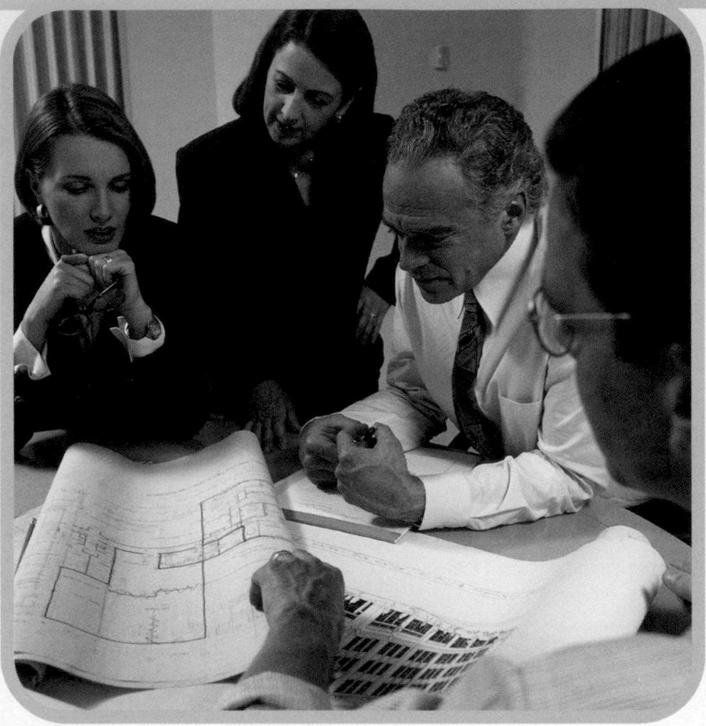

Management by objectives was the driving management philosophy of a particular bank. For example, each month bank branches would be given a new target. One month it would be the number of new savings accounts opened. Another month it would the number of loans sold. Another month it would the number of student accounts opened. Quite what was the plan of head office was unclear, but bonuses for the staff at the branches depended on hitting those targets month after month.

The branch manager at one of the Bournemouth branches, Patricia McGuire, regularly went on 'away' days. At these conferences, the objectives that head office were setting its managers were explained. Patricia was expected to communicate those objectives to her staff - to help get them to see the big picture of how they fitted into the big plan. But many branch managers found it difficult to be motivated by these training sessions. Often, the targets were completely unattainable. Take the target in September for signing up students. Her branch was in Bournemouth, capital city of England for senior citizens. She would be lucky to sign up one student, let alone the target of 50.

At Patricia McGuire's annual performance appraisal, her line manager didn't seem unduly worried that her branch had missed its target for 9 out of the previous 12 months. She concentrated on other aspects of Patricia's work and recommended that she be given her individual bonus for the year. During the interview Patricia expressed her frustration that she had no control over what targets were set for her branch staff. The line manager said that the system was not designed to incorporate feedback from staff further down the line. Head office decided what it wanted and that was what went out to the branches.

(a) Discuss whether the management by objectives approach of the bank was effective. (16 marks)

70 Leadership

Leadership and management

Management has a number of functions. For example, managers, according to the management theorist Henri Fayol, should predict what will happen in the future, plan to achieve their objectives, organise resources, exercise command over staff lower down the hierarchy, co-ordinate day-to-day tasks and monitor how well objectives are being achieved. Peter Drucker, writing 40 years later, added motivating and communicating with staff and giving them training opportunities to this list.

Some writers make no distinction between management and leadership in an organisation. Managers are leaders because of the roles they play. Others, however, suggest that leaders are not necessarily the same as managers. Leaders may perform the same functions as managers. But in addition, they may do some or all of the following.

- Leaders can be **visionaries**, understanding where an organisation is at today and seeing the direction in which an organisation has to change to survive and flourish.
- Leaders tend to be good at carrying through the **process of change**. Because they understand the starting point and the end point, they can chart a route from one to the other. Where others may see only chaos and think the organisation is taking the wrong road, the leader has the ability to see through the details and small setbacks which are a part of any change.
- Leaders are often excellent at **motivating** those around them, allowing them to perform at their best. They are particularly good at motivating others to change both themselves and the organisation.

It could be argued that, in large businesses, leaders devise **strategies** whilst managers are responsible for implementing them. However, sometimes leaders do get involved in implementation because they appreciate that it is just as important to implement change as it is to devise strategies. In small businesses, leaders often have the skills to both devise and carry out a strategy.

The characteristics of leaders

One approach to finding out what makes good leaders is to identify the **qualities**, **characteristics** or **traits** that they should have. A number of characteristics have been suggested.

- Effective leaders have a positive self-image, backed up with a genuine ability and realistic aspirations. This is shown in the confidence they have. An example in UK industry might be Richard Branson, in his various pioneering business activities. Leaders also appreciate their own strengths and weaknesses. It is argued that many managers fail to lead because they often get bogged down in short-term activity.
- Leaders need to be able to get to the 'core' of a problem and have the vision and commitment to suggest radical solutions. Sir John Harvey-Jones took ICI to £1 billion profit by stirring up what had become a 'sleeping giant'. Many awkward questions were raised about the validity of the way things were done, and the changes led to new and more profitable business on a worldwide scale for the firm.
- Studies of leaders in business suggest that they are experts in particular fields and well read in everything else. They tend to be 'out of the ordinary', intelligent, and articulate. Examples might be Anita Roddick, the founder of Body Shop or Bill Gates, the founder of Microsoft.
- Leaders are often creative and innovative. They tend to seek new ideas to problems, make sure that important things are done and try to improve standards.
- Leaders often have the ability to sense change and can respond to it. This is dealt with later in this unit.

Leadership styles

Another approach is to examine different styles of leadership. There is a number of styles that managers might adopt in the work setting.

Autocratic An AUTOCRATIC leadership style is one where the manager sets objectives, allocates tasks, and insists on obedience. Therefore the group become dependent on him or her. The result of this style is that members of the group are often dissatisfied with the leader. This results in little cohesion, the need for high levels of supervision, and poor levels of motivation amongst employees.

Autocratic leadership may be needed in certain circumstances. For example, in the armed forces there may be a need to move troops quickly and for orders to be obeyed instantly.

Figure 1: Leadership traits

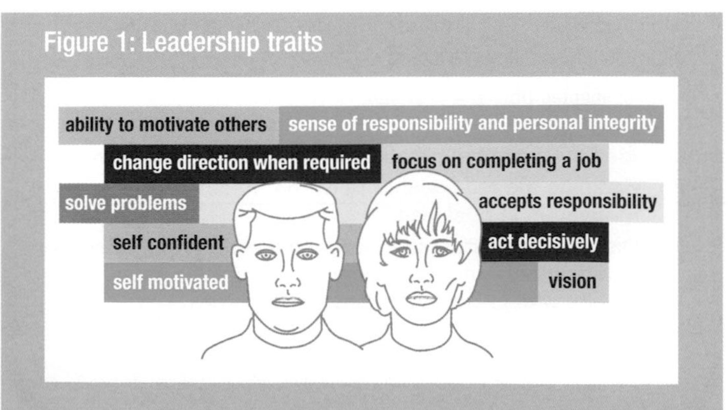

Question 1.

Britain's bosses are becoming more dictatorial in style, causing increased absenteeism among staff and lower productivity, the Chartered Management Institute warned. After surveying more than 1,500 managers, it found most organisations were suffering from overbearing and dogmatic leadership, in spite of overwhelming evidence that the authoritarian approach is ineffective.

Managers were asked to describe the organisation in which they worked. They could choose three characteristics from a list of ten, ranging from 'authoritative', 'risk averse' and 'secretive' to 'accessible', 'empowering' and 'trusting'. The institute said: 'The most widely experienced leadership styles in UK organisations are bureaucratic (40 per cent), reactive (37 per cent) and authoritarian (30 per cent).' Over the same period, the proportion of managers saying they worked in empowering organisations fell from 37 per cent to 25 per cent. The institute said staff in organisations with a dictatorial style were less likely to enjoy their work and more likely to have high rates of sickness absence.

In authoritarian companies, 44 per cent of managers said they got job satisfaction, compared with 71 per cent in other organisations. In innovative and trusting companies, 10 per cent of managers said absence was increasing, compared with 45 per cent in organisations where the culture was suspicious. The most successful businesses had empowering leadership styles. By contrast, 56 per cent of declining companies were stifled by bureaucracy and 26 per cent had a secretive environment.

The institute said organisations should have learned long ago that the authoritarian style was ineffective. 'If not from the management schools, they should have picked up the message from sitcoms such as Blackadder and the Office,' a spokesman said. But whenever organisations failed to meet their targets, it appeared that senior managers responded by creating secretive and bureaucratic environments. This might be due to a shortage of managers with the right mix of skills.

An organisation in difficulty faced more pressure to deliver good results with fewer management resources. Jo Causon, the institute's marketing director, said: 'The effect of management styles on performance can be marked. It has a direct bearing on the levels of health, motivation and commitment linking employers and staff. Of course, improving the sense of wellbeing, determination and productivity is no easy task, but it is one that cannot be ignored.'

The report said: 'It is disappointing that bureaucratic, reactive and authoritarian styles prevail in the UK, when entrepreneurial, accessible and empowering styles are associated with far higher levels of motivation, health and productivity.'

Source: adapted from *The Guardian*, 12.12. 2007.

(a) Identify the different leadership styles in the article.
(b) Examine the relationship between these styles and motivation in business.
(c) Discuss an appropriate leadership style for a business in difficulty facing more pressure to deliver good results with fewer management resources.

Democratic A DEMOCRATIC leadership style encourages participation in decision making. Democratic leadership styles can be persuasive or consultative.

- **Persuasive.** This is where a leader has already made a decision, but takes the time to persuade others that it is a good idea. For example, the owner of a business may decide to employ outside staff for certain jobs and persuade existing staff that this may ease their work load.
- **Consultative.** This is where a leader consults others about their views before making a decision. The decision will take into account these views. For example, the views of the marketing department about whether to launch a new range of products may be considered.

Democratic leadership styles need good communication skills. The leaders must be able to explain ideas clearly to employees and understand any feedback they receive. It may mean, however, that decisions take a long time to be reached as lengthy consultation can take place.

It has been suggested that a democratic style of leadership can be more effective in business for a number of reasons.

- There has been increased public participation in social and political life. Democratic management reflects this trend.
- Increasing income and educational standards means that people now expect greater freedom and a better quality of working life.
- Research suggests that this style is generally more effective. Managers are able to 'tap into' the ideas of people with knowledge and experience. This can lead to better decisions being made.
- People involved in the decision making process are likely to be more committed and motivated, to accept decisions reached with their help, to trust managers who make the decisions and to volunteer new and creative ideas.

Paternalistic PATERNALISTIC leaders are similar to autocratic leaders. They make all the decisions and expect subordinates to obey these decisions. However, whereas an autocratic leader may be uninterested in the well-being of subordinates, a paternalistic leader places a great deal of importance on their welfare. In the past there have been a number of paternalistic leaders, such as Joseph Rowntree and George Cadbury. Examples of their concern for employees included the building of new houses which they could rent at low rates. As with autocratic leaders, paternalistic leaders do not give subordinates control over decision making.

Laissez- faire A LAISSEZ-FAIRE type of leadership style allows employees to carry out activities freely within broad limits. The result is a relaxed atmosphere, but one where there are few guidelines and directions. This can sometimes result in poor productivity and lack of motivation as employees have little incentive to work hard.

Team-based leadership

The growth of flatter and matrix style structures, empowerment, job redesign and team working has affected the type of leadership that managers might use in a business. Managers are more likely today to organise and co-ordinate the workings of a variety of employees at different levels, in different functions and with different skills. In a sense they have become team-based leaders.

Traditional approaches to leadership and management that are linked to authority, status and power are likely to be of limited use to team based leaders. Team leaders are less likely to be individuals who give orders and have a clear understanding of exactly how a task is to be done than people who:

- have the the ability to bring together the right blend of workers to allow business problems to be solved and action implemented;
- can motivate staff in the team to problem solve and accomplish a task;
- know and understand corporate objectives;
- know what resources are available to implement actions in order to achieve objectives;
- evaluate a team and decide if the task has been carried out.

Team-based leadership often happens in businesses where the idea and use of a hierarchy is less relevant. This may happen, for example, in a SINGLE STATUS organisation where every worker is treated the same. They have the same facilities, same dress codes and same terms and conditions of employment. Every worker is made to feel as if they are an important part of the organisation.

Factors affecting leadership styles and approaches

The type of leadership style adopted by managers will depend on various factors. These factors may be **internal** factors, within the business, or **external** factors, from outside the organisation.

The task A certain task may be the result of an emergency, which might need immediate response from a person in authority. For example, if there is an emergency brought on by external factors such as a power failure leading to production ceasing, the speed of decision needed and the action taken may require an authoritarian or autocratic style of leadership.

The tradition of the organisation A business may have developed its own internal culture which is the result of the interactions of all employees at different levels. This can result in one type of leadership style, because of a pattern of behaviour that has developed in the organisation.

The type of labour force A more highly skilled workforce might be most productive when their opinions are sought. Democratic leadership styles may be more appropriate in this case. Certain types of profession in the labour force, for example, may be more used to making their own decisions and require a more democratic style of leadership.

The group size Democratic leadership styles can lead to confusion the greater the size of the group.

The leader's personality The personality of one manager may be different from that of another manager and certain leadership styles might suit one but not the other. For example, an aggressive, competitive personality may be more suited to an authoritarian leadership style. The unit titled 'Individuals in organisations' examines TRAIT THEORIES in detail.

Group personality Some people prefer to be directed rather than contribute, either because of lack of interest or previous experience, or because they believe that the manager is paid to take decisions and shoulder responsibility. If this is the case, then an autocratic leadership style is more likely to lead to effective decision making.

Situation A model of leadership by Ken Blanchard and Paul Hersey suggests that a SITUATIONAL LEADER adopts the most appropriate leadership style for the situation being faced. A leader will have **task behaviour** or **relationship behaviour**. Task behaviour reflects the extent to which the leader has to organise what a subordinate should do. Relationship behaviour reflects

Question 2.

In 2007 a national leadership scheme for the Fire and Rescue Service was launched. The programme aimed at 17,000 managers over four years, would be delivered through training centres, online resources and coaching and mentoring. Des Pritchard, HR director of the Chief Fire Officers' Association, said that the programme would move the service's leadership from a 'transactional' based model to a 'transformational and empowered' one. He said: 'Today's world is much more complex and there are greater demands on leaders. We hope the programme will help them to be more resilient.'

Sue Hopgood, director of organisational development at the Fire Service College, said various reviews had identified that leadership in the service "needed to be developed to be more attund to the twenty-first century". Leaders will be expected to demonstrate core behaviours relating to respect, integrity and trust, service to the public and working with colleagues. Hopgood said the model was unique because "it makes it very clear that the operational domain they work in is as important as their political and leadership domains".

The programme is also part of the Fire and Rescue Service's new diversity strategy. 'Transformational leaders are more likely to bring on board a more diverse workforce. They think differently about recruitment and selection,' Hopgood said.

She admitted that the service 'continues to be a predominantly white male organisation', having just over 2 per cent women and just under 3 per cent BME staff out of a 56,000 strong workforce. Only one out of the 46 fire and rescue services across England currently has a female chief executive. But she is positive that the scheme will help to address the balance. 'Leadership and diversity run alongside each other,' she said.

Source: adapted from *People Management*, 13.12.2007.

(a) Examine the factors that may have influenced the need for a leadership scheme at the Fire and Rescue Service.

how much support is needed and how close personal contact is. Together these will decide which of the following leadership styles will be used.

- **Delegating leadership** is where a leader allows subordinates to solve a problem. For this type of leadership style to work, subordinates need to be mature and require little support at work.
- **Participating or supporting leadership** is where a leader and subordinates work on a problem together, supporting each other. In this situation subordinates are slightly less mature than when a leader delegates and so need more support.
- **Selling or coaching leadership** is where a leader persuades others of the benefits of an idea. Workers are likely to be only moderately mature and require a great deal of support.
- **Telling or directing leadership** is where a leader tells others what to do. Workers are fairly immature. They are told exactly what to do and little contact or support is needed.

Environment CONTINGENCY THEORIES examine how the environment in which the leader operates might determine which particular style of leadership is best suited for a situation. It has been suggested that no leadership style is best in all situations. The style that is most effective will depend on factors such as leadership style, qualities of the followers and aspects of the situation.

The role of leadership in managing change

Leadership is vital in periods of change for businesses. For example, one of the key leadership issues facing growing businesses is how to deal with international markets and globalisation. Leaders may face challenges such as:

- international recruitment to overcome domestic staff shortages;
- cross-border mergers, acquisitions and joint ventures;
- the opening of new markets in Eastern Europe, South East Asia and China;
- European social policy directives, affecting business in member countries;
- developments in information and communications technology.

Earlier it was explained that leaders often have the ability to sense change and respond to it effectively. For example, an effective leader may be able to:

- predict a decline of sales in an important product due to changes in the market or the likelihood of a new production technique being available in the future;
- anticipate possible solutions to changes that may affect a business;
- have a clear vision of the main objectives of a business during periods of change and be able to guide the business to achieve these;
- organise and motivate employees to accept challenges;
- ensure stability and minimise or prevent disruption

There are various stages that leaders work through when managing change.

Preparing for change This involves laying the foundation or groundwork for any changes that may occur in the future. It includes building organisations that are better able to deal with change.

Early stages of implementing change Leaders also play an important role during change implementation. During this period the organisation is often at its most unstable. There may be confusion, fear, reduced productivity and lack of clarity about direction among staff. Employees may want to retain old ways and be unable to look to the future. During this period, leaders may need to:

- acknowledge the feelings and confusion of employees;
- work with employees to create a new vision of the altered workplace;
- help employees to understand the direction of the future.

Focusing only on feelings may not be enough. Leaders often need to initiate the movement into the new practices or situations. However, focusing only on the new vision may result in the perception that the leader is out of touch with the needs of employees. A key part of leadership is knowing when to focus on the difficulties that employees are experiencing, and when to focus on building and moving into the future.

Later stages of implementing change Over time employees become less emotional, more stable and more open to new directions and ways of doing things. This can be a good time for leaders to introduce positive new changes, such as changing unwieldy procedures. Leaders during this stage need to offer hope that the business is working towards being better, by solving problems and improving the quality of work life. While the new vision of the business may have begun when people were struggling with change, this is the time for leaders to make sure that employees 'buy into it', and understand their roles in the changed business.

Why do leaders adopt different styles?

A number of theories have been put forward to explain the most appropriate leadership style when dealing with certain situations or groups at work.

Fiedler In 1976, F. Fiedler argued that 'it is easier to change someone's role or power, or to modify the job he has to do, than to change his leadership style'. From his 800 studies he found who it is difficult for people to change leadership styles – an 'autocrat' will always lead in autocratic style whereas a leader that encourages involvement will tend to be 'democratic'. Different leadership styles may also be effective depending on the situation. He concluded that, as leaders are unable to adapt their style to a situation, effectiveness can only be achieved by changing the manager to 'fit' the situation or by altering the situation to fit the manager. In business it is often difficult to

Table 1

Possible reasons for performance problem	Possible solutions
Is the person fully aware of the job requirements?	Give guidance concerning expected goals and standards. Set targets.
Does the person have the ability to do the job well?	Provide formal training, on-the-job coaching, practice, etc.
Does the person find the task rewarding in itself?	Simplify task, reduce work load, reduce time pressures, etc.
Is good performance rewarded by others?	Reward good performance and penalise poor performance.
Does the person receive adequate feedback about performance?	Provide or arrange feedback.
Does the person have the resources and authority to do the task?	Provide staff, equipment, raw materials; delegate if necessary.
Do working conditions interfere with performance?	Improve lighting, noise, heat, layout; remove distractions etc.

change the situation. Fiedler suggested that a business should attempt what he called leadership match – to choose a leader to fit the situation. Leaders can be either task orientated or relationship orientated. So, for example, a business that faced declining sales might need a very task orientated manager to pull the business around, even if the tradition of the firm might be for a more democratic style of leadership.

Wright and Taylor In 1984, P. Wright and D. Taylor argued that theories which concentrate on the situation or maturity of those led ignore how skillfully leadership is carried out. They produced a checklist designed to help leaders improve the performance of subordinates. It included the following.

- What is the problem? An employee may, for example, be carrying out a task inefficiently.
- Is it serious enough to spend time on? This could depend on the cost to the business.
- What reasons may there be for the problem? How can it be solved? These are shown in Table 1.
- Choosing a solution and evaluating whether it is the most effective one.
- Evaluation of the leader's performance.

This can be used to identify the most suitable leadership style in a particular situation. For example, if the problem above is caused because the employee has been left to make his own decisions and is not able to, a more autocratic leadership style may be needed. On the other hand, if the employee lacks motivation or does not have the authority to make decisions, greater discussion or delegation may be needed.

Likert Rensis Likert identified four styles of leadership:

- exploitative (low concern for people, uses threats, downward communication);
- benevolent (listens to subordinates, uses rewards, decisions still taken by leader);
- consultative (leader makes real efforts to listen to subordinates but still takes decisions);
- participative (encourages decision making by subordinates).

Likert's ideas have also been used to identify two distinct styles of leadership using interviews of leaders and followers.

- Job-centred leader. This leader believes that employees are just a means to an end (production of the product, profit) and that the best way to get them to do what he or she wants is to closely supervise them and use rewards and coercion to communicate with them. This leader uses the legitimate position power as the basis of influencing employees.
- Employee-centred leader. This leader believes that it is necessary to create a supportive work environment in order for workers to be successful in helping the company meet its goals. This leader is concerned with giving employees opportunities for advancement and growth, and for meeting their achievement needs. This leader views employees as part of the team and believes that in order for the company to be successful, the individuals who work there must feel successful too.

Likert did not find that one was better than the other, nor did he recommend one set of behavior over the other.

Blake and Mouton Robert R. Blake and Janse S. Mouton's leadership grid examines two criteria as shown in Figure 2.

- Concern for people – the degree to which a leader

Figure 2: The Blake and Mounton grid

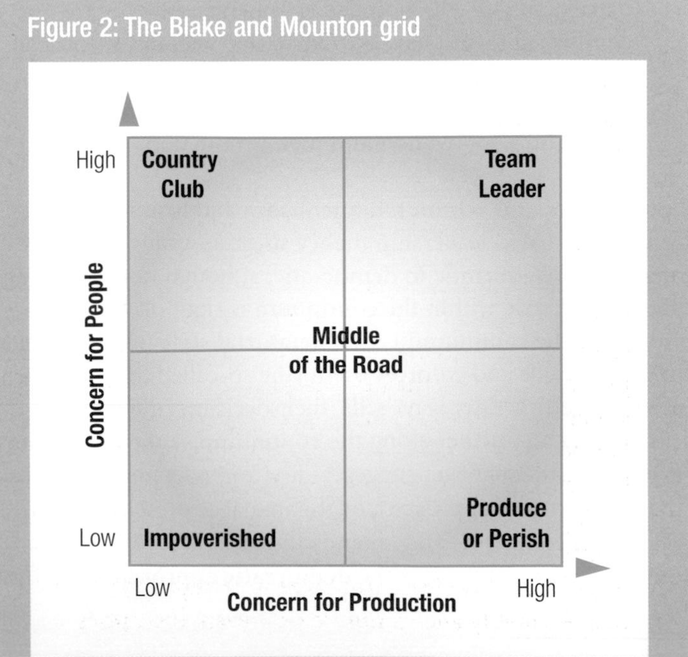

considers the needs of team members, their interests, and areas of personal development when deciding how best to accomplish a task.

- Concern for production – the degree to which a leader emphasises objectives, organisational efficiency and high productivity when deciding how best to accomplish a task.

Using the axis the following five leadership styles were defined.

- **Country Club Leadership – High People/Low Production** These leaders are most concerned about the needs and feelings of members of the team. Leaders assume that as long as team members are happy, they will work hard. This leads to a relaxed work environment, but one in which production suffers due to lack of direction and control.
- **Produce or Perish Leadership – High Production/Low People** These leaders believe that employees are simply a means to an end. Employee needs are secondary to the need for efficient and productive workplace. This type of leader is autocratic, has strict work rules, policies, and procedures, and sees punishment as the most effective means to motivate employees.
- **Impoverished Leadership – Low Production/ Low People** This style tends to be ineffective. Leaders have neither a high regard for creating systems to get the job done, nor for creating a work environment that is motivating. The result is a place of disorganization and dissatisfaction.
- **Middle-of-the-Road Leadership – Medium Production/Medium People** This style my appears to be a balance, but in practice may give away so much of each concern that neither production nor people needs are fully met. Leaders who use this style settle for average performance and feel that this is the most anyone can expect.
- **Team Leadership – High Production/High People** This is the best leadership style. Leaders stress production needs and the needs of the people equally highly. Employees are involved in understanding the business's purpose and determining production needs. When employees are committed to and have a stake in the business, their needs and production needs coincide. This creates a team environment based on trust and respect, which leads to satisfaction, motivation and high production.

Tannenbaum and Schmidt Tannenbaum and Schmidt Continuum-based leadership theory suggests a range of styles ranging from autocratic to democratic, although not suggesting that any one style within the continuum is right or wrong. At one end of the continuum is the **dictatorial style** – the manager makes decisions and enforces them (the so-called tells approach) or, in a slightly gentler way, 'sells' their decision (the tells and sells approach). Further along the continuum, is the **autocratic style**, where the manager suggests ideas and asks for comments (the tells and talks approach), or the manager presents outline ideas, seeks comments and amends the ideas accordingly (the consults approach). Next is the **democratic approach**. Here the manager presents a problem, seeks ideas and makes a decision (the involves approach), or allows employees to discuss the issue and make a decision (the delegates approach). Finally, the continuum ends with the **laissez-faire** approach. Here the manager allows employees to act in whichever way they wish, within specified limits (the abdicates approach).

The continuum is not a static model. It recognises that appropriate style depends on both the leader's personality, values and natural style, and on the employees' knowledge, experience and attitude. Furthermore, the range of situations which present themselves to a leader depend on factors such as the culture of the organisation, time pressure, the amount of authority and the amount of responsibility the leader has, which depends in turn upon the organisation's general environment.

CRITIQUE

The media often suggests that 'heroic' leaders are vital to making a successful business. Such leaders make things happen. They are heroes because they alone have the vision, personality and capability to bring things about in the business, either by themselves or through others. Although not denying that leaders have special qualities, it could be argued that focusing too much on leadership can create problems. For example, this approach may lead to the conclusion that a business without a heroic leader may not be able to function properly. Or it might suggest that the heroic leader is the most important thing to organisational effectiveness. It also perhaps devalues the role and importance of other employees.

There is evidence to suggest that effective businesses are those which are more concerned with the creativity of their products and organisational structures that enable those products to be produced and sold than those that rely heavily on leadership. It could be argued that the ability to teamwork, delegate and manage others effectively is more important in the daily workings of creative organisations than the attributes of heroic leadership, such as vision, command and personality.

Mainstream approaches to leadership also take consensus in organisations for granted, i.e. that employees are generally happy to be at work and that leadership is about providing them with the direction to get the most out of them. Where there is conflict, this is often seen as being related to problems with an individual or about resistance to change. The possibility that there might be underlying conflicts associated with inequalities of wealth, status or power between leaders and subordinates is not considered. Critics argue that although businesses may appear to be consensual, this is because leaders occupy positions in the hierarchy that enable them to suppress conflict or because subordinates have an understanding that compliance or consent is in their own 'best' interests. In other words, the absence of conflict is a consequence of dependence - subordinates depend on managers for terms and conditions, including retaining their jobs, promotion, future employment and references.

KNOWLEDGE

1. Explain the possible differences between a manager and a leader.
2. What are the characteristics or traits of leaders?
3. Explain the difference between autocratic and paternalistic leadership styles.
4. Explain the difference between democratic and laissez-faire leadership styles.
5. What are the implications for leadership of
(a) teamworking; (b) single status structures?

KEYTERMS

Autocratic leadership – a leadership style where the leader makes all decisions independently.

Contingency theories – examine how the environment in which the leader operates might determine which particular style of leadership is best suited to a situation.

Democratic leadership – a leadership style where the leader encourages others to participate in decision making.

Laissez-faire leadership – a leadership style where employees are encouraged to make their own decisions, within limits.

Paternalistic leadership – a leadership style where the leader makes decisions, but takes into account the welfare of employees.

Single status organisation – a business where all employees have equal conditions.

Situational leadership – where a leader adopts a style that suits the situation being faced as a result of the competence and commitment of subordinates.

Trait theories – explain that individuals inherit certain qualities that make them leaders. They identify personalities or characteristics shared by leaders.

Case Study: Martin Guntac

Martin Guntac owns a small chain of four car dealerships in the Yorkshire area. Part of the business is selling cars, both new and second hand. The other half provides servicing and repairs for customers. When he first started the business 30 years ago, he had two employees doing repair work from a run down garage in the back streets of Leeds. Today, he has over 100 employees spread across four premium sites. Each site has a manager, with a head of sales and a head of servicing and repairs underneath them.

Martin relies heavily on the four experienced site managers. They have day-to-day operational control of the business. He monitors their work and keeps a careful check on the performance of each site. Performance is checked both against previous periods and site to site. Martin is capable of making hard decisions. For example, five years ago he sacked one site manager who had been in the post for just 18 months when his site consistently underperformed compared with the other sites in the group.

This was a difficult decision, though, for Martin. He sees himself as a 'people person', and believes strongly in teamworking. Employees are encouraged to develop their own capabilities with a heavy emphasis on staff training and empowerment. Workers are encouraged to make decisions for themselves. Occasionally mistakes are made mainly because of a lack of guidance, but Martin believes firmly that this is an inevitable part of taking responsibility. A staff survey last year showed that over 90 per cent of staff felt 'motivated' at work.

Each week, he has a three hour meeting with the four site managers, his 'board of directors' as he likes to call them. Everything to do with the running of the business is discussed at these meetings. Martin expects his site managers to be frank and there can be major differences of opinion about how to develop the business. Ultimately, he has to make the key decisions but he always consults with others to hear what they have to say.

(a) Discuss the most important factors to have influenced the choice of leadership style by Martin. (12 marks)

(b) Discuss whether the leadership style adopted by Martin is the most suitable for the business. (16 marks)

71 Individuals in organisations

Individuals, groups and organisations

A business is made up of individuals. Individual production workers, office workers or managers etc. belong to groups within the business. Many tasks in modern business are technically complex, such as the production of a vehicle, and can only be carried out in groups using the combined skills of individuals. Other tasks, such as market research, may require people to work together as a co-ordinated 'team'. As well as these formal groups, individuals will also belong to informal groups, for example a group of workers who become friends after joining a company at the same time. Individuals and the groups they belong to make up the business organisation.

No two individuals are the same. They have different characteristics, attitudes, needs and personalities. Why does a business need to know something about these differences? It will help a business to:

- make sure it has chosen the most suitable person for a job from a number of applicants;
- make certain employees' skills are used effectively;
- ensure workers are satisfied and motivated;
- tell how individuals in the workforce will react when faced with a decision or a situation at work.

Physical differences

It is very rare indeed for two individuals physically to be the same in all respects. It is possible, however, to group people based on their shape, size, hair colour etc. Sometimes certain groups are more suitable for a job than others and this may be part of the job description. For example, people wanting to join the police force must be over a minimum height and an applicant to the fire service must have a certain chest expansion. A business, however, must be careful not to restrict physically demanding jobs to men as this type of discrimination is unlawful.

Personality differences

An individual could be described by the way they behave, such as 'happy-go-lucky' or 'quiet'. These give an indication of that person's personality. Psychologists call these words TRAITS. They form the basis of important theories of personality, some of which are used by businesses to make decisions about individuals at work.

Cattell In 1965 Raymond Cattell suggested that people have 16 main traits. To measure these traits he developed a test known as 16 Personality Factor (16PF). Figure 1 shows the 16 traits or factors that are measured in the test. Each one has a scale of 1-10. For example, factor 'A' could be reserved (1), outgoing (10) or somewhere in between. People taking the test choose a point on each scale which reflects their personality. Linking together the 'scores' will give a personality profile.

The 16PF is widely used in the selection of business managers. Kellogg's the cereal manufacturer has used it successfully in the past. By looking at the profiles of successful managers a firm is able to build up a 'suitable' personality profile. When interviewing candidates in future, the business could ask them to fill in a 16PF test and compare their results with the 'ideal profile' to see if the candidate is suitable. Figure 1 shows the results of a study by Makin, Cooper and Cox. The line linking the scores shows the average personality profile of managing directors.

Figure 1: Cattell's 16 Personality Factor questionnaire showing managing directors' average personality profile

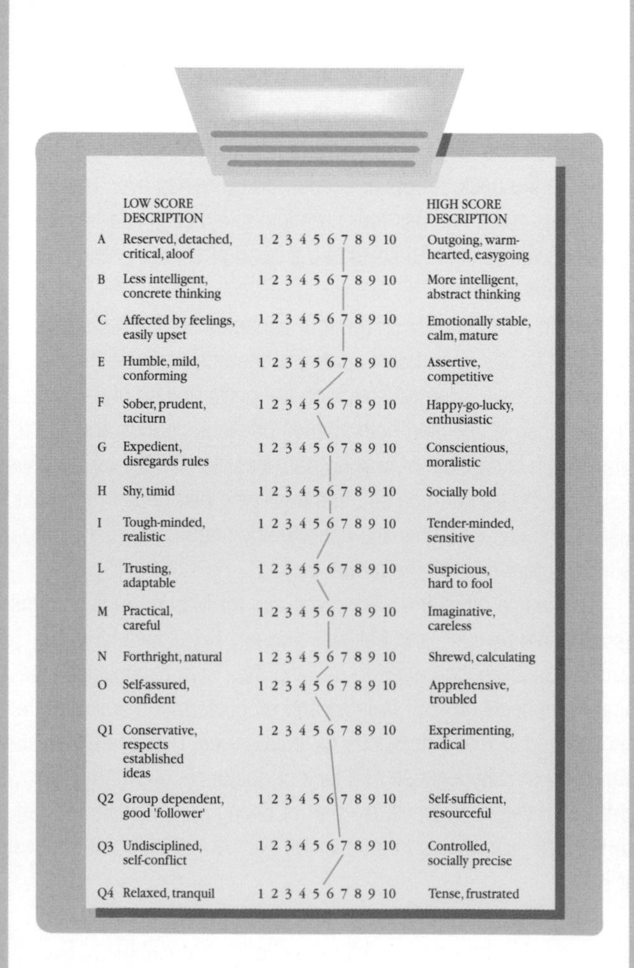

LOW SCORE DESCRIPTION
HIGH SCORE DESCRIPTION
A Reserved, detached, critical, aloof 1 2 3 4 5 6 7 8 9 10 Outgoing, warm-hearted, easygoing
B Less intelligent, concrete thinking 1 2 3 4 5 6 7 8 9 10 More intelligent, abstract thinking
C Affected by feelings, easily upset 1 2 3 4 5 6 7 8 9 10 Emotionally stable, calm, mature
E Humble, mild, conforming 1 2 3 4 5 6 7 8 9 10 Assertive, competitive
F Sober, prudent, taciturn 1 2 3 4 5 6 7 8 9 10 Happy-go-lucky, enthusiastic
G Expedient, disregards rules 1 2 3 4 5 6 7 8 9 10 Conscientious, moralistic
H Shy, timid 1 2 3 4 5 6 7 8 9 10 Socially bold
I Tough-minded, realistic 1 2 3 4 5 6 7 8 9 10 Tender-minded, sensitive
L Trusting, adaptable 1 2 3 4 5 6 7 8 9 10 Suspicious, hard to fool
M Practical, careful 1 2 3 4 5 6 7 8 9 10 Imaginative, careless
N Forthright, natural 1 2 3 4 5 6 7 8 9 10 Shrewd, calculating
O Self-assured, confident 1 2 3 4 5 6 7 8 9 10 Apprehensive, troubled
Q1 Conservative, respects established ideas 1 2 3 4 5 6 7 8 9 10 Experimenting, radical
Q2 Group dependent, good 'follower' 1 2 3 4 5 6 7 8 9 10 Self-sufficient, resourceful
Q3 Undisciplined, self-conflict 1 2 3 4 5 6 7 8 9 10 Controlled, socially precise
Q4 Relaxed, tranquil 1 2 3 4 5 6 7 8 9 10 Tense, frustrated

Question 1.

Ingvar Kamprad is self-made. He decided that working on a farm was not for him and started selling door to door. At 20 he was selling furniture. He called his company IKEA, from his initials, Elmtaryd, the family farm and Agunnaryd, the village where he grew up. Today Kamprad is said to be worth £32 billion. But he is also said to be careful with his money. He drives an 11 year old Volvo and still searches the Internet for cheap air fares. His idea of luxury is Swedish fish roe rather than a yacht. Although disputed, a study has suggested that he controls almost the whole of the private company he founded.

Kamprad is also a ruthless and inventive businessman. In 1956 he invented the flat pack concept of furniture. After starting IKEA he quickly undercut his competitors to gain market share. When he became too busy to operate the shop himself, he invented the retail system where, instead of the business taking goods to the customer, the customer picked up the goods. Today this is one of IKEA's hallmarks. When Kamprad wanted to see how well his sons could perform in business, he gave them each a separate part to run and compete with each other to see who would do best.

Some have argued the working for Kamprad is not easy. He dresses informally and tells his staff to call him by his first name. But it is suggested that he keeps a tight reign on his workforce.

Source: adapted from *The Daily Mail*, 7.4.2004.

(a) **Using the 16PF, examine some of the possible traits of Ingvar Kamprad.**
(b) **Suggest why these traits may be important for establishing a successful business such as IKEA.**

Eysenck In 1975 Hans Eysenck reduced the number of scales upon which personality traits could be measured to two:

- stable-unstable;
- extroverted-introverted.

The stable-unstable scale showed emotional stability. Stable people tended to be calm and reliable, while those with low stability tended to be anxious or reserved. The extroverted-introverted scale described people who were either passive, quiet and withdrawn (introverted) or changeable, outgoing and impulsive (extroverted).

Using these traits, Eysenck built a matrix of an individual's personality. This is shown in Figure 2. Individuals can be placed in one of the four quarters. A stable-introverted person may be calm and reliable, and perhaps suited to a job such as librarian.

Figure 2: Eysenck's matrix

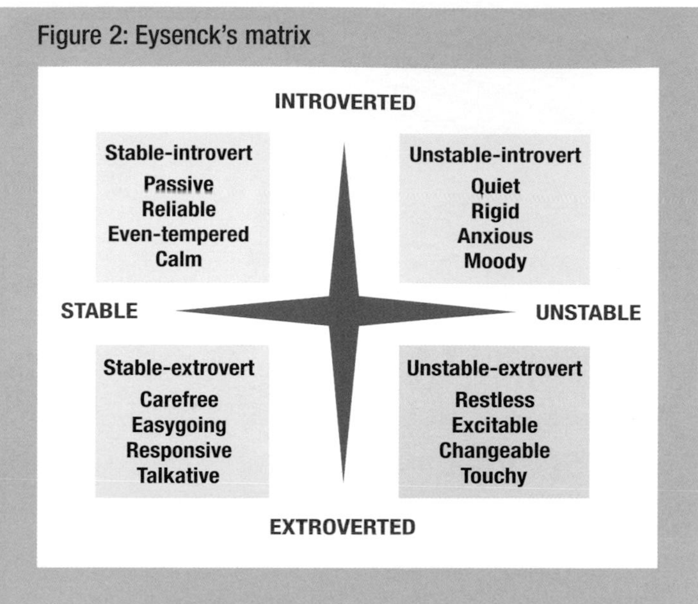

However, if the library needed an injection of new ideas a 'stable-extrovert' may be more suitable.

The matrix can have a number of uses for a business. For example, it could help judge how an employee might deal with a new situation or indicate how well a candidate might suit a particular job. A business may also use the information to build up a team of workers whose personalities complement each other to carry out a task.

Costa and McRae In the early 1990s Eysenck's work was developed by a number of theorists, such as Paul Costa and Robert McRae (1992). They outlined what have come to be known as the 'big five'. The big five are broad personality types or trait clusters. In research studies they have been found consistently to capture the traits that we use to describe ourselves and other people. They are shown in Table 1. Research seems to have reproduced these dimensions, in many different settings, with different people, with different forms of data collection and in different languages.

There are, however, limits to how useful these theories can be. They do not precisely predict what a person will do in any situation, only indicate what a person is likely to do given their personality. Behaviour might, for example, change when faced with stress. Also, people with different personalities may still be able to do a 'good' job when faced with the same situation.

Table 1: Costa and McRae's personality types

Definitions			
extroversion	gregarious, warm, positive	versus	quiet, reserved, shy
agreeableness	straightforward, compliant, sympathetic	versus	quarrelsome, oppositional, unfeeling
conscientiousness	achievement-orientated, dutiful, self-disciplined	versus	frivolous, irresponsible, disorganised
neuroticism	anxious, depressed, self-conscious	versus	calm, contented, self-assured
openness	creative, open-minded, intellectual	versus	unimaginative, disinterested, narrow-minded

Question 2.

Padraig Cruikshank started as a builder from school, working with his father repairing and laying roofs. At 20 he had set up his own business, employing three workers. Two of these workers were friends and the other a friend of his father. Padraig tended to rely on his father's friend for advice on tricky jobs and tried to make sure that all workers had a say if there were problems. As the business expanded and later became a company, Padraig wanted to retain this organisational culture. He offered share options to workers and was keen on the idea of works councils, which he introduced into the business in 2002.

Padraig also felt that it was important to realise that there are sometimes other things in life than work. He knew that some of his father's friends had suffered greatly during the decline of the housing market in the late 1980s. So he tended to take the view that you should 'live for the day'. In 2003 there had been some problems in one of his operations in the Norwich area. There was a rising demand for housing and the local manager had asked workers to work longer hours. They complained that these contravened the European Work Time Directive. Padraig was sure that this did not apply to UK businesses at that time, although it was likely to in future. However, he did have the feeling that any attempt to force longer hours on workers would affect the goodwill he had built up in the company. Padraig visited the local depot where the manager tended to be very anxious about meeting deadlines all the time. Padraig thought that perhaps the answer was to discuss other ways in which deadlines could be met, such as outsourcing, job sharing or flexible hours.

Source: adapted from research information.

(a) Using examples from the data, identify Padraig's personality on Eysenck's two dimensional matrix.

(b) Suggest how such a personality might help the business given the issues that it faces.

Another problem is that they assume an individual will give an honest response. But often it is easy to pick out the acceptable answer or the one that is best in terms of the job. For these reasons, the theories are usually used only for selection and internal promotion.

Personality and stress

Personality and health may be linked in a way that is relevant to business. In 1974, M. Friedman and R. Rosenman claimed to have identified two extreme personality patterns or 'behaviour syndromes', Type A and Type B, as shown in Table 2. These help to explain differences in stress levels at work and allow a 'stress-prone' personality to be identified.

Type A people are more impatient, competitive and aggressive than Type B people, and are more likely to suffer stress-related problems. For example, Friedman and Rosenman found that Type A personalities were three times more likely to suffer heart disease than Type B personalities. Type As thrive on long hours, large amounts of work and tight deadlines. These may be useful social and business characteristics. However, Type As may not be able to stand back from a complex business problem to make an effective decision. They tend to lack the patience and relaxed style required for many management positions. Their impatience can also increase the stress levels of those they work with.

Assessing personality in practice

The work of Cattell and Eysenck tries to 'measure' personality. In business, however, people judge the personality of others in less formal ways, and often fairly quickly. The decision may be based on what they themselves think is important. It could also be influenced by a 'stereotype', where personality is linked to race, sex or age. For example, it may be claimed that female managers are more emotional than male.

It is argued that people get an impression of someone from the first piece of information they receive about that person's characteristics. In an interview, for example, recruiters often make up their minds in the first four minutes and rarely change them. A candidate that did not seem prepared, looked untidy or was abrupt may well have lost the job straight away. People make these decisions because they do not like being uncertain about others. A decision based on first impressions may make the interviewer feel more secure, even if it is wrong. It may take time and further contact before people are seen 'as they really are'. Employers and employees must be prepared to change their minds about people they meet and work with. Only then will they be able to make an 'accurate' assessment of someone's personality.

Differences in intelligence

As well as differing in personality, people differ in intelligence or IQ. There is considerable debate about what intelligence is. One definition, by American psychologist Arthur Jensen, is that it is the ability to discover rules, patterns and principles, and apply these to problems.

Intelligence is usually measured by using IQ tests. They test an individual's ability to reason. A simple IQ test question may ask for the next number in the sequence 1, 3, 6, 10. This tests the ability to find a sequence and to apply it. An IQ 'score' is usually given at the end of the test. A high score is supposed to indicate a higher level of intelligence. Such tests are often criticised, particularly when comparing the intelligence of people in different social groups.

There is a number of factors which are thought to influence

Table 2: Personality characteristics

Type A personality characteristics	Type B personality characteristics
Competitive	Able to take time out to enjoy leisure
High need for achievement	Not preoccupied with achievement
Aggressive	Easygoing
Works fast	Works at a steady pace
Impatient	Seldom impatient
Restless	Not easily frustrated
Extremely alert	Relaxed
Tense facial muscles	Moves and speaks slowly
Constant feeling of time pressure	Seldom lacks enough time

an individual's IQ although there is little agreement on exactly how they affect the IQ.

Culture and class Many researchers argue that IQ tests are biased in favour of the middle classes, since tests are largely constructed by members of this group. Working class people tend to do less well on tests, so comparisons of intelligence between people in these groups are not really valid. It has also been shown that 'Western' IQ tests are not suitable for non-Western people. Cultural differences can mean they often approach and carry out the tests in an inappropriate way.

Genes There is general agreement that intelligence can be inherited. Some psychologists, such as Hans Eysenck in Britain, suggest that some 80 per cent of intelligence is inherited from parents. The rest is influenced by environmental factors such as the environment where we live and grow up, diet, quality of housing and family size. This is strongly contested by other social scientists.

Environment Some argue that differences in IQ are largely due to environmental factors. Research has shown that IQ test results can be affected by the education, motivation and physical health of the person taking the test. They can also be influenced by the person's rapport with whoever is carrying out the test and the language the test is set in.

Businesses today are now less likely to use IQ tests as a means of assessing an individual. Evidence suggests there is little connection between a person's IQ and how well he might do a job. It may be more important for a business to find out about an individual's knowledge and skills (which may include elements of IQ) as this could give a greater understanding of how a person might contribute to the organisation.

Differences in knowledge and skills

A business needs to know what knowledge and skills an employee has so that she can be given a position in the business where she will be of most use. Knowledge can be technical, job specific, vocational or general. To be a plumber, a worker would need the technical knowledge of the trade, e.g. what types of materials and techniques are used for certain jobs. Also, the plumber would need to have knowledge about the way tasks should be carried out and a thorough knowledge of what is involved in the trade – the vocational aspects of being a plumber. In addition, the plumber may need to have more general knowledge, such as the ability to do simple mathematics.

As well as having knowledge, an employee will also need skills. These are the abilities needed to complete a task. The skills required at work can be job specific, communication skills, IT skills, numeracy and literacy skills or problem solving skills. A plumber would not only need to know how to complete a task, but have the appropriate skills to carry it out. The ability to communicate with customers may also be a useful skill.

Businesses want a more qualified and more skilled workforce. They expect workers to update their skills through training, and to develop new and different skills. This makes employees more adaptable and flexible.

It has been suggested that knowledge work and knowledge workers are critical to business success in a changing business environment. Knowledge work requires employees who can:
- use their own existing knowledge;
- acquire new information;
- combine and process information to produce and communicate new information;
- learn continuously from their experiences.

Management theorists such as Peter Drucker and Michael Porter have suggested that knowledge is an important resource for businesses and a source of competitive advantage. They argue that work increasingly involves the processing and production of ideas, images, thoughts, concepts and symbols rather than physical materials. Knowledge workers are most suitable to carry out this sort of work. Knowledge workers are sometimes combined to make knowledge teams.

Problem solving and decision making

Businesses are not only interested in the abilities of their employees, but in the way they use them to solve problems. The way in which an employee prefers to work may cause problems if it differs from the way colleagues work or from what the business expects.

In 1984, Michael Kirton studied the way management initiatives in a business might succeed or fail. He suggested that success may depend on how problem solving was tackled and identified two approaches. ADAPTORS tend to solve problems by using existing or slightly modified approaches. They do not make rapid changes in the way problems are solved. INNOVATORS, however, try to find exciting and possibly unexpected ways of solving problems. Take the example of a small business having problems finding information quickly and easily when it is stored in files. The adaptor might suggest a better method of organising the files. An innovator, however, may feel that replacing the paper filing system with a computer system will be a better solution. These are two extremes. It is likely in business that people will

Question 3.

Today's candidate for most famous knowledge worker might be Bill Gates, the founder of Microsoft. The information revolution has made the management of knowledge vitally important for businesses. Some companies believe that the answer to creating knowledge workers is to recruit the brightest people. This may make sense. A 1995 study in 3,100 US workplaces looked at the relationship between education and productivity. The research showed that, on average, a 10 per cent increase in the workforce's education level led to an 8.6 per cent gain in productivity. This could be compared with a 10 per cent rise in plant and equipment values, which increased productivity by 3.4 per cent.

Another example showing the financial value of people who might be called knowledge workers was the move by institutional investors to have Maurice Saatchi dismissed from Cordiant, the advertising agency (formerly Saatchi & Saatchi). When he left, several directors left in protest and customers such as Mars and BA also defected, leading to a halving of the company's share price. This answers the question often asked by Charles Handy, a management specialist: 'What happens when your assets walk out of the door?' In effect the institutional shareholders thought they owned Saatchi & Saatchi. In fact, they owned less than half of it. Most of the value could be attributed to the human capital of the knowledge workers.

But employing bright people is not a guarantee of success. You might have the best brains, but they must be working for you. Some 150,000 of what might be called 'the brightest workers in the world' left IBM. The problem had been, as IBM later admitted, that many of them were working to their own agenda. Another problem is that some companies believe you can be too intelligent for the job. The most brilliant people are not always easy to manage. However, if the job demands a brilliant mind, then it seems logical to seek out the best.

Source: adapted from *The Financial Times*.

(a) What are the potential problems of knowledge workers for a business?
(b) Why might it make sense to recruit the 'brightest' people to be knowledge workers?
(c) Using evidence from the article, discuss the importance of knowledge workers as assets to a business.

have a combination of the two approaches.

Both these approaches have their strengths and weaknesses. The adaptor can effectively work within the present system, but does not find it easy to seek new solutions. For example, an 'adaptor' working in marketing might look for new product developments using existing products. The innovator, on the other hand, may produce ideas for new products.

This approach often means that the innovator finds it difficult to get ideas accepted. Innovators may be seen as extroverts, generating lists of new ideas, but ignoring the needs of the business. Their attitude can often mean that an adaptor feels uncomfortable working with them. The adaptor, however, may appear conservative and always willing to agree with a superior.

What can managers do to minimise clashes? A study by Makin, Cooper and Cox argued that the solution lies in understanding, together with an acceptance of the other person's position. Knowing someone else's style allows a manager to predict what they are likely to do in any situation.

Differences in emotional intelligence

In 1995 Goleman, an American Harvard Management specialist, coined the term emotional intelligence. It is the ability of a person to sense and understand their own and others' emotions and to apply that understanding to achieve an outcome, for example in a business situation. Successful businesses are able to harness emotional intelligence. Goleman argues that the 'business intelligence' of employees is affected by emotions rather than technical expertise, because emotions drive thinking.

Different individuals will have different emotional intelligence. A study of four year old children found that those who controlled their emotions, and resisted the temptation to eat a marshmallow, performed better on college entry tests fourteen years later. The theory may explain why some employees have problems after early career success. Problems arise because of their inability to understand their impact on others rather than to a lack of expertise. A study by the US company 3M found 90 per cent of the problems which affected its employees' performance were unmeasured. This was because they related to a lack of interpersonal skills, stress, emotional conflicts and personal health, rather than technical failure, absenteeism or poor training.

CRITIQUE

Mainstream approaches to examining individual differences tend to be based around sophisticated techniques of observations, measurement and classification that aim to explain personality and its effects on work organisation and wider society.

According to critical writers this approach fails to address questions such as 'Why is job performance a good thing in itself?', 'What kinds of work should be encouraged?', 'Is personality the cause or consequence of wider social and historical conditions and influences?' and 'Can personality be thought of as a category or entity in its own right?' They argue that these types of question act as a source of motivation and preoccupation for individuals in organisations. They would suggest that there is an anxiety that arises from 'being in the world' and it is to do with developing a clear sense of who we are, i.e. a 'robust identity' and trying to ensure that this identity is confirmed by others. This anxiety can, at times, lead us to try and control others or to crave identity confirmation through consumption of worldly goods or through the marketing of idealised identities (an electronic example of this would be current concerns with communication media such as Facebook and Myspace).

Examining business organisations, many different types of individuals can exhibit a whole variety of behaviours – behaviours that result from identity confirmation strategies and including schizophrenic tendencies and authoritarian and narcissistic personalities. This approach to examining individuals gives us a different way of understanding why organisations can be disorderly, full of conflict, unstable and volatile.

KEYTERMS

Adaptors – individuals who tend to solve problems by using existing or slightly modified approaches already used by the business.

Innovators – individuals who tend to solve problems by finding new, exciting and unexpected solutions to problems in a business.

Traits – a distinguishing feature in character, appearance or habit used in identifying an individual's personality.

KNOWLEDGE

1. State three reasons why businesses need to know about the different characteristics of individuals.
2. What is meant by the 16 Personality Factor?
3. Explain the terms: (a) stable; (b) unstable; (c) extrovert; (d) introvert; in relation to the work of Eysenck.
4. What characteristics might an unstable-extrovert have?
5. How might Eysenck's analysis of personality traits be used by business?
6. State three factors which are thought to influence an individual's intelligence.
7. What are the problems a business might face in using IQ tests?
8. State five differences in skills and knowledge that one employee might have from another.
9. What is meant by the term knowledge worker?
10. Explain the difference between an innovator's and adaptor's approach to problem solving.
11. Why might understanding emotional intelligence be important for a business?

Case Study: *A woman with ideas*

Emma Rickson is a personnel officer in a large advertising agency. She has achieved rapid promotion in the company from her role as a secretary in the sales department to personnel officer with responsibility for recruitment. She did this by completing the Institute of Personnel Management qualifications through evening and weekend courses over a four year period. She was determined to do it and had the intelligence and perseverance finally to achieve her goal.

She has been in personnel for two years and has developed skills and knowledge in many different areas of the profession - in employee legislation, industrial relations issues and in her main interest of recruitment. Emma is outgoing (she had been tested and categorised as stable and extrovert using Eysenck's typology of personality) and popular with her peers. She has always believed in finding new ways to solve particular problems.

The latest problem she faced was the shortage of well-qualified administrative staff who were competent in using the newly-installed computer system. The training given by the company was extremely comprehensive and it was difficult to replace lost employees with the same level of expertise.

Emma recognised that the problem consisted of two main elements. Firstly, not enough men were attracted to this area of work and, second, some of the women who had been trained were leaving to start a family. Due to poor local nursery provision, these women tended to stay at home rather than return to work after having children.

Her plan of action encompassed both aspects of the problem. She devised an educational campaign for the company aimed at men, in order that they might review their own ideas about the suitability of administrative work for males. In it she wanted to emphasise the promotion opportunities in administration work and how it was possible to achieve management status through the administrative route. She showed how administrative work had changed from traditionally repetitive office tasks to ones where high technology and problem solving skills were vital. She targeted the male sector by demonstrating that administrative work required types of skills that were often associated with men. At the same time, she planned to introduce creche facilities for the female employees of the company that would cost them far less than a private nursery and would also be cost effective for the organisation.

Emma drew up her plans and costed them out. The campaign materials and accompanying workshop sessions would be £5,000 for the year. The creche facilities would need capital expenditure of approximately £15,000. The ongoing costs would be met by the employees willing to make use of the service. At present it was costing them £35,000 to recruit and train the staff required for the administration vacancies in the company. She presented her findings to the executive board in a confident and assertive way.

The plan was rejected by senior management as too expensive in the short term and too far fetched. She was told to improve her selection procedures so that she recruited people that would stay. She was also told not to involve herself in other aspects of personnel work that were not her responsibility.

Emma felt saddened and disillusioned by this experience.

(a) Identify TWO characteristics that have gained Emma promotion. (4 marks)

(b) Classify Emma's personality using a suitable method. Explain your answer. (6 marks)

(c) What potential problems might her personality and approach have for the business? (8 marks)

(d) Examine the reasons why Emma's ideas were rejected by management. (10 marks)

(e) Suggest and justify an alternative approach that Emma might have used when putting forward her plan. (20 marks)

72 Groups and teams in business

Working in groups

Working with other people in groups is something that many employees do in business. An employee in a marketing consultancy business may be part of a team developing TV advertisements for a client, part of a group set up to think of ideas to improve working methods and may meet with friends for lunch. Only in a small number of cases will individual employees work on their own, as in the case of a freelance journalist. Even an employee delivering goods on his own from a van will interact with staff and management when he returns to the office or factory.

Individuals may behave differently when working in a group than if they were working on their own. For example, an employee on a building site might want to work at a leisurely pace or find ways to avoid carrying out a task immediately. Group pressure could persuade or embarrass the employee into working harder than he would have wished. The group may want to finish the job early or earn any bonus that is available. In this case the employee's behaviour has changed as a result of being a group member. He is behaving in a way that conforms to the GROUP NORM. In other words, he is behaving in a way that is 'normal' for that group.

There is a certain amount of evidence to support the idea that individual behaviour is influenced by the group. The Hawthorne Studies showed that group behaviour can influence workers' motivation. It is possible to identify certain common features of groups that exist in businesses.

- The behaviour of the group influences all members, e.g. if a decision is made to take industrial action.
- Members of the group have some common interests and objectives, e.g. a production team may want to increase its level of overtime payments.
- Members meet and discuss common interests, e.g. assembly line workers might discuss the latest changes to working conditions.
- There are rules or norms influencing members' behaviour, e.g. members of the finance committee of a business are expected to report back to the managing director after each meeting.

It could be argued that, given the emphasis on team work in many modern organisations, it is essential for businesses to understand how people work in groups. If employees in a group do not work 'well' together, this may reduce productivity and make decision making more difficult.

Types of group

It is possible to distinguish different groups that exist in business. One common method is to divide them into FORMAL and INFORMAL GROUPS.

Formal groups These are groups which are set up by a business specifically to carry out tasks. Formal groups are an actual part of the organisation, with arranged meetings and rules determining their behaviour and actions. Examples of formal groups might be management teams that control one aspect of a business, such as the finance department.

Other examples of formal groups might be groups which are set up to deal with certain problems. For example, a unit might be set up by a business to monitor the introduction of new machinery. The group may include the production manager, an engineer, a supervisor and a number of operators. Its task may be to make sure the changeover is as efficient as possible and it would meet to discuss ways in which this could be achieved.

Formal groups can be **temporary** or **permanent**. A temporary group might be a working party to investigate a computerised information system. Permanent groups include standing committees, such as health and safety committees or a trade union, which is a formal group, but not one created by management. The type of group depends on whether the task involved is recurrent or a 'one-off'.

Informal groups Informal groups are made up of employees with similar interests. They are not a formal part of the business itself. They do not have any formal 'rules', although there are often unofficial norms which influence members' behaviour. An example of an informal group might be a casual meeting over

Exciting Opportunities

The First vacancy is for a person who is dynamic, hardworking, approachable, organised and capable of dealing with the public and their children. They will join the management team and help to develop the future of this growing business, knowledge of the food and beverage industry would also be an advantage. (Hours of business 10am-6pm)

The Second vacancy is for people who like animals and willing to work within their environment. The right person must be outgoing, reliable, friendly and will be expected to work with the public.

Question 1.

(a) Identify the possible:
 (i) formal;
 (ii) informal;
 groups that the successful candidates might belong to, using information in the advertisement.

(b) Explain how belonging to informal groups might help:
 (i) the new employees when settling into their jobs;
 (ii) the business in its relations with the new employees.

Figure 1: The roles of individuals in groups

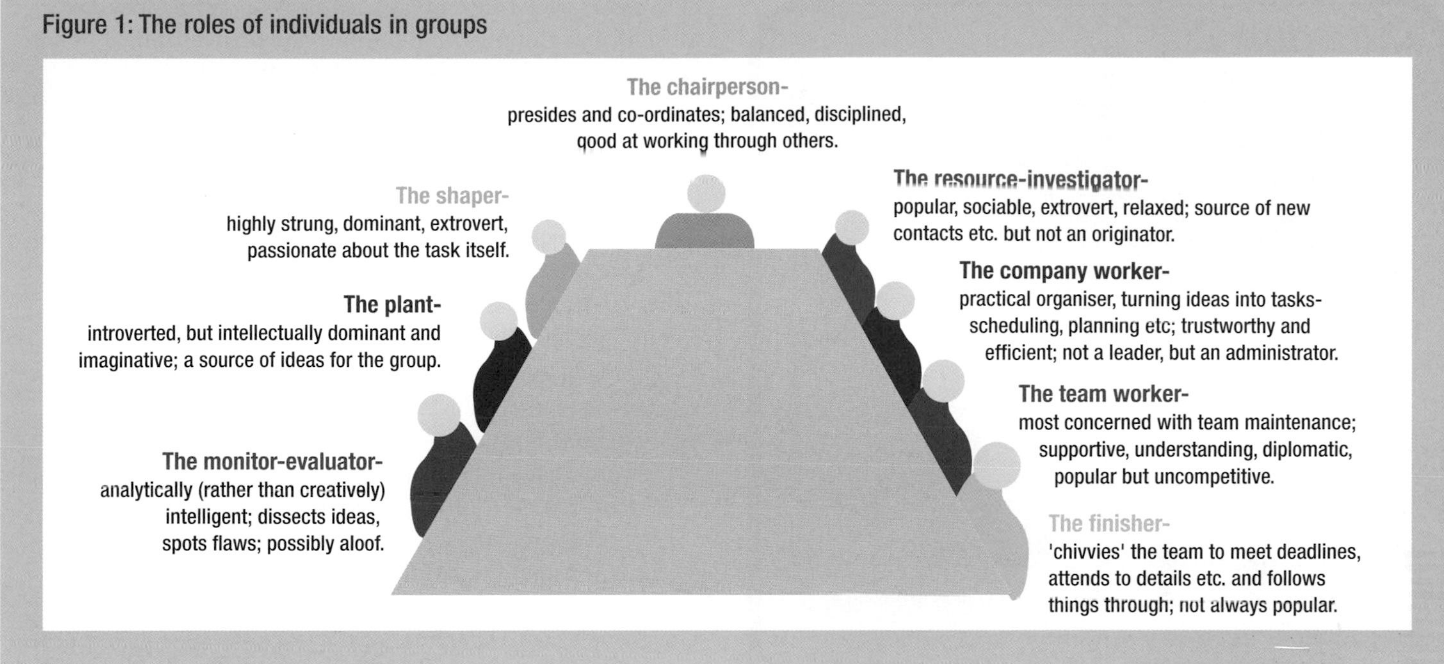

lunch between managers in the production, marketing and finance departments to discuss a new product launch. It could also be a group of hospital workers discussing possible job cuts in their rest room.

The chairperson-
presides and co-ordinates; balanced, disciplined, good at working through others.
The shaper-
highly strung, dominant, extrovert, passionate about the task itself.
The plant-
introverted, but intellectually dominant and imaginative; a source of ideas for the group.
The monitor-evaluator-
analytically (rather than creatively) intelligent; dissects ideas, spots flaws; possibly aloof.
The resource-investigator-
popular, sociable, extrovert, relaxed; source of new contacts etc. but not an originator.
The company worker-
practical organiser, turning ideas into tasks-scheduling, planning etc; trustworthy and efficient; not a leader, but an administrator.
The team worker-
most concerned with team maintenance; supportive, understanding, diplomatic, popular but uncompetitive.
The finisher-
'chivvies' the team to meet deadlines, attends to details etc. and follows things through; not always popular.

There are certain reasons why informal groups exist. It is argued that these groups meet the psychological needs of employees. These might include some of the following.

- The need to be with other people.
- The need for status, determined by membership of various groups. This will also influence the view people have of their personal value and self-esteem.
- The need to feel secure and mutual support. By offering these, groups reduce uncertainty and anxiety.
- The need to solve problems. The group may act as a problem solver for its members.

The informal groups that develop will be determined, to a large extent, by the physical layout required for work. Distance has a powerful influence on who will interact with whom. In general, the more frequent the interactions, the more likely informal groups are to be formed. Informal groups can have considerable influence on group members and the norms and values that a group develops may or may not support those of the organisation.

It may appear that formal and informal groups are separate. This is not the case. Groups that start off as formal often develop powerful informal relations. 'Part' of a company, as well as being a department, may be a department of friends. Japanese organisations, such as Sony, deliberately encourage this. Informal groupings, such as friendships outside work, can provide useful channels of communication for the organisation. The grapevine is a term used for such channels.

It is also possible to divide groups into primary and secondary groups.

- Primary groups are small groups where people can have regular contact, e.g. a small department or office.
- Secondary groups are large groups where people have less regular contact, e.g. a large open-plan office or a large meeting.

A team is a particular type of group. Teams are usually put together for a purpose. For example, a business may have team meetings of workers to discuss production problems or have a team of designers developing a new product. Teams are dealt with later in this unit.

Group decision making

The aims of businesses are to try and create groups that are effective and efficient. If the business can motivate the group to work harder in order to achieve goals, the sense of pride in the group's own competence might create job satisfaction.

There is a number of factors that can help group decision making.

Group members The characteristics and goals of the individual members of the group will help to determine the group's characteristics and goals. An individual is likely to be influenced more strongly by a small group than by a large group. In a large group the person may feel overwhelmed and, therefore, unable to participate effectively in team decisions.

It has been suggested that the effectiveness of a group depends on the blend of the individual skills and abilities of its members. A group might be most effective if it contains:

- a person of originality and ideas;
- a 'get-up-and-go' person with considerable energy, enthusiasm and drive;
- a quiet, logical thinker, who ponders carefully and criticises the ideas of others.

Question 2.

The Waterfront is a hotel in Bournemouth. It considers that its staff are effective because they operate as a team. It has recently been awarded Investors in People status because of its commitment to its employees. Employees are flexible. Staff absences are covered by other staff, so that shortages do not lead to a reduced quality of service. Employees have made a number of suggestions that have solved problems in the hotel. For example, in busy periods some bookings were not taken up. This left empty rooms which could have been filled. One member of staff suggested a reminder be sent in busy periods and this reduced the number of unfilled rooms by 50 per cent.

The hotel had recently promoted its services as a 'wedding centre'. It offered accommodation and a room for the wedding, and provided food for guests. At one reception, however, the owners were on holiday. Staff were unsure who was responsible for ordering flowers. Two sets of flowers were ordered as a result, which raised the costs of the wedding to the hotel. Two of the more senior members of staff also disagreed on the time at which the food would be served.

(a) What might have been the characteristics that made the group at the hotel operate effectively?
(b) Explain the problems that were faced by the group when the new service was introduced.
(c) Examine ways in which the group operation might be improved in future.

This is why groups set up to consider new products often draw members from a number of different departments in the business. This means the group will have a wide range of skills and abilities.

Group roles The most comprehensive study of group roles within a work setting is most probably that of **Meredith Belbin** (1981). He found that successful teams consisted of a mix of individuals, each of whom performed a different role. A summary of these roles is shown in Figure 1.

According to Belbin each person has a preferred role and for a group to be effective all the roles need to be filled. So a business might select people to ensure that they fill one or more of the roles which a group lacks. This is not always possible. Most formal groups within business are predetermined by who has the technical expertise to carry out the task.

How then can a knowledge of these roles help?

- For a group to work efficiently the business must be aware of the roles people prefer. These may become apparent through observation. People should be given tasks which allow them to operate in their preferred roles, whether in a sports team or in a team of medical staff in a casualty department.
- There should be an understanding of why roles that are missing may cause inefficiency. For example, some researchers conducted a study into why some quality circles continued to meet, while others ceased to. They found that all the groups that failed lacked someone who preferred the 'finisher' role. Apparently these groups were good at problem solving and finding solutions but never carried their ideas through.

The group's task The nature of the task may affect how a group is managed. If a job must be done urgently, it is often necessary to dictate how things should be done, rather than to encourage participation in decision making. Jobs which are routine and undemanding are unlikely to motivate individuals or the group as a whole. If individuals want authoritarian leadership, they are also likely to want clearly defined targets.

Group development Groups do not come into existence fully formed. B.Tuckman and N. Jensen (1977) suggested that groups pass through five stages of development. Progress through all stages may be slow, but is necessary for the group to be effective. Some groups get stuck in the middle and remain inefficient.

- **Forming** is when individuals in the group start to find out about each other and are keen to impress other group members. They usually require guidance from a leader about the nature of the group's task.
- **Storming** is a conflict stage. Members bargain with each other and try to sort out what each of them wants individually and as a group. Individuals reveal their personal goals. Hostility may develop if people's goals are different. Individuals may resist the control of other members.
- **Norming** is where group members develop ways of working together. The question of who will do what and how it will be done is addressed. Rules are established. There is greater cohesion and information is passed between group members.
- **Performing** is where the group has developed cohesion. It is concerned with getting the job done and accomplishing its objectives. There is a feeling of interdependence and a commitment to problem solving.
- **Adjourning** is where the group disbands because the task has been achieved or because the members have left.

A group may be ineffective if it has failed to sort out certain issues at earlier stages. For example, problems may result if the issue of leadership has not been decided. Another problem is that people may pull in different directions if the purpose of the group has not been clarified or its objectives agreed.

The characteristics of an effective work group

If a business is to try and improve the effectiveness of groups it must be able to identify the characteristics of an effective work group. These may include some of the following.

- There is a high commitment to the achievement of targets and organisational goals.
- There is a clear understanding of the group's work.
- There is a clear understanding of the role of each person within the group.
- There is free and open communication between members of the group and trust between members.
- There is idea sharing.
- The group is good at generating new ideas.
- Group members try to help each other out by offering constructive criticisms and suggestions.
- There is group problem solving which gets to the root causes of the work problem.
- Group members seek a united consensus of opinion.
- The group is motivated to be able to carry on working in the absence of its leader.

Factors influencing group decision making

There is a number of factors which determine how effective groups are when making decisions.

Size of the group Research has been carried out into the effects of group size on decision making. It has been argued that groups become ineffective once they have 21 members. Other researchers have tried to measure an optimum size for groups. It is felt, in many cases, that the best size is between three and seven members, with five often being quoted as an ideal number.

Why might groups containing these numbers be effective? Larger groups often have communication problems, as more and more people wish to contribute to group discussions. In a small group, the chairperson's role may be fairly informal. When groups get large, however, more formal management may be needed. To address all remarks through the chair in a meeting of four people is perhaps being over-formal. To do so in a meeting of 20 may be a necessity.

The size of the task can determine group size. A group designing and building a motor racing car may require many people, with a variety of skills. Each member is likely to make some contribution to the task of the group. But a group which decides who is to drive the car in a Grand Prix may be small in order to reach a clear decision.

Communication Communication in groups can influence how group decisions are made. A distinction is often made between two types of group.

- Centralised groups are groups where individuals can only communicate with other group members via a central member.
- Decentralised groups are groups where every member can communicate directly with every other member.

Communication in groups can take place in a number of ways.

- The wheel. This is where a person at the centre of the group can communicate with all the other members. They, on the other hand, can only communicate with him or her. If they wish to communicate to other members they can only do so through the same central person. This might be the case in a formal meeting.
- The chain. Information is passed from one individual to the next before it reaches the last person in the group. Any individual only ever communicates with one other person. This might be the case in a police operation, for example.
- The circle. Communication is circular, in other words, messages pass between certain people, who pass it on to others, such as in a large office.
- The all-channel. Every member of the group can communicate directly with every other member, as in an open discussion on where an 'awards' evening should be held.

The degree of centrality is highest in the wheel and is less in the chain and circle. The all-channel has no centre; decisions are made by reaching an agreement. The degree of centralisation can affect the group's efficiency, but this also depends on the complexity of the task. When the task is simple, e.g. deciding on the recruitment policy for a particular job, centralised groups like the wheel are faster and make fewer errors. When the task is more complicated, e.g. organising and putting into practice a recruitment policy for a particular job, decentralised groups may be more suitable.

Leadership It is likely that a group will have a 'leader' to control or guide it. Leadership may be informal, in the sense that one person 'dominates' a group because of their personality, position or access to information. Leaders can also be elected or nominated by the group, such as the chairperson.

There is a number of different leadership styles.

- Autocratic. This involves one-way communication between the leader and others in the group. The leader makes all the decisions and gives out instructions, expecting them to be obeyed by other group members without question. An example might be a powerful head of a large business like Rupert Murdoch.
- Persuasive. The leader makes all the decisions, but believes that other group members need to be motivated to accept them before they will do what she wants them to. She therefore tries to explain her decisions in order to convince them of her point of view, as a teacher or lecturer in a class might.
- Consultative. This involves discussion between the leader and the other group members involved in making a

decision, but the leader retains the right to make the decision herself. By consulting with her group members before making any decision, the leader will take into account their advice and feelings. A council leader might have to operate in this way.
- Democratic. This is an approach where the leader makes a decision based on consensus and agreement within the group. Group members with the greatest knowledge of a problem will have greater influence over the decision. A trade union representative is likely to adopt this style.
- Paternalistic. This is similar to an autocratic style, where a leader makes the decisions. But leaders are also concerned about the welfare of subordinates.

Skills used in groups For individuals to work well in groups, they need to have a variety of skills. These skills can be categorised into three general areas.
- Contribution. Individuals need to communicate their ideas effectively, informing group members of their thoughts, views and motives. They also need to be able to initiate ideas and evaluate both their own contribution and those of others.
- Co-operation. Individuals need to support other group members so that everyone is involved. This is more likely if individuals share their ideas and listen to others. They should also be able to negotiate and consult, so that everyone feels part of the group's activities.
- Production. Group members need to gather information, materials and ideas, and share them with other group members. They need to show the skills of perseverance and reliability especially if the group is struggling with a problem.

Advantages and problems of group decisions

To what extent are groups more effective in making decisions than individuals? There is a number of advantages in allowing groups to make decisions for a business.
- Groups can pool ideas and draw on a variety of expertise. This makes them particularly good at finding errors. For example, in the design and construction of nuclear reactors, a whole variety of groups working on safety aspects are more likely to ensure that all safety measures are thought of and solutions found to safety problems.
- Groups can handle a great deal of information and involved tasks in a shorter period of time than an individual would take. An example might be the design and writing of a computerised information program.
- Group members may support, motivate and help other members when making decisions.
- Groups provide a basis for accountability within a firm. They can also be used as the basis for a bonus system to increase productivity.

Despite these advantages, there are sometimes problems in group decision making.
- Group decisions may take time. When a decision needs to be made quickly, such as a decision to re-order stock, an individual may be more effective from a business point of view. There will be no debate, which will delay any decision that is made.
- Where one person is an obvious expert in the field, that person may make a more accurate and effective decision, for example, a personnel manager in deciding how best to train certain employees.
- There could be conflicting views and personalities within groups. This can lead to a lack of cohesion, with no shared aims or objectives. The result is that the group becomes inefficient in carrying out a task.
- There may be a possibility of 'risky-shift' decisions. Groups may make riskier decisions than individuals would, due to too much group cohesion. For example, a board of directors might decide as a group to take over a potentially profitable, but inefficient, firm. An individual entrepreneur might have considered this decision too risky to take.

Inter-group relations and conflict

One problem that may result for the business from group activity is a conflict between groups. Many managers would agree that some inter-group competition is inevitable and perhaps useful. If there was no competition the business might become stagnant, with few pressures to make changes. This could lead to inefficiency. The other extreme, of very high levels of competition and conflict, may also cause problems. It could lead to anxiety and tension in the workforce which are counter-productive.

Why might conflict result between groups?
- Groups are often in competition with each other over resources. One example might be where the sports and leisure department in a local council needs funds for a swimming pool, but this may result in another group such as the social services department having less. Another example would be where an employee who is an integral part of a production team may have to leave the team at a vital time to attend a health and safety meeting. Conflict results from the groups' competition for the employee's time.
- There may be conflict between groups at different levels in the business organisation. For example, non-graduate entrants to a bank may be restricted because of the promotion or higher pay of graduate entrants.
- Conflict can result when groups have different goals. For example, when there is a divorce of ownership from control, managers may attempt to satisfy their own aims, such as market leadership by a series of price cuts. At the same time they would attempt to make a satisfactory profit for shareholders, who may have wanted the business to maximise profits.
- There are certain psychological factors which can often lead to conflict between groups. When groups are in competition, each will tend to underplay its weaknesses,

Question 3.

IceCool, a major ice cream manufacturer, is concerned with two major business problems - reduced profitability due to rising costs and a lack of appeal among the youth market. It has asked the production and marketing departments for their diagnosis of the problem. Both departments are keen to impress, as it could mean greater resources being dedicated to them if they win the argument.

The marketing department managed to have funds allocated to it so that it could carry out market research on the development of a new ice-cream snack.The results of its work suggest that a market segment of 16-19 year olds would particularly like a dynamic, sports and fitness orientated ice-cream snack - a 'Lucozade Sports' ice cream. The price for this product would have to be in the 80p-90p bracket and the packaging would have to be bright, young and dynamic. The advertising approach would be a nationwide television campaign backed up by national billboard displays. It forecast that the payback period will be two years, but that high profit margins will then be generated for a further two years before going into decline. It has presented its plans to the board of directors.

The production department was far more concerned with the lack of productivity caused by poor capital investment over the last two years. Without any extra allocation of funds, it presented a paper to the board of directors that suggested attacking the problem of poor productivity first so that it might compete more effectively using the product range that was already tried, tested and successful. It was particularly scathing about introducing a new product without solving the underlying problems. Likewise, the marketing department was amazed at the lack of vision from the production department.

(a) Why did conflict arise between the production and marketing departments at IceCool?
(b) What benefits might there be for the company in this conflict?
(c) How can IceCool ensure that the two departments work together when a final decision is made?

overestimate its strengths and degrade the other group. The other group may also be seen as hostile or aggressive. As a result it becomes the enemy – 'them' against 'us'. Because of these two factors, interactions between the two groups become strained and decline.

How can conflict either be avoided or, if it already exists, defused? One method that involves low levels of risk is to get members of one group to work with the other group. This can be achieved by organising joint projects or by some form of exchange. The leaders of the group could initially either work together or exchange roles for this approach to be effective. It can be further developed by communication and swapping of group members. This technique is often used when one organisation takes over another and there is a need to avoid conflict at all levels within the 'new' business. Another possibility is for a business to rotate membership of groups to prevent divisions taking place.

Team building

Businesses often try to improve the productivity and motivation of people working in groups. The 'planned, systematic process designed to improve the efforts of people who work together to achieve goals' is known as TEAM BUILDING.

Team building is based on the idea that before organisations can improve performance, group members must be able to work together effectively. It was first introduced into UK businesses in the 1970s. Exercises were used to help group members develop trust, open up communication channels, make sure everyone understood the goals of the group, help individuals make decisions with the commitment of all members, prevent the leader from dominating the group, openly examine and resolve conflicts and to review work activities. Team building exercises often involve taking groups to outdoor locations and setting them problems to solve. Examples include the pension department at Siemens training in outdoor exercises in Finland and operators at DuPont carrying out charity work such as constructing a play group for disabled children.

A study by W. Dyer (1994) found that many companies said they believed in team building. However, only 22 per cent actually carried out any team building activities. The main reasons suggested for this were that:
- managers did not know how to undertake team building;
- managers did not understand the benefits of spending time on team building and thought it would take too much time;
- team building efforts were not really rewarded in the company;
- people felt their teams were all right;
- people felt team building was not supported by their superiors.

Decision teams and work teams

A distinction can be made between decision teams and work teams in business. A decision team might be a management executive committee, a university academic department or a collection of doctors or lawyers in a clinic. The main function of the team is to make decisions. The team members do not rely on each other to carry out individual tasks. However, they do make decisions about the operation of a department or a business.

In contrast a work team must work together to accomplish a goal. It must co-ordinate its efforts constantly. Examples might be a hospital operating unit or a police SWAT team. Some businesses today organise workers into autonomous work groups. These are groups of employees with a variety of skills who carry out whole tasks, such as manufacturing a complete product. The group exercises a high level of control and makes its own decisions over the work that it carries out.

Knowledge teams

Knowledge teams can be both work teams and decision teams. They are teams of knowledge workers who are collectively

responsible for a product or service. Knowledge work requires employees who can:
- use their own knowledge;
- acquire new information;
- combine and process information to produce and communicate new information;
- learn continuously from their experiences.

Knowledge teams can be made up of specialist workers from a variety of areas or disciplines. The team integrates the work of the specialists. Specialists may only have a small amount of common values, information and skills, so it is important that they communicate and work together. On the other hand, teams are sometimes made up totally of specialists with skills in a particular area. These can be contacted by anyone in the organisation for information that may help to solve problems.

Examples of knowledge teams may be a team responsible for new product development, a management team made up from managers across the business that develops strategic directions or a process improvement team that examines and makes changes to a business's work methods. The advantage of a knowledge team is that a problem can be examined from a variety of perspectives. For example, a business that is trying to cut production costs can take suggestions from finance, marketing and administration staff as well as technical staff.

Effects of team working

The Workers Employment Relations survey of the late 1990s found that up to 65 per cent of workplaces in the UK operate team working at some level, although autonomous work groups are only found in 3 per cent of organisations. Why do businesses introduce team work?
- Team working motivates employees. Edwards and Wright (1998) and Wilkinson (1997), for example, suggested that employees in team situations tend to be more satisfied and motivated than those who are working under more traditional regimes.
- Businesses can use team work as a method to gain a competitive advantage over rivals.
- Team working appears to have a positive influence on employee commitment and identification with the business. Cotton (1993) suggested that self-directed teams have a strong effect on employee attitudes.

Teamworking is not always possible and may not work effectively, however. This may be because work cannot be redesigned for a team. Managers may also fail to implement teamwork properly. Also, certain employees may see team working as simply giving them management responsibilities without the corresponding pay or power.

CRITIQUE

Critical perspectives on teams suggest that rather than team working being seen an improvement in work design which benefits both management and employees, it is a practice that creates, maintains and reproduces unequal social relations. Critical writers contest the 'idealised' picture of teamwork. This can be seen in the 'taken for granted' notions of teamworking creating a win-win work situation. Employees are more satisfied and their work is 'smarter' because they have been treated like adult human beings, with respect, and they are given responsibility and autonomy. This makes it possible for the organisation to be more flexible, innovative and capable of building a future. This rosy picture is obtained by dismissing ideas that do not fit in with mainstream views. For example, some workers actually state that they prefer to be told what to do. The suggestion is that it is irrational to prefer inhumane and alienating repetition to the empowering and democratic self-management found in teams.

KEYTERMS

Formal groups – groups specifically set up by a business to carry out tasks. They have certain formal rules of behaviour.
Group norm – the usual characteristics of behaviour of a group.
Informal groups – groups made up of individuals in business with similar interests. They are not part of the formal business organisation.
Team building – the process designed to improve the effectiveness and motivation of people working together in groups.

KNOWLEDGE

1. 'Group behaviour is different from individual behaviour.' To what extent is this statement likely to be true in business?
2. State four common features that groups in business organisations have.
3. Why might a business set up a temporary formal group rather than making it permanent?
4. Give four advantages for employees of informal group membership.
5. Give six characteristics of effective groups.
6. Briefly explain why optimal group size may be between three and seven members.
7. What is likely to influence the size of a group?
8. Explain the difference between centralised and decentralised group decision making.
9. What are the advantages to the business of group decision making?
10. In what circumstances might individual decision making be more beneficial to a business?
11. What factors within a business might lead to inter-group conflict?
12. What are knowledge teams?

Case Study: Tyler Farndon

Jatinder Dhawan is head of human resources at Tyler Farndon, a manufacturer of mobility products for older people and the disabled. When she says 'the future of the business is too important to be left to management alone' both Nick Gregson, the union official, and Gail Anne Knight, the executive director, agree. The business aims to take the thoughts of its mission statement to provide 'excellent products, ethically produced' into the workplace in as many ways as possible.

Jatinder, Nick and Gail meet on the works council set up in 2000. Part of their discussions involve the progress of the 'Working together, working better' strategy that the business implemented in an attempt to make sure the employee voice at the organisation was being heard. It is an ambitious project, combining flexible work patterns with elements of a single status organisation, where all employees have the same terms and conditions whether they are union members or not. Staff also receive the same annual wage rises, and a bonus if the business is doing well.

The works council has 20 members. It discusses a number of areas, including production, changes in organisation and the development of the business in future. Decisions made by the council are often accepted by employees in the business as they feel that they have been represented in discussions.

Recently, the business has been approached by another company and the possibility of a merger has arisen with a business which specialises in artificial limbs. However, employees feel that the business is doing well and should carry on growing organically. A further option is to transfer some production to an outsourced business and expand into this area itself. Whichever route is taken, the business feels that it would have to be agreed by employees and employers for it to work effectively.

Jatinder regularly meets with other departmental managers of the business to review the human resources needs of their departments. The finance manager tends to take the lead in most of these meetings. He argues that the bottom line of the business must be 'to be profitable'. He will often put pressure on the other department heads to 'remain within budget'. Jatinder has noticed that the head of R&D often seems to get more than other departments. She wonders whether this is because both the finance and R&D heads joined the company together. They have been with the business a long time and often attend conferences where they discuss trends in the industry.

Gail will have to get any decision approved by the other shareholders in the business. Nick will also have to report any decisions back to his union members at meetings. He feels that some expansion is important. But what type? What if his members disagree and feel that some form of industrial action is necessary? He would then need to consult the head office of the union about procedures. Nick has been approached by some employees who say they have heard that any merger is likely to involve redundancy because of the duplication of skills. They thought that everyone was the same at the business, but now managers seemed to be fighting for a strategy which would benefit them.

(a) Identify examples of (i) formal and (ii) informal groups suggested in the article. (6 marks)

(b) Explain how formal and informal groups have influenced communication at the business. (10 marks)

(c) Suggest benefits of team operation and group decision making at the business. (10 marks)

(d) Examine potential areas of conflict between members of groups in the business. (12 marks)

(e) To what extent do you think that the operation of groups and teams is effective at the business? (12 marks)

73 Competitive workforce structures

Adapting organisational structures

The organisational structure of a business may have to change in order to better fit the type of business and the products and services it provides. This is often the case if there are internal changes within the business or changes in external influences. Modern OPEN SYSTEMS THINKING suggests that the design of the organisation must meet the needs of the situation, such as changing lifestyles or customer tastes. A closed system makes little allowance for such changes and often traditional pyramid or hierarchical business structures are rigid with clear boundaries, responsibilities for the way the business works. Open systems thinking favours greater experimentation and innovation in response to changing circumstances. In particular, it sees greater opportunities for employee engagement. This unit considers how a business can adapt its structure to become more competitive.

Centralisation and decentralisation

CENTRALISATION and DECENTRALISATION refer to the extent to which authority is delegated in a business. If there was complete centralisation, subordinates would have no authority at all. Complete decentralisation would mean subordinates would have all the authority to take decisions. Some delegation may always be necessary in all firms because of the limits to the amount of work senior managers can carry out. Tasks that might be delegated include staff selection, quality control, customer relations and purchasing and stock control. Even if authority is delegated to a subordinate, it is usual for the manager to retain responsibility.

In pyramid structures subordinates often have little authority, with most decisions being taken at the top of the organisation. Open systems thinking would suggest that this form of organisation may not suit the various markets that a growing and competitive business could face. Individuals close to comsumers might be better placed to make decisions. Hence regional, divisional, or in some cases for multinational companies' national, operations may become a 'business unit' with its own cost and profit centre. However, it would still remain accountable to the head office. The advantages of centralisation and decentralisation shown in Table 1.

Table 1: Advantages of centralisation and decentralisation

Advantages of centralisation

- Senior management has more control of the business, e.g. budgets.
- Procedures, such as ordering and purchasing, can be standardised throughout the organisation, leading to economies of scale and lower costs.
- Senior managers can make decisions from the point of view of the business as a whole. Subordinates would tend to make decisions from the point of view of their department or section. This allows senior managers to maintain a balance between departments or sections. For example, if a company has only a limited amount of funds available to spend over the next few years, centralised management would be able to share the funds out between production, marketing, research and development, and fixed asset purchases in different departments etc.
- Senior managers should be more experienced and skilful in making decisions. In theory, centralised decisions by senior people should be of better quality than decentralised decisions made by others less experienced.
- In times of crisis, a business may need strong leadership by a central group of senior managers.
- Communication may improve if there are fewer decision makers.

Advantages of decentralisation

- It empowers and motivates workers.
- It reduces the stress and burdens of senior management. It also frees time for managers to concentrate on more important tasks.
- It provides subordinates with greater job satisfaction by giving them more say in decision making, which affects their work, as explained by McGregor's Theory Y.
- Subordinates may have a better knowledge of 'local' conditions affecting their area of work. This should allow them to make more informed, well-judged choices. For example, salespeople may have more detailed knowledge of their customers and be able to advise them on purchases.
- Delegation should allow greater flexibility and a quicker response to changes. If problems do not have to be referred to senior managers, decision making will be quicker. Since decisions are quicker, they are easier to change in the light of unforeseen circumstances which may arise.
- By allowing delegated authority, management at middle and junior levels are groomed to take over higher positions. They are given the experience of decision making when carrying out delegated tasks. Delegation is therefore important for management development.

Delayering

DELAYERING also involves a business reducing its staff. The cuts are directed at particular levels of a business, such as managerial posts. Many traditional organisational charts are hierarchical, with many layers of management. Delayering involves removing some of these layers. This gives a flatter structure. In the late 1980s, the average number of layers in a typical organisational structure was seven, although some were as high as 14. By the early 2000s this was reduced to less than five. The main advantage of delayering is the savings made from laying off expensive managers. It may also lead to better communication and a better motivated staff if they are **empowered** and allowed to make their own decisions.

However, remaining managers may become demoralised after delayering. Also staff may become overburdened as they have to do more work. Fewer layers may also mean less chance of promotion.

Flexible workforces

In the 1950s and 1960s, the UK economy was relatively stable and slow changing. Workers tended to have full-time permanent jobs. However, in the 1970s and 1980s, economic conditions worsened. Primary and secondary industry saw enormous change. Many businesses in these sectors became uncompetitive against foreign firms and closed. There was a rapid shift of output and employment towards the tertiary sector. There was a considerable increase in participation of women in the labour force. Part-time work became far more common.

It was against this backdrop that, in 1985, John Atkinson and the Institute of Manpower Studies put forward the concept of a flexible firm. This was a business which had a 'core' and a 'periphery'.

- The core was made up of workers who organised the essential tasks necessary for the firm's survival. They would tend to be skilled, full-time workers on permanent contracts. Because of their job security, their relatively high pay and their importance to the business, they would tend to be highly motivated.
- The periphery was made up of a variety of workers not central to running the business. They could be employed according to how much demand there was for the firm's products. They could include temporary workers ('temps') on short-term contracts and part-time workers whose hours can easily be increased or decreased. They would also include workers whose jobs had been OUTSOURCED to other businesses. This would include self-employed workers who were paid by the business for doing specific jobs. They might also include **teleworkers** or **home workers**, working from home and operating mainly via computer and email link. It is sometimes argued that peripheral workers are motivated mainly by the pay they receive. Their loyalty to the business employing them is not as great as core workers, since they have insecure jobs and never know whether they will still be in work in 12 months' time.

One of Charles Handy's key concepts is the 'cloverleaf organisation', later called the 'shamrock organisation'. This suggests that there a small core at the centre of a system of 'leaves', made up of outsourced workers, contractors, consultants and temporary workers. The theory has close parallels with Atkinson's flexible firm.

Question 1.

In 2003 The Future Network plc, the international specialist magazine publisher, announced the final stages of the restructuring of its UK business, which began in February 2001. Under the reorganisation plan, Future divided its UK business into three operating divisions – games, computing and entertainment. This was to be accompanied by a reduction in fixed operating costs in the UK by approximately £4 million, through cuts in staffing levels and property overheads.

The changes to the business involved reductions in centralised support services, and in Internet and magazine teams and rationalisation of the company's property portfolio. There was also to be an important change in the way the UK business was managed, by devolving operational responsibility to the individual divisions as profit centres.

Colin Morrison, Chief Operating Officer of The Future Network, said 'This plan is important because of the substantial reduction in our fixed operating costs against a broadly unchanged magazine portfolio. But much more than that, this restructuring and decentralisation plan simplifies our business, and will improve our focus, agility and control. We will now be more streamlined and much better placed to take advantage of our market-leading positions in the important UK market'.

Source: adapted from www.thefuturenetwork.plc.uk.

(a) Describe the organisational changes at The Future Network plc.
(b) Examine the possible benefits and disadvantages for the business of these changes.

Figure 1: Organisation of the flexible workforce

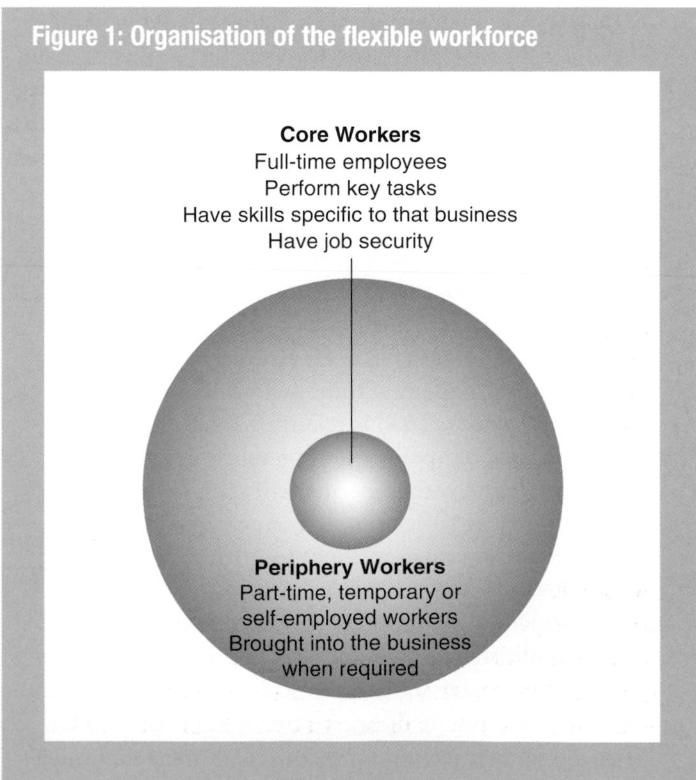

Figure 2: Economically active, employees and full-time employees, UK, millions

Figure 3: Self-employed, part-time employees, workers with second jobs and temporary employees, UK, millions

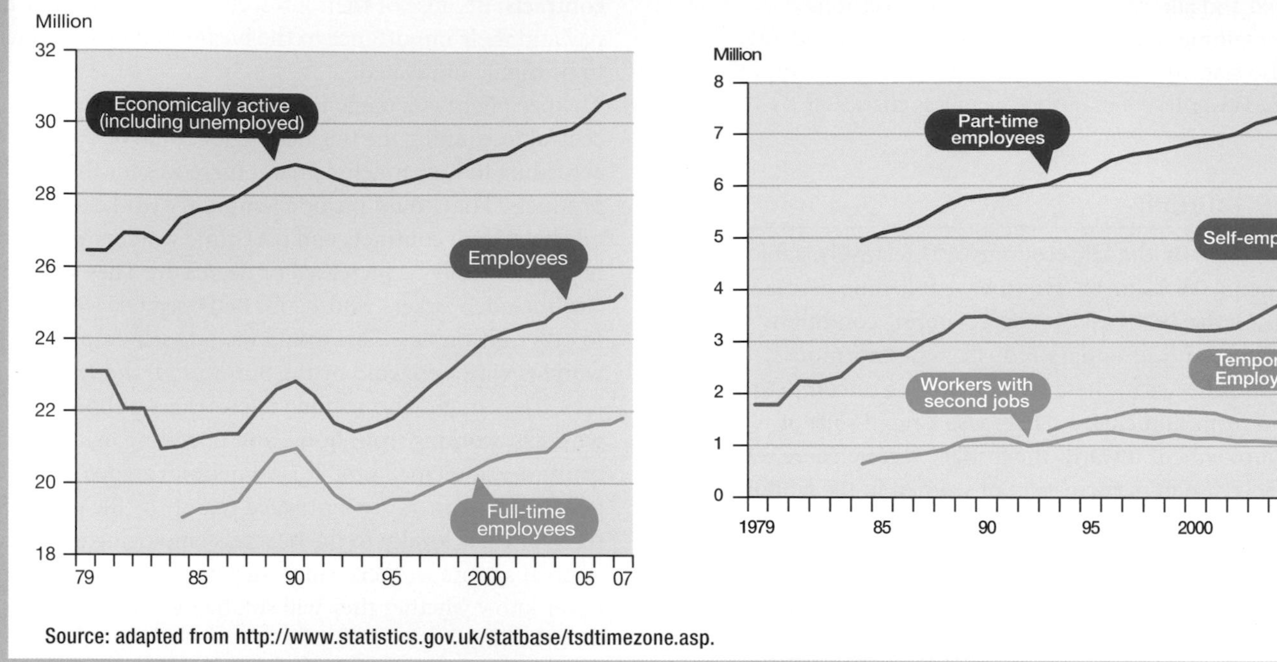

Source: adapted from http://www.statistics.gov.uk/statbase/tsdtimezone.asp.

The advantages and disadvantages of flexible working for businesses

There is a number of advantages of a FLEXIBLE WORKFORCE for a business.

- A flexible workforce allows a business to expand and contract quickly in response to changes in demand for its products. In contrast, a workforce made up of permanent staff is difficult to slim down quickly because of the cost and because of the time it takes to fulfil legal requirements. Businesses may also be reluctant to take on new permanent staff in case demand falls again and they are left with too many staff.
- Some specialist jobs need to be done but it would be wasteful to employ a permanent worker to do them. For example, most small businesses employ accountants to manage their accounts. It is far cheaper to do this than to employ an accountant within the business because the amount of work needed is relatively small.
- In some cases, temporary staff or subcontractors are cheaper to employ than permanent staff. For example, a business may not offer certain benefits to certain staff, although it must be careful not to infringe legislation. If the temporary staff are treated as self-employed or subcontractors, the business may also be able to save on National Insurance contributions. It isn't always cheaper to employ temporary staff and in some cases it may be more expensive because temporary staff or their agencies are able to bid their pay upwards. But temporary staff can be laid off almost immediately they are not needed with little cost, which is not the case for permanent staff.
- Employers are responsible for training their permanent workers. By outsourcing work or employing temporary workers, businesses may be able to pass that cost onto subcontractors or whoever has paid for the training of a temporary worker.
- Employing workers who can job share or work flexible hours may allow a business to operate more efficiently. For example, a business may be able to employ an employee in the day and another in the evening to respond to clients' needs over a longer period. A restaurant may be able to react to increased orders by asking staff to work longer hours at certain times of the week than others.

However, using peripheral workers has its disadvantages.

- Peripheral workers may have less loyalty to the business where they work temporarily. They may be motivated mainly by financial gain.
- Some businesses have found that their outsourced work has been of poor quality, damaging their reputation with customers. The peripheral workers move on and don't have to take responsibility for the poor work. But the business may have lost customers as a result.
- Communication can be a problem. Peripheral workers are not necessarily available when the business would like to communicate with them, although IT and the mobile phone has to some extent solved this problem.
- Employing peripheral workers can be a costly process. For example, a business may put a piece of work out to tender

Question 2.

Colin Traynor, the owner and then manager of Castle Gate Hotel, decided ten years ago to slim his workforce to a minimum and buy in services wherever possible. Twenty two of his fifty permanent staff lost their jobs as work was outsourced. His hotel has a seasonal trade. In July and August, the hotel is fully booked. During the rest of the year, occupancy can fall to as low as 50 per cent despite the hotel being popular with business people and being used as a conference centre. He quickly moved to a model where he employed enough permanent staff to run the hotel at its minimum occupancy levels in the winter and then hired casual labour to cope with the rest of the year. Jobs like laundry, which used to be done in house, were subcontracted to a local firm. Two of the workers in the accounts team lost their jobs and were re-employed by the day as and when they were needed. The marketing of the hotel was contracted out to a local business.

This year, Colin retired and management of the hotel passed to his daughter, Emma. For a long time, she had felt that the quality of service provided by the hotel to its customers was not good enough. Casual staff employed for the peak of the season often showed a lack of knowledge and a lack of commitment. Too much of her time was spent recruiting casual staff. Permanent staff were resentful of casual staff because they were always 'sorting out the mess' created by casual staff. Absenteeism amongst permanent staff was high. Emma was also unhappy with the marketing contract. It was very expensive and she questioned whether the marketing was very effective.

(a) Assess the possible advantages and disadvantages to Castle Gate Hotel of flexible working.

to a subcontractor. It might get the lowest price as a result, but the efficiency gains from putting it out to tender rather than hiring core permanent staff to do the job might be more than outweighed by the costs of the tender process itself.

- Temporary staff can be excellent, well qualified and highly motivated. But equally, some temporary staff are simply workers who have found it difficult to hold down a permanent job. When employing temporary staff, there is no guarantee that they will perform their job as well as would have a permanent member of staff.
- Too many peripheral workers employed alongside core workers can cause demotivation amongst the core workers. Core workers may want to be part of a stable team to form relationships and fulfil some of their higher order needs. Constant turnover of peripheral workers may lead to core workers feeling disorientated.

The impact of flexible working on workers

There are many ways in which workers are affected by flexible work practices. Such practices can affect temporary, part-time or subcontracted employees. However, they might also affect full-time, permanent employees at times.

- For those on temporary contracts and the self-employed, flexible working brings greater insecurity. Temporary workers can lose their jobs at short notice. The self-employed can lose contracts or business overnight. But even workers on permanent contracts face greater uncertainty. They can find themselves being made redundant and their jobs outsourced to a contracting firm. Equally, they can find their pay fringe benefits, such as pensions, and conditions of work worsen to make them 'more competitive' against flexible workers. Insecurity makes most individuals less happy and content and is therefore generally undesirable.
- A more flexible labour force is one where workers can expect their earnings to go down as well as up. It is one where there might be periods of no income coming into the household. It is also one where the individual worker can't expect employers to provide them with a pension. The individual worker therefore must plan to cope with this by saving more and investing in their own personal pension scheme.
- Flexible workers must be prepared to adapt and retrain to a changing job market. A self-employed photographer who finds she can't make a living out of photography may have to find another line of work to survive. Permanent workers are, to some extent, cushioned from this because their employer may pay for retraining and reassign them to other jobs within the business. A flexible market highlights

the need for **lifelong learning** on behalf of workers.
- Flexible workers must be prepared to move quickly from job to job. They must also be prepared to become PORTFOLIO WORKERS. These are workers who don't have a single full-time job but a mix of part-time jobs. A worker might have a cleaning job in the morning and work behind a bar in the evening. Or an individual may do consultancy work for rten days a month, and be a part time non-executive director for one company for six days a month and for another company for four days a month.

Flexible working in the UK

The UK government has increasingly encouraged the growth of flexible working in the last 20 years. Legislation has been introduced to encourage flexible work time, for example. However, it could be argued that it has had limited success as shown in Figures 2 and 3.

- The number of self-employed workers in 2007 was 4.2 million, only slightly higher than in 1990. The growth in self-employment came in the 1980s when it rose from 1.8 million in 1979 to 3.5 million in 1989.
- The number of part-time employees has grown significantly, mainly due to the increased number of women in the workforce. Even so, by 2007, part-time workers represented only one quarter of those economically active.
- The number of portfolio workers (workers with second jobs) has also grown. But in 2007 there were still only 1.1 million such workers, just 3 per cent of those economically active.
- The number of temporary workers has also grown, but in 2004 there were only 1.5 million such workers, just 5 per cent of those economically active.

Most workers today are still on permanent full-time contracts and this is likely to remain so for the foreseeable future. Whilst some industries, such as construction, might have fairly flexible workforces, others such as manufacturing are likely to remain with more traditional work practices.

Flexible working and the Employment Act, 2002

The term 'flexible working' can be used in a different way to the one described above. In the **Employment Act, 2002**, the government gave employees the right to request more flexible working patterns from their employer. Flexible working is then seen as ways in which the employer can give employees choices about when they work. Areas covered by flexible working then include:

- the ability of workers to choose when they start their day and when they finish;
- giving choices about which days of the week an employee works;
- options to move from full-time to part-time working and back again;
- maternity and paternity rights;
- opportunities to take periods of time out for an extended holiday or to look after a child;
- opportunities to job share.

The government argues that flexible working improves productivity. By giving workers greater control over their **work-life balance**, it motivates them to work harder. Labour turnover is also reduced because workers don't have to leave their jobs if their circumstances change and they have to alter their working hours. Reduced labour turnover saves the business the cost of recruiting and training new workers. It also helps retain staff who have received expensive training.

However, many smaller businesses argue that they don't have enough staff to make flexible working practical. If there are only three staff in a business, it may be impossible for one of them suddenly to start working different hours from the other staff. Equally, some aspects, such as better maternity and paternity rights, simply add to the costs of the business.

Knowledge management

Many businesses today see KNOWLEDGE MANAGEMENT as important to their operation. It involves:

- identifying the knowledge of a business, such as the knowledge of employees;
- assessing how the knowledge can be used and planning how to use it effectively;
- ensuring that knowledge is shared by all people in the organisation.

The management of knowledge can have a number of benefits for a business. The speed at which a business gains knowledge and puts it to good use is one way in which it can gain an advantage over its rivals. For example, Sky was the first company to launch digital television in the UK. It could be argued that this will give it an advantage in future as many customers will have 'signed up' and be unwilling to change to another supplier.

It may also prevent a duplication of services. For example, ICL found that several of its businesses were bidding for the same project at the same time without each knowing about the others' activities. It also found 23 different uncoordinated information services for employees, often providing the same information. Knowledge management could have prevented this waste of resources.

Sometimes people leave a business and take years of knowledge and experience with them. It often exists 'in the head' of the employee, who has found the best way to carry out a task or the most suitable skills to use. Making sure that this knowledge is collected and passed on may prevent problems for new employees to the job. It will also reduce time and costs for the business.

CRITIQUE

Some businesses over the last ten years have delayered their organisations to make them into flatter structures. It has often meant taking out layers of middle management. This will affect the hierarchy, span of control and chain of command. The objective is to speed up communication and to provide opportunities for delegation in order to improve responses to market changes, by creating more flexible business organisations with empowered employees. Banks, for example, have moved from traditional, stratified structures with narrow job tasks, into profit-centred, performance-orientated businesses that empower employees to take responsibility. There is also a much greater emphasis on multi-skilled teams and delayered organisations in manufacturing. This has led to greater financial flexibility, employee autonomy, self-monitoring and devolved decision making.

There has been a number of factors have led to changes in the retail sector. Increased globalisation and competition have meant businesses must be able to respond more quickly. As a result they have reduced the number of layers in their hierarchy. Also businesses need to be more aware of consumers' needs. As a result they have restructured into flatter, flexible, team-based organisations. These approaches also attempt to build and develop informal systems to aid the implementation of company objectives. Together, these new strategies have now become **mainstream approaches** to improving business organisational structures.

Although these ideas incorporate a greater sense of human involvement in the way businesses are organised, they do not really examine the power relationship between individuals in an organisation nor the broader power relationships of global organisations and governments. A critical perspective suggests that organisations are more than the structural job roles and functions that make them up. They are about the way managers use power to gain control from their subordinates and how subordinates use their own power to resist. Further, protests from anti-globalisation pressure groups have highlighted how the way businesses are organised can be exploitative of other countries and employees in those countries.

KNOWLEDGE

1. What is open systems thinking?
2. Identify three advantages of (i) centralisation and (ii) decentralisation.
3. How can delayering affect the workforce?
4. What is the difference between the core and the periphery in a flexible firm?
5. What might be the advantages of outsourcing work to a business?
6. What could be the disadvantages to a business of using peripheral workers?
7. What are (a) the advantages and (b) the disadvantages to being a portfolio worker?
8. Why might small businesses suffer from flexible working rights given by the 2002 Employment Act?
9. Suggest three advantages of knowledge management.

KEYTERMS

Centralisation - a type of business organisation where major decisions are made at the centre or core of the organisation and then passed down the chain of command.
Decentralisation - a type of business organisation where decision making is pushed down the chain of command and away from the centre of the organisation.
Delayering - removing layers of management from the hierarchy of an organisation.
Flexible workforce - a workforce that can respond, in quantity and type, to changes in demand a business may face.
Knowledge management - the collection, retention and distribution of vital knowledge that exists within a business.
Open systems thinking - the view that the design of the organisation must meet the needs of the situation.
Outsourced - work which is organised to be carried out workers who are not employees of the business, such as homeworkers or teleworkers.
Portfolio worker - a worker who has a variety of part-time jobs at any one time rather than a single full time job.

Case Study: The growth of teleworking

Teleworking is becoming popular for both employers and employees. The Labour Force Survey (LFS) and other market research estimates suggest that the number of teleworkers in the UK is around 2.2-2.4 million. This is about 7.4-8.6 per cent of the UK working population. The LFS defines teleworkers as 'people who do some paid or unpaid work in their own home who could not do so without using both a telephone and a computer'. This includes:

- people who work in their own home (teleworker homeworkers);
- teleworkers who work elsewhere but use home as a base;
- occasional teleworkers who spend at least one day a week working in their own home or using home as a base.

Lloyds TSB has recognised the benefits of teleworkers. A spokesperson stated 'Under the company's new Work Options scheme, employees can ask to work a variety of ways - job sharing, variable hours, teleworking, reduced hours and term-time working.' These provide staff with a means to 'balance home and work life effectively in a win-win initiative which aims to meet the aims of the business and individuals'. The initiative has been introduced not only to allow staff to work differently but to enable the business to retain skilled workers and attract new employees. The option was not just available to women, men or carers with children, but all staff, whether for study, sport or other commitments.

Source: adapted from www.royaldeaf.org,uk.

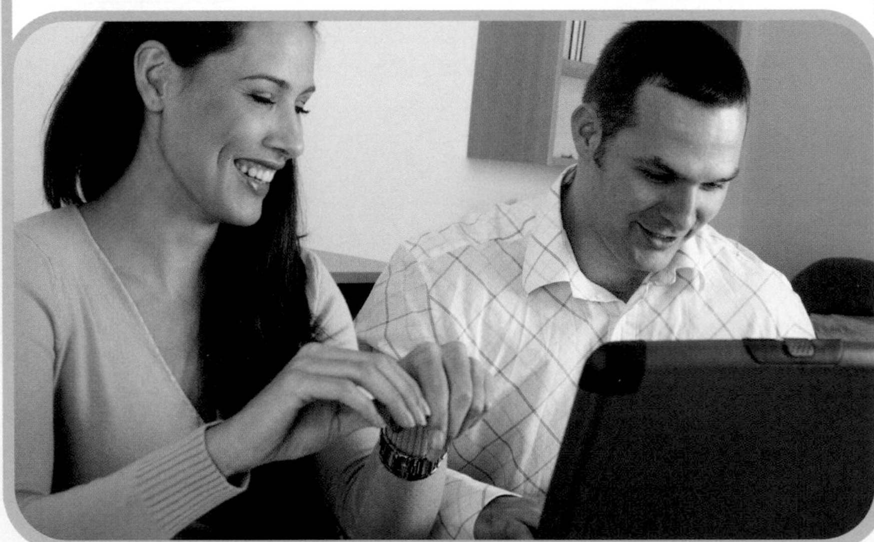

Footballfangs.com is a London based business that offers football kits, fashion clothing and fancy dress outfits for dogs. The business was set up by Tracey Davis and is run by her and her friend from home. They do not employ other full-time or part-time staff. The products are sold online via a website. The business also sells wholesale football shirts for dogs to Premiership and League clubs. All products are imported and sold globally. The website is updated every day and designed and managed in-house.

The business hopes to expand in future. It aims to be the market leader in the UK and Europe and take a sizeable chunk of the US market. It has thought about the possibility of using teleworkers in future to increase sales.

Source: adapted from www.the-bag-lady.co.uk.

Internet service provider, Eclipse Internet, is calling for greater business understanding of the benefits of teleworking. It suggests that the uptake of teleworkers has been slow, rising from one million to three million over a decade since 1997. The major benefit of teleworking is that it allows businesses to cut costs whilst increasing staff productivity and work-life balance. The average cost of a work station in a UK office is £6,422. This rises to £14,778 in London's West End. Providing broadband, a PC/laptop and a phone to an employee's home is an attractive alternative.

Better working styles can lead to better, more productive, workers. On average, 20 per cent of workers spend over an hour a day commuting. Also, according to the Labour Force Survey, more than seven per cent of people spend over two hours a day commuting. With rising petrol, rail and congestion charge costs, cutting commuting time looks more attractive to businesses and employees.

Source: adapted from www.the-bag-lady.co.uk.

Table 2: Teleworkers: employees and self-employed, part-time and full time

Teleworker homeworkers			
			Per cent
	All	*Men*	*Women*
Employees	44	43	45
Self-employed	56	57	55
Full-time	52	74	34
Part-time	47	26	66
Home-based teleworkers			
	All	*Men*	*Women*
Employees	41	40	46
Self-employed	59	60	54
Full-time	81	88	57
Part-time	19	12	43
Occasional teleworkers			
	All	*Men*	*Women*
Employees	84	82	88
Self-employed	16	18	12
Full-time	90	96	78
Part-time	10	4	22

Source: adapted from *Labour Force Survey*.

Table 3: Teleworkers by occupations

Teleworker homeworkers			
			Per cent
	All	*Men*	*Women*
Managers & senior officials	22	28	16
Professional	19	30	10
Associate professional & technical	27	31	23
Administrative & secretarial	24	5	40
Skilled trades	3	*	*
Sales and customer service	*	*	*
Other	5	*	7
Home-based teleworkers			
	All	*Men*	*Women*
Managers & senior officials	21	22	20
Professional	20	19	24
Associate professional & technical	24	21	34
Administrative & secretarial	3	*	9
Skilled trades	23	29	*
Sales and customer service	3	2	5
Other	6	6	6
Occasional teleworkers			
	All	*Men*	*Women*
Managers & senior officials	37	42	28
Professional	33	31	35
Associate professional & technical	17	15	20
Administrative & secretarial	5	*	11
Skilled trades	5	7	*
Sales and customer service	*	*	*
Other	3	3	*

Source: adapted from *Labour Force Survey*.

(a) Examine the benefits to Lloyds TSB of using teleworkers. (8 marks)

(b) Analyse why teleworking is more popular with certain types of occupation. (12 marks)

(c) Discuss whether Footballfangs.com should employ teleworkers in its business in future. (20 marks)

74 Workforce planning

Components of a workforce plan

WORKFORCE PLANNING is the process of determining the labour needs of the business now and in the future, including the number of workers and their skills, and ways of achieving labour targets. It has several aspects.

How many? The business must plan how many workers it needs. A food business that is planning to expand, for example, might require an extra 34 workers next year. When deciding how many staff are needed, the business must take into account whether workers are full or part time and how many hours they will be expected to work.

What skills? The types of workers and their skills must be decided upon. Of the 34 workers, there could be a need for 1 office worker, 15 production workers with no previous qualifications or skills, 2 supervisors with previous experience in the catering trade, and so on.

When needed? The business must decide when new workers will be needed. Is a worker needed immediately or will a vacancy arise in 12 months' time?

Where needed? In larger businesses, there may be many sites where employees are based. So the workforce plan must specify where the employee will be needed.

Achieving targets The human resource plan should identify what changes to staffing will be needed and indicate how this might be achieved. Staffing might need to increase. This can be done in a number of ways.

- Existing staff might have to be **trained** to increase their skills to cope with new demands in their existing jobs.
- Staff might have to be REDEPLOYED (i.e. change their jobs) within the organisation. This is also likely to mean that staff will need to be trained, perhaps to learn different skills.
- New staff may have to be **recruited** from outside the business.

Alternatively, the number of staff required may need to fall. A business may need to **rationalise**.

- This might be achieved through NATURAL WASTAGE. This is where staff who leave because of retirement, to look after children or to get a better job in another business are not replaced.
- A VOLUNTARY REDUNDANCY scheme may be offered to workers. This is where staff are invited to resign from their jobs. Businesses often offer inducements, such as generous redundancy payments, to persuade workers to take voluntary redundancy.
- Those nearing retirement age might be offered an early retirement package. They will be able to draw their pensions now rather than at the age of retirement.
- As a last resort, the business may be forced to make COMPULSORY REDUNDANCIES. This is where selected employees are told they will lose their jobs. A business is legally able to make workers REDUNDANT if their job 'no longer exists' and they do not intend to appoint another worker to do that job.

Assessing and anticipating demand

Businesses use a wide variety of information to calculate their existing and future demand for labour. The starting point is likely to be existing employment patterns. A business knows what it can produce with a given amount of labour. For example, McDonald's knows from previous experience how many staff are needed to run an outlet. A construction company might know how many workers it needs to build a new housing estate. A taxi firm will know how many drivers it needs on a Saturday night. Then, human resource managers can build in a variety of **internal factors** which may influence current or future demand for workers by the business.

Staff turnover STAFF or LABOUR TURNOVER is the proportion of staff leaving a business over a period of time. Staff leave for a variety of reasons. Some may retire and some leave their jobs to look after their children. Others leave because they want a different job. Labour turnover is measured by the formula:

$$\frac{\text{Number of staff leaving over a period of time}}{\text{Average number of staff in post during the period}} \times 100\%$$

Labour turnover varies enormously between different types of job, between industries and between businesses. McDonald's, for example, has a staff turnover of around 100 per cent per quarter in the UK. This means that on average staff only stay three months in their job. Staff turnover for most jobs is much lower than this. Human resource managers have to take staff turnover into account when planning for the future. Businesses with high staff turnover must recruit more frequently than those with low staff turnover. If staff turnover is concentrated amongjust a few jobs in the business, then recruitment will focus on those jobs.

Sales A change in the level of sales for a business is likely to lead to different staffing needs. A business that forecasts a drop in sales of 20 per cent over the next 12 months is likely to need fewer employees. An expanding business is likely to need more.

Question 1.

Penny Dunseith is director of personnel at Pickerell's, a nationwide chain of retailers selling a wide range of goods, including perfumes. Every year she has to present a report to the board of directors outlining the work of the personnel department over the previous 12 months and the personnel issues likely to face it over the next 12 months. In an appendix to the report is a detailed statistical breakdown of staffing requirements. Part of a table from this report is shown in Table 1.

In 2003, she reported that turnover of management the previous year had been 22 per cent, which was roughly what it had been over the previous five years. Turnover of full-time staff below manager level in stores was 38 per cent, whilst for part-time staff excluding weekend staff it was only 52 per cent. Turnover of part time weekend only staff was 125 per cent.

Part-time weekend only staff were mainly 16-25 year old students looking for a little extra money to supplement their pocket money or student grants. In London, there was also a significant minority of young people, mainly from the EU, who had come to the capital to acquire language skills and see the sights. They would often take a weekend job immediately on arrival to start earning some cash and then quickly leave to work more hours.

Ordinary part-time staff who worked during the week as well as weekends were typically again either students, young people from overseas or young females with at least one small child. Full-time staff below manager level were on average five years older than part-time staff. For many, the job was simply one of a succession of jobs, where the worker was constantly looking for a job at the same level offering better pay or working conditions, or nearer to their home. For some, though, it was a stepping stone into management. Penny wanted to devote more resources to training this category of worker, both to reduce staff turnover and to make it easier to recruit at store management level.

Table 1: Average number of employees, 2007

	Number of posts
Full-time store staff below managerial level	6,258
Weekday part-time store staff	4,780
Weekend only part-time store staff	3,524

(a) Assuming that labour turnover rates and overall staffing levels remained the same in 2008 as in 2007, calculate to the nearest whole number the number of staff that need to be recruited in 2008 in the following categories:
(i) full-time staff below manager level;
(ii) weekday part-time store staff;
(iii) weekend only part-time store staff.

(b) How would your answer to 1 (a) differ if, through the provision of extra training in 2008, the labour turnover of full-time staff below manager level fell by 20 per cent?

(c) Suggest why posts filled by students aged 16-25 are likely to have a higher labour turnover than posts filled by young women aged 21-30.

In larger businesses, the type of sales that are expanding and contracting will affect staffing levels. If US sales are falling but UK sales are rising for a fast food chain, then the number of US employees is likely to fall but in the UK numbers will rise. Within a management consultancy firm, expanding contracts for IT consultancy will require more IT experts, while falling contracts for financial consultancy will require fewer accountants.

Functional and strategic decisions Decisions made by one part of a business may affect recruitment. For example, if the marketing department changes its methods of promotion then it may need to employ people with experience in direct marketing or Internet sales. Strategic decisions can also affect recruitment. A decision to diversify into a new product area will mean production and marketing staff with skills currently not in the business may be needed.

In addition to internal influences, there will also be **external influences** from outside the business.

Competition Competition between businesses will affect staffing. In manufacturing today, there is fierce competition between firms in the supply of household goods. Some manufacturers have ceased production in the UK as a result. Others have been forced to become more efficient, producing more output with fewer resources and so bringing down prices. Fewer staff have often been needed. Remaining staff often have to have higher levels of skill and to be flexible.

Technology Changes in technology will probably change the skills needs of a business. In general, improved technology requires more skilled workers to use it. Office technology today requires many white collar workers to be computer literate and able to use software programs. Improved technology is also likely to be labour saving. Fewer workers are needed to produce the same amount of output.

Changing production techniques There can be considerable differences in productivity (output per worker) between businesses. Changing how employees work with existing resources, such as machinery, can considerably improve productivity. Teamworking, for example, can improve productivity. Improved productivity will mean that fewer workers are needed to produce the same amount of output. Equally, they often need greater skills, changing the composition of the workforce.

Legislation There are legal influences on demand. Businesses that only want younger staff may be prevented from doing so by age discrimination legislation.

Assessing and anticipating supply

Understanding how the demand for labour will change over time is only one side of workforce planning. The supply of labour must also be taken into account. Human resource managers must first understand the skills and talents of existing staff. This might be done by conducting a SKILLS AUDIT, a survey of the skills of the workforce. They must also decide whether or not existing employees are likely to remain in their posts or not. They must carry out projections on staff training needs and whether staff can be recruited from within the business or from outside.

Whether a business can meet its future workforce requirements from its existing employees, its **internal supply**, will depend on a number of factors.

Promotion A business may decide to promote employees from inside the organisation. Some businesses encourage internal promotion. The advantage of promoting existing workers is that they already know about the business's practices and culture. They may also be able to adapt more easily to a new job than an outsider. Some workers may also have been 'filling in' temporarily and have experience of the job. Promoting internally would leave a vacancy further down the hierarchy which would need to be filled. This would add costs and time to filling the vacancy.

Staff development and training A business is more likely to be able to find a suitable employee from inside the organisation if it has training and development programmes. Training may provide the skills needed to allow an employee to move to a new position. For example, many larger businesses have graduate training programmes which train employees with degrees for management positions. Businesses that have development programmes which identify how workers can improve, appraise workers' abilities and view the development of employees as important, are more likely to employ an internal candidate. If a business needs to reduce its workforce in a particular department, it may consider retraining its employees and redeploying them to another part of the organisation.

Staff loss and retirement A workforce supply plan should also take into account staff loss and rates of retirement. High rates of labour turnover, as explained earlier, create vacancies. However, they may also lead to large numbers of skilled workers leaving a business which can affect the number of suitable internal candidates for a job. If large numbers of employees are retiring, this may lead to problems when trying to fill senior management posts which require experienced employees. A business may make use of retirement as a means of reducing the workforce if necessary. People can sometimes be encouraged to take 'early retirement', if they are given a financial incentive.

Flexibility A business may be able to change its workforce practices and conditions in order to meet its labour supply requirements. For example, a business may change the number of hours that people work in a period. Employees may be asked to work 1,950 hours in a year rather than 37.5 hours a week. This means that a business can have employees in work for longer than 37.5 hours when they are needed at peak times. If a business wants to add extra responsibility to the role of workers, it may encourage teamwork or the multiskilling of workers. It may also decide to make new jobs part time or to create jobs that can be shared by two people in order to increase the flexibility of the business.

Legal factors If a business finds that its demand for workers is likely to fall in future it may decide to make workers redundant. There are legal conditions which affect how and when workers can be made redundant. They may also be entitled to redundancy or severance payments.

Certain **external factors** will influence the supply of these workers. A business may plan to employ workers from outside the organisation. There are local and national factors that have to be taken into account by a business when planning its external employee requirements.

The availability and price of housing in an area Some employees may not be able to afford housing in a highly priced area such as London, for example. The availability of new housing on a nearby estate may encourage young families with children to move to an area.

The ease and availability of public transport Working at a factory in a remote area may prove difficult for an employee without a car. Areas with efficient rail or bus links may prove popular for some workers. Possible restrictions or charges on cars in city areas may influence external employee supply in future.

Competition The closing or opening of other businesses in an area may either help or hinder external supply of labour. If businesses close, there may be more skilled labour from which to choose. New businesses may reduce the availability of skilled workers. However, they are also likely to train workers, so that it may be possible to 'headhunt' required employees more easily.

Unemployment High rates of unemployment in an area lead to a large supply of workers who are available for work. This increases choice for a business looking to recruit from outside

Question 2.

Seasonal workers employed by Asda at Christmas 2003 would have benefits and job security equivalent to those of full-time colleagues. The new 'seasonal squad' would have the same status as permanent staff, but with a contract to work an annual, rather than weekly, number of hours. The new recruits would be allowed to work for as little as ten weeks of the year. The contracts would cover Christmas, Easter and the school summer holidays. Positions included greeters, porters, checkout operatives and warehouse workers. 'We recognise that people are looking for flexibility across the working year, not just the working week' said Caroline Massingham, Asda retail people director. 'If you're one of the many people that want to balance long periods of leave with a fulfilling job, the options are limited,' she also added.

Asda hoped that more over 50s would be encouraged to join its 22,357 workers in this age group. The supermarket's flexible working package includes one week's leave for new grandparents and up to two years for a career break. It said that since recruiting older workers, it has seen absence levels drop, customer service improve and labour turnover fall.

Source: adapted from *The Guardian*.

BT confirmed plans to open two new call centres in India in 2003 that would create more than 2,000 jobs. The centres would be in Delhi and Bangalore. The cost of opening call centres in India is up to 30 per cent cheaper than in the UK. The two new call centres, which will cost around £3 million to set up, will deal with operations such as telephoning people in the UK to remind them to pay their bills. Last summer, HSBC's Indian call centre employees were praised by the company for being more efficient, polite and enthusiastic than their British counterparts.

Research by recruitment business Adecco suggested British companies will create up to 100,000 call centre jobs in India by 2008. This would slash their wage costs and take advantage of a pool of skilled workers, many of them graduates. Once a call centre is set up, the wage bill makes up two-thirds of its operation costs. Indian call centre workers earn about £1,200 a year, less than a tenth of the £12,000 starting salary of an employee in Britain. But there can be problems. Businesses can have difficulties keeping a grip on everyday operations in a centre so far away from their base and there may be quality control issues.

Source: adapted from *The Guardian*.

(a) Explain why these situations are examples of planning employee supply from outside the organisation.

(b) Examine the factors that might affect the recruitment of workers from outside the organisation in these situations.

the organisation. High rates of national unemployment may make workers more willing to travel.

Availability of skills Specialist skills may be found in particular areas. For example, the area around Stafford, known as the Potteries, traditionally had skilled pottery workers. Some workers made unemployed in shipyard areas such as Tyneside were able to transfer their skills to other related industries when shipyards closed.

The availability of flexible workers Many businesses are taking advantage of the use of teleworkers. These are people who are employed to work at home and make use of technology, such as the fax and computer, to communicate with the business. They work from home which reduces business costs. Some workers are 'employed' by the business, but are not guaranteed work. They are brought in only when required, such as when demand is high. An example might be a delivery firm asking drivers to be 'on call' in case of busy periods. The availability of these workers increases the flexibility of businesses.

Government training and subsidies Government funded training and employment schemes subsidise businesses for taking on young workers for a period of time. This reduces their cost to a business and allows a 'trial run' of a possible employee.

Population and demographic trends Changes in the structure of the population can affect external recruitment. In the UK there is a growing number of older workers who are available for work. The increase in the number of women joining or returning to the workforce is also likely to affect the supply plans from outside the organisation.

Government legislation There are restrictions on the nature and type of advertisements that can be used when recruiting from outside the business. There are also laws which protect the pay and conditions of workers when they are employed.

Costs The earnings of workers from outside the business might affect recruitment. Hiring workers on lower wages can reduce costs. The cost of setting up factories or offices to employ workers must also be taken into account and businesses must assess the relative costs of employees in different areas and with different skills.

Issues in implementing workforce plans

Businesses need to be aware of a number of issues developing and then implementing workforce plans.

Employee/employer relations The ways in which a business meets the targets of its workforce plan can affect employer/employee relations. Internal recruitment can prevent demotivation as staff will see that the business is attempting to reward staff within the business. In addition, training staff to acquire new skills can also reinvigorate staff with new challenges. Staff development and training can also help a business promote employees into more responsible positions. Flexible working conditions can assist employees to develop the work-life balance appropriate to their needs. However, internal recruitment may not suit the needs of employers. Further, if a business fails to employ adequately qualified staff, this can lead to tension and potential difficulties for existing staff who find their workload increased or they are covering for the mistakes of others.

Costs Internal promotion can often be more cost effective and than recruiting a new employee from outside. There are still likely to be interview costs, but relocation costs and the costs involved with a new employee settling in may be prevented. However, when recruiting internally, there may be additional costs associated with training and development and the business may need to weigh up the cost-benefit analysis of different forms of supplying its employees' needs.

Corporate image Businesses are ever more conscious of how their corporate plans are interpreted by the public and what type of image they may generate. This can affect the extent to which the public may want to purchase goods/services from the business and also influence the extent to which potential external candidates may wish to apply for vacancies at the business. Workforce plans must be carefully prepared so that they do not present the business in a poor light. This may be the case if the business is trying to downsize for example.

The value of using workforce plans

Workforce plans are important for all businesses, whether they are expanding or reducing their workforce. They help a business to set out its employee requirements to prevent unforeseen difficulties. For example, a business that is diversifying is unlikely to be successful unless it has planned to recruit staff needed for the areas into which it will move. Plans are also needed so that future budgets can be prepared.

However, workforce plans are only as effective as the quality of information on which they are based and how appropriate the plans are to current and/or future business development. For example, changes in the business environment may require a change in business strategy that may mean a need to redeploy staff to other departments/functions. In addition, increased competition in the market may make a business more vulnerable to the poaching of key staff. If a business is uncertain about the future or its future requirements, this can have an impact on the value of the workforce plans developed.

KEYTERMS

Compulsory redundancy – when employees are dismissed from their job without their consent.
Workforce planning – the process of determining the labour needs of the business now and in the future and how to achieve labour targets.
Natural wastage – the day to day loss of staff by an employer due, for example, to retirement, staff leaving to look after children, sick or elderly relatives, or gaining a better job with another employer.
Redundant – the situation faced by workers when their employment is terminated by an employer that no longer needs them.
Redeployment - the situation faced by workers when their jobs within a business are changed.
Skills audit – a survey of the skills of the workforce.
Staff or labour turnover – the proportion of staff leaving a business over a period of time. It is usually measured as a percentage by dividing the average number of staff employed into the number of staff leaving over a period of time.
Voluntary redundancy – when employees choose or volunteer to lose their jobs, sometimes in return for early retirement benefits or an enhanced redundancy package.

KNOWLEDGE

1. What are the different components of a workforce plan?
2. What internal influences might affect the potential demand for employees in a business?
3. What external influences might affect the potential demand for employees in a business?
4. What internal influences might affect the potential supply of employees to a business?
5. What external influences might affect the potential supply of employees to a business?
6. Explain how a workforce plan might improve employer/employee relations.

Case Study: Stewart and Mathers

Stewart and Mathers is a solicitor, with offices in Lancashire and London. Its head office is situated in Skelmersdale, a 'new town' created to rehouse the overspill of people moving out of Liverpool in the 1960s as inner city housing was knocked down. Skelmersdale is situated next to the M58 and is a half an hour's drive from the cities of Manchester and Liverpool. The planners decided that:

- high private car usage must be catered for, while still encouraging public transport;
- pedestrians and traffic should be separated in the town centre and residential areas;
- industry should be concentrated in separate, but easily accessible, areas;
- open spaces should be provided, but the housing should be designed to foster a close community atmosphere;
- there must be no urban sprawl, and a clear boundary between town and country;
- the town must try and attract a balanced population structure;
- housing in Skelmersdale was to be high density, but without high rise flats;
- residential areas were to be close to the town centre where most facilities were concentrated.

After the year 2004 the business saw a steady growth in its sales of services. Table 2 shows figures relating to the workforce over the period 2004-2008. Stewart and Mathers realised that more cases were being taken out against individuals and companies for accidents which led to personal injury. This mirrored the situation in the USA. Large sums were often paid to employees injured at work, to people who had been hurt in 'road rage' attacks and for complaints against the State for injuries as a result of badly maintained roads or pavements. Most of the decisions in the business were taken by the three partners, two of whom had previous experience of working in other countries. There were ten people in the business who were 'fee earners'.

The organisation decided that it wanted to expand rapidly to take advantage of growing business in this area. It encouraged its administrative staff lower in the hierarchy to train in law qualifications or take the Institute of Law examination. This would allow them to progress to become solicitor's assistants. It advertised widely in the local area to fill vacancies and 'headhunted' graduates of the ILEX (Institute of Legal Secretaries) courses at local colleges who had been trained in basic law skills. It would also be able to take advantage of the government's New Deal by employing young workers for a small number of posts.

However, some of its senior management positions needed to be filled quickly and so the business advertised in national magazines and quality newspapers. If necessary it was prepared to subsidise managers for a short time if they were prepared to move to the area immediately. This might mean that they had to leave property unsold in a different part of the country or leave family and work away from home for a period.

Table 2

	Sales revenue (£m)	Total employees	Employees leaving
2004	1.1	70	3
2005	1.2	72	4
2006	1.4	75	5
2007	1.6	80	5
2008	2.0	100	6

(a) What factors could have affected the promotion of internal employees within the business to higher posts? (6 marks)

(b) Explain how the business may have forecast the increased need for employees after the year 2004. (10 marks)

(c) (i) Calculate the labour turnover of the business over the period 2004-2008. (4 marks)

(ii) Examine the possible effects of changes in labour turnover on the business. (10 marks)

(d) To what extent might the business be able to recruit workers from outside the organisation for:

(i) jobs at the base of the hierarchy;

(ii) managerial jobs? (12 marks)

75 Human resources management

The importance of human resources

It is often the role of the personnel department to plan human resources. Many businesses have shown a renewed interest in the management of human resources in recent years. They have come to realise the importance of employees and their knowledge and skills as an asset of the business. For example, in 1999 every one of Shell's 105,000 employees around the world were asked for their opinions, which were to be used as an 'agenda for change' in the company. Companies such as ICL have come to recognise the importance of retaining and using workers' knowledge. Siemens, the electronics company, has developed its pension department's team building skills in freezing Arctic Circle conditions. It has also used personality tests to evaluate staff. Companies such as Jaguar and Peugeot have made use of psychological testing of managers.

Businesses also seem to be placing greater emphasis on motivation, customer care and training. In the late 1990s BT's 'for a better life' programme encouraged staff to make their own decisions to benefit the customer. In the early twenty first century there was a growing number of employer and union partnerships and works councils in business aimed at improving industrial relations. Many businesses were also moving towards a **flexible workforce**.

Human resource objectives

HUMAN RESOURCE OBJECTIVES are the goals that a business intends to achieve for its human resources. A business may have a number of human resource objectives.

Matching the workforce to the needs of the business This involves getting the right number of people, with the right skills, in the correct part of the business at the right time to meet the strategic objectives of the business. For example, a construction business may be expanding into a new area of buildings and anticipate extra demand for its services. In this case it might set an objective of employing an extra staff to cope with the increased number of clients. But it would also need to set objectives about the type of staff it would need. If it was expanding into more modern designs it might need builders who were skilled at working with large glass constructions. If it was expanding abroad it might need to employ workers in another country.

Minimising labour costs This involves ensuring that labour costs are kept to an acceptable minimum, but without comprising the quality of staff within the business. For example, a manufacturer of electrical components facing a difficult trading period as a result of competition from Internet sales and abroad may set the strategic objective of staying in business for the next three months. It may be forced to reduce it workforce to keep costs down. However, it must be careful that it retains the knowledge of key staff about areas that are expanding and developing in the industry.

Making effective use of the workforce A business may set objectives to ensure that it makes the best use of its employees. One area in which it might set such an objective is in developing the skills of its staff. Training and developing staff so that they reach their full potential can allow the business to maximise returns. For example, a hotel might aim to have all staff qualified with an appropriate vocational course. This could help it to meet customers' needs better, encouraging customer loyalty and return bookings. A business may also set objectives in understanding the needs of employees and what motivates them to commit and achieve in business. For example, it might set targets for the motivation at work of employees in staff surveys. It might aim for 90 per cent of staff to say that they were satisfied that their views were taken into account by the business.

Maintaining good employee/employer relations This could involve developing business organisational structures, procedures, communication systems and employee representation that feel equitable to employees and to which employees can commit. A large plc, for example, involve targets for the number of days lost through disputes or absences from work. A business may also set objectives such as establishing a works council by a particular date or improving communication between management and the workforce.

Human resources management

One of the most important tasks that involves the personnel department in a business is HUMAN RESOURCES MANAGEMENT (HRM). A business is only likely to achieve its objectives if its employees are used effectively. Planning how best to use human resources will help a business to do this. Human resources management has **strategic** implications. It must be integrated into the strategic and corporate planning of the business. It means constantly looking for better ways of using employees to benefit the organisation.

What is involved in the management of human resources? It is often said that it has a 'soft' side and a 'hard' side. This is shown in Figure 1.

The soft side of human resources management

This is mainly concerned with the way in which people are managed. SOFT HRM may include:

- how to motivate and satisfy workers;

Figure 1: Elements of human resources management

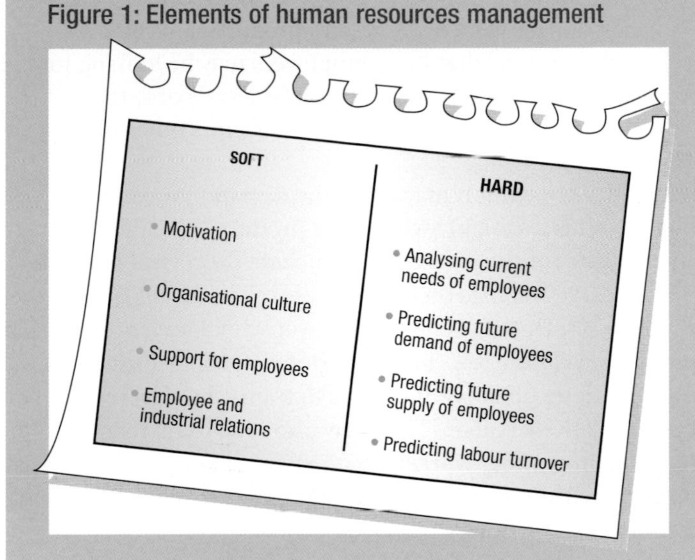

- how to develop an organisational culture or approach in employees, for example good relations with customers, flexibility, or quality at all stages of production;
- how to support and develop employees, for example by training or by improving health and safety;
- the most suitable relationships between employer and the employees or their representatives;
- evaluating alternative policies and their likely costs.

There are various methods that a business could use when managing human resources. Take the example of a hotel with a variety of staff working in different jobs.

Changing business aims into employee goals The hotel may have decided that its main aim was to provide an excellent service to customers. To achieve this aim, goals would have to be set for the behaviour of employees of the hotel, such as always being polite to the customer. It is likely that staff training in customer care would be used to help employees.

Examining the environment There are factors 'outside' a business that could affect human resources management. The hotel would aim to gather as much information as possible to predict the effects of changes in these factors. For example, if health and safety regulations changed that affected the working of the kitchen, staff would need to be aware of these changes and may need training or support to carry them out. Information about external factors can be found from many sources, ranging from industrial journals to competitors' annual reports.

Analysing the current situation It is important for the hotel to be aware of current staff needs. It could do this by using:
- questionnaires to staff and customers;
- interviews with staff;
- discussions with managers;
- performance data;
- recruitment or promotion information.

A questionnaire given to staff and customers at a hotel, for example, might find that customer service is not as good as it could be at the checkout desk because staff are too concerned about getting the paperwork right. A solution might be to simplify the checkout system or use extra staff at busy times. This would help to motivate employees and improve the chances of meeting the goal of improved customer service.

The hard side of human resources management

The hard side of human resources management, HARD HRM, is concerned with quantifying the number and type of employees that a business will need, deciding whether they are available and planning how to get them. This type of human resources management will:
- anticipate the likely future demand for workers;
- analyse current employees and their skills;
- anticipate future supply of workers from inside the business or outside. It will take into account factors such as promotion and labour turnover – the extent to which people leave the business;
- plan how to make up any shortfall of workers or reduce an excess of workers.

The quality of the human resources plan depends on the data on which it is based. A business must have accurate and relevant details for the human resources plan to be effective. For example, details about anticipated future business and the volume of production and sales may be needed. It will then be possible to predict the likely numbers and types of employees that are needed. The human resources plan must also make allowance for changes, such as improvements in technology or new products which might increase or reduce the number of employees needed. The information a business would require to develop an effective human resources plan might include:
- the implications for human resources of changes in corporate strategy, e.g. a possible reduction in the workforce as a result of removing layers of the organisation or deciding to concentrate on core activities of the business;
- the assumptions on which decisions about the workforce have been made, e.g. that there is likely to be growing competition in future;
- all other relevant data that may affect human resources plans, e.g. planned spending on new plant or machinery;
- the timing of changes, e.g. when new products might be introduced;
- anticipated issues in future, e.g. renegotiation of conditions at work;
- a detailed analysis of the current workforce.

Factors affecting human resources management

There are many factors that could affect the management of human resources in a business.

Changing goals of a business If a chemical company, for example, decided that the most effective way to increase profits or turnover was to become more **market orientated**, this is likely to change the personnel the business needs. There would be a need perhaps for employees with market research skills or training in how to promote products. This is an example of how changing goals can affect the demand for labour.

Changes in the market Changes in purchasing patterns of consumers may mean that the demand for labour or labour skills have to change. One example might be the redundancies in the coal industry as a result of demand for cheaper forms of power. Another might be the need to develop good customer relations in fast food retail outlets or financial services as competition has increased.

Changes in the economy can also affect human resource planning. In a recession, a business is likely to reduce its workforce as demand for its products falls.

Technology The introduction of new technology may lead to retraining or a need to recruit workers with specialist skills. For example, many former typists have become computer operators with the introduction of computer systems for storage, retrieval and presentation of information. The business may also have to consider the effect that new technology could have on the motivation of its employees and how to deal with this.

Competition Competition by other firms for workers may affect the supply of labour available to a business. If competitors offer high wages to workers with specialist skills then a business may have to raise its wage levels to recruit the staff it needs.

Competition for customers may also affect a human resources plan. Many firms aim to meet the ISO 9000 quality standard, as customers refuse to use their services without this. An example might be in the electronics industry, where if one firm does not have approval it may lose business to another supplier. A business that obtains the quality standard must employ workers with specialist skills to check the standard is maintained. This can be costly for some small firms.

Population As well as the total population size, the distribution of population in a country can affect the supply of workers available. It is argued that Britain, after the year 2000, faces a number of changes in population distribution that are likely to affect the management of human resources in many businesses.

- **Activity rates.** These are the percentage of any population in the labour force. There has been a growing number of women seeking employment. The activity rates of women of working age are predicted to rise but for men over 25 they are predicted to fall. A growing number of women seeking employment is likely to affect many aspects of human resources management, including how a business recruits workers, work conditions and employee relations.
- **An ageing of the population.** This means that older people are predicted to be a larger percentage of the population. There are also likely to be relatively fewer school leavers and younger workers. A greater proportion of older workers means that more employees may be looking to retire. Older employees may also be less flexible than younger workers and motivated by factors other than money.

An older population may affect the demand for certain goods. Businesses might switch their products to appeal to a more mature consumer. Examples include the revival of 1960s, 1970s and 1980s music on compact disc or to download and the growth in residential care homes. Fewer school leavers mean that employers will have less choice of younger people. Businesses may have to set up apprenticeships to train school leavers as they become relatively scarce. They may also look to fill jobs by recruiting from older workers that may not have previously been considered. B&Q is an example of a business that has a policy of recruiting older workers.

Corporate culture and structure The corporate culture of the organisation is likely to influence human resources management. If a business sees its employees as an asset that need to be trained, developed and motivated then it is likely to regard the management of human resources as important. It would be prepared to spend money and time on developing workers for the benefit of the business. Changes in the hierarchy of a business may affect human resource planning. A removal of a layer of management may mean that fewer employees at this level are required.

Trade unions The relationship between a business and trade unions is likely to affect the management of human resources. In the 2000s it is argued that unions have become more involved in planning. In some businesses unions were derecognised and businesses often negotiated with individuals on terms and conditions of work. The growth of business and union partnerships, union consultation and union recognition in the early twenty first century is likely to have resulted in greater flexibility in human resource management.

Government legislation Government legislation will affect human resource management. Changes to the conditions of part-time workers, the maximum number of hours that can be worked in a week and the minimum wage are all likely to influence the number and type of workers that businesses hire and the way in which labour is used. Government legislation on equal opportunities or a minimum wage has affected the wage costs of businesses and their recruitment and selection procedures. Businesses may also operate a policy where they guarantee disabled workers or ethnic minorities a proportion of jobs.

Finance The finance available to employ, reward or train workers will depend on many factors, such as the overall performance of the business, cash flow and the liquidity of the company. A small business that is building a new factory is unlikely to have funds available to hire new employees, pay large bonuses or carry out extensive training.

The implications of a strategic approach to human resources management

Businesses are increasingly regarding their human resources as an important asset. Developing a human resources management policy is likely to have an number of effects on a business.

- A strategic approach is needed. This means that a business must integrate human resources considerations into its overall corporate planning and strategy. For example, a business that decides to merge with another company must take into account how the workforce needs to change, whether staff need training and assess how motivation may be affected. Alternatively, the hierarchy of the business could be redesigned to suit the needs of employees.
- The business must develop an organisational culture that sees employees as an important part of the company. Managers who are unprepared to listen to employees' views on improvements will prevent the policy from working effectively.
- Motivation, training and support must be given to staff. Staff must be encouraged in the workplace. Businesses may make use of incentives such as bonuses or non-monetary benefits such as job redesign. Training and support must also be given. Marks & Spencer, for example, has employed counsellors to give advice to single parents on coping with children and work.
- Group involvement and participation. Employees must be made to feel part of the business and be committed to its objectives. They must also be prepared to contribute to improvements in quality and productivity.
- Co-ordination with other functions. The management of human resources must be built into all parts of the business, including production, marketing and the finance department, and at all levels in the hierarchy.
- Flexible practices and thinking must be encouraged. Workers must be prepared to change jobs, accept new working methods and conditions. This is dealt with in the next section.
- Recruitment, redundancy and redeployment. Businesses must be able to reduce staff if necessary. Cuts in staff may be achieved in a number of ways. Staff may be allowed to

Question 1.

Newspaper groups are not noted for their training initiatives. There is often too much pressure to meet deadlines. People issues tend to have low priority. But *Metro*, the so-called 'saviour of bored communities', is bucking the trend. Launched in 1999 it reached a 1 million circulation in September 2004. *Metro* was considered to be a classic start-up, explained Steve Auckland, its managing director. 'It was terribly autocratic and people were not the most important aspect of it all' he said. *Metro* prides itself on its different approach to readers. It gives straight talking news and features that fit perfectly into a 20 minute commute to work. Now it wants to take the same approach to human resource management.

Metro's parent company is Allied Newspapers. It persuaded the company to employ a dedicated HR professional. Laura Ashworth was employed in 2003 to look after recruitment, retention and development of the paper's 180 staff. Not all people at the paper were in favour. Some wondered why there should be spending on increased skills when people were leaving to go elsewhere. After her appointment however, attrition rates of staff leaving fell from 25 per cent to 16 per cent.

Auckland argues that even though people leave, it is important to allow them to develop whilst they are at the paper. They then take the good name of the business elsewhere with them. An induction process gives employees in London a three day course and £100 to have a night out of their choice, for example. The aim is to get people to understand the audience – young ABC1 professionals with high incomes – by experiencing their activities. Most newspapers work on the basis that, when you get a job with a national paper, you already have been fully trained. In contrast, *Metro* is committed to giving training to all its employees. More than 80 per cent of staff have had training now, up from 34 per cent in 2003. An internal booklet was developed showing courses that staff could take. They could pick one course relevant to their career and one to their future ambitions.

The business is now moving to the next stage. Managers are being trained in how to conduct appraisal. Members of teams also discuss how their needs can be met by courses in one-to-one discussions with Laura Ashworth. Commercial staff who have reached the top of their grade are also being taken into account. They can arrange special projects, such as a thank you for commercial clients who place large advertising campaigns. Projects that are successful are incorporated into the job of the person involved.

Staff surveys conducted at *Metro* in 2004 showed that 75 per cent of employees understand the goals of the business, compared to 55 per cent in 2003. 72 per cent agree that developing people is now one of the key goals of the business. For every £1 spent on training, the business calculates that there is a 1 per cent improvement in skills. Other surveys have shown that a break is occurring with the 'old school' mentality. Workers, for example, have in the past worked to the stop watch. Now they often stay later than required, just because they want to.

Source: adapted from *People Management*, 13.1.2005.

(a) (i) Explain the type of approach to human resources taken by many publishing companies.
(ii) Identify the approach taken by *Metro* and analyse the potential benefits of this different approach.

(b) To what extent should a new small publishing company follow the current approach of *Metro* to its human resources?

leave without being replaced, known as **natural wastage**. A business may ask for **voluntary redundancies**, where workers agree to leave in return for redundancy payments. The company may also offer **early retirement** to workers close to the compulsory retirement age. If there is no longer enough work, workers may be made redundant. It may also be possible to **redeploy** staff within a business. Training should help workers adapt to working in a different job in a business. Moving to another part of the country may be more difficult.

Human resource strategy – leadership styles

Hard and soft HRM may be linked to leadership styles.

Authoritarian leadership Hard HRM tends to be associated with authoritarian styles of leadership. Authoritarian leaders tend to be TASK-ORIENTATED. This means that they are focused on completing a particular task within limits such as time and cost. They achieve this by structuring the work of their subordinates. Task-orientation can be motivating for subordinates. If a job is going well, subordinates can feel that they are part of a high achieving team. Structure and order can provide a sense of security for workers which is important in motivational needs.

Democratic leadership Soft HRM tends to be associated with democratic styles of leadership. Democratic leaders tend to be PEOPLE-ORIENTATED. They understand that there is a task to be completed. But democratic leaders are as concerned with the needs of subordinates. They listen to subordinates and take their advice. They support subordinates when problems arise with their work or outside of the workplace. By building an atmosphere of trust and respect, where subordinates are encouraged to take initiative, democratic leaders succeed in motivating workers. In all of this, effective communication is essential. A democratic leader who cannot communicate effectively is likely to fail.

Human resource strategy – creating a competitive advantage

Those who advocate an HRM approach argue that it can give a business a competitive advantage. P Boxall, in an article in the *Human Resource Management Journal*, 1996, argues that this competitive advantage comes from two sources.

Human capital advantage HUMAN CAPITAL is the sum of all the education, training, experience and innate skills of a worker or group of workers. Just as individuals with high levels of savings will be able to earn high amounts of interest, so individuals with high levels of human capital will be able to gain high levels of earnings. Businesses offer higher earnings to workers with higher levels of human capital because such workers are more productive. The managing director of a company is paid more than a cleaner because the managing director's much higher level of human capital contributes more to the profit of the company than the cleaner.

The human capital of a worker can be increased through education and training. It can also be increased through giving a worker wider experience. Hence, workers in their 30s tend to have higher levels of human capital than workers in their early 20s starting out their career.

A business can gain a competitive advantage by building up a level of human capital within its workforce which is greater than in its rivals. Using an HRM approach, this is done through managing the HUMAN RESOURCE CYCLE.

- Workers need to be **selected** for their ability to contribute to the strategic goals of the business. Selection is not just about filling vacant posts with workers. It is about questioning whether the post should exist at all, what might the post holder contribute to the business, what qualities and skills should the selectors be looking for, and if no suitable candidates present themselves, what is the most appropriate course of action at that point.
- Workers need to undergo regular **appraisal**. The appraisal should take place in relation to the goals of the business. The appraisal system should therefore be constructed in such a way as to ask how has the individual contributed towards achieving those goals.
- **Reward**s should be given to workers who contribute towards the business achieving its goals.
- Staff **development** should be linked to the needs of the business. What training and experience should an individual receive to better enable them to achieve the goals of the business? With a limited training budget, what is the optimal way to spend that budget in order to secure the firm's objectives?

The human resource cycle of selection, appraisal, rewards and development (also known as the Michigan model) affects the **performance** of employees. The better the selection, the appraisal system, the reward system and staff development, the higher is likely to be the level of human capital in the business. This is what will then give the business its HUMAN CAPITAL ADVANTAGE.

Human process advantage The success of a football team is greater than the sum of the individual human capital of each of

Figure 2: The human resource cycle: the Michigan model of human resource management

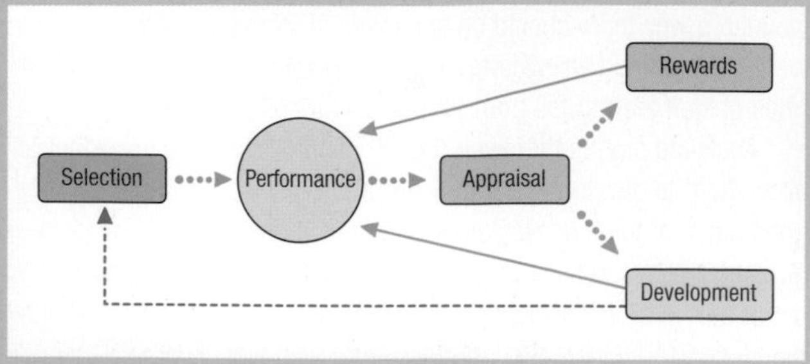

Question 2.

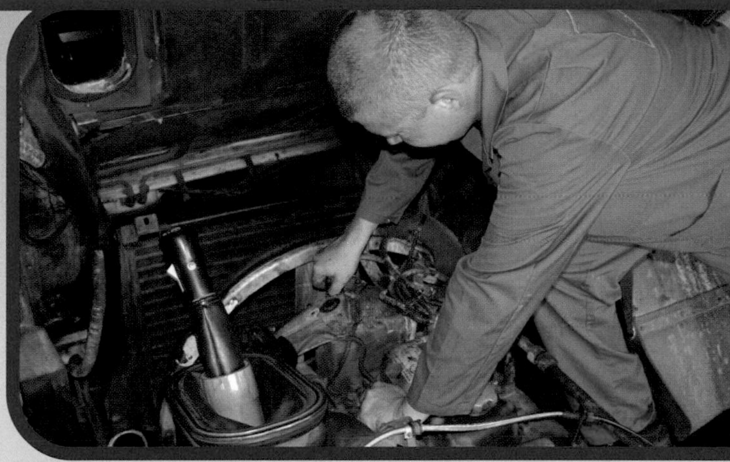

Gerham-Nevis is a motor repair company in the North East area. It has three workshops. Each workshop employs three mechanics and two administration staff. All mechanics work a 38 hour week. At times, there is overtime work which is paid at a higher hourly rate. The two administration staff are paid at a lower rate. There is no system of progression or promotion at the business, although the manager's post at the head office in Newcastle has been filled by an experienced worker from the business each time it has become vacant. A new employee has been hired as a mechanic to take his or her place.

Last year, one of the workers at the Gateshead workshop was given a verbal warning for arriving late in the morning. He got angry and said that mechanics at other garages locally were paid more. Two weeks later, he gave in his notice saying that he had got a better paid job at a garage half a mile away. His post was vacant for three months because, despite advertising it every week in the local newspaper, the company didn't get any suitable applicants. In the end, the company had to take on a trainee. With only two qualified mechanics now at the workshop, productivity fell. Output has still not recovered as the trainee is still learning the trade.

Six months ago, management at Gerham-Nevis decided it needed to differentiate its product more. It took the strategic decision to move into the market for respraying vehicles. For example, some motorists choose to respray their car or motorcycle completely. Gerham-Nevis would also offer a service respraying individual or business vans and trucks with unique designs. Some of the mechanics, however, are opposed to the business moving into this area. They feel that they do not have the necessary skills and are concerned about the extra hours they may be forced to work. Two workers at the Newcastle workshop, in particular, have young children and have to travel to work.

One of the tasks in the office is to collate and deal with all accounts. The owners of the business would like to convert the entire system of invoicing and accounting to a computerised system using a software programme called Sage Line 50. They feel that one of the administration staff could take over this role, although some of them are part time with young children.

(a) Examine the reasons why remuneration at the business may need to change.

(b) Recommend and justify changes that the business could make to its remuneration.

its players. It is about how they play as a team and not just about how they play as individual players. It is also about the network of support from everyone else at a football club. The processes of a business may be as important, if not more important, than the human capital of a business. The processes include:

- the way in which different departments within a business co-operate to achieve the goals of the business;
- the quality of the communication processes, both formal and informal, which determine how knowledge, information and commands are passed through the organisation;
- the relationships between superiors and subordinates and the extent to which both superiors and subordinates are able to use their talents and skills to further the goals of the business;
- the underlying ethos of the business, and whether or not it motivates workers to achieve the goals of the business;
- the way in which a business learns over time, its **organisational learning**, to improve the way in which it conducts business, from R&D to production to marketing to HRM and finance.

HUMAN PROCESS ADVANTAGE is the competitive advantage a business gains over its rivals through the learned interaction of individual workers, which creates a business culture that is independent of any single worker.

Total competitive advantage is the sum of both human capital advantage and human process advantage. Businesses which gain acompetitive advantage through human resource management policies will be more likely to survive and earn high profits than their rivals in the market. To retain that competitive advantage, human resources must be an integral part of the overall strategy of a business. This is the argument that human resource professionals use to justify why human resource management is so important to a business.

Human resource strategy – using remuneration

Remuneration policy is seen in a different way from a Human Resource Management (HRM) perspective. HRM is the process of administering the workforce of a business to achieve its objectives. Remuneration policy is an important part of HRM. Effective remuneration policy, from an HRM perspective, must contribute towards achieving the goals of the business. This is done through ensuring that workers are motivated and are able to employ their skills and talents to the full. From a HRM perspective, the workforce should be highly flexible and adaptable. Team working and ongoing training are likely to be features of a business adopting a HRM approach. Payment systems which contribute towards achieving this will therefore help contribute towards achieving the goals of the business.

There is a number of key features of a payment system

influenced by a HRM perspective.

Pay flexibility Instead of rigid structures, the payment system allows for considerable variation in pay for employees doing the same job. This flexibility allows managers to reward and motivate employees who are performing well. Employee goals, set through an appraisal system, are aligned with the goals of the business. Hence, high performing employees are helping the business to achieve its goals. Flexible pay structures include individual pay bargaining. Where there is collective bargaining, this should be done at local level, with small groups. National or even regional pay agreements should be discouraged.

Job flexibility Jobs are not rigid and do not have fixed job descriptions. Jobs are not boxes on a hierarchy which limit the ability of an employee to contribute to the business. Rather, jobs are flexible, allowing employees to grow into roles and to grow those roles. Their pay is then set according to the contribution they have made to the business and not according to some set amount given on a rigid pay scale. Pay systems then become people-centred rather than job-centred.

Training The development of the individual through experience and training should be linked to the payment system. It might be appropriate to link pay increases with completion of training or gaining qualifications. Part of the pay package might be an allowance for the individual worker to spend on the training which they feel is appropriate for their career needs.

Team working The reward system should encourage team working and team performance where appropriate. For example, the reward system might give bonuses to teams of workers who achieve the objectives they have been set. Or bonuses might be given to teams which have shown flexibility and the ability to adapt.

Decision making Decisions about pay and other rewards should not be decided solely by the HR (or personnel) department. Some responsibility should be devolved to line managers. They are often best placed to operate reward systems tailored to the needs of individual subordinates. For example, a worker might receive a basic pay package which was offered by the HR department when the worker was first appointed to the job. But responsibility for giving bonuses or other rewards might be passed down the line to managers. These managers would have money included in their budgets for this purpose.

Employee needs The reward given to the employee is matched to their needs. For example, many large businesses now operate flexible fringe benefit packages where an employee is given a notional amount of money and can 'buy' fringe benefits from a car, to extra holiday entitlement to private health care insurance and even simply to higher pay. By giving more control to employees of their total remuneration package, workers are able to satisfy more of their needs. This leads to increased commitment to the business and therefore higher motivation. However, the reward given to employees is not just financial. The reward system must take into account the non-financial needs and aspirations of individual employees. So some employees might be motivated by being offered extra training which will help them in their chosen career path. Others may be motivated by the ability to work very flexible hours over the year. Parents who are the main carers of their children might feel high levels of commitment to an employer who allows them to work around the needs of those children.

Recruitment and retention Payment systems should take account of recruitment and retention. In some parts of the business, it might be highly desirable to have stable teams of workers employed over time. The payment system may then give high rewards to these workers relative to the market rate. High relative rewards will discourage workers leaving to find better jobs with another employer. In other parts of the business, it might be healthy to have a regular turnover of staff to bring in new ideas and fresh enthusiasm. Paying the 'going' market rate for the job would then be an appropriate strategy.

Appraisal Many remuneration systems now incorporate appraisal into the process of determining pay through performance related pay. Appraisal is where the performance of an individual worker is reviewed against a set of criteria. Businesses use appraisal to assess the performance of an individual worker over a period of time and to feed back that assessment to the individual. Typically, goals are set for future performance and this may be linked to training needs. Assessment may also be used to discuss career development within the business. Appraisal is not always linked to pay and bonuses. However, for many workers, pay rises or bonuses are conditional upon what takes place within the appraisal process. Fundamentally, using appraisal and performance related pay is an attempt to align the goals of the individual with the goals of the business.

The concepts of 'hard' and 'soft' HRM can be applied to remuneration policy. Where there is a hard approach, payment methods should be linked directly to performance and the contribution of the worker to output and profit. Rewards for success should be clear and transparent to the workforce. Where there is a soft approach, payment methods should be related to the goals of workers as well as those of the business.

For example, with a hard approach to HRM, workers who were taken sick would receive exactly their entitlement under policies laid down by the business. With a soft approach, local managers would be able to 'bend the rules' where they thought this was appropriate. Equally, where a parent had to take a day off work to look after a sick child, the hard approach would be to count it as unpaid leave, or as a day's holiday entitlement. A soft approach might be either to ignore it and for colleagues to cover, or allow the worker to make up the missed hours at another time.

Where a soft approach was associated with democratic leadership, payment systems would reward those who contributed to effective decision making and were good team players. For example, bonus payments for all team members might be linked to their performance as a team. Where a hard approach is associated with autocratic leadership, the leaders of teams alone might receive the bonuses if they motivated their team members sufficiently for the team to achieve its targets.

Human resource strategy – relocation and outsourcing

In the early twentieth century businesses in the UK attempted to reduce costs and improve the flexibility of employees. Faced with growing competition, but also aided by the development of global markets, the Internet and computer technology, businesses attempted to manage their human resources in more efficient ways.

One method favoured by some companies was to relocate businesses in low cost countries, whilst keeping their head offices in the UK. A whole operation might be moved to a country where average earnings were lower than in the UK, employees would be hired in those countries and workers would be made redundant in the UK. This was particularly suitable for operations such as call centres where skills were easily transferrable and there was no need for direct contact with consumers. One of the problems faced with such a reorganisation was control from a distance, although it could be argued that this is no different from the challenges facing a multinational business operating in many countries.

Increasingly businesses have also outsourced operations. In some cases this might be to teleworkers working from home, using computers to communicate with employers. Operating from home might reduce costs for the business, although this type of work might only be suitable for certain operations. If these employees were part time or employed on flexible contracts, as explained earlier, this might improve efficiency and reduce costs even further. In some cases businesses have even outsourced entire operations to other businesses which might be able to produce goods or provide services more effectively.

Advantages of human resources management

There are certain advantages to a business in taking a strategic approach to managing human resources.

- It may allow a business to gain a competitive advantage over rivals. A business which has a well trained, motivated and planned workforce and a human resources policy may be more efficient than competitors.
- It can solve human resources problems that occur in the business such as high rates of turnover and absenteeism.
- Effective human resources management will make the most efficient use of workers and reduce the potential costs of the business.

Question 3.

In 1999 B&Q opened its first store in China. By 2003 it had 8 stores and aimed to open more in future. It was not the policy of the business to saturate overseas businesses with too many expats. Rather their role was to transfer skills, to train and coach local successors, and then move on. These individuals maintain links with the UK through B&Q's central international HR team.

B&Q does not simply transfer UK HR policy to other countries such as China. Instead HR management focusses on meeting local requirements. Human resources in China tends to be a policing and administrative function, so finding people with the right experience proved difficult. The company designed an application form asking candidates about their skills and aspirations. Many ignored the form and simply attached a letter with interesting but irrelevant information. So whilst attracting a large number of candidates it was often difficult to assess them. Despite being warned that the process would not work in China, B&Q has successfully introduced performance appraisal. The company also sends between 12 and 15 people to the UK each year for a two week period so they can learn about the business.

Source: adapted from *People Management*.

(a) Explain the possible benefits of B&Q's human resource approach in China.

(b) Examine the problems B&Q may have faced with managing human resources in the country.

- A business will be able to anticipate changes to its workforce requirements and plan for these. It will also be able to manage change more effectively.
- Industrial relations problems may be prevented if employers and employees are working towards the same goals.
- Human resources management aims to provide long-term benefits for the business. Employing part time workers in a crisis may solve a short-term problem. But a planned, flexible workforce will give benefits to the business over a longer period.

The problems of human resources management

There is a number of problems a business will face when managing its employees.

- Problems with predicting the behaviour of people. A business may have filled a position, but after being appointed the individual may decide he does not want the job. This could mean another costly and time-consuming series of interviews for the firm.
- Problems with predicting external events. Sometimes it is difficult to predict exactly how many employees are required. We have seen that many factors can affect human resource planning. For example, the opening up of markets in the Far East, such as China, or the expansion of the EU into Eastern Europe in the 2000s could have meant

changing plans for businesses aiming to break into these markets. It is likely that employees with knowledge of the business and language of these countries would have been in demand.

- Planning has to be constantly monitored. It is unwise for a business to plan its human resource needs and not alter them in the light of changing events. Planning has to be checked, revised and updated as other factors change.
- Human resources management must be well thought out or it is likely to lead to industrial relations problems. Cuts in the workforce or wage reductions that are not negotiated could affect workers' motivation and may even lead to industrial action.

KEYTERMS

Hard HRM – a human resource management perspective which sees human resources as no different from other resources available to the business, such as financial or physical resources. Their costs, requirements and contribution and can be quantified and businesses can manipulate these to achieve their aims and objectives.

Human capital – the sum of all the education, training, experience and innate skills of a worker or group of workers; the higher the level of human capital of workers, the higher on average will be the rewards they will be able to earn by hiring themselves out to employers.

Human capital advantage – the competitive advantage that a business gains by having a workforce with a higher level of human capital than its rivals. This advantage can be gained through the human capital cycle of selection, appraisal, rewards and development leading to improved performance of workers.

Human process advantage – the competitive advantage a business gains over its rivals through the learned interaction of individual workers which creates a business culture which is independent of any single worker.

Human resource cycle – the process through which human resources are recruited, selected, rewarded and appraised by a business.

Human resource objectives – the goals that a business intends to achieve from its human resources. A business may have a number of human resource objectives

Human resources management – an integrated approach which ensures the efficient management of human resources. It is part of the overall business plan..

People-orientated leadership – where a leader focuses on the needs of subordinates and gives them some autonomy to decide how best a task should be completed. People-orientated leaders tend to be democratic.

Soft HRM – a human resource management perspective which prioritises the needs and development of employees in order to motivate them and make them committed to achieving the goals of a business.

Task-orientated leadership – where a leader focuses on completing tasks rather than on the needs of the individual workers who will help complete the task. Task-orientated leaders tends to be autocratic.

KNOWLEDGE

1. What is human resources management?
2. State four objectives a business could have for its human resources.
3. Explain the difference between the soft and hard side of human resources management.
4. Briefly describe five factors that might affect the managing of human resources by a business.
5. 'A business that does not manage its human resources effectively may face industrial relations problems.' Explain this statement.
6. State:
   (a) five implications of taking a strategic approach to HRM;
   (b) four advantages of human resources management;
   (c) four problems of human resources management; for a business.
7. What is the relationship between the hard and soft side of HRM and leadership styles?
8. What are the steps in the human resources cycle?
9. How can the human resources cycle affect human capital advantage?
10. List three ways in which rewards can take into account employees' needs.
11. How can payments be structured to improve recruitment and retention?
12. What is the relationship between appraisal and rewards?
13. Briefly explain the relationship between:
    (a) the hard side of human resource management and remuneration;
    (b) the soft side of human resource management and remuneration.
14. Identify three problems a business faces in managing its human resources.

Case Study: A five star strategy

Claridges is one of London's most luxurious hotels. It has changed little in 50 years, retaining the feel of glittering chandeliers and society afternoon tea. But behind the opulent surface there appeared to be human resources issues to be dealt with.

Sara Edwards took over as HR Director in 1998. Claridges was battling to maintain its place in the market. Other hotels offered luxury service. Cheaper hotels were shooting up all the time. Visits were down. Occupancy rates were falling at the hotel, complaints were high and staff turnover was running at 73 per cent. She argued that people weren't enjoying the experience at the hotel and staff weren't enjoying working there. A staff satisfaction survey revealed the extent of the problems. Only 47 per cent of staff bothered to respond. Of those that did, only 67 per cent said they felt proud to work for the business. Most felt a mistrust of management. As a result, the executive team came up with a new vision for the business, based on seven values. Edwards argued 'If you don't get it right for the employees, you won't get it right with the guests'.

By the end of 2002 staff turnover had fallen to 27 per cent. Pride at working in the hotel had risen to 99 per cent and every member of staff responded to the survey.

What was the secret behind such a change in employees' views? The seven core values of:

- commitment;
- passion;
- team spirit;
- interpersonal relations;
- service perfection;
- maximising resources;
- responsibility of actions;

were at the heart of the matter. They were depicted as a rainbow and this image helped to reinforce the idea that staff should have fun as well as doing their job. This was a novel idea for a hotel that had traditionally been seen as 'straight-laced'.

To train staff in the new philosophy, managers were taken off site on an away day. Each was asked to give a five minute performance to demonstrate one of the values. Edwards argued that the business had to do something very significant to show that things were going to be different, but fun as well. A new reward scheme 'Going for Gold' built on the idea of the 'rainbow values'. Staff demonstrating special value for the business were given a gold card and had a lucky dip. Prizes ranged from a limo home to a night in a penthouse which would normally cost £3,850.

The 450 employees in the business were encouraged to look to the future. Internal recruitment used to be rare, but after the changes, anyone taken on was viewed as someone who could eventually do a more skilled job. Staff were also encouraged to move across departments to develop their skills. New jobs were advertised in a newsletter. People who did not get the job were given training, as they had shown aspirations to improve.

People who visited the hotel after the changes said that they recognised the same faces. This seemed to imply that people were staying longer in their jobs. This helped to maintain standards in the business. Another scheme was designed to improve staff pride. Employees were invited to experience staying as guests at the hotel for a night. One employee who stayed felt that it brought home why Claridges was unique and reminded the employee why they worked at the hotel.

Such reminders were important after the September 11 terrorist attacks in New York. Many hotels experienced falls in trade. Claridges called a meeting and a plan of action was drawn up. Employees were kept informed at all times and redundancies were kept to a minimum.

Source: adapted from *People Management*, 8.4.2004.

(a) Identify examples of the hard and soft side of human resource management at the hotel. (6 marks)

(b) Explain the factors which may have influenced the change in approach to human resources management. (10 marks)

(c) Examine how the changes in the management of human resources may have affected the business. (10 marks)

(d) Evaluate the effectiveness of human resources management at the hotel using appropriate methods. (14 marks)

76 Communication

What is communication?

COMMUNICATION is about sending and receiving information. Employees, managers and departments communicate with each other every day in business. For example, in a sole trader organisation, the owner may inform the workers verbally that an order for goods has to be sent out in the next two days. In a company, the personnel manager might send a 'memo' to all departments informing them about training courses that are available.

Good communication is vital for the efficient running of a business. A company exporting goods abroad is likely to have major problems if it fails to give the exact time of departure to its despatch department. Similarly, problems will also arise if instructions are not clear and goods are delivered to the wrong address.

Effective communication will only happen if information is sent, received and then understood. Some examples of information and methods of communicating in business might be:

- information on how to fill out expenses claims forms in a memo sent from the accounts department;
- verbal comments made by a manager to an employee informing them that continued lateness is likely to result in disciplinary action by the company;
- employment details given to a new employee on a written contract of employment;
- information on sales figures sent from the sales manager to the chief executive by email or saved as a spreadsheet on computer disk;
- face-to-face negotiations between management and employee representatives over possible rewards for agreeing to changes in work practice;
- a group meeting taking place to discuss how quality could be improved in a work section;
- an order for 20 books faxed to a publisher from a bookshop;
- an advertisement for a salesperson placed on a company website on the Internet.

The communication process

Communication within business can take many forms. There are, however, some common features of all communications that take place in the workplace. Figure 1 shows an example.

Who sends and receives information? Information must be sent by a **sender** and received and understood by the **receiver**, the person or group to whom the information is sent. Communication can take place between managers and employees, as well as between representative bodies, such as trade unions. Information is also passed to people and organisations outside the company. For example, company newspapers not only inform employees about the firm, but present a picture to the outside world of its operations.

What message is being communicated? For communication to be effective the correct message must be sent and received. Messages can be sent for a number of reasons.

- To provide information about the company. Management might inform the workforce about production levels achieved during the previous year. Some information is required by law, for example, the business has to tell employees about their conditions of employment.
- To give instructions, for example, to instruct market research to be carried out.
- To persuade people to change attitudes or behaviour, for example, to warn an employee who is consistently late of the likely action.

Figure 1: An example of information passing through the communication process

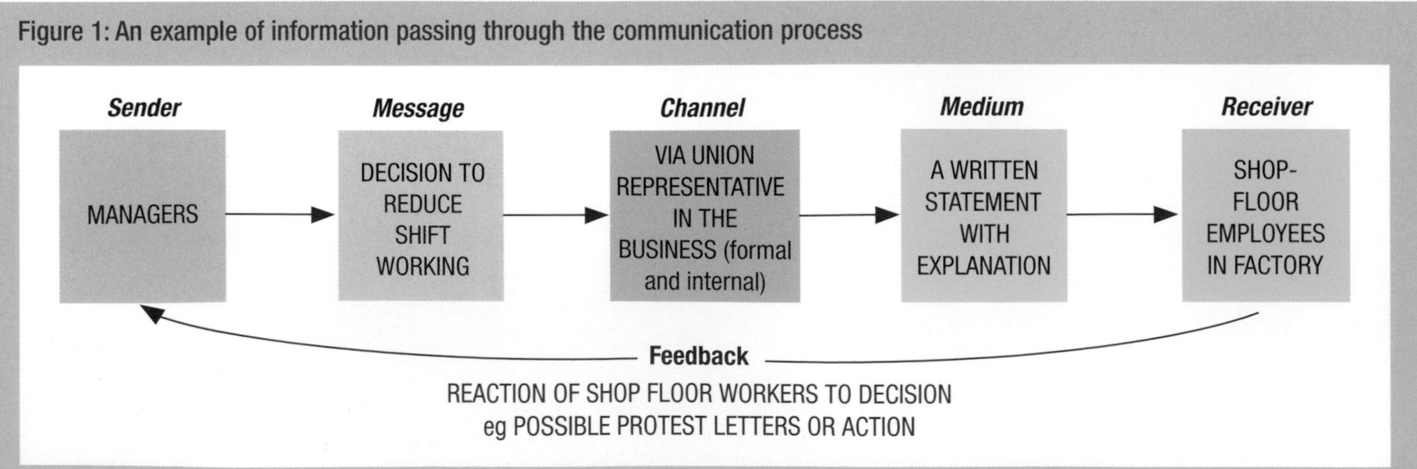

Figure 2: Vertical and lateral communication

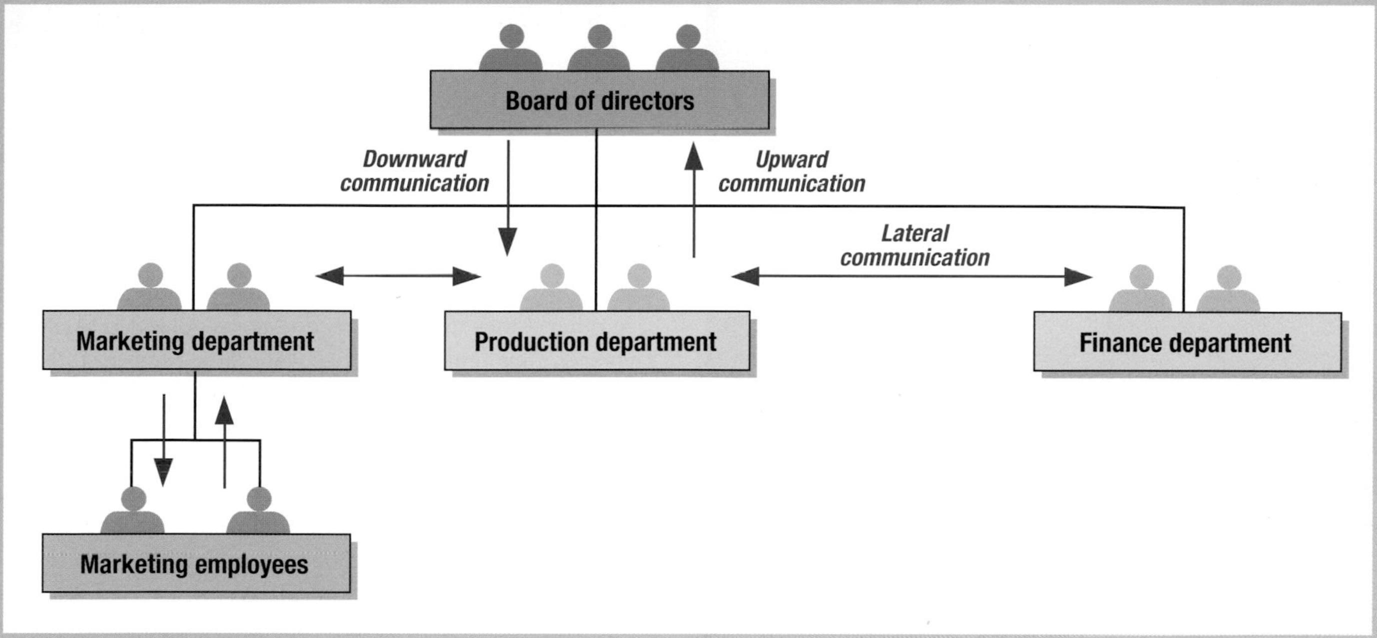

What channel is being used? Communication can be along different routes or CHANNELS OF COMMUNICATION in the organisation. Sometimes this can be between a manager and a subordinate (vertical) or between two departments (horizontal). As well as this formal type of communication, information is often passed informally between departments and employees. Communication can also be to other people within the organisation (internal) or to those outside the organisation (external).

What medium is being used? Information can be communicated in a variety of ways or through different COMMUNICATION MEDIA. These vary from written methods, such as annual reports, to oral methods such as discussions, to the use of information and communication (ICT) technology, such as a fax machine, email or the Internet.

What feedback is given? Communication is not complete until the message is received and the receiver confirms that it is understood through feedback of some sort, for example written or verbal confirmation.

Formal and informal communication

Within a business there are both formal and informal channels of communication.

Formal communication Formal channels of communication are recognised and approved by employers and employee representatives. Examples of formal channels would be a personnel department giving 'notice' to an employee about redundancy, meetings between managers and trade union representatives or team meeting held each week.

Informal communication Informal communication is through non-approved channels. This can both help and hinder formal communications. Information that is communicated through the grapevine may become distorted. This might, in extreme situations, cause industrial relations disputes. However, the grapevine can be acknowledged by management and actively approved of. Some firms issue a 'leak' along the grapevine to see what reaction it might provoke, making changes based on the reaction of employees to proposals, before issuing final instructions. **Rumours**, such as of a launch of a new product by a competitor, can be useful to a business.

Research has shown that effective communication requires both formal and informal channels. Formal statements can then be supported by informal explanations. A business might inform employees that it is introducing new machinery and then management may discuss this with employees and their representatives to find the best way to do it.

Vertical and lateral communication

Information can be communicated vertically (downwards or) upwards and laterally. These different channels of communication are shown in Figure 2.

Vertical communication VERTICAL COMMUNICATION can be downwards or upwards. Downwards communication has, in the past, been used to tell employees about decisions that have already been made. It may be important as it:

- allows decisions by managers to be carried out by employees;

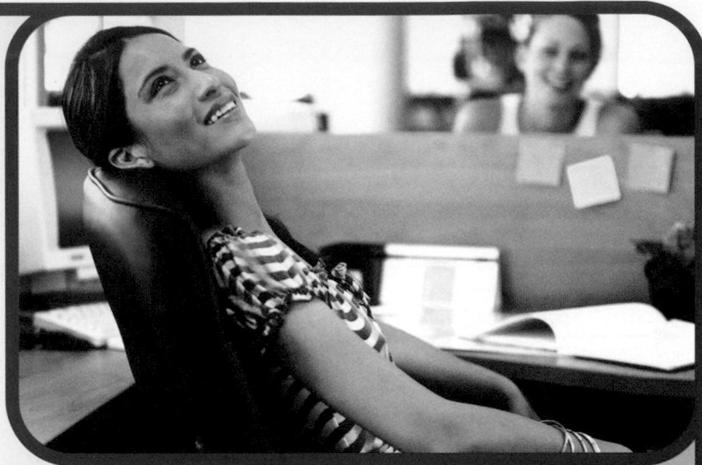

Question 1.

Leila likes her work routine. She gets up at 6.00 each day and is in her open plan office by 7.30. The first thing she does is make a cup of coffee and have a chat with Elle, another early bird into the office. Then she replies to any emails which came in overnight. By 8 o'clock, she is looking at her diary and reminding herself of her priorities for the day. The office is now filling up and Leila knows that for the next hour, colleagues will be dropping by her desk to say good morning, get clarification about the day's work or chat about problems. Her secretary comes in at 8.30 and she always briefs her on the day ahead. When she is not talking, she is reading briefings and memos which don't require too much concentration. 9.00 to 11.00 is Leila's time to write reports for clients based on site visits. Then it is time for a coffee and chat by the coffee machine. Often there are internal meetings in the late morning. The afternoon is typically spent on site visits to external clients. Depending on when the visit finishes, she might go home or pop back to the office to deal with emails and begin writing up the report on her visit.

(a) Explain the meaning of the following using examples from the passage to illustrate your answer.
(i) Internal and external communication.
(ii) Messages, senders, receivers and feedback.
(iii) Channels of communication.
(iv) Medium of communication.
(v) Formal and informal communication.
(vi) Vertical and lateral communication.

- ensures that action is consistent and co-ordinated;
- reduces costs because fewer mistakes should be made;
- should lead to greater effectiveness and profitability as a result of the above.

There is evidence, however, that the flow of information upwards can also help in decision making.

- It helps managers to understand employees' views and concerns.
- It helps managers to keep more in touch with employees' attitudes and values.
- It can alert managers to potential problems.
- It can provide managers with the information that they need for decision making and gives feedback on the effects of previous decisions.
- It helps employees to feel that they are participating and can encourage motivation.
- It provides feedback on the effectiveness of downwards communication and how it can be improved.

Lateral communication LATERAL COMMUNICATION takes place when people at the same level within an organisation pass information. An example might be a member of the finance department telling the marketing department about funds available for a sales promotion. One problem that firms sometimes face is that departments may become hostile towards each other if they don't understand the problems that each face. The marketing department may want these funds, but this might adversely affect the firm's cash flow.

It is also possible to make the distinction between **line communication** and **staff communication**. Line communication has authority behind it. Staff communication does not. An example of staff communication may be where a manager attempts to persuade a worker that it is a 'good idea' to do something. Communication can also be **internal**, to people inside the organisation, or **external**, to those outside.

Communication media

There is a number of methods or media that can be used to communicate information in businesses. Many of these methods can be delivered via electronic media. These are explained in the next section.

Written communication The letter is a flexible method which provides a written record. It is often used for communications with others outside the organisation. It can also be used internally where a confidential written record is needed, e.g. to urge employees against strike action, to announce a redundancy etc.

A **memorandum** is the same as a letter, but is only used for internal communications.It is sent via the internal mail system. Memoranda are useful for many sorts of message, particularly for confirming telephone conversations. Sometimes they are used instead of a telephone. One criticism often made of firms is that they have too many 'memos', when short written notes would do the same job. Some businesses send 'memos' via e-mail. This allows a person to send a message to another person's computer. The memo can then be called up and read by the person receiving it.

Reports allow a large number of people to see complex facts and arguments about issues on which they have to make a decision. A written report does not allow discussion or immediate feedback, as does a meeting, and it can be time-consuming and expensive to produce. However, it does have advantages for passing messages to groups. First, people can study the material in their own time, rather than attending a meeting. Second, time that is often wasted at meetings can be better used. Third, the report is presented in an impartial way, so conflict can be avoided.

Routine information can be communicated through the use of **forms**. A well designed form can be filled in quickly and easily.

They are simple to file and information is quickly retrieved and confirmed. Examples of forms used in business include expense forms, time sheets, insurance forms, and stock request forms.

The **noticeboard** is a method which cheaply passes information to a large number of people. The drawbacks to noticeboards are that they can become untidy or irrelevant. In addition, they rely on people reading them, which does not always happen.

Larger companies often print an internal magazine or newspaper to inform employees about a variety of things. These may include staff appointments and retirements, meetings, sports and social events, results and successes, customer feedback, new products or machinery and motivating competitions, e.g. safety suggestions. The journal usually avoids being controversial. It may not deal with sensitive issues, such as industrial relations or pollution of the environment, and may stop short of criticising management policy or products. It is designed to improve communication and morale, and it may be seen by outsiders (especially customers) who might get a favourable impression of the business.

Face-to-face communication Face-to-face communication involves an oral message being passed between people talking to each other. Examples might be:

- a message passed between two workers about how long is left before lunch;
- an instruction given to an employee to change jobs in a job rotation scheme;
- a warning given by a health and safety officer to a worker.

Group meetings involve face-to-face communication. Meetings can take a number of forms. They may be formal meetings which are legally required, such as the Annual General Meeting of a limited company. They might also be meetings of groups within the business to discuss problems, such as collective bargaining negotiations or meetings of quality circles. Team briefings are also a common method of face-to-face communication in business. Many meetings, however, are simply informal discussions taking place to pass information between employees or managers, such as a 'chat' over lunch.

Face-to-face communication has several advantages. It:

- allows new ideas to be generated;
- allows 'on the spot' feedback, constructive criticism and an exchange of views;
- encourages co-operation;
- allows information to be spread quickly among people.

However, face-to-face communication, such as meetings, can have problems, especially if:

- the terms of reference (defining the purpose and power of the meeting) are not clear;
- the people attending are unskilled or unwilling to communicate;
- there is insufficient guidance or leadership to control the meeting;
- body language creates a barrier.

Oral communication Oral communication can take place other than in face-to-face situations in a business. The telephone is a common method of oral communication between individuals in remote locations or even within an organisation's premises. It provides some of the interactive advantages of face-to-face communication, while saving the time involved in travelling from one place to another. It is, however, more 'distant' and impersonal than an interview for the discussion of sensitive matters and does not provide written 'evidence'. This disadvantage can be overcome by written confirmation.

Sometimes messages can be communicated to groups of employees through a public address system. This might operate through loudspeakers placed at strategic points, e.g. in workshops or yards, where staff cannot be located or reached by telephone.

Information and communication technology

Rapid developments in technology have greatly changed the way businesses communicate with each other. It is now possible to deliver messages instantly, over great distances and to a number of people at the same time via a variety of electronic media.

The Internet The INTERNET is a vast source of information for businesses and individuals who have access to a computer. The introduction of broadband in the UK means that websites containing images and text can be quickly viewed and information can be downloaded. The Internet is useful for external communication, although it might also be useful for internal communication in certain circumstances. For example, businesses can:

- advertise jobs to employees inside and outside the business;
- allow people to view financial reports or company mission statements;
- allow customers to buy products and pay using credit card details;
- gain market research information;

as well as providing stakeholders with a large amount of information about the company.

One major problem with online communication and the sending of messages via the internet is junk mail, known as spam.

Intranets Information on the internet is available to the public. This makes it impossible to send confidential messages. A business intranet is under the control of the company using it so information sent can be controlled. For example, a company with 150 administration staff may all be linked by an intranet. They can send messages and access common information. It is suggested that the biggest savings from the intranet will come from the distribution of standard information throughout an organisation. For example, information such as the internal phone numbers, diaries and timetables quickly become out of date. In electronic format, however, they could be revised as soon as a change occurs and made available to all staff through a 'browser'. Intranets may also be extended into 'extranets'. These could include other business stakeholders, such as customers and suppliers, as well as the staff of a business. For example, suppliers might be able to view their stockholdings held by a company's warehouse to make sure they are provided when required.

Email Many businesses have email addresses. They allow businesses and individuals to communicate immediately with others via word processed text or images that are contained on a computer. Information sent from one email address, via a computer, modem and telephone to another address is stored by the 'server'– a computer dedicated to storage and network facilities. It stays in that address until it is picked up by the receiver. The advantage of email is that long documents can be immediately sent to other people anywhere in the world without them being there.

Mobile phones Many companies and individuals now have mobile phones. These are portable telephones which can be carried around by the user. Telephone calls can be made and received from most areas, often in different countries. They are particularly useful for employees who work outside the office or factory and who move around. Urgent messages can be sent and received immediately. Companies such as Orange and Vodafone offer a variety of services, including receiving and storing messages.

Answerphones Answerphones record messages when the receiver is unable to answer the telephone. They allow important messages to be stored and received if, for example, an employee is away from her desk. They also allow messages to be sent from one company or person to another outside normal office hours. The information will be received when work starts the next day. This is particularly useful when there are time differences between countries. Some people find answerphones impersonal and may not leave a message.

Paging devices These are devices which are useful for people who work outside a business and move around a lot, such as sales representatives. They may also be used by workers in a large organisation, such as a doctor in a hospital. A 'bleeper' alerts the receiver to a message waiting for him on a prearranged telephone number.

Videoconferencing and teleconferencing Videoconferencing is a method of communication which allows individuals in different locations to interact as if they were in the same room. Individuals can see each other on monitors with the use of cameras and talk to each other via telephone lines. This is particularly useful when employees need face-to-face interaction, but work in locations that are distant from each other. It also saves the time taken to get to a central meeting place. Teleconferencing is where many people are linked together via telephone lines. Each person can talk to all others as if they were in the same location.

Laptop computers The development of portable computers means that business people can work in different locations to their office. They allow people to continue working during train journeys, for example, and to email text and images to others via satellite link. They prevent working time from being wasted. They also have the advantage of immediate sending and receiving of information at a variety of locations. Some laptop computers have to be plugged into a telephone terminal to receive email, which can be a problem.

Multi-media communications Businesses are now able to communicate information through a mixture of media. They combine visual images, written text and audio transmissions. This is known as multi-media. Many multi-media programmes are interactive, so that an individual can enter into dialogue with the information that is contained in the programme. The use of multi-media as a business communication tool is particularly useful in the area of training. Individual employees can interact with ideas and concepts developed in the multi-media training package at their own pace.

Electronic noticeboards Businesses are making more use of electronic noticeboards. These communicate the latest information to employees via visual display units located in public places around the business, such as in reception. Their advantage over normal noticeboards is that they can be kept up to date. The main disadvantages are that they are limited to particular locations in the business and the information may not be relevant to everyone who sees it.

Fax machines Faxes are similar to email, but the information is already on paper in the form of text or images. This information is read by a fax machine, converted into audio signals, and sent down a telephone line to another fax machine. The machine then reconverts the signals into text and graphics. The advantages of fax machines are that they send messages instantly and that the receiver does not have to be there to receive the message. A disadvantage compared to email is that it can take a long time to process a large document via the fax. The information also has to be printed out or written before it can be sent.

Barriers to communication

Effective communication will take place if the message is received and understood by the receiver. There is a number of factors that might prevent this from happening. Solutions to some of these problems may simply be using tactics to change how the communication takes place. However, in other cases company-wide strategies may be needed.

Form of the message If the message is unclear or unexpected the receiver is unlikely to understand it or remember it. The rate at which we forget is considerable. We have probably forgotten

half of what we hear within a few hours of hearing it, and no more than 10 per cent will remain after two or three days. To ensure a message is communicated effectively the sender must make sure it:
- does not contain too much information;
- is not poorly written;
- is not presented too quickly;
- is not presented in a way that the receiver does not expect;
- conveys the information that he actually wants to communicate;
- is written in a way that the receiver will understand.

Jargon A word or phrase which has a technical or specialised meaning is known as jargon. The terms understood by a certain group of people may be meaningless to those who don't have this knowledge. One example of this was in Schools of Motoring, where for many years drivers were given the instruction 'clutch in' or 'clutch out', which nearly always confused the trainee. Later the instruction was changed to 'clutch down' and 'clutch up'. Technical information about a product which is not understood by the marketing department may result in misleading advertising and poor sales. Being careful that the communication is written appropriately for the receiver may help to prevent this, for example through editing or rewriting.

The skills of the sender and receiver The ability of the sender to explain a message and the receiver to understand it are important in communication. If an order must be sent out by a certain date, but the sender simply asks for it to be sent as early as possible, communication would not have been effective. If the receiver does not understand what stocks to take the order from, incorrect goods may be sent. Solving such a problem may simply mean checking that both sender and receiver the message and that it is carefully explained. However, if either lacks the skills required then training may be required.

Choice of communication channel or medium Sometimes the channel or medium chosen to send the message may not communicate the information effectively. An example of this might be where a manager attempts to pass a message to an employee, but would have been more successful if the message had gone through a representative. Another example is that safety campaigns are sometimes unsuccessful because slogans and posters are used to persuade individual employees about the importance of safe working practices rather than changes being discussed.

Incorrect target for the message Businesses sometimes send the wrong information to the wrong person. This can result in costly delays and errors and perhaps a poor image in the eyes of the public.

Stereotypes, perceptions and attitudes How employees perceive other people can affect how they interpret the message that is sent. Employees are more likely to have confidence in people they trust, because of past experience of their reliability. On the other hand, if an employee has learned to distrust someone, then what she says will be either ignored or treated with caution. The way employees view things can be affected by being part of a group.

People can also have beliefs about others. This may result in stereotyping of some people. It is possible that, if one person stereotypes another, this may affect how they interpret a message. So, for example, if a manager takes the view that younger people are less knowledgable than older people, this may affect the manager's judgment on a younger employee's opinions.

Training workers to behave objectively when dealing with colleagues can prevent such problems. However, preconceptions might be difficult to remove unless everyone in the business is committed to this approach and it is supported and led by management.

Layers in the hierarchy The length of chain of command or distance can affect communication. If information is passed down by word of mouth through a number of receivers, it is possible for the message to be distorted. This may result in the wrong emphasis or wrong information being received by the individual or group at the end of the communication chain. Industrial relations problems in business have sometimes been a result of a long chain of command. A long chain of command may also prevent effective feedback. Some businesses have delayered their organisations. Removing a layer of the hierarchy

Question 2.

Juan Parente moved from Madrid to Leeds 10 years ago, first to work in the kitchens of a Spanish restaurant and then to open his own restaurant. A year ago, he employed Jason Belfield as an assistant chef. Initially, everything went well but, three months ago, Jason began being late for work once or twice a week. Juan took Jason aside and gave him a severe reprimand, but Jason found it difficult to understand everything Juan was saying because he spoke English with a Spanish accent and included Spanish words in sentences. As time went on, Juan became more angry with Jason's timekeeping and informed him that he may be faced with disciplinary action. Matters came to a head when Jason arrived an hour late on a day when the restaurant was fully booked for the evening and another member of the kitchen staff was off sick. For Juan, the reputation of the restaurant was at stake.

Jason began to dislike working at the restaurant. Three months ago, Jason's mother had fallen seriously ill and he had found it difficult juggling work with hospital appointments and caring for her. He had confided in Emily, another assistant chef, but she did not tell Juan about Jason's problem. The day the restaurant was fully booked Juan was incensed by Jason's lateness, but Jason could only think of his mother lying ill at home. At that moment in time, he didn't care about the restaurant and its reputation.

(a) Explain what barriers to communication existed between Juan and Jason.

(b) Discuss how these barriers to communication could have been overcome for the benefit of both Juan and Jason.

could help to ensure that the message is communicated more quickly and becomes less distorted.

Breakdown of the channel This could be due to technical problems. For example, a business may rely on its management information system on the computerised network. If this breaks down, businesses might have problems dealing with enquiries. Banks, for example, are unable to tell customers what their balances are if computer terminals are not working.

Different countries, languages and cultures A business may have a problem sending a message from one country to another because of time differences. This is particularly a difficulty if an urgent decision is needed. Languages may also be different. The use of ICT, as explained later, may help to prevent this problem to some extent. There could be problems if communication about technical details needed to be explained. The solution may be to ensure communications are multilingual.

Individual cultural traits can also sometimes affect communication. A study of North and South American business people found that they each had different 'conversation distances'. In meetings, problems developed as South American business people came towards people they were talking to, while North Americans retreated. This is often problem for multinational organisations, where operations in different countries behave in different ways. Establishing a common corporate culture and training workers in a shared corporate culture which everyone understands may help to prevent this difficulty.

Intermediaries When there are intermediaries, messages can become distorted, as in a game of 'Chinese whispers'. The more complex the message, the more likely it is to be altered as it passes through a chain of communication. For example, the managing director of a company telling the board of directors that there 'may be redundancies in the future' could easily leak out and become, after many tellings, that there 'will be large scale redundancies now'.

Too many meetings In large businesses, there tends to be far more meetings per employee than in small businesses. Meetings are essential for effective communication. However, they can be unproductive. Some employees will be invited to a meeting although they will have little interest or understanding of the issues to be discussed. Meetings tend to go on far too long, with some employees talking too much and not concentrating on the issues in hand. Meetings may also involve unproductive travel. For example, a meeting of seven employees from different sites in the UK may take place at head office. Those involved may spend a whole day in travelling to and from a meeting which lasts perhaps only four hours. Those attending meetings will also need to be paid travel expenses, further adding to costs.

There are several possible solutions to these problems. Businesses can adopt policies which limit the number and length of meetings and the number of employees taking part. Equally, it is becoming increasingly easy to arrange telephone or video conferences to link up employees in different parts of the country or the world or simply a large site. Some businesses are able to hold meetings online through their company intranets sites or using email.

Lack of common sense of purpose When workers lack a common sense of purpose, they can often misinterpret messages. For example, an administrator in the accounts department may receive a message from the finance director that late payment of invoices must be chased up more vigourously. The administrator may know that the business is experiencing cash flow problems and therefore needs to increase its inflow of cash quickly. At the same time, the marketing director is trying to expand sales to existing customers. In the event, the measures taken are too tough. Long standing large customers are threatened with being taken to court if they don't pay now, while other late paying customers are refused further trade credit. Although invoices are now paid more promptly, the company loses customers and the marketing director is furious. The administrator has misunderstood the message given because she failed to reconcile the goals of the marketing director with those of the finance director.

Equally, different stakeholders often have different aims and objectives, which can lead to problems. For example, local residents fighting against the siting of a waste disposal factory in an area might interpret figures on pollution caused by the factory differently to the owners of the factory. The owners might argue that the figures for pollution are acceptable, whereas local residents might not.

Over-reliance on written communication In a small business, it is easy for workers to talk to each other face to face on a day-to-day basis. In a large company, with perhaps thousands of employees and a number of different site locations, face-to-face contact becomes more difficult. Hence, workers rely much more heavily on written communication, including email. Written communication, however, has its limitations. Messages can be misinterpreted because, unlike face-to-face communication, feedback is often slow and the signals that come from body language are missing. In large businesses, there can be an over-reliance on written communication.

Use of information and communication technology Although new technologies can help communication, there are problems both with the amount of information sent and the use of **information and communication technology** (ICT).

- **Information overload.** Large amounts of information can be sent instantly by such media as fax, email and the Internet. This may result in information overload. Individuals and organisations may not be able to fully process all of the information that is sent. As a result, effective communication may not take place.
- **Introduction.** Electronic media can sometimes create problems when they are first introduced. Staff need

training, which is time consuming. Mistakes can be made if information is not stored, as there may be no written record. There may also need to be a change in working methods and employees may work at a slower pace as they get used to the new methods and equipment.

- **Misuse of new technology.** There is evidence to suggest that employees spend more time using the Internet and email facilities than is necessary. 'Browsing' the Internet and constantly checking email for new messages can waste time. Employees may also use the technology for non-business messages.
- **Confidentiality.** Electronic media often send messages that can be seen be people other than the intended receiver. This can be a problem if the sender wants the message to remain confidential.
- **Viruses.** Computer viruses can damage information kept on computers, although it is possible to protect information by using software.

Preventing technical problems which result in communication breakdowns may simply require regular updates of machinery and software or effective maintenance. But training may also be needed to ensure that employees know how to use communication media effectively. As communication technology changes rapidly, training needs regularly updating.

Factors affecting choice of medium

There is a number of factors that affect which medium a business will use in any situation.

- Direction of communication. Some methods may only be suitable for downward communication, such as films and posters. Other methods are useful for upwards communication only, such as suggestion schemes. Many methods are useful for both.
- Nature of the communication. The choice of communication method may depend on the nature of the message being sent. For example, a comment from a manager to a subordinate about unsatisfactory work may need to be confidential. It is important for the manager to choose a method which does this.
- Many messages are best sent by the use of more than one communication medium. Company rules, for example, might most effectively be communicated verbally on an induction course and as a written summary for employees to take away as a reminder.
- Costs. Films, videos and some tapeslides can be expensive. A business must decide whether the message could be sent just as well by other media.
- Variety. If, for example, a company tries to communicate too many messages by means of a noticeboard, then employees may stop reading it. To make sure messages are sent effectively, a variety of media should be used.
- Speed. If something needs communicating immediately then verbal or electronic communications tend to be quickest.
- Is a record needed? If it is, there is no point in verbally passing on the information. If it is communicated verbally, it may need written confirmation.
- Length of message. If the message is long, verbal communication may mean the receiver does not remember everything that has been said. If a simple yes or no answer is needed, written communication might not be suitable.
- Who will receive the message? The sender must consider how many people will receive the message. She must also take into account where the receiver will be and whether there is access to a means of communication.

Management information systems

A management information system (MIS) in a business is an ICT system that supplies information and communication services. It usually takes the form of integrated programmes and applications that deal with:

- order transactions;
- project planning;
- co-operative work support, such as networked schedules and diaries;
- personnel and customer databases;
- programmes to assist decision making, which pull together key performance indicators of the organisation.

The applications use both automated and manual procedures. In a well designed MIS, the different applications are not independent. They are interconnected subsystems that form a coherent, overall, integrated structure for information and communication services. An effective MIS system can help an organisation improve productivity. It should increase the amount and speed of information that can be communicated and also help to improve the quality and scope of management decisions.

Communication networks

Communication takes place between different individuals and parts of a business and between a business and outside bodies. There are advantages and disadvantages to a business of using different types of COMMUNICATION NETWORK.

The circle In a circle, sections, departments etc. can communicate with only two others, as shown Figure 3a. This type of communication may occur between middle managers from different departments at the same level of the organisation. The main problem with this type of network is that decision making can be slow or poor because of a lack of co-ordination. If middle managers from different departments had been given the task of increasing sales and profits in the short term, they may have difficulty developing a strategy that all would agree on.

The chain The chain (Figure 3b) is where one person passes information to others, who then pass it on. This approach tends to be the formal approach adopted by hierarchical organisations, such as the Civil Service. The main advantage is that there is a leader/co-ordinator at the top of the hierarchy who can oversee communications downwards and upwards to different areas of the business. One problem may be the isolation felt by those at the bottom of the network. Their motivation may be less than others if they feel at the periphery. This network does not encourage lateral communication.

The wheel In the wheel pattern (Figure 3) there is a person, group or department that occupies a central position. This network is particularly good at solving problems. If, for example, the North West region of an insurance company had been asked to increase sales by central office, then the North West regional manager would be at the centre of policy initiative communicating with local managers about the best way forward. The leader in this network is the regional manager.

A connected or 'all channel' network The 'all channel' communication system (Figure 3d) might be used in small group workings. With its participatory style, and more open communication system, the connected network provides the best solutions to complex problems. This type of network might be used, for example, when a department needs to 'brainstorm'. Its disadvantages are that it is slow and that it tends to disintegrate under time pressure to get results when operated in a group.

One solution to the problem of passing complex communications has been solved by the use of information and communication technology. A complex connected network can be set up where instructions and information are passed between many people or departments, or even parts of a business overseas.

Figure 3: Communication networks

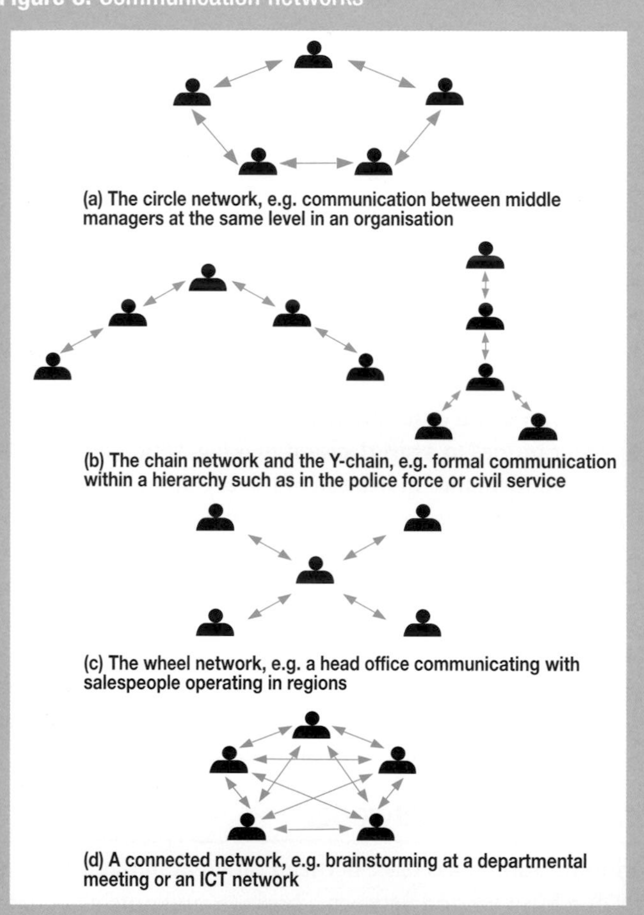

(a) The circle network, e.g. communication between middle managers at the same level in an organisation

(b) The chain network and the Y-chain, e.g. formal communication within a hierarchy such as in the police force or civil service

(c) The wheel network, e.g. a head office communicating with salespeople operating in regions

(d) A connected network, e.g. brainstorming at a departmental meeting or an ICT network

KEYTERMS

Communication – the sending and receiving of messages between two or more individuals, groups or organisations.
Channel of communication – the route by which a message is communicated from sender to receiver.
Communication media – the written, oral or technological methods used to communicate a message.
Internet – the worldwide web, which allows information to be accessed and communicated by computer throughout the world.
Lateral communication – when there is communication between employees and departments at a similar level in the organisational hierarchy.
Vertical communication – when there is communication up and down the hierarchy.

KNOWLEDGE

1. Why is good communication important for a business?
2. Why might a business want feedback in the communication process?
3. Explain the difference between:
   (a) formal and informal communication;
   (b) lateral and vertical communication;
   (c) internal and external communication;
   (d) the channel of communication and the medium of communication
4. How might upward communication be useful to a business?
5. How does effective communication motivate workers according to (a) Maslow and (b) Herzberg?
6. How might (a) working in a team and (b) single status organisations improve communication?
7. Explain why the following might be a barrier to communication within a business:
   (a) a subordinate who does not trust the judgment of his boss;
   (b) a long chain of command;
   (c) a place of work in the UK where for half the workers English is not their first language;
   (d) management deciding that quality is the main priority in production whilst production workers are mainly motivated by their pay.
8. Explain why a large business might face more communication problems than a small business because of the following:
   (a) the amount of information available;
   (b) the length of the chain of command;
   (c) the increased percentage of written rather than oral communication;
   (d) use of ICT;
   (e) meetings;
   (f) cultural and linguistic differences.

Case Study: Jennings Brewery Distribution Depot

'If there's something wrong, I was usually the last person to know about it; messages from the pubs never seemed to be getting through to the right people.' This was one of the first comments Jerome Rogers heard when he took over as distribution manager of Jenning's Brewery, a medium sized business located in Essex, which served the East Anglia region.

The comment was made by one of the local planners in the large distribution depot of the brewery. Jerome was carrying out a series of interviews with his staff to find out both his own workforce's and the publicans' views about how the depot was operating.

The present system was that when the telephone rang in the office with an order any one of the four assistants would answer it. The load planners would then try to group orders together, but there were no regular delivery rounds. The supervisor prided himself on getting orders out quickly – he would give them out on a random basis to the delivery workers who, therefore, rarely made regular visits to one set of pubs.

Through his interviews, Jerome detected a number of problems with the system. He had previously worked in a small brewery where everyone was on first name terms and where good communications with customers was a major objective. He was surprised with the contrast between Pearson's and his old company.

Jerome felt that some way of informing all employees in the depot about its operation may help to develop a corporate culture of unity. He was also looking for ways to keep in more regular contact with head office so that he might advise them of progress and perhaps receive some help with problems.

Depot organisation

The depot's organisation was divided into three sections.

- In the office were four clerical assistants who took incoming calls from the publicans whom the brewery supplied. The publicans usually phoned in their weekly orders, but would also phone if deliveries were late or incomplete.
- Also in the office, but in a sectioned off area, were four load planners who worked at computer terminals, sorting and organising the delivery loads between pubs.
- In the rest of the depot there were 65 delivery employees who carried out the deliveries to the pubs. They communicated with the office via their supervisor, who collected the delivery plans at the start of the day and gave them to the employees making the deliveries.

Results from interviews

- Deliveries were often late. The delivery workers were not very motivated by the work and would 'spin out' a delivery in order to earn overtime.
- Communication between the office and the delivery workers was poor, resulting in poor relations between the two groups.
- Within the office the two groups appeared to work in isolation. Each did not know what the other group was doing.
- Publicans felt that there was a lack of interest in their problems. If publicans phoned in on Friday with a rush order, or to find out why a delivery had not been made, they got the impression that no-one wanted to help them.
- If there was a problem it was impossible to contact the delivery employees. For example, if someone in the depot noticed stock was left behind, he or she could not contact the driver to return to make up the incomplete order.
- There was often no written record of the orders that were phoned in by the publicans.

(a) Identify the communication problems that exist at Jenning's Brewery. (4 marks)

(b) Explain why these problems exist. (8 marks)

(c) Explain how the business might inform the workforce about possible solutions to the communication problems. (8 marks)

(d) Suggest possible solutions to the communication problems at the business. (10 marks)

(d) Assess the effects on the business of these solutions. (10 marks)

77 Representation at work

Employers and employees

EMPLOYERS are businesses or other organisations, such as government, which hire workers to work for them. An employee is a worker hired to work for a business or other organisation. Both employers and employees may feel that it is important for workers' views to be heard and taken into account in the workplace. Workers may be more motivated and employers may benefit as a result, for example. Workers therefore need effective EMPLOYEE REPRESENTATION at work. They need groups or forums both within and outside the organisation to speak with authority on their behalf.

INDUSTRIAL DEMOCRACY is where employees are given the right to elect representatives who will be directly involved in the internal decision making of the business. There is a variety of ways in which employees can be represented in an organisation.

Trade unions

These are perhaps the best known of the representative bodies. TRADE UNIONS are organisations of workers who join together to further their own interests. Trade unions have existed in the UK for over 200 years. Early unions were made up of workers with similar skills and interests, for example the General Union of Operative Spinners set up in 1829. Over time, their **objectives** or goals have remained broadly the same, although the importance of any single objective may differ from union to union. Their main objectives are to:

- secure high wages and maximise other financial and non-financial benefits for their members;
- prevent the loss of their members' jobs;
- gain safe working conditions;
- see that their members are entitled to welfare benefits if they fall ill, become unemployed or retire;
- provide a range of other services which might increase the welfare of their members;
- fight for causes, such as improved public services or nuclear disarmament or the election of a political party which their members support.

The functions of trade unions

Trade unions have a number of functions. These functions allow unions to achieve their objectives.

- They negotiate with employers on behalf of their members in the workplace. This is known as **collective bargaining**. Negotiations include everything from pay rates to conditions of service, redundancies and health and safety.
- They represent individual members in cases such as discrimination and dismissal. This may involve negotiating with the employer. If this fails, the union may pay to have the member represented at an **employment tribunal** or a

Question 1.

Eurotunnel is the operator of the high speed shuttle service which links the UK to France. It has a 99 year lease to operate the Channel Tunnel link, running freight trains and maintaining the infrastructure. It employs 3,400 people, of which about 1,400 are based in the UK on British contracts. To harmonise the workforce, management set up a company council in 1992.

Until June 2000 the company only recognised the council for consultation. But after the Employment Relations Act, 1999, it signed a recognition agreement with the T&G (Transport and General Workers Union) and a single partnership deal to cover all non-managerial employees and a joint management-union negotiating forum. The company suggested that the threat of industrial action and having to negotiate with many different unions swayed its decision, and the fact that the costs involved of action and negotiations would affect a company already £6.5 billion in debt. There were now two negotiating bodies - the council, representing all employees, and the TU forum, representing union members with sole negotiating rights over pay and conditions.

Two surveys were carried out, one just before recognition and the other 18 months after. Certain results were found.

- About 35 per cent of employees said they were union members in the second survey, but only 12 per cent in the first.
- Over 50 per cent of employees said there was an active union presence in the second survey compared to 6 per cent in the first.
- In the first survey there had been strong support for unions in all sections at Eurotunnel. Most said that unions would improve their pay and benefits (over 70 per cent), work conditions (75 per cent), health and safety, and grievances. In the second survey fewer than a third agreed that the T&G had been effective in representing employee interests and only 10 per cent said that the union had improved pay and benefits.
- Most employees wanted the council to be retained. But this was not a vote to replace the TU forum, as employees agreed the council had largely been ineffective as well.

Source: adapted from *People Management*.

(a) (i) Explain how the role of trade unions changed at Eurotunnel.
(ii) Examine the reasons for these changes.
(b) Discuss to what extent employee representation was affected as a result of the changes at Eurotunnel.

court of law.
- They provide members with a range of benefits. These vary enormously from union to union, but they tend to include free legal representation and access to cheap insurance and credit cards.
- They act as a **pressure group** to influence the behaviour of businesses in general, as well as to affect government and the law. Since the beginning of the twentieth century, major trade unions have sponsored Labour MPs and the trade union movement still plays an important role within the Labour Party.
- Trade unions are also responsible, along with management, for INDUSTRIAL RELATIONS. They communicate their members' wishes to employers and try to negotiate the most favourable conditions. However, successful industrial relations means that each party must take into account the wishes of the other when bargaining. It may not be in members' interests for a union to push for a longer work break if this reduces the efficiency of the business, perhaps resulting in job losses in future. However, it may not be in employers' interests to reduce breaks, even if this cuts costs, if it results in worker dissatisfaction.

The organisation of trade unions

In 2008, there were 174 trade unions in the UK. They vary enormously in size and in the way they are organised. However, they can grouped into different **types** of union.

Craft or skill unions These unions represent workers who have a particular craft or skill. For example, musicians can join the Musicians Union, journalists can join the National Union of Journalists and bakers can join the Bakers, Food and Allied Workers Union. Craft unions are the oldest type of union in the UK.

Industrial unions These unions represent workers in a single industry. They don't necessarily represent all the workers in the industry, but they don't accept members from outside of that industry. Examples are the National Union of Mineworkers, the Firebrigades' Union and the National Union of Teachers.

General unions General unions represent workers from different industries and different types of workers. General unions, traditionally, recruited from unskilled workers. However, over the past 20 years there has been a trend for unions to merge to create general unions which represent both skilled and unskilled workers, and blue-collar and white-collar workers. An example in 2007 was the creation of Unite. With its two million members, Unite would be the main trade union in the manufacturing, transport, finance, food and agriculture and printing industries.

White-collar unions These unions represent white-collar workers. Until the 1950s and 1960s, most union members were blue-collar workers. Hence, white-collar unions were seen as a separate type of union. Today, most union members are white-collar workers. It can be argued that all white-collar unions, such as Unison or the National Union of Teachers, can be placed into one of the three types of Craft, Industrial and General Union.

The organisation of a trade union varies. However, in a typical trade union there will be both voluntary and full-time trade union workers. **Shop stewards** or **trade union representatives** are ordinary workers elected within a place of work by members. This group of workers is sometimes called a **branch** of the union. The role of shop stewards is to represent workers' interests to management on issues such as pay, redundancies and working conditions. They also represent the interests of their members at local, regional or national meetings of the union. Shop stewards are typically unpaid volunteers who work for the union in their own time.

Full-time officials are paid officials of the union who work full time for the union. They will be based in offices of the union. They specialise in a particular type of union work, such as recruitment, training or legal advice. The most important full-time official will be the leader of the union, whose title varies from union to union, but is often called the **General Secretary** of the union. The General Secretary is elected by a postal ballot of all members.

Changing industrial relations and the effects on business

Industrial relations have changed over the last 40-50 years. This has been caused by changes in the power and role of trade unions, legislation and views on human resources management. These changes have affected businesses in a variety of ways.

Membership and union density Trade union membership has been in decline since the late 1970s as shown in Figure 1. Trade

Figure 1 Trade unions membership and number of unions 1975-2008

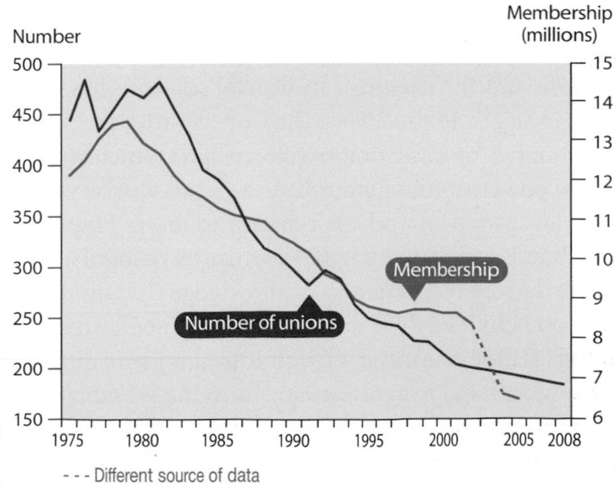

Source: adapted from dti, Certification Office, BERR.

unions have traditionally been strong in primary and secondary industries and public sector services. Also, membership in the past tended to be dominated by male workers. But changes in the make-up of the workforce have altered the pattern of trade union membership. There has been a significant reduction in employment in primary and secondary industries, which has contributed to a decline in overall membership of unions in the UK. Partly this has been due to growing competition from foreign companies and the trend towards globalisation. The largest growth in the workforce has come from private sector service industries where trade unions have traditionally been weak. Moreover, there has been a shift in employment between males and females. In the past there were far more male than female trade union members partly because primary and secondary industries were male dominated. Jobs created in the last 20 years have been predominantly in the service sector and have been often taken by female workers.

Trends in union membership can be seen in the changes in UNION DENSITY, the proportion of any workforce that belongs to a trade union, in the UK. The formula for calculating union density is:

$$\text{Union density} = \frac{\text{number of union members}}{\text{number of workers in the workforce}} \times 100\%$$

Figure 2 shows that trade union density has fallen consistently. It fell from 32 per cent at the end of 1997 to around 27 per cent in 2006. This was because over the period the number of union members fell, but the number of workers in the workforce rose. In contrast, union density amongst female workers was greater in 2006 than in 1997. It has been suggested that the fall in union membership and union density have contributed to a reduction in the power of trade unions. Figure 3 shows that trade union density for both men and women is far greater in the public sector than in the private sector. This might suggest that unions could have greater influence on employers in the public sector.

Legislation Another important factor in changing the power of trade unions and the nature of industrial relations has been legislative changes. In the 1980s, the Conservative government passed a number of trade union 'reform' laws which effectively curbed the power of trade unions. As a result, workers saw unions as less powerful and less relevant to them. Employers, on the other hand, were encouraged to refuse to **recognise** unions in their workplace (i.e. refuse to acknowledge that unions could negotiate on behalf of their members through collective bargaining). Trade unions as a result found it more difficult to recruit members and to represent them in the workplace.

However, in the late 1990s and the early twenty-first century changes in legislation may have led to unions regaining some of their ability to influence business. For example, the **Employment Relations Act, 1999** allowed employees to vote for trade union recognition. Employers could be compelled to recognise unions for collective bargaining under certain conditions. Applications for union recognition are made to the **Central Arbitration Committee** (CAC). This is an independent body designed to provide guidance on union recognition and make judgments about recognition if disputes occur between employees and employers. This Act led businesses to increasingly recognise unions in the early twenty-first century.

Human resource management Human resource management philosophy in the last two decades has emphasised the need for individual pay bargaining and flexible workforces. Traditional union goals of nationwide pay agreements with workers getting the same rate of pay whatever their performance were seen as outdated. Moreover, the 'them and us' philosophy, associated

Figure 2 Trade union density, 1995-2006

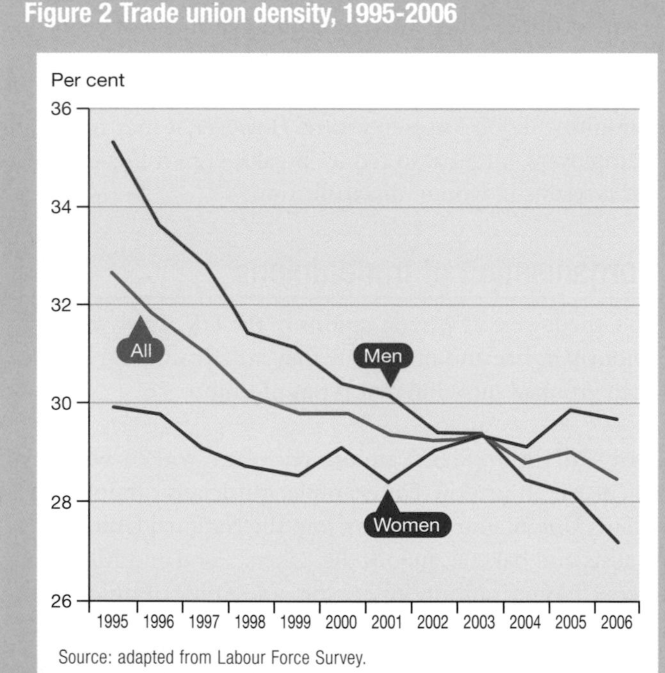

Source: adapted from Labour Force Survey.

Figure 3 Trade union density by sector, 2006

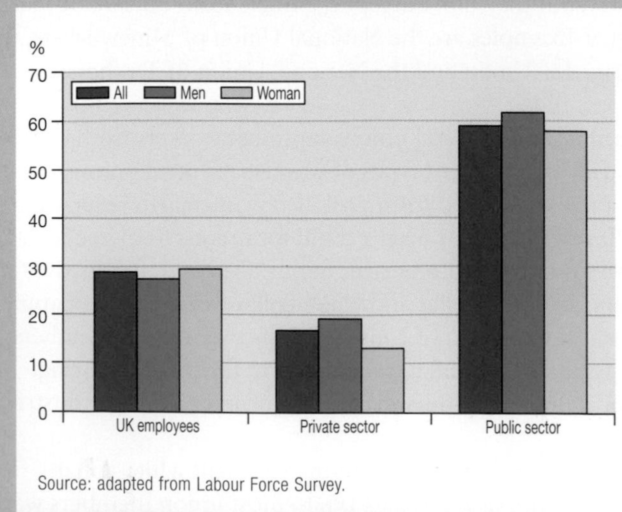

Source: adapted from Labour Force Survey.

with traditional trade unionism, was seen as contrary to a human resource management perspective, which suggested that the goals of workers should be aligned with the goals of the business. Existing employers were therefore encouraged by this to abandon or limit collective bargaining agreements. New businesses may have not recognised trade unions. The number of workers covered by collective bargaining agreements fell from 71 per cent to below 35 per cent in the 25 years before 2006. All this meant that trade unions may have found it more difficult to recruit members in private sector industry.

The overall result is that trade unions are active and recognised in a smaller percentage of businesses than they were 30 years ago. In some businesses, workers are unrepresented and are subject to individual bargaining procedures. Where trade unions are recognised, there has been a significant change in industrial relations.

- Industrial action is rarer. Confrontational approaches to problems are less common. Trade unions in particular recognise that it is in their interests to reach negotiated settlements. There is a much greater realism on the part of trade unions that their actions can make businesses less competitive, putting their members' jobs at risk. Equally, more businesses have recognised that by working with rather than against trade unions, they can improve industrial relations. Trade unions can play a useful role in channelling workers' demands and in reducing the number of negotiating partners for the business. They can also exercise some discipline over their members, helping them to see what is reasonable and unreasonable.
- Some businesses have formalised their relationships with unions by signing a **partnership agreement**. Such agreements lay out medium to long-term plans for industrial relations. They vary from business to business. But they typically cover pay, conditions of work, employment and training. For example, a business may agree that there will be no compulsory redundancies in return for trade unions agreeing to changes in working practices. Or a more flexible working year for workers might be agreed in the context of a three year pay deal.
- In a few high profile cases, some businesses and unions have signed a SINGLE UNION AGREEMENT. A business agrees to recognise only one trade union for collective bargaining purposes. In return, that trade union agrees to a range of conditions about how it will operate. For example, it might sign a NO STRIKE AGREEMENT where it agrees never to bring its members out on strike. Or it might agree to **flexible working practices**. Single union agreements are controversial amongst trade unions. Other trade unions will be excluded from representing workers in that business. If every business concluded single union agreements, there would be major winners and losers amongst trade unions for members. What is more, many trade unionists see single union agreements as a 'sell out' to management. They argue that workers' interests are damaged because a union, to get a single union agreement, has to agree to unfavourable terms with the employer. In practice, single union agreements and no strike agreements have not given businesses a clear competitive advantage. For this reason, they remain the exception rather than the norm in British industry.

The number of unions The number of trade unions in the UK has fallen greatly since the 1970s. In 1975 there were 446. This had fallen to 213 in 2002. In 2008 there were 174 listed by the Certification Officer. This has been almost entirely due to merger activity. As union membership has shrunk and total subscriptions have fallen, trade unions have found it more difficult financially to cope. By combining, they have been able to spread their overhead costs more and so survive financially. Equally, it can be argued that larger trade unions are able to give a better service to their members than very small trade unions. They are able to employ specialist staff and campaign more effectively than smaller unions. It can also be argued that very small unions do not have the industrial strength to be as effective in collective bargaining as larger unions.

Figure 4 Union collective agreements, coverage and presence

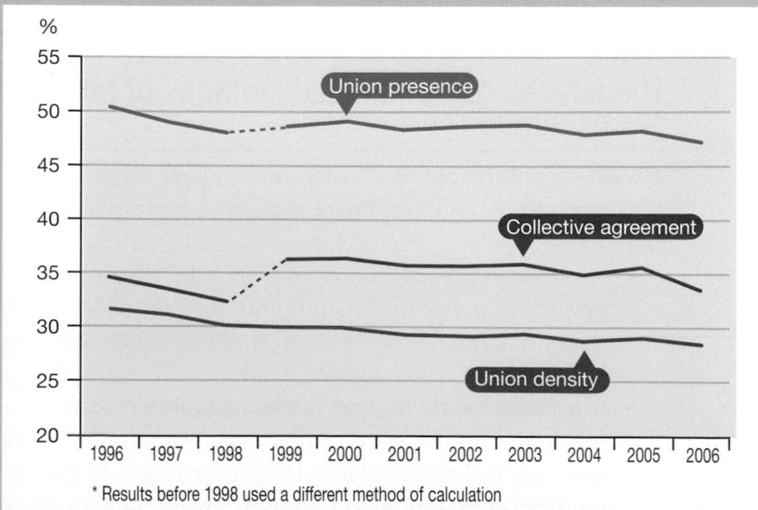

Staff associations

Staff associations represent workers, but tend to perform only some of those functions carried out by trade unions. These might include consultation and bargaining with management. Their members are often made up of workers in a particular business. Examples of staff associations are the Retail Book, Stationery and Allied Trades Employees Association (RBA) or the Balfour Beatty Group Staff Association. In some cases staff associations develop into trade unions. Some associations are affiliated to the TUC, such as the Gallaher Sales Staff Association.

Professional associations

Professional associations perform similar functions to trade unions and sometimes become TUC members. They represent 'professional' occupations. Examples include the British Dental Association, the Prison Officers Association and the Professional Footballers' Association. Some associations, such as the British Medical Association (BMA), represent their members in collective bargaining with employers. They are also responsible for the setting and maintaining of standards. For example, the BMA insists on certain qualifications before admitting employees to its membership. For this reason professional associations tend to be associated with 'white-collar' workers and higher paid groups of employees.

The TUC

The Trades Union Congress (TUC) is an organisation which represents all major trade unions in the UK. In 2008 its 66 affiliated unions had nearly seven million members. There were also around 180 unions outside the TUC.

Each year a conference is held and TUC policy is decided. Member unions send delegates to the conference, the number sent depending on the size of the union. The conference also elects the General Council of the TUC. This is responsible for carrying out policy and running TUC affairs in between conferences. A General Secretary is elected, who is often seen as the mouthpiece of the TUC and is directly involved in TUC negotiations with member unions and government. The TUC has a permanent staff which deals with the day to day issues in between the annual Congress.

In the 1980s and early 1990s the TUC was excluded from consultation by government. Since the mid-1990s, however, it has been involved in a number of new initiatives. For example, it has worked with government and the CBI to encourage **partnerships** in business.

In 2008 the main functions of the TUC were to:
- bring Britain's unions together to draw up common policies and avoid clashes with each other;
- lobby government to implement policies that will benefit people at work;
- campaign on economic and social issues;
- represent working people on public bodies and British workers in international bodies in the European Union and the International Labour Organisation;
- carry out research on employment related issues;
- run training and education programmes for union representatives;
- help unions develop new services for their members;
- build links with other trade union bodies worldwide.

Employers' organisations

Just as certain bodies represent workers, there are organisations which help and support employers. They are often useful for small firms that may be negotiating with a large union. These organisations give advice to employers about collective bargaining and help with technical problems and overseas trade. They may also provide research and training facilities and act as a pressure group for industries. Examples include the Newspaper Society (NS) and the Engineering Employers' Federation (EEF).

The CBI

The Confederation of British Industry (CBI) was formed in 1965. It has a similar role to the TUC, but voices the opinions of employers rather than union members. CBI membership is drawn from private sector industry, service and commercial enterprises, major public sector employers, and some employers' associations, trade associations and Chambers of Commerce.

The internal organisation of the CBI is complex, but it has a ruling council which decides on policy. It also employs permanent staff, headed by the Director General. Detailed policy proposals are examined by standing committees. The CBI is organised to deal with local and area issues through its regional councils. These aim to keep in touch with the needs of small firms and local employers and help them solve their day to day business problems. The membership services of the CBI are wide ranging, both nationally and locally, and are backed up by skilled professional advice from lawyers, accountants and tax specialists.

What role does the CBI have? It attempts to represent its members' interests in a number of ways.
- Government policy. Just like the TUC, it attempts to influence government policy.
- Services. It provides legal, financial and economic advice to its members.
- Local businesses. It provides support and advice to local businesses through its regional offices.
- Through its office in Brussels, the CBI acts in the interests of British industry in the European Union.
- Trade unions. The CBI works with the TUC on consultative bodies such as ACAS.
- Other groups. The CBI provides information for a variety of other organisations and the public in general.

The advantages and disadvantages of employee representation

Advantages Employee representation can have certain advantages for employees. There may also be advantages for employers.
- Representation can lead to workers achieving higher rewards or better work conditions, for example, if a strong union or employee association supports their claims for higher wages.
- If workers feel their views are being represented to employers, and employers are paying attention to them, they may feel more valued. This in turn leads to greater motivation for employees. Employers may benefit from higher output as a result. It can also lead to benefits such as

lower absenteeism and lower turnover of staff.

- Representation can lead to a greater use of the ideas of the workforce. Employee representation can increase the ability of employees to contribute effectively to the business. It encourages a greater interchange of information and ideas within a business. With more information and ideas, it may be easier to make the correct decision on any issue. For example, employees may be able to assess changes in the workplace more easily than employers who are not directly involved in the day-to-day operation of certain aspects of the business.
- Employers may be more sympathetic to the needs of employees. This may help when making decisions. For example, it may put them in a better position to decide if changes are going to cause disruption or unrest.
- It can help a business to develop a common culture and allow a business to achieve its objectives.

Disadvantages Employee participation can also have its disadvantages for both employees and employers.

- The decision making process can be slowed down. If employee's views are constantly being taken into account, it may take several times as long to come up with a decision compared to employers simply making a decision that best suits their needs. This is particularly important at times of crisis when decisions have to be made quickly or even instantly.
- It can be expensive and time consuming. There may be constant meetings with employee representatives. Employees may need to be given time off for union training or meetings, which can delay production.
- It may lead to conflict. Employees represented by a strong organisation at work are likely to have more influence than individual workers. Employers' objectives and those of employees may differ. This could lead to industrial action.
- Some employees will pursue their own interests at the expense of the interests of the business when given the opportunity. Employee respresentation can give them more opportunity to do this.
- Employee representation may encourage workers to believe they have more power than they actually have. This may lead to demotivation when they feel that their advice is not being acted upon.

Question 2.

The Employment Relations Acts of 1999 and 2004 were legislation that enable union recognition. In some cases it would be statutory, for example if certain conditions are met, such as the union having 10 per cent membership and be likely to attract the majority of support in a ballot. In 2006 employees at Newsquest Printing Limited in Colchester, voted 100 per cent in favour of union recognition for Amicus (which became part of the trade union Unite in 2007). Amicus had recognition at the majority of Newsquest's printing plants throughout the UK and there were negotiations taking place at other Newsquest sites to establish recognition agreements. Even though 80 per cent of the workers in the 'bargaining unit' were Amicus members, the company still wanted a ballot. Amicus Branch Organiser, Dave Monaghan, was confident that Amicus could win but the result was even better than he had expected. There was a 91.4 per cent turnout and of the 53 votes cast, all were in favour of recognition. Amicus National Officer, Steve Sibbald, said 'I can't recall the last time we had a 100 per cent vote in favour. There are many occasions when it is over 90 per cent but the unanimous endorsement is better than we could have hoped for. We will now be working hard to establish sound and lasting structures within the company in order to promote a mutually beneficial relationship.'

Source: adapted from www.berr.gov.uk, www.amicustheunion.org.

(a) Explain the factors that may have influenced employee representation at Newsquest Printing Limited.

(b) Discuss whether employee representation will benefit the business in future.

KEYTERMS

Employee – a worker hired to work for a business or other organisation.

Employers – businesses or other organisations which hire workers to work for them.

Employee representation – the 'standing in' for employees and speaking with authority on their behalf.

Industrial democracy – where workers are given the right to elect representatives who will be directly involved in the internal decision making of a business, including the highest levels of the business.

No strike agreement – an agreement between unions and an employer that industrial disputes will not lead to any form of strike action by employees.

Single union agreement – an agreement between an employer and a trade union that only that trade union will be recognised for collective bargaining purposes; it effectively means that other trade unions cannot organise in that business and the business only has to negotiate with one union.

Trade unions – organisations of workers which exist to promote the interests of their members.

Industrial relations – the relationship between employers and employees, particularly groups of workers represented by a union.

Union density – the percentage of any given workforce that belongs to a trade union.

KNOWLEDGE

1. What is the difference between an employee and an employer?
2. State three objectives of trade unions.
3. State three functions of trade unions.
4. Explain two ways in which changes in union density have affected employee presentation.
5. How did the Industrial Relations Act, 1999 affect employee representation?
6. Explain the difference between a professional association and an employers' association.
7. What are the main functions of the TUC?
8. What are the main functions of the CBI?
9. State three advantages of employee representation.
10. State three disadvantages of employee representation.

Case Study: Ryanair

Ryanair is a fast-growing Irish airline company. It has based its success on offering low fares for a basic service. Costs compared to a traditional airline are low per passenger mile travelled and food, for example, is not offered for free on any flight.

The company has had a difficult relationship with trade unions. Its policy is not to recognise trade unions. Instead, it prefers to bargain with individual employees, or use the Employee Representative Committees it has established to communicate with workers. It has gained a reputation for dealing aggressively with trade unions that attempt either to gain recognition or influence the activities of the company. It has also been argued that individual employees who attempt to organise collectively are dealt with in a punitive manner.

For example, in January 2005, The Irish Airline Pilots Union (IALPA) argued successfully before the Labour Court in Ireland that Ryanair pilots should be given a copy of their Terms and Conditions of Employment. This ruling also meant that a complaint of victimisation in the workplace could be heard by an Irish Rights Commissioner. The complaints centred around training for flying new aircraft. Pilots had been informed by Ryanair that if they joined a trade union over the next five years they would have to commit to paying a bond of €15 000 (£10 000) for training to fly the new aircraft which is being introduced into the Ryanair fleet. If they did not undertake the training, the pilots were told they faced redundancy when the older aircraft were phased out. Others reported threats including no pay increases, no promotions, cancellation of staff travel and increased restrictions on taking holidays.

'Ryan be fair', a website critical of Ryanair employment practices, also claimed in 2004 that Ryanair was recruiting in Eastern Europe to cut wages. It said that an 'English language school' had been established in Poland where participants paid €1,900 (£1 200) for a place on a course. Some of the participants were then offered a three year employment contract with a firm called 'Crewlink', which in turn leased out the workers to Ryanair. They received two-thirds of the pay of normal European Ryanair cabin crew staff.

Ryanair claims that its average wages per employee are higher than comparable unionised airlines. In September 2004, for example, it claimed that its staff earned an average of €50,582 a year, compared to the heavily unionised Scandinavian airline SAS which paid €50,425. Trade unions pointed out that Ryanair tends to contract out a number of services which use a high proportion of low-paid workers compared to normal airlines. Not directly employing the same proportion of relatively lowly-paid ground staff would automatically boost the average wage at Ryanair.

Ryanair also claims that its employment practices have benefited customers through lower prices. Speaking about a dispute with Siptu, an Irish trade union representing baggage handlers at Dublin Airport, Michael O'Leary, Chief Executive of Ryanair, said 'Siptu is the union that was quite happy to have £200 airfares and a monopoly (of airline flights) in and out of Ireland'. Driving down costs is central to the Ryanair strategy of competing against other low-cost airlines. The 21 per cent increase in productivity achieved by staff in 2003 compared to the 3 per cent pay increase they received was one part of this relentless drive to cut costs.

Sources: adapted from www.ryan-be-fair.org, Airwise News, 6.9.2004.

(a) Analyse two possible objectives of trade unions dealing with Ryanair. (8 marks)

(b) To what extent should trade unions involved with Ryanair consider the interests of passengers? (12 marks)

(b) Discuss whether Ryanair's anti-union stance is beneficial to the stakeholders of the company. (20 marks)

78 Industrial democracy, bargaining, consultation and participation

Employer and employee conflict

Conflict can exist between different groups and individuals working in business. One type of conflict which may lead to major problems is between the objectives of employers and employees. Conflict between these two groups may result from a number of factors.

- Rates of pay. Employers could attempt to keep wage costs down to remain competitive, whereas unions could try to maximise employees' rewards.
- The introduction of machinery. For example, a business may want to introduce machinery which requires workers to learn new production techniques. Employees, however, may feel that this extra responsibility is an unwanted burden.
- Flexible working. Businesses often require a more flexible workforce. A printing works might decide to operate a 24 hour shift, for example, to cope with extra work. Employees may be unwilling to work at night.
- Work conditions. Workers may feel that better canteen facilities are needed, but employers could see this as an unnecessary increase in costs.

The aim of **industrial relations** procedures is to make sure that each party finds an acceptable solution to any conflict that may exist. Successful industrial relations should prevent the need for industrial action by employers' or employees' groups.

Collective bargaining

COLLECTIVE BARGAINING is one way of minimising conflict in the workplace. It involves determining conditions of work and terms of employment through **negotiations** between employers and employee representatives, such as trade unions. These bodies represent the views of all their members and try to negotiate in their interests. One individual employee working for a large company would have little or no influence in setting their wages or conditions. The representative body has more strength and influence and can negotiate for its membership. Without such a bargaining process, employers and managers would be able to set wages and conditions without taking into account employees' interests.

For collective bargaining to take place:

- employees must be free to join representative bodies, such as trade unions;
- employers must recognise such bodies as representative of workers and agree to negotiate with them;
- such bodies must be independent of employers and the state;
- bodies should negotiate in good faith, in their members' interests;
- employers and employees should agree to be bound by agreements without having to use the law to enforce them.

The result of collective bargaining is a COLLECTIVE AGREEMENT. These agreements are usually written and are signed by the parties and will be binding. Collective agreements can either be **substantive agreements** or **procedural agreements**. Substantive agreements are concerned with terms and conditions of employment. They include pay, work conditions and fringe benefits. Procedural agreements set out how the parties in the bargaining should relate to each other on certain issues. They include negotiating, redundancy, dismissal, recruitment and promotion procedures.

The number of workers covered by collective agreements fell from 71 per cent in 1984 to 35 per cent in 2002. There were many reasons for this including legislation, union membership, union organisation and the type and nature of employment. Collective bargaining is one method by which a business can achieve greater industrial democracy. This is a term which is used in different contexts, but, by analogy with political democracy, generally refers to a situation where workers are entitled to a significant voice in the decisions affecting the business in which they work. This is dealt with again later in this unit.

Question 1.

According to the GMB trade union, Asda the supermarket chain has withdrawn a 10 per cent pay offer to more than 700 workers at a goods distribution centre in the north-east of England. Asda said it had put forward a package of changes to workers' terms and conditions covering areas such as overtime, holiday and premium rates, with savings being used to increase basic pay. The changes would also have seen a move away from collective bargaining to settle pay negotiations to individual bargaining. However, when balloted, the workforce had rejected the package.

Asda has two depots in Washington, Tyne and Wear, one which it has always owned and the one at the centre of the dispute, which it bought several years ago. The two depots have different terms and conditions and the dispute is understood to have arisen from efforts to put both on a similar footing.

Labour relations are a sensitive area for Asda. Its US parent, Wal-Mart, has a reputation of being staunchly anti-union. Earlier this week, Wal-Mart said it was closing a store in Canada just six months after workers there won the right to join a union.

Source: adapted from *The Guardian*, 12.2.2005.

(a) Explain what it would have meant for the workers at the Asda depot in Tyne and Wear to have moved from collective bargaining to individual bargaining.

(b) What might be the advantages and disadvantages to (a) Asda and (b) the depot workers to have changed to an individual bargaining system?

Levels of negotiation

Negotiations can take place at a number of different levels.

International bargaining Large multinational companies operate in many different countries. Some have considered the possibility of negotiating the same conditions for all employees in the business, no matter what country or factory they work in. This has the advantages that conditions can be standardised and workers in one country will not feel envious of those in another. The major problem of this approach is the inflexibility it causes.

National level Employers and employees may agree a deal which applies to all employees. Negotiations may take place to set wage or salary scales, or to discuss national conditions of work. For example, an agreement could be reached on the number of hours that teachers or lecturers should work a year, or their length of holidays, between teachers' unions and the government. A private sector example might be negotiations between the train union RMT and Virgin Trains over health and safety conditions.

Local level Discussions may take place at a local level, so that any settlement can reflect local conditions. An example of local negotiations might be wages or salaries based on the area of operation. From time to time the weightings given to local authority workers for working in the London or surrounding areas are revised. These weightings are added to workers' salaries to take into account the higher cost of living in the area. A locally based engineering company may negotiate with regional union representatives about the need to reduce the workforce because of falling sales. Again, this is likely to take place at local level.

Factory or plant-wide level Negotiations at factory or plant-wide level can take place over a variety of aspects of work. They may involve the personnel department, departmental managers, shop stewards and employee representatives.

Examples of matters that might be agreed upon could be:

- productivity targets;
- the introduction of new machinery;
- hours of work and flexibility within the plant;
- health and safety conditions.

Individualised bargaining Individualised bargaining is where the result of negotiations is the agreement between the employee and the employer in the contract of employment. Union representatives are not involved in negotiations. This means that the employee does not receive advice and does not have the backing of an influential group when discussing terms and conditions. However, it may mean that both sides in the negotiations have greater flexibility.

The negotiation process

For negotiation to be successful in collective bargaining, an agreement must be reached which satisfies all parties. This is far more likely to be achieved if a pattern is followed during negotiation.

The agenda A meeting between all parties involved in negotiation needs an agenda. This will outline what is to be discussed and all parties must agree to it. The order of items on the agenda may influence the outcome of negotiations. If, for instance, all the employees' claims come first and all the management's points come later, then anything that is agreed at the beginning of the meeting cannot be accepted until the management side is given. An agenda that places management and employee items in alternate and logical order can make negotiations easier.

Information Both parties need 'facts' to support their arguments. Negotiators have to collect the information they need, analyse it and make sure that each member of the negotiating team has a say in its interpretation. Often managers make information about a company's financial position available to representatives before meetings. This ensures that both parties have the correct information on which to base discussions.

Strategy It is important for each side in the negotiations to prepare a strategy. This will help them to achieve their objectives. Developing a strategy could include the following stages.

- Agreeing objectives. What do negotiators seek to achieve? The objectives set by employers or unions should, if achieved, lead to improvements. For example, a change in employment rules might improve efficiency or motivation. Negative objectives that emphasise not 'losing ground' are not usually helpful.
- Allocating roles. Who will do what in the negotiations? Negotiators need specific roles. For example, there may be a chairperson to lead the discussion, someone to put the case and a specialist to provide advice.
- Predict what the other side might do. Strategies are unlikely to remain the same during negotiations. Their chances of success are improved if the negotiators have tried to predict what they will hear from the opposition. Negotiators must be prepared not only to put forward their own arguments, but also to respond to arguments put to them.

Unity Because negotiation involves different sets of interests, each team must work out a united position before negotiations begin. If the group's position changes, all members must agree. It is important that a group shows unity at all times during negotiations or its position may become weaker.

Size of the group The number of people representing each side will influence the negotiations. The larger the group the greater the problem of managing communications between group members. When asked to suggest a number, most experienced negotiators opt for three or four in each group. Meetings of fewer people may be accused of 'fixing' an outcome.

Stages of the negotiation Negotiators begin by making it clear that they are representing the interests of others. They often emphasise the strength of their case and start by saying they are unwilling to move from that position. The displays of strength are necessary to convince themselves and the 'opposition' that they are willing to fight for their position. By the time this part of the negotiations starts, both sides should be very clear on the matters that divide them. After the differences have been explored, the next stage is for negotiators to look for solutions that might be more acceptable to each party. Each party will sound out possibilities, float ideas, ask questions and make suggestions. No firm commitments are made at this stage. Negotiations are likely to be more successful if each group is willing to change its position.

Decision making The next stage is to come to some agreement. The management may make an offer.The decision about what to offer is the most difficult and important task in the whole process. The offer may be revised, but eventually it will be accepted or rejected. Agreement is usual in all but a small minority of situations. Employees do not really wish to disrupt an organisation. Even if they take strike action, they will eventually return to the firm. The management need the employees to work for them. They have to reach an agreement no matter how long it takes.

Written statement Producing a brief written statement before the negotiation has ended will make it clear what both parties have decided, if agreement has been reached.

Commitment of the parties So far, agreement has been reached between negotiators only. This is of no value unless the groups represented by the negotiators accept it and make it work.

Employee representatives have to report back to their members and persuade them to accept the agreement. Management representatives may also have to do the same thing. Once the terms have been agreed by both employees and employers, the negotiating process is complete. It is the joint responsibility of both parties to carry out and monitor the agreement.

Consultation

Negotiation, as we have seen, is an activity by which the two parties make agreements which may cover pay and conditions at work and relations between management and employees. JOINT CONSULTATION, by contrast, is the process where management representatives discuss matters of common interest with employee representatives before negotiating or making a decision. There are three types of consultation.

Pseudo-consultation Pseudo-consultation is where management makes a decision and informs employees of that decision through their representatives. Employees have no power to influence these decisions. Some have suggested that it would be more accurately described as information-giving.

Classical consultation Classical consultation is a way of involving employees, through their representatives, in discussions on matters which affect them. This allows employees to have an influence on management decisions. Unions may be involved, for example, in restructuring.

Integrative consultation Pseudo and classical consultation do not directly involve employees in decisions which affect them. Integrative consultation is a more democratic method of decision making. Arguably it is neither consultation nor negotiation. Management and unions discuss and explore matters which are of common concern, such as ways of increasing productivity or methods of changing work practices. The two groups come to a joint decision having used, in many cases, problem solving techniques. An example of an integrative approach to consultation might be the use of quality circles in a number of UK businesses and in foreign firms setting up in the UK.

The Advisory, Conciliation and Arbitration Service (ACAS)

Sometimes parties fail to reach agreements after consultation and negotiation. In these situations the Advisory, Conciliation and Arbitration Service (ACAS) can be of great value to both sides.

During the period of industrial action in the 1970s, groups of employers and employees called for the setting up of a conciliation and arbitration service, independent of government control and of civil service influence. The result was ACAS, which took up its formal duties in September 1974. ACAS is a public body funded by tax, with over 900 staff employed in 11 regional centres and a head office in London. It has a chief executive and a council made up of 12 members ranging from union members to academics. Its main role is to prevent and resolve problems in the workplace. It provides a wide range of services to employers and employees in business.

Industrial disputes ACAS has conciliation duties. It can intervene in industrial disputes at the request of either management or unions. Its role is to try and encourage a settlement that all parties may agree to, using procedures that both parties accept.

Arbitration and mediation ARBITRATION is where both parties in a dispute put forward their case to ACAS. ACAS then independently assesses each case and recommends a final decision. Mediation is where ACAS makes recommendations about a possible solution and leaves the parties to find a settlement.

Advisory work ACAS carries out advisory work with employers, trade unions and employers' associations. This can be short

Question 2.

In January 2005, WM Morrison, the supermarket group, was pressed into rewriting a recognition agreement with the Transport & General Workers Union (T&G). The issue started in January 2004 when 87 per cent of the 1,600 T&G members working at two distribution centres at Wakefield and Northwich rejected a pay offer. Under the terms of the existing agreement, Morrisons had the right to refer any dispute to binding arbitration, where both sides were bound to accept the results of arbitration. Morrisons duly referred this dispute to arbitration. The arbiter confirmed the offer that Morrisons had originally made, much to the disappointment of the T&G.

The T&G responded by attempting to renegotiate the recognition agreement to remove the binding arbitration clause. Morrisons refused. Then the company invited other trade unions to 'bid' for T&G members. This meant asking other trade unions to enter negotiations with Morrisons with a view to changing the union to which existing T&G members belonged. Not surprisingly, the T&G were outraged by such action and in June 2004 conducted a ballot of the 1,600 members for strike action. Over 90 per cent of members supported full strike action.

With the strike ballot result in their pocket, the T&G returned to the negotiating table with Morrisons. In November 2004, the company agreed to remove the binding arbitration clause. It also offered substantial pay increases to the workers. Some drivers received as much as a 15 per cent pay increase taking their pay to £8.33 an hour.

The T&G said that it was very pleased with the outcome. It would now target the 400 non T&G workers at the two sites and hopefully persuade them to join the union. The aim was to get 100 per cent membership of the T&G in the workforce.

Source: adapted from Timesonline, 12.1. 2005, Personnel Today, 12.1.2005, T&G News, January/February 2005.

(a) Suggest why binding arbitration was unpopular with T&G members at the two Morrisons distribution depots.

(b) Discuss whether binding arbitration would always have acted against the interests of the union members at Morrisons.

visits to answer specific questions or long-term, in-depth, projects and surveys. The questions ACAS deal with are wide ranging and can include issues such as contracts of employment, industrial relations legislation, payment systems and personnel policies.

Codes of practice ACAS issues codes of practice. These contain practical guidance on how to improve industrial relations between employers and employees.

Enquiries ACAS has carried out enquiries into the flexible use of labour, appraisal systems, labour turnover, employee involvement, handling redundancy and the use of quality circles. Much of this research is published by ACAS as advisory booklets. Employers use them to help improve industrial relations and personnel management practices.

Individual cases ACAS investigates individual cases of unfair discrimination and unfair dismissal.

Tribunals Employment tribunals hear a wide range of employment disputes, including unfair dismissal and discrimination. ACAS operates independently from the tribunals. Its role is to offer conciliation on disputes, with the aim of settling the matter without a tribunal hearing. This is known as alternative dispute resolution (ADR). The **Employment Rights (Dispute Resolution) Act, 1998** set up an ACAS arbitration scheme designed to find other methods than the courts for solving disputes.

ACAS has developed its services to meet the needs of a changing industrial relations climate. While the bulk of its work continues to be conciliation, mediation and arbitration, it has steadily developed advisory and training services. ACAS has also become more involved in helping business to improve personnel and management practices. These include:

- effective recruitment and selection of employees;
- setting up and operating equal opportunities policies;
- improving communications and joint consultation;
- developing the skills of managers to help them introduce changes in work organisation.

The role of the Central Arbitration Committee

The **Employment Relations Act, 1998** set out a process for unions to be recognised automatically or where a majority of workers voted for it. The Central Arbitration Committee (CAC) is a permanent independent body responsible for union recognition. It has a number of functions.

- It judges applications relating to the statutory recognition and derecognition of trade unions when recognition or derecognition cannot be agreed voluntarily.

- It helps to determine disputes between trade unions and employers over the disclosure of information for collective bargaining.
- It handles claims and complaints regarding the establishment and operation of European works councils in Great Britain.
- It provides voluntary arbitration in industrial disputes.

In the case of union recognition, the CAC would first encourage parties to settle the matter themselves. If this failed, it could award recognition or the union could hold a ballot. The CAC has the power to instruct the employer to co-operate with the ballot or risk a fine.

Employee participation and industrial democracy

Employees are increasingly participating in the operation of businesses and decision making. Decision making is often more accurate and effective when those involved in carrying out instructions have a say in the decision. Many businesses today recognise the value of their employees' views and contributions when deciding on objectives and strategies. The participation of employees in business decision making can take many forms.

Autonomous work groups Autonomous working groups and cells are increasingly being used by businesses to improve performance. They are groups of employees who operate without direct supervision from superiors, making their own decisions about the allocation of tasks, selection and training of new group leaders and methods of working, for example.

Teamworking Teamworking is where employees work together on tasks rather than individually. Teams can take a variety of forms. There may be permanent teams that meet from time to time, such as a management team or a quality circle. They might be permanent teams that are set up and work together constantly each day, such as an autonomous production work group or cell. They might be teams set up for a specific purpose over a particular time period, such as a team to investigate a production problem or whether market research supports a new product.

It is argued that working in teams motivates workers, especially if they are empowered to make decisions. Decisions might benefit from the input of a number of people with different skills. Responsibility for tasks might be shared and productivity improved. However, there can be conflict, differences of ideas, time consuming meetings and slow decisions, which may lead to problems for a business.

Employee shareholders Employees are stakeholders of businesses. In some cases they might also be shareholders. They might own shares in the company they work for as part of an incentive scheme or they might buy shares in other companies on a stock market. Shareholders in limited companies may be able to influence the decisions that are made depending on the percentage of shares that they have. For example, in some limited companies, employee groups may own a percentage of shares and have some influence at annual general meetings.

It could be argued that greater industrial democracy, where employees have a significant say, may exist in a number of situations.

European works councils Works councils are bodies set up by businesses which allow employees and employers to consult, discuss and pass information about decisions which concern the business. In September 1996, the European Works Council Directive came into force, which was adopted in the UK in 2000. It obliges multinational companies operating across the EU to set up groups and forums to inform and consult with employees, known as EUROPEAN WORKS COUNCILS (EWC).

Any company can set up a works council. But EWCs must be set up in companies that employ at least 1,000 workers in Europe and have at least 150 employees in each of at least two member states. Even before 2000, many multinationals in the UK had to set up EWCs because the number of their employees elsewhere in Europe took them over the threshold. Most of these companies included their UK employees as a matter of good business.

Question 3.

Merseyrail had a poor history of industrial relations in the 1990s. This resulted in some well publicised stoppages and industrial action when the franchise was operated by MTL. ACAS helped set up a Committee of Enquiry into industrial relations at the company. As a result of its findings, an ACAS-led joint working group was set up. It comprised managers from the company and representatives of train worker unions such as RMT, ASLEF and TSSA. The group's task was to develop proposals that would improve industrial relations. These included awareness policies, and procedures, roles and responsibilities of industrial relations. ACAS also advised the company to bid for a Department of Trade and Industry grant to help improve employer-employee relations, including joint training. The bid was successful.

Logics Resource Services (LRS) had experienced a number of employment tribunal cases at which ACAS had provided conciliation services. The company approached ACAS to develop preventative action. This included a new handbook with discipline and grievance procedures. Once the procedures were agreed, they had to be accepted by staff who were then trained in the new procedures. Problems had occurred in the business as a result of the rapid growth of the company through mergers, which led to a variety of disciplinary systems being in place. The involvement of ACAS led to a legitimising of the new system for employer and employee. The new system resulted in a fall in enquiries regarding disciplinary matters and industrial claims, and also an improvement in employer-employee relations.

Source: adapted from ACAS report, April 2002-March 2003.

(a) Identify the services offered to companies by ACAS using examples from the article.

(b) Examine the benefits to the companies of involving ACAS in discussions.

Special negotiating bodies are set up to determine the scope, functions and make-up of the EWC. Typically EWCs negotiate in areas of the business such as business structure, the economic and financial position, development, production and sales, employment, organisational change, mergers, cutbacks, closure and collective redundancies.

Research has indicated that councils have a number of benefits for businesses including:
- increased trust between managers and employees;
- greater employee involvement;
- a better understanding by employees of the factors affecting management decisions;
- helping to build a positive corporate culture;
- showing a company's concern for its employees.

Employee owned businesses Some businesses are owned by their employees. These include worker co-operatives and democratic employee owned organisations. The employees of the business will be involved in all its main decisions. An example is Arthurlie Taxis in Barrhead. It was created by private hire taxi drivers who formed a company to act as a marketing co-operative and operates the back-up controller and radio service. The individual drivers are all self employed and pay a levy from their earnings to operate the co-operative.

Factors affecting participation and industrial democracy

The extent to which participation and industrial democracy takes place in business may depend on a number of factors.

Legislation UK government legislation and European laws are likely to have an effect. For example, **the Employment Act, 2002** set in place regulations for fixed conciliation to allow quicker and more amicable settlements to disputes. The EU **Information and Consultation of Employees Regulations, 2005** suggested that in certain cases the workforce could make a written request to businesses asking for information and consultation procedures on decisions likely to affect work arrangements, future business developments and restructuring.

Consultative bodies It was suggested that the introduction of **European works councils,** as a result of the UK signing the Social Chapter of the EU, was likely to increase industrial democracy after the year 2000.

Corporate culture Some businesses have developed a culture that recognises the importance of participation and industrial democracy when decisions are made. They value the contribution that employees can make to effective decision making. Businesses that make use of knowledge teams are likely to see participation and industrial democracy as important.

Representation and power In certain parts of the private sector, where unions are weak, or collective bargaining does not take place, industrial democracy may be limited. An example might be where the owner of a small, non-unionised business decides to move premises and simply informs the workers that this will take place.

Communication and information technology The introduction of company intranets and other communication technologies has helped to speed up and extend the process of industrial democracy.

Quality standards Organisations may seek a quality award, such as **Investors in People**, for the way in which they work with employees. Consultation, the passing of information and involvement in decision making are standards that businesses have to maintain to keep this award. Such an award may attract customers and good quality candidates.

KNOWLEDGE

1. What factors may lead to conflict between employers and employees?
2. Why is collective bargaining important to employees?
3. What are likely to be the results of collective bargaining?
4. Explain the difference between:
   (a) collective bargaining at national and plant level;
   (b) collective bargaining and individualised bargaining.
5. Briefly explain the stages in negotiation that may help to lead to a satisfactory outcome.
6. Explain the different types of consultation.
7. Briefly explain the main areas of activity that ACAS is involved in.
8. What is the role of a European works council?

KEYTERMS

ACAS – a body which mediates where conflict exists in business.
Arbitration – where both sides in a dispute agree to an independent party making a judgment about how a dispute can be resolved.
CAC – the government body responsible for union recognition.
Collective agreement – an agreement reached through the process of collective bargaining.
Collective bargaining – a method of determining conditions of work and terms of employment through negotiations between employers and employee representatives.
European works councils (EWC) – bodies set up to allow consultation with employees by employers and the passing of information to employees.
Industrial democracy – the different situations in business where employees have a significant say in decisions.
Joint consultation – discussion between management and employee representatives before a decision is taken.

Case Study: **Suma**

Suma is a multimillion pound company, supplying 2,500 customers across the UK and abroad. It has 100 employees and is the largest independent wholesaler in the health food and wholefood trade in the UK. Founded in the 1970s as a workers co-operative, it is owned by its member workers. They run the business in a democratic way.

The 'boss' of the firm is the General Meeting of members. This takes place six times a year. The General Meeting agrees strategies, business plans and major policy decisions. Any member can make proposals to the General Meeting and if passed they are mandatory on all workers. The General Meeting elects six of its number to the Management Committee which meets weekly to implement the Business Plan and other GM decisions. The Management Committee in turn appoints company officers: Personnel, Operations, Finance and Function Area co-ordinators.

The Management Committee monitors the implementation of the Business Plan by the Function Areas. Weekly Business Information covering finances, quality of services and labour productivity indicators are reported to the Management Committee by company officers. The Management Committee then issues Action Points when what is actually happening on the ground differs from what is laid out in the Business Plan.

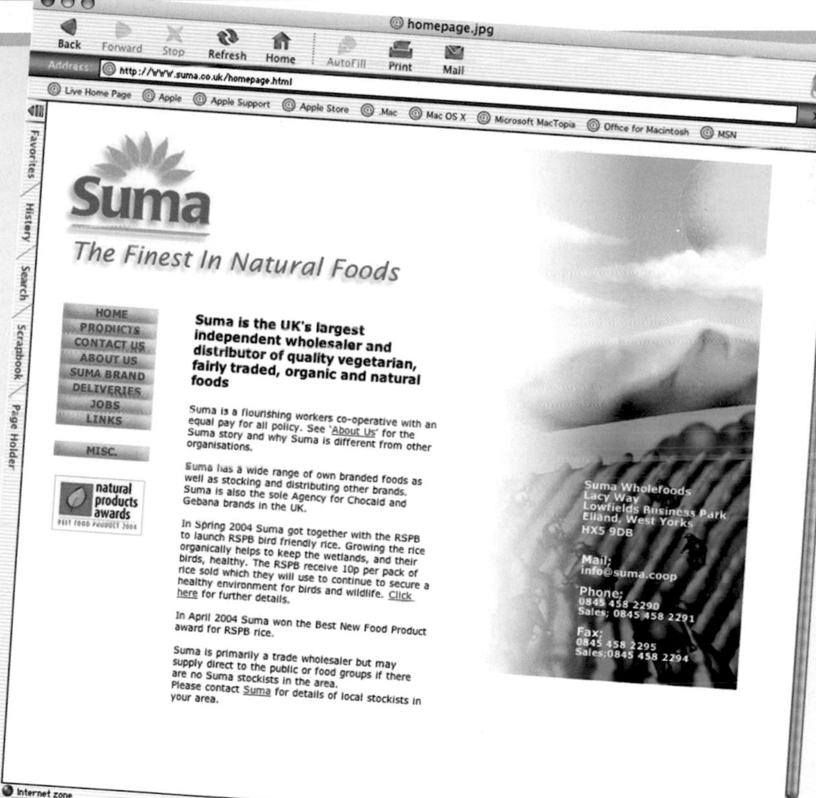

Working at Suma is quite unlike other businesses. Workers must be more self-motivated and take more initiative. Suma departmental co-ordinators do not have an overseer role in the normal sense. Workers support each other to fulfil daily tasks and get home on time. Working as an effective member of a co-operative, not just doing the daily tasks but taking part in the management of the business, is a new skill which all new members have to learn, whether they have been shop floor or management previously. The business can only succeed when all members share this responsibility.

All Suma workers are paid the same daily wage plus allowances and overtime or time off in lieu. It is a good wage for manual warehouse workers and the extra reflects the collective management element of the jobs. In return for the better than average wages, Suma expects much more commitment from its employees. When the need arises, when customer orders are waiting, employees are expected to work until the job is done.

Job variety is important. Drivers will drive for a maximum of three days and then work in the warehouse or office. Office people will do manual work for at least one day a week. Most members will have done a far wider range of jobs and taken on greater responsibilities within Suma than equivalent workers in other businesses. Suma encourages members to take up training and courses to bring in new skills.

Source: adapted from About Us, Suma, www.suma.co.uk.

(a) **Explain why industrial democracy and employee participation can be said to exist at Suma. (8 marks)**

(b) **Discuss the possible advantages and disadvantages to Suma of industrial democracy and employee participation. (12 marks)**

79 Industrial disputes

Industrial action in the UK

Conflict between employees and employers can lead to **industrial action**. Industrial action can be taken by both employers against employees (such as close supervision of work, or a lock-out) and by employees against employers (ranging from an overtime ban to strike action). It is in the interests of both groups to reconcile differences through negotiation and consultation before taking action, although this is not always possible.

The number of stoppages and the number of working days lost through stoppages fell over a period 1982-2006. At its peak in 1984, for example, over 25 million days were lost. By 1989 this had fallen to just over four million and by 2006 was below one million, as shown in Figure 2. In part, this was due to legislation restricting union action. It was also partly due to a change in the attitudes of management and unions towards industrial democracy, which helped to reduce conflict and the number of disputes that arise in business.

Employers' industrial action

Action by management against employees can take a number of forms. Sometimes sanctions can be imposed by individual managers. Some may include, for example, close supervision of employees' work, tight work discipline, discrimination against certain groups, lay offs, demoting workers or speeding up work practices. These actions are usually taken by one member of the management team and will not be repeated in other departments in the company. They might lead to individuals or groups of workers starting grievance proceedings against the manager concerned.

Sanctions can also be organised and carried out throughout the business. Management may use some of the following actions when dealing with trade unions.

The withdrawal of overtime and benefits A business could withdraw all overtime that it offers to workers. This is likely to reduce workers' earnings. The business might also withdraw other benefits it offers to employees, including flexitime, vouchers or other benefits such as leisure club membership.

Lock-outs A LOCK-OUT by employers involves closing the factory for a period of time. Employees' wages may not be paid during this period. This action might adversely affect the image that the public have of the company.

Changing standards and piecework rates Management may change work standards or alter piecework rates when in dispute with employees. This can have the effect of making the employees' task more difficult or reducing the earnings of employees unless they work a lot harder.

Sometimes a management tactic may be to use a strategy of increasing work standards so that unions will call a strike. This might happen when order books are low and stocks are high. By

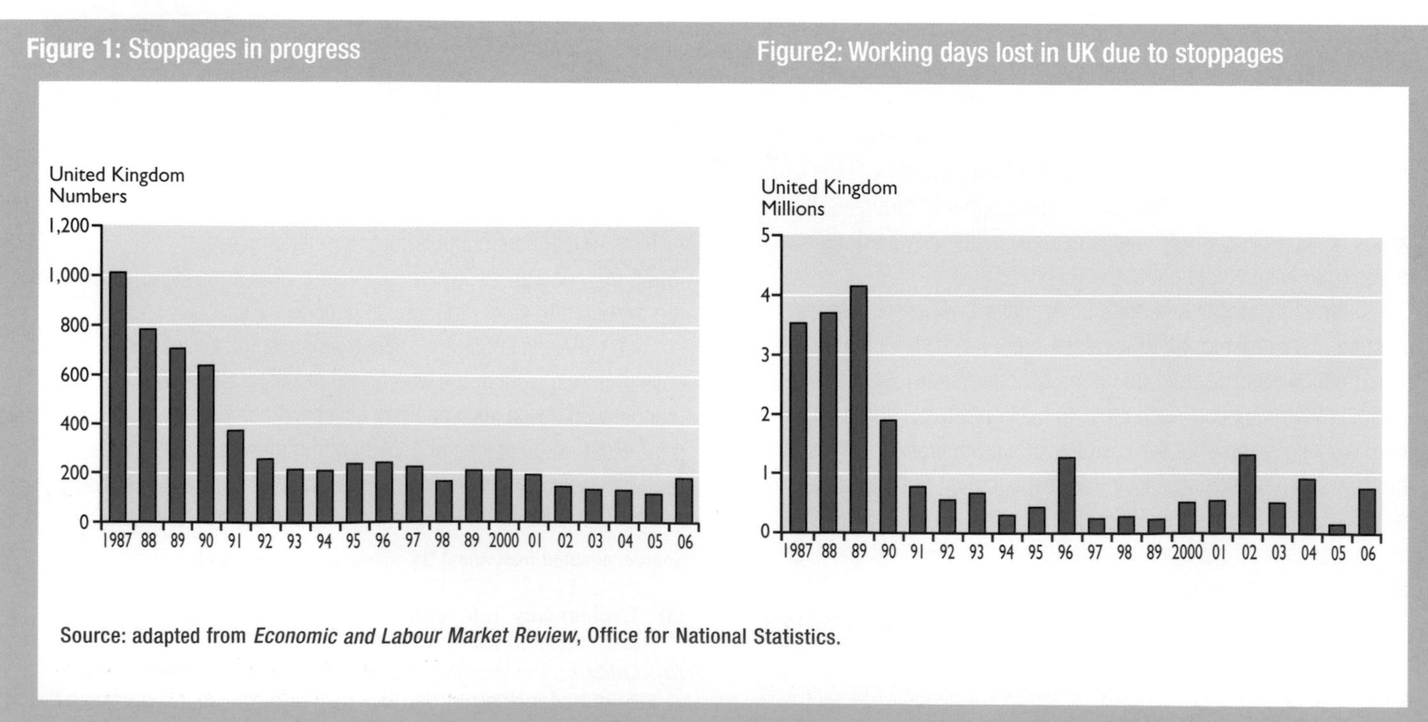

Source: adapted from *Economic and Labour Market Review*, Office for National Statistics.

causing a strike, management does not need to lay anyone off or pay redundancy money. At the same time further stockpiling is reduced.

Closure Management may close down factories and offices or remove plant and machinery from their premises. Some people might not view such activities as industrial action. They may see them as the normal rights of management to shut down uneconomic enterprises or force unco-operative workers to comply with employers' needs in the workplace.

Dismissal In some cases, employers might threaten employees with dismissal. The **Employment Relations Act 1999** set out criteria where it was unfair to dismiss employees for taking industrial action. Employees that are dismissed can take their case to a tribunal, which will judge against the criteria.

Hiring workers If unions take action to withdraw their labour, employers sometimes recruit outside workers or contractors to do their jobs. It has also been suggested that some employers hire 'union busters' to intimidate workers to stop unions winning strike ballots.

The use of courts Businesses might challenge the right of unions and their members to take action through the courts. This might prevent the action taking place. They might also claim damages.

Employees' industrial action

Industrial action used by employees can be wide ranging. It is possible to distinguish between **unorganised** action and **organised** action. Richard Hyman, in his book *Strikes*, wrote that: '... in unorganised conflict the worker typically responds to the oppressive situation in the only way open to him as an individual ... Such reaction rarely derives from any calculative strategy ... Organised conflict, on the other hand, is far more likely to form part of a conscious strategy to change the situation which is identified as the source of discontent.'

Unorganised (or unofficial) action by employees can come in a number of forms.

- High labour turnover.
- Poor time keeping.
- High levels of absenteeism.
- Low levels of effort.
- Inefficient work.
- Deliberate time wasting.
- Unofficial strikes not backed by the employees' union.

These are often taken when workers 'down tools' immediately in reaction to employers' actions.

Such action can be disruptive for a business if it continues for a long period of time. The business, however, can use disciplinary procedures against employees and may even be able to terminate contracts in some cases. However, unofficial action may lead to organised action backed by the union. Organised action can take a number of different forms.

Question 1.

On 18 December 2007 workers at Argos stores in Republic of Ireland held a one day strike. As the threat of a strike grew, it was argued that pressure had been put on seasonal workers and weekend employees not to join the Union, Mandate, for fear of loosing their jobs. The shop steward of the Swords branch of Mandate, said that employeeswere brought into managers offices and had it outlined exactly what joining with Mandate, would mean to their future. Another feature of the strike was the use of workers brought in from Wales and England to cover for Argos employees on strike.

Source: adapted from www.socialistunity.com and ibcom.org/news.

In 2003 workers at the Trellebourg chemical company in Leicester took strike action. This was in response to management action which introduced tags which had to be worn in break time by staff.

Source: adapted from *Labour Research*, November 2003.

Culina Logistics launched an anti-union recognition campaign using the slogan 'vote no way to the TSSA'. According to the union staff were also 'threatened with derisory pay deals, reductions in breaks, loss of bonus schemes' and job losses if TSSA won recognition.

Source: adapted from *Labour Research*, January 2004.

(a) Identify the methods of industrial action being used by employers.
(b) Explain why employers might justify taking such action.

Work to rule or go slow Organised and group industrial action by trade unions against management can take the form of a WORK TO RULE or GO SLOW. A work to rule means employees do not carry out duties which are not in their employment contract. They may also carry out management orders to the letter. This can result in workers strictly observing the safety and work rules which are normally disregarded. Working to rule does not mean that employees are in breach of contract, simply that they carry out tasks exactly according to their contract. This means that tasks are not carried out efficiently. The impact of train drivers working to rule, for example, could mean that trains are late arriving or are cancelled. Drivers may delay taking trains out until rigorous checks are carried out. A go slow is where employees deliberately attempt to slow down production, whilst still working within the terms of their contract.

Overtime ban An overtime ban limits workers' hours to the agreed contract of employment for normal hours. Overtime bans are usually used by trade unions to demonstrate to management that the workforce is determined to take further

Question 2.

In January 2005, firefighters at Glasgow Airport went on indefinite strike and began picketing the airport. The dispute centred around plans by their employer, the British Airports Authority (BAA), to change the way in which fire safety was organised. Up to this point, the 59 firefighters at the airport were responsible both for fire safety on the runways and land of the airport, but also for the airport terminal building. To deal with the airport building, the firefighters had a fire engine crewed by four people fully equipped for firefighting and rescue duties. BAA proposed to transfer responsibility for the terminal building to Strathclyde Fire Service, the fire service provided by the local authority. Staffing levels at the terminal would be reduced to a two person fire safety team which would not be equipped with protective clothing or equipment to carry out any firefighting duties.

The Transport and General Workers' Union (T&G) said the changes would put airport staff and passengers at risk. The response times to any incident in the terminal would increase from two minutes to fourteen minutes.

BAA stated that safety would not be compromised by the changes. It suggested that the main concern of the firefighters was not safety but a loss of 'traditionally high levels' of expensive overtime that would result from the changes. It also said that the fire engine at the centre of the dispute was brought in as an extra precaution during refurbishment in the 1990s when parts of the airport were effectively a building site.

A month after the strike began, the 59 firefighters accepted a compromise solution. The new arrangements would go ahead but eight specialist officers would be recruited to improve fire safety at the terminal. The firefighters would also receive a one-off payment of £1 500 for accepting the changes.

Source: adapted from BBC News World Edition 29.1.2005 and 27.2.2005; Socialist Worker Online, 5.2.2005.

(a) Suggest what the Glasgow firefighters hoped to achieve by going out on strike.
(b) To what extent did the firefighters achieve their possible objectives when the dispute was resolved?

collective action if their demands are not met. An overtime ban does have a disadvantage for workers as it results in lost earnings. It can lead to a reduction in costs for the business, but may also lead to lost production. It can be especially effective where production takes place overnight, for example on large production lines.

Sit-ins and work-ins A SIT-IN or WORK-IN involves a mass occupation of premises by workers. A work-in is where employees continue production with the aim of demonstrating that the factory is a viable concern. It is sometimes used when there is a threat of closure. In a sit-in, production does not continue. The aim is to protest against management decisions and, in the case of factory closure, prevent the transfer of machinery to other factories. A **redundancy sit-in** or work-in is a protest against the closure of a plant or company. A **collective bargaining sit-in** may be used instead of other forms of industrial action such as working to rule, overtime bans and all out strikes, to give employees a position of strength in negotiations.

Sit-ins and work-ins mean the illegal occupation of premises by workers. They also allow workers to gain control over the factory. Why are these tactics used? First, they offer some degree of control over the factory or plant being occupied, which is obviously important in redundancy situations where the removal of plant and machinery to other locations is being threatened. Also by working-in or sitting-in, employees are better able to maintain their group solidarity.

Strikes The ultimate sanction used by trade unions against employers is the strike or industrial stoppage. Stoppages at work are normally connected with terms and conditions of employment. Strikes can be **official** or **unofficial**. Official strikes are where a union officially supports its members in accordance with union rules during a dispute after a ballot for action has been carried out and agreed by union members. Unofficial strikes have no union backing or support. They have, in the past, been called by shop stewards in particular factories, often in response to a particular incident. Such strikes are likely to be short term, local, unpredictable and disruptive for a business.

There is no single reason that explains the trend in stoppages in the UK. A study of strikes in Britain over an extensive time period was carried out by researchers for the government. They discovered that:

- strikes appear to be over major issues;
- strikes are concentrated in a very small proportion of plants – often the larger ones in certain industries and in certain areas of the country;
- industries and regions that have large factories, on average, tend to experience relatively high numbers of strikes. These strikes occur fairly often.

Factors influencing the success of employees' industrial action

Whether industrial action by workers and unions is successful in helping them achieve their aims depends on a number of factors.

Nature and strength of the union A large union negotiating with a small business is more likely to be able to influence the employer. Where large unions are negotiating with large multinational companies or with the government, action may not always be successful.

It has also been argued that unions are less influential if representation in the industry is split. This was perhaps the case when some mine workers left the NUM to form the Union of Democratic Mineworkers. It may also have been a reason for the merger of NALGO, NUPE and COHSE to form the UK's largest union, Unison.

Smaller unions tend to have less influence. The Musicians Union, for example, whilst having rates per hour for performers, is unlikely to be able to force club owners to pay the 'going rate' for performances.

Location and organisation of the workforce It has been suggested that unions are in a stronger bargaining position if a number of their members are employed in the same 'place'. Farm workers, for example, have traditionally been in a weak bargaining position with employers, as few are employed on any one farm. Also, their places of employment are geographically dispersed. This makes meetings and support difficult.

Public support and union views Public support for a dispute may strengthen a union's position. This may be particularly true of public sector workers such as nurses, where the public often 'feel' workers deserve higher wages or not to be made redundant. However, public opinion may change once industrial action begins. This may also be the case in industrial action by railway workers, for example, especially in commuter belts around London. Health unions have, in the past, refused to strike because of the damaging effects on patients.

Management tactics Union action is likely to be less effective if management action can reduce the problems for business. In the car industry, a strike by employees may not affect a producer if there are stocks of cars and orders can still be met.

Management may encourage non-union workers or even union members to cross the picket line, or even be prepared to 'bus in' workers from other areas. The government has, in the past, been prepared to use army vehicles and members of the armed forces when fire service workers have taken industrial action.

Legislation Laws restrict the actions of employers and employee groups such as trade unions. For example, trade unions are liable in certain circumstances for damages during industrial action. Similarly, under certain circumstances, employers cannot make employees involved in industrial action redundant.

Economic climate The state of the economy might affect the relative bargaining strength of employers and employees. For example, take a situation where growth is low in the economy, spending is falling and unemployment is high. There may be excess supply of labour willing to work at cheap wages. So employers may feel that they are in a stronger position. If growth and spending is low in the economy, employers might also feel that they are not in a position to pay high wages. On the other hand, employers may not be able to afford the damaging effects of industrial action during periods of recession.

Question 3.

In December 2003 around 800 staff at Sainsbury's distribution centre in Haydock staged a 24 hour strike after rejecting a pay offer. The centre distributes goods to stores in the north of England. Nearly all workers at the site are members of the union USDAW. A union spokesperson said that the pay offer was significantly behind other warehouse workers in the North West and other Sainsbury's depots. The current offer increased pay from £5.75 to £7.55 an hour, but not to the regional average of £8 an hour, which was initially promised by the company. It was suggested that the company accepted it was paying below the average in 2002. Workers had recently agreed to new working practices at the depot.

Sainsbury's said that it did not expect the walkout to affect customers in supermarkets. The company had contingency plans in place to deal with the action. It argued that the overall package offered to employees was one of the best in the area and that pay offers had been above inflation in the last three years.

Source: adapted from news.bbc.co.uk, breaking.tcm.ie.

(a) Examine the contingency plans that the employer might have to deal with the dispute.

(b) Assess the strengths of employers and employees in the dispute.

Problems of industrial action

There are certain problems which result from industrial action, both for employers and employees.

Employers' problems

- Industrial action can lead to lost production for the business. A go slow or work to rule may reduce output. Strike action could mean that orders are unfulfilled and revenue and profits could fall.
- If industrial action results in production being stopped, then machinery and other resources will be lying idle. A business will have many fixed costs which have to be covered, even if production is not taking place. If output ceases, revenue will not be earned to pay for these costs.
- Industrial action may lead to poor future relationships in a business. Sometimes grievances can carry on after a dispute. This could result in poor motivation and communication.
- Industrial disputes divert managers' attention away from planning. If a business is concerned with solving a dispute that exists now, it may neglect plans for the future.
- Loss of output and delays in production or deliveries caused by action can harm the firm's reputation. This may lead to lost business in future.

Employees' problems

- A work to rule, go slow or strike can lead to a reduction or a loss of earnings.

- Prolonged industrial action may, in some cases, lead to the closure of the business. Employees would then be made redundant.
- Action is likely to place stress on the workforce. It can also cause friction between levels of the hierarchy. For example, managers on the other 'side' in a dispute are unlikely to find their employees motivated.
- If action is unsuccessful, the employees' position may be weaker in future. Members may also leave a union if they feel that it is unable to support their interests.
- Public support may suffer if the action affects people's everyday lives.
- Strike action must conform to current legislation or unions may be liable for damages and employees may be disciplined or dismissed.

Benefits of industrial action

Industrial action is often used as a 'final' measure by unions and employers because of the disruption it causes. There are, however, some benefits for both groups.

- It 'clears the air'. Employers and employees may have grievances. Industrial action can bring these out into the open and, once the dispute is solved, this could improve the 'atmosphere' in the business.
- Introducing new rules. How groups operate in businesses is influenced by rules, such as rates of pay or what is meant by unfair dismissal. Conflict is often about disagreement over these rules. When industrial action has been resolved, this often leads to new rules which each group agrees upon.
- Changing management goals. Management often change their goals and the ways they are achieved after industrial action. For example, a business may have attempted to introduce new working practices without consulting unions, which led to industrial action. In future it may consult with unions before changing work practices.
- Understanding the position of each group. Industrial action often makes the position of employers and employees very clear. It allows each group to hear the grievances of the other, consider them and decide to what extent they agree.

KEYTERMS

Go slow - the reduction of output by workers whilst still carrying on tasks in their contract of employment.
Lock-out - action by employers which prevents employees entering the factory to work.
Sit-in/Work-in - the illegal occupation of premises by workers, which allows workers to gain control of the factory.
Work to rule - when employees do not carry out duties which are not in their employment contract.

KNOWLEDGE

1. Why might the number of days lost through stoppages in the UK have fallen over the last decade?
2. Explain four types of industrial action that employers can take.
3. State six types of employee action.
4. Why might employees be reluctant to use strike action?
5. Explain the difference between a sit-in and a go slow.
6. What factors might influence the success of employees' industrial action?
7. State three problems of industrial action for:
   (a) employees;
   (b) employers.
8. How might industrial action benefit a business?

Case Study: Industrial action

In April 2008 Express Newspapers' journalists called a new three-day strike, after its planned one-day industrial action was cancelled as a 'guerrilla tactic" to frustrate management. Managers had lined up casual staff to cover for the strike and allow the *Daily Express* and *Daily Star* to be published. The new industrial action would take place alongside a 24-hour stoppage announced for the following week. The April 22 and 24 strike could put in jeopardy the *Daily Express* and *Daily Star's* coverage of the Champions League semi finals, which feature Manchester United, Chelsea and Liverpool. Staff voted to strike after Express Newspapers refused to offer more than a 3 per cent pay rise.

In response to the cancellation, Steve Usher, the NUJ chapel representative for the *Daily Star* said 'We suspended today's action because they had already lined up casuals, the Press Association and shuttle buses. They spent a whole lot of money. We thought it would be good to cancel at no cost to us to show them we still mean business. We need a response. This has all got out of hand. It has gone on for too long, but they [management] won't come to us with any meaningful discussions. It has become a battle now.' A union meeting attended by more than 100 NUJ members, passed a resolution calling for a 'genuine partnership' with management.

Source: adapted from *The Guardian*, 11.4.2008.

In 2004 up to 90,000 members of the Public and Commercial Services Union (PCS) began a two day strike sparked by workers' anger over pay. This followed the collapse of pay talks, with the threat of further industrial action to come. The strike forced hundreds of job centres and social security offices to close. Up to 5,000 driving tests were also expected to be cancelled as driving examiners joined the picket line. The PCS claimed the strike was the result of the government's refusal to resolve 'appalling' levels of pay and an unacceptable performance appraisal system in the Department for Work and Pensions (DWP).

The union's general secretary claimed that low pay was endemic in the civil service and called on government ministers to intervene in the dispute. He said that civil servants were sick of a lack of recognition. Workers' anger was worsened by reports that a government inquiry into the civil service was to recommend 80,000 job cuts. The PCS general secretary said the union would oppose any moves to cut jobs because vital services such as the New Deal, immigration and customs were carried out by frontline as well as back-office civil servants.

The DWP described the strike as 'indefensible' and said contingency plans were in place to minimise disruption.

Source: adapted from *The Guardian*,16.2.2004.

(a) Describe the industrial action taken by (i) employees and (ii) employers in the two cases. (6 marks)

(b) Examine the reasons for the industrial action. (10 marks)

(c) Explain the possible benefits and problems of industrial action for both sides. (10 marks)

(d) Assess the factors that might affect the relative strengths and weaknesses in the two disputes. (12 marks)

(e) Evaluate the likelihood of success of the industrial action in each case. (12 marks)

80 The nature of production

What is production?

PRODUCTION takes place when resources, such as raw materials or components, are changed into 'products'. Land, labour, capital and enterprise, the factors of production, are used in the production process. The use of land and a tractor to grow cabbages is an example of production in **primary industry**. An example of **secondary industry** would be the use of wood, plastic, glue, screws, labour, drilling and cutting equipment to manufacture furniture.

Today production is often referred to more generally as those activities that 'bring a product into being'. Activities which are part of **tertiary industry**, such as services, would be included in this definition. A bank might talk about providing a 'product' in the same way as a carpet manufacturer. Examples of products in a bank's product portfolio might include mortgages, current accounts, house insurance and foreign currency. Direct services from the producer to the consumer, such as car repairs or decorating, can also be regarded as production in this sense.

Features of production

Production takes place when a business takes INPUTS, carries out a PROCESS and produces an OUTPUT or product. Production by a jewellery manufacturer may include the following.

- Inputs are the raw materials and components used by a business. These may include gold, silver and precious stones.
- Processes are the methods used to convert raw materials and components into products. Processes might include designing, cutting, bending, soldering and polishing. Such processes are often performed using machines and tools. For example, metal cutters, specialist jeweller's tools, a soldering iron and a small polishing machine might be used.
- Outputs are the products or services produced when inputs are converted. They might include rings, brooches, bangles, bracelets and necklaces.

Planning and controlling production

For production to be effective, it needs to be planned and controlled.

Planning All businesses, whether small or large, need to plan production. Some large firms employ production planners for this task. A number of factors can influence the plan.

- Demand from customers. Businesses get orders from different customers, for different products, with different specifications, at different times. A business must plan which orders should go out first and which can wait.
- The design of a product might affect planning. For example, the design specifications of a product might state that certain materials must be used or certain processes, like high quality finishing, must be carried out.
- Planning must make sure that there are enough resources available. Many businesses purchase stocks of raw materials and components and keep them until they are needed. Others order 'just in time'.

Loading This involves deciding which 'work centres' will carry out which tasks. A work centre may be an employee, a machine, a production cell or a process such as welding.

(a) Using the businesses shown in the photographs, explain what is meant by production.

(b) Explain whether the activities of the business are examples of primary, secondary or tertiary production

Figure 1: Gantt chart showing the sequence of tasks required to produce a batch of 1,000 metal brackets by an engineering company

Task	M	Tu	W	Th	F	M	Tu
Cutting							
Bending							
Welding							
Painting							
Packing							

Sequencing Production usually involves arranging tasks and processes in a sequence. For many products the order of tasks will rarely change, such as in the production of bread. This is often the case when fairly large numbers of the same product are produced. However, when non-standard or customised products are made, the order in which tasks and processes are arranged may need to change.

Scheduling The production schedule will show times when particular tasks and processes should start and finish. This is particularly important when large production projects are being undertaken, such as the construction of a large building. The aim of scheduling is to ensure that resources, such as workers, are not idle whilst waiting for someone else to finish a job before starting their own. **Gantt charts** can be used to help scheduling. A Gantt chart is a visual display showing how tasks might be sequenced over time. The Gantt chart in Figure 1 shows the sequence of tasks required to produce a batch of 1,000 metal brackets by an engineering company.

The chart shows that:

- cutting begins on Monday and takes two days;
- bending, the longest task, begins on Tuesday. It takes three days and can begin before the entire batch has been cut;
- on Thursday welding begins before the entire batch has finished the bending process. Welding takes two days;
- painting begins on Friday even though the whole batch has not been welded and painting the whole batch takes two days;
- packing, which takes only half a day, cannot begin until Tuesday, when the whole batch has been painted.

Dispatching This involves giving instructions about the tasks to be carried out for a particular period. Instructions may be given verbally or in written form.

Progressing This is an ongoing monitoring process. It requires supervisors, teams or managers reporting on the progress of jobs. Managers or teams may have to identify problems and help solve them. They should also try to eliminate bottlenecks and encourage workers, when necessary, to speed up the job.

Added value

A business adds value to raw materials which it uses in the production process. ADDED VALUE can be found in the difference between the cost of purchasing raw materials and the price which the finished goods are sold for. In Figure 2 the builder will use inputs such as land, bricks, wood, tiles, frames, glass and other materials to build a house. The total cost of all the inputs is £31,000. The centre of the diagram shows the various processes required in the construction of the house. These include digging, bricklaying, roofing, tiling, plumbing, joining, painting and other tasks. As a result of these processes an output is produced. In this example the output is a house, which is sold by the builder for £89,000. The **value added** in this case is £58,000 (£89,000 - £31,000).

£58,000 is not the **profit** made by the builder. Part of the £58,000 will be used to pay the wages of employees and business overheads such as insurance, motor expenses and tax. So the

Figure 2: Added value in production

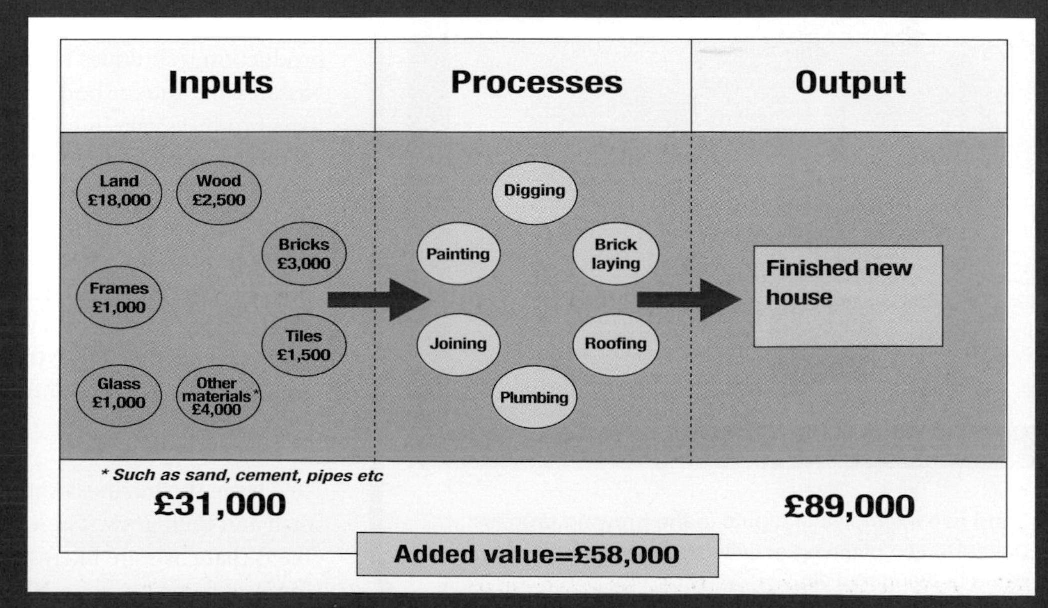

Question 2.

Real ale is the name coined by the Campaign for Real Ale (CAMRA) in 1973 for a type of beer defined as 'beer brewed from traditional ingredients, matured by secondary fermentation in the container from which it is dispensed, and served without the use of extraneous carbon dioxide'. Once the beer has been brewed it is simply placed in the cask in its natural state. Finings, such as isinglass (the swim bladder of fish) or Irish Moss (a seaweed), are placed in the cask to drag down the yeast and clear the beer. Extra hops and sugar may also be added. The cask is sealed and sent off to the pub. In this state it is like a bottle conditioned beer, and like bottle conditioned beers the beer will continue to develop for a certain period of time. All of the steps involved in the production of real ale are shown in Figure 3.

Source: adapted from the *Good Beer Guide*

Figure 3: Production of real ale

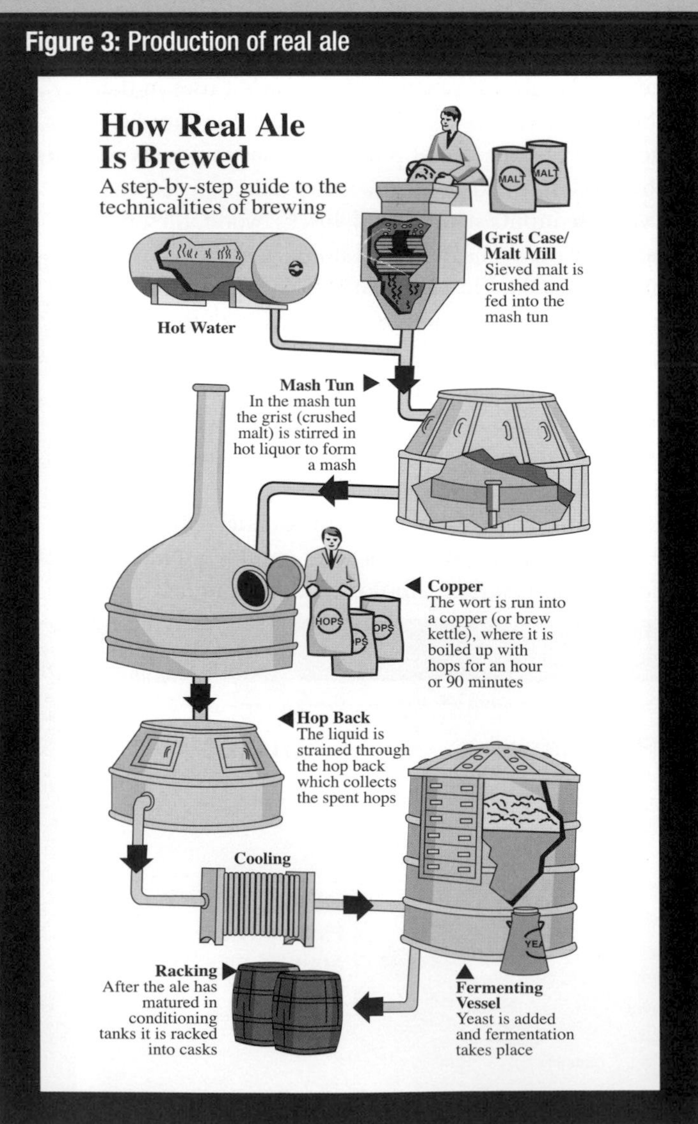
How Real Ale Is Brewed
A step-by-step guide to the technicalities of brewing
Grist Case/ Malt Mill
Sieved malt is crushed and fed into the mash tun
Hot Water
Mash Tun
In the mash tun the grist (crushed malt) is stirred in hot liquor to form a mash
Copper
The wort is run into a copper (or brew kettle), where it is boiled up with hops for an hour or 90 minutes
Hop Back
The liquid is strained through the hop back which collects the spent hops
Cooling
Racking
After the ale has matured in conditioning tanks it is racked into casks
Fermenting Vessel
Yeast is added and fermentation takes place

(a) State two examples of inputs in the brewing process.

(b) Describe two planning activities brewers might use when brewing real ale.

profit figure will be lower than the value added figure. Value added is the difference between the price at which goods or services are sold and the cost of raw materials. Profit is the difference between the price at which goods or services are sold and all costs of production.

For services, it is sometimes more difficult to see how value is added. A supermarket will buy in a product from a producer or wholesaler. It will sell the product for a higher price to customers than it has paid for it. The difference in price is added value. The retailer is adding value because it is providing a service (making the products available in a convenient location) to the customer.

Production decisions

Businesses make a number of important production decisions. A clothing manufacturer, for example, might decide to produce a new range of casual trousers. This could involve using a new type of cloth, changing the layout of the factory, increasing the size of its warehouse, employing more labour and introducing a new quality control system. One production decision will often lead to other decisions having to be made. Decisions made by businesses might include some of the following.

What to produce A business must decide what product it wants to produce. The product may be a new product, that no other business has produced, or an adaptation of its own or a competitor's products. For example, 'Little Feet' are foot shaped plastic moulds which keeps two socks together in the wash. The creator, Andrea Marks, based the design on grips used to hold tea towels in kitchens. Many supermarkets now offer financial services such as savings accounts similar to those of banks.

What production method should be used Businesses choose how best to make their products. Different businesses might use different production methods, even when they make the same products. For example, TVR and Nissan both manufacture cars. TVR hand-builds its cars in a small factory in Blackpool. Its production techniques make more use of skilled workers than Nissan's and the car bodies are made from fibreglass. Nissan mass produces cars in factories around the world. It relies more on robots, computers and other machines than TVR and uses metal for the car bodies.

Where production should be located Business owners have to decide where best to locate their premises. Generally, they will find locations where costs will be lowest. Small business owners may locate near to where they live. Large multinationals may locate production in countries where the government gives them subsidies and grants.

How large the business should be Most businesses start off small and then grow. There are many advantages of growing. One is that costs are likely to fall due to economies of scale. However, some business owners are content to remain relatively small, to avoid the extra responsibilities growth brings for instance.

How to ensure quality Businesses are more likely to be successful if they can produce high quality products. Businesses have to decide how they might improve quality. This might involve using more expensive raw materials, training staff to higher levels or introducing a quality system, such as total quality management (TQM).

KEYTERMS

Input – the raw materials used in production.
Output – the goods or services resulting from production.
Process – the method used to convert inputs to final goods or services.
Production – the transformation of resources into goods or services.
Added value – the difference between the cost of raw materials and the selling price.

KNOWLEDGE

1. State three examples of production in the (a) primary (b) secondary and (c) tertiary industries.
2. State five features of planning and controlling production.
3. Explain how a cereal manufacturer adds value to production.
4. 'The retailer marked up the wholesale price by 10 per cent.' Explain why this is an example of calculating value added.
5. Why is value added not the same as profit?

Case Study: Ben and Jerry's

Ben and Jerry's is a well known brand of luxury ice cream. The brand is now owned by the giant food company, Unilever, but ice cream is still produced in Ben and Jerry's factory in Waterbury, Vermont. The processes involved in the production of Ben and Jerry's ice cream are summarised in Figure 4.

The main ingredient for Ben and Jerry's ice cream is milk and hundreds of family farms in the St Albans area of Vermont supply the St Albans Co-operative Creamery. Here the milk is separated into heavy cream and condensed skimmed milk and then transported by tanker to the Waterbury factory. When the tankers arrive the milk and cream are pumped into four 6,000 gallon storage silos where it is held at a temperature of 36 degrees until it is needed for production. Cartons of ice cream are produced continuously at the Waterbury factory on a production line. Production is highly automated and when production begins the following processes are used.

- **Mixing** This is arguably the most important part of the whole process and is supervised by a mixman. Milk, cream, liquid cane sugar, natural stablizers and egg yolks are mixed together in a 1,000 gallon stainless steel blend tank.
- **Pasteurisation** This involves heating the mix to 180 degrees to kill off any harmful bacteria.
- **Homogenisation** This means breaking down the fat globules in the mix to make them smaller. Now the ice-cream will be smoother, will whip better and won't melt as easily.
- **Cooling** The mix is then left for at least four hours, usually overnight, to let the fat cool and form into crystals.
- **Flavouring** This process is what makes Ben and Jerry's ice cream unique. Flavours, fruit purees, or colours are added at this point to the mix which passes through 500 gallon steel vats. Some examples of flavourings are vanilla, pure peppermint, food extracts, banana puree and even some liqueurs.
- **Freezing** The mix is then pumped through a special barrel

freezer which freezes some of the water in the ice-cream and whips air into it at the same time. Up to half the volume of ice-cream is air. Without it, the ice-cream would be like a frozen ice cube. Ben and Jerry's freezers use liquid ammonia as a freezing agent (40 degrees below zero). Each freezer can handle over 700 gallons of ice cream mix per hour.

- **Chunk feeding** Any fruits, nuts, sweets or biscuit bits are added to the semi-frozen mixture at this point. However, smooth ice creams would by-pass this process.
- **Variegation** This is the process that adds the swirls to Ben and Jerry's ice cream. The frozen mix passes through a variegator where swirls of marshmallow, fudge, peanut butter or caramel, for example, are injected into the ice cream.
- **Packaging** After the chunks and swirls are added, the ice cream is ready for dispensing into pint containers. This is done using an automatic filler. This piece of machinery fills about 120 cartons per minute.
- **Hardening** Before the ice cream can be stored or distributed it needs to be frozen further from its semi-frozen state to a fully frozen state of 10 degrees below zero. A spiral hardner is used in this process where the wind speed temperature inside the machine's tunnel is 60 degrees below zero.
- **Bundler** This is the final stage in the production process and involves shrink wrapping the pint cartons into bundles of eight which are then stacked on pallets ready for transportation to storage.

Source: adapted from www.benjerry.com.

Figure 4: The processes involved in the production of Ben and Jerry's ice cream

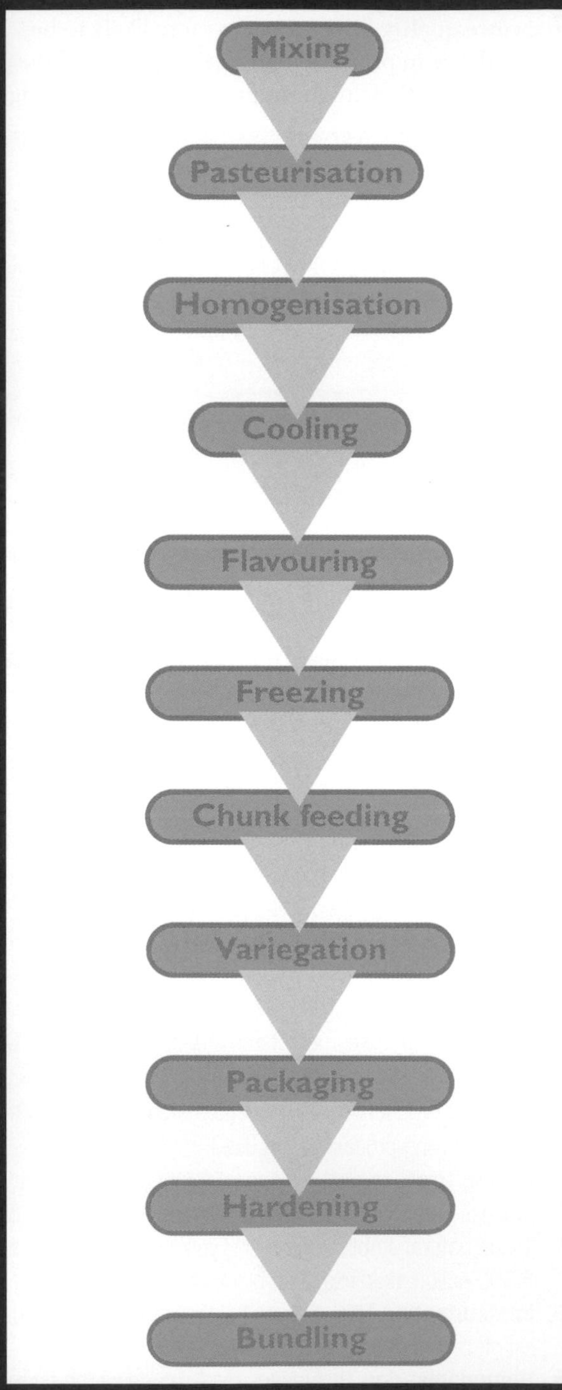

(a) Explain why the production of Ben and Jerry's ice cream is an example of secondary production. (4 marks)

(b) Outline the possible role of a production planner at Ben and Jerry's factory. (6 marks)

(c) Using ice cream production as an example, explain what is meant by (i) inputs (ii) processes (iii) outputs. (12 marks)

(d) Explain how Ben and Jerry's add value when producing ice cream. (8 marks)

(e) Discuss two possible production decisions that Ben and Jerry's might have to make. (10 marks)

81 Types of production

Deciding how to produce

A business must decide on the most suitable method to manufacture its goods or to provide services. It is likely that products which are different will be produced differently. For example, a plastic drinks bottle may be produced using automated machinery, but a wrist watch may be assembled by hand. Products that are similar can also be produced in different ways. The Ford Motor Company and Morgan Cars both produce cars, but different processes are used. Ford builds cars using a production line and semi-skilled labour, but Morgan cars are hand built by skilled workers. There are three important decisions that businesses must make when choosing how to produce. These are shown in Figure 1, along with the factors which influence these decisions. In the diagram it is assumed that the firm has already decided 'what' to produce. When deciding how to produce, the objective of the firm will be to minimise the cost per unit of output, i.e. PRODUCTIVE EFFICIENCY.

What production method will be used? Production is sometimes divided into one of three methods. JOB PRODUCTION is where one job is completed at a time before moving on to another. An example might be a costume made for a television play set in the nineteenth century. BATCH PRODUCTION involves dividing the work into a number of different operations. An example would be bread production, where each batch goes through several different baking stages before it is completed. FLOW PRODUCTION involves work being completed continuously without stopping. The production of cars on a production line might be one example.

Some industries may combine different methods of production. For example, a large brewery may produce 'batches' of beer, but then send them to a bottling line for packaging, where flow production is used. Such combinations are particularly common in the food industry.

Figure 1: Factors which affect the decision about how to produce

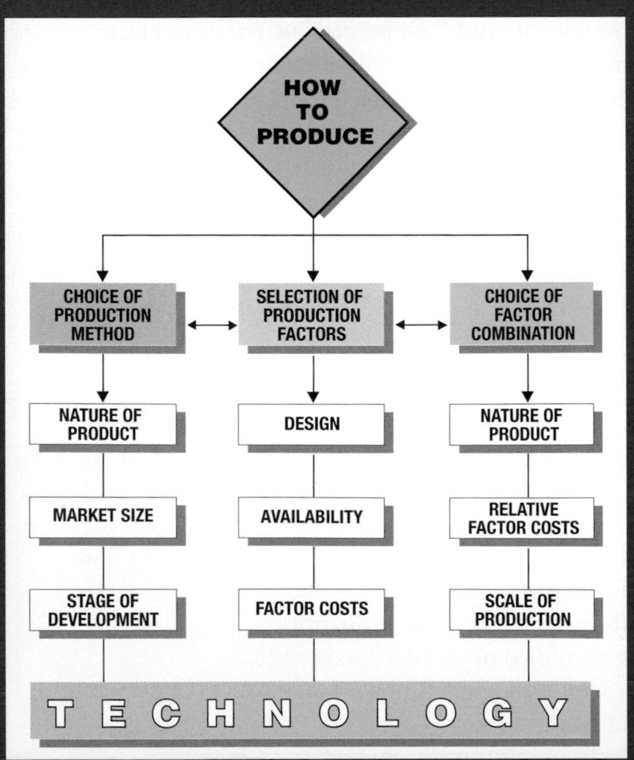

What factors of production will be used? Businesses are often faced with a wide choice between alternative production factors. For example, a builder planning to construct a new house must decide what building materials to buy, which tools to use, which sub-contractors to employ and whether to hire any extra labour. The builder will be faced with a choice in all of these cases. If he decides to hire a labourer, there may be hundreds or even thousands of people to choose from in the area.

How will the factors of production be combined? A third production decision concerns the way in which the available production factors should be combined. For example, should an assembly plant invest in a highly automated assembly operation, or employ a large semi-skilled labour force to undertake the work?

This unit focuses on the types of production a business might choose from.

Job production

Job production involves the production of a single product at a time. It is used when orders for products are small, such as 'one-offs'. Production is organised so that one 'job' is completed at a time. There is a wide variety of goods and services which are produced or provided using this method of production. Small-scale examples include the baking of a child's birthday cake, a dentist's treatment session or the construction of an extension to a house. On a large scale, examples could include the building of a ship, the construction of the Channel Tunnel or the manufacture of specialised machinery. Job production is found in both manufacturing and the service industries. Because the numbers of units produced is small, the production process tends to be labour intensive. The workforce is usually made up of skilled craftsmen or specialists and the possibility of using labour-saving machinery is limited. Many businesses adopt this method of production when they are 'starting up'. The advantages and disadvantages of job production are shown in Table 1.

Table 1: Advantages and disadvantages of job production

Advantages

- Firms can produce unique or 'one-off' orders according to customer needs. For example, a wedding dress may be designed and produced for the individual taste of a client. It is also possible to change the specifications of a job at the last minute, even if the work has actually begun.
- Workers are more likely to be motivated. The tasks employees carry out often require a variety of skills, knowledge and expertise. Their work will be more demanding and interesting. They will also see the end result of their efforts and be able to take pride in their work. Jobs may be carried out by a team of workers aiming to achieve the same objectives. This should help raise the level of job satisfaction.
- The organisation of job production is fairly simple. Because only one job is done at a time, co-ordination, communication, supervision and inspection can take place regularly. Also, it is easier to identify and deal with problems, such as a defective damp proof course in a house or a poorly cooked meal in a restaurant.

Disadvantages

- Labour costs will be high because production tends to be labour intensive. The workforce is likely to be skilled and more versatile. Such employees will be more expensive. The amount of time each employee spends on a particular job will also be long.
- Because there is a variety of work, subject to many specifications, the business would need a wide range of tools, machines and equipment. This can prove expensive. Also, it may not be possible to achieve economies of scale because only one 'job' is produced at a time.
- Lead times can be lengthy. When building a house, the business has to incur costs which cannot be recovered until the house is sold. Sometimes the sale of a house can take a long time.
- Selling costs may also be high. This is likely if the product is highly complex and technical. The sales team will need to be well qualified, able to cope with questions and deal with problems concerning sales and installation. Some firms employ agencies to help reduce their selling costs.
- Once the demand for a firm's product rises, job production may become costly. Firms may prefer to use a method more suited to producing larger quantities. This is not always the case. Even if demand is high, each customer may require a unique order. In addition, many firms believe that the 'personal touch' they can offer in job production is important. As a result, they may choose not to change to other production methods. Other production methods require some degree of product standardisation. This may result in more efficient production, but a loss of 'individuality'.

Table 2: Operations involved in the production of a batch of bread

1. Blend ingredients in a mixing container until a dough is formed.
2. Knead the dough for a period of time.
3. Leave the dough to rise for a period of time.
4. Divide the dough into suitable units (loaves) for baking.
5. Bake the loaves.
6. Allow loaves to cool.

Batch production

Batch production may be used when demand for a firm's product or service is regular rather than a 'one off'. An example might be a furniture factory, where a batch of armchairs is made to a particular design. Production is divided into a number of operations. A particular operation is carried out on all products in a batch. The batch then moves to the next operation. A baker uses batch production when baking bread. The operations in the baking process are broken down in Table 2.

These operations would be performed on every batch of bread. There is some standardisation because each loaf in the batch will be the same. However, it may be possible to vary each batch. The ingredients could be changed to produce brown bread or the style of baking tin could be changed for different shaped loaves.

A great number of products are produced using this method, particularly in manufacturing, such as the production of components and food processing. For example, in a canning plant, a firm may can several different batches of soup, each batch being a different recipe. Products can be produced in very large or very small batches, depending on the level of demand. Larger production runs tend to lower the **unit** or **average cost** of production. New technology is increasingly being introduced to make batch production more efficient. The advantages and disadvantages of batch production are shown in Table 3.

Flow production

Most people will have some idea of flow production from pictures of motor car factories. Production is organised so that different operations can be carried out, one after the other, in a continuous sequence. Vehicles move from one operation to the next, often on a conveyer belt. The main features of flow production are:

- the production of large quantities;
- a simplified or standardised product;
- a semi-skilled workforce, specialising in one operation only;
- large amounts of machinery and equipment;
- large stocks of raw materials and components.

Table 3: Advantages and disadvantges of batch production

Advantages	Disadvantages
• Even though larger quantities are produced than in job production, there is still flexibility. Each batch can be changed to meet customers' wishes. It is particularly suitable for a wide range of similar products. The settings on machines can be changed according to specifications, such as different clothes sizes.	• Careful planning and co-ordination are needed, or machines and workers may be idle, waiting for a whole batch to finish its previous operation. There is often a need to clean and adjust machinery before the next batch can be produced. This can mean delays. In brewing, one day of the week is used to clean equipment before the next batch begins.
• Employees can concentrate on one operation rather than on the whole task. This reduces the need for costly, skilled employees.	• Some machinery may have to be more complex to compensate for the lower skill levels required from the labour force. This may lead to higher costs.
• Less variety of machinery would be needed than in job production because the products are standardised. Also, it is possible to use more standardised machinery.	• The workforce may be less motivated, since they have to repeat operations on every single unit in the batch. In addition, they are unlikely to be involved with production from start to finish.
• It often results in stocks of partly finished goods which have to be stored. This means firms can respond more quickly to an urgent order by processing a batch quickly through the final stages of production.	• If batches are small then unit costs will remain relatively high.
	• Money will be tied up in work-in-progress, since an order cannot be dispatched until the whole batch has been finished.

Question 1.

Alex Stone is a chartered accountant. He runs a small business from an office in Kidderminster producing final accounts for sole traders, partnerships and small private limited companies. He has a client base of around 110 businesses and employs a secretary and a young trainee accountant. In addition to preparing accounts He offers other services such as:

- completing tax returns;
- taxation planning;
- advice on the financial management of businesses;
- advice on investment;
- auditing.

(a) Use this case as an example to explain what is meant by job production.

(b) Explain why job production might help to motivate Alex and his trainee.

Flow production is used in the manufacture of products as varied as newspapers, food and cement. It is sometimes called **mass production**, as it tends to be used for the production of large numbers of standard products, such as cars or breakfast cereals. Certain types of flow production are known as **continual flow production**, because products such as clothing material pass continually through a series of processes. **Repetitive flow production** is the manufacture of large numbers of the same product, such as plastic toy parts or metal cans.

The advantages and disadvantages of flow production are shown in Table 4. In the 1990s flow production processes were changed in an attempt to solve some of the problems. Japanese manufacturers setting up businesses in the UK introduced methods to improve efficiency. Just-in-time manufacturing, for example, helped to reduce the cost of holding stocks. Some vehicle manufacturers attempted to introduce an element of job production into flow processes by **customising** products for clients. For example, a range of different cars was produced on the same production line. Cars in the same model range differed in colour, engine size, trim and interior design.

Process production

PROCESS PRODUCTION is a form of flow production which is used in the oil or chemical industry. Materials pass through a plant where a series of processes are carried out in order to change the product. An example might be the refining of crude oil into petrol.

Flow production relies on the use of computers. Computers send instructions to machines, control production speeds and conditions, and monitor quality. They allow large numbers of products to be produced continuously to exact standards or control continuous production, which requires many processes.

Table 4: Advantages and disadvantages of flow production

Advantages

- Unit costs are reduced as firms gain from economies of scale.
- In many industries the process is highly automated. Production is controlled by computers. Many of the operations are performed by robots and other types of machinery. Once the production line is set up and running, products can flow off the end non stop for lengthy periods of time. This can reduce the need for labour, as only machine supervisors are needed.
- The need to stockpile finished goods is reduced. The production line can respond to short-term changes in demand. For example, if demand falls the line can be shut down for a period of time. If it rises then the line can be opened.

Disadvantages

- The set--up costs are very high. An enormous investment in plant and equipment is needed. Firms must therefore be confident that demand for the product is sufficient over a period of time to make the investment pay.
- The product will be standardised. It is not possible to offer a wide product range and meet different customers' needs. However, modern machinery is becoming more flexible and is beginning to overcome this problem.
- For a number of reasons, worker motivation can be a serious problem. Most of the manual operations required on the production line will be repetitive and boring. Factories with production lines tend to be very noisy. Each worker will only be involved in a very small part of the job cycle. As a result of these problems worker morale may be low and labour turnover and absenteeism high.
- Breakdowns can prove costly. The whole production system is interdependent. If one part of the supply or production line fails the whole system may break down.

Choice of production method

The method of production chosen might depend on a number of factors.

The nature of the product Many products require a specific method of production. For example, in the construction industry, projects such as bridges, roads, office blocks and sewers must be produced using job production. Cereal farming involves batch production. A plot of land undergoes several processes before it 'produces' a crop.

The size of the market Fast-moving consumer goods like soap, confectionery and canned drinks are normally produced using flow production because the market is so big. When the market is small, flow production techniques are not cost effective.

The stage of development a business has reached When firms are first set up, they often produce small levels of output and employ job or batch production methods. As they grow and enjoy higher sales levels, they may switch to flow production.

Technology The current state of technology will affect all decisions concerning how to produce. As technology advances, new materials and machinery become available. Changes in technology often result in firms adopting new methods of production. For example, the development of computers and robotic welders has radically changed the way in which cars are manufactured. Also, car manufacturers are now able to produce different models on the same production line at the same time.

Question 2.

Uniform+ was established in 1997 and has become a leading supplier of workwear, leisurewear and promotional clothing to businesses and organisations across the UK. In 2006, the company moved to a purpose-built freehold head office and factory in Cannock. Uniform+ supplies over 12,000 garments a week to more than 5,500 customers. The company has an excellent reputation in the industry because of their:

- commitment to offering a wide choice of quality clothing at unbeatable prices;
- dedication to providing excellent customer service and value for money;
- fast turnaround and flexibilty to meet customers' needs;
- unique free logo and delivery service.

Like most companies in the clothes industry, Uniform+ uses batch production. The company can meet a wide range of different orders due the flexibility of its machinery and its multi-skilled workforce.

(a) Use the clothes industry as an example to explain what is meant by batch production.

(b) Why is batch production common in the clothes industry?

(c) How do you think Uniform+ has overcome some of the typical problems associated with batch production?

KEYTERMS

Batch production – a method which involves completing one operation at a time on all units before performing the next.
Flow production – very large scale production of a standardised product, where each operation on a unit is performed continuously, one after the other, usually on a production line.
Job production – a method of production which involves employing all factors to complete one unit of output at a time.
Process production – a form of flow production where materials pass through a plant where a series of processes are carried out in order to change the product.
Productive efficiency – production methods which minimise unit costs.

KNOWLEDGE

1. What are the three main decisions which have to be made regarding the method of production?
2. Under what circumstances might a business become more capital intensive?
3. State three types of products which may be manufactured using job production.
4. Describe the advantages and disadvantages of job production.
5. State three products that are generally manufactured using batch production.
6. Describe the advantages and disadvantages of batch production.
7. Describe four features of flow production.

Case Study: Nacional

Nacional is a major breakfast cereal manufacturer in Portugal and forms part of the grain milling Amorim-Lage Group. The popularity of breakfast cereals has grown in Portugal in recent years and one of Nacional's main production facilities was in need of a major update and expansion using new technology and new ideas. Early in 2004, Nacional carried out a major refit and expansion plan that was completed by mid-September. The investment in the new facility was estimated at 11.2 million euros.

Nacional's main product was cornflakes but since the expansion the facility has been able to manufacture a variety of extruded breakfast cereal products for marketing under its own brand names and also for supermarket own-brand labels. The adoption of extrusion techniques (drawing a dough mixture through a shape to produce a continuous strand with an identical cross section which can be cut into shapes such as stars or squares for example) in processing breakfast cereal at the Nacional plant has widened the production possibilities because a variety of grains can now be used. This has allowed the blending of different grains into unique cereal pieces. Extrusion has also made production more efficient by combining several processing steps into a single, continuous flow.

PV Baker has supplied and installed a complete processing plant for Nacional. It incorporates the entire production process, from compounding and mixing the recipe 'dough' through extrusion and cooking to drying and coating the final extruded product shapes. The new facility can make a variety of different products, including corn-balls, coco-balls, choco curls, golden squares, stars and rings, as well as co-extruded filled pillow shapes. All of these extruded shapes, except the pillows, will be coated with a honey, sugar or glucose based glaze.

Most of the products are cut into individual pieces by a die as they leave the extruder. A key design feature of the facility is the ability to change over rapidly between products in response to market demand, including those products involving different raw materials and syrup. For example, to create filled pillow products, which cannot be cut at the die, a mobile crimping unit is wheeled in and out of the line.

Source: adapted from www.foodprocessing-technology.com

(a) State four processes used in the production of breakfast cereals at Nacional. (4 marks)
(b) Explain how Nacional is using both batch production and flow production methods in its factory. (10 marks)
(c) When upgrading its production facilities, what role did technology play at Nacional? (6 marks)
(d) To what extent do you think the 11.2 million euro investment will benefit Nacional? (20 marks)

82 Capacity utilisation

Operational decisions and targets

OPERATIONS MANAGEMENT is the organisation and control of the process by which inputs, such as labour, materials and machinery, are transformed into final products or by which services are provided to customers. Production managers, for example, are responsible for making decisions about:

- what production methods are to be used;
- what levels of input of labour, machinery and materials are needed to produce a given quantity of output;
- how best to utilise the firm's capacity;
- what stock levels are required to support production;
- how to ensure that work is completed on time;
- how best to ensure quality.

Decisions about the entire business that affect production also need to be made. For example:

- What is the optimal size for a business? Should there be five employees, 500 or 500,000?
- Where should production take place? On one or two sites? In the UK or the Far East?

Good operations management can help a business to be more effective. One approach which operations managers are likely to use is to set OPERATIONAL TARGETS. Setting targets can help managers monitor the performance of the production department. A number of key targets might be used, as shown in Figure 1.

Figure 1: Operational targets

Unit costs

Unit cost is the cost of producing a single unit of output. It is the same as average cost. It can be calculated as:

$$\text{Unit cost} = \frac{\text{Total cost}}{\text{Output}}$$

So, for example, if a computer manufacturer produced 12,000 laptop computers in a year at a total cost of £3,480,000, the unit cost would be given by:

$$\text{Unit cost} = \frac{£3{,}480{,}000}{12{,}000} = £290$$

This means that each single laptop computer cost £290 to make.

Production managers may set operational targets for unit costs. These costs can be measured at the end of a production run and compared with the targets. If actual unit costs are higher than the targets, the production manager is likely to search for reasons why so that appropriate action can be taken. Generally, businesses are always looking for ways to *control* or reduce unit costs.

Capacity utilisation

CAPACITY UTILISATION is about the use that a business makes from its resources. If a business is not able to increase output, it is said to be running at full capacity. Its capacity utilisation is 100 per cent. So if a 52 seater coach from London to Edinburgh has 52 passengers, it is operating at full capacity. If it had 32 passengers it would be operating at less than full capacity and so it would have EXCESS, SURPLUS, SPARE or UNUSED CAPACITY.

Businesses do not always operate at full capacity. It may not be possible to keep all resources and machinery fully employed all the time. However, most businesses would wish to be operating at close to full capacity, such as 90 per cent.

In some cases businesses even choose to operate at less than full capacity in order to be flexible. For example, they might want to have capacity to cope with increased orders from regular customers. Without this, a business might let down its customers and risk losing them.

Capacity utilisation can be measured by comparing actual or current output with the potential output at full capacity using the formula:

$$\text{Capacity utilisation} = \frac{\text{Current output}}{\text{Maximum possible output}} \times 100$$

A printing operation might be able to operate for ten hours, six days a week using shifts. If it only had enough work to operate for 48 hours last week, the capacity utilisation would be:

$$\text{Capacity utilisation} = \frac{48}{(10 \times 6)} \times 100 = 80\%$$

Another example might be a printing machine that is capable of printing 10,000 leaflets in a time period but only prints 9,000. It has a capacity utilisation of (9,000 ÷ 10,000) x 100 = 90 per cent. In this case the machine has unused, excess, surplus or spare capacity of 10 per cent.

Costs and capacity utilisation

A business can lower its unit or average costs if it can increase its capacity utilisation. This is because some of its costs are fixed. Higher levels of capacity utilisation and higher levels of output, will make a business more efficient. Table 1 shows capacity utilisation output, variable cost, fixed cost, total cost and average cost (unit cost) for a component manufacturer. When capacity utilisation is raised from 60 per cent to 80 per cent, for example, average cost falls from £2.42 to £2.31. This is because the fixed costs of £50,000 are spread over more units of output. This explains why firms will always be keen to raise capacity utilisation.

Table 1: Capacity utilisation, output, variable cost, fixed cost, total cost, unit cost for a component manufacturer

Actual output (units)	120,000	160,000
Maximum possible output (units)	200,000	200,000
Capacity utilisation	60%	80%
Variable costs (£2 per unit)	£240,000	£320,000
Fixed costs	£50,000	£50,000
Total cost	£290,000	£370,000
Unit cost	£2.42	£2.31

Question 1.

Oliver Handy make mattresses. It is an established business and operates from a small factory in Swindon. It employs twelve staff and has recently appointed a new production manager. In 2006, the then manager retired after 25 years of service to the company. He was replaced by the current manager. Within two months of the new manager arriving some sweeping changes were made to production methods and working practices. The new manager emphasised the importance of production targets, unit costs, staff rewards and operations management. Table 2 shows some financial information for Oliver Handy.

Table 2: Financial information for Oliver Handy

				(£)
	2004	**2005**	**2006**	**2007**
Total output	12,000	13,500	14,000	17,000
Total cost	252,000	297,000	305,200	297,500

(a) What is meant by operations management?
(b) (i) Calculate the unit costs for the four years.
(ii) What impact has the new production manager had on unit costs?
(c) How can setting operational targets help a business like Oliver Handy?

Improving capacity utilisation

A business will make better use of its resources if it increases its capacity utilisation. Its unit costs will be lower and profits will be higher. How can firms increase capacity utilisation?

Reduced capacity A business might decide to cut capacity. It might do this by RATIONALISING, for example. This involves reducing excess capacity by getting rid of resources that the business can do without. There is a number of measures a business might take.

- Reducing staff by making people redundant, employing more part-time and temporary staff and offering early retirement.
- Selling off unused fixed assets such as machinery, vehicles, office space, warehouses and factory space.
- Leasing capacity. Debenhams has leased unused floor space in its stores to other retailers, for example. Parts of a factory could also be leased to another manufacturer. The advantage of this is that the space may be reclaimed if demand picks up again.
- Moving to smaller premises where costs are lower.
- MOTHBALLING some resources. This means that fixed assets, such as machinery, are left unused but are maintained, so that they can be brought back into use if necessary.

Increased sales If a business sells more of its output, it will have to produce more. Therefore capacity utilisation will rise. A business might need to spend money on promotion to increase sales, for example. If these costs are not covered by the extra revenue generated, raising capacity utilisation in this way may not be viable.

Increased usage A problem that many businesses face is dealing with peak demand. Train operators can find that capacity utilisation is close to 100 per cent during the 'rush hour', but perhaps as low as 10 per cent late at night. Such businesses would like to increase capacity utilisation during 'off-peak' hours. This might explain why discounts are offered for 'off-peak' travel.

Subcontracting Capacity utilisation can vary considerably within a business. Where capital equipment has low utilisation rates, it might be more efficient for the business to SUBCONTRACT or OUTSOURCE the work. This means hiring or contracting another business to do work which was previously done in-house.

For instance, a business might run a small fleet of delivery vans which on average are on the road for four hours per day. It is likely that it would be cheaper for the business to sell the vans and employ a company to make the deliveries. The delivery company would be more efficient because it would be running its vans for much longer during the day. There may also be cost savings in terms of staff. If the business employed full-time drivers for the vans, they would have been under-utilised if they only worked four hours per day.

Subcontracting can also lead to other cost advantages. The delivery business will be a specialist business. It should operate its delivery service more efficiently than a business with a few vans and little knowledge of the industry. If nothing else, it should have greater buying power. It might be able, for instance, to negotiate lower prices for its vans because it is buying more vans. If it is a very small business, its hourly wages may be less than, say, a union-negotiated rate at the larger business.

An alternative outsourcing strategy is to take on outsourcing contracts for other businesses. For example, a major manufacturer of soap could accept contracts from rival soap manufacturers to improve its capacity utilisation. Outsourcing then becomes a strategy for increasing demand for the business.

Redeployment If a business has too many resources in one part, it may be possible to deploy them in another part. For example, a bank may ask some of its employees to work in another branch for a short period.

Advantages and disadvantages of working at full capacity

Advantages Working at full capacity has some benefits.

- Average costs will be minimised because fixed costs will be spread across as many units of output as possible. This will help to raise profits.
- Staff motivation might be good if workers feel secure in their jobs.
- A busy operation can improve the company's image. As a result, customers might be more confident when placing orders.

Problems However, there may be some drawbacks when a firm is unable to increase output any more.

- The pressure of working at full capacity all the time might put a strain on some of the resources. For example, workers might be doing too much overtime, resulting in tiredness and stress. This might cause accidents or absence.

Question 2.

Zaman & Nazran is a business which specialises in the manufacture of diecast zinc and aluminium products. It produces components for a variety of industries. Since being founded in the mid-1990s, it has grown to today's workforce of 14 employees. Sales were up 7 per cent last year and 50 per cent up from five years ago. It is confident that in the next five years, it can increase its sales by another 50 per cent.

Table 3 shows the number of hours that machinery and equipment were used during each week between July and August 2008. Management works on the assumption that 60 hours per week represents full capacity for the business. This reflects the maximum number of hours that the existing labour force would be prepared to work, including overtime.

Currently, equipment in a typical week is used to 75 per cent capacity. Working to 100 per cent capacity in any week, such as in the second week of July 2008, is unusual and difficult to maintain because machines break down or employees are off work sick. In fact, in the second week of July, the business was forced to sub-contract some of the work to rival companies because it couldn't cope with delivery deadlines set by customers. Seasonal factors affect demand. Orders often fall in late July and early August because customers tend to produce less due to their workers taking summer holidays.

Management has considered rationalisation to reduce costs. Equally the business is committed to an investment programme to buy the latest equipment, which will increase productive efficiency and allow for expansion of sales in the future.

Table 3

	July				August			
Week	1	2	3	4	1	2	3	4
Hours worked	44	60	47	31	41	45	45	47
Capacity utilisation (%)	73	100	?	?	?	?	?	?

(a) Explain what is meant by:
(i) 'capacity utilisation';
(ii) 'rationalisation'.

(b) Calculate capacity utilisation for weeks 3-4 in July and weeks 1-4 in August.

(c) Analyse two ways in which the business could increase capacity utilisation.

(d) Discuss whether the business would perform better in the long term if it sold off half its plant and equipment, moved to smaller premises, sacked half the workforce and used subcontractors to complete work which it could not manufacture to meet delivery deadlines from customers.

Machines may also be overworked to breaking point.
- The business might lose lucrative orders from new customers.
- There may be insufficient time for staff training and important maintenance work.

Matching production to demand

A production manager has to make sure that production levels tie in with the level of demand. If production levels exceed demand there will be a build up of stocks. This may be expensive because stock holding costs can be very high indeed. Also, if the stocks are not being sold, there will be a drain on resources. However, if production levels are too low, the business may not be able to satisfy demand. This could lead to a loss of trade if customers are kept waiting and decide to buy from a rival. Matching production with demand often means that operational methods should have some flexibility built in. This can be achieved in a number of ways.

Offering overtime Production managers could ask staff to work overtime if orders increase. Overtime is often popular with workers because overtime rates are usually higher than basic wage rates. They may be time and half or double time. However, not all workers will want to work overtime because they have other commitments.

Hiring part-time or temporary staff A business might use temporary or part-time staff to deal with surges in demand. Temporary staff can be 'hired and fired' according to demand levels. They will be employed on very short-term contracts. However, temporary staff will have to be trained and may not be as reliable as permanent staff. Part-time staff are generally more flexible than full-time staff. They can often adapt to changes in the hours they work.

Making flexible use of capital Fluctuations in demand may also mean that capital needs to be flexible. This might be achieved by leasing machinery and equipment in the short-term. For example, vehicles, tools and machinery can be leased to cope with increases in demand.

Using suppliers Businesses will need flexible suppliers. When orders increase a business might need to call on suppliers to make emergency deliveries. Suppliers that cannot offer flexibility and reliability might be avoided.

Adjusting production Production levels can also adjusted to match demand through rationalisation and subcontracting. This is discussed above.

Holding finished stocks A common way of matching production and demand is to hold stocks of finished goods. If demand increases, orders can be satisfied from stocks. If demand falls, then stocks can be accumulated. However, stock holding costs need to be taken into account when using this approach.

Some businesses have to cope with **seasonal demand**. These could be businesses operating farms, hotels and other leisure activities, for example. They have to organise their operations to deal with 'peak' demand in the high season and very low demand out of season. The methods discussed above are likely to be even more important to such businesses.

Non-standard orders

It is not unusual for businesses to receive **non-standard orders**. These are orders for goods that the business does not normally produce. For example, a publisher may be asked for a particular book to be available in the Welsh language. To meet such an order businesses may need to reset machines, use different labour skills, different raw materials and possibly different tools. In the example above the publisher would need to employ someone to translate the text, typeset the whole book again and organise a small production run. To meet non-standard orders extra costs will be incurred and a business may charge a premium price. Non-standard orders might be irritating but refusing such orders might lead to a loss of custom. However, accepting non-standard orders might gain new long-term customers.

KEYTERMS

Capacity utilisation – the use that a business makes of its resources.

Excess or surplus capacity – when a business has too many resources, such as labour and capital, to produce its desired level of output.

Mothballing – when machines, equipment or building space are left unused but maintained so they could be brought back into use if necessary.

Operations management – the organisation and control of the process by which inputs, such as labour, materials and machinery, are transformed into final products or by which services are provided to customers.

Operational targets – the goals set by a business that must be achieved in the production of a product or provision of a service.

Rationalising – reducing the number of resources, particularly labour and capital, put into the production process, usually undertaken because a business has excess capacity.

Subcontracting or outsourcing – hiring or contracting another business to do work which could be done in-house by a business.

KNOWLEDGE

1. State four decisions a production manager might have to make.
2. State four operational targets that might be set by a business.
3. Explain what is meant by unit cost.
4. Why will unit costs fall if capacity is better utilised?
5. State three ways in which a business might reduce capacity.
6. What is meant by redeployment?
7. What are non-standard orders?
8. State four measures that a business might take to help match production with orders.

Case Study: Gibson's Golf Buggies Ltd

Gibson's has manufactured golf buggies for 27 years. The company employs 48 staff and has a factory in Manchester. Its standard product has the following features.

- Double-seated, four-wheeled electric powered
- Twist grip stepless speed control for smooth operation
- Forward/reverse switch conveniently located
- Safe operator controlled speed governor
- Maximum speed restricted to 8mph in consideration of other golfers
- Hill climbing ability: 1:3 gradient
- Battery charging unit simply plugged into rear of buggy
- Two heavy duty batteries - 12V 75 amp/hour coupled in series.

In 2004, the company started to experience some problems. Intense competition from overseas manufacturers, China in particular, resulted in a decline in sales. The company responded by making cost savings and investing in a new marketing campaign. This appeared to halt the decline in sales and boost profit margins. However, the factory was left with a great deal of unused capacity, particularly in the winter when demand always fell. Table 4 shows some production information for Gibson's Golf Buggies Ltd.

Table 4: Gibson's Golf Buggies Ltd

	2003	2004	2005	2006	2007
Output	14,000	12,000	11,000	10,500	10,900
Total capacity	18,000	18,000	18,000	18,000	18,000

(a) Explain what is meant by 'capacity utilisation'. (3 marks)

(b) (i) Calculate the capacity utilisation for Gibson's over the five year time period. (5 marks)
(ii) Comment on the capacity utilisation of Gibson's over this time period. (5 marks)

(c) Why is the capacity utilisation at Gibson's a problem? (6 marks)

(d) How might Gibson's deal with the problem of seasonal demand in the factory? (10 marks)

(e) Evaluate the measures that might be used by Gibson's Golf Buggies Ltd to improve capacity utilisation. (20 marks)

83 Stock control

Operational decisions and stocks

Businesses purchase raw materials, semi-finished goods and components. A washing machine manufacturer, for example, may buy electric motors, circuit boards, rubber drive belts, nuts, bolts, sheet metal and a variety of metal and plastic components. These stocks of materials and components are used to produce products which are then sold to consumers and other businesses. Managing these materials is the responsibility of the production or operations manager. Materials management involves:

- the purchasing of stocks and their delivery;
- the storing and control of stocks;
- the issue and handling of stocks;
- the disposal of surpluses;
- the provision of information about stocks.

The nature of stocks

Businesses prefer to minimise stock holding because it is costly. In practice a variety of stocks are held, for different reasons.

Raw materials and components These are purchased from suppliers before production. They are stored by firms to cope with changes in production levels. Delays in production can be avoided if materials and components can be supplied from stores rather than waiting for a new delivery to arrive. Also, if a company is let down by suppliers it can use stocks to carry on production.

Work-in-progress These are partly finished goods. In a television assembly plant, WORK IN PROGRESS would be televisions on the assembly line, which are only partly built.

Finished goods The main reason for keeping finished goods is to cope with changes in demand and stock. If there is a sudden rise in demand, a firm can meet urgent orders by supplying customers from stock holdings. This avoids the need to step up production rates quickly.

Normally, at least once every year, a business will perform a STOCK TAKE. This involves recording the amount and value of stocks which the firm is holding. A stock take is also required for security reasons – to check that the items actually in stock match the stock records kept by the business. The stock take is also necessary to help determine the value of total purchases during the year for a firm's accounts. A physical stock take can be done manually by identifying every item of stock on the premises. Many firms have details of stock levels recorded on computer.

The cost of holding stocks

In recent years stock management has become more important

Question 1.

(a) Look at the photographs. Explain which of them shows: (i) stocks of raw materials; (ii) work-in-progress; (iii) stocks of finished goods.

(b) Explain why businesses hold stocks of finished goods.

for many firms. Careful control of stock levels can improve business performance. Having too much stock may mean that money is tied up unproductively, but inadequate stock can lead to delays in production and late deliveries. Efficient stock control involves finding the right balance. One of the reasons why control is so important is because the costs of holding stocks can be very high.

- There may be an **opportunity cost** in holding stocks. Capital tied up in stocks earns no rewards. The money used to purchase stocks could have been put to other uses, such as buyingnew machinery. This might have earned the business money.
- Storage can also prove costly. Stocks of raw materials, components and finished goods occupy space in buildings. A firm may also have to pay heating, lighting and labour costs if, for example, a night watchman is employed to safeguard stores when the business is closed. Some products require very special storage conditions. Food items may need expensive refrigerated storage facilities. A firm may have to insure against fire, theft and other damages.
- Spoilage costs. The quality of some stock, for example perishable goods may deteriorate over time. In addition, if some finished goods are held too long they may become outdated and difficult to sell.
- Administrative and financial costs. These include the cost of placing and processing orders, handling costs and the costs of failing to anticipate price increases.
- Out-of-stock costs. These are the costs of lost revenue, when sales are lost because customers cannot be supplied from stocks. There may also be a loss of goodwill if customers are let down.

Stock levels

One of the most important tasks in stock control is to maintain the right level of stocks. This involves keeping stock levels as low as possible, so that the costs of holding stocks are minimised. At the same time stocks must not be allowed to run out, so that production is halted and customers are let down. A number of factors influence stock levels.

- Demand. Sufficient stocks need to be kept to satisfy normal demand. Firms must also carry enough stock to cover growth in sales and unexpected demand. The term BUFFER STOCK is used to describe stock held for unforeseen rises in demand or breaks in supply.
- Some firms stockpile goods. For example, toy manufacturers build up stocks in the few months leading up to December ready for the Christmas period. Electricity generating stations build up stocks of coal in the summer. During the summer, demand for electricity is low so less coal is needed. At the same time, prices of coal during the summer months are lower, so savings can be made.
- The costs of stock holding. The costs of holding stock were described earlier. If stock is expensive to hold then only a small quantity will be held. Furniture retailers may keep low stock levels because the cost of stock is high and sales levels are uncertain.
- The amount of working capital available. A business that is short of working capital will not be able to purchase more stock, even if it is needed.
- The type of stock. Businesses can only hold small stocks of perishable products. The stock levels of cakes or bread will be very small. Almost the entire stock of finished goods will be sold in one day. The 'life' of stock, however, does not solely depend on its 'perishability'. Stocks can become out of date when they are replaced by new models, for example.
- LEAD TIME. This is the amount of time it takes for a stock purchase to be placed, received, inspected and made ready for use. The longer the lead time, the higher the minimum level of stock needed.
- External factors. Fear of future shortages may prompt firms to hold higher levels of raw materials in stock as a precaution.

Stock control

It is necessary to control the flow of stocks in the business. This ensures that firms hold the right amount. Several methods of stock control exist. They focus on the RE-ORDER QUANTITY (how much stock is ordered when a new order is placed) and the RE-ORDER LEVEL (the level of stock when an order is placed).

- **Economic order quantity** (**EOQ**). It is possible to calculate the level of stocks which minimises costs. This is called the economic order quantity. It takes into account the costs of holding stock, which rise with the amount of stock held, and the average costs of ordering stock, which fall as the size of the order is increased. A business must calculate the EOQ to balance these costs.
- **Fixed re-order interval**. Orders of various sizes are placed at fixed time intervals. This method ignores the economic

Figure 1: Stock control

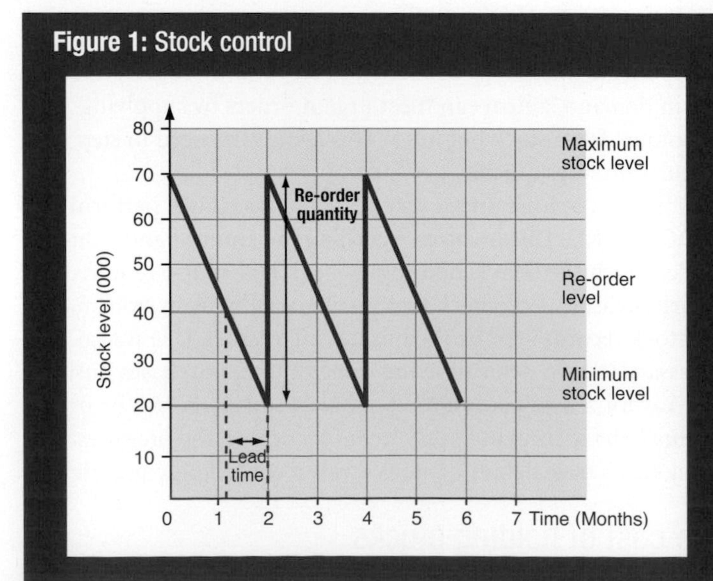

order quantity, but ensures that stocks are 'topped up' on a regular basis. This method may result in fluctuating stock levels.

- **Fixed re-order level.** This method involves setting a fixed order level, perhaps using the EOQ. The order is then repeated at varying time intervals.
- **Two bin system.** This simple method involves dividing stock into two bins. When one bin is empty a new order is placed. When the order arrives it is placed into the first bin and stocks are used from the second bin. When the second bin is empty stocks are re-ordered again.

A stock control system is shown in Figure 1. It is assumed that:

- 50,000 units are used every two months (25,000 each month);
- the **maximum stock level**, above which stocks never rise, is 70,000 units;
- the **minimum stock level**, below which stocks should never fall, is 20,000 units, so there is a buffer against delays in delivery;
- stock is re-ordered when it reaches a level of 40,000 units (the **re-order level**);
- the **re-order quantity** is 50,000 units - the same quantity is used up every two months;
- the **lead time** is just under one month. This is the time between the order being placed and the date it arrives in stock.

This is a hypothetical model which would be the ideal for a business. In practice deliveries are sometimes late, so there is a delay in stocks arriving. Firms may also need to use their buffer stocks in this case. It is likely that re-order quantities will need to be reviewed from time to time. Suppliers might offer discounts for ordering larger quantities. The quantities of stocks used in each time period are unlikely to be constant. This might be because production levels fluctuate according to demand.

Question 2.

Hahmid & Odusanya is a machine fabrications specialist. It makes large parts for machine tools and special parts machines such as those be found on production lines. It holds stocks of steel. The pattern of its stockholding is shown in Figure 2.

Figure 2:

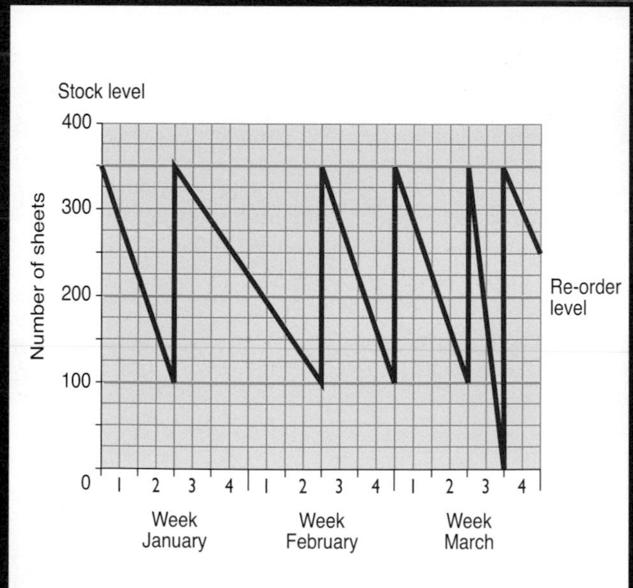

(a) Measured in numbers of sheets of steel, what is (i) the maximum stock level; (ii) the buffer stock level; (iii) the re-order level?

(b) Explaining your reasoning, suggest in which weeks there was (i) an unexpected large rush order; (ii) very disappointing sales.

(c) Explain what might happen to maximum stock levels if the business began to experience cash flow problems.

Too much or too little stock

Why might having too much or too little stock be bad business practice?

Too much stock

- Storage, insurance, lighting and handling costs will all be high if too much stock is held.
- Large stock levels will occupy space in the premises. There may be more productive ways of using this space, such as improving the layout of the factory.
- The opportunity cost will be high. Money tied up in stocks could be used to buy fixed assets, for example.
- Large stock levels might result in unsold stock. If there is an unexpected change in demand, the firm may be left with stocks that it cannot sell.
- Very large stocks might result in an increase in theft by employees. They may feel the business would not miss a small amount of stock relative to the total stock.

Too little stock

- The business may not be able to cope with unexpected increases in demand if its stocks are too low. This might result in lost customers if they are let down too often.
- If deliveries are delayed the firm may run out of stock and have to halt production. This might lead to idle labour and machinery while the firm waits for delivery.
- The firm is less able to cope with unexpected shortages of materials. Again, this could result in lost production.
- A firm which holds very low stocks may have to place more orders. This will raise total ordering costs. Also, it may be unable to take advantage of discounts for bulk buying.

Computerised stock control

Stock control has been improved by the use of computers. Many businesses hold details of their entire stock on computer databases. All additions to and issues from stocks are recorded and up to date stock levels can be found instantly. Actual levels of stock should be the same as shown on the computer printout. A prudent firm will carry out regular stock checks to identify differences.

Some systems are programmed to automatically order stock when the re-order level is reached. In some supermarkets, computerised checkout systems record every item of stock purchased by customers and automatically subtract items from total stock levels. The packaging on each item contains a bar code. When this is passed over a laser at the checkout, the sale is recorded by the system. This allows a store manager to check stock levels, total stock values and the store's takings at any time of the day. Again, the system can indicate when the re-order level is reached for any particular item of stock.

Access to stock levels is useful when manufacturers are dealing with large orders. The firm might need to find out whether there are enough materials in stock to complete the order. If this information is available, then the firm can give a more accurate delivery date.

KEYTERMS

Buffer stocks – stocks held as a precaution to cope with unforeseen demand.

Lead time – the time between the placing of the order and the delivery of goods.

Re-order level – the level of stock when new orders are placed.

Re-order quantity – the amount of stock ordered when an order is placed.

Stock rotation – the flow of stock into and out of stores.

Stock take – the process of counting the amount of stock held at a point in time in order to calculate the total stock level held.

Work-in-progress – partly finished goods.

JIT and stock rotation

In recent years many businesses have changed their approach to stock management. To reduce costs, firms have held low levels of stocks. In some cases holdings of both finished goods and raw materials have been reduced to zero. This approach to stock control is the key feature of just-in-time manufacturing (JIT). It is explained fully in the unit on lean production.

Businesses often use systems to control the flow of stocks in and out of their store areas. This flow of stock is sometimes called STOCK ROTATION. One system used to rotate stock is called First In First Out (FIFO). This means that those stocks which are delivered first are the first ones to be issued. This method is useful if stocks are perishable or if they are likely to become obsolete in the near future. A second method of stock rotation is called Last-In-First-Out (LIFO). This system involves issuing stock from the latest rather than the earliest deliveries. This method might be used if the stocks are difficult to handle and it is physically easier to issue the more recent deliveries. However, when using this method it is important that stocks are not perishable. 'Old' stock could remain in store for long periods before it is finally used.

KNOWLEDGE

1. What are the activities involved in materials management?
2. Why do businesses prefer to minimise stock holdings?
3. What is meant by: (a) components; (b) finished goods?
4. What are the costs of holding stocks?
5. Why are buffer stocks held by firms?
6. Why do some firms stockpile?
7. What is meant by LIFO and FIFO?

Case Study: Regal Jewels

Regal Jewels is a small chain of jewellers. It has nine outlets in the south east. Each shop has a manager and employs one or two other full-time staff with some part time staff who help out at busy times, such as Christmas. The shops stock a wide range of rings, earrings, bracelets, necklaces, gemstones and watches. They also produce specialist, tailor made pieces for wealthy customers. The business has flourished by focusing on the old fashioned virtues of personal service and value for money. All managers are members of the HRD Institute of Gemology, Antwerp (Europe's diamond capital). This is a highly regarded professional qualification and gives the business a great deal of credibility. The shop operates at the top end of the market and most of their pieces sell for over £100 – with many pieces going for £1,000s.

Stock is the most valuable asset for the business. After the last stock take, the total value of stocks held by Regal Jewels was £3,560,000. The stock is purchased centrally by the owner of the business. Regal Jewels uses a number of different suppliers, some of them from overseas. However, there have been one or two problems relating to stock management at the business.

One problem is maintaining the supply the supplier of customised carrier backs. All customers leave the shops with their purchases packaged in a specially designed Regal Jewels bag, adorned with gold ribbon and the business logo. Regular purchases of these carrier bags are made every month. The diagram in Figure 2 shows stocks of the carrier bags for a nine month period.

Another problem faced by the business owner is keeping right up to date with the stocks held in each shop. At the moment a manual, paper-based stock system is used. This is proving to be increasingly cumbersome and inefficient as the business grows. She is thinking of setting up an online stock control system. A new online system has been developed which allows small businesses, such as Regal Jewels, to login and manage their stock levels. It is perfect for a business with more than one location. It is possible to monitor stock movements and react to information delivered to a computer from anywhere in the world. The system has a number of benefits.

- Cost effective (no software to purchase/upgrade).
- No new hardware needed.
- Available from multiple locations.
- Easy to use system/set-up system.
- Free support available (unlike all other systems).
- Time saving (no need to produce your own reports or fill in endless paperwork).
- Up/downsizeable for when your business grows or shrinks.
- Easy to train other members of staff.
- 30 day free trials available.

(a) **Regal Jewels have monthly stock takes.**
(i) What is meant by a stock take? (3 marks)
(ii) Why do you think a stock take is so important for Regal Jewels? (6 marks)

(b) **Discuss two stock holding costs that Regal Jewels will incur. (6 marks)**

(c) **Look at Figure 3. Identify the (i) lead time; (ii) the re-order quantity; (iii) re-order level; (iv) minimum stock level for the carrier bags. (8 marks)**

(d) **In September 2007, Regal Jewels found a new supplier of carrier bags. Why do you think it took this action? (6 marks)**

(e) **Do you think Regal Jewels should introduce the online stock system? (10 marks)**

Figure 3: Stocks of Regal Jewels carrier bags

3,000
2,000
1,000
Re-order level
JAN FEB MAR APR MAY JUN JUL AUG SEP
2007

84 Quality

What is quality?

Consumers, faced with many goods or services at similar prices, are likely to consider QUALITY when making choices. Quality could be described as those features of a product or service that allow it to satisfy customers' wants. Take an example of a family buying a television. They may consider some of the following features:

- physical appearance - they may want a certain style;
- reliability and durability - will it last for 10 years?
- special features - does it have stereo sound?
- suitability - they may want a portable television;
- parts - are spare parts available?
- repairs - does the shop carry out maintenance?
- after sales service - how prompt is delivery?

They may also consider features which they perceive as important, such as:

- image - is the manufacturer's name widely recognised?
- reputation - what do other consumers think of the business or product?

The importance of quality has grown in recent years. Consumers are more aware. They get information through magazines such as *Which*? that contain reports on the quality of certain products. They also have more disposable income and higher expectations than ever before. Legislation and competition have also forced firms to improve the quality of their products.

Businesses, faced with competition, are also concerned about the quality of their:

- design - the ideas and plans for the product or service;
- production processes - the methods used to manufacture the goods or provide the services.

Poor designs may lead to problems with the materials and the functions of the finished good or service. It costs time and money to redesign poor products. Clients are unlikely to use businesses with poor designs again. Problems also occur with poor quality production processes. Faulty products are costly for a business. Machinery that breaks down or constantly needs to be repaired will also be expensive. Late delivery and ineffective productivity that results in poor quality can harm a business's reputation.

Traditional quality control

Traditionally, in manufacturing, production departments have been responsible for ensuring quality. Their objectives might have been to make sure that products:

- satisfied consumers' needs;
- worked under conditions they were likely to face;
- operated in the way they should;
- could be produced cost effectively;

Question 1.

Airbus S.A.S. is the aircraft manufacturing subsidiary of EADS N.V., a pan-European aerospace business. Based at Toulouse, France with significant operations in other European states, Airbus produces around half of the world's jet airliners. Airbus employs around 57,000 people at sixteen sites in four European countries. Airbus' customers expect quality in the aircraft they buy. Safety, reliability, comfort and maintenance costs are key areas where quality is crucial in an airline's judgment of an aircraft. To achieve the very highest standards in these and other aspects of an aircraft's performance the question of quality is addressed by Airbus at every stage, from design to final assembly and beyond. Repeated checks are made. Tests are applied. Airbus ensures every supplier of parts meets the strictest standards on quality. Defective work, parts and materials are rejected.

Delivering aircraft on time, on cost and on quality – getting it right first time – is the goal Airbus continually strives for. Airbus has a network of key employees who identify problems at various stages of design, production and assembly and recommend action to eradicate them, pre-empting possible costly delays at a later point. These employees also ensure continuous improvement in standards and efficiency by pinpointing ways in which people could work better or tools and materials could be improved. As it raises production to meet demand, Airbus knows setting even higher standards in quality is critical to maintaining its success.

Source: adapted from www.airbus.com.

(a) (i) What features do customers of Airbus consider important when buying aircraft?
(ii) Which of the features in (i) do you think is the most important?

(b) What measures does Airbus take to meet the high quality aspirations of customers?

- could be repaired easily;
- conformed to safety standards set down by legislation and independent bodies.

At Kellogg's, the cereal manufacturer, for example, samples of breakfast cereal have, in the past, been taken from the production line every half hour and tested. The testing took place in a food review room twice a day and was undertaken by a small group of staff. Each sample, about 50 in total, was compared with a 'perfect' Kellogg's sample and given a grade between 1 and 10. 10 was perfect but between 9.8 and 7, although noticeable to the trained eye, was acceptable to the customer. Below 7 the consumer would notice the reduction in quality. The cereals were tested for appearance, texture, colour, taste etc. More sophisticated tests were carried out in a laboratory where the nutritional value of a sample, for example, was measured.

QUALITY CONTROL in UK organisations, in the past, often meant **quality controllers** or **quality inspectors** checking other people's work and the product itself after production had taken place. By today's standards this is not quality control, but a method of finding a poor quality product (or a problem) before it is sold to the consumer.

Quality assurance

Today businesses are less concerned about 'Has the job been done properly?' than 'Are we able to do the job properly?' In other words inspection is carried out during the production process. This means that problems and poor quality products can be prevented before final production.

Such a preventative approach has been used by Japanese businesses and is known as TOTAL QUALITY MANAGEMENT (TQM). It is now being adopted by many companies in the UK. It involves all employees in a business contributing to and being responsible for ensuring quality at all stages in the production process. QUALITY ASSURANCE is a commitment by a business to maintain quality throughout the organisation. The aim is to stop problems before they occur rather than finding them after they occur.

Quality assurance also takes into account customers' views when planning the production process. For example, customers may be consulted about their views through market research before a product is manufactured or a service provided. They may also be part of a consultation group involved at the design and manufacturing stage.

Total quality management

Errors are costly for business. It is estimated that about one-third of all the effort of British businesses is wasted in correcting errors. There are benefits if something is done right the first time. Total quality management (TQM) is a method designed to prevent errors, such as the creation of poor quality products, from happening. The business is organised so that the manufacturing process is investigated at every stage. It is argued that the success of Japanese companies is based on their superior organisation. Every department, activity and individual is organised to take into account quality at all times. What are the features of TQM?

Figure 1: The systematic approach to quality management

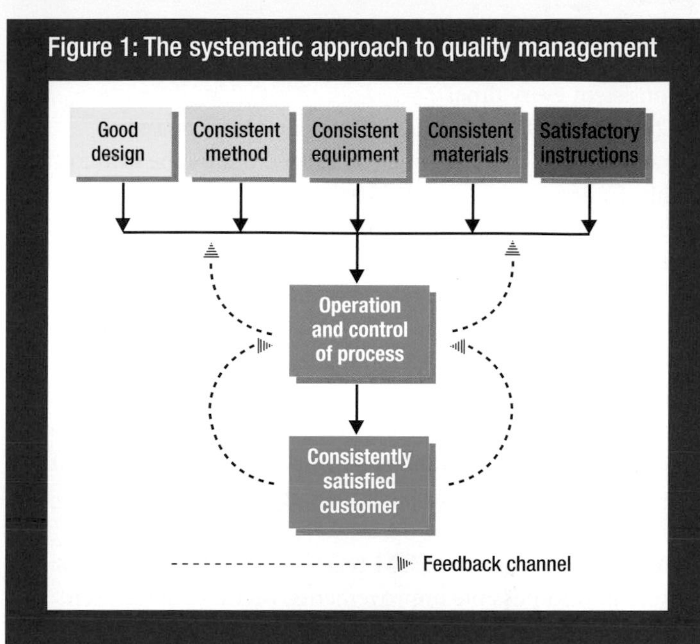

Quality chains Great stress is placed on the operation of QUALITY CHAINS. In any business a series of suppliers and customers exists. For example, a secretary is a supplier to a manager, who is the customer. The secretarial duties must be carried out to the satisfaction of the manager. The chain also includes customers and suppliers outside the business. The chain remains intact if the supplier satisfies the customer. It is broken if a person or item of equipment does not satisfy the needs of the customer. Failure to meet the requirements in any part of the quality chain creates problems, such as delays in the next stage of production.

Company policy, accountability and empowerment There will only be improvements in quality if there is a company-wide quality policy. TQM must start from the top with the most senior executive and spread throughout the business to every employee. People must be totally committed and take a 'pride in the job'. This might be considered as an example of job enrichment. Lack of commitment, particularly at the top, causes problems. For example, if the managing director lacks commitment, employees lower down are unlikely to commit themselves. TQM stresses the role of the individual and aims to make everyone accountable for their own performance. For example, a machine operator may be accountable to a workshop supervisor for his work. They may also be empowered to make decisions.

Control Consumers' needs will only be satisfied if the business has control of the factors that affect a product's quality. These may be human, administrative or technical factors, shown in Figure 1. The process is only under control if materials, equipment and tasks are used in the same way every time. Take an example of a firm making biscuits. Only by cooking in the same way can the quality be consistent every time.

These methods can be documented and used to assess operations. Regular audits must be carried out by the firm to check quality. Information is then fed back from the customer to the 'operator' or producer, and from the operator to the supplier of inputs, such as raw materials. For example, a retailer may return a batch of vehicles to the manufacturer because the gears were faulty. The manufacturer might then identify the person responsible for fitting the gears. An investigation might reveal that the faulty gears were the responsibility of a component supplier. The supplier can then be contacted and the problem resolved. Quality audits and reviews may lead to suggestions for improvements - a different material, perhaps, or a new piece of equipment.

Monitoring the process TQM relies on monitoring the business process to find possible improvements. Methods have been developed to help achieve this. STATISTICAL PROCESS CONTROL (SPC) involves collecting data relating to the performance of a process. Data is presented in diagrams, charts and graphs. The information is then passed to all those concerned.

SPC can be used to reduce variability, which is the cause of most quality problems. Variations in products, delivery times, methods, materials, people's attitudes and staff performance often occur. For example, statistical data may show that worker attitudes may have led to variations in output late on Friday afternoon. Discussion might result in a change in the 'clocking on' and 'clocking off' times to solve the problem.

Teamwork TQM stresses that teamwork is the most effective way of solving problems. The main advantages are:

- a greater range of skills, knowledge and experience can be used to solve the problem;
- employee morale is often improved;
- problems across departments are better dealt with;
- a greater variety of problems can be tackled;
- team 'ideas' are more likely to be used than individual ones.

TQM strongly favours teamwork throughout the business. It builds trust and morale, improves communications and cooperation and develops interdependence. Many UK firms in the past have suffered due to lack of sharing of information and ideas. Such approaches have often led to division between sections of the workforce.

Consumer views Firms using TQM must be committed to their customers. They must be responsive to changes in people's needs and expectations. To do this, information must be gathered on a regular basis and there must be clear communication channels for customers to express their views. Consumers are often influential in setting quality standards. For example, holiday companies issue questionnaires to their customers on the way back from a package holiday. The information can be used to identify the strengths and weaknesses of their operations. Such information can be used to monitor and upgrade quality standards.

Zero defects Many business quality systems have a zero defect policy. This aims to ensure that every product that is manufactured is free from defects. A business that is able to guarantee zero defects in customers' orders is likely to gain a good reputation. This could lead to new clients and improved sales.

Quality circles TQM stresses the importance of teamwork in a business. Many businesses have introduced quality circles into their operations. Quality circles are small groups of staff, usually from the same work area, who meet on a regular and voluntary basis. They meet in the employer's time and attempt to solve problems and make suggestions about how to improve various aspects of the business. Issues such as pay and conditions are normally excluded. After discussions, the team will present its ideas and solutions to management. Teams are also involved in implementing and monitoring the effectiveness of solutions. In

Question 2.

Compsoft is a UK-based company which produces tailor-made data management software for high-growth businesses. One of Compsoft's first products was Delta, a market-leading DOS-based database which is still used by many organisations today. Compsoft also developed Equinox, a rapid application development tool and database environment. Equinox is used by SMEs, blue-chip companies and governmental bodies.

Compsoft is committed to quality assurance and has been awarded ISO 9001, the internationally recognised standard for the quality management of businesses. As a result Compsoft has adopted the BSI framework to monitor its business processes to ensure the quality of service provided to its customers. Some of the basic requirements of certification include:

- adapting a set of procedures that cover all key processes in the business;
- monitoring development processes to ensure they are producing quality products;
- keeping records;
- checking outgoing applications for defects, with appropriate corrective action where necessary;
- regularly reviewing individual processes and the quality system itself for effectiveness;
- facilitating continual improvement.

Regular monitoring ensures that these standards are upheld and that Compsoft remains worthy of its title as an accredited ISO 9001 provider.

Source: adapted from www.compsoft.co.uk.

(a) (i) What is quality assurance?
(ii) How does Compsoft ensure quality in its business?
(b) What role does the BSI play in Compsoft's quality assurance?
(c) What benefits might Compsoft enjoy as a result of ISO 9001 certification?

order for quality circles to be successful certain conditions must exist.

- A steering committee should be set up to oversee the whole quality circle programme.
- A senior manager should ideally chair the committee. Managers must show commitment to the principle of quality circles.
- At least one person on the committee should be accountable for the programme.
- Team leaders should be properly trained.

Using TQM TQM helps companies to:

- focus clearly on the needs of customers and relationships between suppliers and customers;
- achieve quality in all aspects of business, not just product or service quality;
- critically analyse all processes to remove waste and inefficiencies;
- find improvements and develop measures of performance;
- develop a team approach to problem solving;
- develop effective procedures for communication and acknowledgement of work;
- continually review the processes to develop a strategy of constant improvement.

There are, however, some problems.

- There will be training and development costs of the new system.
- TQM will only work if there is commitment from the entire business.
- There will be a great deal of bureaucracy and documents and regular audits will be needed. This may be a problem for small firms.
- Stress is placed on the process and not the product.

ISO standards

Businesses can work to quality assurance **codes of practice**. These show that a production process has been carried out to a certain standard and to the required specification. Once a business has been assessed and has achieved a certain standard, it is regularly checked by the awarding organisation to make sure standards are maintained. ISO 9000 is an international standard which businesses seek to achieve.

The **British Standards Institution** (BSI) is an independent organisation that attempts to set quality standards in industry. The BSI and other independent bodies, such as Lloyds, offer BS EN ISO 9000 registration. The title reflects the European (EN) and international (ISO) recognition for this series. BS EN ISO 9001 gives quality assurance in design, development, production, installation and servicing and is suitable for businesses which have a large element of design in their operations. BS EN ISO 9002 gives quality assurance in production, installation and servicing, for businesses which produce fairly standard products with little or no design. BS EN ISO 9003 gives quality assurance in final inspection and testing. This standard is suitable for small firms or where customers can check quality themselves through inspection.

Firms seeking certification have to show that their methods and procedures meet the recognised standards and comply with requirements. They are inspected on a regular basis to make sure that standards are being maintained. BS EN ISO 9000 certification can help a business to:

- examine and improve systems, methods and procedures to lower costs;
- motivate staff and encourage them to get things right first time;
- define key roles, responsibilities and authorities;
- ensure that orders are consistently delivered on time;
- highlight product or design problems and develop improvements;
- record and investigate all quality failure and customer complaints and make sure that they do not reoccur;
- give a clear signal to customers that it is taking measures to improve quality;
- produce a documented system for recording and satisfying the training needs of new and existing staff regarding quality.

Product standards

Businesses may include signs and symbols on their products which tell a customer about the product's standards. Certain bodies have also been set up to ensure the quality of goods and services.

British Standards Institution Any business can apply to the BSI for an inspection of its product. Those that achieve and maintain a standard can carry the BSI Kitemark. The Kitemark tells the customer that the product has been tested to destruction, to ensure that it meets with certain safety standards. Products that carry a Kitemark include some cricket helmets, kitchen units, child car safety seats, door locks, curtains, and sofa and duvet covers.

The BSI also issues a number of other product standards. These include ensuring:

- products conform to yachting standards;
- the tensile strength of yarns;
- performance levels for the amount of UV light through sunglasses;
- grades of carpet pile, according to quality and durability.

The British Electrotechnical Approvals Board (BEAB) Now part of Intertek, a global leader in testing, inspection and certification, this is a body which inspects domestic electrical equipment. Manufacturers of domestic electrical appliances will be keen for the BEAB to approve their products. Approval can serve as a recognition of quality that customers will recognise.

The Association of British Travel Agents (ABTA) The Association of British Travel Agents is a trade association which has drawn up a code of practice for its members. The code aims to improve the trading standards of activities related to the sale of holidays. Travel agents are allowed to register with ABTA if they agree to follow its code of practice.

The Wool Marketing Board This allows manufacturers to carry labels such as the Wool Mark if their garments are made entirely of pure new wool. Obtaining a trademark is a way for a firm to give quality assurance to customers. If customers know that the quality of a product is guaranteed, they are more likely to buy the product. Also, there is less need to inspect the product, and returns and re-ordering are reduced.

The British Toy and Hobby Association (BTHA) developed the Lion Mark as a symbol of toy safety to be displayed on toy packaging. Toy manufacturers that want to include the Lion Mark must take out a licence with the BTHA. The manufacturer must sign a strict code of practice which sets standards relating to toy safety and advertising, as well as counterfeiting and markings on toy guns. The Lion Mark was adapted by the BTHA and the British Association of Toy Retailers (BATR) for shops. If the symbol is displayed in a shop it indicates that the retailer has agreed to a strict code of practice. They agree only to offer safe toys for sale and to ensure staff are briefed on toy safety matters such as age warnings.

The Consumers Association This is a body which follows up complaints by people about faulty products or services. It also makes recommendations about products and services to customers. These take into account such things as quality, reliability and value for money. Often survey results appear in its *Which?* magazine.

The Institute of Quality Assurance (IQA) The Institute of Quality Assurance is a professional body in the UK whose purpose is the promotion and advancement of quality practices. The IQA has three main objectives.

- To seek the advancement of quality management and practices and help the exchange of related information and ideas.
- To promote the education, training, qualification and development of people involved in quality assurance and the management of quality.
- To provide a range of services to members and, where appropriate, to the community at large.

Some businesses support their products with WARRANTIES. If goods are warranted, it means that the manufacturer will undertake any necessary work arising from a defect in the product 'free of charge'. Warranties are popular with products such as cars and a wide range of electrical appliances.

A number of laws exist which protect consumers from poor trading practices. They have tended to focus on safety aspects and consumer exploitation. However, increasingly UK laws and EU regulations are taking into account product quality. Existing laws are enforced by local inspectors, called **Trading Standards Officers**.

Poka-Yoke

Poka-Yoke (meaning 'inadvertent mistake' and 'prevent' in Japanese) is a quality assurance technique developed by manufacturing engineer Shigeo Shingo. It aims to eliminate defects in products by preventing or correcting mistakes as early as possible. While visiting the Yamada Electric plant in Japan, Shingo was told about a problem with the assembly of a product that had a switch with two push-buttons supported by springs. Sometimes workers assembling the switch would forget to insert a spring under each push-button. The error would not be found until the product reached a customer, which was embarrassing and expensive.

Shingo suggested a solution that became the first poka-yoke technique. In the old method, workers began by taking two springs out of a large parts box and then assembling the switch. In the new approach, a small dish is placed in front of the parts box and the workers' first task is to take two springs out of the box and place them on the dish. Workers then assemble the switch. If springs remain on the dish, workers know they have forgotten to insert them. Poka-yoke techniques fall into two categories.

- A **prevention** device makes it impossible to make a mistake at all. An example is in the design of a 3.5 inch computer disk. The disk is designed to be asymmetrical, so it will not fit into the disk drive in any other way than the correct one. Prevention devices remove the need to correct a mistake, since one has not been made in the first place.
- A **detection** device warns workers when a mistake has been made, so that the problem can be corrected. The small dish used at the Yamada Electric plant was a detection device. Another example would be an alarm that sounds in a car when the seat belt is not fastened.

Costs and benefits of ensuring quality

Firms will want to monitor the costs of quality control carefully. All businesses are likely to face costs when trying to maintain or improve the quality of their products and services.

- The cost of designing and setting up a quality control system. This might include the time used to 'think through' a system and to train staff to use it.
- There might be a cost in terms of lost production. When a business introduces a major new system there may be some serious disruption while the new system is 'bedded-in'. This could lead to a loss of output and damage to customer relations if orders are not met.
- The cost of monitoring the system. This could be the salary of a supervisor or the cost of an electronic sensor.
- There will be costs if products do not come up to standard. Faulty goods may have to be scrapped or reworked. Product failures might also result in claims against a company, bad publicity and a possible loss of goodwill.

- The cost of improving the actual quality. This may be the cost of new machinery or of training staff in new working practices.
- If the whole quality system fails, there may be costs in setting it up again. Time may be needed to 'rethink' or adjust the system. Retraining might also be necessary.
- Quality initiatives will only be successful if the people involved in their implementation are properly trained. This can prove very costly. For example, if TQM is introduced the entire workforce will have to be trained. This may involve sending all staff on specialist training courses or outsourcing training to an expert in TQM.

It has been suggested that between 10-20 per cent of the revenue of a business is accounted for by quality related costs. This means that UK businesses could save billions of pounds by cutting such costs. The vast majority of these costs is spent on appraisal and failure, which add very little to the quality of the product. Eliminating failure will also help to reduce appraisal and failure costs.

Although quality control systems are costly, it is argued that their benefits outweigh the costs. The actual quality of the product should be improved, so customers are more likely to purchase the product. Business costs may be cut if faults in products are identified before the product reaches the market. The costs of failure once the product has reached the market are likely to be much higher than those incurred during manufacture.

Quality, USP and pricing flexibility

Some businesses use quality as a means of developing a unique selling point (USP). If a business can differentiate its product on grounds of quality and persuade the customer that its product is superior to its rivals, it may enjoy some benefits. One of the main benefits is the ability to charge a higher price. If consumers are convinced that a product is superior in quality to those of its rivals, they are often prepared to pay higher prices. This gives a business more flexibility in pricing. For example, Porsche, the performance car manufacturer, has a global reputation for high quality. Consequently it is able to charge premium prices for their range of sports cars.

KEYTERMS

Quality – features of a product that allow it to satisfy customers' needs. It may refer to some standard of [illegible]

Quality assurance – a method of working for businesses that takes into account customers' wants when standardising quality. It often involves guaranteeing that quality standards are met.

Quality chains – created when employees form a series of links between customers and suppliers in business, both internally and externally.

Quality control – making sure that the quality of a product meets specified quality performance criteria.

Statistical process control – the collection of data about the performance of a particular process in a business.

Total quality management – a managerial approach which focuses on quality and aims to improve the effectiveness, flexibility, and competitiveness of a business.

Warranties – guarantees that faulty products will be repaired or replaced within a period of time.

KNOWLEDGE

1. What is meant by the quality of a product?
2. Explain the difference between actual and perceived quality.
3. Explain the difference between quality control and quality assurance.
4. State 5 implications of TQM for a business.
5. Why is teamwork so important in TQM?
6. How does ISO 9000 affect a business?
7. What is the role of the British Standards Institution?
8. Explain the advantage of manufacturing trademarks to a business.
9. What are the costs and benefits of ensuring quality?

Case Study: GNY Building Materials

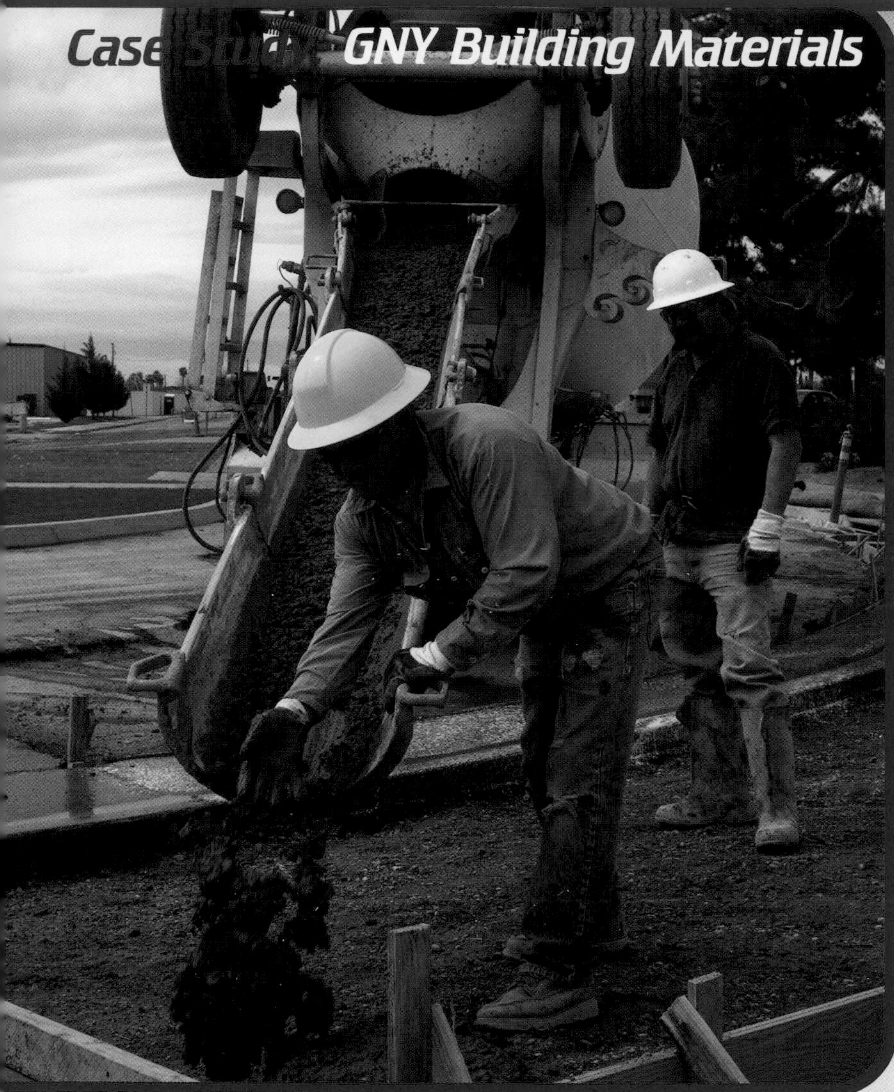

GNY Building Materials is a multi-location ready mix concrete, sand and gravel supplier. It employs over 350 staff and is currently faced with the twin problems of escalating costs and ailing customer service. After an important board meeting it was decided to create a new business culture, a culture which valued quality, customer service and continuous improvement. A business consultant was commissioned to perform a TQM readiness assessment, organise a Quality Steering Committee, train the management and hourly employees in TQM and support the work of the departmentally based Quality Teams and the cross functional Corrective Action Teams.

When the consultant began work it was apparent that the company did not have a history of participative management and reacted slowly to opportunities. Initial interviews confirmed that management was viewed sceptically. Poor internal communication led to employees feeling fear and resentment. Also, the business faced increasingly aggressive competition. A major objective for implementing TQM was to eliminate the waste in delivery and improve the reliability of delivery. The chairman made it plain that the savings from improvements would fund the culture he needed to foster in order to implement TQM.

Implementing TQM

There was a number of steps involved in implementing TQM at the business.

STEP 1 Perform a TQM readiness assessment. Over a five day period all of the senior management team and several hourly employees were interviewed. This highlighted several areas for targeted customer service improvement and cost reduction. TQM training was developed and initial Corrective Action Teams (CATs) were formed.

STEP 2 Communicate the vision to every single employee in the company. The chairman told each employee his vision for the business.

STEP 3 Organise the steering committee and train the management team. Training was further developed in the six TQM training sessions.

By incorporating their culture, credibility was improved. In addition, training improved the application of TQM ideas and broke down barriers to change. Four groups of twenty employees were then trained. The consultant trained in-house trainers to continue the training of employees. A second, but equally important, task continued parallel to the training. The Corrective Action Team (CAT) used the TQM process to improve the customer service levels and eliminate waste in trucking. It used each of the five critical areas in TQM to generate the needed changes in their trucking operations. These were considered to be the following.

- Customer Focus
- Waste Elimination
- Teamwork
- Continuous Improvement
- Problem Solving

Over three months the business generated cost reduction initiatives worth £600,000 and implemented over £300,000 of cost savings. This major victory by hourly and first line management demonstrated the effectiveness of TQM. GNY Building Materials realised a 25:1 payback on its investment in Total Quality Management. Their premier service reputation was restored and it became the preferred supplier to many contractors. According to the chairman, the company has become much more flexible and responsive. Improvements to the bottom line confirm this.

(a) What is a TQM readiness assessment? (4 marks)

(b) Why did GNY Building Materials introduce TQM? (6 marks)

(c) How important was training in the implementation of TQM at GNY Building Materials? (8 marks)

(d) Examine the likely costs incurred by GNY Building Materials when implementing TQM. (10 marks)

(e) Evaluate the benefits to GNY Building Materials of introducing TQM. (16 marks)

85 Customer service

What is customer service?

CUSTOMER SERVICE is about meeting the needs of customers. Customer service can be defined as 'a series of activities designed to enhance the level of customer satisfaction – the feeling that a product or service has met the customer's expectations'. Customer service has become increasingly important in recent years due to market orientation and the belief held by businesses about the importance of customers. If businesses offer good customer service, they are more likely to see customers return. Customers may also recommend products to their friends and relatives if they have enjoyed good customer service. Some businesses aim to exceed customer expectations. This approach should go a long way to satisfying customers.

The nature of customer service can vary quite significantly depending on the type of business providing it. Some examples are given below.

- Being courteous, friendly and helpful to customers.
- Dealing with complaints and problems in a sensitive and practical manner.
- Providing an Internet tracking service so that customers can see how their orders are progressing.
- Providing information, and advice about products.
- Providing assistance such as helping a non-English speaker complete an application form for a sports club.
- Offering extra services, such as a hotel providing free champagne, chocolates, flowers and a bowl of fresh fruit to honeymooners.

Customer service and communication

Call centres Customer service can be provided over the telephone. Many financial institutions such as banks and insurance companies, travel companies and the providers of utilities, use CALL CENTRES to provide customer service. Call centres have large numbers of staff or **call centre agents** who deal with telephone calls from customers. Someone working at a call centre for a bank may deal with a query on a customer's bank statement, for example. People working at call centres generally sit in front of a computer and respond to customers' telephone calls all day. All the information they need to provide customer service, including customers' account details, can usually be accessed from the computer.

However, some customers do not like call centres and their criticisms generally follow a number of common themes, for example:

- operators working from a script – too impersonal;
- non-expert operators;
- incompetent or untrained operators incapable of processing customers' requests effectively;
- overseas locations, with language and accent problems;

Question 1.

Asda, the supermarket chain, provides a variety of customer services.

Instore Greeters Greeters are customer care specialists who are trained to help customers with all their enquiries. ASDA are proud of their warm and friendly Greeters who always give customers a genuine welcome as they walk into the store. They provide a range of help, from selecting the right shopping trolley to suit customers' shopping needs, helping wheelchair users and directing customers to the right aisle.

Trolley range Asda offers customers a wide range of trolleys ranging from smaller smart shoppers to larger 175 litre trolleys with child seats. Its fleet of trolleys also accommodates the elderly and disabled. It has low and high trolleys which attach to wheelchairs along with Senior Citizen trolleys to help less able customers to get around the store.

Electric Karts To help less able shoppers navigate stores Asda introduced Electric Mart Karts to all food stores. ASDA was the first major retailer to introduce them. The Mart Karts are easy to use and all customers are given a demonstration when joining the Asda 'Scooter Club'.

Refund policy If customers are not happy with any purchase of branded items they simply return the product and Asda will offer a full refund or a replacement product. A receipt is preferred but not essential.

Exchange policy When customers purchase an electrical item they can ask for their receipt to be placed into a free Guarantee Wallet. This means that their purchase is guaranteed for a full year. However, customers will need to keep their own receipt to cover the warranty.

Source: adapted from www.asda-corporate.com.

(a) **Using examples from the case, explain what is meant by customer service.**

(b) **How might Asda benefit by training staff in customer service?**

- automated queuing systems. This sometimes results in excessively long hold times;
- a lack of communication between different business departments

Online A growing number of businesses have their own websites and provide customer service online. For example, people can get information about products and services. They can also buy products online. One common customer service is to provide answers to a list of FAQ (frequently asked questions). Also, if a person wants further information from a business they can ask questions using email. Email is increasingly used as a means of responding to customers by businesses. In some cases this has replaced the work of call centres. Many businesses prefer to provide customer service in this way because it is cheaper than answering customers' telephone calls.

Methods of meeting customer expectations

Since the provision of customer service has become increasingly important, businesses have developed different ways of identifying customer expectations and meeting them.

Market research In order to meet customer expectations it is necessary to identify them. One obvious way is to carry out market research to find out exactly what customers expect. A wide range of market research techniques could be used. These include exit surveys, telephone surveys, customer satisfaction questionnaires, focus groups, in-depth interviews and online surveys. Online surveys have become very popular with businesses. They can be used to find out what customers thought about the quality of customer service when buying online or how useful customers found the website, for example.

Customer satisfaction surveys are widely used in leisure and tourism. For example, hotels often leave short questionnaires in their rooms for guests to complete before they leave. Tour operators often ask holidaymakers to complete customer satisfaction surveys on the plane during the journey home. Some businesses employ market research agencies to carry out in-depth customer satisfaction surveys. However, these can be very expensive.

Once information from market research has been gathered and analysed, it can be used to design customer service provision. Some businesses will aim to provide customer service which they hope will exceed customer expectations.

Training Businesses are more likely to meet customer needs if staff are trained to deliver good customer service. Staff who come into direct contact with customers might be trained in a variety of skills to help provide better customer service. Some examples are shown in Figure 1.

A business may use off-the-job or on-the-job training methods when improving staff skills in customer service. Large companies are likely to have their own training facilities and courses, some of which are likely to target customer services.

Figure 1: Training to provide effective customer service

Smaller businesses might rely more on experienced staff to teach new recruits 'good practice' while on the job. There is a number of businesses that provide training courses which focus on customer services. An example is shown in Figure 2. This gives details of an introductory course in customer training provided by Activia.

Training in customer service will help staff to do their job more effectively. Without proper training the quality of customer service is likely to be poorer. Training will also motivate staff. Without training they may become frustrated because they cannot do their jobs properly. Training is also likely to make staff more flexible. For example, staff from one

Figure 2: Introductory training course on customer services provided by Activia

This intensive one day training course teaches delegates the basics of customer service. They will learn how to develop and maintain a positive attitude, show extra attentiveness to customers, use customer-friendly language, and deal effectively with customer complaints and problems. Finally, delegates learn how to build rapport with customers, interpret non-verbal communication skills, provide quality customer service over the telephone and communicate effectively through email.

Source: www.activia.co.uk.

department might cover for an absent colleague in another if they have been widely trained. Training is often necessary to bring staff up to date with new technology or new legislation in customer services. For example, staff in a travel agency might be trained in a new computer-based booking system for clients.

Quality assurance, quality control and quality standards

Another way of meeting customer expectations is to adopt recognised quality standards in customer service. A business might also guarantee quality by taking into account customer needs and ensuring that quality is built into processes and systems used when providing customer service. This is called quality assurance. Some approaches to quality assurance and quality standards are outlined below.

Total quality management One of the main approaches to quality assurance used by businesses today is total quality management (TQM). This involves every single person in a business taking responsibility for quality, including those involved in customer service. TQM makes the customer the centre of attention. One of the advantages of using TQM is that the approach involves collecting data for monitoring purposes. Customer service data can be used to help maintain quality standards and also to improve them in the future. This is explained in the next section.

BS 8477:2007 The British Standard Institution (BSI), a body responsible for setting quality standards in industry, has recently published the first British Standard for customer service. It is the BS 8477:2007 Code of practice for customer service. It sets out essential, basic principles for establishing and maintaining effective customer service and provides recommendations for applying these principles. If businesses are granted certification in this standard, it will help to guarantee standards of customer service.

The Institute for Customer Service This organisation is the professional body for customer service. Their aim is to help members raise their customer service standards and individuals achieve professional recognition. In particular it:

- provides advice and guidance on world-class customer service issues;
- defines professional customer service standards;
- promotes a wide understanding of the nature of competent customer service and how individuals can acquire it;
- spreads authoritative customer service knowledge through breakthrough research papers;
- offers a range of quality products and services to help organisations and individuals improve customer service.

Businesses that become members of this organisation can use its services to help them maintain quality standards in customer service.

Charter mark Charter Mark is the government's national standard for customer service excellence. Charter Mark is a powerful, easy to use tool to help everyone in an organisation focus on and improve customer service. Achievement of the standard is recognised by awarding the right to display the prestigious Charter Mark logo. The Charter Mark is awarded for excellence in the provision of customer services by public sector or a voluntary organisation such as a hospital, a police force, a local authority, a prison, a primary school, a Jobcentre or a museum. To qualify for the Charter Mark organisations have to satisfy six criteria.

Monitoring and improving customer service

Many businesses monitor the quality of their customer service. They may do this by gathering data. The data can be analysed and the results used to make recommendations on how to improve the quality of customer service in the future. Businesses can use a number of methods to gather data.

Questionnaires Many businesses gather data using questionnaires. Customers might be asked to complete questionnaires in a follow-up procedure after a sale has been made. Corkills, the Volkswagen car dealer and service centre in Southport, uses a telephone questionnaire to gather information about customer service after customers have had their cars serviced. Questionnaires can be tailored to the needs of different businesses. Figure 3 shows a questionnaire used by Fred. Olsen Travel to gather information about the quality of its customer service.

Figure 3: Customer service survey used by Fred. Olsen Travel

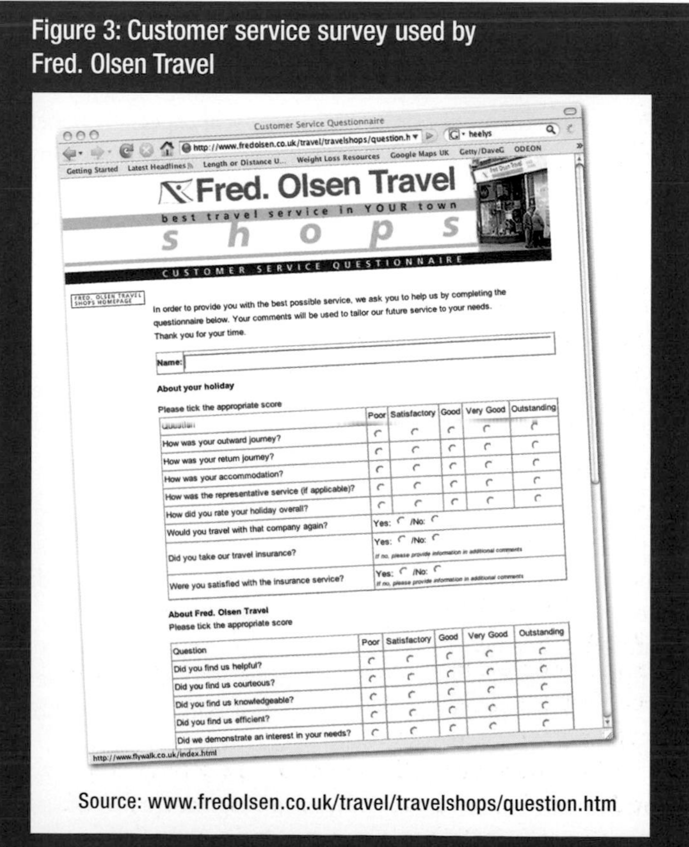

Customer Service Questionnaire

http://www.fredolsen.co.uk/travel/travelshops/question.h

Fred. Olsen Travel

best travel service in YOUR town

shops

CUSTOMER SERVICE QUESTIONNAIRE

FRED. OLSEN TRAVEL SHOPS HOMEPAGE

In order to provide you with the best possible service, we ask you to help us by completing the questionnaire below. Your comments will be used to tailor our future service to your needs. Thank you for your time.

Name:

About your holiday

Please tick the appropriate score

Question	Poor	Satisfactory	Good	Very Good	Outstanding
How was your outward journey?					
How was your return journey?					
How was your accommodation?					
How was the representative service (if applicable)?					
How did you rate your holiday overall?					
Would you travel with that company again?	Yes: /No:				
Did you take our travel insurance?	Yes: /No: If no, please provide information in additional comments				
Were you satisfied with the insurance service?	Yes: /No: If no, please provide information in additional comments				

About Fred. Olsen Travel

Please tick the appropriate score

Question	Poor	Satisfactory	Good	Very Good	Outstanding
Did you find us helpful?					
Did you find us courteous?					
Did you find us knowledgeable?					
Did you find us efficient?					
Did we demonstrate an interest in your needs?					

http://www.flywalk.co.uk/index.html

Source: www.fredolsen.co.uk/travel/travelshops/question.htm

Question 2.

TSO (the stationery office) delivers managed print and publishing services to a variety of private and public sector clients. The company is committed to high quality customer service. It sets targets for performance which are outlined below.

- Answer 80% of our telephone calls in 10 seconds, 90% in 20 seconds and 95% in 30 seconds.
- Achieve an abandon call rate of no more than 2% of call volumes answered.
- Average time to answer a call of 6 seconds.
- Process standard written order requests sent by post within an average of 2 working days of receipt.
- Deliver a service that achieves a benchmarked satisfaction score of 83.1%.
- Achieve a fair outcome for customers when things go wrong and receive less than 1.4% of complaints received against overall despatches.

TSO also gathers data to monitor its performance. An extract from its results is shown in Table 1.

Source: adapted from www.tso.co.uk.

(a) How does TSO monitor performance in customer service?

(b) Comment briefly on TSO's performance in customer service provision in 2006.

(c) What are the main advantages of using quantitative data when monitoring customer performance?

Table 1: Performance standards for TSO customer service – an extract from 2006

		2006											
	Target	Jan	Feb	Mar	Apr	May	Jun	Jul	Aug	Sep	Oct	Nov	Dec
% of calls answered in 10 seconds	> 80.0	91.9	93.6	92.9	93	90.9	92.5	92.9	91.5	90.0	93.0	92.9	94.2
% of calls abandoned	< 2.0	0.7	0.6	0.6	0.7	1.1	0.7	0.6	1.0	1.1	1.0	1.29	2.2
Average time to answer (seconds)	6 max	6	6	6	6	7	7	6	8	10	7	7	7
Complaints - % of orders dispatched	< 1.25	1.2	1.3	1	1.3	0.79	1.08	1.18	1.28	1.12	1.4	1.14	1

Gathering performance data Businesses will especially benefit if they can produce quantitative data when monitoring customer service performance. Quantitative data is much easier and quicker to analyse than other types of data. For example, it is easier to make quick comparisons between different years using numeric performance indicators. Businesses that use quantitative data are likely to set performance targets. At the end of the year actual performance can be compared with the targets. Striving for targets will help to improve performance. An example of quantitative customer service performance data is shown in Table 1 in Question 2.

Recording telephone conversations One common way of monitoring the quality of customer service is to record telephone conversations between customers and staff providing customer service over the telephone. By analysing these recordings a business can identify areas for improvement. For example, a recording of a telephone conversation might reveal that a particular member of staff does not know enough about the products the employer is selling.

Complaints A common way of monitoring the quality of customer service is to keep an up to date record of all complaints from customers relating to customer service. By analysing the nature of complaints a business can take measures to improve the quality of its customer service in the future. Businesses generally take complaints quite seriously. If they fail to respond positively to customer complaints they are likely to lose customers in the future. 'Complaints can be used as business feedback to help drive decision making and customers should be able to complain through a variety of channels', says RightNow Technologies, a customer relations management software producer.

Monitoring and improving the quality of customer services are clearly important issues. Businesses can monitor the quality of customer service by gathering information using the methods described above. They must then take measures to improve the quality of customer service by acting on the results shown by an analysis of that data. This might involve retraining staff, modifying systems or introducing new ways of providing effective customer service.

The benefits of high levels of customer service

It has been argued that customer service is generally the critical factor in determining whether a customer buys and is retained. Consequently, the benefits of providing good quality customer service are huge. Some of the benefits of providing high levels of customer service are outlined below.

- Retaining customers through effective customer service enables easier growth. For example, healthier sales volumes and margins can be sustained and a business can expand as a result of word-of-mouth referrals.
- High levels of customer retention through effective customer service also improves staff morale and motivation. No-one enjoys working for a business where customers are not valued and customer service systems are either ineffective or non-existent. When customers are happy, staff are likely to be happier too. As a result they will be more productive.
- Improved staff morale and motivation resulting from reducing customer dissatisfaction also benefits staff retention and turnover, recruitment quality and costs, stress, grievance, discipline and counselling pressures.
- In some industries, where the product is fairly homogenous, the provision of customer service is one of the few ways in which the product can be differentiated. Consequently, providing good customer service is crucial.
- Reduced customer dissatisfaction will obviously reduce legal action from customers and claims that a business is breaking fair trading laws.
- Retaining customers also enables the business to focus more on proactive opportunities such as growth, innovation and development, rather than reactive tasks such as fire-fighting, crisis management and failure analysis.
- Having a culture of delighting and retaining customers improves the image of a business. A company's reputation in the media, and increasingly on the web in blogs and forums, for example, can be improved. The converse also applies. For example, one disgruntled customer and a reasonable network of web friends may cause a significant public relations headache.

So providing high levels of customer service will increase sales, assist growth, retain customers, improve staff motivation, reduce costs and improve the image of a business.

KEYTERMS

Call centre – an office where large numbers of staff provide customer service over the telephone.
Customer service – a series of activities designed to enhance the level of customer satisfaction.

KNOWLEDGE

1. Give two examples of customer service a bank might provide.
2. How do call centres provide customer service?
3. State two criticisms of using call centres to provide customer service.
4. State two ways in which a business can meet customer expectations in relation to customer service.
5. What is the Charter Mark?
6. State four advantages of using the BS 8477: 2007.
7. State three ways in which a business might monitor the quality of customer service.
8. How can customer service be used to differentiate a product?

Case Study: ScottishPower

ScottishPower uses an intelligent web-based self-service system to enable faster, more accurate answers to customer queries. The system, from Transversal, the UK's leading provider of multi-channel eService solutions for customer-facing websites and contact centres, ensures customers receive rapid responses to their online account queries. 'We are committed to making it easy for our customers to benefit from the flexibility and cost savings of managing their accounts online,' said Nicola Morrison, online manager at ScottishPower. 'As part of our overall aim to be the industry's number one for customer service we needed to ensure that they had fast, accurate answers to their queries. Working with Transversal has not only helped underpin our online growth, but has given us an unparalleled insight into our customers' requirements through the ability to analyse the questions they are asking,' she said. By investigating the type and number of questions asked on its site, ScottishPower has been able to ensure that the right information is immediately available to its customers - without needing to invest in costly market research. For example, after seeing a growing number of queries on energy efficiency, this information was made more visible on the new site.

Increasing the number of its 5.2 million UK customers who manage their gas and electricity accounts online is part of ScottishPower's business strategy to become the UK's best integrated power provider. Some 95 per cent of customer questions are now answered automatically, improving customer service and encouraging consumers to adopt more online services such as meter reading and billing. ScottishPower introduced a new website in February 2007. Customers can enter meter readings online, view and pay bills, change services, update personal details and notify the company when changing address.

Source: adapted from www.e-consultancy.com.

(a) Describe some examples of customer service provided by ScottishPower. (6 marks)
(b) How has the provision of customer service probably changed for ScottishPower in recent years? (6 marks)
(c) How has Transversal helped to improve the quality of customer service at ScottishPower? (10 marks)
(d) How important do you think customer service is to ScottishPower? (10 marks)
(e) Evaluate the benefits to ScottishPower of providing high levels of customer service. (18 marks)

86 Purchasing

The role of suppliers in operations

Suppliers are important business stakeholders and will benefit from the success of a business. However, they can also contribute to that success. Operations managers need to find effective suppliers that provide good quality materials and services at competitive prices. Suppliers also need to be thoroughly reliable and offer some flexibility in their services. Having good suppliers, and maintaining effective relations with them, will help to improve the operational performance of a business

Controlling costs Businesses that use just-in-time (JIT) manufacturing techniques depend very heavily on their suppliers. JIT manufacturers need supplies delivered at regular intervals and at specific times. JIT manufacturers do not hold stocks of materials and components, so a break in supply leaves them vulnerable. If a supplier fails to deliver, or delivers the wrong order, the manufacturer may have to close down production for a time. This could be very expensive. Having good suppliers therefore reduces the costs of holding stock. It can also prevent costly delays.

Reliability and customer satisfaction For JIT manufacturers suppliers need to be 100 per cent reliable. Their role is critical. Many suppliers feeding JIT manufacturers have located their own operations very close to their customers. This helps to reduce the chances of a break in supply and fosters good relations. Even businesses that do not operate JIT will need reliable suppliers. For example, most large supermarkets receive daily deliveries of fresh fish. If these supplies did not arrive on time supermarkets might not be able to offer their customers the range of fish they have come to expect. This could result in lost sales and disgruntled customers.

The need for flexibility In some industries businesses need highly flexible suppliers. One reason for this is because some businesses are subject to sharply fluctuating demand. In the events and hospitality industry it is often very difficult to estimate demand. For example, a catering company providing meals at a cricket match might require additional supplies of food if the attendance was unusually high due to very good weather.

Purchasing

In many businesses it is the purchasing department that has responsibility for working with suppliers. Purchasing involves the buying of materials, components, fuel, tools, machinery, equipment, stationery and services by the business. It also includes adopting any method that allows the firm to obtain the goods and services it needs, such as hiring.

Figure 1: Stages in the purchasing process

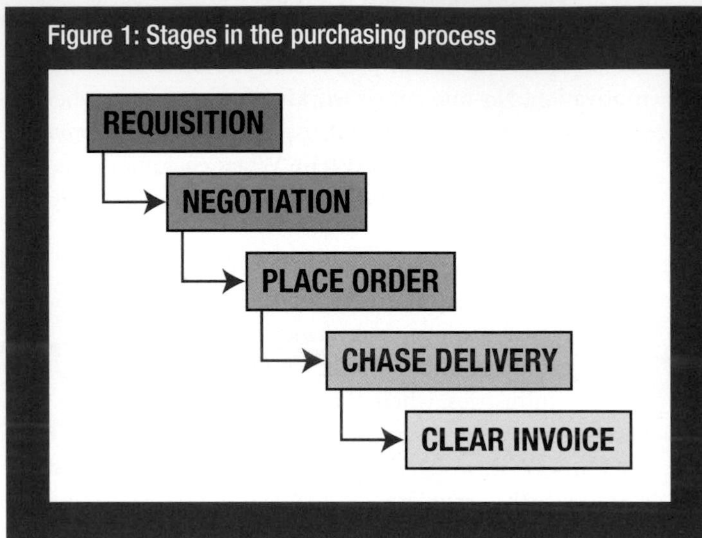

The various stages in the purchasing process are shown in Figure 1. Purchasing usually begins when the purchasing department is notified of a particular need. For example, a firm's stores or a particular department may send a **requisition form** asking for more stationery. The purchasing department will then act on this. Most purchases are repeat purchases from regular suppliers. Orders are placed with the supplier at previously agreed prices and delivery is accepted under previously arranged terms. New products may need different materials and new suppliers. This will involve a period of search and negotiation, as the buyer tries to find the best deal. If there is a delay in delivery, it is the purchasing department's responsibility to find out why and speed up delivery. Once the goods have arrived the invoice is checked and then payment can be made.

In manufacturing the purchasing department works closely with the production and finance departments. Most purchasing is carried out on behalf of the production department. The finance department needs information about purchases to make payments and record the transactions.

The importance of purchasing is likely to vary according to the nature and size of the business. In many service industries purchasing is not very important. This is because materials are only a small fraction of the total cost of the final product. For example, hairdressing involves very little purchasing, as production involves a skill and uses few materials. However, a large manufacturer requires a large amount of materials, components etc. and so the firm will employ a purchasing department made up of specialists.

Centralised and decentralised purchasing

In some businesses, **centralised purchasing** is used. This is where the purchasing for the whole business is carried out by one department. The advantage of this method is that **economies of scale** can be gained as large-scale buyers enjoy lower rates and market power. Also, the same quality and standard of materials can be set throughout the business. The distribution and warehousing of supplies can also be better planned.

Decentralised purchasing may reduce the cost and burden of administration. Purchasing officers in each department may be more in touch with the needs of that department. In retailing, if purchasing is undertaken by each store manager, the needs of each store can be better catered for. The added responsibility might also motivate store managers.

Choosing effective suppliers

It is important for a business to evaluate suppliers. A poor supplier may delay production, which can be costly. When choosing suppliers a business is likely to use a number of **criteria** to evaluate their reliability.

Price For many businesses the price charged by suppliers will be the most important criterion when choosing a supplier. If businesses can lower the costs of raw materials, components and other services they will make more profit. Price will be particularly important if there is little difference in the quality of the material being purchased. For example, when finding an electricity supplier, only the price is likely to be considered.

Payment terms Payment terms can vary enormously. Payment terms usually refer to the length of the credit period and the method by which payment must be made. Businesses will tend to prefer long credit periods – 90 days or more perhaps. The method of payment is not likely to be a big issue today, although not many businesses will want to pay in cash unless there are significant discounts.

Quality Businesses will need good quality materials and services. They cannot produce good quality products themselves if they use poor quality materials. For example, a business that fits high quality kitchens cannot use poor quality tiles and kitchen units.

Capacity If a business is going to buy very large quantities from a supplier, it will want reassurance that the supplier has the capacity to meet demand. If there is a danger that the supplier may run out of capacity, supplies may be threatened which could disrupt production. A business may also consider the capacity of a supplier if it is likely that the business would be expanding in the near future.

Reliability Businesses want suppliers that deliver goods when they say they will. They also want the correct order first time. Suppliers that are late and prone to making mistakes in orders will be avoided.

Flexibility Many businesses prefer suppliers that can offer a flexible service. For example, can they change orders at the last minute or can they deliver a day early? Flexible suppliers make operations management easier when planning production.

Question 1.

McPhersons Ltd is a chain of twenty butchers operating in Scotland and the North of England. Its head office is attached to the shop located in Leeds. All the purchasing is currently undertaken at head office and the meat is delivered in bulk to a warehouse in Leeds. The firm employs a driver to distribute orders to the varios shops twice a week. The board of directors is considering the decentralisation of the purchasing function, since the discounts from bulk buying are not particulary significant. If decentralisation takes place each shop manager will receive a £2,000 p.a. salary increase. The discounts lost from bulk buying are expected to total £20,000 p.a. Cold storage, handling and disitribution costs are expected to fall by £50,000 in total and administration costs will be £5,000 lower in total. It is expected that the quality of the meat will improve when purchasing is the responsibility of the shop managers.

(a) **Advise the company whether or not decentralisation is a worthwhile change in operational policy, in purely financial terms.**

(b) **Explain the non-financial advantages and disadvantages to McPhersons of decentralising purchasing.**

Vendor rating

The measurement of suppliers' performance is called VENDOR RATING. A business must choose criteria which could be used to measure the performance of a supplier.

A simple vendor rating system is shown in Table 1. The supplier is awarded a mark for performance based on five criteria. For example, the supplier has a good price record, scoring 18 out of a possible 20. Adding the scores gives a total vendor rating of 71/100. When deciding which supplier to choose, a firm is likely to pick the one with the highest rating. If a business feels that some criteria are more important than others, it may give them more value using a weighting system. One problem with this system is how to judge a supplier's performance against given criteria. It may be possible to use records. But sometimes evaluation may simply be based on the subjective opinion of a manager.

Table 1: A simple vendor rating system

Criteria	Maximum Score	Actual Score
Quality	20	17
Price	20	18
Delivery	20	10
Communication	20	12
Flexibility	20	14
Total	**100**	**71**

Question 2.

Vi-Spring manufactures high quality beds. A feature of its large range is the ability to offer customers a wide variety of personalised options. It markets its well-known products around the world through a number of large and small retailers. Founded over 100 years ago, the company now employs 180 people and is located in Plymouth, Devon.

The company has recently adopted a just-in-time (JIT) approach to production. Vi-Spring now holds a very low stock of raw materials. Stocks required for production come in on a JIT basis from around two hundred suppliers, of which thirty are key sources. The majority - mainly those providing cotton ticking, padding and webbing - are in the North of England. Delivery of an order is on a next-day basis; other materials are on a longer lead time.

The company prefers to build close and reliable relationships with its suppliers, regarding them as key business partners. If a problem develops, rather than dropping a supplier Vi-Spring will work with it to overcome the issue concerned.

Source: adapted from http://datadialogs.com.

(a) Why is the reliability of suppliers so critical for Vi-Spring?
(b) Do you think Vi-Spring has good relations with its suppliers? Explain your answer.

Table 2: Motives for making and buying

Motives for making
• Making is cheaper.
• There are no suitable suppliers.
• Delivery times cannot be met by suppliers.
• Quality standards cannot be met by suppliers.
• Spare capacity exists in the factory.
• To maintain secrecy.
• To ensure continuity of supply.
• To retain labour during a slack period of trading.
Motives for buying
• Buying is cheaper.
• To increase specialisation.
• Uneconomical to make small quantities.
• Lack of capacity.
• Transfer risk to the vendor.
• Avoid investment in specialist plant or labour.

KEYTERMS

eSourcing – using the Internet in the purchasing process.
Vendor rating – a method of measuring and evaluating the performance of suppliers.

eSourcing

ESOURCING is the use of Internet technologies and electronic communications in the whole purchasing process. It is a systematic approach that can handle all stages in the purchasing process including identifying appropriate suppliers, tendering, negotiation and award and contract management. The various eSource tools available enable buyers and suppliers to connect and agree a contract quickly and efficiently in order to improve the company's competitiveness. eSourcing significantly reduces the length of time spent on the whole purchasing process. It also reduces the need for paper-based systems and labour-intensive processes. In general, eSourcing helps to improve operational efficiency and can benefit both buyers and suppliers. Buyers benefit from eSourcing for following reasons.

- Faster sourcing process and faster results – time reductions of up to 70%.
- Elimination of face-to-face meetings, travel time, and geographical barriers.
- More transparent, uniform and predictable pricing.
- Improved enforcement of corporate purchasing policies.
- Increased process transparency.
- Better supplier measurement.

Suppliers can also benefit from eSourcing for certain reasons.

- More efficient and objective sourcing process and more level playing field.
- Easier to respond – negotiations and travel are eliminated.
- Lower selling costs.
- Improved convenience for buyers, leading to more transactions.

Make or buy?

Another decision which a business often faces is whether to make a component itself or buy it from a supplier. There are reasons for both making a product and buying it in, as shown in Table 2. In recent years businesses have tried to improve their flexibility. One method of doing this is to outsource production. This is where a business uses the services of another firm, to produce its components for example. A business that aims to outsource production will buy in components rather than make its own.

KNOWLEDGE

1. Why is it important to develop effective relations with suppliers?
2. How important is the role played by suppliers for JIT manufacturers?
3. What are the different stages in the purchasing process?
4. What is the difference between centralised and decentralised purchasing?
5. State two benefits of centralised purchasing.
6. State four benefits of eSourcing to buyers.
7. State three benefits of eSourcing to suppliers.

Case Study: IXO Instruments Ltd

Based in Southampton, IXO Instruments Ltd is a privately owned company. It operates in the market for high-value, handheld test instruments. Its products are sold through a network of national catalogue houses, regional stocking distributors and international master distributors. The company has become one of the largest manufacturers and suppliers of test equipment. It has built an enviable reputation for providing innovative products offering unique and patented designs with features, functions and reliability at an affordable price. IXO is ISO 9001:2000 certified. Its products include portable meters for the measurement and testing of light, sound, temperature, humidity, airflow and water quality.

IXO has a supplier base of 120 but is always looking for new suppliers to keep costs down. The family who own the company set demanding financial targets, which often means that managers continually have to cut costs. At the moment a vendor rating system is used to find new suppliers. Recently a new supplier was found for a component in a new printer. The component is a circuit board and is called FFD 339. Table 3 shows some of the information that was used to find the new supplier.

Table 3: Supplier information for FFD 339

Supplier name	Price	Quality	Reliability	Flexibility	Payment terms	Total
Reynolds Ltd	18	8	7	8	6	
AGT	12	8	9	9	5	
Adco	14	6	7	5	8	
Veelle	8	9	9	9	9	
Williams & Co	20	8	6	4	5	

NB All criteria are marked out of 10 except for price which is given more weight and marked out of 20.

Unfortunately, last year, the operations manager had to take early retirement due to ill health. A new manager was appointed and it was apparent that she wanted to make a number of operational changes. She was particularly concerned about the treatment of suppliers. She felt that IXO could not develop effective relations with suppliers if they continually looked for cheaper ones. To improve operational performance with regard to suppliers, she was extremely keen to make use of eSourcing in the organisation.

(a) **(i) How does IXO Instruments Ltd choose effective suppliers? (4 marks)**

(ii) Which is the most important criterion for IXO when choosing suppliers? Explain your answer. (6 marks)

(b) **Which of the suppliers shown in Table 3 would have been selected by IXO Instruments Ltd? Explain your answer. (8 marks)**

(c) **Analyse IXO's current relationship with suppliers. (8 marks)**

(d) **Evaluate the possible benefits to IXO Instruments Ltd if they adopt eSourcing. (14 marks)**

87 Using technology in operations

The nature and impact of technology

One of the most significant factors affecting how businesses have operated in the twentieth century has been the impact of new TECHNOLOGY. It is easy to see its impact when we consider some of the changes that have taken place in business.

- New products, such as camcorders, compact discs, laptop computers and services such as direct purchasing from television.
- New production processes, such as robotic welding, and computer controlled cutting machines.
- New materials such as silicon chips for computer circuit boards and polystyrene for packaging.
- Changes in business operations and new skills. For example, as a result of automatic cash tills in banking, many staff have been retrained to sell financial services.

There are many ways in which technology can be defined. One approach is to say that it is 'a creative process which uses human, scientific and material resources to solve problems and generate better efficiency'. Some examples make this clear. A business that uses video conferencing to communicate with branches spread all over the country is using technology. So is a plant which uses lasers to detect faults in products as they move along the production line.

How does technological progress take place? It is usually by means of **invention** and **innovation**. Invention is the discovery of something new. Some examples include the laser beam developed in 1960 by Dr. Charles Townes and the microprocessor developed in 1971 by Marcian Hoff in the USA. Inventions are then developed into products. The laser beam has been used for cutting in industry, micro-surgery in hospitals and spectacular lighting shows in displays.

Inventions are sometimes made by creative people 'outside' business. For example, the ball point pen was invented by a sculptor, and the pneumatic tyre by a veterinary surgeon. Today, research is carried out by teams of people working for a business, university or the government. The rewards to inventors can be very high, if their inventions can be used commercially and patented.

In business, innovation is the commercial exploitation of an invention. An invention is not usually in a form that consumers will buy. The product must be developed to meet consumers' needs, so that it can be sold profitably by business. UK firms have, perhaps, been reluctant to do this in the past. For example, the first working computers were developed in the 1930s. Since then Japan and America have led the world in hardware production and computer research. Enormous investment is often required to innovate once a technical breakthrough has been achieved.

Type of technology in primary industry

Primary industry has been affected by the introduction of new technology in a number of ways. In agriculture the use of tractors, combine harvesters, lifting equipment, grain drying machines and automatic milking and feeding apparatus have helped to increase output, reduce time and waste, and improve conditions. Agrochemicals and pesticides have raised crop yields. Biological research has helped to develop plants and crops which are more resistant to disease and more attractive to consumers. Genetically modified foods are argued to have better resistance to disease. In extractive industries, such as mining, cutting, lifting and tunnelling machines have all led to increased output.

Question 1.

Barclays, Britain's third biggest bank, is planning to cut 1,100 jobs in its processing centre in Poole, Dorset, over the next three years. The redundancies are the result of automation in more of its systems. For instance, cheques which were previously processed by hand will now be handled by computers. The cutbacks will leave just 850 employees remaining. The bank will also shut its Barclays House operation in Poole and seek out smaller premises in the town or nearby Bournemouth.

Unite, the newly formed union which incorporates finance branch Amicus, expressed concerned about the 'large reduction of jobs in Poole'. Union official Steve Pantak said: 'Unite does, however, have robust agreements in place and the bank's plans are spread over the next three years, so we will be working with the bank to ensure the maximum number of redeployments and voluntary redundancies.

The new premises will be 100,000 sq ft compared with the 300,000 sq ft currently provided by Barclays House. The bank has had operations in Poole since 1976. The job reductions will affect a number of areas, including cheque processing as well as IT support and some human resources functions.

Source: adapted from *The Guardian*, 10.5.2007.

(a) Using this case as an example, explain what is meant by automation.
(b) What problem does this case highlight when introducing new technology?

There have also been improvements in safety equipment and mining conditions for workers. The extraction of oil now takes place on large oil rigs with computer controlled drilling equipment. This improves the speed and accuracy of production. In fishing, the introduction of refrigerated boats has helped to improve **productivity**. Forestry has benefited from cutting, lifting and haulage equipment.

One problem with the use of more efficient technology is that resources are used up more quickly. It may be possible to control this in the case of **renewable resources**, such as timber, by replanting and managed forestry. However, unless new forms of power can be developed, there are likely to be problems in future with extracting large amounts of the world's finite resources such as coal and oil. There have also been criticisms of genetically modified food and its possible effects on humans.

Type of technology in secondary industry

New technology has led to major changes in manufacturing. Many factories and production lines employ complex mechanical, electrical and electronic systems. Even smaller manufacturing businesses have benefited from the introduction of new equipment and processes. Examples of new technology can be found in a number of areas.

Robots Robots are increasingly used on assembly and production lines. They have some form of arm, which moves to instructions given by a computer. Repetitive tasks, such as installing components, can be carried out many times with great accuracy. Such tasks may lead to boredom, lack of motivation, tiredness and human error if undertaken by employees. Robots may also increase the flexibility of a business. For example, in 1998 small robots, each with its own set of paint cans, were installed in the paint shop of the Volkswagen-Audi car plant in Germany. The robot could be activated at a few minutes' notice when a customer wants a colour which is not included in the current program. Using the robot means that customer demand for less popular colours can be satisfied without having to clean out the pipes of the main painting apparatus, which would be costly.

Computer aided design COMPUTER AIDED DESIGN (CAD) is now used by businesses in the design process, before a product is manufactured. Examples of products designed using CAD include vehicle bodies, plastic containers to hold milk and oil, furniture and clothing. Designing on computer allows a business to produce accurate drawings, which can be viewed in 3D and altered cheaply and quickly for a client. Designs can be accurately measured and tested on computer for faults, such as unsuitable components or dimensions, which might have caused problems during manufacture.

Computer numerically controlled machines Products can be manufactured using COMPUTER NUMERICALLY CONTROLLED (CNC) machines. Instructions are given to the CNC machine by the operator. The machine then carries out its instructions, controlled by a computer. An example might be a CNC milling machine which is used to cut out a mould of a mouse in plastic. The computer controls the cutting to produce the shape of a mould. In the textile industry computer controlled sewing, cutting and printing machines are used. Some CNC machines make use of **probes** and **coordinate measuring machines** (CMMs). These are designed to make simple or complex measurements, check batches or components one at a time and inspect geometric or irregular shapes. CMMs are accurate to within a few microns. CNC machines can produce shapes and cut quickly and accurately. They can also carry out repetitive tasks without human error. The instructions can be changed easily to carry out different tasks. For example, JCB uses CNC machines to cut a wide range of patterns from metal plates for its mechanical diggers.

Computer aided manufacture In many factories computers are used to design products and the information is then fed into CNC machines. This automated operation is known as COMPUTER AIDED MANUFACTURE (CAM). For example, a manufacturer of telephones may design a new shape using a CAD software program on computer. The instructions may be taken from the CAD program and inputted into CNC machines. These machines will reproduce the shapes, guided by the information contained in the computer. Other examples of CAM include computer controlled manufacture of plastic bricks at Lego, computer controlled assembly lines at Sony and computer controlled temperatures, flow rates and ingredients for pizza production at McCain Foods. The computer controlled weaving system produced by Bonas stores designs on computer in one part of a factory and sends production information to looms in other parts of the factory. These then weave the designed fabric.

Computer integrated manufacture Some businesses have integrated the entire design and production process. Computers are used to guide and control the production of a good. Employees supervise the manufacturing part of the operation, checking that it is working effectively and repairing faults. This system is known as COMPUTER INTEGRATED MANUFACTURE (CIM). There is a number of stages in the operation. They are shown in Figure 1.

- Orders are received via email, fax or letter and inputted into the system. Costings are carried out on computer using spreadsheet programs. Customers are stored on databases. Accounts are kept on computer and regularly updated. Orders which are received are processed and invoiced at a later date.
- The design department uses CAD packages to design the product for a client, making changes on computer. The instructions to manufacture the design are produced and fed through to the production part of the system.
- Production is planned and scheduled. Parts and materials are ordered as required by the computer, which monitors

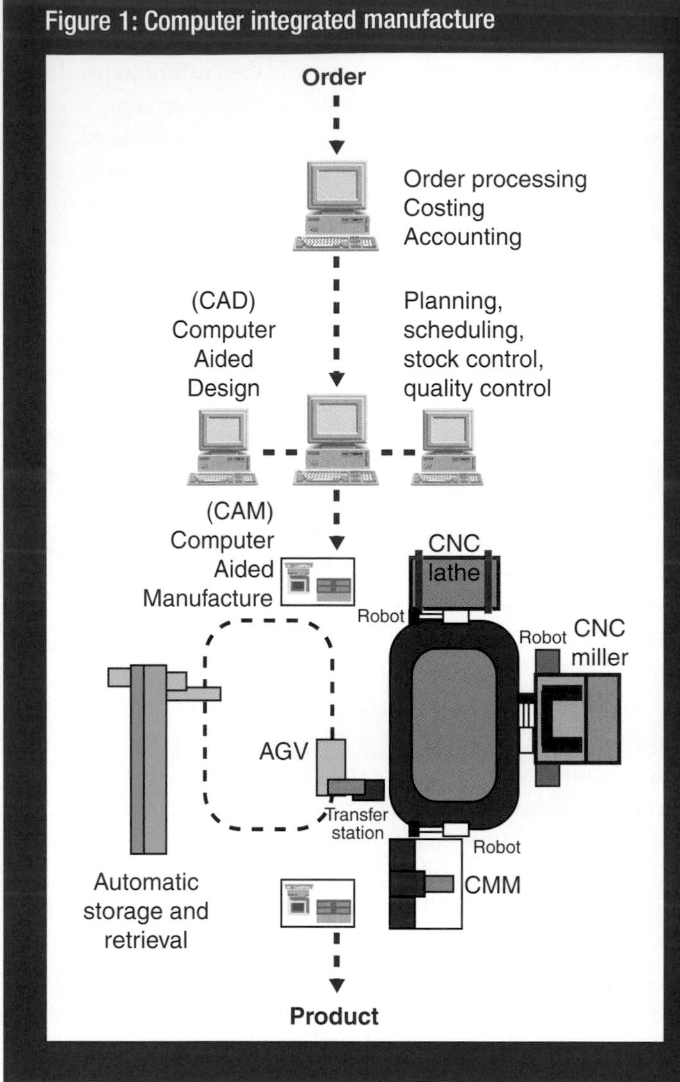

Figure 1: Computer integrated manufacture

stock and automatically reorders where necessary.

- The instructions for production are passed to CNC machines which manufacture the product. CMM machines monitor the quality of the work.
- Robots are used to transfer products from one CNC machine to another.
- Automatically guided vehicles (AGVs) take components to the machines.
- Finished products are taken to the stores or sent for dispatch.

Type of technology in tertiary industry

The supply of services has in the past been relatively more labour intensive than in the primary and secondary sectors. This is because supplying services often requires direct and personal contact with customers. However, today the use of technology in the tertiary industry is becoming more widespread in a number of areas.

Government and private services There is a range of services provided by government or private alternatives. New technology used in health care and dental care has improved services considerably. Developments in new vaccines and drugs have reduced suffering and cured diseases that not long ago may have led to deaths. Surgeons can carry out exact operations using lasers, viewing them on television screens with the use of fibre optics. Replacement teeth can be produced for patients which exactly fit jaw shapes from materials which will last for years. Government information can now be found easily on the Internet.

Financial services Businesses selling financial services match customers with appropriate financial products. For example, client information can be fed into a computer to identify the most suitable insurance policy or savings plan. The sale of financial products such as ISAs, pensions and insurance policies is increasingly carried out on the Internet. Some banks offer online banking services. Many financial organisations now have cash dispensers outside their premises. These can be used by customers who want to take out cash with a minimum of fuss or out of normal working hours. Some banks have cash dispensers inside, and customers can enter the bank in non-business hours using 'swipe cards' to open doors. This gives extra security to customers using the facilities.

Distribution The introduction of containers has made the handling of freight quick and easy. They can be hauled onto trailers and locked in position. This prevents movement during transport and possible damage and theft. At port or rail terminals, containers can be loaded safely and quickly onto trains or ships using cranes. Refrigerated containers allow perishable goods to be transported long distances without deteriorating.

Personal services Dating agencies use computers to match couples using personal information held on databases about clients' characteristics and preferences. Agencies also make use of video technology to record messages from clients. Online dating agencies allow people to register on the Internet.

Post and communication Technology has helped to improve the speed and efficiency of postal and packaging delivery. Many businesses have franking machines that weigh and record the required postage. Bar codes allow a free postal or business service to be provided by firms. A customer can return a leaflet or envelope without charge to a business. Machines at the post office will read the bar code and bill the business providing the service. Post offices make use of video and television to advertise their services.

Most business now make extensive use of email to communicate. Emails can also have attachments. These can be documents that have been scanned or saved as jpeg files. This means that the post does not have to be used, preventing delays in communication.

Hotels, restaurants and transport In the travel industry technology allows customers to travel without a ticket. They can book a flight over the telephone or the Internet using a credit card. The same card is then used to pick up a boarding pass from an airport machine or a check-in counter. Travellers to Australia can obtain an 'electronic visa'. Entry can be organised by giving passport details to a travel agent. These details are sent electronically to the appropriate port of entry. Booking for hotels or theatre tickets can also be made by credit card. Meals at restaurants can be paid for by a 'swipe or switch' card. The transaction is recorded by a machine and the money is automatically transferred from the current account of the customer.

Advertising In advertising, television makes increasing use of advances in filming technology and special effects to make adverts more sophisticated and entertaining. There is also a growing selection of advertising media. For example, advertisers have used electronic messaging on the 'touchlines' of sporting events and in city centres on the sides of buildings. The Internet provides worldwide advertising, but only to Internet users.

Retailing Retailing has benefited in many ways from new technology.

- The packaging of goods has changed greatly in recent years. New materials such as polystyrene and strong plastic wrap have improved the way in which goods are packaged. The materials have been lighter and stronger, have provided better protection, and have been easier to handle. Many firms have redesigned the packaging of goods to increase sales. In some cases new technology has helped. For example, Lucozade and other soft drinks have been packaged in flexible bags instead of cans and bottles.
- There has been a growth in home shopping. Computers and televisions have been linked together to enable shoppers to browse at home and then place orders by telephone or through a link. The Internet is a growing means of direct selling to customers at home.
- Payment has been made easier. Bar codes and hand-held recorders allow customers to register the prices of goods as they shop. This saves time and queues at the checkout. Goods can be paid for by credit or 'swipe cards', increasing security as the customer does not have to carry cash.
- Some supermarkets have unstaffed checkouts where customers can scan their own shopping and choose from a variety of payment methods.

Information and communication technology

INFORMATION AND COMMUNICATION TECHNOLOGY (ICT) is the recording and use of information by electronic means. Some of the uses of **information technology** (IT) have already been explained in the previous sections. However, there are some common uses of ICT which may apply to businesses operating in primary, secondary or tertiary industries.

Administration Many routine tasks can be carried out quickly by computer. These may include customer invoicing or billing. Standard letters or memos may be produced which can be easily changed if necessary. Large amounts of information about customers may be stored on databases.

Personnel Personnel files are now easily kept on databases. They can be regularly updated. Spreadsheets also allow calculations of salaries and deductions.

R&D Computer aided design can be used to research new materials or new product ideas. For example, tests may be carried out on the endurance of materials using a CAD simulation. Recording, monitoring, regulating, forecasting and analysing data are all tasks that can be carried out more easily.

Finance Many firms record all financial transactions on spreadsheets. Some allow instant production of financial information such as profit and loss accounts or income statements, cash flow forecasts, budgets and financial ratios. It is

Question 2.

Coilcolor is one of the largest independent paint coating lines in the UK, specialising in organic coating of steel and aluminium coils. It offers a wide range of protective finishes and colours to suit its customer's requirements. The company has the ability to produce both extremely low and high volume quantities, a wide choice of colours and short lead times. Among their prestigious clients are B&Q, Ikea and Jaguar.

The original stock control and sales processing system was implemented in 1992. Since then Coilcolor's business model has undergone substantial changes. The original system, with its ageing technology base, no longer serviced the demands of this highly competitive industry. Consequently the company had to invest in an upgrade. A company called Computerisation developed two highly sophisticated, bespoke systems for Coilcolor – a Sales Order Processing System and a Stock Control System. The new systems efficiently manage Coilcolor's complex product portfolio. This consists of many product variables including stock code, material, colour etc.

The new systems were created to work alongside Sage MMS, a computerised accounts system. This has reduced administration time and costs by avoiding the need for multiple data entry. Coilcolor has achieved a sustainable competitive advantage through its quick turnaround times within the intensive manufacturing process. Improved administration has enhanced that advantage which was made possible by the implementation of Computerisation's systems. From a customer service aspect its new systems provide the company with the ability to monitor stock efficiently, satisfying customer demand with low minimum order quantities.

Source: adapted from www.computerisation.co.uk.

(a) Explain how Coilcolor makes use of computers in its operations.
(b) What benefits has Coilcolor enjoyed as a result of using computers?

also possible to make checks on outstanding payments that are due from customers so that credit control will be effective.

Communications Developments in information and communications technology mean that information can be collected, stored and sent electronically in a fraction of a second. This saves money and makes sure information is passed correctly. Mobile telephones, faxes and email mean that people can work from a variety of locations. Information can be sent over great distances and at any time. The Internet provides wide ranging communication opportunities, including promotion, online buying and emailing.

Production information Information may be stored about the terms of suppliers. Production costs may be calculated on spreadsheets. The ordering of stocks or components may be carried out by computer. Purchasing may be undertaken using eSourcing, where the whole purchasing process is handled by online purchasing systems.

Stock control Technology is increasingly used to control stock. For example, retailers such as supermarket chains have a very sophisticated stock control system called EPOS (electronic point of sale). The system holds a record of every single stock item in the store. When a customer passes through the checkout every item purchased is subtracted automatically from the stock list. At any time a manager can enter the system to see how much of an item is left in stock. The system may even reorder stock automatically. Businesses may also have systems to reorder stocks online from suppliers, perhaps using intranets or extranets.

Information and sales Many businesses now have their own website on the Internet, providing company information. Some are using sites to provide information or to sell products to customers. A readers' survey by Marketing Technique about use of the Internet by businesses found 75 per cent of respondents worked for companies with their own site. Two-thirds of respondents used the Internet to monitor competitors' activities.

Benefits of new technology

There is a number of benefits to business of using new technology.

Reducing costs One of the main benefits of new technology to businesses is lower costs. If a task or activity is automated, people are replaced by machines which can operate more cheaply. For example, the cost to banks of dispensing cash has fallen considerably since ATMs were introduced.

Improving quality The quality of products is often improved when new technologies are introduced. This is because machines are usually more precise and consistent than humans. For example, robotic welders in car factories can maintain a consistent and high quality weld indefinitely once they have been programmed. This will help to improve the quality of the car.

Increased productivity More can be produced with less and, as a result, businesses may gain higher profits. In addition, fewer of the environment's resources may be used up.

Reducing waste Introducing new technology often results in time being saved and fewer materials being used. For example, technology has created printing machines which waste less paper when printing books or magazines. The ways in which resources are used have attracted a great deal of attention in recent years. As the world's population continues to grow it will be necessary to improve resource use even further.

Improving the working environment Statistics on accidents at work show that the working environment is safer as a result of new technology. Mining and manufacturing in particular have benefited. Modern equipment has made work easier and more tolerable. For example, fork lift trucks mean workers no longer need to load goods by hand. These improvements also help to remove workers' dissatisfaction.

Benefits to society Many new products have come onto the market in recent years. Personal stereo systems, video recorders, satellite and digital television, high performance cars and microwave ovens are some examples. New products mean wider consumer choice and possibly higher living standards. Other developments have helped to make our lives easier, such as ATMs, online shopping and mobile telephones.

Improvements in communications Faster means of transport (such as the jet aircraft), answerphones, email, computer network links and fax machines are all examples of inventions which have helped to improve the speed of communications.

Higher incomes If firms enjoy greater profits they can afford to pay higher dividends to shareholders and higher wages to employees. Also, if efficiency is improved then products may be sold at lower prices. As the country's income increases the government collects more tax revenue. This could be used to improve the quality of public services or alternatively to reduce the overall level of taxation or government borrowing.

Problems with new technology

The introduction of new technology can also cause problems for both business and society.

Cost Development, installation and maintenance can often prove costly. Also, businesses may have to lay off and retrain staff, leading to redundancy payments and retraining costs. If firms borrow to meet these costs, they will have to pay interest. Reorganisation may also be needed. Production may be changed from batch to flow production, job descriptions may be changed and in some cases a larger or smaller plant may be needed.

Labour relations In the past, trade unions have resisted the introduction of some new technology because of the threat to their members' jobs. The growth of union and business partnerships after the year 2000 may have made the introduction of new technology easier.

Job skills New technology creates jobs which require new, technical skills, but replace manual jobs. These new jobs cannot be done by the existing workforce unless it can be retrained. Often, this is not possible.

Breakdowns Automated production lines are interdependent. If one part of the line breaks down the whole process may stop. There may also be teething problems. Breakdowns often occur when technology is first installed. For example, it is argued that the Stock Exchange Automatic Quotation (SEAQ) share dealing system was partially to blame for the 1987 Stock Exchange crash. The system automatically triggered selling instructions, causing big falls in some share prices.

Motivation Some staff may dislike working only with machines. This may affect their motivation.

Management The management of technological change is considered very difficult. One reason is due to the rapid pace of the change. When new technology becomes available business managers have to decide whether or not to purchase it, or wait for the next important breakthrough. Deciding when to invest in new technology is very difficult. The management of the human resources leading up to the change, and during the change, requires great skill. People are often unhappy about change in their lives.

Unemployment and employment Much new technology is labour saving. Tasks once carried out by people will be done by machines. As a result people may become unemployed. For example, in automated production lines tasks such as assembly and quality checks are done by robots and CMMs. One or two employees may act as supervisors. On the other hand technology has to be designed, manufactured, installed, programmed, operated, serviced and replaced, which may create new jobs.

IT problems Computer software can become infected by viruses. A computer virus is a programme written to deliberately damage or destroy software and files. Such viruses are very damaging. It is possible for businesses to use software to check the existence of viruses. They can then be blocked from entering the computer system if included on emails, for example. If a virus has entered the system, it can be removed. Computer software has other problems which can affect a business. They may have to constantly buy the latest software to be compatible with clients or suppliers who use more modern versions. Modern machines may not run older software. New software may not be able to convert older programs.

Leisure time People have gained more leisure time as a result of new technology. They need to learn how to use this extra time in a constructive way. Businesses are taking advantage of this. For example, it is argued that there is enough demand in the UK for many more golf courses.

An ageing population Medicine has benefited greatly from new technology. One effect of this is that the population of many countries is now 'ageing'. As a result the pressure has increased on those in work to support the aged. Demands on public funds will also increase and the government will have to find money for facilities which are needed for the elderly.

Data protection

The rapid development in the use of IT has led to legislation about the collection, storage, processing and distribution of data. **The Data Protection Act 1998** includes eight conditions with which users must comply.

- Personal data should be obtained and processed fairly and lawfully.

KEYTERMS

Computer aided design – the use of computers when designing products.
Computer aided manufacture – the use of computers in the manufacture of products.
Computer numerically controlled machines – machines which have their operations controlled by a computer program.
Computer integrated manufacture – the use of computers to control the entire production process.
Information and communication technology – the recording and use of information by electronic means.
Technology – a creative process which uses human, scientific and material resources to solve problems and improve efficiency.

KNOWLEDGE

1. What is meant by technology?
2. What is the difference between invention and innovation?
3. State four areas of a business that might benefit from new technology.
4. How has new technology been used in marketing?
5. How might a business exporting products abroad make use of new technology?
6. How has information technology been incorporated in production?
7. How has business security used information technology?
8. Why was the Data Protection Act introduced?
9. In what ways has new technology benefited (a) business owners; (b) management?
10. Briefly explain problems that (a) workers and (b) management may face with the introduction of new technology.
11. How might business exploit the Internet?

- Personal data can only be held for specified and lawful purposes.
- Personal data cannot be used or disclosed in any manner which is incompatible with the purpose for which it is held.
- The amount of data held should be adequate, relevant and not excessive.
- Personal data should be accurate and kept up-to-date.
- Personal data should not be kept for longer than is necessary.
- An individual shall be entitled to:
  (a) be informed by any data user if he or she is the subject of personal data and also have access to that data;
  (b) where appropriate, have data corrected or erased.
- Security measures must be taken by data users to prevent unlawful access, alteration, disclosure, destruction, or loss of personal data.

The **1990 Computer Misuse Act** identified certain offences relating to use of computers.

- A person causing a computer to perform a function with intent to secure access.
- Unauthorised access to a computer with the intent to commit a further offence.
- Unauthorised and intentional modification of computer memory or storage media.

An offence is committed if access is unauthorised or if the person knows it is unauthorised. Many codes of practice state that employees may only access information held on a computer which is a relevant part of their work.

There is some legislation regarding the use of the Internet. EU legislation prevents the downloading of copyright music and allows businesses to block downloading, for example. EU legislation in 2003 made it illegal to send junk e-mail, known as spam, by businesses to individuals.

Case Study: Minco Manufacturing

Minco Manufacturing is an American company. It produces over 250,000 fuser rollers a month for more than 400 models of copiers, printers and facsimile machines at its state-of-the-art production plant in Colorado. Its products include sleeved, silicone and hard coated upper fuser rollers, and silicone coated lower pressure rollers.

As a result of adopting 16 new Stäubli robots in its production cells the company has improved product quality and reduced costs. The robots are used for a variety of tasks such as operating lathes. Robots keep labour costs down, allowing Minco to compete internationally. 'By using robots and reducing labour costs, we can compete with companies that make parts in China, for example.' said Brian Duff, manufacturing engineer. 'We are able to keep the work in the United States and still be competitive with the cheaper labour rates in Asian countries.'

'Once the robots have been programmed they just run. ... That frees up the operator to do inspections and move parts in and out of the cell, instead of having all these people loading lathes for 10 to 12 hours a shift,' Duff said. Stäubli robots are known for high-speed performance, and this speed also generated savings. Before the robots were installed, this process required an additional finish turning lathe. We had an operator manually feeding two lathes to work the ends and then feeding a third lathe to do the finish turn work. The finish turning machine was actually capable of twice the production that was possible by hand,' Duff explained. 'With three robotic cells currently running, we've saved three lathes that we can transfer into making another cell.'

They've also saved about 50 per cent more floor space. 'It allows us to design extremely compact work cells,' Duff said.

The quantity of fuser rollers produced and the level of quality needed, demanded repeatability as well as speed. 'Repeatability is key to the robot's performance in this application because of how we are locating the part into the draw tube. If we didn't place the part against the stop very accurately then we would have too much fluctuation and we could not control the quality of the roller,' Duff said. 'We need to meet a length accuracy of less than .005 of an inch, but we're not seeing even that much variation. We're seeing .002 or less.'

After the initial 16 robots are installed, Minco's plan is to integrate robots into other processes that could benefit from automation. Then the company will start replacing their older robots. 'We've talked to Stäubli about adding robots to load the initial paint station. It is very labour-intensive, because every roller we make gets painted. Rollers weigh up to eight pounds so it is exhausting work. We get a lot of operator fatigue and production begins to drop,' he said.

Minco Manufacturing is also considering installing robots to unload rollers off a conveyor after the coating has cured. 'This is very labour intensive, but also has to be done very carefully. At this stage the rollers cannot get nicked or scratched,' Duff said. Robots are also ideally suited for Minco's packaging process.

Source: adapted from www.roboticsonline.com.

(a) Explain how robots are used in operations. (6 marks)
(b) Explain why the introduction of robots is an example of automation. (6 marks)
(c) How will workers benefit from the introduction of more robots? (6 marks)
(d) Discuss the benefits enjoyed by Minco Manufacturing as a result of employing more robots. (10 marks)
(e) Discuss the problems Minco Manufacturing could encounter when making more use of robots. (12 marks)

88 Business size

Defining size

In the UK there are around four million businesses. Their sizes vary. A company like BP has operations around the world, employs thousands of people and has a turnover of billions of pounds. A self-employed joiner may operate in a small workshop, employ one other person and have sales of just a few thousand pounds. Most businesses begin on a small scale and then grow. What is the difference between a large firm and a small firm? When does a small firm become large? How might size be measured?

Turnover Sales revenue that a business earns could be used to measure size. For example, Astra Zeneca, the pharmaceuticals company, is a large business. Its turnover in 2006 was $26,475 million.

The number of employees A business with thousands of employees may be considered large. IBM, the computer manufacturer, for example, employed over 355,000 people in 2006. The term Small and Medium-sized Enterprises (SMEs) is often used when talking about relatively small firms. The EU uses the following criteria to measure firm size:

- micro firm: maximum of 9 employees;
- small firm: maximum of 49 employees;
- medium firm: maximum of 249 employees;
- large firm: 250 or more employees.

The amount of capital employed This measure is based on the amount of money invested in the business. The more money invested the larger the business. For example, in 2006 Melrose, the international engineering group, had capital employed of £255.1 million. Domino's, the pizza company, in comparison, had capital employed of only £12 million (as measured by the value of equity).

Profit Businesses which have higher profits than others may be classed as larger businesses. For example, in 2006 BG, the gas supplier, made a pre-tax profit of £3,103 million. In contrast, William Hill the gaming company, made a pre-tax profit of £292.2 million.

Market share It could be argued that a business with a 43 per cent market share, is larger than one which has a 9 per cent market share in the same industry. Coca-Cola, for example sells over 50 per cent of all cola drinks worldwide.

Market capitalisation This is the current share price multiplied by the number of shares. Table 1 shows the largest five companies in the UK according to this measure.

According to the EU, a firm is considered to be:

Table 1: The largest 5 UK firms (market capitalisation) 4.11.07

Company	Market capitalisation	Industry
1. BP	£119,078m	Oil
2. HSBC	£107,157m	Banking
3. Vodafone	£97,682m	Telecommunications
4. Royal Dutch Shell	£73,733m	Oil
5. Glaxo Smith Kline	£67,402m	Pharmaceuticals

Source: adapted from *The Sunday Times*, 4.11.2007.

- 'small' if it has a turnover of 10 million euros, a balance sheet total of not more than 10 million euros (i.e. capital employed), a maximum of 49 employees and is not more than 25 per cent owned by one or more companies satisfying the same criteria;
- medium-sized if it has a turnover of not more than 50 million euros, a balance sheet total of not more than 43 million euros, a maximum of 249 employees and the same 25 per cent criteria as above;
- large if it exceeds the criteria above.

Problems with measuring size

In practice, measuring the size of a business may not be easy. A highly automated chemical plant may only employ 45 people, but have a turnover of 50 million euros. According to the number of employees, the EU would class it as a small business. However, according to the level of turnover it could be classed as a large business.

Using the level of profit may also be misleading. A large company may have problems and make only a small profit over a period of time and yet still stay in business. One of the problems of using market capitalisation is that share prices change constantly. This means company size is fluctuating all the time. Another problem with this method is that it can only be used for plcs.It is the size of the business relative to its particular sector in an industry that is important. Is it large enough to enjoy the benefits of size in the market? Is it too large or too small in relation to other organisational needs of the business?

Reasons for growth

Most businesses start small and then grow. For example, Sainsbury started as small dairy shop in Drury Street, London in 1869. Today it is one of the UK's largest supermarket chains with a turnover of £18,518 million in 2007. Businesses have to decide about their scale of operations. This means they have to choose how big they want to be. Some businesses prefer to operate on a small scale, however, many others prefer to grow and become much bigger. There are some strong motives for growth.

- Survival. In some industries firms will not survive if they remain small. Staying small might mean that costs are too high because the firm is too small to exploit economies of scale. In addition, small firms, even if they are profitable, may face a takeover bid from a larger firm.
- Gaining **economies of scale**. As firms grow in size they will begin to enjoy the benefits of economies of scale. This means that unit production costs will fall and efficiency and profits will improve.
- To increase future profitability. By growing and selling larger volumes, a firm will hope to raise profits in the future.
- Gaining market share. This can have a number of benefits. If a firm can develop a degree of monopoly power through growth, it might be able to raise price or control part of the market. Some personnel also enjoy the status and power associated with a high market share. For example, it could be argued that Richard Branson enjoys the publicity which goes with leading a large company like Virgin.
- To reduce risk. Risk can be reduced through diversification. Branching into new markets and new products means that if one product fails success in others can keep the company going. For example, tobacco companies have diversified into breweries to guard against a fall in demand for cigarettes.

Question 1.

QinetiQ is a leading international defence and security technology company. It develops innovative technology-based solutions and products and provides technology-rich support services for major government organisations, such as the UK MOD and the US DoD, and for commercial customers around the world. As a leading supplier of defence research to the UK Government, it has built up significant intellectual capital and expertise.

In 2007, QinetiQ generated a turnover of £1,149 million and made a profit of £94.0 million before tax. The value of capital employed by the company was £477.4 million (net assets). The company places a great deal of value on its staff and in 2007 employed more than 13,000 people.

Source: adapted from QinetiQ, *Annual Report and Accounts, 2007.*

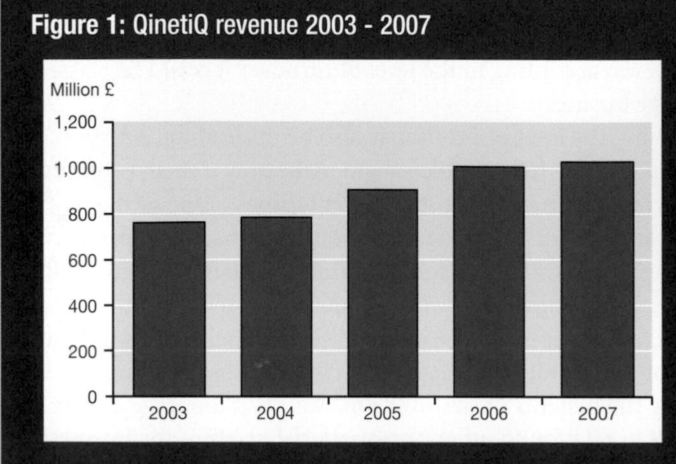

Figure 1: QinetiQ revenue 2003 - 2007

(a) Using evidence from the case determine whether QinetiQ is a small, medium or large business.

(b) During 2007 QinetiQ's share price hit a high of 218p and a low of 161p. The number of shares issued by the company is 660,000,000. (i) Calculate the market capitalisation of QinetiQ based on these two share prices. (ii) Using your answers in (i) explain why market capitalisation may not always be a useful measure of business size.

Methods of growth

There is a number of ways in which a company might grow. **Internal growth** is when a firm expands without involving other businesses. ORGANIC GROWTH means that the firm expands by selling more of its existing products. This could be achieved by selling to a wider market, either at home or abroad. It is likely that internal growth will take a long time for many businesses, but will provide a sound base for development. A quicker alternative is **external growth**. This can be by ACQUISITION or TAKEOVER of other businesses or by MERGING with them. A takeover is when one company buys control of another. A merger usually means that two companies have agreed to join together and create a new third company. In practice these terms are often used interchangeably. In recent decades merger activity has increased greatly leading to a concentration of ownership in many industries. This is discussed in more detail in the unit titled 'Mergers and takeovers'.

It has also been suggested that companies can attempt to grow in one of three ways. Companies can grow by acquisition. For example, AXA, the insurance business, has grown by taking over foreign firms in the US, UK and Japan. However, some companies that have attempted to grow by acquisition have become bigger but not better, and ultimately failed as a result.

Some companies grow by innovating and providing new products. Examples may be Microsoft and Intel. A problem for such companies is that rivals start to copy their ideas, which may slow down growth.

Companies that grow by robust growth might include Coca-Cola and Procter & Gamble. They have long-term growth as an objective, take consumers' needs into account, are prepared to invest in information technology and value the skills of their workforce.

Reasons for the survival of small firms

Despite the advantages of large-scale production, many firms choose to remain small. Also, small firms sometimes have advantages over larger ones.

Personal service As a firm expands it becomes increasingly difficult to deal with individuals. Many people prefer to do business with the owner of the company directly and are prepared to pay higher prices for the privilege. For example, people may prefer to deal directly with one of the partners in an accountancy practice.

Owner's preference Some entrepreneurs may be content with the current level of profits. Some will want to avoid the added responsibilities that growth brings. Others will want to remain below the VAT threshold or will not want to risk losing control of their business.

Flexibility and efficiency Small firms are often more flexible and innovative. They may be able to react more quickly to changes in market conditions or technology. Management can make decisions quickly, without following lengthy procedures.

Lower costs In some cases small firms might have lower costs than larger producers in the same market. For example, large firms often have to pay their employees nationally agreed wage rates. A small firm may be able to pay lower wages to non-union workers.

Low barriers to entry In some types of business activity like grocery, painting and decorating, gardening services and window cleaning, the set up costs are relatively low. There is little to stop competitors setting up in business.

Small firms can be monopolists Many small firms survive because they supply a service to members of the local community which no other business does. People often use their local shop because it provides a convenient, nearby service, saving them the trouble of travelling.

The popularity of small firms in the economy

During the past twenty years there has been a growth in the number of small businesses in the UK. Self-employment has also grown. What factors have led to these trends?

- Rising unemployment has had an important impact. People with redundancy payments have had the capital to set up in business. In some cases unemployed workers saw self-employment as the only means of support.
- The government and local authorities introduced a number of measures to encourage the development of small businesses. **Business start-up schemes** provided funds for small businesses for an initial period. Business Links provide advice on running businesses and obtaining finance. European initiatives have included loans from the European Investment Fund and finance for training from the European Social Fund.
- There have been changes in the structure of the economy. The expansion of the tertiary sector has contributed to the growth in small businesses. Many services can be undertaken more effectively on a small scale.

The growth in the number of small firms has had several effects on the economy.

- Increased flexibility. Smaller firms can adapt to change more quickly because the owners, who tend to be the key decision makers, are close at hand to react to change. For example, a customer may insist that the extension to her house is finished one week before the agreed time. The business owner can put in the extra hours required and perhaps encourage employees to help out. Business owners may also react quickly when some new technology becomes available. This increased flexibility might help the UK economy win more orders from abroad.
- It could be argued that wage levels might fall as a result of more smaller firms. Employees in small businesses often negotiate their own wage rates with the owner. Since they are not in a powerful position on a one-to-one basis, there may be a tendency for initial wage rates and future wage increases to be relatively lower. This will help to keep business costs down.
- More casual and part-time work may have been created. Small firms are often reluctant to employ full-time staff because it is more expensive. For example, part time workers may not be entitled to the same level of holiday pay as full-time workers. Casual and part-time staff also help to improve flexibility. When a business is quiet it can lay off casual staff to reduce costs.
- Staff loyalty may have been improved. In small businesses, relationships between the owners and other staff may be

Question 2.

According to the Sunday Times Fast Track 100, OceanTime 2000 (Ot2k) was the second fastest growing private limited company in 2007. Sales have grown 206% a year from £700,000 in 2003 to £20.1m in 2006. The company employs 78 people.

Hurricanes in the Gulf of Mexico, the high oil price, and a shortage of diving vessels have boosted demand for this Great Yarmouth firm. Trading as Ot2k, the company provides diving, survey and remote-operated-vehicle services to the oil, gas and wind-power industries. A recent project involved inspecting gas installations in Morecambe Bay for Centrica. Founded by Jonathan Soar, Bob MacMillan and John Doherty in 1999, the company recently raised £50m from investors. The full range of services provided by Ot2k included the following.

- Diving - Offshore& Inshore
- Remotely Operated Vehicles - Inspection & Workclass
- Survey - Geophysical & Geotechnical
- Vessel Chartering & Management
- Turnkey Subsea Intervention Packages
- Project Management
- Engineering & Fabrication Services
- Hyperbaric Medical Support

Source: adapted from www.fasttrack.co.uk.

(a) Explain why Ot2k is a medium-sized company.
(b) What evidence is there to suggest that Ot2k has grown quickly?
(c) Explain two possible reasons why Ot2k has grown so quickly.

Figure 2: Share of businesses, employment and turnover by size of business 2005

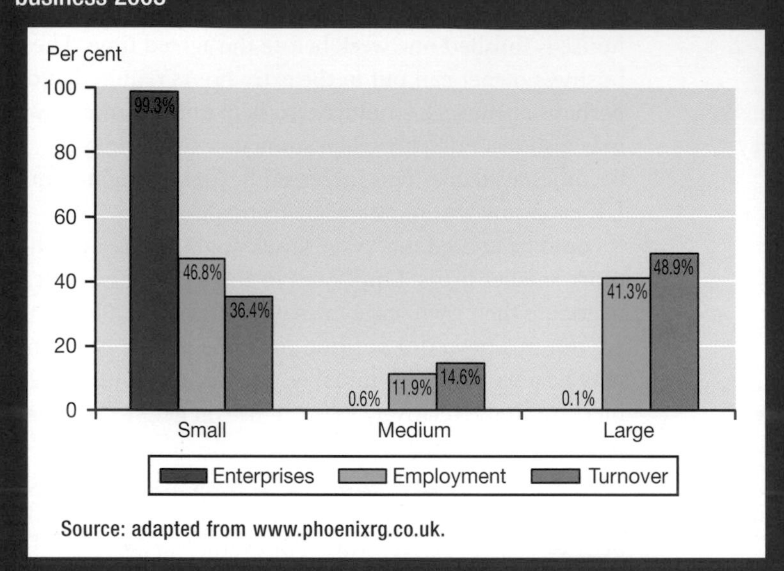

Source: adapted from www.phoenixrg.co.uk.

quite good because they are dealing with each other at a personal level. This might improve motivation and productivity as well as staff loyalty.

- Trade union membership may have declined. In small businesses where relatively fewer workers are employed, trade union membership tends to be lower. This might have implications for the rights of workers in small businesses. It might lead to claims that in some cases, staff are being exploited by small business owners.
- Consumers might benefit from the growth in the number of small firms. More small firms often results in more competition and a wider choice in the market. For example, there has been a growth in the number of computer software producers in recent years. This has led to a variety of 'games' and programs for business and personal use.

The contribution made by SMEs (Small and Medium-sized Enterprises) in the UK is shown in Figure 2.

There were an estimated 4.3 million business enterprises in the UK at the start of 2005, an increase of 59,000 (1.4 per cent) on the start of 2004. Almost all of these enterprises (99.3 per cent) were small (0 to 49 employees). Only 27,000 (0.6 per cent) were medium-sized (50 to 249 employees) and 6,000 (0.1 per cent) were large (250 or more employees). At the start of 2005, UK enterprises employed an estimated 22 million people, and had an estimated combined annual turnover of £2,400 billion. Small and medium-sized enterprises (SMEs) together accounted for more than half of the employment (58.7 per cent) and turnover (51.1 per cent) in the UK. Small enterprises alone (0 to 49 employees) accounted for 46.8 per cent of employment and 36.4 per cent of turnover.

KEYTERMS

Merger – the joining together of two businesses, usually to create a third new company.

Organic growth – growth achieved through the expansion of current business activities.

Takeover or acquisition – the purchase of one business by another.

KNOWLEDGE

1. How can the size of a firm be measured?
2. How is market capitalisation calculated.
3. Why might profit be a misleading measure of a firm's size?
4. State five reasons for growth.
5. What is the difference between internal and external growth?
6. Buying firms to grow quickly can sometimes be a problem. Explain this statement.
7. Explain five reasons why small firms survive.
8. What effect will the growth in the small firms sector have on the flexibility of employers?
9. Look at Figure 2. (i) Which type of firms generate the most turnover in the UK? (ii) Which type of firms employ the most people in the UK?

Case Study: Small firms

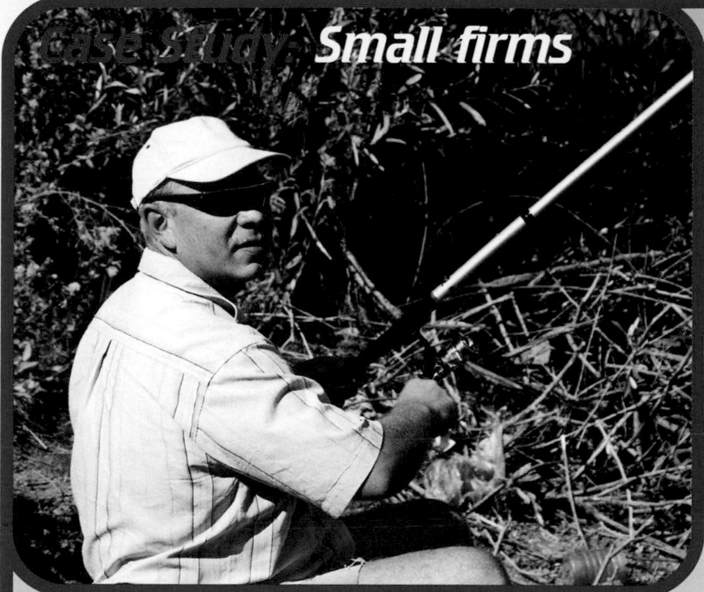

Rodney Wooliscroft owns a fishing tackle business in Kidlington, Oxfordshire. The business is well established and consists of a side street shop in the town centre and a thriving online business. The turnover was around £150,000 per annum up until 2000. However, after this sales started to dip as a result of competition from new, online traders. Rodney had always been reluctant to grow the business because its turnover and profit was sufficient to keep him and his small family very comfortably. Rodney also liked to spend a lot of his spare time fishing. Growing the business would have meant less time fishing. In 2001 Rodney's son became interested in the business and he was encouraged to develop the online service. Rodney knew that if he didn't offer an online service he would struggle to survive. The business now generates a turnover of £190,000 pa which is enough to keep everyone happy. Rodney and his son do not have any other employees and have no plans to grow in the future.

Figure 3: Share of employment in small enterprises (0 to 49 employees) by industry sector, UK private sector, start of 2005

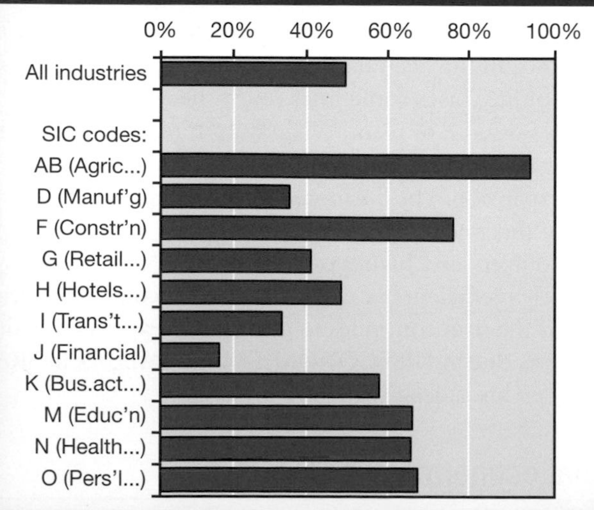

Tianna Nyles runs a financial services business in Harrogate, Yorkshire. She employs a small team of four financial planning advisers with the qualified expertise to provide specialist advice on all aspects of investments, pensions, mortgages and insurance as well as Inheritance Tax and estate planning. Her advisers provide recommendations to suit individual requirements, although many clients have common goals such as:

- To be financially independent and to know they can maintain a chosen lifestyle.
- To ensure their hard earned wealth is preserved for their future security and that of their family and next generation.
- To work with an expert that understands their circumstances and can be trusted to be impartial at all times.
- A need for professional support to organise and manage their financial affairs on an ongoing basis.

Tianna's business is very successful. She does not advertise and relies on 'word of mouth' for all new business. The quality of her personal service is well touted in the town. In 2007 the turnover was £3.4 million and she employed a total of 19 staff.

Source: adapted from DTI statistical press release, 31.8.2006.

(a) Which industrial sectors have a below average number of small firms? (2 marks)

(b) What evidence is there to suggest that the two firms described above are SMEs? (4 marks)

(c) To what extent, if any, are the two businesses above protected by barriers to entry? (8 marks)

(d) Explain why the two firms above are likely to remain small. (10 marks)

(e) Discuss why small firms have managed to survive in such large numbers. (16 marks)

89 Economies of scale and resource mix

Scale of a business

The term SCALE in business means size. When managers and owners talk about increasing the scale of operations they mean that the business should be bigger. Large-scale businesses use more resources and produce more output. They also have higher turnover, enjoy lower unit costs and generally make larger profits. Consequently there are some strong motives for increasing the scale of operations. Unilever, which produces foods, beverages, cleaning agents and personal care products, is a large-scale operator. It is a multi-national company, employs over 180,000 people and enjoyed a turnover of over $50 billion and a profit of over $5 billion in 2006.

Scale and productive efficiency

One objective of production managers is to achieve **productive efficiency**. This occurs when the average cost per unit of output is at its lowest. So if a business produced bolts at 6p per 1,000 when it could produce them at 4p per 1,000, then it would be productively inefficient. It would only be productively efficient if average costs were 4p per 1,000.

There are many reasons why businesses can be productively inefficient. For example, from a production viewpoint, they might:

- not be paying the cheapest price for the materials they buy in;
- be employing more workers than is necessary;
- be using outdated technology;
- hold too much stock;
- have badly organised or inappropriate production methods.

Inefficiency can also be caused by failing to manage human resources effectively. For example, workers might:

- be demotivated and not be working as hard as they could;
- not have received sufficient training;
- apply for a job, but fail to get it despite being the best candidate because of poor recruitment procedures;
- suffer from weak leadership and be less productive;
- be in a poorly organised business where the organisational structure is a barrier rather than a help to efficient working;
- be underemployed and have too little to do because of over recruitment due to poor workforce planning;
- be unable to do their jobs fully because poor workforce planning has led to under-recruitment of staff.

Productive efficiency and economies of scale

The size of a business has a major impact on average costs of production. Typically, there is a range of output over which average costs fall as output rises. Over this range, larger businesses have a competitive advantage over smaller businesses. They enjoy ECONOMIES OF SCALE. In the long run, a business can build another factory or purchase more machinery. This can cause the average cost of production to fall.

In Figure 1 a firm is currently producing in a small plant and its short-run costs are $SRAC_1$. When it produces an output equal to Q_1 its average cost will be AC_1. If it raises production to Q_2, average costs will rise to AC_2. This is the result of the **law of diminishing returns**.

Figure 1: The long-run average cost curve and the effect of economies of scale

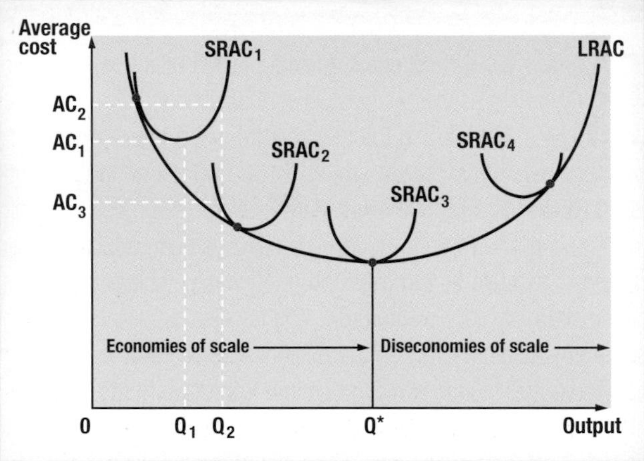

If the firm expands the scale of its operations (which it can do in the long run) the same level of output can be produced more efficiently. With a bigger plant, represented by $SRAC_2$, Q_2 can be produced at an average cost of just AC_3. Long run average costs fall due to economies of scale and will continue to do so until the firm has built a plant which minimises long run average costs. In the diagram this occurs when a plant shown by SRAC3 is built. This is sometimes called the MINIMUM EFFICIENT SCALE of plant. When output reaches Q* in this plant, long run average costs cannot be reduced any further through expansion. The business is said to be **productively efficient** at this point.

At any output level higher or lower than Q*, the business is productively inefficient because average costs could be lower. For example, if the firm continues to grow it will experience rising average costs due to DISECONOMIES OF SCALE, as in $SRAC_4$ in Figure 1. This is dealt with later in the unit.

Internal economies of scale

What are the different economies of scale a firm can gain? INTERNAL ECONOMIES OF SCALE are the benefits of growth that arise within the firm. They occur for a number of reasons.

Purchasing and marketing economies Large firms are likely to get better rates when buying raw materials and components in bulk. In addition, the administration costs involved do not rise in proportion to the size of the order. The cost of processing an order for 10,000 tonnes of coal does not treble when 30,000 tonnes are ordered.

A number of marketing economies exist. A large company may find it cost effective to acquire its own fleet of vans and lorries, for example. The cost to the sales force of selling 30 product lines is not double that of selling 15 lines. Again, the administration costs of selling do not rise in proportion to the size of the sale.

Technical economies Technical economies arise because larger plants are often more efficient. The capital costs and the running costs of plants do not rise in proportion to their size. For example, the capital cost of a double decker bus will not be twice that of a single decker bus. This is because the main cost (engine and chassis) does not double when the capacity of the bus doubles. Increased size may mean a doubling of output but not cost. The average cost will therefore fall. This is sometimes called the **principle of increased dimensions.** In addition, the cost of the crew and fuel will not increase in proportion to its size.

Another technical economy is that of **indivisibility**. Many firms need a particular item of equipment or machinery, but fail to make full use of it. A small business may pay £400 for a laptop computer. The cost will be the same whether it is used twice a week by a part time clerical worker or every day. As the business expands, more use will be made of it and so the **average cost** of the machine will fall.

As the scale of operations expands the firm may switch to mass production techniques. Flow production, which involves breaking down the production process into a very large number of small operations, allows greater use of highly specialised machinery. This results in large improvements in efficiency as labour is replaced by capital.

Businesses often employ a variety of machines which have different capacities. A slow machine may increase production time. As the firm expands and produces more output, it can employ more of the slower machines in order to match the capacity of the faster machines. This is called the **law of multiples.** It involves firms finding a balanced team of machines so that when they operate together they are all running at full capacity.

Specialisation and managerial economies As the firm grows it can afford to employ specialist managers. In a small business one general manager may be responsible for finance, marketing, production and personnel. The manager may find her role demanding. If a business employs specialists in these fields, efficiency may improve and average costs fall. If specialists were employed in a small firm they would be an indivisibility.

Question 1.

Premier Foods, the owner of Branston Pickle, bought the Campbell Soup Company for £450 million ($830 million) in 2006. Premier Foods said the purchase would give it control over well-known brands including Oxo, Batchelors, Homepride and Fray Bentos in the UK and Ireland. After the purchase, Premier Foods said it planned to continue its strategy of acquisitions. The purchase of these brands should help Premier Foods to further exploit economies of scale. 'The Campbell's UK business fits Premier like a glove,' said Robert Schofield, chief executive of Premier foods. 'This acquisition will bring an excellent portfolio of powerful and iconic brands which we intend to drive forward with increased resource and innovation,' he added. The cost of the transaction was met in large by issuing new shares to existing shareholders.

Source: adapted from http://news.bbc.co.uk.

(a) Explain why Premier Foods may be able to exploit (i) marketing economies and (ii) purchasing economies as a result of the acquisition.

Financial economies Large firms have advantages when they try to raise finance. They will have a wider variety of sources from which to choose. For example, sole traders cannot sell more shares to raise extra funds but large public limited companies can. Very large firms will often find it easier to persuade institutions to lend them money since they will have large assets to offer as security. Finally, large firms borrowing very large amounts of money can often gain better interest rates. In the past the government has recognised the problems facing small firms. A number of schemes have been designed to help small firms raise funds.

Risk bearing economies As a firm grows it may well diversify to reduce risk. For example, breweries have diversified into the provision of food and other forms of entertainment in their public houses. Large businesses can also reduce risk by carrying out research and development. The development of new products can help firms gain a competitive edge over smaller rivals.

External economies of scale

EXTERNAL ECONOMIES OF SCALE are the reductions in cost which any business in an industry might enjoy as the industry grows. External economies are more likely to arise if the industry is concentrated in a particular region.

Labour The concentration of firms may lead to the build up of a labour force equipped with the skills required by the industry. Training costs may be reduced if workers have gained skills at another firm in the same industry. Local schools and colleges, or even local government, may offer training courses which are aimed at the needs of the local industry.

Ancillary and commercial services An established industry, particularly if it is growing, tends to attract smaller firms trying to serve its needs. A wide range of commercial and support services can be offered. Specialist banking, insurance, marketing, waste disposal, maintenance, cleaning, components and distribution services are just some examples.

Co-operation Firms in the same industry are more likely to co-operate if they are concentrated in the same region. They might join forces to fund a research and development centre for the industry. An industry journal might be published, so that information can be shared.

Disintegration Disintegration occurs when production is broken up so that more specialisation can take place. When an industry is concentrated in an area firms might specialise in the production of one component and then transport it to a main assembly car plant. In the West Midlands a few large car assembly plants exist, while there are many supporting firms.

Diseconomies of scale

If a business expands, the scale of its operations beyond the minimum efficient scale, diseconomies of scale may result. This is where average costs rise as output rise. There is variety of sources of diseconomies of scale. As shown in Figure 1, long-run average costs start to rise once the output if a business passes Q* on the diagram.

Internal diseconomies of scale Most internal diseconomies are caused by the problem of managing large businesses.

- Communication becomes more complicated and co-ordination more difficult because a large firm is divided into departments.
- The control and **co-ordination** of large businesses is also demanding. Thousands of employees, billions of pounds and dozens of plants all mean added responsibility and more supervision.
- Motivation may suffer as individual workers become a minor part of the total workforce. This can cause poor relations between management and the workforce.
- Technical diseconomies also arise. In the chemical industry, construction problems often mean that two smaller plants are more cost effective than one very large one. Also, if a business employs one huge plant and a breakdown occurs, production will stop. With two smaller plants, production can continue even if one breaks down.

External diseconomies of scale These may occur from overcrowding in industrial areas. The price of land, labour, services and materials might rise as firms compete for a limited amount. Congestion might lead to inefficiency, as travelling workers and deliveries are delayed.

Factors influencing the scale of operation

The scale of operation differs widely from industry to industry. In industries like leather making and furniture manufacture, economies of scale tend to be relatively small. In car assembly or the chemicals industry, they tend to be large. The reasons why they differ are related to the sources of economies of scale.

Technical economies In some industries, there are considerable technical economies. In car manufacturing, for instance, plants need to be a certain size to reach the lowest average cost scale of production. In leather manufacturing, however, even quite small businesses can be highly efficient because the machinery required is relatively little and relatively cheap.

Specialisation In car manufacturing, the organisation of production is complex and there are considerable opportunities to exploit specialisation of labour and capital. In leather manufacturing, the organisation of production is relatively simple with far fewer opportunities to gain the benefits of specialisation.

Purchasing economies Car manufacturers buy billions of pounds of components each year. So there is scope for a large business like Ford to negotiate large discounts compared with a small manufacturer like Morgan cars. In leather manufacturing, the market is much smaller. So no business would ever approach the size of orders that are common in car manufacturing. Hence the difference in purchasing power between small and large firms in the industry is greatly reduced.

Marketing economies In marketing, Ford markets models which sell in their millions around the world. The cost of marketing per car is therefore likely to be far less than, say, for Morgan Motor Company which sells only a few hundred per year. In leather manufacture, it is difficult to mass market any product because leather goods tend to be produced in small quantities to individual designs which are constantly changing. So larger manufacturers are unlikely to have much lower marketing costs per unit sold than small manufacturers.

Because of these factors, leather manufacturers tend not to be large. On the other hand car manufacturers are among the larger companies in the world.

Choosing the optimal mix of resources

A business has to choose an appropriate combination of materials, tools, equipment, machinery and labour before production can begin. The more complex the product, the more difficult this will be. There is often a variety of materials and equipment to choose from. For example, a small manufacturer of jeans has to consider which type of cloth, cotton, stud, zip, sewing machine and labour to use. What influences the factors of production a business chooses?

- The actual design itself may specify which materials to use. For example, a new savoury snack will be made to a strict list of ingredients.
- There may be limited amounts of labour, capital or materials. A company recruiting people with specialist skills may find that supply 'runs out'. It may then have to recruit unskilled workers and train them.
- Businesses will aim to use the cheapest factors, assuming that there is no difference in quality. If there is a difference in quality then the firm must decide which factor most suits its needs and budget. For example, when a company buys a new computer there is a wide range of models to choose from, at a range of different prices. It will have to select a model which suits its needs, and also one which it can afford.

Capital and labour intensity

One of the most important production decisions which operations managers have to make is what combination of capital and labour to use. LABOUR INTENSIVE PRODUCTION techniques involve using a larger proportion of labour than capital. CAPITAL INTENSIVE PRODUCTION techniques involve employing more machinery relative to labour. For example, chemical production is capital intensive, with only a relatively small workforce to oversee the process. The postal service is labour intensive, with a considerable amount of sorting and delivery done by hand.

The optimal resource mix between labour and capital depends on a number of factors.

- The nature of the product. Everyday products with high demand, like newspapers, are mass produced in huge plants using large quantities of machinery. However, in modern economies like the UK an increasing number of the products supplied by businesses are services. Generally, the provision of services is labour intensive.
- The relative prices of the two factors. If labour costs are rising then it may be worth the company employing more capital instead. In countries like China and India where labour is relative cheap, labour intensive production methods are preferred. However, in most developed economies like the UK, labour is more expensive and a great deal of manufacturing is capital intensive.
- The size of the firm. As a firm grows and the scale of production increases, it tends to employ more capital relative to labour. For example, in the UK, Morgan cars, a small sports car manufacturer, uses a labour intensive approach to production. In contrast, Honda, which has a huge car factory in Derby, uses capital intensive production.

Question 2.

In the 1970s, it was argued that large companies could be very profitable if structures were crystal clear and rational. Through these means, human error or deviance could be minimised. But in the 1990s, a variety of studies were conducted which showed that around 1,000 employees in one location is about the maximum size for any company if it is to retain the advantages of economies of scale and minimise the human diseconomies arising from adding more people.

Take the case of IBM, the world's first large computer company. In the 1970s and 1980s, IBM came to symbolise the success of big business. It had pioneered the manufacture of large mainframe computers. But by 1993, it was in trouble, losing £5.6 billion in that year alone. It had failed to move with the times. Part of the business was saying that the future lay with cheap small personal computers. Part of the business was making a profit from computer software. Those at the top failed to listen and persisted in thinking that the future lay with expensive mainframes.

A new chief executive, Lou Gerstner, was appointed. He reduced IBM's workforce by 50 per cent. The company was refocused on providing e-business services and solutions, research and design and semiconductor architecture. Very importantly, the company was segmented into small operational units. IBM employees were remotivated to develop services, discover solutions and be innovative.

Source: adapted from *The Financial Times*, 4.1.2002.

(a) Explain what is meant by 'diseconomies of scale' and, using the example of IBM, explain why they occur.

Table 1: The effect on output as more workers are employed, given a fixed amount of capital

								(Units)
Capital	40	40	40	40	40	40	40	40
No. of workers	1	2	3	4	5	6	7	8
Total output	4	10	18	30	45	52	55	56

Table 2: The benefits and drawbacks of capital and labour intensive strategies

Capital intensive strategies
Benefits
• Generally more cost effective if large quantities are produced.
• Machinery is often more precise and consistent.
• Machinery can operate 24/7.
• Machinery is easier to manage than people.
Drawbacks
• Huge set up costs.
• Huge delays and costs if machinery breaks down.
• Can be inflexible – much machinery is highly specialised.
• Often poses a threat to the workforce and could reduce moral.
Labour intensive strategies
Benefits
• Generally more flexible than capital – can be retrained for example.
• Cheaper for small-scale production.
• Cheaper for large-scale production in countries like China and India.
• People are creative and can therefore solve problems and make improvements.
Drawbacks
• People are more difficult to manage than machines. They have feelings and react.
• People can be unreliable. They may go sick or leave suddenly.
• People cannot work without breaks and holidays.
• People sometimes need to be motivated to improve performance.

The law of diminishing returns

Combining different amounts of labour and capital can affect the productivity of these factors in the short run. As more units of labour are added to a fixed amount of capital, the output of the extra workers will rise at first and then fall. This is shown in Table 1, where the amount of capital is fixed at 40 units. For example, when the second worker is hired the total amount produced (total output) rises by 6 units (10-4). When the third worker is employed, output rises by 8 units (18-10), i.e. a higher amount.

The amount added by each extra worker (the marginal output) continues to rise until the sixth worker is employed. Then output rises by a smaller amount (7 units = 52-45). This is called the law of diminishing returns. Output rises at first because workers are able to specialise in particular tasks, which improves the productivity of extra workers. However, there reaches a point where workers are not able to specialise any more and the productivity of the extra worker begins to fall.

The benefits and drawbacks of capital and labour intensive strategies

Whether a business chooses a capital or labour intensive approach to production, there will be some benefits and drawbacks. These are summarised in Table 2.

KEYTERMS

Capital intensive production – production methods which employ a large amount of machinery relative to labour.
Diseconomies of scale – rising long-run average costs as a firm expands beyond its minimum efficient scale.
Economies of scale – the reductions in cost gained by firms as they grow.
External economies of scale – the cost reductions available to all firms as the industry grows.
Internal economies of scale – the cost reductions enjoyed by a single firm as it grows.
Labour intensive production – production methods which rely on a large workforce relative to the amount of machinery.
Minimum efficient scale (MES) – the output which minimises long-run average costs.
Scale (of a business) – the size of the business.

KNOWLEDGE

1. What is meant by productive efficiency?
2. What are the main sources of internal economies of scale?
3 What are the main sources of external economies of scale?
4. Explain the principle of increased dimensions.
5. Why do diseconomies of scale arise?
6. Explain why the oil extraction industry is dominated by large businesses while hairdressing is dominated by small businesses.
7. State two reasons why a business may use a labour intensive approach to production.
8. State two benefits and two drawbacks of capital intensive production strategies.

Case Study: Timmings plc

Timmings plc manufactures and distributes, through a worldwide network of dealers and distributors, a full line of skid steer and mini skid steer loaders as well as attachments, mobile screening plants and six models of mini excavators. In addition to its industrial and construction products. Timmings has recently added a complete line of potato harvesting, irrigation and handling equipment. The company employs 210 people and turned over £987 million in 2007. Timmings now operates from a large production facility in Birmingham.

Timmings began as a small engineering company in 1978. It repaired agricultural implements for farmers in Hereford and Worcestershire. The business was successful and eventually began making its own agricultural implements after recognising some basic flaws in the machinery it was so often asked to repair. The company grew and by 1996 it had a work force of 240. Between 1978 and 1996 it outgrew its premises in Worcester three times. During this time the company extended its product line and gained a national reputation for high quality agricultural and construction equipment.

In 1996 Timmings moved to a spacious new factory on an industrial estate in Birmingham. The move was the result of receiving a large contract to make and supply potato harvesting equipment. The company expanded by taking on more and more staff. However, in 2001 it began to experience problems recruiting high quality engineers. It was also at this time that the company was sold by the original owners to a large US engineering company. The US parent retained the name of the company and invested very heavily in capital equipment. Around £180 million was spent on CNC machines and robots. Two categories of robot were purchased by Timmings.

- Processing operations robots. These generally perform a specific task such as spot welding or spray painting. These robots are outfitted with a specialised tool to perform the programmed task.
- Assembly line robots. These usually perform a single task in the assembly line process, such as fitting a component. Inspection robots are widely used to examine a finished part or product for defects or irregularities, for example, utilising any number of tools, such as lenses and scanners.

The switch to capital intensive production was met with mixed feelings. For example, all manufacturing robots perform monotonous or repetitive and often dangerous work involving heavy machinery, industrial pollutants, poisonous chemicals or other hazardous materials. However, on the down side some staff may lose their jobs, robots can be expensive to introduce and products may have to become standardised. In the case of Timmings, around 30 staff were laid off.

(a) Using this case as an example, explain what is meant by 'increasing the scale of operations'. (4 marks)

(b) When Timmings began to grow it became more productively efficient. Explain what this means.(6 marks)

(c) Why do you think Timmings plc switched to capital intensive production? (6 marks)

(d) Describe two technical economies of scale that Timmings plc is likely to exploit. (8 marks)

(e) To what extent do you think the benefits of switching to capital intensive strategies outweigh the drawbacks for Timmings? (16 marks)

90 Mergers and takeovers

Reasons for mergers and takeovers

Mergers and takeovers take place when firms join together and operate as one organisation. Why do some businesses act in this way?

- One of the main motives for integration is to exploit the SYNERGIES that might exist following a merger or takeover. This means that two businesses joined together form an organisation that is more powerful and efficient than the two companies operating on their own. Synergy occurs when the 'the whole is greater than the sum of the parts', for example, when 2 + 2 = 5. Synergies may arise from economies of scale, the potential for **asset stripping**, the reduction of risk through diversification or the potential for gains by management.
- It is a quick and easy way to expand the business. For example, if a supermarket chain wanted to open another twenty stores in the UK, it could find sites and build new premises. A quicker way could be to buy a company that already owns some stores and convert them.
- Buying a business is often cheaper than growing internally. A business may calculate that the cost of internal growth is £80 million. However, it might be possible to buy another company for £55 million on the stock market. The process of buying the company might inflate its price, but it could still work out much cheaper.
- Some businesses have cash available which they want to use. Buying another business is one way of doing this.
- Mergers take place for defensive reasons. A business might buy another to consolidate its position in the market. Also, if a firm can increase its size through merging, it may avoid being the victim of a takeover itself.
- In response to economic changes. For example, some businesses may have merged before the introduction of the euro in 1999 in certain European countries or before the expansion of the EU in 2004.
- Merging with a business in a different country is one way in which a business can gain entry into foreign markets. It may also avoid restrictions that prevent it from locating in a country or avoid paying tariffs on goods sold in that country.
- The globalisation of markets has encouraged mergers between foreign businesses. This could allow a company to operate and sell worldwide, rather than in particular countries or regions.
- A business may want to gain economies of scale. Firms can often lower their costs by joining with another firm.
- Some firms are asset strippers. They buy a company, sell off profitable parts, close down unprofitable sections and perhaps integrate other activities into the existing business. Some private equity companies have been accused of asset stripping in recent years.
- Management may want to increase the size of the company. This is because the growth of the business is their main objective.

Merger activity

In the late 1990s and early twenty first century both the number and value of mergers reached record levels. What might have been the reasons for this 'merger boom'?

- There was growth in the UK economy and a buoyant stock market. Higher profits attracted companies to buy shares in or take over other businesses. Companies were also prepared to pay higher prices, which raised the value of mergers and takeovers.
- Faced with greater competition in providing services, there was a number of mergers between financial institutions. Examples of mergers in the financial sector include Lloyds Bank and the TSB and The Royal and Sun Alliance insurance companies.
- Deregulation and liberalisation freed markets. For example, deregulation of the communications industry in the USA allowed an 'alliance' between AT&T and BT. Deregulation of electricity in the UK led to the creation of 14 electricity companies in 1990. By 1998, 12 had either merged together or been bought by outside businesses, mainly because the merged companies would be better able to compete.

Table 1 The largest merger and acquisition deals in Europe since 2000

Rank	Year	Acquirer	Target	Deal Value (US$ Million)
1	2000	Glaxo Wellcome Plc	SmithKline Beecham Plc	75,961
2	2004	Royal Dutch Petroleum Co	Shell Transport & Trading Co	74,559
3	2004	Sanofi-Synthelabo SA	Aventis SA	60,243
4	2006	Pending: E.on AG	Endesa SA	56,266
5	2000	France Telecom SA	Orange Plc	45,967
6	2006	Pending: Suez SA	Gaz de France SA	39,505
7	2006	Merger: Banca Intesa SpA	SanPaolo IMI SpA	37,624
8	2006	Mittal Steel Co. NV	Arcelor SA	32,240
9	2005	Telefónica SA	02 Plc	31,659
10	2006	Merger: Statoil ASA	Norsk Hydro ASA	30,793

Source: adapted from Institute of Mergers, Acquisitions and Alliances Research, Thomson Financial.

- Improvements in information and communication technology meant that it was far easier for businesses to deal with each other. Before, companies in different parts of the country, or in different countries, may have been reluctant to merge because of problems with passing on information. Private company intranets greatly reduced this problem.
- Many firms adopted a company strategy of 'going global'. They wanted operations in many countries and many markets.
- Companies were 'bargain hunting' by taking over companies in Asia. Economic problems in that part of the world meant that companies could be bought relatively cheaply.
- During 2006 and 2007 merger and takeover activity helped to drive the stock market to levels not seen for many years. Many takeovers involved private equity companies taking large plcs into private ownership. For example, Alliance Boots, the high street chemist chain, was bought for £10.6 billion by private equity group Kohlberg Kravis Roberts in 2007.
- One of the biggest takeovers scheduled for 2008 is the acquisition by Carlsberg and Heineken of the UK's largest brewer, Scottish & Newcastle. In January 2008 the board recommended that shareholders should accept the 800p a share offer, valuing the company at £7.8 billion.

Types of merger or integration

As Figure 1 shows, mergers can be classified in a number of ways. Not all mergers fit neatly into these categories, however. HORIZONTAL INTEGRATION occurs when two firms which are in exactly the same line of business and at the same stage of production join together. The merger between BP and Amoco, the two oil companies is an example of a horizontal merger. The benefits of mergers between firms at the same stage of operation include:

Figure 1: A summary of the methods of integration

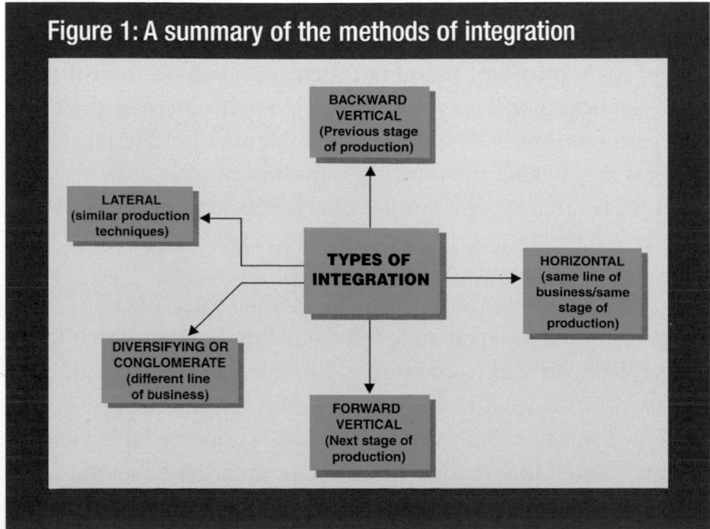

- a 'common' knowledge of the markets in which they operate;
- less likelihood of failure caused by moving into a totally new area;
- similar skills of employees;
- less disruption.

VERTICAL INTEGRATION can be FORWARD VERTICAL INTEGRATION or BACKWARD VERTICAL INTEGRATION. Consider a firm which manufactures and assembles mountain bikes. If it were to acquire a firm which was a supplier of tyres for the bikes, this would be an example of backward vertical integration. The two firms are at different stages of production. The main motives for such a merger are to guarantee and control the supply of components and raw materials and to remove the profit margin the supplier would demand. Forward vertical integration involves merging with a firm which is in the next stage of production rather than the previous stage. For example, the mountain bike manufacturer may merge with a retail outlet selling bikes. Again this eliminates the profit margin expected by the firm in the next stage of production. It also gives the manufacturer confidence when planning production, knowing that there are retail outlets in which to sell. Vertical mergers tend to be rare in the UK.

LATERAL INTEGRATION involves the merging of two firms with related goods which do not compete directly with each other. Production techniques or the distribution channels may be similar. Cadbury-Schweppes is perhaps an example. The two companies used similar raw materials and had similar markets, but did not compete with each other directly.

There are some motives for firms in completely different lines of business to join together. This type of merger is called a CONGLOMERATE or DIVERSIFYING MERGER. A firm might fear a loss of market share due to greater competition. As a result it may try to explore new and different opportunities.

Takeovers

Takeovers amongst public limited companies can occur because their shares are traded openly and anyone can buy them. One business can acquire another by buying 51 per cent of the shares. Some of these can be bought on the stock market and others might be bought directly from existing shareholders. When a takeover is complete, the company that has been 'bought' loses its identity and becomes part of the predator company. Private limited companies, however, cannot be taken over unless the majority shareholders 'invite' others to buy their shares.

In practice, a firm can take control of another company by buying less than 51 per cent of the shares. This may happen when share ownership is widely spread and little communication takes place between shareholders. In some cases a predator can take control of a company by purchasing as little as 15 per cent of the total share issue. Once a company has bought 3 per cent of another company it must make a declaration to the stock market. This is a legal requirement designed to ensure that the existing shareholders are aware of the situation.

Takeovers or mergers can result in situations which may be against consumers' interests. As a result the Department of Trade and Industry might instruct the Competition Commission to investigate the merger. This may result in the government allowing the merger to take place provided certain conditions are met. In extreme cases a merger may be completely blocked. For example, in 2003-04, there was a battle between Tesco, Asda, Sainsbury's and Morrisons to take over supermarket rival Safeway. But the Competition Commission concluded that a Safeway takeover by one of its big rivals would lead to too much concentration in the sector, to the detriment of consumers. It blocked bids by Tesco, Asda and Sainsbury's which cleared the way for Morrisons to buy the company, subject to certain conditions.

Takeovers of public limited companies often result in sudden increases in their share price. This is due to the volume of buying by the predator and also speculation by investors. Once it is known that a takeover is likely, investors scramble to buy shares, anticipating a quick, sharp price rise. Sometimes more than one firm might attempt to take over a company. This can result in very sharp increases in the share price as the two buyers bid up the price.

Hostile and friendly takeovers

Takeovers can be hostile or friendly. A hostile takeover means that the victim tries to resist the bid. Resistance is usually co-ordinated by the board of directors. They attempt to persuade the shareholders that their interests would be best protected if the company remained under the control of the existing board of directors. Shareholders then have to weigh up the advantages and disadvantages of a new 'owner'.

A takeover may be invited. A firm might be struggling because it has cash flow problems, for example. It might want the current business activity to continue, but under the control of another, stronger company. The new company would inject some cash in exchange for control. Such a company is sometimes referred to as a 'white knight'.

The mergers and takeovers described above all refer to public limited companies. It is possible for private limited companies to be taken over. However, an unwanted takeover cannot take place since the shares in private limited companies are not widely available.

Asset stripping

Some takeovers in recent years have resulted in ASSET STRIPPING. The asset stripper aims to buy another company at a market price which is lower than the value of the firm's total assets. It then sells off the profitable parts of the business and closes down those which are unprofitable. Such activity has often been criticised since it leads to unemployment in those sections which are closed down and generates a degree of uncertainty. In 2007, some private equity firms were accused of asset stripping. Indeed, the government was urged to investigate the activities of private equity companies. In one typical case, it was alleged that private equity asset-strippers Permira bought the Homebase DIY chain from Sainsbury's for £745 million. It immediately sold off around 230 Homebase stores for £224 million to rivals B&Q, who promptly closed them down or merged them with any existing B & Q stores nearby, resulting in a wave of redundancies in both companies. Permira then sold what was left of Homebase 18 months later to GUS for £900 million. A 'cool' 600 per cent profit was made on the deal.

Reverse takeovers

REVERSE TAKEOVERS usually occur when a smaller company takes over a larger company. They tend to be friendly takeovers because a small company is unlikely to have sufficient financial resources to take over a much larger company against its will. The larger company may allow the takeover because it feels that the smaller company has a lot to offer in the way of expertise or future potential. Alternatively the larger company may be part of a larger organisation and is up for sale. In 2007, UK-based mobile video company ROK Entertainment Group, completed its reverse takeover of US-based company Cyberfund. ROK will reincorporate in the state of Delaware in US and change its corporate name to ROK Entertainment Group. ROK has three patents and provides a variety of entertainment services including ROK TV.

Another motive for a reverse takeover is to obtain a stock market listing. A large unquoted company might allow a smaller quoted company to 'reverse into it' so that the new company can trade as a plc. For example, Eddie Stobart, the iconic road haulage company, is to list on the London Stock Exchange after reversing into Westbury Property Fund in August 2007. The newly merged company will be known as Stobart Group and be worth about £250 million. It will consist of Eddie Stobart's road and rail operations and Westbury's Runcorn port and Widnes train terminals. The aim is to offer customers integrated sea, rail and road freight transport with the least environmental impact.

Mergers and economies of scale

One of the motives for merging is that costs will be lower if two firms join together. This is because when firms increase their size they gain economies of scale. It is possible that horizontal mergers may benefit most from economies of scale. For example, two banks with similar operations may each have a branch in a high street. If they merge together, costs may be reduced by closing one of the branches.

In 1980 Professor Dennis Mueller studied the effects on efficiency of 800 mergers in seven countries. He found that they were unlikely to lead to economies of scale. He also suggested that small firms would be the main gainers from mergers. A study by Professor Keith Cowling in 1980 supported this view. He investigated the performance over seven years of companies involved in horizontal mergers. The results showed that efficiency gains were no greater than in non-merged businesses and in some cases were worse. This may have been because of a fall in turnover as the merged company 'rationalised' its factory and cut output. Also profits of the combined company may have been lower than what they would have been without the merger.

Many of the businesses involved in mergers and takeovers, however, suggest that cost savings are the main reason for joining together. Some even produce figures to indicate the cost savings they would make. Examples of the economies of scale to be gained were:

- the elimination of duplicated resources. For example, cost savings from the merger between BP and Amoco in 1998 were to be gained from not duplicating oil exploration. The takeover of Amersham in the UK by Nycomed, a Norwegian biotechnical firm, resulted in savings of £9 million one year later;
- the reduction of risk. A small company may be reluctant to operate in a politically unstable country. The BP-Amoco merger may have been willing to do so, because it would have had other projects which may have been profitable if it had problems in certain countries;
- the spreading of the fixed costs of promotion. For example, the design of an advertisement or promotion is a fixed cost. An advertisement may cost £200,000 to make. If it reaches 1 million people in the UK, the average cost is 20p (£200,000 ÷ 1,000,000). If it is shown to 10 million people in the US the average cost falls to 2p;
- the ability to sell a wider range of products because of a wider sales network. This is known as one stop shopping or cross selling. Selling more products from the same distribution network will again reduce the average fixed cost of the sales network;
- the discovery by merged companies which have become global operators that their suppliers have also set up in the many countries in which they operate;
- the fact that larger businesses are in a stronger position to negotiate with suppliers and can negotiate to reduce prices;
- the fact that merged businesses may have COMPLEMENTARY ASSETS. John Kay (1996) suggested that businesses may only be able to operate in certain markets if they have certain assets. For example, a business may advertise nationally to create a brand name. This is unlikely to be successful if it only has shops in Newcastle. It needs a complementary asset such as a chain of national shops.

Joint ventures and alliances

A JOINT VENTURE is where two or more companies share the cost, responsibility and profits of a business venture. The financial arrangements between the companies involved will tend to differ, although many joint ventures between two firms involve a 50:50 share of costs and profits. There are many examples of joint ventures. In 2007, Royal Dutch Shell plc and HR Biopetroleum announced the construction of a pilot facility in Hawaii to grow marine algae and produce vegetable oil for conversion into biofuel. Shell and HR Biopetroleum formed a joint venture company, called Cellana, to develop the project, with Shell taking the majority share. Construction of the demonstration facility on the Kona coast of Hawaii Island began immediately. In another 2007 deal, leading European passenger transport group Arriva plc entered into a new joint venture, which contracted to acquire 49 per cent of Italian bus operator SPT Linea for €6.8 million (£4.7 million). Arriva's Italian business SAB Autoservizi s.r.l. and Lombardy-based Ferrovie Nord Milano Group (FNM SpA), entered into a 50:50 joint venture to acquire the shares in SPT Linea. There is a number of advantages of joint ventures.

- They allow companies to enjoy some of the advantages of mergers, such as growth of turnover, without having to lose their identity.
- Businesses can specialise in a particular aspect of the venture in which they have experience.
- Takeovers are expensive. Heavy legal and administrative costs are often incurred. Also, the amount of money required to take over another company is sometimes unknown.
- Mergers and takeovers are often unfriendly. Most joint ventures are friendly. The companies commit their funds and share responsibility. Such an attitude may help to improve the success of the venture.
- Competition may be eliminated. If companies co-operate

Question 1.

Activision and Blizzard, the gaming companies behind Call of Duty and World of Warcraft, are to merge in a deal worth $18.8 billion (£9.15 billion). US-based Activision also makes console games such as the Tony Hawk series and Guitar Hero. Blizzard is the biggest player in online gaming and World of Warcraft is the global market leader of what are known as massively multi-player online role-playing games. Blizzard is currently owned by the French media group Vivendi. As part of the merger plan, Blizzard will invest $2 billion in the new company, while Activision is putting up $1billion. The merged business will be called Activision Blizzard and its chief executive will be Activision's current CEO Bobby Kotick.

The two firms are hoping that their different strengths will combine to form a business which is powerful on every gaming platform and in every territory. Blizzard is strong in Asia, where its Starcraft series has proved hugely popular. Starcraft, a strategy game first released in 1998, is played by millions of South Koreans in gaming cyber-cafes, and by professional gamers on television. Activision has developed a presence on all three new generation game consoles - Microsoft's Xbox 360, Sony's PlayStation 3 and the Nintendo Wii - with franchises such as Spider-Man and X-Men.

Source: adapted from http://bbc.co.uk.

(a) Using this case as an example, explain what is meant by horizontal integration.
(b) Why do you think Actvision and Blizzard have merged?

in a joint venture they are less likely to compete with each other. However, the venture must not restrict competition to such an extent that consumers' interests are harmed.

There are some disadvantages to joint ventures:

- Some joint ventures fail to achieve the desired results. They are often compromises when an all-out takeover would be better. There may be control struggles. For example, who should have the final say in a 50:50 joint venture?
- It is possible for disagreements to occur about the management of the joint venture. As with any partnership, sometimes there are different views on which course of action to take.
- The profit from the venture is obviously split between the investors. A company might regret this if it became evident at a later date that a particular venture could have been set up by itself.

Alliances may take looser forms than joint ventures. They are usually for three reasons.

- Marketing. For example, McDonald's and Disney have promoted each other's products.
- R&D, where businesses work together to develop a new product. Each business will be able to contribute its individual expertise.
- Information. Supermarkets gather information on customers' buying habits which they share with food manufacturers. This is perhaps a form of **forward vertical integration.**

Demerging

A DEMERGER is where a company sells off a significant part of its existing operations. A company might choose to break up to:

- raise cash to invest in remaining sections;
- concentrate its efforts on a narrower range of activities;
- avoid rising costs and inefficiency through being too large:
- take advantage of the fact that the company has a higher share valuation when split into two components than it does when operating as one.

In 2006, Severn Trent, Britain's second-largest listed water company, demerged its Biffa waste disposal business in the UK. Biffa, valued at around £1 billion, was floated on the stock market on 6 October 2006. The company said there was little synergy between Biffa and its water and waste water business, and shareholders, customers and employees would benefit from dividing the two operations. It also said that £576 million of the proceeds would be returned to shareholders by means of a special dividend.

Management buy-outs

A MANAGEMENT BUY-OUT is where the ownership of a business is transferred to the current management team. The team is likely to buy shares from the existing owners. Funds for the buy-out might be provided by members of the management team itself or by financial institutions, such as banks or venture capitalists. Venture capitalists, such as CinVen, 3i and Schroder Ventures, are specialists who are prepared to take the risk of investing directly in a business. The capital they provide is sometimes called risk capital. Some buy-outs involve these venture capitalists taking complete control. This is known as a leveraged buy-out.

What might account for the popularity of management buy-outs?

- Many buy-outs occur when large companies restructure

Question 2.

GUS was a long-established UK conglomerate founded in 1900 and, for many years, was one of the best performing stocks on the London Stock Exchange. In 2000, the company embarked on a new strategy aimed at delivering long-term shareholder value by focusing on a small number of businesses with above-average growth potential. Other parts of GUS were to be disposed of over time and the proceeds reinvested. By 2003, GUS had been successfully repositioned around three major businesses – Experian, Home Retail Group (formerly Argos Retail Group) and Burberry.

GUS recognised that there were no compelling synergies between these businesses and that their eventual separation was likely to create the most value for shareholders. In December 2005, GUS completed the demerger of Burberry and, in March 2006, announced the separation of its two remaining businesses, Experian and Home Retail Group. GUS believed that Experian and Home Retail Group would achieve their greatest potential and value by becoming independent businesses. It announced a number of expectations of the demerger:

- Enhanced shareholder value.
- Creation of two separately listed companies offering discrete investment propositions, each with clear market valuations.
- Greater flexibility for Experian and Home Retail Group to manage their own resources and pursue strategies appropriate to their markets.
- Sharpened management focus, helping the two businesses maximise their performance and make full use of their available resources.
- Alignment of management rewards more directly with the business and stock market performances, helping to attract, retain and motivate the best people.
- A transparent capital structure and efficient balance sheet for each business.

Source: adapted from www.homeretailgroup.com.

(a) Using this case an example, explain what is meant by a demerger.

(b) 'GUS recognised that there were no compelling synergies between these businesses ...'. Explain what this phrase means.

(c) What are the likely benefits from the demerger?

their operations. They sell off parts of the business which do not fit into their future plans. For example, in 2008, Coventry automotive parts supplier Dunlop Systems & Components was acquired for an undisclosed sum in a management buyout from Trelleborg Automotive UK. The deal cleared the way for the company to focus on developing its business at the niche end of the market. The company supplies air springs and electronically controlled air suspension systems to car, truck and bus manufacturers.

- As part of the privatisation programme the UK government sold businesses to management buy-out teams. For example, in 1996 two rail leasing companies, Porterbrook and Eversholt, were sold to management buy-out teams. So was the British Rail heavy maintenance depot at Eastleigh in Hampshire, for around £10 million.
- If the current owners wish to withdraw from the business. In 2008, host-based printer-driver technology company, Software Imaging, completed a management buyout in what it described as a deal to allow the business to build on its existing success. Backed by the Clydesdale Bank PLC, Software Imaging said that the buyout would enable the company to look at potential acquisitions to complement the existing business and accelerate product development plans to drive future growth. The buyout was led by the company's chief executive officer, Peter Lismer and directors Kevin Jampole and Adam Guy. Technical director and co-founder of the company, Tony Harris, retired as a director, along with fellow co-founders and non-executive directors, John Guy and Dick Hodge.
- To save a business from collapse. In December 2007, Scotland's oldest ski centre was taken over in a management buy-out, according to its website. Liquidators had been appointed for Glencoe Mountain Resort, which took over White Corries when it went into receivership about three years ago. Along with Scotland's other ski centres, Glencoe has suffered from a lack of consistent seasons because of poor snow falls. The resort's website said it was open for business. Invocas were appointed provisional liquidators. It said its primary aim was to safeguard the business.

What might be the advantages of a management buy-out? From the sellers' point of view it lets them raise finance for a possibly ailing firm or subsidiary, which might otherwise have closed down. From the managers' and employees' point of view it would enable them to keep their jobs in the same occupation and area as they had before. It is also argued that the efficiency of the business would be improved by a buy-out. This is perhaps because there is an increased incentive for managers to perform well. Following a buy-out the management team will benefit financially from any profit made by the company, so there is an incentive to keep costs down and motivate the workforce, for example. In addition, the potential for conflict between the owners and the managers is reduced because after a buy-out the owners are the managers.

Generally, it seems that buy-outs are successful as they keep the business going. A study by the Warwick Business School reported that management buy-outs outperformed their industry average for the first three years. However, after that, they tended to underperform. Other, longer term, studies have suggested that performance after the first three years continued to be better than the industry average.

Management buy-ins

MANAGEMENT BUY-INS are where an outside management team takes over a business. Deals of this type are becoming more complex.

Investor buy-outs (IBOs) are where the seller negotiates more closely with the fund provider rather than the management team.

Buy-in management buy-outs (bimbos) are where an external management team, combined with the existing management team, buy the business from its owner.

For example, Murray Johnstone Private Equity Limited and Northern Venture Managers backed the management buy-in of Cego Aluminium Extrusions (Cego) in a £2 million deal. The business was previously owned by Permacell Finesse, part of the Cego Engineering Group, a subsidiary of Laird Group Plc. Cego is a leading manufacturer of specialist aluminium extrusions with annual sales of approximately £9.5 million. The business operates from a factory in Witham, Essex and has approximately 300 customers. It supplies a wide range of extrusions for use in architectural, engineering, office equipment and many other sectors. The management buy-in was led by David Beale, who has extensive experience of the aluminium extrusion industry, having previously been managing director of BOAL (UK) Limited.

Question 3.

Warrington Internet search engine marketing company Latitude Group has undergone a management buyout worth more than £50 million. Private equity investor Vitruvian Partners invested what is believed to be as much as £55 million, which will be used to re-capitalise the business and fund a rapid growth programme. Latitude is the UK's largest independent search engine marketing specialist offering both paid and natural search, with household-name clients including Tesco Finance, House of Fraser, Kwik-Fit Insurance, Crystal Lakes & Ski, Alliance & Leicester, William Hill and Bank of Ireland. Vitruvian Partners is a recently formed London-based private equity firm dedicated to investing in middle-market buyouts, growth buyouts and growth capital across a range of industries in Northern Europe.

Latitude has seen turnover rise from £500,000 in 2002 to more than £30 million in 2006, while headcount has risen from eight in 2002 to more than 100 in 2007. The buy-out was led by chief executive Dylan Thwaites, winner of the Ernst & Young Technology and Communications Entrepreneur of the Year award in 2006. The management team also includes finance officer Julie Moran, operations officer Richard Gregory, and technology officer Rob Shaw. Mr Thwaites said: 'This is a fantastic development for Latitude and its clients. This will help us fund future expansion through acquisition and internal growth.

'We will be looking at new geographic markets and diversification into other digital marketing products including further development of social media and display advertising. All with a view to providing our clients with an even better and more complete service'.

Source: adapted from www.liverpooledailypost.co.uk.

(a) Using this case as an example, explain what is meant by a management buy-out.
(b) What role did Vitruvian Partners play in the buy-out?
(c) How might Latitude benefit from the management buy-out?

KNOWLEDGE

1. Why might firms choose to join together?
2. Why might external growth be quicker than internal growth?
3. Give two examples of:
   (a) horizontal integration;
   (b) vertical integration;
   (c) lateral integration.
4. Why might a firm diversify?
5. Briefly explain how an acquisition is carried out.
6. Why is asset stripping often criticised?
7. What might be a motive for a reverse takeover?
8. Explain why mergers might not result in an improvement in efficiency.
9. What is the difference between a joint venture and a merger?
10. What might be the advantages of demergers?
11. Explain the difference between a management buy-out and a management buy-in.

KEYTERMS

Asset stripping – the selling off of profitable sections and the closing down of loss making sections of a business following an acquisition.
Backward vertical integration – merging with a firm involved with the previous stage of production.
Complememtary assets – assets that a business requires together to be successful.
Conglomerate or diversifying merger – the merging of firms involved in completely different business activities.
Demerger – where a business splits into two or more separate organisations.
Forward vertical integration – merging with a firm involved with the next stage of production.
Horizontal integration – the merging of firms which are in exactly the same line of business.
Joint venture – two firms sharing the cost, responsibility and profits of a business venture.
Lateral integration – the merging of firms involved in the production of similar goods, but not in competition with each other.
Management buy-in – the sale of a business to an outside management team.
Management buy-out – the sale of a business to the existing management team.
Reverse takeover – where a company takes over a larger company than itself.
Synergy – where two or more activities or businesses, combined, create a greater outcome than the sum of the individual parts.
Vertical integration – the merging of two firms at different stages of production.

Case Study: Tesco and Dobbies

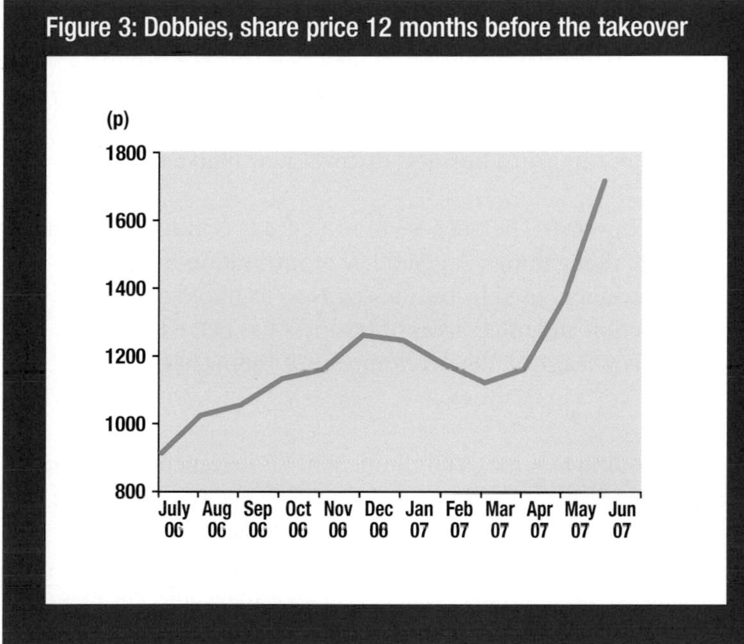

In June 2007, Tesco bought Dobbies Garden Centres for £155.6 million – its first significant deal outside the grocery sector. Tesco paid £15 a share for the Scottish garden centres chain, giving it a foothold in the fast-growing horticultural market. Dobbies is the UK's third largest garden centre chain, with 21 stores based mainly in Scotland and the north of England. The sale will net a windfall of £10 million for James Barnes, the chief executive, who led a management buy-out of the company in 1994 before taking it public three years later. Mr Barnes owns 6.7 per cent of the company. His father and sister own another 2 per cent.

The deal ended the ongoing takeover talks between Dobbies and Apax Partners and also thwarted the ambitions of Sir Tom Hunter, the Scottish entrepreneur, who owns Wyevale Garden Centres and Blooms of Bressingham. The acquisition valued Sir Tom's 10.6 per cent stake in the retailer at nearly £16 million. It is thought that the entrepreneur was 'considering his options' before deciding on his next move. However, observers ruled out the prospect of a bidding war for the garden centre chain. Analysts said that a large stake acquired by Tesco meant that the supermarket group needs backing from just 75 per cent of shareholders to be successful in its bid, therefore precluding Sir Tom from blocking the deal.

Tesco, which approached Dobbies to discuss a potential acquisition early last year, announced the deal after snapping up 22.6 per cent of shares and receiving irrevocable commitments from shareholders over a further 2.7 per cent of the stock.

Richard Ratner, an analyst with Seymour Pierce, said: 'My view is that it is probably all done and dusted, unless the Competition Commission takes the view that they're going to refer it. I can't see why they would, but that's the only thing that could spoil the fun.'

The supermarket group said that the acquisition would give it access to a market for which it was not catering at present and it reflected a strategy of developing the company's non-food operations. Andrew Higginson, the Tesco finance director, said that the supermarket saw potential to expand the range of environmentally-friendly products in Dobbies, adding that it offered a 'big emerging market' in consumer spending.

'I think garden centres can go after that green pound and they are already in an attractive and growing market,' he said. Tesco is keen to capitalise on the current boom in gardening and related 'green' products, including composting kits and water butts. Tesco wants to extend the firm's range of environmentally friendly products to offer wind turbines, home insulation and services such as carbon footprint calculators. It would also seek to expand the chain, particularly in the south of England, to offer 'greater choice and keener pricing'.

Source: adapted from *The Times*, 9.6.2007.

(a) How will James Barnes benefit from the takeover of Dobbies? (4 marks)

(b) (i) Explain the affect on Dobbies' share price of the Tesco bid. (6 marks)

(ii) Explain what might have happened to Dobbies' share price if Sir Tom Hunter and Apax Partners had pursued their interest in the company. (6 marks)

(c) To what extent will Tesco be able to exploit economies of scale as a result of the takeover? (10 marks)

(d) Analyse the benefits to Tesco of taking over Dobbies. (14 marks)

91 Innovation, research and development

Innovation, research and development

Businesses must be able to develop new products, materials, systems and processes and improve existing ones in order to grow and to survive. Today, the pace of technological change, coupled with the rising wants and spending power of consumers, has forced firms to respond by investing in research and development (R&D).

- RESEARCH is the investigation and discovery of new ideas in order to solve a problem or create an opportunity. Methods used to generate new ideas include laboratory research, product evaluation of a business' own and its competitors' products and discussion groups designed to think up new ideas.
- DEVELOPMENT involves changing ideas into products, materials, systems or processes. Quite often a business will identify a number of possible ideas which have scope for development. The first stage is to select the idea which shows the most promise. One of the problems with development is the time scale involved. Some projects take many years to complete and success cannot be guaranteed.
- INNOVATION in business is the commercial exploitation of an invention. It involves committing resources and bringing a new idea to the market. Innovations are intended to make someone better off, and the succession of many innovations grows the whole economy over a period of time.

The purpose of innovation, research and development

Certain purposes of innovation and R&D may be identified.

Solving problems Some R&D is designed to solve problems. For example, in the pharmaceuticals industry most R&D is aimed at developing new drugs and medicines to cure diseases, save or prolong life and reduce human suffering.

Improving quality It is possible to improve the quality of existing products through R&D. In the motor industry a lot of R&D is aimed at improving the safety of cars by improving braking systems for example. Or enhancing the performance of cars by developing new technology, such as the turbo charger. Improving quality is also a means of extending the life cycle of products.

Developing new products One of the main reasons why businesses invest in R&D is to extend their product range or replace products that have come to the end of their life cycle. For example, the development of laptop computers helped to increase the range of products offered by the computer industry. In the electronics industry MP3 players have replaced CDs. The development of new products can help a business discover new markets.

Reducing costs The purpose of some R&D is to find cheaper ways of doing things. A great deal of innovation has focused on the machinery used by businesses. New technology in production and other areas of business has helped to lower costs. For example, the development of robots has reduced labour costs in factories.

Developing new materials Some R&D is designed to develop new materials. Synthetic materials have helped to reduce the use of natural resources. New materials often have features and characteristics which make them better than natural ones. They might be more durable, heat resistant or malleable, cheaper or lighter. DuPont, for example, created Tactel, a lightweight fabric with great strength. Two years after its invention it had captured 50 per cent of the skiwear market. In addition, the development of new materials often results in the creation of new products.

Reducing environmental damage An increasing amount of R&D has been directed at measures to help reduce the damage done to the environment. For example, some businesses are trying to find new ways of reducing energy consumption, cutting toxic emissions and recycling materials.

The cost of innovation, research and development

R&D is often a highly expensive business activity. For example, in the pharmaceuticals industry it can cost up to a £1 billion to

Table 1: The amount of money spent on R&D by the UK's top 10 firms

Rank	Company	R&D (£bn)	Growth	Sector
1	GlaxoSmithKline	3.14	10%	Pharmaceuticals
2	Astra Zeneca	1.97	-11%	Pharmaceuticals
3	BAE Systems	1.45	31%	Aerospace
4	BT	0.73	39%	Telecommunications
5	Ford*	0.69	-10%	Automotive
6	Unilever	0.65	-8%	Food products
7	Rolls Royce	0.35	25%	Aerospace
8	Pfizer*	0.35	-41%	Pharmaceuticals
9	Airbus*	0.34	-1%	Aerospace
10	Royal Dutch Shell	0.34	6%	Oil and gas

* Foreign-owned UK company.
Source: adapted from www.innovation.gov.uk.

bring a single new product to the market. About 45 per cent of all R&D in the UK is in the pharmaceuticals and aerospace industries. Table 1 shows the amount of money spent on R&D by the top 10 UK firms.

The amount of money allocated to R&D by different businesses varies greatly and may depend on a number of factors.

- It is common for businesses to vary their investments according to the funds available in any year. If profits fall for a period of time, R&D spending might fall. Also, a business might be criticised by shareholders if too much profit is allocated to R&D at the expense of dividends.
- Certain industries, such as pharmaceuticals, chemicals, motor cars, computers and defence, tend to have high levels of spending on R&D. This is due to the nature of the industry. For example, new drugs are constantly needed to prevent or cure new or existing illnesses.
- Larger public limited companies tend to be more committed to R&D. They are better able to meet the cost and bear the risk involved than smaller businesses. All the companies listed in Table 1 are plcs.
- Some businesses are committed to high levels of R&D spending because it is part of their corporate objectives and culture. This is certainly the case in pharmaceuticals and aerospace.
- In some industries businesses are forced to invest in R&D to compete. Failure to keep pace with the investment of rivals may mean that a business struggles to survive in the market.
- Businesses are more likely to invest in R&D when the economy is booming. During a recession R&D funding might be cut or frozen.

The benefits of innovation, research and development

Those businesses that do spend on R&D may enjoy a number of benefits.

Competitive edge R&D leads to the development of new products. Firms which are able to develop new products ahead of their rivals will enjoy a competitive advantage in the market. If they can obtain a patent, they will be able to sell the product without competition from other businesses for a period of time. During this time they may be able to raise prices and make **higher profits**. Examples of businesses benefiting from new products include Dyson, the bagless vacuum cleaner manufacturer, and Microsoft, the creators of the world's main operating system for computers.

Improved working environment In some industries, such as mechanical and electrical engineering, research projects are designed to develop new types of machines. Computer controlled machines, for example, have been introduced into many component and textile manufacturers and assembly plants. New technology is capable of cutting costs and raising productivity. In addition, new machinery is often safer, cleaner and more ERGONOMICALLY designed. This helps to make the working environment better for employees.

Question 1.

Wolfson is a global leader in the supply of high performance mixed-signal chips for the digital consumer market. Its products can be found at the heart of consumer electronic applications in the home, in the office and on the move. Wolfson's headquarters are in Edinburgh, where it employs some of the most experienced and innovative designers and engineers in the industry. Over the past few years Wolfson has established an enviable reputation for its audio brand. Many of the world's leading electronics manufacturers are customers, with their chips providing the audio in products such as MP3 players, personal media players, mobile phones, digital cameras, games consoles, flat screen TVs and hi-fi systems. The company has developed a broad range of products and continues to invest heavily in research and development to expand its product portfolio. Wolfson targets growing consumer markets, where added functionality and increased performance are essential to meet customers' expectations. It believes the digital revolution is still in its early stages of development and further advances in technology will allow ever more complex and sophisticated consumer products to be created, providing new opportunities for the company. In 2006 Wolfson spent $29.3 million on research and development. Its turnover was $204.1 million. In 2005 its net profit was $29.0 million.

Source: adapted from Wolfson, *Annual Report and Accounts*, 2006.

(a) Using this case as an example, explain what is meant by innovation and research and development.
(b) How important do you think innovation and R&D is to Wolfson?
(c) What do you think is the main purpose of R&D and innovation to Wolfson?

Image It is often argued that expenditure on R&D helps to enhance a firm's image. Consumers may be impressed by businesses which are committed to R&D. This is because consumers themselves appreciate the benefits of R&D and often recognise that such expenditure is risky. Also, breakthroughs in R&D can be highly prestigious. For example, a pharmaceuticals company developing an effective vaccination to combat Aids would receive a huge amount of positive publicity and recognition.

Motivation Investment in R&D creates opportunities for creativity and invention. Many employment positions in the R&D department will help staff to satisfy their higher order needs, such as self-esteem and self-actualisation. A successful R&D department might also generate a mood of optimism and anticipation in the organisation. This is likely to have a positive effect on the motivation of staff.

Consumer benefits Consumers enjoy an increasing variety of goods and services as new products come onto the market. They are likely to pay lower prices for products because new technology lowers costs. They may also enjoy better quality products resulting from higher grade materials and more effective production methods. New medicines and drugs will improve health.

Risk and innovation

Allocating resources to R&D is extremely risky. Expenditure on R&D does not guarantee new products. Quite often money spent on R&D is wasted. For example, in the pharmaceuticals industry, many of the drugs invented do not reach the market. Trials may be carried out to see whether the drugs have the intended effect and if they have any serious side effects. If drugs fail the trial process they cannot be marketed.

Setting a budget for R&D expenditure is also fraught with uncertainty. R&D departments often spend more than they are allocated. Businesses may have to raise funds externally to finance R&D projects. In recent years a number of pharmaceutical companies have had to use rights issues, to raise extra finance to fund research in medicines and drugs. There are several reasons why setting an R&D budget might be difficult.

- The cost of a scientific research project may be difficult to estimate accurately. This is because researchers will not know when a breakthrough is going to occur. Some research, for example into cancer and aids cures, has been ongoing for many years.
- During an R&D project, there may be unforeseen spending. For example, a business might have to unexpectedly recruit staff with specialist knowledge and experience to further the programme.
- Some R&D programmes run for many years. Therefore their costs tend to rise with inflation. There is a tendency to underestimate inflation and businesses then have to obtain further funding to meet rising costs.

It may be possible to reduce risks by taking out a PATENT. A patent aims to protect the inventor of a new product or manufacturing process. It allows a business to design, produce and sell a new invention and attempts to prevent competitors from copying it. New inventions are protected for 15 years. The developer must make details of the invention available to the Patent Office.

Obtaining a patent can be a lengthy process. To qualify for a patent the invention must be brand new. Checks are then made to ensure it is authentic. The patent is published 18 months after its application and signed and sealed some time after this. The developer must pay annual fees to the Patent Office, which become more expensive after the first four years. This is to encourage production of the new idea. Both the inventor and the consumer can benefit from patents. Some benefits to businesses of patents are:

- a higher level of sales;
- reduced competition;
- legal protection that encourages continued research;
- higher profits, which can be ploughed back into further research and development;
- the benefits to the industry of having the technical information as a result of the patent;
- high risk research and development is encouraged.

Consumers also benefit. New products mean more variety and perhaps a better standard of living. New, more efficient, productive techniques mean lower costs and lower prices.

There is a number of criticisms of the patent system. The granting of sole production and distribution rights to one firm creates a legal monopoly. If this monopoly power is abused then consumers may be exploited.

Implications of innovation strategies

Innovative companies that are committed to high levels of R&D are likely to have differences in the way they operate. The culture of the organisation might be quite different. For example, in companies that emphasise creativity and innovation there is often an informal culture. There may also be more trust and less supervision. If a company pursues innovative strategies there are likely to be implications for other functional areas of the business. The possible implications for finance, marketing and human resources are outlined briefly below.

Finance Innovative companies are likely to have different financial priorities. Inevitably they will spend much larger

Question 2.

In 2006, Rolls-Royce invested a total of £747 million in research and development, of which £395 million was funded from Group resources. Some of the money invested in R&D is being used to address the environmental challenge. During 2006 Rolls Royce launched a new £95 million technology demonstrator programme, the Environmentally Friendly Engine (EFE), which will deliver further improvements in turbine efficiency and combustion emissions. EFE involves a range of industrial and university partners and will validate technologies for pull-through from 2008 into all of their gas turbine products.

Rolls-Royce is a lead partner in the development of the European 'Clean Sky' Joint Technology Initiative. Alongside its industrial partners, it hopes to gain European Commission approval to launch this seven-year programme in mid 2007. In combining this programme with the EFE programme, Rolls Royce will continue with its progress towards achieving the Advisory Council for Aeronautics Research in Europe (ACARE) goals for environmental improvements by 2020. Also, during 2006 Rolls Royce filed a record 330 patent applications.

Source: adapted from www.rolls-royce.com.

(a) Rolls Royce spent a total of £747 million on R&D in 2006. Outline two factors that might influence the amount a business spends on R&D.

(b) Discuss whether some of the R&D expenditure carried out by Rolls Royce was designed to reduce environmental damage.

(c) During 2006 Rolls Royce filed a record 330 patent applications. Explain the purpose of a patent.

amounts on R&D. This may have implications for fund raising. For example, many investors may not be prepared to risk their money in companies that rely heavily on innovation and R&D. This is because they know that R&D can often result in failure. Consequently such companies may struggle to attract funding. They often have to rely more on share capital than on loans when raising money.

Another issue for the finance department is cash flow. R&D has a habit of draining the cash resources of a business. The finance department must monitor cash flow carefully. On the one hand ensuring that the R&D department has enough cash to be effective, but on the other making sure that all of the company's cash does not disappear into a 'black hole'.

Marketing Innovative companies have to work very closely with the marketing department. One of the main sources of new ideas is from customers. Businesses must be responsive to the needs of consumers and R&D projects must address these needs. The marketing department must gather up to date and reliable information from the market and communicate it effectively to R&D centres. Innovative companies will be far more successful if their new products meet the needs of consumers.

When a new product is developed, it may take a time to get accepted in the market. For example, consumers may not believe that a new technical product really works. The marketing department will have to use all their skill to launch the new product successfully. However, once established, innovative products will get good distribution. Large retailers are likely to prefer innovative new products when allocating shelf space to manufacturers.

Human resources Innovative companies may have a more relaxed approach to working. This is to accommodate the needs of their creative people. Working practices may be more flexible and less regimented. Innovative companies may also have to recruit different types of people. They may require a lot of graduates for example. An increasing number of research companies are 'spin-offs' from university departments. For example, privately owned Molecular Profiles was founded in 1997, as a spin-off company from the School of Pharmacy at the University of Nottingham UK. The company specialises in advanced solid state analysis.

Workers in innovative companies are more likely to be involved in the introduction of new methods and working practices. For example, innovative companies may adopt a kaizen (continuous improvement) approach to business, where it is the responsibility of everyone to look for improvements. This view is supported by the management guru Tom Peters. He believes that innovation is the responsibility of everyone in the organisation. In this way, the organisation can harness the creative power of an even wider range of specialists. Also, innovation often comes when people from different backgrounds work in teams. An innovative business must be prepared to adopt such working practices with its employees.

KEYTERMS

Development – the changing of new ideas into commercial propositions.
Ergonomics – the study of people in their working environment and the adaptation of machines and conditions to improve efficiency.
Innovation – the commercial exploitation of an invention.
Patent – a licence which prevents the copying of an idea.
Research – an investigation involving the process of enquiry and discovery used to generate new business ideas.

KNOWLEDGE

1. What is the difference between R&D and innovation?
2. State four purposes of innovation.
3. Why is R&D risky?
4. State four benefits of R&D to a large clothes chain.
5. State three benefits of R&D to businesses.
6. State two industries where R&D expenditure tends to be high.
7. What might be the implications of innovative strategies for human resources?

Case Study: Video games market

By 2011, the worldwide gaming market will be worth $48.9 billion at an annual growth rate of 9.1% from 2006. Key growth engines will include online and wireless games, new-generation consoles, as well as the expanding in-game advertising business. The overall gaming audience continues to expand and become somewhat more female and older than in the past thanks to casual games and games becoming an 'important part of culture'.

Nintendo, which has outsold Sony and Microsoft in the videogame console market, recently became the leader in game revenue, toppling Sony, said iSuppli, a market research agency. Worldwide revenue from Nintendo DS and Wii gaming software amounted to $1.2 billion in the quarter, up more than 31% from the $943.6 million Nintendo enjoyed in the second quarter. In comparison, Sony generated $1 billion in gaming software revenue for its PlayStation 3, PlayStation 2 and PSP players, while Microsoft posted revenue of $317.8 million for Xbox and Xbox 360. In the second quarter, software sales for Sony and Microsoft were $1 billion and $271.9 million, respectively.

Nintendo is expected to maintain its lead, as it ships about 200 additional titles by the end of the year, bringing the number of games to more than 350, many from outside publishers, iSuppli analyst David Carnevale said. In addition, game sales could get a further boost from the expected introduction of a new flagship title for the Wii, called Wii Fit. The game encourages players to engage in full-body exercises using Wii Balance Boards, performing activities including yoga, push-ups, aerobics, and stretching.

Nintendo has achieved mass-market appeal through easy to use games, and the Wii's motion-sensing control that allows players to get more physically involved in games, which could involve swinging a virtual tennis racket or golf club. In contrast, Sony's PlayStation 3 and Microsoft's Xbox 360 are aimed at more serious gamers with cutting-edge titles, such as the popular Halo 3 for the Xbox 360. Microsoft reported recently that sales of Xbox 360 jumped 100% in its fiscal first quarter ended September 30, thanks to the debut of Halo 3. Microsoft hopes the trend will continue through the holiday shopping season.

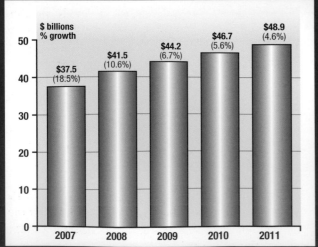

Figure 1: Global video game market – projected growth

Year	$ billions	% growth
2007	$37.5	(18.5%)
2008	$41.5	(10.6%)
2009	$44.2	(6.7%)
2010	$46.7	(5.6%)
2011	$48.9	(4.6%)

Halo 3 has, to date, broken a number of gaming industry records, including the record for first day sales. The title pulled in $170 million on its September 25 launch. Sales of PlayStation 3 software, however, have been suffering due to the console's high price and a lack of compelling titles. The problems have affected third-party game publishers, such as leading game maker Electronic Arts, iSuppli said. EA is losing revenue due to meagre PlayStation 3 sales and the company is rooting for price cuts and improvements to the console in order to encourage software sales. Sony recently cut the price of the PlayStation 3 but, because the company was slow to drop prices and produce compelling games, third-party publishers are flocking to other platforms, the research firm said.

Source: adapted from www.blog.futurelab.net.

(a) (i) Comment on the size and growth potential of the global video games market. (4 marks)
(ii) How has Nintendo become the market leader? (4 marks)
(iii) Why is PlayStation 3 struggling in the market? (4 marks)

(b) What are the purposes of R&D and innovation in the video games market? (8 marks)

(c) In 2007, Sony cut its R&D expenditure on games by nearly 10 per cent to 97.9 billion yen. Explain why R&D in the video games industry is risky. (8 marks)

(d) How might CAD be useful in the video games market? (8 marks)

(e) To what extent are innovations and creativity the keys to success in the video games market? (14 marks)

92 Product design

Product choice

New businesses have to decide what product to manufacture or what service to provide. Once a business is established, it is unlikely to supply exactly the same product or service indefinitely. Over time businesses modify products, withdraw declining products and introduce new ones. They tend to extend product lines and may even diversify into completely different product areas. Decisions to launch new products or adapt existing ones are often complex and outcomes can be uncertain. Most businesses will carry out marketing research before making these decisions. This will help to evaluate the likely success of a new product before production begins.

What influences the products a firm chooses to produce?

The approach of the business Some businesses may be **product orientated**. The nature of the product itself (what it could do and its quality) would be enough to make sure that it sold. For example, when cars were first produced they were unique and a novelty and so the product sold itself. Many firms recognise the need to design products that meet consumers' wishes. These are **market orientated firms**. Increasingly businesses are becoming **asset-led**. They are launching products based on the strengths of the business. For example, a company with a strong brand name for a product may develop other related products.

Competitors' behaviour In order to survive in a competitive market, businesses must supply products which customers prefer at the expense of those supplied by competitors. This may mean developing products which are not available, or copying rivals' ideas and improving them.

Technology New inventions and innovations often result in new products. For example, research has resulted in mobile telephones, flat screen televisions, satellite television with pay per view options, and digital television, with improved picture quality and interactive options. New materials have been created which have led to improved products. Kevlar is a fibre which is used in the manufacture of bullet proof vests because of its resistance to impact. Carbon fibre racing cycles have been created which are lighter and faster than traditional cycles. Totally new products may be created. DVD players play films stored on discs similar to CDs. However, they contain far more information.

Management The choice of product is often made by senior management. It is a crucial decision because it may decide the fate of a company.

Financial viability Do the benefits of new or adapted goods or services outweigh the costs? The benefit to the firm might be the revenue it gains from selling the product. Accountants often act as a constraint on production decisions. They are unlikely to approve funds for products which will make long-term losses.

Approaches to product development

Businesses may prefer to develop a new product which is unique. In practice this is difficult. New product development is expensive and highly risky. As a result most 'new' products tend to be adapted from those which already exist. Product ideas can come from a number of sources.

Ideas from customers The most successful firms will be those which provide products which match the wants of customers. Thus it makes sense to listen to the views of customers when forming ideas for new products. The marketing department is likely to play an important role. Questionnaires and interviews can be used to gather data from customers. However, it is often argued that less structured methods are more appropriate for collecting new ideas. The use of **focus groups**, where seven to ten participants sit to discuss and share ideas about new products, is one approach. Another is to analyse all customer communications, such as complaints and suggestions. It is important for all staff who are in contact with customers to pass on such comments.

Ideas from competitors Companies sometimes rely on copying the products of competitors. This is to avoid the cost and risk of new product development. It is also difficult to be original. A firm will gain a competitive advantage if it can develop a brand new product and be the first in the market. However, a large number of firms wait for competitors to launch new products and then bring out their own versions. Supermarkets often copy famous brand names when launching their own-label brands of goods. In some cases the copying extends to closely imitating the packaging as well as the product. TV companies are quick to bring out their own versions of new quiz games, cookery programmes and other popular TV shows which rival broadcasters launch. Some companies undertake REVERSE ENGINEERING. This process involves taking apart a product to understand how a competitor has made it. A business will closely analyse the product's design and how it has been produced, and identify those key features which are worth copying.

Ideas from staff Businesses may rely on the ideas of their staff for new products. Some staff will work closely with customers and might pass on suggestions for new products as a result of their conversations. Suggestion schemes, where staff might be rewarded for offering new product ideas, are often used.

Ideas from research and development (R&D) Many organisations have research and development facilities. Money is allocated specifically for the invention, experimentation and exploration of new product ideas. This is probably the most expensive source of new ideas. However, the money invested can generate huge returns if a unique product is developed. R&D is discussed in more detail later in this unit.

Ideas from other products Businesses may adapt their own products into new goods or services. They tend to concentrate on best selling brands. Examples might be the development of 'bite sized' versions of well known chocolate bars or diet and low fat versions of drinks or meals.

Product design

In practice, once a business has identified a need for a product, a design brief can be written. This will contain features about a product which the designers can use. For example, a firm aiming to produce a new travel iron may write a design brief such as 'a new travel iron is needed which is compact and possesses all the features of a full-sized model'. Designers can work from this design brief. When designing the new travel iron they may take into account:

- the shape and appearance of the iron;
- whether it fits the intended need;
- how easily and cost effectively it can be produced from the design;
- the dimensions and preferred materials to be used;
- the image it gives when displayed;
- whether the design should create a 'corporate identity', saying something about the image of the company.

The design process

The design process has a number of stages which take the design from an initial idea to a final product. These stages are shown in Figure 1.

Figure 1: Steps in the design process

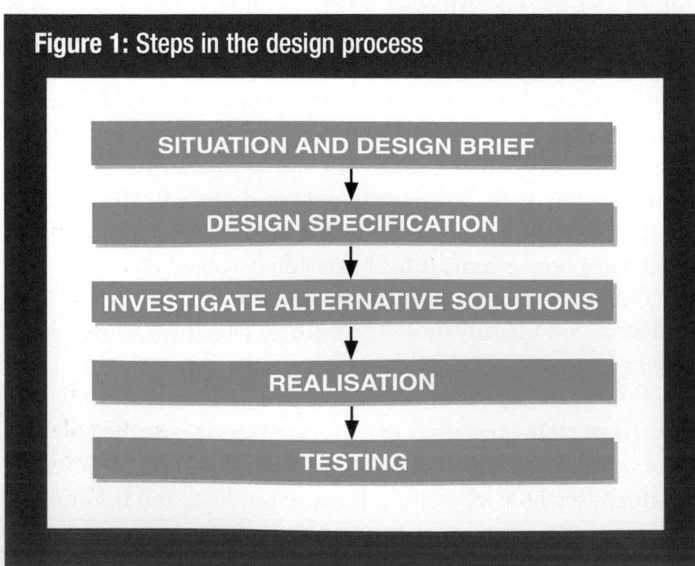

Question 1.

Deborah Brady, a keen equestrian, identified the need for carrying basic equipment while horse riding in a more convenient and comfortable way. The idea was developed during a horse orienteering competition where various equipment including map, phone and pens were used on a regular basis but were difficult to access from a coat or rucksack while 'on the move'. Over a four year period, Deborah developed a range of prototypes in collaboration with local fashion designers and manufactures and with the support of Design Wales and The Wales Innovation Network (WIN) refined the initial concept into a functional activity vest, named 'Q-Pak'. The vest is a multifunctional piece of outdoor apparel incorporating an integral, detachable map case for improved accessibility, together with specifically shaped ergonomic pockets for carrying essential safety equipment and field kit such as compass, space blanket, mobile phone, hand warmer, medical card, whistle, etc. The vest also incorporates high visibility edging to improve safety while on the road.

Although the product was initially designed for use during equestrian orienteering events, further research identified many other sporting activities that would also benefit from a product of this nature including walking, rambling, cycling, mountain biking, climbing, orienteering, fell running, fishing, and rescue units. The product was also entered into the World Invention Show in Geneva in 2005 and was awarded a silver medal in the textile category. The positive feedback gained from the exhibition inspired Deborah to launch the product commercially. The vest, now named the i-Quip Explorer, is marketed by her company, i-Quip Ltd.

Source: adapted from www.designwales.org.uk.

(a) Where did the idea for the i-Quip Explorer come from?
(b) During the design process how did Deborah 'investigate alternative solutions'?
(c) The i-Quip Explorer has ergonomically designed pockets. Explain what this means.

The design process usually begins when a need is found for a new, adapted or redesigned product. Needs may be identified by the marketing department in a **design brief** for the design team, like the one described for the travel iron above.

The next stage is to produce a **design specification and analysis**. One way of achieving this is for the design team, market researchers and the client to meet and discuss their ideas. The design specification and analysis will give a clear description of the purpose of the product, state any functions the product must have and mention constraints, such as cost, size or quality.

Several techniques can be used to produce specifications. One way is to note down all the essential features of a product and to be less interested in those which are only desirable. A pair of walking boots might have essential features such as durability, being waterproof, made of leather and comfortable, and desirable features such as attractiveness, lightness and economy in manufacture. Another technique involves listing all possible alternatives or solutions, even those which initially might be considered unlikely.

Next it is necessary to find some practical solutions to the design brief. Solutions which the design team have suggested should be assessed. Sketches and working examples will help the evaluation. Finally, the team must decide which model or prototype is the most suitable solution to the problem.

The firm can then realise the design solution by making the product. The first production run is likely to be very small because the total design process is not yet complete.

The final stage in the design process is testing. Most designs are tested to check that they satisfy the customer. It is often necessary to refine or modify the product. Sometimes new ideas might be generated once the design solution is in a working situation.

Design features

When designing any product a number of features have to be considered by the designer or design team.

Commercial viability Businesses must be able to produce and sell a product at a profit. Thought must be given to the choice of materials and the production techniques that are used so that production costs can be kept down. If the costs are likely to be too high, the design may well be dropped.

Reliability Designers must ensure their designs satisfy customers' expectations about the reliability of the product. Unreliable products may harm the company's image in the eyes of the consumer. The business will also incur costs if products are frequently returned.

Safety Designers must ensure that their design solutions are safe. Safety is particularly important if products are used by children, the elderly, pregnant women and people with injuries. Safety issues which might be important could include:

- ensuring that products do not contain poisons or dangerous materials such as toxic paint;
- designing products which do not have sharp edges or spikes or providing adequate protection if such features are necessary;
- ensuring that products are finished properly so that edges and faces are smooth and clean;
- incorporating safety features such as child proof caps on bottles;
- ensuring that products are durable because a product which breaks could be dangerous.

Maintenance Technical and mechanical products often need maintenance. Products should be designed so that this can be easily carried out. This is particularly important in the design of machinery.

Environment In recent years consumers have begun to question the effect certain products have on the environment. Designers now have to take this into account.

Convenience and efficiency Products should be designed so that they are convenient and practical to use. For example, some tin openers are 'hand held' whilst others are electrically operated. Consumers are increasingly prepared to pay for products which are easier to use. Businesses also look for machinery and equipment that will lead to a more efficient workforce. Products which are well designed ergonomically should increase efficiency and operator safety and also involve less effort for the user.

Manufacture Designers must ensure that their designs are not

Question 2.

Barbara and Peter Blackburn are gardeners rather than inventors. Their original product was exhibited at the Geneva Inventors and New Products Exhibition in April 2006, where they won a Bronze Medal in their category. This resulted in public, media and trade interest in the product, both in the UK and in Europe. The product started life as a simple frame that had been discarded from another item. It kept open a refuse bag, but needed to be refined in terms of design and materials used. It was the start of the concept of the B-tidy range. After months of building prototypes and using them in their garden, the B-tidy Home and Garden Tidy was developed. The product has had extensive trials with consumers during its development. Market Research indicated very positive potential consumer interest. Blackburn Associates have now developed accessories to complement the Garden & Home Workstation.

The B-tidy range has been manufactured to the highest of standards. Materials used are strong, robust and will withstand the rigors of climate changes. The Home and Garden Tidy solves the two most common problems for gardeners when tidying their gardens – keeping a refuse bag open and upright and keeping tools in one place. It has a robust steel frame with a tough tear resistant waterproof polyethylene pocketed support.

- It will support up to 15 kgs.
- It supports and keeps open any standard size refuse bag.
- It has 8 handy size pockets to keep all those garden tools in one place.
- It can be easily wheeled around the garden.
- Pocketed support easily removes from frame to facilitate removal of heavy bags or for cleaning.
- Convenient working height for standing or kneeling.
- At the end of the day it folds away for easy storage.

Source: adapted from www.b-tidy.co.uk.

(a) Explain how the following design features were important when Barbara and Peter Blackburn developed the B-tidy Home and Garden Tidy. (i) Convenience and efficiency. (ii) Reliability and durability. (iii) Commercial viability.

expensive or technically difficult to make. For example, they may suggest a cheaper material for lining the inside of a suitcase.

Market The designer must consider the marketing mix when designing products. Products are very difficult to market if they are unattractive, clumsy to store and display, expensive to distribute and overpriced.

Aesthetics Designers must consider the colour, size, appearance, shape, smell and taste of products. Many consumers would not wish to be seen wearing poorly designed clothes, for example.

Legal The product should be designed so that it is legally 'fit for purpose'. For example, if a manufacturer claims that a new type of paint is designed to dry within two hours after application, then legally, it must.

Computer aided design

Computer aided design (CAD) is an interactive computer system which is capable of generating, storing and using geometric and computer graphics. It helps design engineers to solve design problems. CAD is used in many industries today. What benefits does CAD offer to a designer?

- CAD has meant huge cuts in lead time, i.e. the length of time between the initial design and actual production. Long lead times result in lower profits as firms lose out to competitors in the race to launch new products.
- A wide range of designs can be shown on the computer screen. Two and three dimensional engineering drawings, wire-framed models, electronic circuit board designs and architectural drawings are examples.
- CAD systems handle repetitive work, allowing the designer more time to concentrate on 'creating' the design. The need for specialists is also reduced, which helps keep down costs.
- Modifications and changes are easily made. The size or shape of a design can be changed in seconds, for example.
- Problems are often more quickly identified. This sometimes prevents the need for expensive reworking later on. Also, the final design, once manufactured, is more likely to be right.
- Increasing use is being made of CAD by businesses. In America, customers entering the Digitoe shoe store in Seattle sit in a seat which has a scanner attached to a computer. The equipment takes detailed pictures of their feet. It sends them to a factory where a shoe mould is made and a pair of custom made leather shoes are produced. The first pair are ready in two weeks, but the moulds can be reused and further pairs can be produced within hours of a new order. This sort of individualised production line, called mass customisation, is a direct result of improvements in CAD and manufacturing software.

Value analysis and value engineering

The aim of VALUE ENGINEERING is to reduce costs and avoid unnecessary costs before production begins. This technique is used by most manufacturers in Japan. It aims to eliminate any costs which do not add value to, or improve the performance of, products and services. VALUE ANALYSIS is a similar process, but is concerned with cost reduction after a product has been introduced.

Value engineering helps businesses to design products at the lowest cost. It is usually carried out by cross departmental teams. Team members might include designers, operations managers, purchasing specialists and cost accountants. The process involves carefully checking the components of a product to find ways to reduce their costs. The team will analyse the function and cost of each element and investigate ways to reduce the number of separate components, using cheaper materials and simplifying processes.

The success of value engineering will often depend on how departments work together. Value engineering cannot be undertaken by an individual. Costs can only be reduced if departments take into account each other's needs. For example, in an effort to cut costs, the quality of a product may suffer to such an extent that the marketing department may find it impossible to sell it. The advantages of value engineering include:

- lower costs, resulting in lower prices for consumers;
- more straightforward methods of manufacture;
- fewer components in products, resulting in lower maintenance and repair costs;
- improved co-operation and communication across departments;
- possible 'spin-offs' for other products.

Value analysis has been used by the government to help improve efficiency in some of its departments. For example, the Edinburgh Healthcare NHS trust set up value analysis groups to look at catering services, portering services and laundry. As a result around £400,000 of savings were made on a budget of £5 million. In addition, the quality of services was also improved in some cases.

The Co-op Bank carried out an ethical and ecological value analysis to estimate the possible costs and benefits of pursuing sustainable development. The bank takes seriously its responsibilities as a practitioner of sustainable development. The bank found that its ethical and ecological positioning makes a sizable contribution to the bank's profitability. Twenty six percent of profits can be assigned to customers who cite ethics as an important factor, and 14 per cent to customers who cite ethics as the most important factor. Recently, the profit attributable to ethically-minded customers was put at between 15 and 18 per cent of the bank's profit before tax.

Lean design

LEAN DESIGN or SIMULTANEOUS ENGINEERING or CONCURRENT ENGINEERING, as it is sometimes known, involves speeding up the whole design process so that a business can bring new products to the market far more quickly. Lean design was first used by Toyota and involves the integration of production and design so that production and design tasks can be undertaken at the same time. Lean design also aims to reduce waste in the design process which may result from a number of factors.

- Looking for information and waiting for test results.
- Generation of unnecessary documents.
- Development of unnecessary physical prototypes.
- Not learning from past design experiences.
- Building in too many features.
- Unused or incomplete designs.
- Underuse of design knowledge.
- Late discovery of manufacturing errors.
- Poor designs.
- Warranty issues.

B/E Aerospace used a lean design approach on a lie-flat first class seat order for Japan Airlines (JAL). The project challenge was how to pack the many internal components of the seat into an extremely tight space, requiring very close collaboration between the industrial designers and the engineers. By using lean design the company was able to reduce waste in its product development process. The lie-flat seat also won B/E Aerospace an award for innovative design. Concept designers and engineers on the seat project avoided data translations by working with CAD software that had functions for concepts and detailed engineering. This let their work proceed concurrently instead of serially – one of the key features of lean design.

KNOWLEDGE

1. How can the behaviour of competitors and the state of technology affect the product a firm chooses to produce?
2. How might a business find out if there is a need for a product?
3. What is meant by a design brief?
4. Describe the stages in the design process.
5. What is meant by a design feature?
6. State six design features that a firm might consider important when designing a product.
7. How does CAD improve business efficiency?
8. How will value analysis benefit consumers?
9. What is the difference between value analysis and value engineering?

KEYTERMS

Lean design (or simultaneous engineering or concurrent engineering) – an approach to product design which involves cutting waste in the design process to reduce the amount of time it takes to design a product.
Reverse engineering – a method of analysing a product's design by taking apart the product.
Value analysis – a procedure to evaluate a product after manufacture to see how costs may be reduced
Value engineering – a procedure designed to reduce and avoid unnecessary costs before production begins.

Case Study: Chrysler

The Chrysler Group of DaimlerChrysler has a strong history of building beautiful and exciting concept vehicles. From 1950 through to 1961, Virgil Exner, Chrysler's first vice president of Styling, led the creation of what he called 'idea cars'. The building of these advanced vehicles helped propel Chrysler to the position of styling leadership it enjoys today. These one-of-a-kind concept vehicles provide unique opportunities to explore new design ideas. Customer reaction to future products can be more effectively gauged as senior management gets comfortable with new design trends. Concept cars may influence new products, as the Portofino influenced the first LH sedans. The Viper and the PT Cruiser concepts were so well received they became production cars. Concept cars also offer engineers a platform to explore advanced technologies on functioning vehicles.

Extracts from Chrysler's design process

Exterior design

Chrysler's world-class designers develop fresh, bold, trend-setting exterior designs. The design process begins with an inspiration that becomes a sketch. Sketches are created along thematic lines using both manual and electronic techniques and the most promising ideas are selected with the guidance of Design Management. Further refinement and development are achieved using state-of-the-art computer rendering tools. Design ideas mature through frequent interaction and feedback from management, engineering platform teams and marketing. As the theme solidifies and the design progresses the finished vehicle takes shape. The designer develops more detailed renderings in multiple views to better illustrate what the vehicle will look like in 3D. Final design themes are then developed into scale and full size clay models.

Interior design

Interior design is critically important to customer satisfaction because the customer interacts in a very personal way with the inside of the vehicle. Interior designers face the difficult challenge of blending aesthetic, functional and ergonomic features, often within tight constraints. Aesthetically, the interior of a vehicle must harmonise with its exterior theme. Functionally, a vehicle interior has to meet many requirements, such as federally-mandated safety standards. Ergonomically, the customer's interaction with the vehicle must be natural and allow for quick response. Controls must be placed within easy reach, instruments clearly visible and placement of components logical.

Conceptual Data Development (CDD)

As more accuracy and quality is required, the designer's initial form is transferred to Chrysler's (CDD) Group. CDD uses CAD software, to further develop the designer's interior and exterior themes. It is this data that links the designer's concept to all other supporting activities in the corporation, such as manufacturing, marketing, finance and purchasing. The CAD operator receives input from various sources: oral direction or sketches from the designer, engineering sections, or scan data from clay models. The design often evolves from a combination of a physical clay model and the CAD data. As more realism is required for full size evaluation, three-dimensional elements such as mirrors, tyres and wheels are developed and added to the CAD data. The final concept data is then sent to engineering for final production surfacing and release.

Source: adapted from www.chrysler.com.

(a) Explain the function of concept cars in Chrysler's design process. (4 marks)

(b) How important is ergonomics in the design of cars? (6 marks)

(c) Explain how the following design features might be important to Chrysler when designing new cars: (i) environment (ii) aesthetics (iii) safety. (12 marks)

(d) How will the use of CAD benefit Chrysler? (8 marks)

(e) To what extent do you think value engineering and value analysis might be used by Chrysler in their design process? (10 marks)

93 Factors affecting location

Making location decisions

Choosing a suitable place to locate a business is an important decision for a business when setting up. This is because it is a long-term decision. Once a business has been set up in a particular location, it is likely to stay there for a period of time. Relocation can be expensive. So a business must find the best possible location when setting up. Business owners may, however, review their location decision from time to time to see if relocation is needed.

Business owners may choose a location near to where they live. But other factors have to be taken into account. Location decisions are likely to be based on the costs and benefits of specific locations. For example, an owner looking to open a restaurant will consider the cost of rent and refurbishment, as well as the proximity to customers and the image a particular location might present. The costs and benefits affecting a location decision may be **quantitative**. This means that they can be measured in monetary terms. An example would be the cost of transporting goods to customers. Other costs and benefits may be **qualitative**. This means that they cannot be measured in monetary terms. An example would be the distance staff have to travel to work.

An increasing number of businesses are being set up at home. This may be because it is cheap and convenient for the owners. Many new businesses are also web-based and can be located anywhere. For example, a business offering educational services over the Internet could be based anywhere in the world.

Technology

Developments in technology have had an impact on business location in recent years. Most businesses now require fast telecommunication links that have the capacity to send and receive voices, text, documents and other images instantly. This usually means that they require access to broadband connections. Developments in technology mean that such links are available almost anywhere and therefore businesses have a wider choice of locations when setting up. Red Gate is a software designer in Cambridgeshire that helps users to run, update and compare databases more efficiently. It delivers its software from its website. Its 200,000 users can download its software and so avoid packaging and shipping costs. Modern telecommunication links might also mean that businesses can set up with less space, as an increasing number of people can work from home.

Many new businesses set up in recent years have produced technological products or offered technology services. Yorkshire-based Sarian Systems, for example, designs and manufactures routers used to process and send data from lottery terminals and cash machines. These companies may operate from **Science Parks.** A Science Park is a business support and technology transfer initiative that:

- encourages and supports the start-up, incubation and growth of innovation-led, high-growth, knowledge-based businesses;
- provides an environment where larger international businesses can develop relations with a particular centre of knowledge creation for their mutual benefit;
- has links with centres of knowledge creation such as universities, higher education institutes and research organisations.

An example of a science park is Aston Science Park based in Aston, Birmingham. Some of the companies located there operate in fields such as software, pharmaceuticals, IT Solutions, E-commerce, multimedia, environmental services and computer hardware.

Location costs

When choosing a suitable location to start a new business, the most important factor is likely to be cost. This is because new businesses are often short of cash and need to minimise location costs. Location costs fall into two categories.

Fixed location costs When setting up a business some 'one-off' costs will be incurred in relation to location. These are fixed costs because they do not vary with output. They might include the following.

Question 1.

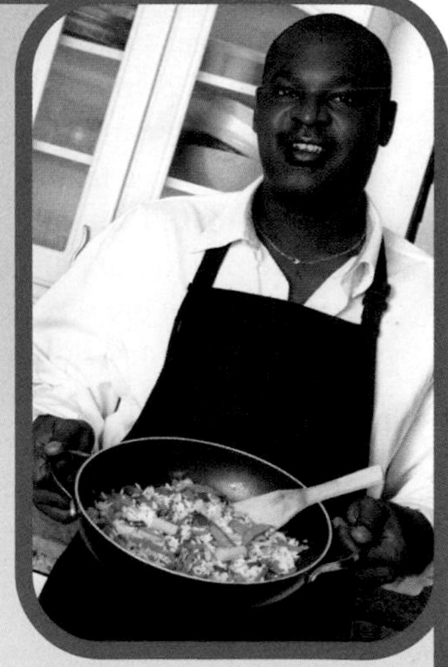

Clevon Guillaume is starting up a business to supply high quality desserts to restaurants and hotels. He was encouraged to do so after winning first prize in a local cooking competition. The awards ceremony was covered in the local press and afterwards Clevon was overwhelmed by the enquiries he got from a range of businesses in the catering industry. One of the tasks he is currently faced with is finding a suitable location. Ideally, he wants to rent a factory unit which can be converted into a working kitchen. He has spoke to a number of estate agents and been in touch with the local Chamber of Commerce.

(a) Identify two (i) qualitative and (ii) quantitative factors that Clevon might take into account when choosing a location.

(b) Which of the above factors do you think might be the most important to Clevon?

- **Search costs.** Finding a suitable location may take time and cost money. These are search costs. They might include the cost of travelling to different sites, fees paid to surveyors for advice or legal searches carried out by solicitors.
- **Planning permission.** It may be necessary to get planning permission when converting premises for business use. This is particularly the case when a property is used for business purposes for the very first time. Obtaining planning permission may incur legal and administration costs.
- **Refurbishment.** Unless new business premises are purpose-built, it will be necessary to pay refurbishment costs. Examples might include painting and decorating, refitting, renovation or wholesale conversion.
- **Purchase cost.** In a minority of cases an entrepreneur might buy a shop, factory, office or other form of premises. This would be a very high cost and because of this many new business owners prefer to start by renting or leasing premises.
- **Government help.** In some cases a new business may choose a location because the government offers to meet some of the costs. The government may offer grants if businesses locate on specific sites – where unemployment is high for example. Grants help to reduce the fixed cost of location.

Other fixed costs relating to location might be ongoing. They do not vary with output but have to be incurred on a regular basis, such as monthly or yearly.

- **Rent or leasing charges.** Rent or leasing charges have to be paid every month and businesses are often tied to long-term agreements that can last five years, for example. Rents can vary significantly. For example, office space in London is more expensive than office space in Glasgow. The rent for a high street shop will be higher than for a side street shop. Business owners will tend to search for premises with lower rents or leasing charges, but the position of premises will also have to be taken into account.
- **Business rates.** Businesses have to pay rates to the local council to pay for amenities such as refuse collection, policing and the fire service. These may vary in different parts of the country. Business rates are usually paid in instalments.
- **Labour.** Some labour costs may be fixed. A certain number and type of staff have to be employed whatever the level of output. Wage rates do vary around the country. For example, wages tend to be higher in London and other parts of the south east.

Variable location costs Variable location costs are those that increase as output rises. Only a minority of location costs are variable.

- **Labour costs.** When businesses expand and sell more, they are likely to need more labour. Businesses that need a large and increasing number of workers might have to consider labour costs carefully. They may decide to locate in regions where labour costs are lower. Some businesses have decided to locate overseas for this reason.
- **Transport costs.** Businesses that use bulky or heavy raw materials may need to locate near to their suppliers. This will help to minimise transport costs. For example, oil refineries are usually located on the coast to avoid the high cost of transport crude oil across land. Businesses that produce bulky or heavy products may need to locate near to their customers. Today this is true, for example, for suppliers to just-in-time manufacturers. In the car industry, some suppliers have chosen to locate close to assembly plants in order to reduce transport costs. The main reason for this is because just-in-time manufacturers require multiple deliveries of small quantities. Transport costs would be considerably higher if suppliers were located some distance away.

Markets

For some businesses, being close to their markets is often the single most important factor in choosing a location. A variety of businesses may be influenced by this factor.

- Businesses that produce products which are more bulky than the raw materials that go into them, such as North Sea oil platforms, are likely to locate close to their market. The components and materials used to assemble North Sea oil platforms are far less bulky than the end product – the platform itself. Therefore, the production of such platforms takes place in locations close to where they will eventually be used – i.e. the North Sea coast – in cities such as Aberdeen. If production was located elsewhere transport costs may be very high. There may also be problems transporting the product to its final destination.
- Suppliers of components and intermediate goods may set up close to their main customers. For example, a number of firms emerged in the Liverpool area supplying shipping companies with packing cases for transportation. After the dock industry declined in Liverpool, some of these companies still existed. The introduction of Just-In-Time (JIT) manufacturing has encouraged component manufacturers to locate nearer to their business customers. The JIT system requires suppliers to provide reliable and immediate delivery. It is likely to be easier to deliver reliably if customers are located less than a mile away, for example.
- Many financial service businesses locate their premises in London. Some would argue that London is the 'financial centre' of the world.
- The growth of the tertiary sector and the decline in 'heavy' industry has resulted in many FOOTLOOSE secondary and tertiary industries. Businesses in these industries are able to locate premises where they wish. Given this freedom, many have chosen to locate near to their markets. The South East of the UK developed a service economy as a result, made up of retailing, financial services, leisure industries and a small amount of 'light' manufacturing.
- Most service industries tend to be located near to markets.

Question 2.

Founded by managing director Anthony Cook when he was only 21, Mobile Fun has capitalised on the mobile-phone craze by selling accessories and ringtones online. Launched in 2000 with virtually no set-up costs, it now offers 5,000 accessories and 100,000 mobile downloads from its headquarters in Birmingham. Goods are despatched to customers using the services outlined below.

- Royal Mail First Class Delivery (UK) – £2.50 per order. Safe & secure shipping. Usually next working day. Please allow up to 5 working days.
- Royal Mail Special Delivery (UK) – £5.95 per order. Guaranteed next working day by 1pm for orders received before 6pm. *(Except Scottish Highlands).
- Royal Mail Saturday Special Delivery (UK) – £7.50 per order. Guaranteed Saturday delivery for 'In stock' items ordered on Thursday evenings & Fridays until 6pm. *(Except Scottish Highlands).
- First Class International Recorded Post (EU) – £10.00 per order. Usually takes 2-5 working days, although varies on customer's local postal service.

Source: adapted from www.fasttrack.co.uk and www.mobilefun.co.uk.

(a) Mobile Fun could be described as footloose. Explain what this means.
(b) (i) Explain why transport is a variable location cost.
(ii) To what extent is Mobile Fun's location influenced by transport costs?

Businesses providing the general public with services like dentistry, dry cleaning and car maintenance must locate their premises in areas which are accessible to people.

- Closeness to the market can also be a SITE FACTOR affecting the location of a business. Site factors affect the choice of one plot of land or one set of premises rather than another after the business has decided to locate in a particular area. For example, WH Smith originally located its outlets in railway stations because its main market was railway passengers buying newspapers and magazines. When it moved out of railway stations, it located its outlets in the nearest available premises. Small retailers supply the needs of local communities. The 'corner shop', for example, relies mainly on customers from a very small local catchment area.

Transport links

The ease of transport can be important in a firm's location decision. Access to motorways, rail networks, ports and airports may all be important. By reducing travel time, motorways may encourage firms to locate premises in areas which might otherwise have been regarded as remote from markets or costly in terms of transport. The building of the M4 between London and South Wales has encouraged location along the 'M4 corridor'.

The accessibility of ports and airports might also be important. This is often true of firms which export their goods. For firms which produce light, low bulk, but high value products, air transport might be the best means of reaching both overseas and domestic markets. More bulky and heavier goods might be transported by sea. Businesses which use a great deal of imported raw materials might also locate close to a port.

The building of the Channel Tunnel improved trade links to the Continent when it was opened. It allowed UK businesses to distribute goods easily and effectively to Europe. It also encouraged firms to locate in the South East if they had markets in Europe. The Channel Tunnel became even more important when trading restrictions with Europe were lifted in 1992. Other regions in the UK have benefited from increased trade with Europe via rail links. However, with increasing congestion on all motorways, firms with European interests have favoured the South East.

Good transport links can also be a factor influencing the choice of site. For example, a business locating in Leeds may choose to build a factory close to the M62/M1 junction rather than North West of the city. In many towns and cities, industrial estates tend to be located close to motorways or railway stations.

Land

When choosing where to locate or relocate premises, firms need to select the 'right' piece of land. This might be a newly completed factory unit, a derelict inner city site, an old factory in need of modernisation or a piece of land never previously used for a business development. When choosing an appropriate piece of land, firms are likely to take into account some combination of the following site factors.

- The cost, relative to other potential sites. A firm must compare purchase prices of alternative sites, consider whether or not renting would be more cost effective and compare the level of business rates in each location.
- Certain businesses may need to locate near to rivers or in coastal areas in order to dispose of waste. Examples might be chemical plants or coal fired power stations.
- The amount of space available for current needs. Some businesses require large areas of land. For example, car manufacturers need sites of several hundred acres.
- Potential for expansion. It is important that firms look into the future when locating premises. When Kellogg's acquired a new cornflake manufacturing plant in Northern Italy, one of the reasons why it favoured Brescia was because of the large amount of adjacent land which they hoped to use in the future for expansion.
- The availability of planning permission. This is particularly important if a firm is going to change the use of some land or premises, or construct new buildings. Local authorities will not always grant planning permission allowing land development, for example in GREEN BELT areas.
- Geological suitability. Some businesses require particular geological features. A nuclear power station must be sited on a geologically stable site.

- Good infrastructure. Facilities such as good road links, appropriate waste disposal facilities and other public utilities are often an important influence.
- Environmental considerations. Today, firms may face pressure from public opinion when locating premises. There can be opposition from pressure groups if they attempt to locate in environmentally sensitive areas.

Some firms in recent years have opted to move their premises out of traditional industrial areas to GREENFIELD sites. These are, literally, rural locations generally found on the outskirts of towns and cities. Here the land tends to be cheaper and more plentiful. However, there may be opposition from environmentalists and greenfield sites can only be developed if there is adequate access. These sites are becoming more popular and are particularly suitable for hi-tech industries. Also, a growing number of wind farms have been located on greenfield sites in recent years. But again there is often strong opposition to the location of such activities on Greenfield sites. For example, in 2008 plans to build one of Europe' largest wind farms, on the Isle of Lewis, were rejected by the Scottish Parliament after they received over 5,000 letters of protest.

The use of BROWNFIELD sites for business location is also increasing. According to the government, a brownfield site is an area of land which was previously used for urban development. Some brownfield sites in the UK have been derelict for many years. One such site is the Greenwich peninsular in London. The site used to house a huge gasworks, but became a rubbish dump and scrapyard for much of South East London. In the late 1990s it was chosen as the location for the Millennium Dome and a number of businesses competed for contracts to build on the land. In recent years property developers have looked to build living accommodation on such sites because the land is often cheap.

Labour

Firms relocating from one part of the country to another will aim to take most of their staff with them. This should cut down on disruption and avoid the need to recruit and train large numbers of new staff. Sometimes, businesses try not to move very far so that staff can travel from their existing homes. For example, the Woolwich Building Society, when relocating from North London, chose Bexley Heath in North Kent – already the home of a large number of its employees.

However, if relocation is a long way from the original position, persuading existing staff to move can be difficult. Selling existing homes, buying new homes, disrupting childrens' education and removal costs can be real obstacles. When choosing a site, firms need to find out whether existing employees can be persuaded to move and whether other sources of labour with the right skills can be recruited locally. Factors that existing staff may feel are important may be the cost of housing, the quality of the local environment, the quality of local schools and perhaps the number of traffic jams in the area.

Labour skills are not evenly distributed throughout the country. If a firm needs a particular type of skilled labour there may be regions which are especially suitable. For example, a firm which is contemplating a new venture in carpet manufacturing might choose Kidderminster as a possible location. Kidderminster is famous for carpet manufacturing and could offer a firm new to the industry a ready supply of appropriately skilled and semi-skilled workers. Other examples of these regional advantages include car workers in the West Midlands, pottery workers in Stoke-on-Trent and steel workers in Sheffield. Where an industry is concentrated in a particular region, advantages, such as expertise in local schools and colleges, research facilities in nearby universities and sympathetic and supportive local government agencies often exist. These are known as external economies of scale.

Government influence

The UK government has influenced the location of business for many decades, probably since the 1920s. There has been a need to revitalise certain areas where key industries have declined. For example, the North East was hit when the shipbuilding industry declined. The North West region suffered when the textile industry collapsed. The main reasons for government intervention in business location are to:

- control development where there is 'business congestion' and adequate employment;
- encourage firms to locate their operations in regions where unemployment is high and business activity is lacking;
- attract foreign businesses to the UK.

The government has attempted to help areas with particular problems in the UK through REGIONAL POLICY. This has involved the use of incentives to attract businesses to regions in need of revitalisation. Incentives have included investment grants, tax breaks, employment subsidies and rent-free factory space.

In the early twenty first century a number of initiatives were used in the UK to encourage businesses to locate in certain areas.

Regional selective assistance This involves discretionary government grants given by the DTI for investment projects that would create or safeguard jobs in ASSISTED AREAS. Assisted areas in the UK are 'locations of considerable development potential. They all have an available workforce, competitive labour costs and high labour flexibility. They share the benefits which Britain as a whole offers the investor in terms of market proximity, good communications, low taxes, the language of business, a deregulated business environment and a government attitude which welcomes investment and enterprise'.

Companies in Scotland accepted £92 million of Regional Selective Assistance (RSA) grant offers in 2006/07, creating or safeguarding more than 9,000 Scottish jobs.

The RSA Annual Summary 2006/07, shows that Scottish firms accounted for 61 per cent (82) of the total number of RSA offers accepted (134). The 134 offers accepted in 2006/07 are related to projects with planned capital expenditure of £416 million. Small and Medium Sized Enterprises (SMEs) accounted for 86 of the RSA offers, accepting total grants of more than £18 million towards investment of £72 million and more than 2,000 associated jobs.

EU structural and cohesion funds The Structural and Cohesion Funds are the European Union's main instruments for supporting social and economic restructuring across the EU. They account for over one third of the European Union budget and are used to tackle regional disparities and support regional development through actions including developing infrastructure and telecommunications, developing human resources and supporting research and development. The European Council of December 2005 agreed a total Structural and Cohesion Funds budget of €308 billion for 2007 to 2013. As a result of the agreement, the UK will continue to receive substantial Structural Funds receipts, amounting to €9.4 billion (2004 prices), for 2007-13. The Structural and Cohesion Funds are divided into three separate funds.

- European Regional Development Fund (ERDF), which provides money for the development of human resources. The money can be used to fund training schemes and is designed to solve labour market problems. For example, a Horizon project in Bristol designed to train childcare workers was funded from this source.
- European Social Fund (ESF), which provides money in the most disadvantaged regions for the development of infrastructure. Examples might be the building of roads and improvements in telecommunications.
- Cohesion Fund which provides funds to strengthen the economic and social cohesion of the EU through the balanced financing of projects, technically and financially independent project stages and groups of projects forming a coherent whole, in the fields of the environment and trans-European transport infrastructure networks .

Regional development agencies Regional Development Agencies (RDAs) are government-funded bodies which promote economic development in the regions. In 2007/08 they had a total budget of £2.297 billion. Under the Regional Development Agencies Act 1998, each Agency has five statutory purposes:

- To further economic development and regeneration
- To promote business efficiency, investment and competitiveness.
- To promote employment.
- To enhance development and application of skill relevant to employment.
- To contribute to sustainable development.

The RDAs' agenda includes regeneration, taking forward regional competitiveness, taking the lead on inward investment and, working with regional partners, ensuring the development of a skills action plan to ensure that skills training matches the needs of the labour market.

Question 3.

The East Durham Enterprise Zone is located in the heart of the thriving North East of England. It is home to some of the region's major industrial estates. Parts of East Durham, around the Peterlee and Seaham areas, have been designated an enterprise zone. Companies locating in this area can benefit from the following.

- Freedom from business rates for 10 years.
- 100 per cent tax allowances on the costs of industrial and commercial buildings.
- A streamlined planning process.
- Possible rent free periods from developers.
- Regional Selective Assistance for most manufacturing and some service type businesses. Applicants must be expanding their business, creating jobs and spending over £0.5 million on equipment, plant and machinery and associated building costs. Typically grants are negotiated at around 15 per cent of eligible expenditure.
- SME Enterprise Grants for SMEs involved in similar activities to those described above. Projects of under £0.5 million can be granted aid to a maximum of 15 per cent of eligible expenditure where job creation exists.
- A Property Development Grant for manufacturing businesses and those providing a service to business on at least a regional scale, which are building new premises. Grants are given towards the cost of various areas of site preparation in the form of £10 per square metre of floorspace constructed to a maximum grant value of £25,000.

One example of a business located in the East Durham Enterprise Zone is Prima Windows. It moved into a 15,000 sq. ft. factory in Seaham Grange in 2002. A total investment of £0.75 million has bought the business a new factory, offices and state of the art CNC machinery for its UPVC profile manufacturing business. The company will increase staff from 25 to 40 and double sales within two years. Director Paul Hewitt said Seaham Grange is a quality estate and the enterprise zone benefits made this a massive investment for the company.

Source: adapted from the East Durham Enterprise Zone website.

(a) Using examples from this case, explain what is meant by an enterprise zone.

(b) Explain three possible reasons why Prima Windows located in Seaham Grange.

Learning and skills council (LSC) This organisation aims to make England better skilled and more competitive. Its single goal is to improve the skills of England's young people and adults to ensure the nation has a workforce of world-class standard.

The LSC is a non-departmental public body which began work in 2001, taking over the roles of the former Further Education Funding Council and Training and Enterprise Councils.

It is responsible for planning and funding high quality

education and training for everyone in England other than those in universities. It has a national office in Coventry and nine regional offices overseeing the work of local partnership teams throughout the county. The annual budget for 2006/07 is £10.4 billion.

The LSC's major tasks are to:

- raise participation and achievement by young people;
- increase adult demand for learning;
- raise skills levels for national competitiveness;
- improve the quality of education and training delivery;
- equalise opportunities through better access to learning;
- improve the effectiveness and efficiency of the sector.

By 2010, the LSC hopes that young people and adults in England will have knowledge and skills matching the best in the world and will be part of a truly competitive workforce.

European Investment Bank (EIB) The EIB grants loans to SMEs anywhere in the UK for investment projects in most industrial sectors. Loans are available from a range of financial institutions. The EIB also provides large loans for capital investment projects in industry or infrastructure. Examples of sectors eligible for EIB loans include advanced technology, environmental protection, transport, telecommunications and energy.

Public sector operations Government might be able to locate offices in areas facing difficulties in order to directly influence employment and spending. Employment might be encouraged from within the local area. For example, the introduction of Welsh, Scottish and London regional assemblies might create jobs in these areas. If regions voted for local assemblies in areas such as the North West, this would also tend to create jobs in regions.

In 2003 the UK government put forward a new approach to regional policy. It aimed to improve gross value added per head of the population in regions. This is a measure of the productivity of workers in the areas. It is not just about the poorest areas, but about improving productivity in all areas.

Industrial inertia

When businesses in the same industry locate in an area with similar businesses this is referred to as INDUSTRIAL INERTIA. Even when the original advantages cease to exist, new firms might still be attracted to the area. An example might be the textile industry in the North West. The original attractions such as coal and water which influenced business to locate in the region have ceased to be important. Newer power sources have been developed and the natural humidity of the area can be recreated by using technology. In addition, natural fibres have been replaced by synthetic materials. However, businesses continue to locate in the area for other reasons, including the availability of skilled workers, support services aimed at the textile industry and perhaps its reputation. Similar reasons might account for the ceramics and pottery industries still existing in the area around Stoke.

Industrial inertia does have some disadvantages. When a region relies heavily on one industry it will suffer if that industry declines. For example, in the 1990s many UK coal mines were closed down in areas where the local pit was the main employer.

Qualitative factors

Qualitative factors are factors which cannot be measured using numbers. There is a variety of qualitative factors which a business might take into consideration when deciding where to set up.

Laws and regulations Any location decision will have legal and regulatory aspects. In many cases, laws and regulations will determine what type of business can occupy what type of premises in what areas. Getting planning permission will be necessary if a business is building new premises. Also, when setting up a new business it may be prudent to get professional advice when in doubt about laws relating to location.

Social, environmental and ethical considerations Many new businesses take social, environmental and ethical considerations into account. For example, a business setting up a market garden to produce organic food may need a plot of land that has been free from pesticides and fertilizers for a period of time. A business setting up a new manufacturing venture may decide to locate a factory in an area where there is high unemployment. It could be argued that the new, younger generation of entrepreneurs, is more likely to take social, environmental and ethical considerations into account because they are more aware of such issues.

Quality of life Evidence suggests that the interests of those making a location decision are very important. Many new businesses, for example, tend to be located where their owner managers live. Small to medium sized businesses, when considering relocating, will typically relocate within a few miles of the present location. Owner managers don't want to move house or locality even if cheaper premises could be found just 50 miles away. The quality of people's living environments is considered to be very important.

Quality of the workforce The quality of the local workforce is important. A business is unlikely to locate to a place where it is unable to recruit the right quality of local labour. In the UK, London and the South East continue to attract new companies because, despite relatively high wages, there is a large pool of highly educated workers from which to draw.

The importance of location

When setting up a business the importance of location is likely to vary. For some businesses location is not a crucial issue. Businesses that are run from home, web-based businesses and businesses that supply national markets, for example, are footloose. This means that they can locate anywhere. They are not tied by any particular location factor.

However, in other cases, finding the right location is vital. A business that needs large areas of land, such as a new golf course, may have to choose a site where land is cheap. A new guest house hoping to attract visitors to an historic city would clearly benefit from a central location in the city. Businesses that export goods would prefer to be located near to ports. A new fast food outlet hoping to attract shoppers and workers would benefit from a prominent position on the high street. These examples show that the importance of location, and the relative importance of different location factors, all depend on the type of business that is being set up.

KNOWLEDGE

1. Under what circumstances will transport costs be particularly influential in business location?
2. State three types of business that will benefit from locating close to the market.
3. For what type of business activity is land an important factor in influencing location?
4. Give three problems that a business might have in transferring its existing labour force to a new location.
5. How might the geographical distribution of labour affect location?
6. What is an enterprise zone?

KEYTERMS

Assisted areas – areas that are designated as having problems by the UK or EU and are eligible for support in a variety of forms.

Brownfield sites – areas of land which were once used for urban development.

Enterprise zones – small inner city areas designated by the government which qualify for financial assistance.

Footloose businesses – businesses that are not tied to a particular location.

Green belt – areas designated by government, usually in agricultural areas, where the development of business is prohibited.

Greenfield sites – areas of land, usually on the outskirts of towns and cities, where businesses develop for the first time.

Industrial inertia – the tendency for firms in the same industry to locate in the same region even when the original locational advantages have disappeared.

Regional policy – measures used by central and local government to attract businesses to 'depressed' areas.

Site factors - factors affecting the choice of a plot or premises rather than an area.

Case Study: Locating a campsite

Gordon Powell left his job at the age of 55 but was not ready for retirement. He wanted to run a business. Gordon enjoyed camping, particularly in the Scottish Highlands and Islands. He planned to move from his home in Doncaster and set up a camp site on the Isle of Skye. Gordon spent eight months planning his business venture. One important issue was the location of the site. He spent four weeks in Skye searching for 'the perfect location'. He thought location would be important because people are more likely to return to the site if the location is attractive. He wanted a site with scenic views close to the sea or a loch. At the end of his four week search Gordon had identified two suitable locations.

- Dunvegan. The pretty village of Dunvegan lies on the east side of the head of Loch Dunvegan, which bites deeply into the Isle of Skye from the north west. It is the largest village on Skye that doesn't stand on the island's east coast. On the village main street is the Giant Angus MacAskill Museum, dedicated to the tallest Scotsman that ever lived. There is also a castle, coral beaches nearby and the views from the village are dominated by the loch and Healabhal Mhòr, a table mountain. The site found by Gordon is about one acre in size, enough for 25 tents and 15 caravans. It also has a derelict farm building which would be suitable for conversion into a toilet block and wash room. However, it would need to be connected to a water supply and the mains electricity.
- Portree. Gordon's second site is three miles from Portree, the largest town on the island. Portree has a harbour, fringed by cliffs, with a pier. Attractions in the town include the Aros Centre and the An Tuireann Arts Centre, both of which celebrate the island's Gaelic heritage. The site is on a cliff top with views across the sea to the island of Raasay. There is a derelict croft which has a water supply and could be converted into a toilet block and washroom. There would also be enough room for a small café. The site is over an acre and could accommodate 34 tents and 20 caravans. However, one problem with this site is the prevalence of the Highland Midge, a biting insect. Midges are particularly bad on Skye and on this side of the island.

Some cost information relating to the proposed locations for the camp site is shown in Table 1.

Map of Skye identifying the two locations

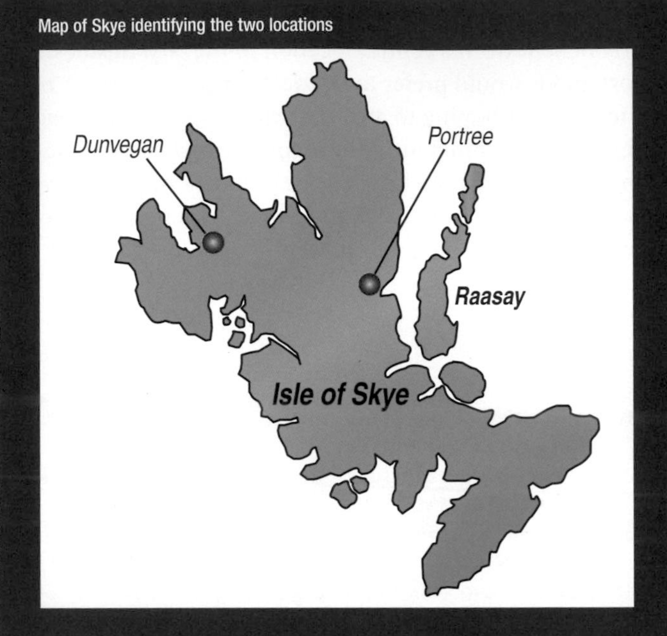

(a) Explain why location is likely to be an important issue for the business in this case. (4 marks)

(b) Do you think Gordon will need to obtain planning permission at all? Explain your answer. (4 marks)

(c) Describe three search costs that Gordon may have incurred when choosing a suitable location for his camp site. (6 marks)

(d) Using this case as an example, explain the difference between 'one-off' fixed costs and 'ongoing' fixed costs, in relation to location. (10 marks)

(e) After a discussion with his accountant, Gordon decided to set up his camp site at Portree. Evaluate whether Gordon should have chosen the Dunvegan site instead. (16 marks)

Table 1: Cost information for the proposed camp site locations

	Dunvegan	Portree
Rent per month	£1,000	£1,200
Toilet block conversion costs	£13,000	£8,000
Other 'one-off' location costs	£2,500	£1,000
Business rates pa*	£2,000	£2,200

* Estimated

94 Location strategies

The effects of expansion on location

If a business is successful the owners will probably want to expand operations. There are motives for growth, such as dominating the market, economies of scale and greater financial security. One of the issues that businesses need to address when growing is location. Most fast growing businesses are likely to outgrow their premises. This means they have to either expand at their current location or relocate to premises which can accommodate a larger scale of operations. Some businesses will have the scope to stay where they are and add to capacity. For example:

- a restaurant may be able to use an upstairs floor to double the number of covers;
- a shop may be able to acquire the premises next door and double capacity. Indeed, there are examples where a shop has acquired many of its neighbours over a period of time;
- a factory may be able to build an extension or occupy adjacent units;
- an office might increase capacity by occupying more floors in an office block.

However, there is likely to come a time for many expanding businesses where relocation is the only option. This might be because there is limited space in the current location, the current premises are unsuitable or expansion requires multiple locations such as a retail chain would. When this happens a business has to make another location decision.

Methods of making location decisions

The decision about where to relocate a business, or a new part of the business, will depend on the costs and benefits of particular sites. Businesses are likely to look at a number of sites, compare the costs and benefits and then make a decision. A decision might be made using a quantitative approach. For example, a business might use investment appraisal techniques when deciding where to locate. However, qualitative factors must not be overlooked.

Quantitative methods

Table 1 shows two possible sites for a business which is considering relocating its premises. It gives the initial cost of the move and then the cost savings to be made in each year compared with the existing site. Three investment appraisal methods can be used to show which, if any, site should be chosen. It is assumed that at the end of five years, the business will be relocating again. So no cost savings will be taken into account after the end of five years.

Payback method With the payback method, the business calculates how long it will take to recoup the initial investment. In location A, the initial cost is £12 million and with annual savings (the equivalent of increased cash flows) of £3 million, the investment will be recouped in 4 years. With location B, the initial cost is higher at £15 million, but the cost savings are £5 million per year. The result is that the investment will be recouped in 3 years. So on the payback method, location B is the preferred location.

Average rate of return (ARR) With the average annual rate of return method, the net return is divided by the initial investment and expressed as a percentage. With location A, there will be a total cost saving (i.e. increased cash flow) over 5 years of £15 million. With an initial cost of £12 million, this gives a return of £3 million (£15 million - £12 million). So the ARR is [(£3 million ÷ £15 million) ÷ 5 years] x 100 per cent, which is 4 per cent. With location B, the cost saving is £25 million over five years with an initial cost of £15 million. So the ARR is [(£10 million ÷ £25 million) ÷ 5 years] x 100 per cent, which is 8 per cent. On the average rate of return method, location B is also the preferred location.

Discounted cash flow With discounted cash flow, the value of future cash flows must be discounted back to the present. The important point about discounted cash flow is that, just as money invested today will grow in value because of compound interest, so the reverse is true: the value of cash available in the future is worth less today. In Table 2, the cost savings (or net cash flows) have been discounted back assuming a discount rate of 15 per cent. The net present value of the cost savings falls the further into the future it occurs. When it is totalled up, the net present value of the cost savings at location A don't cover the initial investment needed. So moving to location A is unprofitable at this rate of discount. On the other hand, moving to location B shows a positive net cash flow. The cost savings outweigh the initial cost of the investment by £1.9 million. So this would suggest that the company should move to location B.

Table 1: Initial costs and cost savings of two new locations

		£ million
	Location A	Location B
Initial cost	12	15
Annual cost savings/increased cash flow		
Year 1	3	5
Year 2	3	5
Year 3	3	5
Year 4	3	5
Year 5	3	5

Table 2: Initial cost and cost savings of two new locations discounted at 15 per cent

	Location A £ millions	Location B £ millions	Discount table 15%	Location A £ millions	£ million Location B £ millions
Initial cost	12	15	1.00	12.0	15.0
Annual cost savings/ increased cash flow					
Year 1	3	5	0.87	2.6	4.4
Year 2	3	5	0.76	2.3	3.8
Year 3	3	5	0.66	2.0	3.3
Year 4	3	5	0.57	1.7	2.9
Year 5	3	5	0.50	1.5	2.5
Total cost savings	15	25		10.1	16.9
Net cash flow	3	10		-1.9	1.9

Whatever the rate of discount used, location B would always be preferred over location A. However, if the rate of discount were much higher than 15 per cent, the discounted cash flow technique would suggest that even location B would give overall negative cash flows and therefore moving would not be profitable.

Qualitative factors

Qualitative factors are factors which cannot be measured using numbers. Qualitative factors are important when making location decisions partly because quantitative methods, such as investment appraisal techniques, cannot capture all the information needed to make a location decision. Qualitative factors are also important because quantitative methods can never give an accurate answer since they are based on assumptions about the future. Forecast revenues one, three or ten years from now, for example, are unlikely to match the actual revenues achieved. The further away in time the forecast, the less likely it is to be accurate. This doesn't mean to say that quantitative techniques are not important. But they must be placed alongside qualitative factors in decision making and their limitations recognised.

There is a variety of qualitative factors which a business might take into consideration when making a location decision.

Laws and regulations Any location decision will have legal and regulatory aspects. In many cases, laws and regulations will determine what type of business can occupy what type of premises in what areas. Getting planning permission will be necessary if a business is building new premises. If two sites are being compared in different countries, the legal frameworks may be very different. For example, one country may have much looser regulation of pollution than another country. Health and safety regulations may differ too.

Social, environmental and ethical considerations Many businesses, particularly larger ones, may take social, environmental and ethical considerations into account. For example, a manufacturer may be reluctant to move away from a local area because it has a long history of involvement with the area, is a major employer and moving away would severely damage the local community. Another business may decide against a particular location because the environmental impact of moving to that location would be too negative. A third business may deliberately choose a location in a high unemployment area as a positive ethical choice to create jobs. Businesses tend to make these choices for two reasons. Some businesses are set up with social, environmental and ethical goals which override the profit motive. Other businesses exploit their social, environmental and ethical decisions to promote themselves to their customers. Equally, businesses may want to avoid negative public relations (PR) which arise when they are accused of acting in an anti-social or unethical way.

Quality of life Evidence suggests that the interests of those making a location decision are very important. Small businesses, for example, tend to be located where their owner managers live. Small to medium sized businesses, when considering relocating, will typically relocate within a few miles of the present location. Owner managers don't want to move house or locality even if cheaper premises could be found just 50 miles away. Large companies will consider whether the managers who have to be sent to a location to run a plant or factory will enjoy the posting. Quality of housing, local schools and the environment are important considerations. So too are factors such as risk to employees. A multinational may choose to locate in China rather than, say, parts of South America or Africa for these reasons.

Political stability In the UK, political stability is taken for granted in most areas. But when large companies make decisions about where to locate around the world, political stability is a key factor. Foreign investment in certain countries may be lower than it would be if there were more political stability in these countries. At worst, political instability can lead to new governments which seize foreign owned assets or suddenly impose high taxes.

Quality of the workforce The quality of the local workforce is important. A business is unlikely to locate to a place where it is unable to recruit the right quality of local labour. China, for example, has attracted a considerable amount of inward investment because it has a relatively well educated labour forceprepared to work for low wages. In the UK, London and the South East continue to attract new companies because, despite relatively high wages, there is a large pool of highly educated workers from which to draw.

Infrastructure Infrastructure, such as roads, railways, airports, hospitals and schools, can play an important part in location decisions. The quality of the infrastructure in a particular location will have an impact on costs and will therefore be part of any quantitative calculation. However, for a multinational company, having a local airport which takes international flights might be an important consideration. For a national company, being near the motorway network might influence a location decision. For a company located in London, which has many workers commuting in every day, nearness to a railway station or a tube station might influence a location decision.

The benefits of optimal location

If businesses make good decisions about location they may find that they have found the **optimal location**. The optimal location is the best possible site for the business. It is the site where costs are minimised and benefits maximised. An optimal location will generate a number of benefits for a business. Some examples are outlined briefly below.

- The best access to markets. Customers will find the location convenient. Consequently businesses will find it easier to attract customers.
- Lowest site costs such as rent, business rates, maintenance and servicing costs.
- Easy access for staff. This is important because travelling to work is becoming increasingly difficult and stressful.
- Good working environment. This will help to improve the quality of life and improve the morale of all those who work there.
- Competitive advantage. If a business occupies the best possible site, it may be at the expense of a competitor. Consequently it will have the advantage over that competitor. Recently, supermarkets have bought up certain plots of land so that rivals cannot use the land to develop a store and compete against them.

Multi-site locations

Some large businesses operate from more than one site. This is quite normal and usually arises for a number of reasons.

- In retailing it is not practical to serve a national market from one giant store. For example, Next, the fashion clothes retailer, could not expect people to travel from all over the country to a centrally located store in, say, Birmingham. The alternative is to operate a chain of stores, each of which serves a local market such as a town or part of a city. This is very common in retailing and there are numerous examples of chain stores – River Island, M&S, Sainsbury, Asda, W H Smiths, Boots, to name but a few. Other types of businesses and franchises such as pub chains, car hire companies, hotel chains, restaurant chains and banks also have multiple outlets for the same reason.
- Large multi-national businesses have operations all over the world. This allows them to serve international markets and exploit local business conditions. For example, Kellogg's operates about 20 factories in countries such as the US (Battle Creek), England, Malaysia, Italy, Germany, Thailand and Australia for this reason.
- Some businesses have different types of operations in a number of different locations. For example, a large manufacturing company might have an assembly plant in one location, components manufacturers in a number of other locations, a head office in London and several warehouses around the country.
- Diversified businesses may have operations all over the place. Companies that grow through acquisition inevitably end up with businesses in multiple locations. For example, Ultra Electronics, a defence and aerospace company, has a large number of businesses operating in three main divisions. The company produces a wide range of

Question 1.

Edney's is a manufacturer of frozen food products. It needs to move because it has outgrown its current premises. It is considering two sites, A and B. Site A has the lowest initial cost at £4.5 million but the move will cause more disruption to production initially than at Site B. In the longer term, however, the financial benefits of Site A are greater than at Site B.

The managing director has asked you to do some calculations on the two sites and make a recommendation about which site should be chosen. He has asked you to consider only any costs and cash flows over a seven year period.

Table 3: Initial costs and net cash flow of two sites, A and B

	Location A £millions	Location B £millions	Discount table Rate of discount at 20%
Initial cost	4.5	6.0	1.00
Net cash flow			
Year 1	1.0	2.0	0.83
Year 2	1.5	2.5	0.69
Year 3	2.0	2.5	0.58
Year 4	2.5	2.5	0.48
Year 5	3.0	2.0	0.40
Year 6	3.0	2.0	0.33
Year 7	3.0	2.0	0.28

(a) **For both sites, calculate (a) the payback time; (b) the average rate of return (ARR); (c) the net present value assuming a rate of discount of 20 per cent.**

(b) **Explain which site you would recommend the company should choose.**

Table 4: Advantages and disadvantages of multi-site locations

Advantages	Disadvantages
• The main advantage of operating with multiple sites is that a business can cover a wider market. Each site can serve a local market and together multiple sites can serve a national market. Retailers and other chains will enjoy high levels of recognition if they can operate outlets all over the country.	• One of the main disadvantages of multi-site operations is that it may be more difficult to exploit economies of scale. For example, it may be difficult to exploit managerial economies because each site will require its own managers. Also, there may be some duplication of resources. For example, every restaurant in a chain will need an electronic cash register. It is unlikely that such a resource will be fully utilised and therefore money is wasted.
• Operating chains allow each outlet to cater for the needs of a local market. It is possible that the needs of a local market in Penrith are slightly different to the needs of a local market in Brighton. Each local outlet can adapt and meet local needs.	• It may become difficult for senior managers to keep a tight control on every single site. This might result in some sites underperforming because there is an inadequate level of control, supervision and accountability. This could lead to diseconomies of scale if a business has too many different sites.
• Manufacturers and other businesses can exploit the advantages that local towns and regions have to offer. For example, a large automotive company may have an assembly plant in the West Midlands where there is a ready supply of trained and experienced labour (the West Midlands has a history of car manufacturing). On the other hand its head office may be in London where it can entertain important visitors, such as customers and potential investors, in one of the most exciting cities in the world.	• Communication is likely to be more difficult. For example, because of geographical distances, senior managers are less able to have face-to-face meetings with workers much lower down the hierarchical structure. There may also be language barriers if sites are spread across the globe.
• Having different sites can allow specialisation to flourish. A company like Ultra Electronics, described above, operates a large number of factories and other business activities across multiple sites. Each site is likely to specialise in a particular product. For example, one of its businesses, Pneumatic Systems, provides leading edge technology in the design development and manufacture of high pressure pneumatic components for the control of gases for critical applications in the aerospace and defence industries. Working as a single specialised operation, Pneumatic Systems will be able to focus more easily and not be distracted by other activities.	• It may be difficult to foster a positive and successful organisational culture when a business operates from multiple sites. What could happen is that each site develops its own unique culture. This might be a problem when bringing together people from different sites for meetings and cross-site ventures, for example.
	• It may be more difficult to standardise systems, procedures and other activities if there are lots of different sites. This could be confusing for customers and also for employees if they have to move around different sites.

electronic, electro-mechanical systems and sub-systems, products and services. It provides these for aircraft, ships, submarines, armoured vehicles, surveillance and communication systems, airports and transport systems. Most of its operations are based in the UK and the US. During 2006 Ultra bought Polyflex Aerospace based in Cheltenham and Winfrith Safety Systems based in Dorset. As Ultra increases the number of its acquisitions, it will have a growing number of sites around the world. The advantages and disadvantages of multi-site location are shown in Table 4.

International location

Multinational companies operate in a number of different locations across the world. International location decisions can be more complex than those made within a country. There is a number of reasons why businesses choose to locate overseas.

Avoiding trade barriers Countries put up trade barriers, such as tariffs (taxes on imports) and quotas (physical limits on the quantity of a product that can be imported). They do this to protect their own national businesses from foreign competition. One way a multinational business can get round such trade barriers is to locate within the country. For example, Japanese car producers set up car plants in both Europe and the USA in the 1980s and 1990s, partly to get around trade barriers put up by EU countries and the US to keep Japanese producers of cars out of their markets.

Financial incentives Businesses may be attracted to a particular country or area if cash or other financial incentives are offered for locating there. Some of the regional aid available in parts of Europe may have influenced the location of Asian multinationals in the 1990s. In some cases governments offer cash, sometimes called 'sweeteners', to businesses if they locate in their country.

Cost of labour Many manufacturing multinational companies have located plants in cheap labour countries such as India or China. Cheap labour then gives them a competitive advantage. However, jobs may be retained in high labour cost countries where high quality labour is needed. Education, training and the skills of the workforce in countries like the UK are vitally important for keeping facilities such as headquarters or research departments in high labour cost countries.

Proximity to markets or suppliers Transport costs can be much greater over larger distances. So multinational companies may have to locate near their markets or their suppliers to remain competitive. A car component manufacturer, for example, may have to set up a factory in the Far East to be near a customer, a car manufacturer. It is not always true, though, that transport costs are significant in international location decisions. If a product is high value, transport costs may be only a small fraction of the final price charged. Equally, transport costs vary according to modes of transport. Sometimes, it can cost less to send an item thousands of miles across the globe by ship than it does to take it from the ship and transport it by lorry for the final 50 miles.

Exchange rate fluctuations Exchange rate fluctuations can be important determinants of location decisions. Businesses trading internationally can experience sudden large movements in exchange rates. Sometimes these movements are beneficial to a business but sometimes they have a negative impact. For example, a UK business may import components from Germany. If the exchange rate of the pound falls sharply against the euro, then the UK business is likely to face a larger bill for imports. One way of getting around this risk is for a company to balance its costs and revenues in a single currency through location decisions. For example, a UK company may export $20 million of goods from UK factories to customers in the USA and import €15 million of goods from a factory it owns in France to the UK. This exposes it to risks of changes in the value of the pound against both the euro and the US dollar. One way around this problem would be to close the factory in France and relocate it to the USA. Then there would be roughly equal and opposite transactions in US dollars, which would considerably reduce the company's exchange rate risks.

Political stability As already mentioned above, political stability is an important qualitative factor in determining decision making. Some countries have very little inward investment by foreign companies because of chronic political instability. Equally, some countries are currently boycotted by western companies because of the nature of their political regimes. To locate in these countries, which may have a poor record on human rights, could attract consumer boycotts or shareholder disapproval.

Language barriers Language can be an important factor in location decisions. One reason why the UK is favoured as a location by US companies is because the UK and the US share a common language. Much of the foreign investment over the past ten years in China has been by companies owned by Chinese people living outside of China. Locating new facilities in China allows them the advantage of low cost labour and they share a common language.

Question 2.

In early 2007, Burberry, the prestigious clothing and accessories company, closed one of its factories in Treorchy, South Wales. It moved production to China, where costs are significantly lower as a result of workers being paid extremely low wages. Profits for the company are likely to soar as the cost of producing one of the famous polo shirts will fall from £11 to about £4.

The closure attracted a huge amount of negative publicity. One of the reasons was the size of the original redundancy offer made to the 300 workers in South Wales. It was a meagre £1000 each; not even enough to buy this year's hottest Burberry accessory the Beaton handbag, priced at a lucrative £1095! It was also reported that the company could lose its royal warrants as the row intensified over the closure. Chris Bryant, Labour MP for Rhondda, allegedly wrote to the Lord Chancellor to demand that MPs have a say in which firms get the warrant. This is currently determined by the Queen and the Prince of Wales. Bryant also called for a Constitutional Affairs Select Committee investigation into the same issue.

Source: adapted from www.burberry.com.

(a) Explain the main reason why Burberry is shifting some production from South Wales to China.

(b) What are the drawbacks of moving production to China?

(c) Burberry operates from multiple sites. Explain one advantage of this.

Inward investment

INWARD INVESTMENT is the flow of foreign funds into a country for the purposes of setting up business operations. In the 1990s the UK attracted billions of pounds of inward investment from foreign companies setting up production plants in the country. The success of the UK in attracting this investment was largely the work of national, regional and local agencies. Examples included English Partnerships, the Commission for the New Towns, the Mersey Partnership and the West Midlands Development Agency. These played vital roles in attracting overseas investment in new factories and decisions by foreign firms to invest in existing operations.

The Thames Valley attracts a high level of inward investment in the UK. For example, in 2006-07, the area received 59 per cent of the total inward investment into the South East of England. Over 50 foreign-owned businesses established a presence in the Thames Valley for the first time. New investment also came from a greater diversity of countries than in previous years, with Australia, Canada, Japan and China making notably more investments. The Thames Valley continues to be attractive to the software industry, with 67 per cent of new investors offering software related products and services. Companies that come to the Thames Valley from overseas have a high success rate. Two examples are ZyXEL Communications, based in Taiwan, and

KEYTERMS

Inward investment – the setting up of businesses or investment in businesses by a company from another country.

Fulcrum Logic, based in New Jersey. Both companies have seen exponential growth since locating in the area.

Inward investment can have a number of benefits to UK industry.

- Foreign businesses which locate in the UK will need supplies, perhaps from UK suppliers of components and specialist commercial services.
- Businesses will recruit workers. Retailers, cinemas, restaurants and other local businesses will gain from the extra spending.
- Some UK businesses may already supply the overseas business. If production is switched to the UK then transport costs may fall and profits rise.
- UK businesses may learn about new production methods and working practices.
- If UK businesses make a good impression with overseas investors, this might generate publicity, which could lead to further investment in the UK.

KNOWLEDGE

1. Why do expanding firms have to consider relocation?
2. Why might quantitative methods help a business to make a more informed decision when choosing a site for location?
3. How can the ARR be used to make a location decision?
4. State four qualitative factors that might affect the location decision.
5. What is meant by the optimal location?
6. State two reasons why a business might operate from multiple sites.
7. State two advantages of operating from multiple sites.
8. State two disadvantages of operating from multiple sites.
9. Explain why governments might offer 'sweeteners' to businesses to locate in their country.
10. Explain why a bank might set up a call centre in India.

Case Study: Debenhams

Debenhams is a leading multi-category retailer in UK, with a unique mix of own brands, international brands and concessions. Its main product categories are women's, men's and children's clothing and accessories, products for the home, health and beauty, lingerie and food services. The original 'Debenham & Freebody' store was based at Number 33 Wigmore Street, London. This site is still used by the company and houses its communications departments, including their Press Office.

The modern Debenhams group grew from the acquisition of department stores in towns and cities throughout the UK. The first of such purchases, Marshall & Snelgrove in Oxford Street, London was acquired in 1919. Later purchases included stores such as Harvey Nichols in London's Knightsbridge and Browns of Chester. Most stores retained their former identities until a unified corporate image was rolled out across the stores.

Debenhams was listed on the London Stock Exchange in 1928 and continued to expand. In 1985 the company was acquired by the Burton group. At this point the company owned 65 stores. Debenhams demerged in 1998 and was once again listed as a separate company.

In 1997, Belinda Earl, who had previously worked for the company, returned to become its Chief Executive. She and Spencer Hawken introduced 'Designers at Debenhams' which brought a variety of well known fashion talents to the stores at affordable prices, shaking off the dated perception of the company. The company expanded rapidly throughout the 1990s and now has a total of 140 stores in the UK and Ireland, with new stores recently opened at the MetroCentre in Gateshead and Hemel Hempstead, Hertfordshire.

The store has been trialling a compact version called 'Desire by Debenhams' which is mainly aimed at the female market with clothing ranges by 'Designers at Debenhams' and cosmetics. Aside from department stores, Debenhams operates a number of other divisions, including 'Debenhams Finance' (offering home, car and travel insurance and bureau de change services) and 'Debenhams Mobile' (offering mobile phones). In 2006 Debenhams bought 9 of the 11 Roches Stores department stores in Ireland and operate them as Debenhams.

Finally, Debenhams also has an international operation. It has 36 international franchises in 16 different countries. For example, it has stores in Dubai, Turkey, Bahrain, Qatar, Sharjah, Indonesia and Kuwait.

Source: adapted from Wikipedia and www.debenhams.com.

(a) How has expansion affected the location of Debenhams? (6 marks)

(b) (i) What might be the optimal location for a Debenhams store? (6 marks)

(ii) What might be the benefits of an optimal location for Debenhams? (10 marks)

(c) Analyse the difficulties Debenhams may encounter in operating multiple sites. (12 marks)

(d) Evaluate the advantages and disadvantages to Debenhams of having international locations. (16 marks)

95 Lean production

What is lean production?

LEAN PRODUCTION is an approach to production developed in Japan. Toyota, the Japanese car manufacturer, was the first company to adopt this approach. Its aim is to reduce the quantity of resources used up in production. Lean producers use less of everything, including factory space, materials, stocks, suppliers, labour, capital and time. As a result, lean production raises productivity and reduces costs. The number of defective products is reduced, lead times are cut and reliability improves. Lean producers are also able to design new products more quickly and can offer customers a wider range of products to choose from. Lean production involves using a range of practices designed to reduce waste and to improve productivity and quality.

Kaizen (continuous improvement)

KAIZEN is perhaps the most important concept in Japanese management. It means continuous improvement. Every aspect of life, including social life, working life and home life, is constantly improved. Everyone in the business is involved. Kaizen is said to be an 'umbrella concept'. A wide range of different production techniques and working practices must be carried out for it to be effective. Figure 1 shows examples of the techniques, principles and practices. They should result in ongoing improvements. This approach argues that a day should not pass without some kind of improvement being made somewhere in the business.

Figure 1: The kaizen umbrella

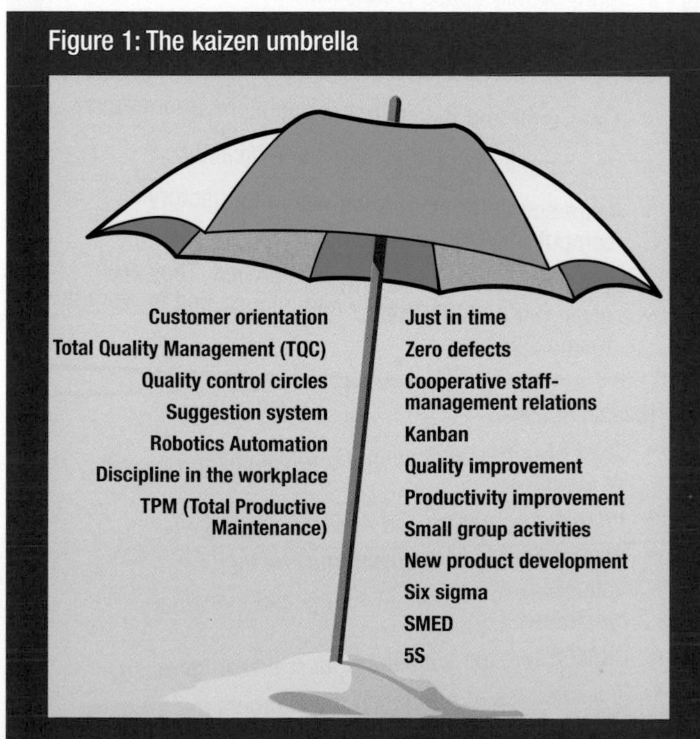

There is a number of features of Kaizen which affect a business.

Continuous improvement Kaizen has been the main difference between the Japanese and the Western approaches to management in the past. The attempts of Western businesses to improve efficiency and quality have tended to be 'one-offs'. In Figure 2 the solid line illustrates the Western approach. Productivity remains the same for long periods of time, then suddenly rises. The increase is followed by another period of stability, before another rise. Increases in productivity may result from new working practices or new technology. The dotted line shows the Japanese approach. Improvements are continuous. They result from changes in production techniques which are introduced gradually.

Eliminating waste The elimination of waste (called muda in Japan) in business practices is an important part of Kaizen. Waste is any activity which raises costs without adding value to a product. Examples may be:

- time wasted while staff wait around before starting tasks, such as waiting for materials to arrive;
- time wasted when workers move unnecessarily in the workplace, such as walking to a central point in the factory to get tools;
- the irregular use of a machine, such as a machine which is only used once a month for a special order;
- excessive demands upon machines or workers, such as staff working overtime seven days a week which causes them to be tired and work poorly.

Firms that adopt the Kaizen approach train and reward

Figure 2: The Western and Japanese approaches to improvement

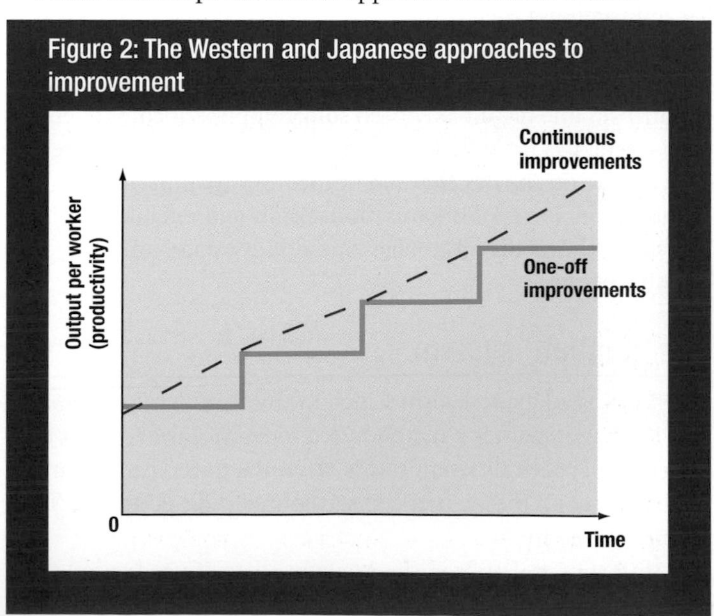

workers to continually search for waste and to suggest how it might be eliminated.

Implementing continuous improvement It is often difficult for workers in a business to look for continuous improvement all the time. Japanese businesses tried to solve this problem by introducing the PDCA (Plan, Do, Check, Action) cycle. It is a series of activities that lead to improvement.

- Plan. Businesses must identify where improvement is needed. Data must be gathered and used to develop a plan which will result in improvement.
- Do. Once the plan has been finalised it must be carried out. The plan is likely to be implemented by workers, on the production line perhaps.
- Check. The next stage in the cycle is to check whether or not there has been an improvement. This task may be carried out by inspectors.
- Action. If the plan has been successful, it must be introduced in all parts of the business.

Just-in-time manufacturing

JUST-IN-TIME (JIT) MANUFACTURING is an important part of lean production and the kaizen approach. It was developed in the Japanese shipbuilding industry in the 1950s and 1960s. The industry recognised that a great deal of money was tied up in stocks. Traditionally, one month's supply of steel was held by a shipyard. However, as the industry became more competitive, shipbuilders insisted that steel suppliers deliver orders 'just-in-time', i.e. a few hours or less before the steel was needed. This reduced the need for high levels of working capital and improved the financial performance of the business. JIT was extended to every stage of production. For example, raw materials were delivered JIT to be made into parts, parts were delivered JIT to be made into goods and goods were produced and delivered JIT to be sold.

JIT was introduced in other Japanese industries, such as the car industry, and then spread to other parts of the world, such as the USA and Europe. JCB has used JIT in its Rochester plant. When JCB excavators are manufactured, every machine on the production line has already been sold. Supplies of components, such as engines from Perkins, and raw materials, such as steel plate, arrive on the day they are needed. JIT manufacturing requires high levels of organisational skills and reliable suppliers.

Table 1 shows the advantages and disadvantages of JIT manufacturing.

The 'Kanban' system

KANBAN is a Japanese term which means signboards or cards. The Kanban system is a method used to control the transfer of materials between different stages of production. The kanban might be a solid plastic marker or coloured ping-pong ball. They might be used to:

- inform employees in the previous stage of production that a particular part must be taken from stocks and sent to a specific destination (conveyance kanbans);
- tell employees involved in a particular operation that they can begin production and add their output to stock (production kanbans);
- instruct external suppliers to send parts to a destination (vendor kanbans).

Kanbans are used to trigger the movement or production of resources. Used properly, they will be the only means of authorising movement. Kanbans are an important part of JIT manufacturing as they prevent the build-up of stock or parts in a factory.

Time-based management

TIME-BASED MANAGEMENT involves reducing the amount of time businesses take to carry out certain tasks, such as launching new products or cutting lead times in production. Time-based management is a feature of lean production because it involves eliminating a type of waste, i.e. time. Time in business is a valuable resource. Productivity can be improved if tasks are carried out more quickly. Time-based management has a number of effects on a business.

Table 1: Advantages and disadvantages of JIT manufacturing

Advantages

- It improves cash flow since money is not tied up in stocks.
- The system reduces waste, obsolete and damaged stock.
- More factory space is made available for productive use.
- The costs of stockholding are reduced significantly.
- Links with and the control of suppliers are improved.
- The supplier base is reduced significantly.
- More scope for integration within the factory's computer system.
- The motivation of workers is improved. They are given more responsibility and encouraged to work in teams.

Disadvantages

- A lot of faith is placed in the reliability and flexibility of suppliers.
- Increased ordering and administration costs.
- Advantages of bulk buying may be lost.
- Vulnerable to a break in supply and machinery breakdowns.
- Difficult to cope with sharp increases in demand.
- Possible loss of reputation if customers are let down by late deliveries.

Focus on customer needs Customers are given a wide range of products to choose from, i.e. different models with different specifications. The same model car can be produced according to different specifications, such as different colours, engine sizes and trims. Manufacturers can achieve this by reducing the length of production runs. Shorter production runs will also allow a firm to cut customer lead times, so customers are not kept waiting.

Use other lean production methods Examples include:
- just-in-time manufacturing;
- simultaneous engineering
- Single Minute Exchange of Dies (SMED);
- flexible manufacturing.

These methods prevent delays on production lines, reduce stock levels and improve scheduling. This means employees are not waiting around for work to arrive.

Machines must be versatile They must be able to produce a variety of products and be adjusted to a range of settings. Settings must be changed quickly and easily to deal with shorter production runs.

Speed up the design process They do this by carrying out a number of design tasks simultaneously. The traditional approach to design is to carry out one task after another. However, time can be saved if design tasks can be completed at the same time. This is called SIMULTANEOUS ENGINEERING. It is a project management approach, not a method of production. Such an approach needs co-ordination and communication between each design team. This approach to speeding up the design process has been called LEAN DESIGN.

Mass producers argue that economies of scale will only be achieved and costs cut if products are standardised and production runs are long. Producing a variety of different models will lead to shorter production runs and higher average costs. Time-based management challenges this view. It may be possible to produce smaller quantities, because costs can be reduced by time savings.

There may be certain advantages for a business using a time-based management system.
- Customers will benefit. A wider range of products will be available and there will be faster delivery times. This might result in higher sales levels for the firm.
- Lean design will result in shorter lead times. This means that resources will be used more effectively and product development will be faster. This will give the business a competitive edge in the market.
- Other lean production techniques will increase efficiency, the quality of products will be improved and waste will be minimised.
- The time spent on a range of production tasks is reduced. This helps to improve productivity and reduce unit costs. As a result manufacturers may offer their products at lower prices or enjoy higher profit margins.

However, it could be argued that some costs might rise as a result of using time-based management. The versatile machinery which this method requires may be more expensive. Staff may also need to be trained in a wider range of skills and tasks to cope with the flexibility in production. Shorter production runs may result in the loss of some economies of scale.

Flexible manufacturing One of the reasons why flow production techniques tend to lead to lower average costs than batch production or job production is because time is not lost changing tools or other equipment to make a new product. For example, a chocolate manufacturer could easily lose a day or two days' production when changing from production of one chocolate bar to another using batch production techniques. Machines have to be completely cleaned to prevent contamination and tooling within the machines has to be changed.

FLEXIBLE MANUFACTURING aims to reduce or even

Question 1.

New Balance Athletic Shoes (UK) Ltd is a US owned company producing a range of high performance athletic shoes. The business has been manufacturing in the UK since 1982 and moved to its current site in Flimby, near Workington, in 1991. New Balance had developed a five year strategic business plan to increase turnover from £70 million to £250 million. In order to achieve this, the manufacturing plant would have to triple the output of the one million pairs of shoes produced in 2005. Land was acquired adjacent to the current site to build another factory unit and the management team was looking for new ways to increase capacity and productivity.

The company employed a consultant to run a series of team workshops with process workers to introduce the basic principles of lean manufacturing. These teams were then challenged to analyse their current process, which led to the development of a new cellular layout requiring 35 per cent less space and only four operatives instead of five. The total work content was balanced between the four operatives to create product flow around the cell. Once the cell footprint had been agreed, a new future state 'ideal' factory layout was developed to convert freed up space into additional cells. The switch to lean production generated a number of benefits for the company.
- Output increased from 10 to 14 pairs of shoes per person per hour.
- Cell teams reduced from five to four people.
- Thirty five per cent reduction in space taken up by manufacturing cell.
- New cells created.
- £1.5 million positive cost variance compared to 2005 manufacturing costs.
- £1.5 million cost avoidance, as there was no longer any requirement to build an additional factory.

Source: adapted from www.mas.dti.gov.uk.

(a) Using this case as an example, explain what is meant by cell production.

(b) Explain why cell production lends itself well to teamworking.

(c) How did the introduction of cell production benefit New Balance Athletic Shoes Ltd?

eliminate changeover time from one product to another so that it becomes as cheap to produce 10 units of one item, 8 of another, and 12 of a third as it is to produce 30 units of the same item. On a car production line, the ideal is for every car produced to be unique. It might be the same model with different specifications. Or it might be two or more models being made at the same time. Flexible manufacturing is achieved by using equipment which can be changed from one use to another use very quickly and ideally instantaneously. It also means that workers must be flexible too, having the skills to deal with different products. Flexible manufacturing requires the back-up of other lean production techniques. For example, on a vehicle production line, if there are 14 different sets of doors fitted during a shift, each a different colour, then there must be just-in-time production techniques used to deliver those doors to that work station at the right time. Otherwise flexible manufacturing would require huge levels of stocks. Similarly, every worker must be responsible for the quality of work done.

Just-in-time production Just-in-time (JIT) manufacturing can be seen as another example of time-based management. JIT cuts the amount of time that stocks are held by a business. In a car manufacturing company, for example, car seats may have been held on average 10 days at the factory in the 1970s before being assembled inside a car. Today, the average stock time held may be three hours because seats are being delivered three times a day to the car plant.

Question 2.

Jenx Ltd is one of the UK's longest established companies designing innovative, therapeutic and development products for children with spinal problems. The company was founded in 1982 and is still run by a Paediatric Physiotherapist and her husband. The company sells its products to over twenty countries worldwide and is committed to a continuous process of review and improvement to offer children the best products available.

After attending a lean training workshop in 2005, Mr Jenkins learned about lean production and the importance of developing an improvement plan. He could see where this could potentially help his business to improve, develop and grow. The key objective from the outset was to involve employees in an improvement programme that allowed them to learn how to make and sustain their own improvements. A team was formed in the machine shop and they were taught the fundamentals of lean manufacturing. This set the foundations for implementing a 5S improvement programme in the machine shop. It was felt that this would help to create a better working environment, improve productivity and provide the best way forward for a programme of change.

As a result of the 15 day 5S Improvement Project, the company has achieved the following.

- Noticeable change in employee commitment and contribution to business improvement.
- Gross value added has increased by £60,000, and productivity by 15 per cent, as a result of the creation of manufacturing cells.
- Distance travelled to manufacture products has reduced from 80 metres to 5 metres (93 per cent).
- Manufacturing finishing cells have been developed and lead times have reduced (60 per cent).
- Stock and WIP (work in progress) has reduced.
- Investment in a new extraction system and sawing equipment has been made.
- Work flow and space utilisation has improved by 20 per cent

Source: adapted from www.mas.dti.gov.uk.

(a) Which lean production method may have been used to reduce stock and WIP?
(b) What is meant by 5S?
(c) How did the implementation of 5S help Jenx Ltd?

Empowerment

Empowerment involves giving employees the power to make decisions in a business. The aim of empowerment is to give employees more control over their own work conditions. Workers in the past have tended to follow the instructions of managers. They were rarely required to think, make decisions, solve problems or work creatively. There was often conflict between management and workers, and little co-operation and team-spirit.

In recent years many businesses have learned that efficiency will improve if workers are given the opportunity to involve themselves in decision making. Workers will be better motivated and the business may gain from the creativity of its workers. Workers may also be more flexible and adaptable. For example, a worker may speak directly to a customer about changes in an order. For empowerment to be successful, managers must have faith in their workforce. They must also trust them and work in partnership without conflict.

Empowerment is not without difficulties. Some workers may not be able to make their own decisions and training may be required to teach them such skills. Managers may resent giving up authority. Some staff may even abuse their power to make decisions.

Teamworking

A growing number of businesses are introducing teamworking into their organisations. This involves dividing the workforce into fairly small groups. Each team will focus on a particular area of production and team members will have the same common aims. Teamworking probably works best in businesses that do not have a hierarchical structure and which have an organisational culture which supports group work. Effective teamworking requires co-operation between workers and management, training for staff and decision making responsibility for workers.

Both the business and its employees might benefit from teamwork. Workers should develop relationships with colleagues and a 'team spirit' which may improve motivation and productivity. Flexibility might improve. For example, team members might be more willing to cover for an absent colleague. Teams might plan their own work schedules, share out tasks, choose their methods of work and solve their own problems. This should lead to quicker decision making and the generation of more ideas. It is also suggested that communication and labour relations may improve as a result of teamworking. However, there may be conflict between team members and managers may resent the responsibility delegated to teams. Teamwork also results to some extent in a loss of specialisation among workers, which is often found in flow or mass production techniques.

Cellular manufacturing

Flow production involves mass producing a standard product on a production line. The product undergoes a series of operations in sequence on a continuous basis until a finished product rolls off the 'end of the line'.

CELLULAR MANUFACTURING or CELL PRODUCTION adopts a different approach and involves dividing the workplace into 'cells'. Each cell occupies an area on the factory floor and focuses on the production of a 'product family'. A 'product family' is a group of products which requires a sequence of similar operations. For example, the metal body part of a machine might require the operations cut, punch, fold, spot weld, dispatch. This could all be carried out in one cell. Inside a cell, machines are grouped together and a team of workers sees the production of a good from start to finish.

Take the example of a furniture manufacturer making parts for a kitchen range in a cell. The raw material, such as wood, would be brought into the cell. Tasks such as turning on a lathe or shaping by routing would be carried out at workstations. The part would then be assembled and passed on to stock. The cell may also be responsible for tasks such as designing, schedule planning, maintenance and problem solving, as well as the manufacturing tasks which are shared by the team.

The advantages of cellular manufacturing include:

- floor space is released because cells use less space than a linear production line;
- product flexibility is improved;
- lead times are cut;
- movement of resources and handling time is reduced;
- there is less work-in-progress;
- teamworking is encouraged;
- there may be a safer working environment and more efficient maintenance.

Benchmarking

BEST PRACTICE BENCHMARKING (BPB) is a technique used by some businesses to help them discover the 'best' methods of production available and then adopt them. BPB involves:

- finding out what makes the difference, in the customer's eyes, between an ordinary supplier and an excellent supplier;
- setting standards for business operations based on the best practice that can be found;
- finding out how these best companies meet those standards;
- applying both competitors' standards and their own to meet the new standards and, if possible, to exceed them.

Figure 3 illustrates the five main steps in BPB. The first step is to **identify** exactly what the company intends to benchmark. Benchmarks that are important for customer satisfaction might include consistency of product, correct invoices, shorter delivery times, shorter lead times and improved after-sales service. For example, Motorola, the communications company, has benchmarked the yield and product characteristics of a range of its activities including its assembly, warehousing and purchasing performance.

The second step involves **choosing a company** to set the benchmark against. This may be done by asking customers who they feel is the best in the field. Business analysts, journalists, stockbrokers or industrialists may also be used. Rank Xerox and Centreparc, the leisure group, have used other parts of their own organisations which have developed a reputation for excellence.

In the third step, information can be **gathered** from a number of sources, such as magazines, newspapers, trade association reports, specialist databases, customers and suppliers. Companies in the same industry often share information. An example may be businesses supplying local markets, such as garden centres. The benefits of this are that the worst performers can get advice from the best and perhaps visit their premises.

The **analysis** of information is best done with quantitative techniques. For example, a firm might compare numerical data relating to delivery times.

The final stage involves **using** the information. Once

Figure 3: A summary of the steps involved in benchmarking

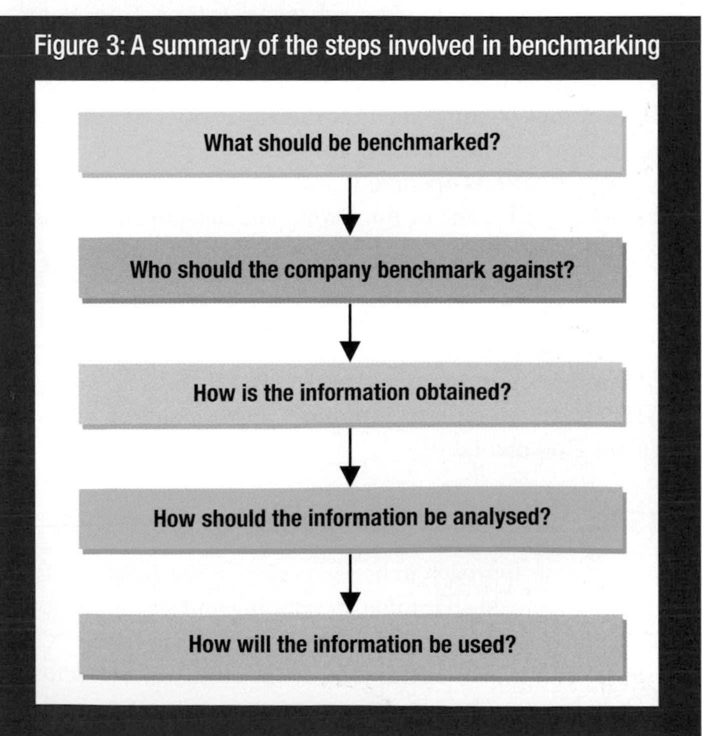
What should be benchmarked?
Who should the company benchmark against?
How is the information obtained?
How should the information be analysed?
How will the information be used?

standards have been found and set, they must be communicated throughout the business. Improvements must be funded, introduced and monitored. Once a company becomes the best in the field others will begin to benchmark against them. This means the company must continue to benchmark its own process.

Six Sigma

Six Sigma is a Japanese method developed by Motorola. It takes its name from the Greek letter 'sigma' used in statistics to indicate standard deviation. It is a statistical approach designed to eliminate defects in processes. A process must not produce more than 3.4 defects per million. A Six Sigma defect is defined as anything that fails to match customer specifications. Six Sigma involves collecting data on performance in processes and then evaluating it. Businesses can reduce variations in performance by using one of two Six Sigma approaches. DMAIC (define, measure, analyse, improve, control) is an improvement system for existing processes that result in too many defects. DMADV (define, measure, analyse, design, verify) is an improvement system used to develop new processes.

Single Minute Exchange of Dies (SMED)

Many manufacturers are under pressure to offer a wider variety of products. This has resulted in companies having to reduce the size of the batches they produce. So it is important to reduce changeover or set-up time. Bottling industries can spend more than 20 per cent of production time on changeovers, for example. Single Minute Exchange of Dies (SMED) is an approach to reduce output and quality losses due to changeovers. It was developed in Japan by Shigeo Shingo and has allowed companies to reduce changeover times from hours to minutes. He developed a method to analyse the changeover process, enabling workers to find out for themselves why the changeover took so long, and how this time could be reduced. There are four key steps in SMED.

- Suppress useless operations and convert IS operations (those which must be done while the machine is stopped) into ES operations (those which can be done when the machine is running).
- Simplify fittings and tightenings.
- Work together.
- Suppress adjustments and trials.

SMED has often resulted in workers approaching changeovers with a 'pit-stop mentality'.

5S (Sort, Set, Shine, Standardise and Sustain)

5S is a Japanese approach to housekeeping in the factory. It is a method of organising, cleaning, developing and sustaining a productive work environment. What does 5S stand for?

- **Sort.** This is about getting rid of the clutter in the factory. Only items such as necessary work tools should be in the factory environment. All other items, such as excess inventory, should be removed.
- **Set in order.** The work area should be organised so that it is easy to find what is needed.
- **Shine.** This is to do with keeping the work area clean. Make it 'shine'.
- **Standardise.** Once the most effective cleaning and sorting methods have been established, they should be used as standards for the whole factory.
- **Sustain.** Mechanisms should be implemented to ensure that the standards achieved are recognised by everyone and used in the future.

This approach has helped businesses to improve efficiency because the work environment is less cluttered and more organised.

KEYTERMS

Best practice benchmarking – imitating the standards of an established leader in quality and attempting to better them.
Cellular manufacturing or cell production – involves producing a 'family of products' in a small self-contained unit (a cell) within a factory.
Flexible manufacturing – a system designed to allow a number of products and product variants to be produced using the same resources over a short space of time.
Just-in-time manufacturing – a production technique which is highly responsive to customer orders and uses very little stock holding.
Kanban – a card which acts as a signal to move or provide resources in a factory.
Kaizen – a Japanese term which means continuous improvement.
Lean design – keeping the resources and time used in the design process to a minimum.
Lean production – an approach to operations management aimed at reducing the quantity of resources used up in production.
Simultaneous engineering – an approach to project management where some, or all of the tasks involved in a project, are carried out at the same time.
Time-based-management – involves setting strict time limits in which tasks must be completed.

KNOWLEDGE

1. What are the aims of lean production?
2. What is meant by the Kaizen umbrella?
3. Explain the purpose of the PDCA cycle.
4. Describe four advantages of JIT manufacturing.
5. What is the purpose of the Kanban system?
6. Describe the three principles of time-based manufacturing.
7. What are the advantages of time-based manufacturing?
8. Give two advantages and two disadvantages of empowerment.
9. Why is teamworking a growing trend in businesses?
10. Describe how cellular manufacturing works.

Case Study: FTL Company Ltd

Family-owned FTL Company Ltd manufactures stainless steel hose assemblies in various types and sizes for a number of industry sectors. The utilities market is the largest share of the business; supported by automotive tuners for power assisted steering applications, payphone handsets, stainless steel metallic hoses and associated pipework. The management team at FTL operates with continuous improvement in mind, and have always encouraged employee involvement in the development of new processes. The company has so far achieved ISO9001:2000 quality standard and is currently working towards BS EN ISO14001.

The company has implemented kaizen principles to reduce costs and improve output. FTL had been successful in winning new contracts which required an increase in production of 50 per cent to support the continued company growth. The company also had an underlying need to reduce waste and improve productivity to respond to competitive pressures and offset recent energy cost increases. FTL therefore decided to bring all of its production in house – a vital step for the company if it was to continue to grow and remain competitive, fighting off competition from India, Turkey and China.

To begin the programme of work, a presentation was delivered to the entire workforce explaining, in simple terms, the need for change. The principles of 'lean' were introduced along with the need for 'total employee involvement'. A kaizen project team was formed comprising operators from the multi-spindle auto-production area, engineers and supervisors. The team was invited to discuss the current method of manufacturing for turned parts and to identify any areas of concern. The major problem area they highlighted was in set-up and changeover times. As a result SMED training was given to the team leading to a full analysis of the process using video footage. Opportunities for improvement were identified, which resulted in a reduction from 27 minutes per shift to 9.5 minutes per shift in set up for turning and grinding.

The team then explored potential improvements in the machine tooling layout and the tooling technology that was being used. A number of improvements were made which extended tool change frequencies further and reduced cycle times from 12 seconds per part to 10 seconds per part. A quality plan was also developed and introduced to ensure that defects were checked for as they happened. The operators were fully trained to carry out the checks independently, giving them greater control of their working environment.

The kaizen team was trained to monitor the machines' ongoing performance and react to any output. Their training also covered how to deliver these results via a Power Point Presentation to management on a monthly basis.

As a result of a 10 day manufacturing efficiency project, FTL has achieved the following.

- 30 new jobs created.
- 65 per cent reduction in set-up times using SMED analysis.
- An additional £72,000 in Gross Value Added.
- 60 per cent increase in people productivity.
- Kaizen activities highlighted a 75 per cent reduction in rework.
- Customer demand is being satisfied from 100 per cent in-house production.
- No loss of customers to low cost labour economies of China, Turkey and India despite increasing competition.
- A quality plan introduced which checks for defects as they happen.
- A self managed Kaizen team has been established to monitor and improve production.
- Staff morale has improved as the multifunctional team has driven improvement - all ideas have been listened to and actions deployed as a team.

Source: adapted from www.mas.dti.gov.uk.

(a) (i) What prompted FTL Ltd to introduce kaizen principles? (4 marks)
(ii) Explain what is meant by kaizen. (6 marks)

(b) Explain the purpose of introducing SMED at FTL. (8 marks)

(c) How important was training when introducing kaizen principles at FTL? (8 marks)

(d) What evidence is there in the case to suggest that FTL is committed to quality? (8 marks)

(e) To what extent has FTL benefited from the introduction of lean production? (16 marks)

96 Resources and waste management

What are resources?

Businesses use resources in production. These are the factors of production in business activity - land, labour, capital and enterprise. This unit deals with land and the materials and resources used by businesses. There are many different materials used in business products. Some are manufactured into other materials or components, which are then used to make different products.

- Silk, a natural resource, is used in the textile industry. Silk fibres are made by caterpillars and are used to make a silk yarn. The yarn is then woven into a fabric. This fabric can be dyed or printed on and used in the manufacture of scarves or shirts, for example.
- Lycra is a SYNTHETIC fibre made from chemicals. It is usually combined with other materials such as wool, nylon, cotton or silk to produce clothes, for example. It allows clothing to stretch and recover its shape.
- Sugar is made by a variety of processes from the natural materials sugar cane or beet. It can be added as a sweetener to products such as jam. When sugar is processed it produces BY-PRODUCTS. These are materials which are created as a 'side effect' of the process. For example, raw sugar is separated from syrup, called molasses, in sugar production. This molasses is used in the food industry and as animal feed.
- Pine is a natural wood used in the production of many items, including tables and chairs, beds, toilet roll holders, children's toys and CD racks.
- Medium density fibreboard (MDF) is produced from waste wood, such as pine or spruce, left over after wooden products are made. Cuttings are combined with water, wax and resin to produce MDF boards. The boards are then used to make products such as furniture, shelving, toys, display stands and flooring.
- Plastics are manufactured from chemicals. Pigments can be added to change their colour and plasticisers make them more flexible. Plastics include polythene (used in bottles, crates and carrier bags), ABS (used in kettles and telephone bodies), polystyrene (used in packaging and model kits) and acrylic (used as a glass substitute in baths, spectacles and street signs).
- Metals may be natural materials found in rocks, such as iron, copper or tin. Carrying out processes can change metal. Heating iron while blowing oxygen on it produces steel. Joining metals into alloys gives the new metal the combined advantages of the original metals. Brass is an alloy of copper, which conducts electricity, and zinc, which is hard but brittle. An alloy of aluminium and copper resists corrosion and is used for outdoor window frames and motor car parts, as it is lightweight and can be shaped.

Waste

In the production of many goods or services some materials are wasted. WASTE also results from production processes. Waste is any material which is no longer useful in a particular production process and has to be disposed of. **The Special Waste Regulations, 1996** classify different types of waste.

Inert waste This includes materials which will not cause environmental pollution and will not have physical, chemical or biological reactions. Examples include stone, brick, most mining waste or subsoil from road widening schemes.

Biodegradable waste Biodegradable waste, such as wood, waste food and garden waste, rots away through the action of living micro-organisms. This can lead to unpleasant smells. Biological reaction may also take place. This can result in landfill gases containing methane and carbon dioxide. Landfill gases are

Question 1.

In 2004 the UK produced about 335 million tonnes of waste. Figure 1 shows the estimated proportion produced by each sector. Estimates shown in the chart are mainly based on data for 2004 except for estimates of sewage sludge which relate to 2005 and construction and demolition waste which relate to 2002/03. The figure for construction and demolition wastes includes excavated soil and miscellaneous materials as well as hard materials, such as brick, concrete and road planings. Waste from the agriculture sector represents less than 1 per cent of total arisings. This waste excludes manure or straw and will come under the same legislative controls as other forms of waste in 2006. Manure and slurry when spread at the place of production, for the benefit of agriculture, is not considered waste.

(a) **How much waste is generated by businesses? Explain your answer.**

(b) **Explain why waste management is important to (i) businesses (ii) the environment.**

Figure 1: Estimated total annual waste by sector

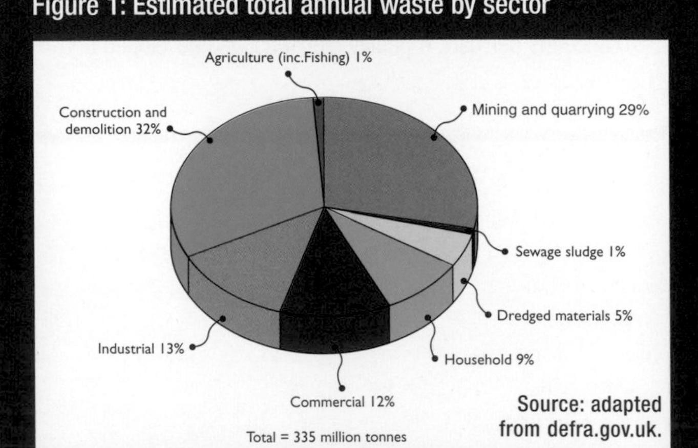

Source: adapted from defra.gov.uk.

thought to be a major factor affecting global warming.

Hazardous waste Hazardous waste can damage health. Clinical waste includes materials from hospitals and vets, which may be contaminated with blood. It must be disposed of by being burned. Special wastes are wastes that appear on an EU list of hazardous wastes and include:

- toxic (poisonous) materials such as lead, rat poison and cyanide;
- materials which cause health risks if inhaled, swallowed or absorbed by the skin, such as asbestos;
- corrosive materials, such as acid, which can burn the skin, eyes and lungs;
- flammable wastes, such as gas cylinders which may ignite.

Businesses must treat some special wastes, such as acids, engine oils and industrial materials, in treatment plants before disposal. Special wastes such as solvents must be disposed of in high temperature incinerators.

Waste management

WASTE MANAGEMENT is a term that describes how businesses deal with waste material. In a small hotel or bookshop, it may just involve making sure that waste material is collected regularly by the local authority. In a chemical processing plant toxic waste may be produced, which must be treated and then disposed of safely. This task might use up a great deal of resources and need continuous monitoring.

Why is waste a problem for a business and for society? For a business, unnecessary waste is expensive. It will raise costs and reduce profit. A firm may try to raise its prices to pay for these extra costs, which might deter customers. For society, some waste is hazardous. If not treated properly it can harm people or the environment. Radioactive waste may kill people if not disposed of carefully. Some resources that are wasted may be non-renewable, such as oil. If waste is reduced, this will mean that such resources will last longer.

Methods of dealing with waste

Waste minimisation Perhaps the best way to reduce business waste is to avoid producing it in the first place. Government measures, such as a landfill tax to make sure businesses meet the cost of waste disposal and environmental effects, have encouraged firms to minimise waste. The government has also helped by setting up special schemes to reduce industrial waste. The Environmental Technology Best Practice Programme (ETBPP), set up in 1994, aimed to encourage practices that would reduce costs by £320 million per annum by the year 2015. Savings could be made as a result of businesses:

- using information from benchmarking publications and case studies and guides on good practice;
- asking advice from an environmental helpline;
- establishing regional waste minimisation projects to reduce costs.

Re-use One way of minimising waste is to re-use materials and products which would otherwise be disposed of. Milk bottles, for example, are collected daily and reused. Plastic containers can be reused for different liquids. Pallets are used again and again by businesses when transporting goods. Charity shops sell second hand clothing. Voluntary groups such as Waste Watch and Going for Green have helped to promote this practice.

Recycling Recycling involves the collection of a waste material such as paper, plastic, glass, aluminium or steel, and producing a new raw material from that waste. For example, Plysu makes containers to hold liquids such as detergents from recycled plastic. It is possible to collect material for recycling in a number of ways.

- Bring systems, where people take materials to collection points, such as bottle banks or clothes banks.
- Collect systems, where households separate certain materials and put them outside the house for collection by voluntary groups, the council and organisations such as the Scout movement. These groups sell the waste collected to businesses for processing.
- Central processing is carried out by or on behalf of local councils. It involves sorting mixed waste at a central processing plant where household refuse is collected. Such plants not only recycle materials but also generate energy. In 2007, Sefton council began a collection scheme whereby households organised their waste into three bins – one for glass, tins and paper; one for compostable refuse such as garden waste; and one for everything else.

Incineration This involves burning waste materials at very high temperatures. It reduces the volume of waste by turning about 70 per cent of it into carbon dioxide gas, other gases and water vapour. The ash that results from burning the waste is often used in the construction industry or taken to landfill sites. Some gases are poisonous and must be prevented from entering the atmosphere by the use of special pollution control equipment. Although new incinerators are expensive, interest in them is increasing because of the rising costs of other methods of disposal.

Landfill Around 90 per cent of all solid waste in Britain is LANDFILLED. This is a fairly safe way of disposing of waste which involves burying it in the ground. This is not without problems. In the past gas has escaped leading to explosions. Today landfill sites contain 'liners', such as clay or polythene to prevent escape. Pipes and pumps are used to release them. In some cases landfill gas is cleaned and used to provide energy for nearby factories or to generate electricity. When a site is full, a top is constructed, which is covered in clay and layers of soil so rain water can drain off. It is then planted with crops or plants.

Composting Composting involves collecting organic waste such as potato peelings, kitchen scraps, grass cuttings and other garden waste and allowing it to decompose. It can then be returned to the soil, where it will act as a natural fertiliser. Composting tends to be carried out in people's gardens rather than as a business activity because compost can vary in standard and there is a problem finding markets for it.

Design Increasingly businesses are considering the impact of waste when designing products and processes. Design teams are developing products and processes which minimise waste in a number of ways.

- Production processes can reduce waste. For example, JIT and kaizen methods have helped to reduce waste in production.
- Firms are using less packaging. For example, single portion yogurt pots now use 5 grams of plastic instead of 12 grams.
- Manufacturers are designing cars which use less fuel. Cars are now more aerodynamic. Components are made from plastic rather than metal or aluminium rather than steel, which makes them lighter.
- The development of concentrated products. For example, in the detergent industry producers sell concentrated fabric conditioner in pouches rather than plastic bottles. A 1 litre bottle of conditioner weighs 70 grams. However, a 12 gram plastic pouch holds 1 litre of conditioner concentrate.
- In the electronics industry designers are continually trying to reduce the size of many products such as computers, mobile phones, hi-fi systems and TVs. Smaller versions use fewer resources.

Benefits and problems of waste management

Businesses which carry out waste management measures may enjoy certain benefits.

- Waste management can help businesses reduce their costs. For example, by minimising waste a business may use fewer resources. In addition, if less waste is generated the cost of disposal will be lower.
- If businesses reduce waste they may be able to offer products at lower prices to consumers. This may give the business a competitive edge.
- By spending money on research and development in waste management businesses may be able to find ways of using their waste productively. For example, they may produce a material from waste which they might be able to sell.
- If a business has a well developed waste management policy, designed to protect employees and the environment from hazardous waste, its image may be improved.
- By reducing certain wastes businesses might be able to reduce the amount of tax they pay. Businesses that use landfill sites to dispose of waste must pay landfill tax.
- An effective waste management policy should help a business to avoid breaking the law regarding waste

Question 2.

Viridor Waste Management is one of the UK's leading waste management companies. Currently operating 25 regional landfill sites, numerous regional recycling facilities and 189 waste processing sites UK-wide, it provides a full range of waste management services. These include the following:

- Recycling
- Composting
- Household waste recycling site management
- Transfer Stations
- Power generation
- Energy from waste incineration
- Clinical and confidential waste services
- Hazardous waste treatment
- Commercial liquid and dry waste collection
- Site restoration and remediation of contaminated land
- Safe and efficient landfill disposal
- Waste auditing and minimisation services

Viridor has recently won Chartered Institute of Waste Management (CIWM) awards for the best-run waste facilities three times in five years, and has been shortlisted twice in the industry's Awards for Excellence. Fifty operational centres are accredited to the ISO 14001 Environmental Management System, the highest recognised international standard, covering over 100 operational facilities. This ensures continual improvement in environmental performance and provides assurance to customers and communities alike.

Table 1: Operational data for Viridor Waste management

Company Turnover	298.9 million (2005/06)
Operational Sites:	189
Clinical Waste Incinerators (with energy recovery):	1
Composting Facilities:	9
Household Waste Recycling Centres:	73
Landfill Sites:	25
Liquid Waste Treatment Centres:	5
Materials Recycling Facilities:	13
Resource Transfer Stations:	22
Transport/Collection Depots:	25
Power Plants	23

Source: adapted from www.viridor-waste.co.uk.

(a) Why do you think companies like Viridor Waste Management have flourished in recent years?

(b) Explain what is meant by (i) hazardous waste, (ii) landfill (iii) composting.

disposal, and thus avoid paying fines.

There are also some disadvantages of waste management.

- Some aspects of waste management are very expensive and contribute to higher business costs. The proper disposal of hazardous waste, such as nuclear waste, can be very expensive.
- Higher business costs resulting from waste management activities may raise the prices of products to customers. This may be a problem if a business is trying to sell goods in overseas markets where foreign laws regarding waste disposal are less restrictive.
- Small businesses might be at a disadvantage. They may not have the resources to spend on waste management which larger companies have.

Factors affecting waste management

Needs of stakeholders Waste management decisions may be complicated. Different business stakeholders can have needs which may conflict. For example, shareholders are keen to maximise returns. They may want a business to maximise profits, which may mean spending less on waste management. However, the local community may want a business to devote more resources to waste management in order to improve the environment. But this could reduce profits. Employees will also be concerned about waste management for health and safety reasons.

There may even be conflict within groups. Some consumers might prefer businesses to keep waste management costs to a minimum, so that prices are kept low. Others may prefer businesses to spend more on waste management activities, even if it means paying higher prices, because of the impact on the environment.

Legislation There is a growing body of UK and EU legislation regarding the disposal and treatment of waste. Complying with the various Acts of Parliament will affect the way businesses handle waste. For example, the government has raised the rate of landfill tax from £14 per tonne in 2003 to £40 per tonne in 2009. As a result, some businesses may have decided to find other methods of disposal or tried to reduce the amount of waste they generated.

Costs As already shown, the disposal and treatment of waste is becoming a highly commercialised activity. Businesses need to consider the costs of different methods of waste management and charges made by different businesses in the industry.

Ethical stance As the importance of image and social responsibility grows, businesses are likely to pay more consideration to waste management. Firms must operate within the law when managing waste. But they may go further. For example, a business might incur extra costs by using recycled materials in production or by ensuring that the liquid waste discharged into rivers was actually cleaner than the minimum legal standard. This type of ethical behaviour might help to improve its image.

Local initiatives In some regions support groups have been established which encourage businesses in their area to reduce waste. For example, the West Midlands Waste Minimisation Club provides support and advice on waste minimisation in the West Midlands area. The existence of such groups is likely to encourage firms to adopt waste minimisation programmes.

Government waste strategy – 2007

In 2007 the UK Government has set out its vision for sustainable waste management in **Waste Strategy for England 2007.** The Government's key objectives are to:

- decouple waste growth (in all sectors) from economic growth and put more emphasis on waste **prevention and re-use;**
- meet and exceed the **Landfill Directive diversion targets** for biodegradable municipal waste in 2010, 2013 and 2020;
- increase diversion from landfill of **non-municipal waste** and secure better integration of treatment for municipal and non-municipal waste;
- secure the **investment in infrastructure** needed to divert waste from landfill and for the management of hazardous waste; and
- get the most environmental benefit from that investment, through increased recycling of resources and recovery of energy from residual waste using a mix of technologies.

KNOWLEDGE

1. State three materials used in:
   (a) the clothing industry;
   (b) the construction industry;
   (c) the car industry;
   (d) the food industry.
2. Give two examples of: (a) inert waste; (b) biodegradable waste; (c) hazardous waste.
3. Why is waste a problem for: (a) a business; (b) society?
4. Why might waste minimisation be the best way to reduce the impact of waste?
5. What is the difference between re-use and recycling?
6. Why is design important in waste management?
7. Suggest four advantages and four disadvantages of waste management.
8. Explain how the needs of stakeholders can affect waste management decisions.
9. State four measures taken by the government to reduce waste.

KEYTERMS

By-products – materials which are produced as a result of a process designed to produce a different material.

Landfill – a way of disposing of waste which involves burying it in the ground.

Synthetic materials – materials which are produced artificially, for example by chemical process, rather than naturally.

Waste – any material which is no longer of use to the system that produced it and which has to be disposed of.

Waste management – the way in which businesses deal with the problem of waste materials.

Case Study: Perth and Kinross Leisure (PKL)

Organisations in the public sector and the private sector have looked to minimise waste in recent years. One example in the public sector is the Perth Leisure Pool which has three pools, a health suite, a crèche and a gym facility. The centre has taken a number of measures to reduce waste in its organisation. For example, recently, it installed colour coded recycling containers in all public areas to encourage visitors to the pool to recycle. This was in response to customer demands. Kerr Smith, the operations manager, said, 'The main driver to get started was in customer feedback'. Having received suggestions that there was possibly more we could do, we arranged a visit from the council's waste advisor to give us suggestions'. In fact the centre had been recycling 'back of house' but felt that the practice should be adopted 'front of house' as well. After the system of different coloured bins was introduced there was a great deal of positive feedback from customers. It was also hoped that awareness would be raised and recycling would increase in the wider community. Kerr said, 'It is still early but the initial signs are that we are reducing general waste. We hope to cut down on the number of general waste collections we have which will reduce the amount of waste we send to landfill and of course save money in the long term.

Perth and Kinross Leisure (PKL) have made some other notable achievements in their bid to minimise waste across their leisure sites. Some examples are outlined below.

- Most of Perth and Kinross leisure centres have public recycling points and the Perth Leisure Pool had one set up in their car park in 2007.
- All PKL centres have plug in time clocks to ensure that non-essential equipment is switched off overnight. This has helped to save £100 per machine per year.
- Centre managers have organised audit tours in buildings to identify where lights can be switched off, heating levels can be reduced or other energy savings can be made.
- One centre has been piloting a waterless urinal system. The initial signs are that it has worked very well. The cost per month of the system is only £20. The centre will save £350 per cistern each year. It is hoped that all centres will adopt this system very soon.
- Perth Leisure Pool has changed its lighting arrays to reduce the consumption of electricity. Also the 10 x 400 watt lamps in the training pool have been replaced by 10 x 250 watt lamps. This saves approximately £400 per year.
- In the Leisure Pool Hall a heat recovery unit has been added to the dehumidifier. This has reduced gas consumption and saved around £600 per year. The payback time for the recovery unit is expected to be around 12-18 months.
- Bells Sports Centre has undertaken an audit carried out by the Carbon Trust. As a result a mechanical and electrical consultant was hired. This led to taps in the centre being replaced by spring loaded push caps. This will help to reduce water consumption.

Source: adapted from www.pkc.gov.uk.

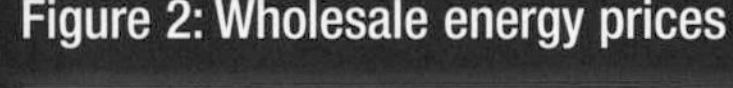

Figure 2: Wholesale energy prices

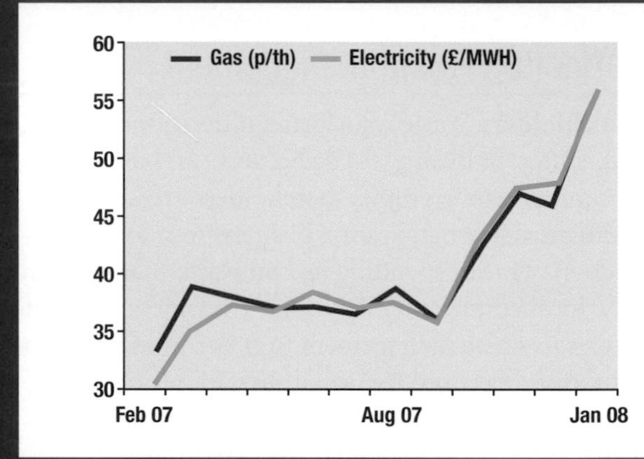

Source: adapted from www.ebusiness-energy.com

(a) State four resources used every day by the Perth Leisure Pool. (4 marks)

(b) Using this case as an example, explain what is meant by waste management. (4 marks)

(c) Why is waste minimisation the best way of dealing with waste? (6 marks)

(d) What is the purpose of the 'audit tours' used by PKL in waste minimisation? (6 marks)

(e) Analyse the benefits of waste minimisation to PKL. (8 marks)

(f) To what extent might a large commercial bank benefit from some of the measures taken by the PKL? (12 marks)

97 Efficiency and strategy

What is efficiency?

The objective of a business might be to be profitable. One way of doing this is to increase efficiency. EFFICIENCY is to do with how well resources, such as raw materials, labour and capital can be used to produce a product or service. Businesses often use costs as an indicator of efficiency. A manufacturer, for example, that finds its **average costs** falling may well be improving efficiency as long as the quality of goods or services does not fall. Generally, as efficiency improves firms become more profitable. However firms may still be profitable without being efficient. This may perhaps be the case with firms that have a great deal of market power. BT, for example, operated profitably in a market free from competition for many years. This does not necessarily mean that increased profits came from being more efficient.

Why might businesses want to measure efficiency?

- To improve control of the business. Information about the efficiency of different parts of a business will allow managers to find strengths and weaknesses.
- To make comparisons. The efficiency of different plants can be compared, for example. The efficiency of the business compared to one of its competitors may also be useful.
- To help negotiations. Efficiency indicators can help a business when discussing wage rates, levels of staff and working practices with trade unions, for example.

How might efficiency be measured? Lower average costs or rising profitability are only **indicators** of efficiency. It is difficult to measure efficient business practice as many factors influence it. It is possible, however, to measure the efficiency of a process or an input such as labour or capital.

Measuring efficiency

How might a business measure the efficiency of a production process or its capital or employees?

Measuring labour productivity Labour PRODUCTIVITY can be found by dividing the output over a certain period by the number of workers employed:

$$\text{Labour productivity} = \frac{\text{Output (per period)}}{\text{Number of employees (per period)}}$$

If a small market garden employs 20 pickers who pick 40,000 lettuces a day, their productivity is 2,000 lettuces per worker each day.

This ratio measures the output per employee and is a useful indication of the efficiency of the labour force. There are, however, problems when calculating the ratio. For example, which workers should be counted? Should the maintenance crew, management, and clerical staff be counted, or should the ratio concentrate on direct labour only, ie shopfloor workers? How should part time workers and the long term sick be treated? How can the ratio accommodate a multi-product plant, where an employee's efforts might contribute to the production of more than one product?

What factors may lead to an improvement in labour productivity?

- There may be a change in the amount or quality of another input. For example, tools and equipment may have been replaced by more up to date and effective ones.
- The way in which labour and shifts are organised could be improved.
- Inefficient businesses with low labour productivity may be closed.
- Some of the improvement may result from increased effort from the workforce.
- The number of workers may be cut.

Measuring capital productivity A business may be interested in the productivity of its capital. This is becoming increasingly likely as more and more firms become capital intensive. A capital productivity ratio can be calculated by dividing output by the amount of capital employed in a given time period.

$$\text{Capital productivity} = \frac{\text{Output}}{\text{Capital employed}}$$

If a factory employed 10 sewing machinists and the total number of garments sewn in a day was 900, the productivity of capital would be 90 garments per machine each day.

Again, improvements in the productivity of capital may not be the result of more efficient capital alone. For example, the performance of an engine can be improved if it is serviced regularly and used carefully.

The labour and capital productivity ratios above are 'partial factor' productivity ratios. They measure the efficiency of just one input. A firm might want to measure the efficiency of the combined inputs it uses.

$$\text{Multi-factor productivity} = \frac{\text{Output}}{\text{Labour + materials + capital + etc.}}$$

This ratio takes into account that efficiency can be influenced by the quality and effectiveness of all inputs.

Measuring value added In recent years some firms have calculated the value added by the business where:

$$\text{Value added} = \text{Sales revenue - external expenditure}$$

Question 1.

In February 2007, Airbus shook the British aerospace sector by unveiling plans to axe 1,600 jobs just months after its UK partner, BAE Systems, sold its 20% stake in the business. The British downsizing was part of a wider shake-up of the troubled pan-European plane-maker involving 10,000 staff cuts, the closure or sale of three plants in France and Germany and plans for widespread outsourcing - some of which is likely to go to lower cost countries such as China. New chief executive, Louis Gallois, brought in to put the company back onto an even keel following new aircraft delays and the impact of a falling dollar, said many of the changes should have been made years ago.

Most of the 1,600 UK job losses will fall on Filton, near Bristol, which manufactures parts for wings, fuel systems and landing gear on Airbus aircraft such as the workhorse A320 jet. Airbus said it would deal with most of the excess jobs through natural wastage, but the Amicus union said it was 'extremely disappointed' by the cuts. Alistair Darling, the industry secretary, 'regretted' the job losses in Britain but said the long-term future for Airbus remained good. Three other sites - Saint-Nazaire-Ville in France plus Varel and Laupheim in Germany will either be sold or closed.

Mr Gallois, who has a reputation for bold and decisive moves following the successful restructuring of the SNCF national railway business, said the financial gains to be obtained at Airbus were a necessity. 'We have no choice ... we have to reduce our costs.' But he also said it was time Airbus operated as a single company. 'We are fighting against history to create one Airbus. And frankly as a newcomer after 10 years (around the aerospace business) I am surprised how difficult it is to find integrated solutions for the management of Airbus'.

Source: adapted from *The Guardian* 28.2.2007.

(a) Using this case as an example, explain what is meant by downsizing.
(b) Why has Airbus decided to downsize its operations?
(c) Airbus plans to outsource some production to China. What is meant by outsourcing?

This is a measure of overall company performance and shows the money available for reinvestment in the business and distribution to shareholders.

In the UK productivity for the whole economy can be measured as gross value added (GVA). This is the value of gross domestic product or national income in the economy plus subsidies minus taxes. Labour productivity can then be measured as GVA per head by dividing this figure by employment.

Assessing business efficiency is a complicated task. A whole variety of measures are required and there is no single indicator which reflects accurately the overall efficiency of a business. A range of financial ratios may also be used to help assess the performance of a business.

Work study

WORK STUDY is an attempt to find the 'best' or most 'efficient' way of using labour, machines and materials. The work of F W Taylor is said to have formed the basis of work study methods.

Work study uses two techniques - method study and work measurement. Method study involves identifying all the specific activities in a job, analysing them, and finding the best way to do the job. This could be an existing job or a new one. Method study will allow a firm to:

- identify an optimum way to carry out a task;
- improve the layout of the factory or the workplace;
- minimise effort and reduce fatigue;
- improve the effectiveness of processes;
- improve the use of labour, machines and materials;
- establish the costs of particular activities to help with accounting;
- achieve results in the least time.

Once the best work method has been found, work measurement can be used to find the effort needed to carry out a task to an acceptable standard. The results can be used to design incentive schemes and determine staffing levels.

How is work measurement carried out? One example might be a worker being observed by a work-study assessor. The assessor might watch a worker set up a cutting machine, cut 10 patterns, reset the machine for a different pattern, and cut 10 more patterns, and record the findings. The performance might be rated against a scale of, say, 0 - 100, such as the British Standard Rating Scale (where 100 is the standard performance of an average, experienced, motivated worker). It is possible for an efficient and motivated worker to exceed 100 on this scale. Work-study assessors are often disliked by employees. Some regard these time and motion officers with suspicion and feel threatened. Workers are sometimes expected to work harder in the future as a result of their observations.

Ergonomics is also an important feature in work study. Machines and the environment should be adapted so that the individual can achieve the best performance. A study of the working area might concentrate on such things as air temperature, humidity, radiation, noise levels and lighting. A study of the positioning of dials might be used when studying machines. EU legislation has laid down a set of rules relating to the use of VDUs by employees, for example.

Improving efficiency

There is a variety of methods that a business might choose which could improve efficiency. Some of the main methods are explained in the sections that follow. The aim of the business when introducing changes to improve efficiency is to increase the productivity of factors of production, reduce costs and raise profits. Increasingly businesses are adopting company-wide approaches which involve the whole business in improving efficiency.

Introducing standardisation

STANDARDISATION involves using uniform resources and activities or producing a uniform product. It can be applied to tools, components, equipment, procedures and business documents.

Changing systems can be very expensive, although there are benefits. A construction firm that builds a range of flats, for example, would benefit if all were fitted with standard cupboards. Savings are made in a number of ways. Bulk purchases can be made, the same tools and procedures could be used for fitting and training time could be reduced. This is an example of internal standardisation. Standardisation can also be more general. For example, efficiency will improve if there are standard components like nuts, bolts, pipes, screws and wire or standard measurements terminology, procedures and equipment.

The creation of the Single European Market in 1992 aimed to standardise regulations, procedures and specifications about quality, health and safety. This has benefited all businesses in EU member countries.

The main disadvantage is that the designers are constrained. They can not change production easily to suit the individual consumer. Designers may also face a more demanding job if they have to design products which must contain certain standard components and dimensions. Standardisation may also lead to inflexibility, which could result in a slower reaction to change.

Changing factory and office layout

The way in which a factory or office is set out can affect efficiency. The machinery and work stations should be set out so that effort and cost are minimised and output is maximised. This will be achieved if:

- the area is safe and secure;
- handling and movement are minimised;
- good visibility and accessibility is maintained;
- flexibility is maximised;
- managers are co-ordinated.

There is no standard method of factory layout because different products need different techniques. Also, different companies producing the same product might choose different methods. For example, both Guinness and Fullers produce beer, but the layouts of their breweries are very different. Fullers uses very traditional brewing techniques. Guinness uses more up to date methods. What are the common types of factory layout?

Process layout This system involves performing similar operations on all products in one area or at one work station. For example, the manufacture of wellington boots involves a mixing process where PVC resin and stabiliser are mixed, a moulding process which takes place on a moulding machine, a trimming operation where the boots have unwanted material cut off, and packaging ready for distribution. Each of these processes is undertaken on all boots at each work station, and work stations are located in different parts of the factory.

This type of layout is often used with batch or cell production because of its flexibility. Planning is needed to avoid machines being overloaded or remaining idle.

Product layout With this method, machinery and tasks are set out in the order required to make the product. The products 'flow' from one machine or task to another. Flow production techniques use this method. It is popular because handling time is reduced and there is greater control. However, it can only be used if there is large demand for the product.

Fixed position layout This involves performing operations on the work-in-progress and then returning it to a fixed location after each process. Alternatively, resources are taken to a site at which production occurs. An example would be the construction of a bridge.

It is not just factories which may change their layout to improve efficiency. For example, some businesses have given more thought to the way their offices should be laid out. Some favour 'open plan' offices. This is where large numbers of employees all work in the same area with no walls or partitions. This could help to improve communication and lead to a 'team spirit' in the organisation. Businesses such as supermarket chains also consider very carefully the best way to lay out their stores. One of their objectives is to ensure that parts of the store do not become congested when the store is busy.

Downsizing

A large number of firms have attempted to improve their efficiency by DOWNSIZING. This term, coined by US management theorist Stephen Roach, has been used to describe the process of reducing capacity, ie laying off workers and closing unprofitable divisions. The advantages of this for businesses may be:

- cost savings and increased profit;
- a leaner, more competitive operation;
- only having efficient, profitable business, with no 'dead horses' to flog;
- profitable businesses not subsidising unprofitable ones.

Downsizing became popular amongst companies in the late 1990s and early twenty first century. Many businesses cut the number of employees, even in developing areas. For example, LogicaCMG, the computer services group, cut 1,400 jobs when it was formed from the merger of UK and Dutch companies in 2002. In 2003 it announced a further 800 job cuts as it aimed to improve cost savings from £60 million to £80 million a year. Despite this enthusiasm, there is some evidence to suggest it is not always the most effective strategy. For example, a report by the Employers Forum on Age (EFA) based on 80 of its members suggested there were few real gains from downsizing. In addition, businesses lost the skills, experience and knowledge of employees. Some companies even hired back redundant staff as consultants. However, downsizing is still a recognised strategy for improving efficiency. In 2008, in response to a 24 per cent fall in the final quarter's profit to $205m (£103m), Yahoo, the Silicon Valley company, announced that it will cut 1,000 jobs, 7% of its workforce, in its biggest downsizing since the collapse of the dotcom boom at the beginning of the decade.

Reengineering

REENGINEERING was defined by Michael Hammer and James Champy (1993) in their book *Reengineering the Corporation* as: 'the fundamental rethinking and radical redesign of business processes to achieve dramatic improvements in critical contemporary measures of performance such as cost, quality, service and speed'.

Table 1: Reengineering

• Businesses should organise their work around processes. Examples of processes that might be redesigned include assembly or purchasing of stocks.
• Traditional methods of improving efficiency involve small changes to existing practices. Reengineering involves radically changing processes or introducing new ones. A business should discard old practices and 'start from scratch'.
• Reengineered processes operate without assembly lines. This allows several jobs to be combined. For example, jobs such as quality checker, paint sprayer and stock orderer may be combined.
• Workers make decisions and are empowered. This should reduce delays in decision making and shorten processes.
• In traditional production, tasks are completed one after the other in a strict sequence. Reengineered processes allow tasks to be completed in a 'natural order', which could be out of sequence.
• Traditional processes produce standardised products, which limits choice. Reengineering allows multiple designs or products, without the loss of scale economies.
• Most large businesses are divided into departments, which have a function. Reengineered processes cross boundaries. For example, the production department might market its own products.
• In traditional processes there is too much checking. Sometimes controls and checks cost more than the money they save. Reengineered processes only employ cost-effective controls and checks.
• Reengineering cuts down on the external contact points. For example, a supplier chasing payment will only have one point of contact. This prevents different people in the business giving out different information.
• Reengineered processes are able to gain the advantages of centralisation and decentralisation.

Features Reengineering has a number of features as shown in Table 1.

What processes are redesigned? These might be processes which are no longer working, for example, a quality assurance system that results in high levels of faulty products, processes which affect customers, such as lead times, and processes which are relatively easy and cheap to redesign.

Effects on a business How might reengineering of processes affect a business?

- Process teams, such as an assembly team, will take the place of functional departments, such as the production department.
- Jobs change from simple tasks to multi-dimensional work. Repetitious assembly line work disappears. It is replaced by individuals working in process teams, responsible for results.
- Workers will be empowered and no longer follow a set of rules laid down by management. They have to think, interact, use judgment and make decisions. Reengineered processes require workers to have an understanding of their jobs.
- Employees will not be promoted because they have a good performance record, but because they have the ability to do another job. Good performance is rewarded by bonuses.
- Employees must believe that they are working for customers and not their bosses.
- Managers no longer issue instructions and monitor the work of subordinates. They assist, guide and help staff to develop.
- Organisational hierarchies become flatter. Staff make decisions for themselves so there is less need for managers. Flatter organisations bring executives closer to customers and workers. Success depends on the attitudes and efforts of empowered workers rather than the actions of task orientated managers. Executives must be leaders who can influence and reinforce employees' values and beliefs.

Agile manufacturing

Some have suggested that businesses need an approach to cope with turbulent markets, competition, changing tastes, fast growth in technology and increasing consumer expectations. Today, customers want to buy products which are custom made and tailored to individual needs. All these trends have led to the development of AGILE MANUFACTURING.

The main aim of agile manufacturing is for a business to be able to perform effectively in a changing market. It will allow customised products to be made with short lead times and without rising costs. Agile manufacturers will be able to adopt new technologies more quickly and have a high degree of flexibility. This will allow large and rapid changes in output, product mixes and delivery dates.

How will a business be able to do this? An agile manufacturer will need flexible people, a reduction in rigid structural hierarchies, broader-based training, flexible production technologies and computer-integrated manufacturing. Radical changes in organisation will also be needed. Figure 1 shows the differences in approach of three production methods. Agile manufacturers need short term relationships with suppliers. This will allow supply contracts to be set up and ended quickly to cope with changes in technology and demand. There is evidence of this happening already, with a growing number of joint ventures across industries. They will also make greater use of **outsourcing**. This involves finding a contractor to supply components or to carry out processes that a business may have undertaken. Car manufacturers often outsource production. Brakes, brakepads, electronics, mirrors, windows and seats are all produced by outside suppliers. It leaves the business more able to concentrate on its 'core' areas. This growth in outsourcing will require quick and effective communication with suppliers and workers. Improved communications technology will allow this.

These ideas have led to the term VIRTUAL COMPANY. It refers to a group of closely linked separate 'entities' which can quickly disband and reform to cope with a turbulent environment.

Knowledge management

'Knowledge management is strategy and processes to enable the creation and flow of relevant knowledge throughout the business to create organisational, customer, and consumer value' according to David Smith of Unilever. The aim of knowledge management is to unlock the information held by individual members of the workforce and share it throughout the company. If this can be done, efficiency should improve. For example, the marketing department may find that customers are unhappy with the stitching on a shirt. If this knowledge was passed to the production department, it may help to reduce returns. Information and communication technology has a vital role to play in the storage, manipulation and presentation of information to all staff in the organisation.

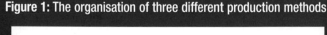

Figure 1: The organisation of three different production methods

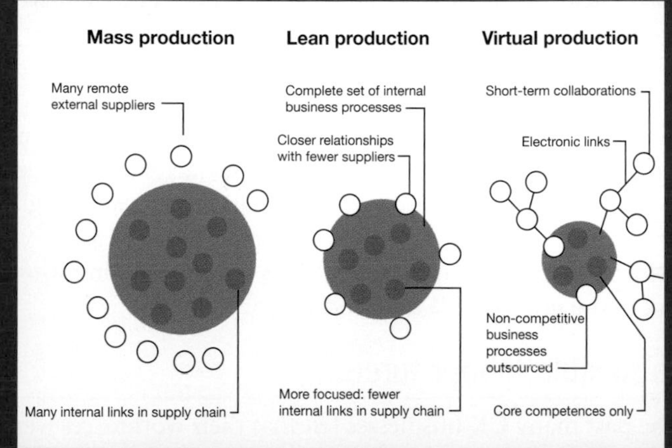

Question 2.

Lowe & Partners Worldwide is a global advertising agency that has over 80 agencies in 54 different countries. In the late 90's and early part of this decade Lowe went through an aggressive merger and acquisition phase and this expansion presented a number of challenges to the computer network such as:

- effective group communication and sharing of information;
- knowledge retention when personnel moved on;
- increased efficiency and uniformity of common business/creative processes.

The creation of a collaborative portal has helped to address these concerns and support creative excellence across the Lowe Network. The portal, branded 'Lowe Go', provides a virtual 'desktop' for Lowe users and supplies fast access to the information, people and business tools needed to add substantial business value.

Before the creation of Lowe Go it was common for knowledge to be kept in personal folders or in users' mail files resulting in a loss of knowledge when employees left the agency. The portal has allowed users to upload case studies and important documents to be used as reference when pitching and on other campaigns. Before Lowe Go there was no easy way to share information and promote creative excellence across the group. Now Lowe share company news, industry news and promote creative excellence throughout the group. This increase in knowledge in turn provides increased accuracy in the business decision making process, and enables any one office to call on the resources and expertise of other people within the Lowe Network.

The key aspect of the portal is the ability to bring people of different communities (account management, planners, creative, finance etc) into one workplace to generate ideas and review new creative work. This helps account directors to gain an insight on how the new advertising campaign is perceived and provides valuable information to a wider audience that was not possible before. For example, posting up the latest Nokia advert (from the DAM), then asking selected users for their feedback results in a more accurate business decision before the advert is previewed to the client. The results/feedback is kept and can be used for future campaigns.

Source: adapted from www.contentmanagement365.com.

(a) Using this case as an example, explain what is meant by knowledge management.

(b) Describe how Lowe & Partners Worldwide captured and shared its knowledge.

(c) What benefits might Lowe enjoy as a result of its commitment to knowledge management?

Tom Peters - 'In Search of Excellence'

Tom Peters and Robert Waterman in their book *In Search of Excellence* identified eight key characteristics of good performing companies from financial statistics and interviews with managers, as shown in Table 2.

Peters later revised his ideas to take into account changes in the business environment.

Table 2: Characteristics of good performing companies

• Large firms were too slow when making decisions, particularly launching new products. They spent too much time analysing data. A better approach was to launch new products quickly, correct problems after and then market the improved version. Cutting lead times was also emphasised by certain managers.
• Successful companies were those which listened to consumers. Customers tended to know what they would buy and firms should supply products which customers want.
• The generation of new ideas was a key factor for success. All employees should be encouraged to try out new ideas even if they did not always work. Mistakes were not criticised in organisations where ideas were encouraged, but viewed as 'good tries'. Employees should operate as though they were running their own small business.
• Top companies recognised the qualities and potential of their workforce. Given the opportunity, workers would act creatively and solve their own problems. If workers generated ideas which management took into account, improvements in productivity would occur.
• Successful businesses stressed values such as continuous innovation, good customer service and dependable quality. Leading by example was also considered important for managers.
• Diversification could weaken a company. Expanding through the development of strengths would be more profitable than trying to do something completely different.
• Organisation charts in leading companies tended to be flatter. Flat structures and a simple chain of command are more effective than matrix structures.
• Successful businesses tended to be decentralised.

- Businesses should revolutionise their approach when adapting to external influences on the business environment.
- Businesses should aim to develop new 'stars' in their product portfolio. Stars are products with a high market share and a high growth potential.
- Businesses, because they cannot control market events, should try to anticipate changes and continually move forward.

Michael Porter - competitive advantage

Michael Porter suggested that businesses could achieve a competitive advantage over rivals by following one of three generic strategies. One of these strategies is cost leadership. A cost leader will be the firm with the lowest unit costs. Low costs may be achieved through the mass production of a fairly standardised product, exploiting economies of scale, automating and reducing overheads. This is dealt with in the unit titled 'Competition and business strategy'.

Peter Senge - the learning organisation

In his book *The Fifth Disciple*, Peter Senge put forward the idea of the learning organisation. According to a definition in the IRS Management Review, a learning organisation is one 'that facilitates the learning of all its members and thus continually transforms itself'. It has been argued that to compete in the uncertain and changing conditions of the global market place, a business needs to be able to learn.

There are two types of learning. **Learning how** involves processes designed to transfer and improve skills that will improve performance. **Learning why** involves looking at how things are happening using diagnostic skills. An example of its operation took place in 1998 when Reed Elsevier, the publishing group, began to prepare for the 'age of the Internet'. The Reed Elsevier Technology Group (RETG) was set up to educate other parts of the group about new technologies. The aim was to ensure that Reed Elsevier's different business units acquired technological expertise themselves. When part of the company acquired some new technological knowledge RETG passed it around the whole organisation. This ensured that something was only learnt once and time was not wasted.

Kaizen

Kaizen means continuous improvement. It is a company wide strategy designed to eliminate waste in business and lead to continual improvement in all aspects of a firm's operations. All staff in the organisation are trained to be on the lookout, all of the time, for ways of making improvements. If small improvements are made continually, their impact over long periods of time will be great. In addition, the company will always be moving forward. Kaizen includes a wide range of different production techniques and working practices, such as quality circles, suggestion schemes, automation, discipline in the workplace, just-in-time manufacturing and zero defects. Businesses which have adopted Kaizen in the UK have enjoyed enormous efficiency gains. For example, GSM Graphic Arts of Thirsk, which makes metal and plastic labels for the motor and electronics industries, operates Kaizen in its factory. In 10 years, GSM improved many aspects of its operations, attracted high profile customers, such as Nissan, GM and Ford, and saw employment grow from 17 to 200. This is dealt with in more detail in the unit titled 'Lean production'.

The flexible labour force

In the past many UK businesses felt that their workforces were too inflexible. Labour productivity in many industries was significantly lower than in other countries. Workforces were uncooperative, resistant to change and lacking in motivation. In order to compete with overseas competition, firms needed to improve the flexibility of the workforce. Methods of improving flexibility included training workers in a number of tasks (multi-skilling), allowing staff to choose their hours of work within limits, using temporary or part-time staff to cope with seasonal demand and outsourcing work to teleworkers or homeworkers. This is dealt with in more detail in the unit titled 'Competitive workforce structures'.

Delayering and empowerment

DELAYERING also involves a business reducing its staff. The cuts are directed at particular levels of a business, such as managerial posts. Many traditional organisational charts are hierarchical, with many layers of management. Delayering involves removing some of these layers. This gives a flatter structure. In the late 1980s, the average number of layers in a typical organisational structure was seven, although some were as high as 14. By the early 2000s this was reduced to less than five. The main advantage of delayering is the savings made from laying off expensive managers. It may also lead to better communication and a better motivated staff if they are empowered and allowed to make their own decisions. However, remaining managers may become demoralised after delayering. Also staff may become overburdened as they have to do more work. Fewer layers may also mean less chance of promotion. Delayering and empowerment are dealt with in the units under the section heading 'People in organisations'.

Quality

It may be possible to improve efficiency by introducing measures to improve the quality of the product or the production process.

- Total Quality Management (TQM) is an approach which aims to reduce the number of errors made in a business. It also encourages staff to continually review and check their work. Fewer errors should improve efficiency because there will be less waste and less repeat work.
- Benchmarking involves a business identifying another organisation which is the very best in a particular field. For example, a business may recognise that a company has a low rate of absenteeism. It could identify the reasons why its absenteeism record is so low and adopt its methods.
- Some businesses adopt recognised quality standards in their operations, such as the BS EN ISO 9000. Once this standard has been awarded, regular checks are made to ensure standards are maintained. Such high standards will tend to pressurise businesses into being efficient. This is dealt with in more detail in the unit titled 'Quality'.

Change in business size

Some businesses believe that they can improve efficiency by growing. This is because larger businesses can exploit **economies of scale**. By exploiting economies of scale businesses will enjoy lower costs. Some mergers and takeovers are motivated by this objective. This is dealt with in more detail in the unit titled 'Economies of scale and resource mix'.

Technological improvements

Investment in new technology will often improve efficiency. New machinery may be quicker, more accurate, be able to carry out more tasks, and work in more extreme conditions than older equipment or labour. Many machines are controlled by computers and can undertake very complex tasks.

- In the primary industry, technology has raised productivity dramatically. The main reason for this is because, in agriculture for example, machinery has replaced people.
- In secondary industry, robots, lasers, CNC machines and automated plants have been increasingly introduced. This has resulted in large increases in efficiency and a reduction in costs.
- Even in the tertiary sector, which tends to be labour intensive, the scope for using technology has increased. For example, a French leisure company has opened a small chain of hotels which are unstaffed for most of the day. People check in using their credit cards and make no contact at all with staff. A small team of staff visit the hotels for a short time each day to clean and service the rooms. Information and communication technology has improved the ability to communicate over large distances.

This is dealt with in more detail in the unit titled 'Introducing technology in operations'.

Relocation

Many businesses relocate some, or parts, of their operations to improve efficiency. The main motive for relocation is to take advantage of cheaper resources in the new locations. For example, some companies have relocated their call centres in India. Call centres are labour intensive and labour is far cheaper in India. Some manufacturers have also switched production. For example, James Dyson, the manufacturer of the Dyson Dual Cyclone vacuum cleaner, decided to switch production from the UK to Malaysia in 2002. The government in the UK also has a record for relocating its activities to save money. For example, the DVLC was relocated in Swansea a number of years ago. Businesses are also 'relocating' some of their business activities onto the Internet. For example, banks offer online banking services, which reduces staffing levels and the need for expensive high street branches.

This is dealt with in more detail in the unit titled 'Location strategies'.

Benefits to stakeholders of improving efficiency

Improvements in efficiency can benefit a number of business stakeholders.

- Shareholders. Improved efficiency will tend to lower costs and raise profits.With greater profits shareholders may be paid higher dividends and higher share prices. Businesses will also have more profit to reinvest. This could help to protect the long term future of the business.
- Customers. If greater efficiency reduces costs businesses may offer products at lower prices. Customers might benefit if the quality of products are improved. Delivery times and customer service might also be better.
- Employees and managers. A more efficient workforce may be better motivated and enjoy more job satisfaction. They may be valued more by employers, get better training, be given opportunities to use their talents and enjoy better working relationships with managers. Employees may also benefit from higher wages and better working conditions.
- Suppliers. Suppliers may benefit from better relationships with businesses and prompter payment. Measures such as just-in-time manufacturing rely heavily on good relationships with suppliers.
- Community. Better efficiency might reduce waste and lower social costs such as pollution.
- Government. If greater efficiency leads to higher profits, the government will gain more tax revenues.

CRITIQUE

There are certain criticisms of modern production and management theories.

- After implementing strategies such as downsizing, delayering, reengineering and outsourcing, a number of businesses have found problems. For example, two thirds of the companies identified by Tom Peters as standard-bearers of excellence in 1982 were in trouble five years later. Michael Hammer admitted that 70 per cent of the firms that claimed to have 'reengineered' themselves failed to improve their market position.
- Michael Hammer admitted that a flaw existed in his own theory. In an article published in The Wall Street Journal in November 1996, he is reported to have told a business conference that he had forgotten about one factor - people. He said: 'I was reflecting my engineering background and was insufficiently appreciative of the human dimension. I've learned that is critical'.
- Reengineering in many businesses has simply meant downsizing. Businesses have tried to cut jobs without appreciating the long term effect of their actions. Job cuts have led to a stressed out, insecure and demotivated workforce.
- Peter Drucker and other management theorists emphasise the role of people as a firm's main asset and the corporation as a social as well as a commercial institution. Approaches which seek to remove employees with important business knowledge may have an adverse effect on the business. This is perhaps why knowledge management was said to be important for businesses in the early twenty first century.
- Many new management theories have been described as 'fads' or 'bandwagons'. They have failed to deliver improvements in profit or positive change. Businesses may simply use whatever theory happens to be in fashion at the time.

KEYTERMS

Agile manufacturing - a strategy which allows a business to react rapidly to changing conditions.
Delayering - the removal of managerial layers in the hierarchical structure.
Downsizing - the process of reducing capacity, usually by laying off staff.
Efficiency - how well inputs, such as raw materials, labour or capital can be changed into outputs, such as goods or services.
Productivity - the ratio of outputs to inputs in a production process, such as the output of a given amount of labour or capital.
Reengineering - redesigning business processes, such as product design, to improve efficiency in the organisation.
Standardisation - the use of uniform resources and activities.
Virtual company - a company which has outsourced every business activity.
Work study - a process which investigates the best possible way to use business resources.

KNOWLEDGE

1. How might a business measure (a) labour productivity and (b) capital productivity?
2. What are the benefits of work study for a business?
3. What are the advantages and disadvantages of standardisation?
4. State four possible effects on businesses of reengineering.
5. Suggest two ways in which a business may become more agile in manufacturing.
6. Describe four of Tom Peters' characteristics of good performing companies.
7. State four benefits of downsizing.
8. State (i) two advantages and (ii) two disadvantages of delayering.
9. Give three examples of labour flexibility.
10. What is the aim of Kaizen?
11. What is the difference between knowledge management and the learning organisation?
12. Suggest two criticisms of modern management theories to improve efficiency.

Case Study: Gregsons

Gregsons is a large mail order company, selling a wide variety of electrical goods such as kettles, irons, food blenders, microwave ovens, TVs, music systems and computers. Its products are advertised heavily in daily newspapers, magazines and on TV. The business sells on price, by offering well known brand names at prices that are typically 20 per cent below those of other outlets. The company operates from a site in Staffordshire where it owns a warehouse and an office block. It is organised into five departments.

- Finance and HR.
- Marketing.
- Goods inward.
- Order-picking and dispatch.
- Logistics.

In 2008 Gregsons attempted to diversify into furniture by mail order. However, this was unsuccessful and it withdrew from the operation after two years at a cost of £5.6 million. In 2008 the directors decided to embark on a new strategy. They decided to improve efficiency across the whole organisation and increase sales by going online. A number of strategic initiatives were implemented.

Reengineering. The entire ordering process was reengineered. Before, orders were received by post or over the telephone and dealt with manually. A new system was introduced which could cope simultaneously with telephone orders and online orders and process them automatically. A voice recognition system is now used for telephone orders. Mail orders are still accepted, but order forms were redesigned to be read by computer. The IT system installed to run the process also allows customers to track their order status on the Internet. Staffing in the department was cut from 120 to 32. However, many of the staff were retrained to work in a new customer services function. The purpose of this function was to deal swiftly and sympathetically with customer complaints and to try to sell more products by developing relationships with customers once an order had been dispatched successfully.

Flexibility. More flexible working practices were introduced. Staff would be able to choose 80 per cent of their hours of work in return for being on call at certain times. One problem that Gregsons experienced was a surge in demand immediately after a TV advert. This often meant that staff were overworked for a period and mistakes were made with order picking and dispatch. Vehicle drivers were also included in this arrangement. Staff would also be trained in more tasks and encouraged to solve their own problems.

Delayering. A delayering process was undertaken. Three management and supervisory layers were 'stripped out'.

Table 3: Key performance indicators 2005 and 2008

	2005	2008
Lead time	10 days	3 days
Order-picking errors	7,350	2,100
Absenteeism	8.70%	5.60%
Customer complaints	1,290	320
Sales revenue	£231m	£275m
Wage bill	£34m	£28m

The purpose of this was to cut costs, improve communications, empower staff and speed up the decision making process. It was also felt that delayering was necessary to help introduce the flexible working practices described above. It was expected that delayering would cut the wage bill by several million pounds per year once voluntary redundancy and early retirement payments had been met.

In 2008, by monitoring a number of key performance indicators, Gregsons was able to conclude that its new strategy was beginning to generate some very encouraging results. Table 3 shows some performance data.

(a) Identify two benefits to Gregsons of delayering. (6 marks)
(b) Using this case as an example, explain what is meant by reengineering. (8 marks)
(c) Identify elements of Tom Peters' 8 key characteristics of good performing companies in the Gregsons case. (10 marks)
(d) Analyse the possible advantages and disadvantages to Gregsons of the flexible working practices introduced. (12 marks)
(e) To what extent might the increase in sales revenue be attributed to the new efficiency strategy? (14 marks)

98 Critical path analysis

The effective management of time

In business there is a well known saying that 'time is money'. One interpretation is that if tasks are completed more quickly, a business will benefit financially. For example, if a business completes an order in five weeks instead of six weeks there will be some real benefits. Once the order is completed resources are available for other tasks, the customer will get the order more quickly and the business can ask for payment earlier. Completing tasks more quickly will improve efficiency and profitability. Therefore it is not surprising that in recent years businesses have adopted methods such as **lean production** to make better use of time. One established method used to improve the management of time and other resources is **critical path analysis**.

Figure 1: A simple network

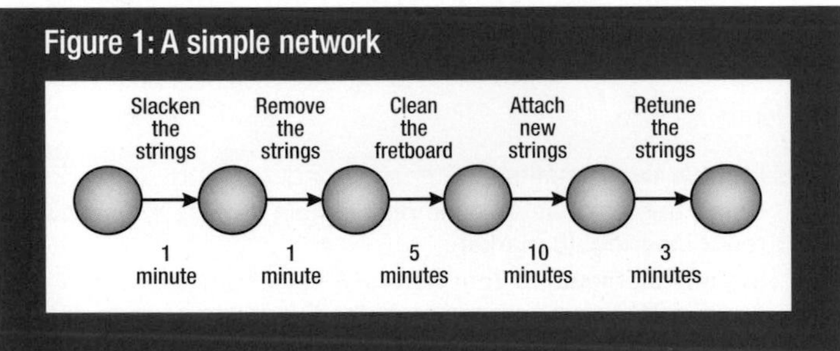

Figure 2: A more complex network

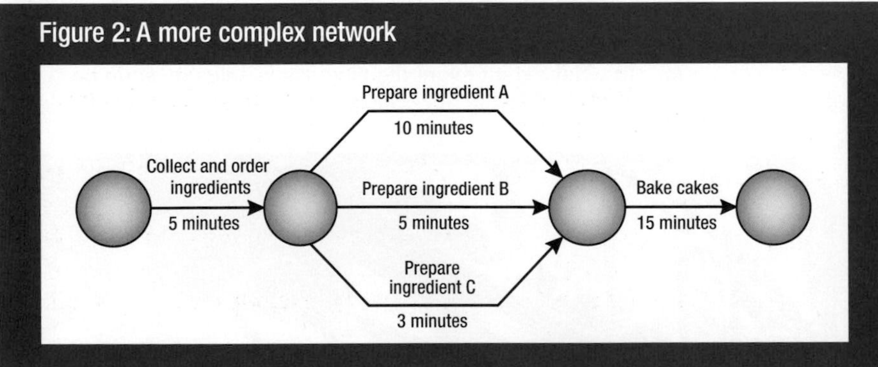

Networks

Many of the operations carried out by businesses are made up of a number of tasks. The operation is only complete when all of the tasks have taken place. For example, the tasks involved in changing a set of strings on a guitar for an instrument repairer might include:

- slackening the strings;
- removing the strings;
- cleaning the fretboard;
- attaching new strings;
- retuning the strings.

These tasks must be carried out in order for the operation to take place. Each task will take a certain amount of time. The operation is shown in Figure 1 on a NETWORK DIAGRAM. The operation takes 20 minutes to carry out (1 minute + 1 minute +5 minutes + 10 minutes + 3 minutes).

Some operations are less simple, with many tasks involved. Figure 2 shows a network diagram for an operation carried out by a cake manufacturer to make cakes for a wedding reception. In this operation some of the tasks can be carried out at the same time. So, for example, some of the ingredients can be prepared at the same time. Ingredient A takes 10 minutes to prepare, which is longer than any of the other ingredients. So the whole operation must take 30 minutes (5 minutes + 10 minutes + 15 minutes). This assumes tasks A, B and C can be carried out at the same time.

Network analysis

Businesses often have to complete large projects, which involve a series of complicated tasks or activities which must be carried out in a certain order. The use of networks helps a business to manage these projects effectively.

Question 1.

An airline company is considering improvements to its turnaround time for planes from the moment a plane arrives at the airport terminal to the time it leaves. Figure 3 shows a network diagram for the turnaround.

(a) What is the minimum amount of time it takes for the turnaround of the aeroplane?

(b) If the company could cut the time it takes to clean a plane from 20 minutes to 14 minutes, would that affect the time change?

Figure 3: Turnaround time for a passenger aircraft

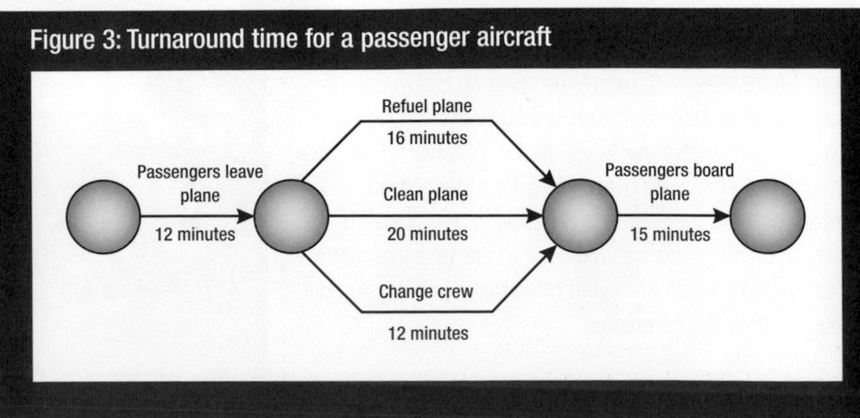

Figure 4: Network for a cottage renovation

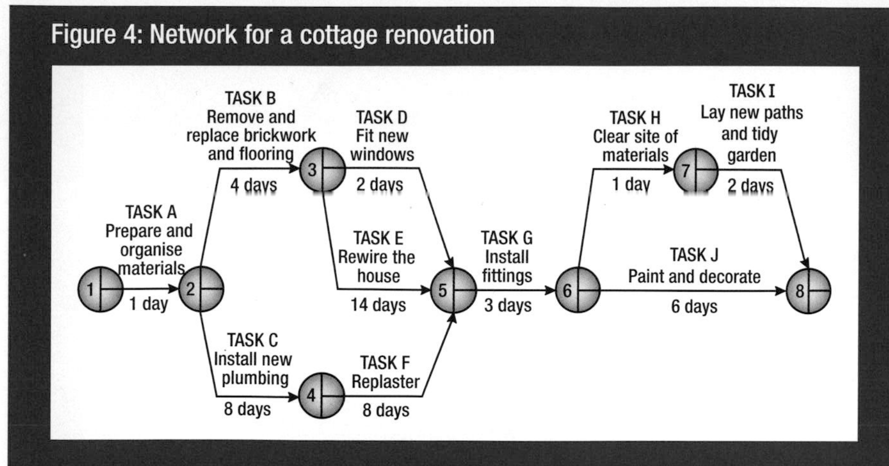

It is vital that a business knows the minimum length of time a project will take to complete. It is also important to know whether a delay in completing individual tasks in an operation will delay the whole project or not. This is known as NETWORK ANALYSIS. It is also called CRITICAL PATH ANALYSIS as it allows a business to find the sequence or 'path' of tasks which are critical to the project and which, if delayed, will cause delays in the entire operation. In practice, businesses may use computers to manage large projects, such as the construction of a road system or hospital, or the manufacture of a large urgent overseas order for new machinery.

Before any project starts, it is important that networks are planned. This involves identifying the tasks that are to take place, how long each will take and the order in which they will take place. This information may be based on previous experience of projects or from research carried out by the business.

Figure 4 shows a network for a construction company which is renovating a cottage. There are certain features to note about the network.

- Arrows and lines show the task or activities to be carried out to complete the project. For example, Task B involves removing and replacing brickwork and flooring in the cottage.
- Some tasks can be carried out together, at the same time. For example, Tasks B and C can take place together but only after Task A has been completed.
- Arrows and lines cannot cross.
- Each task takes a certain amount of time. For example, the business plans to take four days to complete Task B, removing and replacing the brickwork and flooring in the cottage.
- Tasks must be completed in a certain order. Certain tasks are dependent on others being completed. For example, Task D, fitting new windows, and Task E, rewiring, cannot begin until Task B, removing and replacing brickwork and flooring, has taken place.
- Circles on the diagram, called NODES, show the start and finish of a task or activity. For example, Task A, preparing and organising materials, starts at Node 1 and ends at Node 2.
- There is always a node at the start and end of the project.
- Nodes contain information about the timing involved in the project.

Calculating the earliest start times

The first stage in determining the critical path in the network is to calculate the earliest time at which each of the tasks or activities can start, called the EARLIEST START TIME (EST). These are shown in the top right of the nodes. Figure 5 shows the earliest start times for all tasks in the renovation of the cottage.

Node 1 Task A can begin immediately. So 0 is placed in the EST in Node 1.

Node 2 Task A takes 1 day to complete. Tasks B and C, which can be carried out at the same time, can only begin after Task A is completed. So they can only begin after 1 day. This is placed in the EST in Node 2.

Node 3 Task B takes 4 days to complete. Together with the 1 day to complete Task A, this means that Tasks D and E can't start until after 5 days (4 days + 1 day). This is placed in the EST in Node 3.

Node 4 Task C takes 8 days to complete. Together with the 1 day to complete Task A, this means that Task F can't start until after 9 days (8 days + 1 day). This is placed in the EST in Node 4.

Node 5 What will be the earliest start time for Task G which begins at Node 5?

- Tasks A, B and D take 7 days to complete (1 day + 4 days + 2 days);
- Tasks A, C and F take 17 days to complete (1 day + 8 days + 8 days);
- Tasks A, B and E take 19 days to complete (1 day + 4 days + 14 days).

Task G can only begin when all preceding tasks are

Figure 5: Network showing the earliest start times for the cottage renovation

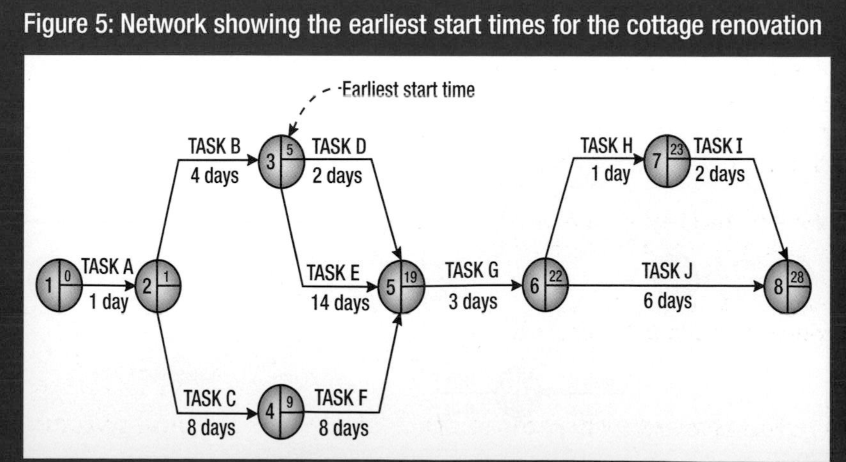

Question 2.

An advertising agency is working on a campaign for a large client for the launch of a new product. It has constructed a network showing the earliest start times for the different phases of the campaign.

(a) Copy out the network in Figure 6 and fill in the earliest start times marked by '?'.

(b) What is the minimum amount of time the campaign will take to complete?

(c) In the one month taken to plan the campaign at the start, the advertising agency revises its estimate of the time taken to plan the newspaper and magazine campaign to 10 months. How will this affect (a) the earliest starting times and (b) the overall time taken to complete the campaign?

Figure 6: Network for an advertising campaign

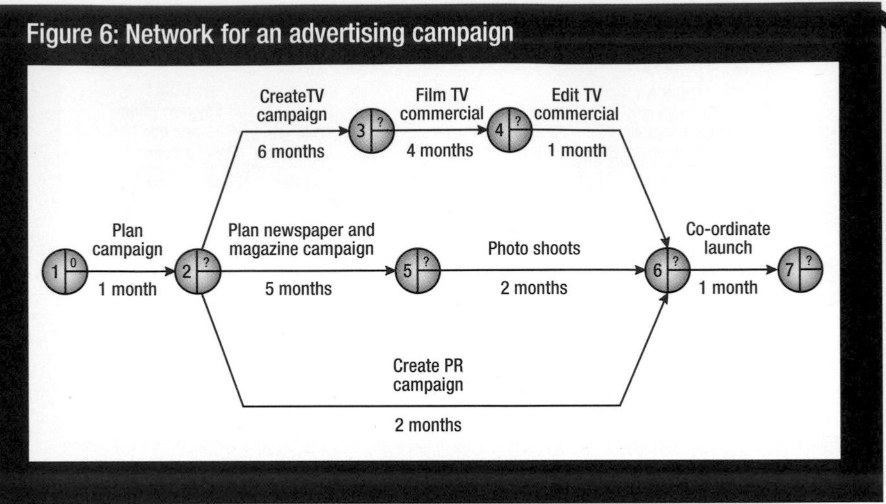

completed. It is dependent on earlier tasks. The longest time to complete these tasks is 19 days. So the EST in Node 5 is 19 days and Task G can't start until after 19 days. This highlights an important rule when calculating earliest start times. Always choose the longest amount of time when placing the ESTs in nodes.

Node 8 Another example of this can be found when calculating the final node, Node 8. Tasks up to Node 6 have taken 22 days to complete. So Tasks H and J can only begin after 22 days. The time taken to complete Task J is 6 days. This is longer than the time taken to complete Tasks H and I, which is 3 days (2 days + 1 day). So the EST placed in Node 8 is 22 days + 6 days = 28 days.

As Node 8 is the final node, then 28 days is the time taken to complete the entire project.

Calculating the latest finish times

The next step involves calculating the latest times that each task can finish without causing the project to be delayed. The LATEST FINISH TIMES (LFTs) of the project to renovate a cottage are shown in Figure 7. They appear at the bottom right of the nodes.

Calculating the latest finish times begins at the final node, Node 8. It has already been calculated that the project will take 28 days. This is placed in the LFT of Node 8. To calculate the LFTs of earlier nodes, use the formula:

LFT at Node - time taken to complete previous task

So the LFT at Node 7, for Task H, is 28 days - 2 days = 26 days.

To calculate the LFT for Task G, to be placed in Node 6, again use the tasks which take the longest amount of time. Task J takes 6 days and Tasks H and I only 3 days (2 days + 1 day). So the LFT at Node 6 is 28 - 6 days = 22 days.

Identifying the critical path

It is now possible to identify the CRITICAL PATH through the network. This shows the tasks which, if delayed, will lead to a delay in the project. The critical path on any network is where the earliest start times and the latest finish times in the nodes are the same. But it must also be the route through the nodes which takes the longest time.

Figure 8 shows the critical path and the tasks which can't be delayed if the renovation of the cottage is to be completed on time. These are tasks A, B, E, G and J. The critical path can be indicated by a broken line or crossed lines, or by some other method, such as highlighting the line in colour, by pen or on computer. Other tasks in the network do not lie on the critical path.

Calculating the float

A business can use the information in the network to calculate the float time in the project. This is the amount of time by which a task can be delayed without causing the project to be delayed. For example, Task I takes 2 days to complete. However, as it does not lie on the

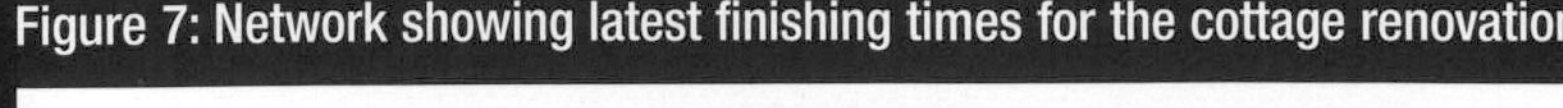
Figure 7: Network showing latest finishing times for the cottage renovation

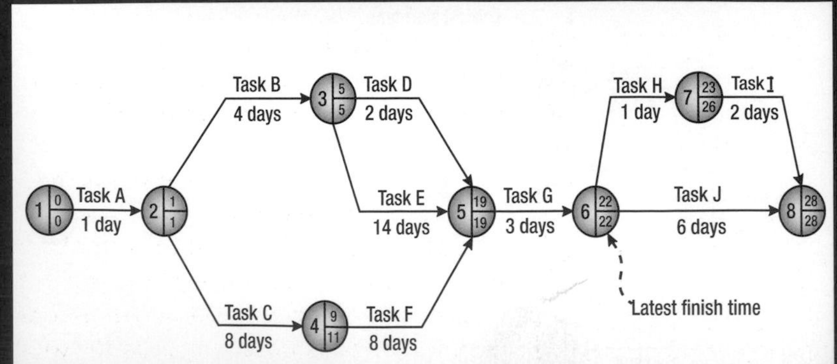

Figure 8: Critical path for the cottage renovation

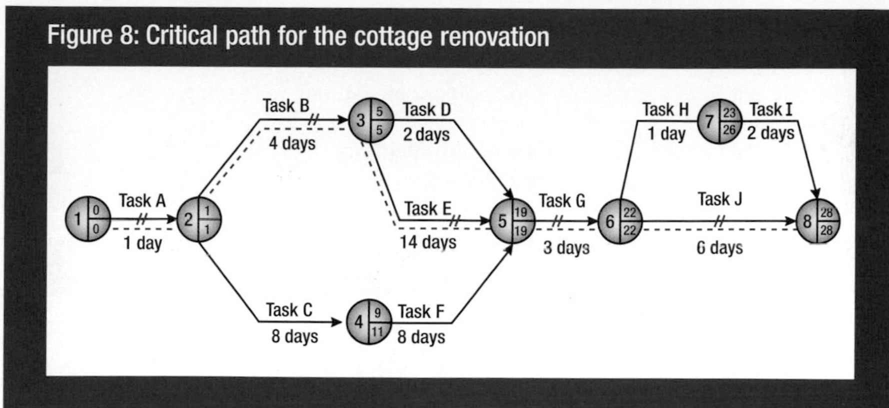

critical path, it is possible that some delay can take place in this task without delaying the whole project. A delay of 1 day, for instance, would not lead to the project taking longer than 28 days.

How much delay can there be in tasks which do not lie on the critical path?

Total float The TOTAL FLOAT is the amount of time by which a task can be delayed without affecting the project. It can be calculated as:

LFT of activity - EST of activity - duration

So for Task B in Figure 8, for example, it would be:

5 days - 1 day - 4 days = 0 days

Activities which lie on the critical path will always have a zero total float value.

For Task C, which does not lie on the critical path, the total float is:

11 days - 1 day - 8 days = 2 days

Table 1 shows the total float for all tasks.

Free float The FREE FLOAT is the amount of time by which a task can be delayed without affecting the following task. It can be calculated by:

EST start of next task - EST start of this task - duration

So for Task C it would be:

9 - 1 - 8 = 0 days

Assessing the value of critical path analysis

Critical path analysis can have a number of benefits for a business.

Efficiency Producing a network can help a business to operate efficiently. For example, a network shows those tasks which can be carried out at the same time. This can help save manufacturing time and the use of resources. Highlighting exactly which delays are crucial to the timing of the project can help a business to meet deadlines. Inability to meet a deadline can be costly for a business. Orders may be lost if goods are not manufactured on time. In the construction industry, clients sometimes have penalty clauses on contracts. These are costs payable by a building company which does not meet its deadlines. Identifying tasks which can be delayed, without affecting the whole project, can help project management. For example, if Task A takes 3 days and Task B takes 4, then a business knows that a delay in Task A will not delay the project. However, it might be able to reduce the length of time that Task B takes to 3 days. This may reduce the length of time the entire project will take. Sometimes building firms earn bonuses for coming in 'on time' or beating deadlines.

Table 1: Float

(days)

Task/activity	LFT	EST	Duration	Total float	EST next	EST this	Duration	Free float
A	1	0	1	0	1	0	1	0
B	5	1	4	0	5	1	4	0
C	11	1	8	2	9	1	8	0
D	19	5	2	12	19	5	2	12
E	19	5	14	0	19	5	14	0
F	19	9	8	2	19	9	8	2
G	22	19	3	0	22	19	3	0
H	26	22	1	3	23	22	1	0
I	28	23	2	3	28	23	2	3
J	28	22	6	0	28	22	6	0

Decision making It can aid decision making in the organisation. The use of business models such as network analysis is argued to be a more scientific and objective method of making decisions. It is suggested that estimating the length of time a project will take, based on past information and an analysis of the tasks involved, should lead to deadlines being met more effectively, as the implications of delays can be assessed, identified and prevented.

Time based management Some businesses operate time based management systems. These are techniques to minimise the length of time in business processes. Identifying tasks which have to be done in order, tasks which can be done together and tasks which may delay the whole project will all help to ensure that the least time

Question 3.

Hurford's is a specialist zinc galvanising business, coating steel components with zinc to prevent them from rusting. A network for one of its processes is shown in Figure 9.

(a) Copy out Figure 9 and fill in the earliest start times for each job on your diagram.
(b) Fill in the latest finishing times on the diagram.
(c) Show the critical path on the diagram.

Figure 9: Network for a zinc galvanising business

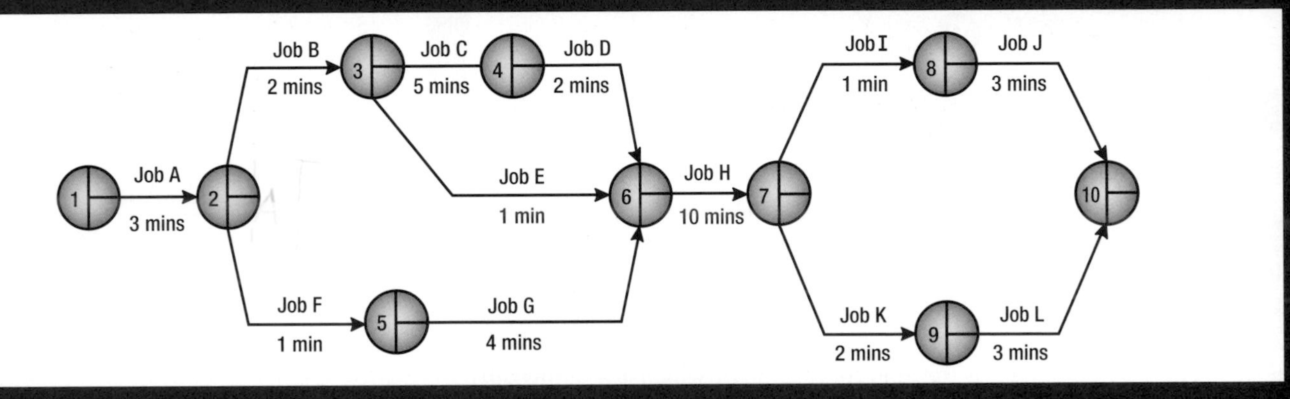

is taken to complete an operation.

Working capital control Identifying when resources will be required in projects can help a business to manage its working capital cycle. Networks allow a business to identify exactly when materials and equipment will be used in a project. They can be purchased when required, rather than holding costly stocks. This is especially important if a business operates a just-in-time system of stock control. If a business has to borrow to purchase materials then charges or interest costs may be reduced if materials are only bought when required. If delays are identified and taken into account then resources can be allocated to other operations until they are needed.

Although critical path analysis is clearly of value, a business must not assume that simply because it produces a network its project will be completed without delay. Information used to estimate times in the network may be incorrect. For example, management might have estimated times based on past performance. But a new project may have special requirements which could take longer. Also, changes sometimes take place when projects are carried out. For example, construction companies may need contingency plans to deal with unforeseen events such as the weather. These would need to be taken into account when producing the network. Large projects may require detailed and extensive networks, calculated on computer.

KNOWLEDGE

1. Why is network analysis also known as 'critical path analysis'.
2. What is shown by a node on a network diagram?
3. Explain the difference between (a) the earliest start time and the latest finishing time; (b) the total float and the free float.
4. Why can network analysis help improve the efficiency of a business?
5. What are the implications of network analysis for working capital control?

KEYTERMS

Earliest start time – how soon a task in a project can begin. It is influenced by the length of time taken by tasks which must be completed before it can begin.

Critical path – the tasks involved in a project which, if delayed, could delay the project.

Critical path analysis/network analysis – a method of calculating the minimum time required to complete a project, identifying delays which could be critical to its completion.

Free float – the time by which a task can be delayed without affecting the following task.

Latest finish times – the latest times that tasks in a project can finish.

Network diagram – a chart showing the order of the tasks involved in completing a project, containing information about the times taken to complete the tasks.

Nodes – positions in a network diagram which indicate the start and finish times of a task.

Total float – the time by which a task can be delayed without affecting the project.

Case Study: Newport Holdings

Newport Holdings manufactures electronic components for domestic appliances. The company has received some large orders recently after a successful sales drive. However, to increase capacity and improve productivity it must replace the entire assembly line with up-to-date technology. The directors are keen to go ahead with the investment, but are worried about the disruption that will be caused. During the construction of the new assembly line production will be zero. The company can hold up to 30 days of stocks so the new line must be up and running within one month. If the new line isn't ready, Newport Holdings will lose approximately £200,000 per day. This will be unacceptable to the directors.

Table 2: The tasks, task order and task times required to construct the new assembly line

Task	Description	Order/dependency	Duration
A	Dismantle old line	Must be done first	3 days
B	Retrain staff	Must follow A	15 days
C	Position lifting gear	Must follow A	2 days
D	Remove roof panels	Must follow A	2 days
E	Lower in new plant	Must follow D	2 days
F	Replace roof panels	Must follow C and E	3 days
G	Install new plant	Must follow F	11 days
H	Test run	Must follow B and G	3 days
I	Safety checks	Must follow H	2 days

Figure 10: Network diagram for the installation of new technology at Newport Holdings

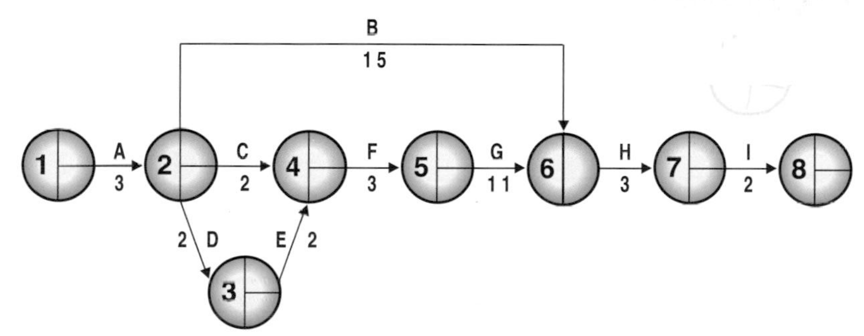

(a) State two objectives of critical path analysis. (4 marks)

(b) For the activities required to install the new technology, calculate the (i) earliest start times (ESTs) and (ii) the latest finish times (LFTs). (12 marks)

(c) Identify the critical path on the network diagram. (4 marks)

(d) Will the construction be completed in time? Explain your answer. (4 marks)

(e) How will the construction time be affected if task B is delayed by 4 days? (6 marks)

(f) Evaluate the advantages and disadvantages to Newport Holdings of using critical path analysis. (10 marks)

99 Operations management techniques

Queueing and simulation

SIMULATIONS are models which try to reproduce in a dynamic way what is going on in reality. Business simulations, such as business games, have become common tools in management training and Business Studies teaching. But simulations can also be used to look at a very specific problem, such as queueing. People who are kept waiting in queues may look for a different place to buy goods and services. Queues also waste resources, such as time spent dealing with customer complaints.

Such problems often result when customers arrive at random. Examples may be people using a cashpoint or a public telephone, patients arriving at casualty or cars arriving at a toll booth. It is the random element which causes the problem. If people used these items regularly it would be easy to decide on the number of staff required to deal with customers without causing delay. This assumes, however, that the service time is constant. This is not always the case. Where the service time is variable, such as at a supermarket checkout, a problem will exist.

Take an example of how a simulation can be used to reduce queuing at checkouts in a supermarket. A number of variables need to be considered.

- The number of customers arriving at the checkouts.
- The number of checkouts in operation.
- The frequency of arrival at checkouts.
- The length of time each customer takes at the checkout.

A simulation will allow a business to work out the number of checkouts it must operate at different times of the day to keep queues at a minimum.

The first stage is to collect information about how the system operates at present. The supermarket collected information about 100 customers who 'checked out' between 5.00pm and 5.30pm. Table 1 shows this information.

Table 1 also shows the **cumulative frequency** of people at the checkout. The information forms the basis of a model which will try to simulate the arrival of customers at checkouts.

Table 1: Information relating to customers arriving at a supermarket checkout

Time between arrivals at checkout (mins)	Frequency (per cent)	Cumulative frequency	Time at check out (mins)	Frequency (per cent)	Cumulative frequency
0	8	8	1	7	7
1	20	28	2	25	32
2	32	60	3	32	64
3	21	81	4	16	80
4	9	90	5	12	92
5	10	100	6	8	100

Random numbers are used to indicate the time between arrivals and the length of time spent at the checkout. Random numbers are obtained from computers and have no pattern provided they are used in a random way. For example a random series of 50 numbers may be:

20	**84**	**27**	**38**	**66**	**19**	**60**	**10**	**51**	**20**
35	**16**	**74**	**58**	**72**	**79**	**98**	**09**	**47**	**07**
98	**82**	**69**	**63**	**23**	**70**	**80**	**88**	**86**	**23**
94	**67**	**94**	**34**	**03**	**77**	**89**	**30**	**49**	**51**
04	**54**	**32**	**55**	**94**	**82**	**08**	**19**	**20**	**73**

Table 2: Cumulative frequencies and allocated random numbers

Time between arrivals (mins)	Cumulative frequency	Random numbers	Time at check out (mins)	Cumulative frequency	Random numbers
0	8	01 - 08	1	7	01 - 07
1	28	09 - 28	2	32	08 - 32
2	60	29 - 60	3	64	35 - 64
3	81	61 - 81	4	80	65 - 80
4	90	82 - 90	5	92	81 - 92
5	100	91 -100	6	100	93 -100

The random numbers are allocated to the 'Time between arrivals' and the 'Time spent at the checkout', according to the cumulative frequencies as shown in Table 2. The simulation can now begin, using the random numbers in the order they are shown above:

Random number 20 - customer 1 arrives after 1 minute
Random number 84 - customer 1 takes 5 minutes to be served
Random number 27 - customer 2 arrives 1 minute after customer 1
Random number 38 - customer 2 takes 3 minutes to be served
Random number 66 - customer 3 arrives 3 minutes after customer 2
Random number 19 - customer 3 takes 2 minutes to be served

Table 3 The results of the simulation showing the arrival times, waiting times, service times and the leaving times of customers

Customer	Random number		Simulated times		Arrived at	Served at	Leaves at	Cust wait (mins)	Checkout wait (mins)
	Arrival	Service time	Between arrival (mins)	Service time (mins)					
1	20	84	1	5	5.01	5.01	5.06	0	1
2	27	38	1	3	5.02	5.06	5.09	4	0
3	66	19	3	2	5.05	5.09	5.11	4	0
4	60	10	2	2	5.07	5.11	5.13	4	0
5	51	20	2	2	5.09	5.13	5.15	4	0
6	35	16	2	2	5.11	5.15	5.17	4	0
7	74	58	3	3	5.14	5.17	5.20	3	0
8	72	79	3	4	5.17	5.20	5.24	3	0
9	98	09	5	2	5.22	5.24	5.26	2	0
10	47	07	2	1	5.24	5.26	5.27	2	0

The simulation can be recorded as shown in Table 3. It is assumed that there is just one checkout in operation to start with. With just one checkout in operation, the average customer waiting time is about three minutes - this might be considered acceptable. Also, the checkout has been working constantly. Let us now run the simulation with two checkouts in operation. The results are shown in Table 4.

Table 4: Results from simulation with two checkouts employed (the random numbers are excluded)

Customer	Simulated times		Arrived at	Checkout number	Served at	Leaves at	Cust. wait	Checkout wait
	Between arrival (mins)	Service time (mins)					(mins)	(mins)
1	1	5	5.01	1	5.01	5.06	0	1
2	1	3	5.02	2	5.02	5.05	0	2
3	3	2	5.05	2	5.05	5.07	0	0
4	2	2	5.07	1	5.07	5.09	0	1
5	2	2	5.09	1	5.09	5.11	0	0
6	2	2	5.11	2	5.11	5.13	0	4
7	3	3	5.14	1	5.14	5.17	0	3
8	3	4	5.17	2	5.17	5.21	0	4
9	5	2	5.22	1	5.22	5.24	0	5
10	2	1	5.24	2	5.24	5.25	0	3

With two checkouts in operation, customers are never kept waiting. However, both checkouts are waiting for customers on many occasions. The results from this simulation can help the supermarket decide whether it wants to operate one or two checkouts. The final decision will also depend on its policy towards customer queueing and staff productivity. For example, if its policy is to keep staff fully employed then it will use just one checkout. Simulations like this may appear cumbersome, but the use of a computer will help speed up the process. They are used quite commonly in business. Other OR techniques are too complex to deal with problems like queueing and congestion. However, simulations are only as good as the data upon which they are based. Inaccurate data could lead to incorrect conclusions being drawn. Also, the data may be expensive to collect in the first place.

Cost-benefit analysis

Many decisions in business are 'financial' decisions. When considering different courses of action decision makers often weigh up the financial costs against the financial benefits. Normally, a business will choose the course of action which generates the greatest net financial benefit. Recently, some firms have begun to consider the costs and benefits of their decisions to the rest of society. Take an example of a chemical company. It is likely to face the 'private' costs of machinery etc., but may also generate pollution into the atmosphere. Pollution is one example of negative externalities or external costs. Similarly, the business will aim to sell its product to earn revenue (a private benefit), but may build a factory and a new road which eases traffic congestion in the area (an external benefit). We can say:

Social costs = private/financial costs + external costs.
Social benefit = private/financial benefit + external benefit.

COST-BENEFIT ANALYSIS is a method used to take into account social costs and benefits when making decisions. A business must place a monetary value on any social costs and benefits which a particular course of action might lead to. For example, consider a business calculating the cost of locating a new factory in a rural area. Part of the external cost might be the potential loss of wildlife. The business must find a way of evaluating this cost in monetary terms. Quite obviously this would be difficult and this is one of the problems with cost-benefit analysis.

Cost-benefit analysis is more commonly used in the public sector. Government investment projects have often been the subject of cost-benefit analysis. For example, the decision whether or not to build a bypass would look at external costs, such as the loss of custom to local businesses when the traffic is diverted. These would be compared with the possible external benefits, such as less congestion and fewer accidents on the local roads. The overall decision would depend on both the external costs and benefits, and the financial costs of constructing the bypass. The abandoning of a Thames crossing at Oxleas Wood because of the impact it would have had on the environment is an example of a project that took social costs and benefits into account.

Question 1.

A warehouse receives lorry loads of corn from local farmers. It currently operates one tipping facility. Table 5 shows the arrival intervals of successive lorries and the times taken to tip their loads.

Table 5: Information regarding the arrival of lorries at a warehouse and the time it takes to tip their loads

Time between arrivals (mins)	Frequency (per cent)	Cumulative frequency	Tipping time (mins)	Frequency (per cent)	Cumulative Frequency
3	5	5	10	12	12
4	10	15	11	20	32
7	45	60	12	30	62
10	30	90	13	28	90
13	10	100	14	10	100

(a) Use a simulation to show the (i) arrival time and (ii) waiting time of ten lorries which begin arriving at 9.00a.m. Use the random numbers in the text on the previous page.
(b) Using another simulation, show the effect of operating two tipping facilities.
(c) Do you think a second tipping facility would be a worthwhile investment? Explain your answer.
(d) Explain one possible disadvantage of using simulation in this case.

Blending

BLENDING is a technique which shows a firm how 'best' to allocate its resources, given a number of constraints. Firms usually aim to allocate resources in a profitable and cost effective way. Blending is one example of LINEAR PROGRAMMING. This method sets out a business problem as a series of linear or mathematical expressions. A linear expression is an equation which links two variables such that their behaviour, if plotted on a graph, would be represented by a straight line. These expressions are then used to find the **optimal** or best solution.

How can firms use blending? It may be used when they are making decisions about production. Take, for example, a firm producing two products, denim jeans and denim jackets with a number of constraints:

- the same resources are used for each product;
- the three main operations in their manufacture are cutting, sewing and studding;
- the time taken for each operation is shown in Table 6;
- in a working day there are 900 minutes of cutting time, 800 minutes of sewing time and 700 minutes of studding time;
- the denim used in jeans costs £5 and in jackets £8;
- jeans sell at £7 per pair and jackets at £11 each.

The firm has to decide what combination of jackets and jeans should be produced to maximise profits, given these constraints.

Table 6: Time taken to carry out operations

			Minutes
	Cutting	Sewing	Studding
Jeans (jn)	3	2	1
Jackets (jk)	1	2	2

The cutting constraint The first step when using this technique is to show the information on constraints as a set of inequalities where ≤ means less than or equal to and means ≥ greater than or equal to. The firm knows that the amount of cutting time needed for jeans is three minutes and for jackets one minute. So the total cutting time is:

$$3jn + 1jk$$

There is also a constraint. The amount of cutting time must be no more than 900 minutes. So:

$$3jn + 1jk \leq 900$$

We can show this on a graph. If the firm used **all** its time for cutting to make jeans (and no jackets were made), it could make:

$$\frac{900 \text{ minutes}}{3 \text{ minutes}} = 300 \text{ jeans}$$

If all the time was used to make jackets (and no jeans were made), it could produce:

$$\frac{900 \text{ minutes}}{1 \text{ minute}} = 900 \text{ jackets}$$

The cutting constraint is shown in Figure 1. The line shows combinations of jeans and jackets that could be cut if all available cutting time is used. So, for example, the firm could make 300 jackets and 200 pairs of jeans. The area inside the line is called the feasible region. It shows all combinations of jackets and jeans that could be cut in the time available, ie when 3jn + 1jk≤900.

Figure 1: The cutting constraint

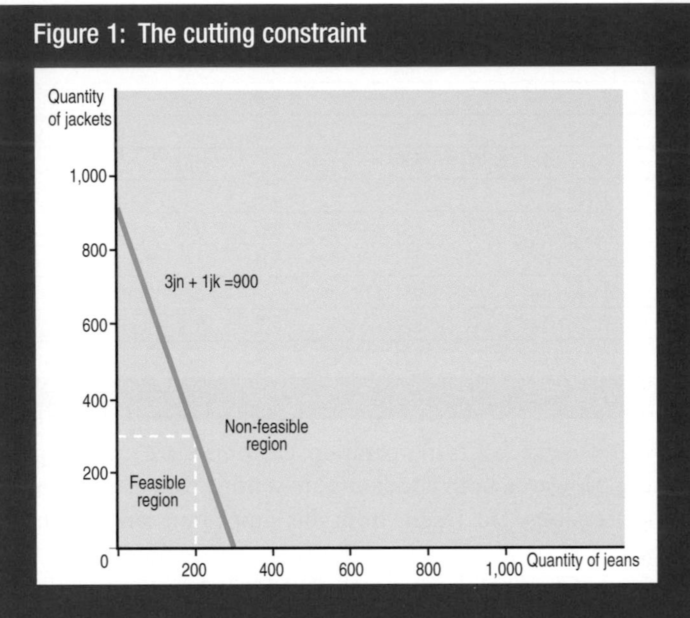

Sewing and studding constraints The time available for sewing is 800 minutes. Sewing jeans and jackets takes 2 minutes each. So:

$$2jn + 2jk \leq 800$$

Similarly, the constraint for studding is 700 minutes. Studding jeans takes 1 minute and jackets 2 minutes. So:

$$1jn + 2jk \leq 700$$

Again we can illustrate these lines on a graph. If all sewing time available was used on jeans **or** on jackets, the firm could make 400 jeans **or** 400 jackets. If all the time available for studding was used on jeans **or** jackets the firm could make 700 jeans or 350 jackets. These two lines are added to the other constraint and are shown in Figure 2. All constraints are now illustrated on the graph. The shaded area represents the feasible region taking all these constraints into account. This shows all the combinations of jeans and jackets that **could** be made.

Figure 2: All constraints and the feasible region

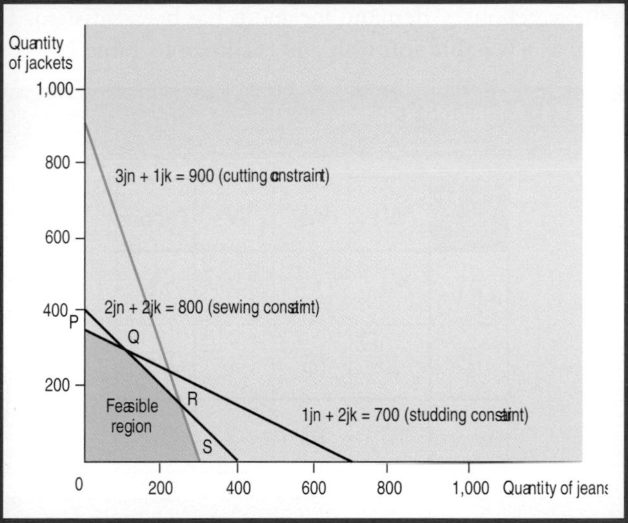

Deciding on a solution How will a firm allocate its resources to maximise profits? This depends on the profit level a firm chooses. The firm knows that the profit made from the sale of a pair of jeans is £7 - £5 = £2. From the sale of a jacket it is £11 - £8 = £3. So the total profit from both is:

$$2jn + 3jk$$

This line can be plotted on the graph. Say that the firm wants to make a profit of £300. This could be gained if the firm produced 150 pairs of jeans and no jackets:

$$£300 = (150 \times 2) + (0 \times 3)$$

or no jeans and 100 jackets:

$$£300 = (0 \times 2) + (100 \times 3)$$

This profit line is shown in Figure 3 (which shows the feasible region PQRS of Figure 2). A higher level of profit can be shown

Figure 3: The optimal or best solution

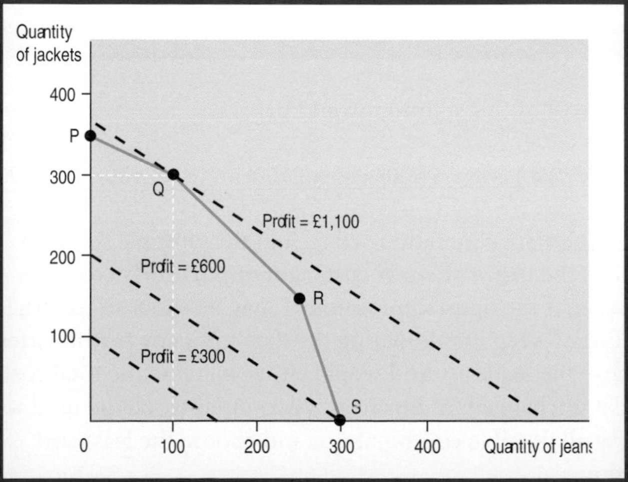

Question 2.

Stonewold Brewery produces two types of ale, best bitter (BB) and strong ale (SA). Three brewing processes are required; malting, mashing and fermenting. The amount of time each process takes and the capacity available is summarised in Table 7. The profit made on a barrel of best bitter and strong ale is £24 and £30 respectively.

Table 7 Time constraints for the three brewing processes

	Malting	Mashing	Fermenting
Hours needed to (BB)	4	8	2
produce 1,000 barrels (SA)	6	4	3
Capacity, total hours available	240	240	150

(a) **Write out the problem as three equations showing the constraints.**
(b) **Draw the constraints on a graph.**
(c) **On the graph, plot a point that shows the allocation of resources that will maximise profit.**
(d) **Calculate the profit that will be earned at this point.**

by moving the line parallel and to the right, e.g. £600. The optimal or best solution for the firm is at Q. If the profit line is moved away from the origin, this is the last point in the feasible region that the profit line would touch. The firm would produce 300 jackets and 100 pairs of jeans. The profit would be £1,100 (300 x £3 + 100 x £2). There is no other combination of jackets and jeans in the feasible region that will earn more profit. Profit will always be maximised on the edge of the feasible region.

Blending can be very useful when firms are deciding how to make best use of their resources. Businesses might use this method to allocate factors of production between different products so that profits are maximised or costs minimised. However, it does have problems. It is a production technique which does not take the demand for products into account. The example used here only uses two products. In practice, firms produce many different products. The **Simplex Method** is used to cope with this, but requires detailed calculations and the use of computers by business.

Transportation

TRANSPORTATION is another linear programming method. It is useful when firms have the problem of transporting items from a number of different origins to various destinations. For example, distribution companies have to decide the most cost effective way to distribute goods from their warehouses to a number of customers. Take an example, where two factories, F1 and F2, supply three warehouses, W1, W2, and W3.

- The output of each factory is constant at 14 and 23 loads per day respectively.
- The warehouses need 16, 18 and 3 loads every day

respectively.
- The transport costs per load are shown in Table 8.

Table 8: Transport costs from factories to warehouses

			£00s per load
		Warehouses	
Factory	W1	W2	W3
F1	3	4	2
F2	1	1	5

The firm must now decide on the most cost effective way of transporting the loads. The first step is to build a model which can be used to help decision making. The information is organised into a matrix as shown in Table 9. This shows that any factory can deliver to any warehouse. The small numbers at the top of each box show the transport cost per load in hundreds of pounds. Notice that the total output of both factories, 37 loads (14 + 23), is the same as the warehouses' demand (16 + 18 + 3).

Table 9: A matrix showing transport costs, factory output and warehousing activities

	W1	W2	W3	Output
F1	[3]	[4]	[2]	14
F2	[1]	[1]	[5]	23
Demand	16	18	3	37

The firm must now decide which factories will supply which warehouses. One way of doing this is to start in the top left hand corner. Say that 14 loads are transported from F1 to W1. This is shown in the top left hand corner in Table 10. This represents the whole of F1's output. If W1, W2 and W3 need supplying, they must be supplied from F2.

Table 10: The start of the solution

	W1	W2	W3	Output
F1	14 [3]	[4]	[2]	14
F2	[1]	[1]	[5]	23
Demand	16	18	3	37

Now assume that F2 sends 2 loads to W1, 18 loads to W2 and 3 loads to W3. All output has been delivered to the warehouses. Also, the warehouses' demand for goods has been satisfied. This is known as a **feasible solution** and is shown in Table 11.

Table 11: A feasible solution

	W1	W2	W3	Output
F1	14 [3]	[4]	[2]	14
F2	2 [1]	18 [1]	3 [5]	23
Demand	16	18	3	37

It is now possible to work out the cost of this solution. The total cost will be:

(14 x £300) + (2 x £100) + (18 x £100) + (3 x £500) = £7,700

It is unlikely that this arbitrary method of deciding on deliveries will give the **least cost solution**. The solution for the firm is shown in Table 12.

Table 12: The least cost solution

	W1	W2	W3	Output
F1	11 [3]	[4]	3 [2]	14
F2	5 [1]	18 [1]	[5]	23
Demand	16	18	3	37

The cost of this solution would be:

(11 x £300) + (3 x £200) + (5 x £100) + (18 x £100) = £6,200

An alternative method used to find this optimal solution involves the use of **shadow costs** and **opportunity costs**. However, if the figures are simple it may be easier to use trial and error - keep manipulating the data until any further attempt to move the loads around would either increase the total cost or leave it unchanged. In business, a computer would be used to look at all possible combinations and choose the least cost solution.

The economic order quantity (EOQ)

Businesses use a number of quantitative techniques to make decisions about their purchases and stock levels. It is possible, for example, for a business to calculate the order size of its stocks, materials or components which minimises total costs. This is called the ECONOMIC ORDER QUANTITY. Total costs are made up of the costs of acquiring stock and the costs of holding stock. Acquisition costs include costs involved with the choice of vendor, negotiation, administration and the inspection of incoming goods.

Acquisition costs, holding costs and total costs are shown in Figure 4. Holding costs rise as order sizes get larger. Holding costs are zero when there are no orders. The larger the order size, the greater the costs of holding it in stock. Acquisition costs fall as order sizes get larger. For example, there is likely to be lower costs in negotiating a few large orders than constantly negotiating many small orders. The order size which minimises total costs will always be at the point where the acquisition cost and the holding cost curves cross each other. This is shown at point EOQ on the diagram.

Figure 4: The economic order quantity

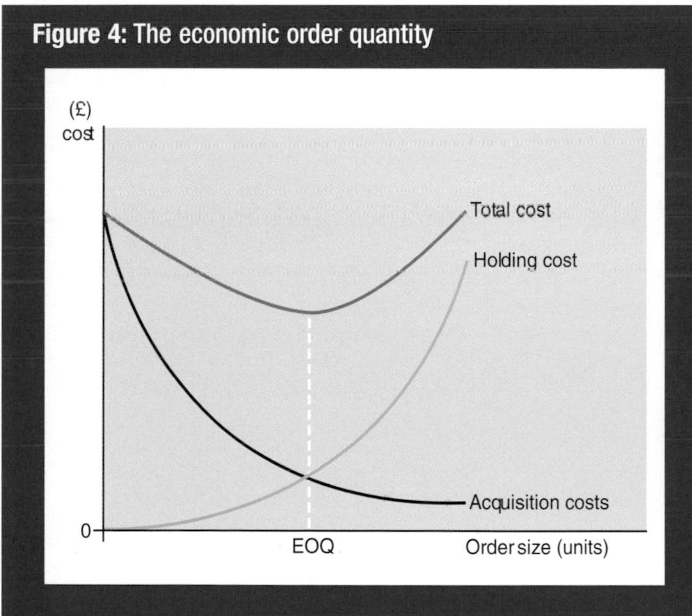

Calculation Say that a builder wants to know what order size of bags of cement will minimise its costs. How can it calculate this? One method used to calculate the EOQ makes the following assumptions.

- Demand for stocks is uniform and does not vary a great deal.
- Store capacity is unlimited.
- Acquisition costs and stock holding costs are not related to the order quantity.
- Material prices are stable.
- Order and delivery quantities are equal.
- Stocks do not fall in value due to deterioration or obsolescence.

Question 3.

Two warehouses W1 and W2 supply three retailers R1, R2 and R3. The supply capacity of the warehouses is 20 and 40 loads per week respectively. The demands of the retailers are 14, 20 and 26 loads per week respectively. The transport costs between the warehouses and retailers are summarised in Table 13.

Table 13

			(£00s)
		Retailers	
Warehouse	R1	R2	R3
W1	1	3	6
W2	4	10	3

(a) Set up a transportation model by constructing a suitable matrix showing, costs, demands, and supply capacities.

(b) Determine the least cost solution for the distribution of loads from warehouses to retailers using your answer to (a) and calculate the cost. (Use trial and error.)

The economic order quantity (Q) can be found using the formula:

$$Q = \sqrt{\frac{2CA}{HP}}$$

where C is the acquisition cost per order, A is the total number of units used each year, H is the holding costs as a percentage of the average stock value and P is the price of each unit.

The building contractor uses 5,000 bags of cement each year which cost £10 each. The holding cost of the cement is 5 per cent of average stock value and acquisition costs are £8. The economic order quantity for cement purchases will be:

$$Q = \sqrt{\frac{2 \times £8 \times 5{,}000}{0.05 \times £10}}$$

$$Q = \sqrt{\frac{80{,}000}{0.5}}$$

$$Q = \sqrt{160{,}000}$$

$$Q = 400 \text{ bags}$$

Thus, the builder will be minimising the total cost of ordering and holding cement if 400 bags are bought each time. In addition, it is possible to calculate the optimum number of orders (A÷Q) by transposing the above formula:

$$\frac{A}{Q} = \sqrt{\frac{HPA}{2C}}$$

$$= \sqrt{\frac{0.05 \times £10 \times 5{,}000}{2 \times £8}}$$

$$= 12.5 \text{ orders per year}$$

Limitations The assumptions on which the economic order quantity formula is based may be unrealistic in practice. The price of many materials, particularly commodities like oil, copper, coffee and cotton, tends to fluctuate with changing market conditions. Businesses are unlikely to have unlimited storage space. Materials, such as perishable goods, may deteriorate if left for a period of time. Changes in these assumptions may lead to different costs for a business, which might affect the EOQ. On the other hand, it could be argued that assumptions are not important, as long as a business realises the limitations and finds the predictions of the model useful.

KEYTERMS

Blending - a graphical approach to linear programming which deals with resource allocation subject to constraints.
Cost-benefit analysis - a technique which involves taking into account all social costs and benefits, when deciding on a course of action.
Economic order quantity (EOQ) - the level of stock order which minimises ordering and stock holding costs.
Linear programming - a technique which shows practical problems as a series of mathematical equations which can then be manipulated to find the optimum or best solution.
Simulation - a technique which imitates what might happen in reality by using random numbers.
Transportation - a method designed to solve problems where there are a number of different points of supply and demand, such as a number of manufacturers distributing their products to a number of different wholesalers.

KNOWLEDGE

1. State three situations where a simulation might be used.
2. Explain what is meant by:
   (a) private costs and private benefits;
   (b) external costs and external benefits.
3. 'The private costs of building a new motorway through a rural area are not the only costs that must be taken into consideration.' Briefly explain this statement.
4. Why are blending and transportation examples of linear programming?
5. Explain briefly two problems that businesses might have when using blending.
6. What does the use of blending show a business?
7. What types of problem does the transportation technique help to solve?
8. Why might a business want to calculate its economic order quantity?
9. State two problems with calculating the economic order quantity.

Case Study: Westmoore Metal Products

Westmoore Metal Products (WMP) is a medium sized engineering company. It employs 45 staff and operates cell production in its factory. Each cell concentrates on a particular family of products. One such cell, the metal rod cell, makes two of the most popular products. These are high precision steel rods for an Austrian customer which makes machine tools. Their component codes are MK and MG.

The metal rod cell contains three machines and employs five staff. The staff organise their own work patterns, but must keep the cell operating for 15 hours per day, 6 days per week. The three machines include a CNC lathe, a CNC milling machine and a vertical profile projector (an inspection machine). To manufacture the MK and MG three key processes are required - turning, milling and inspection. The vertical profile projector is used by other cells for some of the week. The amount of time each process takes and the capacity available is summarised in Table 14. The profit made by each component is £100 for the MK and £80 for the MG.

Westmoore introduced cell production about 5 years ago. One of the problems it had in the factory was a lack of space. In the past the company tended to hold quite high levels of stocks. Westmoore imported most of its steel from northern Spain. Although it is some of the cheapest steel in the world, lead times are long and delivery very unreliable. Thus, the high stock holdings occupy a lot of factory space. At the moment WMP orders about 80 tonnes of steel at a time from its Spanish supplier.

In order to keep stock holding costs to a minimum at WMP, a newly recruited cost accountant has suggested using the economic order quantity (EOQ) to determine the amount of stock to purchase when placing a new order. This takes into account the acquisition cost per order (C), the total number of tonnes used each year (A), the holding cost as a percentage of the average stock value (H) and the price of each tonne (P).

Table 14: Time constraints for the three engineering processes

		Turning	Milling	Inspection
Hours needed to produce one unit	MK	1.5	4	2
	MG	4.5	2	2
Total hours per week available		90	80	50

(a) Write out the problem above as three equations showing the constraints. (3 marks)

(b) Draw the constraints on a graph. (6 marks)

(c) (i) On the graph identify the point which maximises profit. (2 marks)
(ii) State how many of each component should be produced to maximise profit. (1 mark)

(d) Calculate the weekly profit made from the two components at the profit maximising point. (4 marks)

(e) Assuming that C = £100, A = 500 tonnes, H = 20 per cent and P = £200, calculate (i) the EOQ and (ii) the number of orders to be placed during the year. (6 marks)

(f) Using the information in (e), evaluate whether WMP's current ordering policy is cost effective. (12 marks)

100 Aims and vision

Business aims

All businesses have AIMS. An aim is what the business intends to do in the long term – its purpose. Ultimately it is what the business is striving to achieve. Different businesses have different aims. A business might also have more than one aim. What might be the aims of a business?

Profit It could be argued that the main aim of businesses is to make a profit. Some businesses try to PROFIT MAXIMISE. This comes about when the difference between the **revenues** and **costs** is greatest over a period of time. Profit maximisation is most likely to benefit the owners of the business. For a sole trader, the profit is usually equivalent to the wage drawn from the business. The bigger the profit, the more money can be taken. In a company, the level of dividend paid is likely to depend on the profit made. In a public limited company, quoted share prices too are affected by profits. Companies which the stock market thinks will be highly profitable in the future have high share values. Companies which have poor profit forecasts tend to have low share values. Existing shareholders want the price of their shares to be as high as possible.

Shareholder value In the 1980s and 1990s, it became fashionable for large companies to argue that their aim was to maximise SHAREHOLDER VALUE. Shareholder value can be interpreted in different ways. Shareholders make a return from their shares partly through the dividend they receive and partly through increases in value of shares on a stock exchange. Increasing dividends and increasing share price may go together for a growing company. However, companies can pay out too much in dividends in the short-term to please their shareholders at the expense of the long-term success of the business. Profits, instead of being paid out as dividends, can be retained by the company and used for investment. If there is too little investment by the company, it can see sales and profits stagnate and even fall. High dividend payouts can, therefore, **destroy shareholder value** in the longer term. Maximising shareholder value is in the interests of the shareholders. It may even be in the interests of managers too if it secures their jobs.

Survival For some businesses, survival is the main aim. This is particularly true for small businesses just starting up and for larger businesses which have got into financial difficulties. Unless a business survives, it cannot generate benefits for its stakeholders, such as profits for its owners or jobs for employees.

Sales revenue An alternative aim for a business might be SALES REVENUE MAXIMISATION. Earning the highest level possible of revenue over a period of time might lead to high levels of profit, so benefiting the owners of the business. But the owners of a business are not its only stakeholders. In medium to large sized businesses, managers are stakeholders too. They control the day-to-day running of the business. They may have more influence on how the business is run than its owners. Maximising revenue might be more in the interests of managers than maximising profit. The larger the business, the higher the salaries of top managers and their fringe benefits are likely to be. A growing business can be an exciting environment in which to work. There is plenty of opportunity for managers to gain promotion and exercise power over how money is spent, recruitment of staff and new products. The opposite is true in a business which is reducing in size. Job cuts, for instance, are demoralising for all workers. The tendency for managers to pursue revenue maximisation rather than profit maximisation is one of the main reasons why many companies link the **remuneration** (the total pay package) of top managers with profits. It is common today, for instance, for top managers to be given share options. In small businesses, where the owners are the managers, this conflict of interest between them does not arise.

Growth Another aim of a business might be to grow. Revenue is just one measure of the **size** of a business. A business might aim to be the 'number one company in the market', i.e. have the largest market share. There are other measures of growth, such as capital value, and the number of employees it has. If the owners control a business, they might be prepared to sacrifice short-term profits for long-term growth which leads to higher profits in the long term. Maximising growth could

Figure 1: The possible aims of a business

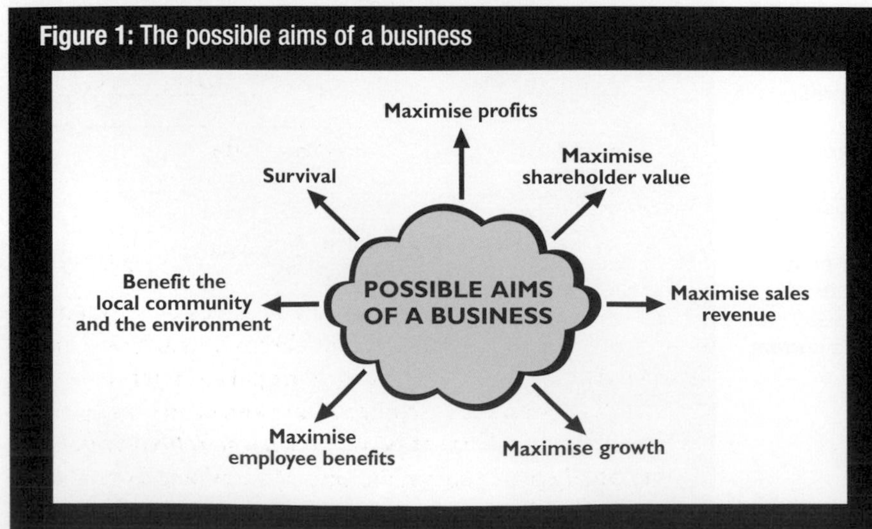

be in their best interests. If managers are in control, growth may become the main business objective because it suits their objectives more than profit maximisation. As already explained, the pay of top managers and their power tends to be linked with business size.

Customer welfare Many businesses state that one of their aims is to benefit their customers. This might be in the form of providing 'best value', or innovative products, or high quality service. Without customers, businesses could not survive. So some argue that customer satisfaction must be an aim of any business.

Employee benefits Employees are stakeholders in a business too. The success of the business is vitally dependent upon the skills and motivation of staff. So it could be argued that the aim of any business must be to benefit employees. The existence of **trade unions** in the workplace can also put pressure on a business to make employee benefits one of its aims.

Benefiting the local community and the environment A few businesses, like The Body Shop, have been set up explicitly with the aim of benefiting the local communities in which they operate and respecting the environment. Equally, some large companies, such as Tesco or BP, have stated aims with regard to community and environmental issues.

What is the main aim of the business?

The main aim of small businesses, such as sole traders or partnerships, is usually to maximise profits. Owners want to maximise the return on their work in a business. There are many exceptions though. For example, doctors working in partnership may make the needs of their patients an important priority.

For companies, though, the situation is more complex. In the UK and the USA, it has been traditional for the needs of shareholders to be most important. So it can be argued that UK and US companies are usually profit maximisers or maximisers of shareholder value. This is true even though there is a **divorce of ownership and control**, where the owners are a different group of people from those who run the company.

In continental Europe and Japan, however, workers, customers and the local community are seen as being much more important stakeholders than in the UK or the USA. So a European or Japanese business may have several aims.

It can also be argued that this is true even in the UK and the USA. According to BEHAVIOURAL THEORIES OF THE FIRM, shareholders, managers, workers, customers, local communities and pressure groups, such as environmental activists, share power within a business. The business aims to reconcile the often **conflicting aims** of each group of stakeholders. For example, it PROFIT SATISFICES, making enough profit to keep shareholders happy, but this is not the maximum level of profit it could make. Instead, it spends more than it otherwise would on environmental projects, or servicing the local community.

Question 1.

Figure 2: Total shareholder return December 2001 to December 2006

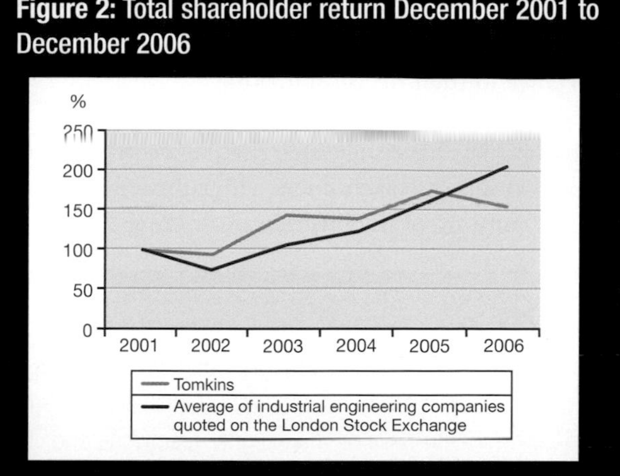

Tomkins is a global engineering and manufacturing group. We manufacture a variety of products for the industrial, automotive and building products markets across North America, Asia and the rest of the world.

Our strategy is focused on the creation of shareholder value by achieving long-term sustainable growth in the economic value of Tomkins. We are targeting growth in revenue and profit through a combination of new product innovation and operational excellence, geographic expansion and strategic bolt-on acquisitions.

(a) Suggest what are the aims of Tomkins as a company.
(b) To what extent has Tomkins achieved its aims between 2003 and 2006?

Table 1: Tomkins-sales, profit, dividends share price per share

	2003	2004	2005	2006
Sales, £ million	2,790	2,721	2,948	3,125
Profit before tax, £ million	193	254	263	245
Dividend per share, pence	12	12.6	13.23	13.89
Ordinary share price, pence	269	254.25	299.75	245.75

Source: adapted from Tomkins, *Annual Report and Accounts*, 2006.

Perhaps it pays better wages to staff than it needs to recruit and motivate them. Senior managers and directors, who have some control over their own pay, are able to negotiate larger remuneration packages than might otherwise be the case.

Over time, the balance of power between stakeholders can change and, therefore, so can the aims of a business. For example, it could be argued that over the past 40 years in the UK the power of employees has gone down as trade union power has decreased. This could be one of the main reasons why the share of profits in the income of the whole UK economy has risen sharply whilst that of earnings has fallen. On the other hand, the power of environmentalists has increased. Forty years ago, few companies acknowledged that the environment was of any importance in their decision making.

Some economists have suggested that, in a company, there are in fact only two sets of stakeholders with sufficient power to influence the running of the business. According to the MANAGERIAL THEORY OF THE FIRM, shareholders and managers share power. Managers have to make enough profit to keep shareholders happy, otherwise they risk losing their bonuses and jobs. But managers have enough day-to-day control to be able to reward themselves more than is strictly necessary.

Question 2.

'GMs's vision is to be the world leader in transportation products and related services. We will earn our customers' enthusiasm through continuous improvement driven by the integrity, teamwork, and innovation of GM people.' (GM is General Motors, the US motor manufacturing company which owns the Vauxhall brand in the UK.)

'McDonald's vision is to be the world's best quick service restaurant experience. Being the best means providing outstanding quality, service, cleanliness, and value, so that we make every customer in every restaurant smile.' (McDonald's is a fast food chain which owns or franchises restaurants throughout the world.)

'Our vision: to become the world's leading company for automotive products and services'. (Ford is one of the world's largest motor car manufacturers.)

'Through becoming the "First Choice" provider of high quality construction, development and consultancy services to selected clients and by continuously developing our products, services and people, we will achieve goals of profitable growth, customer satisfaction and employee fulfilment.' (Simons Group, a UK construction, property development and consultancy group.)

Source: adapted from company websites.

(a) Explain what is meant by a 'vision statement' using examples from the vision statements in the data.

(b) 'Vision statements don't reflect reality.' To what extent is this the case and does it matter?

Vision statements

Large companies may formulate a VISION STATEMENT. This is a statement about what the company wants to be both now and in the future. It is:

- aspirational because it describes the values of the business working to its very best;
- inspirational because it is deliberately designed to motivate staff to achieve the vision and for other stakeholders to with work with the business.

For example, in 2008, the vision statement for Marks & Spencer was 'To be the standard against which all others are measured.' Microsoft's vision was to 'Empower people through great software anytime, anyplace, and on any device'.

Vision statements can seem vague and hopelessly optimistic. For example, it is debatable whether any piece of software will empower people every time it is used. But the purpose of a

KNOWLEDGE

1. What is the difference between maximising profit, maximising sales revenue and maximising shareholder value?
2. Under what circumstances is survival likely to be the main aim of a business?
3. Why might a business aim to (a) maximise employee benefits and (b) maximise customer welfare?
4. Why might the aim of a small business be different from the aim of a large company?
5. What is the difference between managerial theories of the firm and behavioural theories?
6. 'Our vision: to be the UK's foremost provider of computer services in education, to delight our customers and give above average returns to our shareholders.' Explain what is meant by a 'vision statement', using this as an example.

KEYTERMS

Aim – the intention or purpose of a business; what a business is ultimately striving to achieve.

Behavioural theories of the firm – theories which suggest that businesses have multiple aims set by their main stakeholders.

Managerial theories of the firm – theories which suggest that businesses are controlled by managers who run them for their own benefit subject to the need to make enough profit to satisfy shareholders (profit satisficing).

Profit maximisation – earning the highest profit possible over a period of time.

Profit satisficing – making enough profit to satisfy the needs of shareholders whilst pursuing at least one other aim such as rewarding managers and directors.

Sales revenue maximisation – earning the highest possible revenue over a period of time.

Shareholder value – the value of a company to its owners over a period of time as measured by a combination of the size of its dividend payments and the rise in its share price.

Vision statement – a statement about the purpose and values of an organisation, outlining what it would like to be in an ideal world.

vision statement is not to describe the world accurately. It is to present a picture of a place where the business could be in an ideal world. Leaders therefore use vision statements as a way of communicating a message of change and progress. The vision statement shows the direction in which the organisation should be moving to become a better business.

Case Study: Sports Direct International plc

Sports Direct International plc is run by Mike Ashley, now a billionaire having floated a minority stake company on the London stock exchange. The deal valued the company at £2.2 billion, not bad for someone who left school at 16 and began trading from one shop in Maidenhead, Berkshire.

However, City investors have very quickly fallen out of love with the company. The share price of the company had halved within five months of flotation. Investors have complained that they cannot get sensible financial information from the company. The company is also being run in a highly irregular manner for a publicly quoted company. The non-executive chairman of the company, David Richardson, resigned recently in frustration at the way Michael Ashley regularly flouted corporate-governance guidelines.

Sports Direct is successful partly because it sources its stock cheaply, direct from the Far East. It uses those costs to slash the prices of big brands such as Adidas or Nike, making itself one of the most price competitive sports retailers in the country. Mike Ashley has also bought up a number of famous sports brands from sports equipment manufacturers such as as Lonsdale, Slazenger and Karrimor to rival sports retailers such as Gilesports and Lillywhites.

Before flotation, sales and profits rose together. By April 2007, sales were an annual £2 billion with profits before tax of nearly £200 million. However, within months of flotation, the company was issuing a profit warning as England failed to qualify for the World Cup, killing sales of England football shirts and other replica kit.

Michael Ashley was unrepentant, accusing the City of short-termism. 'I am building a long-term business', he said. 'I can't spend all my time worrying if the share price goes up and down. It may drop to 80p, but over three years I am betting it will be nearer 800p. I have built the company over 25 years and I am planning the next 25 years. But all anyone wants to talk to me about is what happened in June' (the time of the World Cup). He went on to say: 'The current share price is pathetic. I can't think of many safer long-term investments at this price. What annoys me the most is that some people are saying they didn't get what they bargained for (when buying shares). In my opinion they got exactly what it said on the tin.'

By his own admission, Michael Ashley is consumed by a 'ferocious' desire to succeed. He believes that one day Sports Direct could be a £4 billion company. His vision for the future is clear. Sports Direct will need to expand into mainland Europe, take 100 per cent ownership of more brands and acquire large strategic stakes in others.

Source: adapted from *The Sunday Times* 29.7.2007; en.wikipedia.org

(a) Evaluate whether Michael Ashley and City shareholders might have different aims for the company. (40 marks)

(b) Discuss what might be included in a vision statement for Sports Direct International. (40 marks)

101 Objectives and mission

Objectives

An OBJECTIVE or GOAL of a business is an outcome which allows a business to achieve its aims. Businesses can have a wide variety of objectives such as:

- to increase pre-tax profits by ten per cent over the next 12 months;
- to increase sales in the USA by five per cent over the next six months;
- to recruit an extra ten highly motivated staff in the marketing department over the next three months;
- to cut carbon emissions in European operations by five per cent over the next 24 months;
- to switch to sourcing 100 per cent organic food over the next three years.

Objectives should be practical outcomes from the operation of a business. One way of summarising this is to use SMART criteria. This says that objectives should be:

S **specific** - they must set out clearly what a business is attempting to achieve;
M **measurable** - they must be capable of being measured so that it can judged whether or not they have been achieved;
A **agreed** - everyone responsible for achieving an objective must have agreed with the objective and understood what it meant;
R **realistic** - the objective must be achievable given the resources available and the market conditions;
T **time specific** - the objective must specify over what period of time it is to be achieved.

Corporate objectives

CORPORATE OBJECTIVES are the objectives set by the most senior management and directors for the company as a whole.

Question 1.

A national brewery has set out its corporate objectives for the next three years. It faces a difficult market with very strong competition from other brewers. Its mass market brands have declined in sales over the past five years, although its specialist brews have increased. Overall, however, sales have been falling at over 2 per cent per year. Over the next two years, the company has set itself the objective of maintaining the value of sales and its market share for all beers. Profits are to rise by 3 per cent per annum.

Andy Snow is in charge of marketing. His job is now to draw up a set of objectives for his department given the corporate strategies. He knows that he needs to focus on issues such as sales volumes, prices, market segments and costs. He must be realistic about his objectives given the difficult trading conditions of the past few years.

(a) Suggest FOUR objectives for the marketing department of the company over the next two years and analyse how each might contribute to the achievement of the corporate objectives.

For example, multinational companies like BP, Wal-Mart (which owns Asda in the UK), Toyota or Vodafone have corporate objectives which cover the performance of the whole of their operations. Corporate objectives will differ from industry to industry. But they might include objectives such as the following:

- for profit before tax to grow by 15 per cent over the next three years;
- for sales revenue to grow by 30 per cent over the next five years;
- to increase market share by five per cent over the next two years;
- for dividends paid to shareholders to increase by six per cent per year over the next four years;
- for operating costs to fall by three per cent over the next 24 months;
- for carbon emissions from company operations to fall by 15 per cent over the next five years.

Corporate objectives for UK and US companies tend to be financial objectives. This is because corporate objectives are aimed at satisfying the needs of the owners of the company, the shareholders. Financial objectives are also easier to quantify at a corporate level than other possible objectives. For example, it is more difficult to quantity something like 'increase the motivation of staff' or 'increase consumer satisfaction with our products' when there are 30,000 staff and 20 million customers worldwide than 'increase profit before tax by two per cent' or 'increase sales by three per cent'.

Functional objectives

Medium to large sized companies are organised on a functional basis. They are organised into **departments**. Each department specialises in performing a particular type of task. There are many ways in which companies can be organised by function but by far the most common is to divide them into marketing, finance, operations and human resources. Depending upon the industry and company, these departments will be given different names. In some companies, there may be additional departments like a legal department where a particular function is very important. In some companies, responsibility for one of these functions may be split between two different departments. Marketing and sales, for example, may be split. In addition, large companies are likely to be split into a number of subsidiary companies, each of which, for example, will have its own marketing department or finance department. So a large company may have 20 different finance departments, 19 in subsidiary companies and one finance department at head office.

FUNCTIONAL OBJECTIVES (sometimes also called DEPARTMENTAL OBJECTIVES) are the objectives of each department. For example, the objectives of the marketing department might be to:

- increase sales by three per cent each quarter;
- stem the fall in sales in Asian market to two per cent per year;
- increase the ratio of visits to the online ordering website to sales placed from one in every ten to one in every eight on the company website;
- increase the sales placed with sales representatives from £50,000 per quarter to £52,000 per quarter;
- increase market share in the Eastern European market from five per cent to six per cent over the next three years.

Functional and corporate objectives

In the best run of companies, functional objectives will be completely tied to corporate objectives. In poorly run companies, functional objectives will lead to outcomes which have little to do with corporate objectives.

For example, a company might set itself the corporate objective of increasing operating profit by 4 per cent per year over the next 36 months. The company has no subsidiary companies and it is organised into four departments: marketing, finance, operations and human resources. Profit is the difference between revenues and costs. So marketing might be given the functional objective of increasing sales revenues by two per cent per year. The operations and human resources department might be given the functional objective of reducing staffing costs by one per cent per year through increased efficiency. Operations might also be given the functional objective of reducing the use of raw materials by one per cent per year whilst producing two per cent more output per year. If these functional objectives are achieved, then this will add up to the corporate objective of increasing operating profit by four per cent per year.

Mission statements

Large businesses often have a MISSION STATEMENT. This is a statement, written by the business of its purpose and primary objectives. It is about the here and now, in contrast to a **vision statement** which is about the future and where the business would like to be. A mission statement should describe in very general terms the core activities of a business. It might also include:

- a reference to the geographic markets in which the business operates;
- objectives of the business such as objectives about sales, profits, market share or shareholder value;
- attitudes and values towards stakeholders such as customers or workers;
- statements about moral or ethical issues.

A mission statement is written to communicate the purpose of a business to stakeholders such as workers and senior management. It should be highly memorable because employees should understand how their work contributes to the purpose of the whole business. Like a vision statement, it should be capable of inspiring those who read it or hear it.

Mission statements vary enormously in what they contain. Some are very brief, one line, one idea statements. Some are very complex. One line, one idea statements, such as 'Too make people happy' can be criticised for being too simple and not saying enough about the mission of the business. Mission statements which have a large number of ideas are probably too complex to serve their purpose. Disney's mission statement is: 'We create happiness by providing the finest in entertainment to people of all ages, everywhere' is an example of a good mission statement. It states the purpose of the company, which is to create happiness by providing entertainment. It says something about its markets which are worldwide and for people of all

Question 2.

Plastering Contractors (Stanmore) Ltd is a company based in the South East of England. It provides a range of specialist construction services including plastering to construction companies. It has a turnover of £50 million and a workforce of around 600 people. Its mission statement is: 'To assemble an able, highly trained, well respected team who, through large-scale operation, offer an excellent and unique service to the construction industry and also provide a just, equal, harmonious working environment with security of employment, job satisfaction and excellent remuneration for every member of staff, whether they be office based or trades workforce.'

Source: adapted from stanmoreltd.co.uk.

(a) Explain what is meant by a 'mission statement', using Plastering Contractors (Stanmore) Ltd as an example.
(b) What aspects of the business does the Stanmore mission statement emphasise?
(c) Given Stanmore's mission statement, what aims might the company have in terms of profit and sales?

KNOWLEDGE

1. Explain the difference between a functional objective and a corporate objective.
2. Why should objectives be SMART?
3. Why might corporate objectives mainly be expressed as financial objectives?
4. What is the purpose of a mission statement?

KEYTERMS

Corporate objectives - the objectives of a medium to large-sized business as a whole.

Functional (or departmental) objectives - the objectives of a department within a business.

Mission statement - a brief statement, written by the business, of its purpose and its objectives, designed to encapsulate its present operations.

Objective or goal - a target of or outcome for a business which allows it to achieve its aims.

SMART - acronym for the attributes of a good objective - specific, measurable, agreed, realistic and time specific.

ages. It is also inspirational, talking about the 'finest' entertainment.

A mission statement should always include something about the general objectives of a business. Specific SMART objectives should then flow out of a mission statement. Objectives about sales, market share and customer satisfaction, for example, can be developed. SMART objectives which contradict a mission statement indicate a business which is unlikely to be performing well. For example, Disney is a successful company in the long term when it earns profit because it creates 'happiness by providing the finest entertainment'. A company like Disney is unlikely to be successful in the long term if its objective is to earn profit with little regard for the happiness of its customers.

Case Study: Sainsbury's

J Sainsbury: mission statement

Our mission is to be the consumer's first choice for food, delivering products of outstanding quality and great service at a competitive cost through working 'faster, simpler and together'.

Source: adapted from company information.

In 2001, Sir Peter Davis, chief executive of Sainsbury's had told shareholders that his 'business transformation' programme would deliver a saving of £600 million every year by the end of the programme in 2004. In October 2004, a new chief executive, Justin King, said the programme had failed. He wrote off £260 million against ineffective supply chain equipment and ineffective IT systems. Worse than that, the failure had lost loyal customers and those still shopping at Sainsbury's were spending less.

At the heart of the problems were four brand new automated warehouses designed to handle all the products being delivered to the Sainsbury's chain in the UK. They should have delivered cost savings through economies of scale in distribution. Instead, they led to a breakdown in communication between the individual stores and the suppliers. IT systems should have matched what was being sold in a store with deliveries from the automated warehouses. What actually happened was that stores were failing to get deliveries on time. The result was 'stockouts': empty shelves in the stores where there should have been products for sale. If it isn't on the shelves, the customer can't buy it and so sales fall. Equally, some Sainsbury's customers got so frustrated by continual stockouts that they abandoned Sainsbury's altogether and did their regular shop at another supermarket.

But there was another problem. Stock was in the system but not in the right place. So, for example, fresh fruit and vegetables which should have been on display for sale in a supermarket was languishing in one of the warehouses undelivered. The result was a considerable increase in wastage. Instead of being bought by customers, it was being thrown away.

When Justin King took over as chief executive in 2004, he quickly appointed Lawrence Christensen, the former operations manager at Safeway, to sort out the supply chain problem. Lawrence Christensen put in place a number of solutions which haven't completely solved the problem but, where fully implemented, have resulted in a fall in stockouts of 75 per cent. He went back to Witron and Siemens, the two groups behind the equipment IT systems, to try to make improvements. He put in extra labour to manually sort products where needed. He is also implementing a 'step change' programme across all Sainsbury's stores to put clear systems in place around deliveries, stock auditing and making sure the inventory was correct.

Sainsbury's supply problems were symptomatic of much wider problems. In the 1990s, it lost market leadership to Tesco. By 2008, Tesco had one third of the grocery market, twice the market share of Sainsbury's. The company has to address the fact that it isn't the cheapest supermarket at which to shop, customers don't seem to value the differences between it and its competitors and yet it aims to be a distinctive mass market grocery retailer. It cannot afford to make mistakes at the functional level if it is to stand any chance of closing the gap between itself and Tesco.

Source: adapted from the *Financial Times*.

(a) A functional objective of the 'business transformation' programme was to deliver savings of £600 million per year. Evaluate the extent to which the failure of the programme might have affected Sainsbury's ability to achieve its corporate objectives. (40 marks)

(b) Evaluate the extent to which Sainsbury's achieved the objectives set out in its mission statement in the early 2000s. (40 marks)

102 Strategy

Strategy

Businesses have **aims** which they hope to achieve through their **objectives**. But objectives are not achieved through chance. Many businesses **plan** how to achieve their objectives. Planning to achieve objectives is known as STRATEGY.

The term 'strategy' in business can be used in a variety of ways.

- Organisations have strategies to achieve their aims. The organisation might be the whole company which then has a **corporate strategy**. Or it might be part of a large business which has a **divisional** or **business unit strategy**. Or it might be a department within a business which has a **departmental strategy**.
- Organisations use strategies to achieve their objectives. Strategies might include **business strategies**. These are concerned with how a business can gain a competitive advantage in the market place. They deal with issues such as product differentiation, cost advantages and market niches. Business strategies are linked to **global strategies** for larger companies.

This unit concentrates on corporate, divisional and departmental strategies. Business strategies and global strategies are discussed in detail in the unit titled 'Competition and business strategies' .

Corporate strategy

CORPORATE STRATEGY deals with how to achieve the main objectives of the whole business. It is concerned with plans and policies which allocate resources in a way which will allow the business to achieve its corporate objectives. It is also concerned with two key issues.

- Whether or not the size of the business will give it the resources to achieve the objectives set.
- What range of activities the business needs to undertake to achieve its goals.

For many businesses, concentrating on a single industry or market is the appropriate corporate strategy. By doing this, they

Question 1.

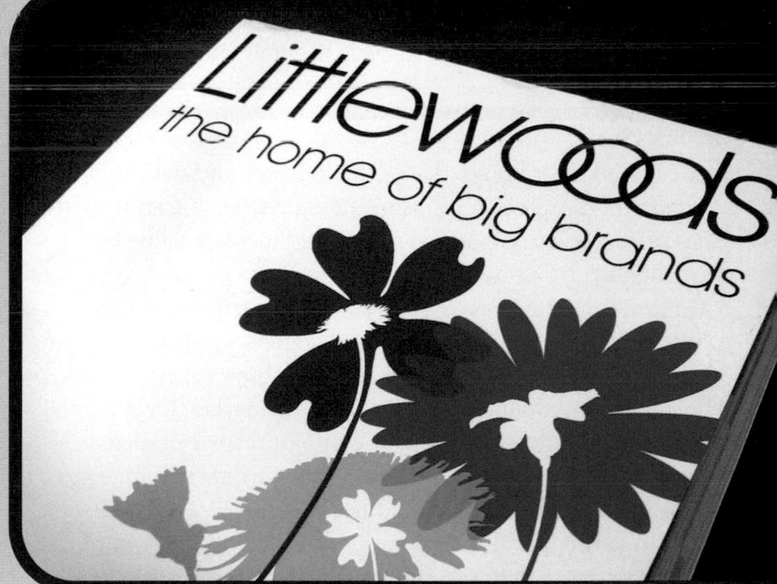

Littlewoods was once one of the UK's largest private limited companies. It owned a football pools company (a form of gambling) and was a major retailer through its home shopping catalogue and a chain of high street stores. The arrival of the National Lottery in 1994 took away much of the market for football pools and, in 2000, Littlewoods sold its pools business for £161 million. The Littlewoods home shopping catalogue and high store stores had also been struggling against fierce competition and was barely profitable at best. In 2002, the rest of the company was sold for £750 million to the Barclay brothers, entrepreneurs who had a track record of turning around ailing companies. In 2003, the Barclay brothers bought the home shopping and catalogues business of GUS plc. This was made up of a number of catalogue brands, including Additions Direct, Great Universal, Marshall Ward, Choice and Kays.

Following a strategic review, the 120 branch high street chain of Littlewoods stores was sold by the Barclay brothers to Associated British Foods for £409 million. Associated British Foods converted some of these into branches of Primark, a clothing subsidiary which it owned. The rest were sold to other retailers. Littlewoods, the retail chain, disappeared from Britain's high streets in 2006.

The Littlewoods catalogue operation was merged with the rest of the company's catalogue brands to form Littlewoods Shop Direct Group with sales of over £2 billion per year. More than £200 million has been spent rationalising and re-organising the portfolio of catalogues, head offices, warehouse operations and call centres. The Littlewoods catalogue itself was relaunched in 2007. Traditionally, the Littlewoods catalogue had a reputation for selling mainly to the lower D and E socio-economic groups. Today, the catalogue has gone up-market. Brands such as Bench, Miss Sixty, Replay and Diesel are now stocked. Trinny and Susannah, famous fashion experts from their TV show, have been recruited to feature in an advertising campaign. Very importantly, large amounts have been invested in developing an online store which is fun and friendly. Today, Littlewoods Shop Direct Group is the UK's fourth largest Internet retailer behind Amazon, Tesco and Argos. It has targets to double Internet sales over the next three years.

Source: adapted from *The Sunday Times*, 8.4.2007; en.wikipedia.org

(a) Corporate strategy is concerned with the size of the business and the markets in which it operates. Explain why (i) selling off the Littlewoods high street chain and (ii) creating Littlewoods Shop Direct Group were examples of corporate strategy.

(b) Evaluate whether the corporate strategy for Littlewoods Shop Direct Group is likely to be successful.

Question 2.

Burberry is a luxury goods brand. It has its roots in the manufacture and sale of trench coats designed with the characteristic Burberry checks. Today it has expanded beyond outerwear to handbags, accessories and other apparel. In 2006-2007, it conducted a major strategic review. Out of this came five strategic themes, to:

- grow and leverage its franchise operations;
- intensify the development of non-apparel (i.e. non-clothes) sales and products;
- accelerate growth from its chain of retail shops;
- invest in under-penetrated areas;
- pursue excellence in its operations.

As part of continued investment in 'under-penetrated areas', the company continues to expand in North America. In 2007-2008, it planned to open another ten new stores in the USA bringing its total to 50. Stacey Cartwright, finance director, said: 'There are still further opportunities beyond that in the US and if you look at our peers they have between 70 and 100 stores there. We would be targeting those sorts of numbers.' The US market is attractive for a number of reasons, not least because it is home to an increasing number of consumers who favour luxury goods and accessories. Some also believe that the Burberry brand is more highly rates overseas than in the UK.

2007 also saw a strategic milestone for the company. For the first time, revenues from its own chain of retail stores exceeded the value of sales of Burberry merchandise through other retail channels.

Source: adapted from Burberry Group plc, *Annual Report and Accounts, 2007*; *The Financial Times*, 25.5.2007.

(a) Explain the link between Burberry opening another ten stores in the USA and its strategic direction.

(b) Evaluate whether expanding further in the USA by opening its own stores might help Burberry to achieve its strategic objectives of raising sales and profits.

can exploit their knowledge of the industry and develop their competitive strategies. A business pursuing such a strategy then has to decide on its optimal size. Could it create value by growing in size or perhaps downsizing?

However, a business may be able to create value for its owners by moving into other markets. It may grow **vertically**, moving into markets which either it sells into or buys from. It may grow **horizontally**, expanding into its existing market. Or it may become a **conglomerate**, moving into unrelated markets. Equally, it may grow **organically** from within. Or it may grow by **taking over** or **merging** with other businesses. A key issue in growth is whether it will create **synergies**. Will the sum of the parts be greater than the individual parts working as completely separate businesses?

Equally, a large business should consider whether it can create value by **divesting** itself of businesses. Parts of the business may be underperforming. This may be because it is in a low profit industry. Or perhaps it is a relatively small part of the whole business and insufficient management time is being devoted to its running. Equally, since the 1990s, there has been a growing trend for businesses to **outsource** functions. The argument is that a business needs to concentrate on its CORE CAPABILITIES (or CORE COMPETENCES): what it is best at doing. For example, a business which specialises in manufacturing canned food does not necessarily have an expertise in logistics (getting raw materials to the business and then transporting finished products to customers). It might be more cost-effective to outsource logistics to a specialist logistics company.

Fifty years ago, it became fashionable for large businesses to be conglomerates. A conglomerate is a business which produces a range of products in widely differing markets. A steel producer which also owns a fast food change would be an example. Today, it is more fashionable for businesses to focus on a narrow range of markets in which senior management have an expertise. A water company should, therefore, concentrate on providing water management services. A train operator should concentrate on providing train services. A key feature of corporate strategy is deciding which part of the business should be retained and which should be sold off or closed down.

Strategic direction and strategic gaps

Corporate and business strategies are corporate and business plans which show how a business can achieve its objectives in the medium to long term. The strategic plan may be to do what the business currently doing, only more effectively. So the business may see itself making the same products in the same places and selling into the same markets in three to five years' time. Alternatively, the strategic plan may be to move the business in a new direction. For example, a UK manufacturer may have a plan which says that the value of products sourced (i.e. made) in the UK should fall from 60 per cent to 25 per cent as production is shifted off shore to low wage economies, such as Eastern Europe or the Far East. Or the plan may be to move into adjacent higher profit margin markets. A fixed line telephone company, for example, may plan to acquire a mobile telephone company in the medium term. So the STRATEGIC DIRECTION of a business is the path which a business plans to follow to achieve its goals.

Once the strategic direction has been established, a detailed set of plans will be produced. These will enable lower and middle management to make the correct decisions to ensure the success of the plan. The period of time for which detailed plans can be made is called the PLANNING HORIZON. This might be from one to three years for a business in a stable market environment.

Sometimes, though, a STRATEGIC GAP may emerge between what a business wants to achieve and its objectives. For example, a company may have as one of its objectives that it will achieve a 20 per cent growth in sales each year. A new strategic plan is worked out and senior managers find that, given the existing strategic direction of the company, it is most unlikely that this objective will be realised over the next three to five years. Senior management, therefore, either has to produce a different strategy to **close the strategic gap**, or it has to modify its objectives. A new strategy might be to expand sales overseas. Or it might be to enter new product markets. Or sales might be increased by spending more on R&D to develop new products in existing markets.

Business unit or divisional strategy

Corporate strategy relates to objectives and plans for the whole company or corporation. It is a term used in connection with medium to large companies. Large companies are often split up into divisions. Some choose to do this geographically with, for example, a North American division, a European division and a division which covers the rest of the world. Others choose to do this by product, for example with a building materials division and an engineering division. Each division (or business unit) will have its own DIVISIONAL or BUSINESS UNIT STRATEGY. Divisions themselves may contain a number of subsidiary companies, each of which will have their own strategies. Business unit or divisional strategies should contribute to the realisation of the objectives of whole company. For example, if an objective of the whole company is to raise worldwide sales by ten per cent over three years, then the strategies of the different divisions of the company must show how this will be achieved.

Functional or department strategies

Medium to large sized companies are organised on a functional basis. They are organised into **departments**. Each department specialises in performing a particular type of task. There are many ways in which companies can be organised by function, but by far the most common is to divide them into marketing, finance, operations and human resources. Depending upon the industry and company, these departments will be given different names. In some companies, there may be additional departments like a legal department where an additional function is very important. In some companies, responsibility for one of these functions may be split between two different departments. Marketing and sales, for example, may be split. In addition, large companies are likely to be split into a number of subsidiary companies, each of which, for example, will have its own marketing department or finance department. So a large company may have 20 different finance departments, nineteen in 19 subsidiary companies and one finance department at head office.

Each of these departments should have a FUNCTIONAL or (DEPARTMENTAL) STRATEGY which details plans of how it will meet its objectives. For example, the operations department may be given a functional objective of cutting costs per unit produced by four per cent over the next three years. It then has to plan how to achieve this objective. It may decide that this can be achieved by sourcing raw materials more cheaply saving two per cent in costs, increasing labour efficiency by five per cent, saving one per cent in costs after the annual pay rise has been taken into account, and reducing wastage saving a further one per cent. These plans together with the objectives form the departmental strategy for the coming 36 months.

Strategy and tactics

Strategies set out the long-term objectives and the plan for how they will be achieved. **Tactics** are short-term strategies to achieve limited objectives. For example, a corporate (or strategic) objective might be to grow the North American market by 50 per cent over the next five years and the plan to achieve the objective is to grow the company both organically and through acquisition. One year into the strategy, a company in the North American market may come up for sale. A tactic might be to take it over to help achieve the corporate objective. Two years into the strategy, a new piece of equipment may come onto the market which would allow the company to improve considerably the quality of its some of its products. A tactic could be to buy the equipment to make the company's products more attractive to customers.

Figure 1: Hierarchy of strategy within a large company

Corporate strategy
|
Business unit or divisional strategy
|
Functional strategy

KNOWLEDGE

1. Explain the possible connection between corporate strategy and downsizing.
2. Why is a long decision to move into a new market an example of corporate strategy?
3. What is the link between corporate strategy and the planning horizon?
4. 'The company intends to close its strategic gap by increasing its marketing spending.' Explain what this means.
5. Explain the difference between corporate strategy and (a) functional strategy; (b) competitive strategy.
6. Explain how business divisional strategies might be linked to corporate strategies.
7. Explain the relationship between a functional objective and functional strategy.
8. What is the difference between a long-term strategy and a tactic?

KEYTERMS

Business unit (or divisional) strategy - strategy of a division or a subsidiary company owned by a parent company.
Core capabilities (or competences) - the most important strengths of a business, which should be central to decision making when corporate strategy is devised.
Corporate strategy - the plans and policies developed to meet a company's objectives. It is concerned with what range of activities the business needs to undertake in order to achieve its goals. It is also concerned with whether the size of the business organisation makes it capable of achieving the objectives set.
Divisional (or business unit) strategy - strategy of a division within a business, such as a geographical division or a product-related division.
Functional (or departmental) strategy - strategy of a department within a business.
Planning horizon - the period of time for which detailed plans have been made which will allow a business to achieve its strategic objectives. This may vary from business to business from a few months to a few years, in part depending upon the pace of change in the markets into which a business sells.
Strategic direction - the path which a business plans to follow to achieve its goals.
Strategic gap - the difference between where a business predicts it will be in the medium to long term and where it wants to be as shown by the objectives it has set itself.
Strategy - planning used to achieve objective by business.

Case Study: Glenaden Shirts

There is almost nothing left today of what was once one of Britain's major industries. But Glenaden Shirts, based in Derry in Northern Ireland, has survived the closure of most of the UK's textile industry. However, survival was a close thing. In 2000, the owner of the Derry factory, Coats Viyella, moved to close it and it was only saved by a management buy-out led by Andrew Lowden, now managing director. Last year, a controlling stake in the company was bought by Amicus Capital, a private equity company, which installed Terry McCartney as Chairman.

Glenaden Shirts has gone from strength to strength since 2000. According to Terry McCartney, 'They're becoming a supplier of branded consumer goods rather than an old-fashioned textile company.' Their location in Northern Ireland puts them at a cost disadvantage to competitors elsewhere in the world. Wages of staff, for example, are many times what would be paid to staff if they were in China or India. However, the company has transformed a cost disadvantage into a marketing advantage. Unlike competitors, it can put a 'Made in Britain' label on its products. 'There are a growing number of consumers who value the Made in Britain label. Its a sort of snobbery I suppose,' says Andrew Lowden. The Made in Britain label particularly helps the 45 per cent of sales overseas. In markets such as the USA and Japan, the label carries considerable cachet. 'A Wall Street banker doesn't want to find what he thought was a British-made shirt was, in fact, made in Taiwan,' says Terry McCartney. In the UK, the company has moved away from supplying mainly City gents in London to marketing its products through a network of independent retailers in cities and towns outside London for professionals who want a tidy work shirt or a fashion piece for a special occasion.

Glenaden makes 300,000 high quality shirts a year. It has two parts to its business. There is a sub-contracting arm which supplies Thomas Pink, the UK's largest upmarket shirt retailer, and other Jermyn Street retailers. There is also an operation which makes shirts for sale under the Thread & Bone label owned by Glenaden. The company took a further step towards achieving its goal this week by buying Coles, an old Jermyn Street brand that had closed its London shops and had become an Internet-based mail-order business. Coles, it believes, will fit neatly into this portfolio.

Source: adapted from *The Financial Times*, 20.1.2007.

Note: Jermyn Street is a street in central London famous for shirtmakers. Just as Saville Row is associated with fine cut suits and tailoring, so Jermyn Street is associated with the production and sale of up-market finest quality shirts.

(a) 'They're becoming a supplier of branded consumer goods rather than an old-fashioned textile company.' Define 'corporate strategy' and suggest what might be the corporate strategy of Glenaden. (40 marks)
(b) Evaluate the success of Glenaden's corporate strategy. (40 marks)

103 Planning

Purpose of corporate plans

Planning is important at every stage of the life of a business and at every level. For example, a small business starting up is far more likely to survive if it has drawn up a business plan than if it hasn't. A department of a large company is more likely to achieve its objectives if it has drawn up a functional or departmental plan. Similarly, a large business is far more likely to achieve its goals if it has drawn up a **corporate plan**.

Corporate plans have a variety of purposes.

- Corporate plans help businesses to define their objectives. In theory, objectives are set before the plan is devised. In practice, objectives may have to be modified if the plan shows that there is little chance of the objectives being met. For example, an objective may be to increase sales in the Far East by 20 per cent per year. But research undertaken whilst drawing up the plan may show that this would lead to the company increasing its market share in the Far East from 10 per cent to 30 per cent which, given the response of competitors, would be almost impossible to achieve. So this sales objective may have to be modified.
- Corporate plans identify the path over time that needs to be taken to achieve corporate objectives. It maps out corporate strategy. For example, a company objective may be to increase sales in the North American market by 50 per cent within four years. The plan may state that the company will have to make an acquisition of an existing company within 2 years to increase its sales by 30 per cent. The other 20 per cent will come from organic, internal growth of the business including the company which has been taken over.
- Corporate plans should identify risks and probabilities. The business environment is constantly changing. Favourable opportunities arise unexpectedly which the company should take advantage of. Equally, the company may be knocked off course by unexpected adverse events. The corporate plan should allow for these eventualities where it is possible to identify the probability of risk and opportunity. The unit called '**Contingency planning**' discusses planning for future crises. Corporate planning, however, cannot effectively deal with opportunities and risks that cannot be identified or quantified. Planning therefore has its limitations.

Developing a corporate plan

There are many ways of developing a corporate plan but one standard model is to develop a strategy systematically as follows.

1. Clarify objectives.
2. Gain information about the business and its external environment by carrying out an audit.
3. Summarise and analyse the results of the audit by carrying out a SWOT analysis.
4. Make plans to achieve the objectives set.
5. Implement the plans.
6. Review and evaluate outcomes.
7. Prepare the next plan.

Each of these stages, shown in Figure 1, will now be considered in detail.

Clarifying the objectives of the business

The first stage of developing a strategy is to identify objectives. Unless objectives are clear, it will be impossible to devise plans to achieve them. There are different types of objective which can be identified for planning purposes.

Strategic objectives STRATEGIC OBJECTIVES are the main objectives of a business. They are the objectives which will help the business achieve its **aims**. They will almost certainly be LONG-TERM OBJECTIVES. This is because it is most unlikely that the aims of a business can be achieved in, say, the next six or 12 months. Long-term objectives tend to be objectives for the next three to five years.

Tactical objectives TACTICAL OBJECTIVES are SHORT TERM OBJECTIVES. They are objectives which will help

Figure 1: Formulating a strategy

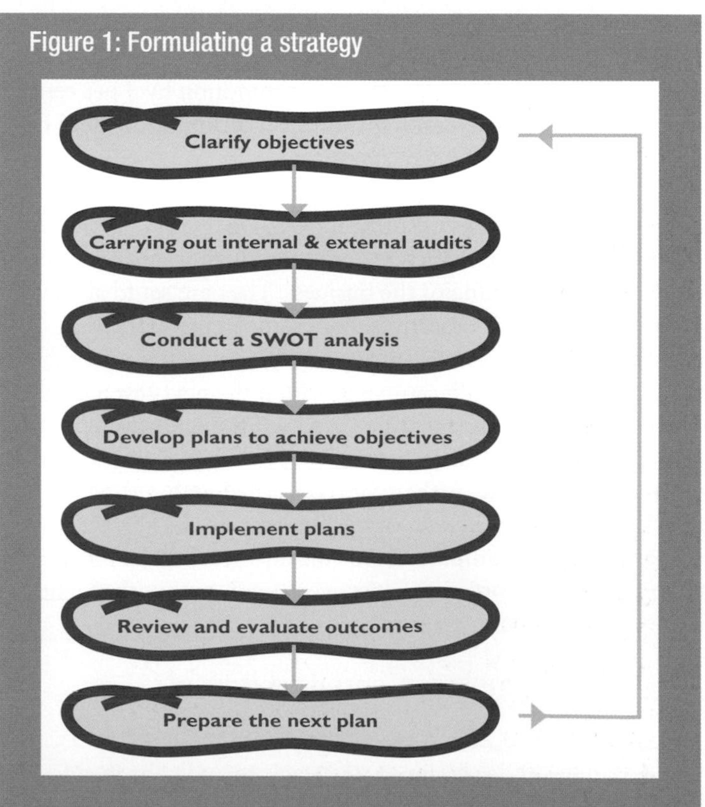

Question 1.

Sixcor is a UK private limited company which manufactures food equipment for sale to businesses in the food processing and food retailing sectors. Last year was a difficult year for the company. Sales were down 5 per cent whilst profits fell from £3.5 million the previous year to £0.1 million. Part of the problem was the strength of the pound. Overseas orders were lost to competitors on price. Those orders which Sixcor did gain were at such low prices that they were barely profitable. In the UK market, Sixcor suffered because of the movement of the economy into a mild recession.

However, problems within the company didn't help the situation. During the year, the company moved to a larger site so that production could be expanded. But there was considerable disruption during the move. An estimated four weeks' production was lost as a result. There were continued difficulties recruiting sufficient skilled production workers and as a consequence some orders were sent out late. The marketing department reported that the failure to deliver some goods on time made it more difficult to get repeat orders, whilst the finance department warned that the situation adversely affected cash flow.

The company continued to roll out new products in response to changing customer needs and to advances in technology. Competitors too, though, were bringing out innovative products, making the trading environment difficult. There was considerable debate at board level about whether the expenditure on research and development for new products was too great or too little. Any increase in spending would hit profits in the short term, but could enhance profits in the long term if it gave the company a competitive advantage.

(a) (a) From the information given list (i) six issues which would be included in an internal audit of the business and (ii) six issues which would be included in an external audit. (b) would any issues be included in a PESTLE analysis?

(b) Which problems facing the company last year were short-term problems and therefore unlikely to affect performance in the long term?

(c) Evaluate the most important problems facing the business in the long term.

achieve the strategic objectives set by the business. For example, a strategic objective might be to increase sales by 10 per cent per year over the next five years. A tactical objective to help achieve this could be to increase spending on promotion by 5 per cent over the next year. Increased spending on promotion would be a TACTIC employed by the business.

Operational objectives OPERATIONAL OBJECTIVES are very short-term objectives which are typically small scale and cover the day-to-day running of the business. They are set to achieve tactical and strategic objectives. For example, the marketing department might set itself the operational objective of finalising an advertising campaign within the next seven days. The production department may set itself the objective of getting an important order out on time in 21 days' time.

Strategic planning is therefore concerned with setting out how the strategic objectives of the business can be achieved over the long term. An annual plan for the business will be more concerned with short-term objectives. It will set out the tactics to be used to achieve this year's part of the strategic plan.

Auditing the business and its external environment

The next stage in developing a strategy is to audit the business and its external environment.

The internal audit An INTERNAL AUDIT is an analysis of the business itself and how it operates. It attempts to identify strengths and weaknesses of its operations. It would cover areas such as:

- products and their cost, quality and development;
- finance including profit, assets and cash flow;
- production, including capacity, quality, efficiency and stock management;
- internal organisation including divisional and departmental structures;
- human resources including skills, training and recruitment.

In a large business, the internal audit might be conducted by outside **management consultants**, brought into the business to conduct an independent analysis.

The external audit An EXTERNAL AUDIT is an analysis of the environment in which the business operates and over which it has little or no control. It can be split into three parts: the market, competition and the political, economic, social and technological environment.

The audit should analyse the **market** or markets in which the business operates. For example, it should analyse:

- the size and growth of the market;
- the characteristics of the customers in the market;

- the products on offer;
- the pricing structure;
- how products are distributed;
- how products are promoted;
- industry practices, such as whether there is a **trade association** or government regulation.

The audit should also analyse the **competition** in the market. The nature of the competitive environment will be important in setting strategy. For example it should analyse:

- the structure of the industry including the number and size of competitors, their production capacity and marketing methods, the likelihood of new entrants to the market or businesses leaving the industry;
- finance including profits of competitors, their investment programmes, costs, revenues, cash flow and assets.

Third, the external audit should use PESTLE ANALYSIS. This is analysis of the political (P), economic (E), social (S), technological (T), legal(L) and environmental (E) issues relevant to the business. It is also sometimes called PEST-G analysis (Political, Economic, Social, Technological and Green factors).

- Politics, government, taxes and the law affect the business. For example, the tax environment will affect the price of goods (through VAT), investment (through corporation tax) and the number of workers employed (through National Insurance contributions and pension legislation).
- The economic environment is very important to the business. Whether the economy is likely to be in boom or recession could have an important impact on sales. Levels of unemployment will affect both customer demand and ability to recruit workers. Inflation will impact on pricing policy. Barriers to international trade will affect exports.
- The social and cultural environment covers areas such as education, demographics (i.e. population), migration, religion, roles of men and women and changing consumer tastes. For example, more and more women going out to work has increased the market size for ready made meals and takeaway food. Increased educational attainment over the past 40 years has increased the skills of the workforce.
- Changes in technology can have a radical impact on businesses. Manufacturing is continuing to be transformed by automated machinery. Computers have eliminated large numbers of jobs in banking and insurance. Quality has been considerably improved through applications of information technology.
- Legilsation can affect businesses. For example, customers and suppliers will have certain rights in law which need to be taken account of when trading. Trade union legislation

Question 2.

Phipps is a company which specialises in producing colour pigments. These are used to colour everything from cans, wrappers, cartons, plastic products, textiles to magazines. It is a global company with customers and plants across the world. Its fastest growing market is in the Far East where it has plants in China and Thailand. But it faces intense competition at the bottom end of its market from Far Eastern producers who have even lower costs of production than Phipps.

Economists are predicting a major slowdown in the world economy over the next 12 months led by a recession in the United States. The Japanese market remains weak following a decade of weak or no economic growth. The combination of weakness in demand in the United States and Japan threatens to make any recession in the Far East severe and deep.

Three weeks ago, Graham Downy, the managing director (MD) of the company for the past ten years, left to take up an appointment with a larger rival company. This has left a major gap in the senior management team. Graham was considered to be an excellent MD and had overseen substantial growth in the company. It could take months to find a suitable replacement.

An audit of two plants in the United States found that management there had allowed a substantial stock of pigment to build up. The management has since been replaced, but decisions about what to do with the excess stock have yet to be taken.

A new pigment suitable for metal coatings is about to be launched. It has superior colour retention qualities, but is more expensive to produce than traditional pigments for metal coatings. A debate about pricing policy is taking place within the company.

(a) What is meant by SWOT analysis?
(b) Use SWOT analysis to discuss the future of Phipps.

will affect employment. Controls on advertising will affect promotion.

- The impact of environmental changes have been felt by some businesses more than others. Extraction companies, such as oil companies or copper mining companies, have been forced to change the way in which they work because of pressure from environmental groups and governments. Businesses need to be seen to be green if only to create a positive public relations image with both their workers and with consumers.

SWOT analysis

The internal and external audits should yield a large amount of information about the business and its external environment. However, this information needs to be summarised. There are many ways of doing this, but one useful way is to complete a SWOT ANALYSIS.

SWOT analysis involves looking at the internal strengths and weaknesses of a business and its external opportunities and threats.

Strengths These are positive aspects of the business arising from the **internal audit**. For example, it might have a loyal customer base, its products may be seen as amongst the best in the market or it might make large profits.

Weaknesses These are the negative aspects of the business arising from the **internal audit**. For example, fault rates in production may be high, recent promotional campaigns may have failed or staff training may be poor.

Opportunities The **external audit** should show up what opportunities are available to the business. For example, there may be an opportunity to expand into a new market with existing products. Or the weakness of a competitor may enable the business to gain market share. Or technological developments may permit the development of new products.

Threats The **external audit** should also show up what threats face the business. For example, falling numbers of customers in the 16-25 age group may threaten the sales of the business. The government may be about to increase the minimum wage, which would push up the wage bill and overall costs for the business. The business may be liable to come under attack from environmental pressure groups because of its poor record on environmental issues.

SWOT analysis is often carried out in brainstorming sessions before being written up. It can be a powerful way of summarising and building upon the results of internal and external audits.

Developing strategies

The next stage is to develop strategies. The business has identified its objectives. It has carried out an audit and analysed its internal strengths and weaknesses, as well as the opportunities and threats posed by the external environment. So it can now plan how to use its strengths and overcome its weaknesses and seize the opportunities presented, whilst countering threats, to achieve its objectives.

Planning can take place at a variety of levels. There could be a 3-5 year plan for a business, prepared by senior management and designed to meet its corporate objectives. This will have far less detail in it than a departmental plan for the next 12 months by the production department designed to meet short-term tactical objectives.

Implementing plans

Plans need to be implemented on a day-to-day basis. The plan should inform workers about the actions they take and the decisions they make. For example, if the plan is to take a product upmarket, then managers should work on improving quality and making sure that the supply channels for the product reflect this. If the plan is to increase profit margins by cutting costs, then a cost reduction plan should be implemented.

Reviewing and evaluating outcomes

Having implemented a strategy, it is important for it to be reviewed. Did it achieve the objectives set? If not, what was achieved? What lessons can be learnt from the failures encountered?

Other methods of developing a corporate plan

There are many different ways of developing a corporate plan. What is outlined above is a progression from:

- strategic objectives, objectives set at a corporate level, to;
- strategic analysis, analysing where the business is now, its markets and the external environment, through tools such as SWOT analysis and PESTLE analysis to;
- making STRATEGIC CHOICES, deciding on where the business is aiming to be, developing strategies to use given corporate objectives and the outcome of strategic analysis to;
- STRATEGIC IMPLEMENTATION, putting the plan into operation, and STRATEGIC MANAGEMENT, following the plan on a day-to-day basis to a;
- STRATEGIC REVIEW, reviewing current strategies and drawing up new strategic plans.

However, there is a wide variety of alternatives ways to create a corporate plan. For example, an alternative strategic framework is shown in Figure 2. It starts from strategic analysis and moves to strategic choice and then to strategic implementation.

Another alternative is shown in Figure 3. It has four stages.

- **Draw** – what are the aims and objectives to be achieved; where does the business want to be in the future?
- **See** – where is the business today and what is the strategic gap between the business today and where it wants to be in the future?

- **Think** – what actions need to be taken to close the strategic gap?
- **Plan** – what resources are needed to execute the plan of action?

Whatever order is used to construct a strategic plan, the key elements are the same: objectives, analysis, implementation and review.

The value of corporate plans

Corporate planning is an essential tool for large companies. It helps them map out a path which will allow them to achieve their objectives and their aims. However, there are many reasons why corporate plans often prove to be a failure.

Unrealistic objectives The objectives may have been unrealistic. There is often a tendency for managers to set objectives which are too ambitious. When set, they impress shareholders or more senior managers. But they prove to be unattainable.

Conflicting objectives The objectives may have been poorly thought out and may conflict. This can often be a problem when different layers of an organisation set objectives. The objectives of the marketing department, for example, may conflict with those of the production department. The overall aim of the business might be to increase profit. The marketing department sets itself the objective of moving its product range upmarket, selling fewer goods but at a high price and profit margin. The production department, on the other hand, sets itself the objective of increasing production to exploit economies of scale, reducing cost per unit and so increasing the potential for profit.

Poor planning Plans to achieve objectives may be badly thought out. For example, the production department may plan to increase production by 20 per cent but fail to build sufficient spending on new equipment into its plan to achieve this.

Poor execution of the plan Even if objectives and plans have been carefully and realistically thought through, workers may not implement them. It could be that the workers lack the skills and training to do so. It could also be that workers are not motivated to implement the plan. Many workers see planning and objective setting as a distraction from the 'real work' of making a sale or getting an order out to a customer. So they do what they think is best, rather than following the plan. The plan may also conflict with the interests of individual workers. For example, a plan may call for a 10 per cent reduction in staff in the production department. But the production manager in charge may resist the job losses to defend his or her staff. Or the production manager may think that making workers redundant will be far more time consuming and less pleasant than getting senior management to change their decision.

Corporate culture Many businesses find it difficult to make planned changes because of the **business** (or **corporate**) **culture** they face. This is a set of ways of doing things and unwritten rules which dominate how the business is run in practice. If the new plan conflicts with the culture of the business, frequently the plan fails. This is one reason why many large businesses stress the importance of a **change culture** in their organisation. Unless staff are prepared to change, there is often little chance of planning being effective because plans often call for change.

Uncontrollable variables Even if a strategy is well executed within a business, events outside the control of the business can

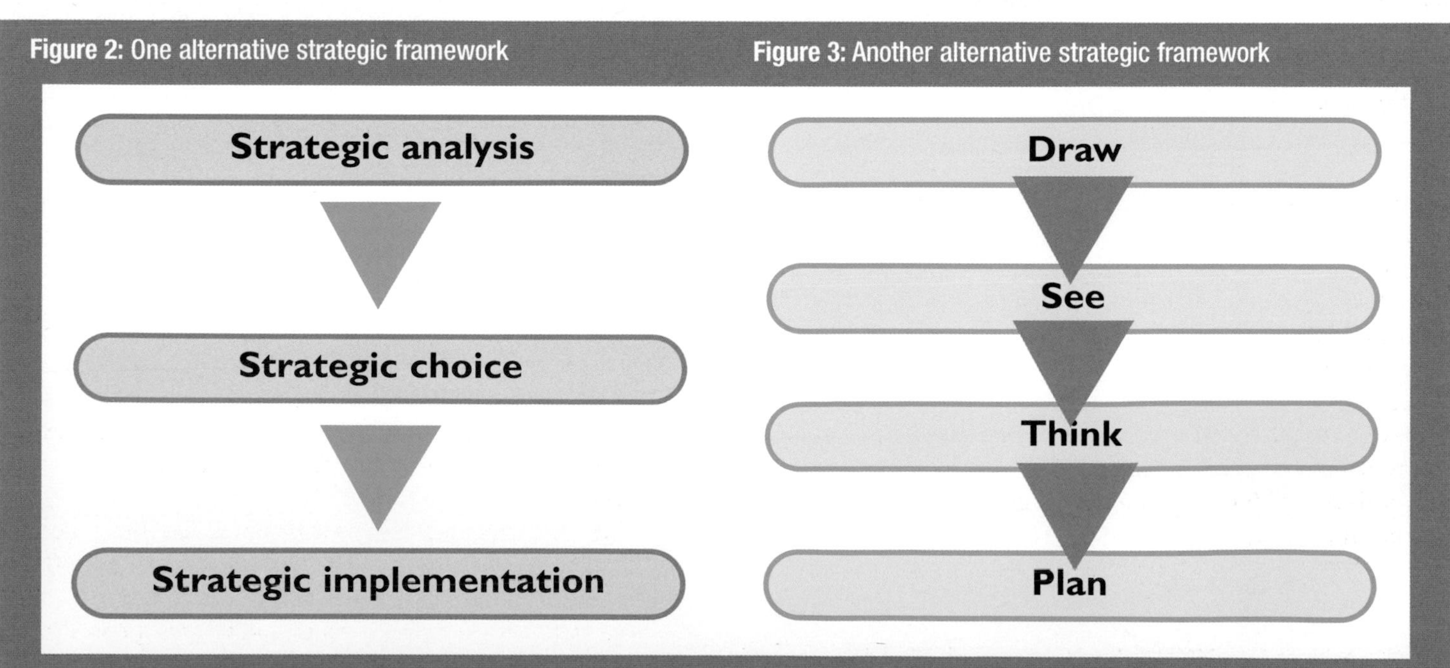

Figure 2: One alternative strategic framework

Figure 3: Another alternative strategic framework

knock the strategy off course. For example, the economy may go into **recession**. This can have a severe effect on sales and profitability. New technology may make existing products obsolete far quicker than expected. Or severe weather conditions may affect production or demand in unexpected ways.

KEYTERMS

External audit - an audit of the external environment in which a business finds itself, such as the market within which it operates or government restrictions on its operations.
Internal audit - an analysis of the business itself and how it operates.
Long-term objective - objective of a business over the next 3-5 years.
Operational objectives - Small scale, short-term objectives to be achieved on a day-to-day basis.
Short-term objectives - objectives of a business which are likely to be achieved within the next 12 months.
Strategic analysis - auditing the internal and external environments of the business to understand where the business is today and how it could develop in the future.
Strategic choices - alternatives which can be taken at a strategic level.
Strategic implementation - putting a strategic plan into operation.
Strategic management - operating a business in accordance with strategic objectives and strategic planning.
Strategic review – evaluating current strategies and drawing up new strategic plans.
Strategic objectives - the main objectives of a business designed to achieve its aims.
SWOT analysis - analysis of the internal strengths and weaknesses of a business and the opportunities and threats presented by its external environment.
Tactical objectives - short-term objectives which help a business to achieve its strategic objectives.
Tactics - short-term, specific ways in which the short term objectives of the business can be achieved.

Corporate plans are all too frequently poorly drawn up or knocked off course by events. Also, in some companies where there is a very strong, successful and entrepreneurial leader, corporate plans don't have much impact on the strategic direction of the company. Such leaders make strategic decisions as opportunities and threats arise, rather than sticking to any plan. So it could be argued that there is little value in drawing up a corporate plan.

However, many corporate plans do provide a successful map for a business to follow. By carefully drawing up the plan and evaluating alternative courses of action, the business has identified a possible successful strategy. Without a plan, outcomes are likely to be much worse. Decisions will be made which have not been carefully analysed and evaluated. Moreover, relatively few companies have leaders who are able to make sound strategic decisions without a planning framework.

So, corporate planning often fails to deliver the anticipated outcomes. But without corporate planning, the outcomes are likely to be even worse for the company.

KNOWLEDGE

1. Briefly explain the purpose of a business plan.
2. Explain the difference between strategic objectives, tactical objectives and operational objectives.
3. What is strategic planning?
4. Explain the difference between an external audit and an internal audit.
5. What is PESTLE analysis?
6. Explain the role of external and internal audits in SWOT analysis.
7. Explain the difference between strategic analysis and strategic implementation.
8. Briefly outline the reasons why a corporate plan may fail.

Case Study: Premier Foods

The company

Premier Foods was a subsidiary of the food company Hillsdown Holdings. It made a range of traditional British food brands including Typhoo Tea. In 1999, it was sold off to a private equity company, Hicks, Muse Tate and Furst. Under the leadership of Robert Schofield, the new company expanded in 2002, buying a number of brands from Nestlé including Branston, Crosse & Blackwell, Sarson's and Sun Pat. In 2003, it bought Ambrosia custard and rice pudding from Unilever. In 2004, the company was floated on the London Stock Exchange and became Premier Foods plc. Within the next three years, the company bought Bird's custard, Angel Delight, Quorn, Cauldron, Oxo, Batchelor's, Homebridge and Fray Bentos.

In November 2006, Premier Foods raised its game substantially by buying the food company RHM for £1.2 billion, taking on £800 million of RHM debt, making the total cost £2 billion. RHM owned a variety of brands but most importantly was the UK's leading maker of bread with brands such as Mother's Pride and Hovis. The stock market liked the deal and at its height valued the company at £2.8 billion. However, since then, problems have emerged and today the stock market valuation of the company is a mere £777 million. What went wrong?

The corporate plan

Premier Foods under Robert Schofield wanted to 'drive value for all our stakeholders' (Annual Report 2006). The corporate plan was to use 'its scale to drive the business, managing costs and driving brands through marketing and innovation' (Annual Report 2006). Increasing the scale of the business through acquisitions would allow economies of scale to be achieved. When acquisitions were made, in the short term, costs could be reduced through closing manufacturing plants where production could be rationalised with other existing plants. For example, following the acquisition of RHM, the company announced the closure of six plants with 1,000 workers. In the longer term, scale would give cost advantages through factors such as greater buying power and lower marketing costs per unit sold. The company estimates that eventually its annual operating costs will be £113 million lower compared to the cost of Premier Foods and RHM operating separately. Premier Foods also uses its expertise in marketing and product innovation to grow sales of its brands organically. So the corporate plan is more brands, more sales per brand and lower average costs. Unfortunately, the plan has been knocked off course.

Wheat prices

One problem has been the doubling of the price of wheat, the most important ingredient in bread. Last summer within a few months the price of wheat doubled from around £100 a tonne to £200 a tonne. On a typical loaf of bread, this increased costs by 7.5p. When retailers then add another 7.5p in profit margin, the price of a loaf of bread goes up by 15p in the shops. Premier Foods has been in a dilemma. Should it try to absorb as much of the extra cost as possible to minimise the price increase to the consumer, but suffer reduced profits as a result? Or should it pass all the increase on in higher prices and risk seeing sales and market share fall?

The competition

When Premier Foods bought RHM in November 2006, RHM had an estimated 19 per cent of the UK market for bread. Within a year, this had fallen to an estimated 16 per cent. In a static market for bread, this means that bread sales at RHM are falling. The most important reason for RHM's loss of market share has been the steady growth of Warburtons, a privately owned company. Five years ago it had less than 15 per cent of the market. Today, it is nearly 23 per cent. It has grown by providing a higher quality bread than its main rivals which it sells at a slightly higher price. Consumers seem to be prepared to pay the higher price for the perceived quality.

Debt problems

In the background to the problems in its core bread operations is the financial position of the company. Premier Food has net debts of nearly £2 billion, built up as the company made its acquisitions. City investors are worried that profits at the company will fall, putting at jeopardy its ability to finance its debt. There is some expectation that Premier Foods may sell off some non-core assets like a French company it owns making part-baked products. But it is unlikely to pay a final dividend this year and there are fears that it will be forced to raise new equity through a rights issue. This would then justify the large fall in the share price in the company seen over the past 12 months.

Source: adapted from *The Sunday Times*, 2.3.2008; Premier Foods, *Annual Report and Accounts*, 2006; en.wikipedia.org.

(a) Using SWOT analysis, evaluate the position in which Premier Foods found itself in March 2008. (40 marks)

(b) Evaluate the strategies that Premier Foods could use to improve its position. (40 marks)

104 Decision making

Why do businesses make decisions?

Businesses are DECISION MAKING units. Making the 'right' decisions help a business to achieve its aims and objectives. Some of the decisions faced by a business might include:

- how much output to produce of different products in a week or a month;
- who should be promoted from the shop floor to a supervisory level;
- whether the price of a product should be raised;
- how the construction of a new warehouse should be financed;
- what should be the design a of a new company logo;
- which supplier should be used to provide components;
- whether a product should be withdrawn from the market;

and many others.

Businesses are forced to make decisions because choices nearly always exist. A business often has to decide which course of action to take from many different possible alternatives. For example, a company that needs to hire a van for a week might have to choose between 10-15 local companies, all of which are able to supply the van to the required specifications. The person responsible for vehicle hire in the company will need to make this decision. A more important decision may have to be made by a business that is rationalising production. The directors and management may need to choose which factory to close from all of those owned by the business.

Decision making is also necessary to solve problems in a business. For example, if the workforce goes on strike the management may have to decide on an appropriate course of action. A business may also have to take decisions to solve problems such as lengthy queues which develop when consumers are buying goods or possible delays which may take place in the construction of a new factory.

All decisions involve some risk. Decisions where the outcome is unpredictable, where many factors can affect success or which affect a large part of a firm's operations for a long period are most risky. A business may be able to minimise the risk by collecting accurate and comprehensive data and by using decision making models. These are dealt with later in this unit.

Types of decision

It is possible to classify the decisions made by businesses in different ways.

Programmed decisions This idea was put forward by H.A.Simon in his 1965 book *The New Science of Management Decisions.* These are repetitive decisions. A set routine for making the decisions will have been established. For example, a supermarket branch manager may have to prepare a rota every week. This will involve decisions about which staff should be on duty during various shifts. The decisions are repetitive (carried out weekly). Also, a procedure is likely to have been developed which specifies exactly how decisions should be made. There may be formal rules which control decisions, such as the minimum number of staff stacking shelves at any one time. The rules will have been developed and improved over time. The decisions may even be carried out on a computer. For these reasons the decisions have been programmed.

Non-programmed decisions Simon argued that these are novel or unstructured decisions. For example, a business may be forced to move its premises because its current location is subject to a compulsory purchase order by a local authority. This is an unusual problem and it is unlikely that a decision making procedure will have been developed to resolve the problem. A decision like this will also have a long lasting effect on the organisation.

In practice decisions will not fall neatly into the two categories above. Many decisions will be partly programmed and partly non-programmed. For example, managers may develop a decision making structure to apply to unforeseen events. Decisions in a business are also likely to be either strategic, tactical or operational.

Strategic decisions STRATEGIC DECISIONS concern the general direction and overall policy of a business. They are far reaching and can influence the performance of the organisation. They will also be **long-term** decisions, which means that they will affect the business for a period of more than one year. Strategic decisions tend to have a high risk because the outcome of the decision is likely to be unknown.

Examples of strategic decisions might include:

- the purchase of Bebo, the social networking website, by the AOL division of Time Warner for $600 in 2008;
- the decision by Thomas Cook, the holiday company, to expand its provision of financial services such as travel insurance, foreign exchange services and credit cards;
- the move by HR Owen, to restructure its car dealership. It has recently sold off 36 sites and concentrated on prime London locations with a handful of other branches in the South East and one in Manchester.

These decisions are all likely to have long term effects on the businesses concerned. They often involve moving into new areas which will require new resources, new procedures and retraining. Whether or not the decisions were the 'right' ones may not be known for several years because it will take time to evaluate their effects on the businesses involved.

Question 1.

Tata, the Indian conglomerate, bought Land Rover and Jaguar from Ford in March 2008 for around $2.65 billion. However, the final sums involved are likely to be significantly more, after factoring in Ford's contribution to pension scheme deficits and its commitment to supply expensive engine and transmission systems to Tata for years to come. It is understood that Tata has raised about $3 billion to fund the deal, including cash to cover working capital requirements. It is also understood that Land Rover and Jaguar employees will be briefed on their futures soon after returning to work following the Easter break. Tata has agreed to keep intact the three manufacturing facilities at Solihull, Castle Bromwich and Halewood, where Ford employs 13,500 people. Unions have been informed that there will be no redundancies.

In 2007, Tata, whose interests run from tea plantations to IT outsourcing, confirmed its global status by buying the Anglo Dutch steelmaker Corus for £6.2 billion. Its international buying spree has also included Tetley, the tea maker, Daewoo's commercial vehicle arm and the Ritz-Carlton hotel in Boston. Winning the Jaguar and Land Rover brands, however, would open a radical new chapter in the company's history.

Although Tata's trucks dominate the highways of India and the company has made passenger cars since 1991, acquiring the marques would represent a foray into uncharted luxury territory.

Source: adapted from *timesonline* 25.03.2008.

(a) Using this case as an example, explain what is meant by a strategic decision.

(b) If Tata were to choose a new supplier for Land Rover parts, why would this be a tactical decision?

Tactical decisions TACTICAL DECISIONS tend to be medium term decisions which are less far reaching than strategic decisions. They are tactical because they are calculated and because their outcome is more predictable. In a business, tactical decisions may be used to implement strategic decisions. For example, as a result of Morrison's strategic decision to take over Safeway, some tactical decisions might have been:

- if any staff will be made redundant or if any staff need to be recruited;
- where duplication occurs, if stores should be closed;
- what should happen to any stores that are closed;
- what retraining of staff might be required and which staff would be retrained;
- what methods of promotion should be used for the new business.

Operational decisions OPERATIONAL DECISIONS are lower level decisions, sometimes called administrative decisions. They will be short term and carry little risk. Such decisions can normally be taken fairly quickly. They require much less thought and evaluation than strategic and tactical decisions. Every day a business makes a large number of operational decisions. Examples might include:

- how many checkouts to have open in a retail outlet at a particular time of day;
- how much time should be allocated to a task in a factory;
- how to stagger breaks for sales staff in a department store so that a minimum number are always on the shop floor;
- when to order new invoices for an office and what quantity to order.

Who makes decisions?

Decisions are made by all staff in a business. However, responsibility for the decision will vary according to the employee's position in the hierarchical structure. A senior manager can delegate decision making powers to a junior manager, but will retain ultimate responsibility for decision making. Also, the size of the company will influence who makes decisions. For example, a sole trader with no employees will make all the decisions. As businesses grow and more staff are employed, decision making is likely to be delegated.

Strategic decisions These are likely to be made by the owners of the business. Such decisions are so important and far reaching that only the owners can be responsible for their outcome. However, in some public limited companies these decisions will be made by the board of directors. Directors are appointed to run plcs in the interests of the owners, the shareholders, who can number thousands. Some important strategic decisions may require the shareholder's consent. For example, shareholders at Hanson, the conglomerate business, were consulted before the group was demerged into four smaller companies in 1996.

Tactical decisions Business managers are likely to make tactical decisions. Such decisions are often required to implement the strategic decisions made by the owners or the senior management team. Important tactical decisions, such as the promotion campaign for a new product, tend to be made by those near the top of the business hierarchy. Less important tactical decisions will often be made by middle or junior managers.

Operational decisions Nearly all employees will be involved in operational decisions. Lower level decisions, such as what task should office staff at an NHS trust hospital perform, are constantly taken by all staff in the business. Sometimes managers may be consulted by their subordinates if they need guidance or approval for a decision.

Question 2.

Sir James Dyson, the vacuum-cleaner entrepreneur, was planning to build a £56m design and engineering school in Bath. However, the project is now under threat ahead of a planning vote by local councillors. Dyson, who wants to build a centre to teach 2,500 teenagers a week and start a diploma to reduce Britain's shortage of engineers, faces an uphill battle for approval. Council officers earlier this month recommended rejection of the scheme on the grounds that it would damage the historic character of the proposed site, a former craneworks. The Environment Agency is also arguing that the centre would pose an increased flood risk to the city. It is the latest setback for the project, conceived four years ago on a site initially suggested by the council. 'Frankly it's bewildering,' said Dyson. 'The same people who offered South Quays, and who we're negotiating with to buy the site, are now jeopardising the school. Why? We have redesigned to the satisfaction of English Heritage and we've safeguarded against flooding. And yet seemingly it's not enough.' However, Dyson, who has lived in and around Bath for the past 40 years, has won support from the government. The project featured in the recent white paper on science and innovation. Dyson's team has rejected other possible sites in Bristol and Swindon. It favours Bath because of its close links to the local university.

Dyson would not say if a 'no' vote would mean the end of the road for his dream. 'We have to wait to see what happens at the meeting', he said. A council spokesman said it would be inappropriate to comment before the meeting.

Source: adapted from the *Sunday Times* 16.03.2008.

(a) Using this case as an example, explain what is meant by an external constraint on decision making.

(b) Describe briefly two pieces of information that Dyson would have needed before deciding to build the school in Bath.

Figure 1: Business organisations in the private sector

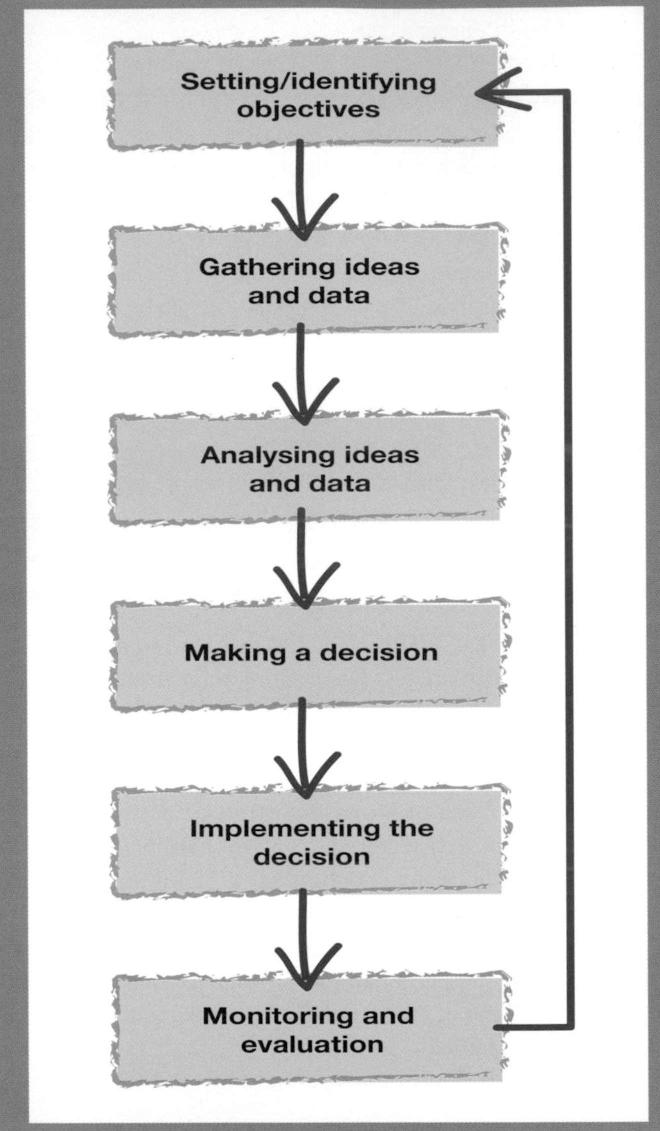

It is argued that delegating decisions to those further down the hierarchy can help motivation. This empowerment of employees can also help to solve problems quickly without the need to consult managers. In the last decade a number of UK businesses have handed decision making to factory, team or group workers, giving them the authority to identify and solve problems before or as they occur. This has led to improvements in both efficiency and quality. The removal of layers of management has also improved decision making in some cases by reducing the number of levels in the chain of command, although this can lead to problems if not supported by retraining and changes in organisational culture.

Intuitive and scientific decision making

Decisions are made in a variety of different ways. In smaller businesses, all types of decision are often made quickly and informally. Owners and managers have a good understanding of what they want to achieve. They then use their knowledge and experience to make decisions. Decision making is often INTUITIVE. Even in large companies, where there is a strong entrepreneurial culture, intuition can play a large role in decision making at the highest level. However, complex decisions will be based on a significant amount of data having been gathered, processed and synthesised. Information management is vital even when decision making seems to be intuitive and informal.

However, the more complex the decision, the more data is likely to be available. There then needs to be more complex ways to analyse and interpret this data. This is the reason why SCIENTIFIC DECISION MAKING methods are used by business. Figure 1 shows such a model. It is based on a number of stages.

Identifying objectives The first stage in the process is to identify the objective a business wants to achieve. The objective might be a corporate objective, such as growth or survival in a poor trading period. These decisions are likely to be complex and might be taken by the board of directors.

For lower level objectives, such as filling a part-time vacancy, decisions may be taken by junior managers. A business's objectives might be different at different stages in its growth. Business activities controlled by local government may have different objectives from public limited companies. The business also needs to develop criteria to measure whether it has achieved its objectives. Quite often the objective is to solve a problem. This might be planning for an uncertain future or dealing with a low level of profitability.

Collecting information and ideas People need information and ideas to make decisions. The amount and nature of the information needed will depend on the decision. For example, the decision whether or not to launch a new product might require some information about possible sales levels and consumer reactions, costs of production and reactions of competitors. It could take several months to collect all this information. Other decisions could perhaps be made from information which the business already has. A decision whether or not to dismiss an employee might be made on the basis of information from the personnel department.

Where does the business get its ideas? It might set up a working party to collect information and ideas from within the firm. The working party would then produce a report or make a presentation to the decision makers. Alternatively, individuals or departments might submit ideas and information. Another way of obtaining information and ideas is to hold discussions amongst staff in the firm.

Analysing information and ideas The next stage in the process is to analyse information to look for alternative courses of action. Possible courses of action may be based on previous ideas or completely new ideas. The aim is to identify which course of action will best achieve the business's objective or solve the problem. It may be possible to test the alternatives before the one that is chosen is carried out.

Making a decision Next the decision has to be made. This is the most important stage in the process. Decision makers have to commit themselves to one course of action. It is difficult to change the decision, so getting it right is vital. For example, once production begins following the decision to launch a new product, it is difficult for the firm to change its mind. If the product does not sell, this can lead to a loss of money. Some decisions can be reversed. For example, if the owner of a shop decides to close on Tuesday afternoons, but then finds the loss of sales is intolerable, the owner can easily reopen again.

Sometimes the decision makers feel that they cannot reach a decision. They may have to obtain more information and complete the previous two stages in the process again.

Communication Once a decision has been made, personnel are informed and the decision is carried out. Quite often the people making the decisions are not those that carry them out. Instructions may be passed by the decision makers to someone else, probably a manager, explaining what action should be taken. For example, if the directors decide to begin selling their products in a new country, instructions must be sent to the marketing manager. In smaller firms decision makers are more likely to carry out their own decisions.

Outcome Once a decision has been carried out it will take time before the results are known. Sometimes this can be quite a long time. For example, the companies which decided to build the Channel Tunnel will not know for several decades whether or not it will be a commercial success.

Evaluate the results Finally, decision makers need to evaluate the outcome of their decisions. This is often presented as a report. It may be necessary to modify the course of action on the basis of the report. For example, it might be necessary to revise the objectives or collect some more information, as shown in Figure 1. There may be problems in following such an approach. Objectives may be difficult to identify or unrealistic. Information may be limited, incorrect or misleading. People making decisions in the process may have different views and this may lead to differences of opinion about what is the best course of action, for example.

Decision making models

The use of MODELS or simulations is widespread in business. Models are replicas or copies of problem areas in business. They are theories, laws or equations, stating things about a problem and helping in our understanding of it. There is a number of common features to models.

- They reflect the key characteristics or behaviour of an area of concern.
- They tend to be simplified versions of areas of concern.
- They simulate the actions and processes that operate in the problem area.
- They provide an aid to problem solving or decision making.
- Models often make use of formulae to express concepts.

Some models can be carried out using computer software. This allows decisions to be made quickly and many variables affecting decisions can be included.

Management science and operations research are areas which often make use of decision making models. For example, linear programming provides a model which allows decision makers to determine optimal solutions to a wide range of business problems. It has been used to make decisions such as:

- how to minimise waste in production;
- how to allocate resources between two competing tasks;
- how to find the least cost mix of ingredients for a product.

Another example in the area of marketing is the use of Ansoff's Matrix. This model is used to help consider the relationship between the strategic direction of the business and its marketing strategy.

A simulation involves trying to mimic what might happen in reality. It allows a business to test ideas and make decisions without bearing the consequences of 'real action' if things go wrong. Imagine a business has a problem. A simulation can be carried out several times, quickly and cheaply, in order to test alternative decisions. There is no risk and resources are not used up. Simulations are often used to deal with problems such as queues in business.

Constraints on decision making

Businesses cannot make decisions with complete freedom. In many situations there are factors which hinder, limit or restrict particular courses of action. These constraintsmay make the decision easier because they eliminate some courses of action. For example, a business may require an agency to carry out market research on its behalf. It may allocate a budget of £5,000 to pay for the research and invite tenders for the work. The tenders received could be:

- Sefton Research Associates – £4,700;
- Aston MR Ltd – £6,100;
- Salford Marketing – £4,900;
- Carlton Marketing – £5,400.

The business can only afford to pay the tenders offered by two of the agencies. Thus its choice is reduced and the decision simplified by its financial constraint. Note, however, that the best quality service may be provided by Aston MR Ltd and so the financial constraint has denied the business using a better quality service.

Internal constraints These may result from the policy of the business itself.

- Availability of finance. Decision makers are often prevented from choosing certain courses of action because the business cannot afford them.
- Existing company policy. For example, to control the wage bill, a firm's policy may be to restrict overtime to a maximum of ten hours per week. The production manager may want to offer workers more overtime to reach a production target. However, she is not able to do so because of the firm's overtime policy.
- People's behaviour. Decisions may be limited by people's ability. For example, a manual worker is unlikely to be able to run a department if the manager is absent. People are also limited by their attitudes. For example, a company may wish to move three people into one office who work in separate offices at the moment, but this could meet with resistance.

External constraints These are limits from outside and are usually beyond the control the control of the business.

- Government and EU legislation. Businesses must operate within the law. For example, a manager may require a driver to deliver some goods urgently to a customer 600 miles away, which would require a 17 hour drive. The law restricts the amount of time a person can drive certain commercial vehicles to about ten hours per day.
- Competitors' behaviour. Say a firm is deciding to introduce a new product. If Mars is enjoying some success with a new product Cadbury's might copy Mars and decide to launch its own version of the product. Because competition has become greater in recent years, this constraint has affected more firms.
- Lack of technology. There are many examples of operations in business that in the past were slow or physically demanding. Today tasks as varied as loading cargo onto ships to computer aided design can be carried on effectively with the use of modern technology.
- The economic environment. It is argued that business activity moves through booms, where demand rises, and slumps. This can affect investment decisions. For example, if a company is deciding whether to build a larger plant, the decision makers may postpone the plan if the economy is in a slump and demand is low. During the recession of the early 1990s a large number of businesses cancelled investment projects.

The quality of decisions

If the right decisions are made the business will benefit. The quality of decisions depends on a number of factors.

Training If people are trained their performance is likely to be better. The people making important decisions in a business should receive training. Courses are offered by business schools and other educational institutions which concentrate on decision making.

Quantity and quality information Decision making will be improved if there is access to information. For example, if a firm is thinking of a price increase, the more information it has on the reactions of customers, the more likely it is to decide whether this is the right course of action. Information technology in business has helped decision makers a great deal. They are able to store more information, retrieve it instantly and change it into a form which is more useful to them.

Inadequate and inaccurate information can lead to the wrong decision being made and may cause serious problems. For example, when an insurance company is setting premiums for motor insurance, if the estimate of the cost of repairing cars is too low then premiums will be set too low. It is also argued that the use of quantitative information helps to improve the quality of the decision.

Ability to use decision making techniques The ability to use decision making techniques will help accurate decisions to be made. For example, one technique used to evaluate the likely returns from choosing a particular course of action is the use of decision trees.

Risk Some decisions involve considerable risk, such as the launching of a new product. It is argued that UK managers are too cautious in their approach to decision making. This is because they prefer to choose courses of action which carry the lowest risk, and avoid taking riskier courses of action which might result in higher profits.

Human element Most decisions are made by people. Different people are likely to make different decisions. How do people differ?

- The level of experience might be different. More experienced decision makers will often, but not always, make much more accurate decisions.
- The attitude to risk may differ. Cautious decision makers will choose different courses of action to 'risk takers'.
- People have different capabilities. Those who are skilled at decision making will enjoy better results than those whose judgements are poor.
- Self-interest may affect the course of action chosen. For example, management and trade unions are likely to reach different conclusions when setting wage levels for the workforce.
- People often have different perceptions. This may influence the decisions they make. For example, two people on an interview panel for a new recruit may have different views of an interviewee's performance.

Interdependence

Businesses are highly interdependent. Many businesses depend on others for supplies of materials and components. Other businesses supply ancillary services, such as cleaning, waste disposal, financial services and maintenance. When making decisions firms should consider how they affect these support services. In recent years some large businesses have put financial pressure on support businesses by delaying payments. This may lead to support services closing down.

Decision makers need to be aware of the interdependence between their own company and their competitors. In highly competitive industries one firm's decisions can affect the behaviour of other firms. For example, in the grocery trade if one supermarket decides to lower the prices of several hundred lines, other supermarkets may have to do the same or risk losing customers. This type of interdependence is particularly important in decisions concerning:

- price;
- launching new products;
- packaging;
- non-price competition;
- introducing new technology;
- exploiting new markets.

KEYTERMS

Decision making – choosing between alternative courses of action.

Intuitive decision-making – where decisions are made based on gut reactions, feelings or intuition rather than using formal models or procedures.

Models or simulations – simplified representations of a business situation or problem.

Operational decisions – lower level, often administrative decisions with little or no risk.

Strategic decisions – decisions concerning policy that have a long term impact on a business. Can be risky.

Tactical decisions – calculated, medium term decisions. May be used to implement strategic decisions.

KNOWLEDGE

1. Why do businesses need to make decisions?
2. Why do decisions involve risk?
3. Explain the difference between programmed and non-programmed decisions.
4. Suggest two examples of a strategic decision.
5. Who makes decisions in business?
6. How might the size of a business affect who makes decisions?
7. What are the common features of scientific models?
8. List three internal and three external constraints on business decisions.
9. State five factors affecting the quality of business decisions.
10. 'Businesses can not make decisions without considering the effects on their suppliers.' Briefly explain this statement.

Case Study: Carparts

Carparts is a national parts distributor for motor cars. It has 112 distribution centres all over the UK. After a period of healthy sales growth in the mid and late 1990s, the company's sales have stagnated. It achieved much of its growth through acquisitions, however, the scope for further acquisitions in the UK has diminished. The company is considering its future and two strategies for further growth have been identified.

- **Set up an online sales service**. This would allow customers to buy spare parts using a computer. One of the main advantages of this is that payment would be received in advance so cash flow would improve. Most of Carparts' existing customers purchase parts on credit. The cost of processing orders would be reduced and new customers might also be attracted. However, there are some disadvantages. Carparts has no experience in computer sales and a lot of money would have to be spent on staff training and computer equipment. Money would also have to be invested in expanding the delivery service since all computer purchases will have to be delivered. This would involve purchasing more delivery vehicles and taking on more staff.
- **Buy AutoPlus, a French distributor of motor car parts**. This would allow Carparts to grow rapidly. AutoPlus is a medium-sized but established distributor in Northern France. Such an acquisition will bring economies of scale to Carparts and allow the company to develop its core activities. However, the company does not have any experience in overseas business development. It is also worried that the products demanded in France might be quite different to the ones bought in the UK due to the differences in motor car models purchased in the two countries.

One of the problems faced by the company is that the board of directors is currently split over which course of action should be taken. Although the company Chairperson has a casting vote, on such an important issue he is reluctant to use it. One factor that will have to be taken into account is the cost of the two options. Setting up an online service will cost around £2.2 million while buying AutoPlus will cost at least £4.5 million. There is also the possibility that another bidder might enter the market for AutoPlus which would drive up the price. However, the purchase of AutoPlus will generate immediate returns whereas revenue from the online business is likely take a while to build up. The directors who favour the online services option have often been criticised for being too risk averse.

On the morning before the final board meeting when the decision will be made, the Chairperson, who is busy making final preparations for the meeting, delegates a number of tasks to his Personal Assistant.

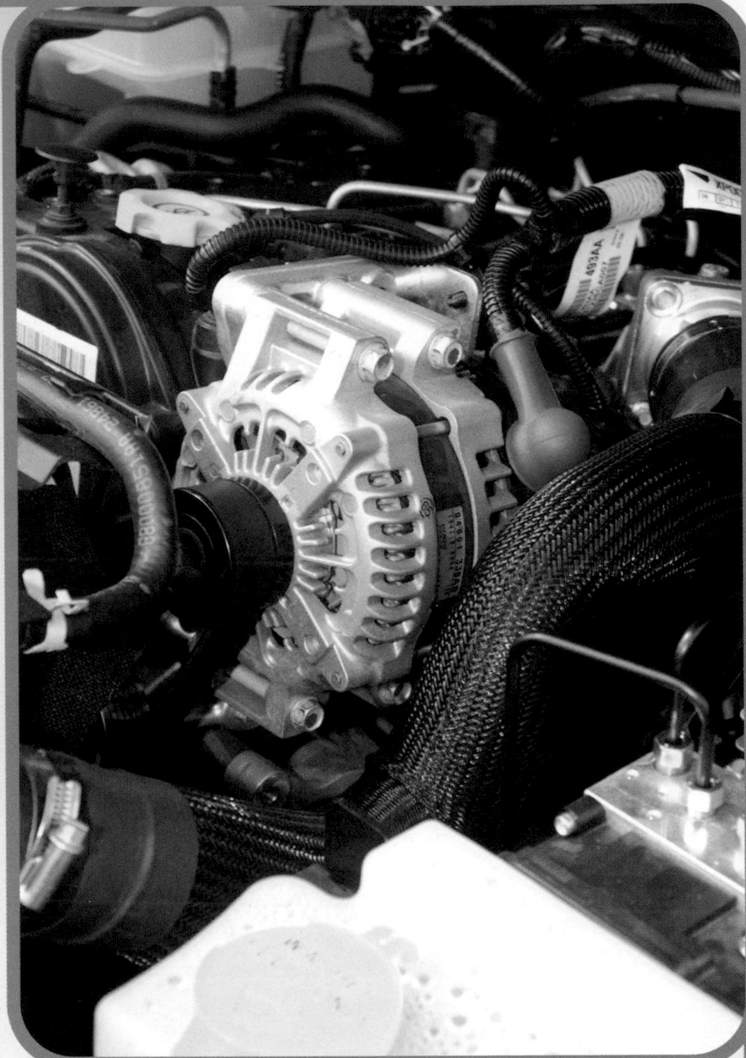

- Book a table in a suitable restaurant for the Chairperson to entertain some important shareholders the next day.
- Choose four distribution centres for the Chairperson to visit at random the day after.
- Decide which branch manager should receive the monthly merit award.

(a) **What is the objective in the decision faced by Carparts? (4 marks)**

(b) **Using examples from the case, explain what is meant by an operational decision. (6 marks)**

(c) **Outline the possible (i) internal and (ii) external constraints that there might be on the decision facing Carparts. (12 marks)**

(d) **Examine the possible difficulties involved in the strategic decisions facing the company. (16 marks)**

(e) **Discuss whether the business has the information required to make the best decision. (40 marks)**

105 Decision trees

Making decisions

Every day, businesses make decisions. Most, if not all, involve some risk. This could be because the business has limited information on which to base the decision. Furthermore, the outcome of the decision may be uncertain. Launching a new product in a market abroad can be risky because a firm may not have experience of selling in that market. It may also be unsure about how consumers will react.

When faced with a number of different decisions a business will want to choose the course of action which gives the most return. What if a printing company had to decide whether to invest £750,000 in a new printing press now or wait a few years? If it bought now and a more efficient machine became available next year then it might have been more profitable to wait. Alternatively, if it waits it may find the old machine has problems and costs increase.

When the outcome is uncertain, decision trees can be used to help a business reach a decision which could minimise risk and gain the greatest return.

What are decision trees?

A DECISION TREE is a method of tracing the alternative outcomes of any decision. The likely results can then be compared so that the business can find the most profitable alternative. For example, a business may be faced with two alternatives - to launch a new product in Europe or in the USA. A decision tree may show that launching a new product in Europe is likely to be more successful than launching a new product in the USA.

It is argued by some that decision making is more effective if a **quantitative approach** is taken. This is where information on which decisions are based, and the outcomes of decisions, are expressed as numbers. In a decision tree, numerical values are given to such information. The decision tree also provides a pictorial approach to decision making because a diagram is used which resembles the branches of a tree. The diagram maps out different courses of action, possible outcomes of decisions and points where decisions have to be made. Calculations based on the decision tree can be used to determine the 'best' likely outcome for the business and hence the most suitable decision.

Features of decision trees

Decision trees have a number of features. These can be seen in Figure 1 which shows the decision tree for a business that has to decide whether to launch a new advertising campaign or retain an old one.

Decision points Points where decisions have to be made in a decision tree are represented by squares and are called decision points. The decision maker has to choose between certain courses of action. In this example, the decision is whether to launch a new campaign or retain the old one.

Outcomes Points where there are different possible outcomes in a decision tree are represented by circles and are called **chance nodes.** At these chance nodes it can be shown that a particular course of action might result in a number of outcomes. In this example, at 'B' there is a chance of failure or success of the new campaign.

Probability or chance The **likelihood** of possible outcomes happening is represented by probabilities in decision trees. The chance of a particular outcome occurring is given a value. If the outcome is certain then the probability is 1. Alternatively, if there is no chance at all of a particular outcome occurring, the probability will be 0. In practice the value will lie between 0 and 1. In Figure 1, at 'B' the chance of success for the new campaign is 0.2 and the chance of failure is 0.8.

It is possible to estimate the probability of events occurring provided information about these events can be found. There are two sources of information which can be used to help estimate probabilities. One source is **backdata.** For example, if a business has opened 10 new stores in recent years, and 9 of them have been successful, it might be reasonable to assume that the chances of another new store being successful are $^{9}/_{10}$ or 0.9. Another source is research data. For example, a business might carry out marketing research to find out how customers would

Figure 1: A simple decision tree based on a decision whether to retain an existing advertising campaign or begin a new one

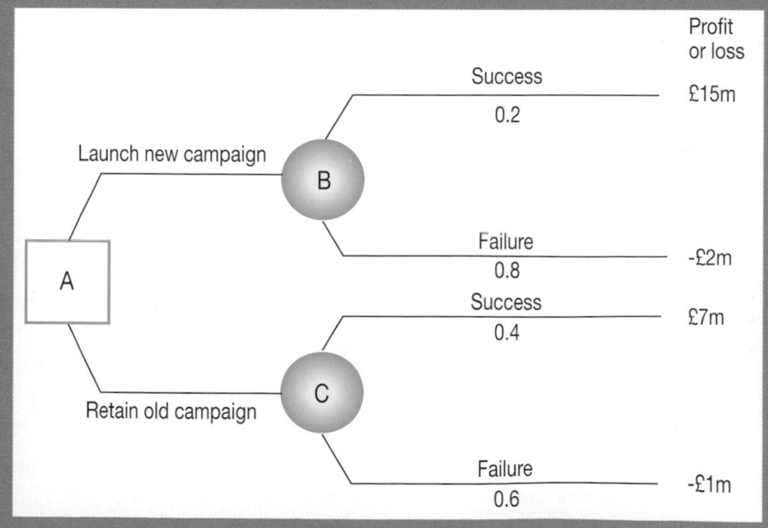

Question 1.

BGS Holdings owns a chain of 32 pubs and bars in the north of England. Due to intense competition, revenue has fallen in the last couple of years. As a means of boosting revenue it has been suggested that the chain, in line with many other competitors, should use 'happy hours' to attract more customers. Traditionally a 'happy hour' is a period of time (not always an hour) where drinks are sold at reduced prices. The problem though is choosing the right 'hour' when prices should be reduced. It is thought not to be a good idea to choose a period of time which is already popular. This is because sales of drinks would already be very high and to cut prices during this time would reduce margins significantly. In order to help make the decision an investigation was carried out in a sample of four pubs. The data gathered during the investigation is shown in Table 1.

Table 1: Happy hour data gathered by BGS Holdings

Happy Hour period	Probability of success	Estimated effect on profit	Probability of failure	Estimated effect on profit	Expected value
3-4pm	0.5	+£1,300	?	-£200	?
4-5pm	0.5	+£1,700	?	-£400	?
5-6pm	0.7	+£400	?	-£1,200	?
6-7pm	0.6	+£1,000	?	-£800	?
7-8pm	0.6	+£1,100	?	-£400	?

(a) Complete Table 1.
(b) On financial grounds, when should the 'happy hour' be arranged?

react to a new product design. 80 per cent of people surveyed may like the product and 20 per cent may dislike it.

Expected values This is the financial outcome of a decision. It is based on the predicted profit or loss of an outcome and the probability of that outcome occurring. The profit or loss of any decision is shown on the right hand side of Figure 1. For example, if the launch of a new campaign is a success, a £15 million profit is expected. If it fails a loss of £2 million is expected.

Calculating expected values

What should the firm decide? It has to work out the expected values of each decision, taking into account the expected profit or loss and the probabilities. So, for example, the expected value of a new campaign is:

		Success		Failure
Expected value	=	0.2 x £15m	+	0.8 x (-£2m)
		(probability) (expected profit)		(probability) (expected loss)
	=	£3m	-	£1.6m
	=	1.4m		

The expected value of retaining the current campaign is:

		Success		Failure
Expected value	=	0.4 x £7m	+	0.6 x (-£1m)
	=	£2.8m	-	£0.6m
	=	2.2m		

From these figures the firm should continue with the existing campaign because the expected value is higher.

Numerous outcomes

It is possible to have more than two outcomes at a chance node. For example, at point 'B' in Figure 1 there might have been 3 outcomes:

- the probability of great success may be 0.2 with a profit of £15 million;
- the probability of average success may be 0.4 with a profit of £6 million;
- the probability of failure may be 0.4 with a loss of -£2 million.

The expected value is now:

= (0.2 x £15 m) + (0.4 x £6 m) + (0.4 x -£2 m)
= £3 m + £ 2.4 m - £0.8 m
= £4.6 m

Decisions, outcomes and costs

In practice businesses face many alternative decisions and possible outcomes. Take a farmer who has inherited some land, but does not wish to use it with his existing farming business. There are three possible decisions that the farmer could make.

- Sell the land. The market is depressed and this will earn £0.6 million.
- Wait for one year and hope that the market price improves. A land agent has told the farmer that the chance of an upturn in the market is 0.3, while the probabilities of it staying the same or worsening are 0.5 and 0.2 respectively. The likely proceeds from a sale in each of the circumstances are £1 million, £0.6 million and £0.5 million.
- Seek planning permission to develop the land. The legal and administration fees would be £0.5 million and the probability of being refused permission would be 0.8, which means the likelihood of obtaining permission is 0.2. If refused, the farmer would be left with the same set of circumstances described in the second option.

If planning permission is granted the farmer has to make a decision (at node E). If the farmer decides to sell, the probability of getting a good price, ie £10 million, is estimated to be 0.4, while the probability of getting a low price, i.e. £6 million, is 0.6. The farmer could also develop the land himself at a cost of £5 million. The probability of selling the developed land at a good price, ie £25 million, is estimated to be 0.3 while the likelihood of getting a low price, ie £10 million, is 0.7.

The information about probability and earnings is shown in Figure 2. What decision should the farmer make? The sale of the land immediately will earn £0.6 million.

The expected value of the second option, waiting a year, is:

Figure 2: The decisions faced by a farmer in the disposal of land

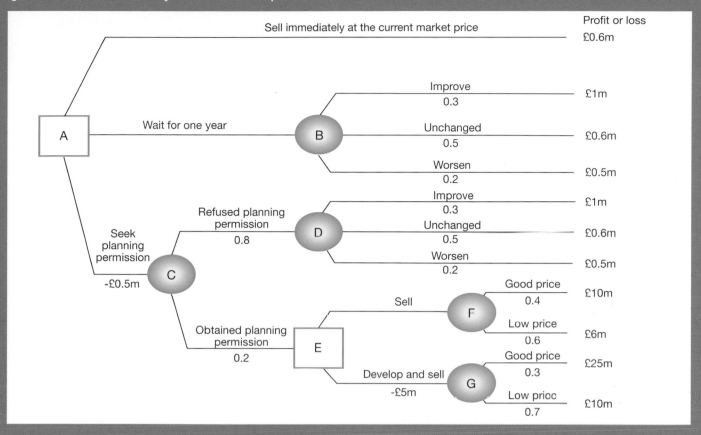

Expected value = 0.3 x £1m + 0.5 x £0.6m + 0.2 x £0.5m
= £0.3m + £0.3m + £0.1m
= £0.7m

Since this earns more than the first option, it would be a better choice. We could show this in Figure 4 (over the page) by crossing the 'selling immediately' path with a //, indicating that the first option will not be taken up. The expected value of the second option (£0.7 million) is shown in the diagram at node B.

A **rollback technique** can then be used to work out the expected value of the third option, seeking planning permission. This means working from right to left, calculating the expected values at each node in the diagram. The expected value at node D is:

Expected value = 0.3 x £1m + 0.5 x £0.6m + 0.2 x £0.5m
= £0.7m

Question 2.

Colin Andrews is the owner of Slade farm near Spalding. He specialises in vegetable crops and allocates about 400 acres of land each year to the production of potatoes and swedes. He decides what crops to plant in October each year.

If Colin plants potatoes he estimates that the probability of a good crop is 0.3, which will generate £50,000 profit. The probability of an average crop is 0.3, which would result in £30,000 profit. The probability of a poor crop is 0.4, which would result in only £10,000 profit.

If swedes are planted, either a good crop or a bad crop will result. He estimates that the probability in each case is 0.5. A good crop will generate a profit of £40,000 and a poor crop only £10,000. Figure 3 is a decision tree which shows this information.

(a) What is happening at points B and C in the decision tree?

(b) Calculate the expected values of each course of action and decide, on financial grounds, which course Colin should take.

Figure 3: The alternative courses of action faced by Colin Andrews

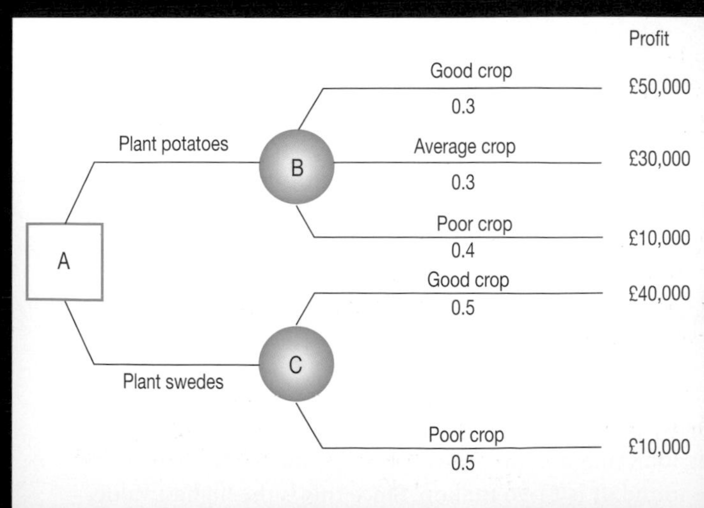

Figure 4: The final solution to the farmer's decision problem (all expected values and unused routes are shown)

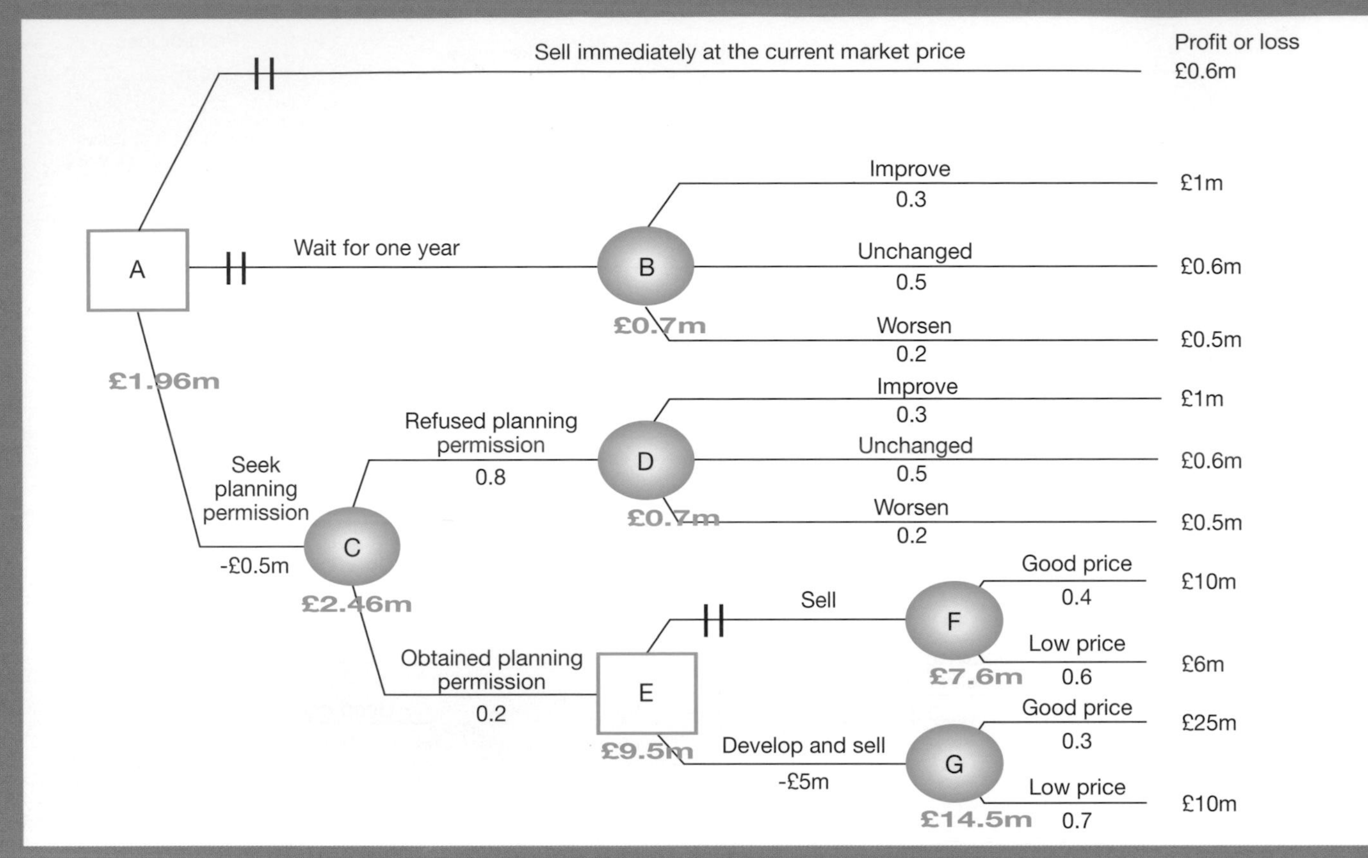

The expected value at node F is:

$$\text{Expected value} = 0.4 \times £10\text{m} + 0.6 \times £6\text{m} = £4\text{m} + £3.6\text{m} = £7.6\text{m}$$

The expected value at node G is:

$$\text{Expected value} = 0.3 \times £25\text{m} + 0.7 \times £10\text{m} = £7.5\text{m} + £7\text{m} = £14.5\text{m}$$

At node E, a decision node, the farmer would choose to develop the land before selling it. This would yield an expected return of £9.5 million (£14.5 million - £5 million) which is higher than £7.6 million, ie the expected return from selling the land undeveloped. Thus, in Figure 4 the path representing this option can be crossed. The expected value at node C is now:

$$\text{Expected value} = 0.2 \times £9.5\text{m} + 0.8 \times £0.7\text{m} = £1.9\text{m} + £0.56\text{m} = £2.46\text{m}$$

Finally, by subtracting the extra cost of seeking planning permission (£0.5 million), the expected value of the final option can be found. It is £1.96 million. Since this is the highest value, this would be the best option for the farmer. This means a // can be placed on the line to node B as £0.7 million is lower than £1.96 million. All of the expected values are shown in Figure 4.

Figure 4 shows profit or loss (taking into account costs) and then the **extra** costs of planning permission are subtracted in the calculation. However, a decision tree may show revenue on the right side instead of profit and **all** costs indicated on the diagram must be subtracted. Whichever is shown, the method of calculation is the same.

Advantages and disadvantages of decision trees

Decision trees can be applied to much more complicated problems. They have some major advantages.

- Constructing the tree diagram may show possible courses of action not previously considered.
- They involve placing numerical values on decisions. This tends to improve results.
- They force management to take account of the risks involved in decisions and help to separate important from unimportant risks.

The technique also has some limitations.

- The information which the technique 'throws out' is not exact. Much of it is based on probabilities which are often estimated.
- Decisions are not always concerned with quantities and

probabilities. They often involve people and are influenced by legal constraints or people's opinions, for example. These factors cannot always be shown by numerical values. Qualitatitive data may also be important.

- Time lags often occur in decision making. By the time a decision is finally made, some of the numerical information may be out of date.
- The process can be quite time consuming, using up valuable business resources. However, computerised decision making models can be used to analyse decision trees which can save some time.
- It is argued that decision makers, in an attempt encourage a particular course of action, may manipulate the data. For example, a manager might be 'biased' when attaching probabilities to certain outcomes. This will distort the final results.
- Decision trees are not able to take into account the dynamic nature of business. For example, a sudden change in the economic climate might render a decision based on a decision tree obsolete.

KNOWLEDGE

1. Why are decision trees useful when a business has to make important decisions?
2. What is meant by a quantitative approach to decision making?
3. What is meant by probability in a decision tree?
4. What is the difference between chance nodes and decision nodes?
5. How is the expected value of a course of action calculated?
6. What are the advantages and disadvantages of using decision trees?
7. State three possible situations where a business might make use of a decision tree.

KEYTERMS

Decision trees - a technique which shows all possible outcomes of a decision. The name comes from the similarity of the diagrams to the branches of trees.

Question 3.

Trumed plc is a medical company that carries out research into new treatments for colds and influenza. It has won a contract from a large pharmaceuticals corporation to carry out research into new treatments. Trumed has identified three distinct research programmes to develop a vaccination to combat the strain. The code names for each programme are VAC1, VAC2 and VAC3. The cost of the programmes, the expected returns and the probabilities of success and failure are illustrated in the decision tree in Figure 5.

Figure 5: The costs, revenues and probabilities of success and failure of each research programme for Trumed plc

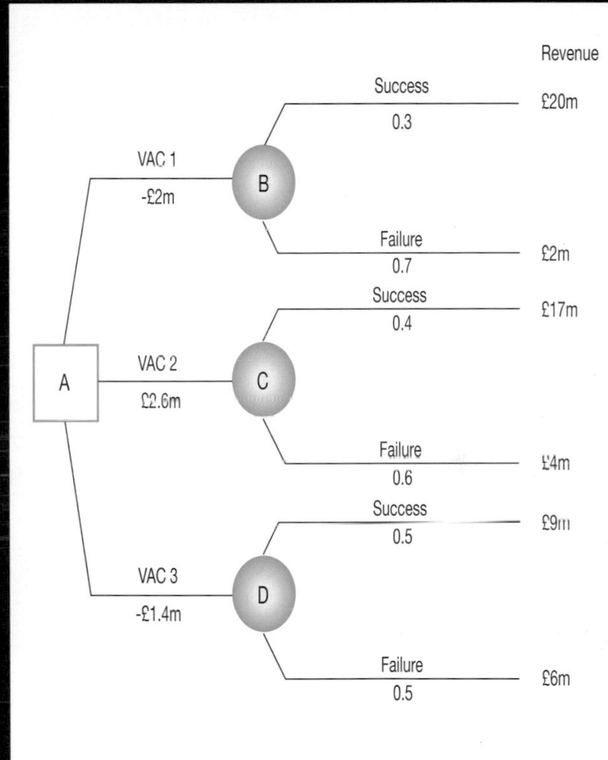

(a) Calculate the expected values of each research programme and advise Trumed which is the best option.

Case Study: ***Opal Media***

Opal Media publishes a number of consumer magazines in the UK. It specialises in magazines for people involved in minority sports such as canoeing, snow boarding, surfing, paragliding, bowling, archery, skydiving and water-skiing. Opal Media currently owns 18 publications. In 2007, the company was concerned that one of its magazines, *Squash Monthly*, was not performing well enough. Its circulation figures had dwindled slowly but consistently over the last ten years. Pat McMahon, head of marketing, believed that the fall in sales was due mainly to the decline in the popularity of the sport. Twenty years ago, *Squash Monthly*, was one of the company's 'stars'. It was now regarded as a 'dog' by many in the department and was barely breaking even.

The board at Opal Media asked Pat to look into the situation and make a recommendation. Pat identified a number of options open to the company. These are outlined below.

Withdraw *Squash Monthly* from the market and replace it with a new magazine The marketing department believes there might be a gap in the market for a magazine devoted entirely to the 2012 Olympics. Obviously this would have a short life cycle because once the event is over sales would fall to zero. However, the amount of publicity that the event would get suggests that the potential for high sales levels for a short period of time could be enormous. It was also felt that competitors would not be interested in a magazine with such a short life cycle.

- With a thorough development programme the new magazine, called *2012*, could be launched in September 2009. The cost of thorough product development would be £400,000 and once launched net revenue of £3.5 million would be generated if the magazine was a complete success. The chances of this were estimated to be 0.5. If the magazine flopped sales would only be £900,000. The chances of this were thought to be 0.2. If the magazine enjoyed moderate success (0.3 chance) sales of £1.8 million would be generated.
- If the product was launched with a rapid development programme it could come out in September 2008. This would cost £100,000. However, with a short development programme the quality would not be as good and as a result advertising revenue would be lower. If the launch was a complete success (0.6 chance) sales revenue of £2.8 million would be generated. If the magazine flopped (0.2 chance) revenue would be £500,000. With moderate success (0.2 chance) revenue would be £1.2 million.

Retain *Squash Monthly* in its existing form and invest £500,000 in an above-the-line promotion This strategy would generate £3.9 million if successful and the chances of success are 0.4. If the investment fails to be a success only £700,000 will be generated.

Retain *Squash Monthly* and develop some extension strategies Two alternative extension strategies were identified by the marketing department.

- Relaunch the magazine with new features, articles and some below-the-line promotion. The cost of this strategy would be £300,000 and if successful would generate revenue of £3 million. The probability of this was estimated at 0.5. If the strategy was unsuccessful only £600,000 would be generated.
- Launch *Squash Monthly* in Canada and America. This would be risky and more expensive but the rewards potentially higher at £8 million if completely successful. The costs would be £600,000 and the chance of complete success is estimated to be 0.3. If the magazine flopped in the new markets the revenue would only amount to £800,000.

Figure 6 The costs, revenues, and probabilities of success and failure of the options open to Opal Media

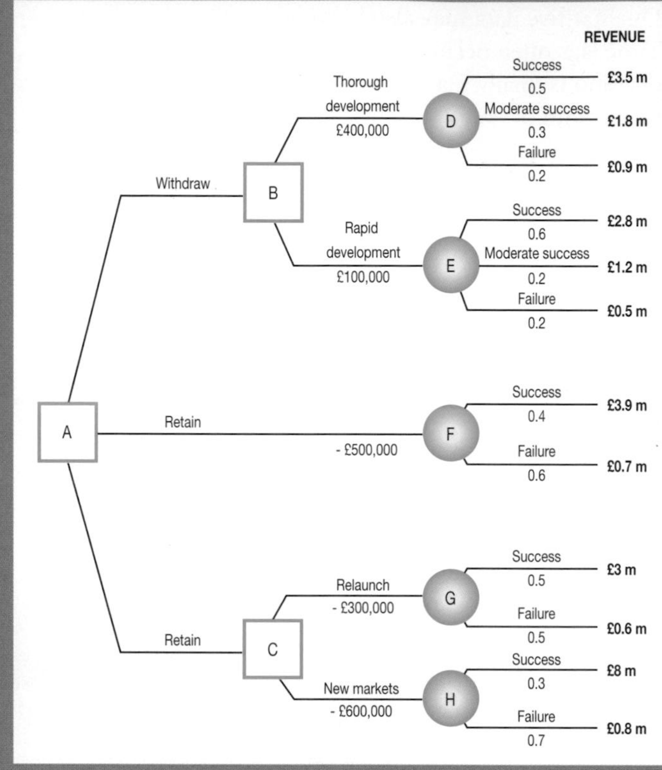

(a) Using this case as an example, explain the difference between a decision node and a chance node in a decision tree. (6 marks)

(b) Calculate the expected values for each option and determine on financial grounds which option Opal Media should select. (14 marks)

(c) Just before the final decision was made by Opal, it was bought to the attention of the marketing department that future exchange rate forecasts would have an impact on the revenues earned in Canada and the USA. It was estimated that the pound would rise against the dollar over the next few years and the revenues earned could fall to £6.5 million and £0.6 million (depending on the success of the launch). Examine how this might this affect the decision. (16 marks)

(d) Evaluate the choice by Opal Media to use decision trees to make a decision about the future of Squash Monthly. (40 marks)

106 Fishbone analysis and force field analysis

Decision making tools

There are many decision making tools available to businesses. For example, there is a wide number of scientific decision models such as

- Ansoff's Matrix (see unit 29);
- Porter's 5 Forces analysis (see unit 129);
- decision trees (see unit 105);
- network analysis (see unit 98).

In this unit, we will look at another two decision making models: fishbone diagrams and force field analysis.

Fishbone diagrams

Fishbone (or cause-and-effect or Ishikawa) diagrams are used to identify the causes of a problem. Fishbone diagrams were popularised by Kaoru Ishikawa, who pioneered quality management processes in Japanese shipyards.

To use the technique, first, the problem is identified. In Figure 1, it is placed on the right hand side of the diagram. Then the causes of the problem are identified. Each major cause (or **general cause**) is placed on one of the arrows which feeds through to the central spine of the diagram. Then smaller arrows may be placed showing the more **refined causes** – the causes of a major cause. The diagram looks like a fishbone and hence the name for it. For example, a company may find that its sales growth is disappointing. On investigation, it finds that a major cause of the failure to grow overall sales is the performance of the Northern sales team. A cause of this poor performance might be the ineffective leadership of the Northern senior sales manager as shown in Figure 2.

The causes may be placed on the diagram as they are discussed in a group. Alternatively, they may be placed systematically on the diagram with each major arrow showing a particularly type of cause. For example, the categories for causes may be:

- the 6 Ms - machine, method, materials, measurement, man, and mother nature (the environment);
- the 8 Ps - price, promotion, people, processes, place/plant, policies, procedures, product;
- the 4 Ss - surroundings, suppliers, systems, skills.

Once the causes have been identified, it is up to the team to tackle some of the causes and bring about the change needed to solve the problem.

Force field analysis

Force field analysis was developed in the 1950s by Kurt Lewin, an American social psychologist. It is used to understand the forces of change. In the model, there are two contrary forces.

Driving forces Driving forces are forces which promote change. For example, a new manager with new ideas might be appointed to a post. Or a competitor might bring out a new model which hits sales of your own product. Or a new government regulation might be introduced which affects the business.

Restraining forces Restraining forces are forces which prevent change. For example, subordinates might not put into practice the orders they have received from more senior managers. Equipment may be too old to produce the outcomes now expected. The economy might be in recession and it might be difficult to increase orders.

In the model, an equilibrium is said to exist when the driving forces equal the restraining forces. At this point, there will be no change. If the driving forces are greater than the restraining

Figure 1: A fishbone diagram

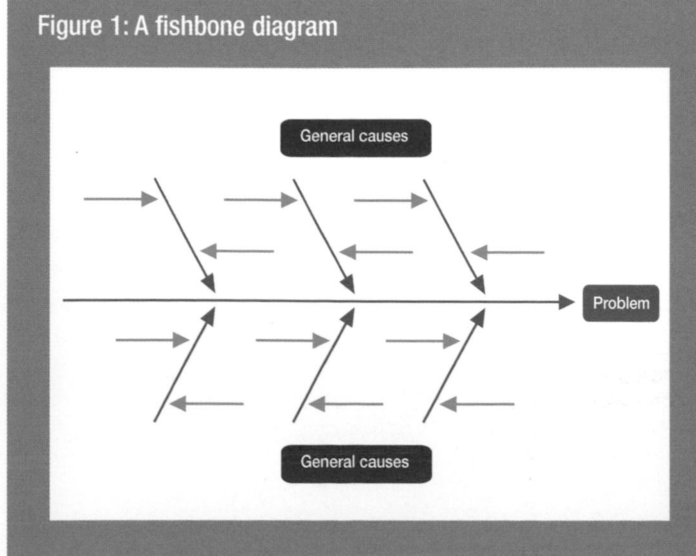

Figure 2: General and refined causes in a fishbone diagram

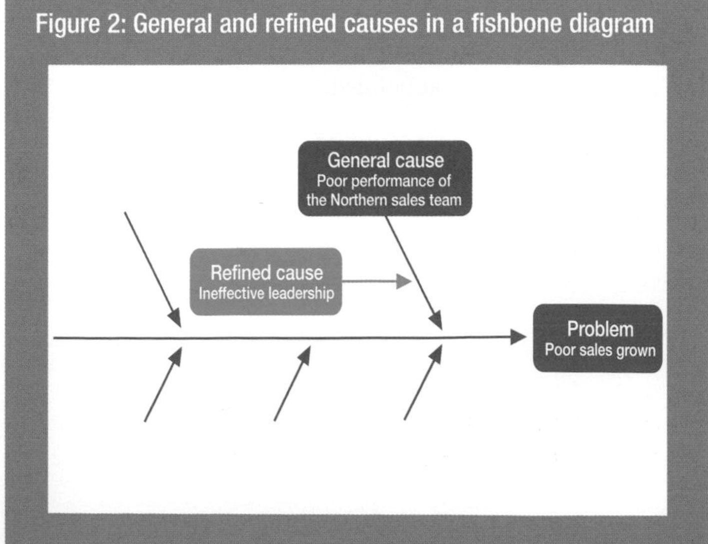

forces, there will be change in the required direction. If the restraining forces are greater than the driving forces, there will be a movement in the opposition direction to what is desired. For example, management may decide that it wants to see sales increase by ten per cent this year. If the economy is in boom, this driving force alone may be enough to secure the ten per cent increase. If the economy is in recession, this may be such a large restraining force that sales actually fall during the year.

Figure 3 shows a force field diagram. To use the model as a management tool, an individual or a team must analyse the following.

- First, it must identify a goal or vision: where does the business, the department, the team or other group want to be?
- It then analyses where it is now in relation to that goal or vision.
- Having understood where it is now and where it wants to be, it should identify the driving forces for change and the restraining forces to change in that situation. The driving forces and restraining forces are given a relative strength on a scale, say from one to five. One might be very weak, five might be very strong.
- To effect change, an imbalance must be achieved in favour of the driving forces. Either the driving forces must become stronger or the restraining forces must be made weaker. It is then up to the management team to introduce changes which will bring this about.

For example, the senior management of a 30 strong sales team may be given the goal of increasing sales by ten per cent over the next year. It decides to use force field analysis to help it understand how this could be achieved. It identifies a number of driving factors which will help it to achieve the goal. The most important, given a '5' rating, is the introduction of a new product in two months' time which should prove popular with customers. However, there is a number of restraining forces. The most powerful restraining force is the performance of the Northern sales team. It has consistently underperformed on sales growth over the past three years despite being given extra training and extra resources. To create the imbalance necessary for change, it is decided that the Northern sales team must be restructured and a new senior area manager appointed.

Figure 3: A force field diagram

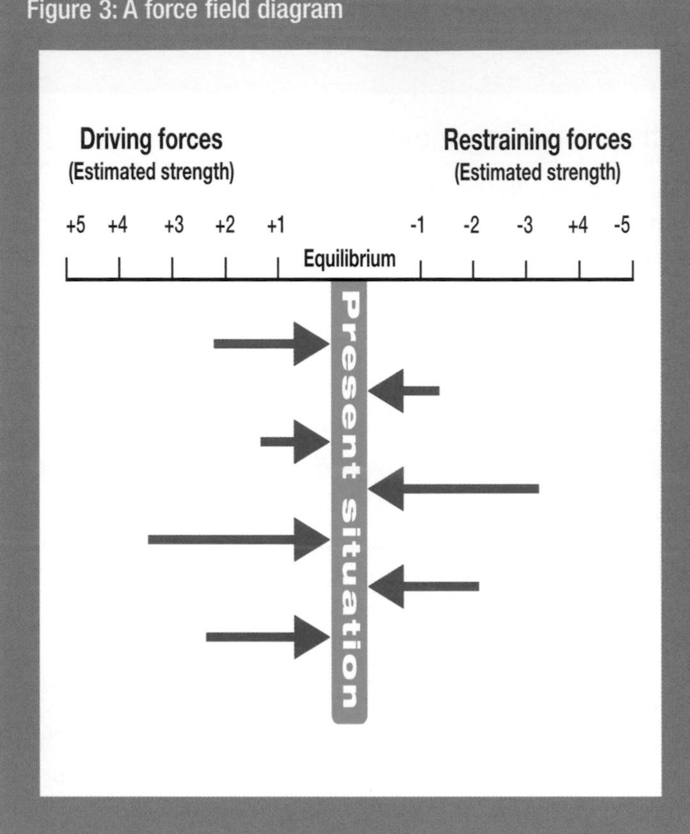

KNOWLEDGE

1. Explain the difference between general and refined causes in a fishbone diagram.
2. In force field analysis, explain the difference between driving and restraining forces.
3. 'For change to occur, there must be an imbalance between driving and restraining forces.' Explain this statement.

Case Study: Delcolt

Delcolt is a furniture manufacturer which specialises in chairs and tables for schools, hospitals, offices and factories. Its manufacturing base is in Sunderland and up until four years ago it sold only into the UK market. At the time, it wanted to expand and thought that it would be easier to do this in Europe than in the UK. So it set up two sales offices, one in Paris, the other in Berlin. Both were operated as profit centres and set profit targets. In the first year, it was recognised that both would make a loss as contacts were built up amongst potential customers. The second year, the profit centres were expected to break even. For the past two years, targets have been set and missed by both profit centres, as can be seen from Table 1.

The sales managers in Paris and Berlin have different ways of working. Henri Ducas in Paris tends to be cautious in his operations. He keeps a tight control on costs and is focussed on meeting targets. Paul Stengelhofen is much less systems-orientated. Gaining a sale is what gives him most satisfaction. The difference showed up just two months ago. Paul Stengelhofen succeeded in selling some furniture to the Lilles office of a German company. Lilles is in Northern France. When Henri Ducas heard about it, he immediately faxed a memo of complaint to Sunderland and Berlin. Henri argued that any sales in France should have gone through the Paris office where they had the expertise to deal with French customers. Paul Stengelhofen simply replied that a 'sale was a sale' and why bother to make a fuss about who dealt with it.

Henri also complains that the French market is much tougher than the German market. There are more competitors in the French market and customers tend to spend less per order than German customers. Therefore he has, in fact, been set much tougher targets than Paul Stengelhofen in the German market. Paul dismisses this and says that Henri's sales team fail to close deals often enough.

Both Henri and Paul have put part of the blame for their failure to achieve their profit targets on the product range of the company. They argue that, whilst it might be attractive to British buyers, it lacks the design flair that is needed in the French and German markets. Their competitors are selling more stylish products and winning orders. They also argue that the product ranges are overpriced. They could clinch far more deals if prices were 20-30 per cent lower. If nothing else, lower prices would overcome some of the customer resistance to the design issues with the range.

Table 1: Delcolt: management accounts for Paris and Berlin offices: 2006-2009

				£
	2006	**2007**	**2008**	**2009**
Paris office				
Sales turnover	30,000	90,000	300,000	500,000
Cost of sales	15,000	45,000	150,000	250,000
Overheads	120,000	150,000	150,000	150,000
Total costs	135,000	195,000	300,000	400,000
Profit	-105,000	-105,000	0	100,000
Target profit	-100,000	0	100,000	200,000
Berlin office				
Sales turnover	40,000	130,000	380,000	660,000
Cost of sales	20,000	65,000	190,000	330,000
Overheads	130,000	150,000	180,000	200,000
Total costs	150,000	215,000	370,000	530,000
Profit	-110,000	-85,000	10,000	130,000
Target profit	-100,000	0	100,000	200,000

(a) Delcolt has a problem. Its French and German operations are failing to make enough profit. Use a Fishbone diagram to discuss the causes of the problem. (40 marks)

(b) Delcolt wants its French and German operations to achieve their profit targets next year. Use force field analysis to discuss a possible solution to this problem. (40 marks)

107 Contingency planning

Crises

Every business faces crises in its day-to-day operations. A CRISIS is usually an unforeseen event which threatens the business in some way. Crises in a business occur for a variety of reasons.

Production Production crises are common in business. On a day-to-day basis, machinery and vehicles may break down, causing production delays. Over a short period a company might receive unexpectedly large orders, causing it to run out of stock of raw materials. More rarely, a fire might destroy premises or flooding might bring work to a halt for several days. In winter, construction businesses, for example, may lose time because of abnormal weather conditions. Snow may also prevent workers getting into work.

Finance Many businesses experience financial crises. A common financial problem is a cash flow crisis. This is when a business does not have enough cash to pay its bills. However, some businesses face a financial crisis because of unforeseen events, such as the sudden loss of a major customer. Another problem that can arise is that a firm's bankers may suddenly decide to withdraw an overdraft facility or recall a large loan, which could force the business into receivership.

Human resources Human resource problems are as common as production and finance problems for businesses. A crisis may take place simply by a worker not turning up for work. In a restaurant, for example, if there are just two cooks in the kitchen and one fails to turn up on a business night, the kitchen might be in crisis. Equally, a sudden walkout by staff over an industrial relations issue can cause chaos within the business. Other events which can cause problems include key workers suddenly leaving for a better job elsewhere, a flu virus sweeping through a workforce leaving many unable to come into work, or the sacking of a popular manager.

Product quality Most businesses at some time experience a problem with the product they make or with the quality of supplies coming into the business. In a bakery, a whole batch of bread might have to be thrown away because it was overcooked. In the car industry, a car model might have to be recalled because a fault is found. Production might come to a sudden stop because supplies of a key component are found to be faulty and unusable.

Public relations Some large businesses have faced public relations crises. A newspaper, for example, may run a story about how a company is sourcing materials from Third World producers which use cheap labour. A television company may broadcast a programme about poor work conditions in one of the company's factories. These stories can have an immediate effect on sales, with some customers boycotting the company.

Environmental issues Some businesses face considerable environmental challenges. Nuclear power, the chemicals industry or any form of mining may suffer crises because of environmental issues. For example, a crisis might occur because of the breakdown of safety equipment, a sudden spillage of waste into a river or a fire which releases toxic chemicals into the atmosphere.

Corporate crises Some crises threaten the business as a whole. For example, a company may suddenly face a takeover bid. Major shareholders may decide to sell their shares, threatening to destabilise the share price.

Contingency planning

Most businesses recognise that crises will arise in the future. However, it could be argued that relatively few have effective plans in place to deal with unforeseen eventualities. Those that do have plans tend to be larger businesses or well planned SMEs. Planning now, about how to do deal with a crisis in the future, is

Question 1.

In February 1997, Aisin Seiki, a brake manufacturer in Japan making parts for Toyota, was completely destroyed by fire. The impact on Toyota was devastating. The brake manufacturer was the sole supplier of brakes to Toyota plants in Japan and Toyota used a just-in-time delivery system for the brakes. Within hours, Toyota plants were running out brake parts and overall, 18 of Toyota's Japanese plants were shut down for almost two weeks. Estimated sales losses were 70,000 vehicles worth $325 million.

The fire didn't just affect Toyota. Hundreds of Toyota's other suppliers were forced to shut down because they could no longer supply Toyota's assembly lines whilst they were out of action.

Toyota resolved the problem in the short term by working with other brake manufacturers that usually supplied Toyota's rivals, Nissan and Honda. These brake manufacturers agreed to supply Toyota with brake parts at a competitive price. In the long term, Toyota has diversified its component purchases to ensure that no single plant can bring Toyota's production to a standstill again.

Source: adapted from www.converium.com.

(a) Explain, using the example of Toyota, why just-in-time manufacturing can lead to a crisis which shuts down a factory.

(b) Discuss whether manufacturers should hold large stocks of components and raw materials to avoid the problem experienced by Toyota.

called CONTINGENCY PLANNING.

The first step in contingency planning is to identify the possible crises that could affect the business. The second step is to think about possible ways of dealing with each crisis. Then the best solution can be identified and plans drawn up showing how the business will respond. In some cases, it may be desirable to carry out practice exercises to familiarise staff with how the crisis will be dealt with. For example, a business may identify fire on the premises as a possible risk which would threaten the lives of employees. Escape routes would then be planned and employees notified of what to do in the event of a fire. There may follow regular fire practices, where staff practise evacuating the building.

Contingency planning is a cost for a business. Management time has to be spent on this activity. Most potential crises are either too trivial or too unlikely to be worth considering. So contingency planning has to be limited to:

- situations where contingency planning is required by law, such as under the Health and Safety Act;
- crises with a relatively high probability of occurring, such as an incident which could potentially generate negative public relations;
- crises with a relatively low probability of occurring, but which if they did occur would have a very high cost for the business.

For example, a particular crisis which could cost a business £5 million might have a 20 per cent probability of occurring in any 12 month period. The cost to the company if the crisis occurred over the next 12 months is mathematically £1 million (£5 million x 20 per cent). If the cost of contingency planning for the event is £5,000, then there is a clear advantage to the business of carrying out contingency planning. Equally, if a particular crisis would cost a business £100 million and there is a probability of 0.1 per cent of the event happening, then the potential cost is £100,000 (£100 million x 0.1) If the cost of carrying out contingency planning for this event is £5,000, then there is still an advantage to the business of doing this despite the low probability of the event. On the other hand, if the cost of a crisis were to be £5 million, but there is a 0.01 per cent chance of the event happening over the next 12 months, then the potential lost is only £500 (£5 million x 0.01 per cent). If the cost of formulating a contingency plan for this event is £5,000, it may not be worth carrying out.

Question 2.

Jocelyn Milne is the office manager at Reid Architecture, a small business employing 100 staff with an Office in Oxford Circus, London. Chatting with staff from some of the businesses nearby, she was shocked to learn that they were working in an area that was a possible terrorist target. A few months ago, she was asked by the firm's professional-indemnity insurers what contingency plans had been put in place should disaster strike. She discovered that nothing had been organised.

As a result, Mark Taylor, a director at the company, began formulating an action plan. 'When we discussed this at board level, everyone had seen what had happened since September 11 and realised how real problems could be. But we didn't quite realise how complex it was to formulate a disaster plan.' On September 11 2001, terrorists flew two planes into the World Trade Centre in New York destroying the building. Taylor had to develop a brief that identified the company's key workers and set out what to do if staff could not get into the building, how to make sure that all important information stored on the computers was saved or retrieved, and how to maintain internal and external lines of communication. He planned for a variety of scenarios, ranging from being evacuated for a day to a week or permanently.

Source: adapted from *The Sunday Times*, 29.6.2003.

(a) Explain why Reid Architecture needed a contingency plan to deal with a situation such as its location being a terrorist target.

(b) Suggest why the measures in the contingency plan drawn up by Reid Architecture, such as making sure all computer data was retrievable, was important to an architectural practice.

Contingency planning and crisis management

Contingency planning and CRISIS MANAGEMENT will involve a number of different areas of the business.

Finance A crisis may have financial implications. For example, if a fire destroys a factory, output will be lost and so revenue will fall. Then there will be costs of rebuilding. The cost of replacing machinery of buildings due to fire and flooding, and the interruption to a business's activity, can be insured against. However, a loss of profit caused as a result of a downturn in the market, the failure of a product due to poor design or industrial action cannot be insured against. A business may also hold contingency funds. These are reserves of cash held back to deal with the financial implications of a crisis. Equally, a business may arrange for an overdraft or loan facility with its bankers to be drawn up in a crisis.

All these methods lead to extra costs for the business. Insurance premiums have to be paid, holding cash means that it cannot be used productively elsewhere in the business and banks charge fees for arranging overdrafts and loan facilities even if no money is borrowed.

Production Potentially, there are many different crises which involve production. A simple problem is machinery breaking down. A business may plan to transfer production to another machine, or it may have a 24 hour 365 day a year call out contract with a machine repair business. A more serious crisis would occur if a large company used just-in-time production techniques and its sole supplier of a key component suffered a fire which stopped all production. The company's contingency plan may identify an alternative source of supply. Or it may have drawn up plans with the supplier to organise a resumption of production within 48 hours by using rented equipment and new rented premises.

Human resource management If a crisis is to be successfully resolved, it must be clear who is responsible for dealing with the crisis. A contingency plan must therefore include the names of who will take charge in the crisis and what roles they will fulfil. Chains of command and channels of communication should be clearly set out. For example, a holiday company may run coach tours in Germany. There is a risk that a coach may suffer a crash, with casualties amongst the passengers. A contingency plan for such a risk may give responsibility for dealing with the problems resulting from the crash to a senior manager. Underneath the senior manager may be another manager responsible for setting up a crisis call centre where relatives can ring to get information. The plan may state that call operatives have the authority to offer relatives affected a free flight to Germany. A more senior employee may have the authority to give out immediate hardship grants of £1,000 to families affected. Meanwhile, it may be planned that a small team will fly out to Germany to deal with victims in hospitals and to deal with the dead. The team would also be responsible for looking after the relatives as they arrive in Germany. An individual may be made responsible for dealing with the press, issuing press releases and giving interviews.

Equally important in a crisis is the motivation of staff. In practice, employees tend to react positively in a crisis. If there is a fire or flood, for example, staff will typically work long hours to deal with the aftermath. However, the contingency plan should consider how employees will be rewarded for their positive response in a crisis. If a fire completely destroys a factory, and it takes three weeks to start up again in new premises, will the staff be paid for those three weeks even though they stay at home not working? Should staff be given a bonus for dealing with a crisis? If temporary staff need to be taken on to deal with a crisis, what in the contingency plan deals with possible friction between existing employees and the new staff leading to poor morale?

Marketing Marketing may pose considerable problems in a crisis. The contingency plan must deal with these marketing challenges. For example, if there is a fire which disrupts production, how will the business look after its customers? The contingency plan may say that supplies should be bought from rival producers and delivered to customers. Or customers may be contacted individually to explain the problems and given a timetable for when supplies will be resumed. Compensation may be offered to customers for the disruption caused by a temporary loss of supply. If the crisis is caused by a fault with a product, the contingency plan may state that all existing supplies will be recalled with the company paying for the recall. Compensation may be offered to customers who have already bought faulty products.

The contingency plan may outline how public relations will be handled in the event of a crisis. An individual may be nominated to deal with the press. The amount of information to be given out may be decided in advance in the contingency plan.

Success and failure

When faced with a serious crisis, such as the destruction of premises, a small business which does not have contingency plans may be forced to cease trading. Even large companies without plans can be forced out of business by a single catastrophe. When a foreign exchange trader working for Barings Bank lost $1 billion, the bank was forced to put itself up for sale to survive. Lesser crises are still likely to harm a business. Fires, floods and faulty products all tend to lead to one-off costs to a business which are not offset by gains elsewhere. Without contingency planning, these costs are likely to be higher than if there is planning in place.

Occasionally, however, crises can have an overall positive impact on a business. An airline, for example, which looks after its customers when it has to suspend flights may gain positive public relations. A devastating fire may be an opportunity to

KEYTERMS

Contingency planning - the creation of plans of how particular crises which might affect a business will be dealt with should they arise.

Crisis - usually an unforeseen event which threatens the business in some way, such as a sudden drop in sales, a fire which destroys premises or the discovery of a fault in a product.

Crisis management - dealing effectively with an unforeseen or unplanned event.

KNOWLEDGE

1. What type of crises might a small engineering company face?
2. Explain how a contingency plan might be drawn up.
3. Should every contingency be considered by a business in contingency planning?
4. How might a business react to a crisis in (a) finance; (b) production; (c) human resources; (d) marketing?
5. Why do contingency plans need to be reviewed regularly?

rebuild to allow more efficient production.

Contingency planning does not guarantee that a business will survive a crisis. For example, a business may have planned for a range of crises, except for the one that actually occurs. Or the plans may have been drawn up too long ago to reflect the current situation in which the business finds itself. The planning itself may have been faulty. When tested, solutions may prove inadequate.

Because of the changing business environment, contingency plans need to be reviewed on a regular basis. Current assumptions about potential crises must be constantly questioned and methods to deal with them constantly updated.

Case Study: Maya Lim

Table 1: Profit and loss account of Maya Lim

Profit and loss account for year ended 31.5.2008	
	£
Turnover	83,890
Cost of sales	41,498
Gross profit	42,392
Expenses	37,720
Net profit	4,672

Maya Lim found her life turned upside down when a leak, followed by an explosion, effectively destroyed her premises which were part of a shopping centre. Maya was ill-prepared for such a disaster. She, along with all the other people in the shopping centre at the time, were safely evacuated so at least there was no loss of life and few injuries. However, her business was one of a number of firms that never recovered.

Part of the problem was that her business had not been doing particularly well financially. Table 1 shows the profit and loss account for her last year of full trading. She had an agreed overdraft limit of £8,000 with her bank and on the day of the explosion, she was overdrawn on her bank account by £7,854. She had also £10,450 of outstanding trade credit, much of it already overdue to her suppliers from the run up to the previous Christmas which had seen very disappointing sales.

In the aftermath of the explosion, Maya, along with other retailers in the centre were unable to visit the premises for a number of days. She didn't know what she was going to find, but it was worse than she imagined. Her entire stock was so damaged that none of it was saleable and fixtures and fittings were not worth salvaging. The small office at the back of the outlet where she kept most of her business records was particularly badly affected. Some of the records were completely destroyed, whilst others were only useable with difficulty.

Maya spent days worrying about what she would find. Seeing the premises in such a condition worried her considerably. She knew she had to decide what to do about her business, but she found she couldn't face up to the difficult decisions that lay ahead. The management of the shopping centre let her know that it would have to be completely rebuilt and so premises would not be available certainly in the short term and possibly for more than a year. So she would have to look for new premises. Then she would have to buy in new stock. But she had no cash. The insurance payout for the damage would take months to come. It would only cover the cost of the stock and fixtures and fittings anyway. She had no insurance for loss of earnings while she couldn't trade. She couldn't see how her bank would increase her overdraft limit. Nor could she see any supplier giving her more trade credit given her existing debts.

By the time her unit in the centre had been repaired, Maya had got a management job paying £30,000 a year and she was no longer interested in taking back the premises.

(a) Explain the nature of the crisis that faced Maya Lim from the perspective of finance, marketing, production and human resources. (40 marks)

(b) Discuss whether any amount of contingency planning would have saved Maya's business in the aftermath of the crisis. (40 marks)

108 Organisational culture

Organisational culture

Every place of work has a slightly different atmosphere. Some are busy, some are friendly, some are disorganised and some are shabby. This reflects the ORGANISATIONAL CULTURE (sometimes also called ORGANISATION CULTURE or CORPORATE CULTURE or BUSINESS CULTURE) of a business. Organisational culture is the values, attitudes, beliefs, meanings and norms that are shared by people and groups within an organisation.

Edgar Schein, a US writer, suggested in 1985 (*Organisational culture and leadership*) that organisational culture existed at three levels within a business. These three levels are shown in Figure 1.

Surface manifestations These are examples of organisation culture which can easily be seen by a wide range of stakeholders. They include:

- artifacts, such as furniture, clothes or tools – wearing a uniform would be an example;
- ceremonials, such as award giving ceremonies or the singing of the company song at the start of work;
- courses, such as induction courses, or ongoing training courses for workers used to instil organisational culture;
- heroes of the business, living or dead, such as Bill Gates, Richard Branson or Walt Disney, whose way of working provides a role model within the business;
- language used in a business specific way, such as Asda referring to its workers as 'colleagues' or McDonald's calling its workers 'crew members';
- mottoes, which are short statements which never change, expressing the values of an organisation such as John Lewis's motto 'Never knowingly undersold';
- slogans, which are short statements that can change over time, such as British Airways 'the worlds favourite airline';
- stories, which tell of some important event which exemplifies the values of the business;
- myths, which are frequently told stories within a business about itself but there is not necessarily any evidence that these stories are literally true;
- norms, which are the ways in which most workers behave, such as not worrying if you turn up for work late, always being prepared to cover for workers who are off sick, or thinking it is acceptable to use the company's telephone to make personal calls;
- physical layout of premises, such as open plan offices, 'hot desking', or allocating the size of an office according to a manager's place in the hierarchy;
- rituals, which are regular events that reinforce the culture of an organisation, such as always supporting Red Nose Day (we are a caring organisation), having a weekly 'dress down day' (we are a relaxed organisation), or holding an annual Christmas party (we are a sociable organisation);
- symbols, which are signs that represent the business, such as McDonald's 'Golden Arches', or the apple logo of Apple computers.

Surface manifestations are a constant reminder to stakeholders of the culture of an organisation. They are visible and frequently used to create and reinforce that culture. However, they are not the culture itself.

Organisational values Organisational values are located below the surface manifestations of organisational culture. They are consciously thought out and expressed in words and policies. The values expressed in a mission statement would be an example. Often these are the values which have come from the top of an organisation. Perhaps they have come from the original founder of the business. Or perhaps they have come from the current senior management which has attempted to impose a culture on the business. Organisational values might reflect the actual culture of a business. But, equally, they might not. Workers at the bottom of the hierarchy might have very different values from the ones that senior management want them to possess.

Basic assumptions Basic assumptions are the organisation's culture. They represent the totality of individuals' beliefs and how they then behave. They are 'invisible' and below the surface and therefore often difficult to see, understand and change.

In practice, there may be discrepancies between the three levels. For example, a company might organise regular social events for employees (a surface manifestation). It might say in documents that it is a 'friendly and caring employer' (its organisational values). Yet, throughout the organisation there might be a culture of competitiveness which tends to make

Figure 1: Organisational culture at three levels

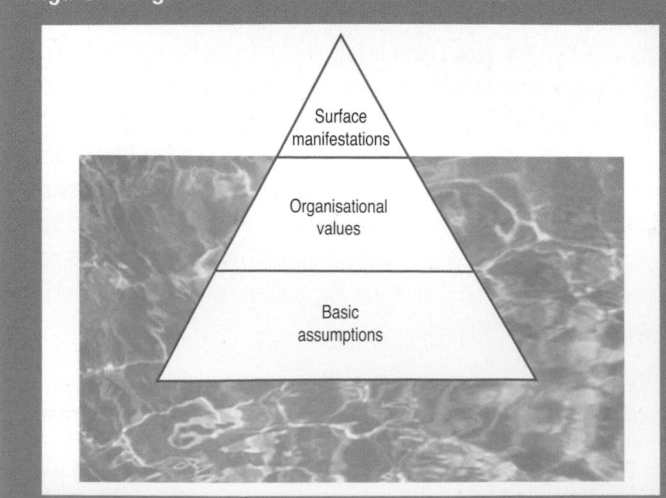

people 'look out for themselves' and makes everyone distrustful of everyone else. In this situation, the actual organisational culture is different from the surface manifestation and the organisational values. In contrast, another organisation might call its employees 'partners' (the surface manifestation). Its mission statement may say that it is committed to 'rewarding employees as well as shareholders' (its organisational values). It may then, year after year, pay employees above the average for the industry and give regular annual bonuses based upon how much profit the business has made during the year (the organisational culture). Here the underlying organisational culture fits with the stated values and the surface manifestation. There is a culture of rewarding employees because they are stakeholders.

Types of organisational culture

There are many ways of classifying organisational culture (i.e. grouping the organisational cultures of different businesses into categories and then describing the general characteristics of those cultures). One attempt to classify organisational culture was made by Charles Handy in *Understanding Organisations* (1981). He argued that there were four main types of organisational culture.

Power culture A power culture is one where there is a central source of power which is responsible for decision making. There are few rules and procedures within the business and these are overridden by the individuals who hold power when it suits them. There is a competitive atmosphere amongst employees. Amongst other things, they compete to gain power because this allows them to achieve their own objectives. This creates a political atmosphere within the business. Relatively young, small to medium sized businesses, where a single owner founded the firm and is still very much in control, could typically have power cultures.

Role culture In a role culture, decisions are made through well established rules and procedures. Power is associated with a role, such as marketing director or supervisor, rather than with individuals. In contrast to a power culture, power lies with the roles that individuals play rather than with the individuals themselves. Role cultures could be described as bureaucratic cultures. The Civil Service could be an example of a role culture.

Task culture In a task culture, power is given to those who can accomplish tasks. Power therefore lies with those with expertise rather than with a particular role, as in a role culture. In a task culture, teamworking is common, with teams made up of the experts needed to get a job done. Teams are created and then dissolved as the work changes. Adaptability and dynamism is important in this culture. Examples of task culture could be businesses which operate cellular manufacturing of components, teamworking in the manufacture of cars, scientific or medical

Question 1.

Dodgeville, Wisconsin USA, is home to the corporate headquarters of Lands' End, the mail order clothing company selling everything from shirts to swimwear. Founded in 1963, it came to the UK in the 1990s setting up in Oakham in Rutland. Just in case you were wondering about why there is an apostrophe at the end of 'Lands', when the first letterhead was produced, the printers put the apostrophe in the wrong place and the company couldn't afford to change it. The story says something about the genuineness of the company and its ability to own up to making mistakes.

Mindy Meads is president and chief executive officer. She is your typical corporate American executive, perfectly pleasant yet unable to see outside the tunnel vision of the company's culture. Asked to describe Lands' End, she replies 'If you were to sum up what Lands' End is for the apparel, it is very high quality, with the fabric we use, some of the workmanship that we put into the product.' Summing up the company ethos, she says: 'We have a very unique culture in our company; so customer driven. Everybody is working together to one goal: to get what the customer wants.'

To illustrate this, she talks about the customer, on the eve of her wedding, ringing and asking a Lands' End saleswoman to give her a 5 a.m. wake-up call. She was happy to oblige. Then there was a rogue batch of turtleneck sweaters. Lands' End voluntarily sent out 800,000 replacements to customers who had already bought the defective product. 'That was quite a bit of money', Mindy Meads conceded, insisting that the goodwill it engendered with customers made it worthwhile. She also talks about Lands' End's stain resistant trousers, perfect for coping with hazardous spills. As the brochure puts it: 'The moment a rogue splash of coffee lands, you'll be thankful for the Teflon technology that causes liquids to simply bead up and roll off.'

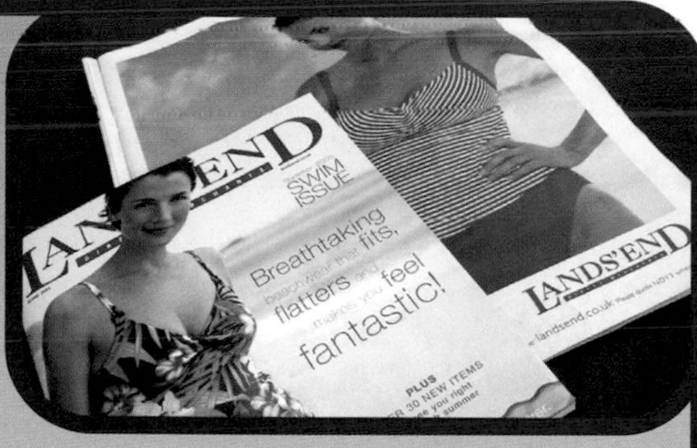

On the Lands' End website, you can find 'The Lands' End Principles of Doing Business'. Included in the eight principles are phrases like 'we do everything we can to make our products better', 'we price our products fairly and honestly', 'we accept any return for any reason, at any time', 'we believe that what is best for our customer is best for all of us' and 'we encourage our customers to shop for our products in whatever way they find most convenient'.

Source: adapted from *The Times*, 6.3.2004.

(a) **What (i) surface manifestations and (ii) organisational values are described in the passage of Lands' End's organisational culture?**

(b) **If the surface manifestations and organisational values permeate the whole organisational culture, what sort of beliefs would you expect Lands' End's workers to have and how would you expect them to behave?**

Question 2.

In 2005, there was a large explosion at the BP oil refinery in Texas City, Texas. Fifteen people were killed and 180 more were injured. A number of enquiries were launched, including one by the US Congress, the equivalent of the UK Parliament and one by BP itself.

Part of the blame for the accident was put by the BP enquiry on the company's global management culture. There was a lack of clear lines of responsibility within BP's refining business. BP managers routinely ignored standard procedures. Guidance from corporate headquarters was too often interpreted as orders and managers had a 'lack of respect for audit findings' that were too often not sent to the appropriate people. Within the refining group, the corporate culture suffered from a 'lack of corporate memory' and 'broken' performance management systems at the highest levels. 'Incompetent' workers were allowed to remain in their posts and 'mavericks' who ignored standard procedures were tolerated, it added.

The congressional investigation suggested, however, that BP managers may have deliberately underspent on maintenance in an effort to meet corporate cost cutting goals. This followed deep cost cutting ordered by BP headquarters after it had acquired the refinery in a merger.

Source: adapted from news.bbc.co.uk, 1.11.2006.

(a) **BP puts safety above profit. Explain, however, why organisational culture might have led to the Texas disaster.**

(b) **Evaluate how BP's organisational culture needs to change to prevent a repetition of the Texas accident.**

(c) **What might be the obstacles to changing BP's organisational culture?**

project research operations or exploration of raw materials.

Person culture A person culture is one where there is a number of individuals in the business who have expertise but who don't necessarily work together particularly closely. The purpose of the organisation is to support those individuals. Examples of person cultures could be firms of accountants, lawyers, doctors or architects.

Changing organisational culture

Some writers, such as Tom Peters and Robert Waterman in *In Search of Excellence* (1982) have claimed that organisational culture can give a business a competitive advantage. Companies such as Microsoft, McDonald's or Virgin have been successful because they had an appropriate organisational culture for their industry. When the organisational culture is not right, then the organisation is likely to suffer from a competitive disadvantage.

For example, in the 1970s and 1980s, Japanese motor manufacturers gained a competitive advantage over their US and European rivals through the introduction of lean manufacturing techniques. Part of this was an attention to quality. Poor quality work became unacceptable within the Japanese car industry. The business used the slogan 'zero defects'. The values were expressed in the work procedures of car plants. But underlying all this was an understanding amongst workers that quality standards had to be met all the time. Quality was put above maximising output. In contrast, US and European manufacturers at the time paid lip service to quality but on the factory floor, poor quality workmanship was a daily fact of life. In the 1990s, US and European car manufacturers copied Japanese lean production techniques simply to survive. Part of that was completely changing the attitudes of workers to quality. Through training and changing the way in which employees worked, quality has improved enormously.

Changing business culture can, however, be difficult. The CULTURE GAP, the difference between the current culture and the culture that is desired by certain stakeholders such as senior management, can be very large. There is a variety of obstacles which need to be overcome if culture is to change.

Workers' and managers' views Both management and workers can be resistant to change. Many will have worked within the business for a long time. They will be used to certain ways of working. Change can threaten this. Change may also threaten their jobs or pay. One way of dealing with such problems is to work with managers and workers to change their attitudes and beliefs. Careful and sensitive implementation of change over a period of time can lead to a change in culture. For example, training can be used to explain why change is needed and how it is to be implemented. Equally, where there are performance-related pay systems, increases in pay or bonuses can be linked to changes in work methods and work attitudes. A more radical method is to make managers and workers redundant who resist change. Or they might be redeployed to jobs where they cannot influence the changes taking place. In extreme cases, businesses have been known to close a whole site and move the work elsewhere. In the UK motor industry, for example, some car plants have been told that unless they make the changes to lean production techniques, they would be closed. Sacking workers is more likely to take place where there is some urgency to change the culture. For example, if managers at a factory are told that they must raise productivity by 40 per cent over the next twelve months or risk closure, this can lead to very rapid change.

Technology and the physical environment Culture can often be maintained and promoted by the physical environment in which the business operates. An office building made up of small rooms will not promote open communication between staff. A production line where workers are stationed in isolation along the line, performing repetitive tasks, is unlikely to promote responsibility and quality assurance. Changing culture often means changing the physical environment in which workers operate. Building a new facility and hiring mostly new workers presents a real opportunity to completely change organisational culture. Few businesses, however, can do this. Instead, they have to make a large number of small changes, such as buying new equipment or moving the office furniture around, to create a change in culture. The inability to make a completely new start means that changes in culture can take a long time. It also explains why some new businesses can be so successful at winning market share from older more established businesses.

The external environment Sometimes it is the external environment which is the obstacle to changing organisational culture. For example, health and safety legislation or employment law might limit the ability of businesses to encourage a new culture within the business. A lack of competition in the market might reinforce a culture of complacency and no change. There were significant changes in those industries that were privatised and opened up to competition in the UK in the 1980s and 1990s. National and regional cultures can also have an important impact on organisational cultures. It can be argued that French companies have different organisational cultures to Japanese or US companies. Trying to make a business more entrepreneurial, for example, might be easier in the USA with its strong focus on individualism than in a country with a strong focus on collectivism.

Effects of organisational culture

Organisational culture affects a business in a wide variety of ways. Three of these ways are on motivation, organisational structures and change.

Motivation Organisational culture affects the motivation of staff. It can have a direct effect because the way in which staff treat each other impacts on motivation. For example, motivation is likely to be greater if the culture of the organisation respects individual workers and their achievements. A highly competitive culture might motivate some workers and demotivate others. Organisational culture can also indirectly affect motivation. An organisational culture which leads to a successful business is likely in itself to motivate staff because they feel part of a successful business.

Organisational structures Organisational culture can affect the organisational structure of a business. In a person culture, for example, the hierarchy is likely to be fairly flat. So in an architects' practice or a doctors' practice there are are unlikely to be many layers of management. This is because a number of key workers, like partners in a doctors practice, share the senior management roles. In a role culture, in contrast, there is likely to be more layers of management. The larger the business, the more layers in the hierarchy there are likely to be as specialist roles are assigned.

New management One way for a business to change is for new management to be appointed. The greater the change needed, the more likely it is that the new management will have to confront the existing organisational culture. The organisational culture is likely to be part of the problem which needs addressing if the business is to be turned around.

Mergers and takeovers When two businesses merge or one takes over another, each business is likely to have a different organisational culture. The process of creating a single business out of the two organisations will therefore involve changing organisational culture. In a takeover, one simple way of making that change quickly is for the senior management in the company being taken over to be made redundant. Without powerful advocates at the top of the organisation, those lower down will find it difficult to resist the change that will be imposed upon them. However, motivation and morale is often low in a company which has been taken over for the first 12-24 months because they are being forced to change.

Advantages of a strong corporate culture

It is argued that there are certain advantages to a business of establishing a strong corporate culture.

- It provides a sense of identity for employees. They feel part of the business. This may allow workers to be flexible when the company needs to change or is having difficulties.
- Workers identify with other employees. This may help with aspects of the business such as team work.
- It increases the commitment of employees to the company. This may prevent problems such as high labour turnover or industrial relations problems.
- It motivates workers in their jobs. This may lead to increased productivity.
- It allows employees to understand what is going on around them. This can prevent misunderstanding in operations or instructions passed to them.
- It helps to reinforce the values of the organisation and senior management.
- It acts as a control device for management. This can help when setting company strategy.

Criticisms of corporate culture

It has been suggested that a business will benefit if management ensures that:

- there is a strong corporate culture:
- the 'culture gap' is kept to a minimum and there is a single corporate culture that all people in the business work towards.

Certain criticisms of this view have been put forward.

Corporate culture and economic performance John Kotter and James Heskett (1992) researched the relationship between corporate culture and economic performance. They tested the idea that a strong culture improves performance by measuring the strength of the culture of 207 large firms from a variety of industries. A questionnaire was used to calculate a 'culture index' for each firm. They then looked for any correlation between a strong culture and the firm's economic performance over an eleven year period. The research did show a positive correlation, but weaker than most management theorists would have expected. Strong culture firms seemed almost as likely to perform poorly as their weak-culture rivals.

Question 3.

Royal Dutch/Shell group, the oil group, believes that managing talent is a matter of 'tugging at the heartstrings' of employees. It argues that young recruits choose companies because of the values, beliefs and the culture of the organisation. As a result, Shell has developed a set of business principles which places honesty, integrity and respect for people at the core of its corporate culture. Shell organises a worldwide survey of all employees to find out how they feel about the company. Michael Osbaldeston, head of Shell Global Learning, says 'The result gives us a clearer picture of how attractive a company Shell is to work for and how we could do better in the future'.

Retaining innovative workers is crucial for the Pentland Group, which designs and produces sportswear such as Speedo and Ellesse. It changed the working environment by incorporating lots of natural light, communal space, coffee bars and a gym into its new building. But it found that this, in itself, was not enough without good management practice. It has just completed a company-wide assessment of its management behaviour. It found that the immediate supervisor is massively influential in terms of people's productivity. 'Good management is fundamental to releasing talented workers to do what they do best and when you do that you retain them' says Chris Matcham, group human resources director.

Source: adapted from Guardian Unlimited.

(a) Explain the features of successful corporate cultures of the businesses in the article.

(b) Suggest possible benefits to these businesses of the corporate cultures they have adopted.

Different perspectives on corporate culture There are other views on the nature of corporate culture.

- A business is made up of sub-cultures which coexist. Sometimes these are in harmony, but sometimes in conflict. There may be differences of interests and opinions among different groups. As a result, cultural practices in companies are interpreted in different ways by employees. These may not always be those intended by management. For example, a profit-sharing scheme may be seen as a sign of equality by one group. Everyone gets a share in the profits, not just management and shareholders. Another group, however, may see it as a bribe for employees to conform with the company.
- The main feature of business life is ambiguity. Companies lack clear centres due to decentralisation, delegation and the employment of temporary and part-time workers. Also, new working practices often leave employees physically separated and socially distant. As a result, employees share some viewpoints, disagree on others and are indifferent to yet others.

These approaches are seen as positive, to meet the requirements of the complexity of business life. The way businesses do things can be interpreted in a variety of ways. Values, beliefs, and norms may not be shared between individual employees or between employees and management. The reason why someone does something in the way they do may not be just because management has created a culture that everyone follows. It may be because of other factors, such as outside influences, internal politics, self- interest, the sub-culture of a group, or different individual personalities.

KEYTERMS

Culture gap - the difference between the current culture and the culture that is desired by certain stakeholders such as senior management.

Organisational or organisation or corporate or business culture - the values, attitudes, beliefs, meanings and norms that are shared by people and groups within an organisation.

KNOWLEDGE

1. Explain the difference between surface manifestations, organisational values and basic assumptions of corporate culture.
2. Explain the differences between a power culture, a role culture, a task culture and a person culture.
3. How can organisational culture give businesses a competitive advantage?
4. How can a culture gap hold back a business?
5. Outline the possible impact of organisational culture on (a) staff motivation and (b) the organisational structure of a business.
6. State five advantages of a strong organisational culture.
7. Explain two criticisms of having a uniform organisational culture within a business.

Case Study: Radigan's

Brian Strode was appointed Chief Executive of Radigan's two years ago. Radigan's is a medium-sized engineering company with 750 employees. Once, the company was much larger, with at its peak some 5,000 employees spread over three sites. Today, the company is based on one site reflecting the need to concentrate resources to gain competitive advantage.

When Brian Strode came into the company, he could see that it faced massive problems. Previous management had underinvested in every part of the business. Equipment was old, products were not at the cutting edge in the field and training of staff was non-existent. It was not surprising that Radigan's was struggling to maintain sales.

When talking to workers and managers about change, most seemed to think that the attitudes of other staff could not be changed. They put forward a variety of reasons why change was almost impossible. Some pointed to the main trade union representing shop floor workers as a major obstacle. They said it would resist any changes in the conditions of service of employees. Others said that staff were too set in their ways to change. They had always done the job like this and it would be impossible to get them to do it a different way. Half the workforce, including most of the managers, were over the age of 45 and there were only two employees under the age of 25. Another problem often cited was the strong division of workers into separate informal groups with distinct identities. Typically, there would be around 10-15 people in a group who took their breaks together, socialised informally together at work and formed friendship patterns outside the workplace. Each group built up a 'them and us' mentality. Each thought it was doing the hardest work in the company whilst other groups were contributing little or nothing to the organisation. Workers on the shop floor saw managers as 'pen pushers' who knew nothing about the 'real' work of the company that they were doing in making products. Managers saw shop floor workers as lazy and inflexible, always ready to find an excuse why something couldn't be done. Overall, most workers were highly cynical about the contribution that other workers made to the company. Equally, most workers and many managers had little idea of the competitive pressures that the company was now facing, particularly from Far Eastern imports.

Looking through the paperwork, Brian Strode could find little that was written down that could inspire change. The company had no mission statement. There was nothing coherent about a vision for the future. Most of what was there seemed to be about reacting to events rather than shaping them. He was surprised that there didn't seem to be much that even supported the very conservative nature of the company.

Looking round the site, Brian observed that everything was very boxed in. The very walls of the factory and offices seemed to emphasis the small group mentality of the workforce. Office staff, for example, were all working in small cramped offices, mostly on their own. Amongst the office staff, there were a lot of posters and stickers on walls or mugs with little work slogans like 'I'm the boss', 'Overworked and underpaid', 'The buck doesn't stop here - keep going' and 'Hard work never killed anyone, but why chance it?'. By 5.30 each evening, the place was deserted. Shop floor workers, office staff and most managers worked to the clock. The minute they were due to leave, they were out like a shot.

Brian set about trying to change the culture of the business. It had to be more responsive to the needs of customers. Costs had to be reduced to maintain sales. Quality needed to be considerably improved. To achieve this, he wanted to see a more flexible and far better trained workforce, probably working in teams and whose goals were aligned to those of the company.

(a) Discuss how Brian Strode could change the organisation's culture from its surface manifestations to its basic assumptions. (40 marks)

(b) To what extent would Radigan be a more successful company if it had a strong organisational culture shared by all staff? (40 marks)

109 Implementing and managing change

What causes change in business?

Businesses today have to operate in rapidly changing markets and conditions. They can no longer rely on a constant stream of customers, the same production process or the same product over a long period of time. They must constantly be aware of, and be prepared to respond to, changes in a number of areas.

Developments in technology The introduction of new technology can affect a business in many ways. There have, for example, been rapid changes in communications technology, production techniques and electronic components in recent years.

Market changes Businesses must respond to changes in the markets in which they sell. There may be competition from new businesses. This has been the case in the energy supply market. Former public sector owned gas and electricity suppliers were privatised and markets opened up to competition. New markets have opened up, such as the mobile phone market for companies such as BT. Competition may also come from new businesses entering a market, such as the offering of financial services by supermarkets. Other factors such as the Single European Market, globalisation, the opening up of markets in eastern Europe and China, the introduction of the euro and the expansion of the EU in 2004 were all likely to change how businesses operate.

Consumer tastes Businesses must also be prepared for changes in the tastes of consumers. Examples might be the purchase of environmentally friendly products, the desire for greater knowledge about products or the need for more efficient methods of shopping, such as purchasing via the Internet.

Legislation Government legislation can force changes in business activity. Taxation of pollution would affect the production methods of many firms. Safety standards, such as EU regulations for VDU users, are also likely to affect how employees operate. Government aid or subsidies may affect the possible location of a business. Legislation on the number of hours employees can work may change work practices.

Changes in the workforce Population changes will affect the age and make-up of the workforce. The ageing of the population in the UK in the early part of the twenty first century was likely to result in changing recruitment policies for businesses. A falling population is also likely to change how a business plans its human resources.

Changes in the economy It is argued that economies go through periods of boom and slump, recession and recovery. This is known as the business cycle. Income, spending, saving, investment and economic variables such as unemployment and inflation are all likely to be different at different stages in the cycle.

The effects of change

The changes illustrated in the last section can have a number of effects on business.

- Product life cycles could become shorter. This means that businesses must constantly be looking to develop new and profitable products or services.
- The role of market research is likely to increase. A business must not be 'surprised' by sudden changes in the market. Research and forecasting techniques should help a firm to predict more accurately the situation in future.
- Research and development will be essential in industries where rapid change is taking place. As well as anticipating market changes, a business must be prepared to respond to the needs of the market with new products, which can compete with those of competitors.
- Retraining of managers and 'shop floor' workers might be necessary. This may be to learn skills associated with new technology or to develop skills to meet changing consumer tastes. Examples may be the education of office staff in communications technology, such as e-mail or videoconferencing or the learning of foreign languages by UK business people wishing to enter foreign markets.
- Businesses must take account of changes in their human resource planning. This could mean employing a more flexible workforce that could be changed quickly to meet the needs of the business, for example employing part time workers, or the use of job sharing. It might also mean employing workers in low cost countries, such as in call centres abroad.
- A business must develop a culture and organisation which is prepared to respond to change.
- Businesses must be aware of competitors' actions and be prepared to react to them. Businesses now benchmark their activities against those of rivals or other companies. Business must also be able to respond to new and emerging markets. These might be new markets abroad or markets for new products within a country.
- Quality is likely to become more important as consumer awareness develops and competition increases. Firms must consider the quality of their products and also their after sales service and customer relations. For example, many businesses have tried to achieve the international BS EN IS0 9000 quality standard.
- Changes in equipment. Rapid change often makes equipment redundant. Businesses may find problems from the inability to read computer disks because software has

been updated to the need for new systems to cope with just-in-time requests. These changes could involve a large amount of spending if businesses do not wish to become outdated.

- Changes in production methods. Rapid changes can sometimes lead to increasing costs. Some businesses have reacted by outsourcing their production to low cost countries. Others have changed the technology they use to reduce costs.

Why manage change?

The management of change in business has grown in importance in recent years. Under pressure from competitors, higher costs and economic conditions, many firms in the UK developed company-wide change programmes.

There are some examples of firms that have made only minor changes to their business operations and remained successful. The Morgan Car Company still retains many of the original production methods and design features that have been part of its operation since the 1930s. It argues that it is exactly these 'original' features that attract consumers. However, most businesses that refuse to change will eventually go out of business.

Resistance to change

Businesses are likely to face some resistance to change from parts of the workforce for a number of reasons.

- Workers and certain levels of management sometimes fear the unknown. They feel safe with work practices, conditions and relationships that they have been used to for a period of time.
- Employees and managers may fear that they will be unable to carry out new tasks, may become unemployed or may face a fall in earnings.
- Individual workers might be concerned that they will no longer work with 'friends', or may be moved to a job which they dislike.

If change is to be carried out effectively, the business must make certain that these fears are taken into account. Only if employees feel they can cope with change, will the business be operating to its potential.

Owners of businesses may also be resistant to change for similar reasons. They might fear operating in unknown markets and conditions. They might not want the cost of any changes. They may also fear that they might not be able to adjust to new situations and be forced out of business.

Resistance may also be found in the **culture** of the organisation. Custom and practice are embedded in systems which reflect the norms, values and beliefs of the organisation. While this may give stability, it presents problems of rigidity when a business needs to change.

Customers and **suppliers** too may resist change. They may be unwilling to change their own practices when the business they are dealing with changes. For example, a company may reorganise its sales force and decide that it will no longer visit clients which give it less than £5 000 worth of orders per year. Instead, it will develop a website and telesales operation to deal with small customers. Inevitably, it will lose some customers which are not prepared to place orders in this way.

In order to deal with resistance to change, many theorists have suggested the need for a multi-step approach. Psychologist

Question 1.

Eversholt Ltd manufactures metal sheets used in the production of a wide range of products. It has recently found that it has been producing increasing amounts of waste metal in its manufacturing processes. As a result charges at landfill sites have risen considerably over the last two years.

Jemma and Niall Kilburn, two of the directors, have come back from a fact finding mission to other countries to see how to make use of recycled waste. In the USA they found a number of businesses which, with the right machinery, were able to move into associated production areas. There was a strong and growing interest in recycled products in the US. Consumers were often prepared to pay a little more knowing their money was helping to preserve the environment. This had led to a growth in a number of new businesses manufacturing recycled metal products.

Jemma and Niall drew up a business plan and presented it to the other directors. They felt that some of them would require a great deal of convincing before the business could make such a great change in direction. The reorganisation also had some wide ranging implications. The recycling machinery would require a large initial investment and would need to have the latest specification to conform to operating standards. Some of the workers at the business would need to be retrained to operate the machines. It was also likely that if the business took off, the operation would need to expand, with everything that would involve.

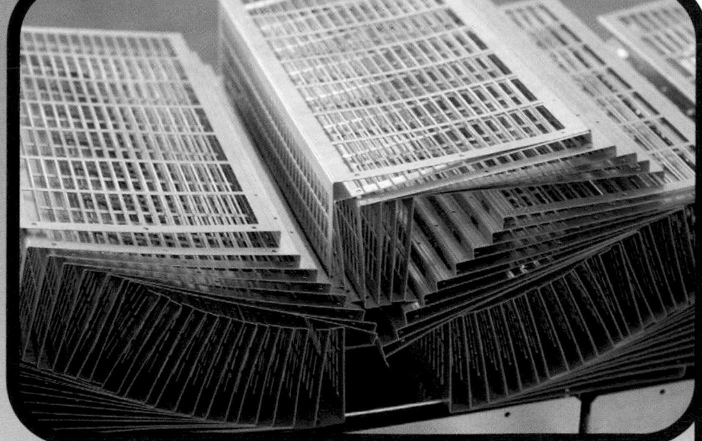

(a) Identify the factors which might have led to change at the business.

(b) Examine the implications for the business of any change in its operations.

Question 2.

Remploy is the UK's largest employer of people with disabilities. It manufactures products as diverse as car headrests, furniture and shower units. It has bucked falling industry trends by achieving a five per cent increase in profits largely by embracing changes in those who make a difference - the workforce.

In the early 2000s the company decided it wanted to increase staff from 12,000 to 25,000 and triple output over a five year period. The personnel director and resource director were asked to work closely to start a major change programme. The idea was that roving internal consultants focus on Remploy sites that had more work than they could cope with. They investigate the 'weakest link' in the production process, then move on to find the next 'weakest link'.

The crux of the change programme was to make sure that every person had a say in how the day to day processes were to be run. This meant that even simple ideas could be shared. For example, one employee suggested sticking coloured tape on the machinists' tables during sewing to improve accuracy and to speed up the process. Staff also wanted to remove a huge overhanging machine so that they could see each other and help to communicate when a constraint in the flow of work had built up.

Assessment is now based on the end product, so that staff have a feeling of ownership and team spirit. Staff morale improved greatly as changes were made with all the factory involved and not just management. The business argues that there were short term benefits but also a long term change in culture. One of the machinists at the company said 'Change is frightening but, because we all have a say, we feel more confident in making those changes'.

Source: adapted from *People Management.*

(a) Identify the approach to managing change at Remploy using examples from the article.
(b) Examine the benefits to (i) employees and (ii) the business of such an approach.

Kurt Lewin emphasised a three step process.

- Introducing an innovation with information aimed to satisfy a need.
- Overcoming resistance by group discussion and decision making.
- Establishing a new practice.

Removing resistance to change

There are certain ways in which resistance to change might be prevented and barriers to change removed.

- There should be clear objectives given to everyone involved in the change. Individual departments or work sections or workers may disagree with the objectives. But it is far worse from a motivational viewpoint for them not to understand why the changes are taking place.
- People who are affected by change might be involved in discussions about the changes that are taking place. This will give them the feeling that they are involved in shaping change and have a stake in its outcome.
- The business should attempt to prevent misinformation and rumours. It may be possible to organise formal meetings where employees are informed about decisions taking place.
- There must be sufficient resources allocated to achieving the change. For example, if an engineering company sets itself the objective of increasing labour productivity (output per worker) by 30 per cent within 12 months but is not prepared to spend any extra on capital investment, it might not be possible to achieve the change. Equally, change often necessitates training of staff. If workers are expected to perform new tasks and new roles, but are given no training, then the level of actual change achieved may be disappointing.
- Following company procedures backed up by the requirements of the law often reduces resistance to change. If workers can see that everyone is being treated equally and that their legal rights are being preserved at all times, they will feel more reassured and less willing to attack the changes being proposed.
- PROJECT CHAMPIONS are usually associated with successful change management. A project champion is someone with power and influence within the organisation that is supporting the change. Project champions are different to project managers, the individuals responsible for managing the change on a day to day basis. Change is often difficult to achieve. Unless there is someone with power and influence to support the project, plans for change can be shelved or fail to be implemented. Project champions maintain motivation for those involved in the project, provide help and advice, secure resources to implement change and push the change agenda with more senior colleagues.
- PROJECT GROUPS are groups of individuals charged with implementing a particular one-off task. The task might be to research a market or consider the impact of new legislation on a business for example. Sometimes, project groups are appointed to implement and manage change. The advantage of creating a project group to implement change is that it makes a group of people responsible for the task. Some project groups include representatives of the main stakeholders in the change. This helps to give the group an insight into the main issues involved in the change. It also creates lines of communication with the stakeholders in the change. By being more involved and better informed, stakeholders are more likely to accept and embrace change.
- The business should try to ensure that its organisational culture fits in with its new operations and organisation. This is discussed in the next section.

Developing an organisational culture for change

An **organisational culture** includes the beliefs, norms and values of a business. It is a generally held view about how people should behave, the nature of working relationships and attitudes. Many companies, especially Japanese firms such as Honda, Toyota and Sony, place great emphasis on all employees understanding the company's 'culture'.

It has been suggested that a business which creates a culture of change is likely to manage it far more effectively. Management at the top must have a clear idea of how they expect the business to change. Structures, methods of training, management styles etc. must then alter to reflect this. Finally a culture must be established where all employed are aware of the new relationship and methods of working.

One model that was widely used to implement change in the 1990s was total quality management (TQM). A feature of TQM is that everyone in the business is responsible for maintaining and improving quality, including the quality of the product, production methods and the supply to the customer. TQM's motto is 'getting it right the first time' and this is applied to external customers and what are known as 'internal customers' - the people employees work with. This approach helps develop a culture where all employees, managers etc. are trying to achieve the same goal, which should motivate, develop teamwork and improve communication, accountability and rewards.

There are those, however, who suggest that organisational culture is not something that can be easily manipulated. They argue that culture depends on human interaction and is continuously being recreated. Hence, to believe that a senior management team can unilaterally change an existing culture according to some blueprint is mistaken. Organisational culture, according to this view does change, but often slowly and in unpredictable ways. There is also a danger of thinking of organisational culture as a single over-arching idea to which all members of the business subscribe. Organisations, however, may have sub-cultures linked to particular groups. There may be conflict between these subcultures. In addition, even if new culture is established, there is no evidence that simply having a new culture improves performance.

Different approaches to managing change

Research by John Storey has suggested that the way businesses manage change can be classified into four different approaches.

A total imposed package One approach to managing change is for people at the 'top' of the business to plan out major restructuring programmes without consultation with workers or worker representatives. The main advantage of this method is that a company can have a 'vision' of where it is going. It can compare where it is 'now' with where it was 'then'. It is possible, using this approach, to prepare departmental action plans, set timetables and measure how far change has been achieved. The business can also make changes without having to take into account the wishes of other groups. The disadvantage of planning change from the top is that middle managers, supervisors and employees may not feel involved.

Imposed piecemeal initiatives A different approach is to have unplanned or piecemeal initiatives designed to bring about change. Initiatives might be introduced by employers to solve particular problems or only at times when they are needed in the business. Examples of initiatives that might take place are:

- the introduction of team meetings or quality circles;
- improvements in technology or channels of communication;
- improvements in incentive payments or rewards;
- improvements in the flexibility of work practices;
- changes in the workforce, such as teleworkers or subcontracting;
- the introduction of performance appraisal.

A problem with piecemeal initiatives is that they sometimes have different objectives. One might be trying to improve management leadership. The other might to trying to encourage greater participation. Another difficulty is that piecemeal initiatives tend to be short lived. In difficult times businesses may decide to drop costly changes.

Negotiated piecemeal initiatives Productivity agreements are often used to help change take place. Unions agree to changes in work practices, usually in exchange for extra payments or improved conditions for workers.These negotiated changes tend to be ad-hoc, without any coordinated policy by the business.

Negotiated total packages This is where a 'total package' for change is put together. It is negotiated by employers and union representatives. It may be in the form of a 'national deal', which involves changes in work practices for all employees in every plant or office in exchange for increased rewards or improved conditions. In practice this method of managing change was rarely used in Britain before the 1990s. However, the changing roles of trade unions and the likelihood of partnerships between business and unions after the year 2000 may have seen this type of negotiation taking place more often.

Evaluating the management of change

Managers will have a clear idea of the improvements to performance that they want from change in business. They may want productivity gains as a result of the use of multi-skilled teams or improved response times to customer demands due to new communication technologies. These are sometimes referred to as **performance indicators**. Performance indicators can be used to evaluate the management of change. Any evaluation strategy will have quantitative and qualitative methods of analysing changes in working practices.

- A rise in output from 10,000 to 15,000 as a result of change or an improvement in average delivery time from two days to 24 hours would be measurable, quantitative improvements.
- Employees' responses to a questionnaire, stating that change had improved their motivation, could be a qualitative method of evaluating the management of change.

KEYTERMS

Project champion – an individual who believes in the objectives of a project, seeks support for it from management and other stakeholders and helps to remove barriers which prevent the project from succeeding.

Project group – a number of individual members of an organisation who have been given responsibility for a one-off task, such as preparing a report or implementing an IT software change.

KNOWLEDGE

1. State five factors that may cause change in a business.
2. How might change affect:
   (a) market research
   (b) research and development;
   in a business?
3. Why is it important for businesses to manage change?
4. How might (a) workers and (b) the culture of the organisation prove resistant to change?
5. How might a project champion help the process of change?
6. What is meant by 'developing an organisational culture for change'?
7. Briefly explain four approaches to change.

Case Study: A successful merger

When Lowke's bought Feraday's, many at Feraday's feared the worst. The company had performed poorly over the past few years and there had been persistent rumours that it would be sold off and broken up. Senior management at Lowke's, however, saw Feraday's as an opportunity to revitalise what had once been one of the best companies in the food processing sector.

From the first, all talk of 'takeover', 'asset stripping' and 'downsizing' was banned. Instead, management was encouraged to talk about 'creating a world class company', 'moving forward', 'expanding the business' and 'taking what is best in our partnership'. There was no immediate move to make anyone redundant, despite the obvious overlap of roles, particularly at senior management levels. Instead, it was made clear to everyone that the new company would take shape after a period of 24 months of intense reflection on how best to create a successful business. The board of directors set the company the goal of raising its sales by 5 per cent within those two years and by 25 per cent within five years. Operating profits were to rise by 5 per cent within two years but by 40 per cent within five years. The strategy to achieve these objectives was left to senior management to devise. However, the Board made it clear that it expected the strategy to evolve from consultation at every level of the new company.

Not everyone was prepared to engage meaningfully in the consultation. Some could not see beyond their own life goals and were simply not interested in the future success of the business. It was impossible to shift them from the 'I've worked here for 20 years, so the company owes me my job with no changes' type attitude. But most could see that change was needed and were prepared to think about how best to achieve that change.

Managers and workers from both companies looked at how each was operating. Sometimes it was clear that one company was performing a task or function more efficiently than the other. This then became the catalyst for change as the whole company standardised on best practice. Where there was overlap and cost savings could be achieved through rationalisation, all workers were consulted and interviewed before any decisions about their personal future was taken. Some didn't want to move forward with the company but were very satisfied with early retirement packages. Others were helped to find jobs and even promotion with other employers. Yet others were offered different jobs within the company. It might be in a different location. Or it might be a different job for which they were offered training to fulfill.

Because there was fairly intense contact between workers within the two companies over the 24 months, it soon became apparent to workers at Feraday's that there was no favouritism being given to either business methods or individual workers at Lowke's. This helped build up a climate of trust which made it easier to secure changes at Feraday's.

Lowke's was a large private limited company whose Board of Directors were committed to long-term growth. They were aware that profits could have been higher in the short term if they had wielded an axe to Feraday's very quickly. The solutions that came out of the consultations were not necessarily very different to what senior managers at Lowke's would have come up with anyway. However, the Board of Directors wanted to preserve as much talent as possible within the new company. It also wanted to avoid the demotivation of staff that often took place after a takeover. The Board was equally aware that takeovers by other companies in the industry had led to problems with both suppliers and customers. For example, the needs of customers could easily be lost by an organisation undergoing radical change. Its model of change, it hoped, would create an organisation which would continue to evolve successfully in future years.

(a) Evaluate the costs and benefits to Lowke's of adopting a fairly lengthy, consultative model of change. (40 marks)

(b) Discuss whether the model of change adopted by Lowke's could be implemented by a public limited company. (40 marks)

110 Economic growth and the business cycle

Economic growth

For the past 50 years, the UK economy has grown at an average rate of 2.5 per cent. This is the long-run trend rate of growth of the UK economy. ECONOMIC GROWTH is measured by changes in the size of NATIONAL INCOME. This is the value of total income in the economy. It is also equal to the value of total spending and total production or output. There is a number of different ways of calculating national income. The method most often used by economists and the media is GROSS DOMESTIC PRODUCT or GDP.

Economic growth means that more is produced. In turn, this means that households and individuals can, on average, consume more goods and services. The standard of living enjoyed by the typical family today is far higher than it was 25 or 50 years ago as Figure 1 shows.

The business cycle

GDP does not rise at a steady rate each year. There are fluctuations and in some years the level of GDP may even fall. These fluctuations tend to occur on a regular basis and follow the same broad pattern. This is known as the BUSINESS CYCLE or TRADE CYCLE or ECONOMIC CYCLE. There are four phases to the business cycle, shown in Figure 2.

Boom In a BOOM, the economy is doing well.

- Output is high and the economy is growing strongly.
- Consumer spending is high. Also consumers are willing to borrow to finance their purchases.
- House prices are likely to be growing, helped by high mortgage lending by banks and building societies.
- Unemployment is low and businesses may find it hard to recruit new workers.
- Wages are likely to be rising at a fast rate, as businesses compete to employ a limited pool of workers.
- Strong growth in demand for goods and services, combined with above average increases in wages, might increase inflation rates. Inflation is the rise in the general level of prices in the economy.
- With many domestic businesses working at full capacity, they could find it difficult to provide all the products that customers want to buy. So demand for imports might grow at a faster than average rate.
- There might be bottlenecks in certain sectors of the economy. This is where customers want to buy products, but they aren't available in sufficient quantities from domestic producers or importers. Delivery times might be longer. In some industries, waiting lists may develop.
- Businesses, encouraged by strong demand, will tend to increase their investment spending to increase their capacity.
- Record numbers of new businesses will be created, attracted by the possibility of earning high profits.

Figure 1: Income (GDP) per person at constant 2003 prices, UK 1956-2007.

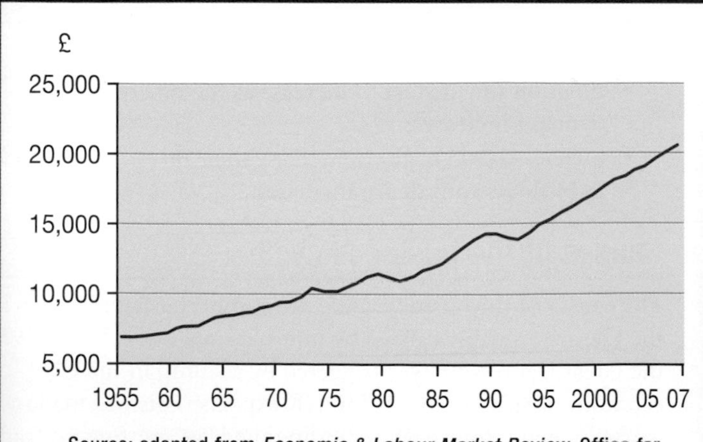

Source: adapted from *Economic & Labour Market Review*, Office for National Statistics.

Downturn In a DOWNTURN or ECONOMIC SLOWDOWN or DOWNSWING, the rate of growth of the economy begins to fall.

- Lower growth in demand will cause unemployment to rise, which in turn will lead to even lower demand growth.
- Wage increases will start to slow and businesses will find it more difficult to push through price increases. So the rate of inflation will start to fall. Some sectors of the economy might be more affected than others.
- Many businesses will see a fall off in growth of sales and some will see an absolute fall.
- Profit growth will falter and could become negative.
- The rate of growth of imports will fall as the the rate of growth in overall spending by UK customers slows.

Recession or depression The bottom of the business cycle has a number of different names. If economic growth becomes negative, i.e. GDP falls, then it tends to be called a DEPRESSION or SLUMP. The last major prolonged depression in the UK economy occurred during the 1930s. However, there were short depressions in 1974-75, 1980-82 and 1990-92.

When GDP is still growing, but at a very low rate at the bottom of the cycle, the media use both the terms

Figure 2: The actual rate of growth measured by changes in GDP fluctuate from year to year round the long run trend rate of growth for the economy. These fluctuations are known as the business cycle. In the business cycle, recessions can either be very mild or deep.

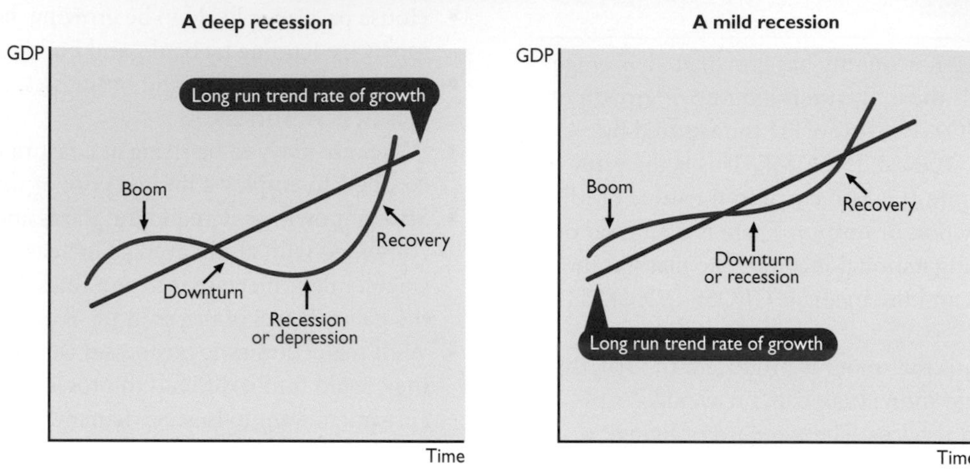

Question 1.

The largest speculatively built office block outside London has opened to lettings in Birmingham. Owned by the private equity firm, Carlyle Group, Colmore Plaza is around 300,000 square feet.

The Birmingham economy has boomed over the last 15 years. It has, for the most part, recovered from the loss of much of its manufacturing industry in the 1970s, 1980s and 1990s. Today, the Birmingham economy is mainly service based. But up until now, Birmingham has had a shortage of modern office space. Offices built in the 1960s and 1970s are often scruffy and lacking in space for cabling. 'Historically there has been a dearth of decent office space in Birmingham', said Philippa Pickavance, a partner at property consultants Drivers Jonas. 'This year and in spring 2009 around 700,000 square feet of space will come onstream. But this is space we need.' Ms Pickavance calculates that 662,000 square feet were let last year in Birmingham, a 12 per cent increase on 2006.

However, the economy could be going into a recession. In turn, this could impact on the ability of Colmore Plaza to attract tenants. So far, one floor of the £150 million building has been rented to Davis Langdon, a project manager. This leaves another 11 floors to rent at target prices of over £30 per square foot. Carlyle Group must be hoping that any dip in growth of the Birmingham economy will be small and short lived.

Source: adapted from *The Financial Times*, 11.3.2008.

(a) Explain the links between economic growth and the building of office space.

(b) Evaluate whether Carlyle Group will have to lower its rents in 2008 and 2009 to attract tenants for its Colmore Plazza building.

downturn and RECESSION. So the word recession can be used both to describe a period of very low growth or a period when GDP is actually falling.

At the bottom of the business cycle:

- unemployment is relatively high and inflation relatively low;
- low increases in demand or, at worst, falls in demand will lead to workers being laid off;
- it will be difficult for businesses to increase their prices without losing sales;
- investment by businesses will be low and there will spare capacity in the economy.

Recovery In a RECOVERY or UPSWING, the economy begins to pick up again, and:

- the rate of growth of GDP starts to increase or moves from being negative to positive;
- unemployment begins to fall as businesses take on more workers to cope with the rise in economic activity;
- inflation might start to increase as the rate of growth of demand increases;
- businesses will begin to increase their investment spending as business confidence increases.

Causes of the business cycle

The causes of the business cycle are complex. Major slumps in the UK are arguably caused by international trade. In the 1930s, the Great Depression was triggered by a slump in the US economy, which led to a fall in UK exports. This was made worse by many countries, including the USA, putting up trade barriers such as taxes on imports (called **tariffs**) or limits on the amount that could be imported (called **quotas**). In the 1970s and 1980s, the two depressions of 1975-6 and 1980-82 were

Question 2.

JCB warned of a 'flat' year ahead because of weakening demand in the US and parts of Europe. John Patterson, the chief executive of Britain's biggest maker of construction equipment, said he was cautious about 2008. There were increasing signs that the slowdown in the economy would affect demand for JCB's productions, used widely in housing and road construction in the US and in important parts of western Europe including the UK.

In the US, the overall market for construction machines slumped 13 per cent in 2007, according to John Patterson, and JCB's US sales fell by almost that amount. There were signs of similar weaknesses in countries such as Spain and Italy. The UK had held up fairly well in 2007, but 'there is a question mark over how the UK market will perform this year' said Mr Patterson.

However, the company highlighted the opportunities outside of these markets, particularly in India, Russia, South America and the Middle East. 'The growth in these places is likely to offset what could be a downturn elsewhere', commented Mr Patterson. He singled out India as the country were JCB had made the most headway recently. In 2007, India, where JCB has three plants, accounted for sales of 17,000 JCB machines, almost a quarter of the world total. This was an increase of 60 per cent since 2006.

Source: adapted from *The Financial Times*, 12.3.2008.

(a) Explain, using a diagram and examples from the data, what is meant by a 'slowdown in the economy'.

(b) Evaluate strategies JCB could use to deal with a slowdown in its western European and US markets.

arguably caused by steep rises in the price of oil on world markets. On the other hand, the depression of 1990-92 was caused by the British government putting up interest rates to 15 per cent to reduce rising inflation. The depression was made worse by an exchange rate of the pound which was too high, hitting exports. Minor downturns since then have had a variety of external causes. For example, the downturn in 2002-2003 was caused by the fall in international spending following the terrorist attacks on the Twin Towers in New York on 9.11. 2001. The downturn in 2008-2009 was caused by a fall in international spending following difficulties in world financial markets. These difficulties were initially caused by problems with bad lending to some homeowners in the USA (so called 'sub-prime mortgage lending).

Even without these external shocks, economies might recover but then go back into recession on a regular basis. There is a number of factors which can cause these regular fluctuations.

Consumer durables During the recession phase of the business cycle, households will delay buying consumer durables. These are consumer products, such as furniture, cookers, carpets, television sets and cars which are used up (or consumed) over a number of years. This causes a fall in growth of demand for these products or even a negative growth in demand, i.e. there is a fall in sales.

As the recession progresses, there comes a point when some households are forced to replace consumer durables. A car, for example, might cost so much to repair this time that it is better to buy a new car. This is often helped by government policy. At the bottom of the cycle, government often cuts interest rates to stop the economy falling further into recession. Consumer durables are often bought on credit. Low interest rates reduce repayments and so encourage consumers to buy.

At the top of a boom, in contrast, the government often raises interest rates to slow down the economy and reduce inflation. This rise in interest rates chokes off demand for credit and so buying of consumer durables falls.

Stock levels At the top of a boom, businesses will expand production. However, small falls in the rate of economic growth will leave them with excess stocks. These might be finished goods which they can't sell. Or businesses might have bought in stocks of raw materials which, because of lower demand for their products, they haven't used up.

Businesses will then start to DESTOCK, i.e. reduce their stock levels. This can have a significant effect on demand. Assume that a business suffers a small fall in sales and ends up with two weeks' worth of extra raw material stocks. At some point it will reduce its stock orders or it might simply cancel stock deliveries for two weeks. This has a knock-on effect on suppliers. A customer that cancels two weeks' worth of orders can lead to a significant downturn in production. This effect is then magnified because reducing stock is an easy way of stemming a cash flow crisis. Businesses in financial trouble in a recession can get much needed cash to survive by running down their stocks. Destocking then fuels a downward spiral in demand in the economy.

At the bottom of the cycle, there is a point when businesses can no longer destock without going out of business. Many will be operating with too little stock for greatest efficiency. So stock buying will start to increase. Once this happens, there is an upward spiral of spending which contributes to recovery and eventually boom.

Investment At the top of a boom, businesses will be investing to expand their capacity. However, growth in production can become unsustainable with bottlenecks emerging. For example, very low unemployment means that some businesses will be unable to recruit all the labour they need. Suppliers may not be able to keep up with all the orders they receive and will delay deliveries. New production capacity, the result of that extra investment, will come onstream which is not fully utilised. At this point, some businesses will cut back on their investment to better match their production and capacity. Also at the top of a boom, the government may have put up interest rates if it feels the need to reduce inflationary pressures in the economy. Higher interest rates increase the cost of borrowing to finance new investment. So some businesses will abandon investment plans.

If investment spending begins to fall, this reduces demand in the economy. Businesses which make investment goods, such as construction companies building offices and factories or machine tool manufacturers, will suffer first. They could lay off workers, which further reduces demand in the economy. This leads to a downward spiral known as a recession.

At the bottom of the business cycle, businesses will have been putting off investment because of financial difficulties. However, there will come a point when they have to invest to replace worn out capital equipment. This decision may be helped by low interest rates set by government more worried about recession than inflation. A small increase in investment starts an upward spiral of demand in the economy. More spending by one business leads to more jobs and more spending.

The impact of the business cycle on business

Changes in the level of economic activity affect all businesses. But some are affected more than others.

Output The major impact of the business cycle is on output and sales. In a boom, output and sales will be growing. In a recession, growth will be sluggish at best. At worst, output and sales will fall. Some businesses will be more affected than others. Businesses that make or sell consumer necessities, such as food, gas or petrol will not be too affected. People will continue to buy these products. Businesses which make luxury products or products whose purchase can be delayed, such as restaurant meals or cars, will suffer more.

Profit In a boom, it is easier for even inefficient businesses to make a profit. Markets are buoyant and there is often little pressure to lower prices.

In a recession, inefficient businesses or those making products that are not necessities can often make losses.

Business start-ups, expansion and closures In a boom, with sales and profits relatively easy to make, there is likely to be a high number of business starts-ups. Existing businesses might expand.

In a recession, businesses are forced to close down or abandon investment and expansion plans. Many businesses will contract in size, closing unprofitable areas. In a prolonged recession, there will be far more businesses closing down than starting up.

Employment In a boom, businesses will tend to take on workers to cope with expanding demand. However, recruitment may be difficult because unemployment is low and there are fewer workers looking for jobs. There will also be pressure on businesses to raise wages to stop staff leaving for better paid jobs.

In a recession, businesses will tend to reduce their workforces. Staff leaving may not be replaced, a process known as **natural wastage**. There may also be a need for compulsory redundancies.

Stocks and investment In a boom, stock levels and investment will be high, as explained above.

In a recession, both will fall, typically at a faster rate than the fall in demand.

Strategic responses to economic growth

Over time, the UK economy is growing in size at an average rate of 2.5 per cent. This presents businesses with considerable opportunities. On average, their sales and profits should be increasing by 2.5 per cent a year after inflation has been taken into account. Unfortunately, the situation facing businesses is far more complex. Over time, the pattern and structure of the economy is also changing.

- Rising incomes lead to demand for some products rising by far more than the average whilst for others they can lead to a fall in demand. For example, sales of jam have been falling for the past thirty years. With more income to spend, consumers prefer to buy other foods. On the other hand, demand for computer equipment has risen by far more than the average over the past 20 years.
- The structure of the economy is changing. Most of the UK's manufacturing industry has disappeared over the past 50 years because goods can be produced more cheaply overseas. New products and new production processes have also transformed what is produced and how it is produced.

Companies have a variety of possible strategies they can use in these circumstances.

- They can move from slow growing markets to fast growing markets in the hope of raising sales. For example, they can buy companies in fast growing markets and sell those parts of their existing business that are in slow growing markets. Or they can expand their own operations into fast growing markets and cut back on investment in those parts of the business which are in slow growing areas.
- Companies can stay in a slow growing market but hope that their competitors will leave it. Or they can take over some of their competitors. Either way, they can increase

both sales and market share. It could also give them greater control of the market and allow them to raise prices and profit margins. So the strategy is for the company to grow at a fast rate whilst the market as a whole is growing slowly.

- Where companies are coming under pressure from cheap foreign competition, they need to reduce their own costs. One way is to increase sourcing of services, components and finished goods from overseas. A UK company then retains high value added processes in the UK.

Over time, companies find it difficult to make the changes needed to cope with profound, long-term changes in the economy as a whole. Most of the top 100 companies quoted on the London Stock Exchange today, for example, will have ceased to exist in 50 years time. They will have shrunk in size, been taken over, been split up or maybe even have disappeared completely.

Strategic responses to the business cycle

When fluctuations in the level of economic growth are very small, most businesses are unlikely to need to make any strategic response. This is because small changes in economic growth don't have much impact on sales for most businesses.

However, if the economy were to go into a severe recession, then many businesses would have to act decisively in order to survive. Sharp downturns in sales should be met by cuts in output and stocks. The business may need to make workers redundant. Companies may have to close down factories, offices and other facilities. Budgets, such as those for marketing and research, may have to be cut because of cash flow problems.

Some businesses, like grocery supermarkets, may feel relatively little impact of a recession because they sell necessities which consumers will continue to buy when their incomes fall. Other businesses, like house builders or furniture manufacturers, may see very sharp falls in orders. This is because consumers will make sharp reductions in purchases of what they see as luxuries like moving house or buying new furniture. Businesses which rely on consumers to buy their goods on credit could also be badly affected because in a recession consumers will be reluctant to take on new debt.

Recessions can be a business opportunity as well as a threat.

- Companies that have the cash may be able to buy up assets at a cheap price. Share prices of other companies are likely to be low. So it might be a good time to expand through acquisitions.
- Businesses which maintain their marketing spending through a recession may be able to gain a competitive advantage over rivals who have been forced to cut their marketing spending.
- Maintaining spending on research and development and on staff training can also give a competitive advantage over rivals which have been forced to cut their spending.
- Some businesses may collapse and exit the market. This is an opportunity for another business to step in and gain the customers that have been abandoned.

KEYTERMS

Boom – the peak of the business cycle, when the economy is growing fast and unemployment is low but when there could be problems with rising inflation.
Business cycle or trade cycle or economic cycle – regular fluctuations in the level of output of the economy, going from boom through recession and depression to recovery.
Destocking – when a business reduces its levels of stock held.
Downturn or downswing or economic slowdown – when the rate of economic growth begins to fall and unemployment begins to rise.
Economic growth – the change in the productive potential of the economy; it is usually measured by changes in national income and in particular GDP.
Gross Domestic Product (GDP) – the commonest way in which national income is measured.
National income – the value of total income in the economy; it is also equal to the value of total spending and total production or output.
Recession or depression or slump – the bottom of the business cycle when economic growth is negative and there is high unemployment. Recession may also be used to describe a period of very slow economic growth.
Recovery or upswing – when the rate of economic growth begins to increase following a recession or depression and unemployment begins to fall.

KNOWLEDGE

1. What is the link between GDP and economic growth?
2. What are the differences between (a) a boom and a depression, (b) a recession and a recovery?
3. What impact might the business cycle have on (a) sales and (b) business start-ups?
4. A company is in a slow growing sector the economy. What might be its strategic response?
5. A company is faced with intense price competition from overseas competitors despite strong growth in the economy as a whole. What should be its strategic response?
6. Explain how a business manufacturing furniture might respond if the economy went into a deep recession and sales of furniture nationally fell by 20 per cent.

Case Study: UK housing

The slide in house prices is gathering momentum, according to Hometrack, the housing data company. Its survey suggests that values have fallen 0.3 per cent since last month, the third consecutive monthly fall and the largest in almost two years. Richard Donnell, direct of research at Hometrack, said: 'The second half of the year has seen a major reversal in confidence on the back of higher interest rates and concerns over the outlook for the financial markets.'

The downturn in the economy is affecting businesses. For example, Taylor Wood, one of Britain's biggest housebuilders, apparently took the decision to freeze all land purchases in mid-October and has completed only on deals agreed before then.

Source: adapted from business.times.online.co.uk 24.12.2007.

The Bank of England governor, Mervyn King, admitted yesterday that the economy might grind to a halt this year. When asked whether a recession was possible this year, he said the Bank's predictions were 'not inconsistent; with two quarters of falling GDP, the technical definition of a recession. He also warned that house prices could fall.

Source: adapted from www.guardian.co.uk 14.2.2008.

Hup Housebuilding plc is a UK regional housebuilding company operating mainly in the North of England. Over the past seven years, it has experienced a boom in sales. It expanded from approximately 1,000 completions of new properties in 2000 to 3,000 completions in 2006. The start of 2007 looked highly promising but conditions in the economy deteriorated suddenly and by the end of the year, the company was experiencing difficulties in selling newly completed properties. Whilst Hup Housebuilding completed almost 3,000 properties in 2007, it had 300 properties left unsold at the end of the year.

Its competitors were in a similar position. They were offering a wide variety of 'deals' to customers to entice them to buy. But they were also cutting back on starting new projects. For the first time in many years, applications for jobs with Hup Housebuilding had gone up. Hup Housebuilding also noticed that land prices were easing.

(a) Evaluate the strategies that Hup Housebuilding could use to cope with a possible recession in the economy in 2008. (40 marks)

(b) Discuss whether a downturn in the housing market could be more of an opportunity than a threat for Hup Housebuilding. (40 marks)

111 Interest rates

Interest and interest rates

If a business or an individual borrows money, they usually have to pay **interest** on the loan. Equally, if they put their savings into a bank or building society, they expect to receive interest.

The INTEREST RATE is the price of borrowing or saving money. For example, if a small business borrows £10,000 from a bank for one year, and the interest rate is 7 per cent, it has to pay £700 in interest. Equally, if a business has £1 million in the bank for a year which it uses as working capital, and the rate of interest the bank offers is 3 per cent, it will earn £30,000 in interest.

Different interest rates

A business might be able to borrow money on overdraft at 6 per cent. If it took out a five year loan, the interest rate might be 7 per cent. A consumer buying a house might be offered a mortgage rate of 8 per cent. The interest rate on a credit card might be 15 per cent.

These are just four of the thousands of interest rates in an economy. Each interest rate is set within a market for money. In each market, there is a **demand** for money. This comes from those who want to borrow money. There is also a **supply** of money from those who want to lend money. The forces of demand and supply will fix the price of money in that market, which is the interest rate.

Many money markets are influenced by the rate of interest set by the central bank of a country. In the UK, the central bank is the Bank of England. It has the power to fix the rate of interest charged and offered by the major banks in the UK on short-term loans and savings. Banks such as Barclays or HSBC will change their BASE RATE when the Bank of England declares a change in interest rates. The base rate of a bank is the rate around which all its other interest rates are structured. For short- term savings with the bank, it will offer interest rates below the base rate. For borrowing, it charges above the base rate. The profit it makes out of borrowing and lending has to come from the difference between the lower rate of interest it gives to savers and the higher rate of interest it charges to borrowers.

Base rates are linked to other rates of interest in the economy. When base rates fall, so do long-term rates of interest. The rate of interest on other types of borrowing, such as borrowing through a credit card, also tends to fall. But there is no direct link between these other interest rates and the base rates set by the Bank of England. So short-term interest rates can change and long-term interest rates can remain unaffected. Sometimes, long-term interest rates can be rising when short-term interest rates are falling. It depends on market conditions.

Effect on business overheads

Changes in interest rates are likely to affect the overheads of a business. Interest charges are part of overhead costs. If interest rates rise, businesses are likely to have to pay higher interest payments on their borrowing. For example, a business might borrow £10,000 on overdraft. The annual payments on this would rise from £600 to £700 if the rate of interest rose from 6 to 7 per cent a year.

Not all borrowing is at variable rates of interest. Variable rates mean that banks or other lenders are free to change the rate of interest on any money borrowed. Many loans to businesses are at fixed rates of interest. This is where the bank cannot change the rate of interest over the agreed term (the time over which the loan will be paid off) of the loan. A rise in interest rates in the economy won't affect the overheads of a business with only fixed term loans. But, if a business wanted to take out new loans, it would have to pay the higher rates of interest the bank or other lender was now charging. So overhead costs would rise.

Question 1.

Dalton's is an industrial manufacturer of canning products. It currently has an overdraft of £1.2 million and loans of £4.3 million. Of these loans:

- £1.3 million are variable rate loans, with interest at 2 per cent above base rate;
- £1 million is at a fixed rate of 8 per cent;
- the remaining £2 million is at a fixed rate of 9 per cent.

(a) Explain why interest on borrowings is an overhead cost for Dalton's.

(b) Base rates in the economy fall from 6 per cent to 5 per cent. As a result the overdraft rates for Dalton's falls from 7 per cent to 6 per cent. Calculating the change in interest payments, explain how this will affect the company's overhead costs.

Question 2.

Bill Lockington was devastated when his business went up in flames. He made a range of tyres, manufactured from existing worn out tyres. His 'retreads' had proved popular with customers because of their high quality and low prices compared with brand new tyres. Due to the high cost of insurance, he was uninsured at the time of the accident and it looked as though ten years' hard work had come to an abrupt end.

However, having got over the psychological shock of seeing £250,000 worth of equipment and stock destroyed overnight, he decided that it was possible to rebuild the business. Two important things had not disappeared. First, he still had a list of customers who wanted to buy his tyres. Second, he had the knowledge and a skilled workforce to produce quality retreads. Low interest rates were vital to success too. He could not have afforded to borrow the money to restart the business if he could not have borrowed at 7 per cent from his bank. The retread business was also highly dependent on buoyant consumer confidence. Low interest rates encouraged customers to buy vehicles and motorcycles and so create the demand for retreads in the longer term.

Even so, he had to make economies. Before the fire, he had built up stocks worth £100,000 of used tyres. Such large levels of stock were unnecessary for the efficient running of the business. His new business started with just £20,000 worth of stock.

(a) Explain carefully how low interest rates affected Bill Lockington's business.

(b) Suggest why he only bought £20,000 worth of stock to restart the business when previously he had held £100,000 worth of stock.

(c) Discuss whether Bill Lockington could have recovered from the fire if interest rates had been high at the time.

Effect on investment decisions

Changes in the rate of interest affect the amount that businesses invest, for example in new buildings, plant and machinery. There are four main reasons for this.

The cost of loans Investment projects are often financed through loans. A rise in interest rates increases the cost of borrowing money. So projects financed this way will find that the total costs have risen, reducing profitability. This might be enough to persuade some businesses to shelve their investment plans. Total investment in the economy will then fall.

Attractiveness of saving Businesses have the alternative of putting their funds into savings schemes rather than investing in machinery or buildings, for example. A rise in interest rates makes putting money into financial assets relatively more attractive. For example, if interest rates rise from 5 to 8 per cent, a business might decide to shelve an investment project and save the funds instead.

Paying off existing loans A rise in interest rates will increase the cost of existing variable rate borrowing. A business could choose to pay off existing loans rather than increase its investment. This will reduce its costs. It also reduces the risk associated with borrowing.

A fall in demand A rise in interest rates is likely to reduce total spending in the economy, as explained below. This might affect the profitability of many investment projects. For example, a business might forecast that an investment project would be profitable with 20,000 sales a year. But if sales were projected to be only 15,000 a year because of a downturn in demand, then the investment project could be unprofitable and might not go ahead.

Effect on demand

The level of interest rates affects aggregate demand (i.e. total demand) for goods and services in the economy. A rise in interest rates will tend to push down aggregate demand. A fall in interest rates will tend to increase demand.

Businesses are directly affected by changes in demand. When demand falls, their sales go down because less is being bought. If demand rises, businesses receive more orders and more sales.

There are many different ways in which changes in interest rates lead to changes in the sales of businesses.

Domestic consumption Consumers will be hit by a rise in interest rates. The cost of loans will rise. This will deter consumers from buying goods bought on credit, such as cars, furniture and electrical equipment. These goods are known as CONSUMER DURABLES because they are 'used up' over a long period.

In the UK, people who have a mortgage (a loan to buy a house) are also likely to see their monthly repayments rise because most mortgages are variable rate loans. Existing mortgage holders will then have less to spend on other goods and services. Some potential new home buyers will be put off because they can't afford the repayments, directly hitting the new housing market. If unemployment begins to rise because of less spending, consumer confidence will fall. This will make consumers even less willing to take out loans and spend.

Domestic investment As explained above, businesses are likely to cut back plans for new investment if interest rates rise. Investment goods, like new buildings or machines, are made by businesses. So these businesses will see a fall in their demand.

Stocks Businesses keep stocks of raw materials and finished goods. Stocks cost money to keep, because a fall in stock levels could be used to finance a fall in borrowing and interest payments. So a rise in interest rates will increase the cost of keeping stock. This will encourage businesses to destock, i.e. reduce their stock levels. This will be especially true if the rise in interest rates has hit demand in the economy. With fewer sales, less needs to be produced. So less stock needs to be kept. But cutting stock reduces orders for businesses further up the chain of production. For example, a retailer cutting stocks affects demand from its suppliers. Destocking due to higher interest rates will therefore cause a fall in demand throughout much of industry.

Exports and imports A rise in interest rates tends to lead to a rise in the value of one currency against others. A rise in the pound, for example, will make it harder for UK businesses to export profitably. At the same time, foreign firms will find it easier to gain sales in the UK domestic market because they will be able to reduce their prices. The result is likely to be a fall in exports and a loss of sales to importers in the domestic market. Both will reduce demand and hit UK businesses.

Variable impact on businesses

Changes in interest rates affect different businesses in different ways. Businesses that are most likely to be affected are those which:

- have high levels of borrowing at variable rates of interest;
- sell consumer goods, typically bought on credit;
- are directly linked to the housing market, such as house builders;
- produce investment goods for other businesses;
- depend on exports or are in markets where competition from imports is particularly strong.

A rise in interest rates might have little impact on some of these. For example, a rise in interest rates might not deter consumers from taking out loans because their confidence is high. Or the rise might have little impact on the value of the pound and so not affect exports and imports. The impact depends very much on what else is happening in the economy.

There are also many businesses that are unlikely to see much change in their demand even if other businesses are suffering. For example, consumers tend not to cut back on their spending on food even when times are hard. So supermarkets are often unaffected by changes in interest rates. A hairdressers or a village post office are unlikely to be much affected either.

Strategy and interest rates

Different businesses should have different strategic reactions to changes in interest rates.

- If interest rate changes are relatively small, then there is little need for businesses to change their strategies at all. When interest rates are low, a movement of 1 or 2 per cent in interest rates is unlikely to have much impact.
- Highly indebted businesses are particularly at risk from interest rate rises. Sharp rises in interest rates over a short period of time can push such businesses towards insolvency. They need to reduce their debt burden as quickly as possible. In the short term, this may mean selling assets, if necessary at the expense of future sales and profits. Some businesses may be able to refinance debt. It could be that shopping around banks or other financial institutions will give a lower rate of interest on borrowings. Alternatively, a company may be able to raise share capital and convert some its debt into equity.
- Significant falls in interest rates should stimulate investment by businesses. With the cost of borrowing significantly cheaper, investment projects, which in the past would have been unprofitable, now become profitable. Extra investment might make a business more competitive and allow it to expand sales or market share with the objective of increasing profit and shareholder value. Conversely, a significant rise in interest rates will increase the cost of borrowing, making investment less profitable. So a business is likely to reduce its investment.
- If rises in interest rates are large enough to cause a sharp downturn in the economy, then businesses exposed to markets most affected by the downturn will need to react. A supermarket chain will not see much impact on sales from a downturn and so need take little action. A furniture manufacturer, on the other hand, could see a large drop in sales. It needs to take immediate action to reduce production levels. It should cut stocks and, if necessary, cut the number of workers it employs. The longer the recession, the deeper it will need to cut.

KEYTERMS

Base rate – the rate of interest around which a bank structures its other interest rates. A rise in the base rate will result in a rise in most saving and borrowing rates and vice versa.

Consumer durables – consumer goods such as televisions, furniture and cars which are used over a long period of time. They are often bought on credit.

Interest rate – the price of borrowing or saving money. There are many different interest rates charged in an economy because there are many different markets for borrowed funds.

KNOWLEDGE

1. A business has borrowed £100,000 on overdraft. Bank base rates rise. How is this likely to affect the amount of interest the business pays?
2. What is the difference between variable and fixed rates of interest for a business that has borrowed money?
3. Explain briefly why the investment plans of a business may change if there is a fall in the rate of interest.
4. (a) How might consumers react to a fall in the rate of interest and (b) why might this benefit businesses?
5. Why might businesses destock if interest rates rise?
6. Why might a fall in interest rates lead to a change in export orders?

Case Study: Fastenings

In 1991 bank base rates had been at the crippling level of 14-15 per cent for nearly two years. The economy was in the midst of a deep, prolonged recession which had begun in 1989. Al Farrall had run his fastening business for 23 years, but he had never known conditions like this.

He manufactured fastenings mainly for the car and furniture industries. Bolts, castor pegs, nuts and pins were the staple products. Like many businesses, he had expanded in the mid-1980s. Furniture sales were booming in the climate of relatively low interest rates. The housing market was also booming, which encouraged home owners to buy new furniture as they moved house.

At the same time, car production picked up, first for the domestic market and then later for export. But, in 1989, the bottom dropped out of this market. Bank base rates had gone from a low of 7.5 per cent in mid-1987 to 14 per cent by mid-1989. Car production fell back and furniture sales slumped. He not only lost sales volumes, but found himself having to offer ridiculously low priced contracts to win orders.

By early 1991, Al's business was facing closure. He had already been forced to cut the workforce from 20 in 1989 to 12 in 1991, helping to swell the ranks of the UK unemployed which had risen from 1.5 million to 3 million over the period. While his workforce shrank, his borrowing just kept growing. With the benefit of hindsight, he knew that he had made a huge mistake to borrow £150 000 to buy new equipment in 1988. A third of his equipment now lay idle because of lack of orders. His borrowings stood at an unsustainable £200,000 given that the business had made a loss of £25 000 in 1990 and was on track to make a loss of £30,000 in 1991. The business desperately needed a cut in interest rates and a return to growth in the economy.

(a) To what extent were Al Farrall's business problems caused by overborrowing in the late 1980s? (40 marks)

(b) Bank base rates fell from 14 per cent in February 1991 to 6 per cent in February 1993. Discuss whether this change could have helped Al's business to survive. (40 marks)

112 Exchange rates

The exchange rate of a currency

An EXCHANGE RATE is the price of one currency against another. For instance, the exchange rate of the pound might be €1 = £0.58 or £1 = US$1.60. At these exchange rates, a business wanting to buy €1 million through its bank would have to pay £580,000 (€1 million x 0.58) plus a commission.

Currencies can change in value. If the exchange rate changed to € = £0.60, the business would now have to pay £600,000 (€ million x 0.60) plus commission.

- A rise in the value of the pound against other currencies means that the pound will buy more foreign currency. For example, if the value of the pound changed from £1 = €1.60 to £1 = €1.75, this would a rise in the value of the pound. Each pound is now worth €0.15 more than before. A rise in the pound is sometimes called an APPRECIATION of the currency.
- A DEPRECIATION or **fall** in the value of the pound would mean that the pound would buy less foreign currency than before. A change from £1 = $1.50 to £1 = $1.30 would be an example. The pound buys $0.20 less than before.

Sometimes, the value of a currency is said to be high. This means that it can buy more foreign currency compared to the recent historical average. For example, the recent historical average value of the pound against the euro might be £1 = €1.40. If the actual value of the pound today were £1 = €1.60, the value of the pound would be high. On the other hand, it would be low if it were well below the £1 = €1.40 level. So, for example, it would be low if the exchange rate were £1 = €1.20.

Changes in exchange rates

Exchange rates are affected by the demand for and supply of currencies. Buyers of one currency demand another currency. Sellers of one currency supply another currency.

Demand for a currency Demand for a currency like the pound, for example, comes from three main sources.

- Exports. A US business buying goods priced in pounds from a UK business would need to buy pounds to pay the invoice. The US business would be buying an export from the UK. So buyers of UK EXPORTS, goods or services sold abroad, would demand pounds.
- Capital transactions. Foreign individuals, businesses or other organisations might want to buy UK owned assets. For instance, a French company might decide to buy a UK company. It would need to buy pounds to buy out the UK company's shareholders. Or a German citizen might want to buy shares on the London stock exchange in Barclays Bank. She would need to exchange euros for pounds to do this.
- Speculation. The largest source of demand for pounds on a day-to-day basis is foreign currency speculation. Dealers in foreign currency buy and sell pounds. They hope to sell at a higher price than they buy, to make a profit.

Question 1.

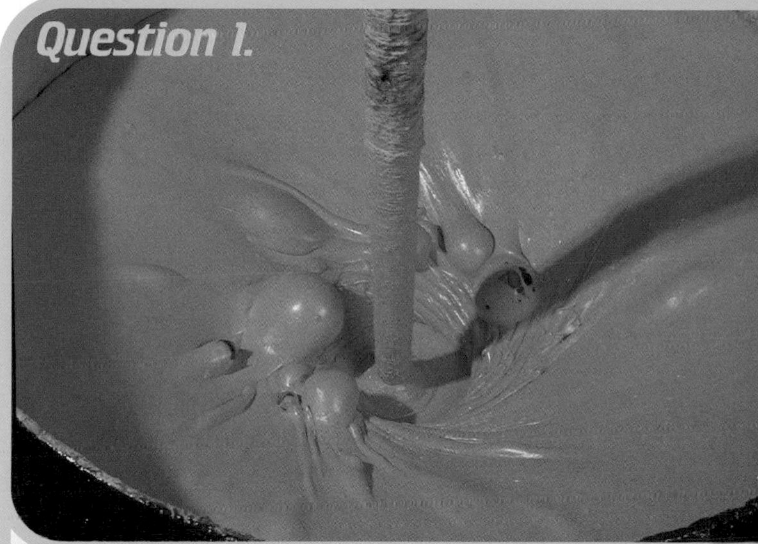

Betteny is a UK paint manufacturer. It produces paint for domestic and industrial use worldwide. The fall in the value of the pound in the early part of this year both against the US dollar and the euro was welcome news to the company. With the pound so high in the previous two years, the company had struggled along with many UK exporters to remain profitable.

The directors of the company had met to discuss their pricing strategy in the light of the fall. On the whole, they decided that they wanted to restore profit margins on export contracts by trying to maintain their prices in pounds sterling. However, the fall in the value of the pound meant that they could afford to offer slightly better prices to overseas customers if it meant that they would win a contract. In the UK market, Betteny would be better able to compete against importers which had eaten into their market share in recent years.

(a) Explain three ways in which the fall in the value of the pound this year could lead to higher profits for Betteny.

Supply of a currency The supply of a currency also comes from three main sources.

- Imports. If a UK company bought components from a United States manufacturer, it would need to buy US dollars and sell pounds to pay the invoice. So UK IMPORTS create a supply of pounds.
- Capital transactions. If UK citizens, businesses or organisations want to buy foreign assets, such as shares,

Question 2.

Rugol & Flynn's is a company which manufactures household goods. The managing director, George Rugol, is an outspoken critic of Britain's failure to join the European Monetary Union. Over the years, he has seen large fluctuations in the value of the pound against European currencies and against the US dollar. Within a matter of weeks, the pound can go up or down against key trading currencies by 5 per cent or more. This is highly disruptive to his business since his company exports mainly to Europe but also to the USA.

George Rugol is very careful to ensure that all export contracts are hedged - that is, the company buys or sells foreign currency in advance so that it knows how much it will receive in pounds on any given order. But this takes both time and money to arrange with its bankers. The company wouldn't have to do this for sales in Europe if the UK used the same currency, the euro, as its main trading partners.

Equally, the business imports raw materials. The exact price to be paid is uncertain because of day-to-day exchange rate fluctuations. Again, the company hedges all contracts but this adds to the costs of the contract.

George Rugol wants it to be as risk free to sell his products to Germany or France as it is to London or Scotland. This means that Britain must adopt the euro.

(a) Rugol and Flynn's signs a contract to export goods to France in one month's time for 50,000 euros. A week later, the value of the pound rises by 5 per cent against the euro. Explain whether the company would gain or lose out as a result?

(b) Explain whether the UK joining the euro would help Rugol and Flynn's with its exports to the USA.

factories or companies, they will need to sell pounds for foreign currency.

- Speculation. Foreign currency speculators dominate day-to-day transactions. They buy and sell, hoping to make a profit.

The rate of exchange changes minute by minute depending upon how much is demanded and how much is supplied. Foreign exchange rates, therefore, tend to be volatile. Figure 1 shows how the pound has changed against the US$ since 1980.

Figure 1: The value of the pound against the dollar

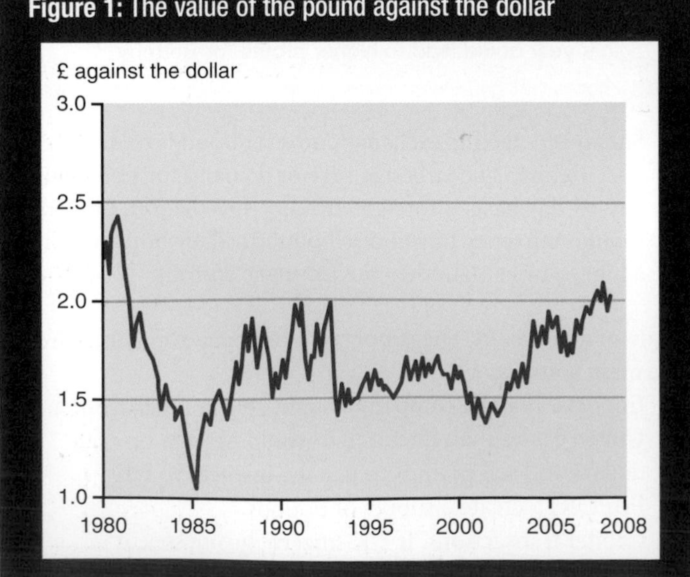

Exports and exchange rate changes

Businesses can be directly or indirectly affected by changes in the exchange rate. Those most affected are likely to be EXPORTING (selling goods and services to foreign governments, businesses and individuals) or IMPORTING (buying goods and services from abroad).

Take a UK company that EXPORTS marmalade abroad. The price of a pot of marmalade is 50p. If the value of the pound is £1 = €1.60, a company abroad buying a pot of marmalade will pay €0.80 for it (1.60 x 0.50p). What if the value of the pound now appreciates (i.e. rises) to £1 = €1.80? How might the UK business react?

Keep the price in pounds the same The UK company could keep the price in pounds the same. So at 50p per pot, it would now cost the foreign company €0.90 (1.80 x 0.50p). This rise in price from €0.80 to €0.90 would affect demand (i.e. the quantity bought). It is likely that the quantity demanded would fall. The UK company would see a fall in sales abroad. By how much depends on how price sensitive was demand. If it was highly price sensitive (i.e. price elasticity of demand is high), the percentage fall in sales would be high. If demand was fairly insensitive (i.e. price elasticity of demand is low), then there would be little effect on sales.

Keep the foreign currency price the same The UK company could keep the foreign currency price the same, i.e. keep the price of the pot of marmalade at €0.80. If it did, the price it would receive in pounds would fall to around 44p (€0.80 ÷ the exchange rate = €0.80 ÷ €1.80). By adopting this pricing strategy, demand for marmalade should remain unchanged. But profits from marmalade sales would fall. It might even be the case that at 44p the business would make a loss on the sale.

So for an exporting business, a **rise** in the value of the pound is likely to result in either a fall in export sales, a fall in profits on those sales, or both. Which of these occurs depends on the pricing policy the exporting company adopts following the appreciation of the currency.

The reverse is true if the value of the pound **falls**. Exporting companies can choose to let the foreign currency prices of their goods fall. This should lead to a rise in export sales. Or they can improve their profit margins by raising the price in pounds to a level where the foreign currency price is unchanged. Or they can do a combination of the two, seeing some increase in sales and some increase in profits.

Imports and exchange rate changes

Businesses that import goods are affected by exchange rate changes too. For example, the marmalade manufacturer might import oranges from Spain. What happens if the value of the pound changes?

A rise in the value of the pound If the price of the pound goes up against the euro, it means that the company can now buy more euros for £1. So the price of imports should fall. For example, assume that it can buy 10 kilos of oranges for €1.60. At an exchange rate of £1 = €1.60, 10 kilos cost £1. But if the exchange rate of the pound now appreciates to £1 = €1.80, the cost of 10 kilos of oranges, still priced at €1.60, falls to around 89p (€1.60 ÷ €1.80).

A fall in the value of the pound The opposite occurs if the value of the pound falls. For example, the pound might depreciate from £1 = €1.60 to £1 = €1.40. Before, 10 kilos of oranges cost €1.60 or £1. After, 10 kilos of oranges still cost €1.60. But the price in pounds is around £1.14 (€1.60 ÷ €1.40). A fall in the value of the pound leads to higher import prices.

As with exports, foreign companies could adjust their own prices to compensate for the change in the exchange rate.

So, if the value of the pound **rises**, import prices in pounds will fall and foreign firms will become more competitive in the UK market. Instead of selling more exports to the UK, however, foreign firms could choose instead to raise prices in their currency. If they raised them so that the price in pounds remained the same, they wouldn't sell any more products to the UK. But they would increase their profit on each sale.

If the value of the pound **falls**, import prices in pounds will go up and foreign businesses will find it more difficult to sell into the UK market. By cutting prices in their own currency, foreign firms can bring the price in pounds back to what it was before. They, however, suffer lower profits as a result.

Direct and indirect effects of exchange rate changes on a business

Businesses can be affected directly and indirectly by changes in the exchange rate.

Directly Businesses might be affected by changes in the exchange rate directly because they sell abroad or buy imports. Many of these businesses are both exporters and importers. For them, exchange rate changes can have complicated effects.

- A UK business that buys roughly the same amount of imports as it exports can be unaffected by an exchange rate change. If the pound falls in value, the extra cost of imports can be offset by rises in the UK price of its exports.
- A UK business that has high levels of exports, but imports little, is likely to benefit from a **depreciation** of the pound. It can either allow foreign currency prices to fall and so become more competitive overseas, or it can increase its prices in pounds and so increase profit margins.
- A UK business that has high levels of exports, but imports little is likely to suffer from an **appreciation** of the pound. Either it will have to put up foreign currency prices and become less competitive or it will have to absorb the exchange rate rise by lowering its prices in pounds, resulting in lower profit margins.

Indirectly UK businesses can also suffer indirectly from exchange rate changes. This is because of the effect of a change in the value of the pound on inflation.

A **depreciation** in the value of the pound will mean that the price of imported goods and services is likely to rise. UK businesses that import these products could pass on some of the rise in price to customers, many of whom will be other businesses. So a business that doesn't import anything may still pay higher prices for supplies because of a fall in the exchange rate.

Similarly, an **appreciation** of the pound can lead to importing businesses passing on the saving made on imports to their customers in the form of lower prices.

Exchange rates and the rate of interest

Changes in interest rates can lead to changes in exchange rates. A fall in interest rates, for example, is likely to lead to a fall in the exchange rate. Lower interest rates discourage saving and investment in a country. So if UK interest rates fall, fewer pounds will be bought to invest in the UK. A rise in interest rates is likely to raise the exchange rate.

How might lower interest rates and exchange rates affect a business? Lower interest rates can **benefit** UK businesses:

- borrowing money in the UK, as they pay back less;
- selling to the UK market, because lower interest rates will encourage UK consumers to borrow and spend more;
- selling exports. They can either sell more, since prices will be cheaper to foreigners, or increase their prices and profit margins.

A fall in interest rates is likely to **harm** UK businesses because:

- inflation in the UK may increase as a result of higher import prices;
- UK businesses that import materials from abroad may be affected by a fall in the exchange rate which causes import prices to rise.

The opposite is true if interest rates rise.

Strategy and exchange rates

Many businesses find that exchange rate changes can have a major effect on their finances. They have to develop strategies to cope with exchange rate changes.

Balancing exports and imports A business could try to balance the value of exports and products that are imported. Some car manufacturers operating in the UK have adopted this strategy. If the value of the pound rises, the manufacturer lowers its export prices in pounds to leave the foreign currency price the same. But the lower revenues it earns in pounds are matched by the lower prices it has to pay for imported products. The net result is that profit is unaffected.

Similarly, if the value of the pound falls, import prices will rise for the business. But it can offset this by raising the price of its exports in pounds, which leaves the foreign currency price to its customers the same.

Becoming more competitive Changes in the value of the pound can affect two main groups of businesses. If the value of the pound rises:

- exporters will find that the foreign currency price of their goods will rise if they maintain existing prices in pounds. This will damage export sales;
- imports are likely to fall in price. This will harm sales of UK businesses that make products competing against imports.

A fall in the value of the pound will help both UK exporters and those UK businesses in competition with imports.

Both exporters and UK businesses that compete against imported products can attempt to become more COMPETITIVE. They can do this in two ways.

First, they can try to reduce their costs so they can reduce their prices to customers. If the value of the pound rises by 10 per cent, for example, UK exporters need to cut their prices in pounds by 10 per cent to maintain the same price in foreign currency. Greater price competitiveness can be achieved by more efficient methods of production. The business might be able to get better prices on the products it buys in from suppliers. The workforce may need to be reduced in numbers, with the remaining workers working more efficiently than before. In a few cases, businesses have been forced to cut the wages of workers to achieve cost savings.

Second, they can become more competitive by adding value to the products they sell. Their products might be more reliable or better designed than those available from overseas competitors. Or the UK business might promise faster delivery times.

Marketing changes One response to a rise in the value of the pound for an exporter would be to pull out of the export market. If the business judged that it simply couldn't compete at the new higher exchange rate, then it should concentrate on the domestic market. The opposite strategic response might come from a UK business which suffers competition from abroad. A rise in the value of the pound will make imports cheaper and so give foreign companies a competitive advantage. To compensate for lower UK sales, the UK business may decide that it must expand into foreign markets and so it will start to export products.

Similarly, if the value of the pound fell, this would make UK products more competitive abroad. This could be a marketing opportunity for existing exporters to expand their markets. It could also be an opportunity for a UK firm which hadn't exported before to seek out new markets abroad.

Joining the euro

At present, the UK is not part of the eurozone. Most of the rest of the European Union has had a singe currency, the euro, since 2001. What would be the implications for British businesses if Britain joined the eurozone and replaced the pound with the euro?

Over 50 per cent of all UK exports and imports go to and come from other European Union countries. Joining the euro would mean that the price of those exports and imports would be fixed for UK businesses. There would be no more appreciation or depreciation of the UK currency against other European currencies. Selling to France or Italy would be the same as selling to Northumberland, London or Northern Ireland. As a result, businesses trading with other euro countries wouldn't have to pay commission to banks to change pounds into foreign currencies. It would also remove the uncertainty caused by changing exchange rates. What will be the exchange rate when payment is made on the import or export contract?

However, UK businesses would still face these risks when selling or buying outside the eurozone. Just as the pound can fluctuate against the US dollar or the Japanese Yen, so does the euro.

KNOWLEDGE

1. What is the difference between an appreciating pound and a depreciating pound?
2. (a) An exporter charges £20 for a product sold to the USA. What would be the price in US$ if the exchange rate were (i) £1 = $1.60; (ii) £1 = $1.85; (iii) £1 = $1.35? (b) At what exchange rate would the exporter be most competitive?
3. The value of the pound changes from £1 = $1.70 to £1 = $1.40. How might a UK exporter to the USA change its prices as a result and what would be the effect on sales?
4. Why might a rise in the value of the pound force UK exporters to become more competitive?
5. How might exchange rate changes affect marketing?

KEYTERMS

Appreciation of a currency – a rise in the value of a currency.

Competitiveness – the extent to which a business or a geographical area such as a country, can compete successfully against rivals.

Depreciation of a currency – a fall in the value of a currency.

Exchange rate – the price of one currency in terms of another currency.

Exports – goods or services produced domestically and sold to foreigners.

Exporting – selling goods and services produced domestically to foreigners.

Imports – goods or services produced outside the country and purchased from foreigners.

Importing – buying goods and services produced outside a country from foreigners.

Imports - goods or services produced outside the country and purchased from foreigners.

Case Study: Hot dogs

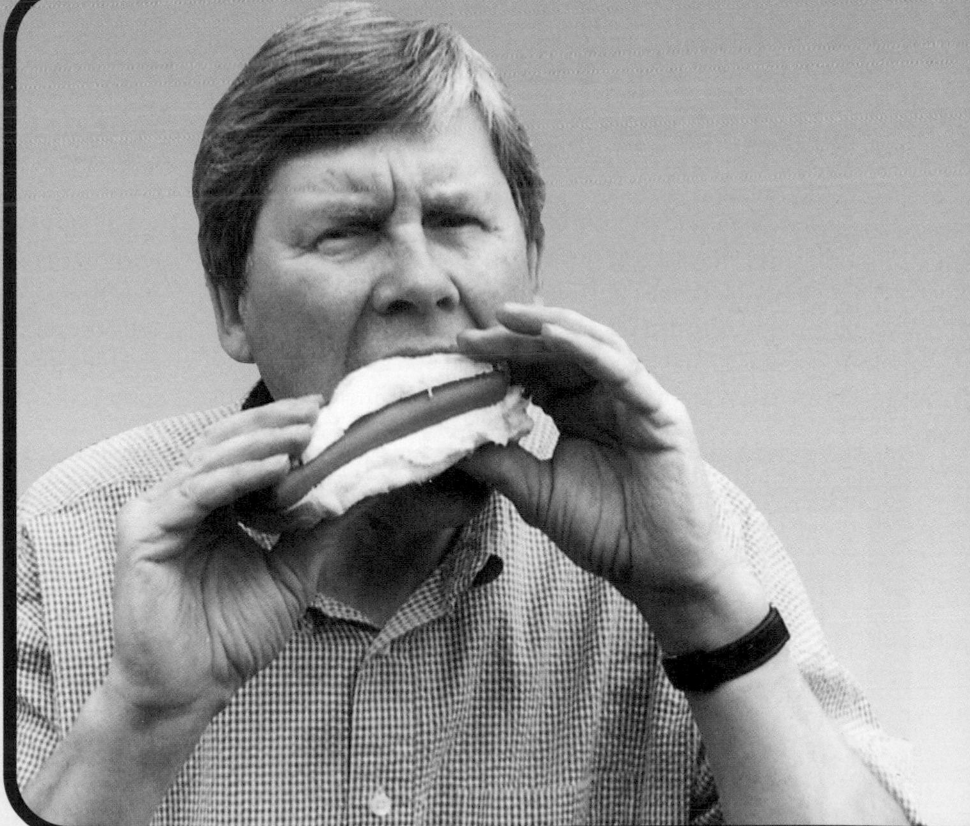

Joseph Wolff is a major importer of hot dogs to the UK. He founded his business 20 years ago and imports mainly from Germany and Denmark. Over the years, he has had to cope with large changes in the value of the pound against both the German deutschmark, the old German currency, and the Danish krona. Today, he is no better off. The German deutschmark has been replaced by the euro. But the Danish krona still exists because Denmark, like the UK, refused to adopt the euro as its currency in 2002 when the euro was launched.

The hot dog business is fiercely competitive. When the pound depreciates in value, Wolff is unable immediately to put up prices to his UK customers. He simply has to see his profit margins reduced. On the other hand, his short-term profit margins improve when the pound appreciates in value against the euro and the krona. Over a longer period of time, he make small price adjustments, but he has to be careful not to put up his prices too much or else he would lose orders from customers.

Over the years, Wolff has tried to reduce exchange rate risks by seeing if he could buy hot dogs from UK sausage manufacturers. The quality of the UK product has been disappointing though. UK manufacturers seem to have little idea of how to make a truly great hot dog.

(a) Discuss the possible impact of changes in the value of the pound on Wolff's hot dog business. (40 marks)

(b) Consider whether Wolff would be better off setting up his own hot dog manufacturing business in the UK. (40 marks)

113 Inflation and deflation

The meaning of inflation

INFLATION is a general **rise** in prices in the economy. A 5 per cent inflation rate over the past 12 months, for example, means that the average increase in prices across the economy during the past year was 5 per cent.

DEFLATION is a **fall** in average prices. Deflation means that, on average, the products are cheaper to buy than before. Note, however, the term 'deflation' is also used to describe a recession in the economy, when the inflation rate is falling but inflation is still positive.

Figure 1 shows inflation since 1959 for the UK economy. There have been considerable fluctuations in the yearly rise in prices, from a low of 0 per cent in 1959 to a high of 24.1 per cent in 1975. At its worst in 1975, a basket of products which cost £1 at the start of the year had risen in price to £1.24 at the end of the year. Today, the Bank of England is given the responsibility of keeping inflation at around 2.5 per cent per year.

Figure 2 shows price changes for Japan since 1990. It experienced deflation in a number of years during the 1990s and 2000s. Average prices were falling in Japan.

The measurement of inflation

In the UK, inflation is usually measured by calculating the change in the CONSUMER PRICES INDEX (CPI). Another commonly used measure of inflation is the RETAIL PRICES INDEX (RPI). Both the CPI and the RPI are measures of average prices calculated from the same data source. Each month, around 12,000 prices of more than 600 goods and services are taken around the UK, and from all different types of business which sell the products to consumers. An average price for that month is then worked out and converted into index number form. The month's figures can then be compared to last month's average price, or that of 12 months ago, to calculate the percentage rise in prices (i.e. the inflation rate) over the period.

Over time, the products which are priced each month change. The exact basket of products is derived from an annual survey of households (the Family Expenditure Survey). Each household taking part has to record everything it spends over a period. From the data, a profile of the 'typical household' in the UK emerges and how it spends its money. Researchers then go out and price up this average basket of products bought by the average family each month.

One key difference between the two measures of inflation, the CPI and the RPI, is that the RPI places more weight on changes in house prices.

The causes of inflation

Inflation can be caused by two main sets of factors – demand and costs.

Demand-pull inflation DEMAND-PULL INFLATION is caused by too much demand in the economy as a whole. Typically, the economy is booming and output (AGGREGATE SUPPLY) is not keeping up with the spending of consumers and businesses (AGGREGATE DEMAND). Shortages may develop in some parts of the economy because businesses are working at maximum capacity. In these circumstances, businesses are under little pressure to give discounts to buyers. So prices rise towards their list price. Many might also put up their list prices without losing customers.

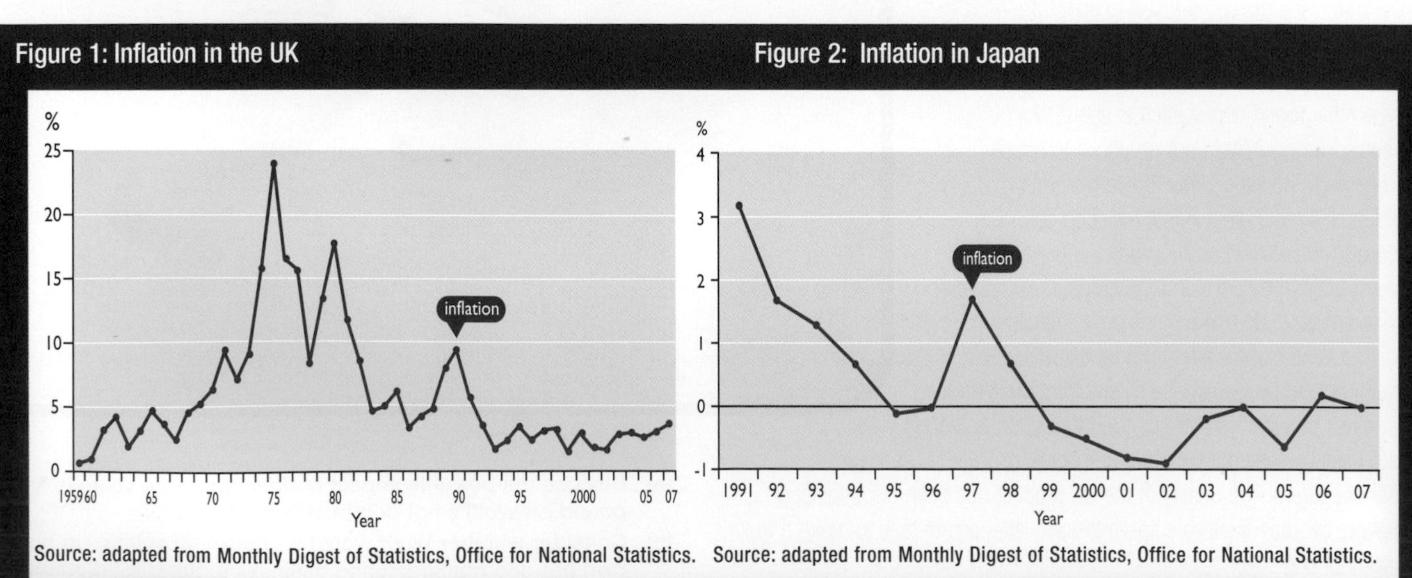

Source: adapted from Monthly Digest of Statistics, Office for National Statistics. Source: adapted from Monthly Digest of Statistics, Office for National Statistics.

Cost-push inflation COST-PUSH INFLATION occurs when costs of production rise without there being a rise in aggregate demand in the economy. Costs may rise for a number of reasons.

- Over the past 50 years, cost-push inflation in the UK has occurred mainly due to sharp rises in the cost of imported goods, such as oil. In 1973-74, for example, the price of oil quadrupled, from around $5 a barrel to $20 a barrel. These 'supply-side shocks' led to large price increases throughout the economy. Inflation in 1975 reached 24.1 per cent, for instance.
- Rises in wages might cause cost-push inflation. In the 1960s and 1970s, there was an increase in trade union militancy. Some argue that this caused wages to rise more than they would otherwise have done. On the other hand, in the 1980s, tough new laws were introduced by government that limited the powers of trade unions and strike action. It can be argued that reducing the power of trade unions reduced cost-push inflationary pressures.
- Other causes of cost-push inflation can be rises in taxes or profits. If the government increases taxes on goods and services, inflation will rise. In 1979, for example, the government increased VAT from 8 per cent to 15 per cent. This added around 5 per cent overnight to the inflation rate for that year. Equally, if the economic climate changes, as it did in the 1980s, and businesses decide that they need to earn more profit, this is likely to come about through price increases.

Wage-price spirals and expectations Cost-push inflation and demand-pull inflation tend to feed off one another. This is known as a WAGE-PRICE SPIRAL. It often starts through a supply-side shock, such as a sudden increase in import prices. Businesses put up their prices to remain profitable. Higher prices lead to workers demanding large pay rises. If they don't get wage rises which are at least as large as the increase in inflation, their standard of living will fall. This is because their wages won't be able to buy as much as before at the new high prices. Large wage increases lead to an increase in aggregate demand as workers spend their pay increases. However, businesses are forced to put up their prices again because their wage costs have increased. This leads to more wage demands and so on.

Wage-price spirals might be restricted by government policy to control inflation. However, at the end of the spiral, inflation tends to stabilise at a certain level anyway, for example 2 per cent in the late 1990s or 5 per cent in the mid-1980s. Stable inflation is maintained through the role of expectations. If all economic agents in the economy expect inflation to be the same as before, then they will act in a way which ensures that it is achieved. For example, if everyone expects inflation to be 2 per cent, then workers will negotiate pay rises of 2 per cent plus a little more to give them higher spending power than before. If workers expect inflation to be 20 per cent, they will negotiate for wage rises in excess of 20 per cent.

Similarly, businesses will base their price rises on expected inflation. If expected inflation is 2 per cent, businesses will tend to raise their prices by a few per cent. If expected inflation is 20

Question 1.

Zeenat is a small garment manufacturer in Nottingham, with 15 employees. It makes up clothes for a variety of buyers, including a couple of high street chains. The past four years have been very difficult for the company. Prices paid have been falling consistently as retailers have increasingly sourced clothes from the Far East. Last month, for example, official statistics were published showing that the price of clothes on the high street had fallen by 1.8 per cent the previous month.

It had all been different when the company was started up ten years previously. Then, prices could be increased each year to cover increased costs such as wage increases or raw material price rises. Today, costs were still going up but prices were falling. Take, for example, the minimum wage which the company has to pay its remaining workers. This had increased by 4 per cent last year and would be going up another 3.5 per cent next year.

(a) Why are falling prices a problem for a company such as Zeenat?

(b) Discuss whether high inflation would pose worse problems for Zeenat than mild deflation would.

per cent, they will put up their prices by around 20 per cent. The whole system can be stable if every economic agent acts on common expectations. But it can be unstable if different economic agents have different economic expectations. For example, a wage price spiral may begin if workers suddenly demand and obtain pay increases of 10 per cent when expected inflation has been 5 per cent.

Inflation, deflation and businesses

Inflation is not necessarily a problem. If prices are rising by a few per cent each year, and the inflation rate is fairly constant, inflation is likely to have little impact on businesses.

The situation is different if inflation is high. At 5 per cent and over, businesses have to be managed to cope with inflation. When inflation gets over, say, 20 per cent per annum, there are serious consequences for businesses. This is particularly true if inflation is fluctuating. For example, if yearly inflation goes from 5 per cent to 25 per cent to 150 per cent and then back down to 10 per cent in a four year period, then a business could easily be forced to close.

Equally, even quite low levels of deflation can have a significant impact on business. So there is considerable difference between 2 per cent inflation per year, which has little or no effect on business, and 2 per cent deflation.

Effects of inflation on businesses

High and particularly fluctuating inflation is likely to be damaging to business for a number of reasons.

Increased costs High or fluctuating inflation imposes a variety of costs on businesses.

- With suppliers' prices rising all the time, but at different rates, time must be spent researching the market for the best deals. Equally, more time has to be spent tracking the prices of competitors to decide when and by how much to increase your own prices. These costs are called **shoe leather costs,** because before the age of the telephone and the Internet, businesses would have to send their employees round on foot to gather this information.
- Raising prices costs money. Customers have to be informed of the new prices. Brochures might have to be reprinted and sent out. Websites might have to be updated. The sales force has to be made familiar with new prices. These costs are called **menu costs** because, for a restaurant, increasing prices means that it has to reprint its menus.
- Management is likely to have to spend more time dealing with workers' pay claims. Instead of being able to sign a two or three year deal, annual pay negotiations are likely to be the norm. If there is **hyperinflation**, where inflation is running into 100 per cent per annum or over, pay negotiations may have to take place each month. There is also a much larger risk of strikes because workers and managers will probably have different views of future inflation rates. Workers will be worried that any deal they make will leave them worse off after inflation. So they might be more willing to take industrial action to get high pay settlements.

Uncertainty With high and fluctuating inflation, businesses don't know what prices will be in three or six months' time, let alone in one or five years. But decisions have to be made now which will affect the business in the long term. For example, businesses need to invest to survive. But how much should they invest? The price of a new machine, a shop or a new computer system will probably be higher in six months than today. But are they worth buying if interest rates are at very high levels? What if the new machine is bought, financed by very high cost borrowing and there is a **recession**, where demand for goods and services falls?

Another problem with uncertainty is linked to entering long-term contracts. A customer might approach a business wanting to buy products on a regular monthly basis for the next two years. How can the supplier put a price on this contract if it doesn't know what the inflation rate will be over the next 24 months?

Borrowing and lending Borrowing and lending becomes an opportunity and a problem for businesses. On the one hand, the real value of debts incurred in the past can become quickly eroded by inflation. If inflation is 100 per cent per annum, the real value of money borrowed a year ago is halved in one year. Inflation initially benefits borrowers and harms lenders.

But in an inflationary environment, interest rates rise to match inflation. If inflation is 100 per cent, interest rates might be 110 per cent. If there is prolonged inflation, interest rates are likely to become INDEX LINKED – linked to the index of prices. So interest might be charged at the rate of inflation plus 5 per cent or plus 10 per cent.

Consumer reactions Consumers react to inflation as well as businesses. Prolonged inflation tends to lead to more saving. Inflation unsettles consumers. They become less willing to borrow money, not knowing what will happen in the future. The value of savings tends to fall as inflation erodes their real value. So people react by saving more to make up savings to their previous real value. Increased saving means less spending and so businesses will sell less.

If inflation is very high, consumers will adopt different spending patterns which may affect businesses. For example, if there is hyperinflation, prices will be changing by the day. Consumers will then tend to spend wages or interest as soon as they receive them. On 'pay day' there can be huge activity in shops. Supermarkets have to be geared up to selling most of the weekly or monthly turnover in just a few hours. Suppliers of fresh produce to supermarkets have to be geared to delivering most of their goods on one day a week.

International competitiveness High inflation poses problems for businesses that buy or sell abroad.

If the inflation rate in the UK is 10 per cent, but is only 2 per cent in France, then UK **exporters** will become uncompetitive against French businesses. For example, if a UK product is priced at 58 pence, it would be sold at €1 in France (assuming the exchange rate is €1= £0.58). Now assume there is inflation in the UK and the manufacturer has to put its prices up by 10 per cent to 63.8p or €1.10. In contrast, competitors in France only experience 2 per cent inflation and put their prices up to €1.02. The UK exporter has therefore lost price competitiveness and will find it harder to sell into the French market.

UK businesses facing competition from French firms will also suffer because French imports to the UK will be relatively cheaper. UK companies might have to put up their prices by 10 per cent because of cost-push pressures in the UK economy when French competitors are only putting up their prices by 2 per cent. UK companies will therefore lose market share in their home market.

Effects of deflation on businesses

Deflation, a general fall in overall prices, can also lead to problems for businesses.

A stagnant economy Deflation tends to be associated with an economy which is not growing in size. It might even be shrinking. This is because falls in price are often associated with falling levels of demand. Consumers are reluctant to spend money. Businesses don't want to increase their investment because their output is stagnant. Demand for exports may also be stagnant, perhaps because of a recession in the world economy. In a stagnant economy, problems could be made worse by rising unemployment. This also tends to reduce the willingness of consumers to spend and borrow. Faced with deflation, businesses will find it difficult to expand their own production. Many could face falling demand for their products if they are selling into markets which are in decline because of changes in spending patterns.

Reducing costs Deflation means that businesses are being forced to cut their prices. When deflation initially occurs, businesses may choose to pay for the price cuts by simply cutting their profits or accepting a loss for the year. But if deflation is prolonged, businesses have to cut their costs to survive. Cost cutting year on year is very difficult. It may be possible to achieve lower costs through more efficient production methods. An alternative is to cut the wages of workers. This is likely to lead to demotivation and threats of industrial action. It is perhaps more difficult to manage a business that continually has to cut its prices than it is to manage one where prices can be slowly pushed upwards.

In recent years, some industries, particularly in the manufacturing sector, have seen the prices of their products fall when prices in the economy as a whole have been rising. They have been suffering from deflation when there has been mild inflation in the whole economy. The cause has been intense price competition, particularly from the Far East and countries like China. They have been forced either substantially to increase their productivity, or to move upmarket where price competition is less intense.

Strategy and inflation

If inflation is low, businesses are unlikely to need to have strategies to cope with changing prices. It is only when inflation rates rise considerably that businesses may need to adapt their strategies. The main strategic responses of businesses to high inflation should be to push up their own prices while at the same time attempting to minimise the rises in their own costs.

Pushing up prices Moderate to high general inflation in an economy is likely to mean that a business is facing increases in its own costs. Suppliers will be pushing up their prices while workers will be demanding higher wages. Businesses can respond strategically to these cost pressures by putting up their own prices and so maintaining their profit margins. Putting up prices will be much easier if competitors are also putting up their prices. Equally, if a business is selling a popular differentiated product, this will reduce the ability of customers to buy elsewhere when prices are raised. However, there is always a danger when putting up prices that sales will fall and market share will be lost.

Reducing costs An alternative strategy to inflationary pressures is to cut costs. For example, a business may buy labour saving equipment in order to cut the cost of labour. It may seek out alternative suppliers willing to charge lower prices. It may look at all its production processes and make changes to increase efficiency in production. Cost cutting is likely to most successful as a strategy when inflation is relatively low. When inflation is relatively high, the best a business might hope to achieve is to have lower cost inflation than its competitors.

KNOWLEDGE

1. What is the difference between inflation and deflation?
2. Explain the problems that a business might face if:
   (a) there is very high inflation of 25 per cent per year;
   (b) there is high inflation and it does not know whether inflation will rise or fall next year;
   (c) it has financial reserves of £2 million deposited with its bank and there is high inflation;
   (d) it is a major exporter and inflation is much lower in other countries;
   (e) prices in the economy are, on average, falling.
3. What strategies might a business use if inflation is high?

KEYTERMS

Aggregate demand – total demand within the economy, which is equal to total output and total spending.

Aggregate supply – total supply within the economy, equal to total output of the economy.

Consumer Prices Index – a measure of the price level used across the EU and used in the UK by the Bank of England to measure inflation.√

Cost-push inflation – inflation which is caused by changes in aggregate supply, typically increases in the price of imports or increases in wages.

Deflation - strictly defined, it is a fall in the general price level within an economy. It is often used, however, to describe a situation when the rate of economic growth is falling or is negative and when inflation is falling.

Demand-pull inflation - inflation which is caused by changes in aggregate demand, such as a large increase in consumer spending, or a sizeable increase in spending by businesses on capital equipment (i.e. investment), or a significant increase in exports.

Index linked – in the context of inflation, adjusting the value of economic variables such as wages or the rate of interest in line with a measure of inflation such as the Retail Price Index.

Inflation - a general rise in prices.

Retail Prices Index (RPI) – a measure of the price level which has been calculated in the UK for over 60 years and is used in a variety of contexts.

Wage-price spiral – the process whereby increases in costs, such as wages, lead to increases in prices and this in turn leads to increases in costs to businesses.

Case Study: McGinnel's

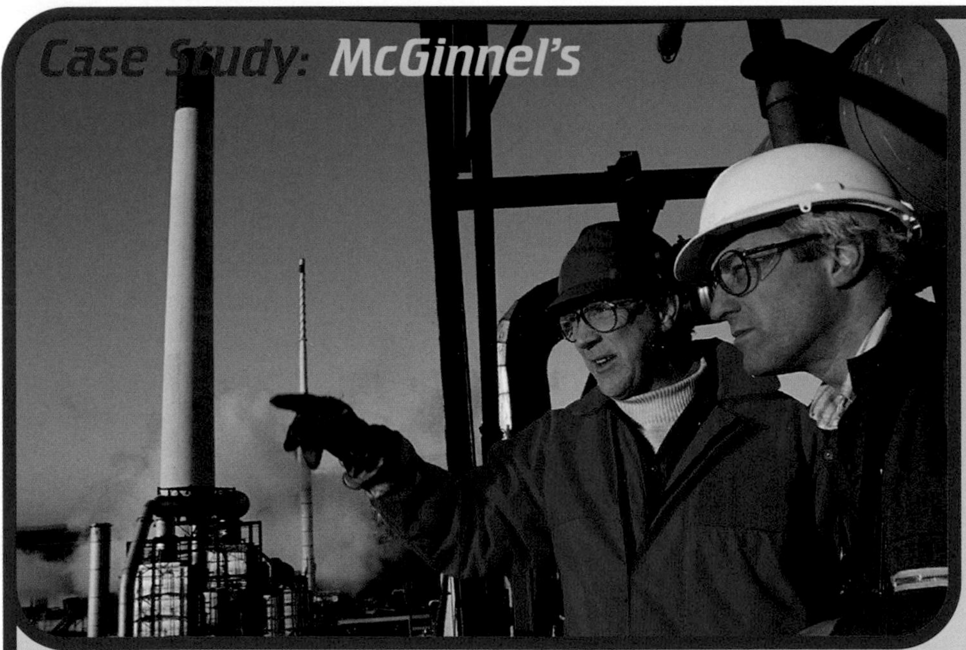

McGinnel's is a small independent oil supply company in the south west of England. It buys oil on the open market from refineries and sells to businesses and home owners with oil fired central heating systems. Its green and white liveried tankers are a familiar sight in its local market.

The single largest cost for the company tends to be the oil it buys. The price of crude oil over the years has fluctuated enormously. The result has been that the cost base of the business has also fluctuated significantly.

Another major cost facing the company has been the wage costs of employees, together with related costs such as National Insurance contributions, pension contributions and training. These costs have tended to rise at roughly the same rate as average inflation in the UK. Although tanker drivers' pay has risen faster than the rate of inflation, this has been, to some extent, offset by rises in productivity. Through improved working practices and the introduction of new technology, fewer staff have been needed to deliver the same amount of oil.

Other costs include running a small fleet of tanker trucks for delivery of oil to customers and the overhead costs of the central office and plant for storing oil. Over time, these costs have risen at a little over the average rate of inflation for the economy.

The price that the company charges its customers is very much affected by the price charged by its competitors, the oil majors such as BP Amoco or Texaco. McGinnel's has survived the competition over the years by giving very slightly better prices to customers than the oil majors. Sometimes this pricing policy has caused financial problems because McGinnel's has had to pay higher prices for its oil supplies, but has been unable to pass on the higher cost because the oil majors have left their prices constant. Equally, McGinnel's has sometimes had a profit windfall when oil prices have dropped but the oil majors have been slow to respond with falls in the price of oil to customers. Over time, though, the oil majors have adjusted their prices in line with changes in the price of crude oil.

More importantly, perhaps, for sales, McGinnel's has offered customers excellent service. It has been prepared, for example, to offer same day delivery to customers who suddenly find they have run out of oil. By being a highly efficient, value for money 'local' company, McGinnel's has built up a very loyal customer base.

(a) To what extent is McGinnel's affected by inflation in the wider economy? (40 marks)

(b) Discuss whether McGinnel's should change its pricing policy to one where its prices change immediately the price of its oil supplies change. (40 marks)

114 Unemployment

Unemployment and underemployment

There are always unemployed workers in a market economy. However, the level of UNEMPLOYMENT can vary as Figure 1 shows. Official statistics on unemployment tend to measure those who do not have a job, but who are actively looking for work.

There are many more, however, who would take on a job if it were available, but are not actively seeking work. The largest group of these **underemployed** people is women who remain at home to look after children. Another large group is the over-50s. Many have taken early retirement because they were made redundant from an existing job. However, they would re-enter the workforce if there were a suitable job available.

Types of unemployment

There is a number of different types of unemployment. Each type is related to a different **cause** of unemployment.

Frictional unemployment Often workers voluntarily leave their jobs or are made redundant before they have another job. Or they may leave one job but their next job only starts in, say, two weeks' time. In between jobs, they are classified as unemployed. This type of unemployment is called FRICTIONAL UNEMPLOYMENT.

Seasonal unemployment In some industries, it is common for workers to be employed only at certain times of the year. In tourism, for example, workers are taken on just for the tourist season. In the construction industry, outdoor construction workers can often be laid off in the winter when building conditions become difficult. In agriculture, extra workers are taken on at harvest time. In general, unemployment tends to go up in the winter and down in the summer because of this SEASONAL UNEMPLOYMENT.

Cyclical unemployment Economies can go from boom to recession. The unemployment caused by the move to recession is called CYCLICAL UNEMPLOYMENT. Usually it occurs because aggregate (or total) demand in the economy stops growing at a rate that is fast enough to maintain current levels of employment. At worst, the economy can go into a depression and aggregate demand can fall. With less demand for goods and services, unemployment will rise.

Figure 1: Unemployment, claimant count, millions, not seasonally adjusted.

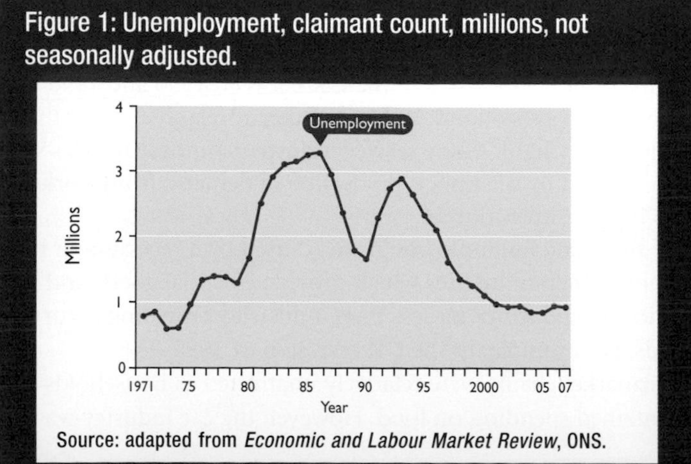

Source: adapted from *Economic and Labour Market Review*, ONS.

Structural unemployment Today, the pace of change in an economy can be very fast. These changes can lead to STRUCTURAL UNEMPLOYMENT. This is unemployment caused by changes in the structure of an economy.

There is a number of different types of structural unemployment.

- **Technological unemployment** is caused by changes in technology which allow different methods of production to be used or permit new goods to be made. For example, computer technology has transformed much of manufacturing. It has reduced the number of workers needed to produce a given output. Equally, it has created jobs in industries such as computer manufacturing. However, the workers who lost their jobs in manufacturing are unlikely to live in the place where the new jobs are created. Even if they were, they might not have the right skills. They might not even want the new jobs if the new jobs are at a much lower rate of pay.
- Where a whole region is affected by a run down of major industries, **regional unemployment** is said to exist. The reason for the run down may be changes in technology. Or it could be that major industries in a region have become uncompetitive. In the UK, for example, much of manufacturing has closed down and the jobs have been transferred to the Far East where wages are much lower. It could be that demand for the product of a region has fallen. Lace making in Nottingham or coal from Wales are examples.
- **Sectoral unemployment** is said to exist when major industries collapse leaving large numbers of unemployed workers.

These different types of structural unemployment are usually linked. Structural unemployment would not exist if there were perfect **mobility of labour** within an economy. If the labour market were perfect, workers would be able to move from job to job instantly. They would have the skills to move from being a coal miner to being a computer technician. They could move from Wales to London. They would also be able to understand that they might have to take a cut in pay to get a job.

In the real world, however, there are barriers to mobility. Workers don't have transferable skills. Housing costs are a major barrier to mobility. Workers might not want to leave the town where they were brought up. There might be discrimination against unemployed workers in their 50s trying to get jobs.

Question 1.

Last year was a watershed year for Gill's, the US fast food chain. For the first time, it made a loss. Outside of the USA, the company is still expanding profitably. But in its core US market, it has experienced significant difficulties. Competition has been intense and US consumers have begun to desert Gill's for fast food chains offering healthier alternatives.

Problems for Gill's have been made worse by a downturn in the US economy which has seen rising unemployment. The result has been that fast food chains have suffered from a lack of lunchtime foot traffic. The company claims that it is fairly recession proof because 'when people are cutting back we tend to be one of the last things to be eliminated because our product is not very expensive'. However, to offset rising unemployment and increased competition, the company recently introduced a $1 menu.

A sign that not everything was well with Gill's was the announcement this year that it would be closing 175 outlets, many in the US where there were simply too few customers due to fierce local competition. Some analysts believe that a more savage cut in capacity in the USA, particularly where Gill's outlets were very close to each other, would boost profits.

(a) Explain why rising unemployment could lead to problems for Gill's.

(b) Discuss whether closing outlets in the USA in a recession would be a sensible strategy for Gill's to adopt.

Effects of unemployment on businesses

Changes in the unemployment levels in a local area, region or country can have major effects on businesses.

Output Rises in unemployment are likely to affect output and sales of businesses. For example, a small town may have a factory that employs 10 per cent of its workers. If that factory closes, shops in the town will almost certainly see a downturn in trade because unemployed workers will spend less. Suppliers to the factory, perhaps in the local area, will also see a fall in sales.

Low unemployment, on the other hand, is associated with rising output as employed workers spend their wages and other firms invest.

Redundancies and recruitment A fall in output because of rising unemployment could lead to businesses making some of their workers redundant. Redundancies have many effects on businesses. It can be costly if redundancy pay is given. It takes management time to organise. It leads to demotivation amongst staff. On the other hand, if a business is able to recruit in a high unemployment period, it could have a large number of applicants from which to choose. High unemployment can also help put downward pressure on pay and reduce the willingness of workers to take industrial action to support a pay claim.

Low unemployment, on the other hand, is associated with recruitment of workers in tight labour markets. So businesses may have relatively few workers applying for a job. There is also upward pressure on wages because the demand for labour is high and the supply relatively low.

Capacity If unemployment is rising and a business is suffering falling orders as a result, it is likely to suffer from excess capacity. Machines will be idle and office and factory space will be underutilised. This can raise average costs because fixed costs won't change, but less will be produced. Eventually, businesses will be forced to cut their excess capacity by closing sites, not replacing equipment and moving to smaller premises.

On the other hand, falling unemployment leading to higher output is likely to increase capacity utilisation and reduce average costs. Eventually, businesses will increase their capacity, which will fuel demand in the economy further.

Government spending and taxes In a downturn, with rising unemployment, government spending will increase. This is because there will be a rise in social welfare payments to the unemployed. The government is unlikely to raise taxes at this point for fear of reducing spending in the economy even further.

However, if unemployment starts to fall, the government may begin to raise taxes to reduce its borrowing. Higher taxes may be targeted at households, which will slow down the pace of recovery. Taxes could also be targeted at businesses. For example, corporation tax, a tax on company profits, might be raised. This would hit profits.

Sectoral and regional effects Some businesses would be more affected than others by rising unemployment. If the rising unemployment was structural, then businesses in certain industries or certain regions would be affected. For example, the decline of heavy industry in the UK between 1950 and 1990 hit regions such as Scotland, Wales, Northern Ireland and Northern England very hard. Many service industries in these regions were then affected by the knock-on decline in demand from workers who became unemployed.

If the rising unemployment was caused by a recession in the economy, then industries which provide essential goods and services would suffer far less than industries providing luxury goods. For example, in the UK recession of 1990-92, supermarket chains were relatively unaffected as households maintained spending on food. However, the car industry was badly affected because many households and businesses delayed buying new cars and made do with their existing vehicles.

Social issues Long-term unemployment tends to create areas of poverty where the unemployed tend to live. Vandalism, crime and other types of antisocial behaviour can result in those areas. This will affect any business located there. For example, business premises may be broken into, equipment stolen, or vandals may set fire to the premises. New businesses thinking of setting up in such areas might be deterred, whilst existing businesses may relocate or shut down, making the problems of unemployment worse.

Strategy and unemployment

If there are small changes in unemployment, then businesses need not change their existing strategies. If there is a large rise in unemployment, this is likely to be associated with a recession and falling demand in the economy as a whole. Different businesses will then be affected in different ways. Businesses which produce essentials like food may see little change in demand for their products. However, businesses making products which see a sharp fall in demand should cut their production too. This could mean making workers redundant and closing factories, outlets and offices. Businesses which fail to make the necessary cuts could themselves become casualties of the recession. Rising unemployment, however, could be an opportunity to pick up workers who are better skilled and motivated.

Large falls in unemployment are likely to be good for most businesses. Demand is likely to be increasing at an above - average rate. Sales will be rising. Businesses should use the opportunity to expand. However, they may have increasing problems recruiting the right sort of workers.

KEYTERMS

Frictional unemployment - when workers are unemployed for short lengths of time between jobs.
Structural unemployment - when the pattern of demand and production changes, leaving workers unemployed in labour markets where demand has shrunk. Examples of structural unemployment are regional unemployment, sectoral unemployment and technological unemployment.
Cyclical unemployment - when there is insufficient demand in the economy for all workers to be able to get a job. Cyclical unemployment occurs in recessions.
Unemployment – when those actively seeking work are unable to obtain a job.

KNOWLEDGE

1. Explain the difference between (a) frictional unemployment and seasonal unemployment; (b) cyclical unemployment and structural unemployment.
2. Explain why 300 workers being made redundant in a small town could affect services industries in the local area.
3. Why might rising unemployment lead to overcapacity in industry?
4. Why might a business be deterred from setting up in an area of high unemployment?

Case Study: UK textile industry

The UK textile industry employs around 300, 000 workers, more than the farming, car manufacturing or chemicals industries. When a car production plant like Dagenham in Essex or Longbridge in Birmingham faces closure, it is national news. But the 41, 000 job losses in the textiles industry last year passed almost unnoticed by the media. One difference between textiles and these other industries is that the textile job losses being experienced are almost all amongst low paid women. In the car production, farming and chemicals industries, the workforce is often made up of better paid male workers.

Maggie Rowley provides an example of the story. She worked as a machinist for Coates Viyella, a major supplier to Marks & Spencer, for 20 years. She was one of 450 women made redundant 18 months ago when M&S moved its manufacturing base for the trousers on which she worked to Morocco. Her factory was one of two in Rossington, an old mining village outside Doncaster. On the one road into the village is the pit where her brothers, all miners, were once employed; one still is, the rest work on chicken farms.

Maggie Rowley was lucky enough to get another textiles job after the factory closed, but it was two bus rides away and only paid at the national minimum wage rate. She was quickly made redundant from that job too and now she works in a lighting components factory. Commenting on her job loss at Coates Viyella, she said that it was caused because 'there was no investment, no training, no planning. Now we're losing a whole industry and it's devastating.'

There are significant centres of textile production around the country with a quarter of the industry based in the East Midlands. In Maggie Rowley's home area, 1,000 textile jobs have gone, plus more jobs lost in Doncaster itself. Closures can hit an area hard. Often, textile plants close in areas where there is already high unemployment, particularly male unemployment. Women working in textiles may well be the only wage earner in their household. They often don't have cars and find it difficult to travel far to get a job.

(a) Discuss the possible effects of textile closures on manufacturing and service businesses in the Doncaster area. (40 marks)

(b) 'There was no investment, no training, no planning.' To what extent can a UK business avoid closing down plants and making workers redundant by investment, training and planning? (40 marks)

115 Taxation

Taxation

TAXATION is the charges that the government makes on the activities, earnings and income of businesses and individuals. The government uses the money raised by taxation to:

- pay for government spending on a wide variety of public sector activities including transport, education, health, defence and housing;
- to affect factors in the economy such as inflation and unemployment;
- to redistribute income, from those with higher incomes, to those who need it most;
- to influence patterns of consumer expenditure.

Taxes are sometimes classified into **direct** and **indirect** taxation. Direct taxes are taxes taken directly from the income of businesses or individuals, such as income tax. An indirect tax is a tax on a good or service, taken from income when it is used or spent, such as VAT.

Types of direct taxation

What are the main types of taxation in the UK?

Income tax This is a tax on the income or earnings of individuals. It includes charges made on the wages or salaries of employees and on the income of sole traders. It includes other earnings, such as the dividends paid to directors or limited companies. People do not pay tax on all their income. There are some allowances, such as a personal allowance on which people do not pay tax. After these allowances are taken into account, tax is charged on the remaining **taxable income**.

Income tax is a **progressive** tax. The more people earn the higher the proportion of their income that is paid in tax. This is because some of their income, their personal allowance, is tax free. Top income earners pay the highest rate of tax at 40 per cent but this top rate is only payable on the proportion of their taxable earnings which exceed around £30,000.

Other factors might also be taken into account when calculating income tax. For example, employees can claim a mileage allowance without tax for using company cars for business purposes. Certain gifts to charities by businesses are not liable for tax.

National Insurance contributions These are payable by employers, employees and the self-employed. They are calculated mostly as a percentage of income. For employers, they act as a tax on employment, adding to the total cost of employing workers. For employees and the self-employed, they are a substantial tax on earnings like income tax.

Corporation tax This is a tax on the profits of private and

Question 1.

Stuart Elliott runs a Victorian Experience tourist attraction in London. Go into the building and you step back in time to the world of Charles Dickens and Sherlock Holmes. He was disappointed with the last government Budget. The Chancellor put up corporation tax rates, although he didn't put up Employers' National Insurance contributions as had been widely predicted.

Of course, there were also all the hidden increases. Whenever Stuart puts up his ticket prices, for example, 17.5 per cent of the increase immediately goes to the Chancellor in extra VAT. When he gives his workers a pay increase, he has to pay over 10 per cent of that increase to the Exchequer in Employers' National Insurance contributions. Like many entrepreneurs, Stuart feels he is overtaxed and doesn't get many benefits from the government.

(a) Explain five different taxes that Stuart Elliott and his business would pay.

(b) Examine how a rise in (a) the rate of corporation tax and (b) Employers' National Insurance contributions would affect the business and the decisions that Stuart might make about its future operations.

public limited companies. There are lower rates for small companies than for larger companies.

A business can claim capital allowances. This is where it is able to claim allowances against certain types of spending, such as building hotels in enterprise zones or expenditure on research and development. It would not have to pay as much corporation tax if it could claim such allowances.

Capital gains tax This is a tax on the sales of capital assets. Capital gains usually involve the sale of shares, although they can involve non-business assets such as rental property owned by individuals.

Inheritance tax This is a tax on money left on death. If a person leaves money to a husband or wife, the transfer of money is tax free. Otherwise, the first approximately £300,000 is tax free and the rest is taxed at 40 per cent.

Types of indirect tax

Value Added Tax (VAT) VAT is charged on goods or services which are made and bought in the UK. There were three rates of VAT in 2008:

- the standard rate was 17.5 per cent. This applies to most goods and services bought in the UK;
- the zero rate of 0 per cent. This applies to certain goods in the UK which are subject to VAT, but at a nil rate. Examples include food, books and children's clothing and footwear;
- the reduced rate of five per cent. This applies to a narrow category of products including womens' sanitary products, children's car seats and installation of energy saving items.

It is often argued that, within the standard rate band, VAT is a **regressive** tax. The more you earn, the less as a proportion of your income you pay in tax. The main reason for this is that higher income earners tend to save more of their income and so don't pay VAT on the income they don't spend. This reduces their average rate of tax on VAT as a proportion of their income.

Customs duty This is a tax on goods and services imported into a country. Customs duties are usually charged as a percentage of the value of the imported goods. They are often placed on imports of foreign businesses, to raise the price of their goods in an attempt to protect home businesses from competition. A problem, however, is that businesses importing supplies have to pay higher prices.

Excise duties Excise duties are a tax on the sale of a narrow range of products including alcohol, cigarettes and petrol and diesel fuel. Because excise duties are very high, they are a substantial money raiser for the government.

Council tax This is a charge paid by residents of domestic housing in the UK to local authorities. The charge people pay is based on the council tax band in which the valuation officer places a dwelling. The bands are based on the size, location, layout and character of the property. The valuations are designed to show what the property would have been sold for on the open market, given certain assumptions. Different local authorities have different bands.

Business rates Business rates, or national non-domestic rates (NNDR), are annual charges on the rateable value of business premises. The rateable value is broadly the yearly rent for which the property could be let out.

Stamp duty This is a tax paid on the purchase of land, property, leases and certain types of shares and securities.

Insurance premium tax Insurance premium tax is a tax on all general insurance such as cars, homes and travel insurance.

Environmental taxes There is a variety of indirect taxes which are used to change the behaviour of individuals and businesses to benefit the environment. The **landfill tax** is a charge on waste disposed in landfill sites. The **aggregates levy** is a tax on sand, gravel and crushed rock extracted in the UK or imported from abroad. The **climate change levy** is a charge on fuels used by business. **Air passenger duty** is a tax on each passenger flying by air. VAT and excise duty on fuel for cars and heavy goods vehicles can also be seen as environmental taxes.

Effects of changes in taxation on business

How might changes in taxation affect businesses in the UK?

Consumer spending Changes in certain types of taxation are likely to increase the income consumers have left after tax. These include reductions in income tax rates, increases in personal allowances and an increase in the limits on which inheritance tax is paid or a reduction in the rate of inheritance tax. If consumers have more income left they might increase spending on the products of businesses. Increases in income tax, National Insurance contributions and council taxes are all likely to leave consumers with less income and could reduce spending on products.

Prices An increase in VAT or excise duty will raise the costs of a business. Businesses often pass this on to customers by raising the price of goods. An increase in customs duty will increase the price of goods being imported into a country.

Business costs, revenue and profits Increases in some taxes might raise the costs of business. For example, VAT will raise costs. A business might try to raise prices to cover this and maintain profit. However, higher prices can reduce sales and so profit could still be affected if revenue falls. Rises in corporation tax, business rates, employers' National Insurance contributions and landfill tax will all tend to reduce business profits. Reductions in taxes are likely to increase the profits of a business.

Business spending and investment Increases in costs and reduced profits mean that businesses have less retained profit. This can affect the ability of the business to pay its debts, buy stocks and meet other expenses. It can also affect whether it invests in new factories or machinery.

Shares Changes in capital gains tax and stamp duty might affect shareholding. For example, an increase in capital gains tax might deter shareholders or delay sales of shares.

Importing and exporting Increases in customs duties can affect businesses. For example, if the UK raised customs duties on imported products a UK business might benefit because as imports against which it competed would then have a higher price. However, UK businesses buying imported supplies would have to pay higher prices.

Business operations and employees Increases in National Insurance contributions of employers might deter employers from recruiting extra workers. Changes in taxation on company cars or mileage allowances might also changes how a business offers these benefits to employees.

Other effects Certain types of business might be affected by changes in tax. For example, an increase in landfill tax might encourage businesses to recycle. A rise in passenger duty could discourage holiday makers and reduce the demand for holidays.

Tax avoidance and evasion Increases in taxation often lead businesses to try to avoid paying the tax. For example, they might not hire workers to avoid higher National Insurance contributions or switch from buying imports to avoid customs duties. In some cases they might even try to evade the law, for example dumping waste in the countryside to avoid landfill taxes, which is illegal.

KEYTERMS

Taxation – the charges made by government on the activities, earnings and income of businesses and individuals.

KNOWLEDGE

1. What is the difference between a direct and an indirect tax?
2. State six types of tax in the UK.
3. Why is income tax progressive and VAT regressive?
4. State three taxes that might reduce company profits if they rise.

Case Study: UK taxation

The Chancellor has launched a review of the competitiveness of the UK's tax system. This is in response to a trend for UK multinational companies to relocate their headquarters to countries that levy lower taxes on profits. Recently, for example, Shire, the UK's third-biggest pharmaceutical company, and United Business Media, the publisher, have relocated to Ireland.

The UK has the lowest corporation tax rates amongst the world's largest economies. But it is finding it difficult to defend itself against the attraction of smaller countries such as Ireland and Switzerland which have even lower corporation tax rates.

The Chancellor can't afford to lose tax revenue from corporation tax. The sort of tax cut that the CBI is urging would see revenues fall by over £1 billion a year. On the other hand, if corporation tax isn't lowered, more companies could leave the UK. Each company that moves overseas means the Exchequer loses corporation tax revenues.

Source: adapted from *The Financial Times*, 30.4.2008.

Rules doubling the amount of passenger duty people pay when taking flights from the UK came into force today. The Chancellor said when announcing the tax increase that airlines should pay more for damaging the environment.

Some airlines have fiercely opposed the increase, saying that it would have no impact on the environment because it would not discourage people from flying. Other airlines have said that it is a tax on a highly successful growing industry which provides employment for the UK economy. They are worried that they will have more empty seats on their planes as a result of the tax increase. City analysts will be looking with interest to see if the airlines attempt to cushion the effect of the tax increase by lowering the pre-tax price of tickets.

Source: adapted from news.bbc.co.uk 1.2.2007.

The cross-party Communities and Local Government Committee has said that local councils should be given more freedom to adjust business rates. The Parliamentary committee made up of MPs said: 'We are dismayed that (the government) proposes to hobble local authorities' ability to raise sums which would enable them – in partnership with local business – to make a meaningful contribution to the economic development of their area.'

Business organisations would fiercely resist giving such powers to local authorities. They fear that councils would substantially increase business rates in order to keep down more high profile council tax rates paid by households.

Source: adapted from *The Financial Times*, 21.1.2008.

(a) Evaluate how raising taxes might affect business decisions to invest in expansion in the UK. (40 marks)

(b 'It would always be better to raise extra taxes on consumers and workers rather than directly on businesses.' Evaluate arguments for and against this statement from a business perspective. (40 marks)

116 Population

The influence of population on business

People are vital to the operation of businesses. They provide organisations with labour. People also demand the goods and services that businesses produce. Changes in total population can affect businesses. A growing population is likely to place greater demand on a country's resources. Businesses are also affected by the structure of the population of the markets within which they operate. A higher proportion of people who are elderly means greater need for support. This unit considers the main trends in these DEMOGRAPHIC FACTORS and how they influence the operation of businesses.

Population size and business

In 2008, the world's population was estimated to be 6.7 billion It is forecast to stabilise at 9-10 billion by the end of the twenty first century.

Different countries have different population sizes. Their populations also grow at different rates. For example, the UK's population in 2008 was estimated to be 60.8 million. Figure 1

Figure 1: Population estimates, UK

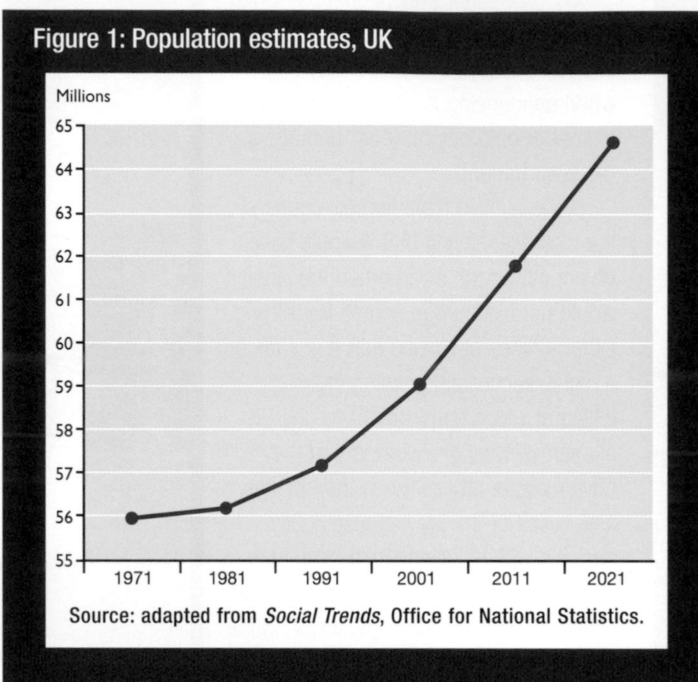

Source: adapted from *Social Trends*, Office for National Statistics.

Question 1.

Figure 2: Population growth rates, 2006

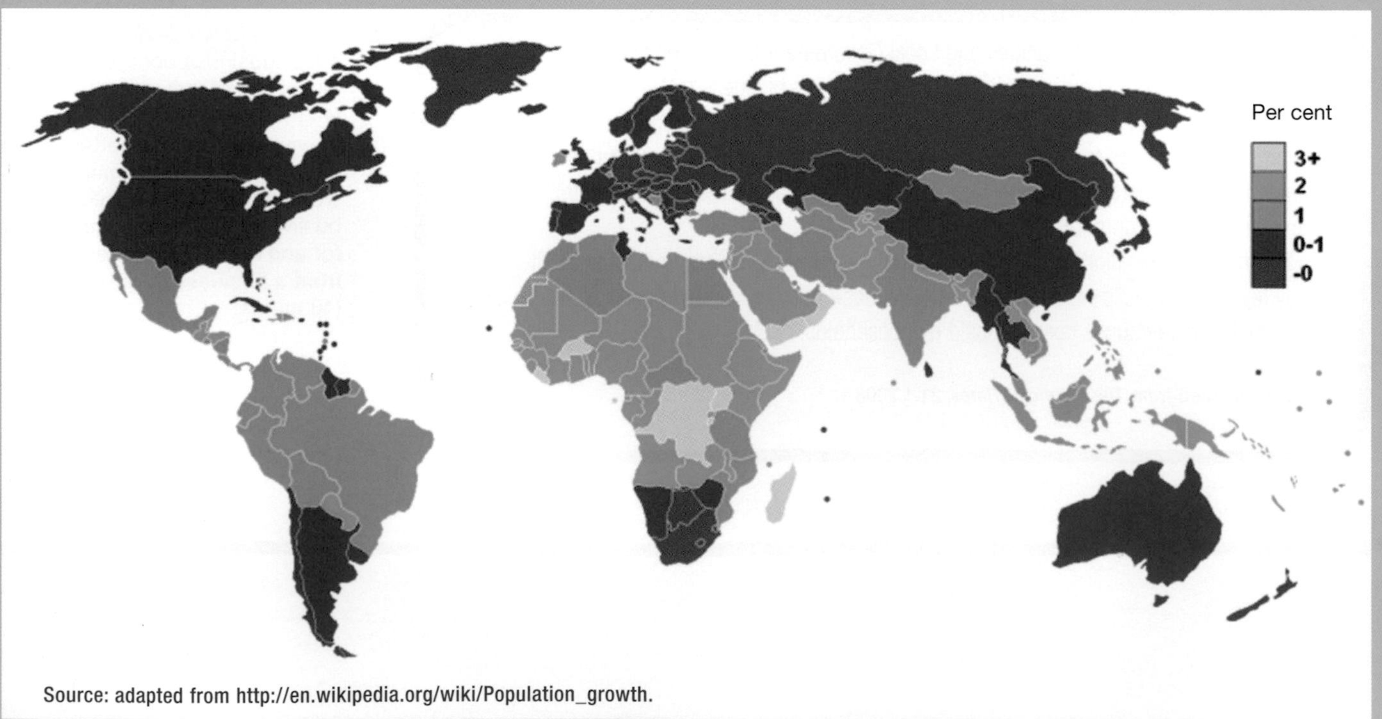

Source: adapted from http://en.wikipedia.org/wiki/Population_growth.

(a) Describe the trends taking place in Figure 2.

(b) Using this information, explain the possible benefits and problems for businesses based in (i) Africa and (ii) eastern Europe.

shows predictions for population growth to the period from 1971 to 2021. Population growth in the UK was around 0.1-0.3 per cent per annum in the early twenty first century. In contrast, Somalia, with a population of 9.2 million, had an annual population growth rate of 3.2 per cent.

What effect might a growing population have on businesses?

- There is likely to be greater demand for goods and services.
- There is likely to be a larger pool of labour.
- There may be growing pressure on resources, if population growth is greater than the growth in output.

The factors affecting population growth and business

What factors might determine the growth of a country's population and how might this affect businesses? It is suggested that there are three main factors which affect population growth - births, deaths, and migration. Table 1 shows how these factors can affect the UK population, both in the past and in the future.

Table 1: Factors affecting population change, UK

Thousands

	1981-1991	1991-2001	2001-2006	2006-2011	2011-2021
Total population at start of period	56,357	57,439	59,113	60,587	62,761
Annual averages					
Live births	757	731	701	780	802
Live deaths	655	631	595	565	551
Net natural change	103	100	106	215	252
Net migration	5	68	189	220	191
Overall annual change	108	167	295	435	443

Source: adapted from *Social Trends 2008*, Office for National Statistics.

The number of births If nothing else changes, a greater number of births will increase the population of a country. A larger number of births may affect businesses in a number of ways. This is discussed in the next section.

The number of deaths If nothing else changes, a smaller number of deaths should increase the population. Furthermore, changes in the number of years people are expected to live can affect businesses. This is also discussed in the next section.

Net natural change This is the difference between the number of births and the number of deaths. A positive number shows that births are greater than deaths. The population is therefore increasing naturally. A negative number shows that births are less than deaths and the population is declining naturally. However, to see whether the population is increasing or decreasing overall, the impact of migration needs to be taken into account.

Migration NET MIGRATION is the difference between the number of people entering a country (immigration) and the number leaving (emigration). **Positive** net migration occurs when more people enter the country than leave it. **Negative** net migration occurs when more people leave the country than enter it.

Changes in immigration and emigration might affect businesses in a country in a number of ways.

- **Immigration.** The effect of immigration on the demand for a business's products may depend upon the age and income levels of immigrants and where they settle. For example, parts of North London reflect immigration from Arab countries. A range of businesses, such as restaurants and supermarkets, have emerged to meet the needs of those settling in that area. The effects of immigration upon labour supply may depend upon the need for businesses to recruit the skills that immigrants possess. Where there are labour shortages, immigration can be a way of filling vacancies. The National Health Service, for example, has often relied upon immigrants to fill posts. Immigrants may also possess entrepreneurial skills which will help them to set up their own businesses.
- **Emigration.** This occurs when people leave a country. Large scale emigration from certain areas or by certain age groups can affect demand for businesses serving particular parts of the country or age groups. Emigration can also affect the pool of qualified workers that businesses can choose from. There are two reasons for this. First, emigrants tend to be mainly young people between the ages of 20 and 40. They are more likely to possess the energy and up-to-date skills and knowledge most in demand by businesses. Second, many emigrants from the UK are amongst the most highly skilled and able employees. They are likely to be tempted away by offers of better salaries and conditions elsewhere.

Age distribution of the population and business

POPULATION STRUCTURE is concerned with the breakdown or distribution of the population according to a variety of categories. This age distribution of the UK population looks at the numbers of people in the total population that fall into different age groups.

The birth rate, death rate and net migration from a country can all affect the age distribution of the population. Changes in these factors can affect businesses in a number of ways.

Birth rate The BIRTH RATE is measured by the number of live births per thousand of the population. The birth rate varies according to many factors. For example, in the UK in the 1970s there was a decline in the birth rate, perhaps due to better contraception and a growing number of women choosing to go out to work. The growing number of births in the 1980s may have been due to the larger number of women of child bearing age. In the late 1990s the birth rate fell. Women in their twenties

Question 2.

Figure 3: Divorces, UK, thousands

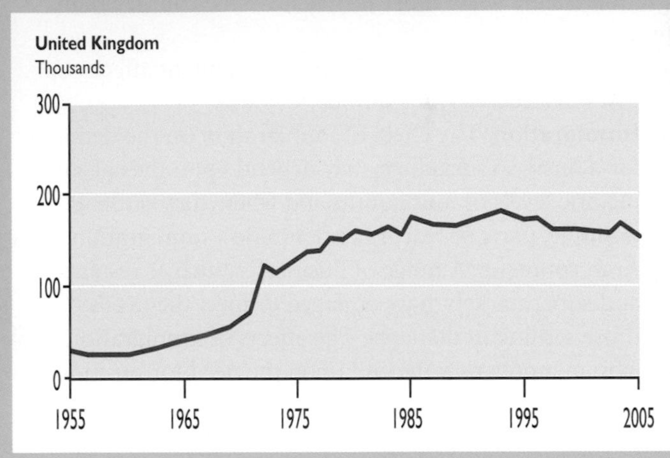

Table 2: Households by size, UK, percentages

	1971	1981	1991	2001	2007
One person	18	22	27	29	29
Two people	32	32	34	35	35
Three people	19	17	16	16	16
Four people	17	18	16	14	13
Five people	8	7	5	5	5
Six or more	6	4	2	2	2
All households (=100%) (millions)	18.6	20.2	22.4	23.8	24.4
Average household size (number of people)	2.9	2.7	2.5	2.4	2.4

Source: adapted from *Social Trends*, Office for National Statistics.

(a) Identify the trends taking place in the data.
(b) Examine how these trends might affect businesses in the UK.

were having 1.3 children on average, compared to 1.9 thirty years earlier. In the early twenty first century the birth rate in the UK, as in other developed countries, was rising slightly. This was predicted to continue to around 2021, when it would fall again.

How might a fall in the birth rate affect businesses?

- It could be argued that the fall in the birth rate in the 1970s should have led to a decline in the demand for baby products. However, increases in real incomes may have offset this, so that businesses selling baby products have continued to be successful.
- A decline in the birth rate does have consequences for the future supply of labour. Falls in the birth rate can lead to a 'demographic timebomb', with shortages of young workers available to businesses. The low number of births in the 1970s led to a smaller proportion of teenagers and people in their 20s in the 1990s. It was suggested that there could be labour shortages in the 1990s as a result. The recession in the early 1990s and falls in demand prevented this to some extent.
- Falls in the birth rate can lead to lower school numbers. This may be reflected in a fall in demand for teachers and for school materials.

An increase in the birth rate may also affect businesses. After the Second World War (1945) there was a large increase in the birth rate. These 'baby boomers' were approaching middle age in the early twenty first century. Many businesses attempted to target these groups. For example, record companies reissued music on CD that these people may have listened to when they were younger, hoping for them to buy again.

The death rate The DEATH RATE is the number of deaths per thousand of the population. The death rate in the UK and other EU nations has been declining steadily since the end of the Second World War. Combined with increases in the population as a whole in the UK, the decline in the death rate has meant steadily increasing numbers of people in older age categories. It is suggested that the number of people aged 60 and above will continue to increase in the future. The UK is said to have an **ageing population**. This means that there is a growing number of older people as a proportion of the population. What will be the effects of this ageing population?

- Changing patterns of demand. Some elderly people enjoy relatively high retirement incomes. This means that the demand for goods and services associated with the elderly is likely to increase. There could be increasing demand for leisure activities for the elderly, medical products, sheltered housing and specialist household goods. An example of a business which has benefited from this change is Saga holidays. It began by specialising in vacations for over 50s. Now it has expanded its activities into financial services.
- Effects on the labour market. Advances in medicine, better sanitation and housing and increasing affluence have all led to people living longer and healthier lives. One of the side effects of this has been an increasing pool of labour amongst those in their 50s, 60s and even 70s.
- Effects on government. An ageing population is likely to mean more demand for state provided services like hospitals and provisions such as bus passes and state pensions. There is also likely to be a need to raise more money from those in work, for example by taxation, to pay for those who are retired. There will be a rise in the DEPENDENCY RATIO. This is the proportion of dependants or non-workers to workers.

Migration If large numbers of younger or older people are emigrating from or immigrating to a country, this can affect its age distribution. For example, the emigration of large numbers of younger people from a country will tend to leave it with an older population, as discussed in the previous section.

Gender distribution of the population and business

There is a higher proportion of women in the UK population than men. In the early twenty first century these ratios were 51.1 per cent and 48.9 per cent. This is despite the fact that more boys than girls are born in the UK. The main reason for this is that the death rate is higher for men than for women. On average, women live longer than men. This means that there are higher proportions of women in older age groupings.

Table 3 shows that over the age of 65, there is a greater population of women than men. The gender imbalance amongst younger age groupings is far less marked. Providing services for older, often single women may represent an increasingly important market for businesses. A change in the ratio of men to women may also affect the birth rate. Fewer women may mean fewer children are born.

Although not directly related to the gender distribution, arguably the single biggest change for businesses in this area has been the increasing number of women entering the labour market. Businesses are increasingly targeting women in their marketing of products such as cars and electrical goods. Women are also obtaining senior posts in management and becoming a relatively larger part of the workforce. Businesses have to respond to this in their recruitment and provision of facilities for women.

Table 3: Population by gender and age, percentages, UK 2011

	%								
	-16	16-24	25-34	35-44	45-54	55-64	65-74	75+	Total (m)
Males	9.5	6.1	6.7	6.9	6.8	5.7	4.2	3.2	30.9
Females	9.1	5.8	6.7	7.0	7.0	6.0	4.6	4.7	31.9

Source: adapted from *Social Trends*, Office for National Statistics.

Geographical distribution of population and business

The movementc of people between countries is called **external migration**. But **internal migration**, the movement of people within a country, may also affect businesses.

Urban and rural location In the UK, approximately 80 per cent people live in urban areas. Within urban areas, inner cities have tended to lose population whilst country towns have tended to increase their population. However, the revitalisation of many inner city areas has more recently seen some flow of particularly young people back into these locations.

Age and location In general, younger people are more likely to live in urban areas than older people. For example, 16 per cent of people in urban areas are aged 18 to 29 compared to 11 per cent in rural areas. In contrast, 15 per cent of people in urban areas are aged over 65 compared to 18 per cent in rural areas.

Age and migration Young people tend to have higher mobility than older people.

How might businesses have been affected? It is possible that businesses may react to demand by younger people in cities. For example, in Inner London house builders have responded to these changes by building houses and flats suited to the needs of younger people. Their marketing of these developments has been geared to the needs of younger buyers. The movement out from cities may encourage support businesses or entertainment to locate in semi-rural or urban fringe areas. Examples may be multiplex cinemas, shopping malls and family orientated pubs.

Other changes in the structure of the population

Households One of the most significant changes in the structure of the population has been changes in the households within which people live. Increasingly people are living in smaller units, especially one person households, and less in extended and nuclear family groups. This has been the result of increases in the number of divorces and older people living longer after their partners have died. Businesses may be able to cater for the needs of people in these groups by developing fast, microwavable food, single accommodation or singles' holidays, for example.

Ethnic minority groups The age structure of ethnic minority groups may vary. For example, people from black groups other than Black African and Black Caribbean are more likely than people from the Chinese group to have been born in the UK. Certain ethnic groups have a younger age structure. 45 per cent of Bangladeshis in the UK are under the age of 16, for instance.

KEYTERMS

Birth rate - the number of live births per thousand of the population.
Death rate - the number of deaths per thousand of the population.
Demographic factors - features of the size, location and distribution of the population.
Dependency ratio - the proportion of dependants or non-workers to workers.
Net migration - the difference between the number of people entering a country (or region) and the number leaving it.
Population structure - the breakdown of the people in a country into groups based on differences in age, gender, geographical location etc.

KNOWLEDGE

1. What does the population growth rate show?
2. Suggest three effects of a growing population on businesses.
3. State three factors that affect population size and growth.
4. What happens to population if net migration is negative?
5. How might immigration affect businesses?
6. State two factors that might cause a fall in the birth rate.
7. How might a fall in the birth rate affect a business?
8. State two benefits to a business of an ageing population.
9. How might a larger proportion of women than men affect population?
10. State two other features of the structure of population that might affect a business.

Case Study: The future of the UK population

The UK population is predicted to continue to increase, reaching 71.1 million in 2031 and 85 million by 2081.

The average age of the whole population will increase. This is because of increased life expectancy and the moving of the large 'baby boomer' generation born in the 1950s and 1960s into old age. For example, in 2006, there were 4.7 million people in the UK aged 75 and over. The number is projected to increase to 5.5 million in 2016 and 8.2 million by 2031, a rise of 76 per cent over 25 years compared to a 17 per cent rise in the population as a whole.

The number of under 16 year olds will increase from 11.6 million to 12.8 million between 2006 and 2031, a rise of 10 per cent, much of the increase accounted for by young immigrants having children.

The average age of the working population will increase. Part of this is due to the fact that the state pension age for both sexes will increase to 68 by 2046 from the current 60 for women and 65 for men.

Of the expected 10.5 million increase in the UK population between 2006 and 2031, 5.6 million is projected to come from the natural increase in the population (births minus deaths) whilst the remaining 4.9 million is net migration (immigration minus emigration).

Source: adapted from *Population Trends*, Spring 2008, Office for National Statistics.

Table 4: Projected population by age, UK, 2006-2031 millions

	2006	2011	2016	2021	2026	2031
Under-16	11.5	11.6	12.1	12.7	12.8	12.8
Working age	37.7	39.0	40.4	41.6	43.0	43.4
Pensionable age	11.3	12.2	12.5	13.0	13.4	14.9

Figure 4: Projected population

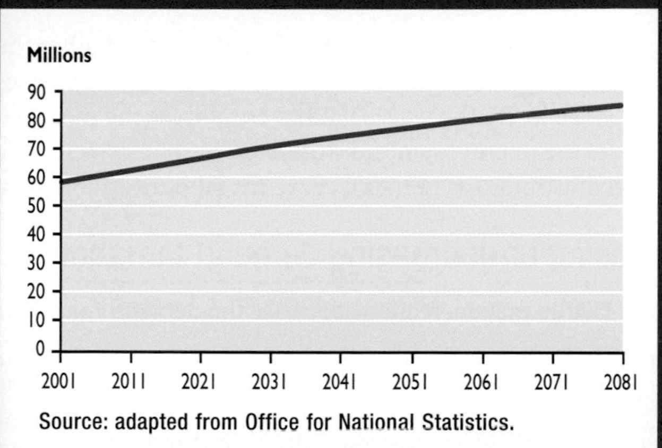

Source: adapted from Office for National Statistics.

Figure 5: Cinema attendance: by age, 2006

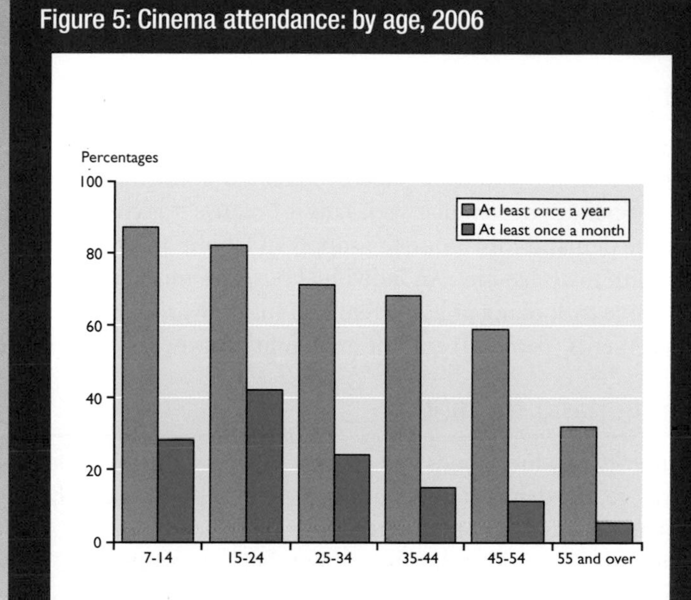

Source: adapted from Film Monitor (January to December 2006).

Table 5: Selected use of the Internet by age, 2007

Percentages

	16-24	25-44	45-54	55-64	65 and over	All aged 16 and over
Finding information about goods and services	83	88	89	86	75	86
Sending/receiving email	84	87	86	86	80	85
Using services related to travel and accommodation	52	67	69	63	56	63
Obtaining information from public authority websites	30	51	49	50	36	46
Internet banking	34	52	46	43	31	45
Looking for information about education	54	38	36	19	-	36
Playing/downloading games/images/films/music	58	40	25	14	-	35
Seeking health-related information	20	31	34	23	18	27

Source: Omnibus Survey, Office for National Statistis.

(a) Discuss the impact of the trends shown in the data on the supply of labour to businesses. In your answer, examine issues such as recruitment, training, and the age profile of the workforce in a business. (40 marks)

(b) Assess, in future, how businesses might change their products and services to take advantage of the trends shown in the data. (40 marks)

117 Labour markets and business

The market for labour

In the markets for goods and services the forces of demand and supply determine prices. It could be argued that the market for labour operates in a similar way. This is because it is concerned with the demand for labour, the supply of labour and the price of labour, the wage rate. An individual business might plan its workforce by looking at its current and future worker requirements (demand) and the availability of workers (supply).

The demand for labour

In order to produce goods and services businesses need labour. Therefore, the demand for labour comes from businesses. The demand curve for labour is determined by the combined behaviour of individual businesses and their approach to employing workers.

To examine the demand for labour it is necessary to consider how businesses reach decisions about taking on extra staff. Most businesses need to make sure that the costs of taking on extra staff are lower than the extra revenue generated by those staff. Take the example of a design business employing another designer at a cost of £2,200 per month. If the additional monthly revenue generated by this designer was more than £2,200 the design business may be satisfied. However, if the extra monthly revenue generated by the new designer was less than £2,200, the design business is unlikely to be satisfied with the decision to take on the new employee.

Table 1 illustrates this. It shows that, at a monthly cost of £2,200, Link Design might be prepared to employ five designers. This is because the first to the fifth designers are all adding more to revenue than they are costing Link Design to employ. However, the sixth designer is adding less to revenue than she is costing the business. Therefore, at a monthly cost per designer of £2,200 Link Design would employ five designers. At a monthly cost of £1,300 per designer it would employ six designers. If the cost per month of employing designers were to rise to £3,100, only four designers would be employed.

Table 1: Employing extra designers at Link Design Ltd

Number of designers employed	Total revenue monthly (£)	Additional revenue from each extra designer (£)
1	3,500	3,500
2	8,000	4,500
3	12,000	4,000
4	15,100	3,100
5	17,300	2,200
6	18,600	1,300

In general, therefore, it could be argued that the higher the wages of employees, the fewer will be employed by businesses. Similarly, the lower the wages paid to employees the more likely businesses are to employ more workers. This is shown in Figure 1, which illustrates the demand curve for labour.

Increasing or decreasing demand for labour

Certain factors may increase or decrease the demand for labour.

Question 1.

Fentons is a dry cleaning business. Table 2 shows information about employees at the business.

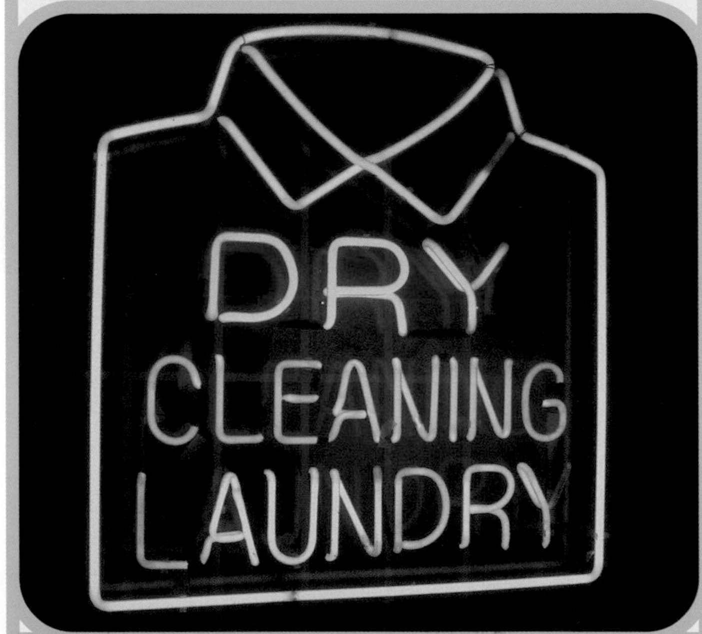

Table 2: Employee information

Number employed	Total revenue annually (£)	Additional revenue from each employee (£)
20	350,000	-
21	390,000	-
22	425,000	-
23	450,000	-
24	470,000	-
25	480,000	-

(a) Complete the third column in the above table for the 21st to the 25th worker.

(b) How many workers would Fentons employ at a cost of: (i) £40,000; (ii) £25,000; (iii) £10,000?

(c) What is the most likely employment level in this business? Explain your answer.

Figure 1: The demand curve for labour

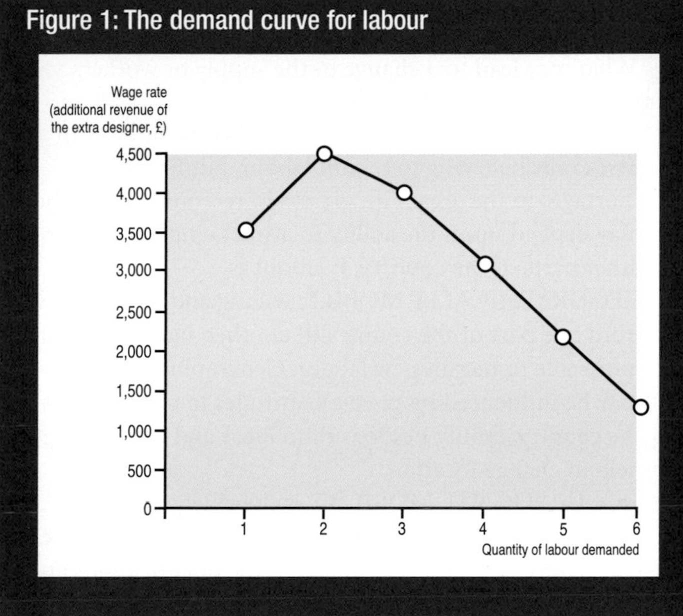

Figure 2: Changes in the demand for labour

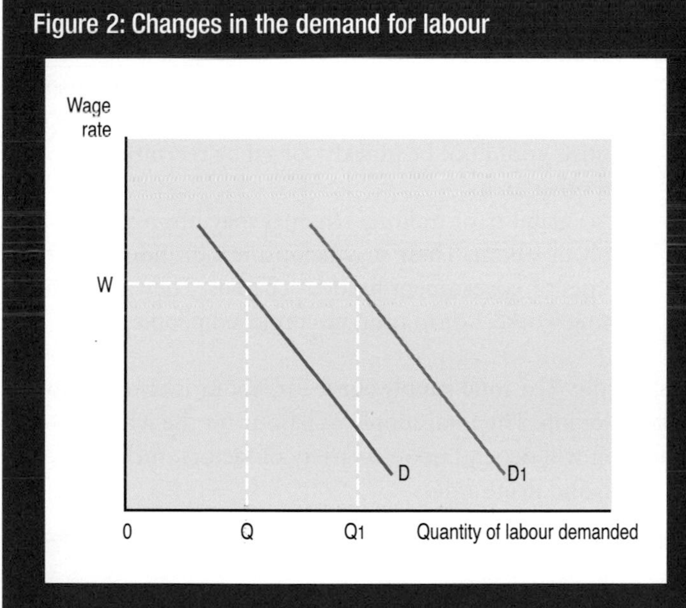

Changes in labour productivity It is suggested that if workers are able to improve their productivity, the business might be more willing to hire extra workers. For example, Link Design employees may increase productivity so that the additional revenue generated by each employee doubled. This would mean that the sixth worker would now add £2,600 extra revenue (£1,300 x 2). If the wage rate was still £2,200 a month, it would be worth the business employing this worker. If workers in the design industry become more productive, then design businesses may be willing to employ more workers.

Demand for the product The demand for labour is said to be a DERIVED DEMAND for the products or services that businesses produce. For example, Link Design may receive a contract to design a national monthly magazine. It may employ more workers as a result. The design industry may need to employ more workers as a result of increased spending by businesses on design and promotion.

Question 2.

BMW, the German car group, was considering plans to increase production of its Mini range at Oxford to about 200,000 a year to meet booming demand in November 2003. Helmut Panke, BMW's chief executive, said that Mini sales could top 165,000 in 2003 after the record of 144,000 in 2002. The company was planning to remove bottlenecks at the plant by a number of means. One option was to lengthen shifts from eight to nine or 10 hours.

Mr Panke told reporters in London that, with an annual productivity increase of 4 per cent, output at BMW car plants could grow by between 40,000 and 50,000 units a year – with minimum investment. Increased output and sales of the Mini, which aimed to launch a convertible model in 2004, were integral to BMW's plans to lift global sales from 1 million to 1.4 million by 2008, including 1,000 new Rolls-Royce Phantoms. The BMW chief hailed the Mini as 'a UK manufacturing success story', belying the myth that Britain's manufacturing sector was in terminal decline.

Source: adapted from *The Guardian*, 13.11 2003.

(a) Identify the factors which may have influenced the demand for labour at BMW.

(b) Examine how these factors might have affected the demand curve for labour in future.

The effect of these changes can be shown by a shift to the right in the demand curve for workers from D to D_1, as shown in Figure 2. Businesses will increase the number of workers employed from Q to Q_1. Falls in productivity and reduced sales of products will move the curve to the left, reducing the demand for workers.

The supply of labour

The supply curve for labour shows the amount of labour which will be supplied to the market at a particular wage rate. It is possible to show how individual workers, workers in an industry and the total supply of workers will react to a particular wage rate.

Individual workers For an individual worker, the supply of labour is the number of hours that he or she is prepared to work. As the REAL WAGE RATE rises, a worker is likely to want to work longer hours. The real wage shows what the wage of the worker can actually buy because it takes into account changes in the prices of goods. This is shown in Figure 3. At a real wage rate of OW, OQ hours are worked. Above OW it has been suggested that an increase in the price of labour may lead to less labour being offered to the market. This is because a higher wage may allow individuals to earn the same amount as on a lower wage,

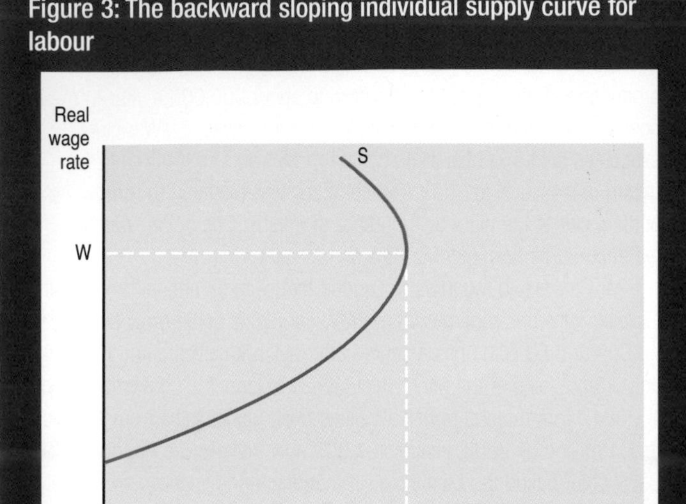

Figure 3: The backward sloping individual supply curve for labour

but by working for less time. So, for example, someone working for 40 hours per week at £25 per hour would earn £25 x 40 = £1,000 per week. If the wage were to be increased to £30 per week, the same person could work for 35 hours per week (£30 x 35 = £1,050) and earn the same quantity. The effect of this tendency for individuals to work less creates the backward sloping individual supply curve for labour, shown in Figure 3.

Supply to an industry It is argued that the supply curve for workers in an industry is generally upward sloping, from left to right. This is shown in Figure 4. More workers are prepared to offer their services to the labour market at higher real wage rates. As real wages rise from OW to OW_1, more workers are prepared to offer their services, OQ to OQ_1.

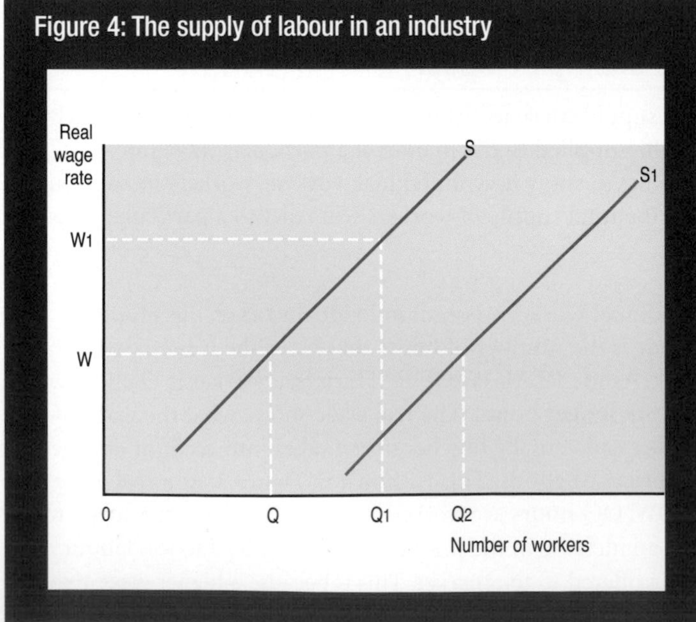

Figure 4: The supply of labour in an industry

Figure 4 also shows shifts in the supply curve. A shift to the right indicates an increase in supply of workers, from OQ to OQ_2. What may lead to a change in the supply of workers to businesses?

- Improvements in geographical mobility. Businesses in Essex may be trying to recruit labour, but find labour shortages in the area. The success in recruiting new labour may depend upon the ability to attract employees from other parts of the country. If labour is GEOGRAPHICALLY MOBILE, willing and able to move from one part of the country to another, businesses may be more able to recruit new labour. Geographical mobility may be influenced by people's attitudes to certain areas of the country, family ties to certain areas and government help to change location.
- OCCUPATIONAL MOBILITY is the extent to which labour is able to move from one occupation to another. Occupational mobility is linked to the qualifications and skills of labour. Highly qualified and skilled employees tend to be able to change occupations more easily. The levels of skills and qualifications required for some occupations are very high. This means that it is not straightforward for those trained in other occupations to move into these jobs. For example, a shortage of forensic scientists could not be quickly solved by recruiting labour from other areas.
- The availability of training schemes may improve the supply of labour. These may be business or industry schemes or government funded schemes. They may retrain existing workers or to train unemployed people.

Total supply The total supply curve for labour is also said to be upward sloping. The total supply of labour for the whole population will depend upon a variety of factors, such as:

- birth and death rates;

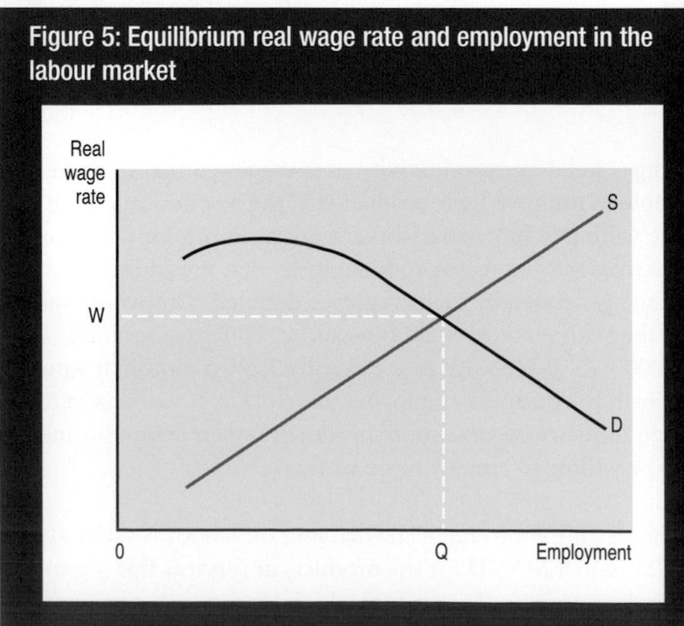

Figure 5: Equilibrium real wage rate and employment in the labour market

- migration;
- the age distribution of the population;
- the number of people physically capable of work.

Wage and employment determination

In highly competitive labour markets the price of labour (the real wage rate) is likely to be determined by the interaction of the demand curve for and supply curve of labour. As in other markets, the equilibrium price is the point at which the demand and supply curves intersect. In competitive labour markets this will determine the rate that wage earners are paid by businesses. This is show in Figure 5. The diagram also shows the number of workers employed at this equilibrium real wage rate.

Labour market conditions and business

Different conditions in the labour market influence the demand and supply of labour by businesses. These conditions are influenced by factors that are often outside the control of businesses. They may lead to situations were there are changes in the demand for or supply of labour. They may also create situations of excess demand or excess supply.

Government intervention in the labour market Governments usually intervene in labour markets in order to pursue 'social' aims, such as ensuring that all employees are paid at least a minimum amount or to prevent discrimination. For example, the **Equal Pay Act of 1970** aimed to prevent businesses paying women less than men for the same or similar work. Some businesses which had previously been paying women less than men, faced increased wage costs as a result. In certain circumstances, this led to a reduction in employment. This can be seen in Figure 6, which shows the demand and supply curves for labour in an industry. The equilibrium wage rate is OW and employment is OQ. The effect of equal pay legislation is to raise the wage rate to OW_1. As a result of the higher wages, workers are prepared to supply OQ_1 labour, but employers only want OQ_2 workers. Unemployment is therefore OQ_1-OQ_2. The OQ_2 workers still employed have higher wages, but OQ-OQ_2 workers have lost their jobs. The analysis will be similar if a **minimum wage** is set above the equilibrium wage rate.

Trade unions and professional groups These organisations seek to further the aims of their members. One of the ways in which they do this is by attempting to increase or maintain the pay levels of their members. The main way in which they attempt to do this is through collective bargaining. Trade unions and professional organisations which are successful may be able to push wage levels above the equilibrium level. The effect of this is similar to that shown in Figure 6.

Unions and professional organisations may also seek to restrict the supply of labour to a particular market. The solicitors' organisation known as the Law Society, for example, has testing examinations which all aspiring solicitors must pass. Many believe that one of the functions which these examinations serve is to restrict the supply of new solicitors. The effect of this is shown on Figure 7. It can be seen that a restriction in the supply of solicitors causes a shift to the left of the supply curve from S to S_1. The result in the fall in the supply of labour is a rise in the equilibrium wage rate from W to W_1. This is because labour is more scarce. The demand for labour by businesses will also fall because of the higher wage rate, from Q to Q_1.

The amount of unemployment At higher levels of unemployment businesses are able to recruit from a larger pool of labour. This means that suitable labour may be more readily available and the increased supply of labour may force down the equilibrium wage. Labour shortages at times of high

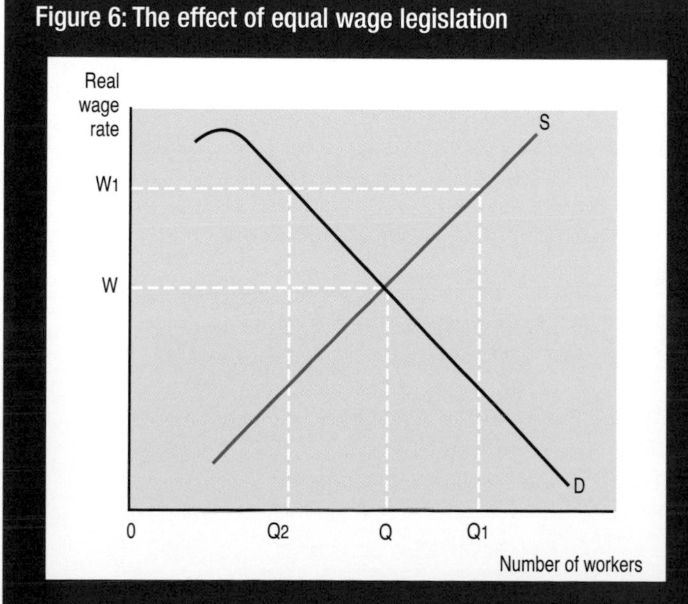

Figure 6: The effect of equal wage legislation

Figure 7: The effect of a restriction in supply on the equilibrium wage rate of labour

Question 3.

The UK has a national minimum wage. This means that businesses cannot pay employees a wage rate below a certain level. From October 2008, these minimum wage rates were:

- main (adult) rate for workers aged 22 and over, £5.73 an hour;
- development rate for workers aged 18-21 inclusive, £4.77 an hour;
- for 16-17 year olds, £3.53 an hour.

Source: adapted from news.bbc.co.uk 5.3.2008.

(a) Assume that the introduction of a minimum wage sets wage rates higher than the equilibrium wage rate paid in the food industry. Using a demand and supply diagram, explain how this might affect the demand for and supply of labour in the industry.

(b) A cafe pays all its kitchen staff, whatever their age, a wage rate of £7.50 an hour. Discuss the effects of the minimum wage rates in 2008 on this business.

employment, either in the economy as a whole or in particular sectors of the economy, are likely to have the opposite effect. This will mean that businesses have a smaller pool of available labour from which to recruit and upward pressure on the equilibrium wage.

KEYTERMS

Derived demand for labour – when the demand for workers by business is the result of demand for the product or service produced by business.

Geographical mobility – the ease with which workers can move from one occupation to another in a different location.

Occupational mobility – the ease with which workers can switch from one type of job, with particular skills, to another requiring different skills.

Real wage rate – the value of the wage rate taking into account the effect of prices. It shows how much the value of the money wage rate can purchase.

KNOWLEDGE

1. What is meant by the demand for labour?
2. What is likely to happen to the demand for labour by businesses if wage rates rise?
3. State two factors that can lead to an increase in the demand for labour by businesses.
4. What happens to the amount of hours individual workers may want to work at higher wages?
5. What happens to the supply of labour by workers as wage rates rise?
6. State two factors that may lead to an increase in the supply of labour by workers.
7. How might a fall in the supply of workers affect: (i) wage rates; (ii) demand by businesses?
8. How might wage legislation affect a business's demand for labour?
9. If unemployment is high, how might this affect recruitment by a business?

Case Study: Building bonanza

Britain is expected to experience a building bonanza over the next five years. Despite fears of a downturn in private sector construction, there will be a surge in schools construction projects for the London Olympics and increased spending on transport. For example, there is a £4.7 billion government programme to renew or rebuild every secondary school in the country.

However, there is a shortage of skilled labour to meet demand. ConstructionSkills, an employer-led sector skills body established by the government, estimates that employment in construction will rise by almost a sixth to 2.8 million workers by 2011 compared with 2.4 million in 2005. 87,600 new recruits will be needed by the industry each year between 2007 and 2011 in order to meet demand. The biggest need is expected to be for skilled trades such as bricklayers, cladders and roofers. ConstructionSkills plans to launch a series of national skills academies on large building sites to provide training for would-be construction workers. The first of these, on a £600 million development in London Bishopsgate, started last year.

A lack of trained labour in recent years has sucked in migrant workers from east European countries, such Ukraine, Poland and Lithuania, to fill gaps on building sites. Trade unions have complained that employers are using these workers to cut costs by paying low wages. Trade unions also complain that some employers are operating illegally by not declaring the workers for tax and National Insurance purposes.

Source: adapted from *The Financial Times*, 3.3.2007.

(a) Using demand and supply diagrams, discuss what it likely to happen to the demand for and supply of labour in the UK construction industry in the next five years. (40 marks)

(b) Evaluate whether wages in the construction industry, as declared to the tax authorities, are likely to rise faster than the national average in the future. (40 marks)

118 Globalisation and multinational companies

What is globalisation?

Over the past 50 years, the rate of growth of exports and imports has been faster than the rate of growth of output round the world. The UK, along with almost all other countries in the world, is becoming ever more integrated with the world economy. This is the process of GLOBALISATION. Globalisation means, for example that

- most of the clothes we buy are made abroad;
- the Chinese buy financial and legal services from the City of London;
- letters from a British hospital might be typed in India before being emailed back to the UK and printed out to be sent to patients.

There are three important aspects of globalisation.

Increased trade in goods and services The volume of trade in both goods and services is rising at a faster rate than the output of individual countries. Barriers to trade, from taxes on imports to transport costs, are coming down. In today's economy, a British firm in Birmingham might as easily buy supplies from a company in Germany or China as one in London. This is leading to the ever greater integration of the world economy.

Increased movements of labour from country to country Increasing numbers of workers are leaving their country of origin to find work in richer countries. For example, an estimated 600,000 workers from Eastern Europe arrived to work in the UK following the accession of countries like Poland to the European Union. Equally, there are an estimated 2 million Britons living abroad. Some have gone to work. Others have retired, for example to Spain and France. Just as migration within a country has increased over the past 50 years, so too has international migration.

Increased movement of financial capital Globalisation has led to increasing movements of financial capital across national boundaries. Each year, US and EU companies are buying up British companies. Equally, British companies are buying up US and other EU companies and expanding abroad. British companies are building factories in China. Japanese companies are building factories in the UK. UK savers are lending money to borrowers in Germany. China is lending money to the United States.

Most of the movement of goods, labour and capital is between the rich, developed countries of the world. But the fastest growing economies are in poorer developing countries. China, with a population of 1.1 billion has been doubling its output every 7 years for the past thirty years. India, with a projected population of 1.4 billion by 2050, is moving towards achieving the same level of economic growth. These EMERGING MARKETS have already had a profound impact on the UK businesses. The UK textile industry, once one of the largest employers in the country, has been almost wiped out by foreign competition. In contrast, China represents one of the UK's fastest growing markets for a wide range of goods and services. Over the next 100 to 200 years, the economies of the largest emerging countries including China and India will far overtake that of the EU in size. The UK, in 2008 the world's 4th largest economy, will inevitably slip down the world's league tables as emerging countries catch us up.

Factors affecting globalisation

It could be argued that certain factors have contributed to the growth of globalisation.

Technological change has played an important role in globalising the world's economy. More powerful computers and communications technology have allowed the easy transfer of data. The Internet has revolutionised the way in which consumers purchase products.

Cost of transportation The cost of transportation has fallen. The single most important factor in the falling cost of transportation has been the revolution in the use of containerised transport. The standard containers in use today were first seen in the 1950s. The ability to load a container at a factory, take it by road or rail to a port, transport it by sea and then deliver it to a customer at the other end has considerably reduced the cost of transport. Today, 90 per cent of all non-bulk cargoes worldwide are moved by container.

Cost of communication The cost of communication has fallen. The cost of making a phone call has fallen over time. Communication has also been revolutionised by the Internet and email which allow very low cost written communication to take place.

Deregulation The deregulation of business. Throughout the 1980s, 1990s and early twenty first century many businesses were privatised in countries throughout the world. In the UK the privatisation of former state owned monopolies allowed competition. The removal of restrictions on foreign businesses operating in eastern European and Asian countries also increased the ability of businesses to operate globally. New markets were opened up to foreign competition.

The liberalisation of trade Trade protection has been reduced due to the operation of organisations such as the World Trade Organisation (WTO). For example, reduction of restrictions on

Question 1.

Goodyear in Wolverhampton was once a major employer in the city. In 1998, it still employed 2,200 workers and the site contained the UK national headquarters offices of the company. By 2004, only 550 workers remained and the UK national headquarters had been moved to Birmingham.

Workers at the site blame the 1998 acquisition by Goodyear of a stake in the Sava Tires in Slovenia in Eastern Europe: Goodyear purchased the rest of the company in 2004. The world's biggest tyre company said at the time that the move was 'to further strengthen its position in the rapidly expanding central and Eastern European market, as well as consolidating its low-cost sourcing capabilities'. Following the acquisition, Goodyear invested more than £55 million in modernisation at Sava Tires. The international company also has another three plants in Eastern Europe and the Middle East: in Debica, Poland; Izmit in Turkey; and Adapazari, also in Turkey. The four plants between them produced around 40 per cent of the 84 million tyres last year. Workers in Eastern Europe are paid a fraction of the wages in the UK. Although wages will eventually catch up, there will be many years to come in which the wage gap will remain substantial.

The security of the remaining 550 jobs at Goodyear Wolverhampton was questionable. All that was left was retread work, storage and the mixing and calendering of tyre ingredients for 'export' to other Goodyear Dunlop factories in the UK. In 2006, another 40 jobs were lost when Goodyear's plant at Wearside in the North East of England was shut due to competition from Eastern European producers. In 2007, however, the now 350 people still employed at the plant received a boost when a new multi-million pound machine, the size of a four storey building, was installed. Gerard Coyne, from the Transport and General Workers' Union, said the investment would give some security for the future.

Source: adapted from the *Express & Star*, 8 April 2004; news.bbc.co.uk 5.4.2006 and 15.3.2007.

(a) Explain why moving production from Wolverhampton to Eastern Europe might improve Goodyear's productive efficiency.

(b) Discuss what might persuade Goodyear to retain remaining production at Wolverhampton.

trade in textiles is likely to have opened up markets in Asia and the West.

Consumer tastes Consumer tastes and their responses have changed. Consumers in many countries are more willing to buy foreign products. Examples might include cars from Korea and Malaysia which are now purchased in Europe. It could also be argued that consumers around the world increasingly have similar tastes. Some food products are sold in many countries with little difference to their ingredients.

Emerging markets The growth of emerging markets and competition. New markets have opened up in countries that have seen a growth in their national income. Examples might include countries in South East Asia and the more successful countries in eastern Europe. As businesses in these countries have become more successful, they have been able to compete in western economies.

The effects of globalisation on business

Globalisation has had many effects upon businesses throughout the world. The impact of globalisation has not been evenly spread. Some businesses, for example those in telecommunications, have witnessed dramatic changes. Others, such as small businesses serving niche markets in localised areas, may have been little affected by globalisation.

There is a number of effects of globalisation upon businesses. Some provide opportunities whilst others present threats.

Competition The impact of globalisation on many larger businesses has been to dramatically increase the level of competition which they face. There is a number of reasons for this.

- Foreign competition has increasingly entered markets previously served mainly or exclusively by domestic businesses.
- Deregulation has meant that many businesses which previously had little or no competition are now opened up to the forces of global competition.
- Globalisation has provided opportunities for new, innovative businesses to enter markets and compete with all comers, including well established industry leaders. For example, Microsoft, Intel, Compaq and Dell, once relative newcomers to the computer industry in the past, were able to compete effectively against the market leader at the time, IBM.

Meeting consumer expectations and tastes Competition by businesses seeking to meet customer needs in increasingly effective ways has raised customer expectations in many markets. Businesses must now meet ever greater consumer demands about quality, service and price. They must also provide the greater choice of products expected by purchasers. The global market has made predicting consumer preferences more difficult. For example, few businesses predicted the huge rise in the popularity of mobile phones or the speed with which consumers would accept the internet.

Economies of scale Businesses able to build a global presence are likely to enjoy a larger scale of operations. This will enable them to spread their fixed costs over a larger volume of output and reduce unit output costs. A larger scale of operations also allows businesses to exercise power over suppliers and benefit from reduced costs. For example, global hotel chains such as Holiday Inn and Marriott are in a position to benefit from volume discounts from catering supply companies.

Choice of location Businesses with a global presence can choose the most advantageous location for each of its operations. When locating its operations, a business may consider:

- reduction of costs. For example, Nike's decision to locate its shoe manufacturing operations in countries such as China and Vietnam was perhaps based on cost reduction factors. Low cast labour has also resulted in some UK businesses locating call centres in India.
- enhancement of the business's performance. Production and service facilities are located in parts of the world which are likely to improve factors such as product or service quality. For example, Microsoft may have taken this into account when deciding to locate its research laboratories in Cambridge.

Mergers and joint ventures Businesses are increasingly merging or joining with others, often in other countries, in order to better provide their goods or services to a global market. Both manufactures and retailers are operating on a global basis. A manufacturer, for example, may merge with another in order to make products in the country in which they will be sold. A DIY retailer may merge with a supplier of toilet seats in another country in order to distribute its products more easily to customers in that country.

Multinational companies

Multinational companies have come to play an increasingly important role in world trade. MULTINATIONAL COMPANIES (or MULTINATIONAL CORPORATIONS or TRANSNATIONAL CORPORATIONS) are companies which have significant production or service operations in at least two countries. These could be primary product companies such as Geest, Exxon Mobil or BP. They could be manufacturing companies like General Motors, Ford, Toyota or Sony. Or they could be service sector companies like Vodafone, Starbucks, the coffee shop chain, Wal-Mart, the world's largest supermarket chain which owns Asda.

Most multinationals operate largely in developed countries. This is where their shareholders, their headquarters, their markets and their production facilities are located. Mergers and takeovers tend to take place between companies in developed countries. A few multinationals, particularly in the primary sector, have large operations in developing countries. Examples are oil companies like Exxon Mobil and Total, and primary food companies like Geest. Many multinationals are seeing growing sales into countries like India and China.

A recent trend is for multinationals owned and controlled in developing countries to take over companies in developed countries. For example, the world's largest steel company in 2007 was Mittal Steel, an Indian company, creating by a series of takeovers of steel companies in the developed world by Mittal Steel. One of the world's largest cement manufacturers is the Mexican company Cemex, which in 2007 had operations in 50 countries across the world and owned 66 cement plants. As the developing world increases its income, more and more multinational companies will be owned by shareholders in the developing world.

Reasons for multinational companies to exist

Why do multinationals exist and what advantages does their size give them? Why are multinational companies growing in size as the world economy grows?

Economies of scale There are many industries where only the largest firms with world wide access to both production facilities and markets can fully exploit economies of scale. Examples of such industries include the oil and motor manufacturing industries. Typically, the amounts of capital needed are so large that small firms find it difficult to compete.

Knowledge and innovation Many multinational companies are storehouses of accumulated knowledge and powerful players in the field of innovation. For instance, it is difficult to imagine how any small enterprise could exploit oil from miles below the sea bed in the deep waters of the North Sea, or produce the technology to put a man on the moon. Genetic engineering or microchips are two examples of where multinationals are in the forefront of bringing new products to the market. Some large retailers have a more successful knowledge of what their customers want to buy than their competitors and have developed highly sophisticated logistics systems to get products from manufacturers to customers.

Branding and marketing Some multinational companies use very little technology. Instead, they rely for their world presence on branding and marketing. At some point in the past, they have produced a highly successful product in a local market. This is then rolled out into other national markets. Coca Cola or McDonald's are two examples of this. Each brand is protected from competition through patents, and heavy use of advertising and other forms of promotion.

Market and political power Some multinationals exploit market power in individual national markets to create a global business. They might have legitimate patents or copyrights or own key resources. Equally, they may build on these by **anti-competitive practices** which attempt to force existing firms out

Question 2.

Martin Winterkorn, the chief executive of the German car manufacturer, speaking at VW's annual press conference, said that the days of building one car for the whole world were 'dead and buried'. For 20 years, the dream of the world's major car manufacturers had been to build a car which could be sold into all national car markets. The car manufacturer to achieve this would, so the thinking went, be able to gain a competitive edge over its rivals because it would be able to get costs down due to economies of scale in production. Selling 30 million vehicles a year of one model would have lower costs per unit than selling 6 million vehicles but in five different models each.

Martin Winterkorn announced that Volkswagen would be introducing 20 new models in the next years, including vans and pick-ups. The plan was to sell 8 million cars a year by 2010, up from 6.2 million in 2007. With Toyota now the world's largest car manufacturing company by sales volume, he said he hoped to beat Toyota in sales and profitability, customer satisfaction and quality. 'In the coming years, we will make the VW group the world's most international carmaker.' It could only happen if customers were offered vehicles appropriate to their needs, which included affordability. 'Our customers in China or India expect us, as a global player, to offer entirely different solutions than we do in the US or Western Europe' he said.

VW's desire to beat Toyota is made more difficult by its extremely weak position in the key US market. It is weighing whether to construct a new factory there to build a mid-sized saloon. A decision on this matter would be made in the summer, executives said.

Source: adapted from *The Financial Times*, 14.3.2008.

(a) Why is motor car manufacturing dominated by multinational companies such as Volkswagen and Toyota?

(b) Explain why a customer in India or China might have to be offered an 'entirely different solution' in terms of model of car than a customer in the UK or the USA.

(c) Volkswagen wants to overtake Toyota as the world's largest car manufacturer. Evaluate ways in which it could gain a competitive advantage over Toyota.

of the market and prevent new firms from entering it. Multinationals also have a long history of subverting and corrupting governments to achieve their aims. They are so large that they have considerable financial resources to be able to use either in bribing government officials and politicians, or maintaining powerful lobby organisations.

Possible advantages of multinational companies to individual countries

Multinational companies can give a variety of benefits to the individual countries in which they operate.

Home countries Individual countries gain international competitiveness if they are the national base for a multinational corporation. This is because a disproportionate amount of spending by the multinational will take place in its home country. Moreover, the resources employed are likely to be the most sophisticated within the organisation. For instance, the multinational will almost certainly have its headquarters in its home country. A disproportionate amount of research and development is likely to take place there. The home country is likely to be used as a production base, with a disproportionate number of production facilities there or with inputs being sourced from other firms in that country. One of the reasons why the developed world traditionally dominated world markets was because hardly any developing countries created successful multinationals. This is now changing with countries such as Taiwan, South Korea, China and India developing their own multinational companies which are outcompeting western companies.

Transfers of capital When Tesco sets up a new chain of supermarkets in Eastern Europe, or Toyota builds a new car plant in the UK, there is a transfer of capital from one country to another. This is called **foreign direct investment (FDI)**. FDI leads to an immediate increase in the resources available within a country. In most cases, they will in the short term lead to a multiplier effect. Construction workers for a new supermarket will spend their wages in local shops and on local produce, boosting national income. In the longer term, an increase in investment pushes the production possibility boundary of an economy outwards, which should lead to higher growth.

Transfers of knowledge With foreign direct investment comes a transfer of knowledge from one country to another. In some cases, industrial secrets are well kept. For example, despite operating in most countries in the world, no one but a few at headquarters knows the formula for Coca Cola. But Coca Cola does transfer knowledge to the local companies it works with about how to operate a bottling and distribution company. When Nissan and Toyota built plants in the UK, their production techniques were widely copied by other car manufacturers operating in the UK. Multinationals with plants in China know that Chinese entrepreneurs and companies will constantly seek to copy and imitate what they see and then pose a real threat to their markets.

Employment Multinationals create jobs wherever they set up operations. They are sometimes criticised for only creating low level jobs for local employees whilst importing more highly skilled labour from abroad. A French hotel chain in the UK, for example, may employ local British labour for cleaning but in practice always has a French worker as the manager of each hotel. However, increasingly multinational companies recognise that creating an international employment base leads to greater productivity. Training local workers to take high level jobs within the company is an investment which strengthens the company. Training given to employees also spills over into the local economy. It raises the level of human capital. Employees leave multinationals to take jobs elsewhere in the economy and sometimes to set up their own businesses.

Taxes Multinationals pay taxes to national economies. This can then pay for government spending in areas such as health and education. Multinationals are often accused of paying as little tax as possible and seeking out locations where taxes are low. A common technique to avoid tax on profits is TRANSFER PRICING. Assume a multinational company has to make a product in country A, a country which charges high taxes on profits. The company will therefore want to make as little profit as possible in country A. The company also has operations in country B, a country which charges low taxes on profits. By selling the product made in country A at an artifically low price to its operations in country B, it can minimise its profits in country A. It then sells the product from country B at the market price, perhaps even back to customers in country A. But then it makes high profits in country B because it has bought the good at an artifically low price from country A. It still has to pay taxes on profits in country B, but its overall tax liability in countries A and B is much lower because of transfer pricing. Inevitably, because multinationals are profit seeking companies, they will seek to minimise their tax liabilities. If Slovakia offers lower taxes than the UK, this will be one factor which a US multinational will take into account when deciding where to put a new plant in the EU. Governments therefore need to weigh up the benefits of attracting investment by offering low taxes against loss of tax revenues. They also need to be robust in their dealings with multinationals to ensure that they pay their fair share of taxes.

Consumer choice Multinationals can bring greater consumer choice to a country. For example, Toyota and Nissan set up manufacturing plants in the UK to sell more cars into the UK market, Coca Cola and McDonald's set up in many countries to sell their products.

Exports Multinationals may increase a country's exports. This then increases the resources available to purchase imports. If it is an energy company like Exxon Mobil, exports of oil may be the main export for an economy.

Economic growth Multinational companies are a key component of the world trading system. By allocating resources in an efficient way, they help promote world growth. For example, multinational companies are one of the elements which explain why China and India are currently growing so fast. Without multinational companies, trade would be reduced and so too, almost certainly, would world GDP.

The possible disadvantages of multinational companies

Some argue that multinationals have a negative impact on individual economies.

Lack of accountability The size of multinationals can make them seem unaccountable to anyone. In practice, multinationals are accountable to many bodies. They are answerable, for instance, to their shareholders. Increasingly, though, they have had to account for their actions to other stakeholders. They have to obey the law of the countries in which they operate, unless government is so corrupt or weak that multinationals can evade the law. They are also subject to scrutiny by pressure groups, such as environmental groups.

Loss of national identity Multinationals are often accused of leading to lowering living standards by destroying native culture. McDonald's, for instance, has encountered opposition in some countries which see US burgers as a threat to national cuisine and eating habits. Globalisation inevitably means that there is a blurring of national identities as standards are accepted throughout the world. Standardisation can give rise to considerable benefits, though, because they allow people and firms to use common equipment, common ways of thinking and doing things, as well as helping in the purchase of products.

Footloose capitalism Multinationals have the power to move production from country to country, creating and destroying jobs and prosperity in their wake. They do this to maximise their profits. For instance, they might close a production facility in a high cost country like the UK or the USA and move it to a

Question 3.

Louis Vuitton and Chanel will this week be competing for the limelight as both open stores in Hong Kong. Louis Vuitton and Chanel are luxury fashion houses, selling very expensive luxury goods to the very rich. Louis Vuitton is re-opening a store that it has over-hauled and expanded. The outlet will be its second-largest worldwide, after its flagship Champs Elysees store in Paris. Louis Vuitton's event will close on Friday night with a party for 2,500 guests held in a golden tent.

Asia is a fast growing market for the luxury fashion market. With a population of 1 billion, and a growth rate which is seeing incomes double every seven years on average, it only needs the smallest fraction of this population to want to shop at a luxury fashion house for it to be a highly lucrative market. The luxury fashion houses are moving from having outlets in 'first tier' cities like Beijing and Shanghai, to 'second tier' cities, large provincial cities which still have a rich elite.

Growth, however, brings its own challenges. Simply taking what works in Paris or London to an Asian city is not necessarily going to be successful. The brand needs to adapt to local culture whilst at the same time retaining its distinctive image. Thibault Villet, President of Coach, the US maker of handbags and other accessories, for example says: 'We are clearly a New York brand and so need to communicate an image in accordance with our DNA. But the right way for us to go local is when we do events, where we certainly want to be working with the local celebrities.'

Another challenge for Asia's fashion development is a shortage of skills. Customers expect sales staff to be knowledgeable, friendly and yet deferential. Inexperienced sales staff can drive customers away. There are likely to be fewer repeat customers and fewer introductions by word of mouth.

A key question is whether image-conscious fashion houses will join the outsourcing bandwagon by shifting production to Asia. Last year, Louis Vuitton made its first manufacturing move outside of Europe by establishing a shoe production venture in Pondicherry, India. About 100 people are employed in its workshop there but the company has no plans to go further. After all, part of the brand image of a luxury Paris or Milan fashion house is that its goods are made by highly skilled craftsmen in France or Italy. No one will pay hundreds of pounds for a handbag if they think it has been made in a sweatshop in Thailand. So the fashion houses have to be ultra-cautious about what functions they outsource to low cost locations.

Source: adapted from *The Financial Times*.

(a) Evaluate the advantages and disadvantages to Louis Vuitton of outsourcing production to a country like India.

(b) To what extent might (i) Hong Kong and (ii) India benefit from having a Louis Vuitton store or production facility located in their country?

low cost country like India or Thailand. Globalisation is inevitably leading to a shifting of production from the developed world to the developing world. This is one key way in which the poor developing countries of the world can increase their living standards. However, multinationals are not the prime cause of this shift in production. Rather, they are responding to market forces in exactly the same way that national companies are so doing. Over the past 30 years, domestic UK companies have increasingly sourced goods from overseas to take advantage of better prices. They have closed their own manufacturing operations, or forced previous UK suppliers to close down through loss of orders.

Destruction of the environment A number of multinationals dominate world extraction industries such as oil or gold mining. These industries are inevitably particularly destructive of the environment. Other multinationals, such as motor manufacturers or even service companies have also been accused of destroying the environment for instance in the way in which they source their raw materials. However, any form of production could be argued to be undesirable from an environmental viewpoint. Moreover, multinational companies often have better environmental records than smaller national companies. They not only have the financial resources to be able to minimise their impact on the environment; they also have the technical knowledge and ability to innovate which can lead to minimising environmental problems.

Exploitation of poor countries The anti globalisation movement portrays multinationals as exploiting poor countries to increase their own profits. Multinationals pay local labour the lowest wage possible. They employ child labour. Conditions of work are very poor. Natural resources are extracted and sold with hardly any compensation going to the local country. Taxes paid are minimal. Goods are sold which show no sensitivity to local culture. As little as possible is put back into the country because this would reduce the amount of profit that can be transferred back to the rich developed home country. It is correct that some individual multinational companies can be severely criticised for their historical record. It is also true that some multinational companies today are more aggressive in their pursuit of profit whatever the consequences than others. However, other multinational companies have an excellent record of dealing fairly with individual countries, local workers and local consumers. It should also be remembered that most activities of multinational companies are focussed in the developed world. So criticism of multinational companies needs to be focussed against individual companies rather than multinational companies as a group.

Corporate social responsibility

Many multinational companies have responded to criticism by implementing **corporate social responsibility (CSR)** procedures. Typically, a member of the board of the company is given responsibility for corporate social responsibility. Targets are drawn up on a wide range of issues such as the environment, employees, suppliers and customers. Policies are then put in place to achieve those targets. Data is gathered to monitor whether targets have been achieved. Sometimes, outside auditors are used to audit results in the same way that outside auditors are used to audit company accounts.

Corporate social responsibility is a way of recognising that a company has a variety of stakeholders, each of whom have different goals. Maximising profit at the expense of the environment or workers' safety is not necessarily the goal for a company to pursue.

Critics of corporate social responsibility argue that targets set are typically arbitrary and are too low to make a substantial impact on the issue concerned. They often argue that only government regulation will force multinational companies to become socially responsible. The answer to issues about, say, illegal logging of forest in Indonesia, is for government to ban the purchase of this product. Otherwise, whilst some multinationals will not buy the timber because of their corporate social responsibility policies, other multinational companies will buy it.

The verdict

Multinationals can be easy targets for those who dislike global capitalism. Individuals are relatively powerless when factories are closed and production is shifted thousands of miles away. New products, such as genetically modified food, can also raise important questions about whether such technologies should be exploited. On the other hand, without multinational companies, there would be far less trade and innovation. World output would almost certainly be considerably lower, arguably leading to lower living standards.

Free market economists would argue that the focus of any debate about multinationals is not whether they should be allowed to exist but about how government, representing all stakeholders in society, can set up regimes which can regulate the activities of multinationals for the benefit of all. For the anti-globalisation movement, multinationals are a symbol of all that is wrong with a world where profit and private greed control how resources are distributed.

KEYTERMS

Globalisation - the integration of the world's economy.
Hypercompetition - the disruption of existing markets by flexible, fast moving businesses.
Multinational - a company which owns or controls production or service facilities outside the country in which it is based.
Transfer pricing - a system operated by multinationals. It is an attempt to avoid relatively high tax rates through the prices which one subsidiary charges another for components and finished products.

KNOWLEDGE

1. What is meant by a global market?
2. State three important aspects of globalisation.
3. Suggest five factors which have contributed to the growth of globalisation.
4. How might globalisation affect the location of a business?
5. Why might globalisation increase competition for businesses?
6. Explain briefly why the following businesses might become a multinational company: (a) an oil company; (b) a mass manufacturing car company; (c) a fast food chain.
7. Outline briefly the role of multinational companies in (a) international trade; (b) transfers of knowledge between countries; (c) creating employment; (d) increasing choice for consumers.
8. Why might a country not benefit from the activities of multinational companies?

Case Study: Bilateral trading

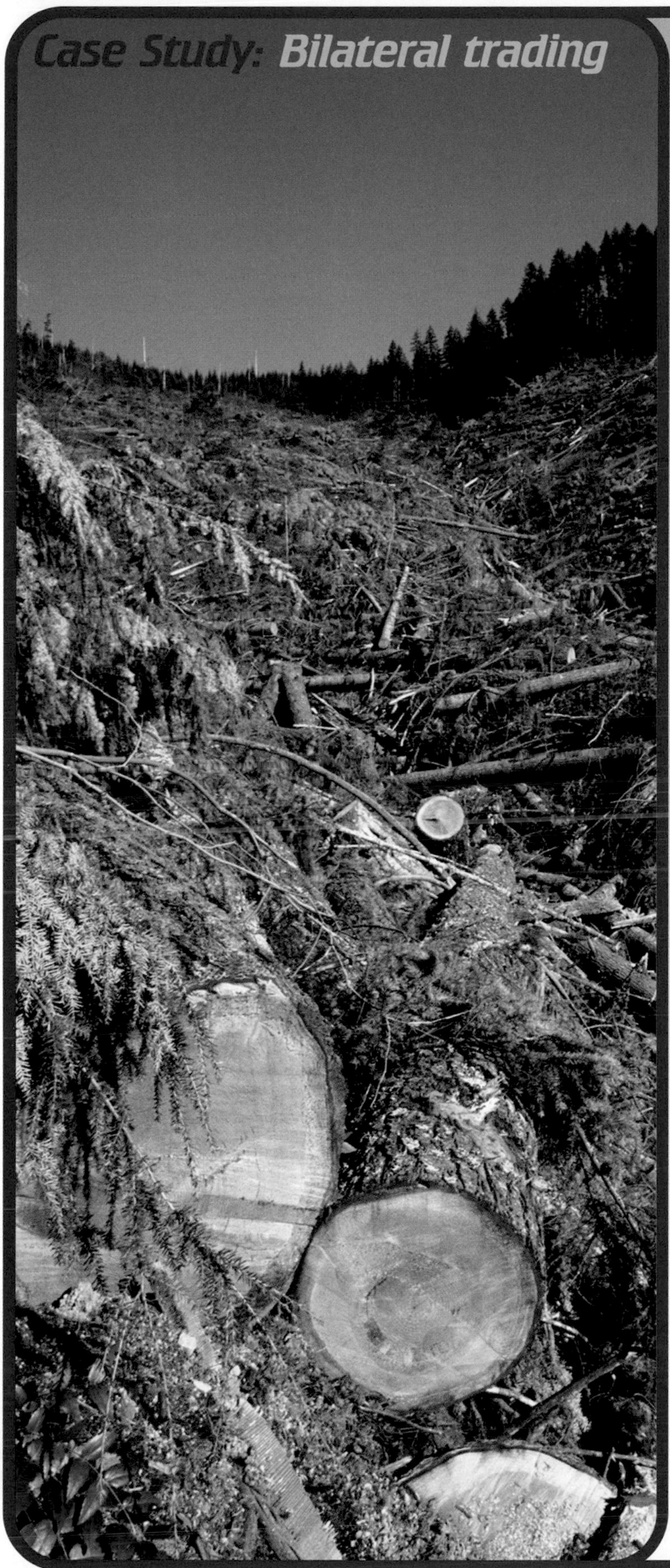

Corporates

Friends of the Earth is a charity which campaigns for solutions to environmental problems. In January 2008, the following was posted on their website about multinational companies.

The balance of power has shifted. Governments are losing control to huge multinational corporations. This process is putting basic human rights and vast areas of the natural world in serious danger. It's time to challenge the rise of corporate power.

Each time we visit the supermarket, pay our taxes or fill up our car we fuel the growth of big companies. Behind the public face of corporations:

- Democracy is eroded. Companies often have more power than governments. They threaten to move their business to get what they want.
- Environments are destroyed. Rainforests are cleared to grow products on our supermarket shelves. Demand for palm oil has decimated forests in Borneo.
- Human rights are abused. People have no say on changes ruining their lives. Communities are thrown off their land or forced to live next to leaking oil pipes.

By law, public companies have to maximise profit and keep investors happy. This means economic growth comes before people and the planet. Did you know that 51 of the world's biggest economies are now corporations?

You shouldn't have to worry about all this when you do your weekly shop. Unfortunately some companies try to claim they are greener than they really are. Corporates have too much power and too little incentive to care about communities and the environment. To head off such accusations, many businesses are adopting voluntary Corporate Social Responsibility (CSR) policies. CSR promises to do more than the legal minimum to protect people and the planet. But CSR is failing because it:

- Doesn't make a difference. Companies don't deliver on promises ....
- Ignore the real problems. Reports gloss over impacts of core business ....
- Is voluntary. There is no enforcement ....

Companies hide behind lobbying groups that fight on their behalf for less regulation. For example, the Confederation for British Industry (CBI) lobbies on behalf of business against laws that would benefit people and the environment.

Corporate power is out of control. The current systems are failing the planet. Governments need to regain control of big business to give rights for people and rules for big business.

Source: adapted from www.foe.co.uk.

Shell and climate change

The *Shell Sustainability Report 2006* stated 'Shell was one of the first energy companies to acknowledge the threat of climate change, to call for action by governments, our industry and energy users, and to take action ourselves. In 1998, we set ourselves voluntary targets for reducing greenhouse gas emissions from our operations. Since then Shell Renewables has built one of the broadest alternative energy portfolios of any major energy company. We have increased the supply of natural gas - the lowest carbon fossil fuel - and of the lower sulphur transport fuels needed by more fuel-efficient modern engines. The expected future costs of emitting CO2 have been included in our investment decisions since 2000. This helps us design new projects so that they remain profitable in the carbon-constrained world that is now emerging.

Partnerships are being pursued to develop lower carbon technologies. Large scale demonstration projects to capture and store CO2 are being given careful consideration. Our retail business runs a services of public campaigns to encourage innovation and promote energy conservation.

We stepped up our appeal to governments in 2006 to lead on this issue and introduce effective policies to combat climate change. The importance of government leadership has become clear. Without policies that reward lower CO2 technologies and create a predictable long-term cost for emitting greenhouse gas emissions, individual companies will have no incentive to make the massive investments needed.

Our appeal to government is fourfold: firstly to involve all major emitting countries and all sectors - not just industry - to avoid distorting competition; secondly, to develop stable, long term greenhouse gas targets to allow companies to plan and invest; thirdly, to use emissions trading systems more widely as a cost-effective way to manage greenhouse gas emissions from industry and to include reductions from CO_2 capture and storage in those schemes; and finally, to design better-targeted support for alternative energy sources, to help them reach the point where they can compete without further subsidies.'

Source: adapted from *The Shell Sustainability Report 2006*, Shell.

Tesco

The Tesco *Corporate Responsibility Review 2006* stated:'We sell a wide range of products, both own-brand and branded, which have palm oil as an ingredient. We do not buy palm oil directly - almost all of the palm oil used by the manufacturers of our own-brand products is bought through three of the world's largest palm oil traders. These three traders are members or affiliate members of the Roundtable on Sustainable Palm Oil (RSPO), which works to help industry identify ways of sourcing this ingredient more sustainably. In June 2006 Tesco too joined the RSPO. We hope that our participation will help the RSPO encourage other palm oil consumers to demand a sustainably sourced supply.

We want to make sure that the timber we buy is from legal, sustainable sources. We will never knowingly purchase timber from illegal sources. All sources of timber for our garden furniture are either Forest Stewardship Council (FSC) approved or members of the Tropical Forest Trust (TFT), committed to achieving the FSC standard through the certification supply programmes of ethical auditors.'

Source: adapted from *Corporate Responsibility Review 2006*, Tesco.

(a) 'Each time we visit the supermarket, pay our taxes or fill up our car we fuel the growth of big companies.' (Greenpeace). Evaluate whether the stakeholders of multinational companies would be better off if they were broken up and considerably reduced in size. (40 marks)

(b) Evaluate the impact of multinational companies like Shell and Tesco on countries in which they are based and on countries from which they purchase supplies. (40 marks)

119 Government policy

The role of government in the economy

Governments play a number of roles in an economy which affect business.

- Government creates the legal and regulatory framework which govern the way in which businesses and individuals relate to each other. In the UK, for example, government gives rights of ownership to private property. This is fundamental to businesses. Without this right, they would not be able to protect their property, from land and buildings, to stocks of goods to intellectual property such as patents and copyright. UK law also regulates contracts. All businesses buy and sell. Without an effective law of contract, this process would become uncertain and discourage businesses from operating. The impact of the law on business is discussed in more detail in the unit titled 'Business and the law'.
- Government provides goods and services from health and education to roads and the police.
- The government uses taxes and spending to influence the way individuals and businesses behave. For example, it taxes cigarettes to discourage individuals from smoking. It subsidises training of workers to encourage individuals to become more skilled.
- It uses its powers of spending and tax to influence the amount of demand in the economy. This can help prevent the economy from suffering a recession or experiencing rising inflation. Some of the same effects can also be had through its power to control the rate of interest.

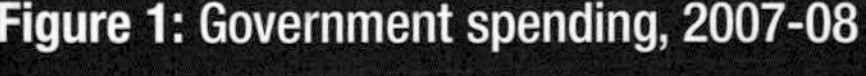

Figure 1: Government spending, 2007-08

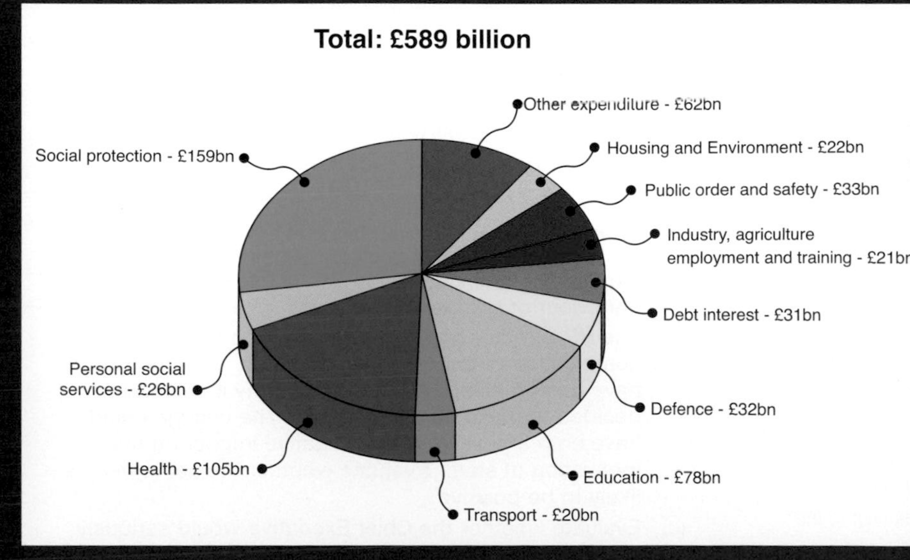

Government provision of goods and services

In the UK, government (i.e. the public sector) accounts for between 40 and 45 per cent of all the goods and services produced in the economy. In addition, it redistributes income through a variety of welfare benefits. Some of the main areas of government spending, shown in Figure 1, are:

- social protection or welfare benefits such as the State old age pension and Child Benefit;
- health which is mainly spending on the National Health Service;
- education including primary and secondary schools as well as universities;
- transport including roads and subsidies for rail transport.

Businesses benefit directly from the provision of goods and services by government. For example, the workers they employ have mainly been educated in the British education system. Roads allow their goods to be transported between business premises. Spending on the police and the judiciary ensure that property rights are respected.

Some of what is provided by government is produced by state owned enterprises and organisations. For example, education in schools is provided mainly by local authorities. But a significant proportion of public sector goods and services are produced by the private sector. For example, new roads are built by private construction companies under contract from government. Tanks and military aircraft are purchased by government from private sector companies. Social services departments purchase residential care for the elderly from private businesses. Supplying products to the public sector is a major sales opportunity for many businesses.

Changing what is bought and how it is produced

In most circumstances, the prime purpose of taxes is to raise revenues that will pay for government spending. But sometimes, taxes are used deliberately to change the behaviour of businesses and consumers. For example:

- taxes on alcohol and tobacco are used to discourage consumption of these drugs;
- taxes on cars and petrol are used to encourage the purchase of 'green' cars and discourage the purchase of cars with high emissions and heavy fuel use; they are are also used to reduce the level of traffic to reduce congestion on roads;

- pollution and environment taxes such as the Landfill Tax are used to encourage businesses to adopt more environmentally friendly practices;
- tax allowances on investment encourage businesses to invest.

Governments also sometimes use **subsidies** to alter behaviour. A subsidy is a grant given to lower the price of a good. For example, governments may subsidise businesses to train workers by paying part of the costs of training. Governments may subsidise some elements of the costs of a business start-up to encourage more people to set up their own business. Governments may also provide subsidies to businesses that set up in a high unemployment area to encourage job creation.

Fiscal policy

FISCAL POLICY is the government use of its spending, taxes and its borrowing to influence economic activity. Fiscal policy can be used to influence the behaviour of individuals and businesses as described above. However, it can also be used to influence the economy as a whole.

When governments increase their spending more than they increase taxes, total spending in the economy rises. For example, if the government increases spending by £20 billion but taxes only rise by £5 billion, then there is an increase in spending by the government sector of £15 billion. The exact impact of this on the economy is complex. However, this net increase in spending will give a boost in the short term to total demand (or **aggregate demand**). The economy will expand. Hence this is called **expansionary fiscal policy**.

Expansionary fiscal policy should be used by government when the economy is going into a **recession**. This is when unemployment is rising and spending is slowing down or even falling. Businesses should therefore benefit from expansionary fiscal policy. This explains why, when trading conditions are difficult, business groups such as the CBI call for the government to adopt expansionary fiscal policies by either increasing its spending or cutting taxes.

Restrictive fiscal policy is the opposite of expansionary fiscal policy. It occurs when the government raises taxes more than any increase in its spending. It reduces demand from government in the economy. It should be used by the government when the economy is overheating at the top of a boom and there is too much spending. Too much spending

Question 1.

Zaphrom is a UK company which manufactures pharmaceutical products. It currently provides 70 cars to its employees, from the Chief Executive to senior managers to sales staff. In his 2008 budget, the Chancellor announced major changes to the tax payable on cars. The tax on cars which emit high levels of CO2 (carbon dioxide) would increase substantially. From April 2009, companies would only be allowed to write off 10 per cent of the value of a car emitting more than 160 gm of CO2 per kilometre compared to 25 per cent as at present. This would substantially increase the cost to the company of owning cars. In addition, from 2010, road tax (the cost of the tax disk on cars) would increase substantially for the first year of a car's life. For example, on the Chief Executive's Land Rover, it would increase from the current £500 to £950. On the Finance Director's Jaguar, it would increase from the current £400 to £750. Given that the company buys cars from new and then sells them after two or three years, this would lead to a significant rise in the cost of the company car fleet.

The HR director, who is responsible for making decisions about the company car fleet, wants to see the car fleet become greener so as to minimise the effects of the Chancellor's budget. Inevitably, some staff will be told that they will no longer be supplied with the model of car they have grown to like. She is going to 'sell' the changes in terms of the company's contribution to reducing greenhouse gas emissions, helping to solve the global warming problem and 'doing our bit' to save the planet. This will go down well with some staff. But she hasn't yet decided how to tell the Chief Executive that he can no longer have his Land Rover. She wonders how he would take it if she suggested he might like to trade it in for a Vauxhall Astra.

Source: adapted from *The Financial Times*, 14.3.2008.

(a) Explain how the Chancellor can use taxes to alter the behaviour of companies on green issues.

(b) The HR Director has chosen to change the composition of the company car fleet. (i) What would have been the impact on the company if she had decided to make no change? (b) The change could have both a positive and a negative impact on the motivation of staff. Evaluate whether the net impact is likely to be positive.

(c) Evaluate whether the Chief Executive would seriously consider making the switch from a Land Rover to a Vauxhall Astra.

Question 2.

The US economy is threatening to slide into a recession. Faltering spending led to fierce lobbying by business groups for the government to give a fiscal boost to the economy. Earlier this month, their lobbying was rewarded when Congress approved a $152 billion package of tax cuts. Tax payers will receive a one-off rebate sometime between May and the end of the summer. Cheques for up to $600 (£300) will be sent to individuals earning up to $75,000 (£37,500) and $1,200 for married couples who earn up to $150,000 (£75,000). Families with children will gain an additional $300 (£150) per child.

The National Retail Federation, representing US retailers, estimates that 40 per cent of the rebates will be spent, with the rest either used to pay off debts or saved. Not every retailer, though, will be a winner from the rebates. Past experience shows that consumers increase their basic spending but don't increase their discretionary spending when given tax rebates in a recession. So consumers will purchase lower-margin food and small basic household items like a new kettle. But they won't go out and buy luxuries like a new $2,000 high definition television. They might buy ice cream from Wal-Mart but they will think twice about going out to a restaurant. Wal-Mart, the largest supermarket chain in the USA, whose core customer is the average to below average income earner, could benefit. Starbucks, the coffee chain, which has already reported fewer customers visiting its outlets, might see little benefit.

Source: adapted from the *Financial Times*, 19.2.2008.

(a) Explain why Wal-Mart could be a beneficiary from the tax rebates but Starbucks and furniture retailers might see little benefit.

(b) A chain of US electrical retailers sells kitchen equipment like fridges, cookers and electric kettles, entertainment equipment such as televisions, games consoles and DVD players, and a range of computers and printers. In February 2008, it was having to make some decisions about its stock levels for the next 9 months. Discuss much stock it should buy and what sort of stock it should hold compared to the nine months to December 2007.

leads to inflation and is unsustainable in the long term.

Using fiscal policy to smooth out booms and recessions in the business cycle benefits business in the long term. It creates a more predictable economic climate which allows businesses to plan with greater certainty. It reduces risk and encourages investment.

Monetary policy

MONETARY POLICY is policy which uses interest rates to influence the economy. Control of interest rates has been given by the UK government to the Bank of England. Each month, the Bank of England has to decide whether to raise interest rates, leave them at the same level or reduce them.

The Bank of England uses interest rates to control inflation in the economy. Rises in interest rates reduce total spending by households and businesses. This reduces total demand for goods and services and moderates the rate of inflation. Falls in interest rates tend to come when the Bank of England believes the rate of inflation will fall below its target level, currently 2 per cent per annum. Falls in interest rates will boost spending by households and businesses.

High levels of inflation in general harm business and business activity. Controlling inflation is therefore important for businesses. Changing the rate of interest also helps smooth out the business cycle.

How businesses might respond to changes in interest rates is covered in more detail in the unit titled 'Interest rates'.

Supply-side policies

Fiscal policy and monetary policy is used to affect aggregate demand. By adjusting its total spending, level of taxes or interest rates, the government can increase or reduce the amount of total spending in the economy. This can then have a short-term impact on economic variables such as inflation, unemployment, and the business cycle.

However, a key long-term aim of the government is to increase the productive capacity of the economy. Growth in capacity is often called the 'underlying rate of economic growth' to distinguish it from growth in GDP. Policies to increase the productive capacity of the economy are called SUPPLY-SIDE POLICIES. This is to distinguish them from fiscal and monetary policies which affect aggregate demand. There are three main ways in which supply-side policies can increase the productive capacity of the economy.

Increasing investment The government can use policies to promote investment by businesses. For example, it can give tax relief on money used to buy investment goods. Or it can give grants to pay for investment. It can also invest itself. Building new roads and bridges or reclaiming derelict land are examples of infrastructure spending which will benefit business.

Improving the quality of the labour force A workforce which is better educated and trained and has more experience will be more productive than one which is less well trained. So the average UK worker might be able to produce more in money terms than the average Indian or Thai worker. Through better education and promoting training, the government can therefore increase long-term economic growth.

Making sure that both capital and labour are fully utilised Businesses can invest in new machines but if those machines stand idle, they won't be productive. Similarly, if workers are out of work or their skills are underutilised, then the economy will not grow as fast as it could. So a key role of government is to ensure that resources are being used productively. Policies which encourage employment, such as the New Deal or increased vocational training, help to achieve this. So do macroeconomic policies which smooth out the business cycle. Sound financial policies which result in low inflation will encourage investment. So too will a legal system which allows businesses to own property, sign enforceable contracts and trade goods without too much fear of crime. Countries that do not have a sound legal and financial framework often fail to grow as fast as they could as a result.

There are other examples of supply-side policies used by government in an effort to increase the efficient use of resources in the economy. For example, there are regular attempts by government to simplify 'red tape', the rules and regulations ranging from tax returns to health and safety inspections to labour laws. Red tape imposes considerable costs on businesses, particularly small businesses. There are also regular changes to amount of tax paid by businesses or workers to encourage them to work more efficiently.

Privatisation

One example of a supply side policy is PRIVATISATION. This was a policy introduced in the 1980s where state owned industries and assets were sold off to the private sector. For example the gas, electricity, coal, water, steel, post office, telecommunications, airline, airports and railway industries were all partly or fully owned by the UK government before 1980. The arguments in favour of NATIONALISATION, the government buying assets from the private sector , owning them and then providing goods and services, are:

- by providing on a large scale, as with the National Health Service, the government can gain economies of scale and so lower costs of production to citizens;
- essential services can be provided which would otherwise not be provided in sufficient quantities by free markets;
- by eliminating the profit made by businesses, the cost to the citizen of those products would be lower.

However, there have been major criticisms of state owned industries and strong arguments in favour of privatisation.

- State owned monopolies did not have the profit or competitive incentives to reduce cost wherever possible. Hence, when industries such as gas and electricity were privatised, their new private owners stripped out huge layers of costs making them far more efficient than before. Despite now earning large profits, the new businesses were able to lower their prices to customers.
- There was no incentive for industries to innovate. Privatised industries have often introduced new services better able to cater for the needs of their customers.
- Government often starved industries of investment because it wanted to reduce its spending. The result was a lack of essential investment in industries such as water and the railways. When these industries passed into private hands, investment increased because the privatised businesses saw that they could increase their profits by investing more.
- As a one-off advantage to taxpayers, the government sold off these assets to the private sector for billions of pounds. This was used to pay off part of the government debt, reducing interest payments and allowing for lower taxes.

Some privatised industries, such as gas, electricity, water, telecommunications and the railways, were privatised in such a way that there was not always enough competition in the industry to prevent the new businesses charging high prices and exploiting customers. For this reason, the industries were given REGULATORY BODIES. These include ofcom for the telecommunications industry and ofwat for the water industry. They have the power to fix maximum prices in the industry. In the case of the telecommunications industry, ofcom has tended to force prices down to take account of increased efficiency in providing telecommunication services. They also have the power to force existing monopoly businesses to open up individual markets to competition. For example, BT has been forced to allow competitors to provide broadband services which use BT landlines to reach customers.

Intervention vs laissez faire

The role of government has changed over time. Traditionally, government had two main functions. One was to maintain armed forces in time of war. The second was to administer justice. Taxes were raised to pay for both of these. Gradually, the role of government has expanded. Today, various branches of government in the UK are responsible not just for defence and the justice system, but also for education, health care, roads, welfare benefits as well as many other areas. Government is also responsible for running the economy as a whole and for regulating many areas of economic and social activity.

There is a debate, however, about the extent to which government should interfere in the workings of the economy and society.

Laissez faire approach The LAISSEZ FAIRE approach is that government should intervene as little as possible. 100 years ago, for example, government did not feel it had any responsibility for unemployment or inflation. There was little regulation of the labour market. 'Red tape' was minimal. Those who favour a laissez faire approach argue as follows.

KNOWLEDGE

1. Why are property rights important for businesses?
2. How do businesses benefit from government spending?
3. Explain the difference between a tax and a subsidy.
4. How might expansionary fiscal policy benefit businesses?
5. What might be the impact on businesses of a fall in the Bank of England's interest rate?
6. How might supply-side policies benefit businesses?
7. What are the possible advantages and disadvantages of privatisation as a supply side policy?
8. Briefly summarise the arguments in favour of (a) a laissez faire approach to the economy and (b) an interventionist approach.

- Government intervention has to be paid for by taxes. The more government intervention, the higher the taxes needed, whether to pay for inspectors to monitor health and safety legislation, or doctors to provide a free health service. The money raised in taxes would be better used if it were in the hands of those being taxed, consumers, workers and businesses. High taxes also discourage investment and enterprise. Foreign companies thinking of setting up in the UK would be discouraged by a high tax regime.
- Government intervention often does more harm than good. For example, attempts to reduce inflation can lead to higher inflation or very high unemployment. Protecting workers rights by setting minimum wages can lead to firms being forced out of business because of higher wage costs and unemployment increasing. Heavy regulation discourages investment and reduces international competitiveness because it adds to the costs of running a business. Foreign businesses wanting to set up in the UK could be discouraged by a heavy regulatory framework.
- Free markets usually provide a better outcome than regulated markets or no markets at all. Everything from health care to railways and even motorways can be more efficiently provided by markets.
- Where free markets fail, it is usually better for government to persuade firms in the industry to regulate themselves, for example by adopting voluntary codes of practice. In advertising, the Advertising Standards Authority regulates advertising without the need for government intervention.

Intervention approach Those who argue in favour of government INTERVENTION would disagree with the laissez faire approach.

- Macroeconomic management of the economy is essential to avoid the dangers of high inflation and high unemployment. Governments have not always been successful at this but a pure laissez faire approach would result in very deep recessions and unsustainable booms.
- Consumers, workers and citizens demand ever more stringent regulation from government. Consumers demand that they are fairly treated by businesses from which they buy goods and services. Workers want protection from employers who treat them unfairly. Citizens want the environment to be clean and healthy.

KEYTERMS

Fiscal policy – the government use of its spending, taxes and its borrowing to influence economic activity.
Monetary policy – government policy which uses monetary variables such as the rate of interest to influence the economy.
Nationalisation – the transfer of firms or assets from private sector ownership to state ownership.
Interventionism – an economic philosophy which argues that government should intervene in the workings of the economy whenever the free market mechanism fails to optimise society's welfare.
Laissez faire – an economic philosophy which says that government should intervene in the workings of the economy as little as possible because free markets are the best way to maximise welfare for society.
Regulatory bodies – bodies set up in the UK by government which oversee the workings of certain privatised industries where competition is restricted.
Supply-side policies – government policies aimed at increasing the productive capacity of the economy.

Case Study: Micro-brewing

Steve Haynes sold his bar when the government announced that a ban on smoking in public places would be introduced. Only a fraction of the sales came from food and he could see that the ban would have a significant impact on his takings. He decided to move into micro-brewing, producing speciality ales sold both to bars and pubs, but also to retailers. Since the smoking ban came into force, his sales to retailers have increased 10 per cent, vindicating his hunch that drinkers would consume more at home.

However, he is angry about the higher-than-inflation increases in tax on beer in the Chancellor's last budget. The Chancellor justified the tax increase by arguing that binge drinking was now too serious a problem and that something had to be done about it. Raising the tax on alcohol would discourage young people from excessive drinking. However, Steve argues that young people don't binge drink on the traditional types of beer that he brews. So why should his beers be taxed more highly?

The last budget also saw slightly higher income taxes on low to medium income earners, the typical customer for his beers. With the economy slowing and consumer debt at record levels, Steve has shelved plans for expansion for the time being. But he is hopeful that extra marketing and greater awareness of his products amongst retailers could at least compensate for the negative trends in the economy.

The Bank of England has cut interest rates by a whole 1 per cent over the past months to counter growing recessionary pressures. This has helped reduce Steve's overheads because he took out a £100,000 variable rate loan to finance the purchase of the micro-brewery. The cost of hops, however, has increased considerably in line with the large increases seen in the price of many agricultural commodities.

(a) Evaluate the impact of the changes in government policy described in the passage on Steve Hayne's micro-brewery business. (40 marks)

(b) Would Steve Hayne's micro-brewery business have higher sales and higher profits if the government cut every tax and every type of government spending by 20 per cent? Justify your answer. (40 marks)

120 The EU and other international trading blocs

Trading blocs

All UK businesses are to some extent affected by what happens in the international economy. They might export or import products. Or they will buy supplies from companies which themselves have used imported products.

The extent to which businesses export and import is affected by the PROTECTIONIST barriers put up by governments. There are many barriers to trade but two of these are tariffs and quotas.

- A TARIFF is a tax on imports. It is sometimes called a customs duty. The higher the taxes on imports, the more expensive imports become. Hence, high tariffs restrict the volume of trade.
- A QUOTA is a limit on the physical number of goods that can be imported over a period of time. For example, a quota might be 1 million passenger cars over a year. Quotas are set to limit the volume of imports.

When there are no protectionist barriers on trade, FREE TRADE is said to exist.

UK Trade with the rest of the world is governed by a complex set of rules, set out in international treaties which the UK has signed. Possibly the most important of these is the treaty it signed when it joined the European Union (EU). The EU is an example of a TRADING BLOC. This is a group of countries which have signed an agreement to reduce or eliminate trading barriers between themselves. There are hundreds of trading blocs in existence round the world today, most of which are relatively unimportant and made up of just two countries. Apart from the EU, the most important trading blocs are:

- NAFTA, the North American Free Trade Agreement, made up of Mexico, the United States and Canada;
- ASEAN, the Association of Southeast Asia Nations, includes Malaysia, the Phillipines, Singapore and Thailand;
- Union of South American Nations, formed by the joining together of two other trading blocs, the Andean Community and Mercusor.

The EU is by far the most developed of today's trading blocs. Most trading blocs are agreements to reduce or eliminate tariffs and quotas over a period of time. In contrast, the EU is a customs union where there is a long term agenda for ever deeper economic and possibly political integration between member countries. In the rest of this unit, we will consider how businesses are affected by the existence of a trading bloc such as the European Union.

The European Union

The UK has been a member of the EUROPEAN UNION (EU)

Figure 1: The EU, 2008

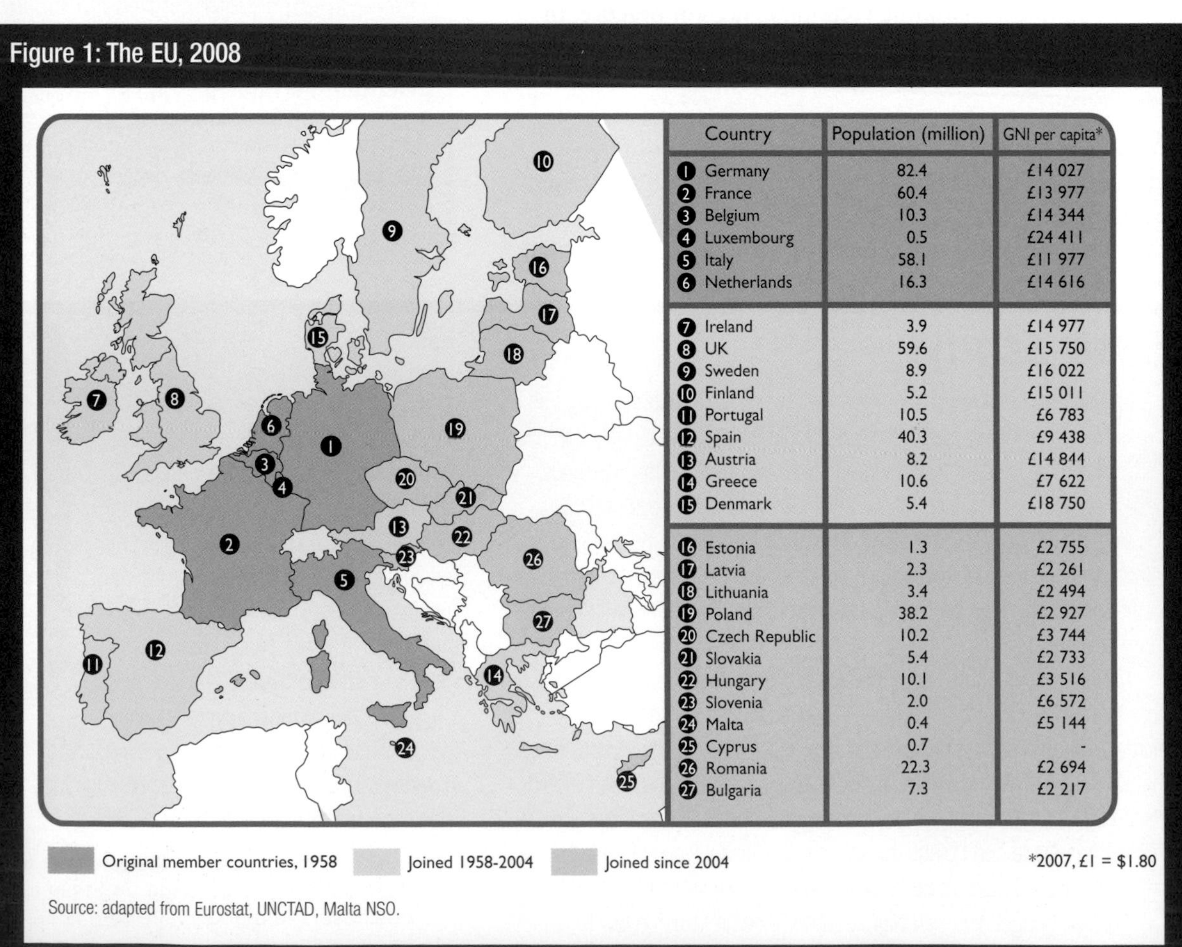

Country	Population (million)	GNI per capita*
1 Germany	82.4	£14 027
2 France	60.4	£13 977
3 Belgium	10.3	£14 344
4 Luxembourg	0.5	£24 411
5 Italy	58.1	£11 977
6 Netherlands	16.3	£14 616
7 Ireland	3.9	£14 977
8 UK	59.6	£15 750
9 Sweden	8.9	£16 022
10 Finland	5.2	£15 011
11 Portugal	10.5	£6 783
12 Spain	40.3	£9 438
13 Austria	8.2	£14 841
14 Greece	10.6	£7 622
15 Denmark	5.4	£18 750
16 Estonia	1.3	£2 755
17 Latvia	2.3	£2 261
18 Lithuania	3.4	£2 494
19 Poland	38.2	£2 927
20 Czech Republic	10.2	£3 744
21 Slovakia	5.4	£2 733
22 Hungary	10.1	£3 516
23 Slovenia	2.0	£6 572
24 Malta	0.4	£5 144
25 Cyprus	0.7	-
26 Romania	22.3	£2 694
27 Bulgaria	7.3	£2 217

Source: adapted from Eurostat, UNCTAD, Malta NSO.

since 1973. Around 60 per cent of UK exports and imports of goods are to and from the EU. So the EU is by far the largest trading partner for the UK.

The UK has been a reluctant partner within the EU. It refused to join when the EU was established in 1956. It has tended to resist changes which would deepen both economic and political integration. For example, the UK refused to join the Single Currency. British businesses are divided about the benefits of the EU. To understand why, it is necessary to know about the history of the EU, its institutions and the costs and benefits for businesses of being within the EU.

1956 The Treaty of Rome In 1956, six European countries, France, Germany, Italy, Belgium, the Netherlands and Luxembourg , signed the Treaty of Rome. This established a Common Market between the countries. There are two aspects to a common market. First, there is a CUSTOMS UNION. This exists when a group of countries remove all barriers to trade of goods and services between themselves but erect a common tariff barrier to products coming in from outside the customs union area. Second, barriers to the mobility of labour and financial capital are removed.

1986 The Single European Act In practice, whilst barriers to trade such as tariffs and quotas had been removed between member countries, there remained many other barriers to trade. For example, individual governments still regularly only gave contracts to domestic suppliers. Banks couldn't operate freely across the whole EU. So in 1986, member countries agreed to deepen economic links by removing these barriers to create a SINGLE EUROPEAN MARKET by December 31st 1992. This would greatly increase market access for businesses in one country to another country.

1991 The Maastricht Treaty This treaty gave greater powers to the EU to create common policies in the areas of social affairs, industrial affairs, education, defence and health. For example, EU legislation states that workers should not work more than 48 hours per week. The Maastricht Treaty also set the EU the goal of creating a monetary union, abolishing individual currencies and creating one currency for the whole union.

2002 The launch of the euro On 1st January 2002, most EU countries replaced their currencies with the euro. This eliminated a major barrier to trade. The UK decided not to participate in the single currency at the time. UK companies therefore still faced exchange rate risks and the cost of exchanging pounds for euros when trading with the rest of Europe. The group of countries which have adopted the single currency is often called the EUROZONE.

Question 1.

In April 2005, a preliminary judgment from the European Court of Justice gave victory to Marks & Spencer (M&S) in a battle over taxes. M&S had wanted to offset the losses it had made in France, Germany and Belgium against profits made in the UK. This would have reduced the amount of corporation tax the company would have paid in the UK by around £30 million. The UK Inland Revenue had declared that the company could not do this. Only losses made in the UK could be offset against profits made in the UK by the company.

The preliminary ruling from the European Court of Justice agreed with M&S that the Inland Revenue's policy breached a core European treaty principle: that member states cannot hinder an EU national in one country from establishing a business in another. The preliminary ruling stated that a group relief scheme that does not allow a parent company to deduct the losses of its foreign subsidiaries under any circumstances is incompatible with European law. The ruling rejected the Inland Revenue argument that a national government cannot offer a tax advantage to a subsidiary based in a foreign country where it has no power of taxation.

However, the ruling does seem to prevent 'double dipping': where a company reclaims tax on the same losses in two countries. The ruling says that where a government allows subsidiaries of foreign companies to claim tax relief on losses made, then those tax benefits must be claimed in that country.

What made the Marks & Spencer case special was that the

company pulled out of continental Europe in the early 2000s because it was making losses on these operations. So it had no prospect of future profits against which it could offset these losses in Belgium, France and Germany.

Source: adapted from the *Financial Times*, 8.4. 2005.

(a) Explain why Marks & Spencer was able to appeal against a UK tax ruling.

(b) Both the Treaty of Rome and the Single European Act mean that 'member states cannot hinder an EU national in one country from establishing a business in another'. How could membership of the EU both (a) benefit and (b) harm the interests of a UK company like Marks & Spencer?

Enlargement since 1973 Between 1956 and 1972, the European Union was made up of just the original six founder countries. Since then, over 20 countries have joined, starting with the UK, Ireland and Denmark in 1973. In 2004, seven countries from Eastern Europe joined, followed by a further two in 2007. More countries wish to join including some of the states of the former Yugoslavia and, more controversially, Turkey.

European institutions

There are four main institutions which govern the EU.

The European Commission The European Commission (EC) is located in Brussels. It is responsible for proposing policy and legislation to the European Council of Ministers. Once accepted, it is then responsible for implementing that policy and legislation.

Question 2.

BWD Entertainment is a UK based media company. Originally a magazine company, it has diversified into radio and trade newspapers and also runs a book publishing business. In the 1990s, it acquired stakes in magazine publishing companies in Spain, the Netherlands and Italy and owns radio companies in both Germany and France.

The directors of the company have recently completed a strategic review and have decided that the new entrants to the EU in Eastern Europe should be targeted for acquisitions. Their economies are likely to grow at a faster rate than the EU average over the next 10-20 years and this should give plenty of scope for increasing sales over time.

They are particularly looking at the largest new entrant country, Poland, with a population of 38.2 million. One strategy would be to buy an established Polish magazine company and use its editorial expertise and distribution system to push a number of new magazines based on ones which have proved popular in the UK, Spain and Italy. A different strategy would be to buy a Polish magazine company which already had strong market share. By giving new finance, BWD would allow the existing Polish management greater opportunities to launch new magazines aimed at the local market. A third possible strategy would be to set up a company from scratch, recruiting editors and other workers from established Polish magazine companies, but also putting in staff from existing BWD operations in other European countries. This would probably be the highest risk strategy.

(a) **Explain why there might be greater scope for marketing magazines in Poland than in, say, the UK or Italy over the next ten years.**

(b) **By considering the possible advantages and disadvantages of each of the three strategic options, discuss which is likely to be the most successful for BWD. In your answer, identify what other information would be needed to make an informed choice.**

The EC is headed by the President of the European Commission who is responsible for acting in the interests of the EU. Commissioners are appointed to represent each member country.

The Council of Ministers The Council of Ministers is made up of ministers from each member country who meet on a regular basis. Twice a year, heads of government from each country also meet at the European Council. The Council of Ministers is the decision making body of the EU. It approves or rejects proposals from the European Commission about new regulations and directives.

The European Parliament The European Parliament is based in Strasbourg. Voters in EU countries elected MEPs, Members of the European Parliament, to sit in the parliament. Its role is to comment on proposals put forward by the European Commission to the Council of Ministers. It does not have the power to make laws as in national parliaments. Its major power, which it has used once, is that it can dismiss the President of the European Commission and European Commissioners.

The European Court of Justice The European Court of Justice is the final court of law within the European Union. Its decisions are binding. Individual citizens and businesses can appeal to the European Court of Justice against decisions made in local or national courts. The European Court of Justice bases its decisions on EU law.

EU laws are called **directives**. In some cases, these have to be agreed by all member countries through the Council of Ministers. In other cases, they can be passed if a majority of countries agree. Directives become EU law by being made law in each individual national parliament. The European Commission then has the power to issue **regulations** based on these directives. Directives tend to be broad and general in nature. Regulations are specific and detailed.

Impact on UK businesses of being part of the EU customs union

UK businesses operate within the EU customs union. This means that, for UK businesses, there is free trade within the European Union. However, businesses outside the European Union may face tariffs or other barriers if they want to sell products in the EU. There are advantages and disadvantages to UK businesses of being part of the EU customs union.

- Firms operating within customs unions have free access to markets which would otherwise be protected by tariffs or quotas. In this way British firms, for example, have access to all other EU markets. For many firms this provides them with the opportunity to operate in EU markets in much the same way that they would at home. A Blackburn based firm would operate in Berlin or Bilbao in much the same way as it would in Brighton or Birmingham.
- Firms will have access to the most appropriate factors of

production. A British firm might purchase cheap land in Southern Portugal for a new factory location, skilled designers from Italy or capital equipment from France.
- Customs unions provide firms with large markets to sell to. The bigger the market a firm is selling to, the greater the economies of scale it is able to benefit from.
- Businesses operating within a common market will be protected from competition from outside this area by an external business. Such protection allows businesses to be sheltered from the potentially damaging effects of competition such as price wars.
- Increased competition from European firms may act as an incentive for British firms to increase efficiency and standards.

There are, however, disadvantages for businesses operating within a customs union or common market.
- Before Britain joined the EU, British firms could buy goods and services from the lowest cost producers around the world. Foodstuffs were imported in huge quantities from New Zealand and the USA in this way. Since joining the EU, however, British firms have had to pay far more for foodstuffs from New Zealand and Australia because of the common external tariff.
- Whilst a British based firm will have free access to other EU markets, businesses based in these markets will also have access to the UK market. Such competition may reduce the market share which domestic businesses have established.
- Protection from external tariffs is not always beneficial to firms operating from within a common market. This is because being sheltered from external competition may result in less incentive for a firm to become more efficient. In the long run, this may lead to a deterioration in the firm's performance.
- Firms may have to adapt their marketing strategies to suit the needs of consumers in each country within the customs union. For example, surveys have found that of the thousands of products commonly sold in European supermarkets, only a small proportion are widely on sale in identical format in at least the four largest countries.

Enlargement of the European Union

Over the past ten years, there has been a considerable enlargement in the EU, taking in much of Eastern Europe. In the future, more countries in Eastern and Southern Europe are likely to join, including possibly Turkey. Enlargement affects UK businesses in a variety of ways.
- Membership of the EU brings down barriers to trade. So it is easier for UK businesses now to export to these countries. On the other hand, it is also easier for businesses in the new member countries to export to the UK. So some UK businesses will gain export business. Other UK businesses will lose sales because of increased exports from the new member countries.
- By being able to import cheaper raw materials from new member countries, some UK businesses will be able to lower their costs. They will therefore become more competitive than before.
- Some production currently in the UK is likely to be relocated to new member countries. Wages paid to workers are typically very much lower. So too are other costs such as the cost of land and taxes paid. By switching to a lower cost production country, UK businesses can become more internationally competitive.
- If a UK business is able to increase sales significantly, average costs of production should fall because of economies of scale. This will give it a further competitive advantage.
- Enlargement has led to a large influx of migrant workers from Eastern Europe. They are prepared to work for low wages in the UK. Some industries, such as agriculture and food processing, are now heavily reliant on these workers. They reduce costs for UK businesses making them more competitive.

The single currency

In 2002, most EU countries abandoned their own currencies and adopted the euro as a single currency. What this means is that a business in Germany can use the same currency to pay for goods bought from France or Spain as it can from other German businesses. The UK, however, did not adopt the euro and retained its own currency, the pound. This has disadvantages for UK businesses.
- UK businesses have to pay banks commission every time they want to change pounds into euros or vice versa. EU businesses trading within the eurozone don't have these charges. Hence, UK businesses are likely to have higher costs when trading with other eurozone countries.
- The value of the pound fluctuates against the euro. So a UK business doesn't know what price it will pay for euros in six months or a year's time. This makes trading with businesses in the eurozone as risky as trading with businesses in other countries like China or the USA. But businesses trading with other businesses in the eurozone don't face these risks because they are all using the same currency, the euro.
- Separate currencies make prices less transparent. This is particularly important for small, unsophisticated businesses. For example, a small London based business knows the monetary value of a product from a Scottish based business when it is quoted at £200 a tonne. But it doesn't necessarily know the monetary value if a German firm quotes a price of €300 a tonne. It is relatively easy to find the exchange rate of pounds for euros. But for a small firm, prices in different currencies may discourage it from buying or selling because it is not immediately obvious what is the price.

Despite these disadvantages, UK businesses are divided about whether the UK should replace the pound with the euro. The main possible economic disadvantage of joining the eurozone concerns the management of the economy. Joining the single currency would mean that the Bank of England would no longer be able to set a separate main interest rate for the UK. The main interest rate for the UK would then be the one set for the whole eurozone by the European Central Bank. This would limit the ability of the UK government to influence inflation and economic growth in the UK. If the UK were in a recession, for example, the Bank of England could no longer set low interest rates to encourage spending to get us out of recession. This would then be bad for UK businesses. However, many economists and businesses do not believe that this would in practice be a serious problem for the UK. The UK is already so tied into the European economy that it has limited room for setting independent policies anyway.

The other major objection to the UK adopting the euro is that it would be another step towards complete European integration. Some UK businesses argue that Britain's membership of the EU increases their costs because of 'red tape': EU regulations make them less internationally competitive. They also argue that UK businesses would do better if EU imports could be kept out through protectionist measures.

KNOWLEDGE

1. What is the difference between a tariff and a quota?
2. Name four world trading blocs.
3. Explain briefly the terms of (a) the Treaty of Rome; (b) the Single European Act; (c) the Maastricht Treaty.
4. Compare the roles of the European Commission, the Council of Ministers, the European Parliament and the European Court of Justice in the EU.
5. What might be the advantages and disadvantages to a UK business exporting metal components to customers in the EU and the USA of being part of the EU customs union?
6. What impact might EU enlargement have on (a) a farmer in Norfolk and (b) a shoe manufacturer in Northampton?
7. Explain how a UK manufacturer might be at a competitive disadvantage because the UK is not part of the eurozone.

KEYTERMS

Customs union – a union of countries which establish free trade amongst themselves and put up a common tariff to imports from outside the union.

Eurozone – the group of countries which have adopted the single European currency, the euro.

European Union – a customs union whose aim is economic integration with a single market and which also has political and defence objectives.

Free trade – the import and export of goods and services with no barriers to trade such as tariffs or quotas.

Protectionism – government policies aimed at limiting the import of products into a country.

Quotas – limits on the physical quantity of products that can be imported into a country.

Single European market – the market for goods and services produced within the European Union, a market which is free of trade barriers and and restrictions to trade.

Tariff – taxes, also called customs duties, on goods imported into a country.

Trading bloc – a group of countries which have signed an agreement to reduce or eliminate tariffs, quotas and other protectionist barriers between themselves.

Case Study: The EU

The EU has taken another step towards possibly introducing a common business tax across Europe. There have been pressures from a number of EU countries to introduce a harmonised corporation tax for businesses operating in two or more EU countries. This is because, at present, businesses are free to locate their headquarters in whichever EU country has the lowest corporation tax. Exactly where a company is financially based has many other implications for the business. So corporation tax levels are just one of many factors which determine location. However, low corporation tax countries like Ireland have seen a slow influx of companies attracted by its tax regime.

A study by the Oxford-based Said Business School estimates that a single EU corporation tax would increase the tax bill for British businesses by £4 billion. This is because the UK is a low corporation tax country and so harmonising the tax across all EU countries would lead to a higher rate of tax.

The UK government is opposed to the proposal.

Source: adapted from *The Times*, 3.4.2007.

The EU is bringing in new health and safety regulations for the industrial use of chemicals. Called Reach (Registration, Evaluation, Authorisation and Restriction of Chemicals), all chemicals of one tonne or more in volume that are manufactured in or imported into the European Union will have to be tested for health and safety. They must also be registered with a new, central European authority, the European Chemicals Agency, in Helsinki, Finland.

For European workers, the new regulations are good news. Trade unionists point out that one in three occupational diseases in the 15 older EU member states is due to exposure to chemicals. Industry currently uses thousands of chemicals, in products ranging from bleach and soap to paints and dyes, which may not have been fully tested and assessed for their effect on human health and the environment.

But it will be costly for business. Estimates suggest that complying with Reach will cost industry within the EU between €2.8 billion and €5.2 billion (£1.8 billion - £3.4 billion) over 11 years. The overall cost is likely to be double this as chemical businesses in non-EU countries will also have to comply with the regulations if they wish to continue selling to the EU.

Source: adapted from *The Guardian*, 24.3.2008.

There are some who would like Britain to leave the EU altogether. Too much red tape, extra competition from abroad and higher taxes are some of the complaints. But talking to businesses on the ground, it becomes clear that the EU has become an integral part of the everyday life of many businesses in the UK.

Take Harry Grant, for example, who runs a farm in Norfolk. He employs 10 Eastern European workers on a regular basis and at the height of the harvesting season this can grow to 40. They work hard and the wages he pays allows him to make a profit in a highly competitive market. Like many farmers, he is totally reliant on Eastern European migrant workers since locally born workers won't take jobs in the industry.

Bill Lewis runs a foundry business in the West Midlands. Around half his output is exported to European markets. If Britain were to leave the EU and tariffs were put on his goods, he wouldn't be able to compete. His customers would buy from other businesses within Europe.

Claire O'Neal is a buyer for a high street chain of fashion stores. Sourcing from countries like China certainly leads to lower costs. But her customers want fashion fast. If there is a new fashion trend, she wants to be able to get garments into the stores within 6 weeks. She can only do that by buying from within the EU or possibly Turkey because of the time it takes to transport the goods. Also, European manufacturers are much more geared up to small production runs and fast turnaround times. Another advantage of buying from within the EU is that paperwork and dealing with regulations is much less.

(a) Evaluate the impact of the EU on UK businesses. (40 marks)

(b) To what extent might a UK withdrawal from the EU, with the EU putting up tariffs and quotas on UK goods, advantage UK businesses? (40 marks)

121 Consumer protection

The growth of protection

At the beginning of the last century consumers and producers were seen as having equal responsibility. Indeed, consumers were expected to ensure that their purchases were satisfactory. This approach can be summarised by the expression caveat emptor, which means - 'let the buyer beware'.

Today, the relationship between consumers and businesses is viewed differently. Many see consumers as being at the mercy of powerful and well organised producers. This has led to a rise in interest about consumer affairs and increasing pressure on governments to pass legislation to protect consumers. Consumer magazines, such as *Which?*, and consumer television programmes, such as 'Watchdog', have lent pressure to this movement seeking to protect the rights of consumers.

There is a number of reasons why consumers may need protecting more than they did in the past.

- Globalisation of world markets. Goods and services from around the world can now easily be sold in countries other than their place of origin. Consumers in the UK might, for example, need protection from goods and services imported from abroad. These products might have been produced to standards which are lower than those imposed on UK and EU businesses. Safety standards of children's toys, for example, have been lower in goods produced in Asia in the past.
- The growth of the Internet. The Internet provides many opportunities for consumers. But it also leads to problems because it is largely unregulated. Goods and services may be purchased, but might not be delivered. Companies might advertise and be paid, but then close down. Financial information, such as credit card details, might be found and used against consumers' wishes. Companies might be able to 'spy' on consumers' buying activities and also send unwanted materials through e-mail.
- The increasing complexity of many goods and services. Technological advances, in particular, have increased the gap between the knowledge of consumers and producers about products. Few consumers have the ability to properly assess the quality of the technology which goes into everyday items such as televisions, microwave ovens or computers. Such ignorance might leave consumers at the mercy of producers.
- The environment within which businesses operate is becoming increasingly competitive. Some believe that this degree of competition encourages businesses to take advantage of consumers. This may be in the form of reductions in the level of service or the quality of goods offered, for example.
- The disposable income of many consumers has increased greatly over the last four to five decades. This means that the average consumer purchases far greater quantities of goods and services than would have been the case in the past. It is argued that more protection needs to be offered to consumers as a result.
- Scientific advances have created a variety of materials that were not previously available. For example, genetically modified products have developed as a consequence of scientific advances in the production of foods. Consumers may need to be protected against any possible harmful effects of such scientific discoveries.

Question 1.

The Consumer Protection Regulations 2008 bring UK law into line with the rest of the EU in this area of law. It introduces a general duty on businesses not to trade unfairly and seeks to ensure that traders act honestly and fairly towards their customers. The regulations only cover business to consumer transactions and not business to business sales. The new regulations will replace part of the Trade Descriptions Act.

A wide range of unfair business practices are to be outlawed. For example, it is now an offence for a business to claim to be a signatory to a code of conduct when it is not. Businesses can no longer claim to be giving extra rights to consumers when these rights already belong to them in law. Firms can no longer say they are about to close down when they have no intention of closing down.

One industry is seriously worried about the new regulations. The multi-million pound psychic industry is afraid it will be become open to prosecution. Everything from horoscopes to tarot cards to seances are commonly sold. For example, psychic mailings, letters promising spiritualist services in exchange for a cheque, are estimated to have cost Britons £40 million in 2006-2007. The problem is that psychic services are often sold to vulnerable individuals, for example following a bereavement. Under the new regulations, any psychic who seeks to mislead, coerce or take advantage of vulnerable individuals for personal gain is open to prosecution.

Psychics say that theirs is a religion. The new law represents an attack on their freedom to practise that religion. But when the Trading Standards Officer calls, psychics will be treated in the same way as double glazing sales people, promoters of prize draws and shops which are forever saying they are closing down and everything must go.

Source: adapted from www.guardian.co.uk, 6.4.2008; www.opsi.gov.uk; www.businesslink.gov.uk

(a) Examine the implications of the suggested change in legislation to:
(i) consumers;
(ii) businesses.

Consumer protection legislation

It could be argued that, in a number of areas, businesses cannot be relied upon to regulate themselves. These include their dealings with employees and other firms, as well as consumers. Governments in the past have found it necessary to regulate businesses, by passing laws which protect consumers from their activities. Some examples in the UK are shown below.

Weights and Measures Act, 1951, 1963 and 1985 These Acts are designed to prevent the sale of underweight or undervolume products. For example, they make it an offence to use false or unfair weighing equipment or to give short measures. All prepacked goods must have information about the net quantity of their contents. The Acts also give inspectors the power to test weighing and measuring equipment.

Trade Descriptions Act, 1968 This prohibits false or misleading descriptions of goods or services. For example, a pair of shoes which are described as made of leather cannot be made of plastic.

Unsolicited Goods and Services Act, 1971 This law seeks to prevent the practice of sending goods to consumers which they had not ordered, and then demanding payment. It states that unsolicited goods need not be paid for and that consumers can keep such goods after six months if the seller does not collect them. This was amended in 2001 to include electronic documents.

Consumer Credit Act, 1974 This aims to protect the rights of consumers when they purchase goods on credit, such as hire purchase or credit sale agreements. For example, it states that consumers must be given a copy of any credit agreements into which they enter. It also ensures that only licensed credit brokers can provide credit. There are many other offences listed which constitute a breaking of the law. These include credit firms sending representatives to people's homes to persuade them to take credit and credit agreements which have high interest rates.

Consumer Safety Act, 1978 This law was passed in order to prevent the sale of goods which might be harmful to consumers. It concentrates, in particular, upon safety matters relating to children's toys and electrical goods.

Sale of Goods Act, 1979 This law states that goods sold to consumers should meet three main conditions. First, that they are of merchantable quality which means that goods should not have any serious flaws or problems with them. Second, that they are fit for the purpose for which they were purchased. For example, paint which is sold to be used outdoors should not begin to peel or flake with the first outbreak of poor weather conditions. Third, that they are as described. Thus, an anorak described as waterproof should not leak in the rain.

Supply of Goods and Services Act, 1982 This seeks to protect users of services, ensuring services are of 'merchantable quality' and at 'reasonable rates'. For example, a holiday firm which booked clients into a four star hotel that turned out to be of lower quality would be in breach of the conditions. Breaches of this and the 1979 Act are subject to civil law. An injured person can sue for breach of the Act.

Consumer Protection Act, 1987 This law was introduced to bring Britain in line with other European Union nations. It ensures that firms are liable for any damage which their defective goods might cause to consumers. For example, a firm supplying defective electrical equipment would be liable for any injuries caused to consumers using that equipment. It also seeks to outlaw misleading pricing, such as exaggerated claims relating to price reductions on sale items. An example might be a statement that a good is '£2 less than the manufacturer's recommended price' when it isn't.

Food Safety Act, 1990 This law ensures that food is safe and does not mislead the consumer in the way it is presented. It is an offence to:

- sell food that does not comply with regulations, ie is unfit to eat or is contaminated;
- change food so that it becomes harmful;
- sell food that is not of the quality stated;
- describe food in a way that misleads.

Breaches of the Act are a criminal offence, punishable by a fine and/or a prison sentence.

Sale and Supply of Goods Act, 1994 This Act amends the Sale of Goods Act, 1979 and the Supply of Goods and Services Act, 1982 in favour of the buyer. For example, consumers now had a right to partial rejection. A buyer of a case of wine may accept ten bottles, but reject the two which do not match the description ordered.

Food Safety (General Food Hygiene) Regulations 1995 These list a whole series of regulations about the preparation and storage of food and equipment.

Food Labelling Reguations, 1996 These specify exactly what information should be included on food labels.

Financial Services and Markets Act, 2000 This set up the Financial Services Authority (FSA). The FSA is an independent body designed to develop confidence and regulate activities, promote public awareness, protect consumers and prevent crime in financial markets and exchanges. For example, it will only allow businesses to trade in financial markets if they meet criteria and it might investigate and prosecute businesses operating outside the rules.

Businesses that break these laws may be liable under **criminal** or **civil law**. Under criminal laws enforced by government, such as the Weights and Measures Acts, businesses can be prosecuted for breaking the law and, if found guilty, may be fined or imprisoned. Under civil law, such as the Sale and Supply of

Goods Acts, a consumer or business may sue a business to gain compensation.

Consumer protection and the European Union

Increasingly the European Union is affecting legislation in member countries. The EU's aim is to harmonise (make the same) consumer laws. It is responsible for a series of directives which all EU nations implement as laws and regulations. Examples include:

- EU directive, Unfair Terms in Consumer Contracts, in April 1993, which led to the **Unfair Terms in Consumer Contracts Regulations, 1994** in the UK. This directive sought to prevent consumers being locked into unfair contracts which undermined their rights;
- the EU directive which led to **The General Product Safety Regulations, 1994** in the UK. These state that all products supplied to customers must be safe;
- EU directives 88/314 and 88/315 leading to the **Price Marking Order, 1991** which states that the selling price of goods must be indicated in writing;
- **Telecommunications (Data Protection and Privacy) Regulations, 1999** which prevent people and businesses from receiving unwanted direct marketing telephone calls or faxes;
- **Consumer Protection (Distance Selling) Regulations, 2000** which relate to sales over the Internet. They require a seller to provide information on the main characteristics of the goods, the price, including any taxes and delivery costs, payment arrangements, guarantees and where to address complaints about the goods;
- **Electronic Commerce (EC Directive) Regulations, 2002** which deal with the protection of consumers involved in e-commerce. For example, online selling and advertising is subject to UK legislation and online traders must give clear information about who they are and how to complete transactions;
- The **Sale and Supply of Goods to Consumers Regulations, 2002** provide minimum rights on faulty goods, such as rights to refunds, compensation and replacements. They are designed to encourage people to shop 'across borders', in other EU countries, knowing there is protection if something is wrong with goods they buy.
- The **Consumer Protection Regulations 2008** introduce a general duty on businesses not to trade unfairly and seek to ensure that traders act honestly and fairly towards their customers. They cover areas such as falsely claiming accreditation to a quality standard, misleading customers about the quality of a good and high pressure sales tactics. The regulations replace part of the Trade Descriptions Act.

Effects of protection on business

The increase in the number of consumer laws and the concern about protecting consumers has a number of possible implications for firms.

Question 2.

The Competition Commission, after a lengthy investigation, has found that there are 'few if any problems' in the UK grocery market. Suppliers, including farmers, had complained to the Competition Commission that the supermarket giants like Tesco forced them to give uneconomic prices for the goods they sold. They suggested that the tough deals negotiated by supermarkets were putting them out of business. At the same time, independent grocery stores complained that the low prices offered by supermarkets were also driving them out of business. They said that customers were getting a poor deal because, with the closure of independents, there was less and less competition in the market.

The Competition Commission has, however, recommended that an ombudsman be appointed to police dealings between the supermarket chains and their suppliers. Those suppliers that felt that supermarkets had acted unfairly could appeal to the ombudsman to investigate their case. The supermarket chains are opposed to the proposal. They say it will increase their costs because they will have to pay for the ombudsman and staff. Instead, they argue that the existing voluntary Code of Practice, which governs the relationship between the grocery chains and their suppliers, should be retained. Suppliers argue that the voluntary Code of Practice doesn't work effectively because suppliers who complain under the Code fear they will have their contracts terminated by their supermarket customer.

Source: adapted from *The Financial Times*, 1.5.2008.

(a) Explain who might benefit and who might lose out if the recommendation to create the post of an ombudsman in the grocery market went ahead.

(b) A new supermarket is opened on the edge of a small town. In the next 12 months, three independent grocery and butcher shops in the centre of town close down. (i) Have consumers benefited by the opening of the supermarket? (ii) Should the Competition Commission recommend that no new supermarkets from the existing four large supermarket chains be opened in the UK? Justify your answer.

- Increases in costs. Improving the safety of a good or ensuring that measuring equipment is more accurate can increase the costs of a firm. For example, an electrical firm producing table lamps may find that its product contravened legislation. The firm would have to change or improve the components used to make the lamps or re-design the lamp itself. Such changes would be likely to raise the firm's costs.
- Quality control. Many firms have needed to improve their quality control procedures as a result of legislation. For example, firms involved in bagging or packaging goods must ensure that the correct quantities are weighed out. Failure to do so could result in prosecution. In addition, businesses must be careful not to sell substandard or damaged products.
- Dealing with customer complaints. Many businesses now have a customer service or customer complaints department to deal with customers. These allow firms to

deal with problems quickly and efficiently and to 'nip problems in the bud' - dealing with any problems before the customer turns to the legal system.
- Changes in business practice. Attempts to ensure that customers are treated fairly by a business may place pressure on it to become more market orientated. The firm would attempt to ensure that it is actually meeting the needs of those people it is attempting to serve. Such a change, for example, may lead to greater use of market research.

Monopolies and mergers

It is argued, by some, that competition between businesses benefits consumers. Such arguments have been one influence upon government's attempts to control monopolies and mergers.

In some cases just one business, a monopolist, controls the market for a particular good or service although this is rare in the UK. Such market strength puts this firm in a position where it has the potential to exploit its consumers. It can also prevent other businesses from competing against it.

A LEGAL MONOPOLY in UK law is defined as any business which has over 25 per cent market share. An example may be Microsoft, in its production of operating systems for computers.

A merger is the joining together of two or more firms. Examples of mergers between well know companies in the early 2000s were Gillette (manufacturers of shaving equipment) with Proctor & Gamble (a multinational household products company) and Royal Bank of Scotland with ABN Amro (a Dutch bank).

Some criticisms of monopolies and mergers for consumers and businesses include the following.
- They raise prices in order to make excess profits.
- They fix prices. When a small group of firms control the market for a product, it is believed that they may act in unison to fix prices at an artificially high level.
- They force competition out. It has been suggested that monopolists sometimes pursue pricing or promotional strategies designed to force competitors out of the market.
- They prevent new firms from entering markets.
- They carry out a range of practices to restrict competition.

Examples include putting pressure on retailers not to stock the goods of rival firms and attempting to prevent suppliers from doing business with new entrants to the market.

There are, however, a number of arguments which support the continued existence of monopolies.
- Because monopolies often operate on a large scale, they are able to benefit from economies of scale. The cost advantages from this can allow monopolies to set prices lower than would be the case if there were a number of firms competing, and still make profits.
- Monopolies can use their large profits to undertake research and development projects. Many of these projects, which result in technological and scientific breakthroughs, could not be afforded by smaller firms.
- Monopolies are much better placed to survive in international markets. It is argued that this is only possible if a firm operates on a large scale.

Anti-competitive practices

ANTI-COMPETITIVE PRACTICES (or RESTRICTIVE TRADE PRACTICES) prevent competition between businesses. Examples of such restrictive practices include the following.
- A business which is a dominant supplier in a particular market may set a minimum price for the re-sale of its products. Such firms may also seek to ensure that retailers stock their products alone. In return, retailers are often given exclusive rights to sell this product within a particular area.
- Firms forming agreements to fix prices and/or limit the supply of a product. Such agreements between firms are often referred to as **collusion**.
- A dominant supplier requiring retailers to stock the full range of its product lines.

It is usually argued that consumers suffer as a result of these practices. For example, if two businesses join together to fix prices so that another business is forced to close, this will restrict consumers' choice. Such practices may benefit those businesses taking part, but will be against the interest of those that are faced with the restrictive practices.

Legislation in the UK

Certain legislation in the UK is designed to protect consumers from the problems created by monopolies, mergers and restrictive practices.

Fair Trading Act, 1973 This Act defined what constitutes a monopoly or merger in the UK. A monopoly is said to exist if a business has a 25 per cent share of the market or greater. A merger is said to exist if the combined total assets of businesses that joined together were greater than a certain value, ie £70 million in 2004. It also set up the **Office of Fair Trading (OFT)**. This was set up as a body to oversee all policy relating to competition and consumer protection. The current role of the OFT is discussed in the next section.

Competition Act, 1998 This Act:
- prohibits agreements, cartels or practices which prevent, restrict or distort competition;
- prohibits conduct which amounts to abuse of a dominant position;

although the government can grant exemptions. It also set up the **Competition Commission**. The current role of the Competition Commission is discussed later.

Enterprise Act, 2002 This Act replaced the provisions of the Fair Trading Act. Many of its new provisions were complementary to those of The Competition Act, which remained in force. The Act:

- set up the OFT as a corporate body in its own right;
- set up a Competition Appeals Tribunal (CAT) and stated how appeals could be made to it;
- made new provisions for merger controls, with decisions taken by the OFT and the Competition Commission. In most cases, mergers would be investigated on a 'competition test' (i.e. turnover over £70 million or 25 per cent of market share). Mergers would be prohibited or remedies required if there was a substantial lessening of competition as a result;
- allowed the OFT and ministers to refer investigations to the Competition Commission;
- outlined rules of investigations for the Competition Commission to decide if actions prevent, restrict or distort competition and how to take action to remedy the adverse effect on consumers;
- created a new criminal offence for individuals operating in certain cartels and investigation powers for the OFT. Cartel activities might involve price fixing, limiting supply, market sharing and bid-rigging;
- set out new competition provisions, for example disqualifying company directors who break competition law;
- outlined new procedures for enforcing consumer legislation, ie allowing the OFT to force businesses breaking the law to stop or be taken to court;
- set out rules for disclosing information by public authorities;
- changed insolvency law.

The Office of Fair Trading

The Office of Fair Trading (OFT) has an important role in promoting and protecting consumers' interests and ensuring that businesses in the UK are fair and competitive. It has a number of functions.

- Competition enforcement. The OFT enforces current legislation, stops cartels, damaging anti-competitive practices and abuses of dominant market positions, promotes a competitive culture, informs businesses about legislation, and works with the European Commission on cases.
- Consumer regulation enforcement. The OFT enforces current legislation and regulations, takes action against unfair traders, encourages codes of practice, gives consumers information to understand the law and works with bodies with enforcement powers.
- Markets and policies initiatives. The OFT can investigate markets and make public its findings. It might then recommend stronger enforcement, a change in regulations or an improvement in consumer awareness.

The OFT has the power to make market investigation references to the Competition Commission. To do this it must have reasonable grounds to suspect that features of the market prevent, restrict or distort competition. It must also publish its reasons. It also has the power to investigate mergers. If it decides that the merger will lessen competition substantially, it can either refer the merger to the Competition Commission or ask the businesses to remedy the problems. There are exceptions, for example if the benefits of the restriction outweigh the adverse effects on consumers.

Question 3.

Utility firm, Npower, is to face an investigation by the energy regulator, Ofgem, over allegations about sales tactics. Following an undercover investigation by the *Sunday Times*, it is alleged that some door-to-door sales staff in London misled potential customers. Householders thought they asking for more information about changing power suppliers when in fact the sales staff were switching them without their consent from their existing suppliers to Npower.

The company issued a statement in which it said: 'Npower management will of course co-operate fully with Ofgem in its investigation. We were very concerned at the actions of a small number of individuals in a London sales team as reported in the *Sunday Times*. We took swift action to take the team off the road and investigate the problem. Following an in-depth investigation by our audit team, disciplinary hearings will be schedules shortly. We cannot prejudge the outcome of these meetings but the penalty for fraudulent activity is dismissal. We have also taken steps to confirm that the systems in place currently are working effectively and we taken the entire Npower sales force off the road to reinforce the standards that we require. Where appropriate we have introduced additional procedures to ensure we operate to the highest standards across all our sales teams.'

Adam Scorer of consumer watchdog Energywatch said: 'More than 100 consumers contact us each month to complain about Npower's marketing tactics. No consumer should be subjected to such bully boy behaviour and such poor service.'

An Ofgem spokesperson said it had the power to fine Npower up to ten per cent of its global income if it upheld the allegations. In the last case of mis-selling in 2002, Ofgem fined London Electricity, now part of EDF, £2 million.

Source: adapted from news.bbc.co.uk, 22.2.2008.

(a) Explain, using the data, why regulators are needed in industries such as power and telecommunications.

(b) Discuss whether the actions of a regulators like Ofgem are likely to make markets more competitive and improve consumer choice.

The Competition Commission

The Competition Commission (CC) also plays an important part in protecting consumers and ensuring businesses do not break consumer legislation. It is an independent body which carries out inquires into mergers and markets referred to it by the OFT, the Secretary of State or regulatory bodies.

The CC has around 50 part-time members, appointed for eight years by the Secretary of State for Trade and Industry. They are appointed for their experience and ability. Members are supported by around 150 staff. The Chairperson of the Competition Commission usually appoints four or five members to undertake enquiries.

The **Enterprise Act 2002** gave the CC powers to investigate mergers and carry out market investigations into anti-competitive practices referred to it. It will then determine whether or not:

- a merger has caused or may be expected to cause a lessening of competition;
- any feature of a market prevents, restricts or distorts competition.

It was also given enforcement powers. For example, if an adverse effect of competition is identified or a merger is found to reduce competition the CC can:

- prohibit a merger from taking place;
- impose remedies which the businesses involved must then agree to carry out.

The CC will take into account any possible benefits of mergers before deciding on remedies.

The Competition Commission has been criticised in the past for a number of reasons.

- It has no powers to investigate on its own, only referrals.
- Investigations have taken a long time to complete.
- The limited number of staff has restricted the number of investigations that can be carried out.
- Many findings have favoured businesses and not consumers.

The European Union

The European Community has rules to ensure free competition in member countries. The European Commission is responsible for applying these rules, working closely with national governments.

- Article 81 of the Treaty of Rome prohibits anti-competitive agreements which may affect trade between member states and which prevent, restrict or distort competition in the single market. The Commission can grant exemptions if there are benefits from the practices, such as improved efficiency or the promotion of research and development.
- Article 82 prohibits the abuse of a dominant position which may affect trade between member states.

In 2004 the EU was to introduce major changes to the 1990 EU Merger Regulations. These set out the EU merger control regime, including how mergers were referred to and investigated by the European Commission. The changes included:

- a revision of merger regulation, including a simplification in the system of referrals to the European Commission by member states for investigation and vice versa, and allowing the Commission to impose higher fines on businesses that do not provide required information for investigations;
- setting guidelines on the appraisal of horizontal mergers, ie mergers between competitors;
- setting non-legislative measures to improve decision-making, to be contained in a set of 'best practices'.

Regulatory bodies

During the 1980s and 1990s, former state monopolies were sold off as part of the government's privatisation programme. The aim was to increase efficiency in these firms by removing them from the public sector. However, the creation of private monopolies led to concern that these newly privatised firms would take advantage of their market position and exploit consumers. Regulatory bodies have been set up to regulate them as a result.

- Ofwat (the Office of Water Services). This was set up in 1989 to regulate the water and sewerage industry.
- Orr (the Office of the Rail Regulator). This was set up in 1993 to regulate the rail industry.
- Ofgem (the Office of Gas and Electricity Markets). This was set up in 1999 from the former regulatory bodies for the gas (Ofgas) and electricity (Offer) industries. It regulates the gas and electricity markets.
- Ofcom (the Office of Communications) regulates both the telecommunications industry (landlines and mobiles) as well as the broadcasting industry (radio and television).

The regulatory bodies have many different powers, but perhaps two main functions.

- To operate a system of price controls. The regulatory authorities for water, gas and electricity and telecommunications have operated according to a Retail Price Index RPI plus or minus formula. This allows the business to set its prices based on average rises in prices, which are then adjusted upwards or downwards. So if the regulator felt that prices needed to be controlled and reduced it is likely to set a RPI minus figure.
- To help bring about the introduction of competition wherever this might be possible. In some respects, this is more difficult than implementing price controls. This is because telephone lines, gas pipelines, water pipes and the National Grid are examples of **natural monopolies**. If every house, factory and office were connected with a number of different water pipes or telephone lines from which to choose, the costs within these industries would rise significantly. It therefore makes sense for the regulated business to operate such services.

However, there is no reason why other businesses should not be allowed to transmit their power, gas, telephone calls or water down the existing National Grid, gas pipeline network, telephone lines and water pipes. Indeed, this is the way

KEYTERMS

Legal monopoly – in the UK, any business with over 25 per cent of the market.
Anti-competitive practices or restrictive trade practices – any attempt by businesses to prevent competition.

in which competition has been introduced into these industries. A range of rail passenger businesses such as Virgin and First North Western are, for example, able to operate services on railways lines controlled by Railtrack.

Regulating other businesses

Other businesses are also controlled by regulatory bodies. The Financial Services Authority (FSA) is responsible for regulating the performance and behaviour of businesses operating in the financial services industry, such as insurance and pensions companies. This is an industry which has aroused suspicion in the past due to scandals regarding the mis-selling of pensions to consumers, for example. The FSA was set up as an independent non-government body but given statutory powers under the **Financial Services and Markets Act 2000.**

It is the threat of government regulation which causes many industries to 'keep their own house in order' by establishing their own regulatory bodies. The Advertising Standards Authority is an example of a self-regulatory body for the advertising industry. The European Petroleum Industry Association (EUROPIA) regulates conduct by businesses operating in the European petroleum producing industry.

KNOWLEDGE

1. What is meant by the term caveat emptor?
2. For what reasons might consumers need more protection today?
3. List five main consumer protection acts.
4. In what ways might businesses be affected by consumer protection legislation?
5. What are the possible advantages and disadvantages of monopolies?
6. How is a monopoly defined by UK law?
7. What is the role of the Competition Commission?
8. How does EU legislation affect monopolies and mergers?
9. What are the main bodies set up to regulate the former state monopolies?
10. State two other industries that are regulated.

Case Study: Airline Cartel

European and US antitrust officials have raided the offices of British Airways, Lufthansa, Air France-KLM, Cargolux and other air-cargo companies as part of a transatlantic cartel probe. The raids followed allegations that the airlines had violated Article 81 of the EC treaty which outlaws cartels, price fixing and market sharing.

The rise in fuel prices over the previous 18 months has pushed up passenger and freight charges across the airline industry, leading cargo operators to impose surcharges on customers. Surcharges have also been imposed for new security measures. Groups representing customers said that these surcharges could sometimes exceed the actual transport cost. They also said that the surcharges had been very similar across different airlines.

If found guilty, the airlines face a maximum fine of ten per cent of global annual turnover from the European Commission. In addition they could be fined by US anti-trust authorities. All the airlines whose offices were raided denied operating any form of anti-competitive practices and have promised to co-operate fully with the competition authorities. The European Commission stressed that 'the fact that the European Commission carries out such inspections does not mean that the companies are guilty of anti-competitive behaviour'.

Source: adapted from the *Financial Times* 15.2.2006; www.theAustralian.news.com.au 16.2.2006; www.ogisticsmanager.com 15.2.2006.

British Airways was today fined £270m after admitting price fixing on fuel surcharges on its long-haul flights. The Office of Fair Trading imposed a fine of £121.5 million after British Airways admitted that between August 2004 and January 2006 it colluded with Virgin Atlantic over the surcharges, added to ticket prices in response to rising oil prices, which increased from £5 to £60. The OFT said that on at least six occasions Virgin and BA discussed or informed each other about proposed changes to the surcharges, rather than setting levels independently as required by competition law.

Within hours of the OFT announcement, British Airways was hit by a $300m fine from the US Department of Justice. It was fined not just for fixing fuel surcharges for passengers but also for colluding with other airlines over cargo fuel surcharges. Korean Air was also fined $300m as part of the conspiracy. US Attorney General William W Mercer said: 'When British Airways, Korean Air and their co-conspirators got together and agreed to raise prices for passenger and air cargo fares, American consumers and businesses ended up picking up the tab for their illegal conduct. Today's enforcement actions demonstrate that the anti-trust division will investigate and prosecute illegal cartel activity - here and abroad - in order to ensure that American consumers and businesses are not harmed by illegal cartel activities.'

Source: adapted from Guardian Unlimited, 1.8.2007.

(a) Discuss the possible impact on both consumers and business customers of the decision by regulatory authorities to fine airlines. (40 marks)

(b) Evaluate whether consumers would be better off if there were no laws or regulations covering monopoly and anti-competitive practices. (40 marks)

122 Protection at work

Why is protection needed?

Why might a business protect its employees? There are certain laws protecting people in the workplace. Legislation has laid down rules about:

- health and safety;
- employment protection (dismissal, redundancy and leave of absence);
- wage protection;
- recruitment, selection and training.
- data about employees.

This legislation provides guidelines and acts as a constraint on how a business makes decisions. In addition, from a purely practical point of view, it makes sense for a business to protect its workers. Satisfied employees are far more likely to help a business achieve its goals. A business may also feel it has a moral obligation to protect employees. As their employer, it should look after their interests in the workplace.

Health and safety at work

Providing a healthy and safe environment can mean many things. It could include some of the following.

- Providing and maintaining safety equipment and clothing.
- Maintaining workplace temperatures.
- Ensuring adequate work space.
- Ensuring adequate washing and toilet facilities.
- Guaranteeing hygienic and safe conditions.
- Providing breaks in the work timetable.
- Providing protection for the use of hazardous substances.
- Providing protection from violence, threats or bullying.
- Providing a relatively stress free environment.

It is likely that the conditions for a healthy and safe environment will vary depending on the nature of the task carried out. Ensuring the health and safety of a mine worker will require different decisions by a business from protecting an office worker. Although both must be protected from adverse effects of equipment, for example, protection is likely to be different.

Businesses must protect people outside the workplace who might be affected by activities within it, eg those living near a chemical or industrial plant. They must also protect visitors or customers to shops or premises.

Health and safety legislation

In the UK, laws to protect employees have been passed for over 100 years. There are also many regulations concerning health and safety at work which are updated from time to time as work conditions change. In addition, businesses may follow codes of practice designed to protect workers.

The Health and Safety at Work Act, 1974 The aim of the **Health and Safety at Work Act, 1974** is to raise the standard of safety and health for all individuals at work, and to protect the public whose safety may be put at risk by the activities of people at work.

Every employer is required to prepare a written statement of their general policy on health and safety. Employees must be advised of what the policy is. Management have the main responsibility for carrying out the policy. In the case of negligence, proceedings can be taken against an individual manager as well as against the business. The Act also places a duty on employees while they are at work to take reasonable care for the safety of themselves and others. The employee is legally obliged to comply with the safety rules drawn up by management. Employers or employees who fail to comply can be taken to court and fined. Part of the Act requires a business to give training, information, instruction and supervision to ensure the health and safety at work of employees.

The Act is backed up by the Health and Safety Executive (HSE) and the Health and Safety Commission (HSC), which are responsible for seeing that the Act is carried out. Health and safety inspectors are appointed to make sure the law is being carried out. They have the power to enter employers' premises, carry out examinations and investigations, take measurements, photographs and recordings, take equipment and materials and examine books and documents. The HSE/HSC have the power to issue **codes of practice** to protect people in various situations, for example:

- the protection of individuals against ionising radiation;
- the control of lead pollution at work;
- time off for training of safety representatives;
- control of substances hazardous to health (various).

The Health and Safety at Work Act is the main Act which allows new regulations to be brought in as appropriate.

Question 1.

John Smart was employed by Jones and Hadden, a paper merchant in Oxford. The company buys paper in bulk from foreign mills and distributes it to users in the UK. Trade and paper prices began to fall and the company was looking for ways of cutting costs. John had been employed as warehouse manager to control the arrival and delivery of paper. With no prior consultation, one Monday in March, a director informed John that his services were no longer required. John was told that he was to be made redundant at the end of the week. The following week the company employed a younger man to do John's job, at a far lower salary.

(a) Comment on the fairness of John's dismissal.

(b) What advice would you give John about his next course of action?

Table 1: UK/EU health and safety regulations

Manual Handling Operations Regulations, 1992 (Directive 90/269/EEC) Relate to the transport and handling of loads.
Workplace (Health, Safety and Welfare) Regulations, 1992 (Directive 89/654/EEC) Relate to the requirements of conditions at work, such as maintenance, ventilation, space and rest facilities.
Personal Protective Equipment at Work Regulations, 1992 (Directive 89/656/EEC) Relate to protective clothing and equipment.
Health and Safety (Display Screen Equipment) Regulations, 1992 (Directive 90/270/EEC) Relate to the use of computer screens.
Safe Use of Work Equipment, Provision and Use of Work Equipment Regulations, 1998 (Directive 89/655/EEC) Relate to the safe use of equipment and machinery.
The Management of Health and Safety at Work Regulations, 1999 (Directive 89/391/EEC) Relate to the assessment of risk and the implementation of health and safety arrangements to keep employees safe.
The Maternity and Parental Leave Regulations, 1999 (Directive 96/34/EEC) Relate to time off work for mothers and fathers when children are born.
Control of Asbestos at Work Regulations, 2002 Relate to the assessment and control of risk associated with asbestos on premises.
The Control of Substances Hazardous to Health Regulations, 2003 Relate to the handling, use and control of substances used in production which might affect the health of workers, such as nuclear fuel or chemicals.
The Work at Height Regulations 2005 (and amendments 2007) Relate to those who work at height. Place duties on employers to protect employees by ensuring risks and equipment are assessed and controlled and work is planned and organised.

UK and EU regulations There is a number of regulations relating to health and safety in the UK. Regulations are introduced to cope with new work situations. Increasingly UK regulations are influenced by European Union (EU) directives, which are agreed by member countries of the EU.

The **Working Time Regulations, 1998** were important regulations introduced into the UK as a result of an EU directive which addressed concerns over the problems caused by long work hours. They provided a number of rights for most employees including:

- a maximum working week of 48 hours a week;
- 4 weeks annual paid leave a year;
- 11 consecutive hours' rest in any 24 hour period;
- a 20 minute rest break after 6 hours' work;
- a limit of an average 8 hours' work in any 24 hours for night workers.

The regulations were amended in 2003 to include some groups that were previously excluded, such as 'non-mobile workers in road, rail and sea transport'. In 2003 the UK was the only EU country with an opt-out clause, which allowed employees to work longer than the 48 hour a week limit if they and their employer both agree.

Table 1 shows some examples of regulations which affect UK and EU businesses.

Employment protection

Employees are entitled to a contract of employment when they are first appointed to a job. The contract of employment is an agreement between the employer and the employee on the terms and conditions under which the employee will work. An employee may be able to claim for a breach of contract by the employer. Employees are also protected by legislation against discrimination.

The **Employment Relations Act, 1999** stated that employees who have worked for an employer for a year had a right not to be unfairly dismissed. It also aimed to introduce 'family friendly policies', such as parental leave for people adopting a child, and to remove limits on awards for unfair dismissal. Certain people cannot claim unfair dismissal, such as an independent contractor or freelance agent, who are not employees.

There is a number of reasons why employees might be dismissed which may be **unfair** dismissal under the conditions of the Act (and its amendments).

- Because they were trying to become or were a member of a trade union. Alternatively, because they refused to join or make payments to a union.
- On the grounds of pregnancy, even though she was able to do the job.
- Making workers redundant without following the correct procedure. This is dealt with later.
- As a result of a transfer of a business, such as when one business is bought by another. However, if the business can prove it was for economic, technical or organisational reasons, it may be considered fair.
- For refusing to work on a Sunday. The **Sunday Trading Act, 1994** gives shop workers the right not to be dismissed for refusing to work on Sundays.

There are reasons why dismissal may be **fair**. The employer must have a valid reason and must act 'reasonably' when dealing with this reason.

- The employee is incapable of doing the job or is unqualified.
- 'Misconduct' of the employee, such as persistent lateness (minor) or theft (major).
- The employer is unable to employ the worker. For example, a lorry driver may no longer be employed if he has lost his driving licence.
- Any other substantial reason. For example, false details may have been given on the job application form.
- Redundancy can take place if the employer needs to reduce the workforce. This could be because a factory has closed or there is not enough work to do. The job must have **disappeared**. In other words, it is not redundancy if

another worker is hired as a replacement. Certain procedures must be followed by employers. They must consult with trade unions over any proposed redundancy. If the union feels the employer has not met requirements, it can complain to a tribunal. Employees are entitled to a period of notice, as well as a redundancy payment based on how long they have been in continuous employment.

If a worker feels that he has been unfairly dismissed, he can take his case to an **employment tribunal**. This is dealt with in the next section. For example, a tribunal may decide that an employee who resigns as a result of the employer's actions has been **constructively** dismissed. To do this the employer must have acted in a way that is a substantial breach of the employment contract. An example might be where the employer demoted a worker to a lower rank or lower paid position for no reason.

Unfair dismissal - what to do

If an employee feels that he has been unfairly dismissed, what can he do about it? It may be possible for a worker and a business to settle the dispute voluntarily. If not, the employee may decide to complain to an **employment tribunal.** Figure 1 shows the stages involved in this.

The complaint must be received within three months of the end of contract. A notice of application is sent to the employer asking if they wish to contest the case. Details of the case are then sent to the **Advisory, Conciliation and Arbitration Service** (ACAS). Its role is to help settle the dispute before it reaches a

Figure 1: How a complaint against unfair dismissal is dealt with

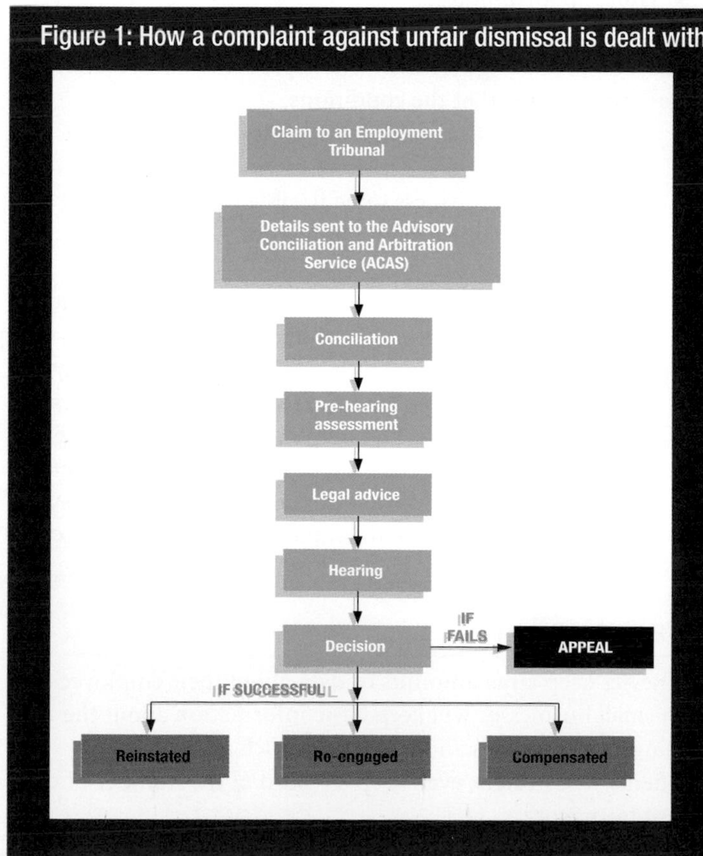

tribunal through conciliation.

Before the complaint does reach a tribunal, there may be a pre-hearing assessment. If either party has a case that is not likely to succeed, they can be told and also informed that they may be liable for costs. The aim of this stage is to 'weed out' hopeless cases.

Once a complaint goes to a hearing at a tribunal, the employee is entitled to legal advice. After the hearing the tribunal will make a decision. If this is in favour of the employee then the tribunal can order:

- the employee to be reinstated in the same job;
- the employee to be re-engaged in another job;
- compensation to be paid.

It is possible to appeal against a tribunal's decision. This will be heard by the Employment Appeal Tribunal. An employee who disagrees with the decisions of an **employment tribunal** and an appeal tribunal may take his or her case to the European Court of Justice (ECJ). This is the highest court of appeal under EU law. If a case is upheld, then UK businesses must comply with its decision as the UK is an EU member.

Wage protection

The main legislation relating to pay in the UK is the **Wages Act, 1986.** This sets out conditions for payments to workers and deductions from wages. Wages are defined as any sum paid to the worker by the employer in connection with the job. This includes fees, bonuses, commission, sick pay, gift tokens or vouchers. Certain payments, such as redundancy payments, expenses or loans are not included.

Deductions made from wages that are covered by the Act include:

- those that must be taken or are agreed upon, such as income tax or National Insurance;
- those shown in the contract of employment;
- those agreed by the worker in writing, such as trade union payments;

providing that these are the agreed amounts. If the employer deliberately decides not to pay part of a worker's wages, then employees can complain to a tribunal. This is a similar process to complaints about dismissal.

Wage protection is also provided through Acts which apply to other areas of employment protection. For example:

- the equal treatment of men and women is covered by the **Equal Pay Act, 1970**
- payment during maternity or paternity leave is covered in the **Employment Act, 2002.**

The minimum wage

The **National Minimum Wage Act, 1998** introduced a minimum wage for workers in the UK. It is unlawful to pay a worker below the rate set for the minimum wage. The National Minimum Wage is lower for young workers below the age of 22.

Why did the government want to introduce a minimum wage?

- To prevent poverty. It would prevent workers being paid

Question 2.

The government has announced an increase in the national minimum wage from October from £5.52 to £5.73 for workers over 22, while for 18 to 21-year-olds it will increase from £4.60 to £4.77.

Industry would have liked to see much lower increases. For example, the British Retail Consortium (BRC) said that its members would find it difficult to absorb the new costs. Since 1999, when it was first introduced, the national minimum wage has risen faster than the rate of average earnings increases. Even though this year's increase is in line with the increase in average earnings, Richard Dodd, head of media for the British Retail Consortium, said: 'The danger is it will affect the growth of retail employment, so fewer jobs will be created. Obviously there's a whole range of costs that are rising for retailers which are creating pressures for them and things like rents, rates, service charges, tax bills and fuel bills are all amongst them.' He said that in the retail sector expenses such as training and overtime could be cut back to make way for the increasing cost of paying workers the new minimum wage.

Trade unions welcomed the announced increased. The TUC general secretary, Brendan Barber, said: 'The Low Pay Commission (LPC) was right to withstand pressure from business warning of economic trouble ahead. The truth is that employers will be able to absorb these sensible increases without too much difficulty. The LPC must continue to recommend the highest minimum wage increases that can be sustained as it provides very important protection for low paid workers.'

Paul Myners, chairman of the Low Pay Commission, which sets the minimum wage, said: 'Despite many predictions to the contrary, job numbers in the industries most affected by the minimum wage have grown, and grown significantly, over the same period.'

Source: adapted from www.cv-library.co.uk 28.3.2008; www.guardian.co.uk 5.3.2008.

(a) How does the national minimum wage affect low paid workers?

(b) Discuss, using evidence from the data, the possible impact of the rise in the national minimum wage in October 2008 on a chain of department stores.

very low wages by employers.
- To reduce inequality between the pay of men and women. Women often work in low paid full time or part time jobs.
- To benefit businesses. Greater equality and fairness should motivate employees, reduce staff turnover and improve workers' productivity.

Some businesses argue that raising the wages of low paid workers increases their costs. To pay the higher wages, a business may need to make other workers unemployed or take on fewer new workers, particularly younger workers or people just starting work.

The Social Chapter

The European Union's Social Chapter is an attempt to encourage minimum wages and conditions of work in member countries. It was argued that a business may attempt to respond to falling profits or greater competition by cutting costs. This could lead to poor pay and work conditions for employees. To prevent this, member countries outlined an agreement which covered such areas as:
- a limit on hours of work;
- 'fair and reasonable' rewards;
- minimum wages;
- free collective bargaining;
- access to training;
- workers' involvement in company decision making;
- health and safety;
- union recognition;
- equal opportunities.

The UK signed up to the EU Social Chapter in 1997, with the election of a Labour government. The previous Conservative government argued that the conditions:
- restricted a business's ability to reduce wages when necessary;
- did not allow a business to be flexible when employing workers and making them redundant;
- would increase costs.

When the UK signed up, UK laws would have to be changed to comply with the conditions of the Social Chapter. For example, the number of hours to be worked by most employees must be limited to 48 hours, part-time and full-time workers would be given equal rights, and employees would have a right to paid holidays each year. Other changes would include the introduction of **European works councils** (EWC) in businesses, to negotiate workers' wages with employers, and the setting of a minimum wage as discussed in the previous section.

Data protection

Businesses keep large amounts of data about their employees. Even small businesses will keep basic information about the earnings of employees and deductions such as pension payments. They might even keep a record of the number of days absent from work.

Large public limited companies will have a huge amount of

information about the many employees who work for the organisation. This might include numerical information such as salaries. It might also include written reports, such as an annual review of an employee's progress written by his or her manager. Their application forms are also likely to be kept on record, as well as any disciplinary procedures that have been carried out as a result of their behaviour at work.

Much of the data held by businesses about employees is sensitive, personal information. Increasingly it is being stored on computer files or disks. Businesses must make sure that this information is protected so that it is only available to those with the authority to see it.

The **Data Protection Act, 1998** protects information about employees which is kept by businesses. Any business processing data about employees must comply with a number of principles. There are eight principles put in place to make sure that the information is handled properly. They say that data must be:

- fairly and lawfully processed;
- processed for limited purposes;
- adequate, relevant and not excessive;
- accurate;
- not kept for longer than is necessary;
- processed in line with employees' rights;
- secure;
- not transferred to countries without adequate protection.

Employees have the right to see information that employers keep about them under the Act. They can also request that incorrect information is removed, prevent the processing of information under certain circumstances, stop direct marketing to themselves using the information and claim compensation for misuse.

Question 3.

In 2003 Black & Decker, the tool manufacturing company, introduced software which would allow it to monitor e-mails sent by its employees. A spokesperson for the company said that it had become increasingly aware of the dangers of email misuse as it raises serious issues regarding employee productivity, corporate privacy and legal liability. The software, Mailmeter, will allow the company to generate reports about the amount of e-mail traffic and the domain names of the computers sending and receiving e-mails, without reading the content of e-mails. It is often suggested that using such software helps IT departments to adhere to the law regarding employee privacy.

However, if the business does deem it necessary to analyse e-mail content for disciplinary procedures it must be aware of the data protection law. It must follow strict guidelines if any use of information that is found is to be considered lawful.

Source: adapted from *Computer Weekly*, 28.4.2003.

(a) Explain ways in which the use of the software by Black & Decker might:

(i) help it comply with the law relating to the protection of employees;

(ii) lead to the breaking of the law regarding the protection of employees.

To what extent will a business protect its employees?

There are strong arguments to support the protection of employees by their employers.

- Businesses that protect their employees are likely to have a healthy and motivated workforce, free from accidents, injury and illness.
- A business which breaks the law may be ordered to pay compensation and fined. Over the period 1993-2003 a TUC report stated that unions had won over £3 billion injury compensation for workers. In 2001, £305 million was paid out in injury cases for over 39,000 employees.
- The loss of employees due to lack of protection may require costly recruitment of new employees.
- The work of injured employees may need to be covered by part time employees, which is an extra cost.
- Employees off sick or injured may cause disruption, lost production, the missing of deadlines or serious delays.
- Poor work conditions may affect the productivity of employees and the business, and profits.
- Businesses that do not protect employees may get a poor reputation, which could affect the quality of future applicants.

However, some businesses still fail to protect their employees adequately. Perhaps the main reason for this is the cost involved in protection. Buying safety equipment, changing work practices to ensure safety, setting up safety courses, ensuring legislation is met, and filling in the many forms associated with ensuring safety are time consuming and costly activities. Small businesses in particular find it difficult to keep up with constant changes in safety laws and requirements. They might even decide that it is worth taking the risk that accidents will not occur or that they will not be found out breaking the law. As long as these things do not happen, they can save money by not spending to protect their workers completely.

KNOWLEDGE

1. State five types of health and safety dangers that may exist in business.
2. Briefly explain three pieces of legislation regarding health and safety at work.
3. Under what circumstances might dismissal be:
   (a) fair;
   (b) unfair?
4. What is the role of an industrial tribunal in protecting the employee at work?
5. 'An employee without a strong case for unfair dismissal may face problems if a tribunal finds against them.' Explain this statement.
6. State two pieces of legislation affecting the wages of employees in UK businesses.
7. What does the European Social Chapter aim to achieve?
8. Discuss two effects that signing the Social Chapter may have on the business of a country that signed the agreement.
9. What is meant by data protection?
10. State three advantages to a business of protecting its workers.

Case Study: Airline Cartel

Wienerberger Ltd, the world's largest clay brick and tile manufacturer, has pleaded guilty to two breaches of the Control of Substances Hazardous to Health Regulations 2002. This follows an incident on May 15, 2007 at its Todhills Works, Country Durham, which resulted in one of its employees being hospitalised after inhaling fumes. The company had failed to carry out an assessment of the risks from metal fumes from doing a job and hadn't taken steps to control any resultant exposure. Bishop Auckland Magistrates' Court imposed total fines of £2,000 and ordered £8,516 in costs to be paid.

Source: adapted from Health and Safety Executive Press Release, 11.4.2008.

Everest Ltd, Potters Bar, was fined £6,000 with £15,963.25 costs at Luton Magistrates' Court today after pleading guilty to breaching health and safety law including Work at Height Regulations 2005. The prosecution arose following inspections in 2006 when workers were working at height from mobile tower scaffolds without suitable protection to prevent them from falling. The same company was recently fined £4,000 when one of its employees fell from the platform on which he wasworking.

Source: adapted from Health and Safety Executive Press Release, 30.4.2008.

Businesses are wasting thousands of pounds on excessive health and safety measures thanks to bad advice from rogue consultants, an influential group of MPs has warned. The cross-party Work and Pensions Select Committee's report on health and safety in workplaces said that the government should introduce a system for regulating experts to stop firms introducing unnecessary red tape.

Source: adapted from *The Scotsman*, 20.4.2008

Bob Edmiston, one of the Midland's richest entrepreneurs, has called for the regulatory burden on small businesses to be lifted. He said: 'I think our bureaucracy has just gone crazy. In industrial tribunals there is no consequence of people bring vexatious claims, which are totally untrue. These things have happened in the past and can ruin an employer. I've had a managing director have to spend a week preparing before a tribunal and then the person dropped out. That's alright for a big company with a human resources department, but it could be ruinous for a smaller one. All this makes it very difficult for a small company. I'm all in favour of protecting employees and health and safety, but this has all gone too far. Bureaucracy is my biggest bugbear. If you're having to look over your shoulder all the time, it takes away the time you can spend on a business. Managing people becomes your biggest role.'

Source: adapted from *The Birmingham Post*, 15.4.2008.

(a) 'Health and safety legislation should be repealed because it is damaging business interests.' Do you agree? Justify your answer using evidence from the data. (40 marks)

123 Equal opportunities

What are equal opportunities?

Businesses make choices when recruiting staff and also when selecting staff for training or promotion. Choosing one candidate rather than another is known as DISCRIMINATION. If a man is chosen rather than a woman, when they are both equally qualified, the business has discriminated in favour of the man and against the woman.

Some discrimination is legal and may be considered reasonable. For example, a business may choose a candidate for the post of quality controller in a meat factory because he has ten years experience, rather than a school leaver. However, if another person with experience did not get the job because she was a woman, or from an ethnic minority, this is illegal in the UK. It could also be said to be unreasonable. The rest of the unit will use the term discrimination in this way. Discrimination occurs not only in selection, but in areas such as training, promotion and wages.

EQUAL OPPORTUNITIES mean that everyone has the same chance. In other words, a candidate or employee is not discriminated against because of their sex or race. UK legislation helps to promote this. So do EU laws. These are examples of **individual labour laws** aimed at protecting individuals at work. **Collective labour laws** deal with legislation affecting employee groups such as trade unions.

Why are businesses concerned about equal opportunities? Giving everyone the same chance can affect the productivity, costs and organisation of a business.

Reasons for discrimination

There are certain groups of individuals in society and in business that are arguably discriminated against. Such groups may include:

- women;
- people from ethnic minorities;
- disabled people;
- older people.

Discrimination may occur because of **unproven** ideas or stereotypes about certain groups, such as the following examples.

- Women might not want to take too much responsibility at work because of home commitments; women who are married are less likely to want to be relocated; women with children may be less reliable than men because their main responsibility is to their children.
- Members of certain ethnic minority groups could be difficult to employ because of problems with religious holidays.
- A person in a wheelchair may be less capable than a non-disabled person.
- Older people may be less adaptable, are not interested in coping with new technology and might work more slowly.

All these and many other unproven ideas can affect the way people view these groups during recruitment and selection, and when they are employed.

Women at work

Women form a large and increasing proportion of the working population. In 1979 women accounted for around 38 per cent of all people of working age in employment. By 2007, this had risen to nearly 46 per cent. There is still evidence to suggest that women are discriminated against in the work force.

- There are differences between the earnings of men and women. In 2007, the mean average hourly earnings of men excluding overtime were £14.98. For women it was £12.40 an hour.
- Certain industries, such as construction, still tend to have male majorities. Figure 1 shows that certain occupations, such as administration and secretarial work, tend to have greater percentages of females than males employed. Occupations in which females are mainly employed tend to be lower paid and occupations that are male dominated tend to be more highly paid.
- Occupations in which women are mainly employed tend to be low paid. Male dominated occupations tend to be more highly paid. For example, in 2002, 75 per cent of working women were in the five lowest paid sectors. In engineering and construction, 97 per cent of modern apprentices are men, earning £115 a week. In social care, 89 per cent of apprentices are women, earning around £60 a week.
- In 2007, 57 per cent of women in employment worked full time. For men, the figure was 89 per cent.
- The rate of employment among women with children under five is approximately three quarters that for women with no children. This perhaps suggests the problem finding jobs for women with young children.

On the other hand, it could be argued that the differences between men and women at work are getting smaller.

- There has been a growth in women's employment opportunities in recent years. The need for a more flexible workforce, equal opportunities legislation, demographic changes and the awareness of the role of women in the workforce have meant that business increasingly look to women to fill vacancies.
- Having children is perhaps less of a constraint than it used to be. Some businesses offer creche facilities or allow work at home to encourage women workers with children. Some women choose to pursue a career instead of having children or return to work after childbirth. Women are remaining in education longer or returning to study. This makes them

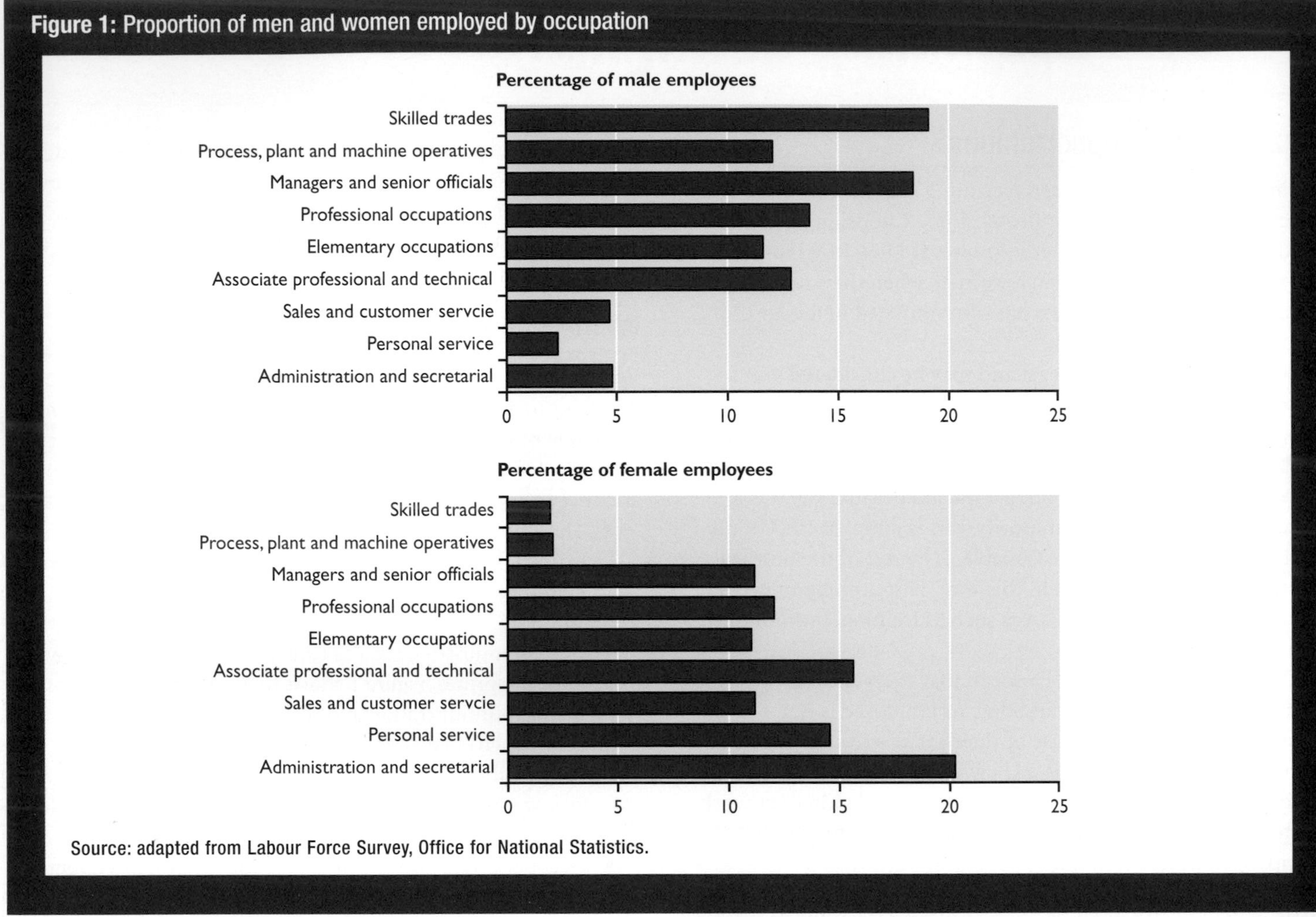

Figure 1: Proportion of men and women employed by occupation

Source: adapted from Labour Force Survey, Office for National Statistics.

more qualified for higher grade posts.

- The 'gender gap' in activity rates is getting smaller as Figure 2 shows. The proportion of women in employment or seeking work rose from 66 per cent to 73 per cent between 1984-2007. Over the same period it fell from 84 per cent to 83 per cent for men.

Legislation and guidance

In the UK, legislation and regulations exist to promote sexual equality at work.

Equal Pay Act The **Equal Pay Act 1970** stated that an employee (whatever their gender) doing the same or 'broadly similar' work as a member of staff of the opposite sex is entitled to equal rates of pay and conditions. The Act aimed to eliminate discrimination in wages and other conditions of work, such as holidays, overtime, hours and duties. The Equal Pay Act was amended in 1983 to allow female employees to claim equal pay for work of 'equal value' to that done by a man. The 1970 Act ruled that an employee should be paid equal pay for work which is 'like work' or 'work rated as equivalent' to that of another employee. But the 1983 amendment made it possible for equal pay to be claimed for work of equal value in 'terms of the

Figure 2: Economic activity rates by gender, aged 16+

Per cent
100
90
80
70
60
50
Males aged 16-64
Females aged 16-59
1971 75 80 85 90 95 00 05 07

Source: adapted from *Labour Market Statistics*, www.statistics.gov.uk.

demands made on her'. Such demands could include the effort, skills and decisions made by an employee. Whether the work was of equal value or not would be determined by job evaluation.

Sex Discrimination Act The **Sex Discrimination Act 1975** made it generally unlawful to discriminate either directly or indirectly against someone on grounds of their sex or being married. Direct discrimination is where an employer treats someone less favourably than another person because of their sex. An example could be where a woman was not employed because it was felt she would not fit in because of her gender. It would also include harassment at work. Indirect discrimination is where an employment condition is applied equally to men and women, but one gender has less chance of complying with it. An example might be if an employer insists on an employee being over, say, six feet tall when it is not necessary for the job. Discrimination is unlawful in areas such as job advertisements, selection, interviews, promotion, training, dismissal and terms of employment. In 1986 the Act was updated, removing restrictions on women's hours of work. This meant that women were more able to take jobs with flexible hours or shift work.

European Union law Businesses in the UK must also comply with European Union (EU) law concerning discrimination. **Article 141 of The Treaty of Rome**, for example, states that 'men and women should receive equal pay for equal work'. The **Equal Pay Directive** explains that equal pay means 'for the same work or for work which equal value is attributed'. **The Equal Treatment Directive** deals with all aspects of employment, promotion, training , work conditions and dismissal. It states that there should be 'no discrimination on grounds of sex, either directly or indirectly, particularly with reference to marital or family status'. Other influential directives include **The Parental Leave Directive**, which allows parental leave and unpaid leave to look after sick or disabled dependants, and **The Part-Time Workers Directive**, which states that part-time workers should be paid on a pro-rata basis to full-time workers. The **European Court of Justice** (ECJ) hears cases and passes rulings relating to sex discrimination in EU member countries.

Effects on business Legislation can have a number of implications for businesses. For example:

- advertisements must not discriminate on the basis of sex or marital status. This means that job titles should be sexless, as in 'cashier' or 'salesperson';
- there is a greater need for job analysis, job descriptions and person specifications. In particular, a person specification must not restrict the job to men or women, unless it is essential;
- interviews must be carried out in a structured way to help to limit any prejudice that an interviewer may have;
- people can not be selected for dismissal because they are male or female.

If employees feel that they have been discriminated against they can take their case to an **employment tribunal.** Under the **Employment Act 2002**, employees can use a questionnaire to request key information from their employer when they are deciding whether to bring a case. They might also take their claim to **court**. Businesses found to be discriminating might be ordered to put into practice measures to prevent it occurring. In some cases they may also be asked to pay compensation.

Question 1.

Advice page

'I work next to a male colleague in my office. He is on the same scale as me and is the same age. But I have recently found out that he is being paid far more than me. I have asked my employers about this. But I was told that although the job we do is similar in terms of decisions and responsibility, we do not do exactly the same job and so I do not have a case.'

'I recently arranged with my employers to have time off work to give birth to my daughter. I agreed a date when I would return to work. However, during the time I was off work my employers say that there has been a reorganisation in the department. All the other employees have a job. But the employers said that they were looking to make some staff redundant and as I was unlikely to be able to carry out the same duties as before with a young child to look after I no longer had a job.'

'Our employers have told us that the image of the company needs to be improved. They want staff to wear specially designed woollen jackets bearing the company logo. They say that these are smart and will help to promote the company image. However, the jackets are very heavy and will be extremely uncomfortable to wear in summer. The employers have stated that all women staff must wear the jackets. But they argue that men do not need to wear the jackets, as jackets are part of suits men wear, which are smart enough.'

Source: adapted from *Labour Research*.

(a) Suggest how the female employees in these businesses might argue a case of discrimination against their employers in a tribunal.

Equality and Human Rights Commission Employees can request help from the Equality and Human Rights Commission (EHRC), which has replaced the Equal Opportunities Commission (EOC). The Equality and Human Rights Commission is a government agency which:

- works with employers towards eliminating discrimination;
- tries to promote equal opportunities;
- helps employees making complaints;
- investigates complaints of discrimination;
- issues notices preventing a business from discriminating;
- reviews the Equal Pay Act.

In 1997 the EOC drew up a statutory code of practice on

Question 2.

In the 1990s targets were set for public services, such as the armed forces, the fire service and the immigration service, to employ workers from ethnic minority groups. The change in public services policy aimed to employ the same percentage of ethnic minorities as there were in the population, around 6 per cent. Nationally just 2 per cent of police officers were made up from ethnic minorities. In areas where ethnic minorities made up a higher percentage of the population, targets would be higher. For example, in parts of London they made up nearly 20 per cent of the population.

By 2003 it was suggested that nearly a third of public bodies had failed to comply with the requirement of the amended Race Relations Act. This set targets for improving race equality in services such as police forces. 1 in 10 public bodies had done nothing to comply with the law. Some organisations, however, had been successful in meeting the requirements. Examples included the London Fire Brigade, which had raised its profile amongst ethnic minorities by holding open days, events and visits in mosques and at festivals. It had also introduced mentoring to promote awareness and help employees from ethnic minorities to become integrated.

Source: adapted from *The Independent*, 30.10.2003.

(a) **Explain why it could be argued that discrimination exists in public services.**

(b) **Explain why the changes made by the London Fire Brigade may prove successful in removing discrimination against ethnic minorities.**

Figure 3: Rates of employment, unemployment and economic inactivity by ethnic group, 2002-2005

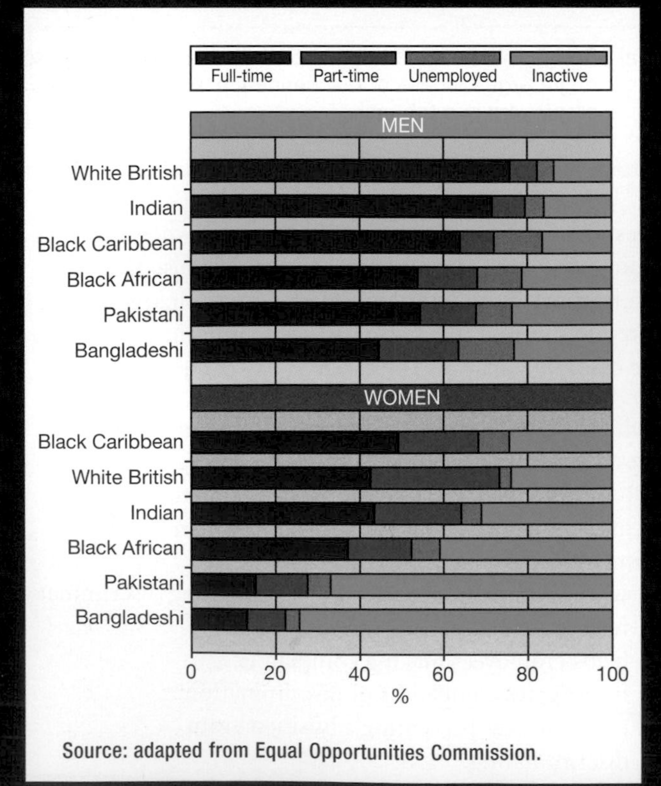

Source: adapted from Equal Opportunities Commission.

equal pay. This contained descriptions of how businesses could organise their pay systems to avoid unfair discrimination. In 2003 this was updated to take into account verdicts in recent cases of discrimination at tribunals and in courts.

Ethnic minorities

There is evidence that certain ethnic groups are discriminated against, often in recruitment and selection. Figure 3 shows that unemployment rates of ethnic minority groups are higher than those of whites and economic activity rates and employment rates are lower.

Legislation and guidance

Race Relations Act, 1976 An awareness of the position of ethnic groups and attempts to deal with DIVERSITY ISSUES have led to anti-discrimination legislation. The **Race Relations Act 1976** makes it generally unlawful to discriminate directly or indirectly on grounds of race. Racial grounds included colour, race, nationality or ethnic origin. Direct discrimination is where a person is treated less favourably compared to someone else on racial grounds. An example would be a person not being employed because it was felt they belonged to a racial group that might be unreliable. Indirect discrimination is where an employment condition is applied equally but a racial group has less chance of complying with it. An example would be not allowing the wearing of turbans, which would rule out Sikhs from being employed.

Under the Act an employer cannot discriminate on grounds of race:

- in making arrangements for deciding who should be offered the job;
- in the terms offered;
- in refusing or deliberately omitting to offer employment.

Effects on business The implications for the employer are similar to those of the Sex Discrimination Act. Advertisements should be worded so that there is no indication that some ethnic groups are preferred to others. Writing a job description and person specification will also be useful. The use of selection tests should be monitored. Many tests discriminate against people from minority backgrounds in the way they are designed. Also, people from some ethnic backgrounds may be at a disadvantage because the method of testing is alien to their culture.

The Act was amended in 2002. Protection was extended against racial discrimination by public authorities and public authorities, such as police forces and health trusts, were required to promote racial equality. In 2003 it was amended further to take into account the requirements of the **EU Race and Ethnic Origin Directive 2000**. For example:

- a wider definition of indirect discrimination would be used and people could make a claim against an employer even before they had been put at a disadvantage;
- people from ethnic groups had a legal right to claim against racial harassment.

Question 3.

Figure 4: People who think their job application was affected because they were too old, by age and sex, GB

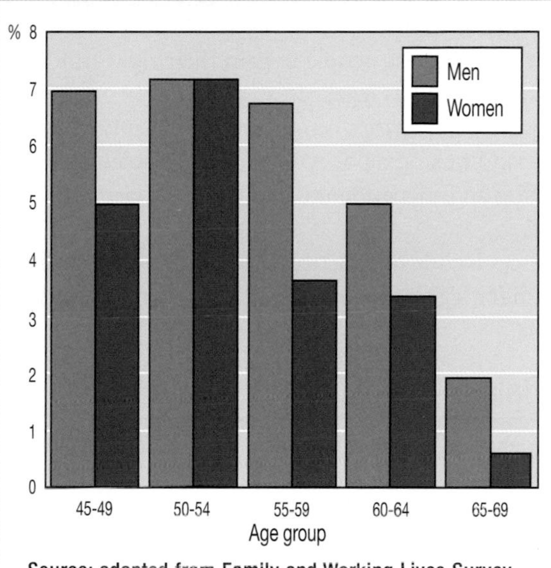

Source: adapted from Family and Working Lives Survey.

Figure 5: Percentage of older people with health problems, by age and sex, GB

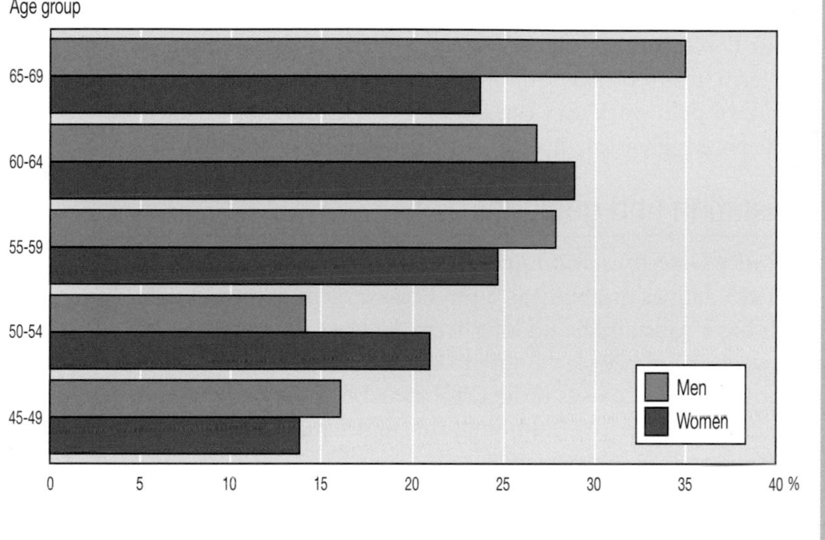

(a) Describe the trends taking place in Figures 4 and 5.

(b) How might these trends explain why age discrimination takes place?

Employees who feel that they have been discriminated against on grounds of race can take their case to an employment tribunal. In 2001 there were nearly 4,000 claims, a 280 per cent increase from 1997. However, the success rate at hearings was only 16 per cent compared to 65 per cent for redundancy cases and 28 per cent for sex discrimination.

Equality and Human Rights Commission The Equality and Human Rights Commission (which has replaced the Commission for Racial Equality), promotes 'fair treatment and equal opportunities for everyone regardless of race, colour, nationality or ethnic origin'. Its tasks include:

- giving information to staff who think they have been racially harassed;
- working with businesses to promote practices that ensure equal treatment;
- running campaigns to encourage organisations and people to create a just society;
- making sure all laws take into account race relations legislation.

It has the power to advise and assist people with complaints about racial abuse, conduct formal investigations and take legal action against advertisements and applications that racially discriminate.

The Equality and Human Rights Commission produces a **Race Relations Code of Practice** which gives practical guidance to help employers, trade unions, employment agencies and employees understand the provisions of the **Race Relations Act**. It provides guidance on:

- types of unlawful discrimination, such as an employer

Figure 6: Percentage of those either unemployed or wanting a job for all working aged people (16-59/64) by whether disabled or not disabled

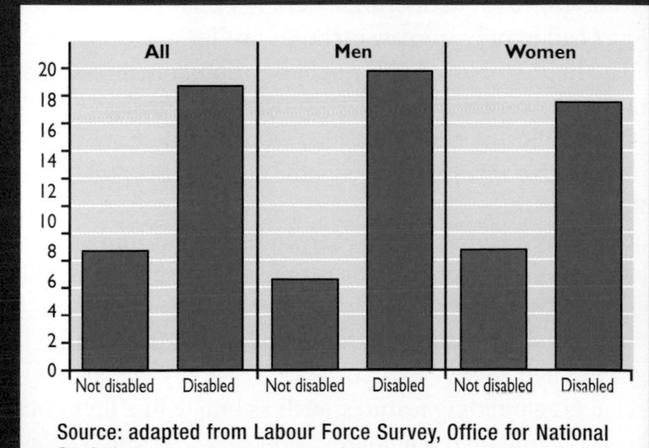

Source: adapted from Labour Force Survey, Office for National Statistics.

demanding higher language standards than are needed for the effective performance of the job;
- selection criteria that are relevant to the job to prevent subjective and racial discrimination occurring;
- training opportunities to gain the skills required for a job.

Disabled people

There are many different ways of defining disabled people. The Labour Force Survey (adjusted) defines them as 'those with a long-term health problem/disability that limits the kind or amount of paid work they can do'. Figure 6 shows that disabled people have higher unemployment rates than non-disabled.

Legislation and guidance

Disability Discrimination Act The **Disability Discrimination Act, 1995** defines disability as 'a physical or mental impairment which has a substantial and long-term (at least 12 months) adverse effect on people's ability to carry out normal day-to-day activities'. The Act makes it unlawful for a business (with 15 or more employees in 2003, although this figure may change) to discriminate against a person in:
- recruitment;
- selection or dismissal;
- the terms of employment offered;
- promotion, transfers, training or other benefits.

A business would discriminate if it treats one person **less favourably** than others for a reason relating to disability, unless the treatment is **justified**.

What is less favourable treatment? An example of discrimination might be if two people applied for a job as a translator, but a disabled person in a wheelchair did not get the job because of his disability, even though he was the better translator. Discrimination would also take place if a business asked the disabled person for a driving licence when no driving was involved in the job of translator. To avoid discrimination, a disabled person must be given the job if he is the best candidate.

When is less favourable treatment justified? There must be relevant and substantial (i.e. not trivial) reasons to treat people less favourably to avoid discrimination. For example, if the employer had to move to new premises just for one disabled candidate to be employed, this might be a substantial reason not to employ the worker. However, employers must make 'reasonable' adjustments for disabled workers. These are adjustments that involve relatively little cost or disruption. They might include:
- changing fixtures, fittings, furniture and equipment, such as modified telephones for people with hearing difficulties or workstations for people in wheelchairs;
- improving access to a building, such as adding a ramp for a wheelchair user;
- changing building features, such as braille in a lift to help a visually impaired employee;
- changing work conditions, such as allowing absences for treatment;
- providing extra training.

The Equality and Human Rights Commission The Equality and Humans Rights Commission (which has replaced the Disability Rights Commission) has a responsibility to eliminate discrimination against disabled people. Its main roles involve:
- providing advice and information for disabled employees, including a helpline;
- supporting disabled people to gain their rights under legislation as well as legal cases;
- organising conferences, campaigns and events to change the law and business policy to protect disabled people;
- providing an independent conciliation service for disabled people.

It also produces a code of practice which outlines the rights of employees under legislation and how business can meet these requirements.

Older people

There is evidence to suggest that older people are discriminated against.
- Age Concern suggests that the employment rate for people between the age of 50 and pension age is 70.9 per cent compared to 74 per cent for all adults under state pension age.
- Older workers are more likely to be working part-time. This is particularly the case for people over state retirement age. This might be because of choice. But it may also be because businesses are less wiling to employ older workers full-time.
- Older workers are less likely to receive training. In the early 2000s employees aged 16-19 were over twice as likely to have received job-related training than those aged 50-59/64.

Legislation and guidance

In the past, the main protection for older employees was against redundancy. For example, if they were made redundant they were often entitled to severance pay. In difficult periods, older people may be the first to be made redundant. They are sometimes persuaded to accept voluntary redundancy by taking early retirement.

There was also no specific protection against age discrimination when seeking employment and in training or promotion. However, cases taken to an employment tribunal have been won using sex or race discrimination in relation to age. For example, a case by an employee against the Civil Service bar on people aged over 32 was judged to discriminate against black people, since black employees were older than white employees at the time due to adult immigration.

Today, the **Employment Equality (Age) Regulations 2006** make it unlawful for employers to discriminate against a person on the basis of age. For example, it is unlawful not to give a job to a person aged 55 simply because of their age. Older workers cannot be harassed in the workplace, for example by being called names which relate to their age. They also cannot be victimised, for example by being refused training or promotion on grounds of age. However, there are exemptions in the Regulations. For example, young workers aged 18-21 can be given a lower National Minimum Wage than older workers. Employers can set a compulsory retirement age for their workers so long as that is no lower than age 65.

Some argue that there are actually advantages to a business in employing workers 'over 40'.

- The over 40s have greater experience and better judgement in decision making.
- The over 40s have already satisfied many of their needs for salary and status and are able to concentrate more on job responsibilities.
- The over 40s have a greater 'social intelligence' and the ability to understand and influence others.

B&Q, the chain of DIY stores, has recognised the benefits of employing older people, and has adopted a policy of hiring over 50s in its stores.

Why might businesses have equal opportunities policies?

Certain businesses operate an **equal opportunities policy**. This means that the business is committed to giving all applicants an equal chance of, say, selection, no matter what their sex, sexuality, race, age, marital status, religion or disability. The aim of such a policy is to remove discrimination in all areas of the business, including promotion, training and financial rewards, so that the culture of the organisation is not to exclude any employees whatever their race, colour, nationality or gender. Examples of employers that operate such a policy have included Ford and Kingfisher the retail group.

How will such a policy affect business?

- A business is far more likely to employ the 'best' person for the job if everyone is given an equal opportunity. The quality of applicants may also improve.
- Equal opportunities for training are likely to lead to a better qualified workforce in key positions, although the cost of training could increase.
- Workers may become better motivated if, for example, the chances of promotion are equal. They are also more likely to remain with the business, reducing staff turnover and costs.
- Production may need to be reorganised. This might include more flexible hours, job rotation or even job sharing. For example, an office job could be carried out by a mother in the morning (when children are at school) and by a male in the afternoon. A more flexible workforce may be better able to respond to change.
- There may be extra wage costs. Paying women equal wages to men will raise the total wage bill.
- Extra facilities may be needed. This can vary from ramps for wheelchairs to children's creches.
- Recruitment, selection and training procedures may have to change.
- The image of the business or jobs in it may have to change. This could improve the image to the customer. Rank Xerox, for example, found that jobs in the business were often seen as 'men's' jobs or 'women's' jobs and tried to change this.

It is argued that POSITIVE ACTION by employers is an important part of a good equal opportunities policy. Positive action describes a range of measures that can be taken to provide equality of opportunity. Examples of positive action are training to meet the needs of racial groups and encouragement to apply for particular jobs. Positive action is only lawful if people of particular groups are **under-represented** in work.

Effective equal opportunities policies must also take into account discrimination against which there is no legislation. It is suggested that employers discriminate against candidates with regional accents in interviews. A survey of recruitment specialists found that they felt Liverpool, Manchester and Birmingham accents were negative. 'Upper class accents' led to hostility in Scotland. Discrimination also takes place against people who employers perceive as being 'fat'. One NHS Trust, for example, set a size limit when recruiting which would have ruled out any candidate over 5 feet 10 inches, weighing over 12 stone 12 pounds.

Sexual orientation

The **Employment Equality (Sexual Orientation) Regulations 2003** came into force in 2003 in the UK to comply with an EU directive. They outlaw discrimination in employment based on sexual orientation towards people of the same sex, the opposite sex or the same sex and the opposite sex. This can be:

- direct discrimination (where someone is treated less favourably than another on grounds of sexual orientation);
- indirect discrimination (where a criterion or practice places people of a particular sexual orientation at a disadvantage);
- harassment or victimisation of people of a particular sexual orientation.

There are some exemptions, for example where the employer applies a particular sexual orientation to avoid conflict with religious convictions.

KEYTERMS

Discrimination – to make a selection or choice from alternatives, such as an applicant for a job. The term is often used to mean an illegal or unreasonable selection in the context of equal opportunities.
Diversity issues – relating to the proportion of the workforce that is made up of different ethnic groups.
Equal opportunities – where everyone has the same chance. In business this can mean the same chance of selection, promotion etc.
Positive action – measures geared towards improving the employment opportunities and training of groups that are under-represented at work.

KNOWLEDGE

1. State four groups that are often discriminated against by businesses.
2. Why might there have been an improvement in employment opportunities for women?
3. What are the main points of:
   (a) The Equal Pay Act;
   (b) The Sex Discrimination Act;
   (c) The Race Relations Act;
   (d) The Disability Discrimination Act?
4. What effect might equal pay legislation have on wages and opportunities for women in the UK?
5. State three ways in which an employer might avoid discriminating against minority groups when recruiting for jobs.
6. What advantages might candidates over 40 have for a business when compared to younger applicants?

Case Study: Sex discrimination in the city

The outgoing Equal Opportunities Commission, to be folded into the new Commission for Equality and Human Rights in a few months' time, has published a final report. The Commission found discrimination is still widespread in politics, employment and public services. For example, only 20 per cent of MPs are women. Retired women have 40 per cent less income than their male contemporaries. Women are paid 38 per cent less per hour than men for working part-time and 17 per cent for working full-time. Jenny Watson, the chairwoman of the Equal Opportunities Commission, said: 'Today, most women work, many men no long define themselves as breadwinners and both sexes often struggle to find the time they need to care for others in their lives. Despite many advances, Britain's institutions have not caught up with these changes. A country that channels women into low-paid work, fails to adequately support families and forces people who want to work flexibly to trade down in jobs pays a high price in terms of child poverty, family and low productivity.'

Source: adapted from *The Guardian*, 24.7.2007.

According to the Equal Opportunities Commission, women in the City are paid 43 per cent less than men, compared with a national pay gap of 22 per cent. A raft of cases taken to industrial tribunals also shows that sexism and discrimination is commonplace in many other ways for women workers in the City of London. City employment lawyers say that more than half their sex discrimination cases are to do with pregnancy and maternity.

Olivia, aged 40, who sued her bank in 2004, said that despite the veneer of equal opportunities 'in many ways, things are worse now for women than they used to be.' The sexism used to be crude and up front. Now, 'the sexism has gone underground and while several of the big banks look like they're making concerted efforts to recruit more women, in my experience, they're still not following through. It just makes it easier for them to fight cases when they can say: "look at our diversity training, we've ticked the box".'

Source: adapted from news.bbc.co.uk 15.6.2007.

Gill Switalski, 51, a top City lawyer has won a claim for sex discrimination after being driven from her job in an 18-month campaign of bullying. An employment tribunal ruled that she was the victim of sex discrimination and harassment by senior management at investment firm F&C. She is now suing the company for £19 million in damages.

Mrs Switalski was allowed to work at home on Fridays to look after her two disabled children. However, when a new manager was appointed, things changed. The new manager became 'fixated' with her working arrangements, repeatedly questioning why she was not in the office on Friday. At the same time, a male colleague, who was also allowed to work from home because he had special-needs children, was not continually interrogated about his work arrangements.

The new manager also continually questioned Mrs Switalski's expenses and quizzed subordinates about her working practices. He is said to have sidelined her in major projects, including the buying of a hedge fund, and she claimed that she was overlooked for top management positions.

F&C has denied any wrongdoing throughout the case.

Source: adapted from *The Telegraph*, 16.3.2008, *The Times*, 18.4.2008.

(a) 'It's more important to be making money than worrying about discrimination legislation.' Evaluate this statement from the perspective of the management of a top City of London financial institution. (40 marks)

(b) Discuss whether equal opportunities legislation is necessary to prevent discrimination in the workplace. (40 marks)

124 Pressure groups

Pressure groups

PRESSURE GROUPS are groups without the direct political power to achieve their aims, but whose aims lie within the sphere of politics. They usually attempt to influence local government, central government, businesses and the media. They aim to have their views taken into account when any decisions are made. Such influence can occur directly, through contact with politicians, local representatives and business people, or indirectly by influencing public opinion.

The use of pressure groups is one way in which stakeholders can exert influence over those making decisions within a business. Pressure groups can represent stakeholders directly involved with the business, such as employees or shareholders. They can also represent those not directly involved in the business, such as local communities or consumer groups.

There are many different types of pressure group and many ways of classifying them. One way is to divide groups into those which have a single cause and those which have a number of different causes.

- Single cause groups include the Campaign for Nuclear Disarmament (CND), Survival International and the NSPCC. Such groups mainly try to promote one cause.
- Multi-cause groups include trade unions, Greenpeace and the Confederation of British Industry. Pressure groups falling into this category tend to campaign on a number of issues. Trade unions, for example, have campaigned on a variety of issues, including the rights of the unemployed and improving the pay and conditions of their members.

Over the last few decades there has been a huge increase in the number of pressure groups and in the scale of their activities. Inevitably this has brought them into much closer contact with businesses. As a result there are now a number of groups which focus their activities upon businesses in general or particular businesses and industries.

- Environmental groups such as Friends of the Earth campaign to prevent businesses from polluting the environment.
- Consumer groups, such as the Consumers' Association seek to protect the rights of consumers in general. Others include The Football Supporters' Federation and rail users' groups.
- Local community groups may, for example, seek to prevent particular business developments or influence the policies of individual firms which operate in their local area.
- Employee groups, such as trade unions and professional associations, try to influence firms on issues such as conditions of work and pay levels.

Pressure groups vary in size. Some, like a local group aiming to divert a by-pass, may be made up of a few local people. Others are national organisations such as Greenpeace or the Royal Society for the Protection of Birds, or international groups such as Amnesty International.

Factors influencing the success of pressure groups

The success of any group, no matter how large or small, will depend on a number of factors.

- Finance and organisational ability. A pressure group with large funds will be able to spend on well organised campaigns. This has been a tactic employed by trade unions and professional groups. A well financed pressure group may also be able to employ full time professional campaigners. Such people are likely to organise more effective campaigns than enthusiasts devoting some of their spare time to such an activity.
- Public sympathy. Capturing the imagination of the public will play an important role in the ability of a pressure group to succeed. The Campaign for Real Ale has been effective in this respect. Almost single handedly they caused a change in the types of beer available in public houses and in the brewing methods of the big brewing companies. As with many successful campaigns, CAMRA's ability to present a clear and simple message to the public was vital.
- Access to politicians. Pressure groups which have access to politicians are able to apply pressure for changes in the law. For example, the International League for the Protection of Horses persuaded the government to ban the export of live horses for human consumption within the EU. Their contacts with politicians were vital in this campaign. The process of applying pressure on politicians is known as lobbying. It has become dominated by skilled professional lobbyists, the fees of whom are out of the range of all but the wealthiest of groups.
- Reputation. Gaining a favourable reputation amongst politicians can be important. The British Medical Association, for example, has a good reputation amongst a variety of politicians and is therefore often consulted on a variety of health matters by the government.

The effects of pressure groups on business

There is a number of ways in which pressure groups can affect firms.

- Pressure groups often seek to influence the behaviour of members of the public about a particular product, business or industry. Friends of the Earth attempts to persuade the public to use cars less and public transport or bicycles more in order to reduce emissions into the atmosphere. This campaign, if successful, would have important

implications for a wide range of firms involved in the transport industry.
- Political parties, through their representatives in Parliament, are able to pass laws which regulate the activities of businesses. Therefore it is not surprising that many pressure groups devote resources to lobbying politicians. An example of this is the attempt by the anti smoking group, Action on Smoking and Health (ASH), to change the law so that all advertising of tobacco is made illegal.
- The actions of pressure groups can reduce the sales of firms. This is often most successfully achieved when efforts are targeted at particular firms. Consumers are then called upon to boycott these firms.
- Firms can face increased costs as a result of the activities of pressure groups. This may involve new production processes or waste disposal methods. Firms may have to counteract any negative publicity from a pressure group. For example, many believe that the campaign to attract visitors to the Sellafield nuclear site was a result of the negative publicity from environmental groups.
- Businesses with a tarnished reputation as a result of pressure group activity may find it more difficult to recruit employees.

How might businesses react to pressure groups?
- By positively responding to the issues raised by pressure groups. It was argued that pressure from Greenpeace contributed to Shell's decision not to dump the Brent Spar oil platform in the North Sea in 1995. Instead it was dismantled and used to build a ferry quay in Norway. Similarly, local pressure groups have been successful in persuading some firms to change building plans and landscape nearby areas.
- Through promotions and public relations. Firms can attempt to counteract negative publicity through their own promotional and public relations work. For example, a number of oil companies which have been criticised for their impact upon the environment have sought to deal with this by promoting the 'greener' aspects of their industry, such as the availability of lead free petrol.
- A number of leading firms either lobby politicians themselves or pay for the services of professional lobbyists to represent their interests.
- Legal action. Where pressure groups make false allegations about a business, this can be dealt with by the legal system. For example, allegations by pressure groups that McDonald's were contributing to the destruction of the Amazonian rainforest were dealt with through legal action in the courts.

KEYTERMS

Pressure groups – groups of people without direct political power who seek to influence decision makers in politics, business and society.

KNOWLEDGE

1. What are the main types of pressure groups?
2. Give three reasons why a pressure group campaign may fail.
3. How can pressure groups affect the sales of a firm's product?

Case Study: Shac

Shac has acquired notoriety for its aggressive campaigning techniques. Not only has it targeted Huntingdon Life Sciences (HLS), but it has deliberately chosen to campaign against all the suppliers to HLS. Its campaign is now an international campaign from the United States to Sweden to Colombia.

It co-ordinates picketing of suppliers. For example, in 17 April 2008, it demonstrated against a number of supplier companies in Hampshire, Surrey and Middlesex. It used its website to report the following. 'Our final stop for the day was GlaxoSmithKline, who are frequent users of HLS, to a point where they would rather pay thousands of pounds for an injunction (to stop picketing) than drop the notorious torture lab. However, something tells me they were starting to have cold feet about their involvement as a customer as worried employees darted quickly from one building to the next and they had organised loads of security, more police than protesters and even safety cones. Your over the top security and running around with papers showing the injunction only makes us more determined, until next time.'

Source: adapted from www.shac.net.

Huntingdon Life Sciences (HLS) is a commercial animal testing laboratory in Huntingdon, near Cambridge. It is the largest commercial laboratory in the UK. It handles animal testing for both human and veterinary medical drug approval, as well as studies on agricultural chemicals, industrial chemicals and foodstuffs. It has clients worldwide, particularly in the UK, the US and Japan.

HLS has been criticised by animal rights and animal welfare supporters because they believe that there is animal abuse taking place at the laboratory. In 1999, video footage was recorded inside HLS which the company agreed showed breaches of animal protection laws. However, HLS claims that these breaches were isolated cases and the staff responsible were sacked and prosecuted. In response, animal rights activists set up a pressure group called SHAC (Stop Huntingdon Animal Cruelty). It aimed to close the HLS facility within three years. It campaigned using traditional techniques, such as picketing the laboratory, lobbying politicians and getting the media to cover its campaign sympathetically. Other action took place, although SHAC disclaimed all knowledge of these activities. They included threats made to members of Huntingdon staff and damage to cars. The managing director of the company was also attacked in his home in 2001. In 2004, the police recorded more than 100 attacks on staff at the company.

Suppliers were also targeted by SHAC for direct legal action. These ranged from suppliers of bottled gas to bankers and stockbrokers who bought and sold its shares. Some direct action included picketing and demonstrations. However, some staff at these companies also received death threats, had their cars vandalised and were intimidated. One campaign against a farm which breeds guinea pigs for use in animal experiments included the owner and family being bombarded with hate mail, telephone calls, hoax bombs and arson attacks.

The direct action against suppliers has been successful to some extent. Many suppliers targeted pulled out of their contracts with Huntingdon, although the company has managed to replace these suppliers with new ones. In the case of banking, the UK government authorised the Bank of England to run bank accounts for the company.

The UK government has provided more general support to HLS. In 2005, it tabled a new bill to make it a criminal offence to cause 'economic damage' though campaigns of intimidation. Companies which deal with the animal research industry will be protected from intimidation. Police will also be given powers to arrest anyone protesting outside the homes of scientists and to ban protesters from approaching a person's property for three months. HLS has lobbied government for stronger measures to be put in place, but accepts that the new law will help it fend off pressure from groups like SHAC.

Source: adapted from www.answers.com/topic/huntingdon-life-sciences; news.telegraph.co.uk 31.1.2005; en.wikipedia.org.

Two key messages in Shac's campaign are about freedom and action. On its website in 2008, for example, it says that: 'We strongly believe that you are either with us or against us. You either want life or death for the animals inside Huntingdon. The same people who are against us now would have criticised the campaigns against Apartheid, Poll Tax and many other just causes. Those who freed slaves over 100 years ago and the suffragettes who fought for women's' right to vote didn't ask for their right and freedoms by saying "Please sir ..." Instead they fought hard with many personal sacrifices and they won. We say to our critics what have you achieved after more than 150 years of doing things by official channels? Our message is simple: "You waste your time talking to liars with a vested interest if you want, but we will carry on saving lives, closing places, decimating animal abusers and winning".

Source: adapted from www.shac.net, May 2008.

Animal experimentation is controversial, but many scientists argue that it is necessary for research. Huntingdon Life Sciences (HLS), for example says: 'There are stages in any research programme when it is not enough to know how individual molecules, cells or tissues behave. The living body is much more than just a collection of these parts, and the need to understand how they interact or how they are controlled is essential. There are ethical limits to the experiments that we can perform in people, so the only alternative is to use the most suitable animal to study a particular disease or biological function.'

HLS argues that animal research has contributed to 'an ever growing number of successes and advances in the field of human medicine. For many years, humans have benefited from the healthcare advances that animal based research has achieved.' It also argues that 'key-hole surgery, organ transplantation, skin grafting and the latest research into the prevention of genetic diseases are all benefiting from animal research.'

Source: adapted from www.huntingdon.com.

(a) Discuss whether the pressure group, SHAC, has adopted an effective strategy to achieve its aims. (40 marks)

(b) You are the managing director of a small company. An animal research laboratory has approached you with a view to a contract to supply it with chemicals. Evaluate whether or not you should accept the contract and, if so, under what terms. (40 marks)

125 Business ethics

Ethics

ETHICS is about morality and doing 'what is right' and not 'what is wrong'. All businesses have to make many ethical decisions. Some are affected by the law. For example, it is illegal for businesses to dump waste by the roadside or send their drivers out on the road in unroadworthy vehicles. However, many ethical decisions have to be made without the help of the law. For example, should an employer allow a worker to take a day off work to look after a sick child and still be paid? Should a company stop buying goods from a factory in the Far East where it knows that work conditions are poor and wages are very low?

Making ethical decisions can be complicated because of differences of opinion. Some argue that it is wrong for businesses to manufacture toy guns to sell to children. Others suggest that they do no real harm. Muslim restaurant owners might face a dilemma about whether to sell alcoholic drink because the Koran forbids the drinking of alcohol. Other restaurant owners might not face such an ethical dilemma. Despite these differences, in many situations most people often take the same ethical stance. For example, most would agree that a company should not use employees' money in a pension fund to bail it out if it is making a loss.

Ethical issues

All businesses have to make ethical decisions. Should a self-employed plumber charge a senior citizen extra when a job takes longer than estimated? Should a finance manager delay payments if the business has cash flow difficulties?

Over the past 20 years, a number of issues have arisen for large firms which require decisions based on ethics.

The environment In countries like the UK or the USA, the law prevents businesses from polluting or destroying the environment. However, businesses must decide whether to adopt even more stringent measures to protect the environment. For example, should a business recycle materials, especially if this will lower profits? Multinational businesses often face lower environmental standards in Third World countries. Should they lower their own environmental standards in the Third World to take advantage of this?

Animal rights Some companies, such as pharmaceutical companies or cosmetics manufacturers, might use animals to test products. Animal rights groups argue this is unethical. Other companies, particularly food manufacturers or oil groups, can destroy habitats and endanger animals. Wildlife conservation groups argue against farming which destroys forests or oil installations, which can pollute the environment leading to the destruction of animal life.

Question 1.

Huntingdon Life Sciences (HLS) is a company which carries out scientific experiments on animals for commercial clients. Since the 1990s, it has been embroiled in a long running dispute with animal rights activists, led by SHAC (Stop Huntingdon Animal Cruelty) which want to close the company down. The long-term term aim of the animal rights activists is for all animal experimentation to be banned. Once Huntingdon Life Sciences has been closed, they will turn their attention to other companies engaged in animal experimentation in pursuit of that aim.

What has been unusual about the dispute is its length and ferocity. The company's main laboratory in Huntingdon is picketed every week. Workers and managers have been subject to threatening telephone calls. The managing director has been attacked with baseball bats at his home. Failing to close down the company, the protesters turned to shareholders and financial companies dealing with Huntingdon. Shareholders were picketed outside their homes. Stockbrokers and bankers were subject to a campaign of abuse. The result was that most shareholders sold their shares in the company, and the banks and stockbrokers in the UK refused to deal any more with Huntingdon. Today, the company's banking facilities are provided by the Bank of England. The campaign has spread to the USA where customers and financial institutions dealing with the company have been targeted. SHAC continues to organise demonstrations against any company which supplies HLS both in the UK and the USA as well as continental countries such as Sweden and France. The purpose of these demonstrations is to 'shame' the company into ceasing to have any commercial contact with HLS.

(a) Discuss whether Huntingdon Life Sciences can ever be an 'ethical' company.

(b) Evaluate whether customers, such as pharmaceutical companies developing new drugs, should continue to use Huntingdon Life Sciences.

Workers in the Third World A number of companies have been criticised for exploiting workers in Third World countries. Companies manufacture in the Third World because it reduces their costs. However, there is an ethical question about the extent to which low costs should be at the expense of low paid workers.

Corruption In some industries, such as defence, bribes might be used to persuade customers to sign contracts. It has been suggested that this takes place in the Third World, where civil servants or government ministers want money from any deal to buy arms. The ethical question is whether it is right to use bribes even if a business knows that its competitors do.

New technologies Some industries are at the cutting edge of science and technology. Most new products developed, such as DVD players or a new chocolate bar, do not cause problems. But since the 1950s, nuclear power generation has been an issue. In the

1990s, GM crops hit the headlines. In the future, many biological processes, such as cloning, could arouse strong ethical reactions.

Product availability If a poor family cannot afford an expensive car, most would not see this as an ethical issue. But if an Aids sufferer in South Africa cannot afford drugs for treatment because pharmaceutical businesses charge such a high price, many would argue that it is an ethical issue. The direction of research is also important. Companies might research new drugs for complaints suffered by only a few in the industrialised world. Or they might research illnesses such as malaria which kill millions each year in the Third World. The choice that businesses make is an ethical issue.

Trading issues Some countries have been condemned internationally for the policies pursued by their governments. They may even have had sanctions or trade embargoes placed upon them. Companies must decide whether to trade with or invest in these countries.

Codes of practice

In recent years, some large businesses have adopted ETHICAL CODES OF PRACTICE. These lay down how employees in the business should respond in situations where ethical issues arise. Ethical codes will differ from one business and one industry to another. However, they may contain statements about:

- environmental responsibility;
- dealing with customers and suppliers in a fair and honest manner;
- competing fairly and not engaging in practices such as collusion or destroyer pricing;
- the workforce and responding fairly to their needs.

Question 2.

Tate & Lyle is to adopt the Fairtrade label for all its retail sugar (packets of sugar sold to consumers) in the UK. It said the change would expand the UK Fairtrade sugar sector, currently only a few million pounds a year, by £80 million by the end of 2009. This will add another household name to the rapidly growing UK market for Fairtrade-branded products following announcements in recent years from companies such as Marks and Spencer.

Harriet Lamb, executive director of the Fairtrade Foundation, said: 'In terms of size and scale, this is the biggest ever Fairtrade switch by a UK company and it's tremendous this iconic brand is backing Fairtrade.'

Fairtrade certification is given when a product meets agreed environmental, labour and developmental standards. Usually, Fairtrade agreements for commodities like bananas or coffee guarantee farmers in developing countries a minimum price above market levels. However, in this case, the deal will involve Tate & Lyle paying sugar-growers a 'social premium' that can be used for community projects such as schools and health clinics. The premium is initially likely to be about £2 million a year, paid to Tate & Lyle's suppliers in Belize in central America. It will affect Belize Sugar Industries, the country's sole sugar processor, and about 6,000 small-holder sugar can growers.

The impact on Tate & Lyle is difficult to quantity. The agreement does not cover the company's much large operation selling industrial sugar to other companies. Nor has Tate & Lyle said what proportion of total cost for retail sugar is accounted for by the cost of the sugar imported from Belize.

(a) Assess the possible advantages and disadvantages to Tate & Lyle of adopting Fairtrade.

Ethical objectives

Ethical codes of practice may develop from **ethical objectives** of businesses. Ethical objectives may be **explicit**. For example, a large business may have as its stated objectives that:

- it will not test its products on animals;
- it will deal with suppliers fairly;
- it will not accept bribes from customers.

Explicit objectives will have been carefully thought out. Partly this is because the business could get bad publicity if it went against its stated ethical objectives.

However, most businesses have **implicit** ethical objectives. Most businesses aim to deal fairly with customers for example. However, implicit ethical objectives are not written down. Instead, they form part of the **corporate culture** of the organisation. They are part of the unwritten rules about how the business deals with its stakeholders, such as customers, suppliers and workers.

Ethics and profitability

As with social responsibility, there might be a conflict between ethical objectives and profitability. Acting ethically when not required to do so by the law can have a negative impact on profit in two ways.

- It can raise costs. For example, paying higher wages than is necessary to Third World workers increases costs. Having to find other ways than animal experiments to test a new drug might add to costs. Adopting an ethical code of practice can raise costs. Staff have to be made aware of it and trained to implement it. It takes management time to prepare a code of practice.
- It can reduce revenues. A business might lose a contract if it refuses to give a bribe. Selling medicines to the Third World at low prices might increase sales, but total revenue is likely to be lower. Refusing to develop GM crops might mean a competitor getting into the market first and becoming the market leader. Acting ethically might even mean the destruction of the company. For example, a cigarette manufacturer which took full account of the costs it causes to customers would probably decide to cease trading.

However, adopting an ethical stance can produce benefits.

- Some companies have used their ethical stance for marketing purposes. In the UK, for example, the Co-operative Bank and The Body Shop have both increased sales by having a strong ethical stance and

drawing in customers which are attracted by this. But adopting an ethical stance is no guarantee of success. Since the mid-1990s, The Body Shop has had disappointing sales growth. An ethical stance which may catch the mood of today's customers may not interest them ten years later.
- For most companies which have taken ethics seriously, it is the equivalent of an insurance policy. They don't want to be caught out behaving unethically and face serious penalties for breaking the law or see sales fall as customers protest against this behaviour. In 2002, two major companies paid the price for unethical behaviour. Enron, a large US energy trading company, collapsed. It was found to have manipulated its accounts to inflate its profits. Senior management had acted unethically by hiding this from shareholders and government. This also led to the collapse of one of the world's top five accounting firms, Arthur Anderson. It had audited Enron's accounts and was accused of hiding the irregularities. As a result, it began to lose its major customers and decided to close down.

Ethics has become a serious issue for large companies. Customers and society have become less tolerant of businesses which behave in a way they see as unethical. However, most companies tend to follow trends and adopt ethical policies which will prevent them from coming to harm in the marketplace or by law. A few have adopted an aggressive ethical stance which sometimes has led to them gaining more customers. Often, small to medium sized businesses do not have management time or resources to draw up an ethical code of practice. Their ethical stance and behaviour is influenced by the society in which they operate.

Should businesses be expected to act ethically?

There is considerable debate about how businesses should actually behave.

Some argue that businesses have a responsibility to act ethically. Those who hold this view stress the fact that firms do not operate in isolation. They are a part of society and have an impact upon the lives of those communities in which they operate. As such they should act in a responsible manner and consider the possible effects of any decisions they make. This means that profit making should not be the only criterion used when making decisions. Other factors which firms might consider include the effect of their decisions upon the environment, jobs, the local community, consumers, competitors, suppliers and employees.

Others argue that businesses should not be expected to act ethically. There are two main views in support of this argument. The first is from supporters of free market economics. They argue that the primary responsibility of businesses is to produce goods and services in the most efficient way, and make profit for shareholders. Firms should attempt to do this in any way they can, providing it is legal. Only by doing this will the general good of everyone be served. If firms are expected to act 'ethically', then consumers may suffer because the ethical behaviour could lead to inefficiency, higher costs and higher prices.

A second argument is that in most cases it is naive to expect businesses to act ethically. Whenever there is a conflict between acting ethically and making greater profits, the vast majority of firms will choose the latter. Those firms which do act in an ethical manner only do so because it is profitable. This view is often held by those who favour government intervention to regulate business. They argue that it is necessary for the government to force firms to behave responsibly through a variety of laws which it must enforce.

Are businesses becoming more ethical?

It could be argued that businesses are increasingly taking a more 'caring' attitude. The growth of companies producing health care products which are not animal tested, the use of recyclable carrier bags and the sale of organically grown vegetables by many retailers could all be an indication of this. Some pension funds and a number of investment schemes are now termed 'green'. They will only invest savers' money in companies which promote the environment.

Others argue that ethical attitudes have failed to penetrate the boardrooms of the UK and that firms continue to act unethically in a variety of ways. An extensive survey undertaken by the University of Westminster found that junior executives and women took the moral 'high ground', with more concern about green issues, staff relations and trade with countries that had records of abusing human rights. This was in contrast to the greed driven motives of company directors, the majority of whom were old and male. One respondent summed up the climate. 'In general, business ethics does not come very high in the scale of human behaviour. Professional standards and levels of caring sometimes leave a lot to be desired.'

One explanation for the findings of the survey is that business culture continues to be driven by short-term profit. This suggests that the stakeholders such as shareholders and directors hold most influence in setting the objectives of the business. These groups tend to be most interested in the profit of the business.

KEYTERMS

Ethics - ideas about what is morally correct or not.
Ethical code of practice - a statement about how employees in a business should behave in particular circumstances where ethical issues arise.

KNOWLEDGE

1. Give two examples of ethical decisions an oil production company might have to make.
2. Explain which types of companies might be particularly affected by ethical issues relating to:
   (a) the environment; (b) animal rights issues; (c) Third World labour; (d) bribery; (e) new technologies; (f) access to products; (g) trading with politically unacceptable countries.
3. What might be contained in an ethical code of practice?
4. To what extent can businesses increase profits by becoming more ethical?
5. 'Businesses should not be expected to act ethically.' Explain the two sides to this argument.

Case Study: Nike

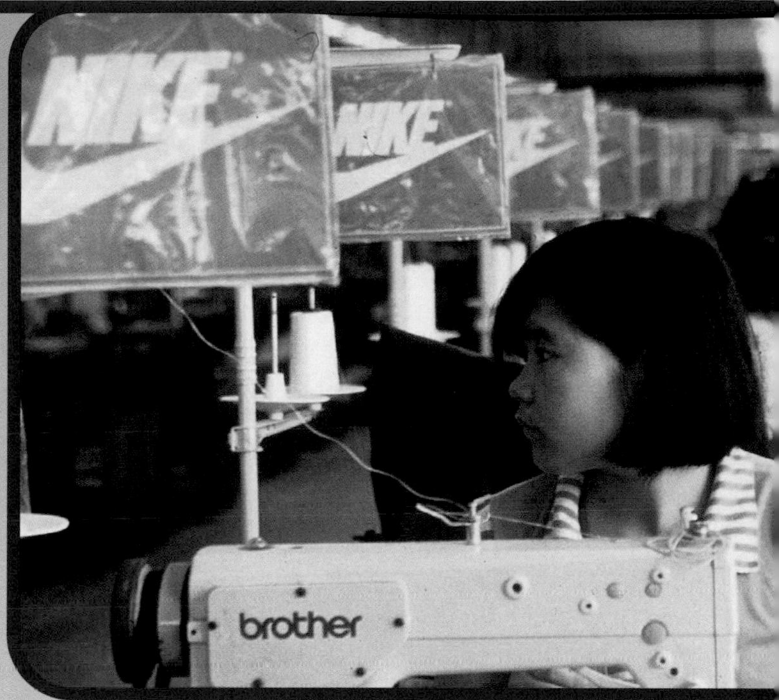

Nike is the world's number one trainer brand. It doesn't manufacturer anything though. It designs shoes and markets them. Production is subcontracted to hundreds of factories round the world. In 2008, around 800,000 workers, 80 per cent of them women aged between 18 and 24 and living in Third World countries, made Nike footwear and apparel.

So how did such a successful company come to face a protracted negative ethical campaign? It started in 1992 when Jeff Ballinger, a US based activist working in Indonesia, published a damning report about conditions in the country's factories, detailing labour abuses, unsanitary conditions and forced overtime. Nike, as a high profile US company, became a symbol for the activists wanting to change the system. Student groups in the US lobbied for independent monitoring of factories of companies selling goods on US campuses, threatening Nike's share of a $2.4bn business in college wear. Activist groups such as Global Exchange bombarded the media with anti-Nike stories.

Nike's initial response was stumbling but it soon gathered pace. In 1992, the company implemented a code of conduct that dealt explicitly with labour rights. There followed a series of initiatives: Ernst & Young, the international firm of auditors, began monitoring labour conditions in 1994; Nike joined President Bill Clinton's Fair labour Campaign in 1996. The company asked Andrew Young, a prominent black American who had been Ambassador to the United Nations, to review factories in Vietnam, China and Indonesia. The company also set out to improve the lives of workers. It launched lending programmes for workers, adult education and better factory monitoring. By 2007, it was committing itself by 2011 to 'improving working conditions in our contract factories through a holistic, integrated business approach to our supply chain'. In particular, it would eliminate excessive overtime in contract factories; implement management training on workers' rights, women's rights and freedom of association and collective bargaining in contract factories; and work with other companies on compliance issues in 30 per cent of their supply chain. Nike is also one of the few companies which publicly disclose the exact location of their contract factories worldwide.

Despite all these initiatives, Nike continues to receive criticism. In 2000, for example, a BBC documentary accused Nike of using child labour in Cambodia. The company as a result reviewed all 3,800 workers records and interviewed those it suspected were under age. But it couldn't verify that all the workers were adult. As a result, it pulled out of production in Cambodia in an attempt at damage limitation. Oxfam Community Aid Abroad, the Australian-based organisation that closely monitors Nike, alleges that 'workers producing for companies like Nike, FILA, adidas, Puma, New Balance and Asics commonly face low wages, long hours, verbal abuse, dangerous working conditions, denial of trade union rights and high levels of sexual harassment'.

Nike itself admits that it is not perfect. In its first 'corporate responsibility report', published in October 2001, it said that making Nike trainers was 'tedious, hard and doesn't offer a wonderful future'. It knew far too little about what happened in the factories it uses. Finally it admitted that its monitoring system did not work well enough. By the time it published its 2005-06 Corporate Responsibility Report, Nike was being much more assertive about its ability to create a supply chain where contract factories could be made to comply with Nike imposed rules about the use of labour.

Nike knows that it will now continue to be targeted by activists unless it uses factories with Western style conditions of work, if not pay. To do that could turn a highly profitable company into one making huge losses, unable to compete against other companies continuing to use cheap Third World labour. It also knows that almost all large clothing manufacturers, or giant retailers such as Wal-Mart (which owns Asda), routinely buy from Third World 'sweatshop' factories where conditions of work are just as poor, if not poorer, than Nike factories. However, perhaps more so than other businesses, it is addressing issues in a realistic way and attempting to put itself ahead of competitors in the corporate social responsibility stakes.

Source: adapted from *The Financial Times*; www.wikipedia.org; www.oxfam.org.au; www.nikebiz.com.

(a) Discuss whether, from an ethical standpoint, Nike should source its products mainly from low cost locations in the Third World rather than from factories in the USA. (40 marks)

(b) Evaluate the costs and benefits to Nike of working with other companies to monitor conditions in its supply chain. (40 marks)

126 Business and the environment

The costs and benefits of business activity

When businesses produce and sell products or services it is relatively easy for them to see the costs involved and the benefits they will gain. These costs are known as PRIVATE COSTS. They might include such things as the wages paid to employees, the cost of an advertising campaign or the purchase of raw materials. The PRIVATE BENEFITS to the business and its owners include the total revenue earned from sales, any resulting profit and the dividends paid to shareholders.

A business may find, however, that it creates other costs. Take a factory producing cement which is located in a small 'scenic' town. The firm may dispose of some of its waste in a local river or discharge dust into the atmosphere. Lorries making deliveries to the factory may disturb the local residents. The factory may be sited close to a local beauty spot, ruining the view. These are all examples of spillover effects or EXTERNALITIES. So the costs to the whole of society, the SOCIAL COSTS, are made up of the private costs of the business plus **negative externalities** (the costs to the rest of society). Social and environmental audits take into account the social costs of business activity.

There may also be **positive externalities** which result from the business. It may create other jobs in the area for companies producing components or design a factory that complements the landscape. The firm may create skills which can be used for other jobs in the area. We can say that SOCIAL BENEFITS to society are the private benefits to business plus positive externalities (the benefits to the rest of society).

There are obvious problems that result from negative externalities. Many externalities affect the environment. Furthermore, when firms set their prices these usually only reflect the private costs of production. Prices will not, therefore, reflect the cost of pollution, noise etc. As a result of this firms may not be concerned about negative externalities as they do not have to pay for them. For example, a chemical company may produce toxic waste from its production process. It might be faced with two choices - disposing of this waste in a nearby river without treating it, or treating it and removing any toxins. The first measure would cost next to nothing, but the second measure could be relatively expensive. The rational choice for the firm, assuming this is legal, is to dispose of the waste untreated in the river. However, for other users of the river, such as anglers and water sports enthusiasts, this decision would have serious effects.

In order to assess the impact of business activity, cost - benefit analysis is sometimes used, particularly for large projects.

Environmental costs

There are many different types of negative externality that may result from business activity. Some are dealt with in other units, e.g. consumer exploitation and employee exploitation. This section will focus on environmental costs.

Air pollution This is pollution from factories, machines or vehicles emitting poisonous gases into the atmosphere. We need only look into the sky above some factories to see evidence of this. Other forms of air pollution may be catastrophes such as at the Chernobyl nuclear plant in 1986, when massive quantities of radioactive materials were released into the atmosphere and surrounding countryside. The results were seen in many countries in Europe.

What are the main causes of air pollution?

- Acid rain. Thousands of acres of forests have been destroyed by acid rain, as a result of sulphur dioxide emissions into the atmosphere.
- Chlorofluorocarbons (CFCs). The use by some firms of CFCs in aerosols and refrigerators has contributed to the breakdown of the earth's ozone layer. The ozone layer acts as a filter for the sun's rays. Without it, exposure to sunlight can increase the risk of skin cancer.
- Carbon dioxide (CO_2) and other gases. There has been a growing awareness that the release of CO_2, and other gases such as methane and nitrous oxide, into the atmosphere is causing a 'greenhouse effect'. The build-up of these gases is associated with the rise in the use of cars and with the generation of electricity with fossil fuels such as coal.

Scientists argue that the 'greenhouse effect' could result in the earth's atmosphere warming up (**global warming**) to such an extent that the polar ice caps melt. This could lead to significant areas of land being submerged by rising sea levels. The

Question 1.

In 1991 Shell, the owner of the Brent Spar oil platform, was looking for ways to dispose of the structure. With the approval of the UK government, it decided to sink it in a deep part of the Atlantic. Sinking it in its place of operation in the North Sea would have caused a hazard to shipping and would have caused further environmental damage to an already polluted area. In 1995 the platform was towed to the Atlantic for sinking. Pressure from groups such as Greenpeace led to Shell abandoning the plan to dump the platform. In 1998 Shell decided to dismantle the platform and use the parts to construct a ferry quay in Norway. Shell had already spent £20 million preparing the platform for sinking. It would cost £26 million for the recycling of the structure.

Using examples from the article, outline the possible:
(a) private costs;
(b) negative externalities;
(c) positive externalities;
of the proposed methods of disposal of the Brent Spar oil platform.

Figure 1: Air pollutants

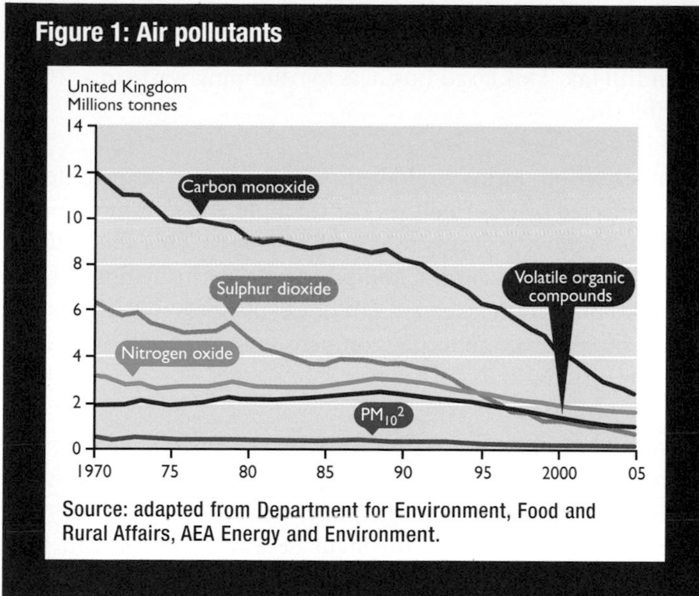

Source: adapted from Department for Environment, Food and Rural Affairs, AEA Energy and Environment.

Figure 2: River water quality

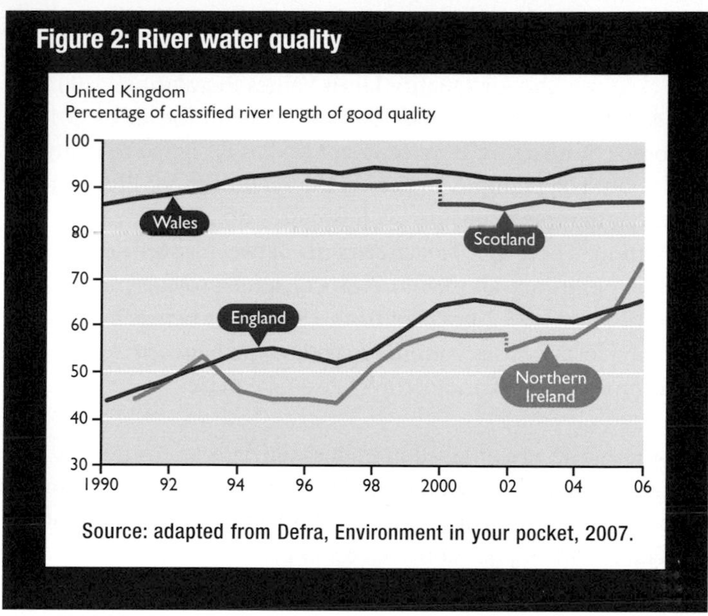

Source: adapted from Defra, Environment in your pocket, 2007.

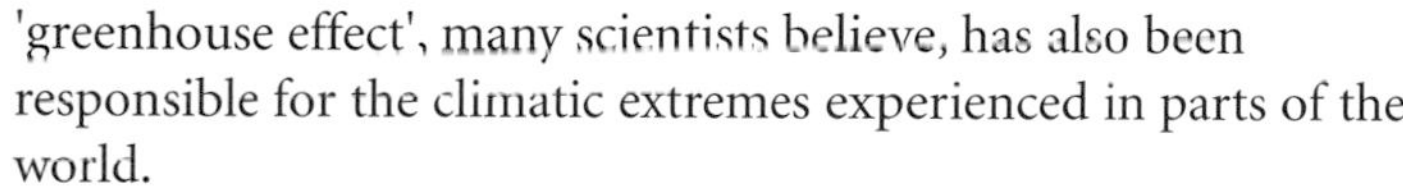

'greenhouse effect', many scientists believe, has also been responsible for the climatic extremes experienced in parts of the world.

Figure 1 shows the emissions of air pollutants in the UK. It suggests that concern over their effect on the environment has led to an effort to cut emissions.

Water pollution Water pollution can occur in a number of ways. Many industries, such as brewing and chemical manufacturing, use water in production. Their plants are usually located by rivers and it is fairly easy, therefore, for them to dispose of waste into nearby water. It is also possible for our drinking water from reservoirs to be polluted by chemicals used in agricultural production. People are starting to drink bottled water or have water filters fitted to their water supply in the home as a result.

The sea has also been polluted over many years. Industries sited near to the coast have used the sea as a dump for their waste. The effluence and cargo of ships are also sometimes dropped into the sea. The North Sea, for example, is one of the most polluted seas in the world as a result of years of discharges from a variety of industries. These have included sewage and the by-products of chemical production. A number of beaches in the UK are unsafe for bathing, according to the European Union, which grades the quality of beaches. Figure 2 shows that there has been an improvement in river quality in the UK since 1990.

Congestion and noise Business activity has resulted in more roads becoming congested with traffic. For example, many firms now transport their goods by rail rather than road. Recent estimates have put the cost of this congestion on British roads as high as £15 billion.

Some business activity can also result in noise pollution. For example, a decision by an airport to open a new runway would affect noise levels experienced by local residents.

Destruction of the environment One example of this is logging and associated industries, which have been responsible for the destruction of sections of the Amazonian rainforests. Another example might include the effects of new buildings in a rural area. A new housing estate in a village, for example, may deprive villagers and visitors of previously unspoilt countryside. It may also increase noise and congestion levels in the village.

Waste disposal Many business operations result in waste products. This may be in the form of waste chemicals resulting from the manufacture of plastics or waste materials from the manufacture of wooden products. The packaging used in products can also be waste and needs to be disposed of.

It has been suggested that some water operators in the UK impose external costs. If a company does not maintain its pipes and leaks occur, this can result in hosepipe bans. It also means that it has to take more water from reservoirs and rivers because of the waste water it has created by leakages.

The impact on the environment of business is not always negative. In derelict urban areas, for example, businesses have converted rundown buildings into office space and have landscaped waste land around the site. Also, some of the buildings may be thought to have architectural merit.

Controlling environmental costs

Because of concern about the impact of business on the environment, attention has been focused on how pollution, congestion and other environmental costs can be controlled. There is a number of ways this can be done.

Government regulation Various pieces of legislation exist in the UK and Europe to prevent the pollution of the environment by business activity. For example, in the UK **The Environment Act, 1995** set up the Environment Agency to the monitor and control pollution. It also set up regulations concerning contaminated land, abandoned mines, national parks, air quality and waste. EU directives often become regulations in the UK. For example, the **Air Quality Limit Values Regulations, 2003** sets targets for reductions in levels of ozone in the air by 2010.

Some countries have government bodies designed to control pollution. For example, in the US the Environment Protection Agency attempts to ensure US businesses do not contravene legislation. There are also agreements between countries to control pollution. The Kyoto Protocol agreed to cut greenhouse gas emissions by 5.2 per cent from 1990 levels between 2008 and 2012. In certain cases voluntary agreements between governments and manufacturers also take place.

Taxation The aim of taxation in this context is to ensure that the social cost of any pollution caused by a firm is paid for. This means that the government must estimate the actual cost to society of different types of pollution. As a result prices would more accurately reflect the true cost of using environmental resources. So, for example, a firm which produced a £5 product with 'environmentally unfriendly' packaging might be taxed 50p for this packaging, raising the price to £5.50. There are two advantages to this. First, the tax revenue might be used to minimise the impact of this packaging on the environment. Second, it might act as an incentive for the firm to produce more environmentally sensitive packaging, so that the tax is either reduced or removed.

In this example the consumer pays for the environmentally unfriendly packaging in the form of a price rise. Some would argue that the firm itself should pay for such costs. In this way, the price would remain at £5.00, but the firm would be taxed 50 pence for externalities created by its packaging. The consumer would not directly suffer as a result of the taxation.

Increases in fuel prices in the UK have been justified by governments on the grounds that consumers should pay prices which accurately reflect the impact of car use on the environment. In the late 1990s the UK government introduced a **landfill tax**. This taxed business for dumping waste in a landfill site.

Compensation Firms could be forced by law to compensate those affected by externalities. For example, it is common for airports to provide grants to nearby residents. This allows them to purchase double glazing and other types of insulation, which provides protection from aircraft noise. Business may also be forced by court action to pay compensation to people affected by their actions.

Government subsidies This involves governments offering grants, tax allowances and other types of subsidy to businesses in order to encourage them to reduce externalities. Such subsidies can allow environmentally desirable projects, which otherwise might not be profitable, to go ahead. For example, a business may be given a grant so that it can build a recycling plant for plastics. This should encourage domestic and industrial users to recycle rather than dump plastic products.

Government subsidies could also be used to encourage more environmentally friendly habits amongst consumers. For example, many councils are attempting to encourage the use of bicycles through schemes such as setting up cycle lanes and giving grants to employees wishing to use bicycles for travelling to and from work.

Road pricing and charges Charging road users could be used to reduce pollution and congestion. There is a long history of charging for motorways in European countries such as France, Spain and Italy. In the UK the first toll motorway was opened in 2004, with travellers and business users paying to travel around

Question 2.

Electricity prices in the UK could rise as a result of plans to cut carbon dioxide emissions beyond EU targets. The UK energy minister, Stephen Timms, said 'Our suggestion is that industrial electricity prices will increase ... by something like 6 per cent, not just in the UK but in major European industrial economies. The comparable figure for domestic bills would be about 3 per cent ... '.

The government had plans to cut carbon dioxide emissions by a fifth by 2010 in preparation for a new EU scheme on emissions trading to start in 2005. The initiative introduces caps on the amount of carbon dioxide emitted by industry. The scheme would force EU companies to pay to pollute. It will be mandatory for around 12,000 factories, of which 2,000 are in the UK. Under the scheme, the government would set emission limits on industry and allow companies to trade the right to produce emissions. Carbon emission limits for power stations have been cut so that, by 2007, their allocations will be 2.75 million tonnes of carbon dioxide below the government's updated energy projections for the sector..

Britain only imports around 2 per cent of its electricity and exports much less than that. The government said the fact that UK producers do not face competition from generators not affected by the EU scheme means they are better placed to absorb the costs of reducing their emissions.

The overall number of allowances for UK industry have been set at a level beyond the Kyoto Protocol commitment. Industry voiced its displeasure at this. 'Emissions trading is the right approach, but if we go too far and other countries don't make similar commitments, we are going to put our hard-pressed manufacturers in an extremely difficult position in global markets' said Digby Jones, the director general of the Confederation of British Industry. But Friends of the Earth pointed out that the UK will not be introducing the toughest limits in Europe. It said some countries, such as Spain and Ireland, will have to take tougher action simply to meet Kyoto targets. Germany was also expected to follow the UK in going further than its Kyoto target.

Source: adapted from *The Guardian*, 19.1.2004.

(a) Explain the types of control on environmental costs mentioned in the article.

(b) Discuss to what extent the competitiveness of UK industry would be affected by these controls.

Question 3.

Marks & Spencer, the UK high street retailer, has caught the mood of the moment by announcing yesterday that it would charge for carrier bags in its grocery departments from November. Bags will now cost 5p each. The Daily Mail and the Women's Institute immediately gave their support to the move. Both Gordon Brown, the Prime Minister, and David Cameron, the leader of the oppositions, have said they would like to see retailers abandon giving away single use plastic bags.

Groundwork, an environmental charity which has been working with M&S, and which will receive all the revenues from the sale of M&S grocery plastic bags, said: 'Not only will this scheme reduce the amount of food carrier bags sent to landfill sites but it will also help improve the quality of life in towns and cities across the country.'

Adam Jones, UK sales director of Papier-Mettler, the company which supplies M&S with plastic bags, commented there was 'never a dull moment' in the world of plastic bags.

However, there is some controversy about the environmental impact of banning plastic bags. If it leads to far more paper bags being used, then paper bags are far more energy-intensive to produce than thin plastic bags.

The announcement by M&S led to other retailers giving reminders about their own initiatives. Aldi, the supermarket chain, already charges for bags. Tesco said its bags were degradable. Sainsbury said it was concentrating on encouraging recycling.

Charging for plastic bags, based on experience from the UK and other countries, is likely to lead to a drop of at least 90 per cent in the number of bags used. Cynics have noted eliminating the use of plastic bags will add to company profits.

Source: adapted from *The Financial Times*, 29.2.2008.

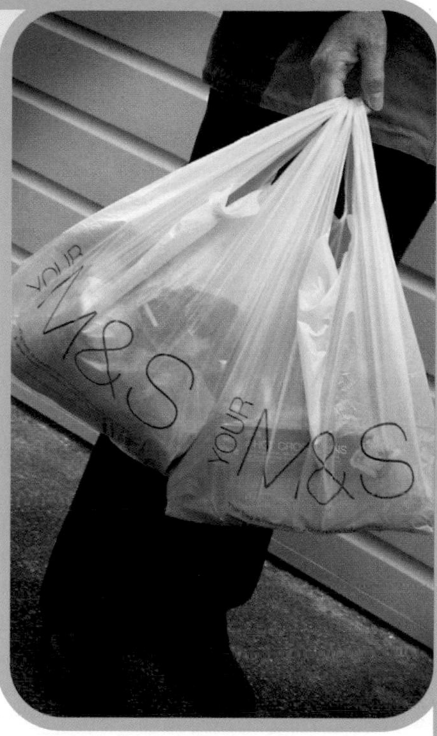

(a) Why might the move by M&S to charge for grocery plastic bags be an example of effective marketing for the company?

(b) Evaluate whether it would benefit both businesses and the environment if the government banned the giving away of free plastic bags by retailers such as supermarket chains, clothes retailers, DIY stores and music shops.

Birmingham to reduce traffic on the M6. In 2003 a Congestion Charge was introduced on most vehicles entering the centre of London.

Park and ride schemes These are also designed to encourage a reduction in car use in city areas. They are often run by local authorities. Car users, for a fee, can park their cars outside the city areas and are taken by bus or rail into and out of the city. A single bus, if full, reduces traffic in the city area and also reduces the need for inner city car parking spaces.

Pollution permits In both the USA and the European Union, pollution permits have been introduced. These allow businesses a certain amount of emissions. If the business reduces its pollution below a certain level, it can save the allowance for later or even sell it. Some have argued that Western economies should adopt the same approach to developing countries as they pollute the atmosphere across the world.

Working together It may be possible for business and/or government to work together to control the effect of business action on the environment. Examples might be:
- the sharing of best practice on environmental controls;
- producing environmental codes of practice;
- developing waste strategies.

Education Governments and other agencies, such as charities, could try to influence consumers and producers through educational and promotional campaigns.

Consumer pressure Consumers have forced a number of firms to consider the impact of their activities on the environment. There is evidence that a new breed of consumer is emerging, who considers factors other than price and quality when buying products. Such consumers take into account the effect on the environment and society of those products which they purchase. So, for example, such a consumer may not buy aerosols containing CFCs, furniture made from trees which have been chopped down in the Amazon rainforest or cosmetics which have been tested on animals.

Although this approach has influenced a wide range of firms, it does have one major problem. Consumers often do not have sufficient information with which to evaluate the impact of business activity upon the environment. Such information is often not disclosed to members of the public. Also, many firms have not been slow to realise that presenting themselves as being environmentally conscious can be very good for sales. However, the actual record of such firms with regard to the environment may well fall short of the claims which they make for themselves. For example, a battery producing company placed an environmentally friendly label on its products. However, this had to be removed when it was revealed that batteries use up more energy in their construction than they create in their use.

Environmental audits An ENVIRONMENTAL AUDIT is one method by which consumers have a fairer chance of assessing the environmental impact of a firm. This could be much like the financial audits which all companies are at present required to have by law. An environmental audit can be one part of a wider social audit. This perhaps indicates the growing pressure put on firms to be concerned about their impact on the environment.

Conservation

All businesses depend, to a greater or lesser degree, on the use of non-renewable resources. These are resources which cannot be replaced and which might in some cases, with current usage, run out within the next 100 years. Such resources range from raw materials, like oil, iron, copper and aluminium, to living creatures.

Conservation ranges from banning the use of such resources altogether, to encouraging businesses to use them sparingly. There is a number of measures which seek to conserve non-renewable resources.

- Recycling schemes. Bottle banks set up to help the recycling of glass are now a common sight in supermarket car parks. Not only do glass recycling schemes help to conserve natural resources, but they can be profitable for those companies involved. Recycling schemes also exist in the paper, plastics and aluminium industries.
- Multilateral agreements. These are agreements between a number of countries which seek to limit the use of natural resources. Agreements now exist which place limits on the amount of fishing and whaling which countries are allowed to carry out. In addition, some countries now have import bans on commodities such as ivory which come from endangered species.
- Government subsidies. These have been used to encourage farmers to conserve the countryside through retaining features such as dry stone walls and hedgerows, for example.

The business response to environmental issues

Environmental issues offer both threats and opportunities to businesses. Businesses which stand to gain the most from growing environmental regulation are those selling pro-environmental and anti-pollution products. These businesses range from engineering companies selling equipment designed to reduce emissions, to service companies which advise other businesses on how they can comply with regulations, to businesses selling environmentally friendly products, such as managed wood.

Those which stand to lose the most are companies which are high polluters and who face competition from other businesses which don't face similar problems. For example, a specialist chemicals company may cease trading because there are many good substitutes to its products which have only a fraction of the environmental impact in production. Or a heavily regulated UK company may face competition from a Third World producer whose government places little restriction on its activity.

Marketing Environmental issues can be a highly effective marketing tool for some businesses. Companies such as the Co-operative Bank and The Body Shop have made a particular point of pursuing environmentally friendly policies. Many businesses on their packaging or in their advertising claim to be environmentally friendly in some way. However, some businesses have found that environmental issues pose a marketing threat. Oil companies, for example, are accused by environment pressure groups such as Greenpeace or Friends of the Earth of harming the environment. In the 1990s, when Shell planned to dispose of a disused oil platform by sinking it in the middle of the Atlantic, environmental pressure groups organised a consumer boycott of Shell petrol stations in Germany. This anti-marketing pressure was successful enough to influence the business to abandon its plans. Perrier was one of the leading brands of bottled water in Europe in the 1990s and in the UK was the top brand by sales. However, a contamination scare affected the image of the brand. Such examples show that businesses must take quick and positive action when an environmental issue suddenly arises. It also shows that some businesses have to work constantly to improve their environmental image.

Finance In some cases, responding to environmental concerns or new laws and regulations can have a positive financial impact on a business. Energy saving measures, for example, can lead to a business having lower costs than before because of previous inefficiencies. In most cases, though, taking environmental action is likely to lead to higher costs. If all businesses in the industry also face these higher costs, prices are likely to rise to reflect the higher costs. Profits would then be largely unaffected. But if higher costs fall more heavily on one business than another, then some will gain a competitive advantage and others lose it. This in turn will have different impacts on profitability. Installing expensive new equipment will also have a negative impact on cash flow. In the nuclear power industry and the car industry, businesses must also make investment decisions knowing that there will be heavy costs at the end of a product's life. In the case of the nuclear power industry, this is in terms of decommissioning plant. For motor manufacturers, they have to take back old cars for recycling. This will affect the outcomes of appraisal methods like the payback method and discounted cash flow.

Operations management Pollution controls and other environmental measures could have an impact on how a product is made. This could range from changes in the type of materials used, to production methods to storage and after-sales service. For example, asbestos was widely used in industry years ago but its use today is severely restricted. Industries such as electricity generation and chemicals have had to introduce much cleaner production methods to reduce emissions. The landfill tax encourages businesses to reduce the amount of waste they produce.

Human resources Environmental concerns and policies have human resource implications. Staff will need to be recruited and trained to deal with ever increasing government regulations concerning the environment. Some businesses may choose to outsource the guidance they need. Larger businesses are likely to put environmental policies in place. This could include an environmental audit where key measures relating to the impact of the business on the environment are audited each year and the results are made public. Implementing policies means that staff throughout the organisation are aware of the policies and what they must do to comply with the policies. As with any policy, unless there are good procedures and training in place to ensure compliance, staff will tend to interpret the policies as they see fit. Effective communication up and down the hierarchy is therefore essential. The very small minority of businesses which make environmental concerns an important business objective can use this as a way of motivating staff. Over time, it will tend to attract employees who are interested in this aspect of business. However, a tension between meeting financial targets such as profits targets and meeting environmental targets is likely to arise. For a business to survive, it must at least break even. In this sense, financial targets tend to be more important than environmental targets. This tension between targets could demotivate staff who want to see environmental targets as the most important for the business.

KEYTERMS

Environmental audit – measures of performance of a business against environmental criteria, such as levels of C02 emissions.
Externalities – occur when private costs are different to social costs and private benefits are different to social benefits.
Private benefits – the benefit of an activity to an individual or a business.
Private costs – the cost of an activity to an individual or a business.
Social benefits – the benefit of an activity to society as well as to a business.
Social costs – the cost of an activity to society as well as to a business.

KNOWLEDGE

1. Give an example of:
   (a) a private cost;
   (b) a positive externality;
   (c) a private benefit.
2. State five examples of negative externalities that may be created by a business.
3. Briefly explain the effect that:
   (a) a tax on a business;
   (b) a subsidy from government to a business;
   might have on the creation of negative externalities.
4. Why might a business be concerned about the views consumers have about how it affects the environment?
5. Briefly explain three consequences of following an environmentally friendly policy for a business.
6. 'Conservation can be profitable for a business.' Explain this statement with an example.
7. State five examples of businesses that may develop as a result of the growth of concern over the effect of businesses on the environment.

Case Study: Supermarket recycling disappoints

The big food retailers are letting both their customers and the environment down according to a report published by the Local Government Association. The study saw a range of common food items being bought from eight retailers: Asda, Lidl, Marks & Spencer, Morrisons, Sainsbury's, Tesco, a local high street and a large market. The content and the packaging of the items were weighed. The packaging was then analysed as to whether or not it could be recycled. Lidl came out as having the heaviest packaging at 799.5g per basket. M&S came out worst for recycling. 40 per cent of its packaging couldn't be recycled.

The Local Government Association said: 'People are working to increase their recycling rates, but their efforts are being hamstrung by needlessly overpackaged products. Many supermarkets are taking action to cut back on excessive packaging, but there is an urgent need to do more. Councils and taxpayers are facing fines of up to £3 billion if we do not dramatically reduce the waste thrown into landfill.'

Friends of the Earth said the results of the survey were very disappointing. 'Despite constant green claims, supermarkets continue to act as a hindrance, not a help, when it comes to green consumer action. Packaging urgently needs to be minimised and made from materials that are easy to reuse, recycle or compost'.

Marks & Spencer's head of corporate social responsibility Mike Barry said: 'We've set ourselves clear and demanding targets to reduce our packaging and only use materials that can be easily recycled or composted. Whilst we've made good progress over the last 12 months, we know there's still much more yet to do in both areas.' The retailer added that councils needed to be more consistent about what was recyclable, pointing out that some councils allowed cardboard to be put in recycling boxes, whilst others did not.

Table 1: % of packaging that is recyclable

Ranking	Retailer	%
1	Local market	79
2	Local retailers	79
3	Asda	70
4	Sainsbury's	70
5	Morrisons	68
6	Tesco	62
7	Lidl	61
8	M&S	60

Source: adapted from www.timesonline.co.uk; www.telegraph.co.uk; www.brandrepublic.com 23.10.2007.

(a) **Evaluate whether it is in the commercial interests of supermarket chains to reduce the packaging on their products and make the packaging recyclable. (40 marks)**

127 Corporate responsibility

Social responsibility and business ethics

Businesses act in the interests of their owners. But social custom, the law and the market force them also to acknowledge responsibilities to their other **stakeholders**, such as their workers, their customers and suppliers and the communities in which they operate. Equally, businesses have to act within an ethical framework. If nothing else, businesses should operate within the law.

However, there is a considerable difference between businesses in the way in which they operate in these areas. Businesses like the Co-operative Bank or The Body Shop make a point of acting in a socially responsible and ethical way. Other businesses like arms manufacturers, by the very nature of the products they make, can be accused of being socially irresponsible.

For many businesses, there is a direct trade-off between the interests of different stakeholders. The opportunity cost for a business which spends £1 million a year supporting charity projects in the local area could be £1 million which is not paid in dividends to shareholders, or £1 million which is not paid to employees in higher wages. The best case scenario for a business is when acting in a socially responsible and ethical way brings benefits to all stakeholders. For example, a doughnut manufacturer may have a policy of sponsoring children's sporting activities. If sales rise as a result, the owners and employees can benefit through higher dividends and more jobs. The local community also benefits from the sponsorship of its young people. Even then, there could be disadvantages. The sponsorship may encourage customers to eat more doughnuts, which could be argued to be unhealthy. The sugar used in the product might have been produced by child labour. There will also be those who will accuse the company of sponsoring children's sporting activities as a mere PR (public relations) exercise.

Many businesses do not have a carefully thought out attitude to social responsibility and ethics. However, large companies are increasingly being forced by the law and by pressure groups to develop policies in these areas. For example, some companies have published social and environmental audits (see below). Others have developed ethical codes of practice.

For some businesses, attitudes to social and ethical responsibility form part of the wider culture of the business. If there is a strong culture of caring towards all the stakeholders, there is more likely to be a strong social and ethical culture. In businesses where the emphasis is mainly on financial targets, social and ethical issues may play little part in decision making.

In some companies, there could also be a clash of cultures between different layers of the organisation, or different parts of the company. Newly appointed senior executives, for example, may put social and ethical policies in place. But these may not filter down the organisation hierarchy. Or head office in London may follow a strong ethical stance but a subsidiary of the company in another country may conceal from head office poor work conditions and the use of labour on very low wages in its factories in order to boost profits.

Changing business culture is often difficult, whether it is aimed at increasing profitability, cutting costs or adopting more ethical codes of conduct. In an autocratic organisation, change is only encouraged if it comes from above. Change may then encounter resistance as it passes down the management hierarchy. Ultimately it may be frustrated because of the unwillingness to change of those at the bottom of the hierarchy. With more democratic leadership, there will be an increased emphasis on consultation, delegation and empowerment. But this too can frustrate change. If social responsibility and ethics are not seen as high priority by all within the organisation, it becomes very difficult for a few, even if they are at the top of the hierarchy, to get their message across. Delegating responsibility and empowering workers is only successful if those workers share the same goals as the business. Getting everyone to share those goals can take a long time.

Corporate social responsibility (CSR)

Some large businesses have responded to concerns about CORPORATE SOCIAL RESPONSIBILITY, their responsibility not just to their shareholders but to all stakeholders, by auditing relevant activities. These audits may then be made available to the public in a Corporate Responsibility Report, in the same way that the financial accounts of the company are published. Auditing involves inspecting evidence against established standards. Auditors can then say that the evidence presented by the business is 'true and fair'.

In accounting, standards for accounting audits are set by accounting bodies such as the Accounting Standards Board. In contrast, social and environmental auditing is voluntary and there is no body which draws up rules about how audits should take place. At present, companies are free to choose what standards they should be measured against and who the auditors will be. Indeed, the vast majority of businesses do not undertake any social or environmental accounting.

Businesses which do compile social and environmental audits use a wide range of measures, which differs from business to business. An oil company, for example, may measure the number of oil spills for which it is responsible. This would not be appropriate for a drinks company which might use other indicators such as levels of air pollution created by its breweries and distilleries. Social and environmental audits might include some of the following.

Employment indicators How well does the business treat its staff? This might include indicators about pensions, healthcare benefits, trade union representation, training and education, number of accidents involving staff, payment of minimum wages, equal

Question 1.

Lucent Technologies was a US manufacturer of telecommunications equipment. It was created by a demerger with AT&T, a large US telecommunications company, in 1996. In 2006, Lucent merged with Alcatel, the French telecommunications equipment company.

Whilst still an independent company, Lucent was pursuing a strategy of selling into the Chinese telecommunications market. As part of its marketing effort, it invited Chinese officials to the USA. The US Department of Justice in an investigation found that the company spent more than $10 million (£5 million) on about 315 trips for 1,000 Chinese government officials and telecoms executives. The problem was that they 'spent little or no time' touring Lucent's production facilities. Instead, they enjoyed sightseeing in Hawaii, Las Vegas, the Grand Canyon, Niagara Falls, Disneyland and Universal Studies. Despite paying for travel, hotels and meals, Lucent also gave some Chinese officials a daily cash allowance of $500 to $1,000. As for relatives or associates of the invited Chinese officials, these were offered 'educational opportunities' both in the USA and back in China. The total cost of these 'educational opportunities' to Lucent was over $100,000.

Lucent was last December was fined $2.5 million by the US Department of Justice under the Foreign Corrupt Practices Act for attempting to bribe Chinese officials to place orders with the company.

Source: adapted from *The Financial Times*, 6.3.2008.

(a) Explain why Lucent was fined $2.5 million.
(b) Discuss whether European and US businesses should be allowed by their governments to use bribery to win contracts in emerging markets such as China and India.

opportunities and the level of women in higher management or director positions.

Human rights indicators How well does the company perform on human rights issues? For example, does it encourage its workers to join trade unions and give those trade unions negotiating rights with the company? Does it have works councils? Does it or its suppliers use child labour? Does the company operate in, buy supplies from or sell products to countries which have poor human rights records? Does it discriminate on grounds of race, gender or age when recruiting or promoting staff?

The communities in which the business operates What impact does the business have on the life of the communities in which it operates? For example, how much does it give to charities? How much is spent on local schools, hospitals and housing?

Business integrity and ethics How ethical is the business in its activities? For example, have there been any cases of trading which breaks legislation involving the company? Did the company make political contributions and to whom? Was the company involved in cases associated with unfair competition?

Product responsibility What was the social impact of the products sold by the business? For example, were there customer health and safety issues? Was after-sales service adequate? Was advertising true and fair? Did the company manage its information on customers and suppliers in such a way as to preserve their privacy?

The environment These indicators can form a separate **environmental audit**. Some businesses may only compile an environmental audit and not include any of the other social indicators described above. Indicators might include the amount of energy or other raw materials such as water or pesticides used by the business. How much waste or effluent was produced? What were levels of greenhouse gas or ozone-depleting emissions? What percentage of materials used were recycled? What was the company's impact on bio-diversity? What impact did it have on protected and sensitive areas? How many times was it fined during the period for failure to comply with environmental regulations and what was the total level of fines?

Some of these measures are **financial**, i.e. they are measured in money terms. Many, however, are **non-financial**. For this reason, it is difficult to get a quick and easy overall measure of how well a business is doing from its social and environmental audit. In contrast, with a financial audit like a set of financial accounts, it is possible, for example, to look at the profit and loss account and say that the business has performed better or worse in terms of revenues, costs and profit. The data from social audits are therefore more difficult to assess and compare from year to year than from financial accounts.

Exposing social costs or just PR?

Social and environmental auditing can be controversial. Those in favour argue that businesses should be encouraged to conduct social and environmental audits for a number of reasons.

- It helps both businesses and their stakeholders to understand the **social costs** of their activities and not just the private costs shown in their financial statements.
- It is a way for management of a business to manage the business in a more socially responsible way and identify issues of **market failure.**
- It allows the stakeholders of a business to evaluate its success using wider criteria than simply financial measures.
- It might be used to plan more effectively for the future. For example, a business might be able to identify new markets, different sources of supply, and different production methods which might suit the needs of its stakeholders, including customers.
- It might prevent some stakeholders, such as pressure groups, from distorting facts to suit their own agendas.

Many pressure groups, however, argue that social and environmental auditing is inadequate. Businesses have the freedom to choose on what they report. It can also be difficult for auditors to verify the statistics produced by the company. In the case of illegal trading, for example, it is in the interests of both the employees and those they are trading with to keep illegal deals away from the eyes of auditors. Investigative journalism also uncovers instances of issues such as use of child labour and poor working conditions in Third World factories which have not been reported in the official social audit. So **social and environmental** audits may be misleading.

Pressure groups would like to see tough uniform standards for social and environmental audits with which all businesses would have to comply. Then it would be possible to compare the performance of one business with another. It would also force businesses to account for externalities which at present they prefer to ignore or, at worst, conceal from their stakeholders.

Current social auditing, pressure groups would argue, is little more than a PR (public relations) exercise. To make themselves look socially and environmentally aware, companies publish social and environment audits. They can use this when talking to the press, to their shareholders and to pressure groups to say that they understand the issues and are taking tough action to combat externalities.

Voluntary social auditing might also be an obstacle to the introduction by government of tougher laws and regulations on social and environmental issues. Companies could argue that their social audits show that they are responsible organisations which have the best interests of the community amongst their goals. Introducing laws and regulations would mean more red tape and higher costs to business without necessarily improving current practice. On the other hand they may be more concerned with maximising shareholder value. Social auditing is therefore an obstacle to what might really be needed – tough laws and regulations to control anti-social businesses.

KEYTERMS

Corporate social responsibility – the responsibility that a business has towards all stakeholders and not just to owners or shareholders.

KNOWLEDGE

1. To whom might a business have social responsibilities?
2. To what extent do all businesses have a strong social and ethical culture?
3. What might be the conflict between implementing ethical decisions and delegation?
4. What is an audit?
5. Why are recognisable and accepted standards important in auditing?
6. What measures might be used when conducting a social and environmental audit?
7. What are the arguments (a) in favour of and (b) against conducting social and environmental audits?

Case Study: BAT

British American Tobacco is one of the world's largest cigarette manufacturers. In its *Social Report 2005* it said: 'Our vision is to achieve leadership of the global tobacco industry through strategies focussed on growth, productivity and responsibility supported by a winning organisation. By growth we do not mean 'selling smoking', but growth in our share of the global market, growth in profit, and continuing growth in shareholder value. By productivity, we mean using resources smartly, enabling additional money to be generated for reinvestment to strengthen our competitive position and performance. We believe that because our products pose risks to health, it is all the more important that our business is managed responsibly and we see responsibility as fundamental to building long-term shareholder value. Through dialogue with our stakeholders and by listening and responding, we are working to pursue our commercial objectives in ways consistent with changing expectations of a modern tobacco business. Our Business Principles are Mutual Benefit, Responsible Product Stewardship and Good Corporate Conduct. In our Social Report, we aim to demonstrate how we are working to live by them.'

Source: adapted from British American Tobacco, *Social Report* 2005.

Table 1: British American Tobacco: key statistics 2003, 2006

	2003	2006
Gross turnover (including duty, excise and other taxes)	£25 622 million	£25 189 million
Operating profit	£2 781 million	£2 622 million
Profit after tax	£788 million	£2048 million
Worldwide excise and tax contribution	£14 360 million	£16 143 million
Group environmental, health and safety expenditure	£34.8 million	£23.6 million
Group charitable and community donations	£12.7 million	£17.6 million
Employees (including associate companies)	86 941	97 431
Factories	87 in 66 countries	52 in 44 countries

Source: adapted from British American Tobacco, Social Report 2003/4; *Social reporting 2006: Progress and review.*

Can the maker of a lethal product be socially responsible? Martin Broughton, the outgoing chairman of British American Tobacco, says of corporate social responsibility (CSR) that: 'To say it's not important for controversial industries to operate responsibly is a very strange way of looking at life. I think because the product is controversial and dangerous, it is more important that the industry is in responsible hands than in what you might call a 'normal' industry.'

BAT's claims of responsibility, however, face an obvious credibility gap. A survey of MPs and non-governmental organisations has just named it the worst of Britain's top 50 companies for corporate social responsibility. 'It would seem that no matter what tobacco companies try to do on the subject of CSR, it's the nature of the product that is the key issue and the two are incompatible', says BPRI, the WPP group consultancy that carried out the survey.

Source: adapted from *The Financial Times*, 28.9.2004

Table 4: Diversity and opportunity: composition of management (including the board of directors), male and female ratios

		Management trainees	Level 1 (junior management)	Level 2 (middle management)	Level 3 (senior management)	Level 4 (senior management)
2003	Male	0.61	0.73	0.78	0.87	0.94
	Female	0.39	0.27	0.22	0.13	0.06
	Male to female ratio	1.6:1	2.7:1	3.6:1	6.7:1	15.7:1
2006	Male	0.54	0.69	0.75	0.84	0.93
	Female	0.46	0.31	0.26	0.16	0.07
	Male to female ratio	1.2:1	2.3:1	2.9:1	5.1:1	13.3:1

Source: adapted from British American Tobacco, Social Report 2003/4; *Social reporting 2006: Progress and review.*

British American Tobacco (BAT) supports community and charitable projects. On its website in 2008, it said that: 'We recognise the role of business as corporate citizens and our companies have long supported local community and charitable projects. We approach corporate social investment (CSI) as an end in itself, rather than as a way to promote ourselves, and our companies have always been closely identified with the communities where they operate.'

It went on to say that 'Our global CSI expenditure in 2006 .... was £17.6 million ... of which £3 million was spent in the UK.'

BAT encourages its companies to focus their CSI activities around the three themes of sustainable agriculture, civic life and employment. For example, 'Sustainable agriculture covers CSI contributions to the social, economic and environmental sustainability of agriculture. It includes activities such as efforts to improve bio-diversity and access to water, afforestation, programmes to prevent child labour, grants for agricultural research or training to help farmers grow non-tobacco crops.'

Table 3: Total amount of waste generated by BAT by type and destination. (Destination = method by which waste is treated, including composting, reuse, recycling, recovery, incineration or landfilling.)

	2002	2006	
	Metric tonnes	Metric tonnes	% change
Non-hazardous waste			
Sent to landfills	50,701	23,449	-53.8
Recycle	98,909	108,290	9.5
Incinerated	1,456	611	-58.0
Other	4,345	529	-87.8
Total	15,5411	13,2879	-14.5
Hazardous waste			
Sent to approved landfills	110	411	273.6
Recycled	362	816	125.4
Incinerated	263	279	6.1
Other	176	56	-68.2
Total	911	1,562	71.5
Hazardous and non-hazardous waste, total	156,322	134,441	-14.0
Per million cigarettes equivalent produced	0.153	0.127	-5.9

Source: adapted from British American Tobacco, Social Report 2003/4; *Social reporting 2006: Progress and review.*

(a) **Using BAT and its corporate social responsibility reporting as an example, discuss the extent to which 'the maker of a lethal product (can) be socially responsible' (Box 2). (40 marks)**

128 Technology

Technological change

The use of **technology** is one of a number of characteristics which separate human beings from most other animals. Over time, humans have developed a range of technologies, such as the wheel, water power, steam power, electricity and telephony. The latest technology to transform society has been the microchip. This has given rise to computers and information and communication technology. The next major wave of technologies is likely to centre around biotechnology.

It has been argued that technological change is **exponential**. This means that the rate of change accelerates over time. Two thousand years ago, the rate of technological change hardly altered at all over a person's lifetime. One hundred years ago, there was significant change for many people in industrialised countries over their lifetime. Today, major changes take place almost every decade.

Business opportunities

Technological change provides businesses with two main opportunities.

New products In some industries, developing new products is vital to the competitiveness of a business. For example, vehicle, domestic appliance and electronic goods manufacturers all survive by constantly bringing out new and improved products. The **product life cycle** varies from industry to industry. In the car industry, models may be changed every five years, although there will be minor modifications made each year. With a new product like a DVD player, the product life cycle may be less than one year. In these industries, failure to bring out new products based on the latest technology is likely to lead to falling

Question 1.

Ever since General Motors installed the first industrial robot in its Trenton, New Jersey, plant in 1962, the car industry has been in the vanguard of robotics. Robots do not demand pay rises, do not join trade unions and are happy to do dirty, smelly, dangerous jobs. They are also pinpoint accurate time after time, an essential ability if your job is to weld together hundreds of thousands of cars a year. Yet car factory automation seems to have reached its peak for two different reasons.

First, car makers have come to realise that robots are expensive compared to workers. Not only is their initial purchase cost high, but they are costly to maintain. Breakdowns are costly too. 'We had to realise in the car industry that a high degree of automation in the factory will give you reliability problems and then you will have downtimes - and downtimes cost you money', said Noirbert Reithofer, director of production at BMW.

Second, robots have proved too inflexible in final assembly where the variety of options on any individual car explodes. Robots are well suited to making standard movements using standard components. But the complexity of options in final assembly is too great. Even in one of the few areas of final assembly that have been colonised by robots - attaching windscreens - some new factories are reverting to human beings. At the new Honda plant in Swindon, the experience gained with the glazing robot in the old factory gave the company the expertise to fit windscreens manually.

Third, with flexible manufacturing systems, car manufacturers want to be able to switch production from one model to the next relatively quickly. Robots can be too inflexible for this. 'There has been a rebalancing', according to Steve Young, automotive vice-president at consultants AT Kearney. 'There is a better understanding of the real cost of automation from real experience.' In particular, he says, it costs a lot more to reprogram the machine for a new vehicle than was expected - as much as buying the robot in the first place.

Source: adapted from *The Financial Times*.

(a) Explain the link between automation and robots.

(b) What are the main advantages to car manufacturers of using robots?

(c) Why have some car manufacturers begun to use less technology in their plants and relied more on human workers?

sales and the survival of the business may be threatened.

However, in other industries, new technology has little if any impact on the product. Heinz Baked Beans, for example, are sold with the marketing message that they haven't changed over time. Today's baked beans are the same as the 'original'. New technologies can also be fiercely resisted by customers. Foods containing GM (genetically modified) crops have had to be withdrawn from supermarket shelves in the UK because some consumers didn't want to buy the products.

So the introduction of technologically improved products is vital in some industries. At the other other end of the scale, some businesses are successful because the product is the same as before, unaffected by technological change.

Product processes Even though Heinz Baked Beans have not changed over time, the technology used in their production is likely to have changed. Much of manufacturing industry has been transformed over the past thirty years, partly due to the introduction of microchip technology. This has resulted in further AUTOMATION of processes where workers have been replaced by machines.

For example, **computer numerical controlled (CNC)** lathes and milling machines are now standard in UK manufacturing. In design, **computer aided design (CAD)** packages are commonplace. These are programs which allow a design to be completed on a computer rather than on paper. The package is also able to do the numerical calculations necessary for the job. **computer aided manufacturing (CAM) (or CAD/CAM engineering)** links CAD packages with CNC machines. The CNC machines can be programmed from the CAD package. Computers are also used in other departments of manufacturing companies. Accounts are likely to be produced using an accounting program and financial information stored on computer or disks. Deliveries can be tracked online with some delivery companies.

Service industries too have been transformed. Even a traditional restaurant, for example, is likely to use a till which is controlled by a microchip. People might pay for a meal using a swipe card. In the kitchen, cookers, refrigerators and utensils will have changed from thirty years ago. In many service industries, there has been a revolution in the way in which the service is delivered. Computerisation has swept away the keeping of manual records. Email communication is becoming more common than written letters. The Internet allows advertising and sales to be made directly to customers via computer link.

Using technology to change the way in which work is done has several benefits. One is that production becomes more efficient, reducing costs. Another is that the quality of production can be improved. Email allows a faster response time to a query. The use of robots lets car manufacturers achieve zero defects in production. Improved technology can be used to improve the health and safety of workers. By automating dangerous processes, workers can be protected from harm.

Impact of changes in technology

New technology can present businesses with considerable opportunities. But it can also pose a major threat. There is a variety of ways in which this occurs.

Implementing technological change Buying a new computer system, installing a new CNC machine or developing a new product with the latest technology will not necessarily be successful in improving productivity or sales. The introduction of new technology is often a high risk process. Many new products fail. It may prove impossible to integrate the new machine into the existing production process. Computerisation may not save a worker time compared to a pen and paper system.

The introduction of new technology might also affect business organisation. Improvements in communication might mean changes in work practices, such as a reduction in face-to-face meetings. It might also allow a business, for example, to set up in another country and keep in regular contact to better meet the needs of a foreign market.

Managing technological change requires skill and often a certain amount of luck on the part of a business.

Competition and survival It is often expensive to install new technology in production processes. Designing new products containing new technology is also costly. Many businesses don't make enough profit or generate the cash flow to be able to afford this investment. However, they risk being left behind in the market if they don't invest. In the UK, manufacturing companies which have consistently failed to invest have become less and less cost competitive. Many businesses have been forced to close due to competition from cheap labour producers in the Far East. In a competitive market place, the businesses that survive are those which invest enough and manage the new technology successfully.

The workforce New technology will have an impact on the workers in a business. Introducing new technology in production is likely to require **training** of workers. This may be on-the-job training or off-the-job training. Not all workers will necessarily be able to cope with the changes. Some workers, for example, may not have the basic skills needed. Others may be reluctant to change to new ways of working. Management may then have to consider redeployment of some staff. Redundancy may also be a possibility. If the new technology is labour saving, and sales are not increasing, then redundancies may be inevitable.

Change can affect **motivation**. Some workers may be highly motivated by working with new products or new processes. Other workers may find it threatening and demotivating. They may be afraid that they will lose their job or their position in the hierarchy. They may worry about having to work with a new group of people or under a different manager. If the workplace is unionised, these fears may lead to trade unions objecting to the changes and attempting to stop, delay or alter them. Management, therefore, need to handle change with great care.

Business culture Technology has radically transformed business culture: the values, attitudes, beliefs, meanings and norms that are shared by people and groups within an organisation. One fundamental shift has been the transfer of workers from doing heavy manual labour in manufacturing to much lighter work in the service sector. The business culture of a coal mine or a factory is very different from an office, a shop, a care home or a hospital. However, technology has influenced business culture even when the same products are being made. For example, the culture on a car production line is different today than it was 50 years ago. Then, workers were typically unskilled, performing repetitive tasks for which they took little responsibility. Today, far more production is now automated, particularly hazardous and dangerous procedures. Production line workers are given responsibility for quality assurance. They may work in teams. Instead of the technology encouraging a spirit of alienation among workers, it has enabled workers to develop more positive attitudes to work.

KEYTERMS

Automation – the process of the replacement of workers by machines in production.

KNOWLEDGE

1. Give three examples of technological change that has occurred over the past three hundred years.
2. What does it mean to say that the rate of technological change is 'exponential'?
3. How can technological change lead to (a) changes in products and (b) changes in production processes?
4. Why might introducing new technology into a workplace be disruptive to production?
5. What are the human resource implications of introducing new technology?

Case Study: Kesslers International

Kesslers International is one of Europe's biggest makers of display stands for retailers. This is a fast-changing category of product, where success depends on translating design into manufacturing as smoothly as possible. At the company's factory in east London, a piece of metal can be cut into a complex shape on the shop floor using digital instructions generated 20 minutes earlier by a designer sitting at a computer terminal on the other side of a partition. 'We spend half our time working on creative design and the other half turning a concept into a working product without losing the aesthetic appeal', says George Kessler, one of two brothers who run the family-owned company.

Each year the company makes up to 1,000 types of display, selling from just a few pounds to £1,500 each, in production runs that are rarely above a few thousand. The displays use about 70,000 types of component. These are made on a variety of machines, including robot welders, vacuum forming machines, laser cutters, injection moulding systems, silk screen printers and powder coating equipment. About 80 per cent of what it makes will not be repeated the next year because of fashion changes.

The main contacts of customers among Kesslers' 300 employees are with its 30 or so designers and product developers. These people use computer-aided draughting systems to turn ideas into product specifications, normally in a matter of weeks after receiving an order. The close link between the design and manufacturing teams means the company can make late changes to orders on behalf of customers, even a few days before the order is delivered. The customers like the flexibility, for which Kesslers charges extra.

Maintaining such a close link between manufacturing and design requires heavy investment. The company spends up to £500,000 a year on capital equipment and puts another £80,000 a year into training. It is putting its employees through special training courses organised by Cardiff University's lean enterprise implementation group to tutor them in the latest thinking in fields such as just-in-time manufacturing and ways to minimise waste. 'There is absolutely no point in investing in machinery if you don't put substantial sums into improving the capabilities of your employees', says George Kessler.

Source: adapted from *The Financial Times*.

(a) Discuss whether technological change in new products or in business processes is more important for Kesslers. (40 marks)

(b) Evaluate the problems that Kesslers might face in using new technologies in production. (40 marks)

129 Competition and business strategies

Markets and competition

Markets have a number of characteristics.

- A market exists in any place where buyers and sellers meet to exchange goods and services.
- The place may be a physical one, such as a street market, or a supermarket. Equally, many transactions today take place by post, fax, over the phone or on the Internet.
- Markets can be local, national or international.
- Some markets, such as that for cricket bats, are small. In some, such as the car market, sales are so large that they dwarf the output of many countries in the world today.

Almost every business has to compete in the market place. COMPETITION can take a variety of forms depending upon the particular market in which a business operates. One simple way of characterising competition is the 4Ps of marketing. All other things being equal:

- the lower the **price** charged, the more sales there will be;
- businesses which sell superior **products** to their rivals will sell more;
- **promotion** can help increase sales;
- getting products to customers at the right **place** and at the right time will stimulate sales.

Classifying markets: an economics approach

Markets can be classified into a number of different types according to their mix of characteristics.

Perfect competition In perfect competition, there are a large number of small businesses, none of which has any significant market share. They are independent of one another because the actions of one business have no effect on other businesses. In a perfectly competitive market, businesses produce homogeneous (or generic i.e. identical) products so there is no product branding by individual businesses. **Barriers to entry** to the market are low. This means that it is easy for a new business to set up in the market. This allows freedom of entry to new businesses.

The main example of a perfectly competitive market is agriculture. It is called 'perfect' competition because it is at one extreme of the spectrum of competition.

Perfectly competitive businesses, such as farms, have little or no control over the price at which they sell. They are **price-takers.** A farmer taking cattle to market has to accept whatever price is set at the auction. A farmer selling potatoes from a farm shop has to price them at roughly the same price as in local shops. Other commodity industries, like coal, copper or iron ore, tend also to be perfectly competitive. So too do industries such as steelmaking, paper manufacture or ship-building where firms find it difficult to differentiate their products from their competitors.

Monopolistic competition In monopolistic competition, there are many small businesses competing in the market. However, there is a very weak branding of products. As with perfect competition, barriers to entry are low and so new businesses can set up easily. Branding means that businesses can choose the price they set: they are **price-setters**. However, their influence over price is weak because the power to brand is weak. An example of monopolistic competition is the sportswear retail market. There are a few large sportswear chains of shops such as RSB. Equally, there are thousands of independent sportswear retailers. Each shop has a brand image and can choose where it wants to position itself in the market in terms of price, products sold, promotion and location. These will all affect how much each sells. For instance, on price, the higher the price charged, all other things being equal, the lower will be the volume of sales.

Oligopoly In oligopoly, a few businesses dominate the market. For example, there might be 2,000 businesses in the market, but if three of them have 80 per cent of the market between them, then the market would be oligopolistic. Because a few firms dominate the market, the actions of one business affects other businesses. For example, if the market share of one business grows from 25 per cent to 28 per cent, other businesses must have lost market share.

Often oligopolies exist because there are high barriers to entry. In car manufacturing, one barrier to entry is cost: when a car assembly plant can cost billions of pounds and a new model £500 million to develop, it is not surprising that there are relatively few businesses in the market. Another major barrier to entry may be the existence of strong brands, often supported by high levels of marketing expenditure.

Branding is a key characteristic of oligopolistic markets. Brands don't just deter competition. They also allow businesses to charge premium prices and sometimes to earn high profits. So oligopolistic businesses are **price-setters**. Branding, though, most favours the top brand in the market. Being number two or number three in terms of market share tends to make it difficult to charge premium prices and earn high profits.

Monopoly With monopoly, there is just one business in the market. Examples of monopoly include rail companies which have the exclusive right to provide a service along a rail route, or water companies which have the exclusive right to provide water to houses in a particular area. Monopolies exist because there are barriers to entry to the market. National monopolies in the UK today tend to be ones where the government has legally restricted competition to the market. However, there can be local monopolies for other reasons. For example, in rural areas, there may only be one large supermarket which effectively has a monopoly on supermarket grocery sales. Or a bus operator may provide the only service along a route even though other bus operators may be legally entitled to run a rival service. In both these cases, the market is not large enough to allow two businesses to offer a service and make a profit.

Monopolies may be able to exploit their market by charging high prices and earning high profits. For this reason, governments either make monopolies illegal, or monitor their activities to prevent them from exploiting the market. In the UK, a number of industries, such as water, rail and telecommunications, are regulated and maximum prices set down.

Changes in competitive structure

Classifying markets into perfect competition, monopolistic competition, oligopoly and monopoly helps to understand the impact on business of changes in the competitive structure of a market.

New competitors New competitors in a market will have a different impact depending on the number of firms in an industry. If a farm switches to growing wheat, this will have no impact on other wheat farmers. Supply from one farm is too small to affect market price. This is why local farmers often co-operate rather than act as rivals. But a new business entering a local newspaper market, or a local bus market could provoke a fierce response from an existing firm. If a local newspaper is a monopolist with 100 per cent of the market, then a new rival could take away a significant share of its market and at worst even force to it close. In oligopolistic or monopoly markets, where a few businesses or just one business dominate the market, existing firms will react strongly to destroy new entrants. For example, they might engage in **predatory pricing**, lowering their prices to such an extent that the new entrant can't make a profit. Or they might increase their marketing spending to limit the sales of the new entrant. They might use the law to prevent the new entrant from operating effectively. Tying up a new competitor in a law suit for a year, even if it comes to nothing, can lead to mounting costs for the new competitor which force it to leave the market.

Creating a dominant business The fewer the number of large firms in an industry, the more market power each remaining firm is likely to have. So two oligopolistic firms each with 50 per cent of the market are likely to have more market power than four firms with 25 per cent of the market each. Market power enables firms to charge higher prices and enjoy higher profit margins. There is a strong tendency, therefore, in oligopolistic industries for firms to merge. An alternative is for firms to **collude**. Collusion occurs when two or more firms agree, typically, to fix prices and sales between themselves. They have then formed a **cartel**. The most powerful cartels are ones which create an effective monopoly in the market. Cartels today are particularly found in markets where firms find it difficult to differentiate their products from each other. Bus services, cement manufacture and vitamins are all examples of industries where cartels have been found in recent years. Cartels and collusion are illegal in the UK and the EU. This is because they push up prices for customers without giving any benefits to them. The beneficiaries are the firms themselves who can enjoy higher profits.

The process of creative destruction Where the industry or market is effectively a monopoly, and barriers to entry are higher, the only way for the monopoly to be broken might be through the process of **creative destruction**. This is when a new entrant enters the market with a revolutionary new product which in itself creates a new monopoly. In the market for pharmaceutical drugs, for example, the goal of all large pharmaceutical companies is to discover a new 'blockbuster' drug. This is a drug which is far superior to anything else on the market. It can be patented and so rival companies cannot copy it. Then it can be sold at very high prices, earning large profits for its makers. The profits of large pharmaceutical companies are crucially dependent on just a handful of drugs they manufacture.

Question 1.

British manufacturers are combating threats from low-cost producer countries by moving into fields where price competition is less important, according to a survey published today. More companies are competing 'on the basis of customer service and quality and less on price' according to the report. Since 1990, manufacturing has slipped from 21 per cent to 14 per cent of the UK economic output, partly as a result of competition from lower-cost nations. Only 40 per cent of companies surveyed said they suffered from low-cost competition in export markets, compared to 50 per cent three years ago. Over the same period, the proportion moving into 'niche' markets, defined as product areas aimed at specialist needs in which global competition is relatively low, increased from 45 per cent to 55 per cent.

An example of a company that has shifted its strategies to compete in areas other than price is JCB, the earthmoving equipment supplier. In the past decade, the company has launched a range of specialist products such as military trucks and telescopic handlers that can pick up loads in restricted spaces. These sorts of machines are made by few other businesses around the world, which means JCB has relative freedom to set prices backed on manufacturing costs and desired profits.

Source: adapted from *The Financial Times*, 3.3.2008.

(a) 'UK manufacturing companies have been moving from competitive markets to oligopolistic markets'. Explain, using the data, what this means.

(b) What might be the advantages to UK businesses of moving from competitive markets to oligopolistic markets?

(c) How might a company like JCB become the dominant business in its market?

Porter's 5 forces analysis

Another way of looking at the competitive environment is to consider a model put forward by Michael Porter in his book, *Competitive advantage: creating and sustaining superior performance (1985).* In the book, he outlines five forces or factors which determine the profitability of an industry. He argues that the ultimate aim of competitive strategy is to cope with and ideally change those rules in favour of the business. Where the collective strength of those five forces is favourable, a business will be able to earn above average rates of return on capital. Where they are unfavourable, a business will be locked into low returns or wildly fluctuating returns. The five forces, shown in Figure 1, are as follows.

The bargaining power of suppliers Suppliers, like any business, want to maximise the profit they make from their customers. The more power a supplier has over its customers, the higher the prices it can charge and the more it can reallocate profit from the customer to itself. Limiting the power of its supplier, therefore, will improve the competitive position of a business. It has a variety of strategies it can adopt to achieve this. It can grow vertically (backward vertical integration), either acquiring a supplier or setting up its own business by growing organically upwards. It can seek out new suppliers to create more competition amongst suppliers. It might be able to engage in technical research to find substitutes for a particular input to broaden the supply base. It may also minimise the information provided to suppliers in order to prevent the supplier realising its power over the customer.

Bargaining power of buyers Just as suppliers want to charge maximum pricers to customers, so buyers want to obtain supplies for the lowest price. If buyers or customers have considerable market power, they will be able to beat down prices offered by suppliers. For example, the major car manufacturers have succeeded in forcing down the price of components from component suppliers because of their enormous buying power and the relatively few number of major car manufacturers in the world. One way a business can improve its competitive position viz-a-viz buyers is to extend into the buyers' market through forward vertical integration. A car manufacturer might set up its own component manufacturing division, for example. It could encourage other businesses to set up in its customers' market to reduce the power of existing customers. It could also try to make it expensive for customers to switch to another supplier. For example, one way in which games console manufacturers keep up the price of computer games for their machines on which they receive a royalty is by making them technically incompatible with other machines.

Threat of new entrants If businesses can easily come into an industry and leave it again if profits are low, it becomes difficult for existing businesses in the industry to charge high prices and make high profits. Existing businesses are constantly under threat that if their profits rise too much, this will attract new suppliers into the market who will undercut their prices. Businesses can counter this by erecting **barriers to entry** to the industry. For example, a business may apply for patents and copyright to protect its intellectual property and prevent other businesses using it. It can attempt to create strong brands which will attract customer loyalty and make customers less price sensitive. Large amounts of advertising can be a deterrent because it represents a large cost to a new entrant which might have to match the spending to grow some market share. Large sunk costs, costs which have to paid at the start but are difficult to recoup if the business leaves the industry, can deter new entrants.

Figure 1: The five competitive forces that determine industry profitability

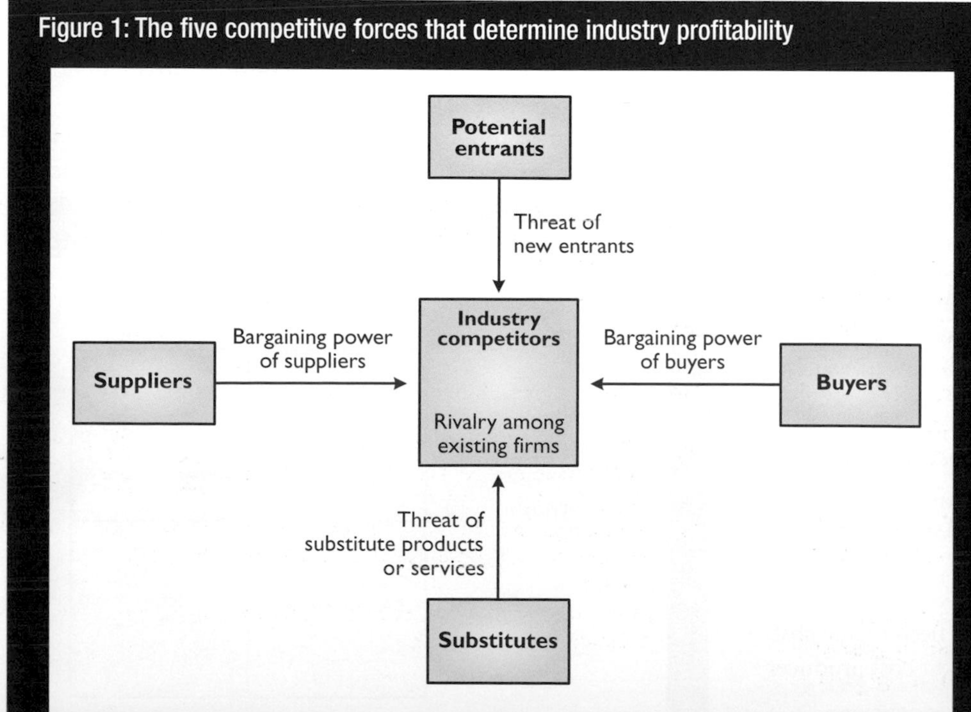

Substitutes The more substitutes there are for a particular product, the fiercer the competitive pressure on a business making the product. Equally, a business making a product with few or no substitutes is likely to be able to charge high prices and make high profits. A business can reduce the number of potential substitutes through research and development and then patenting the substitutes itself. Sometimes, a business will buy the patent for a new invention from a third party and do nothing with it simply to prevent the product coming to market. Businesses can also use marketing tactics to stop the spread of substitute products. A local newspaper, for example, might use predatory pricing if a new competitor comes into its market to drive it out again.

Question 2.

Fudges was founded in 1926 as a bread bakery. By 1988, however, the bakery was in trouble. Bread consumption was in decline and the outlook for the business was bleak. The two brothers who now owned the firm decided that only a fundamental change could save the business. They switched out of bread making and began to sell products that could be transported long distances with a good shelf life. Given their West Country heritage, cheddar wafers seemed a good product to sell along with other biscuits and high quality cakes.

The switch was so successful that the business needed more space for production. In 1998, the business moved to larger premises, buying out the Dorset Village Bakery in Stalbridge. However, the premises were larger than they needed. It decided to use the space they didn't need and the equipment that came with the Bakery to return to bread making. The decision proved disastrous. The bread making side of the business 'haemorrhaged cash'. Bread making was once again abandoned and the company went back to concentrating on its branded biscuit and cake ranges.

All of its 80 lines of wafers, crackers and seasonal offerings are sourced and marketed to reinforce the high-quality, Dorset country brand. The company works closely with suppliers and customers. For example, it has linked with companies like Unilever and Tate & Lyle to produce products featuring Marmite, Colman's mustard and golden syrup. It has just retooled a cutter to change the shape of the Marmite biscuits to look like the iconic tub container in which Marmite is sold. 'A bigger company would not have been able to do that because the volume would not have been large enough', said Mr Fudge, one of the owners.

The competitive advantage of being able to respond quickly with new products is reinforced by Mr Fudge's interest in innovative processes in the bakery, which is full of industrial ovens, long conveyor belts and bespoke machines. However, this sits alongside traditional handbaking techniques. With a staff of 160, all the mixes are weighed and mixed by hand, as is much of the decorating, dipping in chocolate, packing and marzipan ball-rolling. The company did consider moving some production to China. But this would compromise the brand's image of being a Dorset country local product.

Source: adapted from *The Financial Times*, 20.2.2008.

(a) Explain what business strategies Fudges has used to give itself a competitive advantage.

(b) Evaluate whether Fudges could ever gain a competitive advantage in bread making.

Rivalry among existing firms The degree of rivalry among existing firms in an industry will also determine prices and profits for any single firm. If rivalry is fierce, businesses can reduce that rivalry by forming cartels or engaging in a broad range of anti-competitive practices. In UK and EU law, this is illegal but it is not uncommon. Businesses can also reduce competition by buying up their rivals (horizontal integration). Again, competition law may intervene to prevent this happening but most horizontal mergers are allowed to proceed. In industries where there are relatively few businesses, often businesses don't compete on price. This allows them to maintain high profitability. Instead they tend to compete by bringing out new products and through advertising, thus creating strong brands. As a result their costs are higher than they might otherwise be, but they can also charge higher prices than in a more competitive market creating high profits.

Business strategies

BUSINESS or GENERIC STRATEGIES (sometimes also called business level strategies) are strategies which can be used by a business to give a COMPETITIVE ADVANTAGE over business rivals.

There are many different ways of analysing business strategies. However, Michael Porter in the 1985 book argues that there are three ways in which a business can achieve superior performance to competitors. These strategies are summarised in Figure 2.

Cost leadership One way is for the business to become the cost leader in the market. This means being the lowest cost producer for a given quality of product. For example, Wal-Mart in the USA and its subsidiary Asda in the UK have gained market share over time by offering lower prices to customers than competing hypermarket chains. Low cost in itself will not guarantee success. It has to be accompanied by the level of quality of product which a customer expects. So Asda in the UK may have been more successful than its rivals because it has offered a wide range of products, including wellknown branded products, at very low prices. Sainsbury's on the other hand may be regarded as a higher cost, higher price competitor but offering better quality products.

Differentiation A second way is for the business to differentiate its product from rivals. Differentiation is about making a product within a product range different from competitors. It is about giving a product a unique selling point. Differentiation is

Figure 2: Business or generic strategies

COMPETITIVE SCOPE		COMPETITIVE ADVANTAGE: Lower cost	COMPETITIVE ADVANTAGE: Differentiation
	Broad Target	1. Cost leadership	2. Differentiation
	Narrow Target	3A. Cost focus	3B. Differentiation focus

in itself not sufficient to give a competitive advantage. It has to be a differentiated product which customers want to buy. So Heinz or Coca-Cola have been successful because they have products made to unique formulations which customers prefer over other formulations.

Focus A third way is for the business to focus on a particular sector of the market, i.e. to select a market **niche**. There are two forms of focus. **Cost focus** occurs when a business drives down its costs in the market segment to undercut the prices of competitors. **Differentiation focus** occurs when a business sells a unique and differentiated product within the market segment. In many cases, a business adopting a focus strategy will see its main competitors as larger businesses serving the much broader mass market. Because they serve the mass market, they are not always very competitive in individual niche markets. This gives businesses targeting niche markets an opportunity to become more competitive than much larger rivals. However, a focus strategy does not necessarily guarantee success. There may be other highly competitive niche businesses in that market already. Equally, a business may find it difficult either to cut costs compared to mass market businesses or to produce a differentiated product which customers value.

Cost leadership can be developed in the broad market. Wal-Mart has developed its cost strategy in the broad market of retailing. Differentiation too can be developed in the broad market. Coca-Cola has developed its differentiation strategy in the broad market of soft drinks. A business may also seek a competitive advantage in a narrow market. This competitive advantage can be either a cost advantage or a differentiation advantage. For example, BMW has developed a differentiated product in the narrow market for luxury cars.

There are many other ways of considering competitive advantage. Business strategies, for example, can centre around:
- product design and development;
- pricing;
- promotion;
- place in the marketing mix;
- economies of scale;
- quality of production;
- delivery times including just-in-time production;
- the skill and motivation of the workforce;
- a low cost labour force;
- the flexibility of workers;
- an ethical stance for the business.

Global strategy

A GLOBAL or INTERNATIONAL STRATEGY needs to be considered by any business which sells products to overseas customers or which is potentially large enough to move part of its production abroad. A business has four main strategic choices in its global strategy.
- It can export the same products or a service format that have been highly successful in its domestic market. For example, a UK chocolate manufacturer could export a new chocolate bar launched in the UK to Hungary or Thailand. A UK furniture retailer could set up identical stores in France and Germany. The advantage of this strategy is that the product or service has already proved successful in one market and the cost of introducing it into a new overseas market will be less than if the product were adapted. It allows for greater economies of scale to be achieved. Coca-Cola is an example of how successful this strategy can be. However, the main disadvantage is that what is successful in one country may be not appeal to customers in another country.
- A second strategy is to take a successful product in one market and adapt it for overseas markets. For example, McDonald's sells different food in India from France from the USA. The advantage is that there should be more chance that the product will prove attractive to local customers. The main disadvantage, apart from the risk that the product in practice doesn't appeal, is that economies of scale will be lost. Producing a number of slightly different products, each for a different market, is likely to be more costly per unit than a single mass produced product.
- A third strategy is to concentrate on minimising production costs by locating wherever in the world it is least costly to produce. Manufacturing industries in the industrialised countries of the world have been migrating to a small number of developing countries, including China and South Korea, over the past twenty years. They have relocated low skill jobs to countries where workers are paid a fraction of the wages paid to similar workers.
- A fourth strategy is to combine both customising products to local markets with locating where costs are lowest. This is the most difficult strategy to implement because it requires the business to pay attention both to product and to costs.

KEYTERMS

Barriers to entry – factors which make it difficult or impossible for businesses to enter a market and compete with existing producers.

Business or generic strategy – strategies which can be used by a business to give a competitive advantage over business rivals, including pursuing cost leadership, product differentiation or focusing on a market segment.

Competition – rivalry between businesses offering products in the same market; competition may take forms such as price competition, distinctive product offerings, advertising and distribution.

Competitive advantage – an advantage which a business has that enables it to perform better than its rivals in the market.

Global or international strategy – the range of activities across the world a business needs to undertake in order to achieve its goals.

KNOWLEDGE

1. What is the link between competition and the 4Ps?
2. What is the difference between (a) a perfectly competitive market and a monopoly; (b) an oligopolistic market and one with monopolistic competition?
3. Why might a business engage in predatory pricing?
4. What are (a) the benefits and (b) the costs of collusion to a business?
5. What is the process of creative destruction?
6. Explain the benefits a business may obtain if it has market power over the businesses from which it buys.
7. How might the degree of rivalry between firms in an industry affect prices and profits?
8. Explain the difference between competitive advantage and competitive scope.

Case Study: The Nano

In January, talk at North America's biggest automobile show of the year in Detroit was dominated not by any of the new models on display at the show but by a chunky, oblong, little hatchback which just been unveiled half way round the world in India. The car was The Nano, produced by the Indian car manufacturer Tata Motors. It was to go on sale at $2 500 ex tax. Tata Motors was proclaiming it as the car which the emerging middle classes in India could afford to buy. On the day of its launch, Tata's website for the car had 4 million hits; such was the interest in the car.

Low cost cars have already been developed by other car manufacturers, but none has come anywhere near the price of The Nano. Bosch, the German automobile and industrial group, estimated low-cost vehicles prices at less than $7,000 could reach a 13 per cent share of the world market, or about 10 million vehicles, in 2010. The Indian market alone is potentially huge given its current population of 900 million people. It is generating hundreds of thousands of first-time car buyers every year. What's more, there is a culture of frugality in India. Indian suppliers are used to cutting costs, whilst Indian consumers are happy to buy low cost cars.

The Nano doesn't pass EU safety standards and so it couldn't be sold in the UK in the version unveiled in India.

Source: adapted from *The Financial Times*, 4.3.2008.

China is confounding the pundits. Car manufacturers, both Chinese and non-Chinese, had expected the fast-growing demand for cars in China to be weighted towards the small car market. With relatively low incomes and growing congestion in China's cities, the small car seemed to be the obvious choice for the Chinese customer. However, whilst the overall car market has continued to expand at a dramatic rate, demand for small cars is growing far less. Sales of micro and subcompact cars were almost flat last year whilst sales of small-engined vehicles fell by more than 20 per cent.

Chinese consumers appear to be more concerned than car-buyers in other emerging markets about the social status implied by their vehicles. Research by Volkswagen last year found that the average Chinese first-time buyer spent twice his or her annual salary on the vehicle. This has benefited multinational companies like Volkswagen, the market leader, which offers a range of more expensive cars. It has disadvantaged the new generation of Chinese motor manufacturing companies, many of which had hoped to enter the market by selling cheaper, small vehicles to cost-conscious consumers. However, Chinese companies are renowned for copying the successful practices of rivals, especially Western companies. The trend to buy more expensive cars has only given companies like Volkswagen a breathing space. They need to remain at the forefront of innovation and development to provide the Chinese consumer with a car which they aspire to purchase.

Source: adapted from *The Financial Times*, 4.3.2008.

(a) Evaluate how the launch of The Nano has changed the competitive environment for multinational car manufacturers like Volkswagen and Ford. (40 marks)

(b) Discuss how a multinational car company like Volkswagen or Ford should respond to Tata Motor's launch of its Nana car. Use Michael Porter's analysis of business strategies to help you answer this question. (40 marks)

130 Collecting and presenting data

Why do businesses collect data?

Information is a valuable resource in business. Businesses collect large amounts of information or DATA about their own organisations. They may also employ companies, such as Reuters, which specialises in the collection and sale of information. Examples of data that a business might collect include:

- costs of production;
- share prices and exchange rates;
- company reports;
- weekly or monthly sales figures;
- business news, for example about a potential takeover;
- market research findings.

Data are collected by businesses for a number of reasons. Most importantly perhaps, data are required in the decision making process. Managers, employees and others involved in business activity need up to date and accurate data to help them make effective decisions. For example, a business choosing from a number of investment opportunities would require the latest information on the costs and expected return of each project.

Data are required to monitor the progress of a business. Business performance could be gauged by looking at the growth or decline in turnover or profit. Changes in productivity rates can be calculated if a business has data on its inputs and output.

All businesses keep records which contain a wide range of **qualitative** (about nature or characteristics) and **quantitative** (involving measurement) data. These records contain information that is important to the business. Such records might include monthly sales figures, staff files, customer files and market reports. It is important that records are regularly updated so that they are correct when required by the business. Businesses make use of **backdata,** such as sales in previous years, to forecast what might happen in the future.

Data are also used to help control a business. Financial data on payments and receipts are used to control cash flow. A financial controller, for example, might delay payment to a supplier until money is received from customers in order to avoid a cash flow problem.

Why do businesses present data?

Once data has been collected it can be stored, retrieved and presented. The volume of data collected by businesses is enormous and it is important to avoid making mistakes. The development of information and communication technology in recent years has made the handling of data far easier and less prone to error. Data can be stored on computer memory or a disk, 'called up' on a computer screen, manipulated and presented in a variety of styles. Businesses may make use of graphs, charts, tables and other pictorial methods of communicating data. Presenting data in this way:

- can be more concise and easier to understand than written information;
- can take less time to interpret;
- can identify trends clearly;
- may be effective in creating an impact or an image;
- can be used to impress a potential client.

The method of presentation a business chooses will depend on the type of data collected, who and what it is required for and how it is likely to be used. Data can be presented 'internally' and 'externally'. Examples of data presented to those inside a business might be:

- the sales department presenting a breakdown of regional sales figures to senior management to illustrate the popularity of products in an area or the effectiveness of promotion;
- the production manager presenting the accounts department with weekly time sheets to allow the calculation of wages and costs;
- the research and development department providing an analysis of monthly expenditure to enable budgets to be calculated;
- the personnel manager providing an analysis of staff turnover to illustrate possible problems or improvements in human resource management;

Figure 1: Summary results, divisional operating profit and EPS and dividends per share for Johnson Matthey 2007

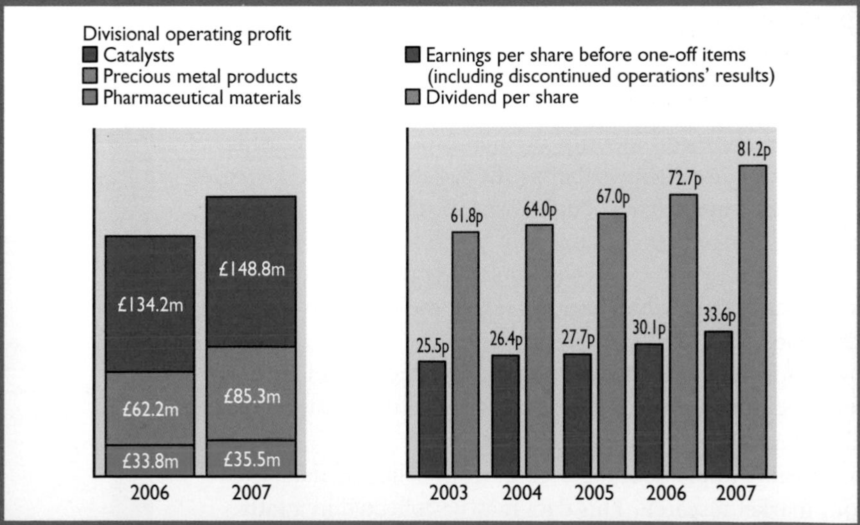

- the market research department providing research data to allow products to be designed to fit consumers' needs.

Examples of data presented to those outside the business could be:

- the accounts department providing Customs and Excise with VAT details to claim back tax on sales which are exempt from VAT;
- the publication of an Annual Report and Accounts to illustrate a company's progress over the last year to shareholders;
- the presentation of a new market range by the marketing department to a potential customer.

Figure 1 shows some business data for Johnson Matthey. Johnson Matthey is a speciality chemicals company and a world leader in advanced materials technology. The data is presented using a variety of methods and shows a number of things. For example, both EPS and dividends per share have increased consistently over the time period. There has been a significant increase in profit from precious metals over the last twelve months. It has increased from £62.2 million to £85.3 million. The table shows that revenue has increased from £4,574 million to £6,152 million.

Bar charts

A BAR CHART is one of the simplest and most common means of presenting data. Numerical information is represented by 'bars' or 'blocks' which can be drawn horizontally or vertically. The length of the bars shows the relative importance of the data. Table 1 shows data on the profit made by Ragwear plc, a manufacturer, over the last six years. They are presented as a bar graph in Figure 2.

Table 1: Profit for Ragwear plc over a six year period

	Yr1	Yr2	Yr3	Yr4	Yr5	£m Yr6
Profit	2.1	2.9	3.8	4.1	3.2	4.9

The main advantage of using a bar chart is that it shows results very clearly. At a glance the reader can get a general feel of the information and identify any trends or changes over the time period. Figure 2 shows that profit has continued to increase over the period apart from a 'dip' in year 5. This might indicate to the firm that trading conditions in year 5 were unfavourable or that the firm's performance was relatively poor. Bar charts are more attractive than tables and may allow the reader to interpret the data more quickly.

The bars in Figure 2 are drawn vertically. They could also, however, be drawn horizontally. They are also two dimensional, but they could have been three dimensional.

It is possible to produce a bar chart from collected data, such as from market research. This data may be collected in a **tally chart** as in Table 2, which shows the results of research into the

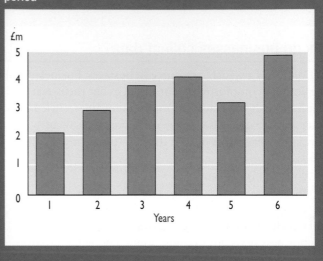

Figure 2: Profit levels for Ragwear plc over a six year period

£m
5
4
3
2
1
0
1 2 3 4 5 6
Years

Table 2: Survey results into the popularity of toothpaste

Brand	Tally marks	Frequency
Colgate	~~||||~~ ~~||||~~ ~~||||~~ etc.	260
Macleans	~~||||~~ ~~||||~~ ~~||||~~ etc.	190
Sensodyne	~~||||~~ ~~||||~~ ~~||||~~ etc.	100
Mentadent	~~||||~~ ~~||||~~ ~~||||~~ etc.	50
Supermarket own brand	~~||||~~ ~~||||~~ ~~||||~~ etc.	230
Aquafresh	~~||||~~ ~~||||~~ ~~||||~~ etc.	20
Oral-B	~~||||~~ ~~||||~~ ~~||||~~ etc.	150
Total		1,000

Figure 3: The popularity of brands of toothpaste from a sample of 1,000 customers

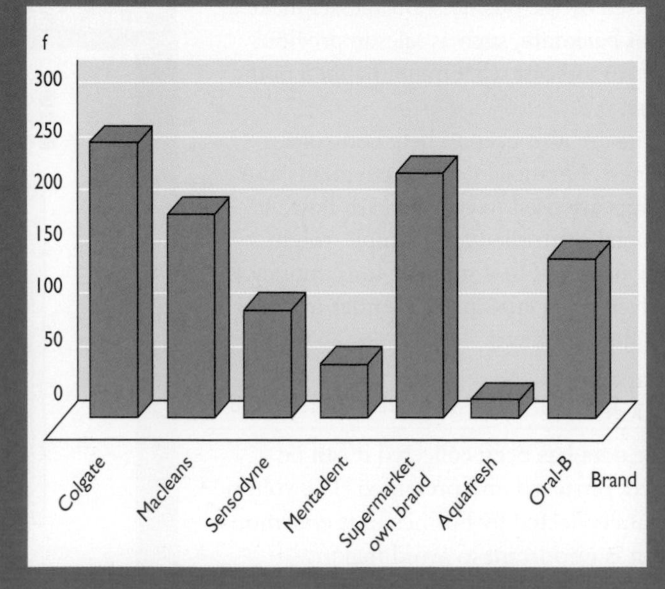

brands of toothpaste bought by a sample of supermarket customers. The total number of times each item occurs is known as the **frequency** (f). So, for example, the most popular from the survey is Colgate and the least popular is Aquafresh. Figure 3 shows the data from Table 2 as a bar chart.

Component bar charts

A COMPONENT BAR CHART allows more information to be presented to the reader. Each bar is divided into a number of components. For example, the data in Table 3 shows the cost structures of five furniture manufacturers in a particular year. The total cost is broken down into labour, materials and overheads.

Table 3: Cost structures of five furniture manufacturers and overheads

£000

	Oakwell	Stretton	Bradford	Jones	Campsfield
Labour	50	36	70	45	90
Materials	18	25	48	23	50
Overheads	10	10	19	9	25

Figure 4: Cost structures and overheads for five furniture manufacturers

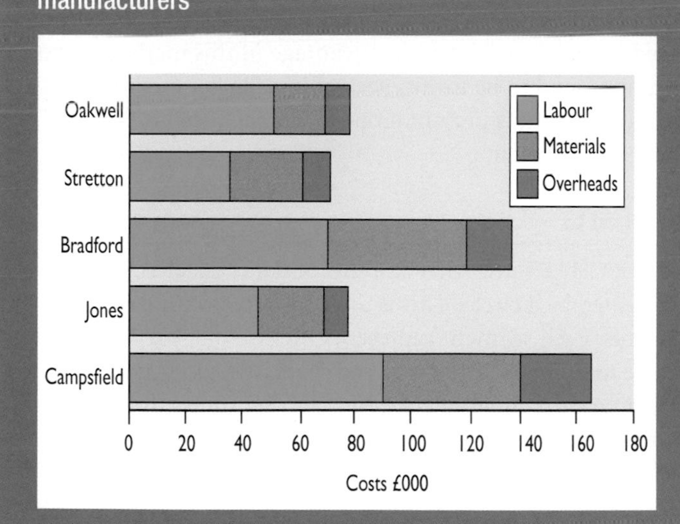

The data in the table are presented as a component bar chart in Figure 4. One advantage this chart has compared to the simple bar chart is that total costs can be seen easily. There is no need to add up the individual costs. It is also easier to make instant comparisons. For example, labour costs are the greatest proportion of total cost at Oakwell. This might suggest to a firm that Oakwell uses a more labour intensive production technique than the others. Also, labour costs at Oakwell are higher than at Stretton, but not as high as at Campsfield. This might indicate that Oakwell is less efficient than Stretton and a much smaller business than Campsfield.

Figure 5 shows three other styles of bar chart, illustrating data for AVC Holdings. This is a company that produces three types of machine tool, code named BAT 4, BAT 3 and BAT 2.

Figure 5: Turnover, profit and labour force data for AVC Holdings, 2004-2008

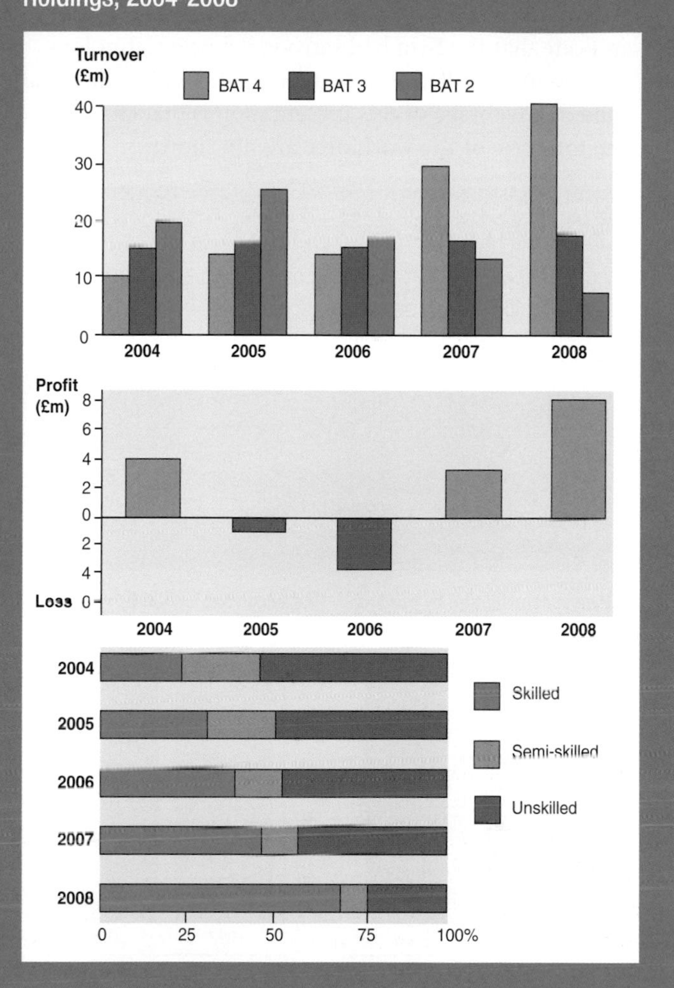

- The top chart is a **parallel** bar chart. It shows the turnover contributed by each of the company's three products. Over the time period the turnover for BAT 4 has increased from £10 million to £40 million. Sales of BAT 3 have remained fairly steady at around £15 million each year. The turnover from BAT 2 has declined from £20 million to £7 million. This type of graph is similar to a component bar chart. The advantage is that it is easier to compare changes between the components, although it is more difficult to compare totals.
- The middle chart is a **gain and loss** bar chart. It shows the profitability of the company over the time period. The performance of AVC Holdings worsened in the first three years and then improved. The profit in 2008 was £8 million. This type of chart distinguishes very clearly between positive and negative values.
- The bottom chart is a **percentage component** bar chart. It shows the breakdown of the workforce in terms of their skill with each section represented as a percentage of the workforce. In 2004 nearly 25 per cent of the workforce

were skilled. In 2008 this had risen to around 70 per cent. The chart also shows that the numbers of semi-skilled workers had fallen as a percentage of the total. This might indicate that the firm had introduced new technology, leading to unskilled staff being replaced with skilled staff. One disadvantage of this presentation is that changes in the total size of the workforce are not shown.

Question 1.

Birmingham-based Cadbury Schweppes is one of the world's largest producer of confectionery and beverages. Some of its brands include Cadbury's Dairy Milk, Cadbury's Crème Egg, Cadbury's Flake, Dr Pepper, Schweppes and Canada Dry. Figure 6 shows some information for the company.

Figure 6: Analysis of confectionery revenue and contribution by region

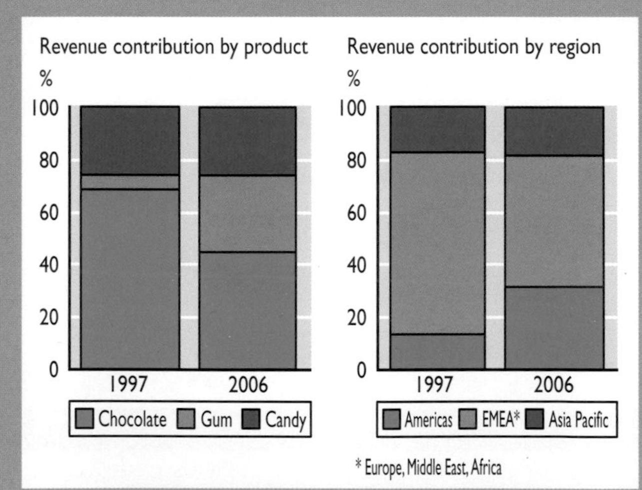

Source: adapted from Cadbury Schweppes, *Annual Report and Accounts*, 2006.

(a) What method of presentation has Cadbury's Schweppes used to present the information shown in Figure 6?
(b) Explain briefly what the two charts show.
(c) Outline one advantage and one disadvantage of using this method of presentation.

A pictograph or pictogram

A PICTOGRAPH or PICTOGRAM is another form of chart. It presents data in a similar way to bar charts. The difference is that data are represented by pictorial symbols rather than bars. Figure 7 shows an example of the orders which GPA Group has received for its aircraft over a nine year time period. The pictograph shows a general decline in orders. This might indicate that there is a general decline in the market or that customers are delaying future orders. One problem with a pictograph is that it is not always easy to 'divide' the symbols exactly. This makes it difficult to read precise quantities from the

Figure 7: A pictograph for GPA Group showing orders for aircraft in March 1999 for each year to 2007

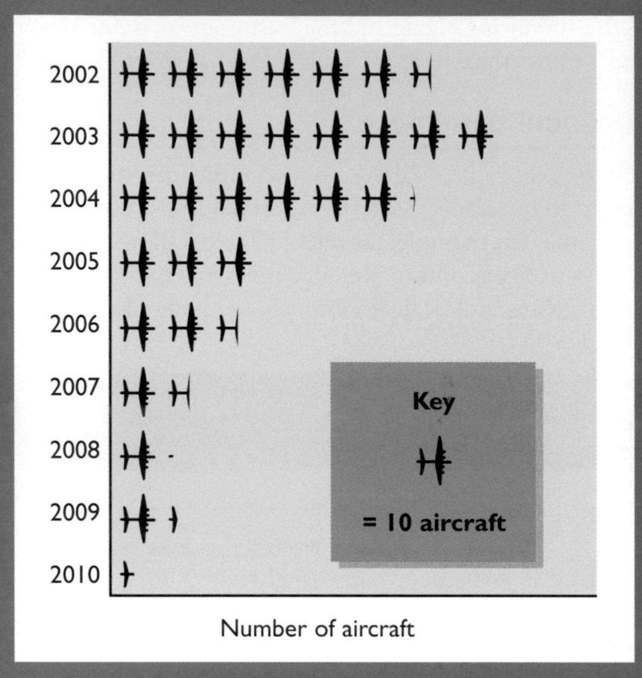

graph. For example, in Figure 7, in 2004 the number of orders is more than 60, but the last symbol is a fraction of an aircraft which makes it difficult to determine the exact size of orders placed in that year. The main advantage of this method is that the graphs tend to be more eyecatching. Such a method might be used in business presentations to attract attention or in reports to the public.

Pie charts

In a PIE CHART, the total amount of data collected is represented by a circle. This is divided into a number of segments. Each segment represents the size of a particular part relative to the total. To draw a pie chart it is necessary to perform some simple calculations. Table 4 shows the details of monthly output at five European plants for a multinational brick producer. The 360 degrees in a circle have to be divided between the various parts which make up the total output of 50,000 tonnes. To calculate the number of degrees each segment will contain, a business would use the following formula:

$$\frac{\text{Value of the part}}{\text{Total}} \times 360°$$

Table 4: Monthly brick output at five European plants

	Bedford	Brescia	Lyon	Bonn	Gijon	Total
Output (tonnes)	10,000	8,000	5,000	15,000	12,000	50,000

Thus, the size of the segment which represents the monthly brick output in Bedford is:

$$= \frac{10,000}{50,000} \times 360^\circ$$

$$= 0.2 \times 360^\circ$$

$$= 72^\circ$$

Using the same method it can be shown that the size of the other segments representing output at the other plants will be: Brescia 58°; Lyon 36°; Bonn 108°; Gijon 86°.

The number of degrees in each segment added together make 360°. A pie chart can now be drawn using a protractor or a spreadsheet or DTP software package on a computer. The pie chart is shown in Figure 8. Bonn makes the largest contribution to monthly output with Gijon second. The company might use this information to compare with monthly production targets.

Pie charts are useful because readers get an immediate impression of the relative importance of the various parts. They can also be used to make comparisons over different time periods. There are however, drawbacks with pie charts.

- They do not always allow precise comparisons to be made between the segments.
- If a total consists of a very large number of components, it may be difficult to identify the relative importance of each segment.
- It is difficult to show changes in the size of the total pie. For example, if the total rises over time it is possible to make the 'pie' bigger. However, the exact size of the increase is often difficult to determine because it involves comparing the areas of circles.

Figure 8: A pie chart illustrating the monthly output (tonnes) at five European plants for a multinational company producing bricks

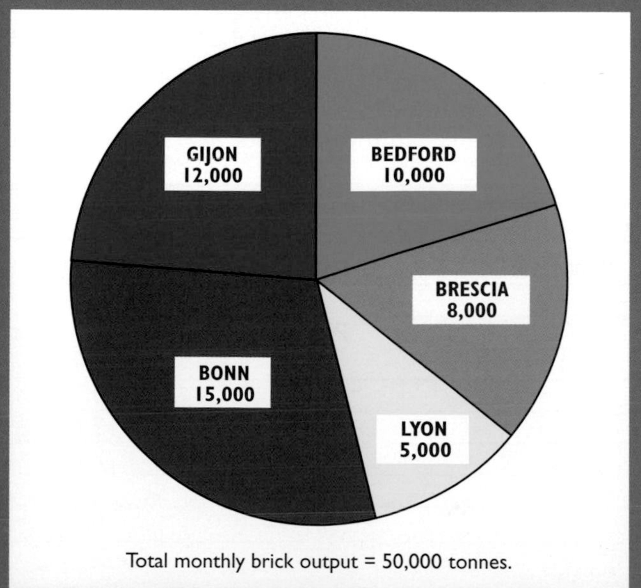

Question 2.

thegamesroom.com was set up in 2001 by Tony Phillips and his best friend from university, Paul Martins. They developed a number of interactive business games which could be played online. After its initial success, a private limited company was formed in 2005 and the company began to expand by developing a wider range of games. However, in 2008 it ran into financial difficulty and invited its financial backer to take a bigger stake in the company. The venture capitalists put in another £2 million and increased their shareholding to 15 million shares. Table 5 shows the number of shares owned by each member of the company in 2005 and 2008.

Table 5: The number of shares owned by members of thegamesroom.com

	2005 (Millions)	2008 (Millions)
Mr A Phillips	8.5	8.5
Mrs B Phillips	2.5	2.5
Mr P Martins	4.0	4.0
Venture capitalist	5.0	15.0

(a) Produce two pie charts to show the shareholding of each member of thegamesroom.com for 2005 and 2008.

(b) Discuss the advantages and disadvantages to the business of presenting data in this way.

(c) Comment briefly on the implications of the changes shown by the pie charts.

Histograms

Table 6 illustrates some data collected by market researchers on behalf of a cinema chain. It concerns the age profile of a sample of cinema goers on a Saturday. The chart shows the number of viewers in the sample that falls into various age ranges (known as **classes**). The total number of times each item occurs in each class is known as the frequency (f). So the total number of viewers in the 10-19 age range is 290. This type of data is usually shown as a HISTOGRAM as in Figure 9. A histogram looks similar to a bar chart, but there are some differences.

- In a histogram it is the **area** of the bars which represents

Table 6: The age profile of cinema goers on a Saturday

Age range	Frequency
0-9	180
10-19	290
20-29	500
30-39	400
40-49	350
50-59	280
60-79	200
Total	2,200

the frequency. In a bar chart it is the length or height of the bars. For example, in Figure 9, all the columns have the same width except for the last one where the age range covers two decades and not one. This means that the frequency in the figure is not 200 as shown in the table, but 100 (200÷2 = 100). This is because in the table 200 viewers fall into the age range 60 - 79, whereas the histogram shows 100 viewers in the age range 60 - 69 and 100 in the range 70 - 79. However, the area of the last bar coincides with the data in the table, ie it is equal to 200. The total area represented by all columns is equal to the sample size of 2,200.

- Bar charts and histograms can be used for **discrete data** - data which only occur as whole numbers, such as the number of people employed in a store. Histograms are most useful when recording **continuous data** - data which occur over a range of values, such as weight or age.
- Histograms tend to be used for grouped data, for example the number of people between the ages of 0 and 9.

The histogram in Figure 9 shows that the most frequently occurring age range of viewers is 20 - 29. The information might be used by the cinema chain to help plan a marketing strategy. It is possible to show the information in Table 6 by plotting a curve called a frequency polygon. It is drawn using the histogram and involves joining all the mid-points at the top of the 'bars' with straight lines. The frequency polygon for the data in Table 6 is shown in Figure 9. Arguably, the visual pattern of the data is shown more clearly by the frequency polygon.

Figure 9: A histogram representing the age profile of a sample of cinema goers on a Saturday – the frequency polygon is also shown

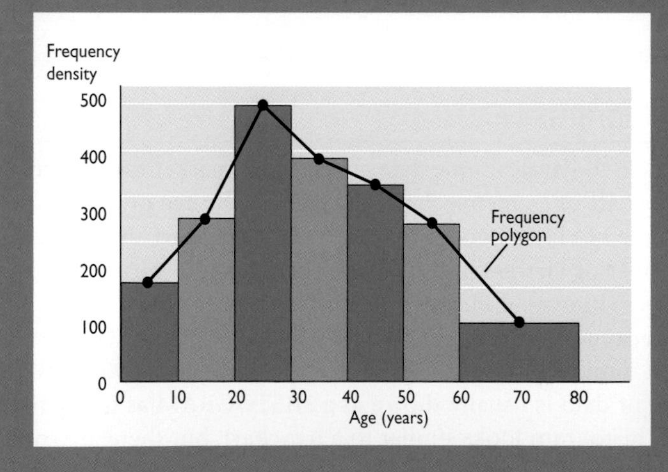

Tables

Tables are used to present many forms of data. They may be used:

- if data are qualitative rather than quantitative;
- where a wide range of variables needs to be expressed at the same time;
- where the numbers themselves are at the centre of attention;
- when it is necessary to perform calculations on the basis of the information.

Some would argue that the use of tables should be avoided if possible. However, a poorly or inaccurately drawn graph would be less effective than a neatly presented table. Table 7 shows the market shares in the global confectionery market. The table shows not only the different competitors operating in the market but also the shares in each of the three main products – chocolate, gum and candy. The table shows that Cadbury Schweppes is the overall market leader with 9.9 per cent of the market. However, Cadbury does not dominate the gum market. Wrigley is the market leader here with 35.9 per cent.

Line graphs

LINE GRAPHS are probably the most common type of graph used by a business. A line graph shows the relationship between two variables. The values of one variable are shown on the vertical axis and the values of the other variable are placed on the horizontal axis. The two variables must be related in some way. The values of the variables can be joined by straight lines or a smooth curve. If **time** is one of the variables being analysed it should always be plotted on the horizontal axis. Output is usually plotted on the horizontal axis. The main advantage of this type of graph is the way in which a reader can get an immediate picture of the relationship between the two variables. Also, it is possible to

Table 7: Market share of the global confectionary market (US $), % share

	Global confectionery market	Chocolate	Gum	Candy
Cadbury Schweppes	9.9	7.5	25.7	7.2
Mars	9.0	14.8	-	3.0
Nestlé	7.8	12.6	0.1	3.2
Wrigley	5.8	-	35.9	2.7
Hershey	5.5	8.2	1.1	2.7
Ferrero	4.4	7.3	-	1.5
Kraft	4.3	7.7	0.1	0.4

Source: adapted from Euromonitor, 2005.

take measurements from a line graph when analysing data. It is much more difficult to do this when reading figures from a table. Quite often more than one line is shown on a line graph so that comparisons can be made. **Economic data** is often presented on a line graph. A line graph showing interest rates over the recent period may influence a business's decision to invest, for example.

Cumulative frequency curves

When collecting data and recording it in a table, it is possible to show CUMULATIVE FREQUENCY. This is the total frequency up to a particular item or class boundary. It is calculated by adding the number of entries in a class to the total in the next class - a 'running total'. Table 8 shows the weights of cereal packages coming off a production line in a particular time period.

The cumulative frequencies in the table can be plotted on a graph. The graph is called an **ogive** and is shown in Figure 11. It can be seen, for example, that 270 packages weigh below 201.5 grams.

A Lorenz curve

A LORENZ CURVE is a special type of line graph. It is a cumulative frequency curve which can be used to show the

Question 3.

The three most popular internet search sites are Google, Yahoo and Microsoft. In May 2007 Microsoft launched an audacious $44.6bn (£22.4bn) bid for Internet rival Yahoo in an attempt to create an online search and advertising group that can rival market leader Google. The deal would bring together one of the Internet's largest and oldest destinations, Yahoo, with Microsoft's MSN platform in the biggest Internet merger since AOL bought Time Warner for $112bn in 2000. Some data relating to the three companies are shown in Figure 10.

Figure 10: Internet search sites - visits and market share

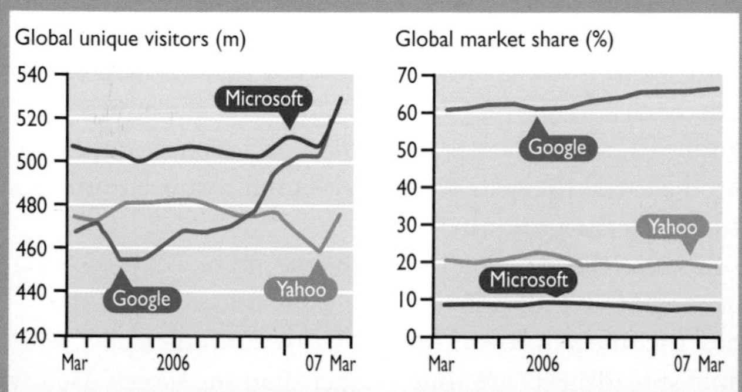

Source: adapted from the Dealogic, comScore.

(a) Describe the information shown in Figure 10.
(b) What are the advantages of presenting data in this way?

Table 8: Cumulative frequency of package weights

Weights falling within these ranges (grams)	Frequency	Cumulative frequency
198-199	30	30
199-200	50	80 (30 + 50)
200-201	150	230 (30 + 50 + 150)
201-202	70	300 (30 + 50 + 150 + 70)
202-203	40	340 (30 + 50 + 150 + 70 + 40)
203-204	5	345 (30 + 50 + 150 + 70 + 40 + 5)

Figure 11: A cumulative frequency distribution (ogive) showing the weights of 345 cereal packages

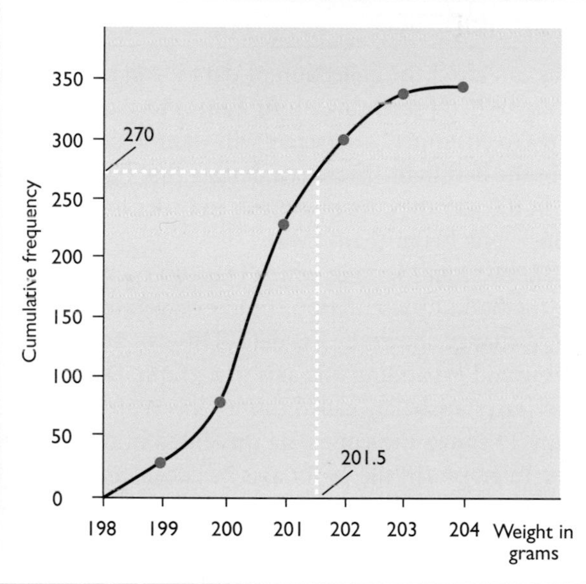

Figure 12: A Lorenz curve illustrating the distribution of hotel business amongst a town's hotels

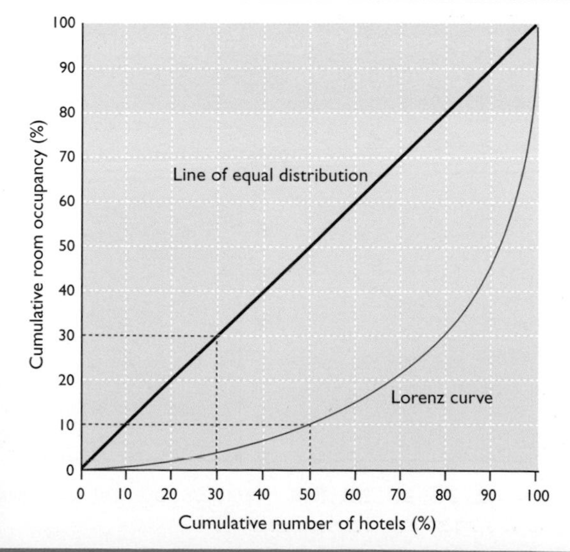

difference between actual distribution and an equal distribution. Figure 12 is a Lorenz curve which illustrates the way in which business is distributed between different hotels in a town. What does the curve show? If business was shared equally between all hotels then the line would be a straight 45° line. So, for example, 30 per cent of the town's hotels would get 30 per cent of all business, measured here as the number of rooms occupied. The Lorenz curve shows the actual distribution of business amongst the town's hotels. For example, 50 per cent of the town's hotels have only 10 per cent of the total hotel business. This obviously indicates a very unequal distribution of business amongst the town's hotels. The further the Lorenz curve is drawn away from the 45° line the more unequal the actual distribution will be. A business might use this to analyse market share. The Lorenz curve is often used to show the distribution of wealth in a particular country.

Bias in presentation

Just as bias can affect the collection of data it can also affect its presentation. When presenting profit figures to shareholders or sales figures to customers, managers will want to show the business in the best light. There is a danger that figures may be distorted in the way they are presented, in order to make performance look better than it was.

There are two main ways in which bias can occur.

- The method of presentation could exaggerate the actual rate of change shown by the data. This can be done by cutting and expanding one axis of a graph. Darrel Huff, an American statistician, called this a 'Gee-Whiz' graph. Figure 13 shows the same data presented in two different ways. In graph (b) the profit axis has been cut and extended. This gives a far better impression of the growth in profit than in graph (a). Similar bias can be introduced into bar charts, pie charts and pictographs.
- A business could leave out figures that do not fit into the 'picture' it wants to portray. For example, in a presentation to customers a firm may show its sales figures have been rising over the past five years, but omit to show that the total market has been increasing at a faster rate. This, in fact, means that the market share of the business has been falling.

Figure 13: The same profit figures for a business presented to show two different pictures

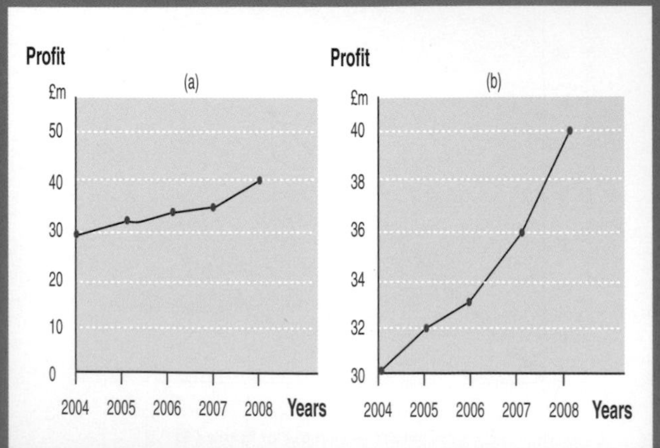

Table 9: An example of a spreadsheet which contains cost data

	A	B	C	D	E	F	G
1		Jan	Feb	March	April	May	June
2	Labour	200	210	230	210	200	230
3	Materials	100	100	110	130	100	110
4	Fuel	35	35	35	30	30	20
5	Overheads	25	25	30	30	35	35
6	Total costs	360	370	405	400	365	395

The formulae for total costs in row 6 is shown below.

6	Total costs	=SUM(B2..B5)	=SUM(C2..C5)	=SUM(D2..D5)	=SUM(E2..E5)	=SUM(F2..F5)	=SUM(G2..G5)

Spreadsheets

Some types of numerical data can be presented effectively using a SPREADSHEET. A spreadsheet allows the user to enter, store and present data in a grid on a computer screen. Just as a word processor is able to manipulate text, spreadsheets can do the same with numerical data. Table 9 shows that the grid is made up of a number of 'cells' or blank boxes. These cells are arranged in rows (information across the spreadsheet) and columns (information down the spreadsheet). Each blank cell is able to carry information which will fall into one of three categories.

- Numerical data - these are the numbers entered by the user which will be manipulated by the program.
- Text - this refers to the words used in the spreadsheet, often headings.
- Formulae - these are the instructions given by the user which tell the computer to manipulate the numerical data, for example, add a column of entries to give a total.

An example of a spreadsheet is illustrated in Table 9. It contains data relating to a firm's production costs. Each column (from B to G) shows the costs of various items each month. Each row shows particular costs over the entire period. For example, row 2 shows the labour costs each month. Row 6 shows the total cost each month. The total cost is automatically calculated by the program.

In this case the formula for cell B6 would be B2 + B3 + B4 + B5 or = SUM (B2..B5). If the business changed any of the entries, the totals in row 6 would change automatically.

Some spreadsheets are much larger than the screen itself with up to 250 columns and 8,000 rows. The screen can only show part of the spreadsheet. Scrolling is used to solve this problem. This enables the user to scan over the entire spreadsheet until the section they need is shown on the screen. The advantages of spreadsheets are listed below.

- Numerical data is recorded and shown in a clear and ordered way.
- Editing allows figures, text and formulae to be changed easily to correct mistakes or make changes in the data.
- It is easy to copy an entry or series of entries from one part of the spreadsheet to another. This is particularly useful when one figure has to be entered at the same point in every column.
- The user can add, subtract, multiply and divide the figures entered on the spreadsheet.
- A spreadsheet can calculate the effect of entry changes easily. This is sometimes referred to as the 'what if' facility, eg what would happen to cell X (total costs) if the entry in cell A (labour costs) increased by 10 per cent? The answer can be found very quickly.
- Some spreadsheet programs allow graphs and diagrams to be drawn from figures in the spreadsheet.

One problem with spreadsheets is in printing the results. Some simple spreadsheets will tend to print everything being used. This can be time consuming and wasteful. Other programs allow the user to print specific rows, columns or cells. Some spreadsheets permit the sheet to be printed sideways to allow for a wide sheet to be printed. A further complication is what should be printed out for some of the cells, eg for a particular cell, should it be the result of a formula or the formula itself?

Databases

A DATABASE is really an electronic filing system. It allows a great deal of data to be stored. Every business which uses computers will compile and use databases. The information is set up so that it can be updated and recalled when needed. Table 10 shows part of a database of a finance company which gives details about their clients. The collection of common data is called a file. A file consists of a set of related records. In the database pictured in Table 10 all the information on Jane Brown, for example, is a record. The information on each record is listed under headings known as fields, eg name, address, age, occupation, income each year. A good database will have the the following facilities.

- 'User-definable' record format, allowing the user to enter any chosen field on the record.
- File searching facility for finding specified information from a file, eg identifying all clients with an income over £24,000 in the above file. It is usually possible to search on more than one criterion, e.g. all females with an income over £24,000.
- File sorting facility for rearranging data in another order, eg arranging the file in Table 10 in ascending order of income.
- Calculations on fields within records for inclusion in reports.

In the world of business and commerce there is actually a market for information held on databases. It is possible to buy banks of information from market researchers who have compiled databases over the years. Names and addresses of potential customers would be information well worth purchasing if it were legally available. The storage of personal data on computer is subject to the **Data Protection Act**. Any company or institution wishing to store personal data on a computer system must register with the Data Protection Office. Individuals have a right under the Act to request details of information held on them.

Table 10: An extract from a simple database

Surname	First name	Address	Town	Age	Occupation	Income p.a.
Adams	John	14 Stanley St	Bristol	39	Bricklayer	£15,000
Appaswamy	Krishen	2 Virginia St	Cardiff	23	Welder	£25,000
Atkins	Robert	25 Liverpool Rd	Cardiff	42	Teacher	£21,000
Biddle	Ron	34 Bedford Rd	Bath	58	Civil servant	£40,000
Brown	Jane	111 Bold St	Newport	25	Solicitor	£22,000

KNOWLEDGE

1. Why is it important for a business to present data clearly, accurately and attractively?
2. What are the main advantages of using bar charts?
3. What is the main disadvantage of using pictographs?
4. State three types of data that component bar charts can be used to illustrate.
5. What is the difference between a histogram and a bar chart?
6. Why are pie charts a popular method of data presentation?
7. What is the main disadvantage of using tables to present data?
8. State two ways in which bias may be shown when presenting data.
9. State the three types of information which a cell in a spreadsheet can carry.
10. What are the main advantages of spreadsheets?
11. What are the advantages of databases for firms?

KEYTERMS

Bar chart - a chart where numerical information is represented by blocks or bars.
Component bar chart - a chart where each bar is divided into a number of sections to illustrate the components of a total.
Cumulative frequency - the total frequency up to a particular item or class boundary.
Data - a collection of information.
Database - an organised collection of data stored electronically with instant access, searching and sorting facilities.
Histogram - a chart which measures continuous data on the horizontal axis and class frequencies on the vertical axis.
Line graph - a line which shows the relationship between two variables.
Lorenz curve - a type of cumulative frequency curve which shows the disparity between equal distribution and actual distribution.
Pictograph or pictogram - a chart where numerical data is represented by pictorial symbols.
Pie chart - a chart which consists of a circle where the data components are represented by the segments.
Spreadsheet - a method of storing data in cells in such a way that a change in one of the entries will automatically change any appropriate totals.

Case Study: BP

BP is Britain's largest company. It operates in the oil sector and employs over 100,000 people worldwide. It has business activities and customers in more than 100 countries across six continents. Every day, it serves millions of customers around the world and its popular brands include BP, Castrol, ARCO, Aral, Ultimate, Connect and am/pm. BP is involved in oil exploration and production, pipelines and shipping, refining, marketing, natural gas and alternative energies.

Table 11: Selective financial information relating to BP

				$m (except per share amounts
	2006	**2005**	**2004**	**2003**
Income statement data				
Sales and other operating revenues from continuing operations	265,906	239,792	192,024	164,653
Profit before interest and taxation from continuing operations	35,158	32,682	25,746	18,776
Profit from continuing operations	22,311	22,448	17,884	12,681
Profit for the year	22,286	22,632	17,262	12,618
Profit for the year attributable to BP shareholders	22,000	22,341	17,075	12,448
Capital expenditure and acquisitions	17,231	14,149	16,651	19,623
Per ordinary share – cents Profit for the year attributable to BP shareholders				
Basic	109.84	105.74	78.24	56.14
Diluted	109.00	104.52	76/87	55.61
Profit from continuing operations attributable to BP shareholders				
Basic	109.97	104.87	81.09	56.42
Diluted	109.12	103.66	79.66	55.89

Figure 14: Historical TSR Performance

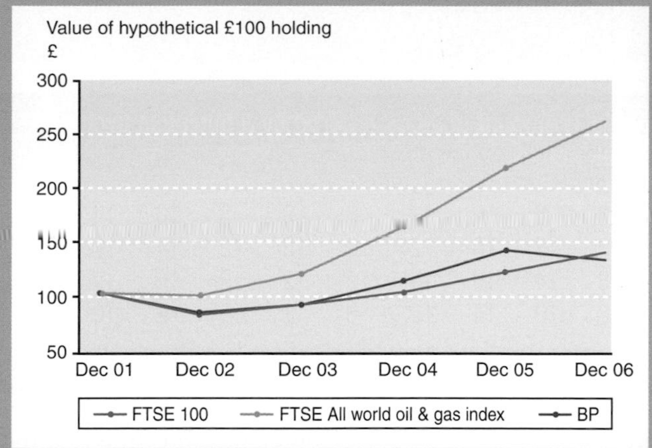

Figure 15: Selective performance data

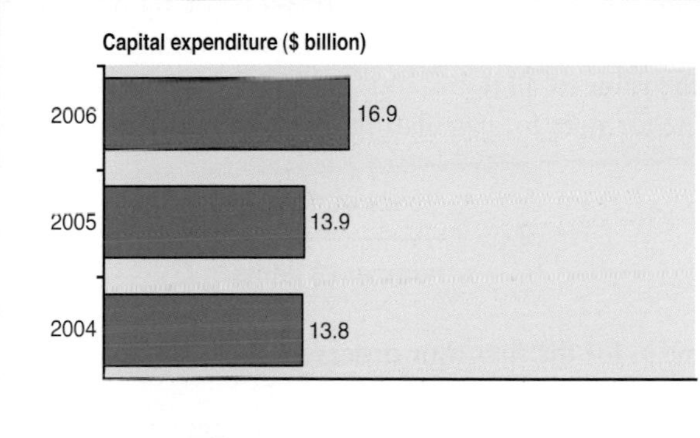

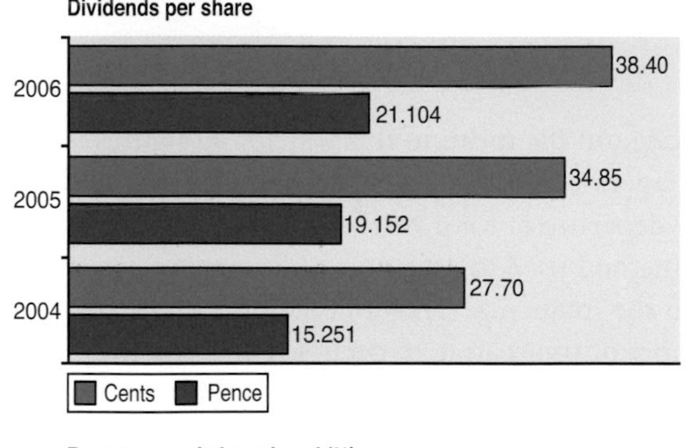

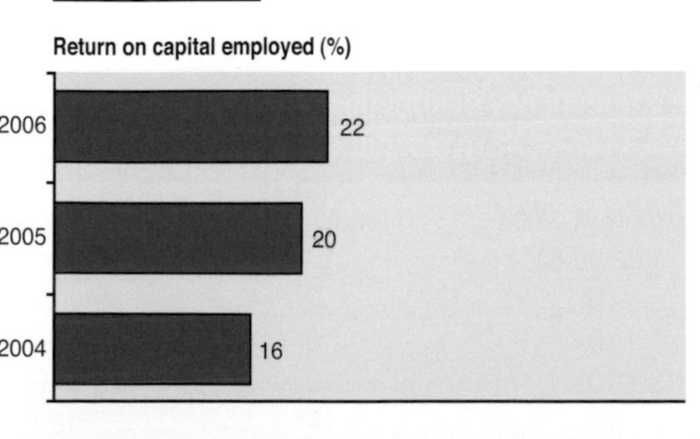

Source: adapted from BP, *Annual Report and Accounts*, 2006.

Figure 16: Selective social responsibility data

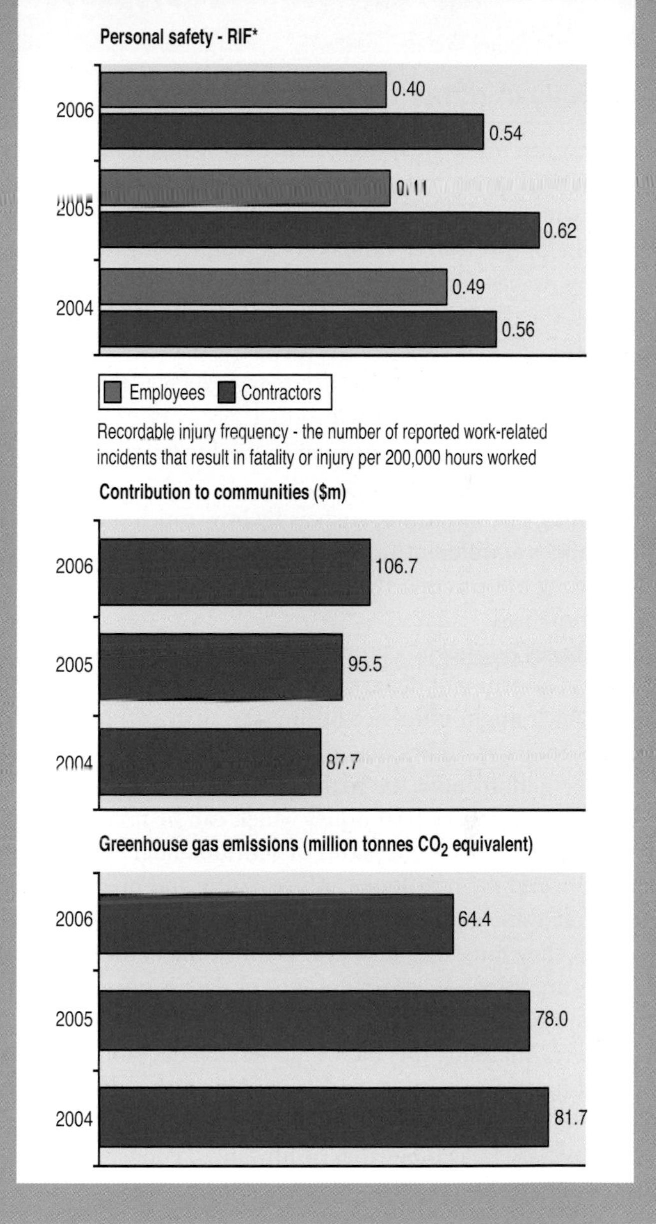

(a) Outline briefly why businesses such as BP present data. (6 marks)

(b) Look at the information in Table 11. Why do you think it has been presented in this way? (4 marks)

(c) (i) What method of presentation is being used in Figure 14? (2 marks)

(ii) Outline one advantage of presenting information in this way. (4 marks)

(iii) What does the information in Figure 14 show? (6 marks)

(d) (i) What methods of presentation are being used in Figures 15 and 16? (3 marks)

(ii) What is shown by the data presented in these figures? (8 marks)

(e) Evaluate the financial performance of BP in recent years. (16 marks)

131 Analysing data

Why analyse data?

A business can make great use of the data which it has collected about such things as costs, sales, markets and profits. Presenting the data will allow a firm to find out important information, such as the proportion of total costs accounted for by employees' wages. However, when looking at more complex problems, the data may need to be analysed in more detail. This can involve:

- finding out the most likely outcome, such as the most likely purchaser of a new product;
- forecasting what may happen in the future, such as the need for extra employees;
- finding out variations, such as by how much output changes at different times of the week, day or year;
- finding out whether the quality of a product is being maintained.

Sometimes businesses can use data which has been analysed for them. Government departments produce information on factors which might influence businesses, such as the rate of inflation. Industry bodies may provide data. For example, ABTA gives information about the market for tourism.

There is a variety of techniques which can be used to analyse data. This unit looks at measures of central tendency and dispersion, and the next looks at forecasting and predicting from data. While these methods can help businesses to make better decisions, they must also take into account the nature of the data they are using. A certain amount of data is unreliable. It may be out of date, collected in a less than thorough way, or incomplete. Analysing this data, and making decisions based on incorrect figures, may cause problems. A firm that decides to increase its stocks because data show they are running low each week, may have large quantities of unwanted goods if the data proves to be incorrect.

Central tendency

Much of the information that a business collects will be too detailed to be useful. It is necessary for this raw data to be organised into a form that decision makers can use more effectively. One method allows the business to discover the most **likely** or **common** outcome from the data. This involves calculating the CENTRAL TENDENCY from the data – usually known as the **average**.

Knowing the most likely outcome will be useful in a number of situations. A business may be interested in:

- the level of stock ordered most often;
- the production level a department achieves most often;
- the average sales each month;
- the average number of days lost through injury.

Table 1 shows the amount of stock ordered by a small business over a period of time. How can the business find the average quantity of stock ordered each week? There are three ways of doing this – finding the **mean**, **median** or **mode**.

Table 1: Amount of stock ordered by a business over a 40 week period

6	8	10	12	8	10	8	10	14	10
10	8	10	12	10	12	12	14	12	12
8	14	10	12	12	12	10	10	12	12
6	10	14	12	8	12	8	12	10	8

Arithmetic mean The arithmetic MEAN is the figure that most people think of as an average. Simply, it can be calculated by adding the value of all items and dividing by the number of items. The formula for calculating the arithmetic mean ($\bar{x}$) is:

$$\bar{x} = \frac{\text{sum of items}}{\text{number of items}}$$

The mean for the first four orders in Table 1 would be:

$$\bar{x} = \frac{6 + 8 + 10 + 12}{4} = \frac{36}{4} = 9$$

Working out the mean in this way for all figures is time consuming. Imagine a multinational adding up the stock needed by every department for a year!

One method used to save time and improve accuracy is to work out the frequency (f) from the figures. The frequency is the number of times an item occurs. The **frequency distribution** for the figures in Table 1 is shown in Table 2.

Table 2: Frequency distribution for stock ordered by a business over a 40-week period

Quantity of stock ordered (x)	Frequency (f)	Quantity (x) x frequency (f)
6	2	12
8	8	64
10	12	120
12	14	168
14	4	56
	Σ f = 40	Σ fx = 420

where Σ = the sum of (adding up all the values)

The mean can be calculated by:

- multiplying the quantity of stock ordered (x) by the frequency (f);
- then adding up all these values and dividing by the total frequency.

The formula for calculating the mean of a frequency distribution is:

$$x = \frac{\Sigma fx}{\Sigma f} = \frac{420}{40} = 10.5$$

Therefore, when the business orders stock, on average it orders 10.5 units. The company might use 10.5 as its average order quantity for stock control.

The advantage of using the mean as a measure of average value is that it takes into account all data. It is also a figure which is generally accepted as representing the average. However, it can be distorted by extreme values, resulting in a figure which is untypical and which may be misleading. For example, if the order in the ninth week had been 94 instead of 14 as in Table 1, the Σfx in Table 2 would have been 500 and the mean would have been 500 ÷ 40 = 12.5.

The median The MEDIAN is the **middle** number in a set of data. When figures are placed in order, the median would be the figure in the middle. For example, the median of the figures 3, 6, 8, 10 and 12 would be 8. The median for 1, 2, 3, 4, 5, 6 would be 3.5, the halfway point. If a business had production figures of 200, 220, 240 and 260 units, the median would be half way between 220 and 240. In this case the median is found by an average of 220 and 240:

$$\frac{240 + 220}{2} = \frac{460}{2} = 230$$

Again, these are simple figures. Businesses, however, have large amounts of data and finding the median may require the use of a formula:

$$\frac{n + 1}{2} \text{ (for odd numbers) or } \frac{n}{2} \text{ (for even numbers)}$$

where n is the number of values or total frequency. In practice, with large numbers of figures, the latter formula is used.

In Table 1 there are 40 values. The median value would be 40 ÷ 2 = the 20th item if they were placed in order from smallest to largest, i.e. 6, 6, 8, 8, 8 etc. The medium value is orders of 10 units. You can see from the cumulative frequency in Table 3 that the 20th item in the cumulative frequency column must have been for an order of ten units.

The median is a useful measure of the average because, unlike the mean, it is not distorted by extreme values. However, the problem with the median is that it ignores all data other than the middle value.

Table 3: Cumulative frequency of stock ordered by a business over a 40 week period

Quantity of stock ordered (x)	Frequency (f)	Cumulative frequency
6	2	2
8	8	10
10	12	22
12	14	36
14	4	40

The mode This is the value that occurs most frequently. From the figures in Table 1, the MODE would be 12 units, as this is the order quantity which occurs most often (14 times). As with the median, the mode is unaffected by mean values and has the added attraction of being easy to calculate. The main problem with the mode value is that it does not take account of all values and might, therefore, prove misleading when taken as a measure of the average. There might also be several modes within a set of data, which will make the measure less useful.

Grouped data

Data is often put into convenient groups, called **classes**. Table 5 shows the results of marketing research into the ages of people buying a particular firm's products. The quantity purchased by each age group (the frequency) is shown in the second column.

How does a business find the average? It is not possible to find the mode, but it is possible to find the **modal group**. This is the group with the highest frequency, in this case consumers between the ages of 30-39 (25).

To find the mean, take points at the centre of each age group,

Question 1.

Ashwear is a company that manufactures a variety of clothing. Table 4 shows information about the cost of its various products.

Table 4

Cost of production	Number of products
£2	4
£4	10
£6	18
£8	8
	40

(a) Calculate:
(i) the arithmetic mean; (ii) the median; (iii) the modal; cost of production.

(b) The firm is considering launching ten new products and has estimated that they will all have a production cost of £10. Calculate the likely effect that this will have on your answers to question (a).

Table 5: Marketing research results showing the ages of people buying a firm's products

Ages of consumers	Quantity purchased (f)	Centre of interval (x)	fx
0 – 9	3	4.5	13.5
10 – 19	10	14.5	145.0
20 – 29	21	24.5	514.5
30 – 39	25	34.5	862.5
40 – 49	22	44.5	979.0
50 – 59	14	54.5	763.0
60 – 69	5	64.5	322.5
	Σ f = 100		Σ fx = 3,600.0

such as 24.5, which is the central point between the ages of 20 and 29. This is shown in column 3. Multiplying the frequency (f) by the central point (x) allows column 4 to be calculated. The **mean** can be found using the formula:

$$x = \frac{\Sigma fx}{\Sigma f} = \frac{3{,}600}{100} = 36$$

where Σ is the sum of all values.

The figure of 36 is an estimate because it has been assumed that the average age of the ten people in the age group 10-19 is 14.5. In fact, it could have been more or less. This is true of all age groups.

The **median** can also only be estimated. To find the median a business would need to calculate a cumulative frequency table. The information in Table 5 has been used to do this in Table 6. Part (a) shows the original table. Part (b) shows how a cumulative frequency table can be calculated. Three goods were bought by consumers under the age of 9. Ten goods were bought by consumers aged 10-19, so 13 goods in all were bought by consumers under the age of 20. The last point is 100, showing

Table 6: Frequency and cumulative frequency tables

(a)		(b)	
Ages of consumers	Quantity purchased	Ages of consumers	Cumulative frequency
0 - 9	3	10 or less	3
10 - 19	10	20 or less	13
20 - 29	21	30 or less	34
30 - 39	25	40 or less	59
40 - 49	22	50 or less	81
50 - 59	14	60 or less	95
60 - 69	5	70 or less	100
	= 100		

Figure 1: A cumulative frequency polygon showing the ages of consumers purchasing a product

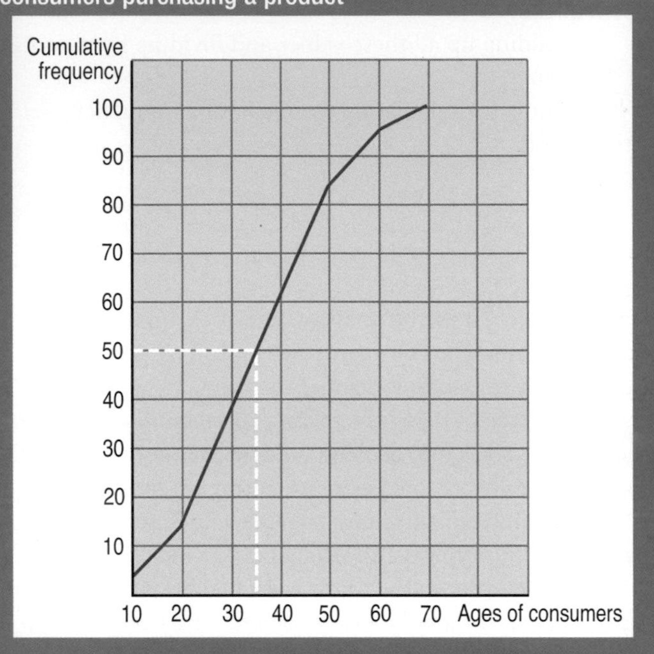

the 100 goods bought altogether by all consumers. It is possible to draw this as a cumulative frequency polygon or ogive as in Figure 1.

What is the median age of consumers buying the products? If there are 100 goods, the median value can be found by drawing a line at 50 to the cumulative frequency curve. This gives a median of 35.

Dispersion

The previous section explained how a business can calculate an

Question 2.

Table 7 shows the salary ranges of employees in a business.

Table 7

Salary range (£)	Number of employees
8,001 - 9,000	6
9,001 - 10,000	15
10,001 - 11,000	40
11,001 - 12,000	25
12,001 - 13,000	10
13,001 - 14,000	4
	100

(a) What is the modal salary group?
(b) Estimate the mean salary. Use approximate mid-class values of 8,500, 9,500 etc.
(c) Estimate the median by drawing a cumulative frequency graph on graph paper.

Table 8: Monthly production figures

												Units
Month	Jan	Feb	Mar	Apr	May	Jun	Jul	Aug	Sep	Oct	Nov	Dec
Sales	40	46	52	54	54	52	58	56	54	56	42	36

average. The business may also be interested in how wide the data are spread - the DISPERSION. It may be that information is widely spread or there is a narrow dispersion. If the data are widely spread, the average is likely to be distant from the rest of the data. If, however, there is a narrow spread, the average will be close to the rest of the data and more typical.

Table 8 shows the monthly output figures for a production plant. In order, the figures will be:

36 40 42 46 52 52 54 54 54 56 56 58

It is possible to calculate the spread in a number of ways.

Range The RANGE is the most simple method. It is the difference between the highest and lowest value. In Table 8 this would be 58 - 36 = 22. The main problem with the range is that it can be distorted by extreme values. Just one rogue figure can vastly increase the value of the range out of all proportion to its size.

Interquartile range The INTERQUARTILE RANGE considers the range within the central 50 per cent of a set of data. It therefore ignores the bottom and top 25 per cent (quarter). This gives it the advantage of being far less prone to distortion by extreme values than is the case with the range.

In order to calculate the interquartile range it is necessary to arrange data with the lowest item first and the highest item last. The first quartile, which is a quarter of the way along, must then be found, followed by the third quartile, which is three-quarters of the way along. The difference between the first and the third quartiles provides the interquartile range.

Using the data in Table 8 it is possible to calculate the first quartile using the formula:

$$\text{First quartile (Q1)} = \frac{n}{4}$$

where n equals the number of values. The first quartile shows the value below which 25 per cent of all figures fall.

So:

$$Q1 = \frac{12}{4} = 3$$

The third quartile can be calculated using the formula:

$$\text{Third quartile (Q3)} = \frac{3(n)}{4} = \frac{3 \times 12}{4} = \frac{36}{4} = 9$$

In the data the third item is 42 and the ninth is 54. So the interquartile range is 54 - 42 = 12. The interquartile range for these production figures is therefore narrower than the range. When dealing with large amounts of data, **deciles** or **percentiles** may have to be used as they give more exact figures. Deciles are the 10, 20 etc. per cent values. In the production figures, the 50th per cent of the values will be 50 per cent of 12 (6), or the sixth value of 52 units of production.

Mean deviation The range and the interquartile range only take into account the spread between two figures in a set of data. However, there are many figures and each will **deviate** from the mean. In business this could be for reasons such as:

- the results from market surveys varying between regions;
- sales varying on a monthly or weekly basis;
- the output from a machine varying in quality as parts begin to wear out;
- the quality of products received from different suppliers varying according to the specifications they have used.

In Table 8 the arithmetic mean of the production figure is:

$$\frac{600}{12} = \frac{\text{(total production over the period)}}{\text{(the number of months)}} = 50 \text{ units}$$

The deviation of each production total from the mean is shown in Table 9.

Table 9

		Units
Months	Production (x)	Deviation $(x-\bar{x})$
Jan	40	-10
Feb	46	- 4
Mar	52	+2
Apr	54	+4
May	54	+4
Jun	52	+2
Jul	58	+8
Aug	56	+6
Sep	54	+4
Oct	56	+6
Nov	42	- 8
Dec	36	-14
	Σ (x) = 60	$\Sigma (x-\bar{x}) = 72$ (ignoring signs)

The MEAN DEVIATION provides one figure, by averaging the differences of all values from the mean. It is usual to ignore the plus and minus signs and use the formula:

$$\text{Mean deviation} = \frac{\Sigma (x-\bar{x})}{n}$$

where Σ = the total of all values
$(x-\bar{x})$ = the difference between the mean and the value ignoring the sign
n = the number of values.

The mean deviation for the monthly production figures in Table 9 would be:

$$\frac{72}{12} = 6$$

This is the average deviation of all values from the mean. The larger the mean deviation, the wider the spread or dispersion. As a method of calculating dispersion, mean deviation has problems, notably the removal of the plus and minus signs. The next section shows two other measures of dispersion, the **variance** and the **standard deviation**, which attempt to deal with this.

Question 3.

Table 10 shows the petrol consumption per annum for area sales representatives working for Quantex plc, a producer of office equipment.

Table 10: Monthly figures

Gallons per annum

Region	North West	North East	North West	South East	South Midlands	West Midlands	East	Wales	Scotland
No. of gallons used	1,200	1,360	1,140	1,000	1,150	1,300	1,250	2,000	

(a) Calculate the mean deviation from the figures.
(b) Calculate the;
(i) range; (ii) interquartile range from the figures.
(c) Which of your answers to (b) do you think is of more use to the business?

The variance and the standard deviation

Both the range and the interquartile range are basic measures of dispersion. They only take into account the spread between two figures in a set of data. The mean deviation is also of limited use because of cancelling out of positive and negative deviations. A more sophisticated measure of dispersion is needed if businesses are going to be able to gain accurate and useful conclusions from a set of raw data.

By using the VARIANCE a business can look at the average of the spread of all data from the mean. Table 11 shows the figures for production from Table 9. To remove the plus and minus figures the deviations have to be squared, rather than ignoring the signs as in the mean deviation calculation. This is shown in the fourth column of Table 11.

The variance can be calculated by:

$$\frac{\Sigma (x-\bar{x})^2}{n} = \frac{568}{12} = 47.333$$

Table 11

Months	Production figures	Deviations from mean $(x-\bar{x})$	Deviations squared $(x-\bar{x})^2$
Jan	40	-10	100
Feb	46	- 4	16
Mar	52	+2	4
Apr	54	+4	16
May	54	+4	16
Jun	52	+2	4
Jul	58	+8	64
Aug	56	+6	36
Sep	54	+4	16
Oct	56	+6	36
Nov	42	- 8	64
Dec	36	-14	196
			$\Sigma (x-\bar{x})^2 = 568$

The original figures were expressed in units of production, but the variance figures are expressed in units 'squared'. To return to the original units it is necessary to find the square root of the variance. This is known as the standard deviation, i.e.:

$$\sqrt{\frac{\Sigma (x-\bar{x})^2}{n}} = \sqrt{47.333} = 6.88$$

Using the variance and the standard deviation

It is possible to use the variance and standard deviation with far more detailed data. Say that a local council is interested in the age profile of its employees because it is considering the introduction of an early retirement policy, and it wants to calculate the likely costs of such a policy over the next few years. Table 12 shows how it might use the mean and the standard deviation.

- As group data are shown in the table, the total frequency is found by multiplying the mid-point of each age class (column 2) by the frequency (column 3) and then adding these values (bottom of column 4). The mean age is then found by:

$$\frac{\Sigma f(x)}{\Sigma f} = \frac{8,365}{230} = 36.4 \text{ years}$$

- The variance is found first by calculating how much each mid-point deviates from the mean (column 5). Next, each of these values must be squared to cancel out the plus and minus signs (column 6). Finally, the frequency of these squared values can be found by multiplying column 6 by column 3 to give column 7.
- The variance is the sum of column 7 divided by the total frequency so:

$$\frac{\Sigma f(x-\bar{x})^2}{\Sigma f} = \frac{37,673}{230} = 164$$

- The standard deviation is:

$$\sqrt{\frac{\Sigma f(x-\bar{x})^2}{\Sigma f}} = \sqrt{164} = 12.8$$

The standard deviation is a measure of the average deviation from the arithmetic mean of a set of values. It is calculated by using the formula:

I standard deviation equals $\sqrt{\frac{\Sigma f(x-\bar{x})^2}{\Sigma f}}$ Σ

Unlike the interquartile range it takes into account all items in a set of data. It is thus much less likely to be distorted by a 'rogue' piece of data within a range. In the example above of the local council, the data had a mean of 36.4 years with a standard deviation of 12.8 years. This would tell the organisation information about both the average age of its employees and the spread of ages.

The standard deviation can be used in a number of ways by a business.

- To establish whether the results of a market research survey are significant and show variations from what was expected.
- To find out the quality of batches of products being bought (e.g. grain being bought by a flour mill) where it would be impossible to check all the batches.
- To check on the standards of output of a production line.
- To identify the likely range of productivity in a workforce where it would be impossible to carry out a work study of all those employed.

Index numbers

When faced with large amounts of data, it may be difficult for firms to see exactly what is happening. Also, figures are often for very large amounts and are measured in different values. This makes interpretation and comparison a problem.

One method to help a business analyse and interpret data is the use of INDEX NUMBERS. Table 13 shows the production figures and unit costs for a company manufacturing small components. It is not easy to immediately see the changes in production or costs from the data. Changing these figures into index numbers will make them easier to interpret.

The first stage in working out an index is to decide on a BASE YEAR. This is given a value of 100 and acts as the base from which all other figures in the index can be compared. In the example, 2005 is taken as the base year and has a value of 100 in the index. Next, all other figures must be changed into index figures based upon the base year.

Table 12

1 Age class	2 Age class mid-point (x)	3 Frequency (f)	4 Mid-point x frequency (fx)	5 Deviation from mean $(x-\bar{x})^2$ mean = 36.4	6 Deviations squared $(x-\bar{x})^2$	7 Frequency of deviations squared $f(x-\bar{x})^2$
16-20	18	25	450	-18.4	338.6	8,456
21-25	23	29	667	-13.4	179.6	5,208
26-30	28	32	896	-8.4	70.6	2,259
31-35	33	36	1,188	-3.4	11.6	418
36-40	38	27	1,026	1.6	2.6	70
41-45	43	23	989	6.6	43.6	1,003
46-50	48	18	864	11.6	134.6	2,423
51-55	53	17	901	16.6	275.6	4,685
56-60	58	13	754	21.6	466.6	6,066
61-65	63	10	630	26.6	707.6	7,076
		Σ f = 230	Σ fx = 8,365			$\Sigma f(x-\bar{x})^2$ = 37,673

Table 13: Production levels and unit costs of a small component manufacturer

Year	2005	2006	2007	2008	2009	2010
Production levels (units)	25,000	24,350	25,500	26,300	26,950	25,950
Unit Costs (£)	1.23	1.25	1.24	1.27	1.30	1.31

For production levels in 2006, this is:

$$\frac{\text{Number produced in 2006}}{\text{Number produced in 2005}} \times 100 = \frac{24{,}350}{25{,}000} \times 100 = 97.4$$

In 2007, it would be:

$$\frac{\text{Number produced in 2007}}{\text{Number produced in 2005}} \times 100 = \frac{25{,}500}{25{,}000} \times 100 = 102$$

A similar process would be carried out for the material costs. The results are shown in Table 14 and Figure 2.

Table 14: Index numbers for production levels and unit costs of a small component manufacturer

Year	2005	2006	2007	2008	2009	2010
Production levels	100	97.4	102.0	105.2	107.8	103.8
Unit costs	100	101.6	100.8	103.3	105.7	106.5

It is now easier for the business to analyse this data. It could use the results in a number of ways.

- To identify trends and forecasts.
- The percentage increase in production or costs can be calculated. For example, between 2005 and 2010, the index of unit costs rose from 100 to 106.5 or 6.5 per cent.
- To compare figures that are measured in different values. The production levels of the business are measured in units and costs are expressed in money values. It is possible to compare the trends in both on the same graph. This is particularly useful for the business. Between 2009 and 2010, for example, production had started to fall whereas material costs were continuing to rise, although not at as great a rate.
- Presenting the data in a clear and easy way for shareholders or managers.

Problems of index numbers

A business will need to take care when producing its index.

- Updating the base year. From time to time a business will need to change its base year, which will affect index figures in the years that follow. After a number of years the firm will no longer be interested in comparing this year's figures with those of, say, ten years ago (the base year). It will want to compare this year's figures with a more recent base year. So for example, in Table 13 if the base year was 2008 instead of 2005, the index of production in 2009 and 2010 would be:

$$2009 \quad \frac{26{,}950}{26{,}300} \times 100 = 102.5$$

$$\text{and } 2010 \quad \frac{25{,}950}{26{,}300} \times 100 = 98.7$$

- Choice of base year. A firm must be careful to choose a base year which is representative. If a year is chosen when costs, prices or output are high, then index figures in later years will be lower than if a more appropriate year was picked. A base year when figures were low will inflate index numbers in following years.
- Nothing has been said so far about the importance of different items that make up an index. A firm's unit costs would be made up of many different items. This is dealt with in the next section.

A weighted index

A more accurate index would take into account that changes in some items are more important than in others. The costs of a

Figure 2: Index of production and unit costs of a small component manufacturer

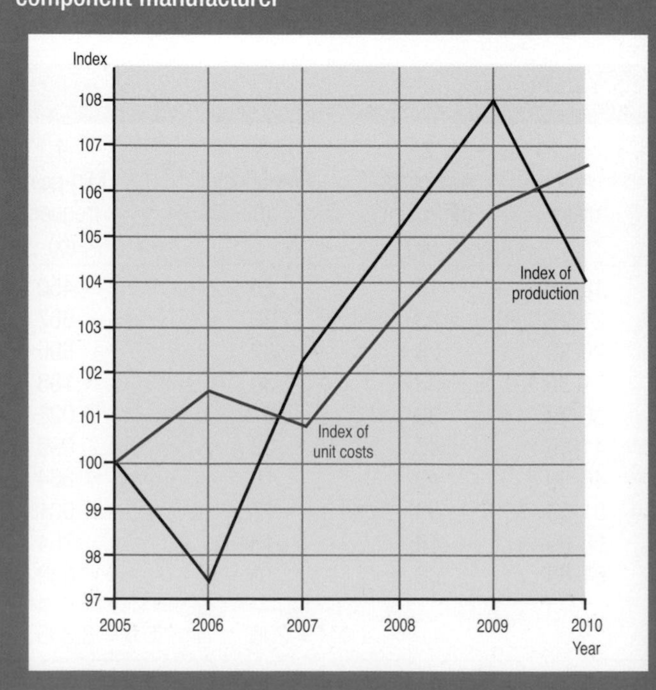

business may be made up of labour, capital, electricity, etc. The firm might be able to construct an index showing how costs change over a period. However, if it spends more on, say, machinery than labour, then the figures for spending on capital must be WEIGHTED.

Table 16 shows a business which spends different amounts on various costs of production over a period. Using year X as the base year, the index of the total cost is calculated by:

$$\frac{\text{Year Y index}}{\text{n items}} = \frac{424}{4} = 106 \text{ or } 6 \text{ per cent}$$

where n = total amount.

This says nothing, however, about the weightings of the different costs. Looking at Table 16, it is possible to work out the proportion of spending on each item in year X.

Total wage costs	=	20 per cent (100,000 ÷ 500,000) x 100
Rent/Rates	=	10 per cent
Materials	=	50 per cent
Production costs	=	20 per cent

A business can now calculate a weighted index using these figures. This is shown in Table 17. The index in year Y is multiplied by the weighting, so the weighted index of, say, total wage costs is 103 x 20 per cent = 20.6.

The weighted index is now 105. When the percentage spent on each item is taken into account, the increase in prices is 5 per cent rather than 6 per cent, as shown in Table 16.

Table 16

				£ per annum
	Year X	Year Y	Year X index	Year Y index ([Costs in year X ÷ costs in year Y] x 100)
Wage costs	100,000	103,000	100	103
Rent/rates	50,000	55,000	100	110
Materials	250,000	260,000	100	104
Production costs	100,000	107,000	100	107
Total costs	500,000	525,000	400 ÷ 4 =100	424 ÷ 4 =106

Table 17

	Weighting	Year Y index	Weighted Year Y index (weighting x Year Y index)
Total wage costs	20%	103	20.6
Rates/rents	10%	110	11.0
Materials	50%	104	52.0
Production costs	20%	107	21.4
			105.0

A weighted index over time

The example so far has only dealt with an index over two years. Table 18 shows calculations for another 2 years based on changes in the index numbers. The proportion spent on each item is assumed to remain the same. This is known as the **base year** or **Laspeyre** method of calculation.

It is also possible to recalculate the index each year based on the weightings in the current year. This is known as the **Paasche** method and can be useful if weightings change frequently. In Table 18 the weighting in year A (the most recent year) may have been:

Total wage cost	=	15 per cent
Rents/rates	=	10 per cent
Materials	=	45 per cent
Production costs	=	30 per cent

The index numbers for each year would have been multiplied by current percentages and not the weightings for the base year. So, in year A the weighted index using the Paasche method would be:

Total wage cost	106 x 15%	=	15.9
Rents/rates	108 x 10%	=	10.8
Materials	110 x 45%	=	49.5
Production costs	115 x 30%	=	34.5
			110.7

Question 4.

A manufacturing company in the South East employs 100 workers. It has become concerned at the level of pay increases over recent years. Table 15 shows the average level of wages for some groups in the business.

Table 15

				£
	2005	2006	2007	2008
Managers	25,000	30,000	32,000	35,000
Administration	10,000	10,500	11,000	12,000
Production	12,000	15,000	16,800	18,000

(a) Using 2005 as a base year, calculate the index for each category.

(b) If 5 per cent of workers are employed as managers, 25 per cent in administration, 55 per cent in production (the other 15 per cent being cleaners etc.), calculate the total cost in 2008 of each category.

(c) How could the business use the index in future pay bargaining?

Businesses can use weighted indexes in a number of ways, especially when there is a number of items which they wish to include in an index. For example, a business which sells five products and wishes to construct a single index, to show its changes in sales over the last ten years, may consider using one. Products with high sales levels could be given a higher weighting than those with low sales levels. In this way, a weighted index, would more accurately reflect overall changes in sales.

Well known indices used to measure inflation are the Consumer Prices Index (CPI) and the Retail Prices Index (RPI). They measure the rate of inflation by finding out how the average household spends its money and monitoring any falls or rises in the prices of those goods and services. The CPI, the measure used in the UK, is an example of a **weighted index** as it gives greater importance to some items than it does to others. For example, a rise in the price of petrol might be given a higher weighting than a rise in the price of soap. A change in the price of a product with a high weighting will consequently have a relatively greater impact upon the index than will a similar change in the price of a product with a low weighting.

Table 18

	Year X Index	Year Y Index	Year Z Index	Year A Index
Total wage costs	100	103 x 20% = 20.6	105 x 20% = 21	106 x 20% = 21.2
Rent/rates	100	110 x 10% = 11.0	110 x 10% = 11	108 x 10% = 10.8
Materials	100	104 x 50% = 52.0	106 x 50% = 53	110 x 50% = 55.0
Production costs	100	107 x 20% = 21.4	110 x 20% = 22	115 x 20% = 23.0
Weighted index	100	105.0	107.0	110.0

KEYTERMS

Base year – a period, such as a year, a month or a quarter, which other figures are compared to, It is given a value of 100 in the index.
Central tendency – a measure of the most likely or common result from a set of data (the average).
Dispersion – a measure of the spread of data.
Index number – an indicator of a change in a series of figures where one figure is given a value of 100 and others are adjusted in proportion to it. It is often used as an average of a number of figures.
Interquartile range – the range between the central 50 per cent of a set of data.
Mean – the value in a set of data around which all other values cluster; commonly used in business as the average of a set of data.
Mean deviation – the average deviation of all figures from the mean, which ignores plus and minus signs in its calculation.
Median – the value which occurs in the middle of a set of data when the data is placed in rank order.
Mode – the most commonly occurring item in a set of data.
Range – the difference between the highest and the lowest values in a set of data.
Variance – the average deviation of all figures from the mean, which removes plus and minus signs by 'squaring' the deviation figures.
Weighting – a process which adjusts an index number to take into account the relative importance of a variable.

KNOWLEDGE

1. Why might businesses need to analyse data?
2. What are the differences between the mean, median and mode as measures of central tendency?
3. How is the mean of grouped data calculated?
4. List five measures of dispersion that might be used in analysing data.
5. Explain two possible uses in business of the standard deviation.
6. Why might a business use index numbers rather than actual figures?
7. State three uses that a business might have for index numbers.
8. Why might weighted index numbers be more useful than a simple index?
9. Explain the difference between the Laspeyre and Paasche methods of calculating a weighted index.

Case Study: EcoFibre Ltd

EcoFibre Ltd is a manufacturer of cereal products. Four years ago it launched a range of cereal bars after research indicated a growing trend towards more healthy 'snack eating' amongst its potential customers. One of its products, Nutrafibre, is a low sugar grain and muesli bar. The product was well received in tests. But it has not been selling as well as the business would like. So EcoFibre has developed a marketing campaign to inform customers of the possible benefits of reduced sugar intake.

Table 19 shows the results of a market research survey of 1,000 customers into the amount of this product they would buy in a period of time, before and after the promotion campaign.

The business will now analyse the information. It is particularly interested in the average or mean quantity purchased per year and the standard deviation before and after the campaign.

The business is also concerned generally about customer spending on the range of cereal bars. It has collected the information in Table 20. It aims to calculate a weighted index of expenditure to examine how overall spending on the range has changed. It will use Year 1 as the base year.

Table 19: Market research results

Quantity of Nutrafibre purchased in a year	Before the campaign	After the campaign
1-10	16	36
11-20	44	44
21-30	84	112
31-40	142	162
41-50	204	182
51-60	160	184
61-70	138	136
71-80	114	92
81-90	62	30
91-100	36	22
	1,000	1,000

Table 20: Expenditure on products in the cereal bar range

				£000
Product	Year 1	Year 2	Year 3	Year 4
A	30	45	45	60
B	10	22	24	22
C	60	60	45	42
D	10	12	14	16
E	50	55	50	40
F	40	48	50	44
	200			

(a) What is meant by:
- **(i) the mean quantity purchased; (3 marks)**
- **(ii) the standard deviation; (3 marks)**
- **(iii) a weighted index of expenditure? (3 marks)**

(b) Using the information in Table 19, calculate:
- **(i) the modal group before and after the promotion campaign; (2 marks)**
- **(ii) the mean quantity of Nutrafibre purchased before and after the promotion campaign (use the central points as 5, 15, 25, 35, etc.) (8 marks)**

(c) (i) Calculate the standard deviation of Nutrafibre purchased before and after the promotion campaign. (8 marks)
- **(ii) Using your calculation of the mean and standard deviation values, evaluate the success of the promotion campaign. (8 marks)**

(d) (i) Calculate a weighted index of expenditure for years 1-4 using the information in Table 20. (8 marks).
- **(ii) Using your calculations discuss whether the business has cause for concern. (12 marks)**

132 Study skills

Studying and assessment

Study skills are the skills that a student needs to plan, organise and carry out their work effectively. They also help a student to answer questions and carry out tasks which are designed to test their abilities. This unit and the next are set out like a manual. They provide guidance and examples to help students when working in term time or when taking examinations. Examples are shown in italics. The units could be used:

- at the start of the course to get ideas on the best way to study;
- constantly throughout the course when studying;
- before examinations during revision preparation.

Action planning

Studying is more effective if there is a plan or strategy. An action plan can be formally written out, but it does not have to be. For any piece of work, it is important for a student to plan:

- how long it will take, bearing in mind any deadline;
- where the student will work;
- when the student will work;
- in what order tasks will be carried out;
- factors likely to affect the work, such as unforeseen occurrences.

A plan can be made for an individual piece of work, work over a term, coursework or project work, revision or an entire scheme of work. It is important for a student to develop a **routine** of work that is effective. It is also important for students to be **committed** to complete the plan. The table below shows a possible action plan that may be used for study, work or revision.

Title and nature of work	What needs to be done? What is the focus? How will it be judged?
Start and finish date	What is the deadline? How long will it take?
Collecting information	Where from? How can it be obtained? What help is needed? How long will it take? How will it be used?
Carrying out the work	Where? When? How long? Who with? What order? Continuous or broken down? Help needed? What factors might affect the work? Possible changes?
Review	Did the plan work? Was the outcome successful? How could it have been done better? Was everything covered?

Time management

An important part of the action plan is planning how long to study or work. Certain factors must be considered when deciding how much time to take when studying.

When to start and when to finish There is a deadline for most pieces of work. This is the date by which they have to be completed. It is important to start early enough and to leave enough time to finish the work. Some people work faster than others. This will affect the time they allocate.

How long the work will take Some pieces of work will take longer than others. Short answer questions will perhaps take less time than an essay. A piece of coursework or project work may take months. So will revision. Some people work more quickly than others, which may reduce the time taken.

How long to work The length of time spent on work can affect its quality.

- Spending a greater amount of time preparing and planning may improve a piece of work.
- The time spent writing may also improve work.
- Working for too long can be tiring and work may suffer. Sometimes it is better to take a short break.
- Some work, such as coursework and revision, cannot be done all at once and must be broken up.
- It is useful to try to break up revision, by learning as you go along. There is likely to be too much to learn in one session at the end. Spreading the work also allows practice.

When to study This will depend on the time available. Some people have a free choice of time. They could work in free time in the day, at lunchtime, in the evening or at weekends. People with part-time jobs or with great commitments may find it more difficult. They may have to work when they can. Sometimes there may be free time which could be usefully used, such as travelling to school or college on a bus or train. Students should also consider that it may not be useful to work:

- late at night because they are tired;
- after strenuous exercise because it may be difficult to concentrate;
- when they are doing lots of other things.

Where to study

It is important to consider where to work. Some students will work better in certain environments than others. Should you work at home or in a different place such as school, a library or another person's house? Issues to consider might be:

- the availability of materials. A library will have books you can use. It may also have a facility to find book titles, newspapers and magazines, perhaps on CD Rom, and access to the Internet. If you keep all your materials at home, it may be better to work there;
- ease of access. Working at home allows easy access to drinks and food. Some people may also want to take a break to watch television or do something else;
- comfortable or not? Working in a familiar environment, such as home, can make work easier. Other people prefer to work in a more 'academic' atmosphere;
- alone or in a group? Some people prefer to work alone. Others like to work with someone else, even if they are doing their own work. Sometimes group activities demand that people work together;
- silent or not? Some people prefer to work in silence as they concentrate better. Working in a library would allow this. Others prefer things to be happening around them.

Other learning considerations

There are other factors that students may want to take into consideration when working.

- Some people prefer to sit on a hard chair. Some prefer to be more comfortable and sit on a soft or relaxing chair.
- Some people like to listen to music whilst they are working. Others prefer silence.
- Some people prefer bright lighting so that everything is clear. Others work better in dimmed lighting.
- Some people prefer to carry out several tasks or activities at once. Others prefer to do one task and then move on to another.
- Some people prefer to eat or chew while they are working as it helps them to concentrate. Others don't.
- Some people learn better by moving around from time to time and some by standing up.

Learning and memory strategies

Different people learn in different ways. Some people learn and remember more easily when they hear something. Others prefer to see it written down and to read it. Some prefer a diagram or picture. Each of these styles of learning may be useful in different circumstances. If a student finds learning something difficult in one way, he or she might try another.

Written methods In many cases students will have to read information and take notes. This is often the most common form of learning on a course at advanced level.

A possible technique used to read information is to:

- choose a section of written material that you will read and quickly scan through it to get the overall idea;
- read the material more slowly;
- put the written material aside and recite the key ideas or points that you have read;
- check that you have covered the main points;
- if you have missed anything, re-read the information.

Often in work or for revision students have to condense large amounts of information into shorter note form. This makes it easier to remember. Steps to note taking may involve the following:

- reading the information and making sure that you understand it first;
- dividing up the information into topic headings and subheadings;
- making suitable notes that are clear and easy to read, and are in a logical order;
- underlining or highlighting important words or key phrases that will trigger memory of the point;
- using page references to the written material;
- leaving space for additions;
- creating an index for your notes, either using a card system or a computer package and updating the order.

Once you have a set of notes you can use the reading technique above to make sure you understand them or for revision.

Example – Business failure

In January 2008, Martha Williams walked out of her farm office for the last time. Her market garden business had ceased trading that day – it had run out of cash. In four weeks' time the assets would be auctioned off and the proceeds used to pay creditors. Heath Farm Food Supplies had become another victim of the 'credit crunch'. Martha needed to borrow around £40,000 to keep the business running until the spring when produce such as lettuces, spinach, watercress, rocket and other salad leaves would be ready to sell and generate much needed cash. Unfortunately, Martha could not find a single bank, or any other financial institution, that would lend her the money.

It all started to go wrong for Martha in early 2007. Against the advice of her accountant, Martha decided to purchase some new harvesting equipment rather than lease it. Martha believed that the long term cost of leasing was far too high and would eat savagely into profits. However, the £45,000 cost of the equipment left the business very short of working capital. Martha argued that a good harvest would pay for it and the loan of £30,000 was easily affordable at current interest rates.

Unfortunately, during March and April a very dry spell of weather had an adverse affect on yields. In a six week period not a single drop of rain fell. This reduced yields by 40 per cent and put back the beginning of the harvest by five weeks. As a result Martha had to extend the bank overdraft by about £10,000. At about the same time interest rates started to rise. The Monetary Policy Committee increased rates three times in 2007. This raised costs for Heath Farm Food Supplies and the business was beginning to struggle. Martha realised that a problem existed and took some appropriate action. She decreased drawings, laid off a member of staff, cancelled all but essential spending and chased up a few long standing debts. This helped for a while but later in the year things got very tight. 'The problem is the yields' said Martha. 'They were 40 per cent down in the spring and since then they haven't recovered enough'.

In January 2008, the business received another very serious setback. One of its main customers, a local supermarket chain, had gone into receivership. The supermarket owed Heath Farm £24,000. This had been due in December 2007 and Martha had been waiting tentatively for the cheque to arrive. She knew that the customer had been struggling and in some ways was half expecting the news. However, it wasn't the end of the world. Provided some long-term funding could be raised Heath Farm Food Supplies would soon begin to flourish, Martha thought. However, she hadn't counted on the 2008 'credit crunch'.

Notes – Business failure (Heath Farm Food Supplies)

- *Heath Farm Food Supplies closes down in 2008 due to the 'credit crunch' – it couldn't raise £40,000 to boost cash flow.*
- *Early 2007, £45,000 equipment purchased with £30,000 loan – tight working capital.*
- *Poor weather reduces yields – bank overdraft extended to £10,000.*
- *Interest rates rise – business starts to struggle and action is taken to help improve cash flow.*
- *January 2008 - bad debt of £24,000 – can't raise cash – business collapses.*

Oral methods It is sometimes easier to remember or understand something if you hear it. When you meet people do you remember their name? If so you may have a strong oral memory. Strategies for learning might include:

- answering questions asked by another person;
- making oral notes onto a tape recorder and playing them back regularly;
- constantly repeating phrases or key words, perhaps in an order;
- make up a **mnemonic**, rhyme or phrase which can be repeated. For example, PESTLE analysis considers the Political, Economic, Sociological, Technological, Legal and Environmental factors that can affect a business.

Pictorial/visual When you meet people do you remember their face? If so you may have a strong visual memory.Visual material can provide an instant 'picture' of information. Sometimes it is easier to see relationships by means of visual representation. Visual information may make use of some of the note taking techniques explained above. It may also make use of photographs. Examples of visual presentation include the following.

(a) Mind maps. *Promotion methods.*
(b) Family trees. *The sources of funds.*
(c) Flow diagrams. *The stages in the design process.*
(d) Horizontal family trees. *Herzberg's two-factor theory.*
(e) Block diagrams. *Calculating profit and loss.*
(f) Method of loci. This involves taking a room you know and imagining certain key words in parts of the room. *Types of integration.*

Learning by doing You may think that you know something or know how to do it. But you might only find out if you test yourself by doing something. It may be possible to test yourself by using:

- classroom or homework activities you have already completed earlier in the course;
- activities in textbooks or workbooks;
- applying ideas in a project or a piece of coursework;
- past examination questions;
- your own activities.

(a) Mind maps

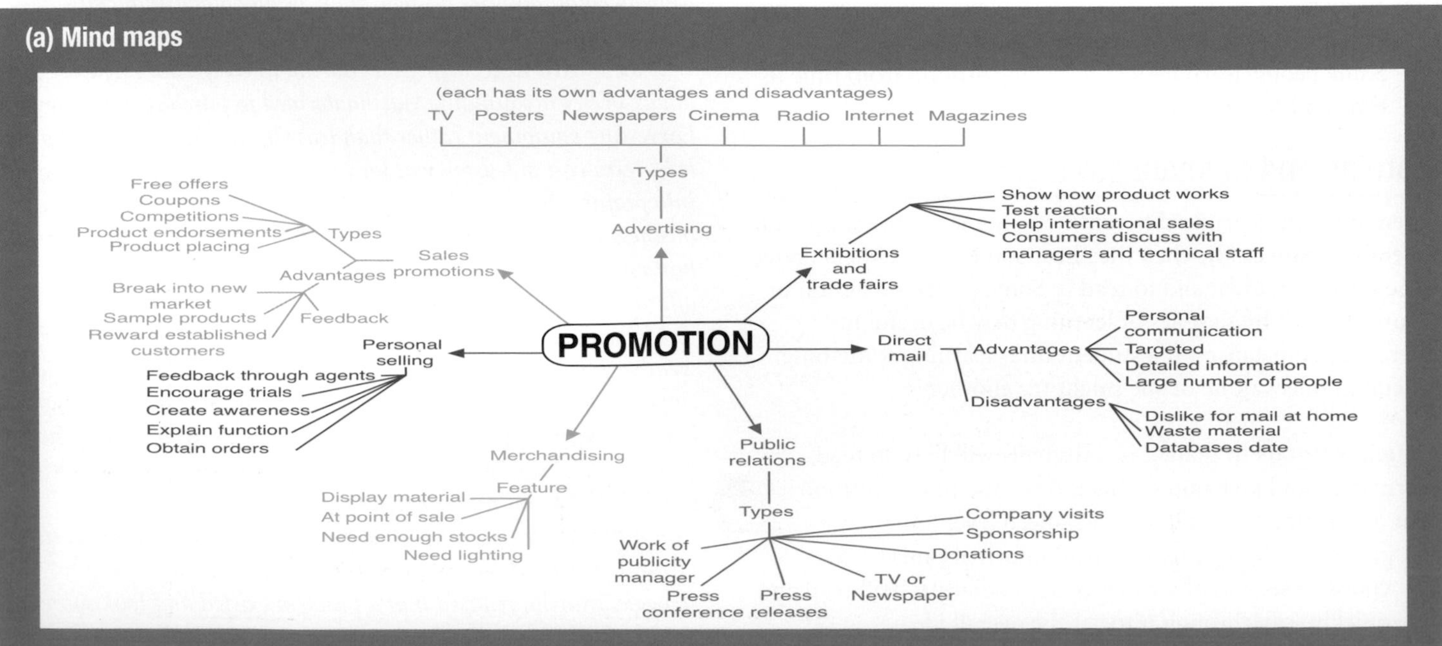

(b) Family trees

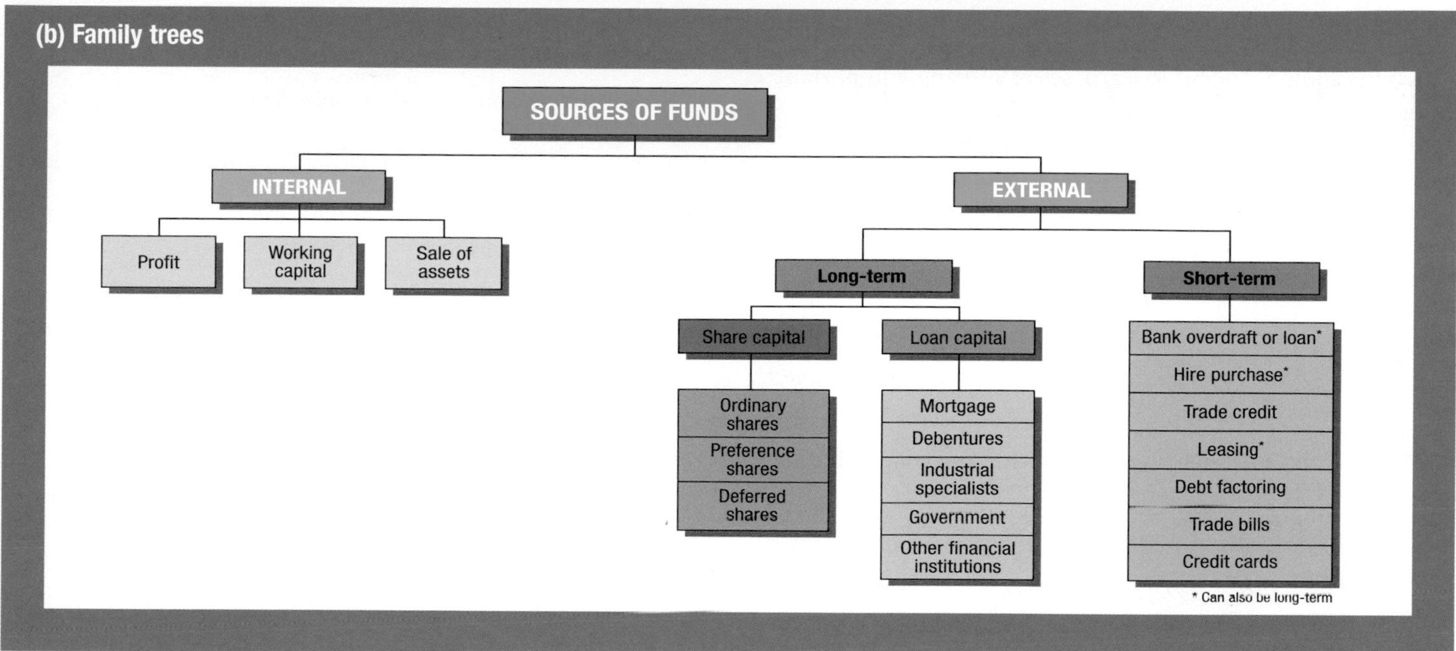

(c) Flow diagrams

(d) Horizontal family trees

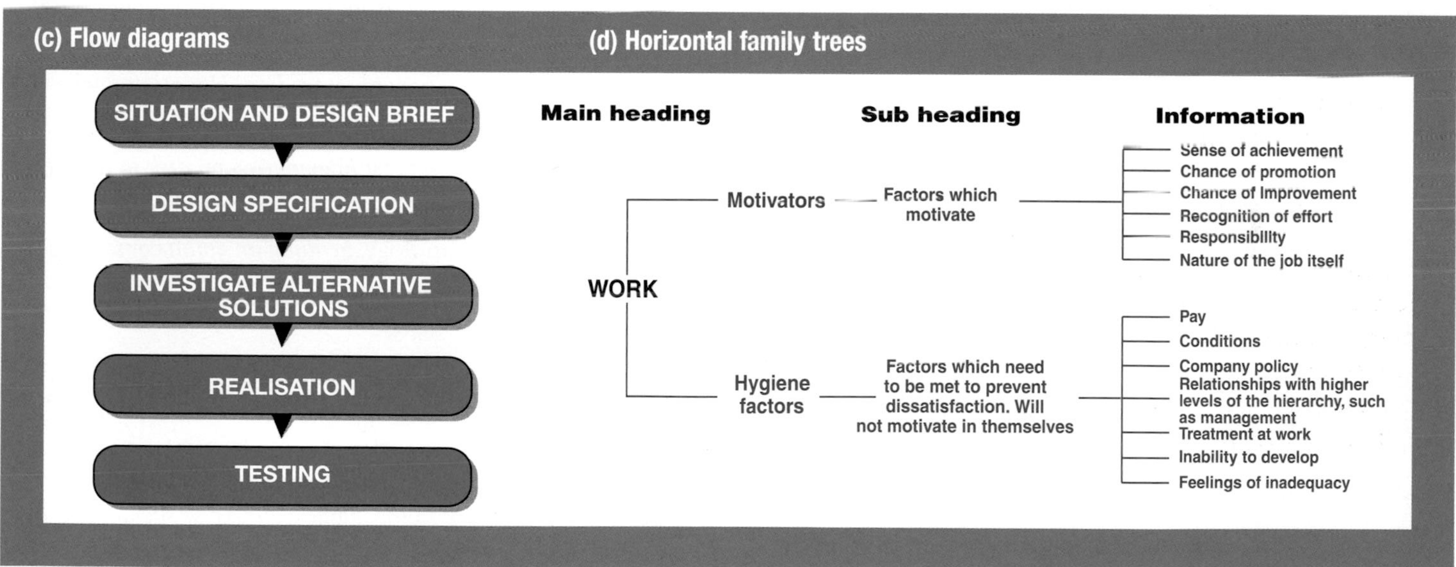

(e) Block diagrams

(f) Method of loci

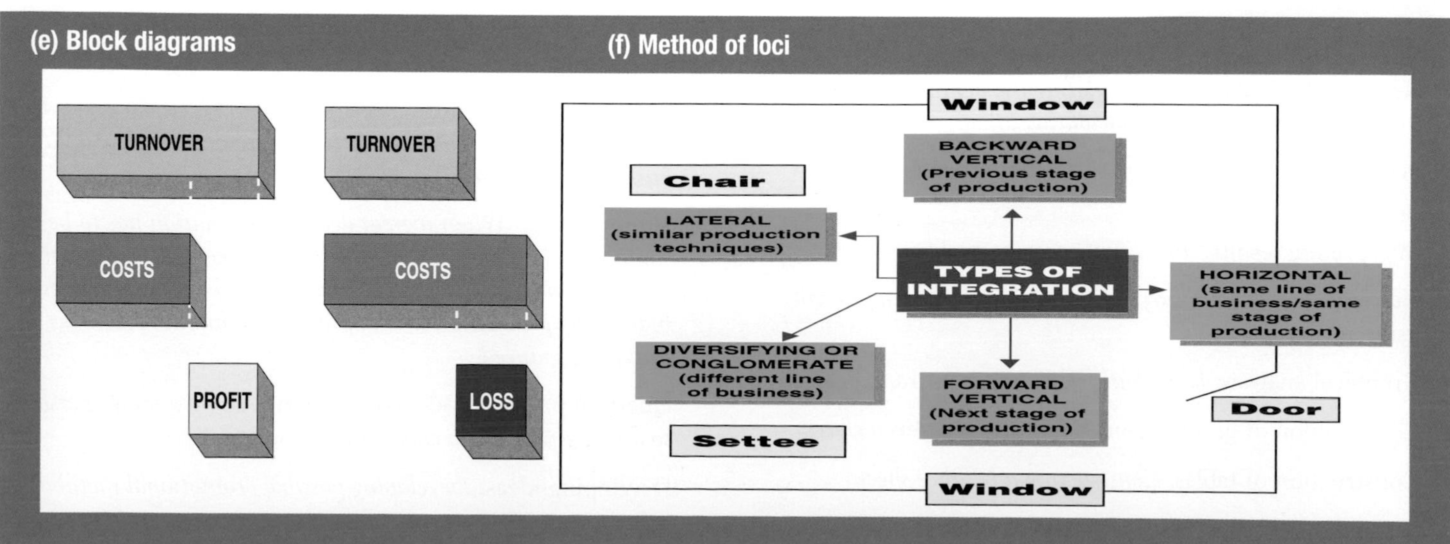

Key skills

Key skills allow a student to learn, select and apply important competences. Key skills at advanced level include communication, application of number, information technology, working with others, improving own learning and performance, and problem solving. All of these skills can be developed by a student taking a course in Business Studies. Some examples of each key skill are shown below.

Communication

- Debates. *Discussing the extent to which business ethics should influence profit.*
- Role play. *An interview scenario or a meeting with a pressure group.*
- Group discussions. *Discussing how a business might promote a new product.*
- Interviews. *A one-to-one interview with a manager about a business problem.*
- Oral presentations. *Presenting the results of marketing research.*
- Passing information. *A memo to staff about reorganisation following the introduction of new technology.*
- Written analysis. *A report recommending action to solve problems identified in the profit and loss account and a balance sheet or a strategy to deal with entry into foreign markets.*
- Written and visual presentations. *Producing a business plan or charts showing the market share of businesses in an industry.*
- Summarising information. *Producing a business organisational chart or a summary of performance from financial ratio data.*
- Written responses. *A letter to a dissatisfied customer.*
- Communication using technology. *An email to the manager showing sales figures on a spreadsheet.*

Application of number

- Numerical calculations. *Calculating the depreciation of assets using different methods or calculating labour turnover.*
- Planning information. *Preparing information for a sales revenue budget.*
- Interpreting results. *Identifying gearing problems from ratios.*
- Numerical analysis. *Carrying out an investment appraisal using various methods.*
- Graphical analysis. *Identifying stock problems from a chart.*
- Construction of graphs. *Constructing a break-even chart.*
- Construction of tables. *Constructing a balance sheet.*
- Collection and presentation of data. *Collecting and presenting sales figures used to produce product life cycle diagrams or market research information showing customers' responses.*
- Forecasting. *Estimating future sales figures from a trend.*

Information technology

- Searching for information. *Finding information on a CD Rom or an Internet website.*
- Reviewing and selecting information. *Selecting appropriate information from the Internet to show accidents at work.*
- Written presentation and manipulation of information. *Writing a report using appropriate software on the impact on the business of the euro.*
- Visual presentation of information. *Illustrating the number of full-time, part-time and outworkers in a business as percentages in a pie chart.*
- Calculation using data. *Calculating cash flow using a spreadsheet.*
- Collection of data. *Entering marketing research information into a database.*
- Manipulation and management of data. *Updating stock figures over time on a spreadsheet to show stock balances.*
- Transfer of data. *Storing cost information on disk so that it can be used for financial calculations by someone else.*
- Communication technology. *Sending an email containing ideas for a new product.*

Working with others

- Discussions. *Discussing possible effects on a business of lean production methods.*
- Group debates. *Debating if multinational businesses should take their profits back to the 'home' country or spend it in foreign countries in which they operate.*
- Searching for information. *Investigating, in a group, a great deal of information such as changes in government legislation over a period.*
- Collecting information. *Investigating, in a group, a great deal of information such as the effects of government policy on a business over a year.*
- Summarising. *When a great deal of information has to be summarised, each group member could take one aspect. For example, when looking at changes in a business, summaries of marketing, production and approaches to human resources could be produced.*
- Question practice and cross checking. *Using another person to ask questions or to check your answers.*
- Developing ideas. *Developing possible promotional methods using discussion sessions.*

- Using outside sources of information. *Discussing the effects of pedestrianisation of a town on a local retailer.*

Improving own learning performance

- Identifying areas to improve. *Areas might include knowledge, memory, time management, work and resource management, such as where to find information and what resources to use, interpreting questions, answering questions, working with others, the work environment, motivation.*
- Evaluating work. *This could include own evaluation, others' opinions, evaluation against criteria, past experience of problems.*
- Identifying methods of improvement. *This could include more practice, changing the method of learning, identifying strengths and applying to other areas, reorganisation of environment such as changing the place or time of work, changing attitudes, changing resources.*
- Identifying help. *Sources of help could be resources, other people, self-help.*

Problem solving

- Identifying problems. *Identify the need to change operations or strategy as a result of variance analysis.*
- Identifying the possible solutions to a problem. *Identifying the different strategies that a business might use to effectively manage change.*
- Choosing solutions from alternatives. *Choosing the most effective advertising campaign using decision trees or the most effective method of work using critical path analysis.*
- Evaluating solutions. *Evaluate the reorganisation of a business to improve productivity using mean and standard deviation calculations.*
- Using IT. *Using spreadsheet calculations to solve problems by identifying the most cost effective or profitable solution.*
- Problem solving in students' own work. *Identifying and solving problems involved in coursework, such as collection of data, storage of data and presentation of data.*

133 Assessment

Assessment criteria/objectives

It is possible to use a range of criteria when assessing the performance of students. This means that examiners or assessors want students to demonstrate a range of different skills. In order to be successful students must:

- understand the skills required by examiners or assessors;
- recognise the skill that is being assessed in a particular question;
- demonstrate all of the skills assessed by the examiner;
- practice skills before the examination.

The criteria used by examiners may fall into the following categories.

Knowledge Students have to demonstrate that they:

- understand business theories and concepts;
- recognise and understand business terms;
- interpret information given in a business context.

Students can recognise questions which test knowledge by looking at the command words in the question. Such words are explained in the next section. An example of a question assessing knowledge might be: *What is meant by best practice benchmarking?*

Application and understanding This assessment criterion requires students to apply theories and concepts in both familiar and unfamiliar situations. This might involve:

- using a business formula in appropriate circumstances, for example, calculating the current ratio for a business;
- using a theory to explain why a business has chosen a particular course of action, for example, using McGregor's Theory Y to explain why a business has introduced quality circles;
- using a business theory to suggest a suitable course of action for a business, for example, suggesting that a chainstore uses loyalty cards to increase repeat sales.

Questions requiring application can again be recognised by looking at the command word. An example of a question requiring application might be: *Explain why the business has cut its research and development budget.*

Analysis Students have to demonstrate that they can break down information and understand the implications of what they have been presented with. Students will encounter both qualitative and quantitative information and will need to:

- identify causes and effects and interrelationships, for example, recognise from a graph that sales are falling and could be a result of new competition in the market;
- break down information to identify specific causes or problems, for example, realise that a business is suffering from inefficiency because according to the information staff motivation has fallen, equipment is worn and working practices are outdated;
- use appropriate techniques to analyse data, for example, use ratio analysis to assess the solvency of a business;
- use appropriate theories, business cases/practices to investigate the question, for example, use elasticity theory to show that raising price may be ineffective.

Questions requiring analysis can be recognised by looking at the command word. An example of a question requiring analysis might be: *Examine the factors which have influenced the firm's decision to close its Cardiff factory.*

Evaluation Evaluation involves making a judgment. Evaluation questions are often used to award the highest grades in examinations. Students might be expected to:

- show judgment in weighing up the relative importance of different points or sides of an argument, in order to reach a conclusion;
- comment on the reliability of information or evidence;
- distinguish between fact and opinion;
- distinguish between relevant and irrelevant information;
- draw conclusions from the evidence presented;
- show judgment on the wider issues and implications.

Questions requiring evaluation can be identified by looking at the command word. For example, *To what extent has the decision to delayer the business been successful?*

When evaluating it is often possible for a student to draw a number of different conclusions. Examiners may be less concerned with the particular conclusion drawn. Very often in business studies there is no 'right' answer. They are more interested in whether students have actually made a judgment and also the quality of their argument in support of the judgment.

Synthesis Opportunities to demonstrate this particular skill may be limited. Synthesis is required in long written answers such as essays, project work or report writing. It involves bringing together a wide range of information in a clear and meaningful way. In particular, students must:

- develop points and themes in a way which builds on previous material and ends with a rounded conclusion;
- produce an argument in a logical sequence;
- provide a clear summarised argument which draws on all the individual elements.

Examiners will tend to look for evidence of synthesis in essays and report writing questions. The sections below on essay writing and report writing will explain how students can demonstrate synthesis.

Quality of language Codes of Practice may require the

assessment of candidates' quality of language wherever they are required to write in continuous prose. In these circumstances students are required to:

- avoid errors in grammar, punctuation and spelling;
- provide well structured arguments which are consistently relevant;
- write in sentences and paragraphs which follow on from one another smoothly and logically;
- express complex ideas clearly and fluently.

Command, directive or key words

When presented with a task or question as part of internally assessed work or externally assessed examinations:

- how do you know what the question is asking?
- how do you know what the assessor or examiner wants you to do?

In many forms of assessment certain **command, directive or key words** in a question will tell the student what is expected of them. Sometimes two or more words appear together in a question. They must all be taken into account when giving the answer.

Information and knowledge Certain command words are designed to find out what a student knows about the subject.

- Define - to state the exact meaning of a term or a phrase. *Define what is meant by marketing research.*
- Describe - to give an account or a portrayal of something. *Describe the hierarchy and span of control of the business.*
- Give - to write down or say something. Sometimes followed by 'an example' or 'an account of'. *Give an example of a private limited company.* May also be followed by 'reasons for' which may involve greater analysis.
- How - to present an account of something. *How has the business raised funds to buy new machinery?*
- Identify - to pick from a variety of information. *Identify three reasons for the merger.*
- Illustrate - to show clearly, often with the use of an example. *Illustrate the main methods used to promote the product.*
- Outline - to give a short description of the main aspects or features. *Outline the view of workers by management.*
- State - to write down or say something. Sometimes followed by what that 'something' should be. *State three features of an effective leader.*
- Summarise - to provide a brief account covering the main points. *Summarise the approach to quality at the business.*
- What - to clarify something. *What is meant by a stakeholder?*
- Which - to select from certain options or to indicate a choice. *Which location did the business find most suitable?*

Application and explanation Certain command words are designed to allow the student to apply knowledge to a given situation, to work out why something has happened and to give reasons for something that has happened.

- Account for - to give reasons for. *Account for the growth in part time workers over the period.*
- Analyse - to examine the importance of certain things in detail, show relationships and make criticisms if applicable. *Analyse the approach to lean production of the organisation.*
- Apply - to bring knowledge to bear on a situation. Note that sometimes the word does not appear in the question. For example, 'Using examples from the article, explain how the business might promote its product' requires an application of knowledge to a particular situation. *Apply the Boston Matrix to the product mix of the company.*
- Calculate - to work out mathematically, usually numerically, but sometimes from a graph for example. *Calculate the return on net assets for the business.*
- Compare and contrast - to show the similarities and differences between two or more things. *Compare and contrast the approaches to recruitment of the two companies.*
- Distinguish - to show the differences between two or more things. *Distinguish between job and batch production.*
- Examine - to investigate closely to find out the 'truth' of the situation as if carrying out an inquiry. *Examine the factors that may have led to cash flow problems.*
- Explain - to make clear a concept, idea or viewpoint. It may involve giving an illustration of the meaning or examples. Note that it is sometimes followed by the word 'why' (see below). *Explain the pricing strategies used by the business.*
- Explore - to investigate or examine in detail, as explained above. *Explore the ways in which a business is affected by changes in interest rates.*
- Investigate - to carry out a detailed examination. *Investigate the factors that may have led the business to go into liquidation.*
- Suggest or give reasons for - to explain why, giving a justification. *Suggest reasons why the business chose to reduce its workforce.*
- Why - to present reasons for something. *Explain why labour turnover has increased.*

Evaluation Certain command words are designed to allow students to make a judgment or to evaluate a judgment that has taken place.

- Assess - an invitation to measure or place a value on the importance of something. *Assess whether the change to just-in-time manufacturing is likely to be successful.*
- Comment on - to give an opinion about the extent to which something has occurred. *Comment on the environmental policy of the organisation.*
- Criticise or critically analyse - to pass judgment on a debatable area. *Critically analyse the growing globalisation of business.*
- Determine - to settle, decide, or find out the nature of. *Determine the most suitable new location for the business.*
- Do you think - to comment on or give an opinion on the

basis of evidence. *Do you think the decision of the business to expand was a suitable strategy in the circumstances?*

- Discuss - to consider a contentious statement or to review an area which might have two or more views. *Discuss whether the business should have introduced group decision making.*
- Evaluate - to make an appraisal of something and to find out how important it is. *Evaluate the strategy used by the business over the period.*
- To what extent (does/do) - to make a judgment or to measure. *To what extent has the change in corporate culture been successful?*

Levels of response

Examiners and assessors may award marks according to the levels of response demonstrated by the student in the answer. The higher the level of response the more marks are awarded to students. An example of different levels that might be identified is shown below.

Level 4 This is the most sophisticated of responses and attracts the most marks. At this level students must provide good evidence of the appropriate skill. Responses must be accurate, extensive, balanced and logical. For example, in evaluation, judgments must be well made and supported by logical arguments. Students must draw original conclusions from the evidence and show awareness of underlying and related themes or issues.

Level 3 At this level student responses are classified as good but with some weaknesses. For example, with regard to knowledge of the subject, to attain level 3 a student must demonstrate that his or her knowledge is satisfactory or better. However, there may be some weaknesses or perhaps the focus is too narrow.

Level 2 If students show that they have clearly used a particular skill, but evidence is limited and there are obvious weaknesses, the response may be classified as level 2. For example, a level 2 response in evaluation would mean that a student has made judgments but they are not well supported by arguments. The evidence will be generally too limited and often below average.

Level 1 This is the most basic of student responses. Some marks will be awarded if a student can demonstrate that they have at least tried to provide some evidence of a particular skill. For example, in analysis a level 1 response would involve some attempt at analysis of data, but lacking in insight and depth.

Level 0 There are no relevant points made and no application, analysis or evaluation.

This approach may be used by examiners when assessing performance in all of the above criteria, even quality of language. However, examiners do not expect students to offer level 4 responses in all of their answers. It depends on the type of question being asked. For example, level 4 responses may only be required in essays, report writing questions and parts of structured questions in decision making case studies. Some examination questions may only require level 1 or level 2 responses. If this is the case, the answers required at level 1 and level 2 may be slightly different from the descriptions above. For example, a question which offers just 4 marks in an examination may require the responses described below.

- Level 2. Students must develop in detail at least one of the relevant factors identified and show some clarity in their explanations.
- Level 1. Students must identify at least one relevant factor and demonstrate some limited attempt at development.

The levels of response required are not normally shown on examination papers. However, students will understand that those questions which carry more marks will require higher levels of response.

Structured questions

The main features of structured questions are as follows.

- They contain several parts.
- The parts normally follow a sequence or pattern.
- Some of the parts may be linked in some way.
- They are generally accompanied by some data to provide students with a stimulus.
- The whole question may require students to demonstrate all skills covered by the assessment criteria, but only one part may be testing a particular skill.
- The parts of the question generally get more demanding as students work through it.
- Different parts may be assessed at different levels of response.

Structured questions are broken down into 'parts'.

First part The first part of the structured question is usually the easiest. This may help students to 'settle' into a question and perhaps give them some confidence. The first part of a structured question:

- is usually designed to test knowledge of a business concept or business term;
- may require a student to perform a simple skill, e.g. a calculation;
- may require a student to give a straightforward explanation or definition;
- usually requires students to provide a basic level response.
- would carry only a few marks.

Examples

(a) Explain the term 'working capital'.

(a) Distinguish between job analysis and job evaluation.

Middle part The middle part of structured questions may vary.

There is no set pattern and this gives examiners and assessors some flexibility when setting structured questions. However, the middle part of structured questions:

- may contain two or more parts;
- usually test knowledge, application, analysis and sometimes evaluation;
- may require students to perform simple or more difficult calculations;
- may require a mixture of straightforward explanation and more complex analysis;
- may carry more marks than the first part.

Examples

(b)(i) Calculate the gross profit margin and the net profit margin for the business.

(ii) Comment on your findings in (i).

(b)(i) Explain the meaning of the term price inelastic.

(ii) To what extent is the concept of price elasticity helpful to a business?

(c) Analyse the possible reasons why increasing numbers of companies are introducing flexible working practices.

(c) Examine the possible implications of the data for:

(i) employees;

(ii) a large manufacturer planning to export for the first time.

Final part This part of the question is usually the most demanding part. The final part of the structured question:

- will nearly always require a higher level response;
- will usually test knowledge, application, analysis and evaluation;
- will usually carry a higher mark allocation;
- may not be broken down into smaller parts.

Examples

(d) Assess the view that business advertising practices should be more heavily regulated.

(d) Evaluate the non-financial factors which might influence the firm's decision to relocate its operations.

(d) Discuss the factors that have influenced the business to change its marketing strategy.

Data response questions

Data response or case study questions are used to test student skills in unfamiliar circumstances. The key features of data response questions include:

- the provision of qualitative or quantitative data, or both, to provide a stimulus for students;
- hypothetical or real case study data;
- the use of structured questions;
- opportunities for students to demonstrate knowledge, application, analysis and evaluation.

Hints

- Always read the data at least twice.
- Use a felt pen to highlight important words, sentences or key numerical information.
- Read the structured questions very carefully, perhaps highlighting command words and other key terms.
- Some of your answers must be related to the data provided.
- Some of your answers must use ideas, concepts and theories not mentioned in the data.
- Answer the parts of the question in order.
- Allocate your time according to the number of marks offered for each part.
- Show all your working out when performing calculations.
- Always attempt all parts of the questions.
- Do not use bullet points when writing your answers.

Answering the first part The information below contains data from a case study question. The data is just a small extract from the question.

The directors are recommending a final dividend of 18p, making a full year dividend of 27p, an increase of 8 per cent over the previous year. The Directors will consider further limited reductions of dividend cover in the medium-term, allowing real dividend growth to be maintained.

(a) Explain the term 'dividend cover'

- To begin with it is helpful to highlight the key words in the question and the key words in the data as shown above. This might help students to focus.
- To pick up all marks in this case it would be necessary to use a couple of sentences to explain the term and then give the formula which is used to calculate the dividend cover.
- The explanation needs to be crisp, clear and uncomplicated. Students need to demonstrate in their answer that they understand the term. The formula can be added at the end.
- A student could give a numerical illustration here. *For example, if a business made a total dividend payment of £300 million and net profit for the year was £500 million, dividend cover would be given by:*

$$\frac{\text{Net profit}}{\text{Dividends}} = \frac{£500m}{£300m} = 1.67 \text{ times}$$

Answering the middle part The data below is from another case study.

One of the things troubling Renton's is the accumulation of stock. Both stocks of raw materials and stocks of finished goods have been building up over recent years. The build up of finished goods is linked to poor sales performance. However, there seems no real reason why stocks of raw materials should have grown. The suggestion made by the production manager to introduce just-in-time methods may be worth considering.

Renton's current assets and current liabilities 2005 - 2008

				(£)
	2005	2006	2007	2008
Raw materials	21,000	22,900	26,600	34,200
Finished goods	31,300	36,800	42,300	49,600
Other current assets	42,300	41,200	44,900	43,800
Current liabilities	109,900	113,500	119,400	138,600

(b) (i) Use ratio analysis to show how the build up of stocks is causing liquidity problems for Renton's.
(ii) Analyse the advantages and disadvantages to Renton's of introducing just-in-time methods.

- Again the first step is to highlight the key words in the question as shown above.
- The question cannot be answered without reference to the data. The first part of the question requires students to analyse the data using a quantitative technique (ratio analysis)
- Students need to calculate the current ratio and/or the acid test ratio to comment on Renton's liquidity position.
- To earn all the marks in this question the student would need to perform the calculations correctly, interpret the results appropriately and draw a meaningful conclusion.
- In this case both the current ratios and the acid test ratios are below the 'ideal' range of 1.5:2 and 1:1 respectively. The acid test ratio is particularly low. This suggests that Renton's has liquidity problems.

The second part of this question requires more analysis.

- Again, begin by highlighting the key words in the question and data as above.
- Before writing the answer it is helpful to jot down a few key points for analysis, such as two advantages and two disadvantages of JIT. Advantages could be less money tied up in stock, more space for other activities or less waste stock. Disadvantages might be vulnerability to a break in supply, loss of flexibility in production or increased ordering and administration costs. These points are not likely to be in the case material. Students will have to bring in outside knowledge. There is nothing to be gained from identifying lots of advantages and disadvantages. The quality of application and analysis will generate marks for this question.
- Marks will be awarded for knowledge, application and analysis. Evaluation marks might also be awarded at this stage.

Answering the final part It is important that students leave enough time to answer this part properly as it usually carries high marks. The data below contains an extract from another case study.

It has been suggested that the economy will grow at a slower rate next year – around 2 per cent. Currently interest rates are historically higher than they have been in the recent past, for example in 2002-03. However, they are predicted to come down in future. The use of credit cards to finance spending is likely to continue and the amount spent using this method of payment may fall due to the higher interest rates.

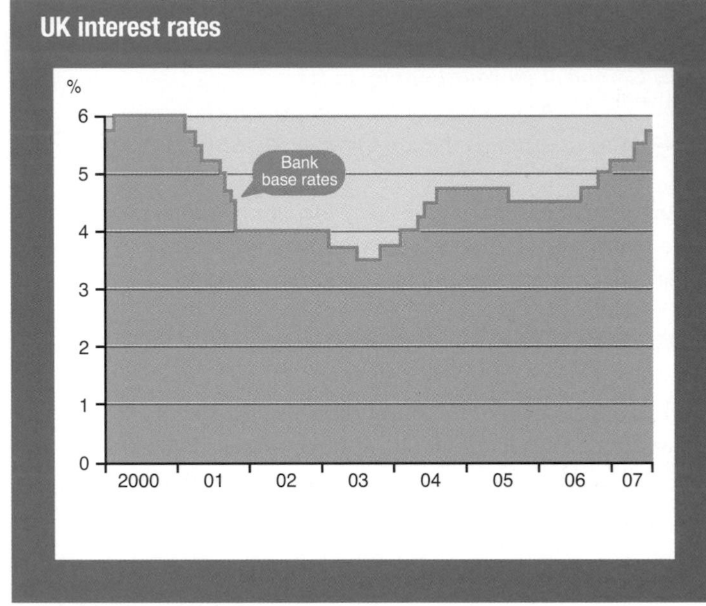

(d) To what extent do external factors, such as those mentioned in the case, influence the performance of a business?

- Students will need to introduce a lot of their own material into their answers.
- Before writing, students should jot down a plan. A plan for this question might appear as follows.
  1. *Explain how external factors, e.g. interest rates, affect businesses.*
  2. *Identify two other factors which might affect businesses, e.g. consumer confidence, borrowing.*
  3. *Analyse the two factors.*
  4. *Evaluate, for example, by saying that external factors have a great influence because they are beyond the control of businesses. However, a good business will include their effect in its forecasting.*
- If the above plan is executed effectively the student will demonstrate all the skills required.
- Students should remember that it is not necessary to identify and list lots of factors. Listing is a low order skill and more marks are awarded for application, analysis and evaluation.

Decision making and problem solving case studies (unseen)

These are often in the form of extended case studies. They can be demanding and require a slightly different approach to answering than shorter data response questions.

- The case material tends to be hypothetical but is usually based on a real life situation.
- The case material tends to focus on a single business.
- The volume of material given is much greater.
- There tends to be some financial information in the case material.
- The case often emphasises analysis and evaluation skills.
- Many of the case questions require an integrated approach when answering. This means that students will need to embrace the full range of the specification in their answers. A single answer may need to address issues such as marketing, production, human resources, finance and external factors all at the same time.
- Questions set usually require students to make decisions or solve problems. For example, a question may require students to suggest a suitable future strategy for a business.
- One question will often require students to use a quantitative technique when answering.
- Examiners often want students to be critical.

Hints

- Skim read the case material to get a feel for the business, its people, its circumstances and its objectives (see section below on things to think about).
- Read again thoroughly, highlighting key information.
- Look at the numerical information and analyse it briefly, without performing any calculations.
- Make brief notes on the key objectives and key themes.
- Read the questions, highlighting command words and other key terms.
- Identify some business theories you might consider discussing in your answers. Questions will probably not request specific theories. The onus is on students to introduce relevant theories.
- Re-read the hints on answering data response questions above.

Issues to think about when planning answers

- People. Business is about people and your answers need to reflect this. Consider the age, family circumstances, the attitudes and personal interests of the people involved in the case material. What motivates them? What is their background? What are their objectives? What are their strengths and weaknesses? These are some of the people issues which students need to consider when shaping their answers.
- Situation. It is important to think about the context in which the business is set. Examples of issues to consider include the type of business organisation (Ltd, plc or sole trader), the prevailing culture, the type of industry, the nature of competition, the size, its financial position, its age, history and potential. It is often helpful to liken the case material to a business which actually exists in a similar context. However, this may not always be possible.
- Objectives. Answers to questions are bound to be linked to what the business is trying to achieve in its given context. A business may be trying to survive following a recession, it may be trying to break into new markets, it may be trying to raise finance for a big investment project, it may be trying to change its culture or take over another business. It is often useful to consider, and distinguish between, short-term and long-term objectives.
- Theories. Students should introduce business theories into their answers. There may be little or no guidance as to what theories are required. Students need to be on the lookout for opportunities to introduce some business theory into every answer they write. For example, if a business is considering a price change, price elasticity theory could be introduced. If a business is merging with another, economies of scale may be discussed. If a business is downsizing the effect on staff might be discussed, in which case motivational theories such as Herzberg or Maslow might be applied.
- Be critical. Be prepared to challenge statements or claims made in a case study if relevant and applicable. Students with an enquiring and critical approach will be rewarded.

Example 1

Most of the structured questions in decision making/problem solving case studies usually require lengthy answers with analysis and evaluation. Therefore it is important to plan before writing an answer. Below is an extract from part of an extended case study. The case study is about Henshaws Ltd, a components manufacturer for the computer industry. It has faced difficulties in recent years due to escalating costs. It is considering ways of improving efficiency and reducing costs.

One option currently being considered by Henshaws Ltd is to outsource its marketing activities. The directors of the company have not been impressed with the performance of this department. Their expenditure has consistently exceeded their budget and they seem to get new business and then lose it. In addition, communications between the department and others in the organisation have not been good. Two of the four company directors have long claimed that the company's strength is in manufacturing high quality components, although the other two directors argue that the company must avoid clinging to 'past glories' and move forward with the times. A number of marketing agencies have given presentations to the board of directors and a decision about whether to outsource marketing is imminent.

(b) Assess the likely advantages and disadvantages to Henshaws Ltd of outsourcing its marketing function.

- To answer this question it is necessary to identify and analyse two or three advantages, identify and analyse two or three disadvantages and then evaluate by making a judgment about whether Henshaws should outsource marketing or not.
- Although the question does not specifically ask for a judgment examiners are probably expecting one. This is because the mark allocation may be quite high.
- A plan should be drafted which might look like this:

Adv. 1. Costs fall.
2. More focus on manufacturing.
3. More effective marketing by specialists.

Disadv. 1. Redundancies.
2. Loss of control of a vital function.
3. Long-term marketing costs might rise.

Eval. Yes - outsource because current marketing is expensive, ineffective and is causing problems. Henshaws will then be more focused and able to exploit its strengths.

- In the answer it is necessary to analyse the above advantages and disadvantages in detail explaining their relevance.
- In the evaluation some students may suggest that Henshaws should not outsource its marketing function. This does not matter. Examiners just want students to make a judgment and support it with a coherent and plausible argument. Remember that these case studies are decision making case studies and therefore a decision must be made!

Example 2

Some quantitative analysis is usually required in extended case studies. It may be quite complex and students often make the mistake of spending too long on this section.The data below contains an extract from an extended case study about a business which is considering a new investment. Arpan Shrinath & Co manufactures training shoes and Arpan is deciding which investment project to go ahead with.

Project 1. *Arpan has considered buying a large delivery van and undertaking his own distribution. At the moment he pays a local company to distribute training shoes to his customers. This has proved expensive and often ineffective.*

Project 2. *A new moulding machine has just been launched on the market by a German machine manufacturer. It is computer numerically controlled and would help to improve the quality of Arpan's products. It would also be more productive than his existing machine.*

Project 3. *Arpan is becoming increasingly concerned that his office staff are working in conditions which are too cramped. Staff frequently complain and he is aware of inefficiencies due to a lack of space. He is considering the construction of a purpose built annex to the factory where office staff can work more effectively.*

Expected returns

	Cost	Year 1	Year 2	Year 3	Year 4	Year 5	Year 6	Total
Project 1	£15,000	£4,000	£4,000	£4,000	£4,000	£4,000	£4,000	£24,000
Project 2	£40,000	£12,000	£10,000	£10,000	£9,000	£9,000	£9,000	£59,000
Project 3	£30,000	£7,000	£7,000	£7,000	£7,000	£7,000	£7,000	£42,000

The table above shows the costs and expected returns for each of these projects over a 6 year period.

(c) Calculate the (i)payback; (ii)average rate of return for the three investment projects and decide which project is the most attractive. Take into account your results from the calculations and any other information you feel is appropriate.

- This question requires knowledge and understanding of investment appraisal techniques. Provided students have revised the quantitative techniques required they just need to apply the appropriate formulae.
- It is often helpful to produce calculations (or the results of calculations) in tables. One way in which the answers to the above question might be presented is:

	Project 1	Project 2	Project 3
Cost	£15,000	£40,000	£30,000
Total return	£24,000	£59,000	£42,000
Total profit	£9,000	£19,000	£12,000
Profit p.a.	£1,500	£3,167	£2,000
ARR	10%	7.9%	6.6%
Payback	3.75 years	3.88 years	4.29 years

- According to the calculations above project 1 appears the most attractive. It has the highest ARR and also the shortest payback period.
- There is likely to be other information in the case which will influence the decision here. For example, if customers are complaining about the quality of products, Arpan might decide to buy the new machine to improve quality, even though the projected financial returns are slightly lower.
- This question is likely to offer a high mark allocation. The calculations alone would not generate all the marks. Students must bring in other information from the case, use their own ideas and also evaluate.
- Some thought must be given to the setting out of numerical answers. Good presentation is important. Avoid

deletions and sprawling calculations. Space answers generously and underline final answers.

Example 3

The final question in an extended case study often requires students to suggest a strategy or give an overall view. The question might also carry higher marks. A possible question might be:

(d) Taking the whole case into account, do you consider that the board of directors should discontinue production at the Newport factory?

- Again, planning is very important here. A lengthy answer is required with relevant points being identified, thorough analysis and evaluation. Students need to bring together a range of relevant points and make a decision.
- Timing is also crucial. Students must ensure that they leave sufficient time to plan and write the answer to this final, and important, question properly.
- Students may use some of the material generated in other answers in the case. But obviously repetition must be avoided.
- Again, it probably does not matter in this question whether students suggest that production is discontinued or not. Examiners want to see a well structured, logical argument with a meaningful conclusion drawn.
- Remember to consider the people, the situation, the objectives and to introduce theories.

Pre-seen case studies

A pre-seen case study is a method of assessment which involves giving students case study material before the day of the examination. This allows students to prepare more thoroughly for the examination by analysing the information and forming ideas in advance.

- Case study material may be issued a number of weeks before the day of the examination.
- The structured questions relating to the case study will not be known until the day of the examination.
- Additional information regarding the case may also be supplied within the question structure.
- The nature of the material provided in the case is likely to be the same as any other case study, but perhaps in more detail. Students should read the previous sections on data response and decision making questions.

Hints

- The general approach to pre-seen case studies is little different from those which are not pre-seen. The only important difference is that students have a great deal of time to study the data. Again, the hints in previous sections on answering data questions should be read.
- There is much more time to read the material so more time can be spent highlighting key words and terms. Students could also note theories, issues or themes which are relevant.
- Any words, terms or theories which are unfamiliar or forgotten can be looked up in the text book. For example, if the case contains an extract from a balance sheet, it might be helpful to consult the balance sheet unit to reinforce understanding of balance sheet terms and structure.
- It is helpful to try and predict possible questions which the examiner might set. This will allow students to prepare answers.
- Try to identify trends, patterns and links in the data and account for them.
- Get help from friends and parents.
- When answering the questions in the examination it is very important to answer the ones set. Students should not try to reproduce their own 'model answers'.

Essay writing

An essay is an assessment method used to find out how students can respond in depth to an open question. It involves writing in continuous prose and provides an opportunity to explain something in detail.

- The quality of grammar, vocabulary, sentence construction and spelling is particularly important.
- A strong emphasis is usually placed on analysis, evaluation and synthesis.
- Essay questions may be integrated and synoptic. This means that students must consider the full range of the specification areas when writing answers. Essays based on one section of a specification or syllabus, such as marketing, may draw on all areas within it.
- The length will vary depending on the time allocated.
- They require a great deal of thought and planning before writing begins.
- The use of real world examples to illustrate points is essential.
- The use of diagrams, such as the Boston Matrix, is encouraged.
- There is rarely a 'right' answer. It is possible for two students to put forward opposing arguments and for both to be awarded high marks. It is the quality of the argument which is important, not the nature of it.

Planning

- Read the question very carefully.
- Highlight the command words and other key words to help provide focus.
- Planning could be in two stages. Stage one might involve a two or three minute session where students jot down an explosion of points and issues they think might be relevant.
- Stage two would then involve sorting points into an

appropriate order and planning out a structure which will accommodate an argument.

Introduction

- It is common to begin with a short introduction where key terms are defined and the question is put into context. Some general information may also be given. An introduction should be no more than a third of a side long, for example.

The main body

- When writing the main body of an answer it is important to follow the plan and write in detail, ensuring that evidence of analysis and evaluation is provided.
- It is vital to answer the question. It is better to write one side of relevant material than five sides of 'waffle'.
- Never use bullet points in essays.
- Never use subheadings in essays.
- Never write lists in essays. Extra marks are not awarded for identifying a large number of relevant points.
- Remember to include real world examples where appropriate.
- It is inadvisable to switch emphasis during the essay. It is best to stick to the plan.
- Diagrams, graphs and other illustrative material may be used but make sure they are clearly labelled and explained in the text.

Conclusion

- It is important to write a conclusion. It may be a statement which answers the question 'in a nutshell', drawing on the points analysed in the main body.
- Conclusions should not repeat material used elsewhere.
- The best conclusions are those which demonstrate evaluation and synthesis.
- Students are often required to make a judgment or give an opinion. Do not 'sit on the fence'.

Example

It has been argued that the productivity of UK businesses falls well behind that of its overseas rivals. Suggest possible reasons why this might be the case and examine the measures which might be taken by UK businesses to improve productivity?

- Essay questions can carry a relatively high number of marks.
- The words highlighted in the title are productivity, UK businesses, overseas rivals, suggest possible reasons, examine, measures and improve productivity.
- The following ideas may be suggested for the essay.
  Define productivity, labour, capital, Rover productivity poor, Nissan good, lack of investment, lack of funds, lack of R&D, dividends too high, too short-termist. Standardisation, re-engineering, kaizen, JIT, outsourcing, virtual companies, TQM, benchmarking, work study, culture, trade unions, weak management, quality circles, technology, training, labour flexibility, delayering, downsizing.
- The ideas generated may not be in any particular order. The focus in the above responses appears to be on production and ways of improving efficiency.
- Another two or three minutes spent planning might deliver the following essay structure.

Introduction

- ➤ *Define productivity - output in relation to inputs.*
- ➤ *An example of evidence which might support the statement is the low productivity of Rover compared with, say, Japanese car makers.*
- ➤ *Suggest that there is a number of approaches to improving productivity, some specific and some strategic.*

Main body

- ➤ *Analyse three possible reasons why productivity is lower in UK.*
- ➤ *Low investment, therefore inadequate and dated technology.*
- ➤ *Lack of R&D because the City wants higher dividends NOW.*
- ➤ *Trade unions may have resisted changes which might improve productivity.*
- ➤ *Explain that measures designed to improve efficiency might be specific or strategic.*
- ➤ *Analyse three specific measures - JIT, benchmarking and new technology.*
- ➤ *Analyse three strategic measures - kaizen, re-engineering and TQM.*

Conclusion

- ➤ *Argue that the statement is probably right for the reasons given. Evaluate by saying that one particular reason may be more important, e.g. lack of investment.*
- ➤ *Argue that the methods employed to improve efficiency depend on the individual firms and their needs.*
- ➤ *Evaluate by suggesting that particular methods may be more suitable, if, for example, a business has dated machinery new technology may have a very significant impact on productivity.*
- ➤ *sArgue that all measures will require co-operation of staff if they are to be successful.*

- When the essay is finished it is important to read through it and check for errors such as spelling, grammar and punctuation. However, avoid frantic crossing out at the last minute because this tends to have a negative effect on presentation.

Report writing

A business report is a formal method of communication. It is a written document designed to convey information in a concise but detailed way. A report is written in a structured way so that information is broken down into manageable parts. The end section of the report is very important. It will contain recommendations for action that a business should take.

- A report begins with a formal section showing who the report is for, who has written it, the date it was written and the title.
- A report is broken into a series of sections. Each section might address a particular issue.
- Each new section should begin with a clear heading and each section could be numbered.
- Each section can be broken down into sub-sections, which again can be numbered. Each sub-section may be a single paragraph.
- Information should be written in sentences and not in note form. Sections will require application, analysis and evaluation.
- Numerical information such as tables, graphs and charts should be shown in an appendix. Similarly, calculations should be shown in an appendix.
- The conclusion is very important and should aim at bringing together points raised and analysed in previous sections. No new material should be introduced at this stage. A conclusion is often an action plan or a series of recommendations.

Features Sometimes examiners require a report in a data response question. Students may be required to write reports based on a wide range of numerical data presented to them in tables or charts. It is this latter style which is the focus of attention here. It is sometimes called the numerical report. In a numerical report:

- information is presented in a number of tables or charts, perhaps five or six distinct pieces of data;
- the data will relate to a particular business and its market, there may also be some general economic data;
- students are required to interpret and analyse the data;
- some data may not be very helpful and should therefore be ignored, because examiners deliberately give more information than is required to force students to be selective;
- the report question will normally be very specific and require students to make a decision, i.e. make recommendations;
- students are often allocated a role when writing the report;
- the structure of the report will often be indicated in the question.

Hints

- Read the introduction and become familiar with the type of business, its market and circumstances.
- Read the tables of data and begin to form views about what they show.
- Make brief notes and comments adjacent to tables and graphs relating to trends and patterns shown by the data.
- Decide whether any data is irrelevant.
- Try to spot links between the different tables of data.
- Start to plan the report structure by identifying some appropriate section headings, **but do not use a heading for each piece of data**. Identify four or five key issues.
- Identify the points to be raised in each section.
- Decide what your conclusions and recommendations will be. Remember that there is not likely to be a right or wrong answer, but you must make a judgment.
- Write the report using the structure outlined above and remembering that the student is playing a role.
- Remember to analyse and evaluate throughout, and also, that the conclusion requires synthesis.

Example

Moa Kuk Ltd is a family business which imports a wide range of oriental soft furnishings and household artifacts. The business has two large stores in London. The second store was opened two years ago and has very quickly returned a profit. Moa Kuk, the managing director, believes that the company could grow very quickly and become a successful franchising operation.

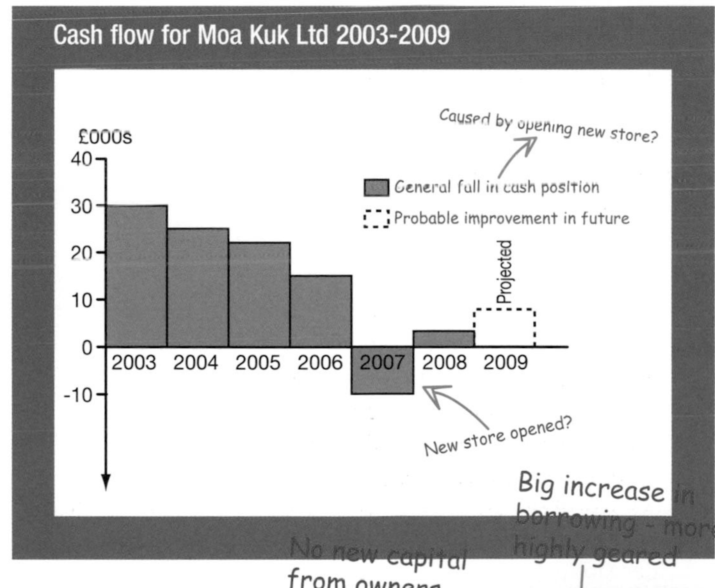

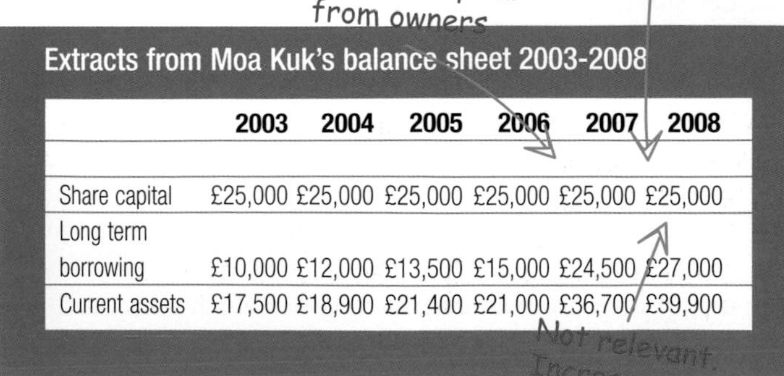

Extracts from Moa Kuk's balance sheet 2003-2008

	2003	2004	2005	2006	2007	2008
Share capital	£25,000	£25,000	£25,000	£25,000	£25,000	£25,000
Long term borrowing	£10,000	£12,000	£13,500	£15,000	£24,500	£27,000
Current assets	£17,500	£18,900	£21,400	£21,000	£36,700	£39,900

You are employed by a firm of business consultants. You have been asked to write a report to assess whether or not Moa Kuk should set up a franchising operation or grow independently.

- The question is likely to carry a relatively high number of marks.
- Begin to think of suitable section headings for the report structure. We only have an extract from a question here, but the limited information does provide some guidance for appropriate headings. For example:
  - *The financial position of Moa Kuk Ltd*
  - *The advantages of franchising*
  - *The disadvantages of franchising*
  - *Recommendations*
- Write brief notes by each data box. These are shown in the graph and the table.
- A plan can be drawn up for the first section.
  - *Cash flow has deteriorated over the period particularly in the last two years when the new store was opened.*
  - *The owners have not contributed any more capital to the business over the period.*
  - *The development of the business has been funded by increased borrowing.*
  - *Borrowing has increased steadily over the period making the company more highly geared.*
- A plan should be drawn up for the other sections in the answer. For example, the information may lead to a conclusion that: *Moa Kuk Ltd is not really in a financial position to fund independent growth. Therefore setting up a franchising operation may well be an effective strategy.*
- There will obviously be other points to consider based on other data which is not provided here.

Project/Coursework

A project or piece of coursework usually involves:

- extended research carried out over a period of time within a real business setting;
- the investigation of a problem or decision that the business is facing;
- the use of both qualitative and quantitative data and analysis in researching and analysing the problem or decision;
- the application of a range of business knowledge, skills and methods to the problem or decision;
- the identification of a number of feasible strategies that the business might pursue;
- evaluation of these strategies and making recommendations about which strategy should be pursued and why;
- the production of an extended report which presents the research and findings and use of a range of methods of presentation to enhance the quality of the report.

Unlike other elements of Business Studies examinations, this work is carried out over a period of time during the course. There will be a deadline by which time the project has to be completed, but it is largely the student's responsibility to set up and carry out the investigation and to produce the report by that deadline. The required length of the report is laid down by the awarding body.

Assessment The teacher is the first assessor for project work. He or she will mark the project as a whole and award marks based upon the assessment criteria set by the awarding body. This will vary between different examinations, but typically covers the following skills:

- the way the problem or decision has been explained and objectives for the project set;
- the use made of relevant business knowledge, ideas and concepts in tackling the problem;
- applying appropriate research methods;
- carrying out relevant analysis using both qualitative and quantitative information;
- evaluating evidence to draw conclusions and make recommendations;
- presentation of evidence in a structured way that shows a logical development of ideas;
- employing a good quality of language including spelling, punctuation and grammar.

There may then be some internal moderation of your teacher's marking by another teacher or lecturer in the school or college to check that all the teachers are marking in a consistent way. Finally a sample of projects will be sent to an external moderator, employed by the awarding body, who will check that the marking has been carried out to the criteria set by the examining body.

Hints

- Choose an organisation for your project with which you have contact, perhaps through family or friends and which will allow you access to the information you require. Your teacher may also have established initial contact with a number of organisations which will provide appropriate projects.
- Don't be too ambitious with your choice of problem. *How might Marks & Spencer improve its profitability?* would be too much of a challenge, whereas *How might Marks & Spencer's Wilmslow branch increase its sales of microwave meals?* might be a more realistic title.
- Produce a project/coursework action plan before you start your research - *what are your objectives? what information do you want to collect? what will be the sources of information? who do you want to talk to? when will you collect the information? what analysis will you carry out? when does the report have to be completed?*
- When carrying out your research within an organisation you will need to collect background information about the organisation as well as information specific to your project.
- Listen carefully and give yourself time each day to write up your notes - you will find that you will collect much more data than you will need, but you won't know which is relevant until you write up the project.
- When you analyse of the data, use the concepts and techniques that you have been learning in your lessons and explain in the project why you are using a particular technique as a means of analysis.

- Try to use both quantitative as well as qualitative analysis if the project lends itself to both.
- There are always alternative strategies for solving a problem - one alternative is always for an organisation to do nothing. You must present alternatives and evaluate their strengths and weaknesses.
- Make your recommendations and relate these back to your project objectives. It does not matter if the organisation would not necessarily follow your advice; but your recommendation should be firmly backed by evidence from your analysis.
- There will always be more that you could have done, but keep to the time deadline and keep to the word limit.

Example

What is the feasibility of extending a 9-hole golf course to 18 holes?

This is an example of a project title that a student has negotiated with the local golf club where she plays as a junior member.

Objectives For this particular project the student, in discussion with the organisation, might set the following objectives:

- to identify the potential demand for an 18-hole course;
- to explore the local competition for the golf club;
- to examine the financial feasibility of building an 18-hole extension;
- to identify possible sources of finance for the extension to 18 holes;
- to make recommendations to the club on whether they should go ahead.

This is a piece of coursework that provides a reasonable problem for the student to tackle; it has scope for both qualitative and quantitative research and analysis and allows the student to make a clear choice at the end. By negotiating the objectives with the club, the student can hope to receive good access to the necessary people to talk to and the club's financial information. Access to accurate financial data is often the major constraint the students face when carrying out project research.

The scope of the project does not require the student to explore the legal background to expanding the golf course. This is a reasonable limitation that makes the project more manageable and the student would not be penalised for this provided the objectives and limitations of the project are made clear at the start.

Collecting information The student might plan to collect a range of data from primary and secondary sources. **Primary research** might include:

- a survey of existing members to establish their demand for an 18-hole course;
- a survey of potential members who might use the course if it had 18 holes;
- interviews with club officials who would be responsible for carrying out the extension;
- identifying the costs of building an extension;
- identifying the costs and availability of different sources of finance;

Secondary research might include:

- identification of the demand for golf through national statistics;
- identification of the location, size and facilities of other golf courses in the area;
- looking at the club's existing financial position through its published income and expenditure statements;
- looking at economic trends that might affect the future costs and revenue for a golf club;
- making use of any previous data that the club had collected if this problem had been considered previously.

Analysis Once the above research has taken place, the student would be in a position to carry out the following analyses of the information collected:

- a forecast of likely demand for the 18-hole course and thereby of the revenue that the club might generate;
- a forecast of the likely flow of expenditures on the project in order to set up and maintain the extended course;
- a cash flow for the project over the next 5/10 years;
- using the pay-back method or discounted cash flow method, an analysis of the financial benefits of the project when compared to other possible investments;
- a comparison of the costs and benefits of different sources of funding for the extension of the course.

Evaluation Before making his/her final recommendation, the student would need to consider the following questions, making use of evidence drawn from the information and analyses presented in the report.

- Does the decision to expand the course fit into the overall strategy of the club?
- On purely financial grounds, is the expansion a viable option? Are there better financial options for the club, eg leaving the money in a high interest bearing account?
- Can the club raise the necessary finance for the expansion? Would the costs of increased borrowing outweigh the benefits?
- How reliable are the forecasts of the demand and revenue figures and the cost and expenditure figures? How accurate is the research on demand? What might change to increase the cost estimates?
- What other external and internal factors would the club need to take into account before making a final decision?

This evaluation would help to provide the basis upon which the student is making their final recommendation as well as pointing forward to other areas that might be considered in a longer report. It should not be seen as a sign of weakness that the report writer asks such questions of their own work. It shows that he or she understands both the strengths and weaknesses of their final decision. It is important to remember that there is no correct answer in report or coursework writing.

Index

Index